D1622874

Strategic Management Model

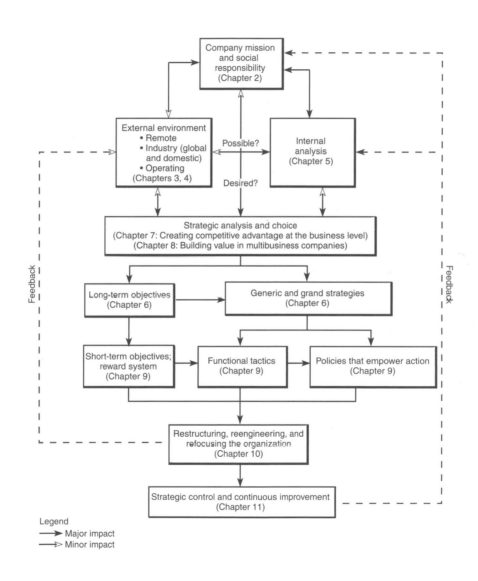

Company mission
and social
responsibility
(Chapter 2)

External environment
• Remote
• Industry (global
and domestic)
• Operating
(Chapters 3, 4)

Possible?

Desired?

Internal
analysis
(Chapter 5)

Strategic analysis and choice
(Chapter 7: Creating competitive advantage at the business level)
(Chapter 8: Building value in multibusiness companies)

Long-term objectives
(Chapter 6)

Generic and grand strategies
(Chapter 6)

Short-term objectives;
reward system
(Chapter 9)

Functional tactics
(Chapter 9)

Policies that empower action
(Chapter 9)

Restructuring, reengineering, and
refocusing the organization
(Chapter 10)

Strategic control and continuous improvement
(Chapter 11)

Feedback

Feedback

Legend
→ Major impact
⇢ Minor impact

Strategic Management

Strategic Management

Formulation, Implementation, and Control

Eighth Edition

John A. Pearce II
College of Commerce and Finance
Villanova University

Richard B. Robinson, Jr.
Moore School of Business
University of South Carolina

Boston   Burr Ridge, IL   Dubuque, IA   Madison, WI   New York   San Francisco   St. Louis
Bangkok   Bogotá   Caracas   Kuala Lumpur   Lisbon   London   Madrid   Mexico City
Milan   Montreal   New Delhi   Santiago   Seoul   Singapore   Sydney   Taipei   Toronto

McGraw-Hill Higher Education

A Division of The McGraw-Hill Companies

STRATEGIC MANAGEMENT: FORMULATION, IMPLEMENTATION, AND CONTROL

Published by McGraw-Hill/Irwin, a business unit of The McGraw-Hill Companies, Inc., 1221 Avenue of the Americas, New York, NY, 10020. Copyright © 2003, 2000, 1997, 1994, 1991, 1988, 1985, 1982 by The McGraw-Hill Companies, Inc. All rights reserved. No part of this publication may be reproduced or distributed in any form or by any means, or stored in a database or retrieval system, without the prior written consent of The McGraw-Hill Companies, Inc., including, but not limited to, in any network or other electronic storage or transmission, or broadcast for distance learning.

Some ancillaries, including electronic and print components, may not be available to customers outside the United States.

This book is printed on acid-free paper.

domestic   1 2 3 4 5 6 7 8 9 0 DOW/DOW 0 9 8 7 6 5 4 3 2
international   1 2 3 4 5 6 7 8 9 0 DOW/DOW 0 9 8 7 6 5 4 3 2

ISBN 0-07-248846-8

Publisher: *John E. Biernat*
Senior sponsoring editor: *Andy Winston*
Editorial coordinator: *Sara E. Ramos*
Marketing manager: *Lisa Nicks*
Producer, Media technology: *Jennifer Becka*
Senior project manager: *Kimberly D. Hooker*
Production supervisor: *Rose Hepburn*
Senior designer: *Jennifer McQueen*
Supplement producer: *Matthew Perry*
Senior digital content specialist: *Brian Nacik*
Cover design: *Kiera Cunningham*
Typeface: *10/12 Times New Roman*
Compositor: *Shepherd Incorporated*
Printer: *R. R. Donnelley*

Library of Congress Cataloging-in-Publication Data
Pearce, John A.
      Strategic management: formulation, implementation, and control/John A. Pearce II,
   Richard B. Robinson, Jr.—8th ed.
         p. cm.
      Includes bibliographical references and indexes.
      ISBN 0-07-248846-8 (alk. paper)—ISBN 0-07-119868-7 (international : alk. paper)
      1. Strategic planning. I. Robinson, Richard B. (Richard Braden), 1947-II. Title.
   HD30.28 .P3395 2003
   658.4'012—dc21
                                                                2002067164

INTERNATIONAL EDITION ISBN 0-07-119868-7
Copyright © 2003. Exclusive rights by The McGraw-Hill Companies, Inc. for manufacture and export. This book cannot be re-exported from the country to which it is sold by McGraw-Hill. The International Edition is not available in North America.

www.mhhe.com

To Susan McCartney Pearce,
David Donham Pearce, Mark McCartney Pearce,
Josephine Elizabeth Robinson,
Katherine Elizabeth Robinson,
John Braden Robinson—
for the love, joy, and vitality that they give to
our lives.

Preface

This eighth edition of *Strategic Management: Formulation, Implementation, and Control* is both the culmination of over 20 years of work by many people and a major revision designed to accommodate the needs of strategy students in the 21st century. These are exciting times and they are reflected on the many new developments in this book and the accompanying McGraw-Hill supplements. This preface describes what we have done to make the eighth edition uniquely effective in preparing students for strategic decisions in tomorrow's fast-paced global business arena. It also allows us the opportunity to recognize many outstanding contributors.

The eighth edition of *Strategic Management: Formulation, Implementation, and Control* is divided into 11 chapters that provide a thorough, state-of-the-art treatment of the critical business skills needed to plan and manage strategic activities. Each chapter has been filled with new, current real-world examples to illustrate concepts in companies that students recognize and regularly read about in the news around the world. Strategic ramifications of topics like executive compensation, E-commerce, the Internet, entrepreneurship, ethics, continuous improvement, virtual organization, cultural diversity, outsourcing, strategic alliances, and global competition can be found across several chapters. While the text continues a solid academic connection, students will find the text material to be practical, skills oriented, and relevant to their jobs.

We are excited and honored to be selected by *BusinessWeek* as its exclusive partner among strategic management textbooks. Their editors were very comfortable with the framework we use to explain strategic management and our emphasis on practical, relevant coverage. We were thrilled to have unlimited access to the world's best business publication to create examples, illustration modules, and various cases. The result is an extensively enhanced text and cases benefiting from hundreds of contemporary examples and illustrations provided by *BusinessWeek* writers worldwide. You will see *BusinessWeek*'s impact on our discussion case feature, our Strategy in Action modules, our cases, and our website. Of course, we are also pleased with several hundred examples blended into the text material, which came from recent issues of *BusinessWeek* or www.businessweek.com.

AN OVERVIEW OF OUR TEXT MATERIAL

The eighth edition continues to use a model of the strategic management process as the basis for the organization of the text material. Previous adopters have identified that model as a key distinctive competence for our text because it offers a logical flow, distinct elements, and an easy-to-understand guide to strategic management. The model has been modestly refined to reflect strategic analysis at different organizational levels as well as the importance of internal analysis in the strategic management process. Adopters see quickly and feel comfortable that the model and subsequent structure continue to provide a student-friendly approach to the study of strategic management.

We reduced the number of chapters to 11 to accommodate excellent reviewer suggestions about a simplified organization and focused coverage of strategic management topics. We reduced the overall text length while ensuring state-of-the-art topical coverage.

Focused wording, elimination of seldom used reference lists and other features have helped ensure a more concise, readable coverage of strategic management.

The first chapter provides an overview of the strategic management process and explains what students will find as they use this book. The remaining 10 chapters cover each part of the strategic management process and techniques that aid strategic analysis, decision making, implementation, and control. The literature and research in the strategic management area have developed at a rapid pace in recent years in both the academic and business press. This eighth edition includes several upgrades designed to incorporate major developments from both these sources. While we include cutting-edge concepts, we emphasize straightforward, logical, and simple presentation so that students can grasp these new ideas without additional reading. The following are a few of the revisions that deserve particular note:

Corporate Social Responsibility

This eighth edition gives added emphasis to the issue of corporate social responsibility. Many collegiate business schools have decided that stand-alone courses in business ethics and social responsibility are no longer necessary. Such decisions make it important that all other business courses accept a greater role in discussing the relevant topics. Our revision helps professors fulfill this obligation by presenting a balanced discussion and useful guidelines to students and managers on key topics in corporate social responsibility.

Agency Theory

Of the recent approaches to corporate governance and strategic management, probably none has had a greater impact on managerial thinking than agency theory. While the breadth and measurement of its usefulness continue to be hotly debated, students of strategic management need to understand the role of agency in our free enterprise, capitalistic system. This edition presents agency theory in a coherent and practical manner. We believe that it arms students with a cutting-edge approach to increasing their understanding of the priorities of executive decision making and strategic control.

Resource-Based View of the Firm

One of the most significant conceptual frameworks to systematize and "measure" a firm's strategic capabilities is the resource-based view (RBV) of the firm. The RBV has received major academic and business press attention during the last decade helping to shape its value as a conceptual tool by adding rigor during the internal analysis and strategic analysis phases of the strategic management process. This edition provides a revised treatment of this concept in Chapter 5. We present the RBV in a logical and practical manner as a central underpinning of sound strategic analysis. Students will find several useful examples and a straightforward treatment of different types of "assets" and organizational capabilities culminating in the ability to determine when these resources create competitive advantage. They will see different ways to answer the question "what makes a resource valuable?" and be able to determine when that resource creates a competitive advantage in a systematic, disciplined, creative manner.

Value Chain Analysis

Outsourcing is becoming a standard business practice in virtually every facet of business operations. This trend enhances the usefulness of the value chain approach in strategic analysis. We have simplified our treatment of this useful conceptual framework and added several contemporary examples to enable students to quickly incorporate the value chain perspective into their strategic thinking process. Chapter 5 includes new Strategies in Action about the use of a value chain perspective at Volkswagen and about its contribution to the impressive strides that UPS is making in overtaking FedEx in the domestic and international package transportation industry.

Executive Compensation

While our text has led the field in providing a practice-oriented approach to strategic management, we have redoubled our efforts to treat topics with an emphasis on application. Our new section on executive compensation in Chapter 9 is a clear example in the eighth edition. You will find an extended discussion of executive bonus options that provides a comparison of the relative merits of the five most popular approaches in use today.

Balanced Scoreboard

A recent evolution in the motivation that underpins strategic management is reflected in the adoption of the Balanced Scoreboard approach to corporate performance evaluation. While the maximization of shareholder wealth retains the top spot in executive priorities, the guideline is now widely accepted that strategic initiatives must produce favorable outcomes over a range of stakeholder objectives. We try to help our readers gain an appreciation for this perspective in our eighth edition.

Bankruptcy

Many times revisions in this book are driven by changes in business trends. Nowhere is that more evident than in our discussion of company bankruptcy. In the 1980s bankruptcy was treated as a last option that precluded any future for the firm. In the first decade of the 2000s the view has dramatically changed. Bankruptcy has been elevated to the status of a strategic option, and executives need to be well versed in its potentials and limitations, as you will see in Chapter 6.

Strategic Analysis and Choice

We have divided the discussion of strategic analysis and choice into two chapters. Chapter 7 examines the single business setting. Chapter 8 looks at the multibusiness company and the diversification decision. We have added an interesting new section delineating the advantages of diversification and the case against it. *BusinessWeek* has helped us add numerous outstanding examples to these two chapters from business writers around the world. DaimlerChrysler, Nokia, Caterpillar, and Amazon.com are just a few of the names students will quickly recognize in coverage that illustrates and helps them more easily understand how strategic analysis is conducted and choices made.

Strategy Implementation

New Chapter 9 focuses on reward systems, short-term objectives, and empowerment mechanisms as part of strategy implementation. It eliminates approximately ten pages of previous discussion of functional tactics that have served as a convenient but sometimes unnecessary review of functional courses leading up to the capstone strategy class. Doing so allows students to move quickly into strategy implementation considerations from an executive perspective.

Structuring an Effective Organization

Chapter 10 provides a new perspective on the issue of organizational structure as a central mechanism for strategy implementation, particularly in larger companies. It explores three fundamental driving forces on contemporary organizational structure—globalization, the Internet, and speed. From this beginning, it covers research by academics and prominent business analysts to identify guidelines relevant to matching structure to strategy in the 21st century. Carly Fiorina's pioneering new structure at Hewlett-Packard provides a starting point, six contemporary guidelines to structuring an effective organization are explored in-depth providing students with useful conceptual tools to take into their post-graduation companies and contribute to specific structural challenges. A concise appendix is provided to Chapter 10 detailing the pros and cons of different basic organizational structures. It is included there rather than in the chapter to increase the readability and contemporary focus of the chapter material.

Organizational Leadership

New Chapter 10 has added coverage of outsourcing, virtual organizations, and the recruitment/development process as key contemporary considerations in building effective management teams. How to get and keep top management talent is an issue of critical importance examined in this new edition.

Strategic Control and Continuous Improvement

New Chapter 11 offers a major revision in our treatment of these topics. First, a reduced and concise treatment of four broad strategic controls used in the formulation and implementation phases of strategic management are discussed and illustrated. Second, the link between quality/continuous improvement initiatives and the strategic management process receive new, in-depth treatment in this chapter. ISO9001 and Six Sigma are examined as contemporary approaches to the continuous improvement of a company's value chain and a mechanism to guide strategic control. The experiences of several well known companies in adopting these tools help illustrate their value in a comprehensive strategic management commitment. Finally, the increasingly popular use of the balanced scoreboard approach is also explored in this new chapter because of its value in supporting strategic control and continuous improvement.

OUR STRATEGIC ALLIANCE WITH *BUSINESSWEEK*

Thanks to the leadership at McGraw-Hill and *BusinessWeek,* we have completed a strategic alliance of our own that benefits every professor and student who uses this book. Our book is *BusinessWeek*'s exclusive partner among strategic management textbooks in the collegiate market. We have long felt *BusinessWeek* to be the unquestionable leader among business periodicals for its coverage of strategic issues in businesses, industries, and economies worldwide. Personal surveys of collegiate faculty teaching strategic management confirmed our intuition: While there are many outstanding business magazines and new publications, none match the consistent quality found in *BusinessWeek* for the coverage of corporate strategies, case stories, and topics of interest to students and professors of strategic management.

Through this partnership, we get unconditional access to *BusinessWeek* material for this book and the insights of their writers and editorial staff in the use of their cutting-edge stories and topical coverage. *BusinessWeek* gets to become more involved in the educational market as a supplements provider and they get increased exposure to strategic management teachers and students entering the business world. They plan to make their publication available on very favorable terms with the expectation that those initial users will roll over into long-term subscribers. From our point of view, this is a unique four-way win-win; teachers, students, authors, and *BusinessWeek* all stand to gain in many ways. We are most proud of their selection criteria: they judged this strategy book as providing the most logical, proven framework to explain strategic management while prioritizing practical, frequent illustrations. The most direct way you can see the impact of the *BusinessWeek* alliance is in three book features: discussion cases, Strategy in Action modules, and 25 short cases.

The Discussion Case Feature

We pioneered the cohesion case innovation several years ago and continue to be pleased by notes and comments from adopters who consider it very useful. For this eighth edition, we created a *BusinessWeek* Discussion Case at the end of each chapter that illustrates key topics from that chapter. In this way, we examine a variety of companies across the 11 chapters. We think that you will find the variety of exciting companies covered, in combination with the depth of the *BusinessWeek* research that underlies these stories, to make this feature a true pedagogical innovation once again. Amazon.com, Toyota-Japan, DaimlerChrysler, Caterpillar, and General Electric are just a few of the exciting situations examined in depth by *BusinessWeek*'s senior staff and shared in detail with students in a very readable fashion.

Strategy in Action Modules

Another pedagogical feature we pioneered, Strategy in Action modules, has become standard in most strategy books. While such affirmation is pleasing, we have long seen the need to obtain quality illustrations to be a difficult permissions and editorial task. No more. Our strategic alliance with *BusinessWeek* lets us once again pioneer an innovation. We have worked with *BusinessWeek* field correspondents worldwide to fill over 60 new *BusinessWeek* Strategy in Action modules with short, hard-hitting current illustrations of key chapter topics. We are the only strategy book to have *BusinessWeek*–derived illustration modules, and we are energized by the excitement, interest, and practical illustration value our students tell us they provide.

Short Cases

As professors of strategy management, we continually look for content or pedagogical developments or enhancements that make the strategy course more valuable. We have been concerned for some time about the length of cases typically available for classroom use. On the one hand, length often accommodates a breadth of information that in turn assures a class discussion that covers "all the bases." It even honors the professorial instruction we both experienced as students that "it is your job to extract the relevant information" from the lengthy case. The answer, we have long felt, is to have a blend of cases in terms of length. Some long cases are needed so that the professor can cover many issues within a company and allow for a truly comprehensive strategic analysis. Some shorter cases also play a role by facilitating a focus on one incident, or allow for a discussion of only 20 to 30 minutes so that the case topic can be used in concert with other materials, or provide a springboard for discussion of "real time" situations, perhaps supplemented by website and Internet-derived information. In brainstorming this issue in focus groups and with *BusinessWeek*'s staff, we created the idea of short cases based on solidly developed *BusinessWeek* articles. These short cases generate useful class discussions while allowing coverage of other material during the case portion of the course or as a supplement and source of variety during the text portion of the course. We think you will find it useful. We have included 25 such cases in the eighth edition while continuing to include 25 longer cases.

CASES IN THE EIGHTH EDITION

We are pleased to offer 50 excellent cases in this edition. As noted above, these include 25 traditional cases and industry notes that adopters expect in a strategic management textbook. The remaining 25 cases are short cases built on solidly developed *Business-Week* articles from the most recent editions of that magazine. Both sets of cases present companies, industries, and situations that are easily recognized, current, and interesting. We have a good mixture of small and large firms, start-ups and industry leaders, global and domestically focused companies, and service, retail, manufacturing, technology, and diversified activities.

Students will feel comfortable with cases about Napster and MP3, North Face, MTV, ZAP, and Avid Technology. The rise of WalMart, the fall of Kmart, the comeback of Caterpillar, the question mark at Tyco, and the telecom mess offer interesting current situations with fundamental strategic issues. Impressive strategic leadership from Carly Fiorina at HP and Meg Whitman at eBay highlight overdue progress in breaking the "glass ceiling." Hyundai, Ryanair, Volkswagen, Nokia, Swatch, ABB, and easyJet are but a few of our cases that take students into strategic management settings around the globe.

Students get to examine numerous industry situations through this 50 set case selection including the personal computer, telecom, automotive, retailing, package transportation, electric vehicles, music, and global watch industries. There are also several opportunities to incorporate the Internet's evolution and the strategic implications within several industries and facing specific companies like *The Wall Street Journal,* Microsoft, and MTV. We have selected many companies well known to students like Cisco, Microsoft, Wal-Mart, Toys "R" Us, AOL, Ford, *USAToday,* UPS, and Boeing. Finally, we include a revision of our popular Wendy's case series both to accommodate a request for its retention by previous adopters and to allow new students to honor the recently deceased Dave Thomas by studying his extraordinary track record as a master strategist in the fast-food industry.

OUR WEBSITE

A substantial website has been designed to aid your use of this book. It includes areas accessible only to instructors and areas specifically designed to assist students. The instructor section includes downloadable supplements, which keep your work area less cluttered and let you quickly obtain information. *BusinessWeek* provides access to the article archives through the instructor website. The site offers an elaborate array of linkages to company websites and other sources that you might find useful in your course preparation. The student resources section of the website provides interactive discussion groups where students and groups using the book may interact with other students around the world doing the same thing. Students are provided company and related business periodical (and other) website linkages to aid and expedite their case research and preparation efforts. Practice quizzes and tests are provided to help students prepare for tests on the text material and attempt to lower their anxiety in that regard. Access to *BusinessWeek* articles that update the cases and key illustration modules in the book are provided. We expect students will find the website useful and interesting. Please visit us at www.mhhe.com/pearce8e.

SUPPLEMENTS

Components of our teaching package include a revised, comprehensive instructor's manual, test bank, PowerPoint presentation, and a computerized test bank. These are all available to qualified adopters of the text.

Professors can also choose between two simulation games as a possible package with this text: The International Business Management Decision Simulation (McDonald/ Neelankavil), or the Business Strategy Game (Thompson/Stappenbeck).

- The International Business Management Decision Simulation is also a Windows-based simulation that provides an international business analysis and plan simulation allowing students to create multinational business plans and compete with other student groups. Fifteen countries representing three regions of the world along with four product categories are included in the simulation. Students assess business plans by using the financial reports contained in the simulation.

- The Business Strategy Game provides an exercise to help students understand how the functional pieces of a business fit together. Students will work with the numbers, explore options, and try to unite production, marketing, finance, and human resource decisions into a coherent strategy.

ACKNOWLEDGMENTS

We have benefited from the help of many people in the evolution of this project over eight editions. Students, adopters, colleagues, reviewers, and business contacts have provided hundreds of insightful comments, suggestions, and contributions that have progressively enhanced this book and its supplements. We are indebted to the researchers and practicing managers who have accelerated the development of the literature on strategic management.

We are particularly indebted to the talented case researchers who have produced the cases used in this book, as well as to case researchers dedicated to the revitalization of case research as an important academic endeavor. First-class case research is a major avenue through which top strategic management scholars should be recognized.

The following strategic management scholars have supported this project in its current edition through their case research efforts. We have personally made sure that the dean at each of the case author's respective institutions is aware of the value that their faculty member's case research provides the strategic management literature and field:

Sherri Anderson
Sonoma State University

David J. Arnold
Global Research Group

Kevin Baker
Roanoke College

F. Barry Barnes
Nova Southeastern University

Alan Bauerschmidt
University of South Carolina

Robert Birney
Alverno College

James Camerius
Northern Michigan University

Rachel Canetta
University of Denver

Joyce Claterbos
University of Kansas

James Clinton
University of Northern Colorado

Isaac Cohen
San Jose State University

Mary Crossan
University of Western Ontario

Carol J. Cumber
South Dakota State University

Peter Davis
Memphis State University

Pat DeMouy
University of South Carolina

Robert Dennehy
Pace University

John Dory
Pace University

Alan Eisner
Pace University

Eisenhower Etienne
Langston University

Armand Gilinsky
Sonoma State University

Shanthi Gopalakrishnan
New Jersey Institute of Technology

Philip Goulet
University of South Carolina

Paula Harveston
Berry College

Amy Hillman
University of Western Ontario

Lawrence R. Jauch
University of Louisiana at Monroe

Caren-Isabel Knoop
Global Research Group

Nirmalya Kumar
International Institute for Managerial Development

Jerome Kuperman
Minnesota State University

Rico Lam
University of Houston—Clear Lake

Joseph Lampel
New York University

Geoffrey Lantos
Stonehill College

Steven Leatherworth
Pace University

Mingfang Li
Cal State—Northridge

Wei Lu
University of Western Ontario

Rickey Madden
Catawba College

James Maddox
Friends University

Richard McCline
San Francisco State University

Robert McGinty
Eastern Washington University

Keith Moody
Pace University

Piero Morosini
International Institute for Management Development

Allen Morrison
University of Western Ontario

Mark Perry
University of Western Ontario

Barbara Petzall
Maryville University—St. Louis

Brian Rogers
International Institute for Managerial Development

Tracy A. Sutter
Oklahoma State University

Norihito Tanaka
Kanagawa University

Marilyn Taylor
University of Missouri at Kansas City

Wu Warlin
University of Western Ontario

Margaret Ann Wilkinson
University of Western Ontario

Thomas D. Wolterink
Grand Valley State University

Joan Winn
University of Denver

Shen Zhang
University of Western Ontario

The development of this book through eight editions has benefited from the generous commitments of time, energy, and ideas from the following colleagues. The valuable ideas, recommendations, and support from these outstanding scholars, teachers, and practitioners have added quality to this book (we apologize if affiliations have changed):

Mary Ackenhusen
INSEAD

A. J. Almaney
DePaul University

James Almeida
Fairleigh Dickinson University

B. Alpert
San Francisco State University

Alan Amason
University of Georgia

Sonny Aries
University of Toledo

Katherine A. Auer
The Pennsylvania State University

Amy Vernberg Beekman
George Mason University

Patricia Bilafer
Bentley College

Robert Earl Bolick
Metropolitan State University

Bill Boulton
Auburn University

Charles Boyd
Southwest Missouri State University

Jeff Bracker
University of Louisville

Dorothy Brawley
Kennesaw State College

James W. Bronson
Washington State University

Eric Brown
George Mason University

Robert F. Bruner
INSEAD

William Burr
University of Oregon

Gene E. Burton
California State University–Fresno

Edgar T. Busch
Western Kentucky University

Charles M. Byles
Virginia Commonwealth University

Gerard A. Cahill

Jim Callahan
University of LaVerne

James W. Camerius
Northern Michigan University

Richard Castaldi
San Diego State University

Gary J. Castogiovanni
Louisiana State University

Jafor Chowdbury
University of Scranton

James J. Chrisman
University of Calgary

Neil Churchill
INSEAD

J. Carl Clamp
University of South Carolina

Earl D. Cooper
Florida Institute of Technology

Louis Coraggio
Troy State University

Jeff Covin
Indiana University

John P. Cragin
Oklahoma Baptist University

Larry Cummings
Northwestern University

Peter Davis
Memphis State University

William Davis
Auburn University

Julio DeCastro
University of Colorado

Philippe Demigne
INSEAD

D. Keith Denton
Southwest Missouri State University

F. Derakhshan
California State University–San Bernardino

Brook Dobni
University of Saskatchewan

Mark Dollinger
Indiana University

Jean–Christopher Donck
INSEAD

Max E. Douglas
Indiana State University

Yves Doz
INSEAD

Julie Driscoll
Bentley College

Derrick Dsouza
University of North Texas

Thomas J. Dudley
Pepperdine University

John Dunkelberg
Wake Forest University

Soumitra Dutta
INSEAD

Harold Dyck
California State University

Norbert Esser
Central Wesleyan College

Forest D. Etheredge
Aurora University

Liam Fahey

Mary Fandel
Bentley College

Mark Fiegener
Oregon State University

Calvin D. Fowler
Embry-Riddle Aeronautical University

Debbie Francis
Auburn University–Montgomery

Elizabeth Freeman
Southern Methodist University

Mahmound A. Gaballa
Mansfield University

Donna M. Gallo
Boston College

Diane Garsombke
University of Maine

Betsy Gatewood
Indiana University

Bertrand George
INSEAD

Michael Geringer
Southern Methodist University

Manton C. Gibbs
Indiana University of Pennsylvania

Nicholas A. Glaskowsky, Jr.
University of Miami

Tom Goho
Wake Forest University

Jon Goodman
University of Southern California

Pradeep Gopalakrishna
Hofstra University

R. H. Gordon
Hofstra University

Barbara Gottfried
Bentley College

Peter Goulet
University of Northern Iowa

Walter E. Greene
University of Texas–Pan American

Sue Greenfeld
California State University–San Bernardino

David W. Grigsby
Clemson University

Daniel E. Hallock
St. Edward's University

Don Hambrick
Columbia University

Barry Hand
Indiana State University

Jean M. Hanebury
Texas A&M University

Karen Hare
Bentley College

Earl Harper
Grand Valley State University

Samuel Hazen
Tarleton State University

W. Harvey Hegarty
Indiana University

Edward A. Hegner
California State University–Sacramento

Marilyn M. Helms
University of Tennessee–Chattanooga

Lanny Herron
University of Baltimore

D. Higginbothan
University of Missouri

Roger Higgs
Western Carolina University

William H. Hinkle
Johns Hopkins University

Charles T. Hofer
University of Georgia

Alan N. Hoffman
Bentley College

Richard Hoffman
College of William and Mary

Eileen Hogan
George Mason University

Phyllis G. Holland
Valdosta State University

Gary L. Holman
St. Martin's College

Don Hopkins
Temple University

Cecil Horst
Keller Graduate School of Management

Mel Horwitch
Theseus

Henry F. House
Auburn University–Montgomery

William C. House
University of Arkansas–Fayetteville

Frank Hoy
University of Texas–El Paso

Warren Huckabay

Eugene H. Hunt
Virginia Commonwealth University

Tammy G. Hunt
University of North Carolina–Wilmington

John W. Huonker
University of Arizona

Stephen R. Jenner
California State University

Shailendra Jha
Wilfrid Laurier University–Ontario

C. Boyd Johnson
California State University–Fresno

Troy Jones
University of Central Florida

Jon Kalinowski
Mankato State University

Al Kayloe
Lake Erie College

Michael J. Keefe
Southwest Texas State University

Kay Keels
Louisiana State University

James A. Kidney
Southern Connecticut State University

John D. King
Embry-Riddle Aeronautical University

Raymond M. Kinnunen
Northeastern University

John B. Knauff
University of St. Thomas

Rose Knotts
University of North Texas

Dan Kopp
Southwest Missouri State University

Michael Koshuta
Valparaiso University

Jeffrey A. Krug
The University of Illinois

Myroslaw Kyj
Widener University of Pennsylvania

Dick LaBarre
Ferris State University

Joseph Lampel
New York University

Ryan Lancaster
The University of Phoenix

Sharon Ungar Lane
Bentley College

Roland Larose
Bentley College

Anne T. Lawrence
San Jose State University

Joseph Leonard
Miami University–Ohio

Robert Letovsky
Saint Michael's College

Michael Levy
INSEAD

Benjamin Litt
Lehigh University

Frank S. Lockwood
University of Wisconsin

John Logan
University of South Carolina

Sandra Logan
Newberry College

Jean M. Lundin
Lake Superior State University

Rodney H. Mabry
Clemson University

Donald C. Malm
University of Missouri–St. Louis

Charles C. Manz
Arizona State University

John Maurer
Wayne State University

Denise Mazur
Aquinas College

Edward McClelland
Roanoke College

Bob McDonald
Central Wesleyan College

Patricia P. McDougall
Indiana University

S. Mehta
San Jose State University

Ralph Melaragno
Pepperdine University

Richard Merner
University of Delaware

Linda Merrill
Bentley College

Timothy Mescon
Kennesaw State College

Philip C. Micka
Park College

Bill J. Middlebrook
Southwest Texas State University

Robert Mockler
St. John's University

James F. Molly, Jr.
Northeastern University

Cynthia Montgomery
Harvard University

W. Kent Moore
Valdosta State University

Jaideep Motwani
Grand Valley State University

Karen Mullen
Bentley College

Gary W. Muller
Hofstra University

Terry Muson
Northern Montana College

Daniel Muzyka
INSEAD

Stephanie Newell
Bowling Green State University

Michael E. Nix
Trinity College of Vermont

Kenneth Olm
University of Texas–Austin

Benjamin M. Oviatt
Georgia State University

Joseph Paolillo
University of Mississippi

Gerald Parker
St. Louis University

Paul J. Patinka
University of Colorado

James W. Pearce
Western Carolina University

Michael W. Pitts
Virginia Commonwealth University

Douglas Polley
St. Cloud State University

Carlos de Pommes
Theseus

Valerie J. Porciello
Bentley College

Mark S. Poulous
St. Edward's University

John B. Pratt
Saint Joseph's College

Oliver Ray Price
West Coast University

John Primus
Golden Gate University

Norris Rath
Shepard College

Paula Rechner
University of Illinois

Richard Reed
Washington State University

J. Bruce Regan
University of St. Thomas

H. Lee Remmers
INSEAD

F. A. Ricci
Georgetown University

Keith Robbins
Winthrop University

Gary Roberts
Kennesaw State College

Lloyd E. Roberts
Mississippi College

John K. Ross III
Southwest Texas State University

George C. Rubenson
Salisbury State University

Alison Rude
Bentley College

Les Rue
Georgia State University

Carol Rugg
Bentley College

J. A. Ruslyk
Memphis State University

Ronald J. Salazar
Idaho State University

Uri Savoray
INSEAD

Jack Scarborough
Barry University

Paul J. Schlachter
Florida International University

John Seeger
Bentley College

Martin Shapiro
Iona College

Arthur Sharplin
McNeese State University

Frank M. Shipper
Salisbury State University

Rodney C. Shrader
Georgia State University

Lois Shufeldt
Southwest Missouri State University

Bonnie Silvieria
Bentley College

F. Bruce Simmons III
The University of Akron

Mark Simon
Georgia State University

Michael Skipton
Memorial University

Fred Smith
Western Illinois University

Scott Snell
Michigan State University

Coral R. Snodgrass
Canisius College

Rudolph P. Snowadzky
University of Maine

Neil Snyder
University of Virginia

Melvin J. Stanford
Mankato State University

Romuald A. Stone
James Madison University

Warren S. Stone
Virginia Commonwealth University

Ram Subramanian
Grand Valley State University

Paul M. Swiercz
Georgia State University

Robert L. Swinth
Montana State University

Chris Taubman
INSEAD

Russell Teasley
University of South Carolina

James Teboul
INSEAD

George H. Tompson
University of New Zealand

Melanie Trevino
University of Texas–El Paso

Howard Tu
Memphis State University

Craig Tunwall
Ithaca College

Elaine M. Tweedy
University of Scranton

Arieh A. Ullmann
SUNY–Binghamton

P. Veglahn
James Madison University

George Vozikis
University of Tulsa

William Waddell
California State University–Los Angeles

Bill Warren
College of William and Mary

Kirby Warren
Columbia University

Steven J. Warren
Rutgers University

Michael White
University of Tulsa

Randy White
Auburn University

Sam E. White
Portland State University

Frank Winfrey
Kent State University

Joseph Wolfe
University of Tulsa

Robley Wood
Virginia Commonwealth University

Edward D. Writh, Jr.
Florida Institute of Technology

John Young
University of New Mexico

S. David Young
INSEAD

Jan Zahrly
Old Dominion University

Alan Zeiber
Portland State University

We are affiliated with two separate universities, both of which provide environments that deserve thanks. As the Endowed Chair of the College of Commerce and Finance at Villanova University, Jack is able to combine his scholarly and teaching activities with his coauthorship of this text. He is grateful to Villanova University and his colleagues for the support and encouragement they provide.

Richard appreciates the support provided within the Moore School of Business by Mr. Dean Kress. Mr. Kress provides multifaceted assistance on projects, classes, and research that leverages the scope of what can be accomplished each year. Moore School colleagues in the management department along with Dean Joel Smith and Program Director Hoyt Wheeler provide encouragement while staff members Cheryl Fowler, Susie Gorsage, and Carol Lucas provide logistical support for which Richard is grateful.

Leadership from Irwin/McGraw-Hill deserves our utmost thanks and appreciation. Gerald Saykes got us started and continues his support. Andy Winston's editorial leadership has enhanced our quality and success. Editorial and production assistance from Sara Ramos helped this to become a much better book. The Irwin/McGraw-Hill field organization deserves particular recognition and thanks for the success of this project.

We also want to thank the *BusinessWeek* editors who listened to the strategic alliance proposal, selected our book, and are proving to be excellent strategic partners.

We hope that you will find our book and ancillaries all that you expect. We welcome your ideas and recommendations about our material. Please contact us at the following addresses:

Dr. John A. Pearce II
College of Commerce and Finance
Villanova University
Villanova, PA 19085-1678
610-519-4332
john.pearce@villanova.edu

Dr. Richard Robinson
College of Business Administration
University of South Carolina
Columbia, SC 29205
803-777-5961
Robinson@sc.edu

We wish you the utmost success in teaching and studying strategic management.

Jack Pearce and Richard Robinson

About the Authors

John A. Pearce II, PhD, is the holder of the College of Commerce and Finance Endowed Chair in Strategic Management and Entrepreneurship at Villanova University. Previously, Dr. Pearce was holder of the Eakin Endowed Chair in Strategic Management at George Mason University and was a State of Virginia Eminent Scholar. In 1994, he received the Fulbright U.S. Professional Award for service in Malaysia. Professor Pearce has taught at Penn State, West Virginia University, the University of Malta, where as a Fulbright Senior Professor in International Management he served as the Head of Business Faculties, and at the University of South Carolina where he was Director of PhD Programs in Strategic Management. He received a PhD degree in Business Administration from the Pennsylvania State University.

Professor Pearce is coauthor of 36 books that have been used to help educate more than one million students and managers. He has also authored more than 250 articles and professional papers. These have been published in journals that include the *Academy of Management Journal, California Management Review, Journal of Applied Psychology, Journal of Business Venturing, Sloan Management Review,* and *Strategic Management Journal.* Several of these publications have resulted from Professor Pearce's work as a principal on research projects funded for more than $2 million. He is a recognized expert in the field of strategic management, with special accomplishments in the areas of strategy formulation, implementation, control, management during recessions, mission statement development, competitive assessment, industry analysis, joint ventures, and tools for strategy evaluation and design.

A frequent leader of executive development programs and an active consultant to business and industry, Dr. Pearce has a client list that includes domestic and multinational firms engaged in manufacturing, service, and nonprofit industries.

Richard B. Robinson, Jr., PhD, is the Business Partnership Foundation Fellow in Strategic Management and Entrepreneurship in the Moore School of Business, University of South Carolina. He also serves as Director of the Faber Entrepreneurship Center at USC and Assistant Director of the Center for Manufacturing and Technology in USC's College of Engineering and Information Technology. Dr. Robinson received his PhD in Business Administration from the University of Georgia. He graduated from Georgia Tech in Industrial Management.

Professor Robinson has coauthored over 30 books addressing strategic management and entrepreneurship issues that students and managers use worldwide. He has authored over 300 articles, professional papers, and case studies that have been published in major journals including the *Academy of Management Journal, Academy of Management Review, Strategic Management Journal, Academy of Entrepreneurship Journal,* and the *Journal of Business Venturing.*

Dr. Robinson has previously held executive positions with companies in the pulp and paper, hazardous waste, building products, lodging, and restaurant industries. He currently serves as a director or adviser to entrepreneurial companies that are global leaders in niche markets in the log home, building products, animation, and computer chip thermal management industries. Dr. Robinson also supervises over 50 student teams each year that undertake field consulting projects and internships with entrepreneurial companies worldwide.

Brief Contents

Contents

Strategic Management

Part One

Overview of Strategic Management

The first chapter of this book introduces strategic management, the set of decisions and actions that result in the design and activation of strategies to achieve the objectives of an organization. The chapter provides an overview of the nature, benefits, and terminology of and the need for strategic management. Subsequent chapters provide greater detail.

The first major section of Chapter 1, "The Nature and Value of Strategic Management," emphasizes the practical value and benefits of strategic management for a firm. It also distinguishes between a firm's strategic decisions and its other planning tasks.

The section stresses the key point that strategic management activities are undertaken at three levels: corporate, business, and functional. The distinctive characteristics of strategic decision making at each of these levels affect the impact of activities at these levels on company operations. Other topics dealt with in this section are the value of formality in strategic management and the alignment of strategy makers in strategy formulation and implementation. The section concludes with a review of the planning research on business, which demonstrates that the use of strategic management processes yields financial and behavioral benefits that justify their costs.

The second major section of Chapter 1 presents a model of the strategic management process. The model, which will serve as an outline for the remainder of the text, describes approaches currently used by strategic planners. Its individual components are carefully defined and explained, as is the process for integrating them into the strategic management process. The section ends with a discussion of the model's practical limitations and the advisability of tailoring the recommendations made to actual business situations.

Strategic Management

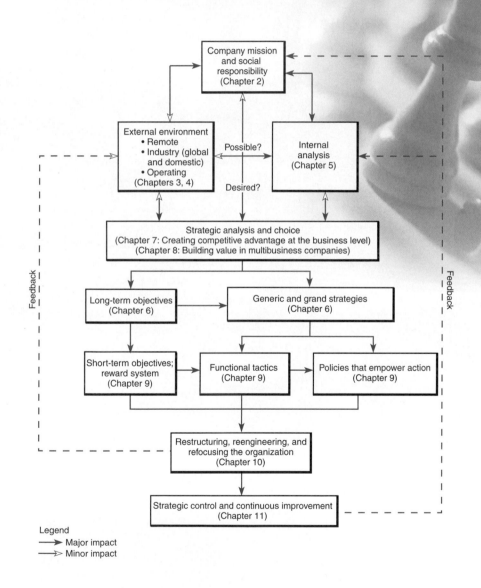

Legend
→ Major impact
⟶▹ Minor impact

THE NATURE AND VALUE OF STRATEGIC MANAGEMENT

Managing activities internal to the firm is only part of the modern executive's responsibilities. The modern executive also must respond to the challenges posed by the firm's immediate and remote external environments. The immediate external environment includes competitors, suppliers, increasingly scarce resources, government agencies and their ever more numerous regulations, and customers whose preferences often shift inexplicably. The remote external environment comprises economic and social conditions, political priorities, and technological developments, all of which must be anticipated, monitored, assessed, and incorporated into the executive's decision making. However, the executive often is compelled to subordinate the demands of the firm's internal activities and external environment to the multiple and often inconsistent requirements of its stakeholders: owners, top managers, employees, communities, customers, and country. To deal effectively with everything that affects the growth and profitability of a firm, executives employ management processes that they feel will position it optimally in its competitive environment by maximizing the anticipation of environmental changes and of unexpected internal and competitive demands.

Broad-scope, large-scale management processes became dramatically more sophisticated after World War II. These processes responded to increases in the size and number of competing firms; to the expanded role of government as a buyer, seller, regulator, and competitor in the free enterprise system; and to greater business involvement in international trade. Perhaps the most significant improvement in management processes came in the 1970s, when "long-range planning," "new venture management," "planning, programming, budgeting," and "business policy" were blended. At the same time, increased emphasis was placed on environmental forecasting and external considerations in formulating and implementing plans. This all-encompassing approach is known as strategic management.

Strategic management is defined as the set of decisions and actions that result in the formulation and implementation of plans designed to achieve a company's objectives. It comprises nine critical tasks:

1. Formulate the company's mission, including broad statements about its purpose, philosophy, and goals.

2. Conduct an analysis that reflects the company's internal conditions and capabilities.

3. Assess the company's external environment, including both the competitive and the general contextual factors.

4. Analyze the company's options by matching its resources with the external environment.

5. Identify the most desirable options by evaluating each option in light of the company's mission.

6. Select a set of long-term objectives and grand strategies that will achieve the most desirable options.

7. Develop annual objectives and short-term strategies that are compatible with the selected set of long-term objectives and grand strategies.

8. Implement the strategic choices by means of budgeted resource allocations in which the matching of tasks, people, structures, technologies, and reward systems is emphasized.

9. Evaluate the success of the strategic process as an input for future decision making.

As these nine tasks indicate, strategic management involves the planning, directing, organizing, and controlling of a company's strategy-related decisions and actions. By *strategy,* managers mean their large-scale, future-oriented plans for interacting with the competitive environment to achieve company objectives. A strategy is a company's game plan. Although that plan does not precisely detail all future deployments (of people, finances, and material), it does provide a framework for managerial decisions. A strategy reflects a company's awareness of how, when, and where it should compete; against whom it should compete; and for what purposes it should compete.

Dimensions of Strategic Decisions

What decisions facing a business are strategic and therefore deserve strategic management attention? Typically, strategic issues have the following dimensions.

Strategic Issues Require Top-Management Decisions   Since strategic decisions overarch several areas of a firm's operations, they require top-management involvement. Usually only top management has the perspective needed to understand the broad implications of such decisions and the power to authorize the necessary resource allocations. As top manager of Volvo GM Heavy Truck Corporation, Karl-Erling Trogen, president, wanted to push the company closer to the customer by overarching operations with service and customer relations empowering the work force closest to the customer with greater knowledge and authority. This strategy called for a major commitment to the parts and service end of the business where customer relations was first priority. Trogen's philosophy was to so empower the work force that more operating questions were handled on the line where workers worked directly with customers. He believed that the corporate headquarters should be more focused on strategic issues, such as engineering, production, quality, and marketing.

Strategic Issues Require Large Amounts of the Firm's Resources   Strategic decisions involve substantial allocations of people, physical assets, or moneys that either must be redirected from internal sources or secured from outside the firm. They also commit the firm to actions over an extended period. For these reasons, they require substantial resources. Whirlpool Corporation's "Quality Express" product delivery program exemplified a strategy that required a strong financial and personnel commitment from the company. The plan was to deliver products to customers when, where, and how they wanted them. This proprietary service uses contract logistics strategy to deliver Whirlpool, Kitchen Aid, Roper, and Estate brand appliances to 90 percent of the company's dealer and builder customers within 24 hours and to the other 10 percent within 48 hours. In highly competitive service-oriented businesses, achieving and maintaining customer satisfaction frequently involve a commitment from every facet of the organization.

Strategic Issues Often Affect the Firm's Long-Term Prosperity   Strategic decisions ostensibly commit the firm for a long time, typically five years; however, the impact of such decisions often lasts much longer. Once a firm has committed itself to a particular strategy, its image and competitive advantages usually are tied to that strategy. Firms become known in certain markets, for certain products, with certain technologies. They would jeopardize their previous gains if they shifted from these markets, products, or technologies by adopting a radically different strategy. Thus, strategic decisions have enduring effects on firms—for better or worse.

Global Strategy in Action
Revising Toyota's Image

Exhibit 1–1

BusinessWeek The hearty appetite for fancy German metal has Toyota Motor Co. (TM) spooked. "Higher-priced sedans are a traditional base of strength for Toyota," says Yasuhiko Fukatsu, managing director for domestic luxury sales. "But BMW and Mercedes-Benz are doing a better job attracting younger buyers." Toyota also is increasingly worried about a resurgent Nissan Motor Co. (NSANY), which is staging a comeback in the sedan niche.

Toyota's answer: Run its rivals off the road. To do so, it is unleashing on Japan a dozen-plus new or improved vehicles. Besides updating such midrange standbys as the Camry, Toyota is bulking up on eye-candy luxury models, most of which sell for $30,000 to $60,000. Among them: fully loaded versions of the muscular and decidedly BMW-ish Verossa, the remodeled Lexus ES 300 (known in Japan as the Windom), and a Mercedes-like sedan called the Brevis. Toyota is even debating marketing cars at home under the Lexus badge, which now exists only overseas.

Aging customers are a problem for Toyota everywhere, but nowhere more than in Japan. Most of the folks buying such luxury Toyota sedans as the best-selling Crown are graying executives who started out with entry-level Toyotas in the 1950s and 1960s. By contrast, upwardly mobile Japanese wouldn't be caught dead in a Crown, a $30,000 sedan often used as a taxi. Consider Shunsuke Kurita, a 46–year-old interior designer who drives a black 1999 BMW 318i. "It's a status symbol more than anything else, but I figure a BMW has better resale value than domestic cars," he says. "Toyota sedans have a fuddy-duddy image."

Still, why all the fuss? After all, foreign imports account for less than 10% of the Japanese auto market. Well, what worries Toyota is that up-and-coming Japanese drivers will develop the kind of loyalty to their German imports that their parents had to Toyota. Were that to happen, Toyota could lose out on future sales to drivers now in their late thirties and early forties.

Source: Extracted from C. Dawson, "Toyota: Taking on BMW," *BusinessWeek,* July 30, 2001.

Exhibit 1–1, Global Strategy in Action, is a *BusinessWeek* excerpt that provides an excellent example of a firm's strategy tied to its image and competitive advantage. For years, Toyota had a successful strategy of marketing its sedans in Japan. With this strategy came an image, a car for an older customer, and a competitive advantage, a traditional base for Toyota. The strategy was effective, but as its customer base grew older its strategy remained unchanged. A younger customer market saw the image as unattractive and began to seek out other manufacturers. Toyota's strategic task in foreign markets is to formulate and implement a strategy that will reignite interest in its image.

Strategic Issues Are Future Oriented Strategic decisions are based on what managers forecast, rather than on what they know. In such decisions, emphasis is placed on the development of projections that will enable the firm to select the most promising strategic options. In the turbulent and competitive free enterprise environment, a firm will succeed only if it takes a proactive (anticipatory) stance toward change.

Strategic Issues Usually Have Multifunctional or Multibusiness Consequences Strategic decisions have complex implications for most areas of the firm. Decisions about such matters as customer mix, competitive emphasis, or organizational structure necessarily involve a number of the firm's strategic business units (SBUs), divisions, or program units. All of these areas will be affected by allocations or reallocations of responsibilities and resources that result from these decisions.

Strategic Issues Require Considering the Firm's External Environment All business firms exist in an open system. They affect and are affected by external conditions that are largely beyond their control. Therefore, to successfully position a firm in competitive situations, its strategic managers must look beyond its operations. They must consider what relevant others (e.g., competitors, customers, suppliers, creditors, government, and labor) are likely to do.

Three Levels of Strategy

The decision-making hierarchy of a firm typically contains three levels. At the top of this hierarchy is the corporate level, composed principally of a board of directors and the chief executive and administrative officers. They are responsible for the firm's financial performance and for the achievement of nonfinancial goals, such as enhancing the firm's image and fulfilling its social responsibilities. To a large extent, attitudes at the corporate level reflect the concerns of stockholders and society at large. In a multibusiness firm, corporate-level executives determine the businesses in which the firm should be involved. They also set objectives and formulate strategies that span the activities and functional areas of these businesses. Corporate-level strategic managers attempt to exploit their firm's distinctive competencies by adopting a portfolio approach to the management of its businesses and by developing long-term plans, typically for a five-year period. A key corporate strategy of Airborne Express's operations involved direct sale to high-volume corporate accounts and developing an expansive network in the international arena. Instead of setting up operations overseas, Airborne's long-term strategy was to form direct associations with national companies within foreign countries to expand and diversify their operations.

Another example of the portfolio approach involved a plan by state-owned Saudi Arabian Oil to spend $1.4 billion to build and operate an oil refinery in Korea with its partner, Ssangyong. To implement their program, the Saudis embarked on a new "cut-out-the-middleman" strategy to reduce the role of international oil companies in the processing and selling of Saudi crude oil.

In the middle of the decision-making hierarchy is the business level, composed principally of business and corporate managers. These managers must translate the statements of direction and intent generated at the corporate level into concrete objectives and strategies for individual business divisions, or SBUs. In essence, business-level strategic managers determine how the firm will compete in the selected product-market arena. They strive to identify and secure the most promising market segment within that arena. This segment is the piece of the total market that the firm can claim and defend because of its competitive advantages.

At the bottom of the decision-making hierarchy is the functional level, composed principally of managers of product, geographic, and functional areas. They develop annual objectives and short-term strategies in such areas as production, operations, research and development, finance and accounting, marketing, and human relations. However, their principal responsibility is to implement or execute the firm's strategic plans. Whereas corporate- and business-level managers center their attention on "doing the right things," managers at the functional level center their attention on "doing things right." Thus, they address such issues as the efficiency and effectiveness of production and marketing systems, the quality of customer service, and the success of particular products and services in increasing the firm's market shares.

Exhibit 1–2 depicts the three levels of strategic management as structured in practice. In alternative 1, the firm is engaged in only one business and the corporate- and business-level responsibilities are concentrated in a single group of directors, officers, and managers. This is the organizational format of most small businesses.

Alternative 2, the classical corporate structure, comprises three fully operative levels: the corporate level, the business level, and the functional level. The approach taken throughout this text assumes the use of alternative 2. Moreover, whenever appropriate,

EXHIBIT 1–2
Alternative Strategic
Management
Structures

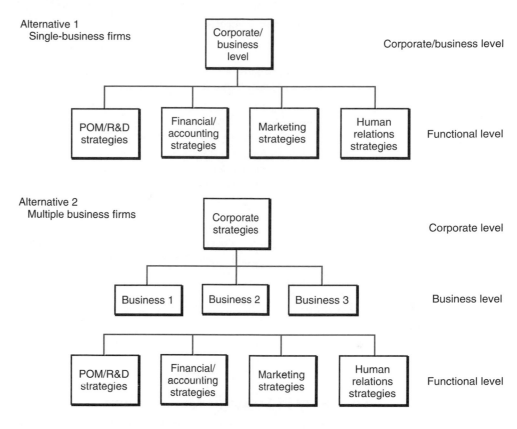

Alternative 1
Single-business firms

| Corporate/business level | | | | Corporate/business level |

POM/R&D strategies — Financial/accounting strategies — Marketing strategies — Human relations strategies — Functional level

Alternative 2
Multiple business firms

Corporate strategies — Corporate level

Business 1 — Business 2 — Business 3 — Business level

POM/R&D strategies — Financial/accounting strategies — Marketing strategies — Human relations strategies — Functional level

topics are covered from the perspective of each level of strategic management. In this way, the text presents a comprehensive discussion of the strategic management process.

Characteristics of Strategic Management Decisions

The characteristics of strategic management decisions vary with the level of strategic activity considered. As shown in Exhibit 1–3, decisions at the corporate level tend to be more value oriented, more conceptual, and less concrete than decisions at the business or functional level. For example, at Alcoa, the world's largest aluminum maker, chairman Paul O'Neill made Alcoa one of the nation's most centralized organizations by imposing a dramatic management reorganization that wiped out two layers of management. He found that this effort not only reduced costs but also enabled him to be closer to the front-line operations managers. Corporate-level decisions are often characterized by greater risk, cost, and profit potential; greater need for flexibility; and longer time horizons. Such decisions include the choice of businesses, dividend policies, sources of long-term financing, and priorities for growth.

Functional-level decisions implement the overall strategy formulated at the corporate and business levels. They involve action-oriented operational issues and are relatively short range and low risk. Functional-level decisions incur only modest costs, because they are dependent on available resources. They usually are adaptable to ongoing activities and, therefore, can be implemented with minimal cooperation. For example, the corporate headquarters of Sears, Roebuck & Company spent $60 million to automate 6,900 clerical jobs by installing 28,000 computerized cash registers at its 868 stores in the United States. Though this move eliminated many functional-level jobs, top management believed that reducing annual operating expenses by at least $50 million was crucial to competitive survival.

EXHIBIT 1–3   Hierarchy of Objectives and Strategies

Ends (What is to be achieved?)	Means (How is it to be achieved?)	Strategic Decision Makers			
		Board of Directors	Corporate Managers	Business Managers	Functional Managers
Mission, including goals and philosophy		✓✓	✓✓	✓	
Long-term objectives	Grand strategy	✓	✓✓	✓✓	
Annual objectives	Short-term strategies and policies		✓	✓✓	✓✓

Note: ✓✓ indicates a principal responsibility; ✓ indicates a secondary responsibility.

Because functional-level decisions are relatively concrete and quantifiable, they receive critical attention and analysis even though their comparative profit potential is low. Common functional-level decisions include decisions on generic versus brandname labeling, basic versus applied research and development (R&D), high versus low inventory levels, general-purpose versus specific-purpose production equipment, and close versus loose supervision.

Business-level decisions help bridge decisions at the corporate and functional levels. Such decisions are less costly, risky, and potentially profitable than corporate-level decisions, but they are more costly, risky, and potentially profitable than functional-level decisions. Common business-level decisions include decisions on plant location, marketing segmentation and geographic coverage, and distribution channels.

Formality in Strategic Management

The formality of strategic management systems varies widely among companies. *Formality* refers to the degree to which participants, responsibilities, authority, and discretion in decision making are specified. It is an important consideration in the study of strategic management, because greater formality is usually positively correlated with the cost, comprehensiveness, accuracy, and success of planning.

A number of forces determine how much formality is needed in strategic management. The size of the organization, its predominant management styles, the complexity of its environment, its production process, its problems, and the purpose of its planning system all play a part in determining the appropriate degree of formality.

In particular, formality is associated with the size of the firm and with its stage of development. Methods of evaluating strategic success also are linked to formality. Some firms, especially smaller ones, follow an *entrepreneurial* mode. They are basically under the control of a single individual, and they produce a limited number of products or services. In such firms, strategic evaluation is informal, intuitive, and limited. Very large firms, on the other hand, make strategic evaluation part of a comprehensive, formal planning system, an approach that Henry Mintzberg called the *planning mode.* Mintzberg also identified a third mode (the *adaptive mode*), which he associated with medium-sized firms in relatively stable environments.[1] For firms that follow the adaptive mode, the identification and evaluation of alternative strategies are closely related to existing strategy. It is not unusual to find different modes within the same organization. For example, Exxon might follow an entrepreneurial mode in developing and evaluating the strategy of its solar subsidiary but follow a planning mode in the rest of the company.

[1] H. Mintzberg, "Strategy Making in Three Modes," *California Management Review* 16, no. 2 (1973), pp. 44–53.

The Strategy Makers

The ideal strategic management team includes decision makers from all three company levels (the corporate, business, and functional)—for example, the chief executive officer (CEO), the product managers, and the heads of functional areas. In addition, the team obtains input from company planning staffs, when they exist, and from lower-level managers and supervisors. The latter provide data for strategic decision making and then implement strategies.

Because strategic decisions have a tremendous impact on a company and require large commitments of company resources, top managers must give final approval for strategic action. Exhibit 1–3 aligns levels of strategic decision makers with the kinds of objectives and strategies for which they are typically responsible.

Planning departments, often headed by a corporate vice president for planning, are common in large corporations. Medium-sized firms often employ at least one full-time staff member to spearhead strategic data-collection efforts. Even in small firms or less progressive larger firms, strategic planning often is spearheaded by an officer or by a group of officers designated as a planning committee.

Precisely what are managers' responsibilities in the strategic planning process at the corporate and business levels? Top management shoulders broad responsibility for all the major elements of strategic planning and management. It develops the major portions of the strategic plan and reviews, and it evaluates and counsels on all other portions. General managers at the business level typically have principal responsibilities for developing environmental analysis and forecasting, establishing business objectives, and developing business plans prepared by staff groups.

A firm's president or CEO characteristically plays a dominant role in the strategic planning process. In many ways, this situation is desirable. The CEO's principal duty often is defined as giving long-term direction to the firm, and the CEO is ultimately responsible for the firm's success and, therefore, for the success of its strategy. In addition, CEOs are typically strong-willed, company-oriented individuals with high self-esteem. They often resist delegating authority to formulate or approve strategic decisions.

However, when the dominance of the CEO approaches autocracy, the effectiveness of the firm's strategic planning and management processes is likely to be diminished. For this reason, establishing a strategic management system implies that the CEO will allow managers at all levels to participate in the strategic posture of the company.

In implementing a company's strategy, the CEO must have an appreciation for the power and responsibility of the board, while retaining the power to lead the company with the guidance of informed directors. The interaction between the CEO and board is key to any corporation's strategy. Empowerment of the board has been a recent trend across major management teams. Exhibit 1–4, Strategy in Action, presents descriptions of the changes that companies have made in an attempt to monitor the relationships between the role of the board and the role of CEO.

Benefits of Strategic Management

Using the strategic management approach, managers at all levels of the firm interact in planning and implementing. As a result, the behavioral consequences of strategic management are similar to those of participative decision making. Therefore, an accurate assessment of the impact of strategy formulation on organizational performance requires not only financial evaluation criteria but also nonfinancial evaluation criteria—measures of behavior-based effects. In fact, promoting positive behavioral consequences also enables the firm to achieve its financial goals. However, regardless

Strategy in Action
The Progress of Board Empowerment

Exhibit 1–4

Company	Innovation
Dayton Hudson Corporation	Requires the inside directors to conduct an annual evaluation of the CEO.
Medtronic	Solicits opinions on board procedures by requiring all directors to complete a questionnaire, then the full board reviews the results at an annual meeting and tries to make improvements.
Stanhome	Developed a formal document that specifies the board's purpose, size, proportion of outside directors, annual calendar, and expectations of directors and management.
Mallinckrodt	Separated the roles of chair and CEO.
Lukens	Formed a committee of outside directors to study a major acquisition proposal, hold discussions with management, and recommend action to the full board.
Campbell Soup Company	Designated a lead director with the title of vice chairman.
Monsanto	Increased the proportion of the board's time that would be focused on strategic direction and considered specific capital proposals within that framework.
General Motors	Developed an explicit set of guidelines that outline how the board will function and be structured.

Source: Reprinted by permission of *Harvard Business Review.* An exhibit from "Empowering the Board," by Jay W. Lorsch, January–February 1995. Copyright © 1995 by the President and Fellows of Harvard University, all rights reserved.

of the profitability of strategic plans, several behavioral effects of strategic management improve the firm's welfare:

1. Strategy formulation activities enhance the firm's ability to prevent problems. Managers who encourage subordinates' attention to planning are aided in their monitoring and forecasting responsibilities by subordinates who are aware of the needs of strategic planning.

2. Group-based strategic decisions are likely to be drawn from the best available alternatives. The strategic management process results in better decisions because group interaction generates a greater variety of strategies and because forecasts based on the specialized perspectives of group members improve the screening of options.

3. The involvement of employees in strategy formulation improves their understanding of the productivity-reward relationship in every strategic plan and, thus, heightens their motivation.

4. Gaps and overlaps in activities among individuals and groups are reduced as participation in strategy formulation clarifies differences in roles.

5. Resistance to change is reduced. Though the participants in strategy formulation may be no more pleased with their own decisions than they would be with authoritarian decisions, their greater awareness of the parameters that limit the available options makes them more likely to accept those decisions.

Risks of Strategic Management

Managers must be trained to guard against three types of unintended negative consequences of involvement in strategy formulation.

First, the time that managers spend on the strategic management process may have a negative impact on operational responsibilities. Managers must be trained to minimize that impact by scheduling their duties to allow the necessary time for strategic activities.

Second, if the formulators of strategy are not intimately involved in its implementation, they may shirk their individual responsibility for the decisions reached. Thus, strategic managers must be trained to limit their promises to performance that the decision makers and their subordinates can deliver.

Third, strategic managers must be trained to anticipate and respond to the disappointment of participating subordinates over unattained expectations. Subordinates may expect their involvement in even minor phases of total strategy formulation to result in both acceptance of their proposals and an increase in their rewards, or they may expect a solicitation of their input on selected issues to extend to other areas of decision making.

Sensitizing managers to these possible negative consequences and preparing them with effective means of minimizing such consequences will greatly enhance the potential of strategic planning.

Executives' Views of Strategic Management

How do managers and corporate executives view the contribution of strategic management to the success of their firms? To answer this question, a survey was conducted that included over 200 executives from the Fortune 500, Fortune 500 Service, and INC 500 companies.[2] Their responses indicate that corporate America sees strategic management as instrumental to high performance, evolutionary and perhaps revolutionary in its ever-growing sophistication, action oriented, and cost effective. Clearly, the responding executives view strategic management as critical to their individual and organizational success.

THE STRATEGIC MANAGEMENT PROCESS

Businesses vary in the processes they use to formulate and direct their strategic management activities. Sophisticated planners, such as General Electric, Procter & Gamble, and IBM, have developed more detailed processes than less-formal planners of similar size. Small businesses that rely on the strategy formulation skills and limited time of an entrepreneur typically exhibit more basic planning concerns than those of larger firms in their industries. Understandably, firms with multiple products, markets, or technologies tend to use more complex strategic management systems. However, despite differences in detail and the degree of formalization, the basic components of the models used to analyze strategic management operations are very similar.

Because of the similarity among the general models of the strategic management process, it is possible to develop an eclectic model representative of the foremost thought in the strategic management area. This model is shown in Exhibit 1–5. It serves three major functions. First, it depicts the sequence and the relationships of the major components of the strategic management process. Second, it is the outline for this book. This chapter provides a general overview of the strategic management process, and the major components of the model will be the principal theme of subsequent chapters. Notice that the chapters of the text that discuss each of the strategic management process components are shown in each block. Finally, the model offers one approach for analyzing the case studies in this text and thus helps the analyst develop strategy formulation skills.

[2] V. Ramanujam, J. C. Camillus, and N. Venkatraman, "Trends in Strategic Planning," in *Strategic Planning and Management Handbook,* ed. W. R. King and D. I. Cleland (New York: Van Nostrand Reinhold, 1987), pp. 611–28.

EXHIBIT 1–5 Strategic Management Model

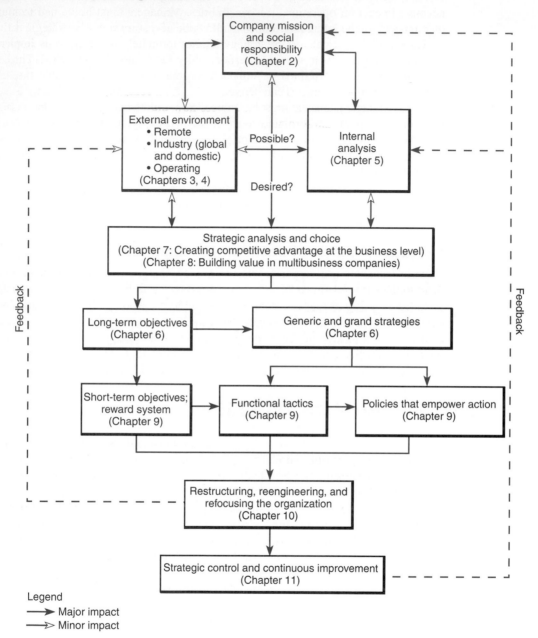

Components of the Strategic Management Model

This section will define and briefly describe the key components of the strategic management model. Each of these components will receive much greater attention in a later chapter. The intention here is simply to introduce them.

Company Mission

The mission of a company is the unique purpose that sets it apart from other companies of its type and identifies the scope of its operations. In short, the mission describes the company's product, market, and technological areas of emphasis in a way that reflects the values and priorities of the strategic decision makers. For example, Lee Hun-Hee, the new chairman of the Samsung Group, revamped the company mission by stamping his own brand of management on Samsung. Immediately, Samsung separated Chonju Paper Manufacturing and Shinsegae Department Store from other operations. This corporate act of downscaling reflected a revised management philosophy that favored specialization, thereby changing the direction and scope of the organization.

Social responsibility is a critical consideration for a company's strategic decision makers since the mission statement must express how the company intends to contribute to the societies that sustain it. A firm needs to set social responsibility aspirations for itself, just as it does in other areas of corporate performance.

Internal Analysis

The company analyzes the quantity and quality of the company's financial, human, and physical resources. It also assesses the strengths and weaknesses of the company's management and organizational structure. Finally, it contrasts the company's past successes and traditional concerns with the company's current capabilities in an attempt to identify the company's future capabilities.

External Environment

A firm's external environment consists of all the conditions and forces that affect its strategic options and define its competitive situation. The strategic management model shows the external environment as three interactive segments: the remote, industry, and operating environments.

Strategic Analysis and Choice

Simultaneous assessment of the external environment and the company profile enables a firm to identify a range of possibly attractive interactive opportunities. These opportunities are *possible* avenues for investment. However, they must be screened through the criterion of the company mission to generate a set of possible and *desired* opportunities. This screening process results in the selection of options from which a *strategic choice* is made. The process is meant to provide the combination of long-term objectives and generic and grand strategies that optimally position the firm in its external environment to achieve the company mission.

Strategic analysis and choice in single or dominant product/service businesses center around identifying strategies that are most effective at building sustainable competitive advantage based on key value chain activities and capabilities—core competencies of the firm. Multibusiness companies find their managers focused on the question of which combination of businesses maximizes shareholder value as the guiding theme during their strategic analysis and choice.

Long-Term Objectives

The results that an organization seeks over a multiyear period are its *long-term objectives.* Such objectives typically involve some or all of the following areas: profitability, return on investment, competitive position, technological leadership, productivity, employee relations, public responsibility, and employee development.

Generic and Grand Strategies

Many businesses explicitly and all implicitly adopt one or more *generic strategies* characterizing their competitive orientation in the marketplace. Low cost, differentiation, or focus strategies define the three fundamental options. Enlightened managers seek to create ways their firm possesses both low cost and differentiation competitive advantages as part of their overall generic strategy. They usually combine these capabilities with a comprehensive, general plan of major actions through which their firm intends to achieve its long-term objectives in a dynamic environment. Called the *grand strategy,* this statement of means indicates how the objectives are to be achieved. Although every grand strategy is, in fact, a unique package of long-term strategies, 14 basic approaches can be identified: concentration, market development, product development, innovation, horizontal integration, vertical integration, joint venture, strategic alliances, consortia, concentric diversification, conglomerate diversification, turnaround, divestiture, and liquidation.

Each of these grand strategies will be covered in detail in Chapter 6.

Action Plans and Short-Term Objectives

Action plans translate generic and grand strategies into "action" by incorporating four elements. First, they identify specific functional *tactics and actions* to be undertaken in the next week, month, or quarter as part of the business's effort to build competitive advantage. The second element is a clear time frame for completion. Third, action plans create accountability by identifying who is responsible for each "action" in the plan. Fourth, each "action" in an action plan has one or more specific, immediate objectives that are identified as outcomes that action should generate.

Functional Tactics

Within the general framework created by the business's generic and grand strategies, each business function needs to identify and undertake activities unique to the function that help build a sustainable competitive advantage. Managers in each business function develop tactics that delineate the functional activities undertaken in their part of the business and usually include them as a core part of their action plan. *Functional tactics* are detailed statements of the "means" or activities that will be used to achieve short-term objectives and establish competitive advantage.

Policies That Empower Action

Speed is a critical necessity for success in today's competitive, global marketplace. One way to enhance speed and responsiveness is to force/allow decisions to be made whenever possible at the lowest level in organizations. *Policies* are broad, precedent-setting decisions that guide or substitute for repetitive or time-sensitive managerial decision making. Creating policies that guide and "preauthorize" the thinking, decisions, and actions of operating managers and their subordinates in implementing the business's strategy is essential for establishing and controlling the ongoing operating process of the firm in a manner consistent with the firm's strategic objectives. Policies often increase managerial effectiveness by standardizing routine decisions and empowering or expanding the discretion of managers and subordinates in implementing business strategies.

The following are examples of the nature and diversity of company policies:

A requirement that managers have purchase requests for items costing more than $5,000 cosigned by the controller.

The minimum equity position required for all new McDonald's franchises.

The standard formula used to calculate return on investment for the 43 strategic business units of General Electric.

A decision that Sears service and repair employees have the right to waive repair charges to appliance customers they feel have been poorly served by their Sears appliance.

Restructuring, Reengineering, and Refocusing the Organization

Until this point in the strategic management process, managers have maintained a decidedly market-oriented focus as they formulate strategies and begin implementation through action plans and functional tactics. Now the process takes an internal focus—getting the work of the business done efficiently and effectively so as to make the strategy successful. What is the best way to organize ourselves to accomplish the mission? Where should leadership come from? What values should guide our daily activities—what should the organization and its people be like? How can we shape rewards to encourage appropriate action? The intense competition in the global marketplace has made this tradition "internally focused" set of questions—how the activities within their business are conducted—recast themselves with unprecedented attentiveness to the marketplace. *Downsizing, restructuring,* and *reengineering* are terms that reflect the critical stage in strategy implementation wherein managers attempt to recast their organization. The company's structure, leadership, culture, and reward systems may all be changed to ensure cost competitiveness and quality demanded by unique requirements of its strategies.

Strategic Control and Continuous Improvement

Strategic control is concerned with tracking a strategy as it is being implemented, detecting problems or changes in its underlying premises, and making necessary adjustments. In contrast to postaction control, strategic control seeks to guide action on behalf of the generic and grand strategies as they are taking place and when the end results are still several years away. The rapid, accelerating change of the global marketplace of the last 10 years has made continuous improvement another aspect of strategic control in many organizations. *Continuous improvement* provides a way for managers to provide a form of strategic control that allows their organization to respond more proactively and timely to rapid developments in hundreds of areas that influence a business's success.

An early entrant, Yahoo emerged as an Internet giant. Yet, despite the success of its product, the management team never developed a strategy to ensure sustainable growth. Ignoring both threats from the AOL–Time Warner merger and opportunities in a merger with eBay, Yahoo misjudged its strategic environment. Even after Yahoo's revenues had significantly decreased, it did not shift its strategy to be less reliant on online advertising. As you will read in Exhibit 1–6, E-commerce Strategy in Action, Yahoo's e-commerce strategy was significantly undermined by its management's failure to see fundamental shifts in its industry.

Strategic Management as a Process

A *process* is the flow of information through interrelated stages of analysis toward the achievement of an aim. Thus, the strategic management model in Exhibit 1–5 depicts a process. In the strategic management process, the flow of information involves historical, current, and forecast data on the operations and environment of the business. Managers evaluate these data in light of the values and priorities of influential individuals and groups—often called *stakeholders*—that are vitally interested in the actions of the business. The interrelated stages of the process are the 11 components discussed in the previous section. Finally, the aim of the process is the formulation and implementation of strategies that work, achieving the company's long-term mission and near-term objectives.

Viewing strategic management as a process has several important implications. First, a change in any component will affect several or all of the other components. Most of the arrows in the model point two ways, suggesting that the flow of information usually is reciprocal. For example, forces in the external environment may influence the nature of a company's mission, and the company may in turn affect the external environment and

E-commerce Strategy in Action

Inside Yahoo!

Exhibit 1–6

BusinessWeek The first sign that the game had changed for Yahoo! Inc. (YHOO) came just days after its stock hit an all-time high—of $237.50. An investment banker had a juicy tip that chief rival America Online Inc. (AOL) was about to buy old-media giant Time Warner Inc. The move would rearrange the planets in the media universe—and rock Yahoo's world.

The next morning, CEO Timothy A. Koogle, President Jeffrey Mallett, and co-founder Jerry Yang held a council of war at the company's Santa Clara (Calif.) headquarters. Should Yahoo stick to its guns and remain an independent assembler of news and entertainment supplied by others? Or should it take advantage of its $110 billion market cap to make an old-media purchase of its own? They would not follow AOL's lead. All of Yahoo's chips would remain on the Net.

It was Yahoo's first big mistake. Over the next 13 months, Yahoo's management troika would commit a series of blunders that would downgrade the No. 1 Internet portal from powerhouse to Milquetoast. Corner-office intrigue, consensus management in gridlock, a souring economy, and plain old bad judgment would conspire to send Yahoo's revenues plummeting.

Yahoo's problems couldn't be fixed by a little cost-snipping and an upsurge in the economy. Its reliance on advertising revenues turned into a liability as dot-com advertisers die off like mayflies and corporate advertisers pony up 50% less for online ads than they did a year ago. Meanwhile, AOL Time Warner boasts a $221 billion market cap and controls a vast empire of online properties, maga-zines, movie studios, and book publishers. Its advertising and commerce revenues rose 10% last quarter.

Yahoo got a second chance to alter its fate. Again, it blew it. Seeking to beef up its e-commerce revenues, Yahoo began negotiating to buy Web auction leader eBay Inc. in late March 2000. But as acquisition talks heated up, so did Yahoo's internal politics. Koogle wanted the deal. But Mallett was concerned about having eBay CEO Margaret C. Whitman in Yahoo's executive lineup. Koogle and Mallett also differed on the strategic importance of the deal. "Tim could see the wisdom of challenging the Yahoo culture through a deal with eBay. Others were more threatened." With Koogle outnumbered, the potential deal unraveled. "This was Yahoo's most fundamental problem. It was always management by persuasion, not management by dictation," says former manager Rich Rygg. And Yahoo paid for it. Yahoo's fortunes flagged. If the merger had gone through, Yahoo would not have to rely on advertising for 90% of its revenues.

Yahoo's take-the-money-and-run style, along with its dearth of media veterans, prevented it from spotting fundamental changes in the Net advertising market. Together, Koogle and Mallett will be remembered as the management duo that built Yahoo into one of the mightiest Internet companies. But the bad mix of Koogle's disengagement and Mallett's headstrong ways kept them from anticipating vital adjustments, and this left the company vulnerable when Yahoo's world began to spin out of control.

Source: Excerpted form Ben Elgin, "Inside Yahoo!," *BusinessWeek*, May 21, 2001.

heighten competition in its realm of operation. A specific example is a power company that is persuaded, in part by governmental incentives, to include a commitment to the development of energy alternatives in its mission statement. The company then might promise to extend its R&D efforts in the area of coal liquefaction. The external environment has affected the company's mission, and the revised mission signals a competitive condition in the environment.

A second implication of viewing strategic management as a process is that strategy formulation and implementation are sequential. The process begins with development or reevaluation of the company mission. This step is associated with, but essentially followed by, development of a company profile and assessment of the external environment. Then follow, in order, strategic choice, definition of long-term objectives, design of the grand strategy, definition of short-term objectives, design of operating strategies, institutionalization of the strategy, and review and evaluation.

The apparent rigidity of the process, however, must be qualified.

First, a firm's strategic posture may have to be reevaluated in response to changes in any of the principal factors that determine or affect its performance. Entry by a major new competitor, the death of a prominent board member, replacement of the chief executive officer, and a downturn in market responsiveness are among the thousands of changes that can prompt reassessment of a firm's strategic plan. However, no matter where the need for a reassessment originates, the strategic management process begins with the mission statement.

Second, not every component of the strategic management process deserves equal attention each time planning activity takes place. Firms in an extremely stable environment may find that an in-depth assessment is not required every five years. Companies often are satisfied with their original mission statements even after a decade of operation and spend only a minimal amount of time addressing this subject. In addition, while formal strategic planning may be undertaken only every five years, objectives and strategies usually are updated each year, and rigorous reassessment of the initial stages of strategic planning rarely is undertaken at these times.

A third implication of viewing strategic management as a process is the necessity of feedback from institutionalization, review, and evaluation to the early stages of the process. *Feedback* can be defined as the collection of postimplementation results to enhance future decision making. Therefore, as indicated in Exhibit 1–5, strategic managers should assess the impact of implemented strategies on external environments. Thus, future planning can reflect any changes precipitated by strategic actions. Strategic managers also should analyze the impact of strategies on the possible need for modifications in the company mission.

A fourth implication of viewing strategic management as a process is the need to regard it as a dynamic system. The term *dynamic* characterizes the constantly changing conditions that affect interrelated and interdependent strategic activities. Managers should recognize that the components of the strategic process are constantly evolving but that formal planning artificially freezes those components, much as an action photograph freezes the movement of a swimmer. Since change is continuous, the dynamic strategic planning process must be monitored constantly for significant shifts in any of its components as a precaution against implementing an obsolete strategy.

Changes in the Process

The strategic management process undergoes continual assessment and subtle updating. Although the elements of the basic strategic management model rarely change, the relative emphasis that each element receives will vary with the decision makers who use the model and with the environments of their companies.

A recent study describes general trends in strategic management, summarizing the responses of over 200 corporate executives. This update shows there has been an increasing companywide emphasis on and appreciation for the value of strategic management activities. It also provides evidence that practicing managers have given increasing attention to the need for frequent and widespread involvement in the formulation and implementation phases of the strategic management process. Finally, it indicates that, as managers and their firms gain knowledge, experience, skill, and understanding in how to design and manage their planning activities, they become better able to avoid the potential negative consequences of instituting a vigorous strategic management process.

Summary

Strategic management is the set of decisions and actions that result in the formulation and implementation of plans designed to achieve a company's objectives. Because it involves long-term, future-oriented, complex decision making and requires considerable resources, top-management participation is essential.

Strategic management is a three-tier process involving corporate-, business-, and functional-level planners, and support personnel. At each progressively lower level, strategic activities were shown to be more specific, narrow, short term, and action oriented, with lower risks but fewer opportunities for dramatic impact.

The strategic management model presented in this chapter will serve as the structure for understanding and integrating all the major phases of strategy formulation and implementation. The chapter provided a summary account of these phases, each of which is given extensive individual attention in subsequent chapters.

The chapter stressed that the strategic management process centers on the belief that a firm's mission can be best achieved through a systematic and comprehensive assessment of both its internal capabilities and its external environment. Subsequent evaluation of the firm's opportunities leads, in turn, to the choice of long-term objectives and grand strategies and, ultimately, to annual objectives and operating strategies, which must be implemented, monitored, and controlled.

Questions for Discussion

1. Find a recent copy of *BusinessWeek* and read the "Corporate Strategies" section. Was the main decision discussed strategic? At what level in the organization was the key decision made?

2. In what ways do you think the subject matter in this strategic management–business policy course will differ from that of previous courses you have taken?

3. After graduation, you are not likely to move directly to a top-level management position. In fact, few members of your class will ever reach the top-management level. Why, then, is it important for all business majors to study the field of strategic management?

4. Do you expect outstanding performance in this course to require a great deal of memorization? Why or why not?

5. You undoubtedly have read about individuals who seemingly have given singled-handed direction to their corporations. Is a participative strategic management approach likely to stifle or suppress the contributions of such individuals?

6. Think about the courses you have taken in functional areas, such as marketing, finance, production, personnel, and accounting. What is the importance of each of these areas to the strategic planning process?

7. Discuss with practicing business managers the strategic management models used in their firms. What are the similarities and differences between these models and the one in the text?

8. In what ways do you believe the strategic planning approach of not-for-profit organizations would differ from that of profit-oriented organizations?

9. How do you explain the success of firms that do not use a formal strategic planning process?

10. Think about your postgraduation job search as a strategic decision. How would the strategic management model be helpful to you in identifying and securing the most promising position?

Chapter 1 Discussion Case

BusinessWeek

Kraft's Global Strategy: Can Kraft Be a Big Cheese Abroad?

1 When Aussies stroll down the aisles of their local supermarket, what catches their eyes are snacks from Unilever (UL) and Nestlé (NSRGY). Kraft Macaroni & Cheese and Oscar Mayer hot dogs, on the other hand, are hard to find and far from first choice. "They would be classified as a slow-moving line," says Terry Walters, the owner of an IGA store in Cairns, Queensland, about the classic American macaroni-and-cheese dinner. As for hot dogs: "We have the meat pie."

2 Kraft may be ubiquitous in U.S. grocery stores, but overseas it's a far different picture. Kraft isn't one of Walters' top five food suppliers, ranking below even H.J. Heinz Co. (HNZ), despite its ownership of Australia's famed Vegemite spread. Only 27% of its total revenues come from overseas, vs. 44% for Heinz, more than 50% for McDonald's Corp. (MCD), and more than 80% for Coca-Cola Co. (KO)

3 That will have to change. As Kraft embarks on a giant initial public offering, expected in mid-June, its challenge is to once again become a growth company. Widely admired for the astute management of its brand lineup, Kraft's nevertheless stuck in a slow-growth industry in the United States. Smart marketing and methodical cost cutting helped it boost earnings 14.1% last year, but Kraft's sales actually dipped slightly, to $26.53 billion. In fact, Kraft's annual sales have dropped 16.2% since 1994. The company took a big step toward building revenues in December with its $19.2 billion purchase of Nabisco Group Holdings Corp. (NGH-U), whose cookie and cracker brands are growing faster than Kraft's top brands.

4 That deal should boost Kraft's sales to an expected $35.05 billion this year. But analysts say that if Kraft is to spark long-term growth, it must do a better job of tapping foreign consumers. Kraft acknowledged as much when it announced that once the IPO is completed, Betsy D. Holden, CEO of Kraft Foods North America, would share the chief executive office with Roger K. Deromedi, a 13-year Kraft veteran who has been president and CEO of Kraft Foods International Inc. for the past two years. The company declined to comment or make top executives available to *BusinessWeek,* citing the quiet period before the IPO, as did parent Philip Morris Cos. (MO).

5 AMERICAN ICONS. The largest food company in North America by far, Kraft has dominated U.S. grocery-store shelves for decades. Its powerhouse brands are American icons: Philadelphia Cream Cheese, Oreo cookies, Tang, Jell-O, Kool-Aid, Life Savers, Planters peanuts, Lunchables prepackaged meals for kids. Its portfolio comprises a remarkable 61 brands with more than $100 million in sales last year. Supermarket consultants say it would be nearly impossible to run a U.S. grocery store without its products.

6 But these aren't the best of times, even for strong supermarket brands. Shopper loyalty has waned as the grocery chains' in-house brands compete for shelf space, and big brands such as Kraft's tend to be mature. Take salad dressing. Even though Kraft is the market leader, "there's Kraft, there's Wish-Bone, there's Hellmann's," says John P. Mahar, operations director at the Green Hills Farms supermarket in Syracuse, N.Y. "If we have Wish-Bone on sale, shoppers pick up Wish-Bone. They don't care. The majority of Kraft's brands are just another commodity."

7 TOBACCO TAINT. Boosting sales will become even more urgent once Kraft has outside shareholders to answer to. Cigarette maker Philip Morris, which has owned Kraft since 1988, is putting 16.1% of the company on the market in an offering that could raise as much as $8.4 billion. That would be the second-largest IPO on record, behind only AT&T Wireless Group's $10.5 billion stock market debut last year. Philip Morris will remain firmly in control, but its goal is to realize more of Kraft's value by distancing the business from the tobacco taint that has held Philip Morris' stock price down.

8 The first concern for investors might be whether Kraft's co-CEO structure can work. Deromedi, 47, and Holden, 45, who started at Kraft as an assistant product manager in 1982, will both report to Geoffrey Bible, chairman of Philip Morris. Analysts wonder how long the arrangement will last, citing a long list of prominent companies, from

DaimlerChrysler to Citigroup, where co-CEO setups fizzled. "The co-CEO structure calls into question if this is truly an independent company," says Goldman, Sachs & Co. analyst Romitha S. Mally. "At the end of the day, it will be the chairman and the board, which is controlled by Philip Morris, who will be the ultimate decision makers for Kraft."

9   In this case, though, the co-CEOs have well-defined management areas. Another plus: Their personalities seem to complement each other. James J. Drury, vice-chairman of Spencer Stuart, an executive-search firm in Chicago, describes Deromedi, who holds a math degree, as "more focused on problem solving and more likely to make tough decisions in complex situations." Holden, he says, is creative, charismatic, and more people-oriented: "She's more the one to take into consideration how a business situation may impact people."

10   A top task for the new CEOs will be figuring out how to expand outside North America. Overseas, Kraft faces a lineup of tough global competitors—Unilever, Nestlé, Groupe Danone—that were quicker to break into fast-growing markets in Asia, Latin America, and Eastern Europe. Unilever and Nestlé, for example, each get 32% of their sales in developing countries. Western Europe, Kraft's strongest international market, is almost as saturated as the United States. Even in Great Britain, Kraft is only the eighth-largest food company. "A truly global organization would have a quarter to one-third of their business in North America, not three-quarters," says Adrian Richardson, global consumer and retail-sector head at BT Funds Management, a large money manager in Sydney.

11   FORTRESS. One problem is that Kraft's strength, convenience products, doesn't go over well in emerging markets, where scarce shopping dollars are concentrated on necessities. Unilever, for example, sells staples in India such as rice with added protein and salt with iodine. Kraft, on the other hand, has only a tiny presence there. But Kraft plans to jump-start sales in emerging markets by introducing additional snack, beverage, cheese, and other brands in countries where it already has a presence. It also plans to enter countries where it has no operations and to make acquisitions, especially in snacks and beverages, according to its filings with the Securities & Exchange Commission.

Richardson believes Kraft could make up to three significant acquisitions in the next few years to beef up its offshore operations: "If they just build, build, build [new plants], they won't meaningfully move the dial," he says. For Kraft, "the U.S. domestic base is an absolute fortress that provides a very good cash cow" with which to go shopping. "They're not too late."

12   Close to home, Kraft is getting a much-needed shot of adrenaline from the Nabisco purchase. Last year, Kraft's sales dipped 1%, vs. gains of 7.3% at General Mills Inc. (GIS) and 6.3% at Hershey Foods Corp. (HSY) Many older Kraft products are in aging categories with flat or declining volumes, such as cereal and traditional store-bought coffee. But with Nabisco, Kraft picked up faster-growing product lines such as Chips Ahoy! cookies and Ritz crackers that will fuel earnings growth. Overnight, Kraft moved from a 6% to a 20% market share in crackers and cookies, a category that's expanding at more than twice the rate of the food-industry average. Goldman's Mally expects Kraft sales to rise 3.5% in each of the next three years, just ahead of the industry average. And with the cost savings it expects to squeeze from Nabisco, Kraft estimates that its earnings will grow at an above-average 18% to 22% annually over the same period.

13   That additional growth will be needed to cover the cost of the Nabisco deal. The newly public Kraft will carry an $18.5 billion debt load, even after using the offering proceeds to pay off a portion of the $11 billion it borrowed through Philip Morris to buy Nabisco. Next year, $7 billion of this debt comes due, and Kraft won't be able to meet that payment, according to its prospectus. But it says it plans to use its good credit rating to refinance.

14   Kraft has long been a leader in product development—in 1989 it launched the novel Lunchables line that's now a $750 million-a-year product. Innovations like that put Kraft on top of the U.S. food industry. Now investors will be counting on Deromedi and Holden to sprinkle some of that magic overseas.

Source: Julie Forster and Becky Gaylord, "Can Kraft Be a Big Cheese Abroad? It needs more global clout to offset a mature U.S. market," *BusinessWeek,* June 4, 2001.

Part **Two**

Strategy Formulation

Strategy formulation guides executives in defining the business their firm is in, the ends it seeks, and the means it will use to accomplish those ends. The approach of strategy formulation is an improvement over that of traditional long-range planning. As discussed in the next eight chapters—about developing a firm's competitive plan of action—strategy formulation combines a future-oriented perspective with concern for the firm's internal and external environments.

The strategy formulation process begins with definition of the company mission, as discussed in Chapter 2. In that chapter, the purpose of business is defined to reflect the values of a wide variety of interested parties. Social responsibility is discussed as a critical consideration for a company's strategic decision makers since the mission statement must express how the company intends to contribute to the societies that sustain it.

Chapter 3 deals with the principal factors in a firm's external environment that strategic managers must assess so they can anticipate and take advantage of future business conditions. It emphasizes the importance to a firm's planning activities of factors in the firm's remote, industry, and operating environments. A key theme of the chapter is the problem of deciding whether to accept environmental constraints or to maneuver around them.

Chapter 4 describes the key differences in strategic planning and implementation among domestic, multinational, and global firms. It gives special attention to the new vision that a firm must communicate in a revised company mission when it multinationalizes.

Chapter 5 shows how firms evaluate their company's strengths and weaknesses to produce an internal analysis. Strategic managers use such profiles to target competitive advantages they can emphasize and competitive disadvantages they should correct or minimize.

Chapter 6 examines the types of long-range objectives strategic managers set and specifies the qualities these objectives must have to provide a basis for direction and evaluation. The chapter also examines the generic and grand strategies that firms use to achieve long-range objectives.

Comprehensive approaches to the evaluation of strategic opportunities and to the final strategic decision are the focus of Chapter 7. The chapter shows how a firm's strategic options can be compared in a way that allows selection of the best available option. It also discusses how a company can create competitive advantages for each of its businesses.

Chapter 8 extends the attention on strategic analysis and choice by showing how managers can build value in multibusiness companies.

Chapter **Two**

Defining the Company's Mission and Social Responsibility

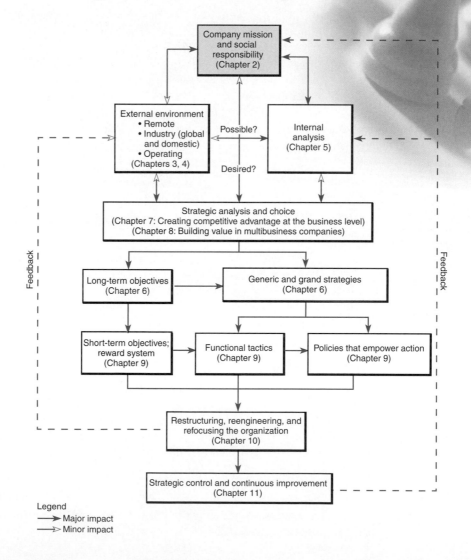

Company mission and social responsibility
(Chapter 2)

External environment
• Remote
• Industry (global and domestic)
• Operating
(Chapters 3, 4)

Possible?

Internal analysis
(Chapter 5)

Desired?

Strategic analysis and choice
(Chapter 7: Creating competitive advantage at the business level)
(Chapter 8: Building value in multibusiness companies)

Long-term objectives
(Chapter 6)

Generic and grand strategies
(Chapter 6)

Short-term objectives; reward system
(Chapter 9)

Functional tactics
(Chapter 9)

Policies that empower action
(Chapter 9)

Restructuring, reengineering, and refocusing the organization
(Chapter 10)

Strategic control and continuous improvement
(Chapter 11)

Feedback

Feedback

Legend
→ Major impact
⇢ Minor impact

WHAT IS A COMPANY MISSION?

Whether a firm is developing a new business or reformulating direction for an ongoing business, it must determine the basic goals and philosophies that will shape its strategic posture. This fundamental purpose that sets a firm apart from other firms of its type and identifies the scope of its operations in product and market terms is defined as the company mission. As discussed in Chapter 1, the company mission is a broadly framed but enduring statement of a firm's intent. It embodies the business philosophy of the firm's strategic decision makers, implies the image the firm seeks to project, reflects the firm's self-concept, and indicates the firm's principal product or service areas and the primary customer needs the firm will attempt to satisfy. In short, it describes the firm's product, market, and technological areas of emphasis, and it does so in a way that reflects the values and priorities of the firm's strategic decision makers. An excellent example is the company mission statement of Nicor, Inc., shown in Exhibit 2–1, Strategy in Action.

The Need for an Explicit Mission

No external body requires that the company mission be defined, and the process of defining it is time-consuming and tedious. Moreover, it contains broadly outlined or implied objectives and strategies rather than specific directives. Characteristically, it is a statement, not of measurable targets but of attitude, outlook, and orientation.

The mission statement is a message designed to be inclusive of the expectations of all stakeholders for the company's performance over the long run. The executives and board who prepare the mission statement attempt to provide a unifying purpose for the company that will provide a basis for strategic objective setting and decision making. In general terms, the mission statement addresses the following questions:

Why is this firm in business?

What are our economic goals?

What is our operating philosophy in terms of quality, company image, and self-concept?

What are our core competencies and competitive advantages?

What customers do and can we serve?

How do we view our responsibilities to stockholders, employees, communities, environment, social issues, and competitors?

FORMULATING A MISSION

The process of defining the company mission for a specific business can perhaps be best understood by thinking about the business at its inception. The typical business begins with the beliefs, desires, and aspirations of a single entrepreneur. Such an owner-manager's sense of mission usually is based on the following fundamental beliefs:

1. The product or service of the business can provide benefits at least equal to its price.

2. The product or service can satisfy a customer need of specific market segments that is currently not being met adequately.

PREAMBLE

We, the management of Nicor, Inc., here set forth our belief as to the purpose for which the company is established and the principles under which it should operate. We pledge our effort to the accomplishment of these purposes within these principles.

BASIC PURPOSE

The basic purpose of Nicor, Inc., is to perpetuate an investor-owned company engaging in various phases of the energy business, striving for balance among those phases so as to render needed satisfactory products and services and earn optimum, long-range profits.

WHAT WE DO

The principal business of the company, through its utility subsidiary, is the provision of energy through a pipe system to meet the needs of ultimate consumers. To accomplish its basic purpose, and to ensure its strength, the company will engage in other energy-related activities, directly or through subsidiaries or in participation with other persons, corporations, firms, or entities.

All activities of the company shall be consistent with its responsibilities to investors, customers, employees, and the public and its concern for the optimum development and utilization of natural resources and for environmental needs.

WHERE WE DO IT

The company's operations shall be primarily in the United States, but no self-imposed or regulatory geographical limitations are placed upon the acquisition, development, processing, transportation, or storage of energy resources, or upon other energy-related ventures in which the company may engage. The company will engage in such activities in any location where, after careful review, it has determined that such activity is in the best interest of its stockholders.

Utility service will be offered in the territory of the company's utility subsidiary to the best of its ability, in accordance with the requirements of regulatory agencies and pursuant to the subsidiary's purposes and principles.

3. The technology that is to be used in production will provide a cost- and quality-competitive product or service.

4. With hard work and the support of others, the business can not only survive but also grow and be profitable.

5. The management philosophy of the business will result in a favorable public image and will provide financial and psychological rewards for those who are willing to invest their labor and money in helping the business to succeed.

6. The entrepreneur's self-concept of the business can be communicated to and adopted by employees and stockholders.

As the business grows or is forced by competitive pressures to alter its product—market—technology, redefining the company mission may be necessary. If so, the revised mission statement will contain the same components as the original. It will state the basic type of product or service to be offered, the primary markets or customer groups to be served, and the technology to be used in production or delivery; the firm's fundamental concern for survival through growth and profitability; the firm's managerial philosophy; the public image the firm seeks; and the self-concept those affiliated with the firm should have of it. This chapter will discuss in detail these components. The examples shown in Exhibit 2–2 provide insights into how some major corporations handle them.

Basic Product or Service; Primary Market; Principal Technology

Three indispensable components of the mission statement are specification of the basic product or service, specification of the primary market, and specification of the principal technology for production or delivery. These components are discussed under one

1. Customer-market	We believe our first responsibility is to the doctors, nurses, and patients, to mothers and all others who use our products and services. (Johnson & Johnson)
	To anticipate and meet market needs of farmers, ranchers, and rural communities within North America. (CENEX)
2. Product-service	AMAX's principal products are molybdenum, coal, iron ore, copper, lead, zinc, petroleum and natural gas, potash, phosphates, nickel, tungsten, silver, gold, and magnesium. (AMAX)
3. Geographic domain	We are dedicated to total success of Corning Glass Works as a worldwide competitor. (Corning Glass)
4. Technology	Control Data is in the business of applying microelectronics and computer technology in two general areas: computer-related hardware and computing-enhancing services, which include computation, information, education, and finance. (Control Data)
	The common technology in these areas relates to discrete particle coatings. (NASHUA)
5. Concern for survival	In this respect, the company will conduct its operation prudently, and will provide the profits and growth which will assure Hoover's ultimate success. (Hoover Universal)
6. Philosophy	We are committed to improve health care throughout the world. (Baxter Travenol)
	We believe human development to be the worthiest of the goals of civilization and independence to be the superior condition for nurturing growth in the capabilities of people. (Sun Company)
7. Self-concept	Hoover Universal is a diversified, multi-industry corporation with strong manufacturing capabilities, entrepreneurial policies, and individual business unit autonomy. (Hoover Universal)
8. Concern for public image	We are responsible to the communities in which we live and work and to the world community as well (Johnson & Johnson)
	Also, we must be responsive to the broader concerns of the public, including especially the general desire for improvement in the quality of life, equal opportunity for all, and the constructive use of natural resources. (Sun Company)

heading because only in combination do they describe the company's business activity. A good example of the three components is to be found in the business plan of ITT Barton, a division of ITT. Under the heading of business mission and area served, the following information is presented:

> The unit's mission is to serve industry and government with quality instruments used for the primary measurement, analysis, and local control of fluid flow, level, pressure, temperature, and fluid properties. This instrumentation includes flow meters, electronic readouts, indicators, recorders, switches, liquid level systems, analytical instruments such as titrators, integrators, controllers, transmitters, and various instruments for the measurement of fluid properties (density, viscosity, gravity) used for processing variable sensing, data collecting, control, and transmission. The unit's mission includes fundamental loop-closing control and display devices, when economically justified, but excludes broadline central control room instrumentation, systems design, and turnkey responsibility.
>
> Markets served include instrumentation for oil and gas production, gas transportation, chemical and petrochemical processing, cryogenics, power generation, aerospace, government, and marine, as well as other instrument and equipment manufacturers.

In only 129 words, this segment of the mission statement clearly indicates to all readers—from company employees to casual observers—the basic products, primary markets, and principal technologies of ITT Barton.

Often the most referenced public statement of a company's selected products and markets appears in "silver bullet" form in the mission statement; for example, "Dayton-Hudson Corporation is a diversified retailing company whose business is to serve the American consumer through the retailing of fashion-oriented quality merchandise." Such an abstract of company direction is particularly helpful to outsiders who value condensed overviews.

Company Goals: Survival, Growth, Profitability

Three economic goals guide the strategic direction of almost every business organization. Whether or not the mission statement explicitly states these goals, it reflects the firm's intention to secure *survival* through *growth* and *profitability.*

A firm that is unable to survive will be incapable of satisfying the aims of any of its stakeholders. Unfortunately, the goal of survival, like the goals of growth and profitability, often is taken for granted to such an extent that it is neglected as a principal criterion in strategic decision making. When this happens, the firm may focus on short-term aims at the expense of the long run. Concerns for expediency, a quick fix, or a bargain may displace the assessment of long-term impact. Too often, the result is near-term economic failure owing to a lack of resource synergy and sound business practice. For example, Consolidated Foods, maker of Shasta soft drinks and L'eggs hosiery, sought growth through the acquisition of bargain businesses. However, the erratic sales patterns of its diverse holdings forced it to divest itself of more than four dozen companies. This process cost Consolidated Foods millions of dollars and hampered its growth.

Profitability is the mainstay goal of a business organization. No matter how profit is measured or defined, profit over the long term is the clearest indication of a firm's ability to satisfy the principal claims and desires of employees and stockholders. The key phrase here is "over the long term." Obviously, basing decisions on a short-term concern for profitability would lead to a strategic myopia. Overlooking the enduring concerns of customers, suppliers, creditors, ecologists, and regulatory agents may produce profit in the short term, but, over time, the financial consequences are likely to be detrimental.

The following excerpt from the Hewlett-Packard statement of mission ably expresses the importance of an orientation toward long-term profit:

> To achieve sufficient profit to finance our company growth and to provide the resources we need to achieve our other corporate objectives.
>
> In our economic system, the profit we generate from our operation is the ultimate source of the funds we need to prosper and grow. It is the one absolutely essential measure of our corporate performance over the long term. Only if we continue to meet our profit objective can we achieve our other corporate objectives.

A firm's growth is tied inextricably to its survival and profitability. In this context, the meaning of growth must be broadly defined. Although the product impact market studies (PIMS) have shown that growth in market share is correlated with profitability, other important forms of growth do exist. Growth in the number of markets served, in the variety of products offered, and in the technologies that are used to provide goods or services frequently lead to improvements in a firm's competitive ability. Growth means change, and proactive change is essential in a dynamic business environment.

Hewlett-Packard's mission statement provides an excellent example of corporate regard for growth:

Objective: To let our growth be limited only by our profits and our ability to develop and produce technical products that satisfy real customer needs.

We do not believe that large size is important for its own sake; however, for at least two basic reasons, continuous growth is essential for us to achieve our other objectives.

In the first place, we serve a rapidly growing and expanding segment of our technological society. To remain static would be to lose ground. We cannot maintain a position of strength and leadership in our field without growth.

In the second place, growth is important in order to attract and hold high-caliber people. These individuals will align their future only with a company that offers them considerable opportunity for personal progress. Opportunities are greater and more challenging in a growing company.

The issue of growth raises a concern about the definition of the company mission. How can a firm's product, market, and technology be specified sufficiently to provide direction without precluding the exercise of unanticipated strategic options? How can a firm so define its mission that it can consider opportunistic diversification while maintaining the parameters that guide its growth decision? Perhaps such questions are best addressed when a firm's mission statement outlines the conditions under which the firm might depart from ongoing operations. General Electric Company's extensive global mission provided the foundation for its GE Appliances (GEA) in Louisville, Kentucky. GEA did not see consumer preferences in the world market becoming Americanized. Instead, its expansion goals allowed for flexibility in examining the unique characteristics of individual foreign markets and tailoring strategies to fit them.

The growth philosophy of Dayton-Hudson also embodies this approach:

The stability and quality of the corporation's financial performance will be developed through the profitable execution of our existing businesses, as well as through the acquisition or development of new businesses. Our growth priorities, in order, are as follows:

1. Development of the profitable market preeminence of existing companies in existing markets through new store development or new strategies within existing stores.
2. Expansion of our companies to feasible new markets.
3. Acquisition of other retailing companies that are strategically and financially compatible with Dayton-Hudson.
4. Internal development of new retailing strategies.

Capital allocations to fund the expansion of existing Dayton-Hudson operating companies will be based on each company's return on investment (ROI), in relationship to its ROI objective and its consistency in earnings growth and on the ability of its management to perform up to the forecasts contained in its capital requests. Expansion via acquisition or new venture will occur when the opportunity promises an acceptable rate of long-term growth and profitability, an acceptable degree of risk, and compatibility with Dayton-Hudson's long-term strategy.

Company Philosophy

The statement of a company's philosophy, often called the *company creed,* usually accompanies or appears within the mission statement. It reflects or specifies the basic beliefs, values, aspirations, and philosophical priorities to which strategic decision makers are committed in managing the company. Fortunately, the philosophies vary little from one firm to another. Owners and managers implicitly accept a general, unwritten, yet pervasive code of behavior that governs business actions and permits them to be largely self-regulated. Unfortunately, statements of company philosophy are often so similar and so platitudinous that they read more like public relations handouts than the commitment to values they are meant to be.

We, the Saturn Team, in concert with the UAW and General Motors, believe that meeting the needs of customers, Saturn members, suppliers, dealers, and neighbors is fundamental to fulfilling our mission.

To meet our customer's needs . . .

- our products and services must be world leaders in value and satisfaction.

To meet our members' needs, we . . .

- will create a sense of belonging in an environment of mutual trust, respect, and dignity;

- believe that all people want to be involved in decisions that affect them, care about their jobs and each other, take pride in themselves and in their contributions, and want to share in the success of their efforts;

- will develop the tools, training, and education for each member, recognizing individual skills and knowledge;

- believe that creative, motivated, responsible team members who understand that change is critical to success are Saturn's most important asset.

To meet our suppliers' and dealers' needs, we . . .

- will strive to create real partnerships with them;

- will be open and fair in our dealings, reflecting trust, respect, and their importance to Saturn;

- want dealers and suppliers to feel ownerships in Saturn's mission and philosophy as their own.

To meet the needs of our neighbors, the communities in which we live and operate, we . . .

- will be good citizens, protect the environment, and conserve natural resources;

- will seek to cooperate with government at all levels and strive to be sensitive, open, and candid in all our public statements.

Saturn's statement of philosophy, presented in Exhibit 2–3, Strategy in Action, indicates the company's clearly defined initiatives for satisfying the needs of its customers, employees, suppliers, and dealers.

Despite the similarity of these statements, the intentions of the strategic managers in developing them do not warrant cynicism. Company executives attempt to provide a distinctive and accurate picture of the firm's managerial outlook. One such statement of company philosophy is that of Dayton-Hudson Corporation. As Exhibit 2–4, Strategy in Action, shows, Dayton-Hudson's board of directors and executives have established especially clear directions for company decision making and action.

Perhaps most noteworthy in the Dayton-Hudson statement is its delineation of responsibility at both the corporate and business levels. In many ways, the statement could serve as a prototype for the three-tier approach to strategic management. This approach implies that the mission statement must address strategic concerns at the corporate, business, and functional levels of the organization. Dayton-Hudson's management philosophy does this by balancing operating autonomy and flexibility on the one hand with corporate input and direction on the other.

As seen in Exhibit 2–5, Global Strategy in Action, the philosophy of Nissan Motor Manufacturing is expressed by the company's People Principles and Key Corporate Principles. These principles form the basis of the way the company operates on a daily basis. They address the principal concepts used in meeting the company's established goals. Nissan focuses on the distinction between the role of the individual and the corporation. In this way, employees can link their productivity and success to the productivity and success of the company. Given these principles, the company is able to concentrate on the issues most important to its survival, growth, and profitability.

Strategy in Action Exhibit 2–6 provides an example of how General Motors uses a statement of company philosophy to clarify its environmental principles.

The corporation will:

Set standards for return on investment (ROI) and earnings growth.

Approve strategic plans.

Allocate capital.

Approve goals.

Monitor, measure, and audit results.

Reward performance.

Allocate management resources.

The operating companies will be accorded the freedom and responsibility:

To manage their own business.

To develop strategic plans and goals that will optimize their growth.

To develop an organization that can ensure consistency of results and optimum growth.

To operate their businesses consistent with the corporation's statement of philosophy.

The corporate staff will provide only those services that are:

Essential to the protection of the corporation.

Needed for the growth of the corporation.

Wanted by operating companies and that provide a significant advantage in quality or cost.

The corporation will insist on:

Uniform accounting practices by type of business.

Prompt disclosure of operating results.

A systematic approach to training and developing people.

Adherence to appropriately high standards of business conduct and civic responsibility in accordance with the corporation's statement of philosophy.

Public Image

Both present and potential customers attribute certain qualities to particular businesses. Gerber and Johnson & Johnson make safe products; Cross Pen makes high-quality writing instruments; Étienne Aigner makes stylish but affordable leather products; Corvettes are power machines; and Izod Lacoste stands for the preppy look. Thus, mission statements should reflect the public's expectations, since this makes achievement of the firm's goals more likely. Gerber's mission statement should not open the possibility for diversification into pesticides, and Cross Pen's should not open the possibility for diversification into $0.59 brand-name disposables.

On the other hand, a negative public image often prompts firms to reemphasize the beneficial aspects of their mission. For example, in response to what it saw as a disturbing trend in public opinion, Dow Chemical undertook an aggressive promotional campaign to fortify its credibility, particularly among "employees and those who live and work in [their] plant communities." Dow described its approach in its annual report:

> All around the world today, Dow people are speaking up. People who care deeply about their company, what it stands for, and how it is viewed by others. People who are immensely proud of their company's performance, yet realistic enough to realize it is the public's perception of that performance that counts in the long run.

Firms seldom address the question of their public image in an intermittent fashion. Although public agitation often stimulates greater attention to this question, firms are concerned about their public image even in the absence of such agitation. The following excerpt from the mission statement of Intel Corporation is an example of this attitude:

Global Strategy in Action
Principles of Nissan Motor Manufacturing (UK) Ltd.

Exhibit 2–5

People Principles
(All Other Objectives Can Only Be Achieved by People)

Selection	Hire the highest caliber people; look for technical capabilities and emphasize attitude.
Responsibility	Maximize the responsibility; staff by devolving decision making.
Teamwork	Recognize and encourage individual contributions, with everyone working toward the same objectives.
Flexibility	Expand the role of the individual: multiskilled, no job description, generic job titles.
Kaizen	Continuously seek 100.1 percent improvements; give "ownership of change."
Communications	"Every day, face to face."
Training	Establish individual "continuous development programs."
Supervisors	Regard as "the professionals at managing the production process"; give them much responsibility normally assumed by individual departments; make them the genuine leaders of their teams.
Single status	Treat everyone as a "first class" citizen; eliminate all illogical differences.
Trade unionism	Establish single union agreement with AEU emphasizing the common objective for a successful enterprise.

Key Corporate Principles

Quality	Building profitably the highest quality car sold in Europe.
Customers	Achieve target of no. 1 customer satisfaction in Europe.
Volume	Always achieve required volume.
New products	Deliver on time, at required quality, within cost.
Suppliers	Establish long-term relationship with single-source suppliers; aim for zero defects and just-in-time delivery; apply Nissan principles to suppliers.
Production	Use "most appropriate" technology; develop predictable "best method" of doing job; build in quality.
Engineering	Design "quality" and "ease of working" into the product and facilities; establish "simultaneous engineering" to reduce development time.

We are sensitive to our *image with our customers and the business community.* Commitments to customers are considered sacred, and we are upset with ourselves when we do not meet our commitments. We strive to demonstrate to the business world on a continuing basis that we are credible in describing the state of the corporation, and that we are well organized and in complete control of all things that determine the numbers.

Exhibit 2–7, Strategy in Action, presents a marketing translation of the essence of the mission statements of six high-end shoe companies. The impressive feature of the exhibit is that it shows dramatically how closely competing firms can incorporate subtle, yet meaningful, differences into their mission statements.

Company Self-Concept

A major determinant of a firm's success is the extent to which the firm can relate functionally to its external environment. To achieve its proper place in a competitive situation, the firm realistically must evaluate its competitive strengths and weaknesses. This

As a responsible corporate citizen, General Motors is dedicated to protecting human health, natural resources, and the global environment. This dedication reaches further than compliance with the law to encompass the integration of sound environmental practices into our business decisions.

The following environmental principles provide guidance to General Motors personnel worldwide in the conduct of their daily business practices:

1. We are committed to actions to restore and preserve the environment.

2. We are committed to reducing waste and pollutants, conserving resources, and recycling materials at every stage of the product life cycle.

3. We will continue to participate actively in educating the public regarding environmental conservation.

4. We will continue to pursue vigorously the development and implementation of technologies for minimizing pollutant emissions.

5. We will continue to work with all governmental entities for the development of technically sound and financially responsible environmental laws and regulations.

6. We will continually assess the impact of our plants and products on the environment and the communities in which we live and operate with a goal of continuous improvement.

idea—that the firm must know itself—is the essence of the company self-concept. The idea is not commonly integrated into theories of strategic management; its importance for individuals has been recognized since ancient times.

Both individuals and firms have a crucial need to know themselves. The ability of either to survive in a dynamic and highly competitive environment would be severely limited if they did not understand their impact on others or of others on them.

In some senses, then, firms take on personalities of their own. Much behavior in firms is organizationally based; that is, a firm acts on its members in other ways than their individual interactions. Thus, firms are entities whose personality transcends the personalities of their members. As such, they can set decision-making parameters based on aims different and distinct from the aims of their members. These organizational considerations have pervasive effects.

Ordinarily, descriptions of the company self-concept per se do not appear in mission statements. Yet such statements often provide strong impressions of the company self-concept. For example, ARCO's environment, health, and safety (EHS) managers were adamant about emphasizing the company's position on safety and environmental performance as a part of the mission statement. The challenges facing the ARCO EHS managers included dealing with concerned environmental groups and a public that has become environmentally aware. They hoped to motivate employees toward safer behavior while reducing emissions and waste. They saw this as a reflection of the company's positive self-image.

The following excerpts from the Intel Corporation mission statement describe the corporate persona that its top management seeks to foster:

Management is self-critical. The leaders must be capable of recognizing and accepting their mistakes and learning from them.

Open (constructive) confrontation is encouraged at all levels of the corporation and is viewed as a method of problem solving and conflict resolution.

Decision by consensus is the rule. Decisions once made are supported. Position in the organization is not the basis for quality of ideas.

A highly communicative, open management is part of the style.

Management must be ethical. Managing by telling the truth and treating all employees equitably has established credibility that is ethical.

Allen-Edmonds

Allen-Edmonds provides high-quality shoes for the affluent consumer who appreciates a well-made, finely crafted, stylish dress shoe.

Bally

Bally shoes set you apart. They are the perfect shoe to complement your lifestyle. Bally shoes project an image of European style and elegance that ensures one is not just dressed, but well-dressed.

Bostonian

Bostonian shoes are for those successful individuals who are well-traveled, on the "go" and want a stylish dress shoe that can keep up with their variety of needs and activities. With Bostonian, you know you will always be well dressed whatever the situation.

Cole-Hahn

Cole-Hahn offers a line of contemporary shoes for the man who wants to go his own way. They are shoes for the urban, upscale, stylish man who wants to project an image of being one step ahead.

Florsheim

Florsheim shoes are the affordable classic men's dress shoes for those who want to experience the comfort and style of a solid dress shoe.

Johnston & Murphy

Johnston & Murphy is the quintessential business shoe for those affluent individuals who know and demand the best.

Source: "Thinking on Your Feet, the Johnston & Murphy Guerrilla Marketing Competition" (Johnston & Murphy, a GENESCO Company).

We strive to provide an opportunity for rapid development.

Intel is a results-oriented company. The focus is on substance versus form, quality versus quantity.

We believe in the principle that hard work, high productivity is something to be proud of.

The concept of assumed responsibility is accepted. (If a task needs to be done, assume you have the responsibility to get it done.)

Commitments are long term. If career problems occur at some point, reassignment is a better alternative than termination.

We desire to have all employees involved and participative in their relationship with Intel.

Newest Trends in Mission Components

Recently, three issues have become so prominent in the strategic planning for organizations that they are increasingly becoming integral parts in the development and revisions of mission statements: sensitivity to consumer wants, concern for quality, and statements of company vision.

Customers

"The customer is our top priority" is a slogan that would be claimed by the majority of businesses in the United States and abroad. For companies including Caterpillar Tractor, General Electric, and Johnson & Johnson this means analyzing consumer needs before as well as after a sale. The bonus plan at Xerox allows for a 40 percent annual bonus, based on high customer reviews of the service that they receive, and a 20 percent penalty if the feedback is especially bad. For these firms and many others, the overriding concern for the company has become consumer satisfaction.

In addition many U.S. firms maintain extensive product safety programs to help assure consumer satisfaction. RCA, Sears, and 3M boast of such programs. Other firms including Calgon Corporation, Amoco, Mobil Oil, Whirlpool, and Zenith provide toll-free telephone lines to answer customer concerns and complaints.

EXHIBIT 2–8
Key Elements of Customer Service–Driven Organizations

1. A mission statement or sense of mission makes customer service a priority.
2. Customer service goals are clearly defined.
3. Customer service standards are clearly defined.
4. Customer satisfaction with existing products and services is continuously measured.
5. Ongoing efforts are made to understand customers to determine where the organization should be headed.
6. Corrective action procedures are in place to remove barriers to servicing customers in a timely and effective fashion.
7. Customer service goals have an impact on organizational action.

Source: An excerpt from "Peters, 1987," p. 78. Reprinted from *Business Horizons*, July–August 1995. Copyright 1995 by the Foundation for the School of Business at Indiana University. Used with permission.

The focus on customer satisfaction is demonstrated by retailer J.C. Penney in this excerpt from its statement of philosophy: "The Penney Idea is (1) To serve the public as nearly as we can to its complete satisfaction; (2) To expect for the service we render a fair remuneration, and not all the profit the traffic will bear; (3) To do all in our power to pack the customer's dollar full of value, quality, and satisfaction."

A focus on customer satisfaction causes managers to realize the importance of providing quality customer service. Strong customer service initiatives have led some firms to gain competitive advantages in the marketplace. Hence, many corporations have made the customer service initiative a key component of their corporate mission. Some key elements of customer service–driven organizations are listed in Exhibit 2–8.

Quality

"Quality is job one!" is a rallying point not only for Ford Motor Corporation but for many resurging U.S. businesses as well. Two U.S. management experts fostered a worldwide emphasis on quality in manufacturing. W. Edwards Deming and J. M. Juran's messages were first embraced by Japanese managers, whose quality consciousness led to global dominance in several industries including automobile, TV, audio equipment, and electronic components manufacturing. Deming summarizes his approach in 14 now well-known points:

1. Create constancy of purpose.

2. Adopt the new philosophy.

3. Cease dependence on mass inspection to achieve quality.

4. End the practice of awarding business on price tag alone. Instead, minimize total cost, often accomplished by working with a single supplier.

5. Improve constantly the system of production and service.

6. Institute training on the job.

7. Institute leadership.

8. Drive out fear.

9. Break down barriers between departments.

10. Eliminate slogans, exhortations, and numerical targets.

11. Eliminate work standards (quotas) and management by objective.

CADILLAC

The Mission of the Cadillac Motor Company is to engineer, produce, and market the world's finest automobiles known for uncompromised levels of distinctiveness, comfort, convenience, and refined performance. Through its people, who are its strength, Cadillac will continuously improve the quality of its products and services to meet or exceed customer expectations and succeed as a profitable business.

MOTOROLA

Dedication to quality is a way of life at our company, so much so that it goes far beyond rhetorical slogans. Our ongoing program of continued improvement out for change, refinement, and even revolution in our pursuit of quality excellence.

It is the objective of Motorola, Inc., to produce and provide products and services of the highest quality. In its activities, Motorola will pursue goals aimed at the achievement of quality excellence. These results will be derived from the dedicated efforts of each employee in conjunction with supportive participation from management at all levels of the corporation.

ZYTEC

Zytec is a company that competes on value; is market driven; provides superior quality and service: builds strong relationship with its customers; and provides technical excellence in its products.

12. Remove barriers that rob workers, engineers, and managers of their right to pride of workmanship.

13. Institute a vigorous program of education and self-improvement.

14. Put everyone in the company to work to accomplish the transformation.

Firms in the United States responded aggressively. The new philosophy is that quality should be the norm. For example, Motorola's production goal is 60 or fewer defects per every billion components that it manufactures.

Exhibit 2–9, Strategy in Action, presents the integration of the quality initiative into the mission statements of three corporations. The emphasis on quality has received added emphasis in many corporate philosophies since the Congress created the Malcolm Baldrige Quality Award in 1987. Each year up to two Baldrige Awards can be given in three categories of a company's operations: manufacturing, services, and small businesses.

Vision Statement

Whereas the mission statement expresses an answer to the question "What business are we in?" a company *vision statement* is sometimes developed to express the aspirations of the executive leadership. A vision statement presents the firm's strategic intent that focuses the energies and resources of the company on achieving a desirable future. However, in actual practice, the mission and vision statement are frequently combined into a single statement. When they are separated, the vision statement is often a single sentence, designed to be memorable. For example:

Federal Express: "Our vision is to change the way we all connect with each other in the New Network Economy."

Lexmark: "Customers for Life."

Microsoft: "A computer on every desk, and in every home, running on Microsoft software."

OVERSEEING THE STRATEGY MAKERS

Who is responsible for determining the firm's mission? Who is responsible for acquiring and allocating resources so the firm can thoughtfully develop and implement a strategic plan? Who is responsible for monitoring the firm's success in the competitive marketplace to determine whether that plan was well designed and activated? The answer to all of these questions is strategic decision makers. As you saw in Exhibit 1–5, most organizations have multiple levels of strategic decision makers; typically, the larger the firm, the more levels it will have. The strategic managers at the highest level are responsible for decisions that affect the entire firm, commit the firm and its resources for the longest periods, and declare the firm's sense of values. In other words, this group of strategic managers is responsible for overseeing the creation and accomplishment of the company mission. The term that describes the group is *board of directors*.

In overseeing the management of a firm, the board of directors operates as the representatives of the firm's stockholders. Elected by the stockholders, the board has these major responsibilities:

1. To establish and update the company mission.

2. To elect the company's top officers, the foremost of whom is the CEO.

3. To establish the compensation levels of the top officers, including their salaries and bonuses.

4. To determine the amount and timing of the dividends paid to stockholders.

5. To set broad company policy on such matters as labor–management relations, product or service lines of business, and employee benefit packages.

6. To set company objectives and to authorize managers to implement the long-term strategies that the top officers and the board have found agreeable.

7. To mandate company compliance with legal and ethical dictates.

In the current business environment, boards of directors are accepting the challenge of shareholders and other stakeholders to become active in establishing the strategic initiatives of the companies that they serve.

This chapter considers the board of directors because the board's greatest impact on the behavior of a firm results from its determination of the company mission. The philosophy espoused in the mission statement sets the tone by which the firm and all of its employees will be judged. As logical extensions of the mission statement, the firm's objectives and strategies embody the board's view of proper business demeanor. Through its appointment of top executives and its decisions about their compensation, the board reveals its priorities for organizational achievement.

AGENCY THEORY

Whenever there is a separation of the owners (principals) and the managers (agents) of a firm, the potential exists for the wishes of the owners to be ignored. This fact, and the recognition that agents are expensive, established the basis for a set of complex but helpful ideas known as *agency theory*. Whenever owners (or managers) delegate decision-making authority to others, an agency relationship exists between the two parties. Agency relationships, such as those between stockholders and managers, can be very effective as long as managers make investment decisions in ways that are consistent with stockholders' interests. However, when the interests of managers diverge from those of owners, then managers' decisions are more likely to reflect the managers' preferences than the owners' preferences.

In general, owners seek stock value maximization. When managers hold important blocks of company stock, they too prefer strategies that result in stock appreciation. However, when managers better resemble "hired hands" than owner-partners, they often prefer strategies that increase their personal payoffs rather than those of shareholders. Such behavior can result in decreased stock performance (as when high executive bonuses reduce corporate earnings) and in strategic decisions that point the firm in the direction of outcomes that are suboptimal from a stockholder's perspective.

If, as agency theory argues, self-interested managers act in ways that increase their own welfare at the expense of the gain of corporate stockholders, then owners who delegate decision-making authority to their agents will incur both the loss of potential gain that would have resulted from owner-optimal strategies and/or the costs of monitoring and control systems that are designed to minimize the consequences of such self-centered management decisions. In combination, the cost of agency problems and the cost of actions taken to minimize agency problems, are called *agency costs*. These costs can often be identified by their direct benefit for the agents and their negative present value. Agency costs are found when there are differing self-interests between shareholders and managers, superiors and subordinates, or managers of competing departments or branch offices.

How Agency Problems Occur

Because owners have access to only a relatively small portion of the information that is available to executives about the performance of the firm and cannot afford to monitor every executive decision or action, executives are often free to pursue their own interests.[1] This condition is known as the *moral hazard problem* or *shirking*.[2]

As a result of moral hazards, executives may design strategies that provide the greatest possible benefits for themselves, with the welfare of the organization being given only secondary consideration. For example, executives may presell products at year-end to trigger their annual bonuses even though the deep discounts that they must offer will threaten the price stability of their products for the upcoming year. Similarly, unchecked executives may advance their own self-interests by slacking on the job, altering forecasts to maximize their performance bonuses; unrealistically assessing acquisition targets' outlooks in order to increase the probability of increasing organizational size through their acquisition; or manipulating personnel records to keep or acquire key company personnel.

The second major reason that agency costs are incurred is known as *adverse selection*. This refers to the limited ability that stockholders have to precisely determine the competencies and priorities of executives at the time that they are hired. Because principals cannot initially verify an executive's appropriateness as an agent of the owners, unanticipated problems of nonoverlapping priorities between owners and agents are likely to occur.

The most popular solution to moral dilemma and adverse selection problems is for owners to attempt to more closely align their own best interests with those of their agents

---

[1] Substitute the terms *managers* for *owners* and *subordinates* for *executives* for another example of agency theory in operation.
[2] Shirking is described as "self-interest combined with guile."

through the use of executive bonus plans.[3] Foremost among these approaches are stock option plans, which enable executives to benefit directly from the appreciation of the company's stock just as other stockholders do. In most instances, executive bonus plans are unabashed attempts to align the interests of owners and executives and to thereby induce executives to support strategies that increase stockholder wealth. While such schemes are unlikely to eliminate self-interest as a major criterion in executive decision making, they help to reduce the costs associated with moral dilemmas and adverse selections.

Problems That Can Result from Agency

From a strategic management perspective there are five different kinds of problems that can arise because of the agency relationship between corporate stockholders and their company's executives:

1. Executives pursue growth in company size rather than in earnings. Shareholders generally want to maximize earnings, because earnings growth yields stock appreciation. However, because managers are typically more heavily compensated for increases in firm size than for earnings growth, they may recommend strategies that yield company growth such as mergers and acquisitions.

In addition, managers' stature in the business community is commonly associated with company size. Managers gain prominence by directing the growth of an organization, and they benefit in the forms of career advancement and job mobility that are associated with increases in company size.

Finally, executives need an enlarging set of advancement opportunities for subordinates whom they wish to motivate with nonfinancial inducements. Acquisitions can provide the needed positions.

2. Executives attempt to diversify their corporate risk. Whereas stockholders can vary their investment risks through management of their individual stock portfolios, managers' careers and stock incentives are tied to the performance of a single corporation, albeit the one that employs them. Consequently, executives are tempted to diversify their corporation's operation, businesses, and product lines to moderate the risk incurred in any single venture. While this approach serves the executives' personal agendas, it compromises the "pure play" quality of their firm as an investment. In other words, diversifying a corporation reduces the beta associated with the firm's return, which is an undesirable outcome for many stockholders.

3. Executives avoid risk. Even when, or perhaps especially when, executives are willing to restrict the diversification of their companies, they are tempted to minimize the risk that they face. Executives are often fired for failure, but rarely for mediocre corporate performance. Therefore, executives may avoid desirable levels of risk, if they anticipate little reward and opt for conservative strategies that minimize the risk of company failure. If they do, executives will rarely support plans for innovation, diversification, and rapid growth.

However, from an investor's perspective, risk taking is desirable when it is systematic. In other words, when investors can reasonably expect that their company will generate higher long-term returns from assuming greater risk, they may wish to pursue the greater payoff, especially when the company is positioned to perform better than its competitors that face the same nominal risks. Obviously, the agency relationship creates a problem—should executives prioritize their job security or the company's financial returns to stockholders?

[3] An in-depth discussion of executive bonus compensation is provided in Chapter 9.

4. Managers act to optimize their personal payoffs. If executives can gain more from an annual performance bonus by achieving objective 1 than from stock appreciation resulting from the achievement of objective 2, then owners must anticipate that the executives will target objective 1 as their priority, even though objective 2 is clearly in the best interest of the shareholders. Similarly, executives may pursue a range of expensive perquisites that have a net negative effect on shareholder returns. Elegant comer offices, corporate jets, large staffs, golf club memberships, extravagant retirement programs, and limousines for executive benefit are rarely good investments for stockholders.

5. Executives act to protect their status. When their companies expand, executives want to assure that their knowledge, experience, and skills remain relevant and central to the strategic direction of the corporation. They favor doing more of what they already do well. In contrast, investors may prefer revolutionary advancement to incremental improvement. For example, when confronted with Amazon.com, competitor Barnes & Noble initiated a joint venture website with Bertelsmann. In addition, Barnes & Noble used vertical integration with the nation's largest book distributor, which supplies 60 percent of Amazon's books. This type of revolutionary strategy is most likely to occur when executives are given assurances that they will not make themselves obsolete within the changing company that they create.

Solutions to the Agency Problem

In addition to defining an agent's responsibilities in a contract and including elements like bonus incentives that help align executives' and owners' interests, principals can take several other actions to minimize agency problems. The first is for the owners to pay executives a premium for their service. This premium helps executives to see their loyalty to the stockholders as the key to achieving their personal financial targets.

A second solution to agency problems is for executives to receive backloaded compensation. This means that executives are paid a handsome premium for superior future performance. Strategic actions taken in year one, which are to have an impact in year three, become the basis for executive bonuses in year three. This lag time between action and bonus more realistically rewards executives for the consequences of their decision making, ties the executive to the company for the long term, and properly focuses strategic management activities on the future.

Finally, creating teams of executives across different units of a corporation can help to focus performance measures on organizational rather than personal goals. Through the use of executive teams, owner interests often receive the priority that they deserve.

THE STAKEHOLDER APPROACH TO COMPANY RESPONSIBILITY

In defining or redefining the company mission, strategic managers must recognize the legitimate rights of the firm's claimants. These include not only stockholders and employees but also outsiders affected by the firm's actions. Such outsiders commonly include customers, suppliers, governments, unions, competitors, local communities, and the general public. Each of these interest groups has justifiable reasons for expecting (and often for demanding) that the firm satisfy their claims in a responsible manner. In general, stockholders claim appropriate returns on their investment; employees seek broadly defined job satisfactions; customers want what they pay for; suppliers seek dependable buyers; governments want adherence to legislation; unions seek benefits for their members; competitors want fair competition; local communities want the firm to be a responsible citizen; and the general public expects the firm's existence to improve the quality of life.

According to a survey of 2,361 directors in 291 of the largest southeastern U.S. companies:

1. Directors perceived the existence of distinct stakeholder groups.

2. Directors have high stakeholder orientations.

3. Directors view some stakeholders differently, depending on their occupation (CEO directors versus non-CEO directors) and type (inside versus outside directors).

The study also found that the perceived stakeholders were, in the order of their importance, customers and government, stockholders, employees, and society. The results clearly indicated that boards of directors no longer believe that the stockholder is the only constituency to whom they are responsible.

However, when a firm attempts to incorporate the interests of these groups into its mission statement, broad generalizations are insufficient. These steps need to be taken:

1. Identification of the stakeholders.

2. Understanding the stakeholders' specific claims vis-à-vis the firm.

3. Reconciliation of these claims and assignment of priorities to them.

4. Coordination of the claims with other elements of the company mission.

Identification   The left-hand column of Exhibit 2–10 lists the commonly encountered stakeholder groups, to which the executive officer group often is added. Obviously, though, every business faces a slightly different set of stakeholder groups, which vary in number, size, influence, and importance. In defining the company, strategic managers must identify all of the stakeholder groups and weigh their relative rights and their relative ability to affect the firm's success.

Understanding   The concerns of the principal stakeholder groups tend to center on the general claims listed in the right-hand column of Exhibit 2–10. However, strategic decision makers should understand the specific demands of each group. They then will be better able to initiate actions that satisfy these demands.

Reconciliation and Priorities   Unfortunately, the claims of various stakeholder groups often conflict. For example, the claims of governments and the general public tend to limit profitability, which is the central claim of most creditors and stockholders. Thus, claims must be reconciled in a mission statement that resolves the competing, conflicting, and contradicting claims of stakeholders. For objectives and strategies to be internally consistent and precisely focused, the statement must display a single-minded, though multidimensional, approach to the firm's aims.

There are hundreds, if not thousands, of claims on any firm—high wages, pure air, job security, product quality, community service, taxes, occupational health and safety regulations, equal employment opportunity regulations, product variety, wide markets, career opportunities, company growth, investment security, high ROI, and many, many more. Although most, perhaps all, of these claims may be desirable ends, they cannot be pursued with equal emphasis. They must be assigned priorities in accordance with the relative emphasis that the firm will give them. That emphasis is reflected in the criteria that the firm uses in its strategic decision making; in the firm's allocation of its human, financial, and physical resources; and in the firm's long-term objectives and strategies.

EXHIBIT 2–10

A Stakeholder View of Company Responsibility

Source: William R. King and David I. Cleland, *Strategic Planning and Policy.* © 1978 by Litton Educational Publishing, Inc., p. 153. Reprinted by permission of Van Nostrand Reinhold Company.

Stakeholder	Nature of the Claim
Stockholders	Participation in distribution of profits, additional stock offerings, assets on liquidation; vote of stock; inspection of company books; transfer of stock; election of board of directors; and such additional rights as have been established in the contract with the corporation.
Creditors	Legal proportion of interest payments due and return of principal from the investment. Security of pledged assets; relative priority in event of liquidation. Management and owner prerogatives if certain conditions exist with the company (such as default of interest payments).
Employees	Economic, social, and psychological satisfaction in the place of employment. Freedom from arbitrary and capricious behavior on the part of company officials. Share in fringe benefits, freedom to join union and participate in collective bargaining, individual freedom in offering up their services through an employment contract. Adequate working conditions.
Customers	Service provided with the product; technical data to use the product; suitable warranties; spare parts to support the product during use; R&D leading to product improvement; facilitation of credit.
Suppliers	Continuing source of business; timely consummation of trade credit obligations; professional relationship in contracting for, purchasing, and receiving goods and services.
Governments	Taxes (income, property, and so on); adherence to the letter and intent of public policy dealing with the requirements of fair and free competition; discharge of legal obligations of businesspeople (and business organizations); adherence to antitrust laws.
Unions	Recognition as the negotiating agent for employees. Opportunity to perpetuate the union as a participant in the business organization.
Competitors	Observation of the norms for competitive conduct established by society and the industry. Business statesmanship on the part of peers.
Local communities	Place of productive and healthful employment in the community. Participation of company officials in community affairs, provision of regular employment, fair play, reasonable portion of purchases made in the local community, interest in and support of local government, support of cultural and charitable projects.
The general public	Participation in and contribution to society as a whole; creative communications between governmental and business units designed for reciprocal understanding; assumption of fair proportion of the burden of government and society. Fair price for products and advancement of the state-of-the-art technology that the product line involves.

Coordination with Other Elements   The demands of stakeholder groups constitute only one principal set of inputs to the company mission. The other principal sets are the managerial operating philosophy and the determinants of the product-market offering. Those determinants constitute a reality test that the accepted claims must pass. The key question is: How can the firm satisfy its claimants and at the same time optimize its economic success in the marketplace?

EXHIBIT 2–11
Inputs to the Development of the Company Mission

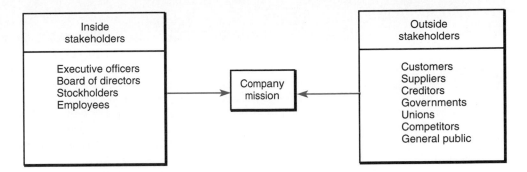

Social Responsibility

As indicated in Exhibit 2–11, the various stakeholders of a firm can be divided into inside stakeholders and outside stakeholders. The insiders are the individuals or groups that are stockholders or employees of the firm. The outsiders are all the other individuals or groups that the firm's actions affect. The extremely large and often amorphous set of outsiders makes the general claim that the firm be socially responsible.

Perhaps the thorniest issues faced in defining a company mission are those that pertain to responsibility. The stakeholder approach offers the clearest perspective on such issues. Broadly stated, outsiders often demand that insiders' claims be subordinated to the greater good of the society; that is, to the greater good of outsiders. They believe that such issues as pollution, the disposal of solid and liquid wastes, and the conservation of natural resources should be principal considerations in strategic decision making. Also broadly stated, insiders tend to believe that the competing claims of outsiders should be balanced against one another in a way that protects the company mission. For example, they tend to believe that the need of consumers for a product should be balanced against the water pollution resulting from its production if the firm cannot eliminate that pollution entirely and still remain profitable. Some insiders also argue that the claims of society, as expressed in government regulation, provide tax money that can be used to eliminate water pollution and the like if the general public wants this to be done.

The issues are numerous, complex, and contingent on specific situations. Thus, rigid rules of business conduct cannot deal with them. Each firm *regardless of size* must decide how to meet its perceived social responsibility. While large, well-capitalized companies may have easy access to environmental consultants, this is not an affordable strategy for smaller companies. However, the experience of many small businesses demonstrates that it is feasible to accomplish significant pollution prevention and waste reduction without big expenditures and without hiring consultants. Once a problem area has been identified, a company's line employees frequently can develop a solution. Other important pollution prevention strategies include changing the materials used or redesigning how operations are bid out. Making pollution prevention a social responsibility can be beneficial to smaller companies. Publicly traded firms also can benefit directly from socially responsible strategies.

Different approaches adopted by different firms reflect differences in competitive position, industry, country, environmental and ecological pressures, and a host of other factors. In other words, they will reflect both situational factors and differing priorities in the acknowledgment of claims. Obviously, winning the loyalty of the growing legions of consumers will require new marketing strategies and new alliances in the 21st century. Many marketers already have discovered these new marketing realities by adopting strategies called the "*4 E's*": (1) make it easy for the consumer to be green, (2) empower

Global Strategy in Action
Occidental Petroleum Accepts Corporate Social Responsibility

Exhibit 2–12

BusinessWeek In Colombia, Los Angeles–based Occidental Petroleum Corp. is clearing the land for an exploratory oil well to be drilled. The government believes the land holds more than half of Colombia's oil reserves and has contracted Occidental to find it. The nature-worshipping U'wa adamantly oppose the exploration. But Occidental emphatically denies that the U'wa will be affected either. The company has held dozens of meetings with community groups and says it is trying to meet all their concerns. Occidental has spent some $140,000 on educational, environmental, agricultural, and basic infrastructure projects in communities closest to the project.

The plight of indigenous groups is penetrating the boardrooms of multinationals, which are being forced to respond as never before to protect their reputations and brand names. Nowhere are the issues more contentious than in investments, such as Occidental's, that involve extracting natural resources in developing nations. Many of these projects have long been marred by corruption, military atrocities, ecological damage, and social upheaval.

Activists and environmental groups have put heavy pressure on multinationals, governments of developing nations, and the World Bank—which funds many such projects—to show there are humane, eco-friendly, and equitable ways to drill and mine in poor nations. On top of this, oil and mining companies now have to answer to institutional investors. And they must meet increasingly stringent environmental and social standards to get financial backing and political-risk guarantees from the World Bank for overseas projects.

The result is shaping up as a new era of corporate responsibility. Multinationals are hiring human-rights advisers, drafting and enforcing codes of conduct, appointing outside monitors, and improving operating practices. They are developing global standards of conduct, such as procedures for security of their installations. They are putting local people on boards of directors and urging government ministers and generals to adhere to international human-rights standards, lest their misdeeds reflect poorly on the investors, too.

Only a handful of multinationals have gotten serious about cleaning up their corporate practices. Even if companies are well-intentioned, the real test is whether the new standards and codes will mean anything in practice.

Source: An excerpt from P. Raeburn and S. Prasso, "Whose Globe?," *BusinessWeek*, November 6, 2000.

consumers with solutions, (3) enlist the support of the consumer, and (4) establish credibility with all publics and help to avoid a backlash.

As presented in Exhibit 2–12, Global Strategy in Action, Occidental Petroleum faces issues of corporate social responsibility in addressing the needs of the many stakeholders involved in the firm's oil exploration in developing countries. The article outlines the many parties that have potential to be impacted by the company's endeavors, including local inhabitants and government, environmental groups, and institutional investors. The article also describes how multinational corporations are acting to benefit the local communities, to restructure their organizations, and to implement codes of conduct to address the needs of the many stakeholders.

British Petroleum' CEO, John Browne, faces the social responsibility questions asked of all leaders of global firms. Global Strategy in Action Exhibit 2–13 presents Browne's view that for his global company to thrive, so must the communities in which his company does business.

Despite differences in their approaches, most American firms now try to assure outsiders that they attempt to conduct business in a socially responsible manner. Many firms, including Abt Associates, Dow Chemical, Eastern Gas and Fuel Associates, Exxon, and the Bank of America, conduct and publish annual social audits. Such audits attempt to evaluate a firm from the perspective of social responsibility. Private consultants often conduct them for the firm and offer minimally biased evaluations on what are inherently highly subjective issues.

BusinessWeek Making globalization work humanely is quickly becoming the dominant issue of our time. From Boston to Bangkok, trade, investment, and information technology are exploding across borders and overwhelming governments' ability to provide social safety nets and public services to cushion the impact on people. A political backlash is building in Asia, Europe, and Latin America. Although international corporations cannot shoulder all the *responsibility*, no challenge is more central to global management than finding a balance between the relentless pressure for short-term profits and broader social *responsibilities*.

What's a chief executive to do? To what degree should companies take on the *responsibility* heretofore shouldered by governments? To what degree can they? One chief executive, John Browne of British Petroleum Co., has a clear philosophy and strategy. Browne believes that for BP to thrive, so must the communities in which it does business. To make that happen, Browne has insisted that the economic and social health of the villages, towns, and cities in which BP does business be a matter of central concern to the company's *board* of directors. He has also made social investment for the long term an important variable in compensating BP employees around the world.

AMBITIOUS GOALS

What to do and how to do it is left to local BP business units. But regular reviews of their activities are held by regional executives. In such areas as job training for local employees and building schools, ambitious goals are set, and performance is measured against them. Involved in the process along with BP employees and *board* directors are local residents whose views are regularly surveyed.

BP's community investments are extensive. In Vietnam, the company is providing computer-based technology to control the damage from recurrent flooding. In Turkey, BP recently financed the replanting of a forest around the Black Sea that had been destroyed by fire. In Zambia, it has supplied 200 solar-powered refrigerators to help doctors store antimalaria vaccines. In South Africa, it has supported the development of small business in urban areas such as Soweto. In Colombia, it is turning its own waste material into bricks for local homebuilding.

In addition, accidents in the workplace, noxious emissions, and oil spills are subject to monitoring and quantification. Ernst & Young verifies company recordkeeping. There is constant pressure to eliminate accidents.

NOT CHARITY

So far, the strategy has not impaired BP's bottom line. To the contrary. "These efforts have nothing to do with charity," says Browne, "and everything to do with our long-term self-interest I see no trade-off between the short term and the long. Twenty years is just 80 quarters. And our shareholders want performance today, and tomorrow, and the day after."

Corporations would do well to take a page out of Browne's playbook: think long-term, invest heavily in the communities that you do business in, be obsessive about achieving profits, and fully integrate social *responsibility* into your policies on governance and compensation.

Source: Jeffrey E. Garten, "Globalism Doesn't Have to Be Cruel," *BusinessWeek,* February 9, 1998.

Corporate Social Responsibility and Profitability

Few trends could so thoroughly undermine the very foundations of our free society as the acceptance by corporate officials of a social responsibility other than to make as much money for their stockholders as possible.

Milton Friedman, Capitalism and Freedom, *1962*

In the four decades since Milton Friedman wrote these words, the issue of *corporate social responsibility* (CSR)—the idea that business has a duty to serve society as well as the financial interest of stockholders—has remained a highly contentious one. Yet managers recognize that deciding to what extent to embrace CSR is an important strategic decision.

There are three principal reasons why managers should be concerned about the socially responsible behavior of their firms. First, a company's right to exist depends on its responsiveness to the external environment. Second, federal, state, and local governments threaten increased regulation if business does not evolve to meet changing social standards. Third, a responsive corporate social policy may enhance a firm's long-term viability. Underscoring the importance of these factors to the firm is the implicit belief that long-run profit maximization is inexorably linked to CSR.

The Debate

Should a company behave in a socially responsible manner? Coming down on one side of the question are those who, like Friedman, believe that a business bears a responsibility only for the financial well-being of its stockholders. Implicit in this statement is the idea that corporate actions motivated by anything other than shareholder wealth maximization threatens that well-being. On the other side, proponents of CSR assert that business does not function in a vacuum; it exists to serve, depends upon its environment, cannot be separated from it, and therefore has a responsibility to ensure its well-being. The environment is represented not only by stockholders/owners and employees, but also by such external stakeholders as customers, unions, suppliers, competitors, government agencies, local communities, and society in general.

The second argument for CSR suggests that stockholders' interests may transcend the financial. Many stockholders expect more from the companies in which they invest than simple appreciation in the economic value of the firm.

The third argument in favor of CSR is that the best way for a company to maximize shareholder wealth is to act in a socially responsible manner. It suggests that when a company behaves responsibly, benefits accrue directly to the bottom line. It also implies that when a company does not behave responsibly, the company and its shareholders suffer financially.

When discussing business ethics, the terms illegal and unethical are often used synonymously. Exhibit 2–14, E-commerce Strategy in Action, presents an argument that eBay is acting unethically by allowing, and profiting from, the sale of "murderabilia" on their website. eBay's lack of prevention is perceived by some critics as "morally reprehensible" and socially irresponsible. Since there are no laws against this type of sale on the Internet, it is not illegal. However, corporate social responsibility is an element of strategic decision making that eBay cannot ignore. If websites are not responsive to society, they increase the odds that people will turn to legislation to discipline corporate behavior.

CSR and the Bottom Line

The goal of every firm is to maintain viability through long-run profitability. Until all costs and benefits are accounted for, however, profits may not be claimed. In the case of CSR, costs and benefits are both economic and social. While economic costs and benefits are easily quantifiable, social costs and benefits are not. Managers therefore risk subordinating social consequences to other performance results that can be more straightforwardly measured.

The dynamic between CSR and success (profit) is complex. While one concept is clearly not mutually exclusive of the other, it is also clear that neither is a prerequisite of the other. Rather than viewing these two concepts as competing, it may be better to view CSR as a component in the decision-making process of business that must determine, among other objectives, how to maximize profits.

Attempts to undertake a cost-benefit analysis of CSR have not been very successful. The process is complicated by several factors. First, some CSR activities incur no dollar costs at all. For example, Second Harvest, the largest nongovernment, charitable food

E-commerce Strategy in Action

eBay's "Murderabilia"?

Exhibit 2–14

BusinessWeek Serial killer Angel Resendez-Ramirez smiles as he sits behind bulletproof glass on Death Row in a maximum-security prison. He has admitted to murdering 12 women across the U.S., yet he jokes and revels in his fame. Locks of his hair and shavings from the callouses on his feet have been sold on Internet auction site eBay for $9.99 a pop. He gets a cut from dealers each time a little piece of him is sold. Tom Konvicka's mother was one of the victims. When Resendez-Ramirez was caught and locked up, Konvicka remembers feeling relief that his mom's murderer was being brought to justice. Now, he's disgusted. Serial killers shouldn't profit from their murders. Their victims are dead and gone and they're still here and making a profit on what they've done.

In Texas, as in most other states, there's nothing to prevent criminals from selling "murderabilia" on the Internet. eBay and other sites don't prevent it, either. In fact, there's little to discourage the sale of a whole range of questionable items online. As the Internet has grown in popularity, it's a ready-made market connecting individuals with a vast audience of potential buyers—all protected by a cloak of semi-anonymity and the hands-off policies of Web auction sites. That wide-open flea market has produced a cornucopia of items for sale that are in bad taste or unethical.

A growing chorus of ethicists, lawmakers, consumer groups, and Internet activists say something needs to be done—either stepped-up monitoring by auction sites themselves, or statutes that police the Netways. By refusing to take responsibility for what is sold on their site, they're cashing in on an overall lack of social accountability the Internet offers. While the sale of murderabilia is not illegal, it's morally reprehensible.

Problem is, when it comes to the Web, it's sometimes difficult to tell what's illegal, what ought to be illegal, and what's just in bad taste. It's clearly against the law to sell things such as endangered species and certain kinds of firearms. But how do you prevent minors from buying alcohol and pornography in a realm where nobody knows their age? Selling body organs online isn't necessarily a crime, but a doctor who participates could breach professional ethics. And how do you prevent the trafficking in items like neo-Nazi paraphernalia that are illegal in some places but not in others?

Given all the confusion, society's first line of defense could be auction site operators—but they're having none of it. eBay has a laissez-faire attitude about what is sold on the site. The company claims it's all part of eBay's philosophy of building a community based on trust. However, by not screening items, eBay skirts potential liability and high monitoring costs.

Now that Net auctions have become such a magnet for potentially dicey items, some states and federal agencies are stepping up their efforts to stop abuses. FBI's Internet Fraud Complaint Center gets more than 1,000 complaints of online auction fraud each month—most of them involving eBay traffic. Agents have begun turning some of these cases over to local law enforcement authorities. In October, state elections officials in Illinois and New York temporarily shut down Voteauction.com, an Internet site where Americans could sell their votes to the highest bidder. Authorities say they are keeping close watch and will nab all who accept money for their votes—and the people who pay them—charging them with violating state and federal election laws. The very nature of the Web makes the unthinkable more possible. Absent the Internet, many people might not have been exposed to the opportunity to revel in Nazi items or bloody murder photos, or be offered an easy chance to buy them without fear of social backlash. eBay is a magnet for people who previously didn't have many outlets because you're immediately linked up to millions of people.

The Web amplifies ethical dilemmas, too. Consider MedicineOnline.com, a site that connects plastic surgery doctors and patients on the Net. The site asks doctors to provide info about their education and experience—including their history of malpractice suits—but takes no responsibility for the veracity of that information. By contrast, a regular hospital is legally bound to take responsibility for the credentials and services of doctors who practice there. That's eBay's answer, too: Since it does not sell anything itself, it's not responsible for what is sold on the site. eBay asks sellers to report any breach of guidelines—in other words, to police the site themselves.

For now, eBay plans to continue to rely on its guidelines—and on its community of members—to blow the whistle on anything beyond the pale. However, with creeps and criminals like Resendez-Ramirez virtually on the loose, eBay's self-monitoring system may not be enough.

Source: An excerpt from Marcia Stepanek, "Making a Killing Online," *BusinessWeek,* November 20, 2000.

distributor in the nation, accepts donations from food manufacturers and food retailers of surplus food that would otherwise be thrown out due to overruns, warehouse damage, or labeling errors. In 10 years, Second Harvest has distributed more than 2 billion pounds of food. Gifts in Kind America is an organization that enables companies to reduce unsold or obsolete inventory by matching a corporation's donated products with a charity's or other nonprofit organization's needs. In addition, a tax break is realized by the company. In the past, corporate donations have included 130,000 pairs of shoes from Nike, 10,000 pairs of gloves from Aris Isotoner, and 480 computer systems from Apple Computer.

In addition, philanthropic activities of a corporation, which have been a traditional mainstay of CSR, are undertaken at a discounted cost to the firm since they are often tax deductible. The benefits of corporate philanthropy can be enormous as is shown by the many national social welfare causes that have been spurred by corporate giving. A few of these causes are described in Exhibit 2–15. While such acts of benevolence often help establish a general perception of the involved companies within society, some philanthropic acts bring specific credit to the firm.

Second, socially responsible behavior does not come at a prohibitive cost. One needs only to look at the problems of A. H. Robbins Company (Dalkon Shield), Beech-Nut Corporation (apple juice), Drexel Burnham (insider trading), and Exxon *(Valdez)* for stark answers on the "cost" of social responsibility (or its absence) in the business environment.

Third, socially responsible practices may create savings and, as a result, increase profits. SET Laboratories uses popcorn to ship software rather than polystyrene peanuts. It is environmentally safer and costs 60 percent less to use. Corporations that offer part-time and adjustable work schedules have realized that this can lead to reduced absenteeism, greater productivity and increased morale. DuPont opted for more flexible schedules for its employees after a survey revealed 50 percent of women and 25 percent of men considered working for another employer with more flexibility for family concerns.

Proponents argue that CSR costs are more than offset in the long run by an improved company image and increased community goodwill. These intangible assets can prove valuable in a crisis, as Johnson & Johnson discovered with the Tylenol cyanide scare in 1982. Because it had established a solid reputation as a socially responsible company before the incident, the public readily accepted the company's assurances of public safety. Consequently, financial damage to Johnson & Johnson was minimized, despite the company's $100 million voluntary recall of potentially tainted capsules. CSR may also head off new regulation, preventing increased compliance costs. It may even attract investors who are themselves socially responsible. Proponents believe that for these reasons, socially responsible behavior increases the financial value of the firm in the long run. The mission statement of Johnson & Johnson is provided as Exhibit 2–16, Strategy in Action.

Performance   To explore the relationship between socially responsible behavior and financial performance, an important question must first be answered: How do managers measure the financial impact of corporate social performance?

Critics of CSR believe that companies that behave in a socially responsible manner, and portfolios comprising these companies' securities, should perform more poorly financially than those that do not. The costs of CSR outweigh the benefits for individual firms, they suggest. In addition, traditional portfolio theory holds that investors minimize risk and maximize return by being able to choose from an infinite universe of investment opportunities. Portfolios based on social criteria should suffer, critics argue, because they are by definition restrictive in nature. This restriction should increase portfolio risk and reduce portfolio return.

Now that U.S. companies are adopting strategic philanthropy, they are assuming an activist stance on social issues. As a result, many causes, including the following, have become national movements.

HUNGER

Before the new approach to corporate philanthropy, the foundations of food companies gave cash donations to anti-hunger organizations. But when the ranks of the hungry increased tenfold in the 1980s, contributions managers in companies such as General Mills, Grand Metropolitan, Kraft General Foods, and Sara Lee decided to play a larger role *and* establish a rallying point around which disparate units of their companies could come together. Marketers arranged for a portion of product sales to be donated to antihunger programs, human resources staffs deployed volunteers, operating units provided free food, and CEOs joined the board of Chicago-based Second Harvest, the food industry's anti-hunger voice. As a result of those efforts, a complex infrastructure of food banks and soup kitchens was developed.

COMMUNITY AND ECONOMIC DEVELOPMENT

Major banks such as Bank of America, Chase Manhattan, Citicorp, Morgan Guaranty, and Wells Fargo explored how philanthropy could be tied to marketing, human resources, government affairs, investment, and even trust management. Their business managers were concerned about the Community Reinvestment Act, which requires lenders to be responsive to low-income communities. Philanthropy managers point out that by going beyond the CRA requirements, they develop positive relationships with regulators while scoring public relations points. For example, at least 60 banks in the United States have created community development corporations to assist run-down neighborhoods.

LITERACY

The effort to increase literacy in the United States is the favorite cause of the communications industry. Print media companies such as McGraw-Hill, Prentice Hall, the *Los Angeles Times,* the *Washington Post,* and the *New York Times* are trying to halt the drop in readership, and broadcasters and cable companies are compensating for their role in the decline of literacy. Those companies have mobilized their marketing, human resources, and lobbying power to establish workplace literacy programs. While human resources budgets fund such programs, philanthropy dollars go mostly to volunteer organizations.

SCHOOL REFORM

About 15 percent of the country's cash gifts go to school reform, and a recent study estimated that at least one-third of U.S. school districts have partnership programs with business. The next step toward reform, promoted by the Business Roundtable, is for companies to mobilize their lobbying power at the state level to press for the overhaul of state educational agencies.

AIDS

AIDS is a top cause for insurance companies, who want to reduce claims; pharmaceutical companies, who want public support for the commercialization of AIDS drugs; and design-related companies, who want to support the large number of gays in their work force. Those industries put the first big money into AIDS prevention measures, and they've helped turn the American Foundation for AIDS Research into an advocate for more and better research by the National Institutes of Health.

ENVIRONMENTALISM

Environmental support varies across industries. In high-tech companies, environmentalism is largely a human resources issue because it's the favorite cause of many employees. Among the makers of outdoor apparel, environmentalism is largely a marketing issue, so companies donate a portion of the purchase price to environmental nonprofits. In industries that pollute or extract natural resources, environmentalism is often a government affairs matter.

Source: Reprinted by permission of *Harvard Business Review.* An excerpt from "The New Corporate Philanthropy," by Jay W. Lorsch, May–June 1994. Copyright © 1994 by the President and Fellows of Harvard University, all rights reserved.

Several research studies have attempted to determine the relationship between corporate social performance and financial performance. Taken together, these studies fail to establish the nature of the relationship between social and financial performance. There are a number of possible explanations for the findings. One possibility is that there is no meaningful correlation between social and financial performance. A second possibility is

"We believe our first responsibility is to the doctors, nurses and patients, to mothers and fathers and all others who use our products and services. In meeting their needs everything we do must be of high quality. We must constantly strive to reduce our costs in order to maintain reasonable prices. Customers' orders must be serviced promptly and accurately. Our suppliers and distributors must have an opportunity to make a fair profit.

We are responsible to our employees, the men and women who work with us throughout the world. Everyone must be considered as an individual. We must respect their dignity and recognize their merit. They must have a sense of security in their jobs. Compensation must be fair and adequate, and working conditions clean, orderly and safe. Employees must feel free to make suggestions and complaints. There must be equal opportunity for employment, development and advancement for those qualified. We must provide competent management, and their actions must be just and ethical.

We are responsible to the communities in which we live and work and to the world community as well. We must be good citizens—support good works and charities and bear our fair share of taxes. We must encourage civic improvements and better health and education. We must maintain in good order the property we are privileged to use, protecting the environment and natural resources.

Our final responsibility is to our stockholders. Business must make a sound profit. We must experiment with new ideas. Research must be carried on, innovative programs developed and mistakes paid for. New equipment must be purchased, new facilities provided and new products launched. Reserves must be created to provide for adverse times. When we operate according to these principles, the stockholders should realize a fair return."

that the benefits of CSR are offset by its negative consequences for the firm, thus producing a nondectectable net financial effect. Other explanations include methodological weaknesses and/or insufficient conceptual models or operational definitions used in the studies. However, among experts, a sense remains that a relationship between CSR and the bottom line does exist, although the exact nature of that relationship is unclear.

CSR Today

A survey of 2,737 senior U.S. managers revealed that 92 percent believed that business should take primary responsibility for, or an active role in, solving environmental problems; 84 percent believed business should do the same for educational concerns.[4] Despite the uncertain impact of CSR on the corporate bottom line, CSR has become a priority with American business. Why? In addition to a commonsense belief that companies should be able to "do well by doing good," at least three broad trends are driving businesses to adopt CSR frameworks: the resurgence of environmentalism, increasing buyer power, and the globalization of business.

The Resurgence of Environmentalism   In March 1989, the Exxon *Valdez* ran aground in Prince William Sound, spilling 11 million gallons of oil, polluting miles of ocean and shore, and helping to revive worldwide concern for the ecological environment. Six months after the *Valdez* incident, the Coalition for Environmentally Responsible Economies (CERES) was formed to establish new goals for environmentally responsible corporate behavior. The group drafted the CERES Principles to "establish an environmental ethic with criteria by which investors and others can assess the environmental performance of companies. Companies that sign these Principles pledge to go voluntarily beyond the requirements of the law."

---

[4] Rosabeth Moss Kanter, "Transcending Business Boundaries: 12,000 World Managers View Change," *Harvard Business Review* 69, no. 3 (May–June 1991), pp. 151–64.

Increasing Buyer Power   The rise of the consumer movement has meant that buyers—consumers and investors—are increasingly flexing their economic muscle. Consumers are becoming more interested in buying products from socially responsible companies. Organizations such as the Council on Economic Priorities (CEP) help consumers make more informed buying decisions through such publications as *Shopping for a Better World,* which provides social performance information on 191 companies making more than 2,000 consumer products. CEP also sponsors the annual Corporate Conscience Awards, which recognize socially responsible companies. One example of consumer power at work is the effective outcry over the deaths of dolphins in tuna fishermen's nets.

Investors represent a second type of influential consumer. There has been a dramatic increase in the number of people interested in supporting socially responsible companies through their investments. Membership in the Social Investment Forum, a trade association serving social investing professionals, has been growing at a rate of about 50 percent annually. As baby boomers achieve their own financial success, the social investing movement has continued its rapid growth.

While social investing wields relatively low power as an individual private act (selling one's shares of Exxon does not affect the company), it can be very powerful as a collective public act. When investors vote their shares in behalf of pro-CSR issues, companies may be pressured to change their social behavior. The South African divestiture movement is one example of how effective this pressure can be.

The Vermont National Bank has added a Socially Responsible Banking Fund to its product line. Investors can designate any of their interest-bearing accounts with a $500 minimum balance to be used by the fund. This fund then lends these monies for purposes such as low-income housing, the environment, education, farming, or small business development. Although it has had a "humble" beginning of approximately 800 people investing about $11 million, the bank has attracted out-of-state depositors and is growing faster than expected.

Social investors comprise both individuals and institutions. Much of the impetus for social investing originated with religious organizations that wanted their investments to mirror their beliefs. At present, the ranks of social investors have expanded to include educational institutions and large pension funds.

Large-scale social investing can be broken down into the two broad areas of guideline portfolio investing and shareholder activism. Guideline portfolio investing is the largest and fastest-growing segment of social investing. Individual and institutional guideline portfolio investors use ethical guidelines as screens to identify possible investments in stocks, bonds, and mutual funds. The investment instruments that survive the social screens are then layered over the investor's financial screens to create the investor's universe of possible investments.

Screens may be negative (e.g., excluding all tobacco companies) or they may combine negative and positive elements (e.g., eliminating companies with bad labor records while seeking out companies with good ones). Most investors rely on screens created by investment firms such as Kinder, Lydenberg Domini & Co. or by industry groups such as the Council on Economic Priorities. In addition to ecology, employee relations, and community development, corporations may be screened on their association with "sin" products (alcohol, tobacco, gambling), defense/weapons production, and nuclear power.

In contrast to guideline portfolio investors, who passively indicate their approval or disapproval of a company's social behavior by simply including or excluding it from their portfolios, shareholder activists seek to directly influence corporate social behavior. Shareholder activists invest in a corporation hoping to improve specific aspects of the company's social performance, typically by seeking a dialogue with upper management.

If this and successive actions fail to achieve the desired results, shareholder activists may introduce proxy resolutions to be voted upon at the corporation's annual meeting. The goal of these resolutions is to achieve change by gaining public exposure for the issue at hand. While the number of shareholder activists is relatively small, they are by no means small in achievement: Shareholder activists, led by such groups as the Interfaith Center on Corporate Responsibility, were the driving force behind the South African divestiture movement. Currently, there are more than 35 socially screened mutual funds available in the United States alone.

The Globalization of Business   Management issues, including CSR, have become more complex as companies increasingly transcend national borders: It is difficult enough to come to a consensus on what constitutes socially responsible behavior within one culture, let alone determine common ethical values across cultures. In addition to different cultural views, the high barriers facing international CSR include differing corporate disclosure practices, inconsistent financial data and reporting methods, and the lack of CSR research organizations within countries. Despite these problems, CSR is growing abroad. The United Kingdom has 30 ethical mutual funds and Canada offers 6 socially responsible funds.

CSR's Effect on the Mission Statement

The mission statement not only identifies what product or service a company produces, how it produces it, and what market it serves, it also embodies what the company believes. As such, it is essential that the mission statement recognize the legitimate claims of its external stakeholders, which may include creditors, customers, suppliers, government, unions, competitors, local communities, and elements of the general public. This stakeholder approach has become widely accepted by U.S. business. For example, a survey of directors in 291 of the largest southeastern U.S. companies found that directors had high stakeholder orientations. Customers, government, stockholders, employees, and society, in that order, were the stakeholders these directors perceived as most important.

In developing mission statements, managers must identify all stakeholder groups and weigh their relative rights and abilities to affect the firm's success. Some companies are proactive in their approach to CSR, making it an integral part of their raison d'être (e.g., Ben & Jerry's ice cream); others are reactive, adopting socially responsible behavior only when they must (e.g., Exxon after the *Valdez* incident).

Social Audit

A *social audit* attempts to measure a company's actual social performance against the social objectives it has set for itself. A social audit may be conducted by the company itself. However, one conducted by an outside consultant who will impose minimal biases may prove more beneficial to the firm. As with a financial audit, an outside auditor brings credibility to the evaluation. This credibility is essential if management is to take the results seriously and if the general public is to believe the company's public relations pronouncements.

Careful, accurate monitoring and evaluation of a company's CSR actions are important not only because the company wants to be sure it is implementing CSR policy as planned, but also because CSR actions by their nature are open to intense public scrutiny. To make sure it is making good on its CSR promises, a company may conduct a social audit of its performance.

Once the social audit is complete, it may be distributed internally or both internally and externally, depending on the firm's goals and situation. Some firms include a section in their annual report devoted to social responsibility activities; others publish a separate periodic report on their social responsiveness. Companies publishing separate social audits include General Motors, Bank of America, Atlantic Richfield, Control Data, and Aetna Life and Casualty Company. Nearly all Fortune 500 corporations disclose social performance information in their annual reports.

Large firms are not the only companies employing the social audit. Boutique ice cream maker Ben & Jerry's, a CSR pioneer, publishes a social audit in its annual report. The audit, conducted by an outside consultant, scores company performance in such areas as employee benefits, plant safety, ecology, community involvement, and customer service. The report is published unedited.

The social audit may be used for more than simply monitoring and evaluating firm social performance. Managers also use social audits to scan the external environment, determine firm vulnerabilities, and institutionalize CSR within the firm. In addition, companies themselves are not the only ones who conduct social audits; public interest groups and the media watch companies who claim to be socially responsible very closely to see if they practice what they preach. These organizations include consumer groups and socially responsible investing firms that construct their own guidelines for evaluating companies.

The Body Shop learned what can happen when a company's behavior falls short of its espoused mission and objectives. The 20-year-old manufacturer and retailer of naturally based hair and skin products had cultivated a socially responsible corporate image based on a reputation for socially responsible behavior. In late 1994, however, *Business Ethics* magazine published an exposé claiming that the company did not "walk the talk." It accused the Body Shop of using nonrenewable petrochemicals in its products, recycling far less than it claimed, using ingredients tested on animals, and making threats against investigative journalists. The Body Shop's contradictions were noteworthy because Anita Roddick, the company's founder, made CSR a centerpiece of the company's strategy.[5]

Summary

Defining the company mission is one of the most often slighted tasks in strategic management. Emphasizing the operational aspects of long-range management activities comes much more easily for most executives. But the critical role of the mission statement repeatedly is demonstrated by failing firms whose short-run actions have been at odds with their long-run purposes.

The principal value of the mission statement is its specification of the firm's ultimate aims. A firm gains a heightened sense of purpose when its board of directors and its top executives address these issues: "What business are we in?" "What customers do we serve?" "Why does this organization exist?" However, the potential contribution of the company mission can be undermined if platitudes or ambiguous generalizations are accepted in response to these questions. It is not enough to say that Lever Brothers is in the business of "making anything that cleans anything" or that Polaroid is committed to businesses that deal with "the interaction of light and matter." Only if a firm clearly articulates its long-term intentions can its goals serve as a basis for shared expectations, planning, and performance evaluation.

A mission statement that is developed from this perspective provides managers with a unity of direction transcending individual, parochial, and temporary needs. It promotes a sense of shared expectations among all levels and generations of employees. It consolidates values over time and across individuals and interest groups. It projects a sense of worth and intent that can be identified and assimilated by outside stakeholders, that is, customers, suppliers, competitors, local committees, and the general public. Finally, it asserts the firm's commitment to responsible action in symbiosis with the preservation and protection of the essential claims of insider stakeholders' survival, growth, and profitability.

[5] Jon Entine, "Shattered Image," *Business Ethics* 8, no. 5 (September/October 1994), pp. 23–28.

Questions for Discussion

1. Reread Nicor, Inc.'s mission statement in Exhibit 2–1, Strategy in Action. List five insights into Nicor that you feel you gained from knowing its mission.

2. Locate the mission statement of a company not mentioned in the chapter. Where did you find it? Was it presented as a consolidated statement, or were you forced to assemble it yourself from various publications of the firm? How many of the mission statement elements outlined in this chapter were discussed or revealed in the statement you found?

3. Prepare a two-page typewritten mission statement for your school of business or for a firm selected by your instructor.

4. List five potentially vulnerable areas of a firm without a stated company mission.

5. Define the term *social responsibility*. Find an example of a company action that was legal but not socially responsible. Defend your example on the basis of your definition.

6. Name five potentially valuable indicators of a firm's social responsibility and describe how company performance in each could be measured.

Chapter 2 Discussion Case

BusinessWeek

Inside a Chinese Sweatshop

1 Liu Zhang (not his real name) was apprehensive about taking a job at the Chun Si Enterprise Handbag Factory in Zhongshan, a booming city in Guangdong Province in southern China, where thousands of factories churn out goods for Western companies. Chun Si, which made Kathie Lee Gifford handbags sold by Wal-Mart Stores Inc. as well as handbags sold by Kansas-based Payless ShoeSource Inc., advertised decent working conditions and a fair salary. But word among migrant workers in the area was that managers there demanded long hours of their workers and sometimes hit them. Still, Liu, a 32–year-old former farmer and construction worker from far-off Henan province, was desperate for work. A factory job would give him living quarters and the temporary-residence permit internal migrants need to avoid being locked up by police in special detention centers. So in late August 1999, he signed up.

2 Liu quickly realized that the factory was even worse than its reputation. Chun Si, owned by Chun Kwan, a Macau businessman, charged workers $15 a month for food and lodging in a crowded dorm— a crushing sum given the $22 Liu cleared his first month. What's more, the factory gave Liu an expired temporary-resident permit; and in return, Liu had to hand over his personal identification card. This left him a virtual captive. Only the local police near the factory knew that Chun Si issued expired cards, Liu says, so workers risked arrest if they ventured out of the immediate neighborhood.

3 HALF A CENT. Liu also found that Chun Si's 900 workers were locked in the walled factory compound for all but a total of 60 minutes a day for meals. Guards regularly punched and hit workers for talking back to managers or even for walking too fast, he says. And they fined them up to $1 for infractions such as taking too long in the bathroom. Liu left the factory for good in December, after he and about 60 other workers descended on the local labor office to protest Chun Si's latest offenses: requiring cash payments for dinner and a phony factory it set up to dupe Wal-Mart's auditors. In his pocket was a total of $6 for three months of 90–hour weeks—an average of about one-half cent an hour. "Workers there face a life of fines and beating," says Liu. Chun Kwan couldn't be reached, but his daughter, Selina Chun, one of the factory managers, says "this is not true, none of this." She concedes that Chun Si did not pay overtime but says few other factories do, either. In a face-to-face interview in August, she also admitted that workers have tried to sue Chun Si.

4 Liu's Dickensian tale stands in stark contrast to the reassurances that Wal-Mart, Payless, and other U.S. companies give American consumers that their goods aren't produced under sweatshop conditions. Since 1992, Wal-Mart has required its suppliers to sign a code of basic labor standards. After exposés in the mid–1990s of abuses in factories making Kathie Lee products, which the chain carries, Wal-Mart and Kathie Lee both began hiring outside auditing firms to inspect supplier factories to ensure their compliance with the code. Many other companies that produce or sell goods made in low-wage countries do similar self-policing, from Toys 'R' Us to Nike and Gap. While no company suggests that its auditing systems are perfect, most say they catch major abuses and either force suppliers to fix them or yank production.

5 What happened at Chun Si suggests that these auditing systems can miss serious problems—and that self-policing allows companies to avoid painful public revelations about them. Allegations about Chun Si first surfaced this May in a report by the National Labor Committee (NLC), a small anti-sweatshop group in New York that in 1997 exposed Kathie Lee's connection to labor violations in Central America. For several months, Wal-Mart repeatedly denied any connection to Chun Si. Wal-Mart and Kathie Lee even went so far as to pass out a press release when the report came out dismissing it as "lies" and insisting that they never had "any relationship with a company or factory by this name anywhere in the world."

6 But in mid-September, after a three-month *BusinessWeek* investigation that involved a visit to the factory, tracking down ex-Chun Si workers, and obtaining copies of records they had smuggled out of the factory, Wal-Mart conceded that it had produced the Kathie Lee bags there until December, 1999. Wal-Mart Vice-President of Corporate Affairs Jay Allen now says that Wal-Mart denied

using Chun Si because it was "defensive" about the sweatshop issue.

7   Wal-Mart Director of Corporate Compliance Denise Fenton says its auditors, Pricewaterhouse Coopers LLP (PWC) and Cal Safety Compliance Corp., had inspected Chun Si five times in 1999 and found that the factory didn't pay the legal overtime rate and had required excessive work hours. Because the factory didn't fix the problems, she says, Wal-Mart stopped making Kathie Lee bags there. Kathie Lee, who licenses her name to Wal-Mart, which handles production, concurred with the chain's action at Chun Si, says her lawyer Richard Hofstetter. Payless also stopped production there after an investigation, a spokesman says.

8   Still, the auditors failed to uncover many of the egregious conditions in the factory despite interviews with dozens of workers, concedes Fenton. Charges NLC Executive Director Charles Kernaghan: "The real issue here is why anyone should believe their audits."

9   A SECOND LOOK. And it's not just Wal-Mart. The NLC's report, entitled Made in China, detailed labor abuses in a dozen factories producing for household-name U.S. companies (www.nlcnet.org). After it came out, bootmaker Timberland Co. asked its auditors to revisit its plant, also in Zhongshan. They found that the factory hadn't fixed most of the violations cited the first time, despite repeated assurances to Timberland that it had. Similarly, in mid-September, Social Accountability International (SAI), a New York group that started a factory monitoring system last year, revoked its certification of a Chinese factory that makes shoes for New Balance Athletic Shoe Inc. after auditors reinspected the plant following the NLC report. "The auditors found that indeed there were many violations they had not picked up the first time," says SAI President Alice Tepper Marlin.

10   Because such efforts to reassure consumers have proven so unsatisfactory, a handful of companies, including Nike Inc. and Reebok International Ltd.—so far, the companies most tarnished by anti-sweatshop activists—have concluded that self-policing isn't enough. They—along with Kathie Lee—helped form the Fair Labor Assn., created in 1998 after a White House-sponsored initiative. The FLA now has a dozen members and is setting up an independent monitoring system that includes human rights groups.

11   Wal-Mart and many other companies, though, reject such efforts, saying they don't want to tell critics or rivals where their products are made. Yet without independent inspections, such companies leave themselves open to critics' accusations that self-policing doesn't work. "The big retailers, such as Wal-Mart, drive the market today, yet . . . they're not committed to changing the way they do business," says Michael Posner, head of New York-based Lawyers Committee for Human Rights and an FLA board member. Wal-Mart's Allen says that after three years of talks, the company may soon set up independent monitoring with the Interfaith Center on Corporate Responsibility, a religious group in New York City.

12   Certainly, what happened at Chun Si illustrates the inadequacy of many labor-auditing systems in place today. Wal-Mart uses nine auditing firms, including PWC. Like other big accounting firms, PWC has a booming labor-auditing business inspecting many of the thousands of factories making toys and clothes made by Wal-Mart and other companies. After Kathie Lee's drubbing by sweatshop critics, she hired Cal Safety, a Los Angeles-based labor-auditing firm, to do separate audits of the factories that produce the clothing and accessories bearing her name. According to Wal-Mart's Fenton, Cal Safety inspected the factory four times from March to December of last year, and PWC inspected it once, in September. The auditors found that Chun Si had numerous problems, including overtime violations and excessively long hours, says Fenton.

13   But otherwise, concedes Fenton, the audits missed most of the more serious abuses listed in the NLC report and confirmed by *BusinessWeek,* including beatings and confiscated identity papers. (Wal-Mart declined to allow *BusinessWeek* to talk in detail to Cal Safety or PWC, citing confidentiality agreements. Randal H. Rankin, head of PWC's labor practices unit, insists his audit did catch many of the abuses found by the NLC, though he wouldn't provide specifics, also citing Wal-Mart's confidentiality agreement. Cal Safety President Carol Pender says her firm caught some, though not all, of the abuses.)

14   All the while, evidence was piling up at the local labor office in Zhongshan. There, officials received a constant stream of worker complaints—several a month since the factory opened 10 years ago, says Mr. Chen, the head of the local labor office, who declined to give his

full name. "Since they opened their factory, the complaints never stopped," he says. Officials would call or go to the factory once a month or so to mediate disputes, but new complaints kept arising, he says. Neither Wal-Mart's nor Kathie Lee's auditors discovered this history.

15 Chun Si also tried to hoodwink the auditors, according to the workers *BusinessWeek* interviewed. After Cal Safety's initial inspection in March, 1999, Wal-Mart (through its U.S. supplier, which placed the order with the factory) insisted that Chun Si remedy the violations or it would pull the contract. Cal Safety found little improvement when it returned in June, as did PWC in September.

16 DOUBLE STANDARD. Chun Si then took drastic steps, apparently in an effort to pass the final audit upon which its contract depended. In early November, management gave a facelift to the two attached five-story factory buildings, painting walls, cleaning workshops, even putting high-quality toilet paper in the dank bathrooms, according to Liu and Pang Yinguang (also not his real name), another worker employed there at the time whom *BusinessWeek* interviewed in mid-September. Management then split the factory into two groups. The first, with about 200 workers, was assigned to work on the fixed-up second floor, while the remaining 700 or so worked on the fourth floor, leaving the other floors largely vacant. Managers announced that those on the fourth floor were no longer working for Chun Si but for a new factory they called Yecheng. Workers signed new labor contracts with Yecheng, whose name went up outside the fourth floor.

17 The reality soon became clear. Workers on the fourth floor, including Liu and Pang, were still laboring under the old egregious conditions— illegally low pay, 14–hour days, exorbitant fees for meals—and still making the same Kathie Lee handbags. "It felt like being in prison," says Pang, 22. But those on the second floor now received the local minimum wage of $55 a month and no longer had to do mandatory overtime. A new sign went up in the cafeteria used by workers on all floors explaining that the factory was a Wal-Mart supplier and should live up to certain labor standards. Liu says there was even a phone number workers could call with problems: 1-800-WM-ETHIC. "When we saw the Wal-Mart statement, we felt very excited and happy because

we thought that now there was a possibility to improve our conditions," says Liu.

18 LAST STRAW. Instead, they got worse. On Nov. 28, a second notice went up stating that starting on Dec. 10, all workers would be required to pay cash for dinner rather than just have money subtracted from their paychecks as before, say Liu and Pang. With up to 80% of workers already skipping breakfast to save money, the upper-floor employees were aghast, says Liu. "If we had left the factory then, we wouldn't have had even enough money for a bus ticket home," he says. "But if we stayed, we knew we wouldn't have enough money to eat."

19 A group of workers, including Liu and Pang, met around a small pond on the factory grounds on one of the following evenings. They knew that workers had fruitlessly complained before to the local labor office. So they decided on a plan to smuggle out documents to prove Chun Si's illegal fees and sub-minimum wages. On Dec. 1, 58 workers overcame their fears of retaliation and marched out the factory gates, down to the labor office.

20 Faced with the throng of workers, local labor officials visited Chun Si and forced the factory to immediately pay the workers and return the illegally collected fees. But the officials also told these workers they would have to give up their jobs at Chun Si. Days later, some 40 labor officials returned, ordered Chun Si to properly register or shut down the so-called Yecheng factory, and fined the company about $8,500. Shortly after the blow-up, Wal-Mart ended production at Chun Si.

21 Kernaghan and other labor activists concede that Chun Si is an extreme example of working conditions in China today. Yet many experts think most factories in China producing for Western companies routinely break China's labor laws. Some Western companies' monitoring efforts do catch and fix some of these problems. But unless companies and governments alike take more serious steps, labor watchdogs will give little credence to company claims that they're doing the best they can.

Source: Dexter Roberts and Aaron Bernstein, "A Life of Fines and Beating: Wal-Mart's self-policing in the Chun Si factory was a disaster. What kind of monitoring system works?" *BusinessWeek,* October 2, 2000.

Chapter **Three**

The External Environment

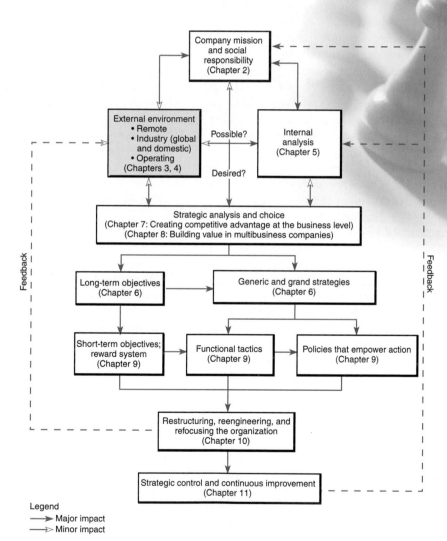

Company mission and social responsibility
(Chapter 2)

External environment
• Remote
• Industry (global and domestic)
• Operating
(Chapters 3, 4)

Possible?

Desired?

Internal analysis
(Chapter 5)

Strategic analysis and choice
(Chapter 7: Creating competitive advantage at the business level)
(Chapter 8: Building value in multibusiness companies)

Long-term objectives
(Chapter 6)

Generic and grand strategies
(Chapter 6)

Short-term objectives; reward system
(Chapter 9)

Functional tactics
(Chapter 9)

Policies that empower action
(Chapter 9)

Restructuring, reengineering, and refocusing the organization
(Chapter 10)

Strategic control and continuous improvement
(Chapter 11)

Feedback

Feedback

Legend
⟶ Major impact
⟶ Minor impact

A host of external factors influence a firm's choice of direction and action and, ultimately, its organizational structure and internal processes. These factors, which constitute the *external environment,* can be divided into three interrelated subcategories: factors in the *remote* environment, factors in the *industry* environment, and factors in the *operating* environment.[1] This chapter describes the complex necessities involved in formulating strategies that optimize a firm's market opportunities. Exhibit 3–1 suggests the interrelationship between the firm and its remote, its industry, and its operating environments. In combination, these factors form the basis of the opportunities and threats that a firm faces in its competitive environment.

EXHIBIT 3–1
The Firm's External Environment

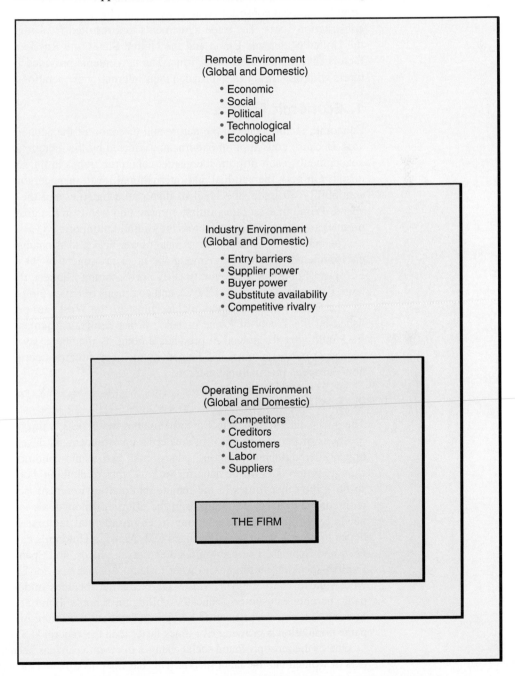

---

[1] The operating environment is sometimes referred to as the *task* or *competitive* environment.

REMOTE ENVIRONMENT

The remote environment comprises factors that originate beyond, and usually irrespective of, any single firm's operating situation: (1) economic, (2) social, (3) political, (4) technological, and (5) ecological factors. That environment presents firms with opportunities, threats, and constraints, but rarely does a single firm exert any meaningful reciprocal influence. For example, when the economy slows and construction starts to decrease, an individual contractor is likely to suffer a decline in business, but that contractor's efforts in stimulating local construction activities would be unable to reverse the overall decrease in construction starts. The trade agreements that resulted from improved relations between the United States and China and the United States and Russia are examples of political factors that impact individual firms. The agreements provided individual U.S. manufacturers with opportunities to broaden their international operations.

1. Economic Factors

Economic factors concern the nature and direction of the economy in which a firm operates. Because consumption patterns are affected by the relative affluence of various market segments, each firm must consider economic trends in the segments that affect its industry. On both the national and international level, managers must consider the general availability of credit, the level of disposable income, and the propensity of people to spend. Prime interest rates, inflation rates, and trends in the growth of the gross national product are other economic factors they should monitor.

The emergence of new international power brokers has changed the focus of economic environmental forecasting. Among the most prominent of these power brokers are the European Economic Community (EEC, or Common Market), the Organization of Petroleum Exporting Countries (OPEC), and coalitions of developing countries.

The EEC, whose members include most of the West European countries, was established by the Treaty of Rome in 1957. It has eliminated quotas and established a tariff-free trade area for industrial products among its members. By fostering intra-European economic cooperation, it has helped its member countries compete more effectively in non-European international markets.

2. Social Factors

The social factors that affect a firm involve the beliefs, values, attitudes, opinions, and lifestyles of persons in the firm's external environment, as developed from cultural, ecological, demographic, religious, educational, and ethnic conditioning. As social attitudes change, so too does the demand for various types of clothing, books, leisure activities, and so on. Like other forces in the remote external environment, social forces are dynamic, with constant change resulting from the efforts of individuals to satisfy their desires and needs by controlling and adapting to environmental factors. Teresa Iglesias-Soloman hopes to benefit from social changes with *Ninos,* a children's catalog written in both English and Spanish. The catalog features books, videos, and Spanish cultural offerings for English-speaking children who want to learn Spanish and for Spanish-speaking children who want to learn English. *Ninos'* target market includes middle-to-upper-income Hispanic parents, consumers, educators, bilingual schools, libraries, and purchasing agents. Iglesias-Solomon has reason to be optimistic about the future of *Ninos,* because the Hispanic population is growing five times faster than the general U.S. population.

One of the most profound social changes in recent years has been the entry of large numbers of women into the labor market. This has not only affected the hiring and compensation policies and the resource capabilities of their employers; it has also created or greatly expanded the demand for a wide range of products and services necessitated by their absence from the home. Firms that anticipated or reacted quickly to this social change offered such products and services as convenience foods, microwave ovens, and day care centers.

A second profound social change has been the accelerating interest of consumers and employees in quality-of-life issues. Evidence of this change is seen in recent contract negotiations. In addition to the traditional demand for increased salaries, worker demands such benefits as sabbaticals, flexible hours or four-day workweeks, lump-sum vacation plans, and opportunities for advanced training.

A third profound social change has been the shift in the age distribution of the population. Changing social values and a growing acceptance of improved birth control methods are expected to raise the mean age of the U.S. population, which was 27.9 in 1970, and 34.9 in the year 2000. This trend will have an increasingly unfavorable impact on most producers of predominantly youth-oriented goods and will necessitate a shift in their long-range marketing strategies. Producers of hair and skin care preparations already have begun to adjust their research and development to reflect anticipated changes in demand.

A consequence of the changing age distribution of the population has been a sharp increase in the demands made by a growing number of senior citizens. Constrained by fixed incomes, these citizens have demanded that arbitrary and rigid policies on retirement age be modified and have successfully lobbied for tax exemptions and increases in Social Security benefits. Such changes have significantly altered the opportunity-risk equations of many firms—often to the benefit of firms that anticipated the changes.

The problems of monitoring social changes are multiplied many times as businesses venture into international markets. One simple but poignant example is described in Strategy in Action Exhibit 3–2.

Translating social change into forecasts of business effects is a difficult process, at best. Nevertheless, informed estimates of the impact of such alterations as geographic shifts in populations and changing work values, ethical standards, and religious orientation can only help a strategizing firm in its attempts to prosper.

3. Political Factors

The direction and stability of political factors are a major consideration for managers on formulating company strategy. Political factors define the legal and regulatory parameters within which firms must operate. Political constraints are placed on firms through fair-trade decisions, antitrust laws, tax programs, minimum wage legislation, pollution and pricing policies, administrative jawboning, and many other actions aimed at protecting employees, consumers, the general public, and the environment. Since such laws and regulations are most commonly restrictive, they tend to reduce the potential profits of firms. However, some political actions are designed to benefit and protect firms. Such actions include patent laws, government subsidies, and product research grants. Thus, political factors either may limit or benefit the firms they influence.

As described in Exhibit 3–3, Global Strategy in Action, the direction and stability of political factors are a major consideration when evaluating the remote environment. Specifically, the article addresses the fact that the legal basis of piracy is political. Microsoft's performance in the Chinese market is greatly affected by the lack of legal enforcement of piracy and also by the policies of the Chinese government. Likewise, the government's actions in support of its competitor, Linux, have limited Microsoft's ability to penetrate the Chinese market.

Political activity also has a significant impact on two governmental functions that influence the remote environment of firms: the supplier function and the customer function.

BusinessWeek India's sacred cows can stop fretting: McDonald's won't be requiring their services. The burger behemoth announced it will open its first franchises in India early next year—but without Big Macs. Deferring to the country's Hindu tradition, which prohibits the consumption of beef, the company instead will serve chicken and fish, as well as vegetable burgers. It's the first time the fast-food company has excluded beef from its menu. New Delhi consultant Dilip Cherian thinks other multinationals should follow McDonald's culturally sensitive lead: "It's not going to be one grand American burger that sweeps through India," he says.

Source: Keith H. Hammonds, ed., "In India, Beef-Free Mickey D," *BusinessWeek,* April 17, 1995.

Supplier Function

Government decisions regarding the accessibility of private businesses to government-owned natural resources and national stockpiles of agricultural products will affect profoundly the viability of the strategies of some firms.

Customer Function

Government demand for products and services can create, sustain, enhance, or eliminate many market opportunities. For example, in the same way that the Kennedy administration's emphasis on landing a man on the moon spawned a demand for thousands of new products; the Carter administration's emphasis on developing synthetic fuels created a demand for new skills, technologies, and products; the Reagan administration's strategic defense initiative (the "Star Wars" defense) sharply accelerated the development of laser technologies; Clinton's federal block grants to the states for welfare reform led to office rental and lease opportunities; and the war against terrorism during the Bush administration created enormous investment in aviation.

4. Technological Factors

The fourth set of factors in the remote environment involves technological change. To avoid obsolescence and promote innovation, a firm must be aware of technological changes that might influence its industry. Creative technological adaptations can suggest possibilities for new products, for improvements in existing products, or in manufacturing and marketing techniques.

A technological breakthrough can have a sudden and dramatic effect on a firm's environment. It may spawn sophisticated new markets and products or significantly shorten the anticipated life of a manufacturing facility. Thus, all firms, and most particularly those in turbulent growth industries, must strive for an understanding both of the existing technological advances and the probable future advances that can affect their products and services. This quasi-science of attempting to foresee advancements and estimate their impact on an organization's operations is known as *technological forecasting*.

Technological forecasting can help protect and improve the profitability of firms in growing industries. It alerts strategic managers to both impending challenges and promising opportunities. As examples: (1) advances in xerography were a key to Xerox's success but caused major difficulties for carbon paper manufacturers, and (2) the perfection of transistors changed the nature of competition in the radio and television industry, helping such giants as RCA while seriously weakening smaller firms whose resource commitments required that they continue to base their products on vacuum tubes.

BusinessWeek One box that solves two problems. That was Microsoft's hope for Venus, a $240–$360 gadget running Windows CE software that turns Chinese TV sets into Internet appliances. Venus would solve two problems by making it both easier and cheaper for Chinese consumers to access the Web. Venus was the key to penetrating China, because it would make Windows nearly ubiquitous in living rooms from Shenzhen to Shanghai.

Fast-forward to late 2000: Venus seems more like one box containing two disasters. Of the three main Chinese companies that signed up to sell Venus boxes, two have pulled them from the market. Only Legend Computer is still selling the units in China—and it ships most of its supply to Southeast Asia. Why has Venus fizzled? Zhang blames both a lack of online content and the relatively high cost of Internet access. But others say Microsoft misjudged the willingness of Chinese to buy what is essentially low-rent technology. And with PCs selling for as little as $600, there isn't much reason to buy Venus.

The Venus project is not the only misfire in Microsoft's China strategy. Microsoft continues to battle software pirates, a poor image with Chinese authorities and consumers, and a growing threat from local rivals offering inexpensive Linux-based service. Microsoft won't release its China revenues, but analysts say they're probably under $100 million this year—less than the company makes in Hong Kong. "We are much smaller than we expected," says Microsoft General Manager Jack Gao.

Increasingly, Microsoft must contend with companies offering Linux, the open-source operating system. The threat is perhaps more political than anything else. Beijing likes to set one foreign company against another—as it has done with Boeing and Airbus. By playing up the potential of Linux, the government may be telling Microsoft that it had better play by its rules.

But Microsoft faces no greater competitor than the thieves who have elevated software piracy to a fine art. Last year, overall sales of computer hardware in China topped $18 billion. But software sales were a measly $2.1 billion. In other countries, the ratio is closer to even. Blame the shortfall on the pirates. Because of all the counterfeiting, Microsoft sold only 2 million licensed copies of its software in China during the year ending in June.

Chinese aren't ready to give up on counterfeit versions of Windows either. "We have a lot of users," says Jack Gao ruefully. "But we don't have a lot of customers." With Beijing intent on developing a local software industry, he says, cracking down on the pirates is in China's interest, too. That will take time. For now, a more humble Microsoft will have to keep trying to win friends in the emerging market it values most.

Source: An excerpt from B. Einhorn and A. Webb, "Microsoft Misfires in China," *BusinessWeek,* December 18, 2000.

The key to beneficial forecasting of technological advancement lies in accurately predicting future technological capabilities and their probable impacts. A comprehensive analysis of the effect of technological change involves study of the expected impact of new technologies on the remote environment, on the competitive business situation, and on the business-society interface. In recent years, forecasting in the last area has warranted particular attention. For example, as a consequence of increased concern over the environment, firms must carefully investigate the probable effect of technological advances on quality-of-life factors, such as ecology and public safety.

As discussed in Exhibit 3–4, E-commerce Strategy in Action, by combining the powers of Internet technologies with the capability of downloading music in a digital format, Bertelsmann has found a creative technological adaptation for distributing music online to millions of consumers whenever or wherever they might be. The ease and wide availability of Internet technologies is increasing the marketplace for online e-tailers. Bertelsmann's response to the shifts in technological factors enables it to distribute music more rapidly to a growing consumer base.

5. Ecological Factors

The most prominent factor in the remote environment is often the reciprocal relationship between business and the ecology. The term *ecology* refers to the relationships among human beings and other living things and the air, soil, and water that support them.

E-commerce Strategy in Action
Bertelsmann's Online Joint Venture

Exhibit 3–4

BusinessWeek On April 2, 2001, Bertelsmann, AOL Time Warner Inc., and London-based EMI Group announced they are teaming up with RealNetworks Inc. on a new online venture called MusicNet. The deal is Middelhoff's latest gambit to ensure that Bertelsmann will play a big role in the digital music business—even if Napster doesn't make it. MusicNet is designed to be a digital music wholesaler. It will act as an intermediary between recording companies and online retailers, providing technology that allows fans to listen to music tracks over the Internet or download songs they can replay and keep. Most important, MusicNet will provide technology allowing recording companies to protect their copyrights and collect royalties. "MusicNet turns into a black box for companies like us that want to offer music services but don't want to have to build all that," says Barry M. Schuler, chairman and CEO of AOL, which plans to use MusicNet as the basis for its own music subscription service.

The MusicNet deal broadens Bertelsmann's digital distribution base. Bertelsmann will own 20% of MusicNet, the same stake as the other recording companies. So Bertelsmann can be sure its music catalog will also be sold on AOL and any other subscription services based on MusicNet. Meanwhile, eCommerce chief Schmidt is making plans for an alternative consumer service called Be Music, which will use MusicNet to make Bertelsmann music available to customers on PCs, mobile phones, and other devices. Bertelsmann's BMG Entertainment, Warner Music Group, and EMI will provide MusicNet with their vast catalogs, accounting for more than 50% of the music market and including artists from Bjork to Madonna. With that kind of critical mass, other record companies will feel pressure to distribute their catalogs via MusicNet. That in turn could push the fragmented music industry toward some kind of technical standard for music sales on the Internet.

If it can overcome the huge technical hurdles, Napster could have enough music from Warner, Bertelsmann, and EMI to convert at least some of its 72 million registered users to paying subscribers. "That's more than enough to build a viable business," says Mark Mulligan, London-based analyst for Jupiter Media Metrix Inc.

Surely many Napster users will bolt to outlaw services if they have to start paying. Even if Napster can get one quarter to pay an average of $5 a month, though, it can generate more than $1 billion a year in revenue. Middelhoff hopes to end the legal challenges, then exercise an option to take a 58% stake and control what is still the media industry's most powerful online draw.

Many in the music industry are still hoping that Napster will die a slow death. Yet none has found an alternative with such powerful popular appeal. "The music business will be transformed by this long-term," says AOL's Schuler.

Source: An excerpt from Jack Ewing, Amy Borrus, Arlene Weintraub, and Jay Greene. "Sold on a Digital Music Dream, An online joint venture could make it come true for Bertelsmann," *BusinessWeek*, April 16, 2001.

Threats to our life-supporting ecology caused principally by human activities in an industrial society are commonly referred to as *pollution*. Specific concerns include global warming, loss of habitat and biodiversity, as well as air, water, and land pollution.

The global climate has been changing for ages; however, it is now evident that humanity's activities are accelerating this tremendously. A change in atmospheric radiation, due in part to ozone depletion, causes global warming. Solar radiation that is normally absorbed into the atmosphere reaches the earth's surface, heating the soil, water, and air.

Another area of great importance is the loss of habitat and biodiversity. Ecologists agree that the extinction of important flora and fauna is occurring at a rapid rate and if this pace is continued, could constitute a global extinction on the scale of those found in fossil records. The earth's life forms are dependent on a well-functioning ecosystem. In addition, immeasurable advances in disease treatment can be attributed to research involving substances found in plants. As species become extinct, the life support system is irreparably harmed. The primary cause of extinction on this scale is a disturbance of natural habitat. For example, current data suggest that the earth's primary tropical forests, a prime source of oxygen and potential plant "cure," could be destroyed in only five decades.

Air pollution is created by dust particles and gaseous discharges that contaminate the air. Acid rain, or rain contaminated by sulfur dioxide, which can destroy aquatic and plant

BusinessWeek

Outdoor clothing company Patagonia Inc. has worked hard to be one of the greenest businesses around. It was the first apparel maker to sell synthetic fleece sweaters and warm-up pants made from recycled soda bottles. Last year, it switched to organic cotton for shirts and trousers—and ate half of the 20% markup that organic production added to the garments' cost. Its glossy catalog, printed on recycled paper that is 50% chlorine-free, uses pictures of adventurers in wild places to promote environmental causes.

But Patagonia still has a troubled conscience. In a surprisingly public mea culpa, the company's fall catalog opens with a letter to customers that is a stark critique of Patagonia's reliance on waterproof coatings such as Gore-Tex, which contains chemical toxins, and bright dyes based on strip-mined metals. It is only by using such "dirty" manufacturing processes, the company confesses, that it can offer the "bombproof" outdoor gear and striking colors that customers love. As the letter laments: "The production of our clothing takes a significant toll on the earth."

Turns out it's not easy being green. Patagonia and a handful of other companies that have made protection of the environment a central tenet of their businesses are running into a new wave of polluting problems that require tougher trade-offs than those of the past. Whether it's Ben & Jerry's Home-made coping with massive amounts of high-fat dairy waste, Stonyfield Farm searching for an affordable way to convert to organic fruit for its yogurt, or Orvis, the fishing-gear maker, trying to build a new headquarters that won't threaten bear habitats, green pioneers are struggling for ways to balance *environmental principles* with profit goals.

None are backing off their commitment to the environment. Instead, the greenest companies are testing the limits of what can be done cleanly. "We want it all," Yvon Chouinard, Patagonia's president, told a meeting of the company's suppliers last year. "The best quality and the lowest environmental impact." But it's getting tougher to push the green envelope without compromising business goals. "Our whole system of commerce is not designed to be ecologically sustainable," says Matthew Arnold, director of Washington-based Management Institute for Environment & Business. "These guys are showing the limits of the system to respond."

And customers have made it clear that quality comes first, even if it means passing up the chance to have less impact on the environment. Patagonia surveys show that just 20% of its customers buy from the company because they believe in its environmental mission.

Source: Paul C. Judge in Boston, "It's Not Easy Being Green," *BusinessWeek*, November 24, 1997.

life, is believed to result from coal-burning factories in 70 percent of all cases. A health-threatening "thermal blanket" is created when the atmosphere traps carbon dioxide emitted from smokestacks in factories burning fossil fuels. This "greenhouse effect" can have disastrous consequences, making the climate unpredictable and raising temperatures.

Water pollution occurs principally when industrial toxic wastes are dumped or leak into the nation's waterways. Since fewer than 50 percent of all municipal sewer systems are in compliance with Environmental Protection Agency requirements for water safety, contaminated waters represent a substantial present threat to public welfare. Efforts to keep from contaminating the water supply are a major challenge to even the most conscientious of manufacturing firms. As described in Exhibit 3–5, Strategy in Action, highly reputed "green" supporter Patagonia has judged itself to be guilty of water pollution.

The Patagonia story is especially interesting because of the "green" fervor with which the company pursues its manufacturing objectives. It provides some details on the difficulties that Patagonia faces in its attempts to do what many ecological activists believe should be a national mandate for all corporations.

Land pollution is caused by the need to dispose of ever-increasing amounts of waste. Routine, everyday packaging is a major contributor to this problem. Land pollution is more dauntingly caused by the disposal of industrial toxic wastes in underground sites. With approximately 90 percent of the annual U.S. output of 500 million metric tons of hazardous industrial wastes being placed in underground dumps, it is evident that land pollution and its resulting endangerment of the ecology have become a major item on the political agenda.

EXHIBIT 3–6
Environmental Costs and Competitiveness

Source: Excerpted from Benjamin C. Bonifant, Matthew R. Arnold, and Frederick J. Long, "Gaining Competitive Advantage through Environmental Investments," p. 39. Reprinted from *Business Horizons,* July–August 1995. Copyright 1995 by the Foundation for the School of Business at Indiana University. Used with permission.

Several recent efforts to quantify environmental spending have suggested that enormous costs are being incurred. A 1990 study by the U.S. EPA concluded that environmental spending was approaching 2 percent of GNP. Manufacturers then used this information to support their claim that regulation was harming industrial growth and putting the nation at a competitive disadvantage vis-à-vis foreign suppliers. The claims, however, simply did not hold up to closer inspection. First, only a small share of pollution abatement and control spending was incurred by industrial facilities. By one estimate (one used as a source for the EPA study), manufacturers incurred a total of $31.1 billion in environmental costs in 1990. This amounted to only 1.1 percent of product shipments. The costs identified by the EPA resulted from such areas as the requirement for catalytic converters on all automobiles ($14 billion in 1990), the construction and operation of public sewer systems ($20 billion), and the disposal of household wastes ($10 billion).

Even if environmental spending made up only 1 percent of costs, it would not be unreasonable for manufacturers to claim that these costs had a significant influence on competitiveness if international competitors were not required to meet similar requirements. Comparisons of international spending suggest, however, that manufacturers in important production areas around the world are experiencing costs similar to those faced by U.S. producers. Pollution control's share of capital expenditures in Germany was 12 percent in 1990, matching the costs incurred by American manufacturers. Similarly, recent environmental spending by U.S. pulp and paper manufacturers is closely matched by key competitors in Canada and Sweden.

These comparisons suggest that although pollution abatement expenditures are clearly a material part of total costs, the impact of these costs on competitiveness is mild. In fact, no clear link can be made between environmental regulation and measurably adverse effects on net exports, overall trade flows, or plant location decisions. It appears that little advantage has been gained by foreign firms based on the environmental requirements in the areas of their production.

As a major contributor to ecological pollution, business now is being held responsible for eliminating the toxic by-products of its current manufacturing processes and for cleaning up the environmental damage that it did previously. Increasingly, managers are being required by the government or are being expected by the public to incorporate ecological concerns into their decision making. For example, between 1975 and 1992, 3M cut its pollution in half by reformulating products, modifying processes, redesigning production equipment, and recycling by-products. Similarly, steel companies and public utilities have invested billions of dollars in costlier but cleaner-burning fuels and pollution control equipment. The automobile industry has been required to install expensive emission controls in cars. The gasoline industry has been forced to formulate new low-lead and no-lead products. And thousands of companies have found it necessary to direct their R&D resources into the search for ecologically superior products, such as Sears's phosphate-free laundry detergent and Pepsi-Cola's biodegradable plastic soft-drink bottle.

Environmental legislation impacts corporate strategies worldwide. Many companies fear the consequences of highly restrictive and costly environmental regulations. However, some manufacturers view these new controls as an opportunity, capturing markets with products that help customers satisfy their own regulatory standards. Other manufacturers contend that the costs of environmental spending inhibit the growth and productivity of their operations. Exhibit 3–6 takes a deeper look into the costs of environmental regulations.

The increasing attention by companies to protect the environment is evidenced in the attempts by firms to establish proecology policies. One such approach to environmental activism is described in Global Strategy in Action Exhibit 3–7.

"The ongoing occurrence of environmental incidents has become unacceptable in the public's mind," says George Pilko, president of Houston-based Pilko & Associates, an environmental consulting firm. That's why companies today are taking a proactive stance when it comes to managing environmental issues. The public just won't tolerate any more Love Canals, Bhopals, or major oil spills. "You've got strong public sentiment, increasingly stringent enviromental regulations at the local, state, and federal level, stricter enforcement of existing regulations, and an exponential rise in environmentally oriented lawsuits.

Companies need to make sure they have an environmental policy that clearly explains their commitment to being proactive and is communicated clearly to all employees. Companies also should be aware of the effectiveness of their current programs and when they stand relative to their competitors. In fact, a Pilko & Associates survey of 200 senior executives representing large industrial firms found that 40 percent of the respondents believed their company was doing an excellent job of managing their environmental problems, while only 8 percent thought their competitors were doing an excellent job.

For those CEOs or senior executives interested in getting out the message that they are serious about dealing with the environment. Pilko advises them to ask themselves the following 10 questions:

1. Do you have a clearly articulated environmental policy that has been communicated throughout the company?

2. Have you had an objective, third-party assessment of the effectiveness of your environmental problems?

3. Have you analyzed how your company's environmental performance compares with that of the leading firms in your industry?

4. Does your company view environmental performance not just as a staff function but as the responsibility of all employees?

5. Have you analyzed the potential impact of environmental issues on the future demand for your products and the competitive economics in your industry?

6. Are environmental issues and activities discussed frequently at your board meetings?

7. Do you have a formal system for monitoring proposed regulatory changes and for handling compliance with changing regulations?

8. Do you routinely conduct environmental due-diligence studies on potential acquisitions?

9. Have you successfully budgeted for environmental expenditures, without incurring surprise expenses that materially affected your profitability?

10. Have you identified and quantifled environmental liabilities from past operations, and do you have a plan for minimizing those liabilities?

Source: Excerpted from Julie Cohen Mason, "Taking a Step in the Right Direction," p. 23. Reprinted by permission of the publisher from *Management Review,* December 1991, © 1991 American Management Association, New York. All rights reserved.

Despite cleanup efforts to date, the job of protecting the ecology will continue to be a top strategic priority—usually because corporate stockholders and executives choose it, increasingly because the public and the government require it. As evidenced by Exhibit 3–8, the government has made numerous interventions into the conduct of business for the purpose of bettering the ecology.

Benefits of Eco-Efficiency

Many of the world's largest corporations are realizing that business activities must no longer ignore environmental concerns. Every activity is linked to thousands of other transactions and their environmental impact; therefore, corporate environmental responsibility must be taken seriously and environmental policy must be implemented to ensure a comprehensive organizational strategy. Because of increases in government regulations and consumer environmental concerns, the implementation of environmental policy has become a point of competitive advantage. Therefore, the rational goal of business should be to limit its impact on the environment, thus ensuring long-run benefits to both the firm and society. To neglect this responsibility is to ensure the demise of both the firm and our ecosystem.

EXHIBIT 3–8
Federal Ecological
Legislation

Centerpiece Legislation

National Environmental Policy Act, 1969   Established Environmental Protection Agency; consolidated federal environmental activities under it. Established Council on Environmental Quality to advise president on environmental policy and to review environmental impact statements.

Air Pollution

Clean Air Act, 1963   Authorized assistance to state and local governments in formulating control programs. Authorized limited federal action in correcting specific pollution problems.
Clean Air Act, Amendments (Motor Vehicle Air Pollution Control Act), 1965 Authorized federal standards for auto exhaust emission. Standards first set for 1968 models.
Air Quality Act, 1967   Authorized federal government to establish air quality control regions and to set maximum permissible pollution levels. Required states and localities to carry out approved control programs or else give way to federal controls.
Clean Air Act Amendments, 1970   Authorized EPA to establish nationwide air pollution standards and to limit the discharge of six principal pollutants into the lower atmosphere. Authorized citizens to take legal action to require EPA to implement its standards against undiscovered offenders.
Clean Air Act Amendments, 1977   Postponed auto emission requirements. Required use of scrubbers in new coal-fired power plants. Directed EPA to establish a system to prevent deterioration of air quality in clean areas.

Solid Waste Pollution

Solid Waste Disposal Act, 1965   Authorized research and assistance to state and local control programs.
Resource Recovery Act, 1970   Subsidized construction of pilot recycling plants; authorized development of nationwide control programs.
Resource Conservation and Recovery Act, 1976   Directed EPA to regulate hazardous waste management, from generation through disposal.
Surface Mining and Reclamation Act, 1976   Controlled strip mining and restoration of reclaimed land.

Water Pollution

Refuse Act, 1899   Prohibited dumping of debris into navigable waters without a permit. Extended by court decision to industrial discharges.
Federal Water Pollution Control Act, 1956   Authorized grants to states for water pollution control. Gave federal government limited authority to correct specific pollution problems.
Water Quality Act, 1965   Provided for adoption of water quality standards by states, subject to federal approval.
Water Quality Improvement Act, 1970   Provided for federal cleanup of oil spills. Strengthened federal authority over water pollution control.
Federal Water Pollution Control Act Amendments, 1972   Authorized EPA to set water quality and effluent standards; provided for enforcement and research.
Safe Drinking Water Act, 1974   Set standards for drinking water quality.
Clean Water Act, 1977   Ordered control of toxic pollutants by 1984 with best available technology economically feasible.

Stephen Schmidheiny, chairman of the Business Council for Sustainable Development, has coined the term *eco-efficiency* to describe corporations that produce more-useful goods and services while continuously reducing resource consumption and pollution. He cites a number of reasons for corporations to implement environmental policy: customers demand cleaner products, environmental regulations are increasingly more stringent, employees prefer to work for environmentally conscious firms, and financing is more readily available for eco-efficient firms. In addition, the government provides incentives for environmentally responsible companies.

Setting priorities, developing corporate standards, controlling property acquisition and use to preserve habitats, implementing energy-conserving activities, and redesigning products (e.g., minimizing packaging) are a number of measures the firm can implement to enhance an eco-efficient strategy. One of the most important steps a firm can take in achieving a competitive position with regard to the eco-efficient strategy is to fully capitalize on technological developments as a method of gaining efficiency.

Four key characteristics of eco-efficient corporations are:

- Eco-efficient firms are proactive, not reactive. Policy is initiated and promoted by business because it is in their own interests and the interest of their customers, not because it is imposed by one or more external forces.

- Eco-efficiency is designed in, not added on. This characteristic implies that the optimization of eco-efficiency requires every business effort regarding the product and process to internalize the strategy.

- Flexibility is imperative for eco-efficient strategy implementation. Continuous attention must be paid to technological innovation and market evolution.

- Eco-efficiency is encompassing, not insular. In the modern global business environment, efforts must cross not only industrial sectors but national and cultural boundaries as well.

INTERNATIONAL ENVIRONMENT

Monitoring the international environment, perhaps better thought of as the international dimension of the global environment, involves assessing each nondomestic market on the same factors that are used in a domestic assessment. While the importance of factors will differ, the same set of considerations can be used for each country. For example, Exhibit 3–9, Global Strategy in Action, lists the economic, political, legal, and social factors that international expert Arvind Phatak uses to assess international environments. However, there is one complication to this process, namely, that the interplay among international markets must be considered. For example, in recent years, conflicts in the Middle East have made collaborative business strategies among firms in traditionally antagonistic countries especially difficult to implement.

INDUSTRY ENVIRONMENT

Harvard professor Michael E. Porter propelled the concept of industry environment into the foreground of strategic thought and business planning. The cornerstone of his work first appeared in the *Harvard Business Review,* in which Porter explains the five forces that shape competition in an industry. His well-defined analytic framework helps strategic managers to link remote factors to their effects on a firm's operating environment.

Global Strategy in Action
Used to Assess the International Environment

Exhibit 3–9

ECONOMIC ENVIRONMENT

Level of economic development

Population

Gross national product

Per capita income

Literacy level

Social infrastructure

Natural resources

Climate

Membership in regional economic blocs (EU, NAFTA, LAFTA)

Monetary and fiscal policies

Wage and salary levels

Nature of competition

Currency convertibility

Inflation

Taxation system

Interest rates

LEGAL ENVIRONMENT

Legal tradition

Effectiveness of legal system

Treaties with foreign nations

Patent trademark laws

Laws affecting business firms

POLITICAL SYSTEM

Form of government

Political ideology

Stability of government

Strength of opposition parties and groups

Social unrest

Political strife and insurgency

Govermental attitude towards foreign firms

Foreign policy

CULTURAL ENVIRONMENT

Customs, norms, values, beliefs

Language

Attitudes

Motivations

Social institutions

Status symbols

Religious beliefs

Source: Arvind V. Phatak, *International Management* (Cincinnati, OH: South-Western College Publishing, 1997), p. 6.

With the special permission of Professor Porter and the *Harvard Business Review,* we present in this section of the chapter the major portion of his seminal article on the industry environment and its impact on strategic management.[2]

OVERVIEW

The nature and degree of competition in an industry hinge on five forces: the threat of new entrants, the bargaining power of customers, the bargaining power of suppliers, the threat of substitute products or services (where applicable), and the jockeying among

[2] M. E. Porter, "How Competitive Forces Shape Strategy," *Harvard Business Review,* March–April 1979, pp. 137–45.

current contestants. To establish a strategic agenda for dealing with these contending currents and to grow despite them, a company must understand how they work in its industry and how they affect the company in its particular situation. This chapter will detail how these forces operate and suggest ways of adjusting to them, and, where possible, of taking advantage of opportunities that they create.

HOW COMPETITIVE FORCES SHAPE STRATEGY

The essence of strategy formulation is coping with competition. Yet it is easy to view competition too narrowly and too pessimistically. While one sometimes hears executives complaining to the contrary, intense competition in an industry is neither coincidence nor bad luck.

Moreover, in the fight for market share, competition is not manifested only in the other players. Rather, competition in an industry is rooted in its underlying economics, and competitive forces exist that go well beyond the established combatants in a particular industry. Customers, suppliers, potential entrants, and substitute products are all competitors that may be more or less prominent or active depending on the industry.

The state of competition in an industry depends on five basic forces, which are diagrammed in Exhibit 3–10. The collective strength of these forces determines the ultimate profit potential of an industry. It ranges from intense in industries like tires, metal cans, and steel, where no company earns spectacular returns on investment, to mild in industries like oil-field services and equipment, soft drinks, and toiletries, where there is room for quite high returns.

In the economists' "perfectly competitive" industry, jockeying for position is unbridled and entry to the industry very easy. This kind of industry structure, of course, offers the worst prospect for long-run profitability. The weaker the forces collectively, however, the greater the opportunity for superior performance.

Whatever their collective strength, the corporate strategist's goal is to find a position in the industry where his or her company can best defend itself against these forces or can influence them in its favor. The collective strength of the forces may be painfully apparent to all the antagonists; but to cope with them, the strategist must delve below the surface and analyze the sources of competition. For example, what makes the industry vulnerable to entry? What determines the bargaining power of suppliers?

Knowledge of these underlying sources of competitive pressure provides the groundwork for a strategic agenda of action. They highlight the critical strengths and weaknesses of the company, animate the positioning of the company in its industry, clarify the areas where strategic changes may yield the greatest payoff, and highlight the places where industry trends promise to hold the greatest significance as either opportunities or threats.

Understanding these sources also proves to be of help in considering areas for diversification.

CONTENDING FORCES

The strongest competitive force or forces determine the profitability of an industry and so are of greatest importance in strategy formulation. For example, even a company with a strong position in an industry unthreatened by potential entrants will earn low returns if it faces a superior or a lower-cost substitute product—as the leading manufacturers of vacuum tubes and coffee percolators have learned to their sorrow. In such a situation, coping with the substitute product becomes the number one strategic priority.

EXHIBIT 3–10 **Forces Driving Industry Competition**

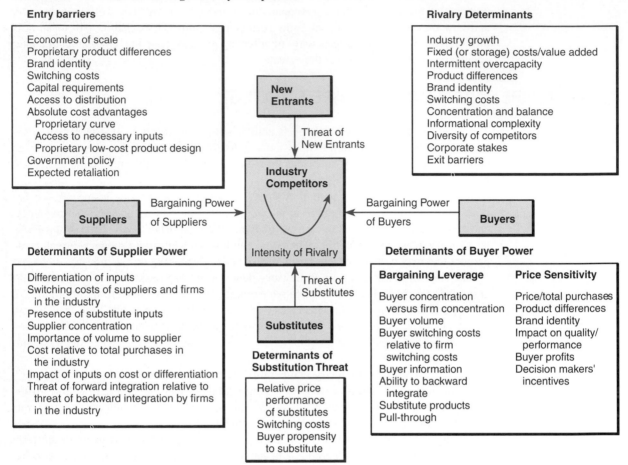

Entry barriers

Economies of scale
Proprietary product differences
Brand identity
Switching costs
Capital requirements
Access to distribution
Absolute cost advantages
  Proprietary curve
  Access to necessary inputs
  Proprietary low-cost product design
Government policy
Expected retaliation

Rivalry Determinants

Industry growth
Fixed (or storage) costs/value added
Intermittent overcapacity
Product differences
Brand identity
Switching costs
Concentration and balance
Informational complexity
Diversity of competitors
Corporate stakes
Exit barriers

New Entrants

Threat of New Entrants

Industry Competitors

Intensity of Rivalry

Suppliers

Bargaining Power of Suppliers

Buyers

Bargaining Power of Buyers

Threat of Substitutes

Substitutes

Determinants of Supplier Power

Differentiation of inputs
Switching costs of suppliers and firms
  in the industry
Presence of substitute inputs
Supplier concentration
Importance of volume to supplier
Cost relative to total purchases in
  the industry
Impact of inputs on cost or differentiation
Threat of forward integration relative to
  threat of backward integration by firms
  in the industry

Determinants of Substitution Threat

Relative price
  performance
  of substitutes
Switching costs
Buyer propensity
  to substitute

Determinants of Buyer Power

Bargaining Leverage	**Price Sensitivity**
Buyer concentration	Price/total purchases
versus firm concentration	Product differences
Buyer volume	Brand identity
Buyer switching costs	Impact on quality/
relative to firm	performance
switching costs	Buyer profits
Buyer information	Decision makers'
Ability to backward	incentives
integrate	
Substitute products	
Pull-through	

Different forces take on prominence, of course, in shaping competition in each industry. In the oceangoing tanker industry, the key force is probably the buyers (the major oil companies), while in tires it is powerful OEM buyers coupled with tough competitors. In the steel industry the key forces are foreign competitors and substitute materials.

Every industry has an underlying structure, or a set of fundamental economic and technical characteristics, that gives rise to these competitive forces. The strategist, wanting to position his or her company to cope best with its industry environment or to influence that environment in the company's favor, must learn what makes the environment tick.

This view of competition pertains equally to industries dealing in services and to those selling products. To avoid monotony, I refer to both products and services as *products.* The same general principles apply to all types of business.

A few characteristics are critical to the strength of each competitive force. They will be discussed in this section.

A. Threat of Entry

New entrants to an industry bring new capacity, the desire to gain market share, and often substantial resources. Companies diversifying through acquisition into the industry from other markets often leverage their resources to cause a shake-up, as Philip Morris did with Miller beer.

The seriousness of the threat of entry depends on the barriers present and on the reaction from existing competitors that the entrant can expect. If barriers to entry are high and a newcomer can expect sharp retaliation from the entrenched competitors, he or she obviously will not pose a serious threat of entering.

There are six major sources of barriers to entry:

1. Economies of Scale

These economies deter entry by forcing the aspirant either to come in on a large scale or to accept a cost disadvantage. Scale economies in production, research, marketing, and service are probably the key barriers to entry in the mainframe computer industry, as Xerox and GE sadly discovered. Economies of scale also can act as hurdles in distribution, utilization of the sales force, financing, and nearly any other part of a business.

2. Product Differentiation

Brand identification creates a barrier by forcing entrants to spend heavily to overcome customer loyalty. Advertising, customer service, being first in the industry, and product differences are among the factors fostering brand identification. It is perhaps the most important entry barrier in soft drinks, over-the-counter drugs, cosmetics, investment banking, and public accounting. To create high fences around their business, brewers couple brand identification with economies of scale in production, distribution, and marketing.

3. Capital Requirements

The need to invest large financial resources in order to compete creates a barrier to entry, particularly if the capital is required for unrecoverable expenditures in up-front advertising or R&D. Capital is necessary not only for fixed facilities but also for customer credit, inventories, and absorbing start-up losses. While major corporations have the financial resources to invade almost any industry, the huge capital requirements in certain fields, such as computer manufacturing and mineral extraction, limit the pool of likely entrants.

4. Cost Disadvantages Independent of Size

Entrenched companies may have cost advantages not available to potential rivals, no matter what their size and attainable economies of scale. These advantages can stem from the effects of the learning curve (and of its first cousin, the experience curve), proprietary technology, access to the best raw materials sources, assets purchased at preinflation prices, government subsidies, or favorable locations. Sometimes cost advantages are enforceable legally, as they are through patents. (For analysis of the much-discussed experience curve as a barrier to entry, see Exhibit 3–11, Strategy in Action.)

5. Access to Distribution Channels

The new boy or girl on the block must, of course, secure distribution of his or her product or service. A new food product, for example, must displace others from the supermarket shelf via price breaks, promotions, intense selling efforts, or some other means. The more limited the wholesale or retail channels are and the more that existing competitors have these tied up, obviously the tougher that entry into the industry will be. Sometimes this barrier is so high that, to surmount it, a new contestant must create its own distribution channels, as Timex did in the watch industry in the 1950s.

In recent years, the experience curve has become widely discussed as a key element of industry structure. According to this concept, unit costs in many manufacturing industries (some dogmatic adherents say in all manufacturing industries) as well as in some service industries decline with "experience," or a particular company's cumulative volume of production. (The experience curve, which encompasses many factors, is a broader concept than the better-known learning curve, which refers to the efficiency achieved over time by workers through much repetition.)

The causes of the decline in unit costs are a combination of elements, including economies of scale, the learning curve for labor, and capita-labor substitution. The cost decline creates a barrier to entry because new competitors with no "experience" face higher costs than established ones, particularly the producer with the largest market share, and have difficulty catching up with the entrenched competitors.

Adherents of the experience curve concept stress the importance of achieving market leadership to maximize this barrier to entry, and they recommend aggressive action to achieve it, such as price cutting in anticipation of falling costs in order to build volume. For the combatant that cannot achieve a healthy market share, the prescription is usually, "Get out."

Is the experience curve an entry barrier on which strategies should be built? The answer is: not in every industry. In fact, in some industries, building a strategy on the experience curve can be potentially disastrous. That costs decline with experience in some industries is not news to corporate executives. The significance of the experience curve for strategy depends on what factors are causing the decline.

A new entrant may well be more efficient than the more experienced competitors: if it has built the newest plant, it will face no disadvantage in having to catch up. The strategic prescription, "You must have the largest, most efficient plant," is a lot different from "You must produce the greatest cumulative output of the item to get your costs down."

Whether a drop in costs with cumulative (not absolute) volume erects an entry barrier also depends on the sources of the decline. If costs go down because of technical advances known generally in the industry or because of the development of improved equipment that can be copied or purchased from equipment suppliers, the experience curve is not an entry barrier at all–in fact, new or less-experienced competitors may actually enjoy a cost advantage over the leaders. Free of the legacy of heavy past investments, the newcomer or less-experienced competitor can purchase or copy the newest and lowest-cost equipment and technology.

If, however, experience can be kept proprietary, the leaders will maintain a cost advantage. But new entrants may require less experience to reduce their costs than the leaders needed. All this suggests that the experience curve can be a shaky entry barrier on which to build a strategy.

While space does not permit a complete treatment here, I want to mention a few other crucial elements in determining the appropriateness of a strategy built on the entry barrier provided by the experience curve:

> The height of the barrier depends on how important costs are to competition compared with other areas like marketing, selling, and innovation.
>
> The barrier can be nullified by product or process innovations leading to a substantially new technology and, thereby, creating an entirely new experience curve. New entrants can leapfrog the industry leaders and alight on the new experience curve, to which those leaders may be poorly positioned to jump.
>
> If more than one strong company is building its strategy on the experience curve, the consequences can be nearly fatal. By the time only one rival is left pursuing such a strategy, industry growth may have stopped and the prospects of reaping the spoils of victory may long since have evaporated.

6. Government Policy

The government can limit or even foreclose entry to industries, with such controls as license requirements and limits on access to raw materials. Regulated industries like trucking, liquor retailing, and freight forwarding are noticeable examples; more subtle government restrictions operate in fields like ski-area development and coal mining. The government also can play a major indirect role by affecting entry barriers through such controls as air and water pollution standards and safety regulations.

The potential rival's expectations about the reaction of existing competitors also will influence its decision on whether to enter. The company is likely to have second thoughts if incumbents have previously lashed out at new entrants, or if:

The incumbents possess substantial resources to fight back, including excess cash and unused borrowing power, productive capacity, or clout with distribution channels and customers.

The incumbents seem likely to cut prices because of a desire to keep market shares or because of industrywide excess capacity.

Industry growth is slow, affecting its ability to absorb the new arrival and probably causing the financial performance of all the parties involved to decline.

B. Powerful Suppliers

Suppliers can exert bargaining power on participants in an industry by raising prices or reducing the quality of purchased goods and services. Powerful suppliers, thereby, can squeeze profitability out of an industry unable to recover cost increases in its own prices. By raising their prices, soft-drink concentrate producers have contributed to the erosion of profitability of bottling companies because the bottlers—facing intense competition from powdered mixes, fruit drinks, and other beverages—have limited freedom to raise their prices accordingly.

The power of each important supplier (or buyer) group depends on a number of characteristics of its market situation and on the relative importance of its sales or purchases to the industry compared with its overall business.

A *supplier* group is powerful if:

1. It is dominated by a few companies and is more concentrated than the industry it sells.

2. Its product is unique or at least differentiated, or if it has built-up switching costs. Switching costs are fixed costs that buyers face in changing suppliers. These arise because, among other things, a buyer's product specifications tie it to particular suppliers, it has invested heavily in specialized ancillary equipment or in learning how to operate a supplier's equipment (as in computer software), or its production lines are connected to the supplier's manufacturing facilities (as in some manufacturing of beverage containers).

3. It is not obliged to contend with other products for sale to the industry. For instance, the competition between the steel companies and the aluminum companies to sell to the can industry checks the power of each supplier.

4. It poses a credible threat of integrating forward into the industry's business. This provides a check against the industry's ability to improve the terms on which it purchases.

5. The industry is not an important customer of the supplier group. If the industry is an important customer, suppliers' fortunes will be tied closely to the industry, and they will want to protect the industry through reasonable pricing and assistance in activities like R&D and lobbying.

C. Powerful Buyers

Customers likewise can force down prices, demand higher quality or more service, and play competitors off against each other—all at the expense of industry profits.

A *buyer* group is powerful if:

1. It is concentrated or purchases in large volumes. Large-volume buyers are particularly potent forces if heavy fixed costs characterize the industry—as they do in metal

containers, corn refining, and bulk chemicals, for example—which raise the stakes to keep capacity filled.

2. The products it purchases from the industry are standard or undifferentiated. The buyers, sure that they always can find alternative suppliers, may play one company against another, as they do in aluminum extrusion.

3. The products it purchases from the industry form a component of its product and represent a significant fraction of its cost. The buyers are likely to shop for a favorable price and purchase selectively. Where the product sold by the industry in question is a small fraction of buyers' costs, buyers are usually much less price sensitive.

4. It earns low profits, which create great incentive to lower its purchasing costs. Highly profitable buyers, however, are generally less price sensitive (i.e., of course, if the item does not represent a large fraction of their costs).

5. The industry's product is unimportant to the quality of the buyers' products or services. Where the quality of the buyers' products is very much affected by the industry's product, buyers are generally less price sensitive. Industries in which this situation exists include oil-field equipment, where a malfunction can lead to large losses and enclosures for electronic medical and test instruments, where the quality of the enclosure can influence the user's impression about the quality of the equipment inside.

6. The industry's product does not save the buyer money. Where the industry's product or service can pay for itself many times over, the buyer is rarely price sensitive; rather, he or she is interested in quality. This is true in services like investment banking and public accounting, where errors in judgment can be costly and embarrassing, and in businesses like the mapping of oil wells, where an accurate survey can save thousands of dollars in drilling costs.

7. The buyers pose a credible threat of integrating backward to make the industry's product. The Big Three auto producers and major buyers of cars often have used the threat of self-manufacture as a bargaining lever. But sometimes an industry so engenders a threat to buyers that its members may integrate forward.

Most of these sources of buyer power can be attributed to consumers as a group as well as to industrial and commercial buyers; only a modification of the frame of reference is necessary. Consumers tend to be more price sensitive if they are purchasing products that are undifferentiated, expensive relative to their incomes, and of a sort where quality is not particularly important.

The buying power of retailers is determined by the same rules, with one important addition. Retailers can gain significant bargaining power over manufacturers when they can influence consumers' purchasing decisions, as they do in audio components, jewelry, appliances, sporting goods, and other goods.

D. Substitute Products

By placing a ceiling on the prices it can charge, substitute products or services limit the potential of an industry. Unless it can upgrade the quality of the product or differentiate it somehow (as via marketing), the industry will suffer in earnings and possibly in growth.

Manifestly, the more attractive the price-performance trade-off offered by substitute products, the firmer the lid placed on the industry's profit potential. Sugar producers confronted with the large-scale commercialization of high-fructose corn syrup, a sugar substitute, learned this lesson.

Substitutes not only limit profits in normal times but also reduce the bonanza an industry can reap in boom times. The producers of fiberglass insulation enjoyed unprecedented demand as a result of high energy costs and severe winter weather. But the industry's ability to raise prices was tempered by the plethora of insulation substitutes, including cellulose, rock wool, and Styrofoam. These substitutes are bound to become an even stronger force once the current round of plant additions by fiberglass insulation producers has boosted capacity enough to meet demand (and then some).

Substitute products that deserve the most attention strategically are those that *(a)* are subject to trends improving their price-performance trade-off with the industry's product or *(b)* are produced by industries earning high profits. Substitutes often come rapidly into play if some development increases competition in their industries and causes price reduction or performance improvement.

E. Jockeying for Position

Rivalry among existing competitors takes the familiar form of jockeying for position—using tactics like price competition, product introduction, and advertising slugfests. This type of intense rivalry is related to the presence of a number of factors:

1. Competitors are numerous or are roughly equal in size and power. In many U.S. industries in recent years, foreign contenders, of course, have become part of the competitive picture.

2. Industry growth is slow, precipitating fights for market share that involve expansion-minded members.

3. The product or service lacks differentiation or switching costs, which lock in buyers and protect one combatant from raids on its customers by another.

4. Fixed costs are high or the product is perishable, creating strong temptation to cut prices. Many basic materials businesses, like paper and aluminum, suffer from this problem when demand slackens.

5. Capacity normally is augmented in large increments. Such additions, as in the chlorine and vinyl chloride businesses, disrupt the industry's supply-demand balance and often lead to periods of overcapacity and price cutting.

6. Exit barriers are high. Exit barriers, like very specialized assets or management's loyalty to a particular business, keep companies competing even though they may be earning low or even negative returns on investment. Excess capacity remains functioning, and the profitability of the healthy competitors suffers as the sick ones hang on. If the entire industry suffers from overcapacity, it may seek government help—particularly if foreign competition is present.

7. The rivals are diverse in strategies, origins, and "personalities." They have different ideas about how to compete and continually run head-on into each other in the process.

As an industry matures, its growth rate changes, resulting in declining profits and (often) a shakeout. In the booming recreational vehicle industry of the early 1970s, nearly every producer did well; but slow growth since then has eliminated the high returns, except for the strongest members, not to mention many of the weaker companies. The same profit story has been played out in industry after industry—snowmobiles, aerosol packaging, and sports equipment are just a few examples.

An acquisition can introduce a very different personality to an industry, as has been the case with Black & Decker's takeover of McCullough, the producer of chain saws.

Technological innovation can boost the level of fixed costs in the production process, as it did in the shift from batch to continuous-line photo finishing in the 1960s.

While a company must live with many of these factors—because they are built into the industry economics—it may have some latitude for improving matters through strategic shifts. For example, it may try to raise buyers' switching costs or increase product differentiation. A focus on selling efforts in the fastest-growing segments of the industry or on market areas with the lowest fixed costs can reduce the impact of industry rivalry. If it is feasible, a company can try to avoid confrontation with competitors having high exit barriers and, thus, can sidestep involvement in bitter price cutting.

INDUSTRY ANALYSIS AND COMPETITIVE ANALYSIS

Designing viable strategies for a firm requires a thorough understanding of the firm's industry and competition. The firm's executives need to address four questions: (1) What are the boundaries of the industry? (2) What is the structure of the industry? (3) Which firms are our competitors? (4) What are the major determinants of competition? The answers to these questions provide a basis for thinking about the appropriate strategies that are open to the firm.

Industry Boundaries

An industry is a collection of firms that offer similar products or services. By "similar products," we mean products that customers perceive to be substitutable for one another. Consider, for example, the brands of personal computers (PCs) that are now being marketed. The firms that produce these PCs, such as AT&T, IBM, Apple, and Compaq, form the nucleus of the microcomputer industry.

Suppose a firm competes in the microcomputer industry. Where do the boundaries of this industry begin and end? Does the industry include desktops? Laptops? These are the kinds of questions that executives face in defining industry boundaries.

Why is a definition of industry boundaries important? First, it helps executives determine the arena in which their firm is competing. A firm competing in the micro-computer industry participates in an environment very different from that of the broader electronics business. The microcomputer industry comprises several related product families, including personal computers, inexpensive computers for home use, and workstations. The unifying characteristic of these product families is the use of a central processing unit (CPU) in a microchip. On the other hand, the electronics industry is far more extensive; it includes computers, radios, supercomputers, superconductors, and many other products.

The microcomputer and electronics industries differ in their volume of sales, their scope (some would consider microcomputers a segment of the electronics industry), their rate of growth, and their competitive makeup. The dominant issues faced by the two industries also are different. Witness, for example, the raging public debate being waged on the future of the "high-definition TV." U.S. policymakers are attempting to ensure domestic control of that segment of the electronics industry. They also are considering ways to stimulate "cutting-edge" research in superconductivity. These efforts are likely to spur innovation and stimulate progress in the electronics industry.

Second, a definition of industry boundaries focuses attention on the firm's competitors. Defining industry boundaries enables the firm to identify its competitors and producers of substitute products. This is critically important to the firm's design of its competitive strategy.

Third, a definition of industry boundaries helps executives determine key factors for success. Survival in the premier segment of the microcomputer industry requires skills that are considerably different from those required in the lower end of the industry. Firms that compete in the premier segment need to be on the cutting edge of technological development and to provide extensive customer support and education. On the other hand, firms that compete in the lower end need to excel in imitating the products introduced by the premier segment, to focus on customer convenience, and to maintain operational efficiency that permits them to charge the lowest market price. Defining industry boundaries enables executives to ask these questions: Do we have the skills it takes to succeed here? If not, what must we do to develop these skills?

Finally, a definition of industry boundaries gives executives another basis on which to evaluate their firm's goals. Executives use that definition to forecast demand for their firm's products and services. Armed with that forecast, they can determine whether those goals are realistic.

Problems in Defining Industry Boundaries

Defining industry boundaries requires both caution and imagination. Caution is necessary because there are no precise rules for this task and because a poor definition will lead to poor planning. Imagination is necessary because industries are dynamic—in every industry, important changes are under way in such key factors as competition, technology, and consumer demand.

Defining industry boundaries is a very difficult task. The difficulty stems from three sources:

1. The evolution of industries over time creates new opportunities and threats. Compare the financial services industry as we know it today with that of the 1990s, and then try to imagine how different the industry will be in the year 2020.

2. Industrial evolution creates industries within industries. The electronics industry of the 1960s has been transformed into many "industries"—TV sets, transistor radios, micro- and macrocomputers, supercomputers, superconductors, and so on. Such transformation allows some firms to specialize and others to compete in different, related industries.

3. Industries are becoming global in scope. Consider the civilian aircraft manufacturing industry. For nearly three decades, U.S. firms dominated world production in that industry. But small and large competitors were challenging their dominance by 1990. At that time, Airbus Industries (a consortium of European firms) and Brazilian, Korean, and Japanese firms were actively competing in the industry.

Developing a Realistic Industry Definition

Given the difficulties outlined above, how do executives draw accurate boundaries for an industry? The starting point is a definition of the industry in global terms; that is, in terms that consider the industry's international components as well as its domestic components.

Having developed a preliminary concept of the industry (e.g., computers), executives flesh out its current components. This can be done by defining its product segments. Executives need to select the scope of their firm's potential market from among these related but distinct areas.

To understand the makeup of the industry, executives adopt a longitudinal perspective. They examine the emergence and evolution of product families. Why did these product families arise? How and why did they change? The answers to such questions provide executives with clues about the factors that drive competition in the industry.

Executives also examine the companies that offer different product families, the overlapping or distinctiveness of customer segments, and the rate of substitutability among product families.

To realistically define their industry, executives need to examine five issues:

1. Which part of the industry corresponds to our firm's goals?

2. What are the key ingredients of success in that part of the industry?

3. Does our firm have the skills needed to compete in that part of the industry? If not, can we build those skills?

4. Will the skills enable us to seize emerging opportunities and deal with future threats?

5. Is our definition of the industry flexible enough to allow necessary adjustments to our business concept as the industry grows?

Industry Structure

Defining an industry's boundaries is incomplete without an understanding of its structural attributes. *Structural attributes* are the enduring characteristics that give an industry its distinctive character. Consider the cable television and financial services industries. Both industries are competitive, and both are important for our quality of life. But these industries have very different requirements for success. To succeed in the cable television industry, firms require vertical integration, which helps them lower their operating costs and ensures their access to quality programs; technological innovation, to enlarge the scope of their services and deliver them in new ways; and extensive marketing, using appropriate segmentation techniques to locate potentially viable niches. To succeed in the financial services industry, firms need to meet very different requirements, among which are extensive orientation of customers and an extensive capital base.

How can we explain such variations among industries? The answer lies in examining the four variables that industry comprises: (1) concentration, (2) economies of scale, (3) product differentiation, and (4) barriers to entry.

Concentration

This variable refers to the extent to which industry sales are dominated by only a few firms. In a highly concentrated industry (i.e., an industry whose sales are dominated by a handful of companies), the intensity of competition declines over time. High concentration serves as a barrier to entry into an industry, because it enables the firms that hold large market shares to achieve significant economies of scale (e.g., savings in production costs due to increased production quantities) and, thus, to lower their prices to stymie attempts of new firms to enter the market.

The U.S. aircraft manufacturing industry is highly concentrated. Its concentration ratio—the percent of market share held by the top four firms in the industry—is 67 percent. Competition in the industry has not been vigorous. Firms in the industry have been able to deter entry through proprietary technologies and the formation of strategic alliances (e.g., joint ventures).

Economies of Scale

This variable refers to the savings that companies within an industry achieve due to increased volume. Simply put, when the volume of production increases, the long-range average cost of a unit produced will decline.

Economies of scale result from technological and nontechnological sources. The technological sources are a higher level of mechanization or automation and a greater up-to-dateness of plant and facilities. The nontechnological sources include better managerial coordination of production functions and processes, long-term contractual agreements with suppliers, and enhanced employee performance arising from specialization.

Economies of scale are an important determinant of the intensity of competition in an industry. Firms that enjoy such economies can charge lower prices than their competitors. They also can create barriers to entry by reducing their prices temporarily or permanently to deter new firms from entering the industry.

Product Differentiation

This variable refers to the extent to which customers perceive products or services offered by firms in the industry as different.

The differentiation of products can be real or perceived. The differentiation between Apple's Macintosh and IBM's PS/2 Personal Computer was a prime example of real differentiation. These products differed significantly in their technology and performance. Similarly, the civilian aircraft models produced by Boeing differed markedly from those produced by Airbus. The differences resulted from the use of different design principles and different construction technologies. For example, the newer Airbus planes followed the principle of "fly by wire," whereas Boeing planes utilized the laws of hydraulics. Thus, in Boeing planes, wings were activated by mechanical handling of different parts of the plane, whereas in the Airbus planes, this was done almost automatically.

Perceived differentiation results from the way in which firms position their products and from their success in persuading customers that their products differ significantly from competing products. Marketing strategies provide the vehicles through which this is done. Witness, for example, the extensive advertising campaigns of the automakers, each of which attempts to convey an image of distinctiveness. BMW ads highlight the excellent engineering of the BMW and its symbolic value as a sign of achievement. Some automakers focus on roominess and durability, which are desirable attributes for the family segment of the automobile market.

Real and perceived differentiations often intensify competition among existing firms. On the other hand, successful differentiation poses a competitive disadvantage for firms that attempt to enter an industry.

Barriers to Entry

As Porter noted earlier in this chapter, barriers to entry are the obstacles that a firm must overcome to enter an industry. The barriers can be tangible or intangible. The tangible barriers include capital requirements, technological know-how, resources, and the laws regulating entry into an industry. The intangible barriers include the reputation of existing firms, the loyalty of consumers to existing brands, and access to the managerial skills required for successful operation in an industry.

Entry barriers both increase and reflect the level of concentration, economies of scale, and product differentiation in an industry, and such increases make it more difficult for new firms to enter the industry. Therefore, when high barriers exist in an industry, competition in that industry declines over time.

In summary, analysis of concentration, economies of scale, product differentiation, and barriers to entry in an industry enables a firm's executives to understand the forces that determine competition in an industry and sets the stage for identifying the firm's competitors and how they position themselves in the marketplace.

Industry regulations are a key element of industry structure and can constitute a significant barrier to entry for corporations. Escalating regulatory standards costs have been a serious concern for corporations for years. As legislative bodies continue their strong hold on corporate activities, businesses feel the impact on their bottom line. In-house counsel departments have been perhaps the most significant additions to corporate structure in the past decade. Legal fees have skyrocketed and managers have learned the hard way about the importance of adhering to regulatory standards. Exhibit 3–12 presents some key principles that enable corporations to abide by the ever-increasing regulations while keeping costs down, maintaining competitiveness, and enhancing creativity.

Competitive Analysis

How to Identify Competitors

In identifying their firm's current and potential competitors, executives consider several important variables:

1. How do other firms define the scope of their market? The more similar the definitions of firms, the more likely the firms will view each other as competitors.

2. How similar are the benefits the customers derive from the products and services that other firms offer? The more similar the benefits of products or services, the higher the level of substitutability between them. High substitutability levels force firms to compete fiercely for customers.

3. How committed are other firms to the industry? Although this question may appear to be far removed from the identification of competitors, it is in fact one of the most important questions that competitive analysis must address, because it sheds light on the long-term intentions and goals. To size up the commitment of potential competitors to the industry, reliable intelligence data are needed. Such data may relate to potential resource commitments (e.g., planned facility expansions).

Common Mistakes in Identifying Competitors

Identifying competitors is a milestone in the development of strategy. But it is a process laden with uncertainty and risk, a process in which executives sometimes make costly mistakes. Examples of these mistakes are:

1. Overemphasizing current and known competitors while giving inadequate attention to potential entrants.

2. Overemphasizing large competitors while ignoring small competitors.

3. Overlooking potential international competitors.

4. Assuming that competitors will continue to behave in the same way they have behaved in the past.

5. Misreading signals that may indicate a shift in the focus of competitors or a refinement of their present strategies or tactics.

6. Overemphasizing competitors' financial resources, market position, and strategies while ignoring their intangible assets, such as a top-management team.

7. Assuming that all of the firms in the industry are subject to the same constraints or are open to the same opportunities.

8. Believing that the purpose of strategy is to outsmart the competition, rather than to satisfy customer needs and expectations.

EXHIBIT 3–12
Innovation-Friendly Regulation

Source: Reprinted by permission of *Harvard Business Review.* An excerpt from "Green and Competitive," by Michael E. Porter and Claas van der Linde, September–October 1995. Copyright © 1995 by the President and Fellows of Harvard University, all rights reserved.

Regulation, properly conceived, need not drive up costs. The following principles of regulatory design will promote innovation, resource productivity, and competitiveness.

Focus on Outcomes, Not Technologies.

Past regulations have often prescribed particular remediation technologies, such as catalysts or scrubbers for air pollution. The phrases "best available technology" (BAT) and "best available control technology" (BACT) are deeply rooted in U.S. practice and imply that one technology is best, thus discouraging innovation.

Enact Strict Rather Than Lax Regulation.

Companies can handle lax regulation incrementally, often with end-of-pipe or secondary treatment solutions. Regulation, therefore, needs to be stringent enough to promote real innovation.

Regulate as Close to the End User as Practical, While Encouraging Upstream Solutions.

This will normally allow more flexibility for innovation in the end product and in all the production and distribution stages. Avoiding pollution entirely or, second best, mitigating it early in the value chain is almost always less costly than late-stage remediation or cleanup.

Employ Phase-In Periods.

Ample but well-defined phase-in periods tied to industry-capital-investment cycles will allow companies to develop innovative resource-saving technologies rather than force them to implement expensive solutions hastily, merely patching over problems.

Use Market Incentives.

Market incentives such as pollution charges and deposit-refund schemes draw attention to resource inefficiencies. In addition, tradable permits provide continuing incentives for innovation and encourage creative use of technologies that exceed current standards.

Harmonize or Converge Regulations in Associated Fields.

Liability exposure in the United States leads companies to stick to safe, BAT approaches, and inconsistent regulation on alternative technologies deters beneficial innovation. For example, one way to eliminate refrigerator cooling agents suspected of damaging the ozone layer involves replacing them with small amounts of propane and butane. But narrowly conceived safety regulations covering these gases seem to have impeded development of the new technology in the United States, while several leading European companies are already marketing the new products.

Develop Regulations in Sync with Other Countries or Slightly Ahead of Them.

It is important to minimize possible competitive disadvantages relative to foreign companies that are not yet subject to the same standard. Developing regulations slightly ahead of other countries will also maximize export potential in the pollution-control sector by raising incentives for innovation.

Make the Regulatory Process More Stable and Predictable.

The regulatory process is as important as the standards. If standards and phase-in periods are set and accepted early enough and if regulators commit to keeping standards in place for, say, five years, industry can lock in and tackle root-cause solutions instead of government philosophy.

Require Industry Participation in Setting Standards from the Beginning.

U.S. regulation differs sharply from European regulation in its adversarial approach. Industry should help in designing phase-in periods, the content of regulations, and the most effective regulatory process.

(continued)

EXHIBIT 3–12
(continued)

> **Develop Strong Technical Capabilities among Regulators.**
>
> Regulators must understand an industry's economics and what drives its competitiveness. Better information exchange will help avoid costly gaming in which ill-informed companies use an array of lawyers and consultants to try to stall the poorly designed regulations of ill-informed regulators.
>
> **Minimize the Time and Resources Consumed in the Regulatory Process Itself.**
>
> Time delays in granting permits are usually costly for companies. Self-regulation with periodic inspections would be more efficient than requiring formal approvals. Potential and actual litigation creates uncertainty and consumes resources. Mandatory arbitration procedures or rigid arbitration steps before litigation would lower costs and encourage innovation.

OPERATING ENVIRONMENT

The operating environment, also called the *competitive* or *task environment,* comprises factors in the competitive situation that affect a firm's success in acquiring needed resources or in profitably marketing its goods and services. Among the most important of these factors are the firm's competitive position, the composition of its customers, its reputation among suppliers and creditors, and its ability to attract capable employees. The operating environment is typically much more subject to the firm's influence or control than the remote environment. Thus, firms can be much more proactive (as opposed to reactive) in dealing with the operating environment than in dealing with the remote environment.

1. Competitive Position

Assessing its competitive position improves a firm's chances of designing strategies that optimize its environmental opportunities. Development of competitor profiles enables a firm to more accurately forecast both its short- and long-term growth and its profit potentials. Although the exact criteria used in constructing a competitor's profile are largely determined by situational factors, the following criteria are often included:

1. Market share.
2. Breadth of product line.
3. Effectiveness of sales distribution.
4. Proprietary and key-account advantages.
5. Price competitiveness.
6. Advertising and promotion effectiveness.
7. Location and age of facility.
8. Capacity and productivity.
9. Experience.
10. Raw materials costs.
11. Financial position.

EXHIBIT 3–13
Competitor Profile

Key Success Factors	Weight	Rating*	Weighted Score
Market share	0.30	4	1.20
Price competitiveness	0.20	3	0.60
Facilities location	0.20	5	1.00
Raw materials costs	0.10	3	0.30
Caliber of personnel	0.20	1	0.20
	1.00†		3.30

*The rating scale suggested is as follows: very strong competitive position (5 points), strong (4), average (3), weak (2), very weak (1).
†The total of the weights must always equal 1.00.

12. Relative product quality.

13. R&D advantages position.

14. Caliber of personnel.

15. General images.

16. Customer profile.

17. Patents and copyrights.

18. Union relations.

19. Technological position.

20. Community reputation.

Once appropriate criteria have been selected, they are weighted to reflect their importance to a firm's success. Then the competitor being evaluated is rated on the criteria, the ratings are multiplied by the weight, and the weighted scores are summed to yield a numerical profile of the competitor, as shown in Exhibit 3–13.

This type of competitor profile is limited by the subjectivity of its criteria selection, weighting, and evaluation approaches. Nevertheless, the process of developing such profiles is of considerable help to a firm in defining its perception of its competitive position. Moreover, comparing the firm's profile with those of its competitors can aid its managers in identifying factors that might make the competitors vulnerable to the strategies the firm might choose to implement.

2. Customer Profiles

Perhaps the most vulnerable result of analyzing the operating environment is the understanding of a firm's customers that this provides. Developing a profile of a firm's present and prospective customers improves the ability of its managers to plan strategic operations, to anticipate changes in the size of markets, and to reallocate resources so as to support forecast shifts in demand patterns. The traditional approach to segmenting customers is based on customer profiles constructed from geographic, demographic, psychographic, and buyer behavior information, as illustrated in Exhibit 3–14.

Enterprising companies have quickly learned the importance of identifying target segments. In recent years, market research has increased tremendously as companies realize the benefits of demographic and psychographic segmentation. Research by American Express showed that competitors were stealing a prime segment of the company's business, affluent business travelers. AMEX's competing companies, including Visa and

EXHIBIT 3–14
Major Segmentation Variables for Consumer Markets

Source: *Marketing Management,* 10/e, by Kotler, © 2000. Adapted by permission of Prentice Hall, Inc., Upper Saddle River, NJ.

Variable	Typical Breakdowns
Geographic	
Region	Pacific, Mountain, West North Central, West South Central, East North Central, East South Central, South Atlantic, Middle Atlantic, New England.
County size	A, B, C, D.
City or SMSA* size	Under 5,000; 5,000–20,000; 20,000–50,000; 50,000–100,000; 100,000–250,000; 250,000–500,000; 500,000–1,000,000; 1,000,000–4,000,000; 4,000,000 or over.
Density	Urban, suburban, rural.
Climate	Northern, southern.
Demographic	
Age	Under 6, 6–11, 12–19, 20–34, 35–49, 50–64, 65+.
Sex	Male, female.
Family size	1–2, 3–4, 5+.
Family life cycle	Young, single; young, married, no children; young, married, youngest child under 6; young, married, youngest child 6 or over; older, married, with children; older, married, no children under 18; older, single; other.
Income	Under $10,000; $10,000–$15,000; $15,000–$20,000; $20,000–$25,000; $25,000–$30,000; $30,000–$50,000; $50,000 and over.
Occupation	Professional and technical; managers, officials, and proprietors; clerical, sales; craftspeople, foremen; operatives; farmers; retired; students; housewives; unemployed.
Education	Grade school or less; some high school; high school graduate; some college; college graduate.
Religion	Catholic, Protestant, Jewish, other.
Race	White, Black, Oriental.
Nationality	American, British, French, German, Scandinavian, Italian, Latin American, Middle Eastern, Japanese.
Psychographic	
Social class	Lower lowers, upper lowers, working class, middle class, upper middles, lower uppers, upper uppers.
Lifestyle	Straights, swingers, longhairs.
Personality	Compulsive, gregarious, authoritarian, ambitious.
Behavioral	
Occasions	Regular occasion, special occasion.
Benefits	Quality, service, economy.
User status	Nonuser, ex-user, potential user, first-time user, regular user.
Usage rate	Light user, medium user, heavy user.
Loyalty status	None, medium, strong, absolute.
Readiness stage	Unaware, aware, informed, interested, desirous, intending to buy.
Attitude toward product	Enthusiastic, positive, indifferent, negative, hostile.

*SMSA stands for standard metropolitan statistical area.

Mastercard, began offering high-spending business travelers frequent flier programs and other rewards including discounts on new cars. In turn, AMEX began to invest heavily in rewards programs, while also focusing on its strongest capabilities, assets, and competitive advantage. Unlike most credit card companies, AMEX cannot rely on charging interest to make money because its customers pay in full each month. Therefore, the company charges higher transaction fees to its merchants. In this way, increases in spending by AMEX customers who pay off their balances each month are more profitable to AMEX than to competing credit card companies.

Assessing consumer behavior is a key element in the process of satisfying your target market needs. Many firms lose market share as a result of assumptions made about target segments. Market research and industry surveys can help to reduce a firm's chances of relying on illusive assumptions. Firms most vulnerable are those that have had success with one or more products in the marketplace and as a result try to base consumer behavior on past data and trends.

Geographic

It is important to define the geographic area from which customers do or could come. Almost every product or service has some quality that makes it variably attractive to buyers from different locations. Obviously, a Wisconsin manufacturer of snow skis should think twice about investing in a wholesale distribution center in South Carolina. On the other hand, advertising in the *Milwaukee Sun-Times* could significantly expand the geographically defined customer market of a major Myrtle Beach hotel in South Carolina.

Demographic

Demographic variables most commonly are used to differentiate groups of present or potential customers. Demographic information (e.g., information on sex, age, marital status, income, and occupation) is comparatively easy to collect, quantify, and use in strategic forecasting, and such information is the minimum basis for a customer profile.

Psychographic

Personality and lifestyle variables often are better predictors of customer purchasing behavior than geographic or demographic variables. In such situations, a psychographic study is an important component of the customer profile. Advertising campaigns by soft-drink producers—Pepsi-Cola ("the Pepsi generation"), Coca-Cola ("the real thing"), and 7UP ("America's turning 7UP")—reflect strategic management's attention to the psychographic characteristics of their largest customer segment—physically active, group-oriented nonprofessionals.

Buyer Behavior

Buyer behavior data also can be a component of the customer profile. Such data are used to explain or predict some aspect of customer behavior with regard to a product or service. As Exhibit 3–14 indicates, information on buyer behavior (e.g., usage rate, benefits sought, and brand loyalty) can provide significant aid in the design of more accurate and profitable strategies.

A second approach to identifying customer groups is by segmenting industrial markets. As shown in Exhibit 3–15, there is considerable overlap between the variables used to segment individual and industrial consumers, but the definition of the customer differs.

EXHIBIT 3–15
Major Segmentation Variables for Industrial Markets

Source: Adapted from Thomas V. Bonoma and Benson P. Shapiro, *Segmenting the Industrial Market* (Lexington, MA: Lexington Books, 1983).

Demographic

Industry: Which industries that buy this product should we focus on?
Company size: What size companies should we focus on?
Location: What geographical areas should we focus on?

Operating Variables

Technology: What customer technologies should we focus on?
User-nonuser status: Should we focus on heavy, medium, light users or nonusers?
Customer capabilities: Should we focus on customers needing many services or few services?

Purchasing Approaches

Purchasing-function organization: Should we focus on companies with highly centralized or decentralized purchasing organizations?
Power structure: Should we focus on companies that are engineering dominated? Financially dominated? Other ways dominated?
Nature of existing relationships: Should we focus on companies with which we have strong existing relationships or simply go after the most desirable companies?
General purchase policies: Should we focus on companies that prefer leasing? Service contracts? Systems purchases? Sealed bidding?
Purchasing criteria: Should we focus on companies that are seeking quality? Service? Price?

Situational Factors

Urgency: Should we focus on companies that need quick and sudden delivery or service?
Specific application: Should we focus on certain applications of our product, rather than all applications?
Size of order: Should we focus on large or small orders?

Perfect Characteristics

Buyer-seller similarity: Should we focus on companies whose people and values are similar to ours?
Attitudes toward risk: Should we focus on risk-taking or risk-avoiding customers?
Loyalty: Should we focus on companies that show high loyalty to their suppliers?

3. Suppliers

Dependable relationships between a firm and its suppliers are essential to the firm's long-term survival and growth. A firm regularly relies on its suppliers for financial support, services, materials, and equipment. In addition, it occasionally is forced to make special requests for such favors as quick delivery, liberal credit terms, or broken-lot orders. Particularly at such times, it is essential for a firm to have had an ongoing relationship with its suppliers.

In the assessment of a firm's relationships with its suppliers, several factors, other than the strength of that relationship, should be considered. With regard to its competitive position with its suppliers, the firm should address the following questions:

Are the suppliers' prices competitive? Do the suppliers offer attractive quantity discounts?

How costly are their shipping charges? Are the suppliers competitive in terms of production standards?

In terms of deficiency rates, are the suppliers' abilities, reputations, and services competitive?

Are the suppliers reciprocally dependent on the firm?

4. Creditors

Because the quantity, quality, price, and accessibility of financial, human, and material resources are rarely ideal, assessment of suppliers and creditors is critical to an accurate evaluation of a firm's operating environment. With regard to its competitive position with its creditors, among the most important questions that the firm should address are the following:

Do the creditors fairly value and willingly accept the firm's stock as collateral?

Do the creditors perceive the firm as having an acceptable record of past payment?

A strong working capital position? Little or no leverage?

Are the creditors' loan terms compatible with the firm's profitability objectives?

Are the creditors able to extend the necessary lines of credit?

The answers to these and related questions help a firm forecast the availability of the resources it will need to implement and sustain its competitive strategies.

5. Human Resources: Nature of the Labor Market

A firm's ability to attract and hold capable employees is essential to its success. However, a firm's personnel recruitment and selection alternatives often are influenced by the nature of its operating environment. A firm's access to needed personnel is affected primarily by three factors: the firm's reputation as an employer, local employment rates, and the ready availability of people with the needed skills.

Reputation

A firm's reputation within its operating environment is a major element of its ability to satisfy its personnel needs. A firm is more likely to attract and retain valuable employees if it is seen as permanent in the community, competitive in its compensation package, and concerned with the welfare of its employees, and if it is respected for its product or service and appreciated for its overall contribution to the general welfare.

Employment Rates

The readily available supply of skilled and experienced personnel may vary considerably with the stage of a community's growth. A new manufacturing firm would find it far more difficult to obtain skilled employees in a vigorous industrialized community than in an economically depressed community in which similar firms had recently cut back operations.

Availability

The skills of some people are so specialized that relocation may be necessary to secure the jobs and the compensation that those skills commonly command. People with such skills include oil drillers, chefs, technical specialists, and industry executives. A firm that seeks to hire such a person is said to have broad labor market boundaries; that is, the geographic area within which the firm might reasonably expect to attract qualified candidates is quite large. On the other hand, people with more common skills are less likely to relocate from a considerable distance to achieve modest economic or career advancements. Thus, the labor market boundaries are fairly limited for such occupational groups as unskilled laborers, clerical personnel, and retail clerks.

EMPHASIS ON ENVIRONMENTAL FACTORS

This chapter has described the remote, industry, and operating environments as encompassing five components each. While that description is generally accurate, it may give the false impression that the components are easily identified, mutually exclusive, and equally applicable in all situations. In fact, the forces in the external environment are so dynamic and interactive that the impact of any single element cannot be wholly disassociated from the impact of other elements. For example, are increases in OPEC oil prices the result of economic, political, social, or technological changes? Or are a manufacturer's surprisingly good relations with suppliers a result of competitors', customers', or creditors' activities or of the supplier's own activities? The answer to both questions is probably that a number of forces in the external environment have combined to create the situation. Such is the case in most studies of the environment.

Strategic managers are frequently frustrated in their attempts to anticipate the environment's changing influences. Different external elements affect different strategies at different times and with varying strengths. The only certainty is that the impact of the remote and operating environments will be uncertain until a strategy is implemented. This leads many managers, particularly in less-powerful or smaller firms to minimize long-term planning, which requires a commitment of resources. Instead, they favor allowing managers to adapt to new pressures from the environment. While such a decision has considerable merit for many firms, there is an associated trade-off, namely that absence of a strong resource and psychological commitment to a proactive strategy effectively bars a firm from assuming a leadership role in its competitive environment.

There is yet another difficulty in assessing the probable impact of remote, industry, and operating environments on the effectiveness of alternative strategies. Assessment of this kind involves collecting information that can be analyzed to disclose predictable effects. Except in rare instances, however, it is virtually impossible for any single firm to anticipate the consequences of a change in the environment; for example, what is the precise effect on alternative strategies of a 2 percent increase in the national inflation rate, a 1 percent decrease in statewide unemployment, or the entry of a new competitor in a regional market?

Still, assessing the potential impact of changes in the external environment offers a real advantage. It enables decision makers to narrow the range of the available options and to eliminate options that are clearly inconsistent with the forecast opportunities. Environmental assessment seldom identifies the best strategy, but it generally leads to the elimination of all but the most promising options.

Exhibit 3–16 provides a set of key strategic forecasting issues for each level of environmental assessment—remote, industry, and operating. While the issues that are presented are not inclusive of all of the questions that are important, they provide an excellent set of questions with which to begin. Appendix 3–A, Sources for Environmental Forecasting, is provided to help identify valuable sources of data and information from which answers and subsequent forecasts can be constructed. It lists governmental and private marketplace intelligence that can be used by a firm to gain a foothold in undertaking a strategic assessment of any level of the competitive environment.

EXHIBIT 3–16
Strategiec
Forecasting Issues

Key Issues in the Remote Environment

Economy

What are the probable future directions of the economies in the firm's regional, national, and international market? What changes in economic growth, inflation, interest rates, capital availability, credit availability, and consumer purchasing power can be expected? What income differences can be expected between the wealthy upper middle class, the working class, and the underclass in various regions? What shifts in relative demand for different categories of goods and services can be expected?

Society and demographics

What effects will changes in social values and attitudes regarding childbearing, marriage, lifestyle, work, ethics, sex roles, racial equality, education, retirement, pollution, and energy have on the firm's development? What effects will population changes have on major social and political expectations—at home and abroad? What constraints or opportunities will develop? What pressure groups will increase in power?

Ecology

What natural or pollution-caused disasters threaten the firm's employees, customers, or facilities? How rigorously will existing environment legislature be enforced? What new federal, state, and local laws will affect the firm, and in what ways?

Politics

What changes in government policy can be expected with regard to industry cooperation, antitrust activites, foreign trade, taxation, depreciation, environmental protection, deregulation, defense, foreign trade barriers, and other important parameters? What success will a new administration have in achieving its stated goals? What effect will that success have on the firm? Will specific international climates be hostile or favorable? Is there a tendency toward instability, corruption, or violence? What is the level of political risk in each foreign market? What other political or legal constraints or supports can be expected in international business (e.g., trade barriers, equity requirements, nationalism, patent protection)?

Techology

What is the current state of the art? How will it change? What pertinent new products or services are likely to become technically feasible in the foreseeable future? What future impact can be expected from technological breakthroughs in related product areas? How will those breakthroughs interface with the other remote considerations, such as economic issues, social values, public safety, regulations, and court interpretations?

Key Issues in the Industry Environment

New entrants

Will new technologies or market demands enable competitors to minimize the impact of traditional economies of scale in the industry? Will consumers accept our claims of product or service differentiation? Will potential new entrants be able to match the capital requirements that currently exist? How permanent are the cost disadvantages (independent of size) in our industry? Will conditions change so that all competitors have equal access to marketing channels? Is government policy toward competition in our industry likely to change?

Bargaining power of suppliers

How stable are the size and composition of our supplier group? Are any suppliers likely to attempt forward integration into our business level? How dependent will our suppliers be in the future? Are substitute suppliers likely to become available? Could we become our own supplier?

(continued)

EXHIBIT 3–16
(continued)

Substitute products or services

Are new substitutes likely? Will they be price competitive? Could we fight off substitutes by price competition? By advertising to sharpen product differentation? What actions could we take to reduce the potential for having alternative products seen as legitimate substitutes?

Bargaining power of buyers

Can we break free of overcommitment to a few large buyers? How would our buyers react to attempts by us to differentiate our products? What possibilities exist that our buyers might vertically integrate backward? Should we consider forward integration? How can we make the value of our components greater in the products of our buyers?

Rivalry among existing firms

Are major competitors likely to undo the established balance of power in our industry? Is growth in our industry slowing such that competition will become fiercer? What excess capacity exists in our industry? How capable are our major competitors of withstanding intensified price competition? How unique are the objectives and strategies of our major competitors?

Key Issues in the Operating Environment

Competitive position

What strategic moves are expected by existing rivals—inside and outside the United States? What competitive advantage is necessary in selected foreign markets? What will be our competitors' priorities and ability to change? Is the behavior of our competitors predictable?

Customer profiles and market changes

What will our customer regard as needed value? Is marketing research done, or do managers talk to each other to discover what the customer wants? Which customer needs are not being met by existing products? Why? Are R&D activities under way to develop means for fulfilling these needs? What is the status of these activities? What marketing and distribution channels should we use? What do demographic and population changes portend for the size and sales potential of our market? What new market segments or products might develop as a result of these changes? What will be the buying power of our customer groups?

Supplier relationships

What is the likelihood of major cost increases because of dwindling supplies of a needed natural resource? Will sources of supply, especially of energy, be reliable? Are there reasons to expect major changes in the cost or availability of inputs as a result of money, people, or subassembly problems? Which suppliers can be expected to respond to emergency requests?

Creditors

What lines of credit are available to help finance our growth? What changes may occur in our creditworthiness? Are creditors likely to feel comfortable with our strategic plan and performance? What is the stock market likely to feel about our firm? What flexibility would our creditors show toward us during a downturn? Do we have sufficient cash reserves to protect our creditors and our credit rating?

Labor market

Are potential employees with desired skills and abilities available in the geographic areas in which our facilities are located? Are colleges and vocational-technical schools that can aid in meeting our training needs located near our plant or store sites? Are labor relations in our industry conductive to meeting our expanding needs for employees? Are workers whose skills we need shifting toward or away from the geographic location of our facilities?

Summary

A firm's external environment consists of three interrelated sets of factors that play a principal role in determining the opportunities, threats, and constraints that the firm faces. The remote environment comprises factors originating beyond, and usually irrespective of, any single firm's operating situation—economic, social, political, technological, and ecological factors. Factors that more directly influence a firm's prospects originate in the environment of its industry, including entry barriers, competitor rivalry, the availability of substitutes, and the bargaining power of buyers and suppliers. The operating environment comprises factors that influence a firm's immediate competitive situation—competitive position, customer profiles, suppliers, creditors, and the labor market. These three sets of factors provide many of the challenges that a particular firm faces in its attempts to attract or acquire needed resources and to profitably market its goods and services. Environmental assessment is more complicated for multinational corporations (MNCs) than for domestic firms because multinationals must evaluate several environments simultaneously.

Thus, the design of business strategies is based on the conviction that a firm able to anticipate future business conditions will improve its performance and profitability. Despite the uncertainty and dynamic nature of the business environment, an assessment process that narrows, even if it does not precisely define, future expectations is of substantial value to strategic managers.

Questions for Discussion

1. Briefly describe two important recent changes in the remote environment of U.S. business in each of the following areas:
   a. Economic.
   b. Social.
   c. Political.
   d. Technological.
   e. Ecological.

2. Describe two major environmental changes that you expect to have a major impact on the wholesale food industry in the next 10 years.

3. Develop a competitor profile for your college and for the college geographically closest to yours. Next, prepare a brief strategic plan to improve the competitive position of the weaker of the two colleges.

4. Assume the invention of a competitively priced synthetic fuel that could supply 25 percent of U.S. energy needs within 20 years. In what major ways might this change the external environment of U.S. business?

5. With your instructor's help, identify a local firm that has enjoyed great growth in recent years. To what degree and in what ways do you think this firm's success resulted from taking advantage of favorable conditions in its remote, industry, and operating environments?

6. Choose a specific industry and, relying solely on your impressions, evaluate the impact of the five forces that drive competition in that industry.

7. Choose an industry in which you would like to compete. Use the five-forces method of analysis to explain why you find that industry attractive.

8. Many firms neglect industry analysis. When does this hurt them? When does it not?

9. The model below depicts industry analysis as a funnel that focuses on remote-factor analysis to better understand the impact of factors in the operating environment. Do you find this model satisfactory? If not, how would you improve it?

10. Who in a firm should be responsible for industry analysis? Assume that the firm does not have a strategic planning department.

Chapter 3 Discussion Case

BusinessWeek

Let's Reinvent the Company

1 On a mild New York City afternoon in late October, dozens of employees crowded into theglobe.com Inc.'s 22nd-floor recreation room. The somber mood was a far cry from November 1998, when the popular Internet community site rocketed to fame with the fastest-rising initial public offering ever. The Ping-Pong table was folded up in a corner and the pool table was covered. The executives wore grim faces—and not just because the stock had plummeted 98% from those halcyon days, to 80 cents a share. They faced the monumental task of reinventing the company they had thought was a New Economy star.

2 Using matter-of-fact PowerPoint slides, newly hired Chief Executive Chuck Peck laid out the details of the company's recently launched strategy: moving beyond consumers and providing Net community services to other websites. The massive restructuring, he said, would slash costs and line up more resources behind the new business-to-business push. But the company's third-quarter results—a loss of $16.6 million on revenues of $6.7 million—showed the toughest job was still ahead, including laying off 41% of the staff. "We've had to overhaul the business," Peck says. Now, it's up to him and the 130 remaining employees to pick up the pieces and reassemble them into a sustainable business.

3 It's a scene now playing at dozens of struggling "business-to-consumer" dot-coms. In a bid to survive, they're exclaiming, "B2C? Not me!" Instead of trying to attract advertisers for fickle Webhead consumers, theglobe.com is offering concrete, useful services to real, paying businesses. In recent months, the flow of consumer companies toward B2B has turned from a trickle to a fire hose. The migrants range from Web delivery service Urbanfetch, which recently shuttered its consumer-oriented video-and-munchies service to become a business courier service, to publicly held search engine Ask Jeeves Inc., which is drastically reorganizing its business to focus on providing search services to other sites. Even e-commerce software makers such as Vignette Corp. and InterWorld Corp. are veering away from selling to consumer sites in favor of courting mainstream businesses.

4 Clearly, one big reason for the switch is that some of those business models never worked and probably never will. Indeed, much of the movement appears born of desperation, as wounded dot-coms try to leap on the next hot trend. Problem is, even that doesn't always work: Skeptical investors have pummeled some B2B wannabes, such as software seller Beyond.com, computer reseller Outpost.com, and online auction house Bid.com International—pushing each of those stocks below $3 a share. "Selling Internet ad space is an entirely different ballgame than selling services to businesses," says Bryan Kester, a project leader with venture-capital firm Redleaf Group Inc.

5 GRAND VISIONS. Still, the redemptive power of the Internet is that it's a ready-made place to quickly reach and serve new kinds of customers. With the rapid pace of change on the Net, business-model mutations are not just possible, but virtually required to stay ahead. "Most Internet companies are changing their business models three or four times each year," says Patricia B. Seybold, CEO of market watcher Patricia Seybold Group. In the end, the success or failure of this massive business-model migration may well determine how powerful the Internet is as a tool for corporate change.

6 The toughest challenge for companies trying to make the shift is determining where to jump. It's often difficult to discern between vibrant business opportunities and flavor-of-the-month Internet fads. When AskMe Corp. CEO Udai Shekawat launched his knowledge-sharing software company in August 1999, he was intent on creating great software. But when the AskMe knowledge-sharing website began seeing a significant jump in traffic and resulting advertising revenues, several company insiders—including Shekawat—began harboring grand visions of becoming an online megaportal. "For a brief time, we were going to take on Yahoo!," he says.

7   But after execs hunkered down over spreadsheets of revenue and market projections, they quickly came to their senses. Shekawat pulled in the reins last January and refocused his techies on writing software. Corporations began requesting AskMe's knowledge-sharing program for their corporate intranets. Today, just six months after garnering all of its revenues from online ads, AskMe gets 90% of its sales from corporate customers. The privately held company projects it will turn a profit in six months.

8   Once companies make their decision, they can't waste any time. The penalties for waiting too long are severe. theglobe.com, for one, couldn't decide how fast to move into B2B services, so even as its online ad revenue stalled, the B2B side didn't pick up the slack. Now, with a severely trimmed workforce and less than $24 million in cash, theglobe.com's future looks iffy. Beyond.com also short-circuited its push to sell to businesses, thanks to a management squabble that kept it from running full-bore with the new plan. One camp wanted to move exclusively into B2B, but CEO Mark L. Breier, a consumer brand maven, wanted to stick with consumers. After mounting losses and executive departures last year, the company finally ditched the consumer push, but now the stock languishes at 63 cents a share.

9   By contrast, moving quickly to latch on to B2B opportunities while they're ripe for the picking pays big dividends. Ask Jeeves first began licensing its software to corporations in 1998, two years after it began. Now, about half of its 750 employees are dedicated to supporting its B2B efforts, which pulled in $13.2 million, or 45% of revenues last quarter. The company expects to be profitable overall by mid-2001, with the B2B side turning a profit by the end of 2001.

10   Given the need for speed, it's crucial for companies to get their staff behind the changes fast. When Paula Jagemann decided last February to spin off a company to provide business services such as website hosting from her consumer-focused OnlineOfficeSupplies.com site, she gathered over 120 employees for several all-hands meetings to spell out her plans. That helped prevent a mass exodus of talent, limiting its attrition rate to about 1% annually. Jagemann expects the new business, part of her holding company, E-Commerce Industries Inc., to pull in $15 million, or half its overall revenues, this year. Says Jagemann: "You almost have to behave like a politician, delivering the same message over and over to your employees."

11   Sometimes they have to behave more like the Grim Reaper. Companies that assume their current staff can adequately address an entirely new market are flirting with failure. OpenTable Corp., for example, cut its teeth as an online restaurant-reservation service for consumers. But after tepid results, executives realized there was a much bigger opportunity in providing Net-based reservations systems and customer analysis tools to restaurants and hotels. So last summer, the company overhauled its management team, including a new CEO and several top lieutenants. But a handful of employees didn't like the moves or the ensuing cultural transformation that made the company less cool. So new CEO Jeffrey B. Edwards fired the malcontents. "We couldn't let that negative attitude linger," he says. Brutal, sure, but that helped persuade investors to kick in an additional $42 million last month, a hefty sum in the current dot-com drought.

12   TRICKY MANEUVERS. Since changing business models isn't cheap, it's just as key to get financial backers on board early. For instance, HomePortfolio.com, which boasts a consumer home furnishings site as well as a B2B services business for furniture manufacturers, needed a cash infusion earlier this year. Execs made no bones about the fact that their true moneymaker would be the B2B business, and that their consumer business would fade. Investors bit, helping HomePortfolio.com raise $48 million in May. "This isn't the summer of VC love anymore," says HomePortfolio.com CEO Dale Williams. "You've really got to keep these people in the loop."

13   Jettisoning the old business, however, remains one of the trickiest maneuvers. When you're starving for cash, it's tempting to try to feed from two different troughs. But it's often tough to juggle two divergent business models aimed at both consumers and businesses. Even while starting to court business buyers last year, Beyond.com spent more than $20 million on consumer-oriented television ads featuring a naked man who was happy he could order from his clothing-optional home. But button-down business buyers may hesitate to make purchases from a company whose icon is a guy with no pants. Says Michael Dunn, CEO of Prophet Brand Strategy, a brand-consulting firm: "Associations with the consumer brand can often be a liability going forward."

14   CROSSING THE CHASM. Indeed, there's no telling which of these transformations will be sustainable and which will prove to be yet another harebrained dot-com scheme. Some companies that have tried to switch have utterly failed: After doing an about-face from a failed strategy to take on Amazon.com Inc., for instance, Value America Inc. tried to offer order-entry and fulfillment services to other businesses after filing for Chapter 11 bankruptcy protection in August. Too late. On Oct. 20, its assets were acquired by technology products distributor Merisel Inc.

15   The companies best prepared to cross the chasm from consumer to B2B e-commerce, say management experts, are those prepared for in-evitable change from the beginning. For one, that means building e-commerce systems that can adapt to changing requirements. Timbuk2 Designs of San Francisco, for instance, had a computer system that allowed consumers to design their own backpacks. But analyst Seybold points out that it was flexible enough for retailers to offer the custom-bag service to consumers as well—providing a whole new revenue stream.

16   Mainly, the key is hiring flexible people. Some Net companies ask job candidates questions that focus on how they would react to turmoil and uncertainty. As the rapidly changing Internet economy continues to force fast changes in strategy, companies need to know how to roll with the punches and run with the new opportunities. "This is where a lot of change-management situations fall on their butt," says Ask Jeeves President Adam Klein.

Source: Ben Elgin, "Let's Reinvent the Company. Online consumer sites are embracing a business-to-business model in desperation," *BusinessWeek*, December 11, 2000.

Chapter **Four**

The Global Environment: Strategic Considerations for Multinational Firms

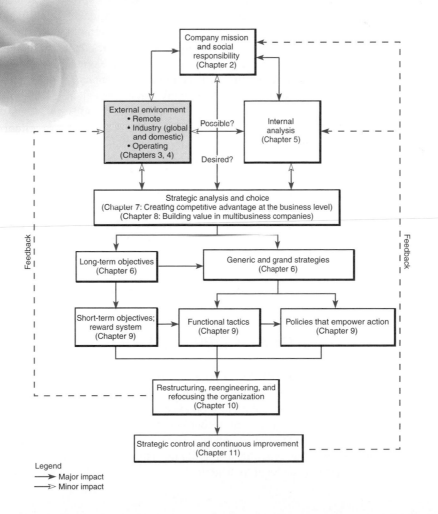

Company mission and social responsibility (Chapter 2)

External environment
• Remote
• Industry (global and domestic)
• Operating
(Chapters 3, 4)

Possible?

Desired?

Internal analysis (Chapter 5)

Strategic analysis and choice
(Chapter 7: Creating competitive advantage at the business level)
(Chapter 8: Building value in multibusiness companies)

Long-term objectives (Chapter 6)

Generic and grand strategies (Chapter 6)

Short-term objectives; reward system (Chapter 9)

Functional tactics (Chapter 9)

Policies that empower action (Chapter 9)

Restructuring, reengineering, and refocusing the organization (Chapter 10)

Strategic control and continuous improvement (Chapter 11)

Feedback

Legend
⟶ Major impact
⟶ Minor impact

Special complications confront a firm involved in the globalization of its operations. *Globalization* refers to the strategy of approaching worldwide markets with standardized products. Such markets are most commonly created by end consumers that prefer lower-priced, standardized products over higher-priced, customized products and by global corporations that use their worldwide operations to compete in local markets. Global corporations headquartered in one country with subsidiaries in other countries experience difficulties that are understandably associated with operating in several distinctly different competitive arenas.

Awareness of the strategic opportunities faced by global corporations and of the threats posed to them is important to planners in almost every domestic U.S. industry. Among corporations headquartered in the United States that receive more than 50 percent of their annual profits from foreign operations are Citicorp, Coca-Cola, Exxon, Gillette, IBM, Otis Elevator, and Texas Instruments. In fact, the 100 largest U.S. globals earn an average of 37 percent of their operating profits abroad. Equally impressive is the impact of foreign-based globals that operate in the United States. Their "direct foreign investment" in the United States now exceeds $90 billion, with Japanese, German, and French firms leading the way.

Understanding the myriad and sometimes subtle nuances of competing in global markets or against global corporations is rapidly becoming a required competence of strategic managers. For example, experts in the advertising community contend that Korean companies only recently recognized the importance of making their names known abroad. In the 1980s, there was very little advertising of Korean brands, and the country had very few recognizable brands abroad. Korean companies tended to emphasize sales and production more than marketing. The opening of the Korean advertising market in the 1990s indicated that Korean firms had acquired a new appreciation for the strategic competencies that are needed to compete globally and created an influx of global firms like Saatchi and Saatchi, J. W. Thompson, Ogilvy and Mather, and Bozell. Many of them established joint ventures or partnerships with Korean agencies. An excellent example of such a strategic approach to globalization by Philip Morris's KGFI is described in Exhibit 4–1, Global Strategy in Action. What is more, the opportunities for corporate growth often seem brightest in global markets. Exhibit 4–2 reports on the growth in national shares of the world's outputs and growth in national economies to the year 2020. While the United States had a commanding lead in the size of its economy in 1992, it was caught by China in the year 2000 and will be far surpassed by 2020. Overall, in less than 20 years, rich industrial countries will be overshadowed by developing countries in their produced share of the world's output.

Because the growth in the number of global firms continues to overshadow other changes in the competitive environment, this section will focus on the nature, outlook, and operations of global corporations.

DEVELOPMENT OF A GLOBAL CORPORATION

The evolution of a global corporation often entails progressively involved strategy levels. The first level, which often entails export-import activity, has minimal effect on the existing management orientation or on existing product lines. The second level, which can involve foreign licensing and technology transfer, requires little change in management or operation. The third level typically is characterized by direct investment in overseas operations, including manufacturing plants. This level requires large capital outlays and the development of global management skills. Although the domestic operations of a firm at

Outside of its core Western markets, Kraft General Foods International's (KGFI) food products have a growing presence in one of the most dynamic business environments in the world—the Asia-Pacific region. Its operations there are expanding rapidly, often aided by links with local manufacturers and distributors.

Japan and Korea, two of the world's fastest-growing economies in the last decade, are important examples. In both countries, local alliances can be crucial to market entry and success. Realizing this fact in the early 1970s, General Foods established joint ventures in both Japan and Korea. These joint ventures, combined with Kraft General Foods International's (KGFI) stand-alone operations, generate more than $1 billion in revenues. In the aggregate, their combined food operations in Japan and Korea are larger than many Fortune 500 companies.

Whereas soluble coffee accounts for just over 25 percent of the coffee consumed in U.S. homes, it fills over 70 percent of the cups consumed in the homes of convenience-minded Japan. Additionally, Japan is the origin of a unique form of packaged coffee—liquid—and a unique channel of distribution—vending machines. Japanese consumers have purchased packaged liquid coffee for years, and it amounts to a $5 billion category. Some 2 million vending machines dispense 9 billion cans of liquid coffee annually—an average of 75 cans per person.

Japan offers a culturally unique distribution channel for coffee products—the gift-set market. Many Japanese exchange specially packaged food or beverage assortments at least twice a year to commemorate holidays as well as special personal or business occasions. The gift-set business has helped Maxim products reinforce their quality image; it also will be a launching pad and support vehicle for Carte Noire coffees.

Outside the Ajinomoto General Foods joint venture, KGFI is developing a freestanding food business under the name Kraft Japan. It is building a cheese business with imported Philadelphia Brand cream cheese, the leading cream cheese in the Tokyo metropolitan market, as well as locally manufactured and licensed Kraft Milk Farm cheese slices. The cheese market is expected to grow approximately 5 percent per year. This is a rapid growth rate for a large food category. In addition to cheese, KGFI also imports Oscar Mayer prepared meats and Jocobs Suchard chocolates.

KGFI's joint venture in Korea, Doug Suh Foods Corporation, is one of the top 10 food companies in the country. Doug Suh manufactures coffees and cereals and has its own distribution network. One of Doug Suh's other businesses in Korea, Post Cereals, is also a strong number two, with a 42 percent category share.

Korea's $400 million coffee market is the fastest-growing major coffee market in the world, expanding at an average annual rate of 14 percent. Growing with the market, Maxim and Maxwell soluble coffees, in both traditional "agglomerate" and freeze-dried forms, account for more than 70 percent of the country's soluble coffee sales. The strength of these brands also brings the company a strong number one position in coffee mix, a mixture of soluble coffee, creamer, and sugar. In addition, its Frima brand leads the market in the nondairy creamer segment.

Beyond Australia, where it has a long-established, wholly owned business, and operations in Japan and Korea, KGFI is targeting many other countries for geographic expansion. In Indonesia, for instance, KGFI has established a rapidly growing cheese business through a licensee and introduced other KGFI products. In Taiwan, the joint venture company, PremierFoods Corporation, holds a 34 percent share of the soluble coffee market and is aggressively developing a Kraft cheese and Jocobs Suchard import business. KGF Philippines, a wholly owned subsidiary, has a leading position in the cheese and powdered soft-drink markets in its country. In the People's Republic of China, the company produces and markets Maxwell House coffees and Tang powdered soft drinks through two successful and rapidly growing joint ventures.

this level continue to dominate its policy, such a firm is commonly categorized as a true multinational corporation (MNC). The most involved strategy level is characterized by a substantial increase in foreign investment, with foreign assets comprising a significant portion of total assets. At this level, the firm begins to emerge as a global enterprise with global approaches to production, sales, finance, and control.

Some firms downplay their global nature (to never appear distracted from their domestic operations), whereas others highlight it. For example, General Electric's formal statement of mission and business philosophy includes the following commitment:

EXHIBIT 4–2   **Projected Economic Growth**

Source: World Bank, *Global Economic Prospects and the Developing Countries.*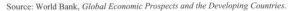

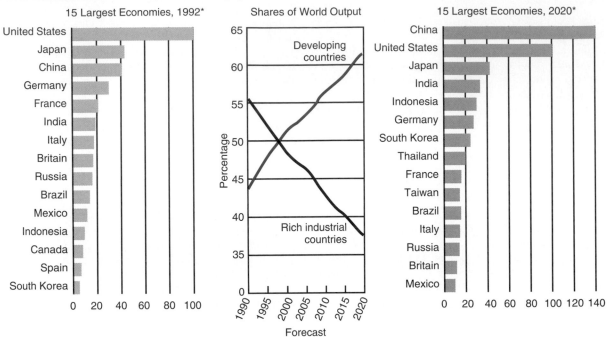

* United States = 100;
Other countries = percentage of U.S.'s GDP

> To carry out a diversified, growing, and profitable worldwide manufacturing business in electrical apparatus, appliances, and supplies, and in related materials, products, systems, and services for industry, commerce, agriculture, government, the community, and the home.

A similar global orientation is evident at IBM, which operates in 125 countries, conducts business in 30 languages and more than 100 currencies, and has 23 major manufacturing facilities in 14 countries.

WHY FIRMS GLOBALIZE

The technological advantage once enjoyed by the United States has declined dramatically during the past 30 years. In the late 1950s, over 80 percent of the world's major technological innovations were first introduced in the United States. By 1990, the figure had declined to less than 50 percent. In contrast, France is making impressive advances in electric traction, nuclear power, and aviation. Germany leads in chemicals and pharmaceuticals, precision and heavy machinery, heavy electrical goods, metallurgy, and surface transport equipment. Japan leads in optics, solid-state physics, engineering, chemistry, and process metallurgy. Eastern Europe and the former Soviet Union, the so-called COMECON (Council for Mutual Economic Assistance) countries, generate 30 percent of annual worldwide patent applications. However, the United States has regained some of its lost technological advantage. Through globalization, U.S. firms often can reap benefits from industries and technologies developed abroad. Even a relatively small service firm that possesses a distinct competitive advantage can capitalize on large overseas operations.

BusinessWeek For most of its 142-year history, Diebold Inc. never worried much about global strategy. As a premier name in bank vaults—and then automated teller machines and security systems—the company focused on U.S. financial institutions, content to let partners hawk what they could abroad. But in 1998, with the U.S. ATM market saturated, Diebold decided it had to be more ambitious. Since then, Diebold has taken off. Sales of security devices, software, and services surged 38% in 2000, to $1.74 billion, led by a 146% jump in overseas sales, to $729 million. The momentum continued in 2001. International sales have gone from 22% of the total to 40% in just two years, and should soon overtake North America.

The ventures overseas have taken Diebold into whole new directions. In China, where it now has half of the fast-growing ATM market, it also is helping the giant International Commercial Bank of China design its self-service branches and data network. In Brazil, Diebold owns and manages a network of 5,000 ATMs—as well as surveillance cameras—for a state-owned bank. In Colombia, it's handling bill collection for a power utility. In Taiwan, where most consumers still prefer to pay bills in cash, Diebold is about to introduce ATMs that both accept and count stacks of up to 100 currency notes and weed out counterfeits. And in South Africa, its ATMs for the techno-illiterate scan fingerprints for identification.

Diebold found it could serve much broader needs in emerging markets than in the United States. Across Latin America, consumers use banks to pay everything from utility bills to taxes. So Diebold ATMs handle these services, 24 hours a day. In Argentina, where filing taxes is a nightmare, citizens now can fill out returns on a PC, store them on a disk, and have their disks scanned on one of 5,000 special Diebold terminals, most of them at banks. Diebold also is landing new contracts across Latin America to manage bank ATM networks.

The $240 million acquisition of Brazil's Procom also gave Diebold an entree into an entirely new line: It landed a huge contract to supply electronic voting machines for Brazil's presidential election last year. Now Diebold is getting into the voting-machine business in the United States, where it expects demand to surge in the wake of the controversial Presidential contest in Florida. Globalization, it seems, can even unveil new opportunities at home.

Source: Excerpt from M. Arndt, P. Engardio, and J. Goodman, "Diebold." *BusinessWeek* (3746), p. 138, August 27, 2001.

As discussed in Exhibit 4–3, Global Strategy in Action, Diebold Inc. once operated solely in the United States, selling ATM machines, bank vaults, and security systems to financial institutions. However, with the U.S. market saturated, Diebold needed to expand internationally to continue its growth. The firm's globalization efforts led to both the development of new technologies in emerging markets and opportunistic entry into entirely new industries that significantly improved Diebold's sales.

In many situations, global development makes sense as a competitive weapon. Direct penetration of foreign markets can drain vital cash flows from a foreign competitor's domestic operations. The resulting lost opportunities, reduced income, and limited production can impair the competitor's ability to invade U.S. markets. A case in point is IBM's move to establish a position of strength in the Japanese mainframe computer industry before two key competitors, Fiyitsue and Hitachi, could dominate it. Once IBM had achieved a substantial share of the Japanese market, it worked to deny its Japanese competitors the vital cash and production experience they needed to invade the U.S. market.

Firms that operate principally in the domestic environment have an important decision to make with regard to their globalization: Should they act before being forced to do so by competitive pressures or after? Should they: (1) be proactive by entering global markets in advance of other firms and thereby enjoy the first-mover advantages often accruing to risk-taker firms that introduce new products or services; or (2) be reactive by taking the more conservative approach and following other companies into global markets once customer demand has been proven and the high costs of new-product or -service introductions have been absorbed by competitors? Although the answers to these questions are determined by the specifics of the company and the context, the issues raised in Exhibit 4–4 are helpful to strategic decision makers faced with the dilemma.

EXHIBIT 4–4
Reasons for Going Global

Source: Betty Jane Punnett and David A. Ricks, *International Business* (Boston: PWS-Kent, 1992), pp. 249–50.

Proactive	
Advantage/Opportunity	**Explanation of Action**
Additional resources	Various inputs—including natural resources, technologies, skilled personnel, and materials—may be obtained more readily outside the home country.
Lowered costs	Various costs—including labor, materials, transportation, and financing—may be lower outside the home country.
Incentives	Various incentives may be available from the host government or the home government to encourage foreign investment in specific locations.
New, expanded markets	New and different markets may be available outside the home country; excess resources—including management, skills, machinery, and money—can be utilized in foreign locations.
Exploitation of firm-specific advantages	Technologies, brands, and recognized names can all provide opportunities in foreign locations.
Taxes	Differing corporate tax rates and tax systems in different locations provide opportunities for companies to maximize their after-tax worldwide profits.
Economies of scale	National markets may be too small to support efficient production, while sales from several combined allow for larger-scale production.
Synergy	Operations in more than one national environment provide opportunities to combine benefits from one location with another, which is impossible without both of them.
Power and prestige	The image of being international may increase a company's power and prestige and improve its domestic sales and relations with various stakeholder groups.
Protect home market through offense in competitor's home	A strong offense in a competitor's market can put pressure on the competitor that results in a pull-back from foreign activities to protect itself at home.

Reactive	
Outside Occurrence	**Explanation of Reaction**
Trade barriers	Tariffs, quotas, buy-local policies, and other restrictive trade practices can make exports to foreign markets less attractive; local operations in foreign locations thus become attractive.
International customers	If a company's customer base becomes international, and the company wants to continue to serve it, then local operations in foreign locations may be necessary.
International competition	If a company's competitors become international, and the company wants to remain competitive, foreign operations may be necessary.
Regulations	Regulations and restrictions imposed by the home government may increase the cost of operating at home; it may be possible to avoid these costs by establishing foreign operations.
Chance	Chance occurrence results in a company deciding to enter foreign locations.

E-commerce Strategy in Action
American E-Tailers Take Europe by Storm

Exhibit 4–5

BusinessWeek After a slow start, U.S. e-commerce giants are taking Europe by storm. "The conventional wisdom that Americans couldn't localize their product in Europe has been proved wrong," says Christian Asmussen.

It's a stunning reversal of fortune. Only a year ago, European Net entrepreneurs were giddy with confidence. They planned to beat back U.S. competitors by moving faster into markets they understood better. Initial public offerings were the talk of London, Amsterdam, and Paris. Startups such as Britain's Boo.com, Freeserve, and lastminute.com seemed destined to be tomorrow's cyberstars.

But Boo has gone broke, Freeserve is on the block, and lastminute's stock is sagging—all while American dot-coms soar. Even America Online Inc. (AOL), which had stumbled in a venture with Bertelsmann, has more visitors throughout Europe than T-Online and is ranked No. 2 in both Britain and Germany. The result is a new hierarchy in Europe. At the top are the phone giants, Deutsche Telekom and France Telecom (FTE), which are able to leverage phone systems to build the leading ISPs. But it's the Americans alongside these titans who are the first continental players—a crucial advantage as Europe's industry consolidates.

European e-tailers now face a nasty shakeout. The Americans are buying: Amazon, for example, has bought online booksellers in Britain and Germany.

Although Europe's e-commerce revenues, at $5.4 billion in 2000, are one-sixth of U.S. levels, growth is likely to prove explosive. Forrester Research Inc., the Boston consultancy, predicts that triple-digit expansion will push total e-business in Europe to $1.6 trillion by 2004. Americans know how to exploit such booming markets, thanks to their experience at home.

While U.S. companies have their critics, retailing expertise honed at home is translating well. Amazon's British site features CDs by local singers, but the back office, distribution, and marketing are imported. "We can adopt about 80% of our American business model," says Steve Frazier, managing director in Britain. Amazon added 400,000 British customers in the first quarter of 2000, increasing revenues 210% from the year before, to $45 million. American e-biz stars also benefit from strong brands built up in the United States. In the nine months since eBay opened in Europe, it has already surpassed QXL in audience—in Germany and Britain—and will take on France next.

Source: Excerpted from William Echikson, "American E-Tailers Take Europe by Storm," *BusinessWeek*, August 7, 2000.

Strategic Orientations of Global Firms

Multinational corporations typically display one of four orientations toward their overseas activities. They have a certain set of beliefs about how the management of foreign operations should be handled. A company with an *ethnocentric orientation* believes that the values and priorities of the parent organization should guide the strategic decision making of all its operations. If a corporation has a *polycentric orientation,* then the culture of the country in which a strategy is to be implemented is allowed to dominate the decision-making process. In contrast, a *regiocentric orientation* exists when the parent attempts to blend its own predispositions with those of the region under consideration, thereby arriving at a region-sensitive compromise. Finally, a corporation with a *geocentric orientation* adopts a global systems approach to strategic decision making, thereby emphasizing global integration.

As described in Exhibit 4–5, E-commerce Strategy in Action, American firms have adopted a regiocentric orientation for pursing strategies in Europe. U.S. e-tailers have attempted to blend their own corporate structure and expertise with that of European corporations. For example, Amazon has been able to leverage its experience in the United States while developing regionally and culturally specific strategies overseas. By purchasing European franchises that have had regional success, E*Trade is pursuing a foreign strategy in which they insert their European units into corporate structure. This

EXHIBIT 4–6   Orientation of a Global Firm

Source: Adapted from Balaji S. Chakravarthy and Howard V. Perlmutter, "Strategic Planning for a Global Business," *Columbia Journal of World Business,* Summer 1985, pp. 5–6. Copyright 1985, Columbia Journal of World Business. Used with permission.

	Orientation of the Firm			
	Ethnocentric	**Polycentric**	**Regiocentric**	**Geocentric**
Mission	Profitability (viability)	Public acceptance (legitimacy)	Both profitability and public acceptance (viability and legitimacy)	Same as regiocentric
Governance	Top-down	Bottom-up (each subsidiary decides on local objectives)	Mutually negotiated between region and its subsidiaries	Mutually negotiated at all levels of the corporation
Strategy	Global integration	National responsiveness	Regional integration and national responsiveness	Global integration and national responsiveness
Structure	Hierarchical product divisions	Hierarchical area divisions, with autonomous national units	Product and regional organization tied through a matrix	A network of organizations (including some stakeholders and competitor organizations)
Culture	Home country	Host country	Regional	Global
Technology	Mass production	Batch production	Flexible manufacturing	Flexible manufacturing
Marketing	Product development determined primarily by the needs of home-country customers	Local product development based on local needs	Standardize within region, but not across regions	Global product, with local variations
Finance	Repatriation of profits to home country	Retention of profits in host country	Redistribution within region	Redistribution globally
Personnel practices	People of home country developed for key positions everywhere in the world	People of local nationality developed for key positions in their own country	Regional people developed for key positions anywhere in the region	Best people everywhere in the world developed for key positions everywhere in the world

strategy requires the combination and use of culturally different management styles and involves major challenges for upper management.

Exhibit 4–6 shows the impacts of each of the four orientations on key activities of the firm. It is clear from the figure that the strategic orientation of a global firm plays a major role in determining the locus of control and corporate priorities of the firm's decision makers.

AT THE START OF GLOBALIZATION

External and internal assessments are conducted before a firm enters global markets. For example, Japanese investors conduct extensive assessments and analyses before selecting a U.S. site for a Japanese-owned firm. They prefer states with strong markets, low unionization rates, and low taxes. In addition, Japanese manufacturing plants prefer counties characterized by manufacturing conglomeration; low unemployment and poverty rates; and concentrations of educated, productive workers.

External assessment involves careful examination of critical features of the global environment, particular attention being paid to the status of the host nations in such areas as economic progress, political control, and nationalism. Expansion of industrial facilities, favorable balances of payments, and improvements in technological capabilities over the past decade are gauges of the host nation's economic progress. Political status can be gauged by the host nation's power in and impact on global affairs.

Internal assessment involves identification of the basic strengths of a firm's operations. These strengths are particularly important in global operations, because they are often the characteristics of a firm that the host nation values most and, thus, offer significant bargaining leverage. The firm's resource strengths and global capabilities must be analyzed. The resources that should be analyzed include, in particular, technical and managerial skills, capital, labor, and raw materials. The global capabilities that should be analyzed include the firm's product delivery and financial management systems.

A firm that gives serious consideration to internal and external assessment is Business International Corporation, which recommends that seven broad categories of factors be considered. As shown in Exhibit 4–7, Global Strategy in Action, these categories include economic, political, geographic, labor, tax, capital source, and business factors.

COMPLEXITY OF THE GLOBAL ENVIRONMENT

Global strategic planning is more complex than purely domestic planning. There are at least five factors that contribute to this increase in complexity:

1. Globals face multiple political, economic, legal, social, and cultural environments as well as various rates of changes within each of them.

2. Interactions between the national and foreign environments are complex, because of national sovereignty issues and widely differing economic and social conditions.

3. Geographic separation, cultural and national differences, and variations in business practices all tend to make communication and control efforts between headquarters and the overseas affiliates difficult.

4. Globals face extreme competition, because of differences in industry structures.

5. Globals are restricted in their selection of competitive strategies by various regional blocs and economic integrations, such as the European Economic Community, the European Free Trade Area, and the Latin American Free Trade Area. Indications of how these factors contribute to the increased complexity of global strategic management are provided in Exhibit 4–8.

CONTROL PROBLEMS OF THE GLOBAL FIRM

An inherent complicating factor for many global firms is that their financial policies typically are designed to further the goals of the parent company and pay minimal attention to the goals of the host countries. This built-in bias creates conflict between the different parts of the global firm, between the whole firm and its home and host countries, and between the home country and host country themselves. The conflict is accentuated by the

Global Strategy in Action

Checklist of Factors to Consider in Choosing a Foreign Manufacturing Site

Exhibit 4–7

The following considerations were drawn from an 88-point checklist developed by Business International Corporation.

Economic factors:

1. Size of GNP and projected rate of growth.

2. Foreign exchange position.

3. Size of market for the firm's products; rate of growth.

4. Current or prospective membership in a customs union.

Political factors:

5. Form and stability of government.

6. Attitude toward private and foreign investment by government, customers, and competition.

7. Practice of favored versus neutral treatment for state industries.

8. Degree of antiforeign discrimination.

Geographic factors:

9. Efficiency of transport (railways, waterways, highways).

10. Proximity of site to export markets.

11. Availability of local raw materials.

12. Availability of power, water, gas.

Labor factors:

13. Availability of managerial, technical, and office personnel able to speak the language of the parent company.

14. Degree of skill and discipline at all levels.

15. Presence or absence of militant or Communist-dominated unions.

16. Degree and nature of labor voice in management.

Tax factors:

17. Tax-rate trends (corporate and personal income, capital, withholding, turnover, excise, payroll, capital gains, customs, and other indirect and local taxes).

18. Joint tax treaties with home country and others.

19. Duty and tax drawbacks when imported goods are exported.

20. Availability of tariff protection.

Capital source factors:

21. Cost of local borrowing.

22. Local availability of convertible currencies.

23. Modern banking systems.

24. Government credit aids to new businesses.

Business factors:

25. State of marketing and distribution system.

26. Normal profit margins in the firm's industry.

27. Competitive situation in the firm's industry: do cartels exist?

28. Availability of amenities for expatriate executives and their families.

use of various schemes to shift earnings from one country to another in order to avoid taxes, minimize risk, or achieve other objectives.

Moreover, different financial environments make normal standards of company behavior concerning the disposition of earnings, sources of finance, and the structure of capital more problematic. Thus, it becomes increasingly difficult to measure the performance of international divisions.

In addition, important differences in measurement and control systems often exist. Fundamental to the concept of planning is a well-conceived, future-oriented approach to decision making that is based on accepted procedures and methods of analysis. Consistent approaches to planning throughout a firm are needed for effective review and evaluation by corporate headquarters. In the global firm, planning is complicated by differences in national attitudes toward work measurement, and by differences in government requirements about disclosure of information.

EXHIBIT 4–8
Differences between Factors That Affect Strategic Management in the United States and Internationally

Source: Adapted from R. G. Murdick, R. C. Moor, R. H. Eckhouse, and T. W. Zimmerer, *Business Policy: A Framework for Analysis,* 4th ed. (Columbus, OH: Grid, 1984), p. 275.

Factor	U.S. Operations	International Operations
Language	English used almost universally.	Use of local language required in many situations.
Culture	Relatively homogenous.	Quite diverse, both between countries and within countries.
Politics	Stable and relatively unimportant.	Often volatile and of decisive importance.
Economy	Relatively uniform.	Wide variations among countries and among regions within countries.
Government interference	Minimal and reasonably predictable.	Extensive and subject to rapid change.
Labor	Skilled labor available.	Skilled labor often scarce, requiring training or redesign of production methods.
Financing	Well-developed financial markets.	Poorly developed financial markets; capital flows subject to government control.
Media research	Data easy to collect.	Data difficult and expensive to collect.
Advertising	Many media available; few restrictions.	Media limited; many restrictions; low literacy rates rule out print media in some countries.
Money	U.S. dollar used universally.	Must change from one currency to another; problems created by changing exchange rates and government restrictions.
Transportation/ communication	Among the best in the world.	Often inadequate.
Control	Always a problem, but centralized control will work.	A worse problem—centralized control won't work; must walk a tightrope between overcentralizing and losing control through too much decentralizing.
Contracts	Once signed, are binding on both parties even if one party makes a bad deal.	Can be avoided and renegotiated if one party becomes dissatisfied.
Labor relations	Collective bargaining; layoff of workers easy.	Layoff of workers often not possible; may have mandatory worker participation in management; workers may seek change through political process rather than collective bargaining.

Although such problems are an aspect of the global environment, rather than a consequence of poor management, they are often most effectively reduced through increased attention to strategic planning. Such planning will aid in coordinating and integrating the firm's direction, objectives, and policies around the world. It enables the firm to anticipate and prepare for change. It facilitates the creation of programs to deal with worldwide development. Finally, it helps the management of overseas affiliates become more actively involved in setting goals and in developing means to more effectively utilize the firm's total resources.

An example of the need for coordination in global ventures and evidence that firms can successfully plan for global collaboration (e.g., through rationalized production) is the Ford Escort (Europe), the best-selling automobile in the world, which has a component manufacturing network that consists of plants in 15 countries.

GLOBAL STRATEGIC PLANNING

It should be evident from the previous sections that the strategic decisions of a firm competing in the global marketplace become increasingly complex. In such a firm, managers cannot view global operations as a set of independent decisions. These managers are faced with trade-off decisions in which multiple products, country environments, resource sourcing options, corporate and subsidiary capabilities, and strategic options must be considered.

A recent trend toward increased activism of stakeholders has added to the complexity of strategic planning for the global firm. *Stakeholder activism* refers to demands placed on the global firm by the foreign environments in which it operates, principally by foreign governments. This section provides a basic framework for the analysis of strategic decisions in this complex setting.

Multidomestic Industries and Global Industries

Multidomestic Industries

International industries can be ranked along a continuum that ranges from multidomestic to global.

A multidomestic industry is one in which competition is essentially segmented from country to country. Thus, even if global corporations are in the industry, competition in one country is independent of competition in other countries. Examples of such industries include retailing, insurance, and consumer finance.

In a multidomestic industry, a global corporation's subsidiaries should be managed as distinct entities; that is, each subsidiary should be rather autonomous, having the authority to make independent decisions in response to local market conditions. Thus, the global strategy of such an industry is the sum of the strategies developed by subsidiaries operating in different countries. The primary difference between a domestic firm and a global firm competing in a multidomestic industry is that the latter makes decisions related to the countries in which it competes and to how it conducts business abroad.

Factors that increase the degree to which an industry is multidomestic include:[1]

The need for customized products to meet the tastes or preferences of local customers.

Fragmentation of the industry, with many competitors in each national market.

A lack of economies of scale in the functional activities of firms in the industry.

Distribution channels unique to each country.

A low technological dependence of subsidiaries on R&D provided by the global firm.

Global Industries

A global industry is one in which competition crosses national borders. In fact, it occurs on a worldwide basis. In a global industry, a firm's strategic moves in one country can be significantly affected by its competitive position in another country. The very rapidly

---

[1] Y. Doz and C. K. Prahalad, "Patterns of Strategic Control within Multinational Corporations," *Journal of International Business Studies,* Fall 1984, pp. 55–72.

expanding list of global industries includes commercial aircraft, automobiles, mainframe computers, and electronic consumer equipment. Many authorities are convinced that almost all product-oriented industries soon will be global. As a result, strategic management planning must be global for at least six reasons:

1. *The increased scope of the global management task.* Growth in the size and complexity of global firms made management virtually impossible without a coordinated plan of action detailing what is expected of whom during a given period. The common practice of management by exception is impossible without such a plan.

2. *The increased globalization of firms.* Three aspects of global business make global planning necessary: (1) differences among the environmental forces in different countries, (2) greater distances, and (3) the interrelationships of global operations.

3. *The information explosion.* It has been estimated that the world's stock of knowledge is doubling every 10 years. Without the aid of a formal plan, executives can no longer know all that they must know to solve the complex problems they face. A global planning process provides an ordered means for assembling, analyzing, and distilling the information required for sound decisions.

4. *The increase in global competition.* Because of the rapid increase in global competition, firms must constantly adjust to changing conditions or lose markets to competitors. The increase in global competition also spurs managements to search for methods of increasing efficiency and economy.

5. *The rapid development of technology.* Rapid technological development has shortened product life cycles. Strategic management planning is necessary to ensure the replacement of products that are moving into the maturity stage, with fewer sales and declining profits. Planning gives management greater control of all aspects of new product introduction.

6. *Strategic management planning breeds managerial confidence.* Like the motorist with a road map, managers with a plan for reaching their objectives know where they are going. Such a plan breeds confidence, because it spells out every step along the way and assigns responsibility for every task. The plan simplifies the managerial job.

A firm in a global industry must maximize its capabilities through a worldwide strategy. Such a strategy necessitates a high degree of centralized decision making in corporate headquarters so as to permit trade-off decisions across subsidiaries.

Among the factors that make for the creation of a global industry are:

Economies of scale in the functional activities of firms in the industry.

A high level of R&D expenditures on products that require more than one market to recover development costs.

The presence in the industry of predominantly global firms that expect consistency of products and services across markets.

The presence of homogeneous product needs across markets, which reduces the requirement of customizing the product for each market. The presence of a small group of global competitors.

A low level of trade regulation and of regulation regarding foreign direction investment.[2]

---

[2] G. Harvel and C. K. Prahalad, "Managing Strategic Responsibility in the MNC," *Strategic Management Journal,* October–December 1983, pp. 341–51.

EXHIBIT 4–9

Factors That Drive Global Companies

Source: Robert N. Lussier, Robert W. Baeder, and Joel Corman, "Measuring Global Practices: Global Strategic Planning through Company Situational Analysis," p. 57. Reprinted from *Business Horizons,* September–October 1994. Copyright 1994 by the Foundation for the School of Business at Indiana University. Used with permission.

1. Global Management Team

Possesses global vision and culture.
Includes foreign nationals.
Leaves management of subsidiaries to foreign nationals.
Frequently travels internationally.
Has cross-cultural training.

2. Global Strategy

Implement strategy as opposed to independent country strategies.
Develop significant cross-country alliances.
Select country targets strategically rather than opportunistically.
Perform business functions where most efficient—no home-country bias.
Emphasize participation in the triad—North America, Europe, and Japan.

3. Global Operations and Products

Use common core operating processes worldwide to ensure quantity and uniformity.
Product globally to obtain best cost and market advantage.

4. Global Technology and R&D

Design global products but take regional differences into account.
Manage development work centrally but carry out globally.
Do not duplicate R&D and product development; gain economies of scale.

5. Global Financing

Finance globally to obtain lowest cost.
Hedge when necessary to protect currency risk.
Price in local currencies.
List shares on foreign exchanges.

6. Global Marketing

Market global products but provide regional discretion if economies of scale are not affected.
Develop global brands.
Use core global marketing practices and themes.
Simultaneously introduce new global products worldwide.

Six factors that drive the success of global companies are listed in Exhibit 4–9. They address key aspects of globalizing a business's operations and provide a framework within which companies can effectively pursue the global marketplace.

The Global Challenge

Although industries can be characterized as global or multidomestic, few "pure" cases of either type exist. A global firm competing in a global industry must be responsive, to some degree, to local market conditions. Similarly, a global firm competing in a multidomestic industry cannot totally ignore opportunities to utilize intracorporate resources in competitive positioning. Thus, each global firm must decide which of its corporate functional activities should be performed where and what degree of coordination should exist among them.

Location and Coordination of Functional Activities

Typical functional activities of a firm include purchases of input resources, operations, research and development, marketing and sales, and after-sales service. A multinational corporation has a wide range of possible location options for each of these activities and

EXHIBIT 4–10
Location and Coordination Issues of Functional Activities

Source: Adapted from Michael E. Porter, "Changing Patterns of International Competition," *California Management Review,* Winter 1986, p. 18.

Functional Activity	Location Issues	Coordination Issues
Operations	Location of production facilities for components.	Networking of international plants.
Marketing	Product line selection. Country (market) selection.	Commonality of brand name worldwide. Coordination of sales to multinational accounts. Similarity of channels and product positioning worldwide. Coordination of pricing in different countries.
Service	Location of service organization.	Similarity of service standards and procedures worldwide.
Research and development	Number and location of R&D centers.	Interchange among dispersed R&D centers. Developing products responsive to market needs in many countries. Sequence of product introductions around the world.
Purchasing	Location of the purchasing function.	Managing suppliers located in different countries. Transferring market knowledge. Coordinating purchases of common items.

must decide which sets of activities will be performed in how many and which locations. A multinational corporation may have each location perform each activity, or it may center an activity in one location to serve the organization worldwide. For example, research and development centered in one facility may serve the entire organization.

A multinational corporation also must determine the degree to which functional activities are to be coordinated across locations. Such coordination can be extremely low, allowing each location to perform each activity autonomously, or extremely high, tightly linking the functional activities of different locations. Coca-Cola tightly links its R&D and marketing functions worldwide to offer a standardized brand name, concentrate formula, market positioning, and advertising theme. However, its operations function is more autonomous, with the artificial sweetener and packaging differing across locations.

Location and Coordination Issues

Exhibit 4–10 presents some of the issues related to the critical dimensions of location and coordination in multinational strategic planning. It also shows the functional activities that the firm performs with regard to each of these dimensions. For example, in connection with the service function, a firm must decide where to perform after-sale service and whether to standardize such service.

How a particular firm should address location and coordination issues depends on the nature of its industry and on the type of international strategy that the firm is pursuing. As discussed earlier, an industry can be ranked along a continuum that ranges between multidomestic at one extreme and global at the other. Little coordination of functional activities across countries may be necessary in a multidomestic industry, since competition occurs within each country in such an industry. However, as its industry becomes

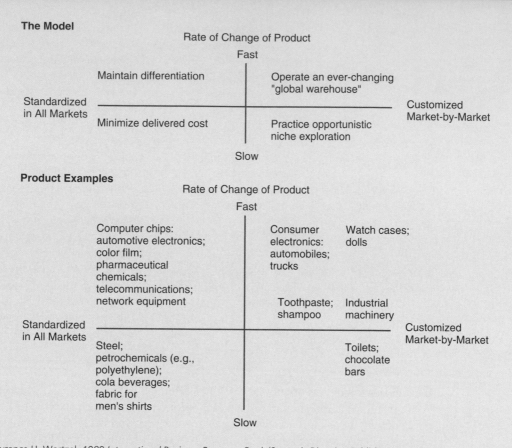

The Model

Rate of Change of Product

Fast

| Maintain differentiation | | Operate an ever-changing "global warehouse" |

Standardized in All Markets ———————————————— Customized Market-by-Market

| Minimize delivered cost | | Practice opportunistic niche exploration |

Slow

Product Examples

Rate of Change of Product

Fast

| Computer chips: automotive electronics; color film; pharmaceutical chemicals; telecommunications; network equipment | | Consumer electronics: automobiles; trucks | Watch cases; dolls |

Toothpaste; shampoo — Industrial machinery

Standardized in All Markets ———————————————— Customized Market-by-Market

| Steel; petrochemicals (e.g., polyethylene); cola beverages; fabric for men's shirts | | | Toilets; chocolate bars |

Slow

Source: Lawrence H. Wortzel, *1989 International Business Resource Book* (Strategic Direction Publishers, 1989).

increasingly global, a firm must begin to coordinate an increasing number of functional activities to effectively compete across countries.

Going global impacts every aspect of a company's operations and structure. As firms redefine themselves as global competitors, work forces are becoming increasingly diversified. The most significant challenge for firms, therefore, is the ability to adjust to a work force of varied cultures and lifestyles and the capacity to incorporate cultural differences to the benefit of the company's mission.

Market Requirements and Product Characteristics

Businesses have discovered that being successful in foreign markets often demands much more than simply shipping their well-received domestic products overseas. Firms must assess two key dimensions of customer demand: customers' acceptance of standardized products and the rate of product innovation desired. As shown in the top figure of Exhibit 4–11, Global Strategy in Action, all markets can be arrayed along a continuum from markets in which products are standardized to markets in which products must be

EXHIBIT 4–12
International
Strategy Options

Source: Adapted from Michael
E. Porter, "Changing Patterns
of International Competition,"
*California Management
Review,* Winter 1986, p. 19.

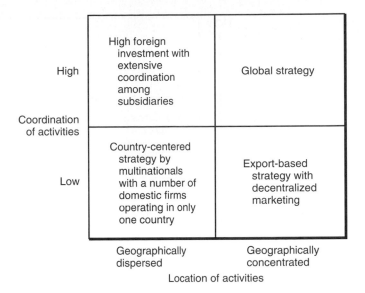

customized for customers from market to market. Standardized products in all markets include color film and petrochemicals, while dolls and toilets are good examples of customized products.

Similarly, products can be arrayed along a continuum from products that are not subject to frequent product innovations to products that are often upgraded. Products with a fast rate of change include computer chips and industrial machinery, while steel and chocolate bars are products that fit in the slow rate of change category.

The bottom figure of Exhibit 4–11 shows that the two dimensions can be combined to enable companies to simultaneously assess both customer need for product standardization and rate of product innovation. The examples listed demonstrate the usefulness of the model in helping firms to determine the degree of customization that they must be willing to accept to become engaged in transnational operations.

International Strategy Options

Exhibit 4–12 presents the basic multinational strategy options that have been derived from a consideration of the location and coordination dimensions. Low coordination and geographic dispersion of functional activities are implied if a firm is operating in a multidomestic industry and has chosen a country-centered strategy. This allows each subsidiary to closely monitor the local market conditions it faces and to respond freely to these conditions.

High coordination and geographic concentration of functional activities result from the choice of a pure global strategy. Although some functional activities, such as after-sale service, may need to be located in each market, tight control of those activities is necessary to ensure standardized performance worldwide. For example, IBM expects the same high level of marketing support and service for all of its customers, regardless of their location.

Two other strategy options are shown in Exhibit 4–12. High foreign investment with extensive coordination among subsidiaries would describe the choice of remaining at a particular growth stage, such as that of an exporter. An export-based strategy with decentralized marketing would describe the choice of moving toward globalization, which a multinational firm might make.

EXHIBIT 4–13
International
Strategy Options

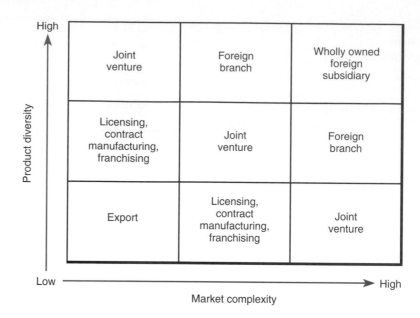

COMPETITIVE STRATEGIES FOR FIRMS IN FOREIGN MARKETS
==

Strategies for firms that are attempting to move toward globalization can be categorized by the degree of complexity of each foreign market being considered and by the diversity in a company's product line (see Exhibit 4–13). *Complexity* refers to the number of critical success factors that are required to prosper in a given competitive arena. When a firm must consider many such factors, the requirements of success increase in complexity. *Diversity,* the second variable, refers to the breadth of a firm's business lines. When a company offers many product lines, diversity is high.

Together, the complexity and diversity dimensions form a continuum of possible strategic choices. Combining these two dimensions highlights many possible actions.

Niche Market Exporting

The primary niche market approach for the company that wants to export is to modify select product performance or measurement characteristics to meet special foreign demands. Combining product criteria from both the U.S. and the foreign markets can be slow and tedious. There are, however, a number of expansion techniques that provide the U.S. firm with the know-how to exploit opportunities in the new environment. For example, copying product innovations in countries where patent protection is not emphasized and utilizing nonequity contractual arrangements with a foreign partner can assist in rapid product innovation. N. V. Philips and various Japanese competitors, such as Sony and Matsushita, now are working together for common global product standards within their markets. Siemens, with a centralized R&D in electronics, also has been very successful with this approach.

Exporting usually requires minimal capital investment. The organization maintains its quality control standards over production processes and finished goods inventory, and risk to the survival of the firm is typically minimal. Additionally, the U.S. Commerce Department through its Export Now Program and related government agencies lowers the risks to smaller companies by providing export information and marketing advice.

Licensing/Contract Manufacturing

Establishing a contractual arrangement is the next step for U.S. companies that want to venture beyond exporting but are not ready for an equity position on foreign soil. Licensing involves the transfer of some industrial property right from the U.S. licensor to a motivated licensee. Most tend to be patents, trademarks, or technical know-how that are granted to the licensee for a specified time in return for a royalty and for avoiding tariffs or import quotas. Bell South and U.S. West, with various marketing and service competitive advantages valuable to Europe, have extended a number of licenses to create personal computer networks in the United Kingdom.

Another licensing strategy open to U.S. firms is to contract the manufacturing of its product line to a foreign company to exploit local comparative advantages in technology, materials, or labor.

U.S. firms that use either licensing option will benefit from lowering the risk of entry into the foreign markets. Clearly, alliances of this type are not for everyone. They are used best in companies large enough to have a combination of international strategic activities and for firms with standardized products in narrow margin industries.

Two major problems exist with licensing. One is the possibility that the foreign partner will gain the experience and evolve into a major competitor after the contract expires. The experience of some U.S. electronics firms with Japanese companies shows that licensees gain the potential to become powerful rivals. The other potential problem stems from the control that the licensor forfeits on production, marketing, and general distribution of its products. This loss of control minimizes a company's degrees of freedom as it reevaluates its future options.

Franchising

A special form of licensing is franchising, which allows the franchisee to sell a highly publicized product or service, using the parent's brand name or trademark, carefully developed procedures, and marketing strategies. In exchange, the franchisee pays a fee to the parent company, typically based on the volume of sales of the franchisor in its defined market area. The franchise is operated by the local investor who must adhere to the strict policies of the parent.

Franchising is so popular that an estimated 500 U.S. businesses now franchise to over 50,000 local owners in foreign countries. Among the most active franchisees are Avis, Burger King, Canada Dry, Coca-Cola, Hilton, Kentucky Fried Chicken, Manpower, Marriott, Midas, Muzak, Pepsi, and Service Master. However, the acknowledged global champion of franchising is McDonald's, which has 70 percent of its company-owned stores as franchisees in foreign nations.

Joint Ventures

As the multinational strategies of U.S. firms mature, most will include some form of joint venture (JV) with a target nation firm. AT&T followed this option in its strategy to produce its own personal computer by entering into several joint ventures with European producers to acquire the required technology and position itself for European expansion. Because JVs begin with a mutually agreeable pooling of capital, production or marketing equipment, patents, trademarks, or management expertise, they offer more permanent cooperative relationships than export or contract manufacturing.

Compared to full ownership of the foreign entity, JVs provide a variety of benefits to each partner. U.S. firms without the managerial or financial assets to make a profitable independent impact on the integrated foreign markets can share management tasks and cash requirements often at exchange rates that favor the dollar. The coordination of manufacturing and marketing allows ready access to new markets, intelligence data, and reciprocal flows of technical information.

For example, Siemens, the German electronics firm, has a wide range of strategic alliances throughout Europe to share technology and research developments. For years, Siemens grew by acquisitions, but now, to support its horizontal expansion objectives, it is engaged in joint ventures with companies like Groupe Bull of France, International Computers of Britain, General Electric Company of Britain, IBM, Intel, Philips, and Rolm. Another example is Airbus Industries, which produces wide-body passenger planes for the world market as a direct result of JVs among many companies in Britain, France, Spain, and Germany.

JVs speed up the efforts of U.S. firms to integrate into the political, corporate, and cultural infrastructure of the foreign environment, often with a lower financial commitment than acquiring a foreign subsidiary. General Electric's (GE) 3 percent share in the European lighting market was very weak and below expectations. Significant increases in competition throughout many of their American markets by the European giant, Philips Lighting, forced GE to retaliate by expanding in Europe. GE's first strategy was an attempted joint venture with the Siemens lighting subsidiary, Osram, and with the British electronics firm, Thorn EMI. Negotiations failed over control issues. When recent events in Eastern Europe opened the opportunity for a JV with the Hungarian lighting manufacturer, Tungsram, which was receiving 70 percent of revenues from the West, GE capitalized on it.

Although joint ventures can address many of the requirements of complex markets and diverse product lines, U.S. firms considering either equity- or nonequity-based JVs face many challenges. For example, making full use of the native firm's comparative advantage may involve managerial relationships where no single authority exists to make strategic decisions or solve conflicts. Additionally, dealing with host-company management requires the disclosure of proprietary information and the potential loss of control over production and marketing quality standards. Addressing such challenges with well-defined covenants agreeable to all parties is difficult. Equally important is the compatibility of partners and their enduring commitments to mutually supportive goals. Without this compatibility and commitment, a joint venture is critically endangered.

Foreign Branching

A foreign branch is an extension of the company in its foreign market—a separately located strategic business unit directly responsible for fulfilling the operational duties assigned to it by corporate management, including sales, customer service, and physical distribution. Host countries may require that the branch be "domesticated"; that is, have some local managers in middle and upper-level positions. The branch most likely will be outside any U.S. legal jurisdiction, liabilities may not be restricted to the assets of the given branch, and business licenses for operations may be of short duration, requiring the company to renew them during changing business regulations.

Wholly Owned Subsidiaries

Wholly owned foreign subsidiaries are considered by companies that are willing and able to make the highest investment commitment to the foreign market. These companies insist on full ownership for reasons of control and managerial efficiency. Policy decisions about local product lines, expansion, profits, and dividends typically remain with the U.S. senior managers.

Fully owned subsidiaries can be started either from scratch or by acquiring established firms in the host country. U.S. firms can benefit significantly if the acquired company has complementary product lines or an established distribution or service network.

U.S. firms seeking to improve their competitive postures through a foreign subsidiary face a number of risks to their normal mode of operations. First, if the high capital investment is to be rewarded, managers must attain extensive knowledge of the market, the host nation's language, and its business culture. Second, the host country expects both a long-term commitment from the U.S. enterprise and a portion of their nationals to be employed in positions of management or operations. Fortunately, hiring or training foreign managers for leadership positions is commonly a good policy, since they are close to both the market and contacts. This is especially important for smaller firms when markets are regional. Third, changing standards mandated by foreign regulations may eliminate a company's protected market niche. Product design and worker protection liabilities also may extend back to the home office.

The strategies shown in Exhibit 4–13 are not mutually exclusive. For example, a firm may engage in any number of joint ventures while maintaining an export business. Additionally, there are a number of other strategies that a firm should consider before deciding on its long-term approach to foreign markets. These will be discussed in detail in Chapter 6 under the topic of grand strategies. However, the strategies discussed in this chapter provide the most popular starting points for planning the globalization of a firm.

Sample Strategies of Global Competitors

It is interesting and informative to study the actual strategies of companies that have recently chosen to globalize their operations. Exhibit 4–14, Global Strategy in Action, provides examples of six different strategies that are being employed by Asian firms: professionalizing management, remaining entrepreneurial, sticking with the core business, bracing for more open markets, going public, and forging strategic alliances. As the details of their strategies make apparent, foreign firms must design plans that will enable them to generate the best mix of global operations and domestic market shares, exactly as U.S. firms are forced to do.

Summary

To understand the strategic planning options available to a corporation, its managers need to recognize that different types of industry-based competition exist. Specifically, they must identify the position of their industry along the global versus multidomestic continuum and then consider the implications of that position for their firm.

The differences between global and multidomestic industries about the location and coordination of functional corporate activities necessitate differences in strategic emphasis. As an industry becomes global, managers of firms within that industry must increase the coordination and concentration of functional activities.

The appendix at the end of this chapter lists many components of the environment with which global corporations must contend. This list is useful in understanding the issues that confront global corporations and in evaluating the thoroughness of global corporation strategies.

As a starting point for global expansion, the firm's mission statement needs to be reviewed and revised. As global operations fundamentally alter the direction and strategic capabilities of a firm, its mission statement, if originally developed from a domestic perspective, must be globalized.

The globalized mission statement provides the firm with a unity of direction that transcends the divergent perspectives of geographically dispersed managers. It provides a basis for strategic decisions in situations where strategic alternatives may appear to conflict. It promotes corporate values and commitments that extend beyond single cultures and satisfies the demands of the firm's internal and external claimants in different countries. Finally, it ensures the survival of the global corporation by asserting the global corporation's legitimacy with respect to support coalitions in a variety of operating environments.

Movement of a firm toward globalization often follows a systematic pattern of development. Commonly, businesses begin their foreign nation involvements progressively through niche market exporting, license-contract manufacturing, franchising, joint ventures, foreign branching, and foreign subsidiaries.

BusinessWeek

STRATEGY 1: PROFESSIONALIZING MANAGEMENT

A sampling of the best emerging Asian companies and their management strategies

Company	Country	Strategy	Revenue
Johnson Electric	Hong Kong	In the business of micromotors, this family company is bringing in outside executives and investing heavily in training.	$250 million ↑ 29%
Taiwan Semiconductor	Taiwan	This highly successful foundry has an American as president. Under him are a handful of Taiwanese with American MBAs.	$740 million ↑ 57%

STRATEGY 2: REMAINING ENTREPRENEURIAL

Company	Country	Strategy	Revenue
Acer	Taiwan	CEO Stan Shih has broken his PC-making company into small, decentralized units so that each can be highly responsive to the market.	$ 3.2 billion ↑ 71%
San Miguel Corp.	Philippines	This beer and food conglomerate is actively spinning off different divisions into separate companies as a way to gain market share and become more efficient.	$ 190 million ↑ 41%

STRATEGY 3: STICKING WITH THE CORE BUSINESS

Company	Country	Strategy	Revenue
Renong Bernard	Malaysia	This group of eight listed companies is now selling off assets to focus on infrastructure. Its leading executives want the company to specialize rather than be a hodgepodge of investments.	$1.3 billion ↑ 19%
Indofood	Indonesia	This Jakarta-based food company made it big at home with its near monopoly in flour milling. Now, it's exporting its noodles to China, Chile, and Poland with the goal of being a global player.	$6.0 billion ↑ 18.9%

STRATEGY 4: BRACING FOR MORE OPEN MARKETS

Company	Country	Strategy	Revenue
Chinatrust	Taiwan	The country's leading credit-card issuer is finding its niche by providing a wide range of services for Taiwanese executives working abroad and other overseas Chinese.	$12.6 billion* ↑ 20%
Thai Farmers Bank	Thailand	Catching up to Citibank in innovative products, the bank is undergoing a reengineering to become more responsive to customers.	$20 billion* ↑ 15.2%

STRATEGY 5: GOING PUBLIC

Company	Country	Strategy	Revenue
Telkom Indonesia	Indonesia	This state-owned company is raising more than $1 billion of equity in Jakarta, New York, and London as part of the government's privatization drive.	$1.8 billion ↑ 30%
China Steel	Taiwan	Once a sleepy state enterprise, this well-run company has been privatized in a major bid to take on the global competition.	$2.9 billion ↑ 34%

STRATEGY 6: FORGING STRATEGIC PARTNERSHIPS

Company	Country	Strategy	Revenue
Legend	China	This emerging computer distributor and manufacturer in China is a marriage of a Hong Kong software house and Beijing's Academy of Sciences.	$480 million ↑ 50%
Mitac	Taiwan	The island's second-largest PC maker manufactures for Compaq, Apple, and AT&T. It is jointly developing desktop computers with Compaq.	$570 million ↑ 50%

*Assets.

Source: Reprinted from November 27, 1995 issue of *BusinessWeek* by special permission, copyright © 1995 by The McGraw-Hill Companies, Inc.

Questions for Discussion

1. How does environmental analysis at the domestic level differ from global analysis?
2. Which factors complicate environmental analysis at the global level? Which factors are making such analysis easier?
3. Do you agree with the suggestion that soon all industries will need to evaluate global environments?
4. Which industries operate almost devoid of global competition? Which inherent immunities do they enjoy?

Components of the Multinational Environment

Multinational firms must operate within an environment that has numerous components. These components include:

1. Government, laws, regulations, and policies of home country (United States, for example).
   a. Monetary and fiscal policies and their effect on price trends, interest rates, economic growth, and stability.
   b. Balance-of-payments policies.
      1. Mandatory controls on direct investment.
      2. Interest equalization tax and other policies.
   c. Commercial policies, especially tariffs, quantitative import restrictions, and voluntary import controls.
   d. Export controls and other restrictions on trade.
   e. Tax policies and their impact on overseas business.
   f. Antitrust regulations, their administration, and their impact on international business.
   g. Investment guarantees, investment surveys, and other programs to encourage private investments in less-developed countries.
   h. Export-import and government export expansion programs.
   i. Other changes in government policy that affect international business.
2. Key political and legal parameters in foreign countries and their projection.
   a. Type of political and economic system, political philosophy, national ideology.
   b. Major political parties, their philosophies, and their policies.
   c. Stability of the government.
      1. Changes in political parties.
      2. Changes in governments.
   d. Assessment of nationalism and its possible impact on political environment and legislation.
   e. Assessment of political vulnerability.
      1. Possibilities of expropriation.
      2. Unfavorable and discriminatory national legislation and tax laws.
      3. Labor laws and problems.
   f. Favorable political aspects.
      1. Tax and other concessions to encourage foreign investments.
      2. Credit and other guarantees.
   g. Differences in legal system and commercial law.
   h. Jurisdiction in legal disputes.
   i. Antitrust laws and rules of competition.
   j. Arbitration clauses and their enforcement.
   k. Protection of patents, trademarks, brand names, and other industrial property rights.
3. Key economic parameters and their projection.
   a. Population and its distribution by age groups, density, annual percentage increase, percentage of working age, percentage of total in agriculture, and percentage in urban centers.

    b. Level of economic development and industrialization.

    c. Gross national product, gross domestic product, or national income in real terms and also on a per capita basis in recent years and projections over future planning period.

    d. Distribution of personal income.

    e. Measures of price stability and inflation, wholesale price index, consumer price index, other price indexes.

    f. Supply of labor, wage rates.

    g. Balance-of-payments equilibrium or disequilibrium, level of international monetary reserves, and balance-of-payments policies.

    h. Trends in exchange rates, currency stability, evaluation of possibility of depreciation of currency.

    i. Tariffs, quantitative restrictions, export controls, border taxes, exchange controls, state trading, and other entry barriers to foreign trade.

    j. Monetary, fiscal, and tax policies.

    k. Exchange controls and other restrictions on capital movements, repatriation of capital, and remission of earnings.

4. Business system and structure.

    a. Prevailing business philosophy: mixed capitalism, planned economy, state socialism.

    b. Major types of industry and economic activities.

    c. Numbers, size, and types of firms, including legal forms of business.

    d. Organization: proprietorships, partnerships, limited companies, corporations, cooperatives, state enterprises.

    e. Local ownership patterns: public and privately held corporations, family-owned enterprises.

    f. Domestic and foreign patterns of ownership in major industries.

    g. Business managers available: their education, training, experience, career patterns, attitudes, and reputations.

    h. Business associations and chambers of commerce and their influence.

    i. Business codes, both formal and informal.

    j. Marketing institutions: distributors, agents, wholesalers, retailers, advertising agencies, advertising media, marketing research, and other consultants.

    k. Financial and other business institutions: commercial and investment banks, other financial institutions, capital markets, money markets, foreign exchange dealers, insurance firms, engineering companies.

    l. Managerial processes and practices with respect to planning, administration, operations, accounting, budgeting, and control.

5. Social and cultural parameters and their projections.

    a. Literacy and educational levels.

    b. Business, economic, technical, and other specialized education available.

    c. Language and cultural characteristics.

    d. Class structure and mobility.

    e. Religious, racial, and national characteristics.

    f. Degree of urbanization and rural-urban shifts.

    g. Strength of nationalistic sentiment.

    h. Rate of social change.

    i. Impact of nationalism on social and institutional change.

Chapter 4 Discussion Case

BusinessWeek

How Well Does Wal-Mart Travel Overseas?

1 In the decade since Wal-Mart Stores Inc. (WMT) began its international exploits with a joint venture in Mexico, its record abroad has been full of merchandising missteps and management upheaval. Such blunders explain why German shopper Claudia Gittel grouses about the meat selection at the Wal-Mart in Esslingen and how the prices were lower when local chain Interspar ran the store. And why rival retailers from Brazil to South Korea scoff at Wal-Mart's product choices and "cookie-cutter" outlets. "We don't see Wal-Mart as a threat anymore," sniffs Hong Sun Sang, assistant manager for E-Mart, a 35-store chain in South Korea.

2 But with its persistence and deep pockets, it would be a mistake to underestimate the world's largest retailer. Just look at the U.S. grocery business, where Wal-Mart is a leader after early stumbles with its huge "supercenters." Likewise, the Bentonville (Ark.) chain has learned some painful lessons about consumers, regulators, and suppliers around the world. Through trial and error, the company has quietly built a powerful force outside the United States. It's now the biggest retailer in Canada and Mexico. Its $32 billion international business equaled 17% of its $191 billion in sales last year, with more than 1,100 stores in nine countries. And its operating profit abroad rose 36% last year, to $1.1 billion, about 12% of total profits. The trend continued in the first half of this year, with international sales rising 9.6% and operating profit jumping 39%.

3 Wal-Mart finally started getting its international act together two years ago after it put then-chief financial officer John B. Menzer in charge of the International Div. The low-key Menzer was credited with tightening financial discipline and boosting return on assets for the parent company. Now he's bringing a similar focus to Wal-Mart's sprawling operations abroad, where he's pushing more authority into the field, working to develop a corps of top managers, and spreading "best practices" from the United States and elsewhere around the world. And for the first time, Wal-Mart is building a global sourcing operation to use its huge sales volumes to command better deals, higher quality, and more innovation from both U.S. and foreign suppliers.

4 The company is backing these efforts with big bucks. Lehman Brothers Inc. estimates that Wal-Mart will devote 26% of its $9 billion in capital expenditures this year to operations abroad, adding about 120 stores. "As a global organization, they've become more savvy," says Ira Kalish, director of global retail intelligence at PricewaterhouseCoopers.

5 Wal-Mart believes that it has no choice but to expand rapidly abroad. Its culture and stock price are built on the expectation of double-digit sales and profit gains year after year. Analysts figure that the company's expanding chain of U.S. supercenters will carry the burden for at least four to eight years. But "someday the United States will slow down, and international will be the growth vehicle for the company," says Menzer.

6 Still, to get there Menzer must clear some high hurdles. The biggest one is Germany, where Wal-Mart bought the 21-store Wertkauf hypermarket chain in 1997 and then 74 unprofitable and often decrepit Interspar stores in 1998. Problems in integrating and upgrading the stores resulted in at least $200 million in losses last year, on roughly $3 billion in sales, estimates analyst Robert Buchanan of A.G. Edwards & Sons Inc. Wal-Mart has stopped predicting when it might make money in Germany. Some analysts believe that it won't break even until at least 2003. "There was a steep learning curve that wasn't expected," says Jim Leach, portfolio manager at shareholder Strong Capital Management.

7 Many of the wounds were self-inflicted. Wal-Mart failed to understand Germany's retail culture, the regulations that can add five years or more to the launch of a new hypermarket, and the stiff competition among some 14 hypermarket chains in a stagnant market. German managers who had been running the Wertkauf and Interspar stores for years didn't always take kindly to American "mentors" who were telling them how to do things when they didn't even speak German. Vendors balked at switching to a new supply system; when Wal-Mart tried to force them to supply its new centralized warehouses, it often found itself with empty shelves.

8 Then, last September, the German Cartel Office compelled Wal-Mart and some rivals to raise prices on milk, butter, and some other staples that they were

found to be selling below cost. Wal-Mart denies that but admits it underestimated the difficulties it would face. "We just walked in and said, 'We're going to lower prices, we're going to add people to the stores, we're going to remodel the stores because inherently that's correct,' and it wasn't," says Wal-Mart CEO H. Lee Scott Jr. "We didn't have the infrastructure to support the kind of things we were doing."

9   FOOD STUFF. Wal-Mart still needs a bigger presence in Germany to compete effectively, many analysts and suppliers contend. They point especially to food, where its market share is put at less than 2%. But Wal-Mart executives insist that they don't need more stores to make the German operation a success. "We have the scale; we just have to operate better," says Menzer.

10   To fix those operational problems, Wal-Mart recently hired a new country head, poaching him from a German tobacco-and-food supplier. Instead of the expensive renovations completed on 24 stores last year, Wal-Mart is carrying out more modest facelifts on 35 outlets this year. And this year it will open its first two new stores since the acquisitions. Wal-Mart is also working more closely with suppliers to boost its centralized distribution effort. About 50% of the products Wal-Mart has targeted for the program now move through central warehouses. Says Menzer: "We set ourselves back a few years, and now we're rebounding."

11   Wal-Mart executives say the German experience helped when they bought the British chain ASDA in 1999. Wal-Mart acquired a strong chain and gave local managers the freedom to run the business. While ASDA is still No. 3 in the grocery market, its share grew from 7.4% in 1995 to 9.6% last year, according to Verdict Research. Wal-Mart gave ASDA better technology for tracking store sales and inventories. And it pulled ASDA into its global buying effort, led by a 40-person unit in Bentonville that helps negotiate prices for products that can be sold in different markets. This enabled ASDA to cut prices on fans and air conditioners, for example, by 50%, boosting sales threefold.

12   Perhaps most important, says ASDA President Paul Mason, "this is still essentially a British business in the way it's run day-to-day." Indeed, one of Menzer's main priorities is to push operational authority to the country chiefs and closer to customers. That has meant cutting the international staff in Bentonville from 450 to 137. Now, Menzer focuses on enforcing certain core Wal-Mart principles, such as "every day low pricing," recently rolled out in Mexico and Argentina. But country managers handle their own buying, logistics, building design, and other operational decisions. "I have the autonomy to do what I need to do to run Wal-Mart Canada," says Mario Pilozzi, president of that business. In contrast, when Wal-Mart entered Canada in 1994, its blueprint specified what to sell and where to sell it—including liquid detergent and Kathie Lee clothing that flopped there. In the past, says CEO Scott, "we could get very specific on what should be on an end cap [a store display at the end of an aisle]. . . . I think we've matured."

13   Still, critics believe that the company retains a headquarters-knows-best mind-set. That raises the question, is Wal-Mart truly a global company, or just a U.S. company with a foreign division? Vijay Govindarajan, a professor of international business at Dartmouth College's Tuck School of Business, says Wal-Mart has few top managers who aren't American and few who speak more than one language and have been posted in several spots abroad. That might be one reason why some competitors scoff at Wal-Mart's claim that it's now sensitive to local tastes. "I get the impression that Wal-Mart is insisting on the American-style layouts and business approach," says Seol Do Won, marketing director at Samsung Tesco Co. in South Korea, which runs seven Home Plus stores. "It's good to introduce global standards, but you also need to adapt to local practice," he says.

14   Menzer insists he's doing just that, and that the lessons are flowing back to Bentonville, too. The U.S. stores and distribution centers, for instance, are now adopting ASDA's system for replenishing fresh food more quickly and in the right quantities. And ASDA's popular line of George brand clothing is being rolled out in the women's department of all U.S. stores this Christmas season. Thomas M. Coughlin, president of the Wal-Mart Stores Div., even removed all the chairs from the room where his managers hold their weekly meeting after he saw ASDA's "air-traffic controllers" room in Leeds. There, managers meet every morning around a high table with no chairs—to keep meetings short and to encourage action—as they pore over figures charted on the walls. As Menzer and Scott have made clear, there's no turning back in Wal-Mart's plan to conquer the world.

Source: Wendy Zellner, "How Well Does Wal-Mart Travel? After early missteps, the retailing giant may finally be getting the hang of selling overseas," *BusinessWeek,* September 3, 2001.

Chapter **Five**

Internal Analysis

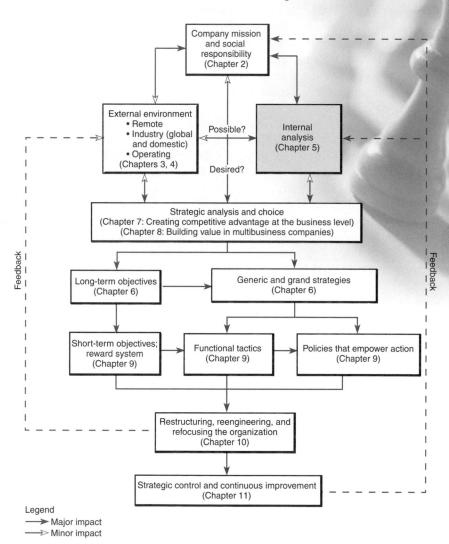

Company mission and social responsibility (Chapter 2)

External environment
- Remote
- Industry (global and domestic)
- Operating
(Chapters 3, 4)

Possible?

Desired?

Internal analysis (Chapter 5)

Strategic analysis and choice
(Chapter 7: Creating competitive advantage at the business level)
(Chapter 8: Building value in multibusiness companies)

Long-term objectives (Chapter 6)

Generic and grand strategies (Chapter 6)

Short-term objectives; reward system (Chapter 9)

Functional tactics (Chapter 9)

Policies that empower action (Chapter 9)

Restructuring, reengineering, and refocusing the organization (Chapter 10)

Strategic control and continuous improvement (Chapter 11)

Feedback

Feedback

Legend
→ Major impact
⇢ Minor impact

Three ingredients are critical to the success of a strategy. First, the strategy must be *consistent* with conditions in the competitive environment. Specifically, it must take advantage of existing or projected opportunities and minimize the impact of major threats. Second, the strategy must place *realistic* requirements on the firm's resources. In other words, the firm's pursuit of market opportunities must be based not only on the existence of external opportunities but also on competitive advantages that arise from the firm's key resources. Finally, the strategy must be *carefully executed.* The focus of this chapter is on the second ingredient: *realistic analysis of the firm's resources.*

Managers often do this subjectively, based on intuition and "gut feel." Years of seasoned industry experience positions managers to make sound subjective judgments. But just as often, or more often, this may not be the case. In fast-changing environments, reliance on past experiences can cause management myopia or a tendency to accept the status quo and disregard signals that change is needed. And with managers new to strategic decision making, subjective decisions are particularly suspect. A lack of experience is easily replaced by emotion, narrow functional expertise, and the opinions of others creating the foundation on which newer managers build strategic recommendations. So it is that new managers' subjective assessments often come back to haunt them.

Strategy in Action Exhibit 5–1 helps us understand this "subjective" tendency among both new and experienced managers. It looks at what happened a few years ago at Navistar when CEO John R. Horne admonished his management team to join him in buying their rapidly deteriorating (in price) stock as a sign to Wall Street that they had confidence in their company. Most managers declined, as their subjective sense of the company's situation and resources was quite negative. Some were reported to have even shorted the stock. The CEO acted virtually alone based on his view that several Navistar resources provided potential competitive advantages. Two years later, Navistar stock was up 400 percent. Subjective assessment had probably been holding the company back. It undoubtedly hit hard in the pocketbooks of several key managers that saw their own stock as an unwise investment.

Internal analysis has received increased attention in recent years as being a critical underpinning to effective strategic management. Indeed many managers and writers have adopted a new perspective on understanding firm success based on how well the firm uses its internal resources—the *resource-based view* (RBV) of the firm. This chapter will start with a look at the RBV to provide a useful vocabulary for identifying and examining internal *resources.* Next the chapter looks at ways managers achieve greater objectivity and rigor as they analyze their company's resources. Managers often start their internal analysis with questions like: "How well is the current strategy working? What is our current situation? Or what are our strengths and weaknesses?" Traditional *SWOT analysis* is then presented because it remains an approach that managers frequently use to answer these questions. More recently, insightful managers have begun to look at their business as a chain of activities that add value by creating the products or services they sell. Associated with this perspective is a powerful concept for introducing rigor and objectivity into internal analysis, the *value chain,* which this chapter will examine in great detail. Finally, objectivity and realism are enhanced when managers use meaningful standards for comparison regardless of the particular analytical framework they employ in internal analysis. We conclude this chapter by examining how managers do this using *past performance, stages of industry evolution, comparison with competitors* or other *"benchmarks,"* industry norms, and traditional *financial analysis.*

Strategy in Action

Navistar: An Objective Internal Analysis Lets It Gun the Engines for the 21st Century

Exhibit 5–1

BusinessWeek As it moved toward a new century, things looked bleak for Navistar International Corp. After decades of crippling labor problems and manufacturing snafus, the $6.4 billion Chicago truck and engine maker had suffered another steep earnings slide last year. Then, in a showdown with United Auto Workers members over costs, CEO John R. Horne had been forced to scrap the company's latest truck introduction. Disheartened investors let the stock drop to $9 a share, just 50¢ above its low.

That's when Horne called his 30 top executives into his office to make a personal plea. Looking for a show of faith in the company, he implored all of them to spend their own money to buy as many shares of Navistar stock as they could. Horne knew it was a lot to ask. Over the previous 10 years, the company—once known as International Harvester—had tallied the worst total return to shareholders of all publicly traded U.S. companies. But he was convinced that if his managers bought, Wall Street would see that as a sign that Navistar's fortunes were turning.

Management's reply was a unanimous no. Many felt that Navistar's shares might drop as low as 6, and all 30 backed away. So Horne bit the bullet alone, buying as much as he could for cash and also turning his 401(k) account entirely into Navistar stock. "I couldn't force them because it was their money," he says. "I laugh at them some now."

All the way to the bank, he might add. By late 2001, Navistar's stock hit 40, a blazing 350% return to shareholders.

What Horne—a 34-year veteran who became president in 1991 and CEO in 1995—convinced himself about was the presence of key resources that were on the verge of becoming distinctive competencies, and key strengths, at Navistar.

TANGIBLE ASSET: CLEANEST BURNING DIESEL ENGINE

Navistar's diesel engine business was the first to be worked over. Horne immediately cut the number of engines in production to two, down from 70 in the mid-80s, for example. And by 1994, with Navistar's balance sheet improving, he introduced a new engine.

Navistar's offering, still the cleanest burning model on the market, quickly attracted major truck manufacturers such as Ford Motor Co. Ford puts the engine in vans and pickups and recently on its hot Expedition sport utility vehicle. Thanks largely to this model, Navistar's share of the diesel engine market rose from 25% in 1990 to 44% in 1998. That's one big reason operating results climbed from a $355 million loss in 1993 to a $349 million profit for the fiscal year ended October 2000.

TANGIBLE ASSET: EXCESS TRUCK AND ENGINE MANUFACTURING CAPACITY

Horne began a wide-ranging overhaul of Navistar's remaining truck and engine manufacturing lines. He started by drastically slicing the number of products Navistar made. Assembly was rationalized too. While Navistar plants used to build multiple trucks for several different markets, today each one specializes in one type of truck with fewer models.

Tackling problems in Navistar's truck and tractor division proved far tougher. Two years ago, for example, Horne laid out a plan to introduce a new generation of trucks. By simplifying the design of components, Horne hoped to bring out a series of truck and trailer models with interchangeable designs and standardized parts, thus cutting costs while reducing errors on the assembly line. Horne's goal: to reduce the 19 heavy-duty and medium truck designs in his main Springfield (Illinois) plant to one or two.

ORGANIZATIONAL CAPABILITY: IMPROVED UNION RELATIONS

Before he got that far, Horne ran smack into the problem that has dogged Navistar for more than a decade: He needed significant concessions from the UAW, which represents almost 80% of Navistar's truck workers. Horne demanded a wage freeze until 2002 and the flexibility to consolidate production. He took a direct approach. "I showed them the books," he says. "They knew survival of the plants depended on the changes."

Union leaders may have known it, but U.S. union members weren't convinced. They rejected the contract outright. Convinced that he could never achieve his profitability goals without the changes, Horne cancelled the new trucks. He took a $35 million charge and made clear his next step would be to look abroad for lower labor costs. By August 1997, the workers folded their cards and approved the plan. Horne's tough stance has paid off. He quickly revived plans for the new truck. And since the new labor contract and other manufacturing changes went into effect last fall, productivity at U.S. plants has already risen 15%.

ORGANIZATIONAL CAPABILITY: NEW PRODUCT DEVELOPMENT PROCESS

Just as important, Horne got Navistar working on new models again for the first time in years. Having brought out few new products during Navistar's long slide, most of the company's models were aging. But to make sure the new products pay off, Horne also introduced tight financial discipline: Today, new projects only win the nod if they can earn a

17.5% return on equity and a 15% return on assets through a business cycle and be available in 2 years or less. *Popular Science* recognized Navistar's revolutionary camless engine technology as "Best of What's New in 2002."

INTANGIBLE ASSET: A VISIONARY LEADER WITH STRONG LEADERSHIP SKILLS

"Horne has done a magnificent job," says David Pedowitz, director of research at New York's David J. Greene & Co. brokerage firm, the largest outside investor with a 5% stake. "For the first time since the breakup of International Harvester, they're in a position to be a world-class competitor."

In the meantime, Horne continues to spread his penny-pinching gospel. Indeed, though he's a big basketball fan, he won't buy courtside seats to see his favorite competitor, Washington Wizards' Michael Jordan, hit the court. When Horne does make it to a home game, it's as a guest. He has other things to do with the fortune he's made in Navistar stock. Like reinvest.

Source: "Navistar: Gunning the Engines," *BusinessWeek*, February 2, 1998; and "Diesels Are the New Thing—Again," *BusinessWeek*, November 13, 2000.

RESOURCE-BASED VIEW OF THE FIRM

Coca-Cola versus Pepsi is a competitive situation virtually all of us recognize. Stock analysts look at the two and frequently conclude that Coke is the clear leader. They cite Coke's superiority in tangible assets (warehouses, bottling facilities, computerization, cash, etc.) and intangible assets (reputation, brand name awareness, tight competitive culture, global business system, etc.). They also mention that Coke leads Pepsi in several capabilities to make use of these assets effectively—managing distribution globally, influencing retailer shelf space allocation, managing franchise bottler relations, marketing savvy, investing in bottling infrastructure, and speed of decision making to take quick advantage of changing global conditions are just a few that are frequently mentioned. The combination of capabilities and assets, most analysts conclude, creates several competencies that give Coke several competitive advantages over Pepsi that are durable and not easily imitated.

The Coke-Pepsi situation provides a useful illustration for understanding several concepts central to the resource-based view (RBV) of the firm. The RBV's underlying premise is that firms differ in fundamental ways because each firm possesses a unique "bundle" of resources—tangible and intangible assets and organizational capabilities to make use of those assets. Each firm develops competencies from these resources and, when developed especially well, these become the source of the firm's competitive advantages. Coke's decision to buy out weak bottling franchisees and regularly invest in or own newer bottling locations worldwide has given Coke a competitive advantage analysts estimate Pepsi will take at least 10 years or longer to match. Coke's strategy for the last 15 years was based in part on the identification of this resource and the development of it into a distinctive competence—a sustained competitive advantage. The RBV is a useful starting point for understanding internal analysis. Let's look at the basic concepts underlying the RBV.

Three Basic Resources: Tangible Assets, Intangible Assets, and Organizational Capabilities

Executives charting the strategy of their businesses historically concentrate their thinking on the notion of a "core competence." Basically, a core competence was seen as a capability or skill running through a firm's businesses that once identified, nurtured, and deployed throughout the firm became the basis for lasting competitive advantage. Executives, enthusiastic about the notion that their job as strategists was to identify and leverage core competencies, encountered difficulty applying the concept because of the generality of its level of analysis. The RBV emerged as a way to make the core competency concept more focused and measurable—creating a more meaningful internal analysis. Central to the RBV's ability to do this is its notion of three basic types of resources that together create the building blocks for distinctive competencies. They are defined below and illustrated in Exhibit 5–2.

Tangible assets are the easiest to identify and are often found on a firm's balance sheet. They include production facilities, raw materials, financial resources, real estate, and computers. Tangible assets are the physical and financial means a company uses to provide value to its customers.

Intangible assets are things like brand names, company reputation, organizational morale, technical knowledge, patents and trademarks, and accumulated experience within an organization. While they are not assets that you can touch or see, they are very often critical in creating competitive advantage.

Organizational capabilities are not specific "inputs" like tangible or intangible assets; rather, they are the skills—the ability and ways of combining assets, people, and processes—that a company uses to transform inputs into outputs. Dell Computer built its first 10 years of unprecedented growth by creating an organization capable of the speedy and inexpensive manufacture and delivery of custom-built PCs. Gateway and Micron have attempted to copy Dell for most of that time but remain far behind Dell's diverse organizational capabilities. Dell subsequently revolutionized its own "system" using the Internet to automate and customize service, creating a whole new level of organizational capability that combines assets, people, and processes throughout and beyond their organization. Concerning this organizational capability, Michael Dell recently said: "Anyone who tries to go direct now will find it very difficult—like trying to jump over the Grand Canyon." Finely developed capabilities, such as Dell's Internet-based customer-friendly system, can be a source of sustained competitive advantage. They enable a firm to take the same input factors as rivals (like Gateway and Micron) and convert them into products and services, either with greater efficiency in the process or greater quality in the output or both.

What Makes a Resource Valuable?

Once managers begin to identify their firm's resources, they face the challenge of determining which of those resources represent strengths or weaknesses—which resources generate core competencies that are sources of sustained competitive advantage. This has been a complex task for managers attempting to conduct a meaningful internal analysis. The RBV has addressed this by setting forth some key guidelines that help determine what constitutes a valuable asset, capability, or competence—that is, what makes a resource valuable.

1. **Competitive superiority: Does the resource help fulfill a customer's need better than those of the firm's competitors?** Two restaurants offer similar food, at similar prices, but one has a location much more convenient to downtown offices than the other. The tangible asset, location, helps fulfill daytime workers' lunch eating needs better than its competitor, resulting in greater profitability and sales volume for the conveniently located restaurant. Wal-Mart redefined discount retailing and outperformed the industry in

EXHIBIT 5–2

Examples of Different Resources

Source R. M. Grant, *Contemporary Strategy Analysis* (Oxford: Blackwell, 2001), p. 140.

Tangible Assets	Intangible Assets	Organizational Capabilities
Hampton Inn's reservation system	Nike's brand name	Dell Computer's customer service
Ford Motor Company's cash reserves	Dell Computer's reputation	Wal-Mart's purchasing and inbound logistics
Georgia Pacific's land holdings	Wendy's advertising with Dave Thomas	Sony's product-development processes
Virgin Airlines' plane fleet	Jack Welch as GE's leader	Coke's global distribution coordination
Coca-Cola's Coke formula	IBM's management team Wal-Mart's culture	3M's innovation process

Classifying and Assessing the Firm's Resources

Resource	Relevant Characteristics	Key Indicators
Tangible Resources Financial Resources	The firm's borrowing capacity and its internal funds generation determine its resilience and capacity for investment.	• Debt/equity ratio • Operating cash flow/free cash flow • Credit rating
Physical Resources	Physical resources constrain the firm's set of production possibilities and impact its cost position. Key characteristics include: • The size, location, technical sophistication, and flexibility of plant and equipment • Location and alternative uses for land and buildings • Reserves of raw materials	• Market values of fixed assets • Vintage of capital equipment • Scale of plants • Flexibility of fixed assets
Intangible Resources Technological Resources	Intellectual property: patent portfolio, copyright, trade secrets Resources for innovation: research facilities, technical and scientific employees	• Number and significance of patents • Revenue from licensing patents and copyrights • R&D staff as a percent of total employment • Number and location of research facilities
Reputation	Reputation with customers through the ownership of brands and trademarks; established relationships with customers; the reputation of the firm's products and services for quality and reliability. The reputation of the company with suppliers (including component suppliers, banks and financiers, employees and potential employees), with government and government agencies, and with the community.	• Brand recognition • Brand equity • Percent of repeat buying • Objective measures of comparative product performance (e.g., Consumers' Association ratings, J. D. Power ratings) • Surveys of corporate reputation (e.g., *BusinessWeek*)

EXHIBIT 5–3
Wal-Mart's Resource-Based Competitive Advantage

Source: Pankaj Ghemawat, "Wal-Mart Stores' Discount Operations," Harvard Business School case number 9-387-018.

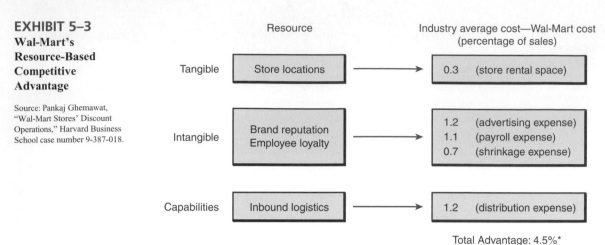

*Wal-Mart's cost advantage as a percent of sales. Each percentage point advantage is worth $500 million in net income to Wal-Mart.

profitability by 4.5 percent of sales—a 200 percent improvement. Four resources—store locations, brand recognition, employee loyalty, and sophisticated inbound logistics—allowed Wal-Mart to fulfill customer needs much better and more cost effectively than Kmart and other discount retailers, as shown in Exhibit 5–3. In both of these examples, *it is important to recognize that only resources that contributed to competitive superiority were valuable.* At the same time, other resources such as the restaurant's menu and specific products or parking space at Wal-Mart were essential to doing business but contributed little to competitive advantage because they did not distinguish how the firm fulfilled customer needs.

2. **Resource scarcity: Is the resource in short supply?** When it is, it is more valuable. When a firm possesses a resource and few if any others do, and it is central to fulfilling customers' needs, then it becomes a distinctive competence for the firm. The real way resource scarcity contributes value is when it can be sustained over time. To really answer this very basic question we must explore the following questions.

3. **Inimitability: Is the resource easily copied or acquired?** A resource that competitors can readily copy can only generate temporary value. It cannot generate a long-term competitive advantage. When Wendy's first emerged, it was the only major hamburger chain with a drive-through window. This unique organizational capability was part of a "bundle" of resources that allowed Wendy's to provide unique value to its target customers, young adults seeking convenient food service. But once this resource, or organizational capability, proved valuable to fast-food customers, every fast-food chain copied the feature. Then Wendy's continued success was built on other resources that generated other distinctive competencies.

Inimitability doesn't last forever, as the Wendy's example illustrates. Competitors will match or better any resource as soon as they can. It should be obvious, then, that the firm's ability to forestall this eventuality is very important The RBV identifies four characteristics, called *isolating mechanisms,* that make resources difficult to imitate:

• **Physically unique resources** are virtually impossible to imitate. A one-of-a-kind real estate location, mineral rights, and patents are examples of resources that cannot be imitated. Disney's Mickey Mouse copyright or Winter Park, Colorado's Iron Horse resort possess physical uniqueness. While many strategists claim that resources are physically unique, this is seldom true. Rather, other characteristics are typically what make most resources difficult to imitate.

- **Path-dependent resources** are very difficult to imitate because of the difficult "path" another firm must follow to create the resource. These are resources that cannot be instantaneously acquired but rather must be created over time in a manner that is frequently very expensive and always difficult to accelerate. When Michael Dell said that "anyone who tries to go direct now will find it very difficult—like trying to jump over the Grand Canyon" (see page 128), he was asserting that Dell's system of selling customized PCs direct via the Internet and Dell's unmatched customer service is in effect a path-dependent organizational capability. It would take any competitor years to develop the expertise, infrastructure, reputation, and capabilities necessary to compete effectively with Dell. Coca-Cola's brand name, Gerber Baby Food's reputation for quality, and Steinway's expertise in piano manufacture would take competitors many years and millions of dollars to match. Consumers' many years of experience drinking Coke or using Gerber or playing a Steinway would also need to be matched.

- **Causal ambiguity** is a third way resources can be very difficult to imitate. This refers to situations where it is difficult for competitors to understand exactly how a firm has created the advantage it enjoys. Competitors can't figure out exactly what the uniquely valuable resource is, or how resources are combined to create the competitive advantage. Causally ambiguous resources are often organizational capabilities that arise from subtle combinations of tangible and intangible assets and culture, processes, and organizational attributes the firm possesses. Southwest Airlines has regularly faced competition from major and regional airlines, with some like United and Continental eschewing their traditional approach and attempting to compete by using their own version of the Southwest approach—same planes, routes, gate procedures, number of attendants, and so on. They have yet to succeed. The most difficult thing to replicate is Southwest's "personality," or culture of fun, family, and frugal yet focused services and attitude. Just how that works is hard for United and Continental to figure out.

- **Economic deterrence** is a fourth source of inimitability. This usually involves large capital investments in capacity to provide products or services in a given market that are scale sensitive. It occurs when a competitor understands the resource that provides a competitive advantage and may even have the capacity to imitate, but chooses not to because of the limited market size that realistically would not support two players the size of the first mover.

While we may be inclined to think of a resource's inimitability as a yes-or-no situation, inimitability is more accurately measured on a continuum that reflects difficulty and time. Exhibit 5–4 illustrates such a continuum. Some resources may have multiple imitation deterrents. For example, 3M's reputation for innovativeness may involve path dependencies and causal ambiguity.

4. **Appropriability: Who actually gets the profit created by a resource?** Warren Buffet is known worldwide as one of the most successful investors of the last 25 years. One of his legendary investments was the Walt Disney Company, which he once said he liked "because the Mouse does not have an agent."[1] What he was really saying was that Disney owned the Mickey Mouse copyright, and all profits from that valuable resource went directly to Disney. Other competitors in the "entertainment" industry generated similar profits from their competing offerings, for example, movies, but they often "captured" substantially less of those profits because of the amounts that had to be paid to well-known actors or directors or other entertainment contributors seen as the real creators of the movie's value.

[1] *The Harbus,* March 25, 1996, p. 12.

EXHIBIT 5–4
Resource
Inimitability

Source: Cynthia A.
Montgomery, "Resources:
The Essence of Corporate
Advantage:" Harvard Business
School Case N1-792-064.

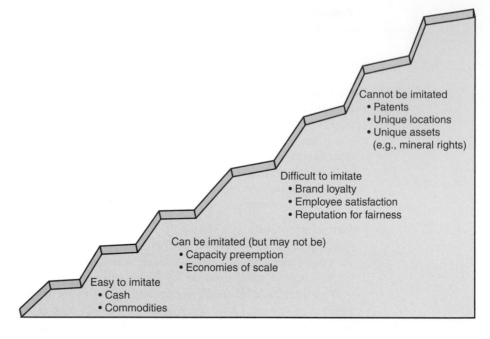

Cannot be imitated
• Patents
• Unique locations
• Unique assets
  (e.g., mineral rights)

Difficult to imitate
• Brand loyalty
• Employee satisfaction
• Reputation for fairness

Can be imitated (but may not be)
• Capacity preemption
• Economies of scale

Easy to imitate
• Cash
• Commodities

Sports teams, investment services, and consulting businesses are other examples of companies that generate sizable profits based on resources (key people, skills, contacts, for example) that are not inextricably linked to the company and therefore do not allow the company to easily capture the profits. Superstar sports players can move from one team to another, or command excessively high salaries, and this circumstance could arise in other personal services business situations. It could also occur when one firm joint ventures with another, sharing resources and capabilities and the profits that result. Sometimes restaurants or lodging facilities that are franchisees of a national organization are frustrated by the fees they pay the franchisor each month and decide to leave the organization and go "independent." They often find, to their dismay, that the business declines significantly. The value of the franchise name, reservation system, and brand recognition is critical in generating the profits of the business.

Bottom line: resources that one develops and controls—where ownership of the resource and its role in value creation is obvious—are more valuable than resources that can be easily bought, sold, or moved from one firm to another.

5. **Durability: How rapidly will the resource depreciate?** The slower a resource depreciates, the more valuable it is. Tangible assets, like commodities or capital, can have their depletion measured. Intangible resources, like brand names or organizational capabilities, present a much more difficult depreciation challenge. The Coca-Cola brand has continued to appreciate, whereas technical know-how in various computer technologies depreciates rapidly. In the increasingly hypercompetitive global economy of the 21st century, distinctive competencies and competitive advantages can fade quickly, making the notion of durability a critical test of the value of key resources and capabilities. Some believe that this reality makes well-articulated visions and associated cultures within organizations potentially the most important contributor to long-term survival.[2]

---

[2] James C. Collins, *Good to Great: Why Some Companies Make the Leap . . . and Others Don't* (New York: HarperCollins, 2001).

6. **Substitutability: Are other alternatives available?** We discussed the threat of substitute products in Chapter 3 as part of the five forces model for examining industry profitability. This basic idea can be taken further and used to gauge the value of particular resources. DeLite's of America was once a hot IPO as a new fast-food restaurant chain focused exclusively on selling lite food—salads, lean sandwiches, and so on. The basic idea was to offer, in a fast-food format, food low in calories and saturated fat. Investors were very excited about this concept because of the high-calorie, high-fat content of the foods offered by virtually every existing chain. Unfortunately for these investors, several key fast-food players, like Wendy's and later McDonald's, Burger King, and Hardees, adapted their operations to offer salad bars or premade salads and other "lean" sandwich offerings without disrupting their more well known fare. With little change and adaptation of their existing facility and operational resources, these chains quickly created alternatives to DeLite's offerings and the initial excitement about those offerings faded. DeLite's was driven out of business by substitute resources and capabilities rather than substitute products.

Using the Resource-Based View in Internal Analysis

To use the RBV in internal analysis, a firm must first identify and evaluate its resources to find those that provide the basis for future competitive advantage. This process involves defining the various resources the firm possesses, and examining them based on the above discussion to gauge which resources truly have strategic value. Four final guidelines have proven helpful in this undertaking:

- *Disaggregate resources*—break them down into more specific competencies—rather than stay with broad categorizations. Saying that Domino's Pizza has better marketing skills than Pizza Hut conveys little information. But dividing that into subcategories such as advertising that, in turn, can be divided into national advertising, local promotions, and couponing allows for a more measurable assessment. Exhibit 5–5 provides a useful illustration of this at Whitbread's Restaurant.

- *Utilize a functional perspective.* Looking at different functional areas of the firm, disaggregating tangible and intangible assets as well as organizational capabilities that are present, can begin to uncover important value-building resources and activities that deserve further analysis. Exhibit 5–6 lists a variety of functional area resources and activities that deserve consideration.

- *Look at organizational processes* and combinations of resources and not only at isolated assets or capabilities. While disaggregation is critical, you must also take a creative, gestalt look at what competencies the firm possesses or has the potential to possess that might generate competitive advantage.

- *Use the value chain approach* to uncover organizational capabilities, activities, and processes that are valuable potential sources of competitive advantage. Value chain analysis is discussed starting on page 137.

Although the RBV enables a systematic assessment of internal resources, it is important to stress that a meaningful analysis of those resources best takes place in the context of the firm's competitive environment. Possessing valuable resources will not generate commensurate profits unless resources are applied in an effective product market strategy; they must be deployed in an optimum way and align related activities for the firm to pursue its chosen sources of competitive advantage. Traditional strategy

EXHIBIT 5–5
**Disaggregating
Whitbread
Restaurant's
Customer Service
Resource**

Source: Andrew Campbell and
Kathleen Sommers-Luchs, *Core
Competency-Based Strategy*
(London: International
Thomson, 1997).

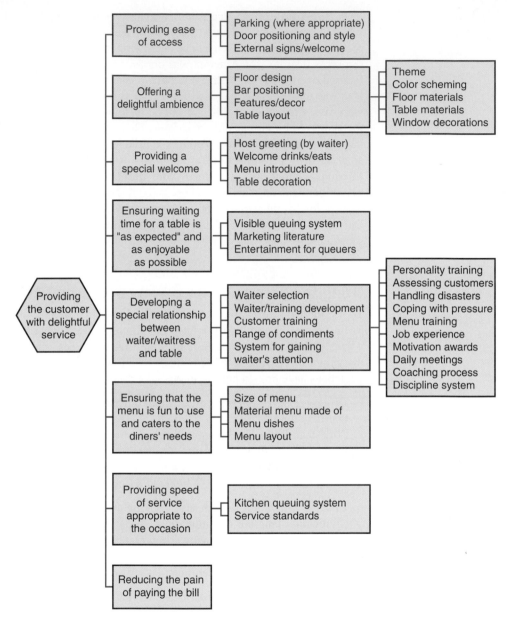

formulation—externally positioning a firm to capitalize on its strengths and opportunities and to minimize its threats and weaknesses—remains essential to realizing the competitive advantage envisioned from an RBV of the firm.[3] The next section examines this traditional approach, often called *SWOT analysis,* as a conceptual framework that may complement the RBV in conducting a sound internal analysis.

[3] Jay B. Barney and Asli M. Arikan, "The Resource-Based View: Origins and Implications," in *Handbook of Strategic Management,* Michael A. Hitt, R. Edward Freeman, and Jeffrey S. Harrison, editors (Oxford, UK: Blackwell Publishers, 2001).

EXHIBIT 5–6
Key Resources across Functional Areas

Marketing

Firm's products-services: breadth of product line.

Concentration of sales in a few products or to a few customers.

Ability to gather needed information about markets.

Market share or submarket shares.

Product-service mix and expansion potential: life cycle of key products; profit-sales balance in product-service.

Channels of distribution: number, coverage, and control.

Effective sales organization: knowledge of customer needs.

Internet usage.

Product-service image, reputation, and quality.

Imaginativeness, efficiency, and effectiveness of sales promotion and advertising.

Pricing strategy and pricing flexibility.

Procedures for digesting market feedback and developing new products, services, or markets.

After-sale service and follow-up.

Goodwill—brand loyalty.

Financial and Accounting

Ability to raise short-term capital.

Ability to raise long-term capital; debt-equity.

Corporate-level resources (multibusiness firm).

Cost of capital relative to that of industry and competitors.

Tax considerations.

Relations with owners, investors, and stockholders.

Leverage position; capacity to utilize alternative financial strategies, such as lease or sale and leaseback.

Cost of entry and barriers to entry.

Price-earnings ratio.

Working capital; flexibility of capital structure.

Effective cost control; ability to reduce cost.

Financial size.

Efficiency and effectiveness of accounting system for cost, budget, and profit planning.

Production, Operations, Technical

Raw materials cost and availability, supplier relationships.

Inventory control systems; inventory turnover.

Location of facilities; layout and utilization of facilities.

Economies of scale.

Technical efficiency of facilities and utilization of capacity.

Effectiveness of subcontracting use.

Degree of vertical integration; value added and profit margin.

Efficiency and cost-benefit of equipment.

Effectiveness of operation control procedures: design, scheduling, purchasing, quality control, and efficiency.

Costs and technological competencies relative to those of industry and competitors.

Research and development—technology—innovation.

Patents, trademarks, and similar legal protection.

(continued)

EXHIBIT 5–6
continued

Personnel

Management personnel.
Employees' skill and morale.
Labor relations costs compared to those of industry and competitors.
Efficiency and effectiveness of personnel policies.
Effectiveness of incentives used to motivate performance.
Ability to level peaks and valleys of employment.
Employee turnover and absenteeism.
Specialized skills.
Experience.

Quality Management

Relationship with suppliers, customers.
Internal practices to enhance quality of products and services.
Procedures for monitoring quality.

Information Systems

Timeliness and accuracy of information about sales, operations, cash, and suppliers.
Relevance of information for tactical decisions.
Information to manage quality issues: customer service.
Ability of people to use the information that is provided.
Linkages to suppliers and customers.

Organization and General Management

Organizational structure.
Firm's image and prestige.
Firm's record in achieving objectives.
Organization of communication system.
Overall organizational control system (effectiveness and utilization).
Organizational climate; organizational culture.
Use of systematic procedures and techniques in decision making.
Top-management skill, capabilities, and interest.
Strategic planning system.
Intraorganizational synergy (multibusiness firms).

SWOT ANALYSIS

SWOT is an acronym for the internal Strengths and Weaknesses of a firm and the environmental Opportunities and Threats facing that firm. SWOT analysis is a widely used technique through which managers create a quick overview of a company's strategic situation. It is based on the assumption that an effective strategy derives from a sound "fit" between a firm's internal resources (strengths and weaknesses) and its external situation (opportunities and threats). A good fit maximizes a firm's strengths and opportunities and minimizes its weaknesses and threats. Accurately applied, this simple assumption has powerful implications for the design of a successful strategy.

Environmental industry analysis in Chapters 3 and 4 provides the information needed to identify opportunities and threats in a firm's environment, the first fundamental focus in SWOT analysis.

Opportunities

An *opportunity* is a major favorable situation in a firm's environment. Key trends are one source of opportunities. Identification of a previously overlooked market segment, changes in competitive or regulatory circumstances, technological changes, and improved buyer or supplier relationships could represent opportunities for the firm.

Threats

A *threat* is a major unfavorable situation in a firm's environment. Threats are key impediments to the firm's current or desired position. The entrance of new competitors, slow market growth, increased bargaining power of key buyers or suppliers, technological changes, and new or revised regulations could represent threats to a firm's success.

Understanding the key opportunities and threats facing a firm helps its managers identify realistic options from which to choose an appropriate strategy and clarifies the most effective niche for the firm. The second fundamental focus in SWOT analysis is the identification of internal strengths and weaknesses.

Strengths

A *strength* is a resource advantage relative to competitors and the needs of the markets a firm serves or expects to serve. It is a *distinctive competence* when it gives the firm a comparative advantage in the marketplace. Strengths arise from the resources and competencies available to the firm.

Weaknesses

A *weakness* is a limitation or deficiency in one or more resources or competencies relative to competitors that impedes a firm's effective performance.

The sheer size and level of Microsoft's user base have proven to be a key strength on which it built its aggressive entry into Internet services. Limited financial capacity was a weakness recognized by Southwest Airlines, which charted a selective route expansion strategy to build the best profit record in a deregulated airline industry.

SWOT analysis can be used in many ways to aid strategic analysis. The most common way is to use it as a logical framework guiding systematic discussion of a firm's resources and the basic alternatives that emerge from this resource-based view. What one manager sees as an opportunity, another may see as a potential threat. Likewise, a strength to one manager may be a weakness to another. Different assessments may reflect underlying power considerations within the firm or differing factual perspectives. Systematic analysis of these issues facilitates objective internal analysis.

The diagram in Exhibit 5–7 illustrates how SWOT analysis builds on the results of an RBV of a firm to aid strategic analysis. Key external opportunities and threats are systematically compared with internal resources and competencies—that is, strengths and weaknesses—in a structured approach. The objective is identification of one of four distinct patterns in the match between a firm's internal resources and external situation. Cell 1 is the most favorable situation; the firm faces several environmental opportunities and has numerous strengths that encourage pursuit of those opportunities. This situation suggests growth-oriented strategies to exploit the favorable match. America OnLine's intensive market development strategy in the online services market is the result of a favorable match of its strong technical expertise, early entry, and reputation resources with an opportunity for impressive market growth as millions of people joined the information highway in the last decade. Its continued strength in interactivity with Net-delivered media is currently a key component of AOL-Time Warner's new growth-oriented strategy in 2004.

EXHIBIT 5–7
SWOT Analysis
Diagram

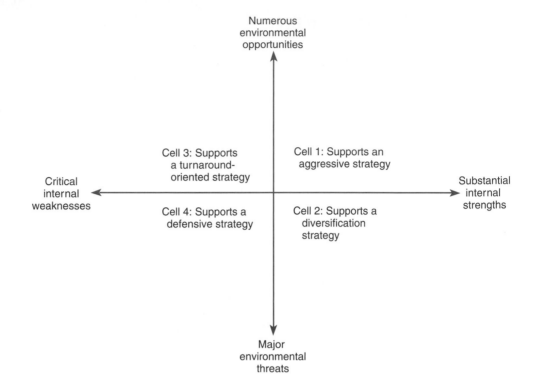

Cell 4 is the least favorable situation, with the firm facing major environmental threats from a weak resource position. This situation clearly calls for strategies that reduce or redirect involvement in the products or markets examined by means of SWOT analysis. Texas Instruments offers a good example of a Cell 4 firm. It was a sprawling maker of chips, calculators, laptop PCs, military electronics, and engineering software on a sickening slid toward oblivion just ten years ago. Its young CEO, Tom Engibous, reinvigorated the ailing electronics giant and turned it into one of the hottest plays in semiconductors by betting the company on an emerging class of chips known as digital signal processors (DSPs). The chips crunch vast streams of data for an array of digital gadgets, including modems and cellular phones. Engibous shed billions of dollars worth of assets to focus on DSPs, which he calls "the most important silicon technology of the next decade." TI now commands nearly half of the $4.4 billion global market for the most advanced DSPs, and it's the No. 1 chip supplier to the sizzling digital wireless phone market.

In Cell 2, a firm whose RBV has identified several key strengths, faces an unfavorable environment. In this situation, strategies would seek to redeploy those strong resources and competencies to build long-term opportunities in more opportunistic product markets. IBM, a dominant manufacturer of mainframes, servers, and PCs worldwide, has nurtured many strengths in computer-related and software-related markets for many years. Increasingly, however, it has had to address major threats that include product commoditization, pricing pressures, accelerated pace of innovation, and the like. Fortunately, Sam Palmisano's determined development of ISSC, better known now as IBM Global Services, has allowed IBM to build a long-term opportunity in more profitable growing markets of the next decade. In the last ten years since Palmisano ran it, Global Services has become the fastest-growing division of the company, its largest employer, and the keystone of IBM's strategic future. The group does everything from running a customer's IT department to consulting on legacy system upgrades to building custom supply-chain management applications. As IBM's hardware divisions struggle against price wars and commoditization and its software units fight to gain share beyond mainframes, it is Global Services that drives the company's growth.

A firm in Cell 3 faces impressive market opportunity but is constrained by weak internal resources. The focus of strategy for such a firm is eliminating the internal weaknesses so as to more effectively pursue the market opportunity. The AOL-Time Warner merger may well have afforded both companies a way to overcome key weaknesses keeping them from pursuing vast 21st-century, Internet-based opportunities. AOL lacks programming content and the ability to sell programming profitably over time. Time Warner is at a loss in managing the complexities of interactive media services.

SWOT analysis has been a framework of choice among many managers for a long time because of its simplicity and its portrayal of the essence of sound strategy formulation—matching a firm's opportunities and threats with its strengths and weaknesses. Central to making SWOT analysis effective is accurate internal analysis—the identification of specific strengths and weaknesses around which sound strategy can be built. One of the historical deficiencies of SWOT analysis was the tendency to rely on a very general, categorical assessment of internal capabilities. The resource-based view came to exist in part as a remedy to this void in the strategic management field. It is an excellent way to identify internal strengths and weaknesses and use that information to enhance the quality of a SWOT analysis. The RBV perspective was presented earlier in this chapter. While the conceptual appeal of the RBV is compelling, many managers remain comfortable with a functional approach to isolate and evaluate internal strengths and weaknesses. The next section describes the functional approach so that you will be aware of how management teams that don't use the RBV identify internal strengths and weaknesses.

While SWOT analysis offers simple, logical approaches to guide internal analysis, managers that endured the downsizing and reengineering of the last decade found the need for an approach that focused them even more narrowly on how work actually took place within their companies as they sought to meet customer needs. What these managers were responding to was the reality that producing goods or services and handling customers often necessitated the simultaneous involvement of multiple functions to be effective. They needed a way to look at their business as a series of activities that took place to create value for a customer—and to use this view as the framework to guide internal analysis. The value chain concept is one such framework.

VALUE CHAIN ANALYSIS

The term *value chain* describes a way of looking at a business as a chain of activities that transform inputs into outputs that customers value. Customer value derives from three basic sources: activities that differentiate the product, activities that lower its cost, and activities that meet the customer's need quickly. *Value chain analysis* (VCA) attempts to understand how a business creates customer value by examining the contributions of different activities within the business to that value.

VCA takes a process point of view: It divides (sometimes called disaggregates) the business into sets of activities that occur *within the business,* starting with the inputs a firm receives and finishing with the firm's products (or services) and after-sales service to customers. VCA attempts to look at its costs across the series of activities the business performs to determine where low-cost advantages or cost disadvantages exist. It looks at the attributes of each of these different activities to determine in what ways each activity that occurs between purchasing inputs and after-sales service helps differentiate the company's products and services. Proponents of VCA believe VCA allows managers to better

EXHIBIT 5–8
The Value Chain

Source: *Harvard Business School on Managing the Value Chain* (Cambridge: HBS Press, 2000).

The Value Chain

Primary Activities

Primary Activities

- **Inbound Logistics**—Activities, costs, and assets associated with obtaining fuel, energy, raw materials, parts components, merchandise, and consumable items from vendors; receiving, storing, and disseminating inputs from suppliers; inspection; and inventory management.
- **Operations**—Activities, costs, and assets associated with converting inputs into final product form (production, assembly, packaging, equipment maintenance, facilities, operations, quality assurance, environmental protection).
- **Outbound Logistics**—Activities, costs, and assets dealing with physically distributing the product to buyers (finished goods warehousing, order processing, order picking and packing, shipping, delivery vehicle operations).
- **Marketing and Sales**—Activities, costs, and assets related to sales force efforts, advertising and promotion, market research and planning, and dealer/distributor support.
- **Service**—Activities, costs, and assets associated with providing assistance to buyers, such as installation, spare parts delivery, maintenance and repair, technical assistance, buyer inquiries, and complaints.

Support Activities

- **General Administration**—Activities, costs, and assets relating to general management, accounting and finance, legal and regulatory affairs, safety and security, management information systems, and other "overhead" functions.
- **Human Resources Management**—Activities, costs, and assets associated with the recruitment, hiring, training, development, and compensation of all types of personnel; labor relations activities; development of knowledge-based skills.
- **Research, Technology, and Systems Development**—Activities, costs, and assets relating to product R&D, process R&D, process design improvement, equipment design, computer software development, telecommunications systems, computer-assisted design and engineering, new database capabilities, and development of computerized support systems.
- **Procurement**—Activities, costs, and assets associated with purchasing and providing raw materials, supplies, services, and outsourcing necessary to support the firm and its activities. Sometimes this activity is assigned as part of a firm's inbound logistic purchasing activities.

identify their firm's strengths and weaknesses by looking at the business as a process—a chain of activities—of what actually happens in the business rather than simply looking at it based on arbitrary organizational dividing lines or historical accounting protocol.

Exhibit 5–8 shows a typical value chain framework. It divides activities within the firm into two broad categories: primary activities and support activities. *Primary activities*

BusinessWeek   Founder Fred Smith and executives running companies controlled by FedEx say they are planning a monumental shift in the FedEx mission. They are accelerating plans to focus on information systems that track and coordinate packages. They are seeking to "morph" themselves from being a transportation company into an information company.

FedEx already has one of the most heavily used websites on the Internet. Company management claims to have 1,500 in-house programmers writing more software code than almost any other non-software company. To complement package delivery, FedEx designs and operates high-tech warehouses and distribution systems for big manufacturers and retailers around the world. For almost two decades, FedEx has been investing massive amounts to develop software and create a giant digital network. FedEx has built corporate technology campuses around the world, and its electronic systems are directly linked via the Internet or otherwise to over 1 million customers worldwide. That system now allows FedEx to track packages on an hourly basis, but it also allows FedEx to predict future flow of goods and then rapidly refigure the information and logistical network to handle those flows.

"Moving an item from point A to point B is no longer a big deal," say James Barksdale, CEO of Netscape and early architect of FedEx's information strategies. "Having the information about that item, and where it is, and the best way to use it. . . . That is value. The companies that will be big winners will be the ones who can best maximize the value of these information systems." Where FedEx's value has long been built on giant airplanes and big trucks, founder Smith sees a time when it will be built on information, computers, and the allure of the FedEx brand name.

If it works, FedEx's value chain will shrink in areas involved with inbound and outbound operations—taking off and landing on the tarmac—and will expand in areas involved with zapping around the pristine and pilot-free world of cyberspace to manage a client's supply chain and its distribution network.

Source: "UPS vs. FedEx: Ground Wars," *BusinessWeek*, May 21, 2001.

(sometimes called *line* functions) are those involved in the physical creation of the product, marketing and transfer to the buyer, and after-sale support. *Support activities* (sometimes called *staff* or *overhead* functions) assist the firm as a whole by providing infrastructure or inputs that allow the primary activities to take place on an ongoing basis. The value chain includes a *profit margin* since a markup above the cost of providing a firm's value-adding activities is normally part of the price paid by the buyer—creating value that exceeds cost so as to generate a return for the effort.

Judgment is required across individual firms and different industries because what may be seen as a support activity in one firm or industry may be a primary activity in another. Computer operations might typically be seen as infrastructure support, for example, but may be seen as a primary activity in airlines, newspapers, or banks. Exhibit 5–9, Strategy in Action, describes how Federal Express reconceptualized its company using a value chain analysis that ultimately saw its information support become its primary activity and source of customer value.

Conducting a Value Chain Analysis

Identify Activities

The initial step in value chain analysis is to divide a company's operations into specific activities or business processes, usually grouping them similarly to the primary and support activity categories shown in Exhibit 5–9. Within each category, a firm typically performs a number of discrete activities that may represent key strengths or weaknesses. Service activities, for example, may include such discrete activities as installation, repair, parts distribution, and upgrading—any of which could be a major source of competitive

EXHIBIT 5–10   The Difference between Traditional Cost Accounting and Activity-Based Cost Accounting

Traditional Cost Accounting in a Purchasing Department		Activity-Based Cost Accounting in the Same Purchasing Department for Its "Procurement" Activities	
Wages and salaries	$175,000	Evaluate supplier capabilities	$ 67,875
Employee benefits	57,500	Process purchase orders	41,050
Supplies	3,250	Expedite supplier deliveries	11,750
Travel	1,200	Expedite internal processing	7,920
Depreciation	8,500	Check quality of items purchased	47,150
Other fixed charges	62,000	Check incoming deliveries against purchase orders	24,225
Miscellaneous operating expenses	12,625	Resolve problems	55,000
	$320,075	Internal administration	65,105
			$320,075

advantage or disadvantage. The manager's challenge at this point is to be very detailed attempting to "disaggregate" what actually goes on into numerous distinct, analyzable activities rather than settling for a broad, general categorization.

Allocate Costs

The next step is to attempt to attach costs to each discrete activity. Each activity in the value chain incurs costs and ties up time and assets. Value chain analysis requires managers to assign costs and assets to each activity, thereby providing a very different way of viewing costs than traditional cost accounting methods would produce. Exhibit 5–10 helps illustrate this distinction. Both approaches in Exhibit 5–10 tell us that the purchasing department (procurement activities) cost $320,150. The traditional method lets us see that payroll expenses are 73 percent [(175 + 57.5)/320] of our costs with "other fixed charges" the second largest cost, 19 percent [62/320] of the total procurement costs. VCA proponents would argue that the benefit of this information is limited. Their argument might be the following:

> With this information we could compare our procurement costs to key competitors, budgets, or industry averages, and conclude that we are better, worse, or equal. We could then ascertain that our "people" costs and "other fixed charges" cost are advantages, disadvantages, or "in line" with competitors. Managers could then argue to cut people, add people, or debate fixed overhead charges. However, they would get lost in what is really a budgetary debate without ever examining what it is those people do in accomplishing the procurement function, what value that provides, and how cost effective each activity is.

VCA proponents hold that the activity-based VCA approach would provide a more meaningful analysis of the procurement function's costs and consequent value-added. The activity-based side of Exhibit 5–10 shows that approximately 21 percent of the procurement cost or value-added involves evaluating supplier capabilities. A rather sizable cost, 20 percent, involves internal administration, with an additional 17 percent spent resolving problems and almost 15 percent spent on quality control efforts. VCA advocates see this information as being much more useful than traditional cost accounting information, especially when compared to the cost information of key competitors or other "benchmark" companies. VCA supporters might assert the following argument that the benefit of this activity-based information is substantial:

> Rather than analyzing just "people" and "other charges," we are now looking at meaningful categorizations of the work that procurement actually does. We see, for example, that a key value-added activity (and cost) involves "evaluating supplier capabilities." The amount spent on "internal administration" and "resolving problems" seems high, and may indicate a

weakness or area for improvement if the other activities' costs are in line and outcomes favorable. The bottom line is that this approach lets us look at what we actually "do" in the business—the specific activities—to create customer value, and that in turn allows more specific internal analysis than traditional, accounting-based cost categories.

Recognize the Difficulty in Activity-Based Cost Accounting   It is important to note that existing financial management and accounting systems in many firms are not set up to easily provide activity-based cost breakdowns. Likewise, in virtually all firms, the information requirements to support activity-based cost accounting can create redundant work because of the financial reporting requirements that may force firms to retain the traditional approach for financial statement purposes. The time and energy to change to an activity-based approach can be formidable, and still typically involves arbitrary cost allocation decisions trying to allocate selected asset or people costs across multiple activities in which they are involved. Challenges dealing with a cost-based use of VCA have not deterred use of the framework to identify sources of differentiation. Indeed, conducting a VCA to analyze competitive advantages that differentiate the firm is compatible with the RBV's examination of intangible assets and capabilities as sources of distinctive competence.

Identify the Activities That Differentiate the Firm

Scrutinizing a firm's value chain may not only reveal cost advantages or disadvantages, it may also bring attention to several sources of differentiation advantage relative to competitors. Dell Computer considers its Internet-based after-sales service (activities) to be far superior to any competitor's. Dell knows it has cost advantage because of the time and expense replicating this activity would take. But Dell considers it an even more important source of value to the customer because of the importance customers place on this activity, which differentiates Dell from many similarly priced competitors. Likewise Federal Express, as we noted earlier, considers its information management skills to have become the core competence and essence of the company because of the value these skills allow FedEx to provide its customers and the importance they in turn place on such skills. Exhibit 5–11 suggests some factors for assessing primary and support activities' differentiation and contribution.

Examine the Value Chain

Once the value chain has been documented, managers need to identify the activities that are critical to buyer satisfaction and market success. It is those activities that deserve major scrutiny in an internal analysis. Three considerations are essential at this stage in the value chain analysis. First, the company's basic mission needs to influence managers' choice of the activities they examine in detail. If the company is focused on being a low-cost provider, then management attention to lower costs should be very visible; and missions built around commitment to differentiation should find managers spending more on activities that are differentiation cornerstones. Retailer Wal-Mart focuses intensely on costs related to inbound logistics, advertising, and loyalty to build its competitive advantage (see Exhibit 5–3), while Nordstrom builds its distinct position in retailing by emphasizing sales and support activities on which they spend twice the retail industry average. The application of value chain analysis to explore Volkswagen's strategic situation in 2003–2004 is described in Exhibit 5–12, Strategy in Action.

Second, the nature of value chains and the relative importance of the activities within them vary by industry. Lodging firms like Holiday Inn's major costs and concerns involve operational activities—it provides its service instantaneously at each location—and marketing activities, while having minimal concern for outbound

EXHIBIT 5–11   Possible Factors for Assessing Sources of Differentiation in Primary and Support Activities

Source: Adapted from *Harvard Business School on Managing the Value Chain* (Cambridge: HBS Press, 2000).

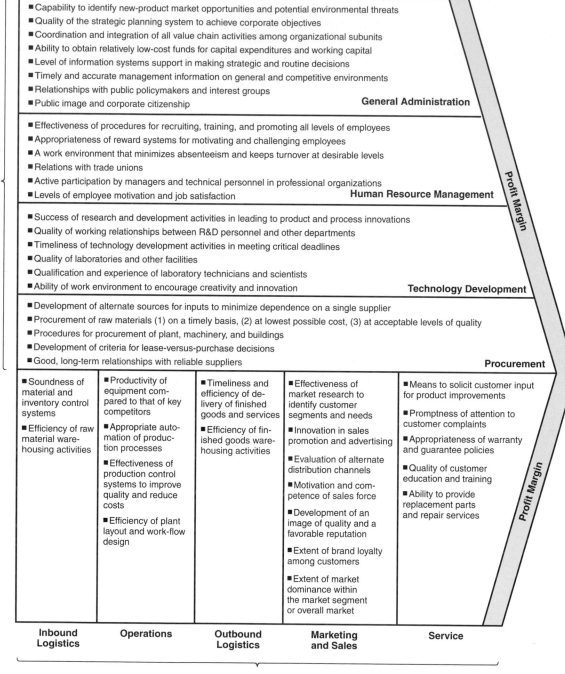

Support Activities

General Administration
- Capability to identify new-product market opportunities and potential environmental threats
- Quality of the strategic planning system to achieve corporate objectives
- Coordination and integration of all value chain activities among organizational subunits
- Ability to obtain relatively low-cost funds for capital expenditures and working capital
- Level of information systems support in making strategic and routine decisions
- Timely and accurate management information on general and competitive environments
- Relationships with public policymakers and interest groups
- Public image and corporate citizenship

Human Resource Management
- Effectiveness of procedures for recruiting, training, and promoting all levels of employees
- Appropriateness of reward systems for motivating and challenging employees
- A work environment that minimizes absenteeism and keeps turnover at desirable levels
- Relations with trade unions
- Active participation by managers and technical personnel in professional organizations
- Levels of employee motivation and job satisfaction

Technology Development
- Success of research and development activities in leading to product and process innovations
- Quality of working relationships between R&D personnel and other departments
- Timeliness of technology development activities in meeting critical deadlines
- Quality of laboratories and other facilities
- Qualification and experience of laboratory technicians and scientists
- Ability of work environment to encourage creativity and innovation

Procurement
- Development of alternate sources for inputs to minimize dependence on a single supplier
- Procurement of raw materials (1) on a timely basis, (2) at lowest possible cost, (3) at acceptable levels of quality
- Procedures for procurement of plant, machinery, and buildings
- Development of criteria for lease-versus-purchase decisions
- Good, long-term relationships with reliable suppliers

Profit Margin

Primary Activities

Inbound Logistics	Operations	Outbound Logistics	Marketing and Sales	Service
■ Soundness of material and inventory control systems ■ Efficiency of raw material warehousing activities	■ Productivity of equipment compared to that of key competitors ■ Appropriate automation of production processes ■ Effectiveness of production control systems to improve quality and reduce costs ■ Efficiency of plant layout and work-flow design	■ Timeliness and efficiency of delivery of finished goods and services ■ Efficiency of finished goods warehousing activities	■ Effectiveness of market research to identify customer segments and needs ■ Innovation in sales promotion and advertising ■ Evaluation of alternate distribution channels ■ Motivation and competence of sales force ■ Development of an image of quality and a favorable reputation ■ Extent of brand loyalty among customers ■ Extent of market dominance within the market segment or overall market	■ Means to solicit customer input for product improvements ■ Promptness of attention to customer complaints ■ Appropriateness of warranty and guarantee policies ■ Quality of customer education and training ■ Ability to provide replacement parts and repair services

Profit Margin

Strategy in Action

Value Chain Analysis Explains Volkswagen's Reasons for Success and Concern

Exhibit 5–12

BusinessWeek Volkswagen CEO Ferdinand Piëch had every reason to feel satisfied. The Austrian engineer and scion of one of Europe's most noted automotive dynasties was less than a year from retirement as chief of the German carmaker. As he looked back, Piëch could boast of one of the great turnarounds in automotive history. Since taking the top job at the Wolfsburg headquarters in 1993, his engineering brilliance had helped resurrect Volkswagen quality and turn models such as the Golf and Passat into all-time best-sellers. Piëch's relaunch of the Beetle cemented VW's hold in the U.S. market. Only VW had successfully revived a communist-era carmaker, Skoda of the Czech Republic. In 2001, as the global car industry lurches through a stressful year, VW saw profits grow above 2000 levels, when they more than doubled, to $1.8 billion, on sales of $76 billion.

Yet Piëch was stressed. Value chain analysis suggested two key value activities had driven his success—product development and operations. It also suggested that two other activities were becoming serious potential drains on the value chain and value he had so meticulously driven—human resource management and marketing and sales.

PRODUCT DEVELOPMENT

Piëch was driven. Unlike many other auto chiefs, he called the shots on product design and engineering. And if you worked for Dr. Piëch, you had better get it right. In Wolfsburg, executives joked that PEP, the acronym for the product development process (*Produktentwicklungsprozess*) really stands for *Piëch entscheidet persönlich*—Piëch decides himself. And he did so fast. He is said to have sketched out the Audi's all-wheel-drive system on the back of an envelope.

Without question, those achievements have been considerable. Volkswagen's four main brands—VW, Audi, Seat, and Skoda—have taken 19% of the European auto market, a gain of some three points in eight years, mostly at the expense of General Motors Corp. and Ford. Not bad for a company that eight years ago suffered from quality problems and a paucity of hit models. In South America, VW vehicles account for one-quarter of car sales, and in China, one-half. The top VW brands in the United States are the Jetta, Passat, and the new Beetle, a remake of the humble bug so beloved of 60s youth. Part of VW success lies in its quirky features. At night, the dashboard instruments the driver looks at, such as the speedometer and clock, light up in red, while those the driver touches, such as the radio, are backlit in blue. "It gives the vehicle some soul, which many of VW's competitors lack horribly," says Wes Brown, a consultant at Nextrend Inc., a Thousand Oaks (Calif.) auto-research firm.

OPERATIONS

When Piëch wasn't drawing up the plans, he was examining them with a gimlet eye. No screaming, of course: That was not the way for Piëch, an Austrian blueblood. One former transmission-plant manager said Piëch would tour the factory quietly, reviewing production data sheets and zeroing in instantly on any numbers suggesting something was amiss in the manufacturing process. "He's the only person whose very presence on the floor would make my stomach begin to hurt," says this manager.

Terrifying, yet inspiring. Under Piëch's tutelage, VW sweated the small stuff. Check this out, says one rival exec: On VW models, the gap between body panels—say between the front fender and wheel panel—had been cut to 1 millimeter. That puts them in a league with the industry's best.

HUMAN RESOURCE MANAGEMENT

In 1993, to buy labor peace, Piëch cut the workweek at VW's German plants from 35 hours to 28.8. That saved 30,000 jobs. But now VW workers can make upwards of $34 an hour. Piëch tried to push through a plan to lower the base wages of new German workers and link them to output instead of hours as this story was published. If this doesn't succeed, VW threatens to put new projects in places such as the Czech Republic, where wages are less than one-third German levels. Cutting such a deal is turning into a hard slog. The unions concede they need to be more flexible. But they are resisting management's demands to increase the workweek to more than 40 hours during peak production without paying overtime.

And investors frustrated with a low stock-PE ratio cannot expect a swift boost to the stock price. The government of Lower Saxony, the biggest investor, worries more about jobs than shareholder value. Five of VW's seven German factories are located in Lower Saxony, and they're among the least productive in Europe. According to World Markets Research Center in London, production at the Wolfsburg plant runs at 46 cars per worker per year, compared with 101 at Nissan Motor Co.'s British factory in Sunderland.

(continued)

MARKETING AND SALES

VW also had gaps in its product lineup. It had nothing to offer in the category of compact minivans—the scaled-down versions of minivans that are popular in Europe. A sport utility vehicle was not scheduled to come out until 2003. "We're [also] missing some niche models—sports car, roadster, another convertible," says Jürgen Lehmann, manager of the Autohaus Moltke dealership in Stuttgart. VW had to sort out these issues while the competition gets tougher.

Bottomline, VW's value chain presents interesting challenges for Piëch's successor, Bernd Pischetsrieder. He inherits extraordinary strengths in product development and manufacturing operations. But for all of the success of the last decade, and an impressive market presence worldwide, he faces emerging value chain weaknesses in human resource management cost considerations and product line gaps in marketing and sales.

Source: "Volkswagen," *BusinessWeek,* July 23, 2001.

logistics. Yet for a distributor, such as the food distributor PYA, inbound and outbound logistics are the most critical area. Major retailers like Wal-Mart have built value advantages focusing on purchasing and inbound logistics while the most successful personal computer companies have built via sales, outbound logistics, and service through the mail order process.

Third, the relative importance of value activities can vary by a company's position in a broader value system that includes the value chains of its upstream suppliers and downstream customers or partners involved in providing products or services to end users. A producer of roofing shingles depends heavily on the downstream activities of wholesale distributors and building supply retailers to reach roofing contractors and do-it-yourselfers. Maytag manufactures its own appliances, sells them through independent distributors, and provides warranty service to the buyer. Sears outsources the manufacture of its appliances while it promotes its brand name—Kenmore—and handles all sales and service.

As these examples suggest, it is important that managers take into account their level of vertical integration when comparing their cost structure for activities on their value chain to those of key competitors. Comparing a fully integrated rival with a partially integrated one requires adjusting for the scope of activities performed to achieve meaningful comparison. It also suggests the need for examining costs associated with activities provided by upstream or downstream companies; these activities ultimately determine comparable, final costs to end users. Said another way, one company's comparative cost disadvantage (or advantage) may emanate more from activities undertaken by upstream or downstream "partners" than from activities under the direct control of that company—therefore suggesting less of a relative advantage or disadvantage within the company's direct value chain.

Compare to Competitors

The final basic consideration when applying value chain analysis is the need to have a meaningful comparison to use when evaluating a value activity as a strength or weakness. Value chain analysis is most effective when comparing the value chains or activities of key competitors. Whether using the value chain approach or an examination of functional areas, or both approaches, the strategist's next step in a systematic internal analysis is to compare the firm's status with meaningful standards to determine which of its value activities are strengths or weaknesses. Four sources of meaningful standards for evaluating internal factors and value activities are discussed in the next section.

INTERNAL ANALYSIS: MAKING MEANINGFUL COMPARISONS

Managers need objective standards to use when examining internal resources and value-building activities. Whether applying the RBV, SWOT analysis, or the value chain approach, strategists rely on four basic perspectives to evaluate where their firm stacks up on its internal capabilities. These four perspectives are discussed in this section.

Comparison with Past Performance

Strategists use the firm's historical experience as a basis for evaluating internal factors. Managers are most familiar with the internal capabilities and problems of their firm because they have been immersed in its financial, marketing, production, and R&D activities. Not surprisingly, a manager's assessment of whether a certain internal factor—such as production facilities, sales organization, financial capacity, control systems, or key personnel—is a strength or a weakness will be strongly influenced by his or her experience in connection with that factor. In the capital-intensive airline industry, for example, debt capacity is a strategic internal factor. Delta Airlines managers view Delta's debt-equity ratio of less than 1.9 brought on by its acquisition of PanAm's international operations as a real weakness limiting its flexibility to invest in facilities because it maintained a ratio less than 0.6 for over 20 years. Continental Airlines managers, on the other hand, view Continental's much higher 3.5 debt-equity ratio as a growing strength, because it is down 50 percent from its 7.0 level five years earlier.

Although historical experience can provide a relevant evaluation framework, strategists must avoid tunnel vision in making use of it. NEC, Japan's IBM, initially dominated Japan's PC market with a 70 percent market share using a proprietary hardware system, much higher screen resolution, powerful distribution channels, and a large software library from third-party vendors. Far from worried, Hajime Ikeda, manager of NEC's planning division at the time, was quoted as saying: "We don't hear complaints from our users." By 2001, IBM, Apple, and Compaq filled the shelves in Japan's famous consumer electronics district, Akihabara. Hiroki Kamata, president of a Japanese computer research firm, reported that Japan's PC market, worth over $25 billion in 2001, saw Apple and IBM compatibles each having more market share than NEC because of better technology, software, and the restrictions created by NEC's proprietary technology. Clearly, using only historical experience as a basis for identifying strengths and weaknesses can prove dangerously inaccurate.

Stages of Industry Evolution

The requirements for success in industry segments change over time. Strategists can use these changing requirements, which are associated with different stages of industry evolution, as a framework for identifying and evaluating the firm's strengths and weaknesses.

Exhibit 5–13 depicts four stages of industry evolution and the typical changes in functional capabilities that are often associated with business success at each of these stages. The early development of a product market, for example, entails minimal growth in sales, major R&D emphasis, rapid technological change in the product, operating losses, and a need for sufficient resources or slack to support a temporarily unprofitable operation. Success at this introduction stage may be associated with technical skill, with being first in new markets, or with having a marketing advantage that creates widespread awareness. Radio Shack's initial success with its TRS–80 home computer was based in part on its ability to gain widespread exposure and acceptance in the ill-defined home computer market via the large number of existing Radio Shack outlets throughout the country.

EXHIBIT 5–13   Sources of Distinctive Competence at Different Stages of Industry Evolution

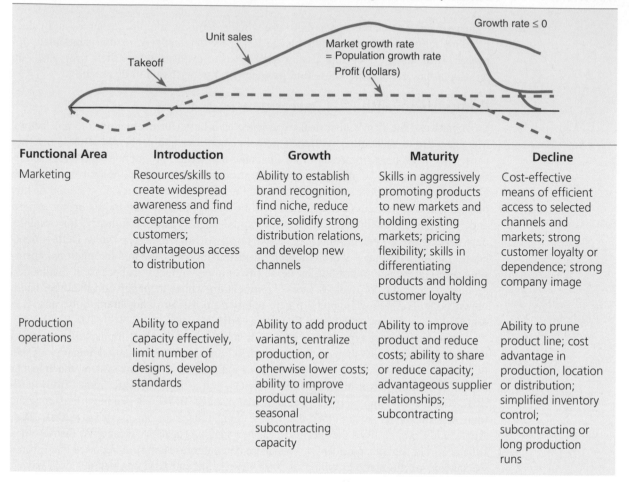

Functional Area	Introduction	Growth	Maturity	Decline
Marketing	Resources/skills to create widespread awareness and find acceptance from customers; advantageous access to distribution	Ability to establish brand recognition, find niche, reduce price, solidify strong distribution relations, and develop new channels	Skills in aggressively promoting products to new markets and holding existing markets; pricing flexibility; skills in differentiating products and holding customer loyalty	Cost-effective means of efficient access to selected channels and markets; strong customer loyalty or dependence; strong company image
Production operations	Ability to expand capacity effectively, limit number of designs, develop standards	Ability to add product variants, centralize production, or otherwise lower costs; ability to improve product quality; seasonal subcontracting capacity	Ability to improve product and reduce costs; ability to share or reduce capacity; advantageous supplier relationships; subcontracting	Ability to prune product line; cost advantage in production, location or distribution; simplified inventory control; subcontracting or long production runs

The strengths necessary for success change in the growth stage. Rapid growth brings new competitors into the product market. At this stage, such factors as brand recognition, product differentiation, and the financial resources to support both heavy marketing expenses and the effect of price competition on cash flow can be key strengths. IBM entered the personal computer market in the growth stage and was able to rapidly become the market leader with a strategy based on its key strengths in brand awareness and possession of the financial resources needed to support consumer advertising. Radio Shack discontinued its TRS–80 due to IBM's strength. Within a few years, however, IBM lost that lead in the next stage as speed in distribution and cost structures became the key success factors—strengths for Dell and several mail order–oriented computer assemblers.

As the industry moves through a shakeout phase and into the maturity stage, industry growth continues, but at a decreasing rate. The number of industry segments expands, but technological change in product design slows considerably. As a result, competition usually becomes more intense, and promotional or pricing advantages and differentiation become key internal strengths. Technological change in process design becomes intense as the many competitors seek to provide the product in the most efficient manner. Where R&D was critical in the introduction stage, efficient production is now crucial to

EXHIBIT 5–13 *continued*

Functional Area	Introduction	Growth	Maturity	Decline
Finance	Resources to support high net cash overflow and initial losses; ability to use leverage effectively	Ability to finance rapid expansion, to have net cash outflows but increasing profits; resources to support product improvements	Ability to generate and redistribute increasing net cash inflows; effective cost control systems	Ability to reuse or liquidate unneeded equipment; advantage in cost of facilities; control system accuracy; streamlined management control
Personnel	Flexibility in staffing and training new management; existence of employees with key skills in new products or markets	Existence of an ability to add skilled personnel; motivated and loyal workforce	Ability to cost effectively, reduce workforce, increase efficiency	Capacity to reduce and reallocate personnel; cost advantage
Engineering and research and development	Ability to make engineering changes, have technical bugs in product and process resolved	Skill in quality and new feature development; ability to start developing successor product	Ability to reduce costs, develop variants, differentiate products	Ability to support other grown areas or to apply product to unique customer needs
Key functional area and strategy focus	Engineering: market penetration	Sales: consumer loyalty; market share	Production efficiency; successor products	Finance, maximum investment recovery

continued success in the broader industry segments. Ford's emphasis on quality control and modern, efficient production has helped it prosper in the maturing U.S. auto industry, while General Motors, which pays almost 50 percent more than Ford to produce a comparable car, continues to decline.

When the industry moves into the decline stage, strengths and weaknesses center on cost advantages, superior supplier or customer relationships, and financial control. Competitive advantage can exist at this stage, at least temporarily, if a firm serves gradually shrinking markets that competitors are choosing to leave.

Exhibit 5–13 is a rather simple model of the stages of industry evolution. These stages can and do vary from the model. What should be borne in mind is that the relative importance of various determinants of success differs across the stages of industry evolution. Thus, the state of that evolution must be considered in internal analysis. Exhibit 5–13 suggests dimensions that are particularly deserving of in-depth consideration when a company profile is being developed.

Benchmarking—Comparison with Competitors

A major focus in determining a firm's resources and competencies is comparison with existing (and potential) competitors. Firms in the same industry often have different marketing skills, financial resources, operating facilities and locations, technical know-how, brand images, levels of integration, managerial talent, and so on. These different internal resources can become relative strengths (or weaknesses) depending on the strategy a firm chooses. In choosing a strategy, managers should compare the firm's key internal capabilities with those of its rivals, thereby isolating its key strengths and weaknesses.

In the home appliance industry, for example, Sears and General Electric are major rivals. Sears's principal strength is its retail network. For GE, distribution—through independent franchised dealers—has traditionally been a relative weakness. GE's possession of the financial resources needed to support modernized mass production has enabled it to maintain both cost and technological advantages over its rivals, particularly Sears. This major strength for GE is a relative weakness for Sears, which depends solely on subcontracting to produce its Kenmore appliances. On the other hand, maintenance and repair service are important in the appliance industry. Historically, Sears has had strength in this area because it maintains fully staffed service components and spreads the costs of components over numerous departments at each retail location. GE, on the other hand, has had to depend on regional service centers and on local contracting with independent service firms by its independent local dealers. Among the internal factors that Sears and GE must consider in developing a strategy are distribution networks, technological capabilities, operating costs, and service facilities. Managers in both organizations have built successful strategies yet those strategies are quite different. Benchmarking each other, they have identified ways to build on relative strengths while avoiding dependence on capabilities at which the other firm excels.

Benchmarking, comparing the way "our" company performs a specific activity with a competitor or other company doing the same thing, has become a central concern of managers in quality commitment companies worldwide. Particularly as the value chain framework has taken hold in structuring internal analysis, managers seek to systematically benchmark the costs and results of the smallest value activities against relevant competitors or other useful standards because it has proven to be an effective way to continuously improve that activity. The ultimate objective in benchmarking is to identify the "best practices" in performing an activity, to learn how lower costs, fewer defects, or other outcomes linked to excellence are achieved. Companies committed to benchmarking attempt to isolate and identify where their costs or outcomes are out of line with what the best practicers of a particular activity experience (competitors and noncompetitors) and then attempt to change their activities to achieve the new best practices standard.

Comparison with key competitors can prove useful in ascertaining whether their internal capabilities on these and other factors are strengths or weaknesses. Significant favorable differences (existing or expected) from competitors are potential cornerstones of a firm's strategy. Moreover, through comparison with major competitors, a firm may avoid strategic commitments that it cannot competitively support. Exhibit 5–14, Strategy in Action, shows how UPS used competitor comparison to assess its strengths and weaknesses in the package transportation industry.

Comparison with Success Factors in the Industry

Industry analysis (see Chapter 3) involves identifying the factors associated with successful participation in a given industry. As was true for the evaluation methods discussed above, the key determinants of success in an industry may be used to identify a firm's internal strengths and weaknesses. By scrutinizing industry competitors, as well as customer needs, vertical industry structure, channels of distribution, costs, barriers

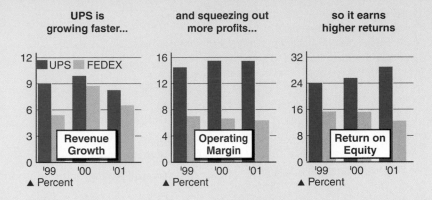

Success Begets Success
Stacking UPS up against FedEx

Data: Banc of America Securities ©BW

Over the past two years, the company has quietly shed its image as the slowpoke of shipping. Be it e-tailing frenzy or dot-com crash, UPS has captured customers by bombarding them with choices: fast flights versus cheap ground delivery, simple shipping or a panoply of manufacturing, warehousing, and supply-chain services. In the United States and several foreign markets, UPS has grabbed a commanding lead over FedEx—and not just in everyday package delivery but in the New Economy services such as logistics. In North America, UPS has even snagged the distinction of preferred carrier to the Web generation: The company handles 36% of all online purchases, versus 13% for FedEx. "UPS is doing things in e-commerce that other companies are just starting to talk about," says Jack R. Staff, chief economist at Zona Research in Redwood City, Calif.

The ascent of UPS charts a reversal of fortune in one of the fiercest rivalries in Corporate America. It was FedEx, after all, that pioneered both overnight delivery of packages and the ability to track their journey using computers. These 1970s' era innovations rocked the shipping industry and helped set the stage for the Internet Revolution of the 1990s. Even now, FedEx rules in certain areas of air freight. Its carefully burnished brand still says "absolutely, positively" to thousands of loyal customers—and not without reason. FedEx is one of America's great success stories, extolled for its customer service.

In the view of many analysts and industry execs, however, UPS now has a pronounced advantage in several hotly contested areas. In addition to its overwhelming lead in ground shipping and its online triumphs, UPS can point to a logistics business that is growing by 40% a year. FedEx is struggling to reverse a decline in this area.

Even in sectors where FedEx still rules, UPS is catching up quickly. FedEx has a commanding lead in the profitable overnight service, for example, delivering more than 3 million such packages daily in 200-plus countries and accounting for 39% of the market. UPS is No. 2, with 2.2 million overnight packages—but its volume has been growing faster than FedEx's for at least three years. In 2000, UPS's overnight business grew at 8%, compared with FedEx's 3.6%. And UPS's operating margin on its domestic air-express service is higher—24% versus 6%—according to Gary H. Yablon, a transportation analyst at Credit Suisse First Boston.

So what accounts for UPS's growth in overnight? The company trumpets its decision in 1999 to integrate overnight delivery into its vast ground-transportation network. UPS, like FedEx, still uses planes to make most such deliveries. But in the past two years, its logisticians have also figured out how to make quick mid-distance deliveries—as far as 500 miles in one night—by truck, which is much less expensive than by air. As a result, UPS's overall cost per package is $6.65, compared with FedEx's $11.89, according to CSFB. Even though FedEx also uses trucks for short hauls, "UPS has a real cost advantage," says John D. Kasarda, director of the University of North Carolina's Frank Hawkins Kenan Institute of Private Enterprise and a former FedEx consultant.

UPS's core strength is its fleet of 152,000 brown trucks, which reach virtually every address in the United States—and increasingly, the world. FedEx has belatedly begun to build its own home-delivery system. But the cost of duplicating a system UPS has spent nearly 100 years building could prove prohibitive. And with $3 billion in cash on

(continued)

hand, UPS could easily wage a price war against FedEx, which isn't generating any spare cash. "This is a game FedEx can't win," says Peter V. Coleman, a transportation analyst at Bank of America Securities. That leaves FedEx dependent on an air-delivery system that is increasingly expensive to operate.

	UPS	FedEx
Founded	1907	1971
Chairman	James P. Kelly	Frederick W. Smith
Headquarters	Atlanta, Ga.	Memphis, Tenn.
2000 Revenue	$29.77 billion	$18.3 billion
Net Income	$2.93 billion	$688 million
Employees	359,000	215,000
Daily Package Volume	13.2 million	5 million
Fleet	152,500 trucks, 560 planes	43,500 trucks, 662 planes

	Unit Cost	Unit Profit	Operating Margin	Avg Daily Volume
Air Deliveries, U.S.				
FedEx	$15.27	$0.93	6%	2,924,000
UPS	$14.60	$3.76	22%	2,162,000
Ground Deliveries, U.S.				
FedEx	$4.77	$0.68	13%	1,541,000
UPS	$4.95	$0.61	11%	10,945,000
Overall Average, including International				
FedEx	$11.89	$0.85	7%	4,788,000
UPS	$6.65	$1.17	15%	14,236,000

Data: Credit Suisse First Boston

to entry, availability of substitutes, and suppliers, a strategist seeks to determine whether a firm's current internal capabilities represent strengths or weaknesses in new competitive arenas. The discussion in Chapter 3 provides a useful framework—five industry forces—against which to examine a firm's potential strengths and weaknesses. General Cinema Corporation, the largest U.S. movie theater operator, determined that its internal skills in marketing, site analysis, creative financing, and management of geographically dispersed operations were key strengths relative to major success factors in the soft-drink bottling industry. This assessment proved accurate. Within 10 years after it entered the soft-drink bottling industry, General Cinema became the largest franchised bottler of soft drinks in the United States, handling Pepsi, 7UP, Dr Pepper, and Sunkist. Exhibit 5–15, Strategy in Action, describes how Avery Dennison used industry evolution benchmarking versus 3M to create a new, successful strategy.

Summary

This chapter looked at several ways managers achieve greater objectivity and rigor as they analyze their company's internal capabilities. Managers often start their internal analysis with questions like: "How well is the current strategy working? What is our current situation? Or what are our strengths and weaknesses?" The resource-based view provides a key, fundamental framework for analyzing firm success based on the firm's internal resources and competencies. *SWOT analysis,* a widely used approach to internal analysis, provides a logical way to apply the results of an RBV. Managers frequently use RBV and SWOT analysis to introduce realism and greater objectivity into their internal analysis. This chapter also described how insightful managers look at their business as a chain of activities that add value creating the products or services they sell—this is called *value chain analysis.* Managers who use value chain analysis to understand the value structure within

BusinessWeek

Avery Dennison has long made adhesives and what it calls "sticky papers" for business customers. Ten years ago, AD decided to take on 3M with its own version of 3M's highly successful Post-It notes and Scotch transparent tape.

How frequently did you buy Avery Notes and Avery Tape? You probably have never heard of them, right? That is because Avery was beat up in that market by 3M and AD exited the business after just a few years. Key strengths, distribution and brand name, that 3M used to build those products were major weaknesses at AD. Plus, in President Charles Miller's way of viewing it, 3M remained aggressive and true to an innovative culture to back its products while AD had grown rusty and "me too" rather than being the innovator it had traditionally been with pressure-sensitive papers. So faced with considerable weakness competing against a major threat, Miller refocused AD on getting innovative in areas of traditional technical strength.

Today, AD has 30 percent of its sales from products introduced in the past five years. It has half the market for adhesive paper stock and 40 percent of the market for coated paper films for package labels. Says Miller, "We believe in market evolution. The best way to control a market is to invent it. With innovative products, superstores aren't able to squeeze margins, as they can in commodity products." New products now pour out of AD labs to position AD strengths against early life cycle stage opportunities.

Source: "The Business Week 50," *BusinessWeek,* March 23, 2001.

their firm's activities and look at the value system, which also includes upstream suppliers and downstream partners and buyers, often gain very meaningful insights into their company's strategic resources, competencies, and options. Finally, this chapter covered four ways objectivity and realism are enhanced when managers use meaningful standards for comparison regardless of the particular analytical framework they employ in internal analysis. This chapter is followed by an appendix covering traditional financial analysis to serve as a refresher and reminder about this basic internal analysis tool.

When matched with management's environmental analyses and mission priorities, the process of internal analysis provides the critical foundation for strategy formulation. Armed with an accurate, thorough, and timely internal analysis, managers are in a better position to formulate effective strategies. The next chapter describes basic strategy alternatives that any firm may consider.

Questions for Discussion

1. Describe SWOT analysis as a way to guide internal analysis. How does this approach reflect the basic strategic management process?

2. What is the resource-based view of the firm? Give examples of three different types of resources.

3. What are three characteristics that make resources more, or less, valuable? Provide an example of each.

4. Apply SWOT analysis to yourself and your career aspirations. What are your major strengths and weaknesses? How might you use your knowledge of these strengths and weaknesses to develop your future career plans?

5. Why do you think value chain analysis has become a preferred approach to guide internal analysis? What are its strengths? Its weaknesses?

Chapter 5 Discussion Case

BusinessWeek

Gap's Internal Analysis: 2002

1   "Give a little bit. Give a little bit of your love to me." So goes the holiday jingle featured in Gap's latest ubiquitous ad campaign. How apt. The fast-growth retailer that Wall Street loved in the 1990s is trying awfully hard to rekindle the old flame.

2   Things sure have changed. Today, "it's awfully easy to hate this company," says Richard Jaffe, an analyst at UBS Warburg. Harsh words. But for the past 18 months, San Francisco-based Gap (GPS) has been disappointing the Street, mainly because it faltered on the most critical piece of the apparel-retail puzzle—fashion. With so many competitors selling the kind of snappy casual clothes that Gap and its Banana Republic and Old Navy offshoots were famous for, the retailer decided it was time for a new approach. But the trendier offerings seemed to turn off mainstream shoppers. Now, the majority of some 29 analysts who cover the company have hold or sell ratings on the stock.

3   However, patient investors might want to look past the dismal news in the next several months and instead focus on how Gap will do next year, say a handful of analysts who recommend its stock. These Gap followers believe that the worst may be over for the retailer because the company is getting a handle on costs and inventory—and has some appealing new fashions for fall 2002. The stock look cheap enough, trading around $13 a share—the lowest since late 1997.

4   BRIGHTER FALL? Over the next 12 months, the clothing retailer will likely have to pull back even more on expansion plans, close underperforming stores, and shrink the size of its larger stores. Gap's management team, headed by retailing guru Mickey Drexler, has publicly acknowledged these weaknesses and the necessity to make changes. Even as many lament the company's recent decline, some analysts still have faith in Drexler's ability to turn Gap around.

5   "I believe in the viability of the brands and the opportunity in the next 12 to 18 months to demonstrate incremental improvement in results," says UBS Warburg's Jaffe. He expects the company's fall 2002 lines to show significant improvement from the too-trendy offerings that will still litter the shelves for most of next year. Jaffe says Gap's ability to tweak offerings to appeal to a broader population is probably still intact.

6   The past several quarters of fashion misfires have been hard lessons for Drexler. But Gap appears to have become more disciplined in ways that will help it get through a few more quarters of disappointing sales. "Into the late '90s, Gap didn't have much use for operational controls. But now that product is falling off, they do," says Kindra Devaney, an analyst with Fulcrum Global Partners.

7   TRIMMING GROWTH. Gap declined to comment for this article. The company, which operates more than 4,000 stores nationwide, used to stuff its shelves with inventory, but it has been paring back over the past year, Devaney says. Its balance sheet has become stronger, as cash flow has increased as less is spent on inventory. "Gap is healthier today than it was 12 to 18 months ago," she says. By sometime in mid-2002, she expects the stock to rise to her price target of $16 a share, a 23% jump from where it trades now, as sales at comparable stores (same Gap-owned stores open at least a year) improve and margins start picking up.

8   Gap also is addressing criticism that it has opened too many new stores. It's pulling back substantially—to 5% to 7% store growth in 2001, from a previously promised 17%. The company expects similar growth in 2002. "They've been taking a look at the big stores and trying to maximize production and downsize their selling footage," Devaney says. Capital expenditures, mainly used for new-store growth, have also come down—to about $1.1 billion this year, from $1.8 billion last year. Gap projects a $650 million capital-spending budget for 2002.

9   If Gap follows through on these plans, momentum in the stock could build quickly. As Gap is the biggest specialty-apparel retailer, with a market cap of $11 billion-plus, a lot of investors are waiting to jump back into it. "Obviously we're keeping an eye on it. I think it has the potential to be a really interesting story," says Angela Auchey Kohler, portfolio manager at Federated Investors.

10   HUGE DISAPPOINTMENT. She's not ready to buy Gap stock just yet, but she's encouraged by the company's ability to control inventory and its brand identities. Kohler says she's waiting to see one month of improved comparable-store sales: "That's all it takes for the stock to shoot up."

11   The going could still be rough in the near term. Gap's fiscal third-quarter sales, ended Nov. 3, were a huge disappointment, declining 17% at stores open at least one year, versus an 8% decrease during the same period last year. The company's reported net loss for the quarter of $46 million before a special charge of $131 million was driven by a decline in gross margins and weaker sales. Compare that to last year's third quarter, when the Gap earned $186 million or 21 cents a share.

12   The fourth quarter, the most important for most retailers, will likely be ugly too, if November is any indication. Total sales for the month fell 14%, to $1.2 billion, compared with last year's $1.4 billion. On average, analysts are expecting Gap to lose 11 cents per share in the fourth quarter.

13   FOREIGN INVASION. Eric Jemetz, senior equity analyst at New Amsterdam Partners, wants to see a turnaround at Old Navy, the Gap unit that has slipped the most in sales, before he considers buying Gap stock again. He also wants to see that Gap can compete abroad and against international retailers moving into the U.S. For one, Swedish-based H&M, which has opened stores in the Northeast, will increase its presence in the states substantially in 2002. "We want to see [Gap] acknowledge that they have this competition coming," Jemetz says.

14   Will Gap be able to reverse its course? Some analysts think the jeans and casual-wear giant is on the right track to reclaiming its place in mass-market apparel. No, it's not a sure bet—far from it. UBS Warburg's Jaffe, who rates the shares a buy, still cautions that the company is in a precarious position. "It's a high-risk gamble," he says.

15   But if Gap gets its fashion knack back and keeps costs under control, investors with a horizon of several years could be rewarded as the retailer gets back on its feet.

Source: Amy Tsao, "How Gap Could Climb Out of Its Hole, *BusinessWeek,* December 17, 2001.

Chapter **Six**

Formulating Long-Term Objectives and Grand Strategies

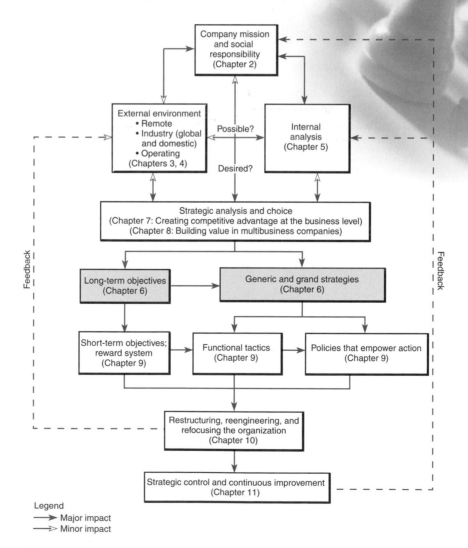

Legend

→ Major impact
⇢ Minor impact

The company mission was described in Chapter 2 as encompassing the broad aims of the firm. The most specific statement of aims presented in that chapter appeared as the goals of the firm. However, these goals, which commonly dealt with profitability, growth, and survival, were stated without specific targets or time frames. They were always to be pursued but could never be fully attained. They gave a general sense of direction but were not intended to provide specific benchmarks for evaluating the firm's progress in achieving its aims. Providing such benchmarks is the function of objectives.[1]

The first part of this chapter will focus on long-term objectives. These are statements of the results a firm seeks to achieve over a specified period, typically three to five years. The second part will focus on the formulation of grand strategies. These provide a comprehensive general approach in guiding major actions designed to accomplish the firm's long-term objectives.

The chapter has two major aims: (1) to discuss in detail the concept of long-term objectives, the topics they cover, and the qualities they should exhibit; and (2) to discuss the concept of grand strategies and to describe the 15 principal grand strategy options that are available to firms singly or in combination, including three newly popularized options that are being used to provide the basis for global competitiveness.

LONG-TERM OBJECTIVES

Strategic managers recognize that short-run profit maximization is rarely the best approach to achieving sustained corporate growth and profitability. An often repeated adage states that if impoverished people are given food, they will eat it and remain impoverished; however, if they are given seeds and tools and shown how to grow crops, they will be able to improve their condition permanently. A parallel choice confronts strategic decision makers:

1. Should they eat the seeds to improve the near-term profit picture and make large dividend payments through cost-saving measures such as laying off workers during periods of slack demand, selling off inventories, or cutting back on research and development?

2. Or should they sow the seeds in the effort to reap long-term rewards by reinvesting profits in growth opportunities, committing resources to employee training, or increasing advertising expenditures?

For most strategic managers, the solution is clear—distribute a small amount of profit now but sow most of it to increase the likelihood of a long-term supply. This is the most frequently used rationale in selecting objectives.

To achieve long-term prosperity, strategic planners commonly establish long-term objectives in seven areas:

Profitability The ability of any firm to operate in the long run depends on attaining an acceptable level of profits. Strategically managed firms characteristically have a profit objective, usually expressed in earnings per share or return on equity.

Productivity Strategic managers constantly try to increase the productivity of their systems. Firms that can improve the input-output relationship normally increase profitability. Thus, firms almost always state an objective for productivity. Commonly used productivity objectives are the number of items produced or the number of services rendered per unit of

---

[1] The terms *goals* and *objectives* are each used to convey a special meaning, with goals being the less specific and more encompassing concept. Most authors follow this usage; however, some use the two words interchangeably, while others reverse the usage.

input. However, productivity objectives sometimes are stated in terms of desired cost decreases. For example, objectives may be set for reducing defective items, customer complaints leading to litigation, or overtime. Achieving such objectives increases profitability if unit output is maintained.

Competitive Position   One measure of corporate success is relative dominance in the marketplace. Larger firms commonly establish an objective in terms of competitive position, often using total sales or market share as measures of their competitive position. An objective with regard to competitive position may indicate a firm's long-term priorities. For example, Gulf Oil set a five-year objective of moving from third to second place as a producer of high-density polypropylene. Total sales were the measure.

Employee Development   Employees value education and training, in part because they lead to increased compensation and job security. Providing such opportunities often increases productivity and decreases turnover. Therefore, strategic decision makers frequently include an employee development objective in their long-range plans. For example, PPG has declared an objective of developing highly skilled and flexible employees and, thus, providing steady employment for a reduced number of workers.

Employee Relations   Whether or not they are bound by union contracts, firms actively seek good employee relations. In fact, proactive steps in anticipation of employee needs and expectations are characteristic of strategic managers. Strategic managers believe that productivity is linked to employee loyalty and to appreciation of managers' interest in employee welfare. They, therefore, set objectives to improve employee relations. Among the outgrowths of such objectives are safety programs, worker representation on management committees, and employee stock option plans.

Technological Leadership   Firms must decide whether to lead or follow in the marketplace. Either approach can be successful, but each requires a different strategic posture. Therefore, many firms state an objective with regard to technological leadership. For example, Caterpillar Tractor Company established its early reputation and dominant position in its industry by being in the forefront of technological innovation in the manufacture of large earthmovers. Exhibit 6–1, E-commerce Strategy in Action, explains that e-commerce technology officers will have more of a strategic role in the management hierarchy of the future, demonstrating that the Internet has become an integral aspect of corporate long-term objective setting. In offering an e-technology manager higher-level responsibilities, a firm is pursuing a leadership position in terms of innovation in computer networks and systems. Officers of e-commerce technology at GE and Delta Air have shown their ability to increase profits by driving down transaction-related costs with Web-based technologies that seamlessly integrate their firms' supply chains. These technologies have the potential to "lock in" certain suppliers and customers and heighten competitive position through supply chain efficiency.

Public Responsibility   Managers recognize their responsibilities to their customers and to society at large. In fact, many firms seek to exceed government requirements. They work not only to develop reputations for fairly priced products and services but also to establish themselves as responsible corporate citizens. For example, they may establish objectives for charitable and educational contributions, minority training, public or political activity, community welfare, or urban revitalization. In an attempt to exhibit their public responsibility in the United States, Japanese companies, such as Toyota, Hitachi, and Matsushita, contribute more than $500 million annually to American educational projects, charities, and nonprofit organizations.

BusinessWeek

Now, in the Internet era, a new type of tech exec is needed. Corporations will need an executive who can harness the latest technology to reach out to customers on one end and suppliers on the other with seamless, up-to-the-minute data communications. In the 21st-century corporation, all managers will have to be tech experts, but the grand high pooh-bah will be somebody we're calling the chief Web officer.

This executive could emerge as the CEO's most important lieutenant, working hand in hand to retool companies into e-businesses. Like today's CIO, the chief Web officer will oversee information systems and strategies—which, by definition, will be based on Internet technology. But, in addition, he or she will create and manage an interwoven web of business relationships made possible by communications technology. Forging flexible e-links between an organization and its partners, suppliers, and customers. Technology and partnerships can't work well without each other—and leaving them in separate hands risks failing to exploit the Net's potential for radically transforming business processes.

For companies that recognize the strategic importance of the Net and appoint leaders to exploit it, the payoff can be enormous. At GE a customer inquiry that used to cost $80 to handle over the phone costs just 50 cents via the Web. With savings like that, analysts figure GE will slash expenses by hundreds of millions this year, while pushing more than $5 billion worth of purchases through the electronic systems. The same goes for Delta Air Lines, where selling a ticket online costs one-quarter as much as a travel agent sale. Delta saved more than $100 million last year thanks to e-commerce, says CFO Edward H. West, who manages the company's online initiatives.

Achieving such results relies on making the Net a strategic priority. But the transition to chief Web officer isn't always easy. Even though CIOs entered the upper ranks of executives in the 90s, the departments they ran were "still the servant of the business," says Harvard Business School professor Robert Austin. Indeed, many CIOs still focus on running internal computer systems, he says, even though "the more exciting stuff is being done elsewhere."

That stuff—websites, e-commerce, online customer support—often bubbles up from skunkworks scattered around a company. Or, it falls under an "e-czar" who bypasses the CIO to report directly to the chief executive. In the coming years, the CIO and e-czar should morph into one. Companies that fail to move in this direction run the risk of turf wars between execs or between line managers launching their own e-commerce initiatives and IT departments charged with keeping corporate digital systems in prime condition.

Source: An excerpt from Andy Reinhardt, "From Gearhead to Grand High Pooh-Bah," *BusinessWeek*, August 28, 2000.

Qualities of Long-Term Objectives

What distinguishes a good objective from a bad one? What qualities of an objective improve its chances of being attained? These questions are best answered in relation to seven criteria that should be used in preparing long-term objectives: acceptable, flexible, measurable over time, motivating, suitable, understandable, and achievable.

Acceptable   Managers are most likely to pursue objectives that are consistent with their preferences. They may ignore or even obstruct the achievement of objectives that offend them (e.g., promoting a high-sodium food product) or that they believe to be inappropriate or unfair (e.g., reducing spoilage to offset a disproportionate allocation of fixed overhead). In addition, long-term corporate objectives frequently are designed to be acceptable to groups external to the firm. An example is efforts to abate air pollution that are undertaken at the insistence of the Environmental Protection Agency.

Flexible   Objectives should be adaptable to unforeseen or extraordinary changes in the firm's competitive or environmental forecasts. Unfortunately, such flexibility usually is increased at the expense of specificity. One way of providing flexibility while minimizing its negative effects is to allow for adjustments in the level, rather than in the nature, of objectives. For example, the personnel department objective of providing managerial development training for 15 supervisors per year over the next five-year period might be adjusted by changing the number of people to be trained. In contrast, changing the personnel department's objective of "assisting production supervisors in reducing job-related injuries by 10 percent per year" after three months had gone by would understandably create dissatisfaction.

Measurable   Objectives must clearly and concretely state what will be achieved and when it will be achieved. Thus, objectives should be measurable over time. For example, the objective of "substantially improving our return on investment" would be better stated as "increasing the return on investment on our line of paper products by a minimum of 1 percent a year and a total of 5 percent over the next three years."

Motivating   People are most productive when objectives are set at a motivating level—one high enough to challenge but not so high as to frustrate or so low as to be easily attained. The problem is that individuals and groups differ in their perceptions of what is high enough. A broad objective that challenges one group frustrates another and minimally interests a third. One valuable recommendation is that objectives be tailored to specific groups. Developing such objectives requires time and effort, but objectives of this kind are more likely to motivate.

Suitable   Objectives must be suited to the broad aims of the firm, which are expressed in its mission statement. Each objective should be a step toward the attainment of overall goals. In fact, objectives that are inconsistent with the company mission can subvert the firm's aims. For example, if the mission is growth oriented, the objective of reducing the debt-to-equity ratio to 1.00 would probably be unsuitable and counterproductive.

Understandable   Strategic managers at all levels must understand what is to be achieved. They also must understand the major criteria by which their performance will be evaluated. Thus, objectives must be so stated that they are as understandable to the recipient as they are to the giver. Consider the misunderstandings that might arise over the objective of "increasing the productivity of the credit card department by 20 percent within two years." What does this objective mean? Increase the number of outstanding cards? Increase the use of outstanding cards? Increase the employee workload? Make productivity gains each year? Or hope that the new computer-assisted system, which should improve productivity, is approved by year 2? As this simple example illustrates, objectives must be clear, meaningful, and unambiguous.

Achievable   Finally, objectives must be possible to achieve. This is easier said than done. Turbulence in the remote and operating environments affects a firm's internal operations, creating uncertainty and limiting the accuracy of the objectives set by strategic management. To illustrate, the rapidly declining U.S. economy in 2000–2001 made objective setting extremely difficult, particularly in such areas as sales projections.

The Balanced Scorecard

The Balanced Scorecard is a set of measures that are directly linked to the company's strategy. Developed by Robert S. Kaplan and David P. Norton, it directs a company to link its own long-term strategy with tangible goals and actions. The scorecard allows managers to evaluate the company from four perspectives: financial performance, customer knowledge, internal business processes, and learning and growth.

EXHIBIT 6–2
The Balanced Scorecard

Source: Robert S. Kaplan and David P. Norton, "Using the Balanced Scorecard as a Strategic Management System," *Harvard Business Review,* January–February 1996, p. 76. Reprinted with permission.

The balanced scorecard provides a framework to translate a strategy into operational terms

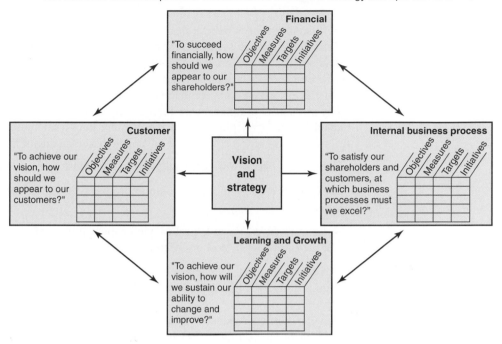

The Balanced Scorecard, as shown in Exhibit 6–2, contains a concise definition of the company's vision and strategy. Surrounding the vision and strategy are four additional boxes; each box contains the objectives, measures, targets, and initiatives for one of the four perspectives:

- The box at the top of Exhibit 6–2 represents the financial perspective, and answers the question "To succeed financially, how should we appear to our shareholders?"

- The box to the right represents the internal business process perspective and addresses the question "To satisfy our shareholders and customers, what business processes must we excel at?"

- The learning and growth box at the bottom of Exhibit 6–2 answers the question "To achieve our vision, how will we sustain our ability to change and improve?"

- The box at the left reflects the customer perspective, and responds to the question "To achieve our vision, how should we appear to our customers?"

All of the boxes are connected by arrows to illustrate that the objectives and measures of the four perspectives are linked by cause-and-effect relationships that lead to the successful implementation of the strategy. Achieving one perspective's targets should lead to desired improvements in the next perspective, and so on, until the company's performance increases overall.

A properly constructed scorecard is balanced between short- and long-term measures; financial and nonfinancial measures; and internal and external performance perspectives.

The Balanced Scorecard is a management system that can be used as the central organizing framework for key managerial processes. Chemical Bank, Mobil Corporation's US Marketing and Refining Division, and CIGNA Property and Casualty Insurance have used the Balanced Scorecard approach to assist in individual and team goal setting, compensation, resource allocation, budgeting and planning, and strategic feedback and learning.

GENERIC STRATEGIES

Many planning experts believe that the general philosophy of doing business declared by the firm in the mission statement must be translated into a holistic statement of the firm's strategic orientation before it can be further defined in terms of a specific long-term strategy. In other words, a long-term or grand strategy must be based on a core idea about how the firm can best compete in the marketplace.

The popular term for this core idea is *generic strategy.* From a scheme developed by Michael Porter, many planners believe that any long-term strategy should derive from a firm's attempt to seek a competitive advantage based on one of three generic strategies:

1. Striving for overall low-cost leadership in the industry.

2. Striving to create and market unique products for varied customer groups through *differentiation.*

3. Striving to have special appeal to one or more groups of consumer or industrial buyers, *focusing* on their cost or differentiation concerns.

Advocates of generic strategies believe that each of these options can produce above-average returns for a firm in an industry. However, they are successful for very different reasons.

Low-cost leaders depend on some fairly unique capabilities to achieve and sustain their low-cost position. Examples of such capabilities are: having secured suppliers of scarce raw materials, being in a dominant market share position, or having a high degree of capitalization. Low-cost producers usually excel at cost reductions and efficiencies. They maximize economies of scale, implement cost-cutting technologies, stress reductions in overhead and in administrative expenses, and use volume sales techniques to propel themselves up the earning curve. The commonly accepted requirements for successful implementation of the low-cost and the other two generic strategies are overviewed in Exhibit 6–3.

A low-cost leader is able to use its cost advantage to charge lower prices or to enjoy higher profit margins. By so doing, the firm effectively can defend itself in price wars, attack competitors on price to gain market share, or, if already dominant in the industry, simply benefit from exceptional returns. As an extreme case, it has been argued that National Can Company, a corporation in an essentially stagnant industry, is able to generate attractive and improving profits by being the low-cost producer.

Strategies dependent on differentiation are designed to appeal to customers with a special sensitivity for a particular product attribute. By stressing the attribute above other product qualities, the firm attempts to build customer loyalty. Often such loyalty translates into a firm's ability to charge a premium price for its product. Cross-brand pens, Brooks Brothers suits, Porsche automobiles, and Chivas Regal Scotch whiskey are all examples.

The product attribute also can be the marketing channels through which it is delivered, its image for excellence, the features it includes, and the service network that supports it. As a result of the importance of these attributes, competitors often face "perceptual" barriers to entry when customers of a successfully differentiated firm fail to see largely identical products as being interchangeable. For example, General Motors hopes that customers will accept "only genuine GM replacement parts."

A focus strategy, whether anchored in a low-cost base or a differentiation base, attempts to attend to the needs of a particular market segment. Likely segments are those that are ignored by marketing appeals to easily accessible markets, to the "typical" customer, or to customers with common applications for the product. A firm pursuing a

EXHIBIT 6–3
Requirements for Generic Competitive Strategies

Source: Free Press *COMPETITIVE STRATEGY: Techniques for Analyzing Industries and Competitors,* pp. 40–41. Reprinted with permission of the Free Press, a division of Simon & Schuster, from *Competitive Strategy: Techniques for Analyzing Industries and Competitors,* by Michael E. Porter. Copyright © 1980 by Michael E. Porter.

Generic Strategy	Commonly Required Skills and Resources	Common Organizational Requirements
Overall cost leadership	Sustained capital investment and access to capital. Process engineering skills. Intense supervision of labor. Products designed for ease in manufacture. Low-cost distribution system.	Tight cost control. Frequent, detailed control reports. Structured organization and responsibilities. Incentives based on meeting strict quantitative targets.
Differentiation	Strong marketing abilities. Product engineering. Creative flare. Strong capability in basic research. Corporate reputation for quality or technological leadership. Long tradition in the industry or unique combination of skills drawn from other businesses. Strong cooperation from channels.	Strong coordination among functions in R&D, product development, and marketing. Subjective measurement and incentives instead of quantitative measures. Amenities to attract highly skilled labor scientists, or creative people.
Focus	Combination of the above policies directed at the particular strategic target.	Combination of the above policies directed at the regular strategic target.

focus strategy is willing to service isolated geographic areas; to satisfy the needs of customers with special financing, inventory, or servicing problems; or to tailor the product to the somewhat unique demands of the small-to-medium-sized customer. The focusing firms profit from their willingness to serve otherwise ignored or underappreciated customer segments. The classic example is cable television. An entire industry was born because of a willingness of cable firms to serve isolated rural locations that were ignored by traditional television services. Brick producers that typically service a radius of less than 100 miles and commuter airlines that serve regional geographic areas are other examples of industries where a focus strategy frequently yields above-average industry profits.

While each of the generic strategies enables a firm to maximize certain competitive advantages, each one also exposes the firm to a number of competitive risks. For example, a low-cost leader fears a new low-cost technology that is being developed by a competitor; a differentiating firm fears imitators; and a focused firm fears invasion by a firm that largely targets customers. As Exhibit 6–4 suggests, each generic strategy presents the firm with a number of risks.

GRAND STRATEGIES

While the need for firms to develop generic strategies remains an unresolved debate, designers of planning systems agree about the critical role of grand strategies. *Grand strategies,* often called master or business strategies, provide basic direction for strategic actions. They are the basis of coordinated and sustained efforts directed toward achieving long-term business objectives.

The purpose of this section is twofold: (1) to list, describe, and discuss 15 grand strategies that strategic managers should consider and (2) to present approaches to the selection of an optimal grand strategy from the available alternatives.

EXHIBIT 6–4
Risks of the Generic Strategies

Source: Free Press *Competitive Advantage: Creating and Sustaining Superior Performance*, p. 21. Adapted with the permission of the Free Press, a division of Simon & Schuster, from *Competitive Strategy: Creating and Sustaining Superior Performance*, by Michael E. Porter. Copyright © 1985 by Michael E. Porter.

Risks of Cost Leadership	Risks of Differentiation	Risks of Focus
Cost of leadership is not sustained: • Competitors imitate. • Technology changes. • Other bases for cost leadership erode.	Differentiation is not sustained: • Competitors imitate. • Bases for differentiation become less important to buyers.	The focus strategy is imitated. The target segment becomes structurally unattractive: • Structure erodes. • Demand disappears.
Proximity in differentiation is lost.	Cost proximity is lost.	Broadly targeted competitors overwhelm the segment: • The segment's differences from other segments narrow. • The advantages of a broad line increase.
Cost focusers achieve even lower cost in segments.	Differentiation focusers achieve even greater differentiation in segments.	New focusers subsegment the industry.

Grand strategies indicate the time period over which long-range objectives are to be achieved. Thus, a grand strategy can be defined as a comprehensive general approach that guides a firm's major actions.

The 15 principal grand strategies are: concentrated growth, market development, product development, innovation, horizontal integration, vertical integration, concentric diversification, conglomerate diversification, turnaround, divestiture, liquidation, bankruptcy, joint ventures, strategic alliances, and consortia. Any one of these strategies could serve as the basis for achieving the major long-term objectives of a single firm. But a firm involved with multiple industries, businesses, product lines, or customer groups—as many firms are—usually combines several grand strategies. For clarity, however, each of the principal grand strategies is described independently in this section, with examples to indicate some of its relative strengths and weaknesses.

Concentrated Growth

Many of the firms that fell victim to merger mania were once mistakenly convinced that the best way to achieve their objectives was to pursue unrelated diversification in the search for financial opportunity and synergy. By rejecting that "conventional wisdom," such firms as Martin-Marietta, KFC, Compaq, Avon, Hyatt Legal Services, and Tenant have demonstrated the advantages of what is increasingly proving to be sound business strategy. A firm that has enjoyed special success through a strategic emphasis on increasing market share through concentration is Chemlawn. With headquarters in Columbus, Ohio, Chemlawn is the North American leader in professional lawn care. Like others in the lawn-care industry, Chemlawn is experiencing a steadily declining customer base. Market analysis shows that the decline is fueled by negative environmental publicity, perceptions of poor customer service, and concern about the price versus the value of the company's services, given the wide array of do-it-yourself alternatives. Chemlawn's approach to increasing market share hinges on addressing quality, price, and value issues; discontinuing products that the public or environmental authorities perceive as unsafe; and improving the quality of its workforce.

These firms are just a few of the majority of American firms that pursue a concentrated growth strategy by focusing on a specific product and market combination. *Concentrated growth* is the strategy of the firm that directs its resources to the profitable growth of a single product, in a single market, with a single dominant technology. The main rationale for this approach, sometimes called a market penetration or concentration strategy, is that the firm thoroughly develops and exploits its expertise in a delimited competitive arena.

Rationale for Superior Performance

Concentrated growth strategies lead to enhanced performance. The ability to assess market needs, knowledge of buyer behavior, customer price sensitivity, and effectiveness of promotion are characteristics of a concentrated growth strategy. Such core capabilities are a more important determinant of competitive market success than are the environmental forces faced by the firm. The high success rates of new products also are tied to avoiding situations that require undeveloped skills, such as serving new customers and markets, acquiring new technology, building new channels, developing new promotional abilities, and facing new competition.

A major misconception about the concentrated growth strategy is that the firm practicing it will settle for little or no growth. This is certainly not true for a firm that correctly utilizes the strategy. A firm employing concentrated growth grows by building on its competences, and it achieves a competitive edge by concentrating in the product-market segment it knows best. A firm employing this strategy is aiming for the growth that results from increased productivity, better coverage of its actual product-market segment, and more efficient use of its technology.

Conditions That Favor Concentrated Growth

Specific conditions in the firm's environment are favorable to the concentrated growth strategy. The first is a condition in which the firm's industry is resistant to major technological advancements. This is usually the case in the late growth and maturity stages of the product life cycle and in product markets where product demand is stable and industry barriers, such as capitalization, are high. Machinery for the paper manufacturing industry, in which the basic technology has not changed for more than a century, is a good example.

An especially favorable condition is one in which the firm's targeted markets are not product saturated. Markets with competitive gaps leave the firm with alternatives for growth, other than taking market share away from competitors. The successful introduction of traveler services by Allstate and Amoco demonstrates that even an organization as entrenched and powerful as the AAA could not build a defensible presence in all segments of the automobile club market.

A third condition that favors concentrated growth exists when the firm's product markets are sufficiently distinctive to dissuade competitors in adjacent product markets from trying to invade the firm's segment. John Deere scrapped its plans for growth in the construction machinery business when mighty Caterpillar threatened to enter Deere's mainstay, the farm machinery business, in retaliation. Rather than risk a costly price war on its own turf, Deere scrapped these plans.

A fourth favorable condition exists when the firm's inputs are stable in price and quantity and are available in the amounts and at the times needed. Maryland-based Giant Foods is able to concentrate in the grocery business largely due to its stable long-term arrangements with suppliers of its private-label products. Most of these suppliers are makers of the national brands that compete against the Giant labels. With a high market share and aggressive retail distribution, Giant controls the access of these brands to the consumer. Consequently, its suppliers have considerable incentive to honor verbal agreements, called *bookings,* in which they commit themselves for a one-year period with regard to the price, quality, and timing of their shipments to Giant.

The pursuit of concentrated growth also is favored by a stable market—a market without the seasonal or cyclical swings that would encourage a firm to diversify. Night Owl Security, the District of Columbia market leader in home security services, commits its customers to initial four-year contracts. In a city where affluent consumers tend to be quite transient, the length of this relationship is remarkable. Night Owl's concentrated growth strategy has been reinforced by its success in getting subsequent owners of its customers' homes to extend and renew the security service contracts. In a similar way, Lands' End reinforced its growth strategy by asking customers for names and addresses of friends and relatives living overseas who would like to receive Lands' End catalogs.

A firm also can grow while concentrating, if it enjoys competitive advantages based on efficient production or distribution channels. These advantages enable the firm to formulate advantageous pricing policies. More efficient production methods and better handling of distribution also enable the firm to achieve greater economies of scale or, in conjunction with marketing, result in a product that is differentiated in the mind of the consumer. Graniteville Company, a large South Carolina textile manufacturer, enjoyed decades of growth and profitability by adopting a "follower" tactic as part of its concentrated growth strategy. By producing fabrics only after market demand had been well established, and by featuring products that reflected its expertise in adopting manufacturing innovations and in maintaining highly efficient long production runs, Graniteville prospered through concentrated growth.

Finally, the success of market generalists creates conditions favorable to concentrated growth. When generalists succeed by using universal appeals, they avoid making special appeals to particular groups of customers. The net result is that many small pockets are left open in the markets dominated by generalists, and that specialists emerge and thrive in these pockets. For example, hardware store chains, such as Home Depot, focus primarily on routine household repair problems and offer solutions that can be easily sold on a self-service, do-it-yourself basis. This approach leaves gaps at both the "semiprofessional" and "neophyte" ends of the market—in terms of the purchaser's skill at household repairs and the extent to which available merchandise matches the requirements of individual homeowners.

Risk and Rewards of Concentrated Growth

Under stable conditions, concentrated growth poses lower risk than any other grand strategy; but, in a changing environment, a firm committed to concentrated growth faces high risks. The greatest risk is that concentrating in a single product market makes a firm particularly vulnerable to changes in that segment. Slowed growth in the segment would jeopardize the firm because its investment, competitive edge, and technology are deeply entrenched in a specific offering. It is difficult for the firm to attempt sudden changes if its product is threatened by near-term obsolescence, a faltering market, new substitutes, or changes in technology or customer needs. For example, the manufacturers of IBM clones faced such a problem when IBM adopted the OS/2 operating system for its personal computer line. That change made existing clones out of date.

The concentrating firm's entrenchment in a specific industry makes it particularly susceptible to changes in the economic environment of that industry. For example, Mack Truck, the second-largest truck maker in America, lost $20 million as a result of an 18-month slump in the truck industry.

Entrenchment in a specific product market tends to make a concentrating firm more adept than competitors at detecting new trends. However, any failure of such a firm to properly forecast major changes in its industry can result in extraordinary losses. Numerous makers of inexpensive digital watches were forced to declare bankruptcy because they failed to anticipate the competition posed by Swatch, Guess, and other trendy watches that emerged from the fashion industry.

A firm pursuing a concentrated growth strategy is vulnerable also to the high opportunity costs that result from remaining in a specific product market and ignoring other options that could employ the firm's resources more profitably. Overcommitment to a specific technology and product market can hinder a firm's ability to enter a new or growing product market that offers more attractive cost-benefit trade-offs. Had Apple Computers maintained its policy of making equipment that did not interface with IBM equipment, it would have missed out on what have proved to be its most profitable strategic options.

Concentrated Growth Is Often the Most Viable Option

Examples abound of firms that have enjoyed exceptional returns on the concentrated growth strategy. Such firms as McDonald's, Goodyear, and Apple Computers have used firsthand knowledge and deep involvement with specific product segments to become powerful competitors in their markets. The strategy is associated even more often with successful smaller firms that have steadily and doggedly improved their market position.

The limited additional resources necessary to implement concentrated growth, coupled with the limited risk involved, also make this strategy desirable for a firm with limited funds. For example, through a carefully devised concentrated growth strategy, medium-sized John Deere & Company was able to become a major force in the agricultural machinery business even when competing with such firms as Ford Motor Company. While other firms were trying to exit or diversify from the farm machinery business, Deere spent $2 billion in upgrading its machinery, boosting its efficiency, and engaging in a program to strengthen its dealership system. This concentrated growth strategy enabled it to become the leader in the farm machinery business despite the fact that Ford was more than 10 times its size.

The firm that chooses a concentrated growth strategy directs its resources to the profitable growth of a narrowly defined product and market, focusing on a dominant technology. Firms that remain within their chosen product market are able to extract the most from their technology and market knowledge and, thus, are able to minimize the risk associated with unrelated diversification. The success of a concentration strategy is founded on the firm's use of superior insights into its technology, product, and customer to obtain a sustainable competitive advantage. Superior performance on these aspects of corporate strategy has been shown to have a substantial positive effect on market success.

A grand strategy of concentrated growth allows for a considerable range of action. Broadly speaking, the firm can attempt to capture a larger market share by increasing the usage rates of present customers, by attracting competitors' customers, or by selling to nonusers. In turn, each of these options suggests more specific options, some of which are listed in the top section of Exhibit 6–5.

When strategic managers forecast that their current products and their markets will not provide the basis for achieving the company mission, they have two options that involve moderate costs and risk: market development and product development.

Market Development

Market development commonly ranks second only to concentration as the least costly and least risky of the 15 grand strategies. It consists of marketing present products, often with only cosmetic modifications, to customers in related market areas by adding channels of

EXHIBIT 6–5
Specific Options under the Grand Strategies of Concentration, Market Development, and Product Development

Source: Adapted from Philip Kotler, *Marketing Management Analysis, Planning, and Control,* 11th ed., 2002. Reprinted by permission of Prentice Hall, Inc., Upper Saddle River, NJ.

Concentration (increasing use of present products in present markets):

1. Increasing present customers' rate of use:
   a. Increasing the size of purchase.
   b. Increasing the rate of product obsolescence.
   c. Advertising other uses.
   d. Giving price incentives for increased use.
2. Attracting competitors' customers:
   a. Establishing sharper brand differentiation.
   b. Increasing promotional effort.
   c. Initiating price cuts.
3. Attracting nonusers to buy the product:
   a. Inducing trial use through sampling, price incentives, and so on.
   b. Pricing up or down.
   c. Advertising new uses.

Market development (selling present products in new markets):

1. Opening additional geographic markets:
   a. Regional expansion.
   b. National expansion.
   c. International expansion.
2. Attracting other market segments:
   a. Developing product versions to appeal to other segments.
   b. Entering other channels of distribution.
   c. Advertising in other media.

Product development (developing new products for present markets):

1. Developing new product features:
   a. Adapt (to other ideas, developments).
   b. Modify (change color, motion, sound, odor, form, shape).
   c. Magnify (stronger, longer, thicker, extra value).
   d. Minify (smaller, shorter, lighter).
   e. Substitute (other ingredients, process, power).
   f. Rearrange (other patterns, layout, sequence, components).
   g. Reverse (inside out).
   h. Combine (blend, alloy, assortment, ensemble; combine units, purposes, appeals, ideas).
2. Developing quality variations.
3. Developing additional models and sizes (product proliferation).

distribution or by changing the content of advertising or promotion. Several specific market development approaches are listed in Exhibit 6–5. Thus, as suggested by the figure, firms that open branch offices in new cities, states, or countries are practicing market development. Likewise, firms are practicing market development if they switch from advertising in trade publications to advertising in newspapers or if they add jobbers to supplement their mail-order sales efforts.

Market development allows firms to practice a form of concentrated growth by identifying new uses for existing products and new demographically, psychographically, or geographically defined markets. Frequently, changes in media selection, promotional appeals, and distribution are used to initiate this approach. Du Pont used market development when it found a new application for Kevlar, an organic material that police, security, and military personnel had used primarily for bulletproofing. Kevlar now is being used to refit and maintain wooden-hulled boats, since it is lighter and stronger than glass fibers and has 11 times the strength of steel.

The medical industry provides other examples of new markets for existing products. The National Institutes of Health's report of a study showing that the use of aspirin may lower the incidence of heart attacks was expected to boost sales in the $2.2 billion analgesic market. It was predicted that the expansion of this market would lower the market share of nonaspirin brands, such as industry leaders Tylenol and Advil. Product extensions currently planned include Bayer Calendar Pack, 28-day packaging to fit the once-a-day prescription for the prevention of a second heart attack.

Another example is Chesebrough-Ponds, a major producer of health and beauty aids, which decided several years ago to expand its market by repacking its Vaseline Petroleum Jelly in pocket-size squeeze tubes as Vaseline "Lip Therapy." The corporation decided to place a strategic emphasis on market development, because it knew from market studies that its petroleum-jelly customers already were using the product to prevent chapped lips. Company leaders reasoned that their market could be expanded significantly if the product were repackaged to fit conveniently in consumers' pockets and purses.

Product Development

Product development involves the substantial modification of existing products or the creation of new but related products that can be marketed to current customers through established channels. The product development strategy often is adopted either to prolong the life cycle of current products or to take advantage of a favorite reputation or brand name. The idea is to attract satisfied customers to new products as a result of their positive experience with the firm's initial offering. The bottom section in Exhibit 6–5 lists some of the options available to firms undertaking product development. A revised edition of a college textbook, a new car style, and a second formula of shampoo for oily hair are examples of the product development strategy.

The product development strategy is based on the penetration of existing markets by incorporating product modifications into existing items or by developing new products with a clear connection to the existing product line. The telecommunications industry provides an example of product extension based on product modification. To increase its estimated 8–10 percent share of the $5–$6 billion corporate user market, MCI Communication Corporation extended its direct-dial service to 146 countries, the same as those serviced by AT&T, at lower average rates than those of AT&T. MCI's addition of 79 countries to its network underscores its belief in this market, which it expects to grow 15–20 percent annually. Another example of expansions linked to existing lines is Gerber's decision to engage in general merchandise marketing. Gerber's recent introduction included 52 items that ranged from feeding accessories to toys and children's wear. Likewise, Nabisco Brands seeks competitive advantage by placing its strategic emphasis on product development. With headquarters in Parsippany, New Jersey, the company is one of three operating units of RJR Nabisco. It is the leading producer of biscuits, confections, snacks, shredded cereals, and processed fruits and vegetables. To maintain its position as leader, Nabisco pursues a strategy of developing and introducing new products and expanding its existing product line. Spoon Size Shredded Wheat and Ritz Bits crackers are two examples of new products that are variations on existing products.

Innovation

In many industries, it has become increasingly risky not to innovate. Both consumer and industrial markets have come to expect periodic changes and improvements in the products offered. As a result, some firms find it profitable to make *innovation* their grand strategy. They seek to reap the initially high profits associated with customer acceptance of a new or greatly improved product. Then, rather than face stiffening competition as the basis of profitability shifts from innovation to production or marketing competence, they search for other original or novel ideas. The underlying rationale of the grand strategy of innovation is to create a new product life cycle and thereby make similar existing products obsolete. Thus, this strategy differs from the product development strategy of extending an existing product's life cycle. For example, Intel, a leader in the semiconductor industry, pursues expansion through a strategic emphasis on innovation. With headquarters in California, the company is a designer and manufacturer of semiconductor components and related computers, of microcomputer systems, and of software. Its Pentium microprocessor gives a desktop computer the capability of a mainframe.

While most growth-oriented firms appreciate the need to be innovative occasionally, a few firms use it as their fundamental way of relating to their markets. An outstanding example is Polaroid, which heavily promotes each of its new cameras until competitors are able to match its technological innovation; by this time, Polaroid normally is prepared to introduce a dramatically new or improved product. For example, it introduced consumers in quick succession to the Swinger, the SX-70, the One Step, and the Sun Camera 660.

Few innovative ideas prove profitable because the research, development, and premarketing costs of converting a promising idea into a profitable product are extremely high. A study by the Booz Allen & Hamilton management research department provides some understanding of the risks. As shown in Exhibit 6–6, Booz Allen & Hamilton found that less than 2 percent of the innovative projects initially considered by 51 companies eventually reached the marketplace. Specifically, out of every 58 new product ideas, only 12 pass an initial screening test that finds them compatible with the firm's mission and long-term objectives, only 7 remain after an evaluation of their potential, and only 3 survive development attempts. Of the three survivors, two appear to have profit potential after test marketing and only one is commercially successful.

Horizontal Integration

When a firm's long-term strategy is based on growth through the acquisition of one or more similar firms operating at the same stage of the production-marketing chain, its grand strategy is called *horizontal integration*. Such acquisitions eliminate competitors and provide the acquiring firm with access to new markets. One example is Warner-Lambert's acquisition of Parke Davis, which reduced competition in the ethical drugs field for Chilcott Laboratories, a firm that Warner-Lambert previously had acquired. Another example is the long-range acquisition pattern of White Consolidated Industries, which expanded in the refrigerator and freezer market through a grand strategy of horizontal integration, by acquiring Kelvinator Appliance, the Refrigerator Products Division of Bendix Westinghouse Automotive Air Brake, and Frigidaire Appliance from General Motors. Nike's acquisition in the dress shoes business and N. V. Homes's purchase of Ryan Homes have vividly exemplified the success that horizontal integration strategies can bring.

Exhibit 6–7, Global Strategy in Action, describes Deutsche Telekom growth strategy of horizontal acquisition. Deutsche Telekom was a dominant player in the European wireless services market, but without a presence in the fast-growing U.S. market. To correct this limitation, Deutsche Telekom horizontally integrated by purchasing the American firm VoiceStream Wireless, a company that was growing faster than most domestic rivals and that owned spectrum licenses providing access to 220 million potential customers.

EXHIBIT 6–6
Decay of New Product Ideas (51 Companies)

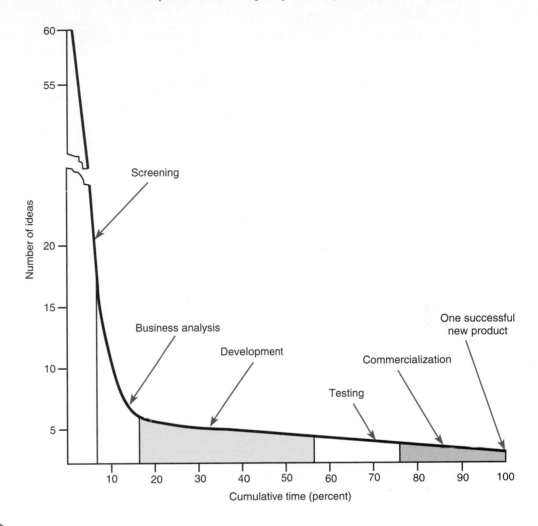

Number of ideas (y-axis)

Screening

Business analysis

Development

Testing

Commercialization

One successful new product

Cumulative time (percent) (x-axis)

Vertical Integration

When a firm's grand strategy is to acquire firms that supply it with inputs (such as raw materials) or are customers for its outputs (such as warehousers for finished products), *vertical integration* is involved. To illustrate, if a shirt manufacturer acquires a textile producer—by purchasing its common stock, buying its assets, or exchanging ownership interests—the strategy is vertical integration. In this case, it is *backward* vertical integration, since the acquired firm operates at an earlier stage of the production-marketing process. If the shirt manufacturer had merged with a clothing store, it would have been *forward* vertical integration—the acquisition of a firm nearer to the ultimate consumer.

Amoco emerged as North America's leader in natural gas reserves and products as a result of its acquisition of Dome Petroleum. This backward integration by Amoco was made in support of its downstream businesses in refining and in gas stations, whose profits made the acquisition possible.

Exhibit 6–8 depicts both horizontal and vertical integration. The principal attractions of a horizontal integration grand strategy are readily apparent. The acquiring firm is able to greatly expand its operations, thereby achieving greater market share, improving economies of scale, and increasing the efficiency of capital use. In addition, these

BusinessWeek Measured against the nation's wireless giants, VoiceStream Wireless Corp. has been a bit of a pipsqueak. So why would Germany's Deutsche Telekom pay an eye-popping $21,639 per subscriber for the little Bellevue, Washington, cell phone company? Simply put, Deutsche Telekom is not buying subscribers in the United States. It's buying potential—in this case, the potential to become a dominant player—not just in the United States, but globally. By the end of 2000, only about 32.5% of the U.S. population will be using some form of wireless compared with 52% in Europe and 60% in Japan. Growth prospects in such a relatively undeveloped market, the German executives reckon, are so high that their company will emerge almost immediately as a formidable rival. U.S. telecom execs say a DT-VoiceStream link will force U.S. players to step up efforts to provide wireless Net service to a broader market, including overseas.

To gain this kind of sway over the lucrative U.S. market and the global market, Deutsche Telekom felt it was worth significantly besting the $4,390 per subscriber Britain's Vodafone paid for AirTouch in 1999 or the estimated $12,400 that the combined Vodafone-AirTouch paid for Mannesmann earlier this year. That has set off a torrent of criticism that it has wildly overpaid for its position. However, Deutsche Telekom's CEO Sommer is confident. Here's what he considered when he agreed to the price: VoiceStream owns licenses in 23 of the top 25 U.S. markets. In wireless lingo, its licenses cover areas with a 220 million subscriber base. Though it has relatively few subscribers signed up and currently does not actually provide service to many of the locales where it holds licenses, it is adding subscribers at a sizzling pace—an 18.5% growth rate that is among the top in the industry.

Wireless companies across the country are taking note, given DT's deep pockets and promise to make a starting investment of at least $5 billion in VoiceStream. With the $5 billion, VoiceStream can accelerate construction of wireless systems in places like California and Ohio. Stanton estimates that the cash infusion will help him push up the roll-out of his service by 6 to 18 months. Also, Deutsche Telekom's cash is expected to allow Voicestream to participate in a major way in the upcoming auction of more spectrum licenses by the FCC.

Source: Excerpted from R. O. Crockett and D. Fairlamb, August 7, 2000, "Deutsche Telekom's Wireless Wager," *BusinessWeek* (3693), pp. 30–32.

benefits are achieved with only moderately increased risk, since the success of the expansion is principally dependent on proven abilities.

The reasons for choosing a vertical integration grand strategy are more varied and sometimes less obvious. The main reason for backward integration is the desire to increase the dependability of the supply or quality of the raw materials used as production inputs. That desire is particularly great when the number of suppliers is small and the number of competitors is large. In this situation, the vertically integrating firm can better control its costs and, thereby, improve the profit margin of the expanded production-marketing system. Forward integration is a preferred grand strategy if great advantages accrue to stable production. A firm can increase the predictability of demand for its output through forward integration; that is, through ownership of the next stage of its production-marketing chain.

Some increased risks are associated with both types of integration. For horizontally integrated firms, the risks stem from increased commitment to one type of business. For vertically integrated firms, the risks result from the firm's expansion into areas requiring strategic managers to broaden the base of their competences and to assume additional responsibilities.

Concentric Diversification

Grand strategies involving diversification represent distinctive departures from a firm's existing base of operations, typically the acquisition or internal generation (spin-off) of a separate business with synergistic possibilities counterbalancing the strengths and

EXHIBIT 6–8
Vertical and Horizontal Integrations

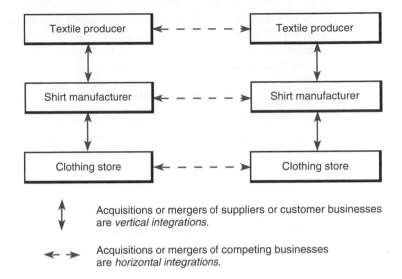

Acquisitions or mergers of suppliers or customer businesses are *vertical integrations*.

Acquisitions or mergers of competing businesses are *horizontal integrations*.

weaknesses of the two businesses. For example, Head Ski initially sought to diversify into summer sporting goods and clothing to offset the seasonality of its "snow" business. However, diversifications occasionally are undertaken as unrelated investments, because of their high profit potential and their otherwise minimal resource demands.

Regardless of the approach taken, the motivations of the acquiring firms are the same:

- Increase the firm's stock value. In the past, mergers often have led to increases in the stock price or the price-earnings ratio.

- Increase the growth rate of the firm.

- Make an investment that represents better use of funds than plowing them into internal growth.

- Improve the stability of earnings and sales by acquiring firms whose earnings and sales complement the firm's peaks and valleys.

- Balance or fill out the product line.

- Diversify the product line when the life cycle of current products has peaked.

- Acquire a needed resource quickly (e.g., high-quality technology or highly innovative management).

- Achieve tax savings by purchasing a firm whose tax losses will offset current or future earnings.

- Increase efficiency and profitability, especially if there is synergy between the acquiring firm and the acquired firm.[2]

Concentric diversification involves the acquisition of businesses that are related to the acquiring firm in terms of technology, markets, or products. With this grand strategy, the selected new businesses possess a high degree of compatibility with the firm's current businesses. The ideal concentric diversification occurs when the combined company

---

[2] Godfrey Devlin and Mark Bleackley, "Strategic Alliances—Guidelines for Success," *Long Range Planning,* October 1988, pp. 18–23.

profits increase the strengths and opportunities and decrease the weaknesses and exposure to risk. Thus, the acquiring firm searches for new businesses whose products, markets, distribution channels, technologies, and resource requirements are similar to but not identical with its own, whose acquisition results in synergies but not complete interdependence.

Conglomerate Diversification

Occasionally a firm, particularly a very large one, plans to acquire a business because it represents the most promising investment opportunity available. This grand strategy is commonly known as *conglomerate diversification.* The principal concern, and often the sole concern, of the acquiring firm is the profit pattern of the venture. Unlike concentric diversification, conglomerate diversification gives little concern to creating product-market synergy with existing businesses. What such conglomerate diversifiers as ITT, Textron, American Brands, Litton, U.S. Industries, Fuqua, and I. C. Industries seek is financial synergy. For example, they may seek a balance in their portfolios between current businesses with cyclical sales and acquired businesses with countercyclical sales, between high-cash/low-opportunity and low-cash/high-opportunity businesses, or between debt-free and highly leveraged businesses.

The principal difference between the two types of diversification is that concentric diversification emphasizes some commonality in markets, products, or technology, whereas conglomerate diversification is based principally on profit considerations.

Several of the grand strategies discussed above, including concentric and conglomerate diversification and horizontal and vertical integration, often involve the purchase or acquisition of one firm by another. It is important to know that the majority of such acquisitions fail to produce the desired results for the companies involved. Exhibit 6–9, Strategy in Action, provides seven guidelines that can improve a company's chances of a successful acquisition.

Turnaround

For any one of a large number of reasons, a firm can find itself with declining profits. Among these reasons are economic recessions, production inefficiencies, and innovative breakthroughs by competitors. In many cases, strategic managers believe that such a firm can survive and eventually recover if a concerted effort is made over a period of a few years to fortify its distinctive competences. This grand strategy is known as *turnaround.* It typically is begun through one of two forms of retrenchment, employed singly or in combination:

1. *Cost reduction.* Examples include decreasing the workforce through employee attrition, leasing rather than purchasing equipment, extending the life of machinery, eliminating elaborate promotional activities, laying off employees, dropping items from a production line, and discontinuing low-margin customers.

2. *Asset reduction.* Examples include the sale of land, buildings, and equipment not essential to the basic activity of the firm and the elimination of "perks," such as the company airplane and executives' cars.

Interestingly, the turnaround most commonly associated with this approach is in management positions. In a study of 58 large firms, researchers Shendel, Patton, and Riggs found that turnaround almost always was associated with changes in top management.[3]

---

[3] Other forms of joint ventures (such as leasing, contract manufacturing, and management contracting) offer valuable support strategies. They are not included in the categorization, however, because they seldom are employed as grand strategies.

1. *The wrong target.* This error becomes increasingly visible as time passes after the acquisition, when the acquiror may realize that anticipated synergies just don't exist, that the expanded market just isn't there, or that the acquiror's and target's technologies simply were not complementary.

   The first step to avoid such a mistake is for the acquiror and its financial advisors to determine the strategic goals and identify the mission. The product of this strategic review will be specifically identified criteria for the target.

   The second step required to identify the right target is to design and carry out an effective due diligence process to ascertain whether the target indeed has the identified set of qualities selected in the strategic review.

2. *The wrong price.* Even in a strategic acquisition, paying too much will lead to failure. For a patient strategic acquiror with long-term objectives, overpaying may be less of a problem than for a financial acquiror looking for a quick profit. Nevertheless, overpaying may divert needed acquiror resources and adversely affect the firm's borrowing capacity. In the extreme case, it can lead to continued operating losses and business failure.

   The key to avoiding this problem lies in the acquiror's valuation model. The model will incorporate assumptions concerning industry trends and growth patterns developed in the strategic review.

3. *The wrong structure.* Both financial and strategic acquisitions benefit by the structure chosen. This may include the legal structure chosen for the entities, the geographic jurisdiction chosen for newly created entities, and the capitalization structure selected for the business after the acquisition. The wrong structure may lead to an inability to repatriate earnings (or an ability to do so only at a prohibitive tax cost), regulatory problems that delay or prevent realization of the anticipated benefits, and inefficient pricing of debt and equity securities or a bar to chosen exit strategies due to inflexibility in the chosen legal structure.

   The two principal aspects of the acquisition process that can prevent this problem are a comprehensive regulatory compliance review and tax and legal analysis.

4. *The lost deal.* Lost deals often can be traced to poor communication. A successful strategic acquisition requires agreement upon the strategic vision, both with the acquiring company and between the acquiror and the continuing elements of the target. This should be established in the preliminary negotiations that lead to the letter of intent.

   The letter must spell out not only the price to be paid but also many of the relational aspects that will make the strategic acquisition successful. Although an acquiror may justifiably focus on expenses, indemnification, and other logical concerns in the letter of intent, relationship and operational concerns are also important.

5. *Management difficulties.* Lack of attention to management issues may lead to a lost deal. These problems can range from a failure to provide management continuity or clear lines of authority after a merger to incentives that cause management to steer the company in the wrong direction.

   The remedy for this problem must be extracted from the initial strategic review. The management compensation structure must be designed with legal and business advisors to help achieve those goals. The financial rewards to management must depend upon the financial and strategic success of the combined entity.

6. *The closing crisis.* Closing crises may stem from unavoidable changed conditions, but most often they result from poor communication. Negotiators sometimes believe that problems swept under the table maintain a deal's momentum and ultimately allow for its consummation. They are sometimes right—and often wrong. Charting a course through an acquisition requires carefully developed skills for every kind of professional—business, accounting, and legal.

7. *The operating transition crisis.* Even the best conceived and executed acquisition will prevent significant transition and postclosing operation issues. Strategic goals cannot be achieved by quick asset sales or other accelerated exit strategies. Management time and energy must be spent to assure that the benefits identified in the strategic review are achieved.

   The principal constraints on smooth implementation are usually human: poor interaction of personnel between the two preexisting management structures and resistance to new systems. Problems also may arise from too much attention to the by now well-communicated strategic vision and too little attention to the nuts and bolts of continuing business operations.

Source: Excerpted from D. A. Tanner, "Seven Deadly Sins of Strategic Acquisition," *Management Review:* June 1991, pp. 50–53. Reprinted by permission of publisher, from MANAGEMENT REVIEW, June 1991, © 1991. American Management Association, New York, All rights reserved.

EXHIBIT 6–10   A Model of the Turnaround Process

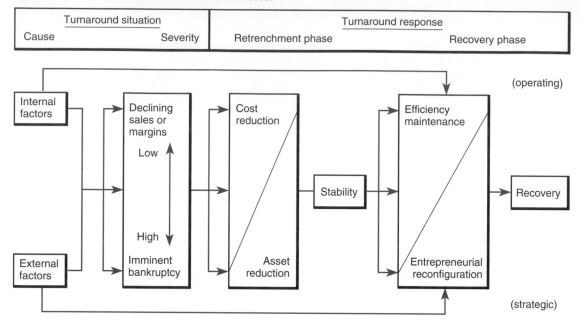

Bringing in new managers was believed to introduce needed new perspectives on the firm's situation, to raise employee morale, and to facilitate drastic actions, such as deep budgetary cuts in established programs.

Strategic management research provides evidence that the firms that have used a *turnaround strategy* have successfully confronted decline. The research findings have been assimilated and used as the building blocks for a model of the turnaround process shown in Exhibit 6–10.

The model begins with a depiction of external and internal factors as causes of a firm's performance downturn. When these factors continue to detrimentally impact the firm, its financial health is threatened. Unchecked decline places the firm in a turnaround situation.

A *turnaround situation* represents absolute and relative-to-industry declining performance of a sufficient magnitude to warrant explicit turnaround actions. Turnaround situations may be the result of years of gradual slowdown or months of sharp decline. In either case, the recovery phase of the turnaround process is likely to be more successful in accomplishing turnaround when it is preceded by planned retrenchment that results in the achievement of near-term financial stabilization. For a declining firm, stabilizing operations and restoring profitability almost always entail strict cost reduction followed by a shrinking back to those segments of the business that have the best prospects of attractive profit margins. The need for retrenchment was reflected in unemployment figures during the 2000–2001 recession. More layoffs of American workers were announced in 2001 than in any of the previous eight years. U.S. companies announced nearly 2 million layoffs in 2001 as the economy sunk into its first recession in a decade.

The immediacy of the resulting threat to company survival posed by the turnaround situation is known as *situation severity*. Severity is the governing factor in estimating the speed with which the retrenchment response will be formulated and activated. When severity is low, a firm has some financial cushion. Stability may be achieved through cost retrenchment alone. When turnaround situation severity is high, a firm must immediately stabilize the decline or bankruptcy is imminent. Cost reductions must be supplemented with more drastic asset reduction measures. Assets targeted for divestiture are those determined to be underproductive. In contrast, more productive resources are protected from cuts and represent critical elements of the future core business plan of the company (i.e., the intended recovery response).

Turnaround responses among successful firms typically include two stages of strategic activities: retrenchment and the recovery response. *Retrenchment* consists of cost-cutting and asset-reducing activities. The primary objective of the retrenchment phase is to stabilize the firm's financial condition. Situation severity has been associated with retrenchment responses among successful turnaround firms. Firms in danger of bankruptcy or failure (i.e., severe situations) attempt to halt decline through cost and asset reductions. Firms in less severe situations have achieved stability merely through cost retrenchment. However, in either case, for firms facing declining financial performance, the key to successful turnaround rests in the effective and efficient management of the retrenchment process.

The primary causes of the turnaround situation have been associated with the second phase of the turnaround process, the *recovery response*. For firms that declined primarily as a result of external problems, turnaround most often has been achieved through creative new entrepreneurial strategies. For firms that declined primarily as a result of internal problems, turnaround has been most frequently achieved through efficiency strategies. *Recovery* is achieved when economic measures indicate that the firm has regained its predownturn levels of performance.

Divestiture

A *divestiture strategy* involves the sale of a firm or a major component of a firm. Sara Lee Corp. (SLE) provides a good example. It sells everything from Wonderbras and Kiwi shoe polish to Endust furniture polish and Chock full o'Nuts coffee. In the 1990s, the company used a conglomerate diversification strategy to build Sara Lee into a huge portfolio of disparate brands. A new president in 1998, C. Steven McMillan, faced stagnant revenues and earnings. So he consolidated, streamlined, and focused the company on its core categories—food, underwear, and household products. He divested 15 businesses, including Coach leather goods in 2000, which together equaled over 20 percent of the company's revenue, and laid off 13,200 employees, nearly 10 percent of the workforce. McMillan used the cash from asset sales to snap up brands that enhanced Sara Lee's clout in key categories, like the $2.8 billion purchase of St. Louis-based breadmaker Earthgrains Co. in 2001 to quadruple Sara Lee's bakery operations.

When retrenchment fails to accomplish the desired turnaround, as in the Goodyear situation, or when a nonintegrated business activity achieves an unusually high market value, strategic managers often decide to sell the firm. However, because the intent is to find a buyer willing to pay a premium above the value of a going concern's fixed assets, the term *marketing for sale* is often more appropriate. Prospective buyers must be convinced that because of their skills and resources or because of the firm's synergy with their existing businesses, they will be able to profit from the acquisition.

The reasons for divestiture vary. They often arise because of partial mismatches between the acquired firm and the parent corporation. Some of the mismatched parts cannot be integrated into the corporation's mainstream activities and, thus, must be spun off. A second reason is corporate financial needs. Sometimes the cash flow or financial stability of the corporation as a whole can be greatly improved if businesses with high market value can be sacrificed. The result can be a balancing of equity with long-term risks or of long-term debt payments to optimize the cost of capital. A third, less frequent reason for divestiture is government antitrust action when a firm is believed to monopolize or unfairly dominate a particular market.

Although examples of the divestiture grand strategy are numerous, CBS, Inc., provides an outstanding example. In a two-year period, the once diverse entertainment and publishing giant sold its Records Division to Sony, its magazine publishing business to Diamandis Communications, its book publishing operations to Harcourt Brace Jovanovich, and its music publishing operations to SBK Entertainment World. Other firms that have pursued this type of grand strategy include Esmark, which divested Swift & Company, and White Motors, which divested White Farm.

Liquidation

When liquidation is the grand strategy, the firm typically is sold in parts, only occasionally as a whole—but for its tangible asset value and not as a going concern. In selecting liquidation, the owners and strategic managers of a firm are admitting failure and recognize that this action is likely to result in great hardships to themselves and their employees. For these reasons, liquidation usually is seen as the least attractive of the grand strategies. As a long-term strategy, however, it minimizes the losses of all the firm's stockholders. Faced with bankruptcy, the liquidating firm usually tries to develop a planned and orderly system that will result in the greatest possible return and cash conversion as the firm slowly relinquishes its market share.

Planned liquidation can be worthwhile. For example, Columbia Corporation, a $130 million diversified firm, liquidated its assets for more cash per share than the market value of its stock.

Bankruptcy

Business failures are playing an increasingly important role in the American economy. In an average week, more than 300 companies fail. More than 75 percent of these financially desperate firms file for a *liquidation bankruptcy*—they agree to a complete distribution of their assets to creditors, most of whom receive a small fraction of the amount they are owed. Liquidation is what the layperson views as bankruptcy: The business cannot pay its debts, so it must close its doors. Investors lose their money, employees lose their jobs, and managers lose their credibility. In owner-managed firms, company and personal bankruptcy commonly go hand in hand.

The other 25 percent of these firms refuse to surrender until one final option is exhausted. Choosing a strategy to recapture its viability, such a company asks the courts for a *reorganization bankruptcy*. The firm attempts to persuade its creditors to temporarily freeze their claims while it undertakes to reorganize and rebuild the company's operations more profitably. The appeal of a reorganization bankruptcy is based on the company's ability to convince creditors that it can succeed in the marketplace by implementing a new strategic plan, and that when the plan produces profits, the firm will be able to repay its creditors, perhaps in full. In other words, the company offers its creditors a carefully designed alternative to forcing an immediate, but fractional, repayment of its financial obligations. The option of reorganization bankruptcy offers maximum repayment of debt at some specified future time if a new strategic plan is successful.

The Bankruptcy Situation

Imagine that your firm's financial reports have shown an unabated decline in revenue for seven quarters. Expenses have increased rapidly, and it is becoming difficult, and at times not possible, to pay bills as they become due. Suppliers are concerned about shipping goods without first receiving payment, and some have refused to ship without advanced payment in cash. Customers are requiring assurances that future orders will be delivered and some are beginning to buy from competitors. Employees are listening seriously to rumors of financial problems and a higher than normal number have accepted other employment. What can be done? What strategy can be initiated to protect the company and resolve the financial problems in the short term?

The Harshest Resolution

If the judgment of the owners of a business is that its decline cannot be reversed, and the business cannot be sold as a going concern, then the alternative that is in the best interest of all may be a liquidation bankruptcy, also known as Chapter 7 of the Bankruptcy Code. The court appoints a trustee, who collects the property of the company, reduces it to cash, and distributes the proceeds proportionally to creditors on a pro rata basis as expeditiously as possible. Since all assets are sold to pay outstanding debt, a liquidation bankruptcy terminates a business. This type of filing is critically important to sole proprietors or partnerships. Their owners are personally liable for all business debts not covered by the sale of the business assets unless they can secure a Chapter 7 bankruptcy, which will allow them to cancel any debt in excess of exempt assets. Although they will be left with little personal property, the liquidated debtor is discharged from paying the remaining debt.

The shareholders of corporations are not liable for corporate debt and any debt existing after corporate assets are liquidated is absorbed by creditors. Corporate shareholders may simply terminate operations and walk away without liability to remaining creditors. However, filing a Chapter 7 proceeding will provide for an orderly and fair distribution of assets to creditors and thereby may reduce the negative impact of the business failure.

A Conditional Second Chance

A proactive alternative for the endangered company is reorganization bankruptcy. Chosen for the right reasons, and implemented in the right way, reorganization bankruptcy can provide a financially, strategically, and ethically sound basis on which to advance the interests of all of the firm's stakeholders.

A thorough and objective analysis of the company may support the idea of its continuing operations if excessive debt can be reduced and new strategic initiatives can be undertaken. If the realistic possibility of long-term survival exists, a reorganization under Chapter 11 of the Bankruptcy Code can provide the opportunity. Reorganization allows a business debtor to restructure its debts and, with the agreement of creditors and approval of the court, to continue as a viable business. Creditors involved in Chapter 11 actions often receive less than the total debt due to them but far more than would be available from liquidation.

A Chapter 11 bankruptcy can provide time and protection to the debtor firm (which we will call the *Company*) to reorganize and use future earnings to pay creditors. The Company may restructure debts, close unprofitable divisions or stores, renegotiate labor contracts, reduce its work force, or propose other actions that could create a profitable business. If the plan is accepted by creditors, the Company will be given another chance to avoid liquidation and emerge from the bankruptcy proceedings rehabilitated.

Seeking Protection of the Bankruptcy Court

If creditors file lawsuits or schedule judicial sales to enforce liens, the Company will need to seek the protection of the Bankruptcy Court. Filing a bankruptcy petition will invoke the protection of the court to provide sufficient time to work out a reorganization that was not achievable voluntarily. If reorganization is not possible, a Chapter 7 proceeding will allow for the fair and orderly dissolution of the business.

If a Chapter 11 proceeding is the required course of action, the Company must determine what the reorganized business will look like, if such a structure can be achieved, and how it will be accomplished while maintaining operations during the bankruptcy proceeding. Will sufficient cash be available to pay for the proceedings and reorganization? Will customers continue to do business with the Company or seek other more secure businesses with which to deal? Will key personnel stay on or look for more secure employment? Which operations should be discontinued or reduced?

Emerging from Bankruptcy

Bankruptcy is only the first step toward recovery for a firm. Many questions should be answered: How did the business get to the point at which the extreme action of bankruptcy was necessary? Were warning signs overlooked? Was the competitive environment understood? Did pride or fear prevent objective analysis? Did the business have the people and resources to succeed? Was the strategic plan well designed and implemented? Did financial problems result from unforeseen and unforeseeable problems or from bad management decisions?

Commitments to "try harder," "listen more carefully to the customer," and "be more efficient" are important but insufficient grounds to inspire stakeholder confidence. A recovery strategy must be developed to delineate how the company will compete more successfully in the future.

An assessment of the bankruptcy situation requires executives to consider the causes of the Company's decline and the severity of the problem it now faces. Investors must decide whether the management team that governed the company's operations during the downturn can return the firm to a position of success. Creditors must believe that the company's managers have learned how to prevent a recurrence of the observed and similar problems. Alternatively, they must have faith that the company's competencies can be sufficiently augmented by key substitutions to the management team, with strong support in decision making from a board of directors and consultants, to restore the firm's competitive strength.

CORPORATE COMBINATIONS

The 15 grand strategies discussed above, used singly and much more often in combinations, represent the traditional alternatives used by firms in the United States. Recently, three new grand types have gained in popularity; all fit under the broad category of corporate combinations. Although they do not fit the criterion by which executives retain a high degree of control over their operations, these grand strategies deserve special attention and consideration especially by companies that operate in global, dynamic, and technologically driven industries. These three newly popularized grand strategies are joint ventures, strategic alliances, and consortia.

Joint Ventures

Occasionally two or more capable firms lack a necessary component for success in a particular competitive environment. For example, no single petroleum firm controlled sufficient resources to construct the Alaskan pipeline. Nor was any single firm capable of processing and marketing all of the oil that would flow through the pipeline. The solution was a set of *joint ventures,* which are commercial companies (children) created and operated for the benefit of the co-owners (parents). These cooperative arrangements provided both the funds needed to build the pipeline and the processing and marketing capacities needed to profitably handle the oil flow.

The particular form of joint ventures discussed above is *joint ownership.* In recent years, it has become increasingly appealing for domestic firms to join foreign firms by means of this form. For example, Diamond-Star Motors is the result of a joint venture between a U.S. company, Chrysler Corporation, and Japan's Mitsubishi Motors corporation. Located in Normal, Illinois, Diamond-Star was launched because it offered Chrysler and Mitsubishi a chance to expand on their long-standing relationship in which subcompact cars (as well as Mitsubishi engines and other automotive parts) are imported to the United States and sold under the Dodge and Plymouth names.

The joint venture extends the supplier-consumer relationship and has strategic advantages for both partners. For Chrysler, it presents an opportunity to produce a high-quality car using expertise brought to the venture by Mitsubishi. It also gives Chrysler the chance to try new production techniques and to realize efficiencies by using the workforce that was not included under Chrysler's collective bargaining agreement with the United Auto Workers. The agreement offers Mitsubishi the opportunity to produce cars for sale in the United States without being subjected to the tariffs and restrictions placed on Japanese imports.

As a second example, Bethlehem Steel acquired an interest in a Brazilian mining venture to secure a raw material source. The stimulus for this joint ownership venture was grand strategy, but such is not always the case. Certain countries virtually mandate that foreign firms entering their markets do so on a joint ownership basis. India and Mexico are good examples. The rationale of these countries is that joint ventures minimize the threat of foreign domination and enhance the skills, employment, growth, and profits of local firms.

It should be noted that strategic managers understandably are wary of joint ventures. Admittedly, joint ventures present new opportunities with risks that can be shared. On the other hand, joint ventures often limit the discretion, control, and profit potential of partners, while demanding managerial attention and other resources that might be directed toward the firm's mainstream activities. Nevertheless, increasing globalization in many industries may require greater consideration of the joint venture approach, if historically national firms are to remain viable.

Strategic Alliances

Strategic alliances are distinguished from joint ventures because the companies involved do not take an equity position in one another. In many instances, strategic alliances are partnerships that exist for a defined period during which partners contribute their skills and expertise to a cooperative project. For example, one partner provides manufacturing capabilities while a second partner provides marketing expertise. Many times, such alliances are undertaken because the partners want to learn from one another with the intention to be able to develop in-house capabilities to supplant the partner when the contractual arrangement between them reaches its termination date. Such relationships are tricky since in a sense the partners are attempting to "steal" each other's know-how. Exhibit 6–11, Global Strategy in Action, lists many important questions about their learning intentions that prospective partners should ask themselves before entering into a strategic alliance.

In other instances, strategic alliances are synonymous with licensing agreements. Licensing involves the transfer of some industrial property right from the U.S. licensor to a motivated licensee in a foreign country. Most tend to be patents, trademarks, or technical know-how that are granted to the licensee for a specified time in return for a royalty and for avoiding tariffs or import quotas. Bell South and U.S. West, with various marketing and service competitive advantages valuable to Europe, have extended a number of licenses to create personal computer networks in the United Kingdom (U.K.).

Objective	Major Questions
1. Assess and value partner knowledge.	• What were the strategic objectives in forming the alliance? • What are the core competencies of our alliance partner? • Which partner contributes key alliance inputs? • What specific knowledge does the partner have that could enhance our competitive strategy? Is that knowledge or some of the knowledge embodied in the alliance? • What are the core partner skills relevant for our product/markets? • Are we realistic about partner skills and capabilities relevant to our strategy and capabilities?
2. Determine knowledge accessibility.	• Have learning issues been discussed in the alliance negotiations? • How have key alliance responsibilities been allocated to the partners? Which partner controls key managerial responsibilities? • Do we have easy geographic access to the alliance operations? • Does the alliance agreement specify restrictions on our access to the alliance operations? • Has our partner taken explicit steps to restrict our access? If yes, can we eliminate these restrictions through negotiation or assignment of managers to the alliance?
3. Evaluate knowledge tacitness and ease of transfer.	• Is our learning objective focused on explicit operational knowledge? • Where in the alliance does the knowledge reside? • Is the knowledge strategic or operational? • Reality check: Do we understand what we are trying to learn and how we can use the knowledge?
4. Establish knowledge connections between the alliance and the partner.	• Do parent managers visit the alliance on a regular basis? • Has a systematic plan been established for managers to rotate between the alliance and the parent? • Are parent managers in regular contact with senior alliance managers? • Has the alliance been incorporated into parent strategic plans and do alliance managers participate in parent strategic planning discussions? • What is the level of trust between parent and alliance managers? • Do alliance financial issues dominate meetings between alliance and parent managers?
5. Draw on existing knowledge to facilitate learning.	• Have the partner firms worked together in the past? • In the learning process, have efforts been made to involve managers with prior experience in either/both alliance management and partner ties? • Are experiences with other alliances being used as the basis for managing the current alliance? • Are we realistic about our partner's learning objectives? • Are we open-minded about knowledge without immediate short-term applicability?
6. Ensure that partner and alliance managerial cultures are in alignment.	• Is the alliance viewed as a threat or an asset by parent managers? • In the parent, is there agreement on the strategic rationale for the alliance? • In the alliance, do managers understand the importance of the parent's learning objective?

Source: Andrew C. Inkpen. "Learning and Knowledge Acquisition through International Strategic Alliances," *Academy of Management Executive* 12, no. 4 (1998), p. 78.

EXHIBIT 6–12
The Top Five Strategic Reasons for Outsourcing

Source: Material prepared for a paid advertising section which appeared in the October 16, 1995, issue of *Fortune* © 1995, Time, Inc. All rights reserved.

1. **Improve Business Focus.**
   For many companies, the single most compelling reason for outsourcing is that several "how" issues are siphoning off huge amounts of management's resources and attention.
2. **Access to World-Class Capabilities.**
   By the very nature of their specialization, outsourcing providers bring extensive worldwide, world-class resources to meeting the needs of their customers. According to Norris Overton, vice president of reengineering, AMTRAK, partnering with an organization with world-class capabilities, can offer access to new technology, tools, and techniques that the organization may not currently possess; better career opportunities for personnel who transition to the outsourcing provider; more structured methodologies, procedures, and documentation; and competitive advantage through expanded skills.
3. **Accelerated Reengineering Benefits.**
   Outsourcing is often a byproduct of another powerful management tool—business process reengineering. It allows an organization to immediately realize the anticipated benefits of reengineering by having an outside organization—one that is already reengineered to world-class standards—take over the process.
4. **Shared Risks.**
   There are tremendous risks associated with the investments an organization makes. When companies outsource they become more flexible, more dynamic, and better able to adapt to changing opportunities.
5. **Free Resources for Other Purposes.**
   Every organization has limits on the resources available to it. Outsourcing permits an organization to redirect its resources from noncore activities toward activities that have the greater return in serving the customer.

Another licensing strategy open to U.S. firms is to contract the manufacturing of its product line to a foreign company to exploit local comparative advantages in technology, materials, or labor. For example, MIPS Computer Systems has licensed Digital Equipment Corporation, Texas Instruments, Cypress Semiconductor, and Bipolar Integrated Technology in the United States, and Fujitsu, NEC, and Kubota in Japan to market computers based on its designs in the partner's country.

Service and franchise-based firms—including Anheuser-Busch, Avis, Coca-Cola, Hilton, Hyatt, Holiday Inns, Kentucky Fried Chicken, McDonald's, and Pepsi—have long engaged in licensing arrangements with foreign distributors as a way to enter new markets with standardized products that can benefit from marketing economies.

Outsourcing is a rudimentary approach to strategic alliances that enables firms to gain a competitive advantage. Significant changes within many segments of American business continue to encourage the use of outsourcing practices. Within the health care arena, an industry survey recorded 67 percent of hospitals using provider outsourcing for at least one department within their organization. Services such as information systems, reimbursement, and risk and physician practice management are outsourced by 51 percent of the hospitals that use outsourcing.

Another successful application of outsourcing is found in human resources. A survey of human resource executives revealed 85 percent have personal experience leading an outsourcing effort within their organization. In addition, it was found that two-thirds of pension departments have outsourced at least one human resource function.

Within customer service and sales departments, outsourcing increased productivity in such areas as product information, sales and order taking, sample fulfillment, and complaint handling. Exhibit 6–12 presents the top five strategic and tactical reasons for exploiting the benefits of outsourcing.

Consortia, Keiretsus, and Chaebols

Consortia are defined as large interlocking relationships between businesses of an industry. In Japan such consortia are known as *keiretsus,* in South Korea as *chaebols.*

In Europe, consortia projects are increasing in number and in success rates. Examples include the Junior Engineers' and Scientists' Summer Institute, which underwrites cooperative learning and research; the European Strategic Program for Research and Development in Information Technologies, which seeks to enhance European competitiveness in fields related to computer electronics and component manufacturing; and EUREKA, which is a joint program involving scientists and engineers from several European countries to coordinate joint research projects.

A Japanese *keiretsu* is an undertaking involving up to 50 different firms that are joined around a large trading company or bank and are coordinated through interlocking directories and stock exchanges. It is designed to use industry coordination to minimize risks of competition, in part through cost sharing and increased economies of scale. Examples include Sumitomo, Mitsubishi, Mitsui, and Sanwa. Exhibit 6–13, Global Strategy in Action, presents a new side to *keiretsus,* namely, that they are adding global partners, including several from the United States. Their cooperative nature is growing in evidence as is their market success.

A South Korean chaebol resembles a consortium or keiretsu except that they are typically financed through government banking groups and largely are run by professional managers trained by participating firms expressly for the job.

SELECTION OF LONG-TERM OBJECTIVES AND GRAND STRATEGY SETS

At first glance, the strategic management model, which provides the framework for study throughout this book, seems to suggest that strategic choice decision making leads to the sequential selection of long-term objectives and grand strategies. In fact, however, strategic choice is the simultaneous selection of long-range objectives and grand strategies. When strategic planners study their opportunities, they try to determine which are most likely to result in achieving various long-range objectives. Almost simultaneously, they try to forecast whether an available grand strategy can take advantage of preferred opportunities so the tentative objectives can be met. In essence, then, three distinct but highly interdependent choices are being made at one time. Several triads, or sets, of possible decisions are usually considered.

A simplified example of this process is shown in Exhibit 6–14. In this example, the firm has determined that six strategic choice options are available. These options stem from three interactive opportunities (e.g., West Coast markets that present little competition.) Because each of these interactive opportunities can be approached through different grand strategies—for options 1 and 2, the grand strategies are horizontal integration and market development—each offers the potential for achieving long-range objectives to varying degrees. Thus, a firm rarely can make a strategic choice only on the basis of its preferred opportunities, long-range objectives, or grand strategy. Instead, these three elements must be considered simultaneously, because only in combination do they constitute a strategic choice.

In an actual decision situation, the strategic choice would be complicated by a wider variety of interactive opportunities, feasible company objectives, promising grand strategy options, and evaluative criteria. Nevertheless, Exhibit 6–14 does partially reflect the nature and complexity of the process by which long-term objectives and grand strategies are selected.

BusinessWeek Amid rolling hills outside Nagoya, Toshiba Corp. recently took the wraps off a new $1 billion chipmaking facility that uses ultraviolet lithography to etch circuits less than one micron wide—a tiny fraction of the width of a human hair.

The Toshiba chip site owes much to a strategic alliance with IBM and Siemens of Germany. In fact, IBM's know how in chemical mechanical polishing, essential to smoothing the tiny surfaces of multilayered chips, played a critical role. "We had little expertise here," concedes Toshiba's Koichi Suzuki.

QUIET CHANGE

What's more, about 20 IBM engineers will show up shortly to transfer the technology back to an IBM-Toshiba facility in Manassas, Virginia. In addition to the semiconductor cooperation, IBM and Toshiba jointly make liquid-crystal display panels—even though they use the LCDs in their fiercely competitive lines of laptop computers. "It's no longer considered a loss of corporate manhood to let others help out," says IBM Asia Pacific President Robert C. Timpson.

For years, many U.S. tie-ups with Japanese companies tended to be defensive in nature, poorly managed, and far removed from core businesses. Now, the alliances are deepening, taking on increasingly important products, and expanding their geographic reach in terms of sales. U.S.-Japanese partnerships are, for example, popping up in Asia's emerging but tricky markets, reducing the risks each company faces.

This deepening web of relationships reflects a quiet change in thinking by Japanese and U.S. multinationals in an era when keeping pace with technological change and competing globally have stretched the resources of even the richest companies. "The scale and technology are so great that neither can do it alone," says Jordan D. Lewis, author of *The Connected Corporation.*

Overall, instances of joint investments in research, products, and distribution by Japanese companies and foreign counterparts, mostly American, have jumped 26%, to 155, in the first quarter of 1996—on top of a 33% increase between 1993 and 1995—according to the Sakura Institute of Research.

ENVY

And while Uncle Sam and U.S. companies with grievances have attacked Japan's system of big industrial groups, called keiretsu, as exclusionary, other chieftains of Corporate America have quietly become *stakeholders* of sorts. The list includes companies as diverse as IBM, General Motors, TRW, Boeing, and Caterpillar.

Many American executives who have established these alliances say they appreciate the attributes of Japan's big industrial groups. U.S. managers have always envied the keiretsu edge in spreading risk over a cluster of companies when betting on a new technology or blitzing emerging markets.

In one industry after another, U.S. and Japanese partners are breaking new ground in their level of cooperation. The impact is felt far beyond the U.S. and Japanese home markets. Take the 50-50 venture between Caterpillar Inc. and Mitsubishi Heavy Industries LTD., part of Japan's $200 billion keiretsu of the same name. Early on, Cat wanted a way to sell its construction equipment in Japan and compete with rival Komatsu Ltd. on its home turf. Mitsubishi wanted to play catch-up with Komatsu, too, and expand its export markets.

Their alliance played a key role in taming Komatsu. But the partners have broader ambitions. Since Cat shifted all design work for its "300" series of excavators to the partnership back in 1987, the venture's two Japanese factories have emerged as Cat's primary source of production for sales to fast-growing Asia. The alliance's products reach the world market through Cat's network of 186 independent dealers in 197 countries.

Source: Brian Bemner in Tokyo, with Zachary Schiller in Cleveland, Tim Smart in Fairfield, William J. Holstein in New York, and bureau reports, "Keiretsu Connections," *BusinessWeek,* July 22, 1996.

In the next chapter, the strategic choice process will be fully explained. However, knowledge of long-term objectives and grand strategies is essential to understanding that process.

SEQUENCE OF OBJECTIVES AND STRATEGY SELECTION

The selection of long-range objectives and grand strategies involves simultaneous, rather than sequential, decisions. While it is true that objectives are needed to prevent the firm's direction and progress from being determined by random forces, it is equally true that objectives can be achieved only if strategies are implemented. In fact, long-term objectives and grand strategies are so interdependent that some business consultants do not distinguish between them. Long-term objectives and grand strategies are still combined

EXHIBIT 6–14   **A Profile of Strategic Choice Options**

	Six Strategic Choice Options					
	1	**2**	**3**	**4**	**5**	**6**
Interactive opportunities	West Coast markets present little competition		Current markets sensitive to price competition		Current industry product lines offer too narrow a range of markets	
Appropriate long-range objectives (limited sample):						
Average 5-year ROI.	15%	19%	13%	17%	23%	15%
Company sales by year 5.	+50%	+40%	+20%	+0%	+35%	+25%
Risk of negative profits.	.30	.25	.10	.15	.20	.05
Grand strategies	Horizontal integration	Market development	Concentration	Selective retrenchment	Product development	Concentration

under the heading of company strategy in most of the popular business literature and in the thinking of most practicing executives.

However, the distinction has merit. Objectives indicate what strategic managers want but provide few insights about how they will be achieved. Conversely, strategies indicate what types of actions will be taken but do not define what ends will be pursued or what criteria will serve as constraints in refining the strategic plan.

Does it matter whether strategic decisions are made to achieve objectives or to satisfy constraints? No, because constraints are themselves objectives. The constraint of increased inventory capacity is a desire (an objective), not a certainty. Likewise, the constraint of an increase in the sales force does not assure that the increase will be achieved, given such factors as other company priorities, labor market conditions, and the firm's profit performance.

Summary

Before we learn how strategic decisions are made, it is important to understand the two principal components of any strategic choice; namely, long-term objectives and the grand strategy. The purpose of this chapter was to convey that understanding.

Long-term objectives were defined as the results a firm seeks to achieve over a specified period, typically five years. Seven common long-term objectives were discussed: profitability, productivity, competitive position, employee development, employee relations, technological leadership, and public responsibility. These, or any other long-term objectives, should be acceptable, flexible, measurable over time, motivating, suitable, understandable, and achievable.

Grand strategies were defined as comprehensive approaches guiding the major actions designed to achieve long-term objectives. Fifteen grand strategy options were discussed: concentrated growth, market development, product development, innovation, horizontal integration, vertical integration, concentric diversification, conglomerate diversification, turnaround, divestiture, liquidation, bankruptcy, joint ventures, strategic alliances, and consortia.

Questions for Discussion

1. Identify firms in the business community nearest to your college or university that you believe are using each of the 15 grand strategies discussed in this chapter.

2. Identify firms in your business community that appear to rely principally on 1 of the 15 grand strategies. What kind of information did you use to classify the firms?

3. Write a long-term objective for your school of business that exhibits the seven qualities of long-term objectives described in this chapter.

4. Distinguish between the following pairs of grand strategies:

   a. Horizontal and vertical integration.
   b. Conglomerate and concentric diversification.
   c. Product development and innovation.
   d. Joint venture and strategic alliance.

5. Rank each of the 15 grand strategy options discussed in this chapter on the following three scales:

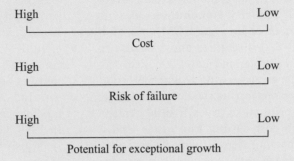

6. Identify firms that use one of the eight specific options shown in Exhibit 6–5 under the grand strategies of concentration, market development, and product development.

Chapter 6 Discussion Case

BusinessWeek

GM's Strategy of Piecemeal Alliances

1 For Fiat, General Motors' purchase of 20% of its auto business on March 13 is just the breather it was seeking. The Italian carmaker gets a deep-pocketed partner with a reputation as an easygoing, hands-off minority stakeholder, leaving Fiat's managers in charge. And GM's prize? It gets small Fiat diesel engines and a chance to trim its costs in Europe and Latin America—not to mention the pleasure of thwarting rival DaimlerChrysler's effort to swallow Fiat whole. Yet GM's minority stake gives it little clout to force the tough cost-cutting Fiat needs, and it leaves GM competing fiercely with its new partner in key European auto segments. Laments one large GM institutional investor: "It looks like a huge victory for Fiat, but it doesn't do very much for GM."

2 In short, it looks like most of GM's growing network of global auto tie-ups: a puzzling mix of missed opportunities and timid half steps. As the global auto industry has consolidated rapidly—with DaimlerChrysler and Ford moving boldly to acquire key players—GM has tiptoed into a series of minority stakes and ad-hoc alliances with rivals. GM hopes to reap the benefits of partnership without the messy culture clash, nationalist backlash, and red ink that a full buyout often entails. Says GM Chief Executive G. Richard Wagoner Jr.: "We think we've hit on the right formula."

3 But its track record suggests a different lesson: little ventured, little gained. Consider GM's stake in struggling Isuzu Motors Ltd. After 29 years as a minority shareholder, GM has gotten some diesel truck engines and co-designed pickup trucks. But Isuzu racked up a $200 million operating loss last year and amassed $8.3 billion in debt. In 1999, GM raised its holdings to 49% from 38%. Grouses the GM investor: "GM never exercised the management due diligence it should have, but it was probably unable to."

4 Even where it has taken control, GM's kid-glove style has brought limited benefit. When it bought half of Saab in 1990, the Swedish carmaker was a money-losing seller of 93,000 cars a year. Cash-strapped itself at first, GM shared

major components between Saab and other GM divisions, improved Saab quality, and eventually rolled out new models. But while Saab's small U.S. sales are rising smartly, it barely ekes out a profit on the 131,000 cars it sells annually worldwide.

5 Still, Wagoner is stepping up GM's efforts to forge alliances. In December, the No. 1 automaker agreed to buy 20% of Fuji Heavy Industries Ltd., maker of Subaru cars, after tripling its holdings in Suzuki Motor Corp., to 10%, in 1998. In 1999, GM bought the remaining half of Saab. It is also negotiating to buy Korea's Daewoo Motor and has inked a technology-sharing deal with Toyota and an engine pact with Honda Motor.

6 GM's strategy has some advantages. Buying a small chunk of a company allows the auto giant inside for a closer look before deciding whether to take a bigger plunge. And taking a small stake in a healthy rival to share the costs of developing new technology or gain access to distribution in another region can help meet a strategic need cheaply.

7 But like elsewhere in life, you get what you pay for. If the partnership isn't a two-way exchange of expertise and capital, the value can be limited. Subaru and Suzuki, for instance, bring GM some small cars without bolstering its know-how. Says Brandies University international marketing professor Shih-Fen Chen: "GM's reliance on Japanese alliances prevents the company from developing its own small cars."

8 Acting as a silent partner is weak medicine indeed when buying into a company that urgently needs fixing. Only a full merger will let GM and Fiat tackle their biggest headache in the European market: overcapacity. To make their alliance pay off, they must quickly ax overlapping models and overhead to cut costs. Since Fiat factories run at just 60% of capacity, some must close. But GM can't make any of that happen—which is just fine with Fiat's managers and the Italian government. DaimlerChrysler execs say privately that they refused to accept such terms.

9 LOPSIDED DEAL. While GM's partial ownership may ultimately lead to a merger, that's at least several years away. By then, both carmakers will have lost the opportunity to fix their European operations while the market was strong. Moreover, the deal gives Fiat the upper hand: It can compel GM to buy the rest of Fiat any time from 2004 to 2009 at a fair-market price. "How do they know where Fiat will be five years from now, especially since they won't have a hand in running it?" says Deutsche Bank Securities Inc. analyst Rod Lache. "That's a pretty big leap of faith." What's more, Fiat can sell its 80% stake to anyone after a year as long as GM has a chance to match terms.

10 In the short run, GM and Fiat plan to gain efficiency by sharing chassis and key components, analysts say. While that's a good idea, getting engineers from different companies and cultures to collaborate is extremely tricky. GM has repeatedly stumbled at the far less complex task of fostering in-house cooperation between its North American and European engineers. The task could be far tougher for GM and Fiat, which will continue to battle in the small and midsize car segments. "If you're competing on 40% of your product [lineup], how willing are you going to be to share product information?" notes Lache.

11 Despite the messy details, merger mania in the auto industry continues at fever pitch. The field of remaining candidates is down to a handful: Daewoo, Mitsubishi Motors, PSA Peugeot Citroen, Volvo truck. That leaves only holdouts BMW and Honda, which are not on the block. But BMW may toss Rover Cars back on the market after trying fruitlessly since 1994 to fix it. Daimler is busily trying to cement a deal with Mitsubishi, and Ford has joined the fray. GM may now seek a partner in its Daewoo buyout attempt. Not everyone has a good economic reason for doing these deals, warns Brandeis' Chen. But until almost everything is snapped up, they're likely to proceed apace.

Source: Kathleen Kerwin, David Welch, and Joann Muller, "For GM, Once Again, Little Ventured, Little Gained. Its small Fiat stake continues a strategy of piecemeal alliances," *BusinessWeek,* March 27, 2000.

Chapter Seven

Strategic Analysis and Choice in Single- or Dominant-Product Businesses: Building Sustainable Competitive Advantages

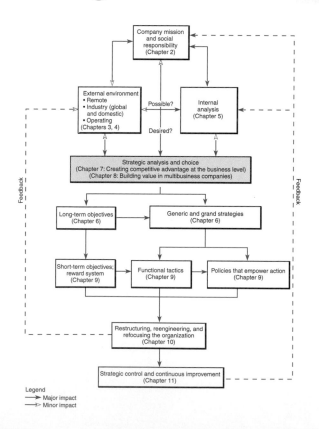

Legend
→ Major impact
⇢ Minor impact

Strategic analysis and choice is the phase of the strategic management process when business managers examine and choose a business strategy that allows their business to maintain or create a sustainable competitive advantage. Their starting point is to evaluate and determine which value chain activities provide the basis for distinguishing the firm in the customer's mind from other reasonable alternatives. Businesses with a dominant product or service line must also choose among alternate grand strategies to guide the firm's activities, particularly when they are trying to decide about broadening the scope of the firm's activities beyond its core business.

This chapter examines strategic analysis and choice in single- or dominant-product/service businesses by addressing two basic issues:

1. **What strategies are most effective at building sustainable competitive advantages for single business units?** What competitive strategy positions a business most effectively in its industry? For example, Scania, the most productive truck manufacturer in the world, joins its major rival Volvo as two anchors of Sweden's economy. Scania's return on sales of 9.9 percent far exceeds Mercedes (2.6 percent) and Volvo (2.5 percent), a level it has achieved most of the last 60 years. Scania has built a sustainable competitive advantage with a strategy of focusing solely on heavy trucks, in a limited geographic area—Europe—and by providing customized trucks with standardized components (20,000 components per truck versus 25,000 for Volvo and 40,000 for Mercedes). Scania is a low-cost producer of a differentiated truck that can be custom-manufactured quickly and sold to a regionally focused market.

2. **Should dominant-product/service businesses diversify** to build value and competitive advantage? What grand strategies are most appropriate? For example, Compaq Computers and Coca-Cola managers have examined the question of diversification and apparently concluded that continued concentration on their core products and services and development of new markets for those same core products and services are best. IBM and Pepsi examined the same question and concluded that related diversification and vertical integration were best. Why?

EVALUATING AND CHOOSING BUSINESS STRATEGIES: SEEKING SUSTAINED COMPETITIVE ADVANTAGE

Business managers evaluate and choose strategies that they think will make their business successful. Businesses become successful because they possess some advantage relative to their competitors. The two most prominent sources of competitive advantage can be found in the business's cost structure and its ability to differentiate the business from competitors. Disney World in Orlando offers theme park patrons several unique, distinct features that differentiate it from other entertainment options. Wal-Mart offers retail customers the lowest prices on popular consumer items because they have created a low-cost structure resulting in a competitive advantage over most competitors.

Businesses that create competitive advantages from one or both of these sources usually experience above-average profitability within their industry. Businesses that lack a cost or differentiation advantage usually experience average or below-average profitability. Two recent studies found that businesses that do not have either form of competitive advantage perform the poorest among their peers while businesses that possess both forms of competitive advantage enjoy the highest levels of profitability within their industry.[1] The average return on investment for over 2,500 businesses across seven industries looked as follows:

---

[1] R. B. Robinson and J. A. Pearce, "Planned Patterns of Strategic Behavior and Their Relationship to Business Unit Performance," *Strategic Management Journal* 9, no. 1 (1988), pp. 43–60; G. G. Dess and G. T. Lumpkin, "Emerging Issues in Strategy Process Research," in *Handbook of Strategic Management,* Hitt et. al., 2002.

Differentiation Advantage	Cost Advantage	Overall Average ROI across Seven Industries
High	High	35.0%
Low	High	26.0
High	Low	22.0
Low	Low	9.5

Initially, managers were advised to evaluate and choose strategies that emphasized one type of competitive advantage. Often referred to as *generic strategies,* firms were encouraged to become either a differentiation-oriented or low-cost-oriented company. In so doing, it was logical that organizational members would develop a clear understanding of company priorities and, as these studies suggest, likely experience profitability superior to competitors without either a differentiation or low-cost orientation.

The studies mentioned above, and the experience of many other businesses, indicate that the highest profitability levels are found in businesses that possess both types of competitive advantage at the same time. In other words, businesses that have one or more value chain activities that truly differentiate them from key competitors and also have value chain activities that let them operate at a lower cost will consistently outperform their rivals that don't. So the challenge for today's business managers is to evaluate and choose business strategies based on core competencies and value chain activities that sustain both types of competitive advantage simultaneously. Exhibit 7–1, Global Strategy in Action, shows Honda Motor Company attempting to do just this in Europe.

Evaluating Cost Leadership Opportunities

Business success built on cost leadership requires the business to be able to provide its product or service at a cost below what its competitors can achieve. And it must be a sustainable cost advantage. Through the skills and resources identified in Exhibit 7–2, a business must be able to accomplish one or more activities in its value chain activities—procuring materials, processing them into products, marketing the products, and distributing the products or support activities—in a more cost-effective manner than that of its competitors or it must be able to reconfigure its value chain so as to achieve a cost advantage. Exhibit 7–2 provides examples of ways this might be done.

Strategists examining their business's value chain for low-cost leadership advantages evaluate the sustainability of those advantages by *benchmarking* (refer to Chapter 5 for a discussion of this comparison technique) their business against key competitors and by considering the impact of any cost advantage on the five forces in their business's competitive environment. Low-cost activities that are sustainable and that provide one or more of these advantages relative to key industry forces should become the basis for the business's competitive strategy.

Low-Cost Advantages That Reduce the Likelihood of Pricing Pressure from Buyers   When key competitors cannot match prices from the low-cost leader, customers pressuring the leader risk establishing a price level that drives alternate sources out of business.

Truly Sustained Low-Cost Advantages May Push Rivals into Other Areas, Lessening Price Competition   Intense, continued price competition may be ruinous for all rivals, as seen occasionally in the airline industry.

BusinessWeek

Honda is hot. In the United States, the Tokyo company can barely keep up with demand for models like the Acura MDX sport utility vehicle and the Odysssey minivan. Four of the top 10 best-selling cars in Japan are Hondas. Honda recently passed rival Nissan to become Japan's second-largest automaker after Toyota.

But the road is not entirely smooth for the Japanese carmaker. Honda Motor Co. has suffered a serious breakdown in Europe. Honda's operations in the Old World reported a loss of nearly half a billion dollars in Britain and the Continent for the year ended March 31. "Our biggest worry is weak sales in Europe," says CEO Hiroyuki Yoshino.

So Yoshino's managers have gone into overdrive to repair the European business. Their game plan includes cost leadership initiatives: boosting capacity at two plants in Britain, heeding European calls for cars with diesel engines, and implementing a hard-nosed cost-cutting program that targets parts suppliers . . . and differentiation opportunities: launching an all-new car for the subcompact market.

Honda has a reputation for tackling all of its challenges head-on. But the European problem, even against the background of record results in the United States, underscores Honda's fragility. Although less than 10% of Honda's global volume—and far less revenue—comes from Europe, the region has outsized importance to Yoshino and his deputies. Why? Because Honda has no safe harbor if its sales in the United States begin to flag, as some analysts expect. The company earns some 90% of its profits in America, a far higher percentage than other Japanese carmakers. "Honda is the least globally diverse Japanese automobile manufacturer," says Chris Redl, director of equity research at UBS Warburg's office in Tokyo. "It's a minor problem for now, but with the U.S. market heading down, it could become a major problem." So a closer look at the cost leadership and differentiation approach at Honda Europe, their confident answer, is as follows.

COST LEADERSHIP

Honda's struggles in Europe today are partly the result of a key strategic error it made when it started making cars in Britain 10 years ago. Company officials didn't foresee the huge runup in the value of the British pound against Europe's single currency, the euro, which made its cars more expensive than competing models manufactured on the Continent. Subpar sales cut output in Britain last year to levels near 50% of capacity: It's impossible to make money at that production level. "Europe is definitely an Achilles' heel for Honda," says Toru Shimano, an analyst at Okasan Securities Co. in Tokyo.

So Honda is increasing purchases of cheaper parts from suppliers outside Britain and moving swiftly to freshen its lineup. Earlier this year, a remodeled and roomier five-door Civic hatchback with improved fuel efficiency rolled off production lines in Britain. To goose output at its British operations, Honda will start exporting perky three-door Civic sedans built at its newest plant to the United States and Japan this year. It also plans to export its British-made CR-V compact SUV to America to augment the Japan-made CR-Vs now being sold there.

DIFFERENTIATION

All of that will help, but Honda's big issue is the hole in its lineup: subcompacts. While 1-liter-engine cars sell poorly in the United States, Europeans and Japanese can't get enough of them. "Honda does not have a product for Europe yet," says UBS Warburg's Redl. It missed out with its 1-liter Logo. "It didn't stand out from the crowd," Yoshino admits.

So the Logo is history, and Honda's new salvation in Europe, due to launch first in Japan on June 21, is an all-new five-door hatchback called the Fit. At 1.3 liters, its engine outpowers Toyota's competing Vitz-class line of cars. Honda says the sporty Fit also boasts a number of nifty features. The only one it would confirm, however, is that owners will be able to flatten all four seats, including the driver's, at the flick of a switch—a selling point for youths keen to load bikes or sleep in it on long road trips.

Source: "Honda's Weak Spot: Europe," *BusinessWeek,* June 11, 2001.

New Entrants Competing on Price Must Face an Entrenched Cost Leader without the Experience to Replicate Every Cost Advantage   EasyJet, a British startup with a Southwest Airlines copycat strategy, entered the European airline market with much fanfare in 2000 with low priced, city-to-city, no frills flights.

EXHIBIT 7–2 **Evaluating a Business's Cost Leadership Opportunities**

Source: Adapted with permission of *Harvard Business School on Managing the Value Chain* (Cambridge: HBS Press, 2000).

A. Skills and Resources That Foster Cost Leadership

Sustained capital investment and access to capital.
Process engineering skills.
Intense supervision of labor or core technical operations.
Products or services designed for ease of manufacture or delivery.
Low-cost distribution system.

B. Organizational Requirements to Support and Sustain Cost Leadership Activities

Tight cost control.
Frequent, detailed control reports.
Continuous improvement and benchmarking orientation.
Structured organization and responsibilities.
Incentives based on meeting strict, usually quantitative targets.

C. Examples of Ways Businesses Achieve Competitive Advantage via Cost Leadership

Technology Development	Process innovations that lower production costs.	Product redesign to reduce the number of components.		
Human Resource Management	Safety training for all employees reduces absenteeism, downtime, and accidents.			
General Administration	Reduced levels of management cuts corporate overhead.	Computerized, integrated information system reduces errors and administrative costs.		
Procurement	Favorable long-term contracts; captive suppliers or key customer for supplier.			
	Global, online suppliers provide automatic restocking of orders based on our sales.	Economy of scale in plant reduces equipment costs and depreciation.	Computerized routing lowers transportation expense.	Cooperative advertising with distributors creates local cost advantage in buying media space and time.	Subcontracted service technicians repair product correctly the first time or they bear all costs.
	Inbound logistics	Operations	Outbound logistics	Marketing and Sales	Service

Profit margin

Analysts caution that by the time you read this, British Airways, KLM's no-frills off-shoot, Buzz, and Virgin Express will simply match fares on EasyJet's key routes and let high landing fees and flight delays take their toll on the British upstart.

Low-Cost Advantages Should Lessen the Attractiveness of Substitute Products A serious concern of any business is the threat of a substitute product in which buyers can meet their original need. Low-cost advantages allow the holder to resist this happening because it allows them to remain competitive even against desirable substitutes and it allows them to lessen concerns about price facing an inferior, lower priced substitute.

Higher Margins Allow Low-Cost Producers to Withstand Supplier Cost Increases and Often Gain Supplier Loyalty over Time Sudden, particularly uncontrollable increases in the costs suppliers face can be more easily absorbed by low-cost, higher margin producers. Severe droughts in California quadrupled the price of lettuce—a key restaurant demand. Some chains absorbed the cost; others had to confuse customers with a "lettuce tax." Furthermore, chains that worked well with produce suppliers gained a loyal, cooperative "partner" for possible assistance in a future, competitive situation.

Once managers identify opportunities to create cost advantage–based strategies, they must consider whether key risks inherent in cost leadership are present in a way that may mediate sustained success. The key risks with which they must be concerned are discussed next.

Many Cost-Saving Activities Are Easily Duplicated   Computerizing certain order entry functions among hazardous waste companies gave early adopters lower sales costs and better customer service for a brief time. Rivals quickly adapted, adding similar capabilities with similar impacts on their costs.

Exclusive Cost Leadership Can Become a Trap   Firms that emphasize lowest price and can offer it via cost advantages where product differentiation is increasingly not considered must truly be convinced of the sustainability of those advantages. Particularly with commodity-type products, the low-cost leader seeking to sustain a margin superior to lesser rivals may encounter increasing customer pressure for lower prices with great damage to both leader and lesser players.

Obsessive Cost Cutting Can Shrink Other Competitive Advantages Involving Key Product Attributes   Intense cost scrutiny can build margin, but it can reduce opportunities for or investment in innovation— processes and products. Similarly, such scrutiny can lead to the use of inferior raw materials, processes, or activities that were previously viewed by customers as a key attribute of the original products. Some mail-order computer companies that sought to maintain or enhance cost advantages found reductions in telephone service personnel and automation of that function backfiring with a drop in demand for their products even though their low prices were maintained.

Cost Differences Often Decline over Time   As products age, competitors learn how to match cost advantages. Absolute volumes sold often decline. Market channels and suppliers mature. Buyers become more knowledgeable. All of these factors present opportunities to lessen the value or presence of earlier cost advantages. Said another way, cost advantages that are not sustainable over a period of time are risky.

Once business managers have evaluated the cost structure of their value chain, determined activities that provide competitive cost advantages, and considered their inherent risks, they start choosing the business's strategy. Those managers concerned with differentiation-based strategies, or those seeking optimum performance incorporating both sources of competitive advantage, move to evaluating their business's sources of differentiation.

Evaluating Differentiation Opportunities

Differentiation requires that the business have sustainable advantages that allow it to provide buyers with something uniquely valuable to them. A successful differentiation strategy allows the business to provide a product or service of perceived higher value to buyers at a "differentiation cost" below the "value premium" to the buyers. In other words, the buyer feels the additional cost to buy the product or service is well below what the product or service is worth compared to other available alternatives.

Differentiation usually arises from one or more activities in the value chain that create a unique value important to buyers. Perrier's control of a carbonated water spring in France, Stouffer's frozen food packaging and sauce technology, Apple's highly integrated chip designs in its Mac computers, American Greeting Card's automated inventory

EXHIBIT 7–3   Evaluating a Business's Differentiation Opportunities

Source: Adapted with permission of *Harvard Business School on Managing the Value Chain* (Cambridge; HBS Press, 2000).

A. Skills and Resources That Foster Differentiation

Strong marketing abilities.
Product engineering.
Creative talent and flair.
Strong capabilities in basic research.
Corporate reputation for quality or technical leadership.
Long tradition in an industry or unique combination of skills drawn from other businesses.
Strong cooperation from channels.
Strong cooperation from suppliers of major components of the product or service.

B. Organizational Requirements to Support and Sustain Differentiation Activities

Strong coordination among functions in R&D, product development, and marketing.
Subjective measurement and incentives instead of quantitative measures.
Amenities to attract highly skilled labor, scientists, and creative people.
Tradition of closeness to key customers.
Some personnel skilled in sales and operations—technical and marketing.

C. Examples of Ways Businesses Achieve Competitive Advantage via Differentiation

						Profit margin
Technology Development	Cutting-edge production technology and product features to maintain a "distinct" image and actual product.					
Human Resource Management	Programs to ensure technical competence of sales staff and a marketing orientation of service personnel.					
General Administration	Comprehensive, personalized database to build knowledge of groups of customers and individual buyers to be used in "customizing" how products are sold, serviced, and replaced.					
Procurement	Quality control presence at key supplier facilities; work with suppliers' new product development activities					
	Purchase superior quality, well-known components, raising the quality and image of final products.	Careful inspection of products at each step in production to improve product performance and lower defect rate.	JIT coordination with buyers; use of own or captive transportation service to ensure timeliness.	Expensive, informative advertising and promotion to build brand image.	Allowing service personnel considerable discretion to credit customers for repairs.	
	Inbound logistics	Operations	Outbound logistics	Marketing and Sales	Service	

system for retailers, and Federal Express's customer service capabilities are all examples of sustainable advantages around which successful differentiation strategies have been built. A business can achieve differentiation by performing its existing value activities or reconfiguring in some unique way. And the sustainability of that differentiation will depend on two things—a continuation of its high perceived value to buyers and a lack of imitation by competitors.

Exhibit 7–3 suggests key skills that managers should ensure are present to support an emphasis on differentiation. Examples of value chain activities that provide a differentiation advantage are also provided.

Strategists examining their business's value chain for differentiation advantages evaluate the sustainability of those advantages by *benchmarking* (refer to Chapter 5 for a discussion of this comparison technique) their business against key competitors and by considering the impact of any differentiation advantage on the five forces in their business's competitive environment. Sustainable activities that provide one or more of the following opportunities relative to key industry forces should become the basis for differentiation aspects of the business's competitive strategy:

Rivalry Is Reduced When a Business Successfully Differentiates Itself   BMW's new Z23, made in Greer, South Carolina, does not compete with Saturns made in central Tennessee. A Harvard education does not compete with a local technical school. Both situations involve the same basic needs, transportation or education. However, one rival has clearly differentiated itself from others in the minds of certain buyers. In so doing, they do not have to respond competitively to that competitor.

Buyers Are Less Sensitive to Prices for Effectively Differentiated Products   The Highlands Inn in Carmel, California, and the Ventana Inn along the Big Sur charge a minimum of $600 and 900, respectively, per night for a room with a kitchen, fireplace, hot tub, and view. Other places are available along this beautiful stretch of California's spectacular coastline, but occupancy rates at these two locations remain over 90 percent. Why? You can't get a better view and a more relaxed, spectacular setting to spend a few days on the Pacific Coast. Similarly, buyers of differentiated products tolerate price increases low-cost–oriented buyers would not accept. The former become very loyal to certain brands.

Brand Loyalty Is Hard for New Entrants to Overcome   Many new beers are brought to market in the United States, but Budweiser continues to gain market share. Why? Brand loyalty is hard to overcome! And Anheuser-Busch has been clever to extend its brand loyalty from its core brand into newer niches, like nonalcohol brews, that other potential entrants have pioneered.

Managers examining differentiation-based advantages must take potential risks into account as they commit their business to these advantages. Some of the more common ways risks arise are discussed next.

Imitation Narrows Perceived Differentiation, Rendering Differentiation Meaningless   AMC pioneered the Jeep passenger version of a truck 40 years ago. Ford created the Explorer, or luxury utility vehicle, in 1990. It took luxury car features and put them inside a jeep. Ford's payoff was substantial. The Explorer has become Ford's most popular domestic vehicle. However, virtually every vehicle manufacturer offered a luxury utility in 2003, with customers beginning to be hard pressed to identify clear distinctions between lead models. Ford's Explorer managers were looking for a new business strategy for the next decade that relied on new sources of differentiation and placed greater emphasis on low-cost components in their value chain.

Technological Changes That Nullify Past Investments or Learning   The Swiss controlled over 95 percent of the world's watch market into the 1970s. The bulk of the craftspeople, technology, and infrastructure resided in Switzerland. U.S.-based Texas Instruments decided to experiment with the use of its digital technology in watches. Swiss producers were not interested, but Japan's SEIKO and others were. In 2005, the Swiss will make less than 5 percent of the world's watches.

The Cost Difference between Low-Cost Competitors and the Differentiated Business Becomes Too Great for Differentiation to Hold Brand Loyalty.   Buyers may begin to choose to sacrifice some of the features, services, or image possessed by the differentiated business for large cost savings. The rising cost of a college education, particularly at several "premier" institutions, has caused many students to opt for lower-cost destinations that offer very similar courses without image, frills, and professors that seldom teach undergraduate students anyway.

Evaluating Speed as a Competitive Advantage

While most telecommunication companies have used the last decade to leap aboard the information superhighway, GTE continued its impressive turnaround focusing on its core business—providing local telephone services. Long lagging behind the Baby Bells in profitability and efficiency, GTE has emphasized improving its poor customer service throughout the decade. The service was so bad in Santa Monica, California, that officials once tried to remove GTE as the local phone company. Candidly saying "we were the pits," new CEO Chuck Lee largely did away with its old system of taking customer service requests by writing them down and passing them along for resolution. Now, using personal communication services and specially designed software, service reps can solve 70 percent of all problems on the initial call—triple the success rate at the beginning of the last decade. Repair workers meanwhile plan their schedules on laptops, cutting downtime and speeding responses. CEO Lee has spent $1.5 billion on reengineering that slashed 17,000 jobs, replaced people with technology, and prioritized *speed* as the defining feature of GTE's business practices.

Speed, or rapid response to customer requests or market and technological changes, has become a major source of competitive advantage for numerous firms in today's intensely competitive global economy. Speed is certainly a form of differentiation, but it is more than that. Speed involves the *availability of a rapid response* to a customer by providing current products quicker, accelerating new product development or improvement, quickly adjusting production processes, and making decisions quickly. While low cost and differentiation may provide important competitive advantages, managers in tomorrow's successful companies will base their strategies on creating speed-based competitive advantages. Exhibit 7–4 describes and illustrates key skills and organizational requirements that are associated with speed-based competitive advantage. Jack Welch, now retired, the CEO who transformed General Electric from a fading company into one of Wall Street's best performers over the last 20 years, had this to say about speed:

> Speed is really the driving force that everyone is after. Faster products, faster product cycles to market. Better response time to customers. . . . Satisfying customers, getting faster communications, moving with more agility, all these things are easier when one is small. And these are all characteristics one needs in a fast-moving global environment.[2]

Speed-based competitive advantages can be created around several activities:

Customer Responsiveness   All consumers have encountered hassles, delays, and frustration dealing with various businesses from time to time. The same holds true when dealing business to business. Quick response with answers, information, and solutions to mistakes can become the basis for competitive advantage . . . one that builds customer loyalty quickly.

[2] "Jack Welch: A CEO Who Can't Be Cloned," *BusinessWeek,* September 17, 2001.

EXHIBIT 7–4 **Evaluating a Business's Rapid Response (Speed) Opportunities**

A. Skills and Resources That Foster Speed

Process engineering skills.
Excellent inbound and outbound logistics.
Technical people in sales and customer service.
High levels of automation.
Corporate reputation for quality or technical leadership.
Flexible manufacturing capabilities.
Strong downstream partners.
Strong cooperation from suppliers of major components of the product or service.

B. Organizational Requirements to Support and Sustain Rapid Response Activities

Strong coordination among functions in R&D, product development, and marketing.
Major emphasis on customer satisfaction in incentive programs.
Strong delegation to operating personnel.
Tradition of closeness to key customers.
Some personnel skilled in sales and operations—technical and marketing.
Empowered customer service personnel.

C. Examples of Ways Businesses Achieve Competitive Advantage via Speed

Technology Development	Use of companywide technology sharing activities and autonomous product development teams to speed new product development.					
Human Resource Management	Develop self-managed work teams and decision making at the lowest levels to increase responsiveness.					
General Administration	Highly automated and integrated information processing system. Include major buyers in the "system" on a real-time basis.					
Procurement	Preapproved, online suppliers integrated into production.					
	Working very closely with suppliers to include their choice of warehouse location to minimize delivery time.	Standardize dies, components, and production equipment to allow quick changeover to new or special orders.	JIT delivery plus partnering with express mail services to ensure very rapid delivery.	Use of laptops linked directly to operations to speed the order process and shorten the sales cycle.	Locate service technicians at customer facilities that are geographically close.	Profit margin
	Inbound logistics	Operations	Outbound logistics	Marketing and Sales	Service	

Product Development Cycles Japanese car makers have focused intensely on the time it takes to create a new model because several experienced disappointing sales growth in the last decade in Europe and North America competing against new vehicles like Ford's Explorer and Renault's Megane. VW had recently conceived, prototyped, produced, and marketed a totally new 4-wheel-drive car in Europe within 12 months. Honda, Toyota, and Nissan lowered their product development cycle from 24 months to 9 months from conception to production. This capability is old hat to 3M Corporation, which is so successful at speedy product development that one-fourth of its sales and profits each year are from products that didn't exist five years earlier.

Product or Service Improvements   Like development time, companies that can rapidly adapt their products or services and do so in a way that benefits their customers or creates new customers have a major competitive advantage over rivals that cannot do this.

Speed in Delivery or Distribution   Firms that can get you what you need when you need it, even when that is tomorrow, realize that buyers have come to expect that level of responsiveness. Federal Express's success reflects the importance customers place on speed in inbound and outbound logistics.

Information Sharing and Technology   Speed in sharing information that becomes the basis for decisions, actions, or other important activities taken by a customer, supplier, or partner has become a major source of competitive advantage for many businesses. Telecommunications, the Internet, and networks are but a part of a vast infrastructure that is being used by knowledgeable managers to rebuild or create value in their businesses via information sharing.

These rapid response capabilities create competitive advantages in several ways. They create a way to lessen rivalry because they have *availability* of something that a rival may not have. It can allow the business to charge buyers more, engender loyalty, or otherwise enhance the business's position relative to its buyers. Particularly where impressive customer response is involved, businesses can generate supplier cooperation and concessions since their business ultimately benefits from increased revenue. Finally, substitute products and new entrants find themselves trying to keep up with the rapid changes rather than introducing them. Exhibit 7–5, Strategy in Action, provides examples of how "speed" has become a source of competitive advantage for several well-known companies around the world.

While the notion of speed-based competitive advantage is exciting, it has risks managers must consider. First, speeding up activities that haven't been conducted in a fashion that prioritizes rapid response should only be done after considerable attention to training, reorganization, and/or reengineering. Second, some industries—stable, mature ones that have very minimal levels of change—may not offer much advantage to the firm that introduces some forms of rapid response. Customers in such settings may prefer the slower pace or the lower costs currently available or they may have long time frames in purchasing such that speed is not that important to them.

Evaluating Market Focus as a Way to Competitive Advantage

Small companies, at least the better ones, usually thrive because they serve narrow market niches. This is usually called *focus,* the extent to which a business concentrates on a narrowly defined market. Take the example of Soho Beverages, a business former Pepsi manager Tom Cox bought from Seagram after Seagram had acquired it and was unable to make it thrive. The tiny brand, once a healthy niche product in New York and a few other east coast locations, muddled within Seagrams because its sales force was unused to selling in delis. Cox was able to double sales in one year. He did this on a lean marketing budget that didn't include advertising or database marketing. He hired Korean- and Arabic-speaking college students and had his people walk into practically every deli in Manhattan in order to reacquaint owners with the brand, spot consumption trends, and take orders. He provided rapid stocking services to all Manhattan-area delis, regardless of size. The business has continued sales growth at over 50 percent per year. Why? Cox says "It is attributable to focusing on a niche market, delis; differentiating the product and its sales force; achieving low costs in promotion and delivery; and making rapid, immediate response to any deli owner request its normal practice."

Two things are important in this example. First, this business focused on a narrow niche market in which to build a strong competitive advantage. But focus alone was

SPEED IN DISTRIBUTION AND DELIVERY

BusinessWeek

Clad in a blue lab coat, a technician in Singapore waves a scanner like a wand over a box of newly minted computer chips. With that simple act, he sets in motion a delivery process that is efficient and automated, almost to the point of magic. This cavernous National Semiconductor Corp. (NSM) warehouse was designed and built by shipping wizards at United Parcel Service Inc. (UPS). It is UPS's computers that speed the box of chips to a loading dock, then to truck, to plane, and to truck once again. In just 12 hours, the chips will reach one of National's customers, a PC maker half a world away in Silicon Valley. Throughout the journey, electronic tags embedded in the chips will let the customer track the order with accuracy down to about three feet. In the two years since UPS and National starting this relationship, the team in brown has slashed National Semiconductor's inventory and shipment costs by 15% while reducing the time from factory floor to customer site by 60%.

INFORMATION SHARING AND TECHNOLOGY

Meanwhile, in the Old Economy, UPS is winning giant customers such as Ford Motor Co., which uses UPS's computerized logistics to route cars more efficiently to its dealerships. In a year, Ford has reduced delivery times by 26% and saved $240 million, says Frank M. Taylor, Ford's vice president for material planning and logistics. "Speed is the mindset at UPS. They'll meet a deadline at any cost," Taylor says. UPS Chairman James P. Kelly chalks it up to the company's slow-and-steady work ethic. "We've spent the past seven years studying where we should be long-term," he says.

While FedEx backpedals in logistics, UPS is in growth mode. And it has figured out how to manage distribution for many companies at one central location—a massive warehouse in Louisville, Ky. Here, UPS handles storage, tracking, repair, and shipping for clients such as Sprint, Hewlett-Packard (HWP), and Nike (NKE) using a mix of high- and low-tech methods. Computerized forklifts scan in new inventory while people in sneakers dash across the vast warehouse to pluck products, box them, and ship them out. In short, UPS uses expensive technology only where it cuts costs.

SPEED IN NEW PRODUCT DEVELOPMENT AND MANAGEMENT DECISION MAKING

Recently retired Volkswagen CEO Ferdinand Piëch has every reason to feel satisfied. The Austrian engineer and scion of one of Europe's most noted automotive dynasties can boast of one of the great turnarounds in automotive history, based on his attention to new product development combined with speed of decision making. Unlike many other auto chiefs, he called the shots on product design and engineering. And if you worked for Dr. Piëch, you had better get it right. In Wolfsburg, executives used to joke that PEP, the acronym for the product development process (*Produkt entwicklungsprozess*) really stood for *Piëch entscheidet persönlich*—Piëch decides himself. And he did it fast. He is said to have sketched out the Audi's all-wheel-drive system on the back of an envelope.

Obsession with detail and speed are key reasons VW has succeeded so brilliantly reviving its fortunes in the United States, where the VW brand was road kill a decade ago. Last year, VW and Audi sales in the United States jumped 14%, to 437,000 units, for a combined 2.5% market share. That's up from a microscopic 0.5% in 1995. Although VW trails its Japanese rivals, it's the only European mass-market carmaker in the United States. Volkswagen's four main brands—VW (VLKAY), Audi, Seat, and Skoda—have taken 19% of the European auto market, a gain of some three points in eight years, mostly at the expense of General Motors Corp. (GM) and Ford. Not bad for a company that eight years ago suffered from quality problems and a paucity of hit models. In South America, VW vehicles account for one-quarter of car sales, and in China, one-half.

CUSTOMER RESPONSIVENESS

Vodafone seemed to be losing ground to aggressive newcomers when Chris Gent, who had been developing Vodafone's international portfolio, took over as CEO in early 1997. He immediately canned the old ad agency and set about building a network of 250 company stores in towns and villages throughout Britain. The idea: to build brand recognition and neighborhood service that would keep customers, especially business users, loyal to Vodafone. Gent's timing couldn't have been better. He had Vodafone ready just as Britain's market was taking off. In the last two years, the combination of lower prices and a booming economy have fueled cell-phone mania in Britain—a phenomenon that Gent and others expect to hit the U.S. soon. In one year, British subscriptions grew by 53%, to 13 million, or 22.4% of the population. Vodafone became an instantly established cell phone provider due to its speed of customer responsiveness through its 250+ company-owned stores.

Source: "UPS vs. FedEx: Ground Wars," *BusinessWeek,* May 21, 2001; "Vodaphone's Wireless Warrior," *BusinessWeek,* May 21, 2001; "Volkswagen," *BusinessWeek,* July 23, 2001.

not enough to build competitive advantage. Rather, Cox created several value chain activities that achieved differentiation, low-cost, and rapid response competitive advantages within this niche market that would be hard for other firms, particularly mass market-oriented firms, to replicate.

Focus allows some businesses to compete on the basis of low cost, differentiation, and rapid response against much larger businesses with greater resources. Focus lets a business "learn" its target customers—their needs, special considerations they want accommodated—and establish personal relationships in ways that "differentiate" the smaller firm or make it more valuable to the target customer. Low costs can also be achieved filling niche needs in a buyer's operations that larger rivals either do not want to bother with or cannot do as cost effectively. Cost advantage often centers around the high level of customized service the focused, smaller business can provide. And perhaps the greatest competitive weapon that can arise is rapid response. With enhanced knowledge of its customers and intricacies of their operations, the small, focused company builds up organizational knowledge about timing sensitive ways to work with a customer. Often the needs of that narrow set of customers represent a large part of the small, focused business's revenues. Exhibit 7–6, Strategy in Action, illustrates how Sweden's Scania has become the global leader in heavy trucks via the focused application of low cost, differentiation, and speed.

The risk of focus is that you attract major competitors that have waited for your business to "prove" the market. Domino's proved that a huge market for pizza delivery existed and now faces serious challenges. Likewise, publicly traded focused companies become takeover targets for large firms seeking to fill out a product portfolio. And perhaps the greatest risk of all is slipping into the illusion that it is focus itself, and not some special form of low cost, differentiation, or rapid response, that is creating the business's success.

Managers evaluating opportunities to build competitive advantage should link strategies to value chain activities that exploit low cost, differentiation, and rapid response competitive advantages. When advantageous, they should consider ways to use focus to leverage these advantages. One way business managers can enhance their likelihood of identifying these opportunities is to consider several different "generic" industry environments from the perspective of the typical value chain activities most often linked to sustained competitive advantages in those unique industry situations. The next section discusses five key generic industry environments and the value chain activities most associated with success.

SELECTED INDUSTRY ENVIRONMENTS AND BUSINESS STRATEGY CHOICES

The analysis and choice of the ways a business will seek to build competitive advantage can be enhanced when managers take industry conditions into account. Chapter 3 discussed ways to examine industry conditions, so we do not repeat that here. Likewise, Chapter 5 showed how the market life cycle concept can be used to examine business strengths. What is important to recognize as managers evaluate opportunities to emphasize a narrow set of core competencies and potential competitive advantages is that different sets appear to be more useful in different, unique industry environments. We examine five "typical" industry settings and opportunities for generating competitive advantages that strategists should look for in their deliberations. Three of these five settings relate to industry life cycle. Managers use these as ways to evaluate their value

Global Strategy in Action
Sweden's Scania Combines Low Cost, Speed, Differentiation, and Focus to Consistently Beat Other Global Truck Manufacturers

Exhibit 7–6

BusinessWeek The preeminent consulting firm McKinsey and Company recently studied the global truck industry to understand which producers had the strongest competitive advantages and why they did. It quickly became a study of the Swedish firm, Scania, and its long time rival, Volvo. On an index that measured value added per hour worked, Scania scored 100 with Volvo close behind. The best Japanese, U.S., and German truck makers trailed by more than 25 points.

Leif Ostling, Scania's burly CEO, attributes the business's success to a determination to stick to its strategy of concentrating on heavy trucks, and rely on its own resources to deliver quality products commanding market-leading prices. McKinsey's analysis broadens the explanation as it sought an answer to how Scania had arrived at its enviable position and what its prospects were for remaining a world leader. McKinsey concluded:

1. Benchmarking: Intense competition between Scania and Volvo in tiny Sweden prepared them both to compete better than other rivals in the global market because the truck industry is much less international than the car industry, leaving newer rivals less competitive even on their home turf. Scania and Volvo have been benchmarking each other for years.

2. Low cost: Scania uses a building principle of maximization of standardization of parts across many brands while also leading the industry in responding to the demand for customization of each vehicle that is sold. How? While every truck is a unique order, Scania uses less than 20,000 components to build their truck compared to 25,000 for Volvo and 40,000 for Mercedes. Fewer parts mean lower development costs, lower manufacturing costs, and lower distribution costs.

3. Speed: Scania produces all main components in house, which allows them to maximize integration of design, development, and production, thus saving time, allowing for greater customization, and fewer parts.

4. Differentiation: There is strong emphasis on customization of each vehicle: "We have to supply a specific truck to a customer's specific needs," said Kaj Holmelius, head of chassis development, pointing to a production line, "Each of these is for a specific order and almost every one will be different in some way when they come off the end of the line. At the same time we want to get as large volumes as possible for individual components."

5. Focus: Scania will not expand into lighter trucks because it would dilute the efficiencies it has wrung out of its modular system. It has no plans to enter the North American market because of very different truck specifications and lower margins. The intention is to grow chiefly in Central and Eastern Europe and in the Pacific region. "We will stick to what we know how to do in limited, margin favorable markets," said Ostling.

The bottom line is, Scania has built a variety of sustainable competitive advantages that promise to keep it on top the world heavy truck market for a long time.

Sources: By Stanley Reed, with Ariane Sains, in Stockholm, "The Young Wallenbergs," *Business Week* International Edition: October 20, 1997; "Scania Pulls Ahead of the Crowd," *Financial Times,* October 16, 1995.

chain activities and then select the ones around which it is most critical to build competitive advantage.[3]

Competitive Advantage in Emerging Industries

Emerging industries are newly formed or re-formed industries that typically are created by technological innovation, newly emerging customer needs, or other economic or sociological changes. Emerging industries of the last decade have been the Internet browser, fiber optics, solar heating, cellular telephone, and on-line services industries.

From the standpoint of strategy formulation, the essential characteristic of an emerging industry is that there are no "rules of the game." The absence of rules presents both a risk and an opportunity—a wise strategy positions the firm to favorably shape the emerging industry's rules.

[3] These industry characterizations draw heavily on the work of Michael E. Porter, *Competitive Advantage: Creating and Sustaining Superior Performance* (New York: Free Press, 1985).

Business strategies must be shaped to accommodate the following characteristics of markets in emerging industries.

Technologies that are mostly proprietary to the pioneering firms and technological uncertainty about how product standardization will unfold.

Competitor uncertainty because of inadequate information about competitors, buyers, and the timing of demand.

High initial costs but steep cost declines as the experience curve takes effect.

Few entry barriers, which often spurs the formation of many new firms.

First-time buyers requiring initial inducement to purchase and customers confused by the availability of a number of nonstandard products.

Inability to obtain raw materials and components until suppliers gear up to meet the industry's needs.

Need for high-risk capital because of the industry's uncertainty prospects.

For success in this industry setting, business strategies require one or more of these features:

1. The ability to *shape the industry's structure* based on the timing of entry, reputation, success in related industries or technologies, and role in industry associations.

2. The ability to *rapidly improve product quality* and performance features.

3. *Advantageous relationships* with key suppliers and promising distribution channels.

4. The ability to *establish the firm's technology as the dominant one* before technological uncertainty decreases.

5. The early acquisition of *a core group of loyal customers* and then the expansion of that customer base through model changes, alternative pricing, and advertising.

6. The ability to *forecast future competitors* and the strategies they are likely to employ.

A firm that has had repeated successes with business in emerging industries is 3M Corporation. In each of the last 20 years, over 25 percent of 3M's annual sales have come from products that did not exist 5 years earlier. Start-up companies enhance their success by having experienced entrepreneurs at the helm, a knowledgeable management team and board of directors, and patient sources of venture capital. Amazon.com's dramatic debut on Wall Street symbolically ushering in the emerging E-commerce industry era for investors will certainly lead to questions about the lasting competitive advantage at Amazon.com. Exhibit 7–7, Strategy in Action, examines whether Amazon.com has the capacity to prevail in this emerging industry.

Competitive Advantage in the Transition to Industry Maturity

As an industry evolves, its rate of growth eventually declines. This "transition to maturity" is accompanied by several changes in its competitive environment:

Competition for market share becomes more intense as firms in the industry are forced to achieve sales growth at one another's expense.

Firms in the industry sell increasingly to experienced, repeat buyers that are now making choices among known alternatives.

Strategy in Action
Does Amazon.com Have a Sustainable Competitive Advantage
in the Emerging "E-Commerce" Industry?

Exhibit 7–7

BusinessWeek When giant retailer Wal-Mart Stores Inc. sued upstart Internet bookseller Amazon.com Inc. in late 1998, jaws dropped. Wal-Mart accused Amazon of raiding its executives to steal its computerized merchandising and distribution trade secrets. The amazing part: Wal-Mart said tiny, money-losing Amazon had caused it "economic damage" and continues to do so. Regardless of the outcome, this case may well signal a watershed in the history of the Internet: the moment when cyberspace retailers began to turn the tables on earthly ones. Indeed, Amazon is blazing a trail in the world of commerce where no merchant has gone before.

Can it shape the E-commerce industry structure? By pioneering—and possibly perfecting—the art of selling on-line, it is forcing the titans of retail to scramble onto the Net. More than that it's jolting them into rethinking whether their traditional advantages—physical size, mass-media branding, and even the sensory appeal of shopping in stores—will be enough to thrive in the New Economy. Says Duke University marketing professor Martha Rogers: "Amazon is an example of how an upstart can redefine its whole industry."

Can it rapidly improve product quality & features? Consider this: Amazon offers an easily searchable trove of 3.1 million titles—15 times more than any bookstore on the planet and without the costly overhead of multimillion-dollar buildings and scads of store clerks. That paves the way for each of its 1,600 employees to generate, on average, $375,000 in annual revenues—almost four times that of No. 1 bricks-and-mortar bookseller Barnes & Noble Inc.'s 27,000 employees. It has 24 inventory turns per year versus 3 for Barnes & Noble, and high cash flow versus low cash flow at B&N.

Can its technology become the dominant one? Amazon's cutting-edge technology gives it a leg up, too, by automatically analyzing past purchases to make recommendations customized to each buyer—a trick that confounds 20th century mass marketing. And with a single mouse click, an order can be placed on its Web site, making shopping a friendly, frictionless, even fun experience that can take less time than finding a parking space at the mall.

Does it have a core group of loyal customers that might buy other things? It has a two-year head start, unheard of in the software industry, on key software that handles millions of transactions and personalizes the customers' experience. It gathers instant information on customer preferences to help understand what else [books and other things] they might want to buy. "We want Amazon.com to be the right store for you as an individual," says founder Jeffrey Bezos. "If we have 4.5 million customers, we should have 4.5 million stores."

While these observations seemed favorable, Merrill Lynch analyst Jonathan Cohen was not. "The company has been able to show it can sell lots of books for less without making money," he said, "and now it has shown it can sell lots of music without making money." Forrester Research CEO George Colony, pointing out entrenched rivals in every sector Amazon.com seeks to enter/redefine, declared that it would soon become known as "Amazon.toast."

Fast forward to late 2001. On any other day, it would've been big news. Pressured to show a path to profits after years of losses, Amazon.com Inc. was to announce that discounter Target Corp. would open an online store on Amazon's home page this fall. Target would pay the e-tailer to sell products such as apparel and jewelry, and would hire it to run the Target Web site. For Amazon, the timing seemed perfect since the deal promised millions in high-margin business. Just one problem: The news crossed the wires at 8:39 A.M. September 11, six minutes before the first hijacked jet crashed into the World Trade Center.

Far from getting a boost from the scarcely noticed deal, Amazon found itself deeper in the soup on concern that Amazon would run out of cash by early 2002. Says Safa Rashtchy, an analyst with U.S. Bancorp Piper Jaffray: "They have to show the Street they can make money." So, Amazon increasingly aims to get other retailers to sell their wares on the Amazon site. "We want to be the place for people to find and discover anything they want to buy online," says Bezos. "But we've never said we had to do it all."

Maybe so. Still, it's a big comedown: Amazon is attempting to become less of an online department store and more a retailing back office. The upstart many people thought would knock off brick-and-mortar giants now aims to be their best friend. What a surprise that one of its major clients would be Wal-Mart. These days, servicing other retailers using its existing logistics, customer service, and Web site operations looks like a surer route to profits than selling lawn furniture. Says Jupiter Media Metrix Inc. analyst Ken Cassar: "Amazon has come to the realization it can't be the dominant force in retail it once hoped."

Source: "Amazon.com: The Wild World of E-commerce," *BusinessWeek,* December 14, 1998. p. 106; "Amazon.com," December 28, 2001.

Competition becomes more oriented to cost and service as knowledgeable buyers expect similar price and product features.

Industry capacity "tops out" as sales growth ceases to cover up poorly planned expansions.

New products and new applications are harder to come by.

International competition increases as cost pressures lead to overseas production advantages.

Profitability falls, often permanently, as a result of pressure to lower prices and the increased costs of holding or building market share.

These changes necessitate a fundamental strategic reassessment. Strategy elements of successful firms in maturing industries often include:

1. *Pruning the product line* by dropping unprofitable product models, sizes, and options from the firm's product mix.

2. *Emphasis on process innovation* that permits low-cost product design, manufacturing methods, and distribution synergy.

3. *Emphasis on cost reduction* through exerting pressure on suppliers for lower prices, switching to cheaper components, introducing operational efficiencies, and lowering administrative and sales overhead.

4. *Careful buyer selection* to focus on buyers that are less aggressive, more closely tied to the firm, and able to buy more from the firm.

5. *Horizontal integration* to acquire rival firms whose weaknesses can be used to gain a bargain price and are correctable by the acquiring firms.

6. *International expansion* to markets where attractive growth and limited competition still exist and the opportunity for lower-cost manufacturing can influence both domestic and international costs.

Business strategists in maturing industries must avoid several pitfalls. First, they must make a clear choice among the three generic strategies and avoid a middle-ground approach, which would confuse both knowledgeable buyers and the firm's personnel. Second, they must avoid sacrificing market share too quickly for short-term profit. Finally, they must avoid waiting too long to respond to price reductions, retaining unneeded excess capacity, engaging in sporadic or irrational efforts to boost sales, and placing their hopes on "new" products, rather than aggressively selling existing products.

Competitive Advantage in Mature and Declining Industries

Declining industries are those that make products or services for which demand is growing slower than demand in the economy as a whole or is actually declining. This slow growth or decline in demand is caused by technological substitution (such as the substitution of electronic calculators for slide rules), demographic shifts (such as the increase in the number of older people and the decrease in the number of children), and shifts in needs (such as the decreased need for red meat).

Firms in a declining industry should choose strategies that emphasize one or more of the following themes:

Strategy in Action

Penn Racquet Sports Seeks Concentric Diversification as the Answer to Declining Sales in a Declining Industry—Tennis Balls

Exhibit 7–8

BusinessWeek Suppose your industry were in free fall. Yet you were the leader in that industry . . . the strongest! What would you do to find more customers? Would you go global in search of sales? Try the Internet? Refocus your business? How about switching species?

That's the drastic move made by Penn Racquet Sports, the nation's No. 1 maker of tennis balls. Penn recently began marketing its fuzzy orbs to some undeniably loyal customers: dogs. *R. P. Fetchem's* is a traditional tennis ball that has been gussied up as a "natural felt fetch toy" for pooches. "Ten times more people own pets than play tennis," explains Penn President Gregg R. Weida. Tennis may be stalled, but pet-pampering is booming. Human beings will shell out $5.95 a box for doggie pasta and will pay $59.95 for a pet canopy bed. Most important to Penn, they buy toys: Last year, owners lavished $41.7 million on dog toys sold in pet stores. While $5 a can might make tennis players gasp, it's no barrier for dog lovers in search of the perfect treat. New York dog owner Joel Katz didn't balk at the Fetchem's price tag. "This guy will do anything for a ball," he said of his cocker spaniel, Max. "He loves them more than food."

Source: "Now, Tennis Balls Are Chasing the Dogs," *BusinessWeek,* July 13, 1998, p. 138.

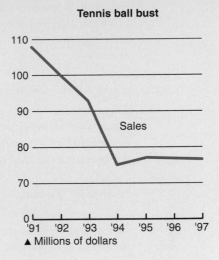

Tennis ball bust

Sales

▲ Millions of dollars

1. *Focus* on segments within the industry that offer a chance for higher growth or a higher return.

2. *Emphasize product innovation and quality improvement,* where this can be done cost effectively, to differentiate the firm from rivals and to spur growth.

3. *Emphasize production and distribution efficiency* by streamlining production, closing marginal productions facilities and costly distribution outlets, and adding effective new facilities and outlets.

4. *Gradually harvest the business*—generate cash by cutting down on maintenance, reducing models, and shrinking channels and make no new investment.

Strategists who incorporate one or more of these themes into the strategy of their business can anticipate relative success, particularly where the industry's decline is slow and smooth and some profitable niches remain. Exhibit 7–8, Strategy in Action, describes how Penn Racquet Sports went from "humans to dogs" to reenergize the declining tennis ball market. At the same time, three pitfalls must be avoided: (1) being overly optimistic about the prospects for a revival of the industry, (2) getting trapped in a profitless war of attrition, and (3) harvesting from a weak position.

Competitive Advantage in Fragmented Industries

A fragmented industry is one in which no firm has a significant market share and can strongly influence industry outcomes. Fragmented industries are found in many areas of the economy and are common in such areas as professional services, retailing, distribution, wood and metal fabrication, and agricultural products. The funeral industry is an example of a highly fragmented industry. Business strategists in fragmented industries pursue low-cost, differentiation, or focus competitive advantages in one of five ways.

Tightly Managed Decentralization

Fragmented industries are characterized by a need for intense local coordination, a local management orientation, high personal service, and local autonomy. Recently, however, successful firms in such industries have introduced a high degree of professionalism into the operations of local managers.

"Formula" Facilities

This alternative, related to the previous one, introduces standardized, efficient, low-cost facilities at multiple locations. Thus, the firm gradually builds a low-cost advantage over localized competitors. Fast-food and motel chains have applied this approach with considerable success.

Increased Value-Added

The products or services of some fragmented industries are difficult to differentiate. In this case, an effective strategy may be to add value by providing more service with the sale or by engaging in some product assembly that is of additional value to the customer.

Specialization

Focus strategies that creatively segment the market can enable firms to cope with fragmentation. Specialization can be pursued by:

1. *Product type.* The firm builds expertise focusing on a narrow range of products or services.

2. *Customer type.* The firm becomes intimately familiar with and serves the needs of a narrow customer segment.

3. *Type of order.* The firm handles only certain kinds of orders, such as small orders, custom orders, or quick turnaround orders.

4. *Geographic area.* The firm blankets or concentrates on a single area.

Although specialization in one or more of these ways can be the basis for a sound focus strategy in a fragmented industry, each of these types of specialization risks limiting the firm's potential sales volume.

Bare Bones/No Frills

Given the intense competition and low margins in fragmented industries, a "bare bones" posture—low overhead, minimum wage employees, tight cost control—may build a sustainable cost advantage in such industries.

Competitive Advantage in Global Industries

A global industry is one that comprises firms whose competitive positions in major geographic or national markets are fundamentally affected by their overall global competitive positions. To avoid strategic disadvantages, firms in global industries are virtually required to compete on a worldwide basis. Oil, steel, automobiles, apparel, motorcycles, televisions, and computers are examples of global industries.

Global industries have four unique strategy-shaping features:

Differences in prices and costs from country to country due to currency exchange fluctuations, differences in wage and inflation rates, and other economic factors.

Differences in buyer needs across different countries.

Differences in competitors and ways of competing from country to country.

Differences in trade rules and governmental regulations across different countries.

These unique features and the global competition of global industries require that two fundamental components be addressed in the business strategy: (1) the approach used to gain global market coverage and (2) the generic competitive strategy.

Three basic options can be used to pursue global market coverage:

1. *License* foreign firms to produce and distribute the firm's products.

2. *Maintain a domestic production base* and export products to foreign countries.

3. *Establish foreign-based plants and distribution* to compete directly in the markets of one or more foreign countries.

Along with the market coverage decision, strategists must scrutinize the condition of the global industry features identified earlier to choose among four generic global competitive strategies:

1. *Broad-line global competition*—directed at competing worldwide in the full product line of the industry, often with plants in many countries, to achieve differentiation or an overall low-cost position.

2. *Global focus* strategy—targeting a particular segment of the industry for competition on a worldwide basis.

3. *National focus* strategy—taking advantage of differences in national markets that give the firm an edge over global competitors on a nation-by-nation basis.

4. *Protected niche* strategy—seeking out countries in which governmental restraints exclude or inhibit global competitors or allow concessions, or both, that are advantageous to localized firms.

Competing in global industries is an increasing reality for many U.S. firms. Strategists must carefully match their skills and resources with global industry structure and conditions in selecting the most appropriate strategy option.

In conclusion, the analysis and choice of business strategy involves three basic considerations. First, strategists must recognize that their overall choice revolves around three sources of competitive advantage that require total, consistent commitment. Second, strategists must carefully weigh the skills, resources, organizational requirements, and risks associated with each source of competitive advantage. Finally, strategists must consider the unique influence that the generic industry environment most similar to the firm's situation will have on the set of value chain activities they choose to build competitive advantage.

EXHIBIT 7–9
Grand Strategy
Selection Matrix

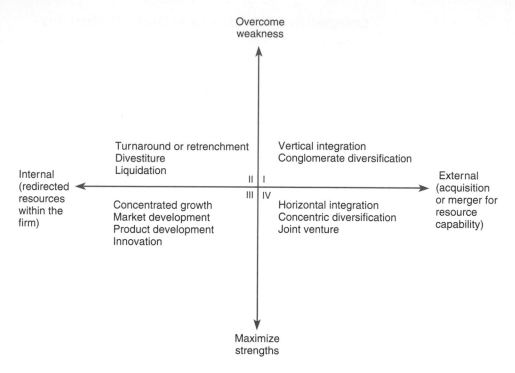

DOMINANT PRODUCT/SERVICE BUSINESSES: EVALUATING AND CHOOSING TO DIVERSIFY TO BUILD VALUE

McDonald's has frequently looked at numerous opportunities to diversify into related businesses or to acquire key suppliers. Its decision has consistently been to focus on its core business using the grand strategies of concentration, market development, and product development. Rival Pepsi, on the other hand, has chosen to diversify into related businesses and vertical integration as the best grand strategies for it to build long-term value. Both firms experienced unprecedented success during the last 20 years.

Many dominant product businesses face this question as their core business proves successful: What grand strategies are best suited to continue to build value? Under what circumstances should they choose an expanded focus (diversification, vertical integration); steady continued focus (concentration, market or product development); or a narrowed focus (turnaround or divestiture)? This section examines two ways you can analyze a dominant product company's situation and choose among the 15 grand strategies identified in Chapter 6.

Grand Strategy Selection Matrix

One valuable guide to the selection of a promising grand strategy is the matrix shown in Exhibit 7–9. The basic idea underlying the matrix is that two variables are of central concern in the selection process: (1) the principal purpose of the grand strategy and (2) the choice of an internal or external emphasis for growth or profitability.

In the past, planners were advised to follow certain rules or prescriptions in their choice of strategies. Now, most experts agree that strategy selection is better guided by the conditions of the planning period and by the company strengths and weaknesses. It should be noted, however, that even the early approaches to strategy selection sought to match a concern over internal versus external growth with a desire to overcome weaknesses or maximize strengths.

The same considerations led to the development of the grand strategy selection matrix. A firm in quadrant I, with "all its eggs in one basket," often views itself as over-committed to a particular business with limited growth opportunities or high risks. One reasonable solution is *vertical integration,* which enables the firm to reduce risk by reducing uncertainty about inputs or access to customers. Another is *conglomerate diversification,* which provides a profitable investment alternative with diverting management attention from the original business. However, the external approaches to overcoming weaknesses usually result in the most costly grand strategies. Acquiring a second business demands large investments of time and sizable financial resources. Thus, strategic managers considering these approaches must guard against exchanging one set of weaknesses for another.

More conservative approaches to overcoming weaknesses are found in quadrant II. Firms often choose to redirect resources from one internal business activity to another. This approach maintains the firm's commitment to its basic mission, rewards success, and enables further development of proven competitive advantages. The least disruptive of the quadrant II strategies is *retrenchment,* pruning the current activities of a business. If the weaknesses of the business arose from inefficiencies, retrenchment can actually serve as a *turnaround* strategy—that is, the business gains new strength from the streamlining of its operations and the elimination of waste. However, if those weaknesses are a major obstruction to success in the industry and the costs of overcoming them are unaffordable or are not justified by a cost-benefit analysis, then eliminating the business must be considered. *Divestiture* offers the best possibility for recouping the firm's investment, but even *liquidation* can be an attractive option if the alternatives are bankruptcy or an unwarranted drain on the firm's resources.

A common business adage states that a firm should build from strength. The premise of this adage is that growth and survival depend on an ability to capture a market share that is large enough for essential economies of scale. If a firm believes that this approach will be profitable and prefers an internal emphasis for maximizing strengths, four grand strategies hold considerable promise. As shown in quadrant III, the most common approach is *concentrated growth,* that is, market penetration. The firm that selects this strategy is strongly committed to its current products and markets. It strives to solidify its position by reinvesting resources to fortify its strengths.

Two alternative approaches are *market development* and *product development.* With these strategies, the firm attempts to broaden its operations. Market development is chosen if the firm's strategic managers feel that its existing products would be well received by new customer groups. Product development is chosen if they feel that the firm's existing customers would be interested in products related to its current lines. Product development also may be based on technological or other competitive advantages. The final alternative for quadrant III firms is *innovation.* When the firm's strengths are in creative product design or unique production technologies, sales can be stimulated by accelerating perceived obsolescence. This is the principle underlying the innovative grand strategy.

Maximizing a firm's strengths by aggressively expanding its base of operations usually requires an external emphasis. The preferred options in such cases are shown in quadrant IV. *Horizontal integration* is attractive because it makes possible a quick increase in output capability. Moreover, in horizontal integration, the skills of the managers of the original business often are critical in converting newly acquired facilities into profitable contributors to the parent firm; this expands a fundamental competitive advantage of the firm—its management.

Concentric diversification is a good second choice for similar reasons. Because the original and newly acquired businesses are related, the distinctive competencies of the diversifying firm are likely to facilitate a smooth, synergistic, and profitable expansion.

The final alternative for increasing resource capability through external emphasis is a *joint venture* or *strategic alliance.* This alternative allows a firm to extend its strengths into competitive arenas that it would be hesitant to enter alone. A partner's production, technological, financial, or marketing capabilities can reduce the firm's financial investment significantly and increase its probability of success.

EXHIBIT 7–10
**Model of Grand
Strategy Clusters**

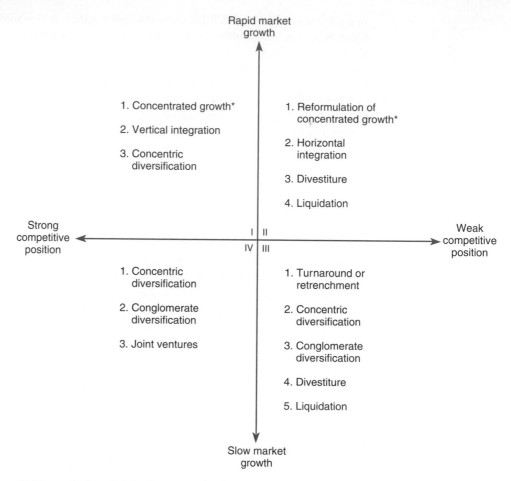

*This is usually via market development, product development, or a combination of both.

Model of Grand Strategy Clusters

A second guide to selecting a promising grand strategy is shown in Exhibit 7–10. The figure is based on the idea that the situation of a business is defined in terms of the growth rate of the general market and the firm's competitive position in that market. When these factors are considered simultaneously, a business can be broadly categorized in one of four quadrants: (I) strong competitive position in a rapidly growing market, (II) weak position in a rapidly growing market, (III) weak position in a slow-growth market, or (IV) strong position in a slow-growth market. Each of these quadrants suggests a set of promising possibilities for the selection of a grand strategy.

Firms in quadrant I are in an excellent strategic position. One obvious grand strategy for such firms is continued concentration on their current business as it is currently defined. Because consumers seem satisfied with the firm's current strategy, shifting notably from it would endanger the firm's established competitive advantages. McDonald's Corporation has followed this approach for 25 years. However, if the firm has resources that exceed the demands of a concentrated growth strategy, it should consider vertical integration. Either forward or backward integration helps a firm protect its profit margins and market share by ensuring better access to consumers or material inputs. Finally, to diminish the risks associated with a narrow product or service line, a quadrant I firm might be wise to consider concentric diversification; with this strategy, the firm continues to invest heavily in its basic area of proven ability.

Firms in quadrant II must seriously evaluate their present approach to the market-place. If a firm has competed long enough to accurately assess the merits of its current grand strategy, it must determine (1) why that strategy is ineffectual and (2) whether it is capable of competing effectively. Depending on the answers to these questions, the firm should choose one of four grand strategy options: formulation or reformulation of a concentrated growth strategy, horizontal integration, divestiture, or liquidation.

In a rapidly growing market, even a small or relatively weak business often is able to find a profitable niche. Thus, formulation or reformulation of a concentrated growth strategy is usually the first option that should be considered. However, if the firm lacks either a critical competitive element or sufficient economies of scale to achieve competitive cost efficiencies, then a grand strategy that directs its efforts toward horizontal integration is often a desirable alternative. A final pair of options involve deciding to stop competing in the market or product area of the business. A multiproduct firm may conclude that it is most likely to achieve the goals of its mission if the business is dropped through divestiture. This grand strategy not only eliminates a drain on resources but also may provide funds to promote other business activities. As an option of last resort, a firm may decide to liquidate the business. This means that the business cannot be sold as a going concern and is at best worth only the value of its tangible assets. The decision to liquidate is an undeniable admission of failure by a firm's strategic management and, thus, often is delayed—to the further detriment of the firm.

Strategic managers tend to resist divestiture because it is likely to jeopardize their control of the firm and perhaps even their jobs. Thus, by the time the desirability of divestiture is acknowledged, businesses often deteriorate to the point of failing to attract potential buyers. The consequences of such delays are financially disastrous for firm owners because the value of a going concern is many times greater than the value of its assets.

Strategic managers who have a business in quadrant III and expect a continuation of slow market growth and a relatively weak competitive position will usually attempt to decrease their resource commitment to that business. Minimal withdrawal is accomplished through retrenchment; this strategy has the side benefits of making resources available for other investments and of motivating employees to increase their operating efficiency. An alternative approach is to divert resources for expansion through investment in other businesses. This approach typically involves either concentric or conglomerate diversification because the firm usually wants to enter more promising arenas of competition than integration or concentrated growth strategies would allow. The final options for quadrant III businesses are divestiture, if an optimistic buyer can be found, and liquidation.

Quadrant IV businesses (strong competitive position in a slow-growth market) have a basis of strength from which to diversify into more promising growth areas. These businesses have characteristically high cash flow levels and limited internal growth needs. Thus, they are in an excellent position for concentric diversification into ventures that utilize their proven acumen. Exhibit 7–8, Strategy in Action, (on p. 205), describes how the number-one tennis ball maker, Penn Racquet Sports, chose concentric diversification from humans to dogs as their best option. A second option is conglomerate diversification, which spreads investment risk and does not divert managerial attention from the present business. The final option is joint ventures, which are especially attractive to multinational firms. Through joint ventures, a domestic business can gain competitive advantages in promising new fields while exposing itself to limited risks.

Opportunities for Building Value as a Basis for Choosing Diversification or Integration

The grand strategy selection matrix and model of grand strategy clusters are useful tools to help dominant product company managers evaluate and narrow their choices among alternative grand strategies. When considering grand strategies that would broaden the scope of their company's business activities through integration, diversification, or joint venture strategies, managers must examine whether opportunities to build value are present. Opportunities to build value via diversification, integration, or joint venture strategies are usually found in market-related, operating-related, and management activities. Such opportunities center around reducing costs, improving margins, or providing access to new revenue sources more cost effectively than traditional internal growth options via concentration, market development, or product development. Major opportunities for sharing and value building as well as ways to capitalize on core competencies are outlined in the next chapter, which covers strategic analysis and choice in diversified companies.

Dominant product company managers who choose diversification or integration eventually create another management challenge. That challenge is charting the future of a company that becomes a collection of several distinct businesses. These distinct businesses often encounter different competitive environments, challenges, and opportunities. The next chapter examines ways managers of such diversified companies attempt to evaluate and choose corporate strategy. Central to their challenge is the continued desire to build value, particularly shareholder value.

Summary

This chapter examined how managers in businesses that have a single or dominant product or service evaluate and choose their company's strategy. Two critical areas deserve their attention: first, their business's value chain; second, the appropriateness of 12 different grand strategies based on matching environmental factors with internal capabilities.

Managers in single-product-line business units examine their business's value chain to identify existing or potential activities around which they can create sustainable competitive advantages. As managers scrutinize their value chain activities, they are looking for three sources of competitive advantage: low cost, differentiation, and rapid response capabilities. They also examine whether focusing on a narrow market niche provides a more effective, sustainable way to build or leverage these three sources of competitive advantage.

Managers in single or dominant product/service businesses face two interrelated issues. First, they must choose which grand strategies make best use of their competitive advantages. Second, they must ultimately decide whether to diversify their business activity. Twelve grand strategies were identified in this chapter along with three frameworks that aid managers in choosing which grand strategies should work best and when diversification or integration should be the best strategy for the business. The next chapter expands the coverage of diversification to look at how multibusiness companies evaluate continued diversification and how they construct corporate strategy.

Questions for Discussion

1. What are three activities or capabilities a firm should possess to support a low-cost leadership strategy? Use Exhibit 7–2 to help you answer this question. Can you give an example of a company that has done this?

2. What are three activities or capabilities a firm should possess to support a differentiation-based strategy? Use Exhibit 7–3 to help you answer this question. Can you give an example of a company that has done this?

3. What are three ways a firm can incorporate the advantage of speed in its business? Use Exhibit 7–4 to help you answer this question. Can you give an example of a company that has done this?

4. Do you think is it better to concentrate on one source of competitive advantage (cost versus differentiation versus speed) or to nurture all three in a firm's operation? What did Caterpillar do in the *BusinessWeek* Discussion Case?

5. How does market focus help a business create competitive advantage? What risks accompany such a posture? How did market focus come into play at Caterpillar?

6. Using Exhibits 7–9 and 7–10, describe situations or conditions under which horizontal integration and concentric diversification would be preferred strategic choices.

Chapter 7 Discussion Case

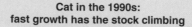

BusinessWeek

Strategic Analysis and Choice in the 1990s at Caterpillar, Inc.

**Cat in the 1990s:
fast growth has the stock climbing**

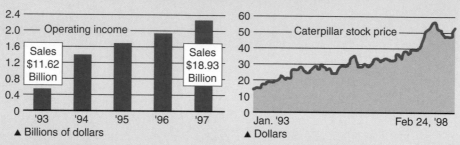

Caterpillar, long the global standard in heavy-duty construction equipment was almost destroyed by the painful industry collapse in the 1980s and subsequent union difficulties. Global demand was dropping fast, and the weak yen allowed Cat's biggest rival, Japan's Komatsu Ltd., to undercut prices by 40%. When Komatsu began to gain share, Cat's CEO Donald Fites—and Cat—got the scare of their lives. And a lengthy, debilitating strike with the United Auto Workers in 1990–91 made matters even more difficult. Fites, who became CEO coming from Caterpillar's marketing organization, took an aggressive stance toward the UAW and sought to craft a strategy for the 1990s that would rebuild Caterpillar as the industry leader. *BusinessWeek*'s De'Ann Weimer visited Caterpillar to report on the strategic analysis and choices Fites made during that time that led to the outstanding turnaround she summarized for you in the chart above. Her findings from mid-1998 illustrate how one company analyzed and chose to build a strategy around key cost, differentiation, and speed competitive advantages in existing markets and eventually new, growth markets.

1   STRATEGIC ANALYSIS. Core operations were too costly—old equipment; slow production processes; numerous dedicated production lines for individual truck and tractor models; product design activities for each model, again quite costly; Problematic union agreement.

2   STRATEGIC CHOICE. **Seek low-cost and speed-enhancing leadership advantages** by integrating production activities across multiple models

to gain economies of scale; speeding up production processes with newer technology; and reducing inventory costs with increased JIT accommodated with speedier production activities:

Fites began by overhauling manufacturing in Cat's core truck and tractor operations. He invested almost $2 billion to modernize his U.S. plants. New state-of-the-art machinery helped Cat **slash time** *out of such mundane tasks as painting, for example, and* **vastly simplified production.** *Today, Cat can build 20 different models from the same basic design. The changes—together with the increased use of temporary workers in its nonunion plants—have also greatly* **improved Cat's flexibility.** *The company can now* **change production levels with a week's notice**—*down from six months at the height of its 1980s crisis. Altogether, Cat's manufacturing time has fallen 75%—one key reason operating margins have exploded, from 5.2% in 1993, to 12.6% in 1997.* **Faster production** *has also allowed Fites to* **slash inventories.** *Gone are the long order backlogs and dealer inventories that weighed heavily on Cat's books; today, it* **refuses orders more than three months in advance.**

3   STRATEGIC ANALYSIS. Caterpillar was getting hurt not only on price, but because many models had changed very little compared to key Japanese competitors. Newer competitors had begun to differentiate themselves based on providing product line extensions with varying product features.

4   STRATEGIC CHOICE. **Seek to differentiate Caterpillar's products** by introducing products that enhance construction efficiency while repre-

senting basic product line extensions or adaptations of Caterpillar's manufacturing and design capabilities.

While aggressively redesigning its manufacturing system, **Cat broadened its products.** *In the last two years, it has introduced 90 offerings—***some all-new, some well-targeted fine extensions** *that enhance construction site efficiency and capabilities in very specific construction tasks. In 1997, for example, Cat introduced a telescopic handler—essentially a tractor with an arm on it that allows masons to work their way up the side of a building eliminating the need for scaffolding so expensive in traditional construction methods.*

5   STRATEGIC ANALYSIS. Caterpillar is a global business. It is affected significantly by currency fluctuations, by development opportunities outside the United States and cyclical downturns, and labor costs in the U.S. versus overseas markets.

6   STRATEGIC CHOICE. **Focus on selected national markets** where establishing **incountry plants** and distribution provide cost advantages while allowing potential synergy across global markets in selected product offerings.

Good timing helped with the turnaround, too. As the combination of reduced costs and the end of recession restored the company's financial health, Fites pushed into new markets. He focused on Asia, where infrastructure development created huge demand. Markets in Latin America, Central Europe, Russia, and other former Soviet states.

7   STRATEGIC ANALYSIS. The heavy construction industry is very cyclical. The global nature of the industry heightens the potential cyclical impact and adds currency risks from fluctuating currency values. Restrictive UAW contracts in the United States add to the cost impact of these risks when demand, and sales, decrease due to global cyclical pressures yet higher labor costs remain built into Cat's cost structure.

8   STRATEGIC CHOICE. **Concentric diversification** into related product-markets that leverage key strengths making engines **into less cyclical markets** than trucks and tractors; and into product-markets that leverage sales and distribution strengths. **Use acquisitions** to accelerate this effort. **Increase global presence of facilities over time** to decrease currency fluctuation impact and reliance on UAW labor.

Some 51% of Cat sales come from overseas—though Fites wants to hit 75% by 2008. To cut the risk of fluctuating currencies—and trim labor costs—Fites has also pushed much manufacturing abroad. Today, roughly half of Cat's 74 plants are abroad, versus just 39% of its 38 plants a decade ago. In the wake of the UAW's rejection of the labor contract—which will prevent Cat from hiring new workers at lower wages or demanding more flexible scheduling in union plants—analysts say the percentage of foreign production could go even higher.

Fites also bulked up in less-cyclical businesses like electric power generation. An offshoot of its long-standing engine business, the move into power gained steam in 1996 when Fites purchased a German maker of engines for generators. Driven by demand for power in developing countries—where governments often don't want to build big power plants—generation has helped boost engines to more than 25% of Cat sales. "They are trending toward smaller, easier-to-operate generators," said Siegfried R. Ramseyer, vice-president of Cat Asia. "This we can do very, very well." He predicted sales could triple in a few years.

The company's largest acquisition to date—the $1.3 billion purchase of Britain's Perkins Engines, which closed in February—was directed at another target altogether: the fast-growing $3.6 billion market for compact construction machinery. These machines, typically operated by one person, are the industry's hottest segment. The star of the category: skid-steer loaders, which break up asphalt, move dirt, and do such a variety of useful things that sales are growing a red-hot 11% a year.

Cat was all but absent in the lucrative small-equipment market, but Fites targeted a 20% share by 2003. He counted on big gains from Perkins, which makes engines for skid-steers. Since engines account for 25% of the costs of a skid-steer, Cat figures that trimming those expenses will allow it to undercut rivals while maintaining margins. Elsewhere, Fites has tapped other new markets by focusing dealers on rental equipment. Initially unpopular with dealers, who must keep rental gear on their books as assets, the change drew lots of smaller customers. The added demand also helped keep prices strong. In 1997, for example, when few companies could do so, Cat raised prices.

WHAT WAS THE RESULT OF CATERPILLAR'S STRATEGIC ANALYSIS AND CHOICE?

9　The reborn company skyrocketed through the upturn with flying colors. Since 1993, when Cat completed its manufacturing overhaul amid soaring demand for construction equipment in the United States and developing nations, sales leaped from $11.6 billion to $18.9 billion, an average of 13% a year. Meanwhile, earnings rose a stunning 45% annually, jumping from just $626 million to $2.3 billion in 1997. Investors won big: In five years, Cat's stock more than tripled.

10　The U.S. market, where Cat sells 49% of its goods, started to slow by 1999. And Asia, Cat's fastest-growing market suffered a headline-grabbing downturn. American dealers quickly started seeing barely used, heavily discounted Cat equipment begin to trickle into the United States from Asia, as customers dumped equipment to raise cash. The slowdown promised the biggest test yet of the "New Cat."

11　The global slowdown in 2000 and recession in 2001 saw Caterpillar's earnings plummet to 1993 levels. The slowdown could hardly have come at a worse time for CEO Gleb Barton, a Caterpillar lifer who moved up to the top job in 2000 with the retirement of Chairman and CEO Donald V. Fites. Under Fites, Caterpillar tallied six consecutive years of record sales and five years in a row of record earnings in the 1990s. But as Barton, 61, wrapped up his second year as boss in 2001 and his 40th year with Cat, it's clear he has his hands full. On Jan. 21, the company said profits fell for the second year in a row, and sales slipped 6% both years. The outsized drop in earnings reflects Cat's increased dependence on engines and other lower-margin products.

12　When it comes to earnings, however, smaller may not be better. Compact gear generally has modest markups. Also, buyers of such gear typically care more about price than service. "At the end of the day, it's the fastest-growing business, and Cat has to be there," says David Raso of Lehman Brothers Inc. in New York. "But it doesn't quite leverage Cat's strength." Lately, Cat's U.S. sales have been driven by the rise of a new distribution channel—equipment-rental companies. Some analysts fear these companies are in for a shakeout, and that could crush demand—and prices—if they are forced to liquidate. And as Cat introduces scaled-down products, competitors are bulldozing their way into its core heavy-equipment business. Moline (Ill.)-based Deere recently came out with its first 55-ton and 75-ton excavators. CNH, which now has global reach and ambitions, also will expand its line of large construction equipment, vows Jean-Pierre Rosso, chief executive of the Dutch company, which has its head office in Racine, Wis. Despite harder times, Cat still dominates, outselling Komatsu and CNH roughly 3 to 1 in heavy equipment. And sooner or later, the North American market will revive. But down cycles can be stubborn. With all of the company's problems, Barton cannot afford a sophomore slump.

Source: "A New Cat on the Hot Seat," *BusinessWeek,* March 9, 1998; "Don't Count Caterpillar Out," *BusinessWeek,* March 20, 2000; and "This Cat Isn't So Nimble," *BusinessWeek,* February 20, 2001.

Chapter **Eight**

Strategic Analysis and Choice in the Multibusiness Company: Rationalizing Diversification and Building Shareholder Value

Company mission and social responsibility (Chapter 2)

External environment
• Remote
• Industry (global and domestic)
• Operating
(Chapters 3, 4)

Possible?

Internal analysis (Chapter 5)

Desired?

Strategic analysis and choice
(Chapter 7: Creating competitive advantage at the business level)
(Chapter 8: Building value in multibusiness companies)

Long-term objectives (Chapter 6)

Generic and grand strategies (Chapter 6)

Short-term objectives; reward system (Chapter 9)

Functional tactics (Chapter 9)

Policies that empower action (Chapter 9)

Restructuring, reengineering, and refocusing the organization (Chapter 10)

Strategic control and continuous improvement (Chapter 11)

Feedback

Feedback

Legend
→ Major impact
⇢ Minor impact

Strategic analysis and choice is more complicated for corporate-level managers because they must create a strategy to guide a company that contains numerous businesses. They must examine and choose which businesses to own and which ones to forgo or divest. They must consider business managers' plans to capture competitive advantage, and then decide how to allocate resources among businesses as part of this phase. This chapter will first examine diversified, multibusiness companies. Specifically, how should the diversified business build shareholder value? For example, MCI has decided to pursue an aggressive diversification program to expand its presence in a variety of different industries; AT&T has recently decided to split into several separate companies while divesting itself of other businesses on three dramatic occasions in the last decade. Why?

A final topic that is important to an understanding of strategic analysis and choice in business organization is the "nonbusiness," behavioral factors that often exert a major influence on strategic decisions. This is true in the single-product business as well as the multibusiness company. What behavioral considerations often influence how managers analyze strategic options and make strategic choices? For example, J. E. Schrempp became CEO of Germany's Daimler Benz as planned, having taken over from his mentor, Edzard Reuter, with whom he had charted a steady 10-year diversification to build a $74 billion company. Three months later, Schrempp reversed the strategy to break up the company, focus on core businesses, and reconstruct a new management team. How could such a dramatic, sudden shift take place? Answering that question requires you to consider behavioral factors as well as strategic issues at Daimler Benz.

RATIONALIZING DIVERSIFICATION AND INTEGRATION

When a single or dominant-business company is transformed into a collection of numerous businesses across several industries, strategic analysis becomes more complex. Managers must deal not only with each business's strategic situation, they must set forth a corporate strategy that rationalizes the collection of businesses they have amassed. Two key audiences are listening. First, managers within the organization want to understand their role and access to resources relative to other businesses within the company. Second, and of greatest importance, stockholders deserve to understand how this collection of businesses is expected to build shareholder value over the long term more effectively than simply investing in separate businesses. In a sense the question is: "Are there compelling reasons why corporate management is better able to invest shareholder value in a variety of other businesses versus allowing shareholders to make that decision themselves?"

Stockholder value in a diversified company is ultimately determined by how well its various businesses perform and/or how compelling potential synergies and opportunities appear to be. Business-level performance is enhanced by sustained competitive advantages. Wise diversification has at its core the search for ways to build value and sustained competitive advantage across multiple business units. We saw several ways opportunities for sharing and building value may be present across different businesses. The bottom line is that diversification that shares skills and core competencies across multiple businesses to strengthen value chains and build competitive advantage enhances shareholder value. And so it is that strategic analysis and choice for corporate managers overseeing multibusiness companies involves determining whether their portfolio of business units is capturing the synergies they intended, how to respond accordingly, and choosing among future diversification or divestiture options. Managers address the following four basic questions to do this.

Are Opportunities for Sharing Infrastructure and Capabilities Forthcoming?

Opportunities to build value via diversification, integration, or joint venture strategies are usually found in market-related, operating-related, and management activities. Each business's basic value chain activities or infrastructure becomes a source of potential synergy and competitive advantage for another business in the corporate portfolio. Morrison's Cafeteria, long a mainstay in U.S. food services markets, rapidly accelerated its diversification into other restaurant concepts like Ruby Tuesdays. Numerous opportunities for shared operating capabilities and management capabilities drove this decision and, upon repeated strategic analysis, accelerated corporate managers' decision to move Morrison's totally out of the cafeteria segment by 2000. Some of the more common opportunities to share value chain activities and build value are identified in Exhibit 8–1.

Strategic analysis is concerned with whether or not the potential competitive advantages expected to arise from each value opportunity have materialized. Where advantage has not materialized, corporate strategists must take care to scrutinize possible impediments to achieving the synergy or competitive advantage. We have identified in Exhibit 8–1 several impediments associated with each opportunity, which strategists are well advised to examine. Good strategists assure themselves that their organization has ways to avoid or minimize the impact of any impediments or they recommend against further integration or diversification and consider divestiture options.

Two elements are critical in meaningful shared opportunities. First, the shared opportunities must be a significant portion of the value chain of the businesses involved. Returning to Morrison's Cafeteria, its purchasing and inbound logistics infrastructure give Ruby Tuesday's operators an immediate cost-effective purchasing and inventory management capability that lowered its cost in a significant cost activity. Second, the businesses involved must truly have shared needs—need for the same activity—or there is no basis for synergy in the first place. Novell, the U.S.-based networking software giant, paid $900 million for WordPerfect, envisioning numerous synergies serving offices globally not to mention 15 million WordPerfect users. Little more than a year later, Novell would sell WordPerfect for less than $300 million, because, as CEO Bob Frankenberg said, "It is not because WordPerfect is not a business without a future, but for Novell it represented a distraction from our strategy." Corporate strategies have repeatedly rushed into diversification only to find perceived opportunities for sharing were nonexistent because the businesses did not really have shared needs. Exhibit 8–2, Strategy in Action, examines just this dilemma at several well-known U.S. companies that have botched their synergy searches.

Are We Capitalizing on Our Core Competencies?

Perhaps the most compelling reason companies should diversify can be found in situations where core competencies—key value-building skills—can be leveraged with other products or into markets that are not a part of where they were created. Where this works well, extraordinary value can be built. Managers undertaking diversification strategies should dedicate a significant portion of their strategic analysis to this question.

General Cinema was a company that grew from drive-in theaters to eventually dominate the multicinema, movie exhibition industry. Next, they entered soft-drink bottling and became the largest bottler of soft drinks (Pepsi) in North America. Their stock value rose 2,000 percent in 10 years. They found that core competencies in movie exhibition—managing many small, localized businesses; dealing with a few large suppliers; applying central marketing skills locally; and acquiring or crafting a "franchise"—were virtually the

EXHIBIT 8–1   Value Building in Multibusiness Companies

Source: Adapted with the permission of *Harvard Business School on Managing the Value Chain* (Cambridge: HBS Press, 2000).

Opportunities to Build Value or Sharing	Potential Competitive Advantage	Impediments to Achieving Enhanced Value
Market-Related Opportunities:		
Shared sales force activities or shared sales office, or both.	Lower selling costs. Better market coverage. Stronger technical advice to buyers. Enhanced convenience for buyers (can buy from single source). Improved access to buyers (have more products to sell).	• Buyers have different purchasing habits toward the products. • Different salespersons are more effective in representing the product. • Some products get more attention than others. • Buyers prefer to multiple-source rather than single-source their purchases.
Shared after-sale service and repair work.	Lower servicing costs. Better utilization of service personnel (less idle time). Faster servicing of customer calls.	• Different equipment or different labor skills, or both, are needed to handle repairs. • Buyers may do some in-house repairs.
Shared brand name.	Stronger brand image and company reputation. Increased buyer confidence in the brand.	• Company reputation is hurt if quality of one product is lower.
Shared advertising and promotional activities.	Lower costs. Greater clout in purchasing ads.	• Appropriate forms of messages are different. • Appropriate timing of promotions is different.
Common distribution channels.	Lower distribution costs. Enhanced bargaining power with distributors and retailers to gain shelf space, shelf positioning, stronger push and more dealer attention, and better profit margins.	• Dealers resist being dominated by a single supplier and turn to multiple sources and lines. • Heavy use of the shared channel erodes willingness of other channels to carry or push the firm's products.
Shared order processing.	Lower order processing costs. One-stop shopping for buyer enhances service and, thus, differentiation.	• Differences in ordering cycles disrupt order processing economies.

EXHIBIT 8–1   *continued*

Opportunities to Build Value or Sharing	Potential Competitive Advantage	Impediments to Achieving Enhanced Value
Operating Opportunities:		
Joint procurement of purchased inputs.	Lower input costs. Improved input quality. Improved service from suppliers.	• Input needs are different in terms of quality or other specifications. • Inputs are needed at different plant locations, and centralized purchasing is not responsive to separate needs of each plant.
Shared manufacturing and assembly facilities.	Lower manufacturing/assembly costs. Better capacity utilization, because peak demand for one product correlates with valley demand for other. Bigger scale of operation improves access to better technology and results in better quality.	• Higher changeover costs in shifting from one product to another. • High-cost special tooling or equipment is required to accommodate quality differences or design differences.
Shared inbound or outbound shipping and materials handling.	Lower freight and handling costs. Better delivery reliability. More frequent deliveries, such that inventory costs are reduced.	• Input sources or plant locations, or both, are in different geographic areas. • Needs for frequency and reliability of inbound/outbound delivery differ among the business units.
Shared product and process technologies or technology development or both.	Lower product or process design costs, or both, because of shorter design times and transfers of knowledge from area to area. More innovative ability, owing to scale of effort and attraction of better R&D personnel.	• Technologies are the same, but the applications in different business units are different enough to prevent much sharing of real value.
Shared administrative support activities.	Lower administrative and operating overhead costs.	• Support activities are not a large proportion of cost, and sharing has little cost impact (and virtually no differentiation impact).
Management Opportunities:		
Shared management know-how, operating skills, and proprietary information.	Efficient transfer of a distinctive competence—can create cost savings or enhance differentiation. More effective management as concerns strategy formulation, strategy implementation, and understanding of key success factors.	• Actual transfer of know-how is costly or stretches the key skill personnel too thinly, or both. • Increased risks that proprietary information will leak out.

BusinessWeek AT&T shelled out $7 billion for NCR Corp. early in the 1990s and finally staked out the strategic beachhead in computers that it had failed, despite billions of dollars spent, to achieve on its own. When AT&T succeeded in taking over computer maker NCR, it figured it had won a major victory in its dream of linking computers and telecommunications. As things turned out, the dream proved to be wishful thinking. Four years and $4 billion in net NCR losses later, AT&T was ready to cut its losses and spin off NCR. AT&T had also invested an additional $3.2 billion into NCR by the time it was spun off to the public. And after its initial emotional IPO market reception in early 1997, NCR stock quickly nosedived as its long-term prospects became more obvious, and unattractive. Analysts and competitors say NCR's computer problems are a lingering result of neglect under AT&T. For starters, NCR's computer sales force was allowed to shrink too much. And though it boasted customers such as H&R Block Inc. and J.C. Penney Co., outsiders say NCR was far too dependent on sales to AT&T. Worse, the phone giant failed to invest enough in the business or expand NCR's computer product lines, especially its Unix-based servers. "What NCR found, because of the AT&T screwup, is that their critical mass in the Unix business is not that big," says Nick Earle, worldwide marketing manager for Hewlett-Packard Co.'s enterprise systems group, a strong NCR rival in both servers and data warehousing.

Although consolidation of health-care providers has made sense for some, it certainly didn't for Dallas-based Medical Care International Inc. and Critical Care America, based in Westborough, Massachusetts. If ever there was a marriage made in hell, this combination of the nation's largest surgery-center chain and largest independent operator of home intravenous services was it. The concept—to create a hospital without walls and enable Medical Care America to profit from the rising demand for low-cost outpatient services—certainly sounded good. But virtually everything that could go wrong in a merger went wrong in this one. Poor timing, faulty due diligence, culture clashes, and big egos doomed the deal from the start. The merger took place just as intensified competition began driving down prices for home infusion services. Critical Care's problems were masked by slow insurer payments and infrequent internal reporting, which made it difficult to spot trends. Less than three weeks after the merger, Chairman and CEO Donald E. Steen announced that third-quarter results would fall below expectations, triggering a free fall in Medical Care America's shares. Management responded by slashing Critical Care's staff, which, in turn, caused it to lose customers. Shareholder lawsuits followed. "The Critical Care merger was bad, really bad," says Steen. "It's something I'm trying to forget." Soon thereafter Medical Care America sold off Critical Care to Caremark International Inc. and six months later sold out to Colurnbia/HCA Healthcare Corp. for $850 million. "This has been a very good merger," Steen says, largely because its broad geographic coverage and supply contracts have enabled it to lower prices.

same in soft-drink bottling. Disney and ABC saw shared core competencies as central in the entertainment industry of the 21st century. AT&T and TCI saw shared core competencies as central to telecommunications success. These and many more companies look to three basic considerations to evaluate whether they are capitalizing on core competencies.

Is Each Core Competency Providing a Relevant Competitive Advantage to the Intended Businesses?

The core competency must assist the intended business in creating strength relative to key competition. This could occur at any step in the business's value chain. But it must represent a major source of value to be a basis for competitive advantage—and the core competence must be transferrable. Honda of Japan viewed itself as having a core competence in manufacturing small, internal combustion engines. It diversified into small garden tools, perceiving that traditional electric tools would be much more attractive if powered by a lightweight, mobile, gas combustion motor. Their core competency created a major competitive advantage in a market void of gas-driven hand tools. When Coca-Cola added bottled water to its portfolio of products, it expected its extraordinary core competencies in marketing and distribution to rapidly build value in this business. Ten years later, Coke sold its water assets concluding that the product did not have enough margin to interest its

Other attempts at expanding by acquiring closely related companies have also bombed. Take, for example, Kmart Corp.'s 1990s acquisitions strategy. Instead of focusing on its core discount business, it lost more ground to Wal-Mart Stores Inc. when it diverted its attention and capital to buying up fast-growing specialized retailers, sometimes paying top dollar. Before long, Kmart had become a $30 billion-sales retail conglomerate with seven specialty store chains and 2,300 Kmart stores. But overhead was higher than rival Wal-Mart and sales per square foot lower. "The Kmart stores were totally neglected," says Trish Reopelle, an analyst with the State of Wisconsin Investment Board. Mid-decade, Kmart was forced to begin selling its specialty stores and CEO Joseph Antonini was out of a job. Kmart has continued to try to avoid bankruptcy protection as it seeks to survive its mistaken pursuit of synergy and diversification.

Few deals made more sense on paper yet so little sense culturally than the merger of Price Club and Costco Wholesale to create Price/Costco Inc., which became the second-largest operator of warehouse clubs after Wal-Mart's Sam's Club. "The economies of the two companies coming together to compete with Sam's Club were compelling," says Jeffrey Atkin, principal of the Seattle money-management firm of Kunath Karren Rinne & Atkin.

The deal had many problems, but the worst were cultural. The Price and Costco people just didn't seem to hit it off. Says analyst Michael J. Shea of Charter Investment Group: "The Price guys had much more of a real estate strip-mall mentality. The Costco guys were the type who started working at grocery stores bagging groceries when they were 10 years old and worked their way up the ladder." In one of the shortest corporate marriages ever, Price and Costco broke up after less than a year. Says analyst Mark Byl, of Laird Norton Trust Co.: "The best thing to happen to that marriage was the divorce."

All this indicates that many large-company CEOs are making multibillion-dollar decisions about the future of their companies, employees, and shareholders in part by the seat of their pants. When things go wrong, as the evidence demonstrates that they often do, these decisions create unnecessary tumult, losses, and heartache. While there clearly is a role for thoughtful and well-conceived mergers in American business, all too many don't meet that description. Moreover, in merging and acquiring mindlessly and flamboyantly, dealmakers may be eroding the nation's growth prospects and global competitiveness. Dollars that are wasted needlessly on mergers that don't work might better be spent on research and new-product development. And in view of the growing number of corporate divorces, it's clear that the best strategy for most would-be marriage partners is never to march to the altar at all.

Sources: "The Case against Mergers," *BusinessWeek*, October 30, 1995; "Is NCR Ready to Ring Up Some Cash?" *BusinessWeek*, October 14, 1996; and "Still Waiting for the New NCR," *BusinessWeek*, December 15, 1997.

franchised bottlers and that marketing was not a significant value-building activity among many small suppliers competing primarily on the cost of "producing" and shipping water. In the last few years, however, Coke has reversed its decision and added the Danske water brand because a rapidly increasing consumer demand has made the value of its extensive distribution network a relevant competitive advantage to the Danske water product line.

Are Businesses in the Portfolio Related in Ways That Make the Company's Core Competence(s) Beneficial?

Related versus unrelated diversification is an important distinction to understand as you evaluate the diversification question. "Related" businesses are those that rely on the same or similar capabilities to be successful and attain competitive advantage in their respective product markets. The discussion case at the end of Chapter 7 described how Caterpillar pursued related diversification into the portable power generation business from its core truck and tractor focus. This related move was very successful in part because Caterpillar's expertise in diesel engine manufacturing, indeed its same engines, could be used to strategic advantage in small scale, portable power generation. Earlier, we described General Cinema's spectacular success in both movie exhibition and soft-drink bottling. Seemingly unrelated, they were actually very related businesses in terms of key core competencies that shaped success—managing a network of diverse business locations, localized competition, reliance on a few large suppliers, and centralized marketing advantages. Thus, the products of various businesses do not necessarily have to be similar to leverage core competencies. While their products may not be related, it is essential that some activities in their value chains require similar skills to create competitive advantage if the company is going to leverage its core competence(s) in a value-creating way.

Situations that involve "unrelated" diversification occur when no real overlapping capabilities or products exist other than financial resources. We refer to this as *conglomerate diversification* in Chapter 6. Recent research indicates that the most profitable firms are those that have diversified around a set of resources and capabilities that are specialized enough to confer a meaningful competitive advantage in an attractive industry, yet adaptable enough to be advantageously applied across several others. The least profitable are broadly diversified firms whose strategies are built around very general resources (e.g., money) that are applied in a wide variety of industries, but are seldom instrumental to competitive advantage in those settings.[1]

Are Our Combination of Competencies Unique or Difficult to Re-create?

Skills that corporate strategists expect to transfer from one business to another, or from corporate to various businesses, may be transferrable. They may also be easily replicated by competitors. When this is the case, no sustainable competitive advantage is created. Sometimes strategists look for a combination of competencies, a package of various interrelated skills, as another way to create a situation where seemingly easily replicated competencies become unique, sustainable competitive advantages. 3M Corporation has the enviable record of having 25 percent of its earnings always coming from products introduced within the last five years. 3M has been able to "bundle" the skills necessary to accelerate the introduction of new products so that it consistently extracts early life cycle value from adhesive-related products that hundreds of competitors with similar technical or marketing competencies cannot touch.

All too often companies envision a combination of competencies that make sense conceptually. This vision of synergy develops an energy of its own leading CEOs to relentlessly push the merger of the firms involved. But what makes sense conceptually and is seen as difficult for competitors to re-create often proves difficult if not impossible to create in the first place. Exhibit 8–3, Strategy in Action, discusses this dilemma, making a case against merger and diversification.

Does the Company's Business Portfolio Balance Financial Resources?

Multibusiness companies usually find that their various businesses generate and consume very different levels of cash. Some generate more cash than they can use to maintain or expand their business while others consume more than they generate. Corporate managers face the very important challenge of determining the best way to generate and use financial resources among the businesses within their company. Faced with this challenge, managers historically looked to balance cash generators and cash users so that, along with outside capital sources, they can efficiently manage the cash flows across their business portfolio.

---

[1] David J. Collis and Cynthia A. Montgomery, *Corporate Strategy* (Chicago: Irwin), 1997, p. 88. "Why Mergers Fail," *McKinsey Quarterly Report*, 2001, vol. 4. "Deals That Create Value," *McKinsey Quarterly Report,* 2001, vol. 1.

BusinessWeek
American companies are in the grip of full-blown merger mania. Each of the last ten years has topped the previous year's merger and acquisition activity. This historic surge of consolidations and combinations is occurring in the face of strong evidence that mergers and acquisitions, at least over the past 35 years or so, have hurt more than helped companies and shareholders. The conglomerate deals of the 1960s and 1970s that gave rise to such unwieldy companies as ITT Corp. and Litton Industries have since been thoroughly discredited, and most of these behemoths have been broken up. The debt-laden leveraged buyouts and bust-ups of the 1980s didn't fare any better, and many surely did a whole lot worse. That era ended not with a whimper but with a bang: In October 1989, when bankers couldn't raise the money for the ill-conceived buyout of UAL Corp., the deal collapsed, dragging the stock market down with it.

During the last decade, chief executives and investment bankers figured that they had finally gotten it right. If UAL marked the end of the 1980s crazy season, then the July, 1991, announcement by Chemical Bank Corp. and Manufacturers Hanover Corp. that they would join in a $2.3 billion stock swap to create the nation's second-largest banking company and produce $650 million in annual expense savings by 1994, seemed to signal that the Age of Reason in mergers and acquisitions had begun. This was to be the era of strategic deals—friendly, intelligent, and relatively debt-free transactions done mostly as stock swaps, which were supposed to enrich shareholders by producing synergies in which two plus two would equal five or more. These synergies would take the form of economies of scale, improved channels of distribution, greater market clout, and ultimately higher profits for surviving companies. Although Harvard University's Michael Porter in a seminal *Harvard Business Review* article argued persuasively that most would-be deal synergies are never realized, the new strategic transactions, Wall Street promised, would be different.

It turns out they're not. Indeed, with investment bankers singing their new, improved siren song, many big company CEOs are demonstrating that they still are as vulnerable to the latest fad as the most naive individual investor. An exhaustive analysis by *BusinessWeek* and Mercer Management Consulting Inc., a leading management consulting firm, of hundreds of deals in this decade indicates that their performance has fallen far short of their promise. Deals that were announced with much fanfare such as AT&T's acquisition of NCR and Matsushita's acquisition of MCA, have since unraveled. Acquisitions by big pharmaceutical manufacturers of drug wholesalers, as well as software and entertainment deals aren't producing the results the acquirers had hoped for. Some recent megadeals like AOL-Time Warner, and Disney's acquisition of Capital Cities/ABC leave many media-industry observers scratching their heads over where the gains are going to come from. "For all these deals to work out, you have to believe that the American public is under-entertained," says Wilbur L. Ross, senior managing director at Rothschild Inc.

These anecdotal findings are supported statistically. The *BusinessWeek*/Mercer analysis indicates that companies performed better in the wake of '90s deals, most of which have been done ostensibly for business reasons, than they did after '80s transactions, a high proportion of which were financially driven. But the analysis also concluded that most of the '90s deals still haven't worked. Of 150 deals valued at $500 million or more, about half destroyed shareholder wealth, judged by stock performance in relation to Standard & Poor's industry indexes. Another third contributed only marginally to it. Further, says James Quella, director of Mercer Management Consulting, "many deals destroy a lot of value." Mergers and acquisitions, he declares, "are still a slippery slope." Key reasons mergers fail were:

Deal performance has been poor because melding two companies is enormously difficult and only a few companies are very good at it. One reason is that buyers often stack the odds against success by rushing headlong into mergers and acquisitions for the wrong reasons in search of synergies that don't exist. To make matters worse, they often pay outlandish premiums that can't be recovered even if everything goes right. And finally—and this is the real deal-killer—they fail to effectively integrate the two companies after the toasts have been exchanged. Good postmerger integration rarely makes a really bad deal work, but bad execution almost always wrecks one that might have had a shot. Says Kenneth W. Smith, a Mercer vice-president based in Toronto: "The deal is won or lost after it's done."

(continued)

Most transactions fall below expectations, but an even greater percentage of companies lose in the M&A game. That's because **a few large, proficient acquirers,** such as General Electric Co. and Dover Corp. (BW—Jan. 23), tend to **do a lot of successful deals while a much larger number of less adept companies execute one or two unsuccessful mergers.** In the 51/2 years ending July 31, 72% of companies that completed six or more deals valued over $5 million each yielded returns above the industry average, compared with 54% of companies that closed just one to five transactions.

Nonacquirers are more likely to outperform their respective industry indices than are **active acquirers.** Only about a fourth of the nation's 500 largest companies have not yet made a single acquisition larger than $5 million in this decade. But over 70% of companies that made no acquisitions larger than $5 million outperformed their respective Standard & Poor's industry indices. Only 50% of all acquirers did better than their industry indices. Many companies—notably Andrew Corp. and Coca Cola Co.—whose industry rivals are bent on growing through acquisition, have delivered superior returns by keeping investment bankers at bay and sticking to their knitting.

Many deals are poorly thought out, founded on dubious assumptions about the potential benefits by CEOs with questionable motivations. "There's tremendous allure to mergers and acquisitions," says Porter. "It's the big play, the dramatic gesture. With the stroke of a pen you can add billions to size, get a front-page story, and create excitement in the markets." Numerous companies have blundered lately when they tried to engineer a major redefinition of their businesses through merger and acquisition—often in response to sea changes in regulation, technology, and even geopolitics. If the spate of copycat deals in computers, telecommunications, media, and technology are any indication, these companies seem to fear they will be left behind forever if they don't do something and do it fast. "Nobody wants to be marooned," says David A. Nadler, chairman of Delta Consulting Group.

Optimism is bolstered by a variety of rationales. One is that vertical integration—linking manufacturing with distribution—will yield vast synergies. On that theory, Merck, Eli Lilly, and SmithKline paid handsomely for drug wholesalers, but the prospects for those deals are looking bleaker and bleaker. Such linkages are behind the Hollywood deals, such as Disney's acquisition of Capital Cities/ABC. "I hate to use the 's' word," says Disney Chairman Michael Eisner, "but that's synergy at work." Others are skeptical. Says Tele-Communications Inc. CEO John C. Malone: "It's an industry that's as certain as betting on a race horse."

Many experts say that the deal-breaker is usually **bad postmerger planning and integration.** If a deal is to stand any chance of success, companies must move quickly and decisively to appoint the new management team, cut costs, reassure customers, and resolve cultural conflicts.

To be sure, some strategic transactions have worked well. The Chemical-Manny Hanny merger; Primerica's acquisition of Travelers Corp.; Toymaker Mattel Corp.'s acquisition of Fisher-Price; and Campbell Soup–Pace Foods have worked. But the kinds of mergers and acquisitions with a better-than-even shot at success are limited indeed. Small and midsize deals—notably leveraged "buildups" in such fragmented industries as funeral homes and health clubs—frequently work. The best acquisitions, says Harvard's Porter, involve "gap-filling," including those in which one company buys another to strengthen its product line or expand its territory. "Globalizing" acquisitions, such as those that enable companies to expand their core business into other countries, may make sense, though culture and language problems undermine many of these deals. Mergers of direct competitors aimed at dominating a market, such as marriages of big banks with overlapping branches, often have worked out.

Source: Phillip L. Zweig in New York, with Judy Perlman Kline in Pittsburgh, Stephanie Anderson Forest in Dallas, and Kevin Gudridge, "The Case against Mergers," *BusinessWeek,* October 30, 1995.

Responding to this challenge during the diversification explosion of the 1970s, the Boston Consulting Group pioneered an approach called *portfolio techniques* that attempted to help managers "balance" the flow of cash resources among their various businesses while also identifying their basic strategic purpose within the overall portfolio. Three of these techniques are reviewed here. Once reviewed, we will identify some of the problems with the portfolio approach that you should keep in mind when considering its use.

EXHIBIT 8–4
The BCG Growth-Share Matrix

Source: The growth-share matrix was originally developed by the Boston Consulting Group.

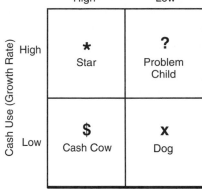

Cash Generation (Market Share)

	High	Low
High	★ Star	? Problem Child
Low	$ Cash Cow	X Dog

Cash Use (Growth Rate)

Description of Dimensions

Market Share: Sales relative to those of other competitors in the market (dividing point is usually selected to have only the two–three largest competitors in any market fall into the high market share region)

Growth Rate: Industry growth rate in constant dollars (dividing point is typically the GNP's growth rate)

The BCG Growth-Share Matrix

Managers using the BCG matrix plotted each of the company's businesses according to market growth rate and relative competitive position. *Market growth rate* is the projected rate of sales growth for the market being served by a particular business. Usually measured as the percentage increase in a market's sales or unit volume over the two most recent years, this rate serves as an indicator of the relative attractiveness of the markets served by each business in the firm's portfolio of businesses. *Relative competitive position* usually is expressed as the market share of a business divided by the market share of its largest competitor. Thus, relative competitive position provides a basis for comparing the relative strengths of the businesses in the firm's portfolio in terms of their positions in their respective markets. Exhibit 8–4 illustrates the growth-share matrix.

The *stars* are businesses in rapidly growing markets with large market shares. These businesses represent the best long-run opportunities (growth and profitability) in the firm's portfolio. They require substantial investment to maintain (and expand) their dominant position in a growing market. This investment requirement is often in excess of the funds that they can generate internally. Therefore, these businesses are often short-term, priority consumers of corporate resources.

Cash cows are businesses with a high market share in low-growth markets or industries. Because of their strong positions and their minimal reinvestment requirements, these businesses often generate cash in excess of their needs. Therefore, they are selectively "milked" as a source of corporate resources for deployment elsewhere (to stars and question marks). Cash cows are yesterday's stars and the current foundation of corporate portfolios. They provide the cash needed to pay corporate overhead and dividends and provide debt capacity. They are managed to maintain their strong market share while generating excess resources for corporatewide use.

Low market share and low market growth businesses are the *dogs* in the firm's portfolio. Facing mature markets with intense competition and low profit margins, they are managed for short-term cash flow (through ruthless cost cutting, for example) to supplement corporate-level resource needs. According to the original BCG prescription, they are divested or liquidated once this short-term harvesting has been maximized.

Question marks are businesses whose high growth rate gives them considerable appeal but whose low market share makes their profit potential uncertain. Question marks are cash guzzlers because their rapid growth results in high cash needs, while their small market share results in low cash generation. At the corporate level, the concern is to identify the question marks that would increase their market share and move into the star group if extra corporate resources were devoted to them. Where this long-run shift from question mark to star is unlikely, the BCG matrix suggests divesting the question mark and repositioning its resources more effectively in the remainder of the corporate portfolio.

The Industry Attractiveness–Business Strength Matrix

Corporate strategists found the growth-share matrix's singular axes limiting in their ability to reflect the complexity of a business's situation. Therefore, some companies adopted a matrix with a much broader focus. This matrix, developed by McKinsey & Company at General Electric, is called the Industry Attractiveness–Business Strength Matrix. This matrix uses multiple factors to assess industry attractiveness and business strength rather than the single measures (market share and market growth, respectively) employed in the BCG matrix. It also has nine cells as opposed to four—replacing the high/low axes with high/medium/low axes to make finer distinctions among business portfolio positions.

The company's businesses are rated on multiple strategic factors within each axis, such as the factors described in Exhibit 8–5. The position of a business is then calculated by "subjectively" quantifying its rating along the two dimensions of the matrix. Depending on the location of a business within the matrix as shown in Exhibit 8–6, one of the following strategic approaches is suggested: (1) invest to grow, (2) invest selectively and manage for earnings, or (3) harvest or divest for resources. The resource allocation decisions remain quite similar to those of the BCG approach.

Although the strategic recommendations generated by the Industry Attractiveness–Business Strength Matrix are similar to those generated by the BCG matrix, the Industry Attractiveness–Business Strength Matrix improves on the BCG matrix in three fundamental ways. First, the terminology associated with the Industry Attractiveness–Business Strength Matrix is preferable because it is less offensive and more understandable. Second, the multiple measures associated with each dimension of the business strength matrix tap many factors relevant to business strength and market attractiveness besides market share and market growth. And this, in turn, makes for broader assessment during the planning process, bringing to light considerations of importance in both strategy formulation and strategy implementation.

The Life Cycle–Competitive Strength Matrix

One criticism of the first two portfolio methods was their static quality—their portrayal of businesses as they exist at one point in time, rather than as they evolve over time. A third portfolio approach was introduced that attempted to overcome these deficiencies and better identify "developing winners" or potential "losers."[2] This approach uses the multiple-factor approach to assess competitive strength as one dimension and stage of the market life cycle as the other dimension.

[2] Attributed to Arthur D. Little, a consulting firm, and to Charles W. Hofer in "Conceptual Constructs for Formulating Corporate and Business Strategies" (Boston: Harvard Case Services, #9-378-754, 1977).

EXHIBIT 8–5
Factors Considered in Constructing an Industry Attractiveness–Business Strength Matrix

Industry Attractiveness	Business Strength
Nature of Competitive Rivalry	**Cost Position**
Number of competitors	Economies of scale
Size of competitors	Manufacturing costs
Strength of competitors' corporate parents	Overhead
Price wars	Scrap/waste/rework
Competition on multiple dimensions	Experience effects
	Labor rates
Bargaining Power of Suppliers/Customers	Proprietary processes
Relative size of typical players	**Level of Differentiation**
Numbers of each	Promotion effectiveness
Importance of purchases from or sales to	Product quality
Ability to vertically integrate	Company image
	Patented products
Threat of Substitute Products/ New Entrants	Brand awareness
Technological maturity/stability	**Response Time**
Diversity of the market	Manufacturing flexibility
Barriers to entry	Time needed to introduce new products
Flexibility of distribution system	Delivery times
	Organizational flexibility
Economic Factors	**Financial Strength**
Sales volatility	Solvency
Cyclicality of demand	Liquidity
Market growth	Break-even point
Capital intensity	Cash flows
	Profitability
Financial Norms	Growth in revenues
Average profitability	**Human Assets**
Typical leverage	Turnover
Credit practices	Skill level
	Relative wage/salary
Sociopolitical Considerations	Morale
Government regulation	Managerial commitment
Community support	Unionization
Ethical standards	**Public Approval**
	Goodwill
	Reputation
	Image

The life cycle dimension allows users to consider multiple strategic issues associated with each life cycle stage (refer to the discussion in Chapter 5), thereby enriching the discussion of strategic options. It also gives a "moving indication" of both issues—those strategy needs to address currently and those that could arise next. Exhibit 8–7 provides an illustration of this matrix. It includes basic strategic investment parameters recommended for different positions in the matrix. While this approach seems valuable, its recommendations are virtually identical to the previous two portfolio matrices.

EXHIBIT 8–6
**The Industry
Attractiveness–
Business Strength
Matrix**

Source: McKinsey & Company
and General Electric.

	High	**Medium**	**Low**
High	Invest	Selective Growth	Grow or Let Go
Medium	Selective Growth	Grow or Let Go	Harvest
Low	Grow or Let Go	Harvest	Divest

Business Strength (vertical axis)

Description of Dimensions

Industry Attractiveness: Subjective assessment based on broadest possible range of external opportunities and threats beyond the strict control of management

Business Strength: Subjective assessment of how strong a competitive advantage is created by a broad range of the firm's internal strengths and weaknesses

BCG's Strategic Environments Matrix

BCG's latest matrix offering (see Exhibit 8–8) took a different approach using the idea that it was the nature of competitive advantage in an industry that determined the strategies available to a companies businesses, which in turn determined the structured of the industry. Their idea was that such a framework could help ensure that individual business' strategies were consistent with strategies appropriate to their strategic environment. Furthermore, for corporate managers in multiple business companies, this matrix offered one way to rationalize which businesses they are in—business that share core competencies and associated competitive advantages because of similar strategic environments.

The matrix has two dimensions. The number of sources of competitive advantage could be many with complex products and services (e.g. automobiles, financial services) and few with commodities (chemicals, microprocessors). Complex products offer multiple opportunities for differentiation as well as cost, while commodities must seek opportunities for cost advantages to survive.

The second dimension is size of competitive advantage. How big is the advantage available to the industry leader? The two dimensions then define four industry environments as follows:

EXHIBIT 8–7
The Market Life Cycle–Competitive Strength Matrix

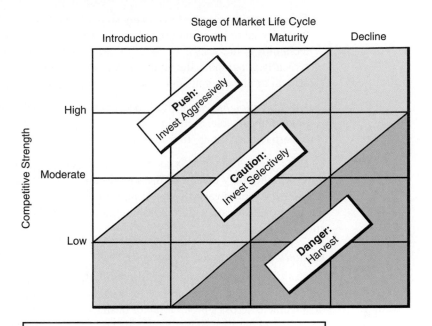

Description of Dimensions

Stage of Market Life Cycle: See page 146.

Competitive Strength: Overall subjective rating, based on a wide range of factors regarding the likelihood of gaining and maintaining a competitive advantage

EXHIBIT 8–8
BCG's Strategic Environments Matrix

Source: R. M. Grant, *Contemporary Strategy Analysis* (Oxford: Blackwell, 2002), p. 327.

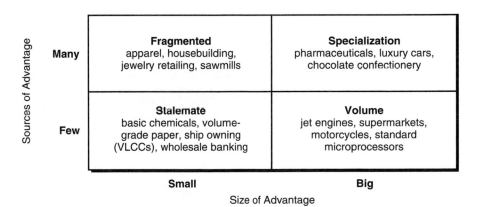

Volume businesses are those that have few sources of advantage, but the size is large—typically the result of scale economies. Advantages established in one such business may be transferable to another as Honda has done with its scale and expertise with small gasoline engines.

Stalemate businesses have few sources of advantage, with most of those small. This results in very competitive situations. Skills in operational efficiency, low overhead, and cost management are critical to profitability.

Fragmented businesses have many sources of advantage, but they are all small. This typically involves differentiated products with low brand loyalty, easily replicated technology, and scale economies minimal. Skills in focused market segments, typically geographic, the ability to respond quickly to changes and low costs are critical in this environment.

Specialization businesses have many sources of advantage, and find those advantages potentially sizable. Skills in achieving differentiation—product design, branding expertise, innovation, first-mover, and perhaps scale—characterize winners here.

BCG viewed this matrix as providing guidance to multibusiness managers to determine whether they possessed the sources and size of advantage associated with the type of industry facing each business; and allow them a framework to realistically explore the nature of the strategic environments in which they competed or were interested in entering.

Limitations of Portfolio Approaches

Portfolio approaches made several contributions to strategic analysis by corporate managers convinced of their ability to transfer the competitive advantage of professional management across a broad array of businesses. They helped convey large amounts of information about diverse business units and corporate plans in a greatly simplified format. They illuminated similarities and differences between business units and helped convey the logic behind corporate strategies for each business with a common vocabulary. They simplified priorities for sharing corporate resources across diverse business units that generated and used those resources. They provided a simple prescription that gave corporate managers a sense of what they should accomplish—a balanced portfolio of businesses—and a way to control and allocate resources among them. While these approaches offered meaningful contributions, they had several critical limitations and shortcomings:

- A key problem with the portfolio matrix was that it did not address how value was being created across business units—the only relationship between them was cash. Because of this, its valued simplicity encouraged a tendency to trivialize strategic thinking among users that did not take proper time for thorough underlying analysis.

- Truly accurate measurement for matrix classification was not as easy as the matrices portrayed. Identifying individual businesses, or distinct markets, was not often as precise as underlying assumptions required.

- The underlying assumption about the relationship between market share and profitability—the experience curve effect—varied across different industries and market segments. Some have no such link. Some find that firms with low market share can generate superior profitability with differentiation advantages.

- The limited strategic options, intended to describe the flow of resources in a company, came to be seen more as basic strategic missions. Doing this creates a false sense of what strategies were when none really existed. This becomes more acute when attempting to use the matrices to conceive strategies for average businesses in average growth markets.

- The portfolio approach portrayed the notion that firms needed to be self-sufficient in capital. This ignored capital raised in capital markets.

- The portfolio approach typically failed to compare the competitive advantage a business received from being owned by a particular company with the costs of owning it. The 1980s saw many companies build enormous corporate infrastructures that created only small gains at the business level. The deconstruction in the 1990s of some "model" portfolio companies reflects this important omission.

Constructing business portfolio matrices must be undertaken with these limitations in mind. Perhaps it is best to say that they provide one form of input to corporate managers seeking to balance financial resources. They should be used merely to provide a basis for further discussion of corporate strategy and the allocation of corporate resources, and to provide a picture of the "balance" of resource generators and users to test underlying assumptions about these issues in more involved corporate planning efforts to leverage core competencies to build sustained competitive advantages. For while the portfolio approaches have serious limitations, the challenge for corporate managers overseeing the allocation of resources among a variety of business units is still to maintain a balanced use of the company's financial resources.

Does Our Business Portfolio Achieve Appropriate Levels of Risk and Growth?

Diversification has traditionally been recommended as a way to manage, or diversify, risk. Said another way, "not having all your eggs in one basket" allows corporate managers to potentially reduce risk to company stockholders. Balancing cyclical revenue streams to reduce earnings volatility is one way diversification may reduce risk. So managers need to ask this question as a part of their strategic analysis and subsequent choice. Likewise, revenue growth can be enhanced by diversification. Many companies in the hazardous waste industry maintained the steady growth investors had come to expect by continuously making acquisitions of other businesses to gain immediate sales growth. Indeed, Exhibit 8–9, Strategy in Action, reports that Generation X managers are much more comfortable with "M&A" diversification growth than their elderly counterparts, with the exception of GE legend Jack Welch.

Both risk and growth are assumptions or priorities corporate managers should carefully examine as they undertake strategic analysis and choice. Is growth always desirable? Can risks truly be managed most effectively by corporate management? Many companies have pursued growth to gain market share without accompanying attention to profitability. Similarly, companies have built diverse business portfolios in part to manage overall risk. In both instances, the outcome is often a later time when subsequent management must "look in the bag" of businesses and aggressively divest and downsize the company until true value-adding activities and synergies linked to sustained competitive advantages are uncovered. Exhibit 8–10, Strategy in Action, shows Finland's Nokia outdistancing Motorola and Ericsson due to the advantage Nokia's focus provides over the others' portfolio problems.

BEHAVIORAL CONSIDERATIONS AFFECTING STRATEGIC CHOICE

After alternative strategies have been analyzed, managers choose one of those strategies. If the analysis identified a clearly superior strategy or if the current strategy will clearly meet future company objectives, then the decision is relatively simple. Such clarity is the exception, however, and strategic decision makers often are confronted with several

Strategy in Action
Generation Xers and Jack Welch Say Mergers and Acquisitions Can Be OK!

Exhibit 8–9

BusinessWeek

FOR GEN X, M&A IS A-OK

Twenty somethings strongly support the mergers-and-acquisitions trend. The young tend to be optimistic, as opposed to those over 65, who grew up in an era when bigger was often not seen as better.

Some have argued that single-product businesses have a focus that gives them an advantage over multibusiness companies like our own—and perhaps they would have, but only if we neglect our own overriding advantage: the ability to share the ideas that are the result of wide and rich input from a multitude of global sources.

GE businesses share technology, design, compensation and personnel evaluation systems, manufacturing practices, and customer and country knowledge. Gas Turbines shares manufacturing technology with Aircraft Engines; Motors and Transportation Systems work together on new propulsion systems; Lighting and Medical Systems collaborate to improve x-ray tube processes; and GE Capital provides innovative financing packages that help all our businesses around the globe. Supporting all this is a management system that fosters and rewards this sharing and teamwork, and, increasingly, a culture that

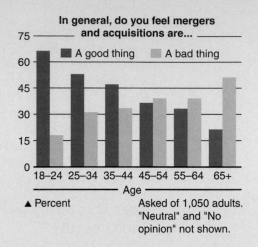

In general, do you feel mergers and acquisitions are...

■ A good thing ■ A bad thing

Age

▲ Percent

Asked of 1,050 adults. "Neutral" and "No opinion" not shown.

makes it reflexive and natural at every level and corner of our Company.

—Jack Welch, Chairman, General Electric Company, 1981–2001

Source: "Up-Front Section," *BusinessWeek,* August 10, 1998, p. 6; Letters to Shareholders, General Electric Company.

---

viable alternatives rather than the luxury of a clear-cut choice. Under these circumstances, several factors influence the strategic choice. Some of the more important are:

1. Role of the current strategy.

2. Degree of the firm's external dependence.

3. Attitudes toward risk.

4. Managerial priorities different from stockholder interests.

5. Internal political considerations.

6. Competitive reaction.

Role of the Current Strategy

Current strategists are often the architects of past strategies. If they have invested substantial time, resources, and interest in those strategies, they logically would be more comfortable with a choice that closely parallels or involves only incremental alterations to the current strategy.

Such familiarity with and commitment to past strategy permeates the entire firm. Thus, lower-level managers reinforce the top managers' inclination toward continuity with past strategy during the choice process. Research in several companies found lower-level

BusinessWeek Focused growth in new geographic cell phone markets and related products, rather than product and technology diversification, is Finland's Nokia's impressive secret.

Six years ago, as an untested CEO, Jorma Ollila bet Nokia, the 133-year-old Finnish conglomerate, on cellular phones, challenging rivals Motorola Inc. and L. M. Ericsson. In the struggle that ensued, Ollila's Finns outdid themselves. Fast and focused, with a canny eye for design, Nokia wrested market share from entrenched competitors and emerged as the most profitable player in the industry.

All told, Nokia is providing troubled Motorola Inc., the leader in old-fashioned analog phones, with a humiliating tutorial on digital communications. Motorola CEO Christopher B. Galvin glumly concedes that "the analog business is trending down." Ollila, for his part, predicts that Nokia will be "No. 1 in the world in the number of phones sold, in growth, and return on capital employed." Rapid growth should about double the worldwide number of cellular subscribers, now equally divided among Europe, Asia, and the Americas, to 550 million by 2001. This benefits the big three—Motorola, Ericsson, and, of course, Nokia—which rule three-quarters of the cellular market with nearly equal shares. Motorola, though, is struggling to escape from dying analog, where prices are collapsing. And Ericsson, while fully in stride with Nokia in digital sets, is far larger and more diverse and is burdened with less profitable old-line businesses.

Source: "Can CEO Ollila Keep the Cellular Superstar Flying High?" *BusinessWeek*, August 10, 1998, p. 55.

Nokia is battling two Goliaths...

	Motorola	Ericsson	**Nokia**
1997 Sales	$29.8	$21.17	**$9.64**
% Increase	+6.5%	+35%	**+34%**
Operating profits*	$1.95	$2.37	**$1.58**
% Increase	Flat	75%	**+98%**

*Billions of dollars

...But its laserlike focus on cell phones...

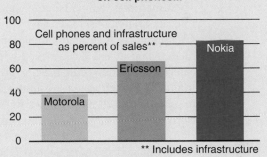

Cell phones and infrastructure as percent of sales**

** Includes infrastructure

...Has earned it a big bang from the phone boom...

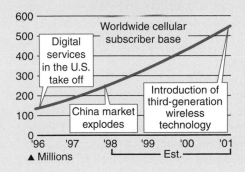

Worldwide cellular subscriber base

Digital services in the U.S. take off

China market explodes

Introduction of third-generation wireless technology

▲ Millions — Est.

...And investors appreciate the difference

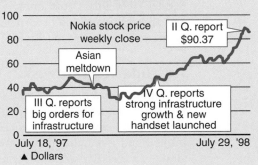

Nokia stock price weekly close

II Q. report $90.37

Asian meltdown

III Q. reports big orders for infrastructure

IV Q. reports strong infrastructure growth & new handset launched

July 18, '97 — July 29, '98

▲ Dollars

managers suggested strategic choices that were consistent with current strategy and likely to be accepted while withholding suggestions with less probability of approval. Research by Henry Mintzberg suggests that past strategy strongly influences current strategic choice. The older and more successful a strategy has been, the harder it is to replace. Similarly, once a strategy has been initiated, it is very difficult to change because organizational momentum keeps it going. Even as a strategy begins to fail due to changing conditions, strategists often increase their commitment to it. Thus, firms may replace top executives when performance has been inadequate for an extended period because replacing these executives lessens the influence of unsuccessful past strategy on future strategic choice.

Degree of the Firm's External Dependence

If a firm is highly dependent on one or more environmental elements, its strategic alternatives and its ultimate strategic choice must accommodate that dependence. The greater a firm's external dependence, the lower its range and flexibility in strategic choice.

Bama Pies is a great family business success story. It makes excellent pies—apple turnovers. For many years, Bama Pies sold most of its pie output to one customer— McDonald's. With its massive retail coverage and its access to alternative suppliers. McDonald's was a major external dependence for Bama Pies. Bama Pies' strategic alternatives and ultimate choice of strategy were limited and strongly influenced by McDonald's demands.

Numerous small software companies and even many larger computer, software, and Internet-related businesses have considerable external dependence on Microsoft's operating system for their main products and services. Decisions to pursue options that put that relationship at risk are weighed with much hesitation because of the impact a negative Microsoft reaction could have on their company's survival. Or consider Amazon.com, the Internet bookseller and e-commerce bellwether company. As Amazon began to build momentum, arch rival Barnes & Noble acquired the leading book distributor Ingram Book Group, which supplied 60 percent of Amazon.com's books. Barnes & Noble promised "no favoritism," but Amazon's high external dependence on Ingram would no doubt be reevaluated and other sources considered even at a higher cost.

While external dependence can restrict options, it isn't necessarily a strategic threat. The last decade has seen firms' efforts to enhance quality and cost include decisions to "sole-source" certain supplies or services, even ones central to the firm's strategic capabilities. This increases "external dependence," but it is seen as a way to "strategically partner" that allows both firms to share information, and improve and integrate product and process design and development, to mention a few benefits that may accrue to both partners. More on this in Chapter 10.

Attitudes toward Risk

Attitudes toward risk exert considerable influence on strategic choice. Where attitudes favor risk, the range of the strategic choices expands and high-risk strategies are acceptable and desirable. Where management is risk averse, the range of strategic choices is limited and risky alternatives are eliminated before strategic choices are made. Past strategy exerts far more influence on the strategic choices of risk-averse managers. Exhibit 8–10, Strategy in Action, shows how the highly focused, risk-tolerant Nokia has flown past risk-averse Motorola in cell phones.

Industry volatility influences the propensity of managers toward risk. Top managers in highly volatile industries absorb and operate with greater amounts of risk than do their counterparts in stable industries. Therefore, top managers in volatile industries consider a broader, more diverse range of strategies in the strategic choice process.

Industry evolution is another determinant of managerial propensity toward risk. A firm in the early stages of the product-market cycle must operate with considerably greater risk and uncertainty than a firm in the later stages of that cycle.

In making a strategic choice, risk-oriented managers lean toward opportunistic strategies with higher payoffs. They are drawn to offensive strategies based on innovation, company strengths, and operating potential. Risk-averse managers lean toward safe, conservative strategies with reasonable, highly probable returns. They are drawn to defensive strategies that minimize a firm's weaknesses, external threats, and the uncertainty associated with innovation-based strategies.

Managerial Priorities Different from Stockholder Interests

Corporate managers are hired, theoretically, to act as agents of shareholders and to make decisions that are in shareholders' best interests. An increasing area of research known as *agency theory* suggests that managers frequently place their own interests above those of their shareholders.[3] This appears to be particularly true when the strategic decisions involve diversification. While stockholder value may be maximized by selling a company, for example, managers in the acquired company may lose their jobs—a potential conflict of interests. In these circumstances, several of the benefits sought through diversification give rise to potential manager-stockholder conflicts. The idea of "sharing core competencies" may encounter resistance from managers suspicious about diluting their valued capability. "Shared infrastructure" usually means fewer managers are needed. "Balancing financial resources" realistically means resources controlled by one management group become shared or diluted to support other businesses.

Similarly, some managers may seek diversification to accelerate sales growth, although continued focus in a narrow market area ensures increased competitive advantage to sustain long-term shareholder value. "Growth" achieved by combining two companies increases the basis on which some managers are compensated, regardless of whether the combination is truly advantageous to stockholders. The bottom line is, particularly where diversification decisions are being made, managerial self-interests can result in strategic choices that benefit managers to the detriment of stockholders. In these situations, strategic decision making can take on a political context like that described in the next section and Exhibit 8–11.

Internal Political Considerations

Power/political factors influence strategic choice. The use of power to further individual or group interest is common in organizational life. A major source of power in most firms is the chief executive officer (CEO). In smaller firms, the CEO is consistently the dominant force in strategic choice. Regardless of firm size, when the CEO begins to favor a particular choice, it is often selected unanimously.

Coalitions are power sources that influence strategic choice. In large firms, subunits and individuals (particularly key managers) have reason to support some alternatives and oppose others. Mutual interest draws certain groups together in coalitions to enhance their position on major strategic issues. These coalitions, particularly the more powerful ones (often called *dominant coalitions*), exert considerable influence on the strategic choice process. Numerous studies confirm the frequent use of power and coalitions in strategic decision making.

[3] K. M. Eisenhardt, "Agency Theory: An Assessment and Review," *Academy of Management Review* 14 (1989), pp. 57–74; B. M. Oviatt, "Agency and Transaction Cost Perspectives on the Manager-Shareholder Relationship: Incentives for Congruent Interests," *Academy of Management Review* 13 (1988), pp. 214–25.

EXHIBIT 8–11   Political Activities in Phases of Strategic Decision Making

Source: Adapted from Liam Fahey and V. K. Naroyanan, "The Politics of Strategic Decision Making," in The Strategic Management Handbook, ed. Kenneth J. Albert (New York: McGraw-Hill, 1983), pp. 20–21.

Phases of Strategic Decision Making	Focus of Political Action	Examples of Political Activity

Identification and diagnosis of strategic issues.	Control of:
	  Issues to be discussed.
	  Cause-and-effect relationships to be examined.
		Control agenda.
		Interpretation of past events and future trends.

Narrowing the alternative strategies for serious consideration.	Control of alternatives.	Mobilization:
		  Coalition formation.
		  Resource commitment for information search.

Examining and choosing the strategy.	Control of choice.	Selective advocacy of criteria. Search and representation of information to justify choice.
Initiating implementation of the strategy.	Interaction between winners and losers.	Winners attempt to "sell" or co-opt losers. Losers attempt to thwart decisions and trigger fresh strategic issues.
Designing procedures for the evaluation of results.	Representing oneself as successful.	Selective advocacy of criteria.

Exhibit 8–11 shows that the *content* of strategic decisions and the *processes* of arriving at such decisions are politically charged. Each phase in the process of strategic choice presents an opportunity for political action intended to influence the outcome. The challenge for strategists lies in recognizing and managing this political influence. For example, selecting the criteria used to compare alternative strategies or collecting and appraising information regarding those criteria may be particularly susceptible to political influence. This possibility must be recognized and, where necessary, "managed" to avoid dysfunctional political bias. Relying on different sources to collect and appraise information might serve this purpose.

Organizational politics must be viewed as an inevitable dimension of organizational decision making that strategic management must accommodate. Some authors argue that politics is a key ingredient in the "glue" that holds an organization together. Formal and informal negotiating and bargaining between individuals, subunits, and coalitions are indispensable mechanisms for organizational coordination. Accommodating these mechanisms in the choice of strategy will result in greater commitment and more realistic strategy. The costs of doing so, however, are likely to be increased time spent on decision making and incremental (as opposed to drastic) change.

Competitive Reaction

In weighing strategic choices, top management frequently incorporates perceptions of likely competitor reactions to those choices. For example, if it chooses an aggressive strategy directly challenging a key competitor, that competitor can be expected to mount an aggressive counterstrategy. In weighing strategic choices, top management must consider the probable impact of such reactions on the success of the chosen strategy.

The beer industry provides a good illustration. Anheuser-Busch dominated the industry, and Miller Brewing Company, recently acquired by Philip Morris, was a weak and declining competitor. Miller's management decided to adopt an expensive advertising-oriented strategy that challenged the big three (Anheuser-Busch, Pabst, and Schlitz) head-on because it assumed that their reaction would be delayed due to Miller's current declining status in the industry. This assumption proved correct, and Miller was able to reverse its trend in market share before Anheuser-Busch countered with an equally intense advertising strategy.

Miller's management took another approach in its next major strategic decision. It introduced (and heavily advertised) a low-calorie beer—Miller Lite. Other industry members had introduced such products without much success. Miller chose a strategy that did not directly challenge its key competitors and was not expected to elicit immediate counterattacks from them. This choice proved highly successful, because Miller was able to establish a dominant share of the low-calorie beer market before those competitors decided to react. In this case, as in the preceding case, expectations regarding the reactions of competitors were a key determinant in the strategic choice made by Miller's management.

Summary

This chapter examined how managers evaluate and choose their company's strategy in multibusiness settings. They look to rationalize their efforts to diversify and their current or anticipated collection of businesses. Doing this means identifying opportunities to share skills and core competencies across businesses or from corporate capabilities to business operational needs. Such opportunities usually arise in marketing, operations, management, or a combination of these activities when a capability in one area contributes to a competitive advantage in another.

Diversified, multibusiness companies face yet another, more complicated process of strategy analysis and choice. This chapter looked at the evolution of this challenge from portfolio approaches to value-based ways to decide which set of businesses maximizes opportunities to build shareholder value.

Critical, often overlooked in the process of strategic analysis and choice, are behavioral considerations that may well determine a company's choice of strategy as much or more so than solely rational analysis. Commitment to the current strategy, external dependence, managerial self-interests, political considerations, and competitive considerations combine to exercise a major influence on how managers eventually evaluate and choose strategies.

Questions for Discussion

1. How does strategic analysis at the corporate level differ from strategic analysis at the business unit level? How are they related?

2. When would multi-industry companies find the portfolio approach to strategic analysis and choice useful?

3. What are three types of opportunities for sharing that form a sound basis for diversification or vertical integration? Give an example of each from companies you have read about.

4. What role might power and politics play in strategic analysis within a multibusiness company? Strategic choice within that same company? Would you expect these issues to be more prominent in a diversified company or in a single–product line company? Why or why not?

5. Several behavioral considerations discussed in this chapter appear to influence strategic analysis and choice within many companies as they seek to chart future direction. From your reading of current business publications, select and explain an example of a company in which one of these behavioral considerations influenced strategic analysis and choice.

Chapter 8 Discussion Case

BusinessWeek

Daimler's Diversification Dance

Chapter 8 has helped you look at companies' decisions to become more diversified, to become multibusiness companies, or to narrow their scope to fewer businesses.

Daimler Benz is an interesting company for you to examine in the *BusinessWeek* Discussion Case because it has had such a varied diversification experience in the decade just ended. You might say that this last decade has been Daimler Benz's *decade-long dance with the diversification devil.*

So *BusinessWeek* reporters take you through *Daimler's Diversification Dance* to illustrate some of the concepts about strategic analysis and choice involving multibusiness companies. They examine it in three phases, or dance steps, ending with the Daimler-Chrysler waltz, which they examined in the greatest detail when it was first consummated. Then, they return three years later to re-examine Daimler's DD at the end of this discussion case.

1   Daimler Benz has "danced" an incredible and varied dance with diversification in the 1990s. You could say there were three segments, steps, or eras to the dance:

- *Obsession* **with Diversification—Be all we can possibly be—in the decade's first half**

- *Revulsion* **with Diversification—Be only what we have to be—in the mid-decade**

- *Simple related* **Diversification—Be the global car company we have to be—decade's end**

OBSESSION WITH DIVERSIFICATION—BE ALL WE CAN POSSIBLY BE—IN THE DECADE'S FIRST HALF

2   Daimler Benz spent billions of dollars on acquisitions in the early 1990s to try to transform itself from an auto maker into a high-tech conglomerate excelling at everything from telecommunications to jet planes. In perhaps the most critical step toward that goal, CEO Edzard Reuter laid out an additional

$1.9 billion—and even billions more later—in a bid to succeed in an industry where his European rivals have failed and become a global heavyweight in microelectronics.

3   Reuter thought he didn't have much choice. Whether in aerospace or autos, Daimler needs to become a leader in microelectronics if it hopes to stay competitive with the United States and Japan. Daimler's new venture would steer clear of standard memory chips, which have led to huge losses. Instead, it will make specialized chips that are custom-designed to control everything from automobile engines to computerized production lines. Daimler executives worried that if they don't make their own chips they will be increasingly dependent on Japanese and American technology for their next generation of products. It would mean sharing sensitive product knowhow with outsiders who design the chips. That's a risk the Germans didn't want to take. One way or another, microelectronics influences two-thirds of Germany's gross national product, said Frank Dieter Maier, head of the new Daimler chip unit. Daimler wasn't alone. Other German industrial giants, such as Siemens and Robert Bosch, also ramped up production of application-specific chips, called ASICs, and other logic products. In fact, the Germans moved toward Japanese-style integration, where systems manufacturers and electronics companies often share space under the same keiretsu roof. Without a competitive chip operation, "Daimler's engineers will lose touch with fast-paced semiconductor developments that have a huge impact on their automotive electronics," said Tomihiro Matsumura, the senior executive vice-president who heads chip operations at NEC Corp.

4   Despite Daimler's deep pockets, Reuter's bet was a risky one. Competition in the multibillion dollar ASIC business gets hotter every day as well-heeled memory-chip makers from South Korea to Tokyo to the Silicon Valley seek to step up production of custom chips. That means learning the hard way. Early in its efforts, when Daimler sold bipolar chips to Mitsubishi Electric, Mitsubishi rejected them, saying they weren't good enough. Daimler engineers redoubled their efforts, revamping test

procedures from start to finish on the production line. Said a hopeful Maier: "It's a learning experience. It will pay off."

5   By the mid-1990s Edzard Reuter was ready to retire at 66 years old having returned Daimler to profitability ($750 million on $74 billion in sales versus a $1.3 billion loss the previous year). He was still passing out copies of his glossy document called The New Age in which Reuter boasted that he had transformed Daimler from a luxury car maker into an "integrated technology group" involved in aerospace, microelectronics, and many kinds of transportation. His heir apparent Jürgen E. Schrempp, had been the leading CEO candidate ever since Reuter appointed him CEO of Deutsche Aerospace (DASA). His mission there was to weld a grab bag of outfits making engines, rockets, planes, and helicopters into a coherent company. That job was a small-scale version of what Reuter has been trying to do with all of Daimler—pool the technical know-how of its autos to avionics units into an integrated high-technology concern, a sort of Teutonic General Electric Co. The effort included pouring $6.25 billion into acquisitions over five years. Reuter left saying the strategy was working. There was little evidence it would pay off soon.

REVULSION WITH DIVERSIFICATION—BE ONLY WHAT WE HAVE TO BE—IN THE MID-DECADE

6   It could have been the smoothest of handovers. When Jürgen E. Schrempp became chief executive of Germany's Daimler Benz, he was expected to inherit a $74 billion industrial empire restored to financial health. His predecessor and mentor, Edzard Reuter, boasted of a return to profitability and promised another boost the next year. But less than three months later, the empire was in disarray. Hit by the soaring German mark, management disputes, and losses from Reuter's own diversification strategy, Daimler was faced with another dangerous slide in profits. Brokers have stamped "sell" recommendations on the stock. In a fight to restore the company's credibility, Schrempp, 50, reversed Reuter's forecast and warned of "severe losses" in his first full year.

7   It turned out that Schrempp, while learning under diversification champion Reuter, had been spending his final year of grooming to become CEO preparing a very different, anti-diversification strategy for Daimler. All that year, Schrempp prepared his strategy, and once in power, he executed it with exacting swiftness. The goal: to reverse his former mentor's grand scheme of building an integrated technology company. First, he streamlined head-office hierarchy, cutting staff by more than 75%. "You have to sweep the stairs from the top down," he says. Then he examined each business unit, grilling frightened managers nearly to tears and set a 12% return-on-capital target for each unit. When the dust had settled, Daimler was down to 23 units from 35 and carried 63,000 fewer people on the payroll within six months after Schrempp became CEO.

8   That year observers described his long-term strategy as:

- Make a decisive break with failed diversification strategy

- Focus on core automotive and truck businesses, which provide most of the group's profits

- Close the money-losing Daimler Benz Industrie unit with sell-offs and transfers of profitable operations to other divisions

- Slim down DASA Daimler Benz Aerospace, reducing its workforce of 40,000 by up to 50%, and step up sourcing of parts from dollar and other weak-currency areas

- Speed up globalization of manufacturing by locating big-ticket plant investments outside Germany

9   By 1997, focus had started to pay off and the "swagger" was back at Mercedes. Take the U.S. market for example. It has been a remarkable turn-around for the German company, whose U.S. sales hit rock bottom in 1991 in the face of a successful onslaught by Japanese luxury brands. But they have since left rivals behind in the slow lane. Bolstered by a stable of new products and aggressive marketing campaigns, Mercedes (and BMW) again rank as the hottest luxury brands in the U.S. They ended 1997 in a dead heat for preeminence among luxury import brands, with BMW's sales of 122,500 vehicles edging out Mercedes' 122,417. And in a luxury-car market that grew just 6% from 1991 to

1997, BMW sales soared 130%, while Mercedes rose 83%. That has allowed the German brands to leapfrog past their top two Japanese rivals, Lexus and Acura. If BMW and Mercedes keep accelerating, they could roar past the faltering U.S. market leaders, General Motors' Cadillac Div. and Ford's Lincoln unit, within the next five years.

10   Competitors now hold Mercedes and BMW up as the standard to beat. "They have clearly reframed the luxury market," says John F. Smith, general manager of GM's Cadillac Div. "I think they've been much more responsive to a variety of consumer tastes." That's just the opposite of the reputations BMW and Mercedes carried at their low point in 1991. Back then, the pair admittedly lost touch with consumers. They paid the price: Sales bottomed out at 53,343 vehicles for BMW and 58,869 for Mercedes—down 45% and 41%, respectively, from their high five years earlier. "The key issue then was to survive," says Michael Jackson, president of Mercedes-Benz of North America.

11   The bottom line was a resounding rejection of the prior diversification strategy choosing instead to focus on stablizing the business around core competencies and capabilities relative to automotive and key transportation products, and to globalize its operations where cost benefits were derived.

SIMPLE RELATED DIVERSIFICATION—BE THE GLOBAL CAR COMPANY WE HAVE TO BE—DECADE'S END

12 CEO Schrempp led an aggressive effort to refocus and simplify Daimler Benz. It worked. But as he looked toward the 21st century's global automotive industry, he had some concerns. Daimler Benz had a limited, upper-scale product line with an industry becoming truly global with overcapacity and increasing full product line competitors. Globally, in 1998 there was plant capacity to build at least 15 million more vehicles each year than could realistically be sold. And overcapacity was expected to balloon to 18.2 million vehicles by 2002. So while he was dismantling Daimler Benz and refocusing it around the automotive industry, Schrempp was thinking about eventually seeking a partner for Daimler that would diversify its product line and

geographic presence in the global automotive industry. He had decided that a carmaker can't compete without a full range of products, and he couldn't stretch the Mercedes brand any further downmarket.

13   But first he had to get Daimler in shape for a merger. Mercedes-Benz was a separate operating company with its own board, run by Helmut Werner, who was a hero in Germany for reviving the Mercedes lineup. Schrempp wanted to give Daimler direct operating control of Mercedes. "We had steps and steps, and layers and layers," Schrempp explains, moving Marlboros around the table to illustrate. "It took months to make a decision." In 1995 and early 1996, talks between Chrysler CEO Eaton and Mercedes CEO Werner about a joint venture for all their international businesses outside Europe and North America had bogged down because of this structure. That failure helped spur Schrempp's reorganization. Although Werner fought to keep Mercedes independent, Schrempp prevailed with the supervisory board. By early 1997, Mercedes was folded into Daimler, Werner was out, and Schrempp was running a car business. A year later the lean, chainsmoking 54-year-old chief executive of Daimler Benz approached Chrysler CEO Robert J. Eaton in his office in Auburn Hills, Michigan with a scheme to merge their two companies. In a steak house with Daimler colleagues after the 17-minute chat, Schrempp worried that he may have been too bold. His fears were unfounded. America's scrappy No. 3 car company and Germany's most revered brand name quickly decided to combine to become the world's fifth-largest carmaker when shares in DaimlerChrysler first traded in November, 1998.

14   Schrempp and Eaton are entering into an unprecedented business experiment. The auto industry has long been among the world's most international. But the DaimlerChrysler merger ushers in a new phase of global competitiveness when the very biggest players in the world's main regions unite as industrial powerhouses of tremendous scope. Schrempp will be judged both on his ability to run this ungainly giant and on whether he can emerge as Europe's most forceful business leader.

15   The megadeal unites two of the world's most profitable auto companies—with combined 1997 net earnings of $4.6 billion. And if ever a merger had the potential for that elusive quality—

synergy—this could be the one. Mercedes-Benz passenger cars are synonymous with luxury and sterling engineering. Chrysler is renowned for its low-cost production of trucks, minivans, and sport-utility vehicles. Chrysler is almost wholly domestic, and Mercedes is increasing global sales—albeit within the confines of the luxury-car market. By spreading Chrysler's production expertise to Daimler operations and merging both product-development forces, the new company could cut costs by up to $3 billion annually—including $1.1 billion in purchasing costs, analysts say. And fundamental synergies are as follows:

Product Synergies: There is almost no product overlap. Mercedes-Benz luxury cars compete in a market beyond Chrysler's mainstream offerings. Chrysler brings strength in minivans, profitable pickups, and sport-utility vehicles. Mercedes has hot-sellers like the E-class sedan and SLK roadster. The only overlapping model: Mercedes M-class, which goes against Jeep Grand Cherokee.

Geographic Synergies: Each company is strong where the other is weak. Chrysler derives 93% of its sales from North America. Mercedes-Benz depends on Europe for 63% of its business. Each company is looking to strengthen its position in its partner's home market and conquer emerging markets together.

One of the biggest opportunities is for the paired company to plunge into new markets that neither could assay alone. Neither has much of a presence in Latin America or Asia, although Daimler does sell heavy trucks there. Chrysler's inexpensive small cars will give Daimler a vehicle to drive into emerging markets. "With our [upscale] product portfolio, we will never be a mass marketer," says a source close to Daimler. "There are some markets where [Mercedes] will never be able to have an impact."

Operational Synergies: Chrysler's slowly improving quality could take a quantum leap forward with help from Daimler engineers. And Daimler's diesel engines, for example, could help Chrysler in its efforts to sell subcompacts and minivans in Europe and elsewhere. Chrysler, for its part, has the industry's best supplier relations, while Daimler still relies on strong-arm techniques to get lower prices from its suppliers. Together, they can save on warehousing and logistics for cars and spare parts in both Europe and the U.S. They also can jointly make internal components like air-conditioning systems and door latches and pool their resources in developing basic technology.

COMBINING DIVERGENT CORPORATE CULTURES: THE KEY CHALLENGE

16   Most rivals were too stunned to react when the merger was first announced. Both Ford and GM declined to comment in the U.S. as did BMW in Germany. On the other hand, many industry watchers immediately questioned whether the enormously divergent cultures of Auburn Hills and Stuttgart won't get in the way of all that synergy. "I can't imagine two more different cultures," says Furman Selz auto analyst Maryann N. Keller. Chrysler's brushes with bankruptcy forged a culture dedicated to speedy product development, lean operations, and flashy design. Daimler remains a buttoned-down, engineering-driven bureaucracy known for conservatively styled products. "The reaction here is shock, excitement, enthusiasm, and concern," said one Chrysler exec.

17   Indeed, most observers feel that Daimler-Chrysler's success hinges on melding two starkly different corporate cultures. Daimler's methodical decision making could squelch Chrysler's famed creativity. Mercedes' reputation for luxury and quality could be tarnished by Chrysler's downmarket image. If they can't create a climate of learning from each other, warns Ulrich Steger, a management professor at IMD, the Lausanne business school, "they could be heading for unbelievable catastrophe."

18   If that happens, it won't be the first time. Big cross-border mergers have a poor track record. In most cases, the hoped-for savings are not realized, the weaker partner is stripped of its best assets, and margins plunge. For instance, BMW's merger with Rover floundered because BMW lacked a clear strategy, and the companies' models cannibalized each other. BMW has asked the British government for aid. Another deal involving a high-profile takeover by an admired foreign company of prized American assets: Sony Corp.'s acquisition of both CBS Records Inc. and Columbia Pictures saw Sony start off mistakenly thinking that it could oversee its freewheeling American companies from afar and with a light touch. It failed to put its own

strong management structure in the U.S. It neglected to build links between Sony's American subsidiaries on the two coasts. It lost control of expenses, and by 1994, Sony was forced to take a $2.7 billion write-off.

19 Sony and Daimler are in different businesses, of course, and no one blueprint applies to all big international mergers. But the most successful global companies, such as Nestlé, ABB Asea Brown Boveri, and General Electric, have put their unambiguous imprint on all their operations by imposing one strong corporate culture with central management for the most critical functions. Someone must articulate overall philosophy and values and establish companywide investment priorities. Someone must set financial and operational performance requirements, compensation policies, and development paths for senior executives. Unless Daimler takes charge of these kinds of tasks immediately, don't be surprised if the deal comes unwound.

20 To avoid a similar fate, Schrempp and Eaton analyzed 50 large-scale mergers from many industries before launching their own. They found that 70% had stumbled, most for lack of clear targets and speed. "What you don't do in the first 12 to 24 months will be very difficult to do later," Schrempp said.

21 That's especially true for two industrial icons from business cultures that couldn't be more different. Chrysler is the very symbol of American adaptability and resilience. Having survived a near-death experience that required a 1979 government bailout, it scrambled under legendary CEO Lee A. Iacocca, and then Eaton, to become one of the world's leanest and nimblest car companies.

22 Daimler Benz, meanwhile, has long represented the epitome of German industrial might, its Mercedes cars the purest examples of German quality and engineering. But despite Schrempp's shakeup at the top, its middle ranks exemplify the hierarchical, procedure-driven German management style that could smother an agile company like Chrysler.

23 He was certainly the dominant player in forging the merger. "I wasn't going to sit passively and be the object of someone else's decision," Schrempp told 1,000 of Munich's glitterati as he introduced the new Mercedes S-Class sedan last month. Schrempp had talked to Ford Motor Co. in 1997, but the U.S. company's family-ownership structure would have complicated a merger. Sources close to Daimler say that Schrempp also approached Honda Motor Co., but found the cultural differences too great.

24 Investors immediately applauded—pushing Chrysler shares up $7\frac{3}{8}$ to $48\frac{13}{16}$ on May 6. "Chrysler has the trucks, vans, and SUVs, and Daimler has the luxury cars," says Seth M. Glickenhaus of Glickenhaus & Co., an investment firm that holds 8 million Chrysler shares. "There are enormous synergies in product." Amid the initial euphoria, *BusinessWeek*'s Jeffrey E. Garten offered perhaps the most objective summary of the cultural challenge to make the DaimlerChrysler merger work: The new company will face massive challenges. DaimlerChrysler will still be only the fifth-largest car company, behind General Motors, Ford, Toyota, and Volkswagen. Its product line, ranging from an $11,000 Dodge to a $130,000 Mercedes, could foster a confused image and culture. The German corporate governance system in which labor and banks hold board seats in order to take a longer-term view could collide with the obsession of American shareholders with immediate returns. Compensation philosophies could be irreconcilable: Just compare Chrysler Chairman and CEO Robert J. Eaton's 1997 pay package of $16 million with that of Daimler chief Jürgen E. Schrempp's $1.9 million. And politically explosive decisions are sure to arise about how to apportion layoffs between America and Germany when downsizing occurs because of the overcapacity in the global auto industry.

25 One final likely outcome from this merger, well before anyone knows if DaimlerChrysler is a success—its very existence could reshape the industry. Look for automakers to scramble for partners to ensure survival as one of the 21st century 20. How that plays out is anybody's guess. "The odd man out here seems to be the Japanese," says Phillippi of Lehman Brothers. "Nissan and Honda in particular have only two legs to stand on: North America and Japan." That won't be enough in this race.

DAIMLERCHRYSLER—2001

26 MARCH 2001. It has been a disastrous run for DaimlerChrysler CEO Jürgen E. Schrempp: expected losses in the billions at Chrysler, a huge

recall at DaimlerChrysler's partner, Mitsubishi Motors Corp., savage attacks in the usually respectful German press. Wrote a commentator recently in the weekly *Die Zeit:* "Should Daimler get rid of Chrysler—or Schrempp?"

27   Schrempp's not going anywhere for now. If anything, he plans to tighten his grip on his global auto empire in a bold attempt to turn this company around for good. The really interesting moves involve the executive suite and Schrempp's own tortured relationship with Chrysler headquarters in Auburn Hills, Michigan. He plans to scrap the automotive and sales councils that Daimler Benz and Chrysler Corp. decided to set up after they merged in 1998. Instead, Schrempp will create a tightly knit executive auto committee headed by him and by Mercedes-Benz chief Jürgen Hubbert. The new committee will make all key strategic decisions and coordinate production and marketing across the group's divisions.

28   It will be an all-German club. Other members will include Daimler hands who helped Schrempp consolidate his power six years ago: Chrysler CEO Dieter Zetsche, commercial vehicles director Eckhard Cordes, Mitsubishi board member Manfred Bischoff, and corporate strategy director Rudiger Grube. The idea is to speed up decision making on everything from overhauling assembly lines and laying off workers to sharing technologies and parts among Chrysler, Mercedes, and Mitsubishi.

29   Another power grab by the *uber*-boss? This time, it makes sense. True, the American absence in the inner circle will be painful to what's left of Chrysler's executive corps. But the only way to boost morale at Chrysler is to get it back on its feet. If the streamlined structured can turn Chrysler around, hurt feelings will fade. While Germans like Schrempp are portrayed as terribly aggressive, their problem to date has been in waiting too long to interfere with foreign subsidiaries. BMW left management of its Rover acquisition in British hands until the brand's value had deteriorated alarmingly. Similarly, if investors want to fault Schrempp for anything, it should be for not stepping in and taking control of Chrysler much earlier. He even left an inexperienced North American executive in charge for nearly a year before bringing in Zetsche. So to analysts, setting up this committee is part of the same take-charge approach Schrempp has shown by sending Zetsche to fix Chrysler, and it's welcome.

30   Of course, Schremmp has yet to find the answer to the most perplexing question: Can anyone run a monster like DaimlerChrysler? No car merger of this kind has ever been tried, so there's no blueprint on the best way to run it. Diffuse decision making certainly didn't do the trick. But Schremmp's central committee risks misreading certain markets and their special demands by making the decisions from too far away. The committee will certainly have to get results fast. Schremmp has agreed to meet six-month performance targets, which could include anything from operating profit to productivity goals. If he misses those targets, the pressure will mount for his removal.

31   NOVEMBER 2001. Just eight months ago, DaimlerChrysler (DCX) CEO Jürgen Schrempp was in the hot seat. Chrysler was expected to lose billions, and some shareholders and commentators were calling for his ouster. But Schrempp dug in his heels, centralized decision making, and agreed to meet tough performance targets: at least $1.1 billion in operating profit this year.

32   Chrysler indeed is losing billions. But thanks to draconian cost-cutting at Chrysler and the consistent strength of the Mercedes-Benz luxury car business, Schrempp still expects the company to meet his 2001 target. Investors were pleased that Chrysler's third-quarter losses, bad as they were, weren't worse. In the meantime, Schrempp has expanded his grip on power. On Sept. 27, DaimlerChrysler's supervisory board extended his mandate by two more years, to 2005

33   September 11 has thrown all these calculations off. Schrempp has already told division chiefs to rethink their numbers in light of the deteriorating economy and get back to him in December—the first sign he may have trouble meeting the 2002 target. Next year will test all of Schrempp's management skills. The company estimates that industry sales will decline by 5% to 8% in the United States and 2% to 3% in Europe. With incentives surging in the U.S. market, Chrysler may have to cut costs even more next year than planned. It already had eliminated 26,000 jobs, slashed procurement costs and cut capacity by 15%. "Like Ford and General Motors, we might have to idle additional plants for two or three weeks, depending on the market," says Schrempp.

34   Schrempp is sticking to his vision of turning DaimlerChrysler into a mighty global group offering a full range of vehicles, from subcompacts to heavy trucks in all major markets. But with Chrysler's outlook deteriorating by the day, balancing long- and short-term goals—especially the interest of Mercedes and Chrysler—will keep getting harder and harder. The survivor still has to learn how to thrive.

Sources: "Schrempp, the Survivor?" *BusinessWeek,* March 5, 2001; "Downshifting Ambitions at DaimlerChrysler," *BusinessWeek,* November 12, 2001.

Part Three

Strategy Implementation

The last section of this book examines what is often called the *action phase* of the strategic management process: implementation of the chosen strategy. Up to this point, three phases of that process have been covered—strategy formulation, analysis of alternative strategies, and strategic choice. Although important, these phases alone cannot ensure success. To ensure success, the strategy must be translated into carefully implemented action. This means that:

1. The strategy must be translated into guidelines for the daily activities of the firm's members.

2. The strategy and the firm must become one—that is, the strategy must be reflected in the way the firm organizes its activities and in the firm's values, beliefs, and tone.

3. In implementing the strategy, the firm's managers must direct and control actions and outcomes and adjust to change.

Chapter 9 explains how organizational action is successfully initiated in four interrelated steps:

1 Creation of clear *short-term objectives* and *action plans.*

2. Development of specific *functional tactics* that create competitive advantage.

3. Empowerment of operating personnel through *policies* to guide decisions.

4. Implementation of effective *reward system.*

Short-term objectives and action plans guide implementation by converting long-term objectives into short-term actions and targets. Functional tactics translate the business strategy into activities that build advantage. Policies empower operating personnel by defining guidelines for making decisions. Reward systems encourage effective results.

Today's competitive environment often necessitates restructuring and reengineering the organization to sustain competitive advantage. Chapter 10 examines how restructuring and reengineering are pursued in three organizational elements that provide fundamental, long-term means for institutionalizing the firm's strategy:

1. The firm's *structure.*

2. The *leadership* provided by the firm's CEO and key managers.

3. The fit between the strategy and the firm's *culture.*

Since the firm's strategy is implemented in a changing environment, successful implementation requires that execution be controlled and continuously improved. The control and improvement process must include at least these dimensions:

1. *Strategic controls* that "steer" execution of the strategy.

2. *Operations control systems* that monitor performance, evaluate deviations, and initiate corrective action.

3. *Continuous improvement* through total quality initiatives a balanced scorecard perspective.

Chapter 11 examines the dimensions of the control and improvement process. It explains the essence of change as an ever-present force driving the need for strategic control. The chapter concludes with a look at the global "quality imperative," which is redefining the essence of control into the 21st century.

Implementation is "where the action is." It is the arena that most students enter at the start of their business careers. It is the strategic phase in which staying close to the customer, achieving competitive advantage, and pursuing excellence become realities. The chapters in this part will help you understand how this is done.

Chapter **Nine**

Implementing Strategy through Short-Term Objectives, Functional Tactics, Reward System, and Employee Empowerment

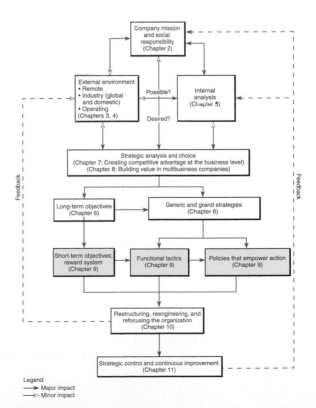

Once corporate and business strategies have been agreed upon and long-term objectives set, the strategic management process moves into a critical new phase—translating strategic thought into organizational action. In the words of two well-worn phrases, they move from "planning their work" to "working their plan" as they shift their focus from strategy formulation to strategy implementation. Managers successfully make this shift when they do four things well:

1. Identify short-term objectives.

2. Initiate specific functional tactics.

3. Communicate policies that empower people in the organization.

4. Design effective rewards.

Short-term objectives translate long-range aspirations into this year's targets for action. If well developed, these objectives provide clarity, a powerful motivator and facilitator of effective strategy implementation.

Functional tactics translate business strategy into daily activities people need to execute. Functional managers participate in the development of these tactics, and their participation, in turn, helps clarify what their units are expected to do in implementing the business's strategy.

Policies are empowerment tools that simplify decision making by empowering operating managers and their subordinates. Policies can empower the "doers" in an organization by reducing the time required to decide and act.

A powerful part of getting things done in any organization can be found in the way its reward system rewards desired action and results. Rewards that align manager and employee priorities with organizational objectives and shareholder value provide very effective direction in strategy implementation.

SHORT-TERM OBJECTIVES

Chapter 6 described business strategies, grand strategies, and long-term objectives that are critically important in crafting a successful future. To make them become a reality, however, the people in an organization that actually "do the work" of the business need guidance in exactly what needs to be done today and tomorrow to make those long-term strategies become reality. Short-term objectives help do this. They provide much more specific guidance for what is to be done, a clear delineation of impending actions needed, which helps translate vision into action.

Short-term objectives help implement strategy in at least three ways. First, short-term objectives "operationalize" long-term objectives. If we commit to a 20 percent gain in revenue over five years, what is our specific target or objective in revenue during the current year, month, or week to indicate we are making appropriate progress? Second, discussion about and agreement on short-term objectives help raise issues and potential conflicts within an organization that usually require coordination to avoid otherwise dysfunctional consequences. Exhibit 9–1 illustrates how objectives within marketing, manufacturing, and accounting units within the same firm can be very different even when created to pursue the same firm objective (e.g., increased sales, lower costs). The third way short-term objectives assist strategy implementation is to identify measurable outcomes of action plans or functional activities, which can be used to make feedback, correction, and evaluation more relevant and acceptable.

EXHIBIT 9–1
Potential Conflicting Objectives and Priorities

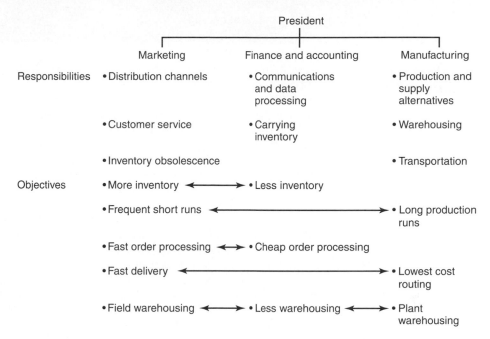

Short-term objectives are usually accompanied by action plans, which enhance these objectives in three ways. First, action plans usually identify functional tactics and activities that will be undertaken in the next week, month, or quarter as part of the business's effort to build competitive advantage. The important point here is *specificity*—what exactly is to be done. We will examine functional tactics in a subsequent section of this chapter. The second element of an action plan is a clear *time frame for completion*—when the effort will begin and when its results will be accomplished. A third element action plans contain is identification of *who is responsible* for each action in the plan. This accountability is very important to ensure action plans are acted upon. Exhibit 9–2, Strategy in Action, illustrates the use of short-term objectives, action plans, and accountability by Kmart's CEO Charles Conaway as he attempted to turn around the dying retailer.

Because of the particular importance of short-term objectives in strategy implementation, the next section addresses how to develop meaningful short-term objectives.

Qualities of Effective Short-Term Objectives

Measurable

Short-term objectives are more consistent when they clearly state *what* is to be accomplished, *when* it will be accomplished, and *how* its accomplishment will be *measured*. Such objectives can be used to monitor both the effectiveness of each activity and the collective progress across several interrelated activities. Exhibit 9–3 illustrates several effective and ineffective short-term objectives. Measurable objectives make misunderstanding less likely among interdependent managers who must implement action plans. It is far easier to quantify the objectives of *line* units (e.g., production) than of certain *staff* areas (e.g., personnel). Difficulties in quantifying objectives often can be overcome by initially focusing on *measurable activity* and then identifying *measurable outcomes*.

Strategy in Action
Short-Term Objectives, Functional Tactics and Action Plans at Kmart

Exhibit 9–2

BusinessWeek

When Charles C. Conaway became Kmart Corp. CEO, he brought along a mania for performance-based analysis. Today, it's hard to miss the point: Conaway's office is dominated by a 20-foot-long mural upon which the CEO tracks quarterly progress on nearly 100 restructuring initiatives, from replenishing shelves to implementing price changes within 48 hours. Beside each project is the cost and benefit to date, plus the name—and phone number—of the manager in charge. "It's the ultimate accountability," Conaway says.

Accountability has been in short supply for years at the foundering discounter, which has seen one turnaround effort after another sputter out as its chronically understocked shelves, tacky merchandise, and poor service drove shoppers to rivals like Wal-Mart Stores Inc. But Conaway, a 40-year-old operations whiz recruited from drug retailer CVS Corp., where he was president and COO, says he's the one to change all that. Since his arrival, Conaway and his band of young management recruits from Wal-Mart, Target, and Coca-Cola (KO) have been attacking the structural problems that led to Kmart's decline. Now that they claim to be making progress on those fronts, they're ready to issue a blue-edged invitation to consumers to try the stores again.

Conaway unveiled a new marketing strategy that draws heavily on the one icon of Kmart's past that still resonates with consumers: the Blue Light Special which was discontinued in 1991. Store managers used the flashing blue police light in the 1960s, 70s and 80s to direct shoppers to unadvertised bargains. By offering a contemporary take on that old device, company officials hope to restore a sense of excitement and reward to shopping at Kmart. "There's a funness to it that, frankly, Kmart didn't have [recently],"

says Steve Feuling, chief marketing officer for Kmart's Blue Light efforts.

The return of the Blue Light via a $25 million advertising blitz, the biggest such initiative in Kmart history, is just a piece of Conaway's overall strategy. After all, the marketing come-on will be wasted if consumers enticed into the stores suffer the same old frustrations. So Conaway has been taking sweeping—and costly—steps to raise service levels, ensure that popular items are in stock, and brighten up the stores.

Conaway's elaborate chart notwithstanding, the payoff still isn't clear. That't why all the resuscitation efforts are overshadowed by a big question: Is there still a role for Kmart between Wal-Mart and Target? "I'm not sure there's room for them," bluntly says the CEO of a major supplier to all three. But Conaway vows it's not too late—as long as Kmart does a better job of staking out its turf between low-price leader Wal-Mart and cheap-chic purveyor Target. Conaway insists the middle ground is wide open for a retailer that relentlessly focuses on moms and two of their key priorities: their kids and their homes. Kmart can meet those priorities with exclusive brands like Martha Stewart and Sesame Street and new licensing and promotional tie-ins with everyone from Walt Disney Co. (DIS) to World Wrestling Federation Entertainment Inc. (WWF) creating a buzz. With research showing that shoppers still have fond memories of the Blue Light Special, the discounter is putting the blue hue at the center of its effort to entice them into the stores more often. TBWA\Chiat\Day, the ad agency best known for its cutting-edge work for Apple Computer, will herald that "The Blue Light Is Back" with ads that place a blue glow in such unexpected settings as the Statue of Liberty's torch or fireflies buzzing in a kid's jar. Kmart's BlueLight.com e-commerce effort

Priorities

Although all annual objectives are important, some deserve priority because of a timing consideration or their particular impact on a strategy's success. If such priorities are not established, conflicting assumptions about the relative importance of annual objectives may inhibit progress toward strategic effectiveness. Facing the most rapid, dramatic decline in profitability of any major computer manufacturer as it confronted relentless lower pricing by Dell Computer and AST, Compaq Computer formulated a retrenchment strategy with several important annual objectives in pricing, product design, distribution, and financial condition. But its highest priority was to dramatically lower overhead and production costs so as to satisfy the difficult challenge of dramatically lowering prices while also restoring profitability.

Exhibit 9–2

already has shown that the theme can click even with more cutting-edge consumers.

Consumers intrigued enough to pay a visit will find that once-dreary stores have been splashed with blue and animated by "celebrity" announcers—Homer Simpson is a possibility—directing shoppers to a central "Blue Light Zone" for the deals. This time around, they're not junky clearance items but coveted products like Sony Playstations, TVs, and Coca-Cola. Also new: a "Blue Light Always" pricing strategy that will slash tags on everyday basics like shampoo, diapers, medicines, and groceries by 2% to 5% to make them competitive with Wal-Mart prices. "Now we're saying we're there for everything you need," says Conaway.

ATTENTION KMART SKEPTICS

Here's how Kmart hopes to get customers into its stores more often

- *Brighter marketing.* It will bathe stores in blue and debut an updated "Blue Light Special" with a $25 million ad blitz.

- *Lower price.* Kmart is matching Wal-Mart (WMT) prices on thousands of basic items.

- *More stock.* It is spending $2 billion to overhaul inventory controls and increase the items it has on hand.

- *Better service.* Employee incentives are helping to raise customer-satisfaction ratings.

Just getting Kmart's best customers to increase their visits from 3.2 per month to 4, as Wal-Mart's core shoppers do, would add $2.8 billion to the top line, says Kmart's chief marketing officer Brent Willis, a recruit from Coke's Latin American unit. "We don't have to take a single customer from Wal-Mart," he says.

To make sure shelves are kept fully stocked, Kmart is spending nearly $2 billion on technology to overhaul its inventory controls. Since October, it's also taken an unusual tack to upgrade service by entering all shoppers willing to dial a hotline in a $10,000 sweepstakes to rate their overall shopping experience. Some 20 million already have responded, generating a database that enables managers to pinpoint performance at the store level and reward cashiers at popular units with as much as $1,200 in quarterly bonuses. Since the program began, Kmart says its satisfaction rating has climbed from 40% to 55%. Conaway's goal is 70%.

Shoppers like Dolores Ronzani, who still smiles at the recollection of booty scored from Blue Light Specials of decades ago, seem receptive to the idea. These days, the 70-year-old widow from Highland Park, Ill., frequents Target, Marshalls, and T.J. Maxx but finds they don't measure up to Kmart in its heyday: "The excitement of the Blue Light Special is missing." If it's excitement she craves, Conaway and Co. aim to provide it in spades.

Source: "Kmart's Bright Idea," *BusinessWeek,* April 9, 2001.

Priorities are established in various ways. A simple *ranking* may be based on discussion and negotiation during the planning process. However, this does not necessarily communicate the real difference in the importance of objectives, so such terms as *primary, top,* and *secondary* may be used to indicate priority. Some firms assign *weights* (e.g., 0 to 100 percent) to establish and communicate the relative priority of objectives. Whatever the method, recognizing priorities is an important dimension in the implementation value of short-term objectives.

Linked to Long-Term Objectives

Short-term objectives can add breadth and specificity in identifying *what* must be accomplished to achieve long-term objectives. For example, Wal-Mart's top management recently set out "to obtain 45 percent market share in five years" as a long-term objective. Achieving that objective can be greatly enhanced if a series of specific short-term objectives identify what must be accomplished each year in order to do so. If Wal-Mart's market share is now 25 percent, then one likely annual objective might be "to have each regional office achieve a minimum 4 percent increase in market share in the next year." "Open two regional distribution centers in the Southwest in 2005" might be an annual objective that Wal-Mart's marketing and distribution managers consider essential if the firm

EXHIBIT 9–3
Creating Measurable
Objectives

Examples of Deficient Objectives	Examples of Objectives with Measurable Criteria for Performance
To improve morale in the division (plant, department, etc.)	To reduce turnover (absenteeism, number of rejects, etc.) among sales managers by 10 percent by January 1, 2004. *Assumption:* Morale is related to measurable outcomes (i.e., high and low morale are associated with different results).
To improve support of the sales effort	To reduce the time lapse between order data and delivery by 8 percent (two days) by June 1, 2004.
	To reduce the cost of goods produced by 6 percent to support a product price decrease of 2 percent by December 1, 2004.
	To increase the rate of before- or on-schedule delivery by 5 percent by June 1, 2004.
To improve the firm's image	To conduct a public opinion poll using random samples in the five largest U.S. metropolitan markets to determine average scores on 10 dimensions of corporate responsibility by May 15, 2004. To increase our score on those dimensions by an average of 7.5 percent by May 1, 2005.

is to achieve a 45 percent market share in five years. "Conclude arrangements for a $1 billion line of credit at 0.25 percent above prime in 2004" might be an annual objective of Wal-Mart's financial managers to support the operation of new distribution centers and the purchase of increased inventory in reaching the firm's long-term objective.

The link between short-term and long-term objectives should resemble cascades through the firm from basic long-term objectives to specific short-term objectives in key operation areas. The cascading effect has the added advantage of providing a clear reference for communication and negotiation, which may be necessary to integrate and coordinate objectives and activities at the operating level.

The qualities of good objectives discussed in Chapter 6—acceptable, flexible, suitable, motivating, understandable, and achievable—also apply to short-term objectives. They will not be discussed again here, but you should review the discussion in Chapter 6 to appreciate these qualities, common to all good objectives.

The Value-Added Benefits of Short-Term Objectives and Action Plans

One benefit of short-term objectives and action plans is that they give operating personnel a better understanding of their role in the firm's mission. "Achieve $2.5 million in 2005 sales in the Chicago territory," "Develop an OSHA-approved safety program for handling acids at all Georgia Pacific plants in 2005," and "Reduce Ryder Truck's average age of accounts receivable to 31 days by the end of 2005" are examples of how short-term objectives clarify the role of particular personnel in their firm's broader mission. Such *clarity of purpose* can be a major force in helping use a firm's "people assets" more effectively, which may add tangible value.

A second benefit of short-term objectives and action plans comes from the process of developing them. If the managers responsible for this accomplishment have participated in their development, short-term objectives and action plans provide valid bases for addressing and accommodating conflicting concerns that might interfere with strategic effectiveness (see Exhibit 9–1). Meetings to set short-term objectives and action plans become the forum for raising and resolving conflicts between strategic intentions and operating realities.

A third benefit of short-term objectives and action plans is that they provide *a basis for strategic control.* The control of strategy will be examined in detail in Chapter 11. However, it is important to recognize here that short-term objectives and action plans provide a clear, measurable basis for developing budgets, schedules, trigger points, and other mechanisms for controlling the implementation of strategy. Exhibit 9–2, Strategy in Action, describes how new Kmart CEO Charles Conaway used short-term objectives as a key basis for strategic control.

A fourth benefit is often a *motivational payoff.* Short-term objectives and action plans that clarify personal and group roles in a firm's strategies and are also measurable, realistic, and challenging can be powerful motivators of managerial performance—particularly when these objectives are linked to the firm's reward structure.

FUNCTIONAL TACTICS THAT IMPLEMENT BUSINESS STRATEGIES

Functional tactics are the key, routine activities that must be undertaken in each functional area—marketing, finance, production/operations, R&D, and human resource management—to provide the business's products and services. In a sense, functional tactics translate thought (grand strategy) into action designed to accomplish specific short-term objectives. Every value chain activity in a company executes functional tactics that support the business's strategy and help accomplish strategic objectives.

Exhibit 9–4 illustrates the difference between functional tactics and corporate and business strategy. It also shows that functional tactics are essential to implement business strategy. The corporate strategy defined General Cinema Corporation's general posture in the broad economy. The business strategy outlined the competitive posture of its operations in the movie theater industry. To increase the likelihood that these strategies would be successful, specific functional tactics were needed for the firm's operating components. These functional tactics clarified the business strategy, giving specific, short-term guidance to operating managers in the areas of marketing, operations, and finance.

Differences between Business Strategies and Functional Tactics

Functional tactics are different from business or corporate strategies in three fundamental ways:

1. Time horizon.

2. Specificity.

3. Participants who develop them.

Time Horizon

Functional tactics identify activities to be undertaken "now" or in the immediate future. Business strategies focus on the firm's posture three to five years out. Delta Air lines is committed to a concentration/market development business strategy that seeks competitive advantage via differentiation in its level of service and focus on the business traveler. Its pricing tactics are often to price above industry averages, but it often lowers fares on

EXHIBIT 9–4
Functional Tactics
at General Cinema
Corporation

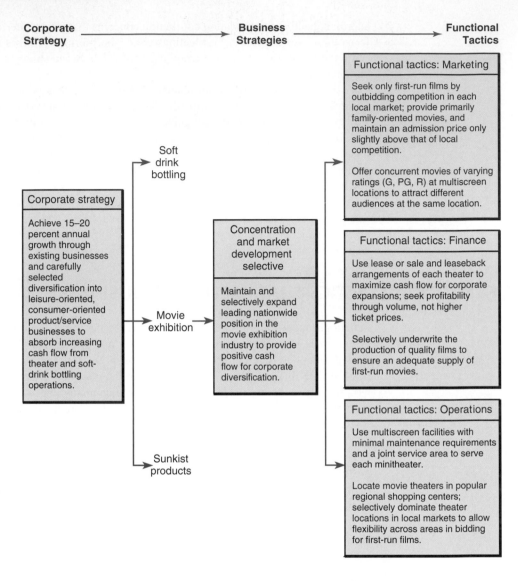

selected routes to thwart low-cost competition. Its business strategy is focused 10 years out; its pricing tactics change weekly.

The shorter time horizon of functional tactics is critical to the successful implementation of a business strategy for two reasons. First, it focuses the attention of functional managers on what needs to be done *now* to make the business strategy work. Second, it allows functional managers like those at Delta to adjust to changing current conditions.

Specificity

Functional tactics are more specific than business strategies. Business strategies provide general direction. Functional tactics identify the specific activities that are to be undertaken in each functional area and thus allow operating managers to work out *how* their unit is expected to pursue short-term objectives. General Cinema's business strategy gave its movie theater division broad direction on how to pursue a concentration and selective market development strategy. Two functional tactics in the marketing area gave managers specific direction on what types of movies (first-run, primarily family-oriented, G, PG, R) should be shown and what pricing strategy (competitive in the local area) should be followed.

Specificity in functional tactics contributes to successful implementation by:

- Helping ensure that functional managers know what needs to be done and can focus on accomplishing results.

- Clarifying for top management how functional managers intend to accomplish the business strategy, which increases top management's confidence in and sense of control over the business strategy.

- Facilitating coordination among operating units *within* the firm by clarifying areas of interdependence and potential conflict.

Exhibit 9–5, Strategy in Action, illustrates the nature and value of specificity in functional tactics versus business strategy in an upscale pizza restaurant chain.

Participants

Different people participate in strategy development at the functional and business levels. Business strategy is the responsibility of the general manager of a business unit. That manager typically delegates the development of functional tactics to subordinates charged with running the operating areas of the business. The manager of a business unit must establish long-term objectives and a strategy that corporate management feels contributes to corporate-level goals. Similarly, key operating managers must establish short-term objectives and operating strategies that contribute to business-level goals. Just as business strategies and objectives are approved through negotiation between corporate managers and business managers, so, too, are short-term objectives and functional tactics approved through negotiation between business managers and operating managers.

Involving operating managers in the development of functional tactics improves their understanding of what must be done to achieve long-term objectives and, thus, contributes to successful implementation. It also helps ensure that functional tactics reflect the reality of the day-to-day operating situation. And perhaps most important, it can increase the commitment of operating managers to the strategies developed.

EMPOWERING OPERATING PERSONNEL: THE ROLE OF POLICIES

Specific functional tactics provide guidance and initiate action implementing a business's strategy, but more is needed. Supervisors and personnel in the field have been charged in today's competitive environment with being responsible for customer value—for being the "front line" of the company's effort to truly meet customers' needs. Meeting customer needs, becoming obsessed with quality service, was the buzzword that started organizational revolutions in the 1980s. Efforts to do so often failed because employees that were the real contact point between the business and its customers were not *empowered* to make decisions or act to fulfill customer needs. One solution has been to empower operating personnel by pushing down decision making to their level. General Electric allows appliance repair personnel to decide about warranty credits on the spot, a decision that used to take several days and multiple organizational levels. Delta Air Lines allows customer service personnel and their supervisors wide range in resolving customer ticket pricing decisions. Federal Express couriers make decisions and handle package routing information that involves five management levels in the U.S. Postal Service.

Strategy in Action
The Nature and Value of Specificity in Functional Tactics versus Business Strategy

Exhibit 9–5

BusinessWeek A restaurant business was encountering problems. Although its management had agreed unanimously that it was committed to a business strategy to differentiate itself from other competitors based on concept and customer service rather than price, it continued to encounter inconsistencies across different store locations in how well it did this. Consultants indicated that the customer experience varied greatly from store to store. The conclusion was that while the management understood the "business strategy," and the employees did too in general terms, the implementation was inadequate because of a lack of specificity in the functional tactics—what everyone should do every day in the restaurant—to make the vision a reality in terms of the customers' dining experience. The following breakdown of part of their business strategy into specific functional tactics just in the area of customer service helps illustrate the value specificity in functional tactics brings to strategy implementation.

Source: Adapted from "How to Have Your Pizza and Eat It, Too," *BusinessWeek,* November 16, 1998; and A. Campbell and K. Luchs, *Strategic Synergy* (London: Butterworth-Heineman, 1992).

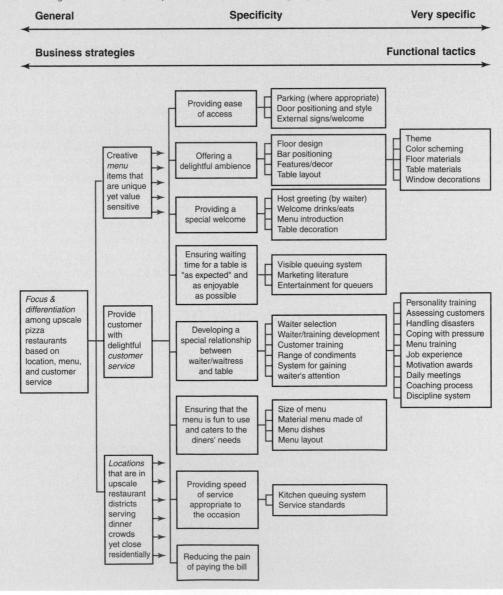

Empowerment is being created in many ways. Training, self-managed work groups, eliminating whole levels of management in organizations, and aggressive use of automation are some of the ways and ramifications of this fundamental change in the way business organizations function. At the heart of the effort is the need to ensure that decision making is consistent with the mission, strategy, and tactics of the business while at the same time allowing considerable latitude to operating personnel. One way operating managers do this is through the use of policies.

Policies are directives designed to guide the thinking, decisions, and actions of managers and their subordinates in implementing a firm's strategy. Previously referred to as *standard operating procedures,* policies increase managerial effectiveness by standardizing many routine decisions and clarifying the discretion managers and subordinates can exercise in implementing functional tactics. Logically, policies should be derived from functional tactics (and, in some instances, from corporate or business strategies) with the key purpose of aiding strategy execution.[1] Exhibit 9–6, Strategy in Action, illustrates selected policies of several well-known firms.

Creating Policies That Empower

Policies communicate guidelines to decisions. They are designed to control decisions while defining allowable discretion within which operational personnel can execute business activities. They do this in several ways:

1. *Policies establish indirect control over independent action* by clearly stating how things are to be done *now.* By defining discretion, policies in effect control decisions yet empower employees to conduct activities without direct intervention by top management.

2. *Policies promote uniform handling of similar activities.* This facilitates the coordination of work tasks and helps reduce friction arising from favoritism, discrimination, and the disparate handling of common functions—something that often hampers operating personnel.

3. *Policies ensure quicker decisions* by standardizing answers to previously answered questions that otherwise would recur and be pushed up the management hierarchy again and again—something that required unnecessary levels of management between senior decision makers and field personnel.

4. *Policies institutionalize basic aspects of organization behavior.* This minimizes conflicting practices and establishes consistent patterns of action in attempts to make the strategy work—again, freeing operating personnel to act.

5. *Policies reduce uncertainty in repetitive and day-to-day decision making,* thereby providing a necessary foundation for coordinated, efficient efforts and freeing operating personnel to act.

---

[1] The term *policy* has various definitions in management literature. Some authors and practitioners equate policy with strategy. Others do this inadvertently by using *policy* as a synonym for company mission, purpose, or culture. Still other authors and practitioners differentiate policy in terms of "levels" associated respectively with purpose, mission, and strategy. "Our policy is to make a positive contribution to the communities and societies we live in" and "our policy is not to diversify out of the hamburger business" are two examples of the breadth of what some call policies. This book defines *policy* much more narrowly as specific guides to managerial action and decisions in the implementation of strategy. This definition permits a sharper distinction between the formulation and implementation of functional strategies. And, of even greater importance, it focuses the tangible value of the policy concept where it can be most useful—as a key administrative tool to enhance effective implementation and execution of strategy.

3M Corporation has a *personnel policy,* called the *15 percent rule,* that allows virtually any employee to spend up to 15 percent of the workweek on anything that he or she wants to, as long as it's product related.

(This policy supports 3M's corporate strategy of being a highly innovative manufacturer, with each division required to have a quarter of its annual sales come from products introduced within the past five years.)

Wendy's has a *purchasing policy* that gives local store managers the authority to buy fresh meat and produce locally, rather than from regionally designated or company-owned sources.

(This policy supports Wendy's functional strategy of having fresh, unfrozen hamburgers daily.)

General Cinema has a *financial policy* that requires annual capital investment in movie theaters not to exceed annual depreciation.

(By seeing that capital investment is no greater than depreciation, this policy supports General Cinema's financial strategy of maximizing cash flow—in this case, all profit—to its growth areas. The policy also reinforces General Cinema's financial strategy of leasing as much as possible.)

IBM had a *marketing policy* of not giving free IBM personal computers (PCs) to any person or organization.

(This policy attempted to support IBM's image strategy by maintaining its image as a professional, high-value, service business as it sought to dominate the PC market.)

Crown, Cork, and Seal Company has an *R&D policy* of not investing any financial or people resources in basic research.

(This policy supports Crown, Cork, and Seal's functional strategy, which emphasizes customer services, not technical leadership.)

Bank of America has an *operating policy* that requires annual renewal of the financial statement of all personal borrowers.

(This policy supports Bank of America's financial strategy, which seeks to maintain a loan-to-loss ratio below the industry norm.)

6. *Policies counteract resistance to or rejection of chosen strategies by organization members.* When major strategic change is undertaken, unambiguous operating policies clarify what is expected and facilitate acceptance, particularly when operating managers participate in policy development.

7. *Policies offer predetermined answers to routine problems.* This greatly expedites dealing with both ordinary and extraordinary problems—with the former, by referring to these answers; with the latter, by giving operating personnel more time to cope with them.

8. *Policies afford managers a mechanism for avoiding hasty and ill-conceived decisions in changing operations.* Prevailing policy can always be used as a reason for not yielding to emotion-based, expedient, or temporarily valid arguments for altering procedures and practices.

Policies may be written and formal or unwritten and informal. Informal, unwritten policies are usually associated with a strategic need for competitive secrecy. Some policies of this kind, such as promotion from within, are widely known (or expected) by employees and implicitly sanctioned by management. Managers and employees often like the latitude granted by unwritten and informal policies. However, such policies may detract from the long-term success of a strategy. Formal, written policies have at least seven advantages:

1. They require managers to think through the policy's meaning, content, and intended use.

2. They reduce misunderstanding.

3. They make equitable and consistent treatment of problems more likely.

4. They ensure unalterable transmission of policies.

5. They communicate the authorization or sanction of policies more clearly.

6. They supply a convenient and authoritative reference.

7. They systematically enhance indirect control and organizationwide coordination of the key purposes of policies.

The strategic significance of policies can vary. At one extreme are such policies as travel reimbursement procedures, which are really work rules and may not be linked to the implementation of a strategy. At the other extreme are organizationwide policies that are virtually functional strategies, such as Wendy's requirement that every location invest 1 percent of its gross revenue in local advertising.

Policies can be externally imposed or internally derived. Policies regarding equal employment practices are often developed in compliance with external (government) requirements, and policies regarding leasing or depreciation may be strongly influenced by current tax regulations.

Regardless of the origin, formality, and nature of policies, the key point to bear in mind is that they can play an important role in strategy implementation. Communicating specific policies will help overcome resistance to strategic change, empower people to act, and foster commitment to successful strategy implementation.

Policies empower people to act. Compensation, at least theoretically, rewards their action. The last decade has seen many firms realize that the link between compensation, particularly executive management compensation, and value-building strategic outcomes within their firms was uncertain. The recognition of this uncertainty has brought about increased recognition of the need to link management compensation with the successful implementation of strategies that build long-term shareholder value. The next section examines this development and major types of executive bonus compensation plans.

EXECUTIVE BONUS COMPENSATION PLANS[2]

Major Plan Types

The goal of an executive bonus compensation plan is to motivate executives to achieve maximization of shareholder wealth—the underlying goal of most firms. Since shareholders are both owners and investors of the firm, they desire a reasonable return on their investment. Because they are absentee landlords, shareholders want the decision-making logic of their firm's executives to be concurrent with their own primary motivation.

However, agency theory instructs us that the goal of shareholder wealth maximization is not the only goal that executives may pursue. Alternatively, executives may choose actions that increase their personal compensation, power, and control. Therefore, an executive compensation plan that contains a bonus component can be used to orient management's decision making toward the owners' goals. The success of bonus compensation as an incentive hinges on a proper match between an executive bonus plan and the firm's strategic objectives. As one author has written: "Companies can succeed by clarifying their business vision or strategy and aligning company pay programs with its strategic direction."[3]

---

[2] We wish to thank Roy Hossler for his assistance on this section.
[3] James E. Nelson, "Linking Compensation to Business Strategy," *The Journal of Business Strategy* 19, no. 2 (1998), pp. 25–27.

BusinessWeek
Microsoft has issued 807 million stock options to employees since 1990—worth $80 billion if they were exercised in late 1998.

Analysts estimate several thousand of Microsoft's 28,000 employees are stock-option millionaires. Even relatively low-level managers can tuck away a small fortune.

The option plan has made some veteran executives fabulously wealthy, including Michel Lacombe, president,

Microsoft Europe, $152 million; Paul Maritz, group vice-president, $176 million; Nathan Myrhvold, chief technology officer, $179 million; Jeffrey Raikes, group vice-president, $237 million.

But the biggest winner is Bill Gates, whose 20.8% stake in Microsoft was worth a staggering $50 billion in 1998.

Source: Table: "The Microsoft Money Machine," *BusinessWeek,* October 26, 1998.

Stock Options

A common measure of shareholder wealth creation is appreciation of company stock price. Therefore, a popular form of bonus compensation is stock options. Stock options currently represent 55 percent of a chief executive officer's average pay package.[4] Stock options provide the executive with the right to purchase company stock at a fixed price in the future. The precise amount of compensation is based on the difference, or "spread," between the option's initial price and its selling, or exercised, price. As a result, the executive receives a bonus only if the firm's share price appreciates. If the share price drops below the option price, the options become worthless. Exhibit 9–7, Strategy in Action, summarizes the Microsoft stock option story.

The largest single option sale of all time occurred on December 3, 1997. Disney Chief Executive Officer Michael D. Eisner exercised more than 7 million options on Disney stock that he had been given in 1989 as part of his bonus plan. Eisner sold his shares for more than $400 million.

Although stock options only compensate an executive when wealth is created for shareholders, some critics question whether options truly gauge executive performance. Those doubting the accuracy of options as performance measures question why an executive should profit by merely riding a bull market where virtually every blue-chip firm's stock appreciates. In essence, they argue that the stock market may lack a correlation with firm operational performance, thus the movement of a company's stock price may be mostly outside the influence of most executives.[5] The case involving Michael King of King World Productions is noteworthy.

Chief Executive Officer Michael King was granted options on December 20, 1995, at the then-market price of $39.50. In about two years the stock rose about 40 percent to $5513/16. Over the same period, the Standard & Poor's 500 stock index gained 61 percent. Although King World shareholders realized wealth creation over this period, the level was mediocre compared to what an average blue-chip stock achieved. While King's wealth increased $24 million, other shareholders would have profited more by investing in a security that mirrored the stock market.

Although the indexing of stock option plans is rare in bull markets, indexing these plans in bear markets is not uncommon. During a bear market, stock prices will decline due to outside factors such as investor uncertainty resulting from volatile international

[4] Gary McWilliams, Richard A. Melcher, and Jennifer Reingold, "Executive Pay," *BusinessWeek,* April 20, 1998, pp. 64–70.
[5] William Franklin, "Making the Fat Cats Earn Their Cream," *Accountancy,* July 1998, pp. 38–39.

markets. In this market environment, some firms will re-price their executives' options at the lower current market value. In truth, the credibility of options may be strengthened at any time by indexing firm stock performance against a peer group of stocks, or against a popular market barometer. "Indexing some of the Chief Executive Officer's options to general stock market measures, such as the Standard & Poor's 500 index, will neither reward them for bull markets, nor penalize them for bear markets; such indexing can help mitigate the effect of overall market moves on executives' pay."[6]

Research suggests that stock option plans lack the benefits of plans that include true stock ownership. Stock option plans provide unlimited upside potential for executives, but limited downside risk since executives incur only opportunity costs. Because of the tremendous advantages to the executive of stock price appreciation, there is an incentive for the executive to take undue risk. Thus, supporters of stock ownership plans argue that direct ownership instills a much stronger behavioral commitment, even when the stock price falls, since it binds executives to their firms more than do options.[7] Additionally, "Executive stock options may be an efficient means to induce management to undertake more risky projects."[8]

By providing stock option plans with a so-called reload feature, firms may reap the previously mentioned benefits of direct executive stock ownership. A *reload* is a bonus of stock options given to executives when options are exercised.[9] In other words, when the executive converts her options into shares, thereby making a very sizable personal investment in the stock of the company, she receives a second bonus grant of stock options to continue to incentivize her to perform. The reload feature allows executives to realize present-day profits, while being rewarded with new options with the potential for future share price appreciation. Because the executive can take advantage of the reload feature only when she is willing to invest her own money into the company, the reload feature achieves the firm's goal of more tightly linking shareholders' and executives' wealth.

Restricted Stock

A restricted stock plan is designed to provide benefits of direct executive stock ownership. In a typical restricted stock plan, an executive is given a specific number of company stock shares. The executive is prohibited from selling the shares for a specified time period. Should the executive leave the firm voluntarily before the restricted period ends, the shares are forfeited. Therefore, restricted stock plans are a form of deferred compensation that promotes longer executive tenure than other types of plans.

In addition to being contingent on a vesting period, restricted stock plans may also require the achievement of predetermined performance goals. Price-vesting restricted stock plans tie vesting to the firm's stock price in comparison to an index, or to reaching a predetermined goal or annual growth rate. If the executive falls short on some of the restrictions, a certain amount of shares are forfeited. The design of these plans motivates the executive to increase shareholder wealth while promoting a long-term commitment to stay with the firm.

---

[6] Nicholas Carr, "Compensation: Refining CEO Stock Options," *Harvard Business Review* 76, no. 5 (September–October 1998), pp. 15–18.
[7] Jeffrey Pfeffer, "Seven Practices of Successful Organizations," *California Management Review,* Winter 1998.
[8] Richard A. DeFusco, Robert R. Johnson, and Thomas S. Zorn, "The Effect of Executive Stock Option Plans on Stockholders and Bondholders," *Journal of Finance* 45, no. 2 (1990), pp. 617–35.
[9] Jennifer Reingold and Leah Nathans Spiro, "Nice Option If You Can Get It," *BusinessWeek,* May 4, 1998, pp. 111–14.

If the restricted stock plan lacks performance goal provisions, the executive needs only to remain employed with the firm over the vesting period to cash in on the stock. Performance provisions make sure executives are not compensated without achieving some level of shareholder wealth creation. Like stock options, restricted stock plans offer no downside risk to executives, since the shares were initially gifted to the executive. Shareholders, on the other hand, do suffer a loss in personal wealth resulting from a share price drop.

Investment bank Lehman Brothers has a restricted stock plan in place for hundreds of managing directors and senior vice presidents. The plan vests with time and does not include stock price performance provisions. It is a two-tiered plan consisting of a principal stock grant and a discounted share plan. For managing directors, the discount is 30 percent. For senior vice presidents, the discount is 25 percent. The principal stock grant is a block of shares given to the executive. The discounted share plan allows executives to purchase shares with their own money at a discount to current market prices.

Managing directors at Lehman are able to cash in on one-half the principal portion of their stock grant three years after the grant is awarded. The rest of the principal and any shares bought at a discount must vest for five years. Senior vice presidents receive the entire principal after two years and any discounted shares after five years. Provisions also exist for resignation. If managing directors leave Lehman for a competitor within three years of the award, all stock compensation is forfeited. For senior vice presidents, the period is two years, and the penalties for jumping to a noncompetitor of Lehman's are not as severe.

Golden Handcuffs

The rationale behind plans that defer compensation forms the basis for another type of executive compensation called *golden handcuffs*. Golden handcuffs refer to either a restricted stock plan, where the stock compensation is deferred until vesting time provisions are met, or to bonus income deferred in a series of annual installments. This type of plan may also involve compensating an executive a significant amount upon retirement or at some predetermined age. In most cases, compensation is forfeited if the executive voluntarily resigns or is discharged before certain time restrictions.

Many boards consider their executives' skills and talents to be their firm's most valuable assets. These "assets" create and sustain the professional relationships that generate revenue and control expenses for the firm. Research suggests that the departure of key executives is unsettling for companies and often disrupts long-range plans when new key executives adopt a different management strategy.[10] Thus, the golden handcuffs approach to executive compensation is more congruent with long-term strategies than short-term performance plans, which offer little staying-power incentive.

Firms may turn to golden handcuffs if they believe stability of management is critical to sustain growth. Jupiter Asset Management tied 10 fund managers to the firm with golden handcuffs in 1995. The compensation scheme calls for a cash payment in addition to base salaries if the managers remain at the firm for five years. From 1995 to 1996, the firm's pretax profits more than doubled, and their assets under management increased 85 percent. The firm's chairman has also signed a new incentive deal that will keep him at Jupiter for four years.

Deferred compensation is worrisome to some executives. In cases where the compensation is payable when the executives are retired and no longer in control, as when the

---

[10] William E. Hall, Brian J. Lake, Charles T. Morse, and Charles T. Morse, Jr., "More Than Golden Handcuffs," *Journal of Accountancy* 184, no. 5 (1997), pp. 37–42.

firm is acquired by another firm or a new management hierarchy is installed, the golden handcuff plans are considerably less attractive to executives.

Golden handcuffs may promote risk averseness in executive decision making due to the huge downside risk borne by executives. This risk averseness could lead to mediocre performance results from executives' decisions. When executives lose deferred compensation if the firm discharges them voluntarily or involuntarily, the executive is less likely to make bold and aggressive decisions. Rather, the executive will choose safe, conservative decisions to reduce the downside risk of bold decision making.

Golden Parachutes

Golden parachutes are a form of bonus compensation that is designed to retain talented executives. A *golden parachute* is an executive perquisite that calls for a substantial cash payment if the executive quits, is fired, or simply retires. In addition, the golden parachute may also contain covenants that allow the executive to cash in on noninvested stock compensation.

The popularity of golden parachutes grew during the last decade, when abundant hostile takeovers would often oust the acquired firm's top executives. In these cases, the golden parachutes encouraged executives to take an objective look at takeover offers. The executives could decide which move was in the best interests of the shareholders, having been personally protected in the event of a merger. The "parachute" helps soften the fall of the ousted executive. It is "golden" because the size of the cash payment often varies from several to tens of millions of dollars.

AMP Incorporated, the world's largest producer of electronic connectors, has golden parachutes for several executives. On August 4, 1998, Allied Signal proclaimed itself an unsolicited suitor for AMP. The action focused attention on the AMP parachutes for its three top executives.

Robert Ripp became AMP's chief executive officer in August 1998. If Allied Signal ousted him, he stood to receive a cash payment of three times the amount of his salary as well as his highest annual bonus from the previous three years. His current salary in 1998 was $600,000 and his 1997 bonus was almost $200,000. The cash payment to Ripp would therefore exceed $2 million. Parachutes would also open for William Hudson, the former chief executive officer, and James Marley, the former chairman. Hudson and Marley were slated to officially retire on June 1, 1999, and August 1, 2000, respectively. Since they remain on the payroll, they stand to receive their parachutes if they are ousted before their respective retirement dates. Hudson and Marley's parachutes are both valued at more than $1 million.

In addition to cash payments, these three executives' parachutes also protect existing blocks of restricted stock grants and nonvested stock options. The restricted stock grants were scheduled to become available within three years. Should the takeover come to fruition, the executives would receive the total value of the restricted stock even if it was not yet vested. The stock options would also become available immediately. Some of the restricted stock was performance restricted. Under normal conditions this stock would not be available without the firm reaching certain performance levels. However, the golden parachutes allow the executives to receive double the value of the performance-restricted stock.

Golden parachutes are designed in part to anticipate hostile takeovers like this. In AMP's case, Ripp's position is to lead the firm's board of directors in deciding if Allied Signal's offer is in the long-term interests of shareholders. Since Ripp is compensated heavily whether AMP is taken over or not, the golden parachute has helped remove the temptation that Ripp could have of not acting in the best interests of shareholders.

By design, golden parachutes benefit top executives whether or not there is evidence that value is created for shareholders. In fact, research has suggested that since high-performing firms are rarely taken over, golden parachutes often compensate top executives for abysmal performance.[11] For example, in 1998, AMP went through a troubled period that included plant closings and layoffs, which depressed its stock price.

Cash

Executive bonus compensation plans that focus on accounting measures of performance are designed to offset the limitations of market-based measures of performance. This type of plan is most usually associated with the payment of periodic (quarterly or annual) cash bonuses. Market factors beyond the control of management, such as pending legislation, can keep a firm's share price repressed even though a top executive is exceeding the performance expectations of the board. In this situation, a highly performing executive loses bonus compensation due to the undervalued stock. However, accounting measures of performance correct for this problem by tying executive bonuses to improvements in internally measured performance.

Traditional accounting measures, such as net income, earnings per share, return on equity and return on assets, are used because they are easily understood, are familiar to senior management, and are already tracked by firm data systems.[12]

Sears, Roebuck and Company bases annual bonus payments on such performance criteria, given an executive's business unit and level with the firm. The measures used by Sears include return on equity, revenue growth, net sales growth, and profit growth.

Critics argue that due to inherent flaws in accounting systems, basing compensation on these figures may not result in an accurate gauge of managerial performance. Return on equity estimates, for example, are skewed by inflation distortions and arbitrary cost allocations.[13] Accounting measures are also subject to manipulation by firm personnel to artificially inflate key performance figures. Firm performance schemes, critics believe, need to be based on a financial measure that has a true link to shareholder value creation.[14] This issue led to the creation of the Balanced Scorecard, which emphasizes not only financial measures, but also such measures as new product development, market share, and safety.

Matching Bonus Plans and Corporate Goals

Exhibit 9–8 provides a summary of the five types of executive bonus compensation plans. The figure includes a brief description, a rationale for implementation, and the identification of possible shortcomings for each of the compensation plans. Not only do compensation plans differ in the method through which compensation is rewarded to the executive, but they also provide the executive with different incentives.

Exhibit 9–9 matches a company's strategic goal with the most likely compensation plan. On the vertical axis are common strategic goals. The horizontal axis lists the main compensation types that serve as incentives for executives to reach the firm's goals. A rationale is provided to explain the logic behind the connection between the firm's goal and the suggested method of executive compensation.

---

[11] Graef S. Crystal, *In Search of Excess* (New York: W. W. Norton & Company, 1991).
[12] Francine C. McKenzie and Matthew D. Shilling, "Avoiding Performance Measurement Traps: Ensuring Effective Incentive Design and Implementation," *Compensation and Benefits Review,* July–August 1998, pp. 57–65.
[13] Fred K. Foulkes, *Executive Compensation: A Strategic Guide for the 1990s* (Boston: Harvard Business School, 1985).
[14] William Franklin, "Making the Fat Cats Earn Their Cream," *Accountancy,* July 1998, pp. 38–39.

EXHIBIT 9–8   Types of Executive Bonus Compensation

Bonus Type	Description	Rationale	Shortcomings
Stock option grants	Right to purchase stock in the future at a price set now. Compensation is determined by "spread" between option price and exercise price.	Provides incentive for executive to create wealth for shareholders as measured by increase in firm's share price.	Movement in share price does not explain all dimensions of managerial performance.
Restricted stock plan	Shares given to executive who is prohibited from selling them for a specific time period. May also include performance restrictions.	Promotes longer executive tenure than other forms of compensation.	No downside risk to executive, who always profits unlike other shareholders.
Golden handcuffs	Bonus income deferred in a series of annual installments. Deferred amounts not yet paid are forfeited with executive resignation.	Offers an incentive for executive to remain with the firm.	May promote risk-averse decision making due to downside risk borne by executive.
Golden parachute	Executives have right to collect the bonus if they lose position due to takeover, firing, retirement, or resignation.	Offers an incentive for executive to remain with the firm.	Compensation is achieved whether or not wealth is created for shareholders. Rewards either success or failure.
Cash based on internal business performance using financial measures	Bonus compensation based on accounting performance measures such as return on equity.	Offsets the limitations of focusing on market-based measures of performance.	Weak correlation between earnings measures and shareholder wealth creation. Annual earnings do not capture future impact of current decisions.

Researchers emphasize that fundamental to these relationships is the importance of incorporating the level of strategic risk of the firm into the design of the executive's compensation plan. Incorporating an appropriate level of executive risk can create a desired behavioral change commensurate with the risk level of strategies shareholders and their firms want.[15] To help motivate an executive to pursue goals of a certain risk-return level, the compensation plan can quantify that risk-return level and reward the executive accordingly.

The links we show between bonus compensation plans and strategic goals were derived from the results of prior research. The basic principle underlying Exhibit 9–9 is that different types of bonus compensation plans are intended to accomplish different purposes; one element may serve to attract and retain executives, another may serve as an incentive to encourage behavior that accomplishes firm goals.[16] Although every strategy option has probably been linked to each compensation plan at some time, experience shows that there may be scenarios where a plan type best fits a strategy option. Exhibit 9–9 attempts to display the "best matches."

[15] Ira T. Kay, *Value at the Top* (New York: HarperCollins, 1992).
[16] James E. Nelson, "Linking Compensation to Business Strategy," *The Journal of Business Strategy* 19, no. 2 (1998), pp. 25–27.

EXHIBIT 9–9   Compensation Plan Selection Matrix

Strategic Goal		Type of Bonus Compensation				Rationale
	Cash	Golden Handcuffs	Golden Parachutes	Restricted Stock Plans	Stock Options	
Achieve corporate turnaround					X	Executive profits only if turnaround is successful in returning wealth to shareholders.
Create and support growth opportunities					X	Risk associated with growth strategies warrants the use of this high-reward incentive.
Defend against unfriendly takeover			X			Parachute helps remove temptation for executive to evaluate takeover based on personal benefits.
Evaluate suitors objectively			X			Parachute compensates executive if job is lost due to a merger favorable to the firm.
Globalize operations					X	Risk of expanding overseas requires a plan that compensates only for achieved success.
Grow share price incrementally	X					Accounting measures can identify periodic performance benchmarks.
Improve operational efficiency	X					Accounting measures represent observable and agreed-upon measures of performance.
Increase assets under management				X		Executive profits proportionally as asset growth leads to long-term growth in share price.
Reduce executive turnover		X				Handcuffs provide executive tenure incentive.
Restructure organization					X	Risk associated with major change in firm's assets warrant the use of this high-reward incentive.
Streamline operations				X		Rewards long-term focus on efficiency and cost control.

Once the firm has identified strategic goals that will best serve shareholders' interests, an executive bonus compensation plan can be structured in such a way as to provide the executive with an incentive to work toward achieving these goals.

Summary

The first concern in the implementation of business strategy is to translate that strategy into action throughout the organization. This chapter discussed four important tools for accomplishing this.

Short-term objectives are derived from long-term objectives, which are then translated into current actions and targets. They differ from long-term objectives in time frame, specificity, and measurement. To be effective in strategy implementation, they must be integrated and coordinated. They also must be consistent, measurable, and prioritized.

Functional tactics are derived from the business strategy. They identify the specific, immediate actions that must be taken in key functional areas to implement the business strategy.

Employee empowerment through policies provides another means for guiding behavior, decisions, and actions at the firm's operating levels in a manner consistent with its business and functional strategies. Policies empower operating personnel to make decisions and take action quickly.

Compensation rewards action and results. Once the firm has identified strategic objectives that will best serve stockholder interests, there are five bonus compensation plans that can be structured to provide the executive with an incentive to work toward achieving those goals.

Objectives, functional tactics, policies, and compensation represent only the start of the strategy implementation. The strategy must be institutionalized—it must permeate the firm. The next chapter examines this phase of strategy implementation.

Questions for Discussion

1. How does the concept "translate thought into action" bear on the relationship between business strategy and operating strategy? Between long-term and short-term objectives?

2. How do functional tactics differ from corporate and business strategies?

3. What key concerns must functional tactics address in marketing? Finance? POM? Personnel?

4. How do policies aid strategy implementation? Illustrate your answer.

5. Use Exhibits 9–8 and 9–9 to explain five executive bonus compensation plans.

6. Illustrate a policy, an objective, and a functional tactic in your personal career strategy.

7. Why are short-term objectives needed when long-term objectives are already available?

Chapter 9 Discussion Case

BusinessWeek

Amazing Amazon.com

Who would believe that you could start a company in your garage and three years later have it worth over $17 billion as a public company with only about $500 million in annual sales and a sizable loss? Jeff Bezos did just that at Amazon.com!

A few stock analysts think Amazon.com is way overvalued; that investors are "nuts" to pay an amount equal to five times Barnes & Noble for this company. You can examine that valuation today as you read this discussion case and see whether they, or the "nutty" investors, were wisest.

Regardless, the value of the Amazon.com story for you is to see why those E-commerce- and Internet-savvy people, many somewhat ahead of the curve in the Internet world of online purchasing, liked the company. And what you will see is that they liked Amazon.com because of the functional tactics and activities—how Amazon.com conducted its business each day.

Those functional activities allowed Amazon.com's strategy to be the first true E-commerce company to become a reality such that these "nutty" investors invested because they could get on the Net and experience those tactics working every day! Amazon.com is a company that *BusinessWeek* journalists Robert Hof, Ellen Neuborne, and Heather Green found to have pioneered and perfected the simple idea of selling online to anyone anywhere in mass before any other business did.

1 Amazon offers an easily searchable trove of 3.1 million titles—15 times more than any bookstore on the planet and without the costly overhead of multimillion-dollar buildings and scads of store clerks. That paves the way for each of its 1,600 employees to generate, on average, $375,000 in annual revenues—more than triple that of No. 1 bricks-and-mortar bookseller Barnes & Noble Inc.'s 27, 000 employees.

2 Amazon's cutting-edge technology gives it a leg up, too, by automatically analyzing past purchases to make recommendations customized to each buyer—a trick that confounds 20th century mass marketing. And with a single mouse click, an order can be placed on its Web site, making

shopping a friendly, frictionless, even fun experience that can take less time than finding a parking space at the mall.

3 Amazon is extending its warm and fuzzy formula far beyond the bibliophile set. In 1999 Amazon debuted a video store, as well as an expanded gift shop—a clear sign that founder Jeff Bezos aimed to make Amazon the Net's premier shopping destination. Buyers who visit the Web site can now find everything from Pictionary games and Holiday Barbies to Sony Walkmen and watches. And Amazon isn't apt to stop there. Not surprisingly, Bezos, who abruptly left a cushy job as a Wall Street hedge-fund manager in 1994 to race across the country and launch Amazon in his Seattle garage, keeps his plans close to the vest. But experts say he's eyeing everything from software and apparel to flowers and travel packages—markets that could pit the upstart against more heavyweights, such as Microsoft Corp. and Nordstrom Inc., as early as next year.

4 Can Bezos, a 34-year-old computer whiz with no previous experience in retail, pull it off? Don't bet against him: In Amazon's first full quarter selling music CDs, it drew $14.4 million in sales, quickly edging out two-year-old cyberleader CDnow Inc. Says analyst Lauren Cooks Levitan of BancBoston Robertson Stephens: "When you think of Web shopping, you think of Amazon first." But as Bezos moves into new markets, he will run smack into traditional retailers that are starting to wield their brands online. A new study by Boston Consulting Group found that 59% of consumer E-commerce revenues—including retail sites and online financial and travel services—are generated by companies such as Eddie Bauer and 1-800-FLOWERS that also sell through traditional channels. Says Carol Sanger, a vice-president at Macy's parent Federated Department Stores Inc.: "We think the brand of Macy's is far more meaningful to the consumer who is looking for traditional department-store goods than any Internet brand name."

5 As if all the rivals aren't scary enough, Amazon faces an even more fundamental uncertainty: Retailing is a business with razor-thin margins,

prompting some analysts to question whether the company will ever be profitable. The theory: Its ambitious growth plans will keep it on the fast track for entering new markets, propelling costs ever upward—and earnings out of reach. Analysts estimate that Amazon will spend nearly $200 million on marketing next year, up 50% over a year ago. "The company has been able to show it can sell lots of books for less without making money, and now it has shown it can sell lots of music for less without making money," says Merrill Lynch & Co. analyst Jonathan Cohen, one of only two analysts with a sell rating on the stock.

6   For every Cohen, though, there are seven analysts who think Amazon ultimately will fulfill investors' seemingly outsized expectations. For one thing, it has an almost unheard-of two-year head start on key software that handles millions of transactions and personalizes the customers' experience. Amazon, for instance, was the first commerce site to use so-called collaborative-filtering technology, which analyzes a customer's purchases and suggests other books that people with similar purchase histories bought: the ultimate in targeted marketing.

7   Besides spurring more purchases, there's another huge bonus for Amazon: It can gather instant feedback on customer preferences to divine what else they might want to buy. Such valuable information has proven forbiddingly effective in capturing new markets online. While it may appear as though the company is careening willy-nilly into new terrain, Amazon is in fact targeting areas its customers have already requested. "We want Amazon.com to be the right store for you as an individual," says Bezos. "If we have 4.5 million customers, we should have 4.5 million stores."

8   Not since superstores and mail-order catalogers came along in the 1980s have merchants faced such a wrenching shift to a new way of doing business. It's a lot like what Wal-Mart did in the past decade: It used computers to transform the entire process of getting products to customers, all the way from the warehouse to Wal-Mart's welcome mats. Now Bezos is using Net technologies to shatter the perennial retail trade-off—he can offer a rich selection and personalized service, while still reaching millions of customers.

9   But technology is just one way Amazon is trying to rewrite the rules of retail. Bookstore and other retail chains largely depend on opening new stores to boost revenues—a huge cost that Amazon completely avoids. In the reverse of traditional retailers, Amazon has relatively high initial costs for things such as computer systems and editorial staff—which partly explain its red ink today. But unlike retailers, who must continually invest in new stores to hike revenues, Amazon can boost sales by simply getting more people to come to its single online store. Says Chief Financial Officer Joy Covey: "I don't think we could have grown a physical store base four times in one year."

10 Of course, for now, Amazon has to spend millions on marketing to bring in new customers—about 24 cents per dollar of revenue last quarter, compared with 4 cents for traditional retailers. But it's little understood just how much leverage Amazon's low capital costs provide to support that spending. Here's how it works: Physical bookstores must stock up to 160 days' worth of inventory to provide the kind of in-store selection people want. Yet they must pay distributors and publishers 45 to 90 days after they buy the books—so on average, they carry the costs of those books for up to four months. Amazon, by contrast, carries only 15 days' worth of inventory and is paid immediately by credit card. So it gets about a month's use of interest-free money.

11 That float—amounting to well over $25 million so far this year—actually provides a large chunk of the cash Amazon needs to cover its operating expenses. In its latest quarter, Amazon used a mere $600,000 in operating cash while jacking up its customer base by 37%, or 1.4 million customers.

12 Even though Amazon is still a long way from making a profit, its basic economics suggest the upstart will someday look more like a fat-cat software company than a scrambling-for-profits retailer. Once Amazon gets enough customers and sales to pay off its initial marketing and technology investments—and as that technology pays off in falling labor costs—additional revenue drops to the bottom line. "Amazon's changing the business model of retailing," says Ann Winblad, a principal at Hummer Winblad Venture Partners.

13   It's no accident that Bezos named Amazon after the river that carries the greatest volume of water. "He wants Amazon to be a $10 billion [in revenues] company," says early investor and board member Tom A. Alberg. To look at Amazon's crowded, grubby Seattle headquarters, you'd never suspect such grand ambitions: It's an unmarked building across from Wigland, the Holy Ghost Revivals mission, and the Seattle–King County needle-exchange program. Unlike most of his Silicon Valley colleagues, Bezos is so cheap that the desks are made of doors and four-by-fours, while computer monitors sit on stacks of phone books. Of course, there's one big bonus: Everyone gets stock options, which have made dozens of Amazonians millionaires. But the usual Valley perks such as free neck massages? Yeah, right.

14   And it's only natural that in a company where everything is being created from whole cloth, the people don't exactly fit either the Silicon Valley or the Microsoft mold. Dogs, sometimes including Bezos' golden retriever, Kamala (named after a minor Star Trek character), and green-haired twentysomethings with multiple piercings run loose, often around the clock. Says Acting Customer Service Director Jane Slade: "We tell the temp agencies, 'Send us your freaks.' "

15   Bezos' executive staff is nearly as eclectic. It's a motley, though whip-smart, band of executives ranging from Microsoft refugees to liberal-arts majors and rock musicians. Ryan Sawyer, for instance, the vice-president for strategic growth, was a Rhodes scholar who studied poetry at Oxford. "They don't care what has been done in the past," says Anne Martin, a principal at BT Alex. Brown Inc., who was on Amazon's IPO road show.

16   And that includes Bezos. What he understood before most people was that the ability of the Web to connect almost anyone with almost any product meant that he could do things that couldn't be done in the physical world—such as sell 3 million books in a single store. Starting the company in his suburban Bellevue (Washington) garage, Bezos interviewed suppliers and prospective employees at, ironically, a nearby cafe inside a Barnes & Noble superstore. Launching Amazon.com quietly in July, 1995, Bezos quickly set out to make the customer's experience as appealing as sipping a latte in a bookstore cafe.

17   Besides the huge selection and simple web pages that load fast, he created a sense of online community. He invited people to post their own reviews of books; some 800,000 are now up. He brought in authors for chats and more: John Updike started a short story, and 400,000 people sent in contributions to finish it.

18   Most important, Bezos made it irresistibly easy to buy a book. After the first purchase, a customer's shipping and credit-card information are stored securely, so the next time, all it takes is a single click to send the books winging their way to a mailbox. And to assure people that their purchase went through, Amazon sent e-mail confirmations of orders—which were often upgraded to priority shipping for free.

19   Rivals have since copied those tactics, but Amazon continues to give customers the red-carpet treatment. This month, it introduced GiftClick, which lets customers choose a gift and simply type in the recipient's e-mail address—Amazon takes care of the rest. The result: Some 64% of orders are from repeat customers, and that's rising steadily. For many, Amazon's a lifeline to literature. Marcia Ellis, an American attorney working in Hong Kong, used to drag home a suitcase full of books when she visited the United States. Now, she orders two books a month online. "Most of the people we know here get books from Amazon," she says.

20   Bezos also was one of the first merchants to leverage the Web's power in unique ways to spread the Amazon brand. Early on, he offered other Web sites the chance to sell books related to their visitors' interests through a link to Amazon. Their inducement: a cut of up to 15% of sales. Now, he has 140,000 sites in the so-called Associates Program.

21   That's what has kept even the online arm of Barnes & Noble at bay. Certainly the No. 1 bookseller, which built its first store 125 years ago, is a savvy merchant, but it proved vulnerable when it came to the ways of the Web. For one thing, it was late in arriving, and its store-trained executives took longer to learn the new rules of e-commerce than Amazon's Net-centric staff. "In the early days, there's a big advantage in not having that

baggage," says William McKiernan, chairman of e-commerce services provider CyberSource Corp.

22   Even after Barnes & Noble went online, it was slower to take advantage of the Net's ability to customize its site to each shopper. That allowed Amazon to use its appealing customer experience as a branding tool far more powerful than conventional advertising. And Barnes & Noble? Despite its well-known name and huge online marketing campaign, only 37% of Internet users recognized the brand without prompting, versus 50% that knew Amazon, according to Intelliquest Information Group.

23   The result: 18 months after Barnes & Noble went online, Amazon.com's $153.6 million in third-quarter sales, up 306% from a year ago, still overwhelm the book giant's online sales by 11 times. And Barnes & Noble's online customer base rose 29%, to 930,000—still less than a quarter of Amazon's.

24   Still, the bottom line is that Amazon needs to get customers to buy more. Indeed, with the bruising price wars that are sure to come, getting each customer to spend a tad extra may be critical for survival. It's just that the next step—the first beyond entertainment media—is a doozy. For one thing, it's unclear that the Amazon brand will extend into, say, toys or consumer electronics. "I get the combination of books and music and videos," says Robert Kagle, a venture capitalist who invests in Internet startups for Benchmark Capital. "Beyond that, I don't know how far their brand goes."

25   Even if the brand does travel well, it's almost guaranteed that other products won't be as profitable. Take CDs: They have lower margins than books. Same for videos. Toys have the disadvantage of not having as established a distribution network as books and music. So Amazon may have to stock more on its own, increasing its inventory costs and skimming off some of that nice float.

26   Already, established competitors are forcing it to do just that. Reel. com says 96% of the 20,000 titles it stocks are on the backlist. Those videos constitute most of its sales—and by far the most profitable portion. "If Amazon wants to ship them in a reasonable time, they'll have to stock them," says Reel.com CEO Julie Wainwright. And some

products, such as cars, real estate, or office products, are simply too cumbersome or expensive to ship. Or they may require too much aftersale support—which makes software a dicey product for Amazon to sell.

27   That's why Bezos will likely branch out beyond retail. In August, he spent $270 million for two companies that steer Amazon even more firmly toward becoming a shopping service rather than just a retailer. One of them, Junglee, has technology that makes it easy to scour the Web for products and compare prices or other features. "We don't even necessarily have to be selling all those things," says Bezos. "We just help people find things that are being sold elsewhere on the Web." Amazon might take a cut of revenues from other retailers if its customers buy their products. Says marketing prof Rogers, who is a partner in consultancy Peppers & Rogers: "Their next mission is to be a service agent."

TENUOUS ADVANTAGE

28 It's a tricky mission. Why? It will be tough to guarantee that the entire customer experience will measure up to Amazon's standard. Any glitches could quickly damage the company's carefully crafted brand name. "In three or four years, they'll be known for 'big,' " says CDnow CEO Jason Olim. "Well, whoop-di-do."

29   In the end, Amazon's success or failure will ride on maintaining a delightful experience for all of those new customers. Indeed, satisfied Amazon customers may well be helping more than most people realize: Analysts say one key to the sky-high stock price, which underwrites so much of its coming opportunity, is that investors can get a personal feel for Amazon's prospects by trying it out—something that's tough to do with most technology companies. Says Halsey Minor, CEO of online network CNET Inc.: "His [Bezos'] greatest advantage is a lot of people who buy his stock buy his books."

Source: Robert Hof, Ellen Neuborne, and Heather Green, "Amazon.com: The Wild World of E-Commerce," *BusinessWeek,* December 14, 1998.

Chapter **Ten**

Implementing Strategy: Structure, Leadership, and Culture

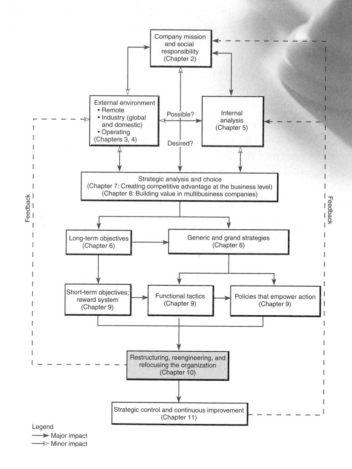

Legend
→ Major impact
⇢ Minor impact

Until this point in the strategic management process, managers have maintained a decidedly market-oriented focus as they formulate strategies and begin implementation through action plans detailing the tactics and actions that will be taken in each functional activity. Now the process takes an organizational focus—getting the work of the business done efficiently and effectively so as to make the strategy work. What is the best way to organize ourselves to accomplish the mission? Where should leadership come from? What values should guide our activities each day? What should this organization and its people be like? These are some of the fundamental issues managers face as they turn to the heart of strategy implementation.

While the focus is internal, the firm must still consider external factors as well. The intense competition in today's global marketplace has led most companies to consider their structure, or how the activities within their business are conducted, with an unprecedented attentiveness to what that marketplace—customers, competitors, suppliers, distribution partners—suggests or needs from the "internal" organization. This chapter explores three basic "levers" through which managers can implement strategy. The first lever is structure—the basic way the firm's different activities are organized. Second is leadership, encompassing the need to establish direction, embrace change and build a team to execute the strategy. The third lever is culture—the shared values that create the norms of individual behavior and the tone of the organization.

Consider the situation facing new Hewlett-Packard CEO Carly Fiorina in 2001. The unfortunate reality for her: HP's lumbering organization was losing touch with its global customers. Her response: As illustrated in Exhibit 10–1, Strategy in Action, Fiorina immediately dismantled the decentralized structure honed throughout HP's 64-year history. Pre-Fiorina, HP was a collection of 83 independently run units, each focused on a product such as scanners or security software. Fiorina collapsed those into four sprawling organizations. One so-called back-end unit develops and builds computers, and another focuses on printers and imaging equipment. The back-end divisions hand products off to two "front-end" sales and marketing groups that peddle the wares—one to consumers, the other to corporations. The theory: The new structure would boost collaboration, giving sales and marketing execs a direct pipeline to engineers so products are developed from the ground up to solve customer problems. This was the first time a company with thousands of product lines and scores of businesses has attempted a front-back approach, a structure that requires laser focus and superb coordination.

Fiorina believed she had little choice lest the company experience a near-death experience like Xerox or, ten years earlier, IBM. The conundrum: how to put the full force of the company behind winning in its immediate fiercely competitive technology business when they must also cook up brand-new megamarkets? It's a riddle Fiorina said she could solve only by sweeping structural change that would ready HP for the next stage of the technology revolution, when companies latch on to the Internet to transform their operations. At its core lay a conviction that HP must become "ambidextrous" excelling at short-term execution while pursuing long-term visions that create new markets. In addition to changing HP's structure, Fiorina also sought to revamp its culture of creativity. Her plan for unleashing a new culture of creativity was what she called "inventing at the intersection." Until 2001, HP made stand-alone products and innovations from $20 ink cartridges to $3 million servers. To revolutionize HP's culture and approach, she launched three "cross-company iniatives"—wireless services, digital imaging, and commercial printing—the first formal effort to get all of HP's separate and sometimes warring "tribes" working together.

Will it work? You are in the position of using hindsight to find out. Regardless, she earned high marks for zeroing in on HP's core problems and for having the courage to

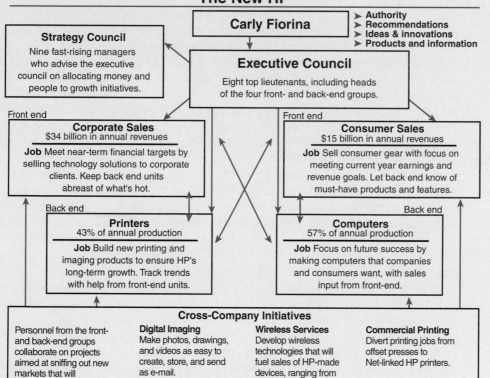

The Fiorina Way

When Fiorina arrived at HP, the company was a confederation of 83 autonomous product units reporting through four groups. She radically revamped the structure into two "back-end" divisions—one developing printers, scanners, and the like, and the other computers. These report to "front-end" groups that market and sell HP's wares. Here's how the overhaul stacks up:

The Old HP
Each product unit was responsible for its own profit/loss performance

- Home PC's, handhelds, laptops
- **CEO**
- Scanners, laser printers, printer paper
- **Executive Council**
- Consulting, security software, unit servers
- Ink cartridges, digital cameras, home printers

The New HP

Carly Fiorina

➤ Authority
➤ Recommendations
➤ Ideas & innovations
➤ Products and information

Strategy Council
Nine fast-rising managers who advise the executive council on allocating money and people to growth initiatives.

Executive Council
Eight top lieutenants, including heads of the four front- and back-end groups.

Front end
Corporate Sales
$34 billion in annual revenues
Job Meet near-term financial targets by selling technology solutions to corporate clients. Keep back end units abreast of what's hot.

Front end
Consumer Sales
$15 billion in annual revenues
Job Sell consumer gear with focus on meeting current year earnings and revenue goals. Let back end know of must-have products and features.

Back end
Printers
43% of annual production
Job Build new printing and imaging products to ensure HP's long-term growth. Track trends with help from front-end units.

Back end
Computers
57% of annual production
Job Focus on future success by making computers that companies and consumers want, with sales input from front-end.

Cross-Company Initiatives

Personnel from the front- and back-end groups collaborate on projects aimed at sniffing out new markets that will create growth.

Digital Imaging
Make photos, drawings, and videos as easy to create, store, and send as e-mail.

Wireless Services
Develop wireless technologies that will fuel sales of HP-made devices, ranging from handhelds to servers.

Commercial Printing
Divert printing jobs from offset presses to Net-linked HP printers.

The Assessment

Benefits

Happier Customers Clients should find HP easier to deal with, since they'll work with just one account team.

Sales Boost HP should maximize its selling opportunities because account reps will sell all HP products, not just those from one division.

Real Solutions HP can sell its products in combination as "solutions"—instead of just PCs or printers—to companies facing e-business problems.

Financial Flexibility With all corporate sales under one roof, HP can measure the total value of a customer, allowing reps to discount some products and still maximize profits on the overall contract.

Risks

Overwhelmed with duties With so many products being made and sold by just four units, HP execs have more on their plates and could miss the details that keep products competitive

Poorer Execution When product managers oversaw everything from manufacturing to sales, they could respond quickly to changes. That will be harder with front- and back-end groups synching their plans only every few weeks.

Less Accountability Profit-and-loss responsibility is shared between the front- and back-end groups so no one person is on the hot seat. Finger-pointing and foot-dragging could replace HP's collegial cooperation.

Fewer Spending Controls With powerful division chiefs keeping a tight rein on the purse strings, spending rarely got out of hand in the old HP. In the fourth quarter, expenses soared as those lines of command broke down.

EXHIBIT 10–2
What a Difference a Century Can Make

Contrasting views of the corporation:		
Characteristic	**20th Century**	**21st Century**
ORGANIZATION	The Pyramid	The Web or Network
FOCUS	Internal	External
STYLE	Structured	Flexible
SOURCE OF STRENGTH	Stability	Change
STRUCTURE	Self-sufficiency	Interdependencies
RESOURCES	Atoms—physical assets	Bits—information
OPERATIONS	Vertical integration	Virtual integration
PRODUCTS	Mass production	Mass customization
REACH	Domestic	Global
FINANCIALS	Quarterly	Real-time
INVENTORIES	Months	Hours
STRATEGY	Top-down	Bottom-up
LEADERSHIP	Dogmatic	Inspirational
WORKERS	Employees	Employees and free agents
JOB EXPECTATIONS	Security	Personal growth
MOTIVATION	To compete	To build
IMPROVEMENTS	Incremental	Revolutionary
QUALITY	Affordable best	No compromise

DATA: *BusinessWeek,* August 28, 2000.

tackle them head-on. And, if it did, the then 46-year-old CEO would become a 21st century management hero for a reinvigorated HP becoming a blueprint for others trying to transform major technology companies into 21st century dynamos. Said Stanford professor Robert Burgelman at the time, "there isn't a major technology company in the world that has solved the problem she's trying to address, and we're all going to learn from her experience."[1]

What CEO Fiorina faced, and Professor Burgelman recognizes, is the vast difference between business organizations of the 20th century and those of today. Exhibit 10–2 compares both on 18 different characteristics. The contrasts are striking, perhaps most so for leaders and managers faced with implementing strategies within them.

Fiorina offers a courageous example of a leader who recognized these compelling differences in the HP of the 20th century and what the HP of the 21st century needed to be. And her decision to adopt a laserlike focus on three key "levers" within HP to attempt to make HP's strategy successful are reflected in the focus of this chapter. Her first lever was HP's *organizational structure,* which was so important from her point of view that, without major change, would mean a partial or complete failure of HP. Her second concern was *leadership,* both from herself and key managers throughout HP. Finally, she knew that the HP *culture,* in this case birth of a new one, was the third critical lever with which to make the new HP vision and strategy have a chance for success.

STRUCTURING AN EFFECTIVE ORGANIZATION

Exhibit 10–2 offers a useful starting point in examining effective organizational structure. In contrasting 20th century and 21st century corporations on different characteristics, it offers a historical or evolutionary perspective on organizational attributes associated with

---

[1] "The Radical," *BusinessWeek,* February 19, 2001.

successful strategy execution today and just a few years ago. Successful organization once required an internal focus, structured interaction, self-sufficiency, a top-down approach. Today and tomorrow, organizational structure reflects an external focus, flexible interaction, interdependency, and a bottom-up approach, just to mention a few characteristics associated with strategy execution and success. Three fundamental trends are driving decisions about effective organizational structures in the 21st century: globalization, the Internet, and speed of decision making.

Globalization   The earlier example at Hewlett-Packard showed CEO Fiorina facing a desperate truth: HP's cumbersome organization was losing touch with its global customers. So she radically reorganized HP in part so multinational clients could go to just one sales and marketing group to buy everything from ink cartridges to supercomputers, in Buffalo or Bangkok. Over two-thirds of all industry either operates globally (e.g., computers, aerospace) or will soon do so. In the last half of the last decade, the percentage of sales from outside the home market for these five companies grew dramatically:

	1995	2000
General Electric	16.5%	35.1%
Wal-Mart	0.0	18.8
McDonald's	46.9	65.5
Nokia	85.0	98.6
Toyota	44.6	53.5

The need for global coordination and innovation is forcing constant experimentation and adjustment to get the right mix of local initiative, information flow, leadership, and corporate culture. At Swedish-based Ericsson, top managers scrutinize compensation schemes to make managers pay attention to global performance and avoid turf battles, while also attending to their local operations. Companies like Dutch electronics giant Philips regularly move headquarters for different businesses to the hottest regions for new trends—the "high voltage" markets. Its digital set-top box is now in California, its audio business moved from Europe to Hong Kong.[2]

Global once meant selling goods in overseas markets. Next was locating operations in numerous countries. Today it will call on talents and resources wherever they can be found around the globe, just as it now sells worldwide. It may be based in the United States, do its software programming in New Delhi, its engineering in Germany, and its manufacturing in Indonesia. The ramifications for organizational structures are revolutionary.

The Internet   The Net gives everyone in the organization, or working with it, from the lowest clerk to the CEO to any supplier or customer, the ability to access a vast array of information—instantaneously, from anywhere. Ideas, requests, instructions zap around the globe in the blink of an eye. It allows the global enterprise with different functions, offices, and activities dispersed around the world to be seamlessly connected so that far-flung customers, employees, and suppliers can work together in real time. The result—coordination, communication and decision-making functions accomplished through and the purpose for traditional organizational structures become slow, inefficient, noncompetitive weights on today's organization.

---

[2] "See the World, Erase Its Borders," *BusinessWeek,* August 28, 2000.

Speed   Technology, or digitization, means removing human minds and hands from an organization's most routine tasks and replacing them with computers and networks. Digitizing everything from employee benefits to accounts receivable to product design cuts cost, time, and payroll resulting in cost savings and vast improvements in speed. "Combined with the Internet, the speed of actions, deliberations, and information will increase dramatically," says Intel's Andy Grove. "You are going to see unbelievable speed and efficiencies," says Cisco's John Chambers, "with many companies about to increase productivity 20 percent to 40 percent per year." Leading-edge technologies will enable employees throughout the organization to seize opportunity as it arises. These technologies will allow employees, suppliers, and freelancers anywhere in the world to converse in numerous languages online without need for a translator to develop markets, new products, new processes. Again, the ramifications for organizational structures are revolutionary.

Whether technology assisted or not, globalization of business activity creates a potential sheer velocity of decisions that must be made which challenges traditional hierarchial organizational structures. A company like Cisco, for example, may be negotiating 50–60 alliances at one time due to the nature of its diverse operations. The speed at which these negotiations must be conducted and decisions made require a simple and accommodating organizational structure lest the opportunities may be lost.

Faced with these and other major trends, how should managers structure effective organizations? Consider these recent observations by *BusinessWeek* editors at the end of a year-long research effort asking just the same question:

> The management of multinationals used to be a neat discipline with comforting rules and knowable best practices. But globalization and the arrival of the information economy have rapidly demolished all the old precepts. The management of global companies, which must innovate simultaneously and speed information through horizontal, global-spanning networks, has become a daunting challenge. Old, rigid hierarchies are out—and flat, speedy, virtual organizations are in. Teamwork is a must and compensation schemes have to be redesigned to reward team players. But aside from that bit of wisdom, you can throw out the textbooks.
>
> CEOs will have to custom-design their organizations based on their industry, their own corporate legacy, and their key global customers—and they may have to revamp more than once to get it right. Highly admired companies such as General Electric, Hewlett-Packard, ABB Ltd., and Ericsson have already been through several organizational reincarnations in the past decade to boost global competitiveness.[3]

Our research concurs with these findings by *BusinessWeek* editors—there is no one best organizational structure. At the same time, there are several useful guidelines and approaches that help answer this question which we will now cover in the next several sections.

Match Structure to Strategy

The recent changes at Hewlett-Packard in Exhibit 10–1, Strategy in Action, illustrate this fundamental guideline. CEO Fiorina adopted the difficult, career-risking path of creating a major new structure at HP because that new structure reflected the needs of HP's strategy for the 21st century. An easier alternative would have been to create a strategy compatible with the existing decentralized structure of 83 semi-autonomous business units that had been in place for over half a century. While easier, however, the result would have been damaging to HP in the long run, perhaps even fatal, because strategic priorities and initiatives would have been guided by structural considerations, rather than the other way around.

---

[3] "The 21st Century Corporation," *BusinessWeek,* August 28, 2000.

The origins of this maxim come from a historical body of strategic management research[4] that examined how the evolution of a business over time and the degree of diversification from a firm's core business affected its choice of organizational structure. The primary organizational structures associated with this important research are still prevalent today—simple functional structures, geographical structures, multidivisional structures, and strategic business units.[5] Four basic conclusions were derived from this research:

1. *A single-product firm or single dominant business firm should employ a functional structure.* This structure allows for strong task focus through an emphasis on specialization and efficiency, while providing opportunity for adequate controls through centralized review and decision making.

2. *A firm in several lines of business that are somehow related should employ a multidivisional structure.* Closely related divisions should be combined into groups within this structure. When synergies (i.e., shared or linked activities) are possible within such a group, the appropriate location for staff influence and decision making is at the group level, with a lesser role for corporate-level staff. The greater the degree of diversity across the firm's businesses, the greater should be the extent to which the power of staff and decision-making authority is lodged within the divisions.

3. *A firm in several unrelated lines of business should be organized into strategic business units.* Although the strategic business unit structure resembles the multidivisional structure, there are significant differences between the two. With a strategic business unit structure, finance, accounting, planning, legal, and related activities should be centralized at the corporate office. Since there are no synergies across the firm's businesses, the corporate office serves largely as a capital allocation and control mechanism. Otherwise, its major decisions involve acquisitions and diverstitures. All operational and business-level strategic plans are delegated to the strategic business units.

4. *Early achievement of a strategy-structure fit can be a competitive advantage.* A competitive advantage is obtained by the first firm among competitors to achieve appropriate strategy-structure fit. That advantage will disappear as the firm's competitors also attain such a fit. Moreover, if the firm alters its strategy, its structure must obviously change as well. Otherwise, a loss of fit will lead to a competitive disadvantage for the firm.

These research-based guidelines were derived from 20th century companies not yet facing the complex, dynamically changing environments we see today. So an easy conclusion would be to consider them of little use. That is not the case, however. First, the admonition to let strategy guide structure rather than the other way around is very important today. While seemingly simple and obvious, resistance to changing existing structures—"the way we do things around here"—continues to be a major challenge to new

---

[4] Alfred D. Chandler, *Strategy and Structure* (Cambridge: MIT Press, 1962); Larry Wrigley, *Divisional Autonomy and Diversification,* doctoral dissertation, Harvard Business School, 1970; Richard Rumelt, "Diversification Strategy and Performance," *Strategic Management Journal* 3 (January–February 1982), pp. 359–69; Richard Rumelt, *Strategy, Structure and Economic Performance* (Boston: HBS Press, 1986). Rumelt used a similar, but more detailed classification scheme; D. A. Nathanson and J. S. Cassano, "Organization, Diversity, and Performance," *Wharton's Magazine* 6 (1982), pp. 19–26; and Christopher A. Bartlett and Sumantra Ghoshal, "Matrix Management: Not a Structure, a Frame of Mind," *Harvard Business Review* 68, no. 4 (1990), pp. 138–45; V. R. Galbraith and R. K. Kazanjian, *Strategy Implementation: Structure, Systems & Processes* (St. Paul, MN: West Publishing, 1986).
[5] Each primary structure is diagrammed and described in detail along with the advantages and disadvantages historically associated with each in an appendix to this chapter.

strategies in many organizations even today as HP again illustrates. Second, the notion that firms evolve over time from a single product/service focus to multiple products/ services and markets requiring different structures is an important reality to accommodate when implementing growth strategies. Finally, many firms today have found value in multiple structures operating simultaneously in their company. People may be assigned within the company as part of a functional structure, but they work on teams or other groupings that operate outside the primary functional structure. We will explore this practice in a subsequent section, but the important point here is that while new and important hybrid organizational structures have proven essential to strategy implementation in the 21st century, these same "innovative" firms incorporate these "older" primary organizational structures in the fabric of their contemporary organizational structure.

Balance the Demands for Control/Differentiation with the Need for Coordination/Integration

Specialization of work and effort allows a unit to develop greater expertise, focus, and efficiency. So it is that some organizations adopt functional, or similar structures. Their strategy depends on dividing different activities within the firm into logical, common groupings—sales, operations, administration, or geography—so that each set of activity can be done most efficiently. Control of sets of activities is at a premium. Dividing activities in this manner, sometimes called "differentiation," is an important structural decision. At the same time, these separate activities, however they are differentiated, need to be coordinated and integrated back together as a whole so the business functions effectively. Demands for control and the coordination needs differ across different types of businesses and strategic situations.

The rise of a consumer culture around the world has led brand marketers to realize they need to be more responsive to local preferences. Coca-Cola, for example, used to control its products rigidly from its Atlanta headquarters. But managers have found in some markets consumers thirst for more than Coke, Diet Coke, and Sprite. So Coke has altered its structure to reduce the need for control in favor of greater coordination/integration in local markets where local managers independently launch new flavored drinks. At the same time, GE, the paragon of new age organization, had altered its GE Medical Systems organization structure to allow local product managers to handle everything from product design to marketing. This emphasis on local coordination and reduced central control of product design led managers obsessed with local rivalries to design and manufacture similar products for different markets—a costly and wasteful duplication of effort. So GE reintroduced centralized control of product design, with input from a worldwide base of global managers, and their customers, resulting in the design of several single global products produced quite cost competitively to sell worldwide. GE's need for control of product design outweighed the coordination needs of locally focused product managers.[6] At the same time, GE obtained input from virtually every customer or potential customer worldwide before finalizing the product design of several initial products, suggesting that it rebalanced in favor of more control, but organizationally coordinated input from global managers and customers so as to ensure a better potential series of medical scanner for hospitals worldwide.

Restructure to Emphasize and Support Strategically Critical Activities

Restructuring has been the buzzword of global enterprise for the last 10 years. Its contemporary meaning is multifaceted. At the heart of the restructuring trend is the notion that some activities within a business's value chain are more critical to the success of the

---

[6] "See the World, Erase Its Borders," *BusinessWeek,* August 28, 2000.

business's strategy than others. Wal-Mart's organizational structure is designed to ensure that its impressive logistics and purchasing competitive advantages operate flawlessly. Coordinating daily logistical and purchasing efficiencies among separate stores lets Wal-Mart lead the industry in profitability yet sell retail for less than many competitors buy the same merchandise at wholesale. Motorola's organizational structure is designed to protect and nurture its legendary R&D and new product development capabilities—spending over twice the industry average in R&D alone each year. Motorola's R&D emphasis continually spawns proprietary technologies that support its technology-based competitive advantage. Coca-Cola emphasizes the importance of distribution activities, advertising, and retail support to its bottlers in its organizational structure. All three of these companies emphasize very different parts of the value chain process, but they are extraordinarily successful in part because they have designed their organizational structures to emphasize and support strategically critical activities. Exhibit 10–3, Strategy in Action, provides some guidelines that should influence how an organization is structured depending on which among five different sources of competitive advantage are emphasized in its strategy.

Two critical considerations arise when restructuring the organization to emphasize and support strategically critical activities. First, managers need to make the strategically critical activities the central building blocks for designing organization structure. Those activities should be identified and separated as much as possible into self-contained parts of the organization. Then the remaining structure must be designed so as to ensure timely integration with other parts of the organization.

While this is easily proposed, managers need to recognize that strategically relevant activities may still reside in different parts of the organization, particularly in functionally organized structures. Support activities like finance, engineering, or information processing are usually self-contained units, often outside the unit around which core competencies are built. This often results in an emphasis on departments obsessed with performing their own tasks more than emphasizing the key results (customer satisfaction, differentiation, low costs, speed) the business as a whole seeks. So the second consideration is to design the organizational structure so that it helps coordinate and integrate these support activities to (1) maximize their support of strategy-critical primary activities in the firm's value chain and (2) does so in a way to minimize the costs for support activities and the time spent on internal coordination. Managerial efforts to do this in the 1990s have placed reengineering, downsizing, and outsourcing as prominent tools for strategists restructuring their organizations.

Reengineer Strategic Business Processes

Business process reengineering (BPR), popularized by consultants Michael Hammer and James Champy,[7] is one of the more popular methods by which organizations worldwide are undergoing restructuring efforts to remain competitive in the 21st century. BPR is intended to reorganize a company so that it can best create value for the customer by eliminating barriers that create distance between employees and customers. It involves fundamental rethinking and radical redesign of a business process. It is characterized as radical because it strives to structure organizational efforts and activities around results and value creation by focusing on the processes that are undertaken to meet customer needs, not specific tasks and functional areas such as marketing and sales.

---

[7] Michael Hammer and James Champy, *Reengineering the Corporation* (New York: HarperBusiness, 1993).

BusinessWeek One of the key things business managers should keep in mind when restructuring their organizations is to devise the new structure so that it emphasizes strategically critical activities within the business's value chain. This means that the structure should allow those activities to have considerable autonomy over issues that influence their operating excellence and timeliness; they should be in a position to easily coordinate with other parts of the business—to get decisions made fast.

Below are five different types of critical activities that may be at the heart of a business's effort to build and sustain competitive advantage. Beside each one are typical conditions that will affect and shape the nature of the organization's structure:

Potential Strategic Priority and Critical Activities	Concomitant Conditions That May Affect or Place Demands on the Organizational Structure and Operating Activities to Build Competitive Advantage
1. Compete as low-cost provider of goods or services.	Broadens market. Requires longer production runs and fewer product changes. Requires special-purpose equipment and facilities.
2. Compete as high-quality provider.	Often possible to obtain more profit per unit, and perhaps more total profit from a smaller volume of sales. Requires more quality-assurance effort and higher operating cost. Requires more precise equipment, which is more expensive. Requires highly skilled workers, necessitating higher wages and greater training efforts.
3. Stress customer service.	Requires broader development of servicepeople and service parts and equipment. Requires rapid response to customer needs or changes in customer tastes, rapid and accurate information system, careful coordination. Requires a higher inventory investment.
4. Provide rapid and frequent introduction of new products.	Requires versatile equipment and people. Has higher research and development costs. Has high retraining costs and high tooling and changeover costs. Provides lower volumes for each product and fewer opportunities for improvements due to the learning curve.
5. Seek vertical integration.	Enables firm to control more of the process. May not have economies of scale at some stages of process. May require high capital investment as well as technology and skills beyond those currently available within the firm.

Business reengineering reduces fragmentation by crossing traditional departmental lines and reducing overhead to compress formerly separate steps and tasks that are strategically intertwined in the process of meeting customer needs. This "process orientation," rather than a traditional functional orientation, becomes the perspective around which various activities and tasks are then grouped to create the building blocks of the organization's structure. This is usually accomplished by assembling a multifunctional, multilevel team that begins by identifying customer needs and how the customer wants to deal with the firm. Customer focus must permeate all phases. Companies that have successfully reengineered their operations around strategically critical business processes have pursued the following steps:[8]

- Develop a flowchart of the total business process, including its interfaces with other value chain activities.

- Try to simplify the process first, eliminating tasks and steps where possible and analyzing how to streamline the performance of what remains.

- Determine which parts of the process can be automated (usually those that are repetitive, time-consuming, and require little thought or decision); consider introducing advanced technologies that can be upgraded to achieve next-generation capability and provide a basis for further productivity gains down the road.

- Evaluate each activity in the process to determine whether it is strategy-critical or not. Strategy-critical activities are candidates for benchmarking to achieve best-in-industry or best-in-world performance status.

- Weigh the pros and cons of outsourcing activities that are noncritical or that contribute little to organizational capabilities and core competencies.

- Design a structure for performing the activities that remain; reorganize the personnel and groups who perform these activities into the new structure.

When asked recently about his new networking-oriented direction for IBM, IBM CEO Gerstner responded: "It's called *reengineering.* It's called *getting competitive.* It's called *reducing cycle time and cost, flattening organizations, increasing customer responsiveness.* All of these require a collaboration with the customer and with suppliers and with vendors."

Downsize and Self-Manage: Force Decisions to Operating Level

Reengineering and a value orientation have led managers to scrutinize even further the way their organizational structures are crucial to strategy implementation. That scrutiny has led to downsizing, outsourcing, and self-management as three important themes influencing the organizational structures into the 21st century. *Downsizing* is eliminating the number of employees, particularly middle management, in a company. The arrival of a global marketplace, information technology, and intense competition caused many companies to reevaluate middle management activities to determine just what value was really being added to the company's products and services. The result of this scrutiny, along with continuous improvements in information processing technology, has been widespread downsizing in the number of management personnel in thousands of companies worldwide. These companies often eliminate whole levels of management. General Electric went from 400,000 to 280,000 employees in this decade while its sales have almost tripled and its profit risen fivefold. Jack Welch's observations about GE's downsizing and the results of *BusinessWeek*'s survey of companies worldwide that have been actively downsizing (which attempts to extract guidelines for downsizing) are shown in Strategy in Action 10–4.

One of the outcomes of downsizing was increased *self-management* at operating levels of the company. Cutbacks in the number of management people left those that remained

---

[8] Judy Wade, "How to Make Reengineering Really Work," *Harvard Business Review* 71, no. 6 (November–December 1993), pp. 119–31.

BusinessWeek GE used to have things like department managers, subsection managers, unit managers, supervisors. We're driving those titles out . . . We used to go from the CEO to sectors, to groups, to businesses. We now go from the CEO to businesses. Nothing else.

—Jack Welch

It's hard to find a major corporation that hasn't downsized in recent years. But simple reductions in staffing don't make for lean management. Here's a checklist, developed by *BusinessWeek* from interviews with executives and consultants, that may tell you if your company needs a diet.

Company Characteristic	Analysis
1. Layers of management between CEO and the shop floor.	Some companies, such as Ameritech, now have as few as four or five where as many as 12 had been common. More than six is most likely too many.
2. Number of employees managed by the typical executive.	At lean companies, spans of control range up to one manager to 30 staffers. A ratio of lower than 1:10 is a warning of arterial sclerosis.
3. Amount of work cut out by your downsizing.	Eliminating jobs without cutting out work can bring disaster. A downsizing should be accompanied by at least a 25% reduction in the number of tasks performed. Some lean companies have hit 50%.
4. Skill levels of the surviving management group.	Managers must learn to accept more responsibility and to eliminate unneeded work. Have you taught them how?
5. Size of your largest profit center by number of employees.	Break down large operating units into smaller profit centers—less than 500 employees is a popular cutoff—to gain the economies of entrepreneurship and offset the burdens of scale.
6. Post-downsizing size of staff at corporate headquarters.	The largest layoffs, on a percentage basis, should be at corporate headquarters. It is often the most overstaffed—and the most removed from customers.

Source: "The 21st Century Corporation," *BusinessWeek,* August 28, 2000.

with more work to do. The result was that they had to give up a good measure of control to workers, and they had to rely on those workers to help out. Spans of control, traditionally thought to maximize under 10 people, have become much larger due to information technology, running "lean and mean," and delegation to lower levels. Ameritech, one of the Baby Bells, has seen its spans of control rise to as much as 30 to 1 in some divisions because most of the people that did staff work—financial analysts, assistant managers, and so on—have disappeared. This delegation, also known as empowerment, is accomplished through concepts like self-managed work groups, reengineering, and automation. It is also seen through efforts to create distinct businesses within a business—conceiving a business as a confederation of many "small" businesses, rather than one large, interconnected business. Whatever the terminology, the idea is to push decision making down in the organization by allowing major management decisions to be made at operating levels. The result is often the elimination of up to half the levels of management previously existing in an organizational structure.

EXHIBIT 10–5
The Product-Team
Structure

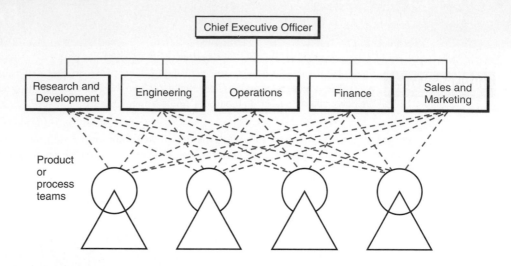

Allow Multiple Structures to Operate Simultaneously within the Organization
to Accommodate Products, Geography, Innovation and Customers

The *matrix organization* described in this chapter's Appendix A was one of the early
structural attempts to do this so that skills and resources could be better assigned and
used within a large company. People typically had a permanent assignment to a certain
organizational unit, usually a functional or staff department, yet they were also frequently
assigned to work in another project or activity at the same time. For example, a product
development project may need a market research specialist for several months and a financial analyst for a week. It was tried by many companies, and is still in use today. The
dual chains of command, particularly given a temporary assignment approach, proved
problematic for some organizations, particularly in an international context complicated
by distance, language, time, and culture.

The *product-team structure* emerged as an alternative to the matrix approach to simplify and amplify the focus of resources on a narrow but strategically important product,
project, market, customer or innovation. Exhibit 10–5 illustrates how the product-team
structure looks.

The product-team structure assigns functional managers and specialists (e.g., engineering, marketing, financial, R&D, operations) to a new product, project, or process team that
is empowered to make major decisions about their product. The team is usually created at
the inception of the new product idea, and they stay with it indefinitely if it becomes a viable business. Instead of being assigned on a temporary basis, as in the matrix structure,
team members are assigned permanently to that team in most cases. This results in much
lower coordination costs and, since every function is represented, usually reduces the number of management levels above the team level needed to approve team decisions.

It appears that product teams formed at the beginning of product-development
processes generate cross-functional understanding that irons out early product or process
design problems. They also reduce costs associated with design, manufacturing, and marketing, while typically speeding up innovation and customer responsiveness because authority rests with the team allowing decisions to be made more quickly. That ability to
make speedier, cost-saving decisions has the added advantage of eliminating the need for
one or more management layers above the team level, which would traditionally have
been in place to review and control these types of decisions. While seemingly obvious, it
has only recently become apparent that those additional management layers were also

BusinessWeek Building teams is a new organization art form for Corporate America. Getting people to work together successfully has become a critical managerial skill. Those companies that learn the secrets of creating cross-functional teams are winning the battle for global market share and profits. Those that don't are losing out.

Take General Motors. Both Ford and Chrysler are picking up market share in the U.S. because each in its own way has discovered how to build product-development teams that generate successful new models. Their method: Bring together people from engineering, design, purchasing, manufacturing, and marketing, and make them responsible as a group for the new car. Then destroy all bureaucracy above them, except for service support. GM has yet to do this. Its team members remain tied to their old structures—the engineers to engineering, purchasing agents to the purchasing department. Decisions aren't made for the good of the new product but to satisfy atavistic requirements of ancient bureaucracies.

Consider Modicon Inc., a North Andover (Massachusetts) maker of automation-control equipment with annual revenues of $300 million. Instead of viewing product development as a task of the engineering function, President Paul White defined it more broadly as a process that would involve a team of 15 managers from engineering, manufacturing, marketing, sales, and finance. By working together, Modicon's team avoided costly delays from disagreements and misunderstandings. "In the past," says White, "an engineering team would have worked on this alone with some dialogue from marketing. Manufacturing wouldn't get involved until the design was brought into the factory. Now, all the business issues are right on the table from the beginning." The change allowed Modicon to bring six software products to market in one-third the time it would normally take. The company still has a management structure organized by function. But many of the company's 900 employees are involved in up to 30 teams that span several functions and departments. Predicts White: "In five years, we'll still have some formal functional structure, but people will probably feel free enough to spend the majority of their time outside their functions."

Eastman Chemical Co., the $3.5 billion unit of Eastman Kodak Co. recently spun off as a stand-alone company, replaced several of its senior vice-presidents in charge of the key functions with "self-directed work teams." Instead of having a head of manufacturing, for example, the company uses a team consisting of all its plant managers. "It was the most dramatic change in the company's 70-year history," maintains Ernest W. Deavenport Jr., president of Eastman Chemical. "It makes people take off their organizational hats and put on their team hats. It gives people a much broader perspective and forces decision-making down at least another level." In creating the new organization, the 500 senior managers agreed that the primary role of the functions was to support Eastman's business in chemicals, plastics, fibers, and polymers. "A function does not and should not have a mission of its own," insists Deavenport. Common sense? Of course. But over the years, the functional departments had grown strong and powerful, as they have in many organizations, often at the expense of the overall company as they fought to protect and build turf. Now, virtually all of the company's managers work on at least one cross-functional team, and most work on two or more on a daily basis. For example, Tom O. Nethery, a group vice-president, runs an industrial-business group. But he also serves on three other teams that deal with such diverse issues as human resources, cellulose technology, and product-support services.

Source: John A. Byrne, "The Horizontal Corporation," *BusinessWeek,* December 20, 1993; and "What GM Needs to Do," *BusinessWeek,* November 1, 1993.

making these decisions with less firsthand understanding of the issues involved than the cross-functional team members brought to the product or process in the first place. Exhibit 10–6, Strategy in Action, gives examples of a product-team approach at several well-known companies and some of the advantages that appear to have accrued.

Take Advantage of Being a Virtual Organization

True 21st century corporations will increasingly see their structure become an elaborate network of external and internal relationships. This organizational phenomenon has been termed the *virtual organization,* which is defined as a temporary network of independent companies—suppliers, customers, subcontractors, even competitors—linked primarily by

EXHIBIT 10–7
General Motors: alliances with competitors

Source: General Motors Corporation Annual Reports; "Carmakers Take Two Routes to Global Growth," *Financial Times* (July 11, 2000), p. 19.

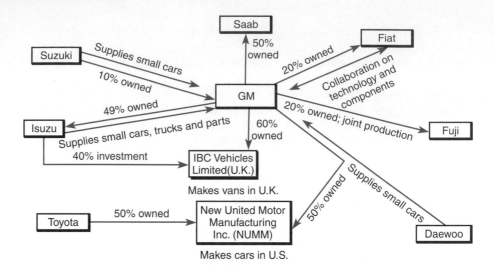

information technology to share skills, access to markets, and costs.[9] Outsourcing along with strategic alliances are integral in making a virtual organization work. Globalization has accelerated the use of and need for the virtual organization.

Outsourcing was an early driving force for the virtual organization trend. Dell does not make PCs. Cisco doesn't make its world renowned routers. Motorola doesn't make cell phones. Sony makes Apple's low-end PowerBook computers. *Outsourcing* is simply obtaining work previously done by employees inside the companies from sources outside the company. Managers have found that as they attempt to restructure their organizations, particularly if they do so from a business process orientation, numerous activities can often be found in their company that are not "strategically critical activities." This has particularly been the case of numerous staff activities and administrative control processes previously the domain of various middle management levels in an organization. But it can also refer to primary activities that are steps in their business's value chain—purchasing, shipping, making certain parts, and so on. Further scrutiny has led managers to conclude that these activities not only add little or no value to the product or services, but that they can be done much more cost effectively (and competently) by other businesses specializing in these activities. If this is so, then the business can enhance its competitive advantage by outsourcing the activities. Many organizations have outsourced information processing, various personnel activities, and production of parts that can be done better outside the company. Outsourcing, then, can be a source of competitive advantage and result in a leaner, flatter organizational structure.

Strategic alliances, some long-term and others for very short periods, with suppliers, partners, contractors, and other providers of world class capabilities allow partners to the alliance to focus on what they do best, farm out everything else, and quickly provide value to the customer. Engaging in alliances, whether long-term or one-time, let each participant take advantage of fleeting opportunities quickly, usually without tying up vast amounts of capital. FedEx and the U.S. Postal Service have formed an alliance—FedEx planes carry USPS next-day letters and USPS delivers FedEx ground packages—to allow both to challenge their common rival, UPS. Exhibit 10–7 shows how General Motors, in its effort to become more competitive globally, has entered into numerous alliances with competitors. Cisco owns only two of

[9] W. H. Davidow and M. S. Malone, *The Virtual Corporation* (New York: Harper, 1992).

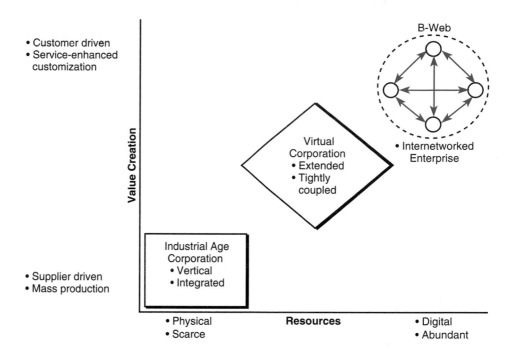

EXHIBIT 10–8
From Traditional Structure to B-Web Structure

Source: Adapted from Don Tapscott, David Ticoll, and Alex Lowry, *Digital Capital: Harnessing the Power of Business Webs* (Boston: Harvard Business School Press, 2000).

34 plants that produce its routers, and over 50 percent of all orders fulfilled by Cisco are done without a Cisco employee being involved.

Web-Based Organizations   As we noted at the beginning of this section, globalization has accelerated many changes in the way organizations structure, and that is certainly the case in driving the need to become part of a virtual organization or make use of one. Technology, particularly driven by the Internet, has and will be a major driver of the virtual organization. Commenting on technology's impact on Cisco, John Chambers observed that with all its outsourcing and strategic alliances, roughly 90 percent of all orders come into Cisco without ever being touched by human hands. "To my customers, it looks like one big virtual plant where my suppliers and inventory systems are directly tied into our virtual organization," he said. "That will be the norm in the future. Everything will be completely connected, both within a company and between companies. The people who get that will have a huge competitive advantage."

The Web's contribution electronically has simultaneously become the best analogy in explaining the future virtual organization. So it is not just the Web as in the Internet, but a weblike shape of successful organizational structures in the future. If there are a pair of images that symbolize the vast changes at work, they are the pyramid and the web. The organizational chart of large-scale enterprise had long been defined as a pyramid of ever-shrinking layers leading to an omnipotent CEO at its apex. The 21st century corporation, in contrast, is far more likely to look like a web: a flat, intricately woven form that links partners, employees, external contractors, suppliers, and customers in various collaborations. The players will grow more and more interdependent. Fewer companies will try to master all the disciplines necessary to produce and market their goods but will instead outsource skills—from research and development to manufacturing—to outsiders who can perform those functions with greater efficiency.[10] Exhibit 10–8 illustrates this

[10] "The 21st Century Organization," *BusinessWeek,* August 28, 2000.

evolution in organization structure to what it calls the B-Web, a truly Internet driven form of organization designed to deliver speed, customized service-enhanced products to savvy customers from an integrated virtual B-Web organization pulling together abundant, world class resources digitally.

Managing this intricate network of partners, spin-off enterprises, contractors, and free-lancers will be as important as managing internal operations. Indeed, it will be hard to tell the difference. All of these constituents will be directly linked in ways that will make it nearly impossible for outsiders to know where an individual firm begins and where it ends. "Companies will be much more molecular and fluid," predicts Don Tapscott, co-author of *Digital Capital.* "They will be autonomous business units connected not necessarily by a big building but across geographies all based on networks. The boundaries of the firm will be not only fluid or blurred but in some cases hard to define."[11]

Remove Structural Barriers and Create a Boundaryless, Ambidextrous Learning Organization

The evolution of the virtual organizational structure as an integral mechanism managers use to implement strategy has brought with it recognition of the central role knowledge plays in this process. *Knowledge* may be in terms of operating know-how, relationships with and knowledge of customer networks, technical knowledge upon which products or processes are based or will be, relationships with key people or a certain person than can get things done quickly, and so forth. Exhibit 10–9, Strategy in Action, shares how McKinsey organizational expert Lowell Bryan sees this shaping future organizational structure with managers becoming knowledge "nodes" through which intricate networks of personal relationships—inside and outside the formal organization—are constantly co-ordinated to bring together relevant know-how and successful action.

Management icon Jack Welch coined the term *boundaryless* organization, to charac-terize what he attempted to make GE become in order for it to be able to generate knowl-edge, share knowledge and get knowledge to the places it could be best used to provide superior value. A key component of this concept was erasing internal divisions so the people in GE could work across functional, business, and geographic boundaries to achieve an integrated diversity—the ability to transfer the best ideas, the most developed knowledge, and the most valuable people quickly, easily and freely throughout GE. Here is his description:

> Boundaryless behavior is the soul of today's GE . . . Simply put, people seem compelled to build layers and walls between themselves and others, and that human tendency tends to be magnified in large, old institutions like ours. These walls cramp people, inhibit creativity, waste time, restrict vision, smother dreams and above all, slow things down . . . Boundary-less behavior shows up in actions of a woman from our Appliances Business in Hong Kong helping NBC with contacts needed to develop satellite television service in Asia . . . And finally, boundaryless behavior means exploiting one of the unmatchable advantages a multibusiness GE has over almost any other company in the world. Boundaryless behavior combines 12 huge global businesses—each number one or number two in its markets—into a vast laboratory whose principal product is new ideas, coupled with a common commitment to spread them throughout the Company.
>
> —Letter to Shareholders, Jack Welch
> Chairman, General Electric Company, 1981–2001

A shift from what Subramanian Rangan calls *exploitation to exploration* indicates the growing importance of organizational structures that enable a *learning organization*

---

[11] Ibid.

BusinessWeek Lowell Bryan, a senior partner and director at consultancy McKinsey & Co., leads McKinsey's global industries practice and is the author of *Race for the World: Strategies to Build a Great Global Firm* and *Market Unbound: Unleashing Global Capitalism.*

Q: How will global companies be managed in the 21st century?

A: Describing it is hard because the language of management is based on command-and-control structures and "who reports to whom." Now, the manager is more of a network operator. He is part of a country team and part of a business unit. Some companies don't even have country managers anymore.

Q: What is the toughest challenge in managing global companies today?

A: Management structures are now three-dimensional. You have to manage by geography, products, and global customers. The real issue is building networked structures between those three dimensions. That is the state of the art. It's getting away from classic power issues. Managers are becoming nodes, which are part of geographical structures and part of a business unit.

Q: What are the telltale questions that reflect whether a company is truly global?

A: CEOs should ask themselves four questions: First, how do people interact with each other: Do employees around the world know each other and communicate regularly? Second, do management processes reflect a network or an old-style hierarchy? Third, is information provided to everyone simultaneously? And fourth, is the company led from the bottom up, not the top down?

Q: Why do multinationals that have operated for decades in foreign markets need to overhaul their management structures?

A: The sheer velocity of decisions that must be made is impossible in a company depending on an old-style vertical hierarchy. Think of a company [like] Cisco that is negotiating

50 to 60 alliances at one time. The old corporate structures [can't] integrate these decisions fast enough. The CEO used to be involved in every acquisition, every alliance. Now, the role of the corporate center is different. Real business decisions move down to the level of business units.

Q: If there is not clear hierarchy, and managers have conflicting opinions, how does top management know when to take a decision? Doesn't that raise the risk of delay and inaction?

A: In the old centralized model, there was no communication be. If you have multiple minds at work on a problem, the feedback is much quicker. If five managers or "nodes" in the network say something is not working right, management better sit up and take notice.

Q: Are there any secrets to designing a new management architecture?

A: Many structures will work. [H]aving the talent and capabilities you need to make a more fluid structure work [is key]. [But] it's much harder to do. The key is to create horizontal flow across silos to meet customers needs. The question is how you network across these silos. [G]etting people to work together [is paramount]. That's the revolution that is going on now.

Q: What is the role of the CEO?

A: The CEO is the architect. He puts in place the conditions to let the organization innovate. No one is smart enough to do it alone anymore. Corporate restructuring should liberate the company from the past. As you break down old formal structures, knowledge workers are the nodes or the glue that hold different parts of the company together. They are the network. Nodes are what it is all about.

Q: How do you evaluate performance in such a squishy system?

A: The role of the corporate center is to worry about talent and how people do relative to each other. Workers build a set of intangibles around who they are. If they are not compensated for their value-added, they will go somewhere else.

Source: *BusinessWeek,* August 28, 2000.

to allow global companies the chance to build competitive advantage.[12] Rather than going to markets to exploit brands or for inexpensive resources, in Rangan's view, the smart ones are going global to learn. This shift in the intent of the structure, then, is to seek information, to create new competences. Demand in another part of the world could be a

[12] Subramanian Rangan, *A Prism on Globalization* (Fountainebleau, FR.: INSEAD, 1999).

new product trendsetter at home. So a firm's structure needs to be organized to enable learning, to share knowledge, to create opportunities to create it. Others look to companies like 3M or Procter & Gamble that allow slack time, new product champions, manager mentors—all put in place in the structure to provide resources, support, and advocacy for cross-functional collaboration leading to innovation new product development, the generation and use of new ideas. This perspective is similar to the boundaryless notion—accommodate the speed of change and therefore opportunity by freeing up historical constraints found in traditional organizational approaches. So having structures that emphasize coordination over control, that allow flexibility (are *ambidextrous*) emphasize the value and importance of informal relationships and interaction over formal systems, techniques and controls are all characteristics associated with what are seen as effective structures for the 21st century.

Redefine the Role of Corporate Headquarters from Control to Support and Coordination

The role of corporate management is multibusiness, and multinational companies increasingly face a common dilemma—how can the resource advantages of a large company be exploited, while ensuring the responsiveness and creativity found in the small companies against which each of their businesses compete? This dilemma constantly presents managers with conflicting priorities or adjustments as corporate managers:[13]

- Rigorous financial controls and reporting enable cost efficiency, resource deployment, and autonomy across different units; flexible controls are conductive to responsiveness, innovation and "boundary spanning."

- Multibusiness companies historically gain advantage by exploiting resources and capabilities across different business and markets, yet competitive advantage in the future increasingly depends on the creation of new resources and capabilities.

- Aggressive portfolio management seeking maximum shareholder value is often best achieved through independent businesses; the creation of competitive advantage increasingly requires the management—recognition and coordination—of business interdependencies.

Increasingly, globally engaged multibusiness companies are changing the role of corporate headquarters from a control, resource allocation, and performance monitoring to one of coordinator of linkages across multiple business, supporter and enabler of innovation and synergy. One way this has been done is to create an executive council comprised of top managers from each business, usually including four to five of their key managers, with the council then serving as the critical forum for corporate decision, discussions, and analysis. Exhibit 10–1, Strategy in Action, at the beginning of this chapter showed this type of forum as central to HP's radical restructuring. GE created this approach over 20 years ago in its rise to top corporate success. These councils replace the traditional corporate staff function of overseeing and evaluating various business units, replacing it instead with a forum to share business unit plans, to discuss problems and issues, to seek assistance and expertise, and to foster cooperation and innovation.

Welch's experience at GE provides a useful example. Upon becoming chairman, he viewed GE headquarters as interfering too much in GE's various businesses, generating too much paperwork, and offering minimal value added. He sought to "turn their role 180 degrees from checker, inquisitor, and authority figure to facilitator, helper, and supporter

---

[13] Robert M. Grant, *Contemporary Strategy Analysis* (Oxford: Blackwell, 2001), p. 503.

of GE's 13 businesses." He said, "What we do here at headquarters . . . is to multiply the resources we have, the human resources, the financial resources, and the best practices . . . Our job is to help, it's to assist, it's to make these businesses stronger, to help them grow and be more powerful." GE's Corporate Executive Council was reconstituted from predominantly a corporate level group of sector managers (which was eliminated) into a group comprised of the leaders of GE's 13 businesses and a few corporate executives. They met formally two days each quarter to discuss problems and issues and to enable cooperation and resource sharing. This has expanded to other councils throughout GE intent on greater coordination, synergy, and idea sharing.

ORGANIZATIONAL LEADERSHIP

The job of leading a company has never been more demanding, and it will only get tougher in the 21st century. The CEO will retain ultimate authority, but the corporation will depend increasingly on the skills of the CEO and a host of subordinate leaders. The accelerated pace and complexity of business will continue to force corporations to push authority down through increasingly horizontal management structures. In the future, every line manager will have to exercise leadership's prerogatives—and bear its burdens—to an extent unthinkable 20 years ago.[14]

John Kotter, a widely recognized leadership expert, predicted this evolving role of leadership in an organization when he distinguished between management and leadership:[15]

> Management is about coping with complexity. Its practices and procedures are largely a response to one of the most significant developments of the 20th century: the emergence of large organizations. Without good management, complex enterprises tend to become chaotic in ways that threaten their very existence. Good management brings a degree of order and consistency to key dimensions like the quality and profitability of products.
>
> Leadership, by contrast, is about coping with change. Part of the reason it has become so important in recent years is that the business world has become more competitive and more volatile. . . . The net result is that doing what was done yesterday, or doing it 5 percent better, is no longer a formula for success. Major changes are more and more necessary to survive and compete effectively in this new environment. More change always demands more leadership.

Organizational leadership, then, involves action on two fronts. The first is in guiding the organization to deal with constant change. This requires CEOs that embrace change, and that do so by clarifying strategic intent, that build their organization and shape their culture to fit with opportunities and challenges change affords. The second is in providing the management skill to cope with the ramifications of constant change. This means identifying and supplying the organization with operating managers prepared to provide operational leadership and vision as never before. Let's explore each of these five aspects to organization leadership.

Strategic Leadership: Embracing Change

The blending of telecommunications, computers, the Internet, and one global marketplace has increased the pace of change exponentially during the last 10 years. All business organizations are affected. Change has become an integral part of what leaders and managers deal with daily.

---

[14] Anthony Bianco, "The New Leadership," *BusinessWeek,* August 28, 2000.
[15] John P. Kotter, "What Leaders Really Do," *Harvard Business Review,* May–June, 1990, p. 104.

The leadership challenge is to galvanize commitment among people within an organization as well as stakeholders outside the organization to embrace change and implement strategies intended to position the organization to do so. Leaders galvanize commitment to embrace change through three interrelated activities: clarifying strategic intent, building an organization, and shaping organizational culture.

Clarifying Strategic Intent

Leaders help stakeholders embrace change by setting forth a clear vision of where the business's strategy needs to take the organization. Traditionally, the concept of vision has been a description or picture of what the company could be that accommodates the needs of all its stakeholders. The intensely competitive, rapidly changing global marketplace has refined this to be targeting a very narrowly defined strategic intent—*an articulation of a simple criterion or characterization of what the company must become to establish and sustain global leadership.* Lou Gerstner is a good example of a leader in the middle of trying to shape strategic intent. "One of the great things about this industry is that every decade or so, you get a chance to redefine the playing field," said Gerstner. "We're in that phase of redefinition right now, and winners or losers are going to emerge from it. We've got to become *the leader in 'network-centric computing.'*" It's an opportunity brought about by telecommunications-based change that will change IBM more than semiconductors did in the 1980s. Says Gerstner, "I sensed there were too many people inside IBM who wanted to fight the war we lost," referring to PCs and PC software, so now he is aggressively trying to shape network-centric computing as the strategic intent for IBM in the next century.

Clarifying strategic intent can come in many different forms. Coca-Cola's legendary former CEO and Chairman Roberto Goizueta said, "Our company is a global business system for which we raise capital to make concentrate and sell it at an operating profit. Then we pay the cost of that capital. Shareholders pocket the difference." Coke averaged 27 percent annual return on stockholder equity for 18 years under his leadership. Travelers Insurance lost $200 million in 1992. Sanford Weill assumed leadership, focusing on a short-term turnaround. Recalling that time, he said, "We sent letters to all suppliers saying: Dear Supplier, either we rebid your business or you lower your costs 15 percent." Within two years, nonpersonnel costs were cut 49 percent in addition to 15,000 jobs. Travelers made $700 million in 1996. Mr. Weill was effective in setting forth strategic intent for Travelers' turnaround. While Coke and Travelers are very different situations, their leaders were both very effective in shaping and clarifying strategic intent in a way that helped stakeholders understand what needed to be done.

Building an Organization

The previous section examined alternative structures to use in designing the organization necessary to implement strategy. Leaders spend considerable time shaping and refining their organizational structure and making it function effectively to accomplish strategic intent. Since leaders are attempting to embrace change, they are often rebuilding or remaking their organization to align it with the ever-changing environment and needs of the strategy. And since embracing change often involves overcoming resistance to change, leaders find themselves addressing problems like the following as they attempt to build or rebuild their organization:

- Ensuring a common understanding about organizational priorities.
- Clarifying responsibilities among managers and organizational units.
- Empowering newer managers and pushing authority lower in the organization.

- Uncovering and remedying problems in coordination and communication across the organization.

- Gaining the personal commitment to a shared vision from managers throughout the organization.

- Keeping closely connected with "what's going on in the organization and with its customers."

Leaders do this in many ways. Larry Bossidy, the CEO who had quadrupled Allied Signal's stock price in the last four years, spends 50 percent of his time each year flying to Allied Signal's various operations around the world meeting with managers and discussing decisions, results, and progress. Bill Gates at Microsoft spends two hours each day reading and sending E-mail to any of Microsoft's 16,000 employees that want to contact him. All managers adapt structures, create teams, implement systems, and otherwise generate ways to coordinate, integrate, and share information about what their organization is doing and might do. Others create customer advisory groups, supplier partnerships, R&D joint ventures, and other adjustments to build an adaptable, learning organization that embraces the leader's vision and strategic intent and the change driving the future opportunities facing the business. These, in addition to the fundamental structural guidelines described in the previous section for restructuring to support strategically critical activities, are the issues leaders constantly address as they attempt to build a supportive organization.

Shaping Organization Culture

Leaders know well that the values and beliefs shared throughout their organization will shape how the work of the organization is done. And when attempting to embrace accelerated change, reshaping their organization's culture is an activity that occupies considerable time for most leaders. Listen to these observations by and about MCI and its CEO Bert Roberts about competing in the rapidly changing telecommunications industry prior to its merger with WorldCom:[16]

> Says Roberts: "We run like mad and then we change directions." Indeed, the ever-changing wireless initiative (reselling wireless services rather than creating its own capacity) illustrates a trait that sets apart MCI from its competitors—a willingness to try new things, and if they don't work, to try something else. "Over at AT&T, people are afraid to make mistakes," says Jeff Kagan, president of Kagan Telecom in Atlanta, Ga. "At MCI, people are afraid not to make mistakes."

It appears that MCI CEO Bert Roberts wanted an organizational culture that was risk taking and somewhat free wheeling in order to take advantage of change in the telecommunications industry. He did this by example, by expectations felt by his managers, and in the way decision making is approached within MCI.

Leaders use reward systems, symbols, and structure among other means to shape the organization's culture. Travelers' turnaround was accomplished in part by changing its "hidebound" culture through a change in its agent reward system. Employees previously on salary with occasional bonuses were given rewards that involved substantial cash bonuses and stock options. Observed a customer and risk management director at drugmaker Becton Dickinson, "They're hungrier now. They want to make deals. They're different than the old, hidebound Travelers' culture."

[16] Alison Sprout, "MCI: Can It Become the Communications Company of the Next Century?" *Fortune,* October 2, 1995, p. 110.

BusinessWeek **EXPERIENCE**

- Multinational Corp.—Worked with top-notch mentors in an established company with global operations. Managed a talented and fickle staff and helped tap new markets.

- Foreign Operation LLC—A stint at a subsidiary of a U.S. company, or at a foreign operation in a local market. Exposure to different cultures, conditions, and ways of doing business.

- Startup Inc.—Helped to build a business from the ground up, assisting with everything from product development to market research. Honed entrepreneurial skills.

- Major Competitor Ltd.—Scooped up by the competition and exposed to more than one corporate culture.

EDUCATION

- Liberal Arts University—Majored in economics, but took courses in psychology (how to motivate customers and employees), foreign language (the world is a lot bigger than the 50 states), and philosophy (to seek vision and meaning in your work).

- Graduate Studies—The subject almost doesn't matter, so long as you developed your thinking and analytical skills.

EXTRACURRICULAR

- Debating (where you learned to market ideas and think on your feet).

- Sports (where you learned discipline and team work).

- Volunteer work (where you learned to step outside your own narrow world to help others).

- Travel (where you learned about different cultures).

Source: "A Résumé for the 21st Century," *BusinessWeek*, August 28, 2000.

As leaders clarify strategic intent, build an organization, and shape their organization's culture, they look to one key element to help—their management team throughout their organization. As Allied Signal's visible CEO Larry Bossidy candidly observed when asked about how after 38 years at General Electric and now at Allied Signal with seemingly drab businesses he could expect exciting growth: "There's no such thing as a mature market. What we need is mature executives who can find ways to grow." Leaders look to managers they need to execute strategy as another source of leadership to accept risk and cope with the complexity that change brings about. So assignment of key managers becomes a leadership tool.

Recruiting and Developing Talented Operational Leadership

As we noted at the beginning of this section on Organizational Leadership, the accelerated pace and complexity of business will increase pressure on corporations to push authority down in their organizations ultimately meaning that every line manager will have to exercise leadership's prerogatives to an extent unthinkable a generation earlier. They will each be global managers, change agents, strategists, motivators, strategic decision-makers, innovators, and collaborators if the business is to survive and prosper. Exhibit 10–10, Strategy in Action, provides an interesting perspective on this reality showing *BusinessWeek*'s version of a résumé for the typical 21st century operating manager every company will be looking for in today's fast-paced, global marketplace.

Today's need for fluid, learning organizations capable of rapid response, sharing, and cross-cultural synergy place incredible demands on young managers to bring important competencies to the organization. Exhibit 10–11 looks at the needs organizations look to managers to meet, and then identifies the corresponding competencies

EXHIBIT 10–11
What Competencies Should Managers Possess?

Source: Ruth L. Williams and Joseph P. Cothrel, "Building Tomorrow's Leaders Today," *Strategy and Leadership* 26 (September–October 1997), pp. 17–23.

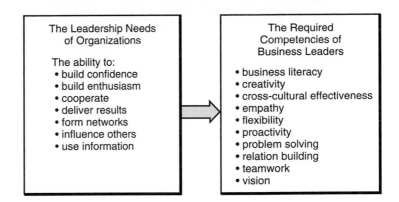

The Leadership Needs of Organizations

The ability to:
• build confidence
• build enthusiasm
• cooperate
• deliver results
• form networks
• influence others
• use information

The Required Competencies of Business Leaders

• business literacy
• creativity
• cross-cultural effectiveness
• empathy
• flexibility
• proactivity
• problem solving
• relation building
• teamwork
• vision

managers would need to do so. Ruth Williams and Joseph Cothrel drew this conclusion in their research about competencies needed from managers in today's fast changing business environment:[17]

> Today's competitive environment requires a different set of management competencies than we traditionally associate with the role. The balance has clearly shifted from attributes traditionally thought of as masculine (strong decision making, leading the troops, driving strategy, waging competitive battle) to more feminine qualities (listening, relationship-building, and nurturing). The model today is not so much "take it on your shoulders" as it is to "create the environment that will enable others to carry part of the burden." The focus is on unlocking the organization's human asset potential.

Researcher David Goleman addressed the question of what types of personality attributes generate the type of competencies described in Exhibit 10–11. His research suggested that a set of four characteristics commonly referred to as emotional intelligence play a key role in bringing the competencies needed from today's desirable manager:[18]

• *Self-awareness* in terms of the ability to read and understand one's emotions and assess one's strengths and weaknesses, underlain by the confidence that stems from positive self-worth.

• *Self-management* in terms of control, integrity, conscientiousness, initiative, and achievement orientation.

• *Social awareness* in relation to sensing others' emotions (empathy), reading the organization (organizational awareness), and recognizing customers' needs (service orientation).

• *Social skills* in relation to influencing and inspiring others; communicating, collaborating, and building relationships with others; and managing change and conflict.

One additional perspective on the role of organizational leadership and management selection is found in the work of Bartlett and Ghoshal. Their study of several of the most successful global companies in the last decade suggests that combining flexible responsiveness with integration and innovation requires rethinking the management role and the distribution of management roles within a 21st century company. They see three critical

---

[17] Ruth Williams and Joseph Cothrel, "Building Tomorrow's Leaders Today," *Strategy and Leadership* 26 (September–October 1997), p. 21.
[18] D. Goleman, "What Makes a Leader?," *Harvard Business Review* (November–December 1998), pp. 93–102.

EXHIBIT 10–12
Management Processes and Levels of Management

Source: C. A. Bartlett and S. Ghoshal, "The Myth of the General Manager: New Personal Competencies for New Management Roles," *California Management Review* 40 (Fall 1997); R. M. Grant, *Contemporary Strategy Analysis* (Oxford: Blackwell, 2001), p. 529.

Attracting resources and capabilities and developing the business	**RENEWAL PROCESS** Developing operating managers and supporting their activities. Maintaining organizational trust	Providing institutional leadership through shaping and embedding corporate purpose and challenging embedded assumptions
Managing operational interdependencies and personal networks	**INTEGRATION PROCESS** Linking skills, knowledge, and resources across units. Reconciling short -term performance and long-term ambition	Creating corporate direction. Developing and nurturing organizational values
Creating and pursuing opportunities. Managing continuous performance improvement	**ENTREPRENEURIAL PROCESS** Reviewing, developing, and supporting initiatives	Establishing performance standards

Front-Line Management   Middle Management   Top Management

management roles: the *entrepreneurial process* (decisions about opportunities to pursue and resource deployment), the *integration process* (building and deploying organizational capabilities), and the *renewal process* (shaping organizational purpose and enabling change). Traditionally viewed as the domain of top management, their research suggests that these functions need to be shared and distributed across three management levels as suggested in Exhibit 10–12.[19]

ORGANIZATIONAL CULTURE

Organizational culture is the set of important assumptions (often unstated) that members of an organization share in common. Every organization has its own culture. An organization's culture is similar to an individual's personality—an intangible yet ever-present theme that provides meaning, direction, and the basis for action. In much the same way as personality influences the behavior of an individual, the shared assumptions (beliefs and values) among a firm's members influence opinions and actions within that firm.

A member of an organization can simply be aware of the organization's beliefs and values without sharing them in a personally significant way. Those beliefs and values have more personal meaning if the member views them as a guide to appropriate behavior in the organization and, therefore, complies with them. The member becomes fundamentally committed to the beliefs and values when he or she internalizes them; that is, comes to hold them as personal beliefs and values. In this case, the corresponding behavior is *intrinsically rewarding* for the member—the member derives personal satisfaction from his or her actions in the organization because those actions are congruent with corresponding personal beliefs and values. *Assumptions become shared assumptions through internalization among an organization's individual members.* And those shared, internalized beliefs and values shape the content and account for the strength of an organization's culture.

[19] C. A. Barlett and S. Ghoshal, "The Myth of the General Manager: New Personal Competencies for New Management Roles," *California Management Review* 40 (Fall 1997), pp. 92–116; and "Beyond Structure to Process," *Harvard Business Review* (January–February 1995).

Leaders typically attempt to manage and create distinct cultures through a variety of ways. Some of the most common ways are as follows:

Emphasize Key Themes or Dominant Values   Businesses build strategies around distinct competitive advantages they possess or seek. Quality, differentiation, cost advantages, and speed are four key sources of competitive advantage. So insightful leaders nurture key themes or dominant values within their organization that reinforce competitive advantages they seek to maintain or build. Key themes or dominant values may center around wording in an advertisement. They are often found in internal company communications. They are most often found as a new vocabulary used by company personnel to explain "who we are." At Xerox, the key themes include respect for the individual and services to the customer. At Procter & Gamble (P&G), the overarching value is product quality; McDonald's uncompromising emphasis on QSCV—quality, service, cleanliness, and value—through meticulous attention to detail is legendary; Delta Airlines is driven by the "family feeling" theme, which builds a team spirit and nurtures each employee's cooperative attitude toward others, cheerful outlook toward life, and pride in a job well done. Du Pont's safety orientation—a report of every accident must be on the chairman's desk within 24 hours—has resulted in a safety record that was 17 times better than the chemical industry average and 68 times better than the all-manufacturing average.

Encourage Dissemination of Stories and Legends about Core Values   Companies with strong cultures are enthusiastic collectors and tellers of stories, anecdotes, and legends in support of basic beliefs. Frito-Lay's zealous emphasis on customer service is reflected in frequent stories about potato chip route salespeople who have slogged through sleet, mud, hail, snow, and rain to uphold the 99.5 percent service level to customers in which the entire company takes great pride. Milliken (a textile leader) holds "sharing" rallies once every quarter at which teams from all over the company swap success stories and ideas. Typically, more than 100 teams make five-minute presentations over a two-day period. Every rally is designed around a major theme, such as quality, cost reduction, or customer service. No criticisms are allowed, and awards are given to reinforce this institutionalized approach to storytelling. L. L. Bean tells customer service stories; 3M tells innovation stories; P&G, Johnson & Johnson, IBM, and Maytag tell quality stories. These stories are very important in developing an organizational culture, because organization members identify strongly with them and come to share the beliefs and values they support.

Institutionalize Practices That Systematically Reinforce Desired Beliefs and Values   Companies with strong cultures are clear on what their beliefs and values need to be and take the process of shaping those beliefs and values very seriously. Most important, the values these companies espouse undergird the strategies they employ. For example, McDonald's has a yearly contest to determine the best hamburger cooker in its chain. First, there is a competition to determine the best hamburger cooker in each store; next, the store winners compete in regional championships; finally, the regional winners compete in the "All-American" contest. The winners, who are widely publicized throughout the company, get trophies and All-American patches to wear on their McDonald's uniforms.

Adapt Some Very Common Themes in Their Own Unique Ways   The most typical beliefs that shape organizational culture include (1) a belief in being the best (or, as at GE, "better than the best"); (2) a belief in superior quality and service; (3) a belief in the importance of people as individuals and a faith in their ability to make a strong contribution; (4) a belief in the importance of the details of execution, the nuts and bolts of doing the job well; (5) a belief that customers should reign supreme; (6) a belief in inspiring people to do their best, whatever their ability; (7) a belief in the importance of informal communication; and (8) a belief that growth and profits are essential to a company's well-being. Every company implements these beliefs differently (to fit its particular situation), and every company's values are the handiwork of one or two legendary figures in leadership positions. Accordingly, every company has a distinct culture that it believes no other company can copy successfully. And in companies with strong cultures, managers and workers either accept the norms of the culture or opt out from the culture and leave the company.

The stronger a company's culture and the more that culture is directed toward customers and markets, the less the company uses policy manuals, organization charts, and detailed rules and procedures to enforce discipline and norms. The reason is that the guiding values inherent in the culture convey in crystal-clear fashion what everybody is supposed to do in most situations. Poorly performing companies often have strong cultures. However, their cultures are dysfunctional, being focused on internal politics or operating by the numbers as opposed to emphasizing customers and the people who make and sell the product.

Managing Organizational Culture in a Global Organization[20]

The reality of today's global organizations is that organizational culture must recognize cultural diversity. *Social norms* create differences across national boundaries that influence how people interact, read personal cues, and otherwise interrelate socially. *Values* and *attitudes* about similar circumstances also vary from country to country. Where individualism is central to a North American's value structure, the needs of the group dominate the value structure of their Japanese counterparts. *Religion* is yet another source of cultural differences. Holidays, practices, and belief structures differ in very fundamental ways that must be taken into account as one attempts to shape organizational culture in a global setting. Finally, *education,* or ways people are accustomed to learning, differ across national borders. Formal classroom learning in the United States may teach things that are only learned via apprenticeship in other cultures. Since the process of shaping an organizational culture often involves considerable "education," leaders should be sensitive to global differences in approaches to education to make sure their cultural education efforts are effective. The discussion case on Hewlett-Packard at the end of this chapter provides some relevant examples of how CEO Carly Fiorina was trying to radically alter HP's organization's culture in 2001.

Managing the Strategy-Culture Relationship

Managers find it difficult to think through the relationship between a firm's culture and the critical factors on which strategy depends. They quickly recognize, however, that key components of the firm—structure, staff, systems, people, style—influence the ways in which key managerial tasks are executed and how critical management relationships are formed. And implementation of a new strategy is largely concerned with adjustments in these components to accommodate the perceived needs of the strategy. Consequently, managing the strategy-culture relationship requires sensitivity to the interaction between the changes necessary to implement the new strategy and

---

[20] Differing backgrounds, often referred to as *cultural diversity,* is something that most managers will certainly see more of, both because of the growing cultural diversity domestically and the obvious diversification of cultural backgrounds that result from global acquisitions and mergers. For example, Harold Epps, manager of DEC's computer keyboard plant in Boston, manages 350 employees representing 44 countries of origin and 19 languages.

EXHIBIT 10–13
Managing the Strategy-Culture Relationship

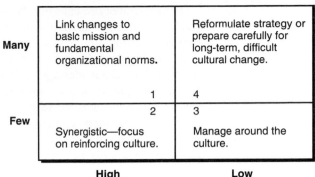

Changes in key organizational factors that are necessary to implement the new strategy

	High	**Low**
Many	Link changes to basic mission and fundamental organizational norms. 1	Reformulate strategy or prepare carefully for long-term, difficult cultural change. 4
Few	2 Synergistic—focus on reinforcing culture.	3 Manage around the culture.

Potential compatibility of changes
with existing culture

the compatibility or "fit" between those changes and the firm's culture. Exhibit 10–13 provides a simple framework for managing the strategy-culture relationship by identifying four basic situations a firm might face.

Link to Mission

A firm in cell 1 is faced with a situation in which implementing a new strategy requires several changes in structure, systems, managerial assignments, operating procedures, or other fundamental aspects of the firm. However, most of the changes are potentially compatible with the existing organizational culture. Firms in this situation usually have a tradition of effective performance and are either seeking to take advantage of a major opportunity or are attempting to redirect major product-market operations consistent with proven core capabilities. Such firms are in a very promising position: they can pursue a strategy requiring major changes but still benefit from the power of cultural reinforcement.

Four basic considerations should be emphasized by firms seeking to manage a strategy-culture relationship in this context. First, *key changes should be visibly linked to the basic company mission.* Since the company mission provides a broad official foundation for the organizational culture, top executives should use all available internal and external forums to reinforce the message that the changes are inextricably linked to it. Second, *emphasis should be placed on the use of existing personnel* where possible to fill positions created to implement the new strategy. Existing personnel embody the shared values and norms that help ensure cultural compatibility as major changes are implemented. Third, *care should be taken if adjustments in the reward system are needed.* These adjustments should be consistent with the current reward system. If, for example, a new product-market thrust requires significant changes in the way sales are made, and, therefore, in incentive compensation, common themes (e.g., incentive oriented) should be emphasized. In this way, current and future reward approaches are related and the changes in the reward system are justified (encourage development of less familiar markets). Fourth, *key attention should be paid to the changes that are least compatible with the current culture,* so current norms are not disrupted. For example, a firm may choose to subcontract an important step in a production process because that step would be incompatible with the current culture.

IBM's strategy in entering the Internet-based market is an illustration. Serving this radically different market required numerous organizational changes. To maintain maximum compatibility with its existing culture while doing so, IBM went to considerable public and internal effort to link its new Internet focus with its long-standing mission. Numerous messages relating the network-centric computing to IBM's tradition of top-quality service appeared on television and in magazines, and every IBM manager was encouraged to go online. Where feasible, IBM personnel were used to fill the new positions created to implement the strategy. But because the software requirements were not compatible with IBM's current operations, virtually all of its initial efforts were linked to newly acquired Lotus Notes.

Maximize Synergy

A firm in cell 2 needs only a few organizational changes to implement its new strategy, and those changes are potentially quite compatible with its current culture. A firm in this situation should emphasize two broad themes: (1) *take advantage of the situation to reinforce and solidify the current culture* and (2) *use this time of relative stability to remove organizational roadblocks to the desired culture.* Holiday Inns' move into casino gambling required a few major organizational changes. Holiday Inns saw casinos as resort locations requiring lodging, dining, and gambling/entertainment services. It only had to incorporate gambling/entertainment expertise into its management team, which was already capable of managing the lodging and dining requirements of casino (or any other) resort locations. It successfully inculcated this single major change by selling the change internally as completely compatible with its mission of providing high-quality accommodations for business and leisure travelers. The resignation of Roy Clymer, its CEO, removed an organizational roadblock, legitimizing a culture that placed its highest priority on quality service to the middle-to-upper-income business traveler, rather than a culture that placed its highest priority on family-oriented service. The latter priority was fast disappearing from Holiday Inns' culture, with the encouragement of most of the firm's top management, but its disappearance had not yet been fully sanctioned because of Clymer's personal beliefs. His voluntary departure helped solidify the new values that top management wanted.

Manage around the Culture

A firm in cell 3 must make a few major organizational changes to implement its new strategy, but these changes are potentially inconsistent with the firm's current organizational culture. The critical question for a firm in this situation is whether it can make the changes with a reasonable chance of success.

A firm can manage around the culture in various ways: create a separate firm or division; use task forces, teams, or program coordinators; subcontract; bring in an outsider; or sell out. These are a few of the available options, but the key idea is to create a method of achieving the change desired that avoids confronting the incompatible cultural norms. As cultural resistance diminishes, the change may be absorbed into the firm.

In the Southeast, Rich's was a highly successful, quality-oriented department store chain that served higher income customers in several southeastern locations. With Wal-Mart and Kmart experiencing rapid growth in the sale of mid- to low-priced merchandise, Rich's decided to serve this market as well. Finding such merchandise inconsistent with the successful values and norms of its traditional business, it created a separate business called Richway to tap this growth area in retailing. Through a new store network, it was able to *manage around its culture.* Both Rich's and Richway experienced solid regional success, though their cultures are radically different in some respects.

BusinessWeek
Behind his gentlemanly demeanor, Jorma Ollila, CEO of Nokia Corp., is a man of extremes. As his wife, Liisa Annikki, tells it, her husband fires up the Finnish sauna a good 15 degrees warmer than she likes it, all the way to 212F—hot enough to boil a pot of tea. It was late March, ice was still floating on Lake Pukala north of Helsinki, and the kids challenged their father to dive in. Emerging from the sauna, Ollila paused, then plunged naked into the icy lake.

Ollila, a 47-year-old former banker, lives by the plunge. He believes people get comfy and complacent and that it takes a dive into the unknown, or a push, to tap into their strongest instincts—those that guide survival. Six years ago, as an untested CEO, he bet the 133-year-old Finnish conglomerate on cellular phones, challenging rivals Motorola Inc. and L. M. Ericsson. In the struggle that ensued, Ollila's Finns outdid themselves. Fast and focused, with a canny eye for design, Nokia wrested market share from entrenched competitors and emerged as the most profitable player in the industry.

The company's startling climb has provided the Continent with something it was sorely lacking: a new high-tech superstar. What's more, that triumph is in a crucial technology—mobile communications. That's the next frontier for the Internet, and one of the few areas where Europe is racing ahead of the U.S.

Smack in the middle of Nokia's success stands Ollila, whose name is accented on the "O." He's a self-avowed nontechie who hasn't even put plumbing in his lakeside cabin. But it's Ollila who is improvising a brand-new style of high-tech management. Refuting the common "slip-and-you-die" thinking, Ollila sticks with slip and you grow.

In a sense, this model is a variation on the man's freezing plunge at the lake. Ollila views disasters as education, and he fires almost no one. While others rush to the world's high-tech hot spots, Ollila created one of his own in an underpopulated stretch between Russia and the Arctic Circle. From there, he nurtures a network of suppliers around the globe. And just when Nokia seems to be performing in top gear, as it is now, Ollila risks disarray by switching the jobs of all his top managers.

Trouble is, Nokia isn't the only one searching for a digital El Dorado in the form of convergence. While Ollila's sharp and nimble Finns ambushed Ericsson and Motorola in the telephone market, they're now converging right into a Silicon Valley traffic jam. To sell pocket-size Net devices, Ollila must maneuver his way among the brightest stars of America's high-tech economy, where everyone from Microsoft Corp. to 3Com Corp. wants to own a piece of the same business.

And few of them are convinced that this next revolution is going to be conducted through mobile telephones. Who's to say, after all, that mobile Web surfers won't use palmtop computers equipped with telephone chips? And there's always the chance the public will shrug at the entire selection of these tiny devices. "You have to think hard," says Richard Howard, director of the wireless research lab at Lucent Technologies Inc.'s Bell Labs. "Do you really need full-motion video in a car phone?"

So despite his laid-back manner, Ollila has no time to catch his breath. He must prepare Nokia for a metamorphosis. Like a snake growing out of its skin, the company has to emerge sleek and strong in the next generation, when simple handsets are stocking stuffers and mobile phones molt into powerful new be-alls. Ollila's tried-and-true motivator is the plunge. In the past, there have been plenty of crises around which to rally the team. Ollila recalls them with great fondness.

So how does Ollila conjure up a sense of fear and urgency? For starters, on July 1, he reached into Nokia's sparkling glass-and-steel headquarters on the shore of the Baltic, took the inner circle of four fortysomething Finns who

(continued)

Reformulate the Strategy or Culture

A firm in cell 4 faces the most difficult challenge in managing the strategy-culture relationship. To implement its new strategy, such a firm must make organizational changes that are incompatible with its current, usually entrenched, values and norms. A firm in this situation faces the complex, expensive, and often long-term challenge of changing its culture; it is a challenge that borders on impossible. Exhibit 10–14, Strategy in Action, describes the exciting success at Finland's Nokia where CEO Jorma Ollila transformed a 133-year-old company into a world technology leader.

When a strategy requires massive organizational change and engenders cultural resistance, a firm should determine whether reformulation of the strategy is appropriate. Are all of the organizational changes really necessary? Is there any real expectation that the run the company's main divisions, and switched all their jobs. His infrastructure executive, Matti Alahuhta, was rotated from his customer-schmoozing position into the marketing vortex of handsets. Asia-Pacific chief Sari Baldauf was told to head up infrastructure, as well as development on Third Generation. Handset chief Pekka Ala-Pietila, who oversaw the spectacular development of the 6100s, became vice-chairman, charged with exploring new ventures. Later this year, Ollila will bring back his chief executive for U.S. operations, Olli-Pekka Kallasvuo, to be chief financial officer. In short, except for Ollila, every top person at the company is getting ready for a brand-new job—all in the name of "removing people from their comfort areas," as Ollila puts it.

Despite the upheaval, Ollila is determined to preserve a corporate culture in Helsinki dominated by Finns. He jokes about this, explaining that the best brains in Silicon Valley, London, or Hong Kong recoil from moving to icy Helsinki, where it's dark all winter. The trick is to give his new recruits autonomy and let them pursue their careers in Nokia's big markets, where taxes are far lower and the lakes thaw by Easter. But Ollila also believes that Nokia draws strength from its understated collegiality, which he associates with the Finnish character. "We don't snap our suspenders," he says in his fluent British English.

The culture Ollila struggles to preserve goes back a ways. Founded in 1865 in a mill town 100 miles north of Helsinki, Nokia has made just about everything at one time or another. Many Finns still associate the name with the rubber snow boots they wore as children. A hundred years later, Nokia had grown into a regional conglomerate.

While Nokia, Ericsson, and Motorola are all preparing to battle one another with Internet phones and intelligent base stations, they've been forced to join forces on the Third Generation. Their worst nightmare: All the new features arrive on schedule—on palmtop computers instead of cell phones. To avoid that scenario, in June the three companies formed a London joint venture with British computer maker Psion PLC. The deal establishes a common software platform—Psion's operating system—for the coming generation of mobile Net devices.

In linking up with tiny Psion, Ollila and his competitors jilted none other than William H. Gates III. Earlier in the year, the Microsoft chairman toured Europe, plugging Microsoft's Windows CE software for Third Generation machines. He lost out. His software, phonemakers complained, was wrenched from the PC and not created for next-generation machines. Gates's loss, though, means that cellular phones could eventually be battling a slew of Microsoft-powered handheld devices in the same mobile market.

Ollila claims not to be worried. "The market will be big enough for all of us," he says. But don't misread the man. He's plenty competitive: He can recite the exact ages of his two sons when they finally beat him in tennis. When it comes time to plunge, Ollila is extreme—a man of fire and ice, leading Nokia into cyberspace.

Source: "Nokia," *BusinessWeek,* August 10, 1998.

changes will be acceptable and successful? If these answers are yes, then massive changes in management personnel are often necessary. AT&T offered early retirement to over 20,000 managers as part of a massive recreation of its culture to go along with major strategic changes in recent years. If the answer to these questions is no, the firm might reformulate its strategic plan so as to make it more consistent with established organizational norms and practices.

Merrill Lynch faced the challenge of strategy-culture incompatibility in the last decade. Seeking to remain number one in the newly deregulated financial services industry, it chose to pursue a product development strategy in its brokerage business. Under this strategy, Merrill Lynch would sell a broader range of investment products to a more diverse customer base and would integrate other financial services, such as real estate sales, into the Merrill Lynch organization. The new strategy could succeed only if Merrill Lynch's traditionally service-oriented brokerage network became sales and marketing oriented. Initial efforts to implement the strategy generated substantial resistance from Merrill Lynch's highly successful brokerage network. The strategy was fundamentally inconsistent with long-standing cultural norms at Merrill Lynch that emphasized personalized service and very close broker-client relationships. Merrill Lynch ultimately divested its real estate operation, reintroduced specialists that supported broker/retailers, and refocused its brokers more narrowly on basic client investment needs.

Summary

This chapter examined the idea that a key aspect of implementing a strategy is the *institutionalization* of the strategy so it permeates daily decisions and actions in a manner consistent with long-term strategic success. The "recipe" that binds strategy and organization involves three key ingredients: *organizational structure, leadership,* and *culture.*

Five fundamental organizational structures were examined, and the advantages and disadvantages of each were identified. Institutionalizing a strategy requires a good strategy-structure fit. This chapter dealt with how this requirement often is overlooked until performance becomes inadequate and then indicated the conditions under which the various structures would be appropriate.

Organizational leadership is essential to effective strategy implementation. The CEO plays a critical role in this regard. Assignment of key managers, particularly within the top-management team, is an important aspect of organizational leadership. Deciding whether to promote insiders or hire outsiders is often a central leadership issue in strategy implementation. This chapter showed how this decision could be made in a manner that would best institutionalize the new strategy.

Organizational culture has been recognized as a pervasive influence on organizational life. Organizational culture, which is the shared beliefs and values of an organization's members, may be a major help or hindrance to strategy implementation. This chapter discussed an approach to managing the strategy-culture fit. It identified four fundamentally different strategy-culture situations and provided recommendations for managing the strategy-culture fit in each of these situations.

The chapter concluded with an examination of structure, leadership, and culture for 21st century companies. Networked organizations, with intense customer focus, and alliances are keys to success. Talent-focused acquisitions, success sharing, and leaders as coaches round out the future success scenario.

Questions for Discussion

1. What key structural considerations must be incorporated into strategy implementation? Why does structural change often lag a change in strategy?

2. Which organizational structure is most appropriate for successful strategy implementation? Explain how state of development affects your answer.

3. Why is leadership an important element in strategy implementation? Find an example in a major business periodical of the CEO's key role in strategy implementation.

4. Under what conditions would it be more appropriate to fill a key management position with someone from outside the firm when a qualified insider is available?

5. What is organizational culture? Why is it important? Explain two different situations a firm might face in managing the strategy-culture relationship.

Chapter 10 Discussion Case

BusinessWeek

Carly Fiorina's Bold Management Experiment at HP

1 Since taking over as chief executive of Hewlett-Packard Co., Carleton S. "Carly" Fiorina has pushed the company to the limit to recapture the form that made it a management icon for six decades. Last November, it looked like she might have pushed too hard. After weeks of promising that HP would meet its quarterly numbers, Fiorina got grim news from the finance department. While sales growth beat expectations, profits had fallen $230 million short. The culprit, in large part, was Fiorina's aggressive management makeover. With HP's 88,000 staffers adjusting to the biggest reorganization in the company's history, expenses had risen out of control. And since new computer systems to track the changes weren't yet in place, HP's bean counters didn't detect the problem until 10 days after the quarter was over. ''It was frantic. The financial folks were running all around looking for more dollars,'' says one HP manager.

2 One might expect a CEO in this spot to dial down on such a massive overhaul. Not Fiorina. After crunching numbers in an all-day session on Saturday and offering apologies for missing the forecast to HP's board at an emergency meeting Sunday, Fiorina told analysts she was raising HP's sales growth target for fiscal 2001 from 15% to as much as 17%. "We hit a speed bump—a big speed bump—this quarter," she said in a speech broadcast to employees a few days later. "But does it mean, 'Gee, this is too hard?' No way. In blackjack, you double down when you have an increasing probability of winning. And we're going to double down."

3 The stakes couldn't be higher—both for Fiorina and for the Silicon Valley pioneer started in a Palo Alto garage in 1938. Just as founders Bill Hewlett and David Packard broke the mold back then by eliminating hierarchies and introducing innovations such as profit-sharing and cubicles, Fiorina is betting on an approach so radical that experts say it has never been tried before at a company of HP's size and complexity. What's more, management gurus haven't a clue as to whether it will work—though the early signs suggest it may be too much, too fast. Not content to tackle one problem at a time, Fiorina is out to transform all aspects of HP at once, current economic slowdown be damned. That means strategy, structure, culture, compensation—everything from how to spark innovation to how to streamline internal processes. Such sweeping change is tough anywhere, and doubly so at tradition-bound HP. The reorganization will be "hard to do—and there's not much DNA for it at HP," says Jay R. Galbraith, professor at the Institute for Management Development in Lausanne, Switzerland.

4 Fiorina believes she has little choice. Her goal is to mix up a powerful cocktail of changes that will lift HP from its slow-growth funk of recent years before the company suffers a near-death experience similar to the one IBM endured 10 years ago and that Xerox and others are going through now. The conundrum for these behemoths: how to put the full force of the company behind winning in today's fiercely competitive technology business when they must also cook up brand-new megamarkets? It's a riddle, says Fiorina, that she can solve only by sweeping action that will ready HP for the next stage of the technology revolution, when companies latch on to the Internet to transform their operations. "We looked in the mirror and saw a great company that was becoming a failure," Fiorina told employees. "This is the vision Bill and Dave would have had if they were sitting here today."

5 At its core lies a conviction that HP must become "ambidextrous." Like a constantly mutating organism, the new HP is supposed to strike a balance: It should excel at short-term execution while pursuing long-term visions that create new markets. It should increase sales and profits in harmony rather than sacrifice one to gain the other. And HP will emphasize it all—technology, software, and consulting in every corner of computing, combining the product excellence of a Sun Microsystems Inc. with IBM's services strength.

6 To achieve this, Fiorina has dismantled the decentralized approach honed throughout HP's 64-year history. Until last year, HP was a collection of 83 independently run units, each focused on a product such as scanners or security software. Fiorina has collapsed those into four sprawling

organizations. See Exhibit 10–1, Strategy in Action, for a diagram showing Fiorina's structural changes at HP). One so-called back-end unit develops and builds computers, and another focuses on printers and imaging equipment. The back-end divisions hand products off to two "front-end" sales and marketing groups that peddle the wares—one to consumers, the other to corporations. The theory: The new structure will boost collaboration, giving sales and marketing execs a direct pipeline to engineers so products are developed from the ground up to solve customer problems. This is the first time a company with thousands of product lines and scores of businesses has attempted a front-back approach, a strategy that requires laser focus and superb coordination.

7   Just as radical is Fiorina's plan for unleashing creativity. She calls it "inventing at the intersection." Until now, HP has made stand-alone products, from $20 ink cartridges to $3 million Internet servers. By tying them all together, HP hopes to sniff out new markets at the junctions where the products meet. The new HP, she says, will excel at dreaming up new e-services and then making the gear to deliver them. By yearend, for example, HP customers should be able to call up a photo stored on the Net using a handheld gizmo and then wirelessly zap it to a nearby printer. To create such opportunities, HP has launched three "cross-company initiatives"—wireless services, digital imaging, and commercial printing—that are the first formal effort to get all of HP's warring tribes working together.

8   Will her grand plan work? It's still the petri-dish phase of the experiment, so it's too soon to say. But the initial results are troubling. While she had early success, the reorganization started to run aground nine months ago. Cushy commissions intended to light a fire under HP's sales force boosted sales, but mostly for low-margin products that did little for corporate profits. A more fundamental problem stems directly from the front-back structure: It doesn't clearly assign responsibility for profits and losses, meaning it's tough to diagnose and fix earnings screwups—especially since no individual manager will take the heat for missed numbers. And with staffers in 120 countries, redrawing the lines of communication and getting veterans of rival divisions to work together is proving nettlesome.

"The people who deal with Carly directly feel very empowered, but everyone else is running around saying, 'What do we do now?'" says one HP manager. Another problem: Much of the burden of running HP lands squarely on Fiorina's shoulders. Some insiders and analysts say she needs a second-in-command to manage day-to-day operations. "She's playing CEO, visionary, and COO, and that's too hard to do," says Sanford C. Bernstein analyst Toni Sacconaghi.

9   Fiorina gets frosty at the notion that her restructuring is hitting snags. "This is a multiyear effort," she says. "I always would have characterized Year Two as harder than Year One because this is when the change really gets binding. I actually think our fourth-quarter miss and the current slowing economy are galvanizing us. When things are going well, you can convince yourself that change isn't as necessary as you thought." Fiorina also dismisses the need for a COO: "I'm running the business the way I think it ought to be run."

10   If Fiorina pulls this off, she'll be tech's newest hero. The 46-year-old CEO already has earned top marks for zeroing in on HP's core problems—and for having the courage to tackle them head-on. And she did raise HP's growth to 15% in fiscal 2000 from 7% in 1999. If she keeps it up, a reinvigorated HP could become a blueprint for others trying to transform technology dinosaurs into dynamos. "There isn't a major technology company in the world that has solved the problem she's trying to address, and we're all going to learn from her experience," says Stanford Business School professor Robert Burgelman.

11   Fiorina needs results—and fast. For all its internal changes, HP today is more dependent than ever on maturing markets. While PCs and printers contributed 69% of HP's sales and three-fourths of its earnings last year, those businesses are expected to slow to single-digit growth in coming years, with falling profitability. Last year, HP was tied with Compaq as the leading U.S. maker of home PCs and sold 60% of home printers, according to IDC. Those numbers make it hard to boost market share. In corporate computing—where the company is banking on huge growth—HP has made only minor strides toward capturing lucrative business such as consulting services, storage, and software. And the failure of Fiorina's $16 billion bid to buy the

consulting arm of PricewaterhouseCoopers LLP leaves her without a strong services division to help transform HP from high-tech's old reliable box-maker into a Net powerhouse, offering e-business solutions.

12   CAREENING. With the tech sector slowing in 2001, this may be the wrong time to make a miracle. In January, HP said its revenue and earnings would fall short of targets for the first quarter, and Fiorina cut her sales-growth estimates to about 5%—a far cry from the mid-teens she had been promising. In late January, the company announced it was laying off 1,700 marketing workers. HP's stock, which has dropped from a split-adjusted $67 in July to less than $40, is 19% below its level when Fiorina took the helm.

13   It's not just Fiorina's lofty goals that are so radical, but the way she's trying to achieve them. She's careening along at Net speed, ordering changes she hopes are right—but which may need adjustment later. That goes even for the front-back management structure. "When you sail, you don't get there in a straight line," Fiorina argues. "You adjust your course to fit the times and the current conditions." Insiders say that before the current slowdown, she expected HP to clock sales growth of 20% in 2002 and thereafter—a record clip for a $50 billion company. Fiorina won't confirm specific growth goals but says the downturn doesn't change her long-term plan.

14   Her overambitious targets have cost her credibility with Wall Street, too. While she earned kudos for increasing sales growth and meeting expectations early on, she has damaged her reputation by trying to put a positive spin on more troubled recent quarters. Hewlett Packard insiders say that while former CEO Lewis E. Platt spent a few hours reviewing the results at the end of each quarter, Fiorina holds marathon, multiday sessions to figure out how to cast financials in the best light. Not everyone is impressed. "I grew up with HP calculators, but they don't work right anymore," jokes Edward J. Zander, president of rival Sun Microsystems. "Everything they mention seems to be growing 50%, but the company as a whole only grows 10%." Fiorina says HP has accurately reported all segments of its business and that she makes no special effort to spin the results. "The calculators still work fine," she says.

15   Fiorina was well aware of the challenges when she joined HP, but she also saw the huge untapped potential. She had grown to admire the company while working as an HP intern during her years studying medieval history at Stanford University. Later, as president of the largest division of telecommunications equipment maker Lucent Technologies Inc., she learned the frustrations of buying products from highly decentralized HP. When HP's board asked her to take over, she jumped at the chance to show off her management chops. While she had spearheaded the company's spin-off from AT&T in 1996, then CEO Richard A. McGinn got all the credit.

16   "PERFECTLY POSITIONED." Soon after signing on, Fiorina decided the front-back structure was the salve for HP's ills. With the help of consultants, she tailored the framework to HP's needs and developed a multiyear plan for rejuvenating the company. Step One would be to shake up complacent troops. Next, Fiorina set out to refine a strategy and "reinvent" HP from the ground up, a task she expected would take most of 2000. Only then—meaning about now—would HP be ready to unleash its potential as a top supplier of technology for companies revamping their businesses around the Web.

17   That's where the cross-company initiatives come in. So far, HP has identified three. There's the digital-imaging effort to make photos, drawings, and videos as easy to create, store, and send as e-mail. A commercial-printing thrust aims to capture business that now goes to offset presses. And a wireless services effort might, say, turn a wristwatch into a full-function Net device that tracks the wearer's heart rate and transmits that info to a hospital. "All the great technology companies got great by seeing trends and getting there first—and they're always misunderstood initially," says Fiorina. "We think we see where the market is going and that we're perfectly positioned."

18   The first chapters of Fiorina's plan came off as scripted. When she replaced 33-year HP veteran Platt on a balmy July day in 1999, Fiorina swept in with a rush of fresh thinking and made headway—for a time. She ordered unit chiefs to justify why HP should continue in that line of business. And she gave her marketers just six weeks to revamp advertising and relaunch the brand. After a few

days on the job, she met with researchers who feared that Fiorina—a career salesperson—would move HP away from its engineering roots. She wowed them. In sharp contrast to the phlegmatic Platt, Fiorina moved through the crowd, microphone in hand, exhorting them to change the world. "There was a lot of skepticism about her," says Stan Williams, director of HP's quantum science research program. "But she was fantastic."

19   If she was a hit with engineers, it took a bit longer to win over HP's executive council. For years, these top execs had measured HP's performance against its ability to meet internal goals, but rarely compared its growth rates to those of rivals. In August, Fiorina rocked their cozy world when she shared details of her reorganization—and of her sky-high growth targets. She went to a whiteboard and compared HP with better-performing competitors: Dell Computer in PCs, Sun in servers, and IBM in services. She issued a challenge: If the executives could show her another way to hit her 20% growth target by 2002, she would postpone the restructuring, insiders say. Five weeks later, the best alternative was a plan for just 16% growth. The restructuring would start by year end.

20   She dove into the details. While Platt ran HP like a holding company, Fiorina demanded weekly updates on key units and peppered mid-level managers with 3 A.M. voice mails on product details. She injected much needed discipline into HP's computer sales force, which had long gotten away with lowering quotas at the end of each quarter. To raise the stakes, she tied more sales compensation to performance and changed the bonus period from once a year to every six months to prevent salespeople from coasting until the fourth quarter. While some commissions were tied to the number of orders rather than the sales amount and contributed to the earnings miss, Fiorina has fixed the problem and accomplished her larger goal of kick-starting sales. "You can feel the stress her changes are causing," says Kevin P. McManus, a vice-president of Premier Systems Integrators, which installs HP equipment. "These guys know they have to perform."

21   This play-to-win attitude has started to take root in other areas. Take HP Labs. In recent years, the once proud research and development center made too many incremental improvements to existing

products, in part because engineers' bonuses were tied to the number, rather than the impact, of their inventions. Now, Fiorina is focusing HP's R&D dollars on "big bang" projects. Consider Bob Rau's PICO software, which helps automate the design of chips used in electronic gear. Rau had worked for years on the project, but the technology languished. Last spring, Rau told Fiorina that the market for such systems was projected to grow to $300 billion as appliance makers built all sorts of Net-enabled gadgets. Within days, Fiorina created a separate division that operates alongside the two back-end groups and has grown to 250 people. Besides Rau's software, it will sell other HP technologies such as new disk drives to manufacturers. "It was like we'd been smothered for four years and someone was finally kind enough to lift the pillow off our face," says Rau.

22   ROUGH EDGES. With Phase One of her transformation behind her, Fiorina launched a formal reinvention process last spring. First up: cutting expenses. Over nine days, a 12-person team came up with ways to slash $1 billion by fiscal 2002. HP could save $100 million by outsourcing procurement. It could trim $10 million by letting employees log their hours online rather than on cardboard time cards. And the company could revamp its stodgy marketing by consolidating advertising from 43 agencies into two. That would save money and, better yet, focus HP's campaigns on Fiorina's big Web plans rather than on its various stand-alone products.

23   But when the big changes really started to kick in, Fiorina's plan started to bog down. In the past, HP's product chieftains ran their own operations, from design to sales and support. Today, they're folded into the two back-end units, leaving product chiefs with a far more limited role. They're still responsible for keeping HP competitive with rivals, hitting cost goals, and getting products to market on time. But they hand those products to the front-end organizations responsible for marketing and selling them.

24   The arrangement solves a number of long-standing HP problems. For one, it makes HP far easier to do business with. Rather than getting mobbed by salespeople from various divisions, now customers deal with one person. It lets HP's expert product designers focus on what they do best and

gives the front-end marketers authority to make the deals that are most profitable for HP as a whole— say, to sell a server at a lower margin to customers who commit to long-term consulting services. "You couldn't miss how silly it was the old way if you were part of the wide-awake club," says Scott Stallard, a vice-president in HP's computing group. "A parade of HP salesmen in Tauruses would pull up and meet for the first time outside of the customer's building."

25   These advantages, though, aren't enough to convince management experts or many HP veterans that a front-back approach will work at such a complex company. How do back-end product designers stay close enough to customers to know when a new feature becomes a must-have? Will executives, now saddled with thousands of HP products under their supervision, give sufficient attention to each of them to stay competitive? And with shared profit-and-loss responsibility between front- and back-ends, who has the final say when an engineer wants to take a flier on expensive research? "You just diffuse responsibility and authority," says Sara L. Beckman, a former HP manager who teaches at the Haas Business School at the University of California at Berkeley. "It makes it easier to say, 'Hey, that wasn't my problem.'"

26   Indeed, the front-back plan is showing some rough edges. While HP cited many reasons for its troubling fourth-quarter results, the reorganization is probably front and center. Freed from decades-old lines of command, employees spent as if they had already hit hypergrowth. In October alone, the company hired 1,200 people. Even dinner and postage expenses ran far over the norm. Such profligate spending was rare under the old structure where powerful division chiefs kept a tight rein on the purse strings. "They spent too much money on high-fives and setting themselves up to grow the following quarter," says Salomon Smith Barney analyst John B. Jones.

27   That situation could improve over time. Fiorina rushed the reorganization into place before the company's information systems were revamped to reflect the changes. Before Fiorina arrived, each product division had its own financial reporting system. It was only on November 1 that HP rolled out a new *uber*-system so staffers could work off the same books. Although it's too soon to say whether it's a winner, HP claims the system will let it watch earnings in powerful new ways. Rather than just see sales for a product line, managers will be able to track profits from a given customer companywide or by region. That way they can cut deals on some products to boost other sales and wind up with a more lucrative relationship.

28   Another restructuring red flag is the way Fiorina now sets strategy, a big departure from "The HP Way"—the principles laid out by the founders in 1957. Based on the belief that smart people will make the right choices if given the right tools and authority, "Bill and Dave" pushed strategy down to the managers most involved in each business. The approach worked. Not only did HP dominate most of its markets, but low-level employees unearthed new opportunities for the company. "HP was always the exact opposite of a command-and-control environment," says former CEO Platt. Although Platt wouldn't comment on Fiorina directly, he says, "Bill and Dave did not feel they had to make every decision." Hewlett Packard's $10 billion inkjet printer business, for example, got its start in a broom closet at HP's Corvallis (Ore.) campus, where its inventors had to set up because they had no budget.

29   EYES ON THE PRIZES. Fiorina isn't waiting for another broom-closet miracle. Since the halcyon mid-90s, the old HP way hasn't worked quite as well. The last mega-breakthrough product HP introduced was the inkjet printer, in 1984. Growth had slowed to just 4% in the six months before Fiorina took over. To give HP better direction, Fiorina has created a nine-person Strategy Council that meets every month to allocate resources, set priorities, and advise her on acquisitions and partnerships. "This is a company that can do anything," Fiorina says. "But it can't do everything."

30   Again, the move makes sense on paper. By steering the entire company, the council can focus HP on a few big Internet prizes rather than myriad underfunded pet projects. But this top-down engine could backfire. Experts point out that except for visionaries like Apple Computer's Steve Jobs or IBM's Thomas J. Watson Jr., it's rare for the suits in the corner office to be able to predict the future— especially in a market as fast-changing as the Net. "If we were to go too far toward top-down, it would not be right for this company," acknowledges Debra L. Dunn, HP's vice-president of strategy.

31   To be sure, Fiorina is quick to embrace ideas from below if she thinks they'll solve a problem. This spring, Sam Mancuso, HP's vice-president of corporate accounts, proposed a team-based plan that advances the front-back approach. Time was, PC salespeople weren't allowed to sell, say, printers. Mancuso has fixed that by pulling together 20-person teams to concentrate on the top 75 corporate customers. The teams create an "opportunity map" for each customer, tracking the total amount of business HP could possibly book. Then the team analyzes what deal would maximize earnings for HP. Mancuso says his operation has boosted sales to top customers by more than 30% since May. "We're taking the handcuffs off, so now we can be more aggressive," Mancuso says.

32   The shackles may be off, but HP still lags its competitors in many areas. For all HP's talk of becoming a Net power, in the fourth quarter, Sun held 39% of the market for Unix servers preferred by e-businesses, according to IDC. HP is in second place with 23% share, a slight improvement over the year before. But it faces growing competition from third-place IBM, which just introduced a product line that many analysts say handily outperforms HP's servers. "HP is just not making much headway," says Ellen M. Hancock, CEO of Exodus Communications Inc. Her company uses 62,000 servers in its Web hosting centers, virtually none of them from HP. And most of HP's Net schemes, such as Cartogra, a service that lets consumers post pictures on the Web, have failed to catch on.

33   Even fans of Fiorina acknowledge she has a ways to go. While wireless juggernaut Nokia Corp. just signed a deal to use HP software, Chairman Jorma Ollila questions how successful Fiorina's turnaround is likely to be. "Carly is very impressive," he says. "But the jury is still out on HP." Says Cisco Systems Inc. CEO John T. Chambers, who named Fiorina to his board on January 10: "I'd bet that Carly will be one of the top 5 or 10 CEOs in the nation. But she has still got to get them running faster." Fiorina wouldn't disagree and says she plans to keep upping her bets. "The greatest risk is standing still," she says. She should hope she has picked the right cards, because she's gambling with Silicon Valley's proudest legacy.

Source: "The Radical," *BusinessWeek,* February 19, 2001.

Appendix

Primary Organizational Structures and Their Strategy-Related Pros and Cons

Matching the structure to the strategy is a fundamental task of company strategists. To understand how that task is handled, we first must review the five basic primary structures. We will then turn to guidelines for matching structure to strategy.

The five basic primary structures are: (1) functional, (2) geographic, (3) divisional, or strategic business unit, (4) matrix, and (5) product team. Each structure has advantages and disadvantages that strategists must consider when choosing an organization form.

FUNCTIONAL ORGANIZATIONAL STRUCTURE

Functional structures predominate in firms with a single or narrow product focus. Such firms require well-defined skills and areas of specialization to build competitive advantages in providing their products or services. Dividing tasks into functional specialties enables the personnel of these firms to concentrate on only one aspect of the necessary work. This allows use of the latest technical skills and develops a high level of efficiency.

Product, customer, or technology considerations determine the identity of the parts in a functional structure. A hotel business might be organized around housekeeping (maids), the front desk, maintenance, restaurant operations, reservations and sales, accounting, and personnel. An equipment manufacturer might be organized around production, engineering/quality control, purchasing, marketing, personnel, and finance/accounting. Two examples of functional organizations are illustrated in Exhibit 10–A.

The strategic challenge presented by the functional structure is effective coordination of the functional units. The narrow technical expertise achieved through specialization can lead to limited perspectives and to differences in the priorities of the functional units. Specialists may see the firm's strategic issues primarily as "marketing" problems or "production" problems. The potential conflict among functional units makes the coordinating role of the chief executive critical. Integrating devices (such as project teams or planning committees) are frequently used in functionally organized firms to enhance coordination and to facilitate understanding across functional areas.

GEOGRAPHIC ORGANIZATIONAL STRUCTURE

Firms often grow by expanding the sale of their products or services to new geographic areas. In these areas, they frequently encounter differences that necessitate different approaches in producing, providing, or selling their products or services. Structuring by geographic areas is usually required to accommodate these differences. Thus, Holiday Inns is organized by regions of the world because of differences among nations in the laws, customs, and economies affecting the lodging industry. And even within its U.S. organization, Holiday Inns is organized geographically because of regional differences in traveling requirements, lodging regulations, and customer mix.

EXHIBIT 10–A
Functional Organization Structures

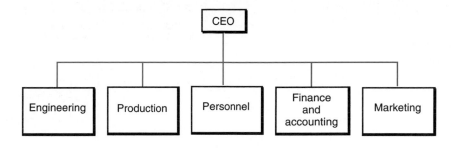

A process-oriented functional structure (an electronics distributor):

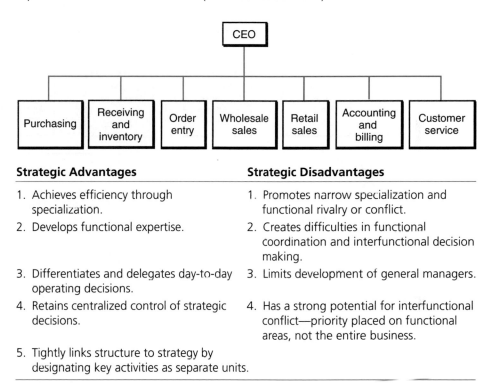

Strategic Advantages	Strategic Disadvantages
1. Achieves efficiency through specialization.	1. Promotes narrow specialization and functional rivalry or conflict.
2. Develops functional expertise.	2. Creates difficulties in functional coordination and interfunctional decision making.
3. Differentiates and delegates day-to-day operating decisions.	3. Limits development of general managers.
4. Retains centralized control of strategic decisions.	4. Has a strong potential for interfunctional conflict—priority placed on functional areas, not the entire business.
5. Tightly links structure to strategy by designating key activities as separate units.	

The key strategic advantage of geographic organizational structures is responsiveness to local market conditions. Exhibit 10–B illustrates a typical geographic organizational structure and itemizes the strategic advantages and disadvantages of such structures.

DIVISIONAL OR STRATEGIC BUSINESS UNIT STRUCTURE

When a firm diversifies its product/service lines, utilizes unrelated market channels, or begins to serve heterogeneous customer groups, a functional structure rapidly becomes inadequate. If a functional structure is retained under these circumstances, production managers may have to oversee the production of numerous and varied products or services, marketing managers may have to create sales programs for vastly different products or sell through vastly different distribution channels, and top management may be confronted with excessive coordination demands. A new organizational structure is often necessary to meet the increased coordination and decision-making requirements that

EXHIBIT 10–B
A Geographic
Organizational
Structure

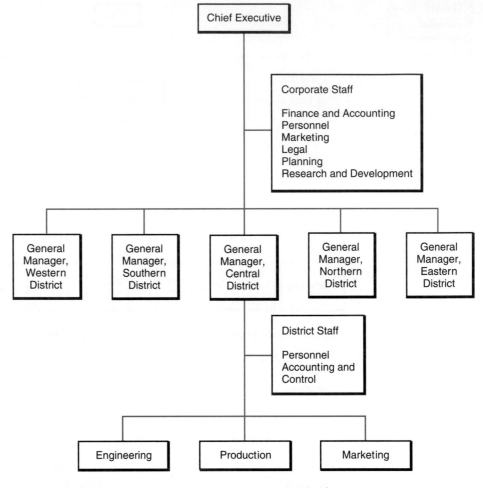

Strategic Advantages	Strategic Disadvantages
1. Allows tailoring of strategy to needs of each geographic market.	1. Poses problem of deciding whether headquarters should impose geographic uniformity or geographic diversity should be allowed.
2. Delegates profit/loss responsibility to lowest strategic level.	2. Makes it more difficult to maintain consistent company image/reputation from area to area.
3. Improves functional coordination within the target market.	3. Adds layer of management to run the geographic units.
4. Takes advantage of economies of local operations.	4. Can result in duplication of staff services at headquarters and district levels.
5. Provides excellent training grounds for higher level general managers.	

result from increased diversity and size, and the divisional or strategic business unit (SBU) organizational structure is the form often chosen.

For many years, Ford and General Motors have used divisional/SBU structures organized by product groups. Manufacturers often organize sales into divisions based on differences in distribution channels.

A divisional/SBU structure allows corporate management to delegate authority for the strategic management of distinct business entities—the division/SBU. This expedites decision making in response to varied competitive environments and enables corporate management to concentrate on corporate-level strategic decisions. The division/SBU usually is given profit responsibility, which facilitates accurate assessment of profit and loss.

Exhibit 10–C illustrates a divisional/SBU organizational structure and specifies the strategic advantages and disadvantages of such structures.

MATRIX ORGANIZATIONAL STRUCTURE

In large companies, increased diversity leads to numerous product and project efforts of major strategic significance. The result is a need for an organizational form that provides skills and resources where and when they are most vital. For example, a product development project needs a market research specialist for two months and a financial analyst one day per week. A customer site application needs a software engineer for one month and a customer service trainer one day per month for six weeks. Each of these situations is an example of a matrix organization that has been used to temporarily put people and resources where they are most needed. Among the firms that now use some form of matrix organization are Citicorp, Matsushita, DaimlerChrysler, Microsoft, Dow Chemical, and Texas Instruments.

The matrix organization provides dual channels of authority, performance responsibility, evaluation, and control, as shown in Exhibit 10–D. Essentially, subordinates are assigned both to a basic functional area and to a project or product manager. The matrix form is intended to make the best use of talented people within a firm by combining the advantages of functional specialization and product-project specialization.

The matrix structure also increases the number of middle managers who exercise general management responsibilities (through the project manager role) and, thus, broaden their exposure to organizationwide strategic concerns. In this way, the matrix structure overcomes a key deficiency of functional organizations while retaining the advantages of functional specialization.

Although the matrix structure is easy to design, it is difficult to implement. Dual chains of command challenge fundamental organizational orientations. Negotiating shared responsibilities, the use of resources, and priorities can create misunderstanding or confusion among subordinates. These problems are heightened in an international context with the complications introduced by distance, language, time, and culture.

To avoid the deficiencies that might arise from a permanent matrix structure, some firms are accomplishing particular strategic tasks, by means of a "temporary" or "flexible" *overlay structure*. This approach, used recently by such firms as NEC, Matsushita, Philips, and Unilever, is meant to take *temporary* advantage of a matrix-type team while preserving an underlying divisional structure. Thus, the basic idea of the matrix structure—*to simplify and amplify the focus of resources on a narrow but strategically important product, project, or market*—appears to be an important structural alternative for large, diverse organizations.

EXHIBIT 10–C
Divisional or
Strategic Business
Unit Structure

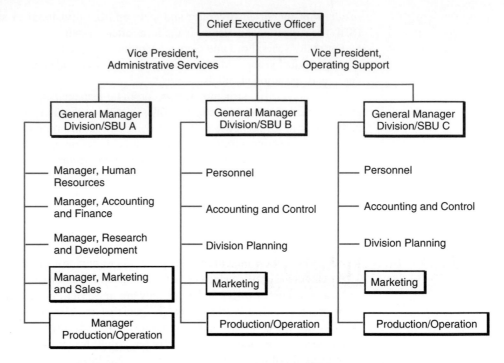

Strategic Advantages	Strategic Disadvantages
1. Forces coordination and necessary authority down to the appropriate level for rapid response.	1. Fosters potentially dysfunctional competition for corporate-level resources.
2. Places strategy development and implementation in closer proximity to the unique environments of the divisions/SBUs.	2. Presents the problem of determining how much authority should be given to division/SBU managers.
3. Frees chief executive officer for broader strategic decision making.	3. Creates a potential for policy inconsistencies among divisions/SBUs.
4. Sharply focuses accountability for performance.	4. Presents the problem of distributing corporate overhead costs in a way that's acceptable to division managers with profit responsibility.
5. Retains functional specialization within each division/SBU.	5. Increases costs incurred through duplication of functions.
6. Provides good training grounds for strategic managers.	6. Creates difficulty maintaining overall corporate image.
7. Increases focus on products, markets, and quick response to change.	

EXHIBIT 10–D
Matrix Organizational Structure

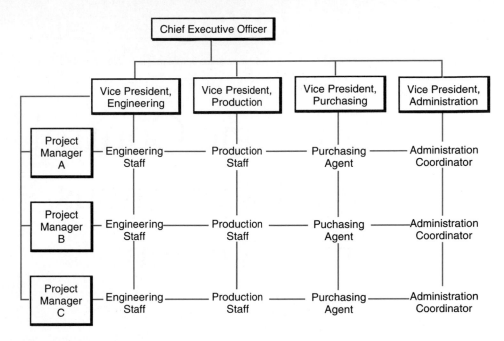

Strategic Advantages

1. Accomodates a wide variety of project-oriented business activity.
2. Provides good training grounds for strategic managers.
3. Maximizes efficient use of functional managers.
4. Fosters creativity and multiple sources of diversity.
5. Gives middle management broader exposure to strategic issues.

Strategic Disadvantages

1. May result in confusion and contradictory policies.
2. Necessitates tremendous horizontal and vertical coordination.
3. Can proliferate information logjams and excess reporting.
4. Can trigger turf battles and loss of accountability.

Chapter **Eleven**

Strategic Control and Continuous Improvement

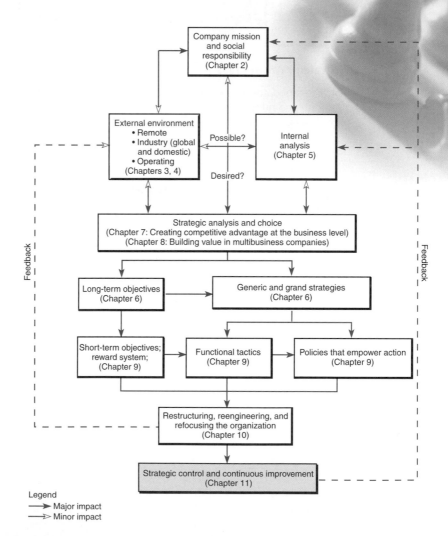

Company mission and social responsibility (Chapter 2)

External environment
• Remote
• Industry (global and domestic)
• Operating
(Chapters 3, 4)

Possible?

Desired?

Internal analysis (Chapter 5)

Strategic analysis and choice
(Chapter 7: Creating competitive advantage at the business level)
(Chapter 8: Building value in multibusiness companies)

Long-term objectives (Chapter 6)

Generic and grand strategies (Chapter 6)

Short-term objectives; reward system; (Chapter 9)

Functional tactics (Chapter 9)

Policies that empower action (Chapter 9)

Restructuring, reengineering, and refocusing the organization (Chapter 10)

Strategic control and continuous improvement (Chapter 11)

Feedback

Feedback

Legend
⟶ Major impact
⟶ Minor impact

Strategies are forward looking, designed to be accomplished several years into the future, and based on management assumptions about numerous events that have not yet occurred. How should managers control a strategy?

Strategic control is concerned with tracking a strategy as it is being implemented, detecting problems or changes in its underlying premises, and making necessary adjustments. In contrast to postaction control, strategic control is concerned with guiding action in behalf of the strategy as that action is taking place and when the end result is still several years off. Managers responsible for the success of a strategy typically are concerned with two sets of questions:

1. Are we moving in the proper direction? Are key things falling into place? Are our assumptions about major trends and changes correct? Are we doing the critical things that need to be done? Should we adjust or abort the strategy?

2. How are we performing? Are objectives and schedules being met? Are costs, revenues, and cash flows matching projections? Do we need to make operational changes?

The rapid, accelerating change of the global marketplace of the last 10 years has made *continuous improvement* another aspect of strategic control in many business organizations. Synonymous with the total quality movement, continuous improvement provides a way for organizations to provide strategic control that allows an organization to respond more proactively and timely to rapid developments in hundreds of areas that influence a business's success. This chapter discusses traditional strategic controls and then explains ways that the *continuous improvement quality imperative* and the balanced scoreboard methodology can be key vehicles for strategic control.

ESTABLISHING STRATEGIC CONTROLS

The control of strategy can be characterized as a form of "steering control." Ordinarily, a good deal of time elapses between the initial implementation of a strategy and achievement of its intended results. During that time, investments are made and numerous projects and actions are undertaken to implement the strategy. Also, during that time, changes are taking place in both the environmental situation and the firm's internal situation. Strategic controls are necessary to steer the firm through these events. They must provide the basis for adapting the firm's strategic actions and directions in response to these developments and changes.

The four basic types of strategic control are:

1. Premise control.

2. Special alert control.

3. Strategic surveillance.

4. Implementation control.

The nature of these four types is summarized in Exhibit 11–1.

Premise Control

Every strategy is based on certain planning premises—assumptions or predictions. *Premise control is designed to check systematically and continuously whether the premises on which the strategy is based are still valid.* If a vital premise is no longer valid, the strategy may have to be changed. The sooner an invalid premise can be recognized and

EXHIBIT 11–1   **Four Types of Strategic Control**

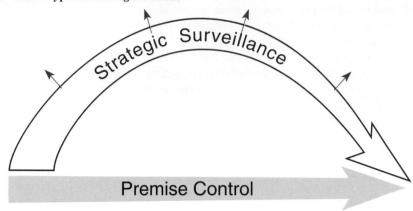

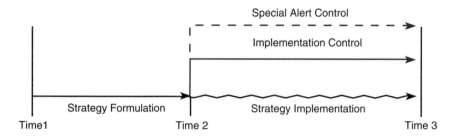

Characteristics of the Four Types of Strategic Control

	Types of Strategic Control			
Basic Characteristics	**Premise Control**	**Implementation Control**	**Strategic Surveillance**	**Special Alert Control**
Objects of control	Planning premises and projections	Key strategic thrusts and milestones	Potential threats and opportunities related to the strategy	Occurrence of recognizable but unlikely events
Degree of focusing	High	High	Low	High
Data acquisition:				
Formalization	Medium	High	Low	High
Centralization	Low	Medium	Low	High
Use with:				
Environmental factors	Yes	Seldom	Yes	Yes
Industry factors	Yes	Seldom	Yes	Yes
Strategy-specific factors	No	Yes	Seldom	Yes
Company-specific factors	No	Yes	Seldom	Seldom

Source: Adapted from G. Schreyogg and H. Steinmann, "Strategic Control: A New Perspective," *Academy of Management Review* 12, no. 1 (1987).

rejected, the better are the chances that an acceptable shift in the strategy can be devised. Planning premises are primarily concerned with environmental and industry factors.

Environmental Factors

Although a firm has little or no control over environmental factors, these factors exercise considerable influence over the success of its strategy, and strategies usually are based on key premises about them. Inflation, technology, interest rates, regulation, and demographic/social changes are examples of such factors.

EPA regulations and federal laws concerning the handling, use, and disposal of toxic chemicals have a major effect on the strategy of Velsicol Chemical Company, a market leader in pesticide chemicals sold to farmers and exterminators. So Velsicol's management makes and constantly updates premises about future regulatory actions.

Industry Factors

The performance of the firms in a given industry is affected by industry factors. These differ among industries, and a firm should be aware of the factors that influence success in its particular industry. Competitors, suppliers, product substitutes, and barriers to entry are a few of the industry factors about which strategic assumptions are made.

Rubbermaid has long been held up as a model of predictable growth, creative management, and rapid innovation in the plastic housewares and toy industry. Its premise going into the 21st century was that large retail chains would continue to prefer its products over competitors' because of this core competence. This premise included continued receptivity to regular price increases when necessitated by raw materials costs. Retailers, most notably Wal-Mart, recently balked at Rubbermaid's attempt to raise prices to offset the doubling of resin costs. Furthermore, traditionally overlooked competitors have begun to make inroads with computerized stocking services. Rubbermaid is moving aggressively to adjust its strategy because of the response of Wal-Mart and other key retailers.

Strategies are often based on numerous premises, some major and some minor, about environmental and industry variables. Tracking all of these premises is unnecessarily expensive and time consuming. Managers must select premises whose change (1) is likely and (2) would have a major impact on the firm and its strategy.

Strategic Surveillance

By their nature, premise controls are focused controls; strategic surveillance, however, is unfocused. *Strategic surveillance is designed to monitor a broad range of events inside and outside the firm that are likely to affect the course of its strategy.*[1] The basic idea behind strategic surveillance is that important yet unanticipated information may be uncovered by a general monitoring of multiple information sources.

Strategic surveillance must be kept as unfocused as possible. It should be a loose "environmental scanning" activity. Trade magazines, *The Wall Street Journal,* trade conferences, conversations, and intended and unintended observations are all subjects of strategic surveillance. Despite its looseness, strategic surveillance provides an ongoing, broad-based vigilance in all daily operations that may uncover information relevant to the firm's strategy. Citicorp benefited significantly from an Argentine manager's strategic surveillance of political speeches by Argentina's former president, as discussed in Exhibit 11–2, Strategy in Action.

Special Alert Control

Another type of strategic control, really a subset of the other three, is special alert control. *A special alert control is the thorough, and often rapid, reconsideration of the firm's strategy because of a sudden, unexpected event.* The tragic events of September 11, 2001, an outside firm's sudden acquisition of a leading competitor, an unexpected product difficulty, such as the poisoned Tylenol capsules—events of these kinds can drastically alter the firm's strategy.

[1] G. Schreyogg and H. Steinmann, "Strategic Control: A New Perspective," *Academy of Management Review* 12, no. 1 (1987), p. 101.

BusinessWeek IMPLEMENTATION CONTROL AT DAYS INN

When Days Inn pioneered the budget segment of the lodging industry, its strategy placed primary emphasis on company-owned facilities and it insisted on maintaining a roughly 3-to-1 company-owned/franchise ratio. This ratio ensured the parent company's total control over standards, rates, and so forth.

As other firms moved into the budget segment, Days Inn saw the need to expand rapidly throughout the United States and, therefore, reversed its conservative franchise posture. This reversal would rapidly accelerate its ability to open new locations. Longtime executives, concerned about potential loss of control over local standards, instituted *implementation controls* requiring both franchise evaluation and annual milestone reviews. Two years into the program, Days Inn executives were convinced that a high franchise-to-company ratio was manageable, and so they accelerated the growth of franchising by doubling the franchise sales department.

STRATEGIC SURVEILLANCE AT CITICORP

Citicorp has been pursuing an aggressive product development strategy intended to achieve an annual earnings growth of 15 percent while it becomes an institution capable of supplying clients with any kind of financial service anywhere in the world. A major obstacle to the achievement of this earnings growth is Citicorp's exposure to default because of its extensive earlier loans to troubled developing countries. Citicorp is sensitive to the wide variety of predictions about impending defaults.

Citicorp's long-range plan assumes an annual 10 percent default on its developing economy loans over any five-year period. Yet it maintains active *strategic surveillance control* by having each of its international branches monitor daily announcements from key governments and from inside contacts for signs of changes in a host country's financial environment. When that surveillance detects a potential problem, management attempts to adjust Citicorp's posture. For example, when a former Argentine president, stated that his country may not pay interest on its debt as scheduled, Citicorp raised its annual default charge to 20 percent of its $500 million Argentine exposure.

SPECIAL ALERT CONTROL AT UNITED AIRLINES

The sudden impact of an airline crash can be devastating to a major airline. United Airlines has made elaborate preparations to deal with this contingency. Its executive vice president, James M. Guyette, heads a crisis team that is permanently prepared to respond. Members of the team carry beepers and are always on call. When United's Chicago headquarters received word of the September 11th hijacking and crash, they were in a "war room" within an hour to direct the response. Beds are set up nearby so team members can catch a few winks; while they sleep, alternates take their places.

Members of the team have been carefully screened through simulated crisis drills. "The point is to weed out those who don't hold up well under stress," says Guyette. Although the team was established to handle flight disasters, it has since assumed an expanded role. The crisis team was activated when American Airlines launched a fare war. And according to Guyette, "We're brainstorming about how we would be affected by everything from a competitor who had a serious problem to a crisis involving a hijacking or taking a United employee hostage."

Such an event should trigger an immediate and intense reassessment of the firm's strategy and its current strategic situation. In many firms, crisis teams handle the firm's initial response to unforeseen events that may have an immediate effect on its strategy. Increasingly, firms have developed contingency plans along with crisis teams to respond to circumstances such as United Airlines did on September 11, 2001 as summarized in Strategy in Action 11–2.

Implementation Control

Strategy implementation takes place as series of steps, programs, investments, and moves that occur over an extended time. Special programs are undertaken. Functional areas initiate strategy-related activities. Key people are added or reassigned. Resources are mobilized. In other words, managers implement strategy by converting broad plans into the concrete, incremental actions and results of specific units and individuals.

Implementation control is the type of strategic control that must be exercised as those events unfold. *Implementation control is designed to assess whether the overall strategy should be changed in light of the results associated with the incremental actions that implement the overall strategy.* The two basic types of implementation control are (1) monitoring strategic thrusts and (2) milestone reviews.

Monitoring Strategic Thrusts or Projects

As a means of implementing broad strategies, narrow strategic projects often are undertaken—projects that represent part of what needs to be done if the overall strategy is to be accomplished. These strategic thrusts provide managers with information that helps them determine whether the overall strategy is progressing as planned or needs to be adjusted.

Although the utility of strategic thrusts seems readily apparent, it is not always easy to use them for control purposes. It may be difficult to interpret early experience or to evaluate the overall strategy in light of such experience. One approach is to agree early in the planning process on which thrusts or which phases of thrusts are critical factors in the success of the strategy. Managers responsible for these implementation controls will single them out from other activities and observe them frequently. Another approach is to use stop/go assessments that are linked to a series of meaningful thresholds (time, costs, research and development, success, and so forth) associated with particular thrusts. A program of regional development via company-owned inns in the Rocky Mountain area was a monitoring thrust that Days Inn used to test its strategy of becoming a nationwide motel chain. Problems in meeting time targets and unexpectedly large capital needs led Days Inn's executives to abandon the overall strategy and eventually sell the firm.

Milestone Reviews

Managers often attempt to identify significant milestones that will be reached during strategy implementation. These milestones may be critical events, major resource allocations, or simply the passage of a certain amount of time. The milestone reviews that then take place usually involve a full-scale reassessment of the strategy and of the advisability of continuing or refocusing the firm's direction.

A useful example of implementation control based on milestone review is offered by Boeing's product-development strategy of entering the supersonic transport (SST) airplane market. Boeing had invested millions of dollars and years of scarce engineering talent during the first phase of its SST venture, and competition from the British/French Concorde effort was intense. Since the next phase represented a billion-dollar decision, Boeing's management established the initiation of the phase as a milestone. The milestone reviews greatly increased the estimates of production costs; predicted relatively few passengers and rising fuel costs, thus raising the estimated operating costs; and noted that the Concorde, unlike Boeing, had the benefit of massive government subsidies. These factors led Boeing's management to scrap its SST strategy in spite of high sunk costs, pride, and patriotism. Only an objective, full-scale strategy reassessment could have led to such a decision.

In this example, a milestone review occurred at a major resource allocation decision point. Milestone reviews may also occur concurrently when a major step in a strategy's implementation is being taken or when a key uncertainty is resolved. Managers even may set an arbitrary period, say two years, as a milestone review point. Whatever the basis for selecting that point, the critical purpose of a milestone review is to thoroughly scrutinize the firm's strategy so as to control the strategy's future.

Implementation control is also enabled through operational control systems like budgets, schedules and key success factors. While strategic controls attempt to steer the company over an extended period (usually five years of more), operational controls provide postaction evaluation and control over short periods—usually from one month to one year. To be effective, operational control systems must take four steps common to all postaction controls:

1. Set standards of performance.

2. Measure actual performance.

3. Identify deviations from standards set.

4. Initiate corrective action.

Exhibit 11–3 illustrates a typical operational control system. These indicators represent progress after two years of a five-year strategy intended to differentiate the firm as a customer-service-oriented provider of high-quality products. Management's concern is to compare *progress to date* with *expected progress.* The *current deviation* is of particular interest, because it provides a basis for examining *suggested actions* (usually suggested by subordinate managers) and for finalizing decisions on changes or adjustments in the firm's operations.

From Exhibit 11–3, it appears that the firm is maintaining control of its cost structure. Indeed, it is ahead of schedule on reducing overhead. The firm is well ahead of its delivery cycle target, while slightly below its target service-to-sales personnel ratio. Its product returns look OK, although product performance versus specification is below standard. Sales per employee and expansion of the product line are ahead of schedule. The absenteeism rate in the service area is on target, but the turnover rate is higher than that targeted. Competitors appear to be introducing products more rapidly than expected.

After deviations and their causes have been identified, the implications of the deviations for the ultimate success of the strategy must be considered. For example, the rapid product-line expansion indicated in Exhibit 11–3 may have been a response to the increased rate of competitors' product expansion. At the same time, product performance is still low; and, while the installation cycle is slightly above standard (improving customer service), the ratio of service to sales personnel is below the targeted ratio. Contributing to this substandard ratio (and perhaps reflecting a lack of organizational commitment to customer service) is the exceptionally high turnover in customer service personnel. The rapid reduction in indirect overhead costs might mean that administration integration of customer service and product development requirements has been cut back too quickly.

This information presents operations managers with several options. They may attribute the deviations primarily to internal discrepancies. In that case, they can scale priorities up or down. For example, they might place more emphasis on retaining customer service personnel and less emphasis on overhead reduction and new product development. On the other hand, they might decide to continue as planned in the face of increasing competition and to accept or gradually improve the customer service situation. Another possibility is reformulating the strategy or a component of the strategy in the face of rapidly increasing competition. For example, the firm might decide to emphasize more standardized or lower-priced products to overcome customer service problems and take advantage of an apparently ambitious sales force.

This is but one of many possible interpretations of Exhibit 11–3. The important point here is the critical need to monitor progress against standards and to give serious in-depth attention to both the causes of observed deviations and the most appropriate responses to them. After the deviations have been evaluated, slight adjustments may be made to keep progress, expenditure, or other factors in line with the strategy's programmed needs. In the unusual event of extreme deviations—generally because of unforeseen changes—management is alerted to the possible need for revising the budget, reconsidering certain functional plans related to budgeted expenditures, or examining the units concerned and the effectiveness of their managers.

EXHIBIT 11–3   Monitoring and Evaluating Performance Deviations

Key Success Factors	Objective, Assumption, or Budget	Forecast Performance at This Time	Current Performance	Current Deviation	Analysis
Cost control: Ratio of indirect overhead cost to direct field and labor costs	10%	15%	12%	+3 (ahead)	Are we moving too fast, or is there more unnecessary overhead than was originally thought?
Gross profit	39%	40%	40%	0%	
Customer service: Installation cycle in days	2.5 days	3.2 days	2.7 days	+0.5 (ahead)	Can this progress be maintained?
Ratio of service to sales personnel	3.2	2.7	2.1	–0.6 (behind)	Why are we behind here? How can we maintain the installation-cycle progress?
Product quality: Percentage of products returned	1.0%	2.0%	2.1%	–0.1% (behind)	Why are we behind here? What are the ramifications for other operations?
Product performance versus specification	100%	92%	80%	–12% (behind)	
Marketing: Monthly sales per employee	$12,500	$11,500	$12,100	+$600 (ahead)	Good progress. Is it creating any problems to support?
Expansion of product line	6	3	5	+2 products (ahead)	Are the products ready? Are the perfect standards met?
Employee morale in service area: Absenteeism rate	2.5%	3.0%	3.0%	(on target)	
Turnover rate	5%	10%	15%	–8% (behind)	Looks like a problem! Why are we so far behind?
Competition: New product introductions (average number)	6	3	6	–3 (behind)	Did we underestimate timing? What are the implications for our basic assumptions?

Correcting deviations in performance brings the entire management task into focus. Managers can correct such deviations by changing measures or plans. They also can eliminate poor performance by changing how things are done, by hiring or retraining workers, by changing job assignments, and so on. Correcting deviations, therefore, can involve all of the functions, tasks, and responsibilities of operations managers. Managers in other cultures, most notably Japan, have for some time achieved operational control by seeking their unit's continuous improvement. Companies worldwide have adapted this point of view that operational control is best achieved through a pervasive commitment to quality, originally called *total quality management* (TQM), which is seen as essential to strategic success into the 21st century.

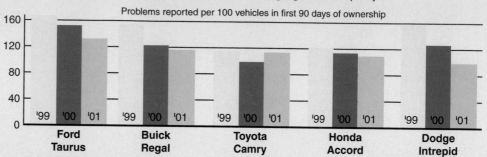

BusinessWeek

Quality Quotients

As they face off with Japan in the midsize sedan market, Detroit's companies are making big strides in quality.

Problems reported per 100 vehicles in first 90 days of ownership

Data: J. D. Power & Associates ©BW

You'd think Ford Motor Co. would learn a lesson about keeping an eye on quality from the $3.5 billion Explorer tire debacle. And, indeed, the automaker went to extraordinary lengths to ensure that its revised 2002 Explorer launched without a hiccup. It even took the unprecedented step of holding up vehicles in the factory for engineers to pore over them for defects. But that wasn't enough. Last May, the new Explorer had to be recalled. It turned out that while redesigning the car, engineers forgot to adjust a rail used to guide the vehicle along an assembly line. The oversight meant that some Explorers limped off the line with nine-inch-long gashes in their tires.

Try as it might, the U.S. auto industry can't shake its karma for shaky quality—even though its cars and trucks are better than ever. *Consumer Reports* recently found that the average number of problems per 100 new vehicles built by General Motors, Ford, and Chrysler dropped from 105 in 1980 to just 23 in 2000. But as the Explorer Redux episode highlights, U.S. cars still are not up to snuff. Despite the improvement, *Consumer Reports* pegs the quality of American vehicles at Japanese levels circa 1985. And the Big Three currently spend about $125 more per vehicle in warranty costs than their Japanese rivals.

Why the gap? It's not that American factory workers are sloppier than their Japanese counterparts. In fact, fewer than 15% of quality problems can be traced to shoddy workmanship or other factory errors, says Sandy Munro, president of Munro & Associates Inc., a Troy (Mich.)-based manufacturing consultant. The real problem, he says, is at the front end of the development process. "It has more to do with who designed it, how they designed it, and what processes and materials they used," Munro contends.

Raiding Toyota

Now, in a drive to reduce costs and boost quality, U.S. carmakers are revamping their approach, trying to root out problems before assembly lines start rolling. They're borrowing strategies invented by the Japanese, or—in the case of Chrysler Corp—raiding Toyota Motor Corp. for quality expertise. And they're bringing suppliers into the design process earlier and treating them like partners, in hopes of spotting problems with components as early as possible.

Detroit is finding, as it did back in the 1970s, that there is no better way to begin than with a close look at Japan. There, top car builders take an evolutionary approach to design, stressing continuous improvement. From year to year, if

THE QUALITY IMPERATIVE: CONTINUOUS IMPROVEMENT TO BUILD CUSTOMER VALUE

The initials TQM have become the most popular abbreviation in business management literature since MBO (management by objectives). TQM Stands for *total quality management,* an umbrella term for the quality programs that have been implemented in many businesses worldwide in the last two decades. TQM was first implemented in several large U.S. manufacturers in the face of the overwhelming success of Japanese and German competitors. Japanese manufacturers embraced the quality messages of Americans

parts are working well, they are kept, not replaced. And by using common components across a range of vehicles, Japanese designs cut down on variability—the old, familiar foe of quality.

In stark contrast, U.S. automakers tend to start with a clean sheet of paper whenever they redesign a vehicle. And this can lead to trouble. When Chrysler introduced the re-designed 1999 Jeep Grand Cherokee, former CEO Robert J. Eaton bragged that there were so few shared bits between the new and old models, they'd all fit in a bag in his hand. He should have kept mum: *Consumer Reports* says the Grand Cherokee's "reliability has been among the worst we've seen."

Another nagging problem at U.S. car shops is an overly narrow focus on component design without enough regard for the larger task of integrating parts on the factory floor. The trouble, points out Jay Baron, director of manufacturing systems group at the Center for Automotive Research in Ann Arbor, Mich., is that good components that don't fit to-gether demand costly last-minute design changes. "This is one area where the Japanese are way ahead of us," says Baron. Instead of striving for perfection in the design of each component, the Japanese fast-forward to the manufacturing phase to make sure the parts fit, and then back up to make necessary adjustments, he says. Now, all three Detroit au-tomakers are beginning to follow suit.

Tricky Problems

Ford, by any calculation, needs the most work. Last year alone, recalls and other quality gaffes cost the company at least $1 billion. Now, Ford is pinning its quality hopes on Six Sigma, a data-driven method pioneered by industrial giants such as AlliedSignal Inc. and Motorola Inc. It's an approach that depends on rigorous statistical analysis to unearth tough problems. And it's already helping crack some tricky ones at Ford. Ill-fitting doors on Ford's top-selling F-150 pickup truck, for example, were blamed for chronic wind noise and leaks. So, after studying the installation of hundreds of such

doors, a Six Sigma team working at Ford's Norforlk (Va.) truck factory discovered that door-fit varied according to the order in which bolts attaching the door to the frame were driven in. The problem implied its own solution. Experiment-ing with various sequences, the team reduced the defects rate by two-thirds—without changing a single part. The change immediately saved $35,000 on the plant floor by eliminating the refitting of bad doors. Larger savings in war-ranty haven't yet been tallied.

Of the Big Three, GM has made the most progress on quality. This year, it climbed to No. 4 on J. D. Power & Asso-ciates' annual overall quality rankings, just a notch behind Nissan Motor Co. Now, GM is looking to close in on the leaders, Toyota and Honda, by working more closely with its suppliers, says GM manufacturing chief Gary Cowger. On some vehicles, GM is even handing over complete design re-sponsibility for its interiors to large suppliers, such as Lear Corp. and Johnson Controls Inc. The subcontractors, GM fig-ures, can better monitor quality by designing and building fully integrated systems—complete seats or dashboards as opposed to just seat frames or speedometers.

At Chrysler, the struggling U.S. unit of Germany's DaimlerChrysler, improving quality is an even more urgent mission. The company's new CEO, former Mercedes chief engineer Dieter Zetsche, has made it a cornerstone of his $3.9-billion turnaround plan. He's overhauling Chrysler's ve-hicle development processes by pulling together teams from all areas of the company—design, engineering, marketing, manufacturing, and purchasing—in a bid to drive out waste. By involving everyone up front, his goal is to avoid the kinds of last-minute design changes that lead to errors later on. Even before Zetsche arrived, Chrysler quality was improving: Its Dodge Intrepid beat out the Toyota Camry and the Honda Accord—long-time leaders in the midsize sedan segment—in J. D. Power's 2001 new car quality survey.

Source: "Detroit Is Cruising for Quality," *BusinessWeek,* September 3, 2001.

W. Edwards Deming and J. M. Juran following World War II, and by the 1970s Japanese products had acquired unquestioned reputations for superior high quality.

Growing numbers of U.S. manufacturers have attempted to change this imbalance with their own quality programs, and the practice has spread to large retail and service companies as well. Increasingly, smaller companies that supply big TQM companies have adopted quality programs, often because big companies have required small suppli-ers to adopt quality programs of their own. Exhibit 11–4, Strategy in Action, describes the aggressive quality imperative thrusted on Detroit automakers in the new century.

TQM is viewed as virtually a new organizational culture and way of thinking. It is built around an intense focus on customer satisfaction; on accurate measurement of every critical variable in a business's operation; on continuous improvement of products, services, and processes; and on work relationships based on trust and teamwork. One useful explanation of the quality imperative suggests 10 essential elements of implementing total quality management, as follows:

1. **Define *quality* and *customer value*.** Rather than be left to individual interpretation, company personnel should have a clear definition of what *quality* means in the job, department, and throughout the company. It should be developed from your customer's perspective and communicated as a written policy.

Thinking in terms of customer value broadens the definition of *quality* to include efficiency and responsiveness. Said another way, quality to your customer often means that the product performs well; that it is priced competitively (efficiency); and that you provide it quickly and adapt it when needed (responsiveness). Customer value is found in the combination of all three—quality, price, and speed.

2. **Develop a customer orientation.** Customer value is what the customer says it is. Don't rely on secondary information—talk to your customers directly. Also recognize your "internal" customers. Usually less than 20 percent of company employees come into contact with external customers, while the other 80 percent serve internal customers—other units with real performance expectations.

The value chain provides an important way to think about customer orientation, particularly to recognize *internal* as well as external (ultimate) customers. Operating personnel are *internal* customers of the accounting department for useful information and also the purchasing department for quality, timely supplies. When they are "served" with quality, efficiency, and responsiveness, value is added to their efforts, and is passed on to their internal customers and, eventually, external (ultimate) customers.

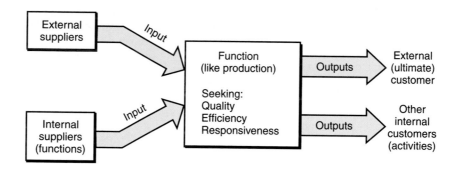

3. **Focus on the company's business processes.** Break down every minute step in the process of providing the company's product or service and look at ways to improve it, rather than focusing simply on the finished product or service. Each process contributes value in some way, which can be improved or adapted to help other processes (internal customers) improve. Examples of ways customer value is enhanced across business processes in several functions are:

	Quality	Efficiency	Responsiveness
Marketing	Provides accurate assessment of customer's product preferences to R&D	Targets advertising campaign at customers, using cost-effective medium	Quickly uncovers and reacts to changing market trends
Operations	Consistently produces goods matching engineering design	Minimizes scrap and rework through high-production yield	Quickly adapts to latest demands with production flexibility
Research and development	Designs products that combine customer demand and production capabilities	Uses computers to test feasibility of idea before going to more expensive full-scale prototype	Carries out parallel product/process designs to speed up overall innovation
Accounting	Provides the information that managers in other functions need to make decisions	Simplifies and computerizes to decrease the cost of gathering information	Provides information in "real time" (as the events described are still happening)
Purchasing	Selects vendors for their ability to join in an effective "partnership"	Given the required vendor quality, negotiates prices to provide good value	Schedules inbound deliveries efficiently, avoiding both extensive inventories and stock-outs
Personnel	Trains workforce to perform required tasks	Minimizes employee turnover, reducing hiring and training expenses	In response to strong growth in sales, finds large numbers of employees and quickly teaches needed skills

4. **Develop customer and supplier partnerships.** Organizations have a destructive tendency to view suppliers and even customers adversarily. It is better to understand the horizontal flow of a business—outside suppliers to internal suppliers/customers (a company's various departments) to external customers. This view suggests suppliers are partners in meeting customer needs, and customers are partners by providing input so the company and suppliers can meet and exceed those expectations.

Ford Motor Company's Dearborn, Michigan, plant is linked electronically with supplier Allied Signal's Kansas City, Missouri, plant. A Ford computer recently sent the design for a car's connecting rod to an Allied Signal factory computer, which transformed the design into instructions that it fed to a machine tool on the shop floor. The result: quality, efficiency, and responsiveness.

5. **Take a preventive approach.** Many organizations reward "fire fighters," not "fire preventers," and identify errors after the work is done. Management, instead, should be rewarded for being prevention oriented and seeking to eliminate nonvalue-added work.

6. **Adopt an error-free attitude.** Instill an attitude that "good enough" is not good enough anymore. "Error free" should become each individual's performance standard, with managers taking every opportunity to demonstrate and communicate the importance of this imperative.

7. **Get the facts first.** Continuous improvement–oriented companies make decisions based on facts, not on opinions. Accurate measurement, often using readily available statistical techniques, of every critical variable in a business's operation—and using those measurements to trace problems to their roots and eliminate their causes—is a better way.

8. **Encourage every manager and employee to participate.** Employee participation, empowerment, participative decision making, and extensive training in quality techniques, in statistical techniques, and in measurement tools are the ingredients continuous improvement companies employ to support and instill a commitment to customer value.

9. **Create an atmosphere of total involvement.** Quality management cannot be the job of a few managers or of one department. Maximum customer value cannot be achieved unless all areas of the organization apply quality concepts simultaneously.

10. **Strive for continuous improvement.** Stephen Yearout, director of Ernst & Young's Quality Management Center, recently observed that "Historically, meeting your customers' expectations would distinguish you from your competitors. The 21st century will require you to anticipate customer expectations and deliver quality service faster than the competition." Quality, efficiency, and responsiveness are not one-time programs of competitive response, for they create a new standard to measure up to. Organizations quickly find that continually improving quality, efficiency, and responsiveness in their processes, products, and services is not just good business; it's a necessity for long-term survival.

Six-Sigma Approach to Continuous Improvement

Sometimes referred to as the "new TQM," Six-Sigma is a highly rigorous and analytical approach to quality and continuous improvement with an objective to improve profits through defect reduction, yield improvement, improved consumer satisfaction and best-in-class performance. Six-Sigma complements TQM philosophies such as management leadership, continuous education and customer focus while deploying a disciplined and structured approach of hard-nosed statistics. Critics of TQM see key success factors differentiating Six-Sigma from TQM.

- Acute understanding of customers and the product or service provided

- Emphasis on the science of statistics and measurement

- Meticulous and structured training development

- Strict and project-focused methodologies

- Reinforcement of the doctrine advocated by Juran such as top management support and continuous education

Companies such as Honeywell (1994), Motorola (1987), GE (1995), Polaroid (1998) and Texas Instruments (1988) have adopted the Six-Sigma discipline as a major business initiative. Many of these companies invested heavily in and pursued this model initially in order to create products and services that were of equal and higher quality than those of its competitors and to improve relationships with customers. Much like TQM, the technique implies a whole culture of strategies, tools, and statistical methodologies to improve the bottom line resulting in tremendous savings, subsequent improvement initiatives, and management action.

A Six-Sigma program at many organizations simply means a measure of quality that strives for near perfection in every facet of the business including every product, process, and transaction. The approach was introduced and established at Motorola in 1987 becoming the key factor in Motorola winning the 1988 Malcolm Baldrige Award for Quality, and has had impressive and undisputed results for many companies who have undertaken it. Allied Signal reported an estimated savings of $1.5 billion in its 1997 annual report while GE's savings in a 1998 annual letter to its shareholders reported benefits exceeding $750 million a year.

How the Six-Sigma Statistical Concept Works

Six-Sigma means a failure rate of 3.4 parts per million or 99.9997%. At the six standard deviation from the mean under a normal distribution, 99.9996% of the population is under the curve with not more than 3.4 parts per million defective. The higher the sigma value, the less likely a process will produce defects as excellence is approached.

If you played 100 rounds of golf per year and played at:
2 Sigma: You'd miss 6 putts per round.
3 Sigma: You'd miss 1 putt per round.
4 Sigma: You'd miss 1 putt every 9 rounds.
5 Sigma: You'd miss 1 putt every 2.33 years.
6 Sigma: You'd miss 1 putt every 163 years!

Source: "When Near Is Not Good Enough," *The Australian CPA,* August 2000.

Many frameworks, management philosophies, and specific statistical tools exist for implementing the Six-Sigma methodology and its objective to create a near perfect process or service. One such method for improving a system for existing processes falling below specification while looking for incremental improvement is the DMAIC process (define, measure, analyze, improve, control).

Define

- Project Definition
- Project Charter
- Gathering Voice of the Customer
- Translating Customer Needs into Specific Requirements

Measure

- Process Mapping (As-Is Process)
- Data Attributes (Continuous vs. Discrete)
- Measurement System Analysis
- Gage Repeatability and Reproducibility
- Measuring Process Capability
- Calculating Process Sigma Level
- Visually Displaying Baseline Performance

THE BIG PICTURE

In 1997 Citibank set about to apply this technique to its non-manufacturing environment by contracting with Motorola University Consulting and Training Services for extensive Six-Sigma training. The goal was to improve Citibank operations globally through defect reduction and process timeline improvement while increasing customer loyalty and satisfaction.

Citibank's mission focused on becoming the premier international financial company in the next millennium requiring excellence in every facet of the business and action on the part of every Citibank employee. This quality initiative began with training 650 senior managers by October 1997 and over 92,000 employees trained worldwide by early 1999.

SIX SIGMA TO THE RESCUE

The initial phase of the Six-Sigma process involved Motorola University training Citibank employees on both Cycle Time Reduction (CTR) and Cross Functional Process Mapping (CFPM). These methodologies essentially set the stage for Six-Sigma by mapping and eliminating wasteful and nonvalue added processing steps from the business. In a nonmanufacturing company, 90 percent of activities may fall into this category. A sigma is a statistical term which measures to what degree a process varies from perfection. A rating of three sigma equals 66,807 defects per million opportunities; a rating of Six-Sigma equals 3.4 defects per million opportunities, or virtual perfection.

Six-Sigma is accomplished using simple tools, including the Pareto chart. The data on the chart identify which problems occur with the greatest frequency or incur the highest cost. It provides the direct evidence of what would be analyzed and corrected first. Typically 20 percent of the possible causes are responsible for 80 percent of any problem.

Citibank undertook the Six-Sigma process to investigate why it was not achieving complete customer satisfaction with a goal to have 10 times reduction in defects and cycle time by December 2000 and 10 times again every two years. Six-Sigma classifies a defect as anything that results in customer dissatisfaction and unhappiness. Indicators of less than optimal status are customer opinions such as:

- You're difficult to do business with;

- You don't fix my problems;

- You're not staying innovative and your systems are not state-of-the-art;

- You are slow and complicated.

Analyze

- Visually Displaying Data (Histogram, Run Chart, Pareto Chart, Scatter Diagram)
- Value-Added Analysis
- Cause and Effect Analysis (a.k.a. Fishbone, Ishikawa)
- Verification of Root Causes
- Determining Opportunity (Defects and Financial) for Improvement
- Project Charter Review and Revision

Improve

- Brainstorming
- Quality Function Deployment (House of Quality)
- Failure Modes and Effects Analysis (FMEA)
- Piloting Your Solution
- Implementation Planning
- Culture Modification Planning for Your Organization

Control

- Statistical Process Control (SPC) Overview
- Developing a Process Control Plan
- Documenting the Process

TEAM APPROACH

A team composed of bankers and operations people identified the entire funds transfer process, tabulating defects and analyzing them using Pareto charts. Highest on the list of defects for this process was the internal callback procedure, which required a staffer to phone back the requester to make sure that the instructions were correct, or had not been altered. "We cut monthly callbacks from 8,000 to 1,000 and we eliminated callbacks for 73 percent of the transactions coming in," says Cherylann Munoz, compliance director of Citibank's Private Bank in the United States and Western Hemisphere.

In Citibank's Global Cash and Trade Organization (GCTO), MU's Six-Sigma methodology helped track defects and documented the results by teaching team members to identify appropriate metrics, determine a baseline, establish appropriate standards, and monitor execution. The employees formed teams to solve any issues they discovered during this analysis.

To reduce the time for opening an account, Citibank formed a cross-functional global team of 80 people. The team first identified sponsors and formed a steering committee to champion the effort. Employees were invited to participate based on their subject matter know-how and ability to assist with the solution. The biggest hurdle for Citibank employees was allocating the time to participate while juggling their daily job responsibilities. Sue Andros, a global process owner in the GCTO responsible for the end-to-end customer experience says process mapping "lets people get to know one another."

"Team members worked well together, since achieving the objectives would make their professional responsibilities easier and would benefit their customers—a win/win situation for everyone," Andros says. "The focus on cycle time and deficiencies has made an impact on how we serve customers. It's not just a matter of doing things faster, it's doing things better. This means eliminating redundancy, minimizing hand-offs, and establishing metrics that reflect performance in the eyes of the customer."

Dipak Rastogi, executive vice president for Citibank's Eastern European/Central Asia and Africa region headquartered in London, agrees with those sentiments. "Introducing quality as a core strategy was viewed as a unique opportunity and differentiating feature not only with regard to our customers, but also our employees," says Rastogi. "When implemented correctly, quality increases customer satisfaction and leads to shorter reaction time and faster introduction of new products—providing a sustainable competitive advantage."

MANAGEMENT COMMITMENT

Teams involved in the Citibank quality initiative needed to have full autonomy to make decisions about changes to the established processes. Senior management sponsored these initiatives or served on steering committees to champion the work and there was an "open door" policy so that teams could gain access to them as needed. According to Peter Klimes, quality director for Citibank in the Czech Republic, the involvement of senior support is a continuous process all the way from setting critical business issues and objectives, to the final improvement implementation. "We have had a well-balanced split between projects initiated by senior management and those initiated by employees," Klimes says. "Our senior operations officer and our corporate bank head were our most active supporters of Six-Sigma projects. Their commitment helps balance back and front office aspects of projects."

Source: "Citibank Increases Loyalty with Defect-Free Processes," *The Journal for Quality & Participation,* Fall 2000, pp. 32–36.

Six-Sigma programs promote an uncompromising orientation of all business processes toward the customer. The first step is always achieving an understanding of customer expectations so that suitable tools can be employed to improve both the internal and external processes. This program does not come fast and cheap, however, management commitment is crucial to the success, and employees must be trained in Six-Sigma methodologies. Exhibit 11–5, Strategy in Action, describes the use of Six-Sigma at Citibank.

ISO 9001 and the Era of International Standards

The ISO 9001 quality management system standard, introduced in 1987, is international in both scope and impact. In early 2000 there were almost 300,000 firms registered in over 143 countries, almost 25,000 of those registered firms in the United States. The trend towards ISO 9001 registration and the creation of additional management system standards such as ISO 14001 (environmental), ISO 18001 (health and safety) and sector-specific standards such as QS-9001 (automotive) and AS-9001 (aerospace) has continued to grow and develop internationally. The standards are voluntary and apply to many kinds of businesses including manufacturers, distributors, services, software developers, public utilities, government agencies, and financial and educational institutions.

The *ISO 9001 standard* focuses on achieving customer satisfaction through continuous measurement, documentation, assessment, and adjustment. A diagram of the approach is provided below. The standard specifies requirements for a quality management system where an organization:

1. Needs to demonstrate its ability to consistently provide product and services that meet customer requirements, and

2. Aims to enhance customer satisfaction through the effective application of the system, including processes for continual improvement of the system and the assurance of conformity to customer requirements.

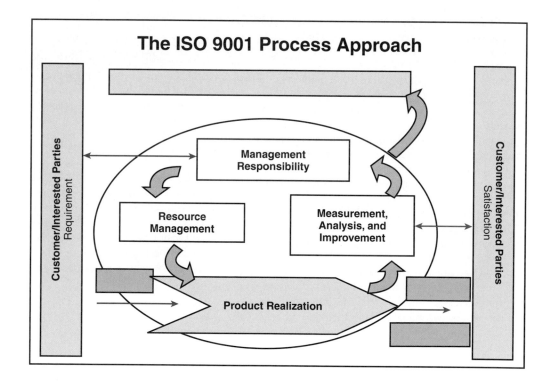

The ISO 9001 Process Approach

Customer/Interested Parties Requirement

Management Responsibility

Resource Management

Measurement, Analysis, and Improvement

Product Realization

Customer/Interested Parties Satisfaction

ISO 9001 has strong commonalities with other quality schemes such as Mil-Q, Deming's 14 points, TQM and the Malcolm Baldrige National Quality Award Criteria. The four focus areas of the ISO 9001 process approach are 1) management responsibility, 2) resource management, 3) product realization, and 4) measurement, analysis, and improvement. ISO 9001 differs from other quality approaches in that it involves formal certification by a sanctioned ISO certification source before a company can claim to meet the standard. Exhibit 11–6, Strategy in Action, describes how well-known golf club maker Ping chose to become ISO 9001 certified.

Upon introduction of the ISO 9001 series of standards, many American and multinational firms not only foresaw the competitive advantage possible by adopting ISO 9001, but also

When John Solheim took the helm at golf equipment maker Ping in 1995, he had a legacy to protect and improve—that of his father, Karsten Solheim. When the employee handbook was written in 1993, Karsten wrote: "It is the customer who keeps us in business, and we must always be sure to give each one first-class treatment. The role of each employee is also very important because dedication to quality assures the success of the company."

The family business was founded over 42 years ago and is based in Phoenix. Today Ping is best known for its custom fit, custom-built golf clubs and competes in a highly innovative and competitive $4 billion golf equipment industry. John wasn't satisfied with the existing standard of quality and set about to find a way to measure the company business against an internationally accepted standard, ISO 9001. "By embarking on this journey, we hoped to measure ourselves against recognized criteria that would reassure us we were doing business appropriately," says Solheim. "We also believed such an accomplishment might help identify areas where we could advance." Both of Solheim's hopes were fulfilled.

THE IMPLEMENTATION AND REGISTRATION PROCESS

After conducting some research, John Solheim decided to pursue registration to both ISO 9001 (quality management system standard) and ISO 14001 (environmental management system standard). This decision was based on several factors:

1. The ISO (International Organization for Standardization) standards are internationally recognized.

2. Attaining registration would provide Ping with a competitive advantage in the marketplace. Ping would be the first competitor in the golf industry to be registered to both ISO 9001 and ISO 14001 standards.

3. Ping wanted the benefits of implementing the management systems such as improved quality, increased environmental awareness, customer satisfaction, and continuous improvement.

Ping began the implementation process in November 1999. The first step was to develop documentation, identify and improve processes and provide training to all personnel involved in the implementation. A preassessment audit acted as a dress rehearsal for employees and heightened their understanding of the requirements as well as identified opportunities for improvement in the existing system.

During this process Ping faced many challenges. First, its workforce consisted of over 1,000 employees who spoke at least six different languages. Additionally, company processes, documentation, and policies were very informal.

Many hours were spent training and developing valuable manuals that are used as reference resources. "The registration process helped me see how everything in the company ties together and our processes really interrelate," said Solheim. "I thought I was fairly well-organized, but the registration audit taught me to dot my I's and cross my T's."

BENEFITS

Ping's steering committee identified many benefits of the ISO 9001 and ISO 14001 registration.

1. Enhanced internal communication and increased focus on customer requirements throughout the organization.

2. The generation of useful information to allow more strategic decision making by all levels of management.

3. Better measurement of the processes that are responsible for quality and the ability to continually improve product quality.

4. Improved customer satisfaction and the continued reputation for quality, innovation, and service in the golf equipment market.

5. Development of a new customer service call system that improved reduced customer response time.

6. Improved environmental performance resulting in reduced emissions.

7. Improved cycle times to meet our customers' demands.

Ping officially achieved registration on October 17, 2000. Ping is now in the process of implementing ISO 9001 and ISO 14001 in its sister company, Ping Europe Ltd., in Gainsborough, United Kingdom. This registration will include the Gainsborough Golf Club, a private 36-hole facility with a driving range and modern clubhouse. Ping believes this will be the first country club to ever be registered to international standards.

Now registered, the company is continuing to focus intensely on continuous improvement of the quality of its systems, operations, service and products in a highly competitive worldwide market. "We continuously hone our ISO 9001 and 14001 systems, strengthening our quality and environmental objectives while looking for improvement opportunities. No one asked us to become ISO registered," Solheim says. "We raised our standards because golfers ultimately decide the fate of our products. Customer satisfaction will be the program's greatest benefit."

Source: Robert T. Driescher, *Quality Progress*, August 2001, pp. 37–41.

saw the value of quality management system implementation in achieving customer satisfaction. As a result, many of these larger firms subsequently imposed the requirements of ISO 9001 on suppliers as a condition to do business and as a way to reduce the supply base to only those suppliers committed to quality and service. It is believed by many that eventually ISO 9001 would reduce and possibly eliminate the need for customer-sponsored audits. In the ISO 9001 registration scheme, third-party auditors employed by registrars conduct ISO 9001 registration audits. National and international accreditation bodies accredit the registrars to certify and publish that the company has met the requirements of ISO 9001.

Customer mandates initially served as an incentive for suppliers desiring to retain existing levels of business with their customers to jump on the ISO 9001 bandwagon and pursue registration. In many cases registration to ISO 9001 gave these suppliers a clear competitive advantage in the marketplace. However in 2001, as many companies continue to pursue and maintain registration, ISO 9001 functions as a way of life for many companies and has become ingrained in daily processes, no longer thought of as a unique or identifiable program. Other companies, who were not pressured to implement ISO 9001, chose to put it into practice as a methodology by which to systematize their operations and to focus on and improve both daily operations and quality levels throughout their organizations.

Nevertheless, along with the establishment of ISO 9001 standards came many misperceptions. Here are just a few of the criticisms targeted at ISO 9001.

- ***ISO 9001 is a European standard and cannot be applicable to American firms.***
  ISO 9001 has traceable American ancestry to military quality systems. The United States is a member of International Organization for Standardization (ISO) and participates in the formulation and continuing committee reviews of ISO 9001.

- ***Implementing ISO 9001 is mandatory if you plan to do business in Europe.***
  This is true for a small number of firms manufacturing a relative handful of products—a list that may continue to grow in the coming years. But the doors to Europe did not slam shut on non-ISO 9001 registered companies in January 1993. Rather, ISO 9001 registration has increasingly become desired, expected and even required in certain markets and industries (i.e., Automotive QS-9001), but growth was driven primarily by customer requirements and competitive pressures.

- ***ISO 9001 is all about paperwork.***
  Ironically, ISO 9001 had in most cases reduced the redundancy and massive manuals and shelves of procedures and books that already exist. Documentation is central to ISO 9001 requirements for the purposes of planning, controlling, training and providing objective evidence of conformance. The goal is to make the documentation support the value-added activity clearly and concisely, eliminating redundancy while supporting usefulness. The standard does not prescribe specific solutions, tactics, strategies or procedures which gives ISO 9001 enormous flexibility.

- ***ISO 9001 is inspection-based as opposed to prevention-based.***
  ISO 9001 requires the quality management system monitor conformance to requirements. This is just one part of the measurement, analysis, and continuous improvement cycle at the heart of the standard. Implementation of the standard alone will not guarantee quality. Management commitment and employee involvement are instrumental in the implementation process.

Since its introduction, international participation in ISO 9001 continues to climb and offers organizations a framework for quality system management. It is no longer new or radical, yet it provides a common language for quality that is easily translatable and applicable across many countries, cultures, and businesses. The focus is not on products and services but rather on the organization's network of activities designed and operated to ensure that output meets the ultimate business objective: satisfying the customer.

The Balanced Scorecard Methodology

A new approach to strategic control was developed in the last decade by Harvard Business School professors Robert Kaplan and David Norton. They named this system the *balanced scorecard.* Recognizing some of the weaknesses and vagueness of previous implementation and control approaches, the balanced scorecard approach was intended to provide a clear prescription as to what companies should measure in order to "balance" the financial perspective in implementation and control of strategic plans.[2]

The balanced scorecard was viewed as a *management system* (not only a measurement system) that enables companies to clarify their strategies, translate them into action, and provide meaningful feedback. It provides feedback around both the internal business processes and external outcomes in order to continuously improve strategic performance and results. When fully deployed, the balanced scorecard is intended to transform strategic planning from a separate top management exercise into the nerve center of an enterprise. Kaplan and Norton describe the innovation of the balanced scorecard as follows:

> The balanced scorecard retains traditional financial measures. But financial measures tell the story of past events, an adequate story for industrial age companies for which investments in long-term capabilities and customer relationships were not critical for success. These financial measures are inadequate, however, for guiding and evaluating the journey that information age companies must make to create future value through investment in customers, suppliers, employees, processes, technology, and innovation.[3]

The balanced scorecard methodology adapts the TQM ideas of customer-defined quality, continuous improvement, employee empowerment, and measurement-based management/feedback into an expanded methodology that includes traditional financial data and results. The balanced scorecard incorporates feedback around internal business process *outputs,* as in TQM, but also adds a feedback loop around the *outcomes* of business strategies. This creates a "double-loop feedback" process in the balanced scorecard. In doing so, it links together two areas of concern in strategy execution—quality operations and financial outcomes—that are typically addressed separately yet are obviously critically intertwined as any company executes its strategy. A system that links shareholder interests in return on capital with a system of performance management that is linked to ongoing, operational activities and processes within the company is what the balanced scorecard attempts to achieve.

Exhibit 11–7 illustrates the balanced scorecard approach drawing on the traditional DuPont formula discussed in Chapter 5 and historically used to examine drivers of stockholder-related financial performance across different company activities. The balanced scorecard seeks to "balance" shareholder goals with customer goals and operational performance goals, and Exhibit 11–7 shows that they are interconnected—

---

[2] This methodology is covered in great detail in a number of books and articles by R. S. Kaplan and D. P. Norton. It is also the subject of frequent special publications by the Harvard Business Review that provided updated treatment of uses and improvements in the balanced scorecard methodology. Some useful books include *Balanced Scorecard: Translating Strategies into Action* (Boston: Harvard Business School Press, 1996); *The Strategy-Focused Organization* (Boston: Harvard Business School Press, 2001). And, in HBR, "Using the Balanced Scorecard as a Strategic Management System," *Harvard Business Review* (January–February, 1996). Numerous useful websites also exist such as www.bscol.com.
[3] Another useful treatment of various aspects of the Balanced Scoreboard to include further learning opportunities you may wish to explore, especially with regard to the use of this approach with governmental organizations, may be found at www.balancedscorecard.org.

EXHIBIT 11–7

Integrating Shareholder Value and Organizational Activities across Organizational Levels

Source: R. M. Grant, *Contemporary Strategy Analysis* (Oxford, UK: Blackwell, 2002), p. 56.

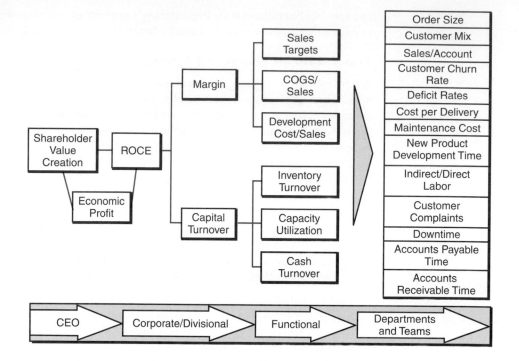

shareholder value creation are linked to divisional concerns for return on capital employed which in turn are driven by functional outcomes in sales, inventory, capacity utilization that in turn come about through the results of departments and teams daily activities throughtout the company. The balanced scorecard suggests that we view the organization from *four* perspectives, and to develop metrics, collect data and analyze it relative to each of these perspectives:

1. *The Learning and Growth Perspective: How well are we continuously improving and creating value?* The scorecard insists on measures related to innovation and organizational learning to gauge performance on this dimension—technological leadership, product development cycle times, operational process improvement, and so on.

2. *The Business Process Perspective: What are our core competencies and areas of operational excellence?* Internal business processes and their effective execution as measured by productivity, cycle time, quality measures, downtime, various cost measures among others provide scorecard input here.

3. *The Customer Perspective: How satisfied are our customers?* A customer satisfaction perspective typically adds measures related to defect levels, on-time delivery, warranty support, product development among others that come from direct customer input and are linked to specific company activities.

4. *The Financial Perspective: How are we doing for our shareholders?* A financial perspective typically using measures like cash flow, return on equity, sales and income growth.

Through the integration of goals from each of these four perspectives, the balanced scorecard approach enables the strategy of the business to be linked with shareholder value creation while providing several measurable short-term outcomes that guide and

EXHIBIT 11–8
Balanced Scorecard for Mobil Corporation's NAM&R

Source: "How Mobil Became a Strategy-Focused Organization," Chapter 2 in R. Kaplan and D. Norton, *The Strategy-Focused Organization* (Boston: Harvard Business School Press, 2001).

		Strategic Objectives	Strategic Measures
Financially Strong	Financial	F1 Return on Capital Employed F2 Cash Flow F3 Profitability F4 Lowest Cost F5 Profitable Growth F6 Manage Risk	• ROCE • Cash Flow • Net Margin • Full cost per gallon delivered to customer • Volume growth rate vs. industry • Risk index
Delight the Consumer Win–Win Relationship	Customer	C1 Continually delight the targeted consumer C2 Improve dealer/distributor profitability	• Share of segment in key markets • Mystery shopper rating • Dealer/distributor margin on gasoline • Dealer/distributor survey

Safe and Reliable
 	
Competitive Supplier
 	
Good Neighbor
On Spec
On Time
	Internal	I1 Marketing
		  1. Innovative products and services
		  2. Dealer/distributor quality
		
		I2 Manufacturing
		  1. Lower manufacturing costs
		  2. Improve hardware and performance
		I3 Supply, Trading, Logistics
		  1. Reducing delivered cost
		  2. Trading organization
		  3. Inventory management
		
		I4 Improve health, safety, and environmental performance
		I5 Quality
			• Non-gasoline revenue and margin per square foot
			• Dealer/distributor acceptance rate of new programs
			• Dealer/distributor quality ratings
			• ROCE on refinery
			• Total expenses (per gallon) vs. competition
			• Profitability index
			• Yield index
			Delivered cost per gallon vs. competitors
			• Trading margin
			• Inventory level compared to plan and to output rate
			• Number of incidents
			• Days away from work
			• Quality Index

Motivated and Prepared	Learning and growth	L1 Organization involvement L2 Core competencies and skills L3 Access to strategic information	• Employee survey • Strategic competitive availability • Strategic information availabiilty

monitor strategy implementation. Kaplan and Norton provide this account of the use of the balanced scorecard at FMC:

> Strategists came up with 5- and 10-year plans, controllers with one-year budgets and near-term forecasts. Little interplay occurred between the two groups. But the [balanced] scorecard now bridges the two. The financial perspective builds on the traditional function

performed by controllers. The other three perspectives make the division's long-term objectives measurable.[4]

Another example that helps you understand the integrating power of the balanced scorecard can be seen at Mobil Corporation's North American Marketing and Refining business [NAM&R]. NAM&R's scorecard is shown in Exhibit 11–8. Assisted by Kaplan and Norton, an unprofitable NAM&R adopted the scorecard methodology to better link its strategy with financial objectives and to translate these into operating performance targets tailored to outcomes in each business unit, functional departments, and operating processes within them. They included measures developed with key customers from their perspective. The result was an integrated system where scorecards provided measurable outcomes through which the performance of each department and operating unit, team or activity within NAM&R was monitored, adjusted, and used to determine performance-related pay bonuses.[5]

The balanced scorecard reflects continuous improvement in management thought about how to better manage organizations. Our coverage of the concept is brief, and you are encouraged to seek additional information and resources suggested in various footnotes or through your own current Web search. Strategic control, continuous improvement, specific measurable feedback and inclusion of everyone in some way responsible for customer satisfaction and organizational success are important developments in the art of strategic management and the science of its succesful application.

Summary

Three fundamental perspectives—strategic control, continuous improvement, and the balanced scoreboard—provide the basis for designing strategy control systems. Strategic controls are intended to steer the company toward its long-term strategic goals. Premise controls, implementation controls, strategic surveillance, and special alert controls are types of strategic control. All four types are designed to meet top management's needs to track the strategy as it is being implemented, to detect underlying problems, and to make necessary adjustments. These strategic controls are linked to the environmental assumptions and the key operating requirements necessary for successful strategy implementation. Ever-present forces of change fuel the need for and focus of strategic control.

Operational control systems require systematic evaluation of performance against predetermined standards or targets. A critical concern here is identification and evaluation of performance deviations, with careful attention paid to determining the underlying reasons for and strategic implications of observed deviations before management reacts. Some firms use trigger points and contingency plans in this process.

The "quality imperative" of the last 20 years has redefined global competitiveness to include reshaping the way many businesses approach strategic and operational control. What has emerged is a commitment to continuous improvement in which personnel across all levels in an organization define customer value, identify ways every process within the business influences customer value, and seek continuously to enhance the quality, efficiency, and responsiveness with which the processes, products, and services are created and supplied. This includes attending to internal as well as external customers. The "balanced scorecard" is a control system that integrates strategic goals, operating outcomes, customer satisfaction, and continuous improvement into an ongoing strategic management system.

[4] R. Kaplan and D. Norton, "Putting the Balanced Scorecard to Work," *Harvard Business Review* (September–October, 1993), p. 147.

[5] "How Mobil Became a Strategy-Focused Organization," Chapter 2 in R. Kaplan and D. Norton, *The Strategy-Focused Organization* (Boston: Harvard Business School Press, 2001). For an online version of the Mobil NAM&R case study, see www.bscol.com.

Questions for Discussion

Questions for Discussion

1. Distinguish strategic control from operating control. Give an example of each.

2. Select a business whose strategy is familiar to you. Identify what you think are the key premises of the strategy. Then select the key indicators that you would use to monitor each of these premises.

3. Explain the differences between implementation controls, strategic surveillance, and special alert controls. Give an example of each.

4. Why are budgets, schedules, and key success factors essential to operations control and evaluation?

5. What are key considerations in monitoring deviations from performance standards?

6. What are five key elements of quality management? How are quality imperative and continuous improvement related to strategic and operational control?

7. How might customer value be linked to quality, efficiency, and responsiveness?

8. Is it realistic that a commitment to continuous improvement could actually replace operational controls? Strategic controls?

9. How is the balanced scorecard approach similar to continuous improvement? How is it different?

Chapter 11 Discussion Case

BusinessWeek

The Web of Quality: Worldwide Links Mean Better Products

1 Just a decade ago, U.S. businesses were crowing about the promise of new quality-improvement programs. Since then, the U.S. quality movement has altered and improved business practices, and many American companies have matched Japan's vaunted quality benchmarks. Industrial offices buzzed with phrases such as "total quality management (TQM)" and "Six-Sigma accuracy." Such catchphrases are heard less frequently because they've been replaced by Internet jargon. And that raises a question: Where does quality stand in the Internet age?

2 Concerns about quality have by no means disappeared. Rather, at most successful companies, quality has become internalized, says quality consultant Joseph A. DeFeo, CEO of Juran Institute Inc. in Wilton, Conn. The special software and management practices associated with the movement are now in everyday use, he says, so quality has become less self-conscious. But it has reemerged as a critical issue because of the rapid development of Internet links among companies. Quality is no longer the concern of just a single factory but of whole supply chains. As companies outsource more of their work, they need to take increasing care to make sure their partners measure up on quality, says Michael J. Burkett, a senior analyst at Boston's AMR Research Inc., a manufacturing consultant.

3 This report explores the role of quality in today's increasingly networked world. The first section looks at how a unit of General Electric Co. is blazing new quality trails in a field it helped pioneer. The second lifts the lid on efforts by Mexico's manufacturers to meet the quality demands of customers in North America and overseas.

GE: ZERO TO 60, NO SKID MARKS

4 Never before has General Electric Co. cranked out gas-powered turbines in such quantities. Given the growing preference for gas-powered generating plants over their much dirtier coal-burning cousins, demand is booming—with no sign of slowing. In May, GE's Power Systems unit installed five times the number of turbines it did a year earlier. Yet despite the problems of grappling with such a huge increase in production, GE has become progressively better at making good on delivery date promises. Indeed, the company has actually delivered many units ahead of schedule (see chart on p. 344). GE Power's success at managing its huge runup in output is a much-discussed success story among GE insiders—and a major reason they view Power Systems head Robert L. Nardelli as a top contender for GE's CEO job when Jack Welch retires.

5 While GE is hardly complaining about this upturn, executives realized that the runup would pose huge risks. In particular, they worried about maintaining their grip on quality, continuing to fill orders on time, and keeping customers happy. The last thing they wanted was to become another example of a company that lost control when it tried to goose production quickly after getting bombarded by orders. The production snafus at Boeing Co. in 1997 offered an ominous example of how things can go wrong in a big rampup. And when GE execs began taking notice in 1998 of industry numbers showing that electrical-power reserves in the United States were shrinking to alarming levels, Boeing's difficulties were painfully fresh.

6 OUTSIDE RISKS. To prepare for the projected hike in orders, GE Power Systems' managers visited companies that had lived through similar explosions in their businesses. They made a point of flying to Seattle to glean insights from Boeing officials. One thing became evident right away: The biggest risk to GE was outside the company. Suppliers that lacked GE's financial resources might not be able to expand production rapidly enough. At Boeing and other casualties of too-fast growth, most breakdowns occurred when

suppliers overestimated their production capacity. Since more than 50% of a turbine's components are purchased from outside vendors, GE wasted no time shoring up its supply chain. In 1998, GE Power Systems launched an exhaustive study of the suppliers that provide key components for the gas turbines. After first screening 250 of its suppliers, it intensively audited 85 that posed the greatest risk. Teams consisting of specialists in supply sourcing, research and development, finance, and management spent up to two weeks at supplier facilities across the United States and around the world.

7   Since the last major rampup in production at Power Systems in the late 80s, GE had two new tools to help it avoid supply-chain problems, says Victor R. Abate, general manager of fulfillment at Power Systems. One was the Internet. But more important was the company's vaunted Six-Sigma program, adopted in 1996. Six sigma is statistics-speak for 99.9999976%. Applied to manufacturing, it means a quality level of no more than 3.4 defects per million products. At GE, the Six-Sigma program also includes guidelines and tools for boosting productivity and wringing inefficiencies out of its manufacturing and service processes. Mark M. Little, a vice-president at GE Power Systems, says that with Six-Sigma's tools, GE no longer has to rely on bludgeoning suppliers to deliver. Instead, GE's auditors have the wherewithal to determine whether suppliers can hand over parts in time.

8   GE's vendor-checkers scrutinize myriad details right down to the individual machine tools that suppliers use to produce turbine parts. GE also evaluates the supplier's suppliers—their production capacity, shipping and delivery systems, and how rigorous their quality programs are. And the exam doesn't end there. Because a supplier might need to boost hiring, GE checks to see whether the company keeps a stack of résumés on hand. In the end, GE eliminated some suppliers and found backups for suppliers with obvious weaknesses. And they tagged some 350 potential problems that continued to be monitored until fixed by the suppliers.

9   INVALUABLE ASSET. Perhaps most important, the initial evaluation allowed GE to establish a framework for ensuring the quality of its supply chain as production rolled forward. Says analyst Nicholas P. Heymann of Prudential Securities Inc., who formerly worked as a GE auditor: "How many companies today have guys that can go into another company and fully assess where the flaws are—and not only that but also fix them? They've executed Six-Sigma all the way through the supplier chain."

10   That was an invaluable asset as orders flowed in and the stress on production systems mounted, both internally and among suppliers. With its new predictive tools, deep knowledge of its suppliers, and the ability to share information quickly via the Internet, GE could identify problems earlier and avoid potentially costly bottlenecks. "Whenever we see variation, we just attack it," Abate says.

11   Example: GE last year realized that a supplier of a core turbine component was poised to fall behind. Although the company was consistently delivering to GE on time, GE's Six-Sigma audit had found the supplier would be unable to keep up as GE went from producing 25 turbines to 45 per quarter in late 1999. GE sent a team to the company, and a settlement was reached: The supplier would lease additional equipment to keep up with GE's production track. "With these very rigorous tools," says Little, "we now know what the leading indicators are, and we can act fast."

12   The Internet has made a big difference, too. When GE engineers are in the field, checking on deliveries at customers sites anywhere in the world, they can report on a problem on their laptops, and this information is available instantly throughout GE Power Systems. Before the Net, the field engineers would typically resolve each problem at the plant site—but GE managers would remain blissfully unaware of the solution, which would have to be engineered all over again the next time.

13   So what's the customer's view of how well GE is coping with its production surges? Duke Energy North America (DENA, a unit of Charlotte-based Duke Energy Corp.) is clearly satisfied. It placed a huge order with GE in the fall of 1998 to outfit nearly two dozen generating plants with gas turbines, four of which will be on line by month's end. Including service agreements, it was a $4 billion order. So far, everything has gone according to schedule or slightly ahead of it, says

James M. Donnell, CEO of DENA. For Duke, there's a lot at stake. With summer already starting to stroke demand for electricity, each day that a gas-turbine plant isn't producing means a huge revenue loss. A 640-megawatt plant running at maximum capacity for 16 hours on a summer day, for example, translates into $1.75 million in gross revenues.

14   For GE the stakes are high, too. The company boasts that it has grabbed a 75% share of current turbine orders. With the power industry relying so heavily on one supplier, more eyes than ever will be watching to see if Power Systems can keep managing the boom.

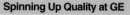

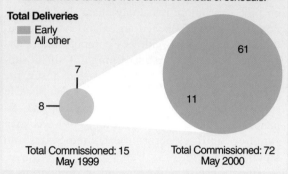

Spinning Up Quality at GE

Thanks to its six-sigma program, turbine production soared and far more turbines were delivered ahead of schedule.

Total Deliveries
- Early
- All other

7

8

61

11

Total Commissioned: 15
May 1999

Total Commissioned: 72
May 2000

Source: Petty, John, When Near Enough is Not Good Enough. Australian CPA, May 2000. Pp. 34–35.

Guide to Strategic Management Case Analysis

THE CASE METHOD

Case analysis is a proven educational method that is especially effective in a strategic management course. The case method complements and enhances the text material and your professor's lectures by focusing attention on what a firm has done or should do in an actual business situation. Use of the case method in a strategic management course offers you an opportunity to develop and refine analytical skills. It also can provide exciting experience by allowing you to assume the role of the key decision maker for the organizations you will study.

When assuming the role of the general manager of the organization being studied, you will need to consider all aspects of the business. In addition to drawing on your knowledge of marketing, finance, management, production, and economics, you will be applying the strategic management concepts taught in this course.

The cases in this book are accounts of real business situations involving a variety of firms in a variety of industries. To make these opportunities as realistic as possible, the cases include a variety of quantitative and qualitative information in both the presentation of the situation and the exhibits. As the key decision maker, you will need to determine which information is important, given the circumstances described in the case. Keep in mind that the results of analyzing one firm will not necessarily be appropriate for another since every firm is faced with a different set of circumstances.

PREPARING FOR CASE DISCUSSION

The case method requires an approach to class preparation that differs from the typical lecture course. In the typical lecture course, you can still benefit from each class session even if you did not prepare, by listening carefully to the professor's lecture. This approach will not work in a course using the case method. For a case course, proper preparation is essential.

Suggestions for Effective Preparation

1. *Allow adequate time in preparing a case.* Many of the cases in this text involve complex issues that are often not apparent without careful reading and purposeful reflection on the information in the cases.

2. *Read each case twice.* Because many of these cases involve complex decision making, you should read each case at least twice. Your first reading should give you an overview of the firm's unique circumstances and the issues confronting the firm. Your second reading allows you to concentrate on what you feel are the most critical issues and to understand what information in the case is most important. Make limited notes identifying key points during your first reading. During your second reading, you can add details to your original notes and revise them as necessary.

3. *Focus on the key strategic issue in each case.* Each time you read a case you should concentrate on identifying the key issue. In some cases, the key issue will be identified by the case writer in the introduction. In other cases, you might not grasp the key strategic issue until you have read the case several times. (Remember that not every piece of information in a case is equally important.)

4. *Do not overlook exhibits.* The exhibits in these cases should be considered an integral part of the information for the case. They are not just "window dressing." In fact, for many cases you will need to analyze financial statements, evaluate organizational charts, and understand the firm's products, all of which are presented in the form of exhibits.

5. *Adopt the appropriate time frame.* It is critical that you assume the appropriate time frame for each case you read. If the case ends in 2000, that year should become the present for you as you work on that case. Making a decision for a case that ends in 1999 by using data you could not have had until 2003 defeats the purpose of the case method. For the same reason, although it is recommended that you do outside reading on each firm and industry, you should not read material written after the case ended unless your professor instructs you to do so.

6. *Draw on all of your knowledge of business.* As the key decision maker for the organization being studied, you will need to consider all aspects of the business and industry. Do not confine yourself to strategic management concepts presented in this course. You will need to determine if the key strategic issue revolves around a theory you have learned in a functional area, such as marketing, production, finance, or economics, or in the strategic management course.

USING THE INTERNET IN CASE RESEARCH

The proliferation of information available on the Internet has direct implications for business research. The Internet has become a viable source of company and industry data to assist those involved in case study analysis. Principal sources of useful data include company websites, U.S. government websites, search engines, investment research sites, and online data services. This section will describe the principal Internet sources of case study data and offer means of retrieving that data.

Company Websites

Virtually every public and private firm has a website that any Internet user can visit. Accessing a firm's website is easy. Many firms advertise their web address through both TV and print advertisements. To access a site when the address is known, enter the address into the address line on any Internet service provider's homepage. When the address is not known, use of a search engine will be necessary. The use of a search engine will be described later. Often, but not always, a firm's web address is identical to its name, or is at least an abbreviated form of its name.

Company websites contain data that are helpful in case study analysis. A firm's website may contain descriptions of company products and services, recent company accomplishments and press releases, financial and stock performance highlights, and an overview of a firm's history and strategic objectives. A company's website may also contain links to relevant industry websites that contain industry statistics as well as current and future industry trends. The breadth of data available on a particular firm's website will vary but in general larger, global corporations tend to have more complete and sophisticated websites than smaller, regional firms.

U.S. Government Websites

The U.S. government allows the public to access virtually all of the information that it collects. Most of this information is available online to Internet users. The government collects a great range of data types, from firm-specific data the government mandates all publicly traded firms to supply, to highly regarded economic indicators. The usefulness of many U.S. government websites depends on the fit between the case you are studying and the data located on the website. For example, a study of an accounting firm may be supplemented with data supplied by the Internal Revenue Service website, but not the Environmental Protection Agency website. A sampling of prominent government websites and their addresses is shown below.

Environmental Protection Agency: www.epa.gov

General Printing Office: www.gpo.gov

Internal Revenue Service: www.irs.ustreas.gov

Libraries of Congress: www.loc.gov

National Aeronautics and Space Administration: www.hq.nasa.gov

SEC's Edgar Database: www.sec.gov/edgarhp.htm

Small Business Administration: www.sba.gov

STAT-USA: www.stat-usa.gov

U.S. Department of Commerce: www.doc.gov

U.S. Department of Treasury: www.ustreas.gov

One of the most useful sites for company case study analysis is the Securities and Exchange Commission's EDGAR database listed above. The EDGAR database contains the documents that the government mandates all publicly traded firms to file including 10-Ks and 8-Ks. A form 10-K is the annual report that provides a comprehensive overview of a firm's financials in addition to discussions regarding industry and product background. Form 8-K reports the occurrence of any material events or corporate changes that may be of importance to investors. Examples of reported occurrences include key management personnel changes, corporate restructures, and new debt or equity issuance. This site is very user friendly and requires the researcher to provide only the company name in order to produce a listing of all available reports.

Search Engines

Search engines allow a researcher to locate information on a company or industry without prior knowledge of a specific Internet address. Generally, to execute a search the search engine requires the entering of a keyword, for example, a company name. However, each search engine differs slightly in its search capabilities. For example, to narrow a search on one search engine may be accomplished differently than narrowing a search on another.

The information retrieved by search engines typically includes articles and other information that contain the entered keyword or words. Because the search engine has retrieved data that contain keywords does not necessarily mean that the information is useful. Internet data are unfiltered, meaning they may not be checked for accuracy before the data are posted online. However, data copyrighted or published by a reputable source may greatly increase the chance that the data are indeed accurate. A list of popular Internet search engines is shown below:

Alta Vista: www.altavista.digital.com

DogPile: www.dogpile.com

Excite: www.excite.com

HotBot: www.hotbot.lycos.com

InfoSeek: www.infoseek.com

Lycos: www.lycos.com

Metacrawler: www.metacrawler.com

WebCrawler: www.webcrawler.com

Yahoo!: www.yahoo.com

Although Yahoo! appears in the above list, it is not a true search engine. Yahoo! actually catalogs websites for users. When keywords are entered into Yahoo!'s search mechanism, Yahoo! will return Internet addresses that contain the keywords. Therefore, Yahoo! is regarded as a very efficient means of locating a firm's website without prior knowledge of its exact web address.

Investment Research Sites

Investment research sites provide company stock performance data including key financial ratios, competitor identification, industry data, and links to research reports and SEC filings. These sites provide support for the financial analysis portion of a case study, but only for publicly traded businesses. Most investment research sites also contain macro market data that may not be company specific, but may still affect many investors of equities.

Investment research sites usually contain a search mechanism if a desired stock's ticker symbol is not known. In this case, the company name is entered to enable the site to find the corresponding equity. Since these sites are geared toward traders who want recent stock prices and data, searching for data relevant to a case may require more elaborate investigations at multiple sites. The list below includes many popular investment research sites:

American Stock Exchange: www.amex.com

CBS Market Watch: cbsmarketwatch.com

CNN FinancialNews: money.cnn.com

DBC Online: www.esignal.com

Hoover's Online: www.hoovers.com

InvestorGuide: www.investorguide.com

Wall Street Research Net: www.wsrn.com

Market Guide: www.marketguide.com

Money Search: www.moneysearch.com

MSN Money: moneycentral.msn.com

NASDAQ: www.nasdaq.com

New York Stock Exchange: www.nyse.com

PC Financial Network: www.csfbdirect.com

Quote.Com: finance.lycos.com

Stock Smart: www.stocksmart.com

Wright Investors' Service on the World Wide Web: www.wisi.com

The Wall Street Journal Online: online.wsj.com/public/us

Zacks Investment Research: my.zacks.com

One site that conveniently contains firm, industry, and competitor data is Hoover's Online. Hoover's also provides financials, stock charts, current and archived news stories, and links to research reports and SEC filings. Some of these data, most notably the lengthy research reports produced by analysts, are fee-based and must be ordered.

Online Data Sources

Online data sources provide wide access to a huge volume of business reference material. Information retrieved from these sites typically includes descriptive profiles, stock price performance, SEC filings, and newspaper, magazine, and journal articles related to a particular company, industry, or product. Online data services are popular with educational and financial institutions. While some services are free to all users, to utilize the entire array of these sites' services, a fee-based subscription is usually necessary.

Accessing these sites requires only the source's address, or the use of a search engine to find the address. The source's homepage will clearly indicate the nature of the information available and describe how to search for and access the data. Most sites have help screens to assist in locating the desired information.

One of the most useful online sources for business research is the Lexis-Nexis Universe. This source provides a wide array of news, business, legal, and reference information. The information is categorized into dozens of topics including general news, company and industry news, company financials that include SEC filings, government and political news, accounting auditing and tax data, and legal research. One particularly impressive service is a search mechanism that allows a user to locate a particular article when the specific citation is known. A list of several notable online data sources is shown below:

ABI/Inform (Proquest Direct): www.il.proquest.com/proquest

American Express: americanexpress.com

Bloomberg Financial News Services: www.bloomberg.com

BusinessWeek Online: businessweek.com

Dow Jones News Retrieval: http://bis.dowjones.com

EconLit: www.econlit.org

Lexis-Nexis Universe: www.lexis-nexis.com

PARTICIPATING IN CLASS

Because the strategic management course uses the case method, the success and value of the course depend on class discussion. The success and value of the class discussion, in turn, rely on the roles both you and your professor perform. Following are aspects of your role and your professor's that, if kept in mind, will enhance the value and excitement of this course.

Students as Active Learners

The case method requires your active participation. This means your role is no longer one of sitting and listening.

1. *Attend class regularly.* Not only is your grade likely to depend on your involvement in class discussions, but the benefit you derive from this course is directly related to your involvement in and understanding of the discussions.

2. *Be prepared for class.* The need for adequate preparation already has been discussed. You will benefit more from the discussions, will understand and participate in the exchange of ideas, and will avoid the embarrassment of being called on when not prepared. By all means, bring your book to class. Not only is there a good chance you will need to refer to a specific exhibit or passage from the case, you may need to refresh your memory of the case (particularly if you made notes in the margins while reading).

3. *Participate in the discussion.* Attending class and being prepared are not enough; you need to express your views in class. You can participate in a number of ways: by addressing a question asked by your professor, by disagreeing with your professor or your classmates (by all means, be tactful), by building on an idea expressed by a classmate, or by simply asking a relevant question.

4. *Participate wisely.* Although you do not want to be one of those students who never raises his or her hand, you also should be sensitive to the fact that others in your

class will want to express themselves. You have probably already had experience with a student who attempts to dominate each class discussion. A student who invariably tries to dominate the class discussion breeds resentment.

5. *Keep a broad perspective.* By definition, the strategic management course deals with the issues facing general managers or business owners. As already mentioned, you need to consider all aspects of the business, not just one particular functional area.

6. *Pay attention to the topic being discussed.* Focus your attention on the topic being discussed. When a new topic is introduced, do not attempt to immediately introduce another topic for discussion. Do not feel you have to have something to say on every topic covered.

Your Professor as Discussion Leader

Your professor is a discussion leader. As such, he or she will attempt to stimulate the class as a whole to share insights, observations, and thoughts about the case. Your professor will not necessarily respond to every comment you or your classmates make. Part of the value of the case method is to get you and your classmates to assume this role as the course progresses.

The professor in a strategic management case course performs several roles:

1. *Maintaining focus.* Because multiple complex issues need to be explored, your professor may want to maintain the focus of the class discussion on one issue at a time. He or she may ask you to hold your comment on another issue until a previous issue is exhausted. Do not interpret this response to mean your point is unimportant; your professor is simply indicating there will be a more appropriate time to pursue that particular comment.

2. *Getting students involved.* Do not be surprised if your professor asks for input from volunteers and nonvolunteers alike. The value of the class discussion increases as more people share their comments.

3. *Facilitating comprehension of strategic management concepts.* Some professors prefer to lecture on strategic management concepts on a "need-to-know" basis. In this scenario, a lecture on a particular topic will be followed by an assignment to work on a case that deals with that particular topic. Other professors will have the class work through a case or two before lecturing on a topic to give the class a feel for the value of the topic being covered and for the type of information needed to work on cases. Still other professors prefer to cover all of the theory in the beginning of the course, thereby allowing uninterrupted case discussion in the remaining weeks of the term. All three of these approaches are valued.

4. *Playing devil's advocate.* At times your professor may appear to be contradicting many of the comments or observations being made. At other times your professor may adopt a position that does not immediately make sense, given the circumstances of the case. At other times your professor may seem to be equivocating. These are all examples of how your professor might be playing devil's advocate. Sometimes the professor's goal is to expose alternative viewpoints. Sometimes he or she may be testing your resolve on a particular point. Be prepared to support your position with evidence from the case.

ASSIGNMENTS

Written Assignments

Written analyses are a critical part of most strategic management courses. Each professor has a preferred format for these written analyses, but a number of general guidelines will prove helpful to you in your written assignments.

1. *Analyze.* Avoid merely repeating the facts presented in the case. Analyze the issues involved in the case and build logically toward your recommendations.

2. *Use headings or labels.* Using headings or labels throughout your written analysis will help your reader follow your analysis and recommendations. For example, when you are analyzing the weaknesses of the firm in the case, include the heading Weaknesses. Note the headings in the cases that follow.

3. *Discuss alternatives.* Follow the proper strategic management sequence by (1) identifying alternatives, (2) evaluating each alternative, and (3) recommending the alternative you think is best.

4. *Use topic sentences.* You can help your reader more easily evaluate your analysis by putting the topic sentence first in each paragraph and following with statements directly supporting the topic sentence.

5. *Be specific in your recommendations.* Develop specific recommendations logically and be sure your recommendations are well defended by your analysis. Avoid using generalizations, clichés, and ambiguous statements. Remember that any number of answers are possible and so your professor is most concerned about how your reasoning led to your recommendations and how well you develop and support your ideas.

6. *Do not overlook implementation.* Many good analyses receive poor evaluations because they do not include a discussion of implementation. Your analysis will be much stronger when you discuss how your recommendation can be implemented. Include some of the specific actions needed to achieve the objectives you are proposing.

7. *Specifically state your assumptions.* Cases, like all real business situations, involve incomplete information. Therefore, it is important that you clearly state any assumptions you make in your analysis. Do not assume your professor will be able to fill in the missing points.

Oral Presentations

Your professor is likely to ask you and your classmates to make oral presentations on a particular case. Oral presentations usually are done by groups of students. In these groups, each member will typically be responsible for one aspect of the overall case. Keep the following suggestions in mind when you are faced with an oral presentation:

1. *Use your own words.* Avoid memorizing a presentation. The best approach is to prepare an outline of the key points you want to cover. Do not be afraid to have the outline in front of you during your presentation, but do not just read the outline.

2. *Rehearse your presentation.* Do not assume you can simply read the outline you have prepared or that the right words will come to you when you are in front of the

class making your presentation. Take the time to practice your speech, and be sure to rehearse the entire presentation with your group.

3. *Use visual aids.* The adage "a picture is worth a thousand words" contains quite a bit of truth. The people in your audience will more quickly and thoroughly understand your key points—and will retain them longer—if you use visual aids. Think of ways you and your team members can use the blackboard in the classroom; a graph, chart, or exhibit on a large posterboard; or, if you will have a number of these visual aids, a flip chart.

4. *Be prepared to handle questions.* You probably will be asked questions by your classmates. If questions are asked during your presentation, try to address those that require clarification. Tactfully postpone more elaborate questions until you have completed the formal phase of your presentation. During your rehearsal, try to anticipate the types of questions that you might be asked.

Working as a Team Member

Many professors assign students to groups or teams for analyzing cases. This adds more realism to the course, since most strategic decisions in business are addressed by a group of key managers. If you are a member of a group assigned to analyze a case, keep in mind that your performance is tied to the performance of the other group members, and vice versa. The following are some suggestions to help you be an effective team member:

1. *Be sure the division of labor is equitable.* It is not always easy to decide how the workload can be divided equitably, since it is not always obvious how much work needs to be done. Try breaking down the case into the distinct parts that need to be analyzed to determine if having a different person assume responsibility for each part is equitable. All team members should read and analyze the entire case, but different team members can be assigned primary responsibility for each major aspect of the analysis. Each team member with primary responsibility for a major aspect of the analysis also will be the logical choice to write that portion of the written analysis or to present it orally in class.

2. *Communicate with other team members.* This is particularly important if you encounter problems with your portion of the analysis. Since, by definition, the team members are dependent on each other, it is critical that you communicate openly and honestly with each other. It, therefore, is essential that your team members discuss problems, such as some members not doing their fair share of work or members insisting that their point of view dominate the team's report.

3. *Work as a team.* Since a group's output should reflect a combined effort, the whole group should be involved in each part of the analysis, even if different individuals assume primary responsibility for different parts of the analysis. Avoid having the marketing major do the marketing portion of the analysis, the production major handle the production issues, and so forth. This will both hamper the group's aggregate analysis and do all of the team members a disservice by not giving each member exposure to decision making involving the other functional areas. The strategic management course provides an opportunity to look at all aspects of the business situation, to develop the ability to see the big picture, and to integrate the various functional areas.

4. *Plan and structure team meetings.* When you are working with a group on case analysis, it is impossible to achieve the team's goals and objectives without meeting outside of class. As soon as the team is formed, establish mutually convenient times for regular meetings, and be sure to keep this time available each week. Be punctual in going to the meetings, and manage the meetings so they end at a predetermined time. Plan several shorter meetings, as opposed to one longer session right before the case is due. (This, by the way, is another way realism is introduced in the strategic management course. Planning and managing your time is essential in business, and working with others to achieve a common set of goals is a critical part of life in the business world.)

SUMMARY

The strategic management course is your opportunity to assume the role of a key decision maker in a business organization. The case method is an excellent way to add excitement and realism to the course. To get the most out of the course and the case method, you need to be an active participant in the entire process.

The case method offers you the opportunity to develop your analytical skills and to understand the interrelationships of the various functional areas of business; it also enables you to develop valuable skills in time management, group problem solving, creativity, organization of thoughts and ideas, and human interaction.

Part Four

Cases

Case 1

BusinessWeek

Ryanair: Europe's Southwest?

1   It's another damp, miserable March day in Dublin, Ireland. But Michael O'Leary bursts into his office with the force of a tropical hurricane. His energy is even more surprising considering he has been up all night birthing six calves at his 250-acre farm an hour outside Dublin. Dressed in old Levis and a rugby shirt and belting out a song by the band U2, the 40-year-old head of Ryanair Holdings PLC is clearly not a conventional corporate chieftain. There aren't too many CEOs who would describe their interests—at least in public—as "smoking, drinking, and chasing women."

2   But then, Ryanair, Europe's first and most successful low-cost carrier, isn't a conventional European airline. "There's no one in Europe doing what Ryanair is doing," says Martin Borghetto, European transport analyst at Morgan Stanley in London.

3   What Ryanair is doing is making air travel within Europe more affordable. O'Leary has transformed Ryanair from a money-losing carrier serving Ireland and Britain into the leader among Europe's six low-fare airlines, with flights to 54 European cities. By emulating the same low-cost, no-frills model pioneered by the U.S.'s Southwest Airlines Co. 30 years ago, O'Leary has made Ryanair one of the world's most profitable airlines. "Ryanair is the best imitation of Southwest Airlines that I have seen," says Southwest founder Herbert D. Kelleher.

4   Europe, long served by entrenched high-fare national carriers, desperately needs airlines such as Ryanair to lower costs for travelers. When Europe's airline industry was deregulated four years ago, O'Leary was first on the spot, offering fares on intra-European flights at an average of half the price of competitors. Now, some Ryanair fares are as low as one-tenth the price of the national carriers.

5   Sounds like a recipe for red ink—but by continually chipping away at internal operating costs, O'Leary has so far managed to undercut rivals and still rake in the profits. Since joining the company a decade ago, first as chief operating officer and then becoming CEO in 1993, O'Leary has increased passenger numbers and profits by an average of 25% annually. Pretax profits last year were $111 million and are estimated to rise to $138 million this year. Operating margins—23% on estimated revenues of $432 million

EXHIBIT 1
Ryanair Performance

Source: Company reports,
Commerzbank.

	Sales	Passengers	Aftertax Profits
		Millions	
1996	$126	3.2	$26
1997	156	3.9	29
1998	209	4.9	43
1999	267	5.6	52
2000	333	7.0	65
2001	432	9.0	90

for the year ended Mar. 31—are higher than all other low-cost carriers in the U.S., including Southwest, and well above the 5% average for big European airlines. "Everyone always says, 'What's your secret?'" O'Leary says. "It's very simple. We're like Wal-Mart in the U.S.—we pile it high and sell it cheap."

SOARING

6 That philosophy has propelled Ryanair into Europe's fastest-growing airline. Last year, it became the first startup to surpass its national carrier, Aer Lingus, in passenger number. Moreover, Ryanair's market value has risen tenfold, to $4 billion, since its 1997 initial public offering—bigger than Sweden's SAS, around the same size as Air France, and only slightly less than British Airways PLC's $5.5 billion. The stock, which trades on Nasdaq and the London and Dublin stock exchanges, is trading around $53, down from its 52-week high of $58 due to the general slump on Nasdaq and world exchanges. But it has held up much better than the Nasdaq's bombed-out tech sector and outstripped most airline stocks, including British Airways.

7 Even so, O'Leary may be about to commit a mistake that has brought down one upstart airline after another on both sides of the Atlantic: overexpansion. In a year when established carriers such as Sabena and Swissair are wading through deep losses, Ryanair is aggressively expanding on the Continent. On Apr. 26, Ryanair began service at Brussels' Charleroi Airport, its first Continental base, offering 30 flights daily to seven European destinations. Ryanair is investing $100 million, creating 100 new jobs, and basing four aircraft at Charleroi.

DEMANDING

8 With fares an average of 80% less than Belgium's flag carrier, O'Leary claims Ryanair will "put Sabena out of its misery." So far, he says demand is ahead of expectations: "We sold more than 50% of the seats on many of these new routes a month before we even started service." O'Leary expects the new base in Brussels to increase traffic fivefold, to 1 million passengers next year, and boost business on the Continent to 40% of Ryanair's traffic by 2003, vs. 20% now. To get there, O'Leary wants to add one new base, five new planes, and six to eight new European routes each of the next five years.

9 Such steady expansion has worked brilliantly out of Dublin and Britain. But as O'Leary delves deeper into Europe, his strategy will be tested. Deep-pocketed competitors with government backing such as Air France and Lufthansa have been steadily beefing up regional service in their respective markets. And with each new Continental base it establishes, Ryanair will have to deal with differing labor and regulatory issues.

10 O'Leary figures his biggest advantage is that Ryanair doesn't really compete head-on with Europe's biggest carriers. It targets the discount market the majors have long shunned in favor of the business-class traveler. "These [low-cost] companies are opening up new segments of the market without really taking clients from the regular carriers," says Air France CEO Jean-Cyril Spinetta. Some 48% of Ryanair's passengers are budget-conscious leisure travelers such as Emanuela Agni, a 34-year-old creative designer at London law firm Allen & Overy. An Italian native, Agni says the cheap fares enable her to fly home a lot more frequently than she otherwise would. "On such a short flight, I couldn't care less about perks," she says. "All I want is lower fares."

11 She's not alone, and fliers now can choose from a number of low-fare carriers. But none has managed to replicate Ryanair's results. Its "cost per available seat mile," the

EXHIBIT 2
How Ryanair Keeps the Cost Down

Source: Company reports, *BusinessWeek.*

Simple Fleet
By flying only Boeing 737s, maintenance costs are kept low. In 1998, the airline ordered 25 737-800s for about $30 million each—$15 million under the list price—from Boeing when it was engaged in a price war with Airbus Industrie.

Secondary Airports
Using airports located outside city centers, many former military airfields, saves time and money. In exchange for bringing in new passengers, Ryanair typically negotiates 15–20-year deals where airport fees on a net basis are little or nothing.

Faster Turnarounds
Less congestion at secondary airports means planes are up in the air 25 minutes after landing, allowing planes to get two flights more per day per aircraft than national carriers flying out of busy mainstream airports.

High Productivity
Revenue per employee is 40% higher than major airlines. This year, Ryanair will carry 9 million passengers with 1,500 employees, while Aer Lingus will carry 6 million passengers with a staff of 7,000.

Online Sales
Since the launch of Ryanair.com in January 2000, 65% of all tickets are sold online, with more than 250,000 bookings each week. Today, agents account for 8% of sales, and their commissions have been slashed to 5% from 7.5%.

No Freebies
Not even peanuts. All drinks and inflight snacks are sold on board, turning a cost into a revenue opportunity. And don't ask for ice. O'Leary saves $50,000 a year by cutting out the cubes.

yardstick used by the airline industry to measure costs, is 30% lower than the average for Europe's major airlines, and its productivity—as measured by the number of passengers per employee—is 40% higher, according to analysts. As a result, Ryanair can break even when its planes are just over half full—an advantage that should help it weather the storm fairly well if an economic downturn materializes in Europe later this year. In contrast, low-cost rivals such as BA's Go need to fly their planes 77% full to break even.

12   O'Leary's biggest cost-saving move is to serve only secondary airports. These out-of-the way terminals are so hungry for business that Ryanair can negotiate airport fees of as little as $1.50 per passenger, plus get marketing and training support for as long as 20 years. That's a fraction of the average rate of $15 to $22 per passenger charged by Europe's major hubs. Because there is so little congestion at these locations, Ryanair's planes are back in the air no more than 25 minutes after landing, allowing it to squeeze two flights more per day from each plane than rivals using the main airports.

13   The company is fielding offers to start service to some 30 of these secondary airports. A handful of them, such as Frankfurt-Hahn, now owned by Fraport, are privatized former NATO bases looking to drum up business. "U.S. tax dollars have financed some of the best-equipped airports in Europe," says Ryanair Chief Financial Officer Michael Cawley, referring to the ex-NATO bases.

14   Ryanair does not offer your typical airport experience. A hop to Paris, for instance, really means a flight to Beauvais, 43 miles north in Picardy, where the terminal looks like a bus depot stuck in the middle of farmland and the baggage handlers are local firemen. Ryanair boasts that all of the airports it serves are linked to the main destination via bus or train. Beauvais passengers, for instance, pay $8.20 to ride a shuttlebus leaving Paris two-and-a-half hours before each departure. But it doesn't always work smoothly: On

EXHIBIT 3
Cheaper than the Competition

Route	Ryanair*	Rival Airline*
London–Biarritz	$66	$542 (Air France)
London–Brussels	74	194 (British Airways)
London–Frankfurt	29	735 (Lufthansa)
London–Oslo	48	804 (SAS)
London–Venice	89	915 (Alitalia)

*Lowest midweek return fare requiring a two-night stay and excluding taxes.

Apr. 9, the bus ran late, leaving passengers booked on a morning flight to Dublin stranded for three hours until the next plane out.

15   The low cost of a Ryanair ticket is what makes such hassles tolerable. To keep delivering on price, Ryanair tries to remove at least one layer of cost from its operations each year. Last year, it cut travel agents' commissions from 7.5% to 5% of the fare and switched to a cheaper computer-reservation system, saving around $6 million. These moves, plus the success of Ryanair.com, a website launched in January 2000, has dramatically cut the airline's dependency on travel agents. Now, 8% of sales are made by agents, 65% are made online, and the rest come through call centers.

COLD CASH

16   O'Leary isn't content just to save money, though. Every potential expense is treated as an opportunity to make money. Free drinks on board? Forget it. Even water will set you back a few dollars. And when the airline's catering company, Gate Gourmet, said it would no longer supply Ryanair with free ice, O'Leary stopped offering ice cubes, a move that should save about $50,000 a year.

17   O'Leary nurtures his reputation as a Robin Hood of the airlines, fighting Europe's big national carriers on behalf of the little guy. Truth is, he now lives like a lord, raising Aberdeen-Angus cattle and thoroughbred horses on his spread in Mullingar, County Westmeath. It wasn't always that way. The eldest of a family of six, O'Leary grew up on a farm in the Irish midlands. He worked two jobs, as a barman and "burger flipper," while studying business at Dublin's Trinity College. Although he never completed his qualifying exams, he worked as a tax consultant, buying and selling property on the side. It was during this time that he met the airline's founder, Tony Ryan, who was running the world's most successful aircraft-leasing firm, Guinness Peat Aviation. He became Ryan's "financial sweeper-upper," advising on tax and investment strategy until Ryan persuaded him to join Ryanair.

18   What a ride it has been since the company's meager beginnings. When Tony Ryan founded Ryanair in 1985, it had just one 15-seat turboprop. A year later, Ryanair broke the British Airways and Aer Lingus duopoly on flights between Dublin and London. But by 1989, Ryanair was in the red, having gone through some $25 million and five CEOs. Ryan turned to O'Leary for advice. "It was a basket case," recalls O'Leary, who told Ryan to shut it down.

19   Instead, Ryan set up a meeting with Southwest's Kelleher, whom he had known for years. In 1990, O'Leary, Kelleher, and new Southwest President and COO Colleen C. Barrett met for dinner at the Palm steakhouse in Dallas. Several cocktails into the discussion, something clicked. "The man's a genius," O'Leary says. Ironically, both Kelleher and Barrett's ancestors come from Kanturk in County Cork, Ireland, the same small town where O'Leary's parents were born. Kelleher recalls that there are 413 people and 21

bars there. "O'Leary and I have a certain kinship," says Kelleher, who is known for his madcap antics, chain-smoking, and fondness for Wild Turkey bourbon.

20   Convinced that he could copy the Southwest model, O'Leary agreed to give running Ryanair a try, provided he got full management control and 25% of any future profits. In short order, he got rid of unprofitable routes and switched from 14 types of aircraft to just one, the Boeing 737, which reduced maintenance costs. Already-low airfares were slashed even further to boost demand. Business-class and frequent-flier programs were abolished. By the end of that first year, Ryanair was turning a profit. By the mid-1990s, profits were growing at such a clip that O'Leary's 25% cut was no longer feasible: The airline needed to plow profits back into the company to grow. To raise capital for expansion, Ryanair went public in 1997, raising around $130 million. O'Leary received a base salary of $340,000 last year and owns an 8% stake in Ryanair that is valued at $250 million.

CREDIBILITY

21   O'Leary brought in new managers as well as shareholders. In 1997, he helped persuade David Bonderman, CEO of investment fund Texas Pacific Group—and who had previously turned around Continental Airlines Inc.—to become chairman of Ryanair. Bonderman, says Cawley, gave Ryanair the credibility it needed in negotiations with Boeing Co. Ryanair bought 15 new 737-800s this year and 13 more are on order through 2003. Cawley won't say exactly how much the airline paid, but analysts estimate it saved close to $15 million off the $45 million sticker price for each aircraft. Ryanair paid 15% of the aircrafts' net purchase price with cash, and borrowed the rest. "Boeing recognized it needed to have a customer in Europe to help it kick Airbus' ass," says Bonderman.

22   After more than a decade at the helm, O'Leary has imprinted his irreverent personality on every aspect of Ryanair. At the airline's cramped and utilitarian headquarters outside the Dublin airport, the company's young staff dress as casually as the CEO. One day a week, O'Leary or one of his seven senior managers pitches in to help check in passengers or load baggage. And every Thursday, Ryanair's baggage handlers take on management in a soccer match. O'Leary has a reputation as an aggressive player.

TOO FAR?

23   The same in-your-face attitude is a feature of the company's advertising campaigns, which O'Leary oversees personally. A recent ad that ran in Ireland, for instance, depicted the Pope claiming that the fourth secret of Fatima was Ryanair's low fares. Besides the "usual collection of loonies" calling in on Irish radio to complain, says O'Leary, his own mother told him that this time he had finally gone too far.

24   Indeed, just as Mum suspected, the Fatima ad got to a lot of people. The Vatican fired off a press release around the globe accusing the airline of blaspheming the Pope. Much to O'Leary's glee, the release attracted the attention of newspapers as far away as India, and generated a ton of free publicity. "I thought I died and went to heaven," says O'Leary. Adds Bonderman: "It's hard to think of another CEO of a company with a $4 billion market cap who would run those ads. They accomplished everything he set out to and more."

25   To be sure, no-frills airlines have had a notoriously checkered existence. With the exception of Southwest, all have fallen victim to either bankruptcy or safety disasters. Britain's Debonair, which filed for bankruptcy in 1999, was Europe's most recent casualty. Richard Branson's Virgin Express is still in business, but it reported losses of nearly

$60 million last year. The biggest challenge for Ryanair, says Bonderman, is maintaining its cost discipline and corporate personality. "We're very conscious that what will screw us up is that we get fat and lazy," admits O'Leary. With such a driven boss, that's not likely to happen soon.

MICHAEL O'LEARY IS NO "LOCAL" IRISH HERO

26 Within Europe, Ryanair CEO Michael O'Leary is a popular guy. Not a week goes by without a new pitch from some European politician hoping to persuade the Irish carrier to begin servicing an airport in his constituency. And in the City, London's financial district, O'Leary's straight talk and stellar financial results have earned him a loyal following. But it's a different story back in Ireland, where O'Leary is viewed with a mix of envy and suspicion.

27 Ryanair may be one of Ireland's top 10 listed companies, but its CEO is no hometown hero. It's not the controversial ads depicting the Pope touting Ryanair fares that have hurt O'Leary's image in Catholic Ireland. And it's certainly not the low airfares. The real problem seems to be O'Leary's success. In Ireland, entrepreneurs don't hold the same cachet as they do in the U.S. And newfound wealth generally is treated with apprehension. Indeed, every time O'Leary sells even the smallest amount of his nearly 8% stake in the airline, he's lambasted by the press which accuses him of "flogging off shares" while expecting his investors to sit tight.

28 It wasn't always that way. In the early years, the company's plucky underdog image played well among the Irish. But now that it has become bigger and more profitable than national carrier Aer Lingus, the airline is not cut any slack. "O'Leary and Ryanair are the strongest evidence of truth in the adage there's no such thing as bad publicity," sniped Ireland's *Sunday Tribune* back in February.

BITTER UNIONS

29 It's O'Leary's tough stance on costs that have gotten him into the most trouble at home. His run-ins with the country's powerful labor unions have irked the largely pro-labor Irish press. In 1998, he refused to recognize the airline's baggage handlers' union and paid for it in the resulting flurry of negative coverage. Shortly afterward, Prime Minister Bertie Ahern publicly attacked O'Leary and Ryanair for practicing "tooth-and-claw capitalism."

30 Indeed, Ireland is the one trouble spot in O'Leary's aggressive expansion plans. Those plans depend on securing favorable long-term deals with airports in exchange for bringing in increased traffic. He has tried unsuccessfully to persuade the state-owned airport authority, Aer Rianta, which also owns Aer Lingus, to offer it the same kind of long-term deals it has secured at lesser known airports in Europe. "Since 1997, our passenger numbers and profits have trebled, but none of that growth has been in Ireland," O'Leary says. "Why? Because the costs here are simply too high."

31 As a result, Ryanair has scaled back its operations in Dublin. It expanded first at London's Stanstead airport and more recently at Brussels' Charleroi, Ryanair's first Continental base. "The deal we got there blows [Aer Rianta] away," O'Leary says. Analysts estimate Ryanair's airport charges in Europe average $1.50 per passenger compared with $13 at Dublin Airport.

32 Now, O'Leary wants a similar offer from Irish airport authorities. He justifies his demand by saying Ryanair is the main reason the amount of traffic at Dublin Airport has

dramatically increased in the past decade. "In many respects, we created the Irish tourism boom that took place between 1985 to 1995, through low fares and increased competition," he says.

CONTINENTAL DRIFT

33   But Aer Rianta isn't swayed. "Sure, they've been phenomenally successful and have contributed to the growth of Dublin Airport," says Aer Rianta spokesman Flan Clune. "But we just can't rewrite our rules to suit Ryanair." That hasn't stopped O'Leary from trying. He's adamant he'll keep on fighting until Aer Rianta gives in.

34   The longer the battle continues, however, the greater the risk that Ryanair turns its home country into an outpost. Over the past four years, Ryanair has not expanded its service and operations in Ireland at all. For a country heavily dependent upon revenues from tourism, that's bad news. If Ryanair expands only on the Continent, Ireland stands to lose jobs, potential tourism income from visiting Europeans, and the business of one of the few super-successful entrepreneurs the country has ever seen.

Source: Adapted by Richard Robinson, University of South Carolina, based on Kerry Capell, "Renegade Ryanair," *BusinessWeek,* International Edition, May 14, 2001.

Case 2

UPS vs. FedEx: Ground Wars

1   Clad in a blue lab coat, a technician in Singapore waves a scanner like a wand over a box of newly minted computer chips. With that simple act, he sets in motion a delivery process that is efficient and automated, almost to the point of magic. This cavernous National Semiconductor Corp. warehouse was designed and built by shipping wizards at United Parcel Service Inc. It is UPS's computers that speed the box of chips to a loading dock, then to truck, to plane, and to truck once again. In just 12 hours, the chips will reach one of National's customers, a PC maker half a world away in Silicon Valley. Throughout the journey, electronic tags embedded in the chips will let the customer track the order with accuracy down to about three feet.

2   While the logistics are extraordinary, they tell only half the story. A similar warehouse in Singapore was constructed seven years ago by UPS rival Federal Express. But FedEx Corp., as it's now called, never managed to make the operation pay off. "They dropped the ball," says Kelvin Phillips, National's director of worldwide logistics. The FedEx team was inflexible, he explains. They forced the chipmaker to ship everything the most expensive way, via overnight air express—even if a shipment didn't require that kind of speed. And under FedEx, the Singapore warehouse never delivered on its promise of streamlining chip inventory. Finally, in 1999, Phillips yanked the business from FedEx and handed it to UPS, which rebuilt the operation from scratch. In the two years since, the team in brown has slashed National Semiconductor's inventory and shipment costs by 15%.

3   The Singapore story is no isolated triumph for UPS. Over the past two years, the company has quietly shed its image as the slowpoke of shipping. Be it e-tailing frenzy or dot-com crash, UPS has captured customers by bombarding them with choices: fast flights vs. cheap ground delivery, simple shipping or a panoply of manufacturing, warehousing, and supply-chain services. In the U.S. and several foreign markets, UPS has grabbed a commanding lead over FedEx—and not just in everyday package delivery but in the New Economy services such as logistics. In North America, UPS has even snagged the distinction of preferred carrier to the Web generation: The company handles 55% of all online purchases, vs. 10% for FedEx. "UPS is doing things in e-commerce that other companies are just starting to talk about," says Jack R. Staff, chief economist at Zona Research in Redwood City, Calif.

4   The ascent of UPS charts a reversal of fortune in one of the fiercest rivalries in Corporate America. It was FedEx, after all, that pioneered both overnight delivery of packages and the ability to track their journey using computers. These 1970s' era innovations rocked the shipping industry and helped set the stage for the Internet Revolution of the 1990s. Even now, FedEx rules in certain areas of air freight. Its carefully burnished brand still says "absolutely, positively" to thousands of loyal customers—and not without reason. FedEx is one of America's great success stories, extolled for its customer service. David Lord, the founder of now defunct dot-com e-tailer Toysmart.com, hails the enthusiasm FedEx brought to his business in its early stages. The shipper went so far as to keep trucks idling outside his small company, ready to move orders as soon as they came in. "I was nobody, but FedEx treated me like a king," he recalls.

5   Nevertheless, on many fronts, UPS is winning the battles. And the companies' diverging fortunes are starting to show up on the bottom line. In revenues, both giants enjoy comparable growth: UPS surged 11% in 2000, to $30 billion, while FedEx's revenues

EXHIBIT 1

Success Begets Success
Stacking UPS up against FedEx

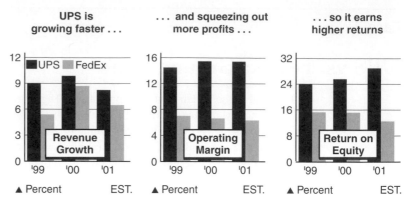

Data: Banc of America Securities ©BW

grew 8.8%, to $18 billion. But in the same period, UPS raked in $2.8 billion in profits, giving it an operating margin of 15.3%. That's roughly double the margin at FedEx, which eked out just $688 million in profits. As the economy slows and competition gets more brutal, both companies are feeling the pain. FedEx's profits were down 4% in its latest quarter, and UPS's were down 8.9% in the quarter ended Mar. 31. FedEx has warned that things will get worse.

6   FedEx Chairman Frederick W. Smith and other top executives declined to discuss these results with *BusinessWeek*. But William G. Margaritis, FedEx's corporate vice-president for worldwide communications and investor relations, insists that the company's performance is up to snuff. "FedEx has a proven track record of delivering solid financial results," he said in a written response to questions from *BusinessWeek*. "Our compound annual earnings-per-share growth rate over the past 10 years is 15.6%."

7   "In the view of many analysts and industry execs, however, UPS now has a pronounced advantage in several hotly contested areas. In addition to its overwhelming lead in ground shipping and its online triumphs, UPS can point to a logistics business that is growing by 40% a year. FedEx is struggling to reverse a decline in this area.

8   Even in sectors where FedEx still rules, UPS is catching up quickly. FedEx has a commanding lead in the profitable overnight service, for example, delivering more than 3 million such packages daily in 200-plus countries and accounting for 39% of the market. UPS is No. 2, with 2.2 million overnight packages—but its volume has been growing faster than FedEx's for at least three years. In 2000, UPS's overnight business grew at 8%, compared with FedEx's 3.6%. And UPS's operating margin on its domestic air-express service is higher—24% vs. 6%—according to Gary H. Yablon, a transportation analyst at Credit Suisse First Boston.

9   In his written response to *BusinessWeek,* Margaritis denied that the company is losing significant ground. "UPS has never caught up and passed FedEx in any arena," he wrote, "certainly not when it comes to reliability, technology initiative, global reach, or brand strength."

10   So what accounts for UPS's growth in overnight? The company trumpets its decision in 1999 to integrate overnight delivery into its vast ground-transportation network. UPS, like FedEx, still uses planes to make most such deliveries. But in the past two years, its logisticians have also figured out how to make quick mid-distance deliveries—as far as 500 miles in one night—by truck, which is much less expensive than by air. As a result, UPS's overall cost per package is $6.65, compared with FedEx's $11.89, according to

EXHIBIT 2
How They Compare

Source: Companies.

	UPS	FedEx
Founded	1907	1971
Chairman	James P. Kelly	Frederick W. Smith*
Headquarters	Atlanta, Ga.	Memphis, Tenn.
2000 Revenue	$29.77 billion	$18.3 billion
Net Income	$2.93 billion	$688 million
Employees	359,000	215,000
Daily Package Volume	13.2 million	5 million
Fleet	152,500 trucks, 560 planes	43,500 trucks, 662 planes

* and founder

CSFB. Even though FedEx also uses trucks for short hauls, "UPS has a real cost advantage," says John D. Kasarda, director of the University of North Carolina's Frank Hawkins Kenan Institute of Private Enterprise and a former FedEx consultant.

11   UPS's core strength is its fleet of 152,000 brown trucks, which reach virtually every address in the U.S.—and increasingly, the world. FedEx has belatedly begun to build its own home-delivery system. But the cost of duplicating a system UPS has spent nearly 100 years building could prove prohibitive. And with $3 billion in cash on hand, UPS could easily wage a price war against FedEx, which isn't generating any spare cash. "This is a game FedEx can't win," says Peter V. Coleman, a transportation analyst at Banc of America Securities. That leaves FedEx dependent on an air-delivery system that is increasingly expensive to operate.

COPYCAT

12   To appreciate how deftly UPS has turned things around, one must consider how badly the company was tripped up by its rival's meteoric success. UPS had experimented with air delivery for decades. But it was 27-year-old Frederick W. Smith, a Yale University graduate and Vietnam War veteran, who got the idea off the ground in 1971. Within five years, Federal Express was soaring—and the package-delivery business would never be the same.

13   UPS didn't counter with its own overnight service until 1988. The explanation for this may lie in its corporate culture. UPS was founded as a messenger service 94 years ago by James E. Casey, who ran the company like a military operation, ordering recruits to be polite at all times and to place speed above all other virtues. To this day, workers at UPS headquarters are forbidden to drink coffee at their desks.

14   This rigid culture didn't breed risk-taking. But by the mid–1980s, FedEx's success had earned a deep respect from its competitor. Not only did UPS begin to ape FedEx's tactics, it was able to duplicate the results—and often at a lower cost. UPS drivers started following their rivals' trucks to learn their methods and to poach customers. "It was warfare," says ex-FedEx exec Christos Cotsakos, now chairman of online broker E*Trade Group Inc. "We were soldiers at FedEx on a holy crusade."

15   Polling its customers, UPS learned that they desired FedEx-style express and tracking services—and that required better information technology. It took UPS 15 years to build a computer system that rivaled FedEx's renowned Cosmos system. But UPS chose a wiser approach. While FedEx forced customers to adopt its proprietary software, UPS designed logistical software that worked with any corporate system. And where FedEx shunned alliances until recently, UPS jumped into partnerships with

giants such as Oracle Corp. and IBM. Its cheaper shipping rates also won UPS the allegiance of dot-com leaders—while they lasted. And when the bubble popped, UPS came to rest on solid brick-and-mortar—namely, Wal-Mart Stores, Ford Motor, and others in that class.

16   Carefully mimicking FedEx, UPS gradually mastered the intricacies of logistics. But retrofitting a computer-centric culture to this erstwhile trucking company proved a Herculean effort. Well into the 1990s, a 1950s' style engineering culture ruled at UPS, complete with myriad rules addressing everything from women's dress to cafeteria protocol. On the road, drivers followed near-military regimens after being drilled on such details as how to quickly buckle and unbuckle seat belts. So when faced with Internet-era business challenges, top execs felt the company needed a fresh start. In 1994, they set up a new logistics group in a building a few miles north of the main campus in suburban Atlanta. Soon, many employees were clamoring to switch over to the new unit. "Everyone knows now that logistics is the place where you can get ahead," confides one junior UPS executive.

17   The new unit quickly paid its way. UPS's logistics revenues—excluding conventional shipping activities—grew 58% last year, topping $1 billion, and is poised for an additional 40% spurt. "I expect UPS to double its logistics business within the next four to five years," says Edward M. Wolfe, a transportation analyst at Bear Stearns & Co. In contrast, he says: "FedEx has lost momentum."

18   FedEx won't break out its results in logistics. But the company tacitly acknowledged a setback when it announced a thorough overhaul of the business late last year. From now on, it will focus solely on providing technology solutions to customers—showing them new ways to track packages, for example. FedEx's Margaritis derides UPS's hands-on approach as old-fashioned "pick-and-pack warehousing." And he says FedEx is reevaluating all of its logistics accounts, looking to weed out ones that don't fit the new strategy.

19   FedEx will have to move fast to avoid more defections from customers such as National Semiconductor. E-tailer SmartHome.com dumped FedEx for UPS because the former "just didn't have the software and systems for us to revolutionize our operations," says Purchasing Director Michael Climo. UPS redesigned SmartHome.com's business from warehouse to website, plugging its package-tracking software into SmartHome.com's site so customers could use the feature without leaving the site. But it studiously left options open—visitors can even select shippers other than UPS. SmartHome staffers used to field about 60 calls a day from customers with shipping queries. Now, those staffers can spend their time making sales pitches.

20   Meanwhile, in the Old Economy, UPS is winning giant customers such as Ford Motor Co., which uses UPS's computerized logistics to route cars more efficiently to its dealerships. In a year, Ford has reduced delivery times by 26% and saved $240 million, says Frank M. Taylor, Ford's vice-president for material planning and logistics. "Speed is the mindset at UPS. They'll meet a deadline at any cost," Taylor says. UPS Chairman James P. Kelly chalks it up to the company's slow-and-steady work ethic. "We've spent the past seven years studying where we should be long-term," he says.

21   While FedEx backpedals in logistics, UPS is in growth mode. And it has figured out how to manage distribution for many companies at one central location—a massive warehouse in Louisville, Ky. Here, UPS handles storage, tracking, repair, and shipping for clients such as Sprint, Hewlett-Packard, and Nike using a mix of high- and low-tech methods. Computerized forklifts scan in new inventory while people in sneakers dash across the vast warehouse to pluck products, box them, and ship them out. In short, UPS uses expensive technology only where it cuts costs.

HUBRIS

22 The story of UPS's remarkable comeback is mirrored—almost blow for blow—by miscalculations and botched opportunities on the part of FedEx. And while FedEx has instituted some promising initiatives in recent months, many analysts believe that it may be too late for FedEx to make up for lost ground.

23 The seeds of FedEx's current woes were sown in the late 1980s. That's when Smith and other top execs—blinded by annual earnings growth averaging 40%—fell into hubris. According to one former executive who asked to remain anonymous, Smith ignored opportunities to build up a residential ground-delivery network, instead putting all of the company's eggs in higher-cost air transport. Says the UNC's Kasarda: "UPS moved quicker into FedEx's turf than FedEx moved into that of UPS." And while Smith's early romance with computers gave him critical traction on the Internet, the technology is now undermining the choicest part of FedEx's operations: overnight delivery, which makes up 50% of its revenues. FedEx's own numbers show that about one-quarter of this business, or 749,000 parcels, are letter-size envelopes. Expand this category to include legal briefs, manuscripts, contracts, and other documents, and the category makes up fully 40% of FedEx's overnight traffic. Virtually all of this material can be transmitted electronically or posted online and downloaded when the need arises.

24 For now, digital delivery is in its infancy, and the impact on FedEx is less than catastrophic. Overnight shipments of letter-sized parcels fell just 2% year-to-year in the quarter ended Feb. 28. But Brian Clancy, a principal at Arlington (Va.) transportation consultant MergeGlobal Inc., expects more precipitous declines. Online security is improving quickly, he notes. And businesses are starting to adopt contractual devices such as digital signatures. As these technologies mature, the electronic transit of everything from real-estate closings to legal settlements is poised to explode—at the expense of shipping. "FedEx is definitely exposed," says Clancy.

25 So is UPS. But since the company still derives most of its business from ground delivery, it is far less dependent on overnight service. And it doesn't share FedEx's worries about the bottom line. Despite operating in the greatest economic boom in its history, FedEx remains narrowly profitable. "The company is woefully underperforming," says BofA analyst Coleman.

26 Margaritis repudiates this critique. He says FedEx anticipated the threat from the Net years ago. "That's why we've expanded into new lines such as home delivery and logistics," he says.

27 In the meantime, FedEx intends to strengthen its own already-formidable position in foreign markets. Right now, only 10% of all deliveries outside the U.S. are overnight. Consultants believe the leader now is Brussels-based DHL International Ltd., controlled by Deutsche Post, which has an estimated 20% to 25% of the international overnight market. But FedEx is tied for second place with TNT Post Group, each with about 10% to 15% of the market. UPS is third, with an 8%-to-12% share. FedEx's intercontinental parcel service grew 11% in the nine months ended Feb. 28. That's faster than any of FedEx's other operations. To juice it even further, FedEx has become the first shipper to gamble on Airbus Industrie's A380–800F air freighter. The triple-decker, which hasn't been built yet, will travel nonstop to just about anywhere in the world within 48 hours while carrying nearly twice the payload of the largest existing jet freighter.

28 FedEx is even making some progress in the ground war with UPS. It recently struck a $7 billion distribution deal with the U.S. Postal Service, hoping to squeeze more revenue out of every plane. The Postal Service will help fill planes that are now flying partially empty. As for FedEx's own trucks, they have served largely as the last leg in overnight

EXHIBIT 3
**In the Air and
on the Ground**

Source: Credit Suisse First
Boston.

FedEx rules the skies, but UPS is bigger on land. Overall, UPS earns more on each package.				
	Unit Cost	**Unit Profit**	**Operating Margin**	**Average Daily Volume**
Air Deliveries, U.S.				
FedEx	$15.27	$0.93	6%	2,924,000
UPS	$14.60	$3.76	22%	2,162,000
Ground Deliveries, U.S.				
FedEx	$4.77	$0.68	13%	1,541,000
UPS	$4.95	$0.61	11%	10,945,000
Overall Average, Including International				
FedEx	$11.89	$0.85	7%	4,788,000
UPS	$6.65	$1.17	15%	14,236,000

delivery. But four years ago, FedEx spent $500 million to buy a ground network to serve businesses. This year, it will shell out an additional $150 million to expand the system in hopes of reaching all U.S. homes by 2002. The strategy, explains Margaritis, is not to compete "head-to-head" with UPS but rather to skim off the best customers with a new portfolio of premium services. FedEx charges extra for those services, which include night and Saturday deliveries—neither of which is now offered by UPS.

29   FedEx recognizes that its dependence on a jet fleet saddles it with the highest cost structure among all shippers. Indeed, the company has largely been cash-flow negative over its 30-year history, due to heavy investments in expansion. The latest drain is FedEx's ground-delivery system. Wall Street, however, is now demanding that the company show positive cash flow. FedEx promises to comply by the end of the year, by cutting costs and squeezing more revenue out of current operations. "Our mantra now is not just to grow, but grow profitably," says Margaritis. At least some of the company's fans are encouraged. "FedEx is on the right path," says Roger Mendel, a vice-president at Northern Trust Corp., which owns 1.1 million FedEx shares.

30   But even Mendel says the company has a lot of work to do. Overseas, rival UPS has scored a major coup: It won six new direct air routes to China from the U.S. Transportation Dept. in January, breaking FedEx's six-year stranglehold on such traffic. As for FedEx's U.S. strategy, analysts say buyers still aren't biting at its premium services.

31   BofA's Coleman sees little evidence that FedEx's new efforts on the ground will pay off. Because it insists on running its four main services as independent businesses, the company misses out on the cost-saving synergies that UPS has mastered. And while FedEx's nascent residential ground-delivery service has captured 11% of the market, it can't keep up with UPS, which spends $70 million-plus a year to expand its ground facilities. Analysts estimate that FedEx is already losing $18 million a quarter on residential ground delivery.

32   No one is counting the wily Smith out of the game altogether. But in the long run, his fleet of red-and-blue planes may prove no match for the countless ranks of UPS's slow-moving brown trucks or its bulging war chest. Like the tortoise in the old fable, UPS is progressing slowly but surely. And in this particular chapter of the story, the hare's stumbles are only helping the tortoise reach his goal.

Source: Adapted by Richard Robinson, University of South Carolina, based on "UPS vs. FedEx: Ground Wars," *BusinessWeek,* May 21, 2001.

Case 3

BusinessWeek

Wine Wars

1   It's a picture postcard of La Belle France: sun-drenched stone houses perched on a hill-side, a soaring Gothic church spire, ripening vineyards. Quinsac, population 1,866, is nestled in the heart of Bordeaux, only a few miles from famed winemaking centers such as Château Latour and Château d'Yquem, whose prized red and white wines fetch $200 or more a bottle.

2   But even if September provides a bumper harvest, Quinsac's winegrowers won't be celebrating. Almost all their grapes will be turned into low-end Bordeaux that sells for less than $5 a bottle in France. Over the past three years, the price of many of their grapes has plummeted by 40%. In Quinsac, where Romans first planted vines and a poem inscribed on a fountain salutes "our wine that soothes the mind," vines are being pulled out to make way for a housing development.

3   Sadly, Quinsac's bitter harvest is shared by much of France's wine country—from the hills of Burgundy to the valley of the Loire. France has dominated the world of wine for centuries and is still No. 1, with $6.5 billion in sales. But the bouquet is fading. The almost medieval system of small, family-owned vineyards is struggling to survive. Huge conglomerates from Australia, California, and elsewhere are outflanking the French. They're spending millions to create consistent brands recognized around the world, while Gallic winegrowers are turning out too much low-quality table wine with mystifying labels.

4   Sure, swank restaurants in New York, London, and Tokyo still stock their cellars with the great French wines. But ordinary consumers don't have the patience to wait for fine Bordeaux wines to mature. They prefer the light, fruity flavors of low-price wine offered by producers in California, Australia, and Chile. These New World vintners are cleaning

EXHIBIT 1
What Ails the French Wine Industry

Source: *BusinessWeek.*

Too Much Regulation
While New World growers are free to plant how they please, France sets strict limits on what types of grapes can be grown in a particular region and how they're planted and picked.

Quantity over Quality
Most French winemakers are paid for the amount of grapes they deliver to a local cooperative, discouraging the careful pruning and limited yields needed to produce high-quality wine.

Too Many Players
The fragmented French wine industry is losing ground to overseas rivals who have created powerful global brands such as Rosemount and Beringer.

Too Confusing
New World wineries make it easy for consumers to understand what they are buying by selling single-grape varietals such as Chardonnay. Most French wines are labeled according to geographical origin. Only connoiseurs can distinguish between dozens of Burgundian villages.

Poor Marketing
Small French winemakers can't afford to keep up with New World competitors on advertising and other promotions. In England, E. & J. Gallo's marketing budget last year reached $2.5 million, more than twice what the entire Bordeaux region spent on marketing.

EXHIBIT 2
Wine Industry Leaders

Source: Direction des Etudes/Centre Français du Commerce Exterieur.

Company	Country	Wine Sales in 2000
1 E&J Gallo Winery	U.S.	$1.5 bil.
2 Foster's Group	Australia	$818 mil.
3 Seagram	Canada	$800 mil.
4 Constellation Brands	U.S.	$712 mil.
5 Southcorp	Australia	$662 mil.
6 Castel Freres	France	$625 mil.
7 Diageo	Britain	$590 mil.
8 Henkell & Sonlein	Germany	$528 mil.
9 Robert Mondavi	U.S.	$506 mil.

*Excluding France's LVMH, which earns more than 75% of its $1.6 billion in wine sales from champagne.

up in the markets that count: North America, Northern Europe, and Asia, where wine consumption is growing steadily, particularly of bottles under $15, while the generic French wines from places such as Quinsac are losing sales. "We are in the front lines in the fight against Australian and American wines," says Thierry Berthelot, commercial director of the Quinsac Wine Cooperative. Overall, French wine exports fell by 5.4% in value last year, to $4.6 billion, and millions of liters of unsold wine are sitting in cellars. France's market share in the U.S. has slipped from 7% to 5% in the past three years, while Australia has tripled its sales since 1995, grabbing almost 3% of the market, estimates Motto Kryla & Fisher LLP, a wine industry consulting firm in Napa Valley.

5   It's the latest chapter in France's ongoing and mostly losing struggle to balance its artisan traditions with the demands of the global market. Big distributors working with supermarket chains want to have reliable wine producers supplying them. Brewers and liquor companies, with deep pockets and marketing reach, are buying up winemakers. Within the past year, a series of takeovers and mergers has created new multinationals. Australia's beer baron, Melbourne-based Foster's Group, bought America's Napa Valley-based Beringer Blass Wine Estates last October for $1.9 billion. In February, Australia's Southcorp, owner of the prestigious Penfolds and more budget-minded Lindemans brands, forked out $725 million to take over family-owned premium winemaker Rosemount. "We've converted from being a cottage industry into a competitive consumer luxury-goods industry," says R. Michael Mondavi, chairman of Robert Mondavi Corp., the world's ninth-largest winemaker with more than $500 million in annual sales.

6   During viticulture's Big Bang, France has stood sulking on the sidelines. Of the world's 10 largest wine companies, only one today is French. While three Australian companies dominate 80% of their home market, Bordeaux alone boasts 20,000 different producers. With the exception of isolated joint ventures such as Baron Philippe de Rothschild's with Mondavi in Chile and California, French wine companies remain provincial. Bordeaux growers find it difficult to cooperate even with Burgundy or Côte du Rhône producers. "We stick to our own home regions just when we must begin to compete in a universe of consumers who dress in Nikes, eat Big Macs, and drink Coca-Cola," laments Jacques Berthomeau, author of an 81-page critique of the French wine industry published on July 31 by the French Agriculture Ministry.

7   Gallic tempers are rising as the bleak scenario unfolds. Angry winegrowers in the Mediterranean region of Languedoc ransacked highway tollbooths last March, demanding higher prices for their grapes. As wine revenues evaporate, southern France is on edge. A year ago, French cheese farmer Jose Bove won widespread popular support by destroying a McDonald's outlet in protest against U.S. sanctions on Roquefort. This

spring, French winemakers derailed an attempt by Mondavi to create a sprawling vineyard in the same Languedoc region. "Each bottle of American and Australian wine that lands in Europe is a bomb targeted at the heart of our rich European culture," says grower Aimé Guibert.

GENERIC FLOOD?

8   Some serious wine lovers—and not just French firebrands—sympathize. Jeffrey Davies, an American wine merchant based in Bordeaux who scouts out producers of small amounts of outstanding wines, worries that the globe will soon be flooded with generic Chardonnays and Cabernet Sauvignons. He yearns to preserve a world in which a Chardonnay produced in Chablis in northern Burgundy tastes drier than a rich, buttery one produced less than 100 miles south in Burgundy's Côte d'Or. "We shouldn't lose these differences," Davies insists.

9   But surviving, much less thriving, will be difficult for the French if they don't wake up to changes in drinking habits, even at home. Few natives still take three-hour lunch breaks, and fewer still down a *petit coup de rouge* at mealtime. The average French person today drinks just 14.5 gallons of wine a year, down from 26.5 gallons in 1960. At the same time, consumption has soared elsewhere, doubling in the U.S. and tripling in Britain. "To many young consumers, tasting cherry and blackberry in a Cabernet is a wonderful thing," asserts Richard Sands, president, chairman, and CEO of Constellation Brands Inc. in Fairport, N.Y. His company has swelled to $700 million a year in sales by recognizing that the palates of consumers who have grown up on soft drinks and Snapple may need coddling.

10   Constellation's breakthrough product? Fruit-flavored wines, such as Chardonnay with peach flavors sold under the Arbor Mist label. While purists are appalled, the launch of the "pop varietal" in gently curved, frosty bottles has spawned a raft of competitors and has been credited by retailers with creating a new class of wine drinkers. Today, Arbor Mist and E. & J. Gallo Winery's Wild Vines sell 7 million cases a year, exceeding U.S. imports of midtier French wines.

11   Even in Britain, Bordeaux' earliest foreign market, the spread of wine drinking beyond the upper classes has meant a switch to American, Australian, and Chilean wines. France's exports to Britain plummeted 16% in value last year. "French wines can be very acidic, while the New World ones are younger and easier to drink," says Fiona Hughes, a 35-year-old buying a bottle of Chilean Cabernet Sauvignon at Berry Bros. & Rudd wineshop in central London.

12   New World producers enjoy many advantages over France. Australian, American, and Chilean winemakers work in steady, hot climates that produce regular harvests and consistent wines. Bordeaux and Burgundy producers must deal with unpredictable weather—resulting in variable vintages—and heavy-handed regulators who control the amount and type of vines they can plant. Strict regulations discourage innovation. Many New World wineries have begun adding oak chips to wine that is fermenting in steel barrels. It's a cheaper way of imparting an oak taste without going to the expense of aging the wine in barrels. In France, that technique is illegal. Irrigation, too, is banned in most of France. "It's like playing rugby when the Australians can pass the ball forward and we can only pass it backwards," complains Jean-Marie Chadronnier, CEO of one of France's largest wine producers, CVBG Companie des Vins de Bordeaux et de La Gironde.

13   When it comes to marketing, the playing field is even more unequal. In Britain, Bordeaux merchant Chadronnier says his $150 million-a-year company can afford only two

salesmen. Southcorp, with $540 million in sales, employs 50. Gallo, the world's largest wine company, spent more than twice as much last year on advertising and promotion in Britain as the entire Bordeaux wine industry, according to the recent French government report. Rather than cooperate, the French often fight among themselves for shelf space. "The people in Bordeaux see Burgundy as the competition," says Victor Motto, partner at Motto Kryla & Fisher. "The people in California see the world as competition."

KUNG FU CACHE

14   The New Worlders are succeeding by injecting pizzazz into the stodgy, snobby wine industry. American vintners have vied with one another to open the most lavish hospitality centers, complete with everything from visiting chefs to aerial trams and art collections. This year, Mondavi opened a "demonstration vineyard" in Walt Disney Co.'s new California Adventure theme park that features not just the vineyard but a movie theater and three tasting rooms. Most French châteaux don't accept visitors without an appointment—and even then, all that most have to show is a musty cellar.

15   The Australians are using star power to attract new wine tasters. Kung fu star Jackie Chan has flogged Lindemans in Asia, and Australian golfer Greg Norman has teamed up with Foster's Beringer to sell Greg Norman Estates wines. In the year and a half since it was launched, the Norman line has become the 10th most-popular Australian brand in the U.S. and sold a respectable 170,000 cases worldwide last year. "It makes a mockery of all the history and the heritage and the 100-year-old vineyards and wonderful châteaux," says Beringer Blass Managing Director Terry Davis.

16   The Australians and Americans are demystifying wine in other ways, too. Compared with French labels, some of the best-selling Aussie brands—Wolf Blass, Penfolds, and Rosemount—are easy to read and remember. What's more, Australian labels tell you exactly what grapes you're getting—a Merlot, Cabernet Sauvignon, or a Chardonnay.

17   In contrast, the French system of labeling by geographic origin rather than type of grape results in widespread confusion. There are 450 different AOC (appelation d'origine contrôllée, or registered origin names). Connoisseurs study for years learning to distinguish between the wines of Burgundy villages such as Vosne-Romanee and Gevry

EXHIBIT 3

Source: *BusinessWeek.*

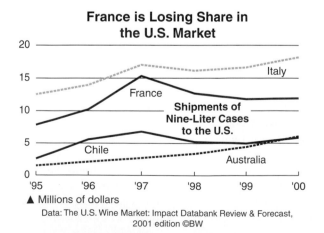

France is Losing Share in the U.S. Market

Shipments of Nine-Liter Cases to the U.S.

Italy

France

Chile

Australia

▲ Millions of dollars

Data: The U.S. Wine Market: Impact Databank Review & Forecast, 2001 edition ©BW

A Tale of Two Labels

Even a beer bum can understand that this popular, well-priced Australian white wine ($10) features the Chardonnay—white wine grape.▶

◀This French wine ($50) also is 100% Chardonnay—but only a connoisseur would know that Champs Cavet is a small piece of land located above a Burgundy village where local *appellation contröllee* rule permit cultivating only Chardonnay. Even then, it would be best to check out Domaine LaTour in a wine rating book, since dozens of producers and merchants sell expensive Puigny–Montrachets that range from the sublime to the substandard

Data: BusinessWeek ©BW

Chambertin, each of which boasts dozens of growers, many bottling their own wines of vastly different quality. "Everyone agrees that we have to simplify the offer," says Allan Sichel, president of the Bordeaux merchant house Maison Sichel.

18   But vested interests resist change. Bordeaux classifications of top-ranking châteaux were made in 1855, and only a single alteration, adding Château Mouton Rothschild to the elite club in 1973, has been made since. "About 500 wines have a classification, and they rake in money while the rest, no matter how good, struggle," says Daniel Cathiard, owner of Château Smith Haut-Lafitte, which was left off the 1855 listing. Generic Bordeaux wines from places such as Quinsac don't have a classification and have no chance of achieving one.

19   The global wine gang can produce large quantities using single grape varietals grown almost anywhere and sold under recognizable brands such as Rosemount's Shiraz and Lindeman's Bin 65 Chardonnay. And they can ensure consistency by blending grapes from different regions. A hailstorm in Monterrey? Mondavi can ship in grapes from fields around nearby Santa Barbara. Even as the economy weakens, the new wine giants use their financial strength to win market share from poorly capitalized French competition. Mondavi increased its marketing budget by 40% this year. "When there is a concern in the economy, people are afraid to buy Château No Name and they come back to the names and the brands they can trust," says R. Michael Mondavi. California winemakers such as Gallo are even pushing its wines in France.

20   Large marketing budgets are crucial, particularly as most wine no longer is bought in specialty liquor shops. Supermarkets sold almost half of the wine in America last year, up from a quarter in 1987. In Britain, big retailers such as Tesco, Sainsbury, and ASDA sell more than 70% of all wine—and their buyers favor suppliers who can provide large volumes, something the French cannot. "When you get to the more esoteric French lines, they are not so accessible to the average drinker," says Nicki Clowes, a Tesco wine buyer.

DRY VS. "LUSCIOUS"

21   Marketing types are working to take the guesswork out of wine buying. New York's Best Cellars Inc. organizes about 100 carefully selected $15-and-under entries not by country of origin or style but rather in eight groupings with names like "fizzy," "soft," "luscious," and "big." The concept has helped it expand into Boston, Seattle, and Washington.

22   Will the French have to resort to such gimmicks to stay in the game? Maybe not. If they can create a range of offerings at different prices around their world-renowned labels such as Château Margaux and Château Cheval Blanc, the elite Châteaux could become like the couture houses, expanding their brand to lower-priced but quality vintages. The Australians are already moving that way. A new drinker can start out with an $11 Penfolds Koonunga Hill, say, and work up to Grange, which goes for $180 a bottle. Southcorp CEO Keith Lambert likens selling wine to selling cars: "People don't remember if it's an E-class or an S-class Mercedes, they just remember it's a Mercedes."

23   But most Bordeaux barons refuse to sully their images. There are almost no ties between the successful top-line growers and the troubled midmarket producers. "We must concentrate on our field of excellence and not spread ourselves too thin," says Paul Pontallier, chief winemaker at Château Margaux. One notable exception: Rothschild uses the $180 Château Mouton Rothschild as the flagship for the more modestly priced Mouton Cadet.

24   More defections may be coming. Some French are disregarding AOC rules and labeling their bottles as table wines. This allows them to plant the grapes they think will produce the best product. Grower Dominique Becot deemphasizes Saint Emilion, putting the locale in small letters on his label, but his critically acclaimed La Gomerie still sells

EXHIBIT 4
Top End Wines

Source: *BusinessWeek.*

Chateau Cheval Blanc	$250
Chateau Latour	$225
Chateau Margaux	$225
Chateau Haut-Brion	$225
Chateau Lafite-Rothschild	$225
Chateau Ausone	$190
Chateau Mouton Rothschild	$180

Note: Wholesale prices per bottle for the first growth 2000 Bordeaux.

for over $100 a bottle. Even in marketing, the French are waking up. The Bordeaux Wine Board has doubled its ad budget in Britain in the past two years. A new campaign features a sexy model dressed in red velvet lingerie hovering over a muscular man. "Let the mood take you to Bordeaux," reads the caption.

25   But advertising alone won't do the trick. Thousands of acres of inferior vines must be ripped up. Hundreds of the 872 French cooperatives must merge or shut down. Bordeaux merchant houses must start cutting deals not only with their Burgundian brothers but with New World partners.

26   Ground zero is the hot southern swath of the country called Languedoc-Roussillon. It produces 9% of the world's grapes and a third of France's total. Massive overproduction of poor wine has been subsidized for years. For a long time, the European Union bought up the region's unsold wine and distilled it into industrial alcohol. Even though farmers were paid to tear up their vines, the flood continues, and an even more painful shakeout looms. Hundreds of millions of liters of unsold Languedoc wine already are stored in cooperative cellars. This year's harvest could triple that amount. "I just don't know how we are going to sell it," admits Jacques Bonnier, director of the cooperative in the village of Aniane.

27   Both the EU and the French government will come under pressure to fork over handouts to struggling vintners and to push for quotas on New World imports. That would surely be a mistake. New competition certainly will force French winemakers to improve, and even some in the wine Establishment welcome such a change. "When I see Gallo trying to sell wine in Paris, I celebrate because it's the only way to wake us up from our slumber," says Philippe Capdouze, president of the Bordeaux wine merchant house FICOFI. And a better bottle of Bordeaux, even if it's picked off a supermarket shelf, would be something just about everybody could celebrate.

MONDAVI'S FORAY INTO FRANCE GOES SOUR

28   David Pearson loves wine and France. The San Diego native studied oenology at the University of California and spent a year after graduation working as an intern on French wine estates. So when Robert Mondavi Corp. asked him in 1998 to head up its Vichon Mediterranean subsidiary, the fresh-faced, French-speaking, 39-year-old Pearson crossed the Atlantic and settled in Southern France. In a hard-pressed region best known for producing oceans of cheap wine, he was confident that New World money and technology could produce superb bottles selling for $60 or more.

29   But this August, the energetic American packed up his belongings and returned to California. An unlikely coalition of local farmers, ecologists, hunters, and communists had painted him as a capitalist plotter and succeeded in killing his ambitious $7.5 million plan to acquire 120 acres of prime grape-growing land on an untamed Mediterranean hillside. "I felt like the Cuban boy Elián González, who became a symbol, in a weird, deformed way, of the clash between two worlds," Pearson laments.

30 Pearson spent his first two years conducting geological surveys to locate top-quality wine real estate. He needed a large tract to produce 260,000 bottles a year, the minimum number that made economic sense for a giant such as Mondavi. He finally settled on a swath of hillside above the 2,000-person village of Aniane, about 15 miles northwest of the regional center of Montpellier. "We saw David and Mondavi as the people who could help us survive the crisis," says Jacques Bonnier, director of the local winegrowers' co-op. In July 2000, Aniane's town council voted to give Mondavi a 99-year lease.

31 A violent backlash ensued. Hunters worried that planting vineyards would frighten away wild boar. Environmentalists railed against razing a forest. Pearson sipped pastis with the locals, reassuring them that the company intended to plant small "islands" of vines and leave much of the natural scrubland untouched. Hunters, he promised, still could roam the hillside during autumn.

32 But the American couldn't shake off one far-reaching charge—that the invading Anglo-Saxons would destroy the village's social cohesion and deform traditional winemaking methods, imposing an alien, money-grubbing industrial model. Leading this crusade was Aimé Guibert, a former businessman whose glove factory had been driven into bankruptcy by Asian competition and whose Mas de Daumas Gassac vineyard produces an internationally renowned red. The 76-year-old Guibert eschews pesticides, harvests his grapes by hand, and traces the origins of his vines back to Palestine at the time of Jesus Christ. "The Mondavis will end up destroying our traditional artisans who make wine, just like McDonald's is destroying French gastronomy," Guibert thunders.

"No Point"

33 In March municipal elections, Aniane's voters threw out the town council and elected as mayor an anti-Mondavi communist, Manuel Diaz. Diaz denounced Mondavi as a menacing multinational similar to Marks & Spencer, which was throwing thousands of French workers out of jobs in order to invest more in its British stores. "When we heard what he was saying, we knew there was no point in staying," Pearson says. In May, Mondavi canceled the vineyard project and is preparing to sell its Vichon brand.

34 Back in Aniane, winegrowers are suffering. Almost 15% of last year's harvest remains unsold. Mayors of 30 other French villages have written Mondavi seeking investment. But it's too late. "For now, we've decided it is too difficult to make wine in France," Pearson says. In September, he becomes managing director of another Mondavi winery near Santa Barbara. The francophile American says he'll miss Southern French cooking—but the wine certainly has left a bad taste in his mouth.

HOW THE FRENCH GAVE THE CALIFORNIA WINE INDUSTRY LEGITIMACY

Much to France's chagrin, a blind taste test 25 years ago in Paris inadvertently launched California's fine wine industry.

35 Sometimes a seemingly inconsequential event can take on huge significance in a nation's commercial and cultural life. We're coming up on the 25th anniversary of one such event—a wine tasting that took place in Paris on May 24, 1976. Long since forgotten by most people, the occasion is being commemorated in Napa Valley as a signal event in the development of California's wine industry. A celebratory dinner in Yountville later this month is expected to attract 1,000 wine industry luminaries.

36   Why all the fuss? The long-ago tasting marked the first time California winemakers realized they were capable of making wines of equal, or of even better, quality than the French.

37   Few expected much from the 1976 Paris tasting. Organized by wine merchant Steven Spurrier, an Englishman who was then only 34 and running a wine school in Paris, it was aimed mainly at capitalizing on the hoopla over the U.S. Bicentennial celebration. The idea was to assemble some of France's greatest experts at Paris' Intercontinental Hotel one afternoon and do a blind tasting of French and California red and white wines.

Bad Rigging

38   Spurrier put the event together in such a rush that there wasn't time to have the California wines shipped through customs. He had to get a group of Californians coming over on a tour to smuggle the bottles into France in their luggage. No one, least of all Spurrier, whose business depended on the goodwill of the French wine industry, expected the California wines to win. "I thought I had it rigged for the French wines to win," admits Spurrier, who now lives in London, where he consults and writes for *Decanter* magazine.

39   What happened next is the stuff of legend in California wine country. The first tasting was of white wines, with four California Chardonnays pitted against six white Burgundies from France. The jury of nine tasters included the *crème de la crème* of France's oenophiles, among them Pierre Tari, secretary general of the Association des Grands Crus Classes, and Raymond Olivier, the dean of French culinary writers.

40   Only one of the haughty French judges had ever even seriously tasted California wines before, Spurrier says, yet the California white wines took three of the top four spots in the blind tasting, with a 1973 Chateau Montelena beating out a 1973 Meursault-Charmes Burgundy for the top rating. A 1974 Roulot Chalone Vineyard Chardonnay from California took third, followed by a 1973 Spring Mountains Vineyard Chardonnay, also from California. A 1973 Batard-Montrachet, which had been classed by the famous wine expert Alexis Lichine as one of the "greatest of all white burgundies," came in a distant seventh.

Alarmed Judges

41   Then came the crucial tasting of the reds, which in wine circles are far more important and prestigious than whites. This time, four Grand Cru Bordeaux squared off against six California Cabernets. Desperately hoping the French would win this round, Spurrier admits he informed the judges that a California white had won the first tasting, rather than wait until the end to announce the results as he should have. The alarmed judges did everything they could to segment what they thought were the California reds and make sure they didn't win.

42   Even so, a 1973 Cabernet from California's Stag's Leap Wine Cellars took the top spot. French wines took the next three—a 1970 Chateau Mouton-Rothschild ranked No. 2, followed by 1970 offerings from Chateau Montrose and Chateau Haut-Brion. A 1971 Ridge Montebello Vineyard Cabernet from California came in fifth.

43   The tasting might have been quickly forgotten. The French certainly weren't going to publicize it. But Spurrier had invited a single journalist, George Taber, a Paris correspondent with *Time* magazine, who wrote a short article about the event under the headline, "The Judgement of Paris." (Taber is now researching a book on the tasting.)

"Seminal Event"

44   The poobahs of French wine were so outraged they banned Spurrier from the nation's prestige wine-tasting tour for a year as punishment for the damage he had done to their image. And when the news hit the U.S., it had an electrifying effect. "It was a seminal event," says Vic Motto, a wine consultant based in Napa Valley. "I cite it every time I speak about the growth of the California wine industry." Adds Ronn Wiegand, chief wine officer at the online wine merchant eVineyard.com: "The French monopoly [on fine wines] was crushed permanently."

45 Until then, the California wine industry was dominated by cheap jug wines, with only a few lonely pioneers struggling to craft higher-quality products. Even most Americans regarded European wines as far superior, and the better California wines had trouble even getting distribution beyond the West Coast. "You had to pound on distributors' doors to get your wine tasted," says Bo Barrett, Chateau Montelena's winemaker. "Once they tasted it, the distributors would give you kind of half compliments like, 'This isn't bad—for a California wine.'"

46 The Paris tasting almost instantaneously gave California's boutique wineries credibility, recalls Warren Winiarski, head of Stag's Leap Wine Cellars. "Here we had a visible endorsement from [French wine] authorities. People were willing to listen who wouldn't listen before. We had people calling us to ask where they could get our wines, both from the trade and among consumers."

Long-Term Ripples

47 Many experts now view the Paris tasting as the key event in the transformation of the California wine industry. Between 1980 and 1990, consultant Motto notes, the number of California wineries tripled, to about 900, as hundreds of ambitious entrepreneurs moved in, bought land and planted vineyards with an eye toward making world-class wines. The economic benefits for the state have been enormous. Even as jug wines have declined in importance, California's annual production of wine has doubled since 1976, to 157 million cases this year, estimates Jon Fredrikson, a Woodside (Calif.) wine consultant.

48 But, as the quality and price of California's wines have climbed, the value of the wine at the producer level has soared more than sevenfold in the same period, to $6.8 billion this year, he estimates. The retail value is roughly double that amount, or about $14 billion this year.

49 On top of that, Golden State wineries have become a major tourist draw. Motto's consultancy estimates that 10 million visitors flock to California wine country annually, with 27% of all tourists to San Francisco now also taking a wine tour. That, in turn, has created a market that supports some of the nation's best restaurants and small hotels.

"Clearly Better"?

50 "When I moved here 43 years ago, there were about 1,000 tourists coming per year, and no good restaurants and no good hotels," recalls Mike Grgich, who was Chateau Montelena's winemaker back in 1976. The tasting transformed his life as well. With his wine dubbed one of the best in the world, he soon got backing to start his own winery, Grgich Hills Cellar in Rutherford. "My life is divided into two parts—before the Paris tasting and after," he says.

51 The tasting, nonetheless, did nothing to dent the French belief that their wines are superior to all others. "With age, French wines are clearly better," sniffs Jean Michel Deluc, head sommelier at ChateauOnline.com, the Paris-based Internet wine merchant, and one of only about 100 Master Sommeliers in France. "There's a tight competition until the wines are 10 to 15 years old, but then the French wines take the lead."

52   To this day, California wines don't do well in France. "To sell wine in France, you have to combat not only the French competition but French chauvinism," Deluc admits.

Wines Worldwide

53   Still, even many American wine experts agree with Deluc's assessment that the best French wines are the best in existence. Wiegand, one of only three people in the world who has earned the twin titles of Master Sommelier and Master of Wine, contends that no California wine approaches the refinement and complexity of, say, a legendary 1945 Chateau Latour. "Of the greatest Cabernet- or Merlot-based wines in the world, the French in my opinion have the top 10 out of 10," he says. "However, once you remove the top 0.5% of wines, California, Australia and Chile come roaring up."

54   Australia and Chile? Yep. Australian winemakers now show every sign of doing to the Americans exactly what they did to the French a quarter century ago. Wiegand notes that in Cabernet tastings these days, Australian wines often best all comers, including the Americans and the French. Indeed, the main significance of the famed Paris tasting isn't so much what it did for California as the way it created opportunity for fine wine production in warm and sunny areas all over the world.

55   All a wine lover anywhere can say about that is *tant mieux*—which is French for "so much the better."

Source: Adapted by Richard Robinson, University of South Carolina, based on "Wine War," *BusinessWeek,* September 3, 2001.

Case 4

BusinessWeek

Sun Microsystems

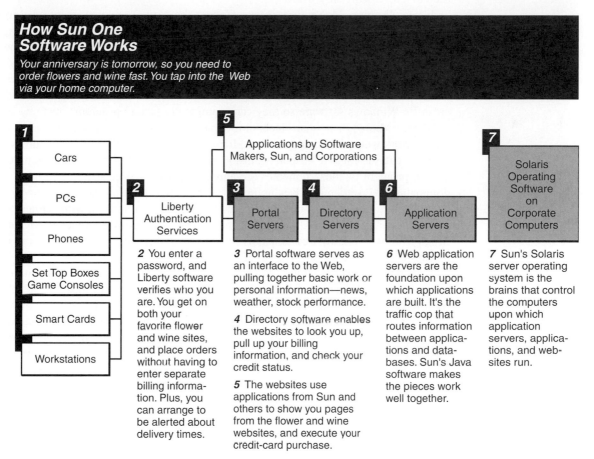

How Sun One Software Works

Your anniversary is tomorrow, so you need to order flowers and wine fast. You tap into the Web via your home computer.

1
- Cars
- PCs
- Phones
- Set Top Boxes Game Consoles
- Smart Cards
- Workstations

5 Applications by Software Makers, Sun, and Corporations

2 Liberty Authentication Services

3 Portal Servers

4 Directory Servers

6 Application Servers

7 Solaris Operating Software on Corporate Computers

2 You enter a password, and Liberty software verifies who you are. You get on both your favorite flower and wine sites, and place orders without having to enter separate billing information. Plus, you can arrange to be alerted about delivery times.

3 Portal software serves as an interface to the Web, pulling together basic work or personal information—news, weather, stock performance.

4 Directory software enables the websites to look you up, pull up your billing information, and check your credit status.

5 The websites use applications from Sun and others to show you pages from the flower and wine websites, and execute your credit-card purchase.

6 Web application servers are the foundation upon which applications are built. It's the traffic cop that routes information between applications and databases. Sun's Java software makes the pieces work well together.

7 Sun's Solaris server operating system is the brains that control the computers upon which application servers, applications, and websites run.

Scott McNealy sees himself as the last challenger to Microsoft's bid for Web domination. Is his plan realistic? Or grandiose bluster?

1   In the 2001 slow economy, Scott G. McNealy says he thinks about quitting his job as chief executive of Sun Microsystems Inc. every single day. With a 2% stake in Sun that's worth $668 million, McNealy would just as soon focus on playing hockey, perfecting his scratch golf game, or hanging out with his three young sons and pregnant wife. Instead he's in the office, coping with the worst tech slump in 16 years. Sun has been losing money for the past two quarters and doesn't expect to see a profit until next summer. That has forced McNealy finally to give up his dream of avoiding layoffs. On Oct. 5, he became one of the last computer executives to hand out pink slips.

2   Why doesn't he just chuck it? He can't, he says, because now he has an even more crucial job ahead of him: Stopping archrival Microsoft Corp. from ruling the Web. "It really is mankind against Microsoft. And mankind needs a bit of a break right now," he says. His words are trademark McNealy—over the top, with a comic twist. And one can't help but wonder if this is just another theatrical moment in the longstanding feud between the two companies. McNealy insists it's not. He drops his usual patter to admit: "I know this sounds like ranting and raving." But he says he's in dead earnest. "This is why I don't quit this job. I've got more than enough money, but I don't want to leave my children to a Microsoft-only world."

3   Especially now. McNealy is incensed about the Nov. 2 announcement of a proposed antitrust settlement that he thinks barely raps Microsoft on the knuckles. "It's garbage," he says. "We've got a much more unfettered monopolist now—one that will hurt innovation and take away people's choice." Like many computer-industry execs, McNealy is dismayed by a settlement he says will do little to curb Microsoft's anticompetitive behavior. If approved by a federal judge, the agreement will allow PC makers to fiddle with Microsoft's Windows software so they can prominently feature programs made by rivals. It will force Microsoft to share technology that lets outside programs, such as streaming media, work well with Windows. And Microsoft will have to disclose its Windows pricing so that it can't use it as a weapon against PC makers who install non-Microsoft products.

4   The problem is, those remedies are aimed at the PC realm, where Microsoft already dominates. The settlement does nothing to keep Microsoft from taking unfair advantage of its Windows monopoly in new markets by packaging Windows with services such as its Passport I.D. authentication, instant messaging, and videoconferencing. McNealy believes Microsoft is now free to use its monopoly unfairly to try to dominate the Internet as thoroughly as it does the PC market.

5   How does he plan to slow it down? By pushing Sun into overdrive to create technology for a new generation of Web services that will compete with those being rolled out by Microsoft. He doesn't have to beat Microsoft—just create a viable alternative. Until now, the Internet has been about websites that people beeline to for stock trades, plane tickets, filling out expense reports, and the like. In the next phase of the Net, these sites will communicate with one another to do a series of tasks on your behalf. If, for example, your flight is delayed, a service would let you know by pager while changing your online calendar and notifying your car service of a new pickup time. That might trigger another service to alert your next business appointment that you will be late.

CRUCIAL FACE-OFF

6   Web services are shaping up to be the next big frontier in computing. Technology leaders foresee a day when all manner of jobs, from managing relationships with customers to coordinating with distributors, will be handled by services delivered over the Net rather than with traditional software programs, phones, and faxes. While it's too early to tell how big the market will be, this is one topic where McNealy and Microsoft agree. "Everything in the world will be in Web services," says Microsoft Chairman William H. Gates III. If he's right, the companies building the underpinnings for these services could become the tech powerhouses for years to come. And if Microsoft wins, it could maintain the kind of hold over the vast reaches of Internet computing that the company now has in the PC world.

7   That's why a face-off with Microsoft is so crucial for McNealy. "I'm the only one left," he says, who can put the technology pieces and partnerships together to offer an alternative to Microsoft. And, he says, he's the only computer exec standing who does not depend on Microsoft in some way. Computer makers rely on Windows for their PCs, servers, and handhelds. Most software makers build their programs to work on Windows. "McNealy sees it as part of his responsibility to maintain the checks and balances in the industry," says John O. Wilkerson, president of global alliances at Electronic Data Systems Corp., a partner of both Sun and Microsoft.

8   That's nonsense, say Microsoft executives. Gates says the antitrust settlement agreement is "fair and reasonable and, most important, is in the best interests of consumers and the economy." Microsoft top brass dismiss McNealy's stand as rhetoric that's "higher than usual and emptier than usual" because he's trying to take the focus off how poorly his company is doing these days. "Scott's a comedian, and he's especially good when he doesn't have any product to sell," says Robert Muglia, a Microsoft group vice-president.

9   There's little question that McNealy would have a better chance against Microsoft if his company's fortunes hadn't taken a dive this year. With its core dot-com and telecommunications markets in tatters, Sun's sales plunged 43% in the quarter that ended on Sept. 30. Faced with vicious price-cutting in the server business by Dell Computer Corp. and a resurgent IBM—Sun's No. 1 rival in corporate computing today—Sun has lost $268 million in the past two quarters. And some of its newer initiatives put it in direct competition with its allies, including software maker Oracle Corp. Meanwhile, Microsoft's Windows server operating system software is gaining market share, rising from 20.6% in 1999 to 27.7% for the first half of this year, according to Gartner Dataquest. Sun's stock price is down from 55 a year ago to 12 today. "I think they're in free fall," says one rival CEO.

NEW SUNRISE?

10   McNealy has been hearing about the demise of Sun since its inception 19 years ago. He concedes that the economic environment is tough, but notes that it's tough on everyone. Sun will weather the downturn, he says, because it has robust technology that companies need to handle their biggest computing chores. He gets backing from analysts, who praise Sun for not cutting its research-and-development spending and believe it will recover next year. Merrill Lynch & Co. predicts that Sun's revenues will rise 20%, to $15.9 billion, next fiscal year, and will deliver $457 million in profits.

11   Vital to a turnaround is Sun's push into Web services. It is pulling together a platform for building Web services called Sun ONE that will compete with Microsoft's services technology, called .NET. These platforms are behind-the-scenes technologies that corporations and independent software makers can use as building blocks for creating services that people subscribe to. Sun's foundation pieces include its Solaris operating system, Java programming language, and software tools. Sun also is merging disparate software into this jumbo package, including its e-commerce software. And it's overhauling all the pieces to comply with new Web-service technology standards by the middle of next year. At that point, Sun hopes to start selling its package of software preconfigured on its computers—along with storage drives and other gear. The goal: giving Web-service providers everything that they need in one easy-to-use package.

12   McNealy will have to move fast if he hopes to keep pace with Microsoft. Once written off as a rich has-been from the PC era, the software giant has come storming back. Last year, blowing past Sun, Microsoft announced .NET, its platform for building Web services. And on Oct. 25, the company released a new version of its PC operating system, Windows XP, that is packed with online services, including Passport, which lets people avoid having to type in a password each time they visit participating websites.

13   While the antitrust settlement does little to slow Microsoft, McNealy says all the scrutiny of the software giant has had one favorable result for him. There's increased support from companies in media, travel, and other markets that share his concerns about

EXHIBIT 1
Sun vs. Microsoft

Server Operating Systems
Microsoft's Windows 2000 dominates the market for sub-$100,000 servers used for lower-level jobs, such as doling out Web pages. But Windows runs less than 1% of the mid- and high-end servers that tackle big jobs. That's where Sun's Solaris system shines.

Advantage: SUN
Microsoft will win lower-end markets, but the most critical computing will be done on high-end computers.

Web Services Platform
Sun's Sun ONE architecture pulls together software, including its Java programming language, to create a foundation for corporations to build Web services. Microsoft's .NET platform does the same thing, and is about a year ahead of Sun ONE.

Advantage: MICROSOFT
Though as Sun ONE rolls out, it could gain ground because of the popularity of Java.

Web Services
Microsoft will offer a vast array of its own services. It already has a service that lets subscribers get traffic alerts wherever they are. Aside from basic offerings such as instant messaging, Sun won't offer services of its own—to avoid competing with its customers.

Advantage: MICROSOFT
With Windows loaded on almost every PC, Microsoft will be able to market its services directly to about 140 million computer buyers next year.

Web I.D.
Some 200 million accounts have been created with Microsoft's identity-authentication service, called Passport. That lets them sign on once to use hundreds of websites. Sun and 34 other companies have created the Liberty Project, which will let each Web service provider choose from many I.D. services.

Advantage: MICROSOFT
Liberty-based services won't be ready for a year or so. Passport should keep its huge lead.

Developer Loyalty
With 7 million developers, Microsoft has the raw-numbers advantage over Sun's Java, which has about 1 million developers. But most of Microsoft's devotees focus on relatively simple PC programs. Big-time Net programs are written using Java.

Advantage: SUN
The Java advantage will help Sun create loyalty with programmers who build next-generation Web services and applications.

Enterprise Applications
Sun's iPlanet suite includes a few programs for buying and selling over the Net. But Sun has never been good at selling software, and software bigs such as SAP and Oracle are likely to sell most of the programs that run on Sun's computers. Microsoft leads Sun in e-commerce software.

Advantage: MICROSOFT
Unless Sun finally gets software right, it may get stuck selling lower-margin hardware.

EXHIBIT 2
Fighting Words

Scott McNealy has never liked Microsoft much, but now his fervor is at an all-time high. Here's a history:

1982
McNealy co-founds Sun on the premise that networked computers that share files and processing power will be more useful than stand-alone PCs.

1993
Sun goes after Microsoft's Windows customers with software for PCs and technology that lets them run PC programs on Sun workstations. McNealy claims it will render Windows "frosting on a road apple," yet Sun makes almost no headway.

1995
After Microsoft scores big with Windows 95, Sun rallies the industry around its Java technology for Web applications. McNealy hypes "Java Stations" that will tap Web servers—minimizing the need for Windows PCs. His pet name for Windows: "Hairball."

1997
Microsoft tweaks Java to make it work better with Windows. Sun sues. When Microsoft calls on Sun to pass stewardship of Java to a standards body, McNealy says: "Having Microsoft give us advice on open standards is like W. C. Fields giving moral advice to the Mormon Tabernacle Choir."'

1998
McNealy tells Congress that Microsoft's hold on software business is like "General Motors having the ability to decide what type of gasoline you put into your car."

2000
Sun is riding high on Internet sales, and Microsoft is facing a court-ordered breakup (*Judge Thomas Jackson*). Still, McNealy warns that Microsoft should be stopped from using the cash hoard from its "ill-gotten" monopoly to buy startups.

2001
The government drops its plans to break up Microsoft. McNealy's worries reach a new high. He says Microsoft's Web authentication service, Passport, will help it dominate the Net. He vows to offer an alternative. "It's mankind against Microsoft," he says.

Microsoft's Web plans. They fear that Passport and other services will allow Microsoft to collect reams of personal data on buyers and their habits that give it a leg up in offering yet more services. Those fears persist even though Microsoft has pledged not to track buying habits or market its own services to Passport subscribers.

14   Still, to combat the perceived threat, McNealy has taken the lead in establishing Project Liberty—an alternative to Passport. Project Liberty is a 34-company standards body that hopes to map out a blueprint so that any company's Passport-like services could hook up to any others. "My concern with Microsoft is that they're going to get between me and my customers," says a telecom executive who is one of Project Liberty's co-founders. "Microsoft has managed to piss off every one of us."

15   "Will all this be enough to restore Sun to its former glory? Probably not. Sun's peak 60% revenue-growth rates are a thing of the past. Because its high-end server technology is more popular with corporations than Microsoft's, Sun should be able to hold or regain market share when the economy recovers. But server margins are tumbling because of increased competition from IBM at the high end and from Windows- and Linux-based servers at the low end. So, to boost profits, Sun will have to do well against Microsoft on its home turf—software.

16   Sun is in a better spot when it comes to Web services. Even though it's trailing Microsoft, its rival Sun ONE contains Java software, which is popular with corporations that

have used it to create Internet programs. That means Sun should be able to gain ground once it has Sun ONE ready next year. The key question: Will Sun ONE be a strong enough alternative to prevent Microsoft from dominating the future of computing? If McNealy falls short, Sun could be well liked by fans but increasingly irrelevant. And Microsoft could be stronger than ever.

17   That would be a devastating defeat for McNealy, who has deeply held beliefs about how companies should do business. His views were formed during his teenage years in suburban Detroit. That's when McNealy watched his father, a vice-chairman at American Motors, lose out to General Motors Corp. and Ford Motor Co. "If he sees someone go over the edge [ethically], it upsets him a lot more than it bothers most people," says his father, Bill. "I think it comes from being around an underdog as a kid and watching us struggle."

18   What upsets McNealy about Microsoft is how it has used its monopoly to beat software competitors such as browser maker Netscape Communications Corp. That, he believes, suppresses innovation by discouraging other tech companies from developing rival products. The losers, he says: consumers and the economy.

19   Sun's philosophy is in stark contrast to Microsoft's. Sun created its Java programming language in 1995 so people could write Web applications that run on any computer. Sun shares management of Java with more than 200 companies that have licensed it. Even though some Java licensees have griped, Sun doesn't control Java in the way Microsoft controls Windows. McNealy's strategy is for Java to fuel overall tech spending and for Sun to grab as much of that new business as possible.

20   Because of Sun's heritage, Web services should have been Sun's game. Since McNealy and three pals formed Sun in 1982, their philosophy was that computers that were networked together would be far more useful than stand-alone PCs. That's why every product in Sun's history has been based on the protocols at the heart of the Internet—the biggest network of all.

21   What went wrong? Sun became a victim of its own success. In the late 1990s, with sales racing, McNealy and his team had their hands full managing the business—no small feat, given that the company's staff grew by 33%, or 10,000, in fiscal 2000. And with cash-flush corporations still pouring money into Java-based projects, Sun execs figured all was well.

HESITATION

22   Meanwhile, Microsoft saw an opportunity to at last become a Net visionary—and executed perfectly. It grabbed the lead in advancing an industry standard called XML. A way of describing digitized data—whether they're specifications for a car part or the format of an insurance claim—XML is critical to Web services, since it lets data be passed among all kinds of computers and software programs. With Microsoft taking the lead, Sun hesitated and fell behind.

23   Microsoft's unveiling of .NET in June 2000, was a wake-up call for Sun. While McNealy immediately dubbed the project ".Not," many Sun insiders were impressed by how much meat there was on Microsoft's plan. They fumed at how .NET seemed to remake Microsoft's image overnight. It was suddenly the leading Web-services pioneer. Some Sun execs feared Web developers might migrate to the .NET camp.

24   Sun got moving, albeit slowly. A nine-person task force led by Chief Technology Officer Greg Papadopoulos began to pull together Sun's Web-services plan. But the company did not fill out the details until last month. In mid-2002, Sun promises to release server software that will let corporate customers offer XML-based Web services to close partners. Technology to take that to the next level, to enable any of these Web services to work with those of any other company, won't be out until 2003. "Sun has not been a leader in Web services at all," says Gartner Group Inc. analyst David Smith. "Microsoft is much more of the visionary than Sun."

25   It's not just in terms of vision that Sun lags, but also in execution. Microsoft has delivered a steady beat of new products based on its .NET strategy. IBM also is ahead of Sun, say analysts. Already, 50,000 of its customers use its technology, called Web-Sphere, as a foundation for creating Internet applications such as programs that manage customer relationships. On May 14, it updated the software so it can be used as a basis for building Web services.

26   McNealy denies Sun is behind Microsoft. Still, he's trying to make Sun think like a software company. On Oct. 5, it announced it was taking over AOL Time Warner's 50% stake in the iPlanet joint venture, maker of website and e-commerce software. That will let Sun merge this group into the rest of the company. Rather than have a separate sales staff, Sun's 12,000 sales reps also will sell software on their rounds.

27   Will the software push work? It's a long shot at best. While Sun is great at creating buzz for a new machine, "we just never have done a good job of marketing software," admits President Edward J. Zander. Consider application-server software, which dishes out applications for such tasks as managing a supply chain over the Web. Sun controlled 40% of the application-server software market in the mid-1990s. Since then, Sun's share has plunged to about 11% as IBM and BEA Systems have taken the lead. That smarts—because these days many developers create Web programs that work on application servers rather than on operating systems, such as Sun's Solaris. "Sun is just way behind," says Scott Hebner, IBM's director of marketing for WebSphere.

TRUST FACTOR

28   While Sun has a long way to go on the software front, interviews with corporate buyers and software developers suggest that, long term, Sun's technology is likely to be a viable alternative to Microsoft's Web services. Telekom Malaysia, for instance, uses Sun ONE technology for its iOffice Web portal for small businesses. It lets 40,000 customers store their phone lists online, make phone calls via the Net, and manage voice-mail, e-mail, and faxes—and have them delivered to their PC or read to them on the phone. Why did Telekom Malaysia not pick Microsoft? Mohamed Roslan Sallehuddin, head of the iOffice business, says "Microsoft was not even considered because their record of technology robustness and support in our company was bad."

29   Sun's biggest advantage may be the trust factor it has engendered through years of backing open industry standards such as Java. Many software developers and corporate customers are confident Sun won't fiddle with Java to cut others out. In contrast, Microsoft critics say it takes advantage of owning Windows to beat other software developers. "Sun is no Mother Teresa, but they have been in a position to take advantage of Java, and they haven't. Scott has to get credit for taking a different tack than Microsoft took," says David A. Litwack, CEO of SilverStream Software Inc. Microsoft's response: It makes it possible for scads of software companies to write programs to run on Windows.

30   Developers of sophisticated corporate software are firmly in the Java camp: It allows them to create programs quickly for a wide variety of computers. A November survey by Evans Data Corp. showed that 55% of developers plan to use Java to develop Web services in the next year, compared with 35% for .NET. That includes some close Microsoft allies: Software giant SAP will use Java in its corporate Web services—even though it does not plan on using other Sun ONE technology. "When we went to our customers, they said: 'Java is what we want,'" says Shai Agassi, CEO of the company's SAP Portals unit.

31   Of course, the success of Java means only that Sun gets to compete—it doesn't guarantee success. And McNealy has plenty of problems to deal with as he prepares for the coming Web-services face-off with Microsoft. One whopper: IBM. Big Blue has been selling its impressive new lineup of powerful servers at cut-rate prices to land big consulting gigs. While Sun's Unix market share declined from 38.9% to 35% between the second quarter of 2000 and this year's second quarter, IBM's lifted from 17% to 21.6%, according to IDC. Sun bounced back from a low of 31.6% in the first quarter, but, still, the price war has slashed Sun's gross margins on servers from 59% at the end of 1999 to 36% in the latest quarter.

32   Meanwhile, makers of PC servers such as Dell Computer Corp. continue to steal share in lower-end markets formerly dominated by Sun. Even though Windows servers have captured only 1% of the market for mid-tier and high-end servers, they have 60% of the market for low-end servers, according to IDC. While Sun's top-end Unix servers have more processing power and are considered more reliable, Windows servers have proved capable of handling demanding corporate computing tasks.

WRIGGLING OUT

33   Sun faces a dilemma. Unlike the PC makers, it designs its own microprocessor and operating-system software. That bill comes to more than $500 million a year. Those expenditures are essential, since they allow Sun to offer a more powerful alternative to Windows. But if Windows servers match Sun's capabilities and eat into Sun's market share, "they won't be able to maintain their margins and make the investments in software to keep up with us," says Microsoft .NET server software chief Paul Flessner.

34   As tough as times are for Sun, McNealy has shown that he can wriggle out of tight spots. In the early 1990s, as PC makers were gobbling up share in the market for technical workstations that made up over 80% of Sun's sales, he spotted the opportunity to expand the server business and struck with textbook efficiency.

35   Now, McNealy doesn't have to beat Microsoft: He just has to slow it down enough to keep it from dominating the Internet. While holding the high moral ground will doubtless help him in his quest, it won't determine who wins and who loses. That will depend on whether Sun's technologies deliver more bang for the bucks than do Microsoft's.

Source: Adapted by Richard Robinson, University of South Carolina, based on "Sun's Defiant Face-Off," *BusinessWeek,* November 19, 2001.

Case 5

BusinessWeek

Best Buy Enters the PC Market

1 Shopping for a personal computer at a Chicago Best Buy store on a recent Sunday, Juan Herrera stopped at the display of a new line of desktops. The prices—from $900 to $1,400—certainly grabbed him, being about $100 less than comparable PCs. Herrera noticed they also had slightly better performance specs than the Hewlett-Packard PCs lined up next to them. But he wondered about the brand: "I never heard the name vpr Matrix before," the 38-year-old postal worker said.

2 Seeking to succeed where virtually every other electronics retailer has failed, Best Buy quietly launched its own brand of PCs under the vpr Matrix name during the week of Jan. 21. The nation's No. 1 consumer-electronics chain is aiming the brand squarely against the key national-brand PCs it sells—H-P, Compaq, and Sony. "Our goal really is to make this a dominant brand in the same way our other brands are," says David Morrish, senior vice-president in charge of computer merchandising at the Eden Prairie (Minn.)–based chain of 470 stores.

OUT IN TWO YEARS?

3 It couldn't have picked a more challenging time. PC sales fell last year—the first time that has happened—and the industry is poised for another round of price wars. Add to that the inherent difficulties of selling a so-called private-label machine, which have already forced retailers Radio Shack, Computer City, and CompUSA out of the business.

4 The hurdles range from building brand awareness and jousting with existing suppliers to managing inventories. Besides, making computers isn't Best Buy's core strength. "They will be out of this in 24 months," predicts David Goldstein, chief executive of Channel Marketing, a Dallas consulting firm.

5 Much like Wal-Mart Stores sells private-label goods such as Sam's Choice detergent, Best Buy is seeking to capitalize on its clout with consumers and capture the higher profit margins such products can bring. At nearly 20%, it already controls the largest share of PC sales at the retail level, followed by Circuit City. But PC gross profit margins are among the lowest earned by electronics retailers, averaging about 8%. By dealing directly with third-party manufacturers, analysts say, Best Buy could potentially gain several percentage points of margin.

MORE LEVERAGE

6 Analysts say Best Buy is also trying to put itself in a stronger position should the HP–Compaq merger go through. It will now have machines to fill the void left on the display shelves if the combined company unifies its product line. Also, having its own line would give Best Buy more leverage against the combined company's increased market clout.

7 Best Buy is moving gingerly. It's using Equus Computer Systems, a Minneapolis-based build-to-order company, to assemble the three models of central processing units it is selling under the Matrix name. People close to Best Buy say Equus is making only about 22,000 units for the retailer for the first quarter.

8   For future orders, the retailer has lined up a major Chinese supplier to do partial assembly of the CPUs, says Best Buy's Morrish. Final assembly, including the faster-changing components, will be done by another U.S. company. Morrish declined to give specifics. Equus also declined to comment.

FULLY LOADED

9   Best Buy isn't targeting the low end of the market, as have other retailers that sold private-label PCs. All three Matrix CPUs have Pentium 4 processors and, depending on the processor speed, sell from $899.99 to $1,299.99. Once bundled with other makers' monitors, keyboards, and printers, the packages sell for about $100 more. All three Matrix CPUs have CD and DVD players, CD burners, and graphics cards that allow digital cameras and camcorders to plug in. Matrix prices run from $100 to $150 below the competing HP and Compaq machines and even further below Sony units.

10   As it develops the line, Morrish says, Best Buy plans to add its own monitors and other peripherals. It also plans to create a unique design, much like Apple, to create a distinctive look. With the music, DVD, and graphics components, Morrish adds, Best Buy is trying to position Matrix as an "entertainment solution" that dovetails with the CDs and other entertainment products the chain sells.

11   In that respect, he explains, Best Buy is attempting to outflank direct PC seller Dell Computer. Dell and Best Buy both aim to launch machines with upgraded components at a faster rate than do HP and Compaq, which would give the chain another advantage, he says.

MARKDOWNS AHEAD?

12   The strategy isn't without risks. The key one, which has dogged retailers that took this route in the past, is profitability. The prices of PCs and components generally tend to go down—and often tumble. This can force the retailer to take aggressive markdowns that eat into profits, says Michael Flink, a former Computer City executive who now works for Levin Consulting of Beachwood, Ohio.

13   Flink says Best Buy won't have the benefit of the markdown allowances that national PC brands give retailers. Morrish counters that Best Buy's inventory-control expertise and knowledge of what its consumers want will help it to escape crippling markdowns.

14   Best Buy also runs the risk of alienating HP, Compaq, or Sony, which could respond by deciding to work more closely with rival Circuit City. Morrish admits the Matrix launch has caused some "stress and strain" with those vendors, but adds: "We are working through the issues." HP and Sony officials declined to comment.

PAYING FOR A NAME

15   Perhaps the biggest test will be whether Best Buy can establish Matrix as a brand that resonates with consumers. By launching Matrix, it's betting that PCs—like the private-label goods sold by Wal-Mart—are becoming more commoditized items that are bought for their features and price more than the brand name. It's also betting that the power of the Best Buy name will give customers the confidence to buy.

16   When Chicago's Herrera shopped for computers at Best Buy, he was looking for national brands. He gave the Matrix machines only a quick glance before heading to HP models. "I'd be willing to pay the higher price for the name," he says.

17   Morrish says Matrix is off to a strong start, however, with Best Buy having sold out of the machines after advertising them for the first time in its circulars on Jan. 27. Matrix may prove to be a success, but history isn't on Best Buy's side.

Source: Adapted by Richard Robinson, University of South Carolina, based on "Robert Berner, "Best Buy's Bid to Be a Player in PCs," *BusinessWeek,* February 1, 2002.

Case 6

BusinessWeek

Carly Fiorina's Proposal: Merge HP and Compaq

1   As Hewlett-Packard Co. Chief Executive Carleton S. Fiorina prepared HP's purchase of Compaq Computer Corp. in summer 2002, there were already red flags flying. In late July, when HP hired Goldman, Sachs & Co. to finalize the deal, the investment bankers' initial feedback was, "Are you sure you want to do this?" Goldman warned the stock would take a 10% to 15% hit right off the bat because of the massive risk of merging two $40 billion behemoths with such a big stake in the hardscrabble PC business. Then, on Sept. 2, two days before the deal was announced, Fiorina had to tweak her presentation to investors after a Goldman stock analyst warned that her pitch was too optimistic. And all the while, Fiorina knew that board member Walter B. Hewlett, the son of HP co-founder William R. Hewlett, might vote the 5.2% stake he controlled against the merger if Wall Street pounded the deal mercilessly.

2   The flags didn't fib. The merger news sent HP's stock skidding down 38% over the next two weeks, and Hewlett was true to his word. On Nov. 6, 2002, he gave Fiorina only a 30-minute warning before announcing he would vote his shares against the deal. That set in motion a bizarre tug-of-war, as Hewlett and Fiorina both hit the road to convince investors they knew what was best for the Silicon Valley icon. Each claimed they were making headway. Indeed, as late as Dec. 6, HP execs were chipper, saying the report being prepared for the David & Lucile Packard Foundation, HP's largest shareholder, with a 10.4% stake, was positive on how the merger would be executed. But on Dec. 7, Fiorina was dealt a body blow. The Packard foundation said it would oppose the deal, uniting the HP heirs against the merger.

3   Fiorina then faced the Herculean task of persuading 67% of the remaining institutional shareholders to vote her way—or face her possible ouster. She had her work cut out for her. In interviews with eight institutional shareholders, *BusinessWeek* learned that four were leaning against the deal, two would probably support the merger, and two were undecided. The eight hold about 7% of outstanding shares. Still, Fiorina felt she could convince investors by the time they voted, which would take place in March 2002. "We started this because we think it's the right thing to do. And the foundation's decision doesn't change that," she said. And if she failed? She said she'll cross that bridge if she came to it. "It is virtually unprecedented for a deal to go to shareowner vote and be voted down," says Fiorina. "If that were to happen, the board and management's credibility would be severely impacted."

4   In the face of daunting odds, Fiorina remained bold and unflinching—the very traits that brought her and HP to this high-wire perch. Ensconced in an HP conference room on a Saturday afternoon—just 24 hours after she received the Packard news—she mapped out why the merger made sense and why she doggedly pursued it even though alarm bells sounded months earlier. "My words to our board and to the Compaq board was that the market was going to hate this deal initially," says Fiorina. "The surprises were in degree." She didn't expect the stock to drop so far, nor did she expect Hewlett would oppose the merger publicly. She called Hewlett's behavior "distracting and disruptive," and an "insult" to the HP board. Some management experts, however, said that if Fiorina knew Hewlett was wavering, she should have scrapped merger talks rather than risk a damaging proxy fight. "You have to question her business judgment," said Charles M. Elson, director of the Center for Corporate Governance at the University of Delaware. "Either [the board] failed to persuade him, or they ignored him. Either way, it's bad."

EXHIBIT 1
Key Players in
the HP–Compaq
Merger

The Opposition

Walter B. Hewlett
The outspoken dissident. The last remaining board member from the founding families went public with his opposition to the Compaq deal on Nov. 6. Now he's actively soliciting other shareholders to vote against the deal.

David Woodley Packard
The son of HP co-founder Dave Packard said he would vote the 1.3% stake he controls against the Compaq deal the day after childhood friend Walter Hewlett announced his opposition. His big problem with the deal: It would require 15,000 layoffs.

Susan Packard Orr
The daughter of Dave Packard and chairperson of the David and Lucile Packard Foundation has been a supporter of Fiorina. But she and the foundation decided to vote against the Compaq merger because of its high risks.

Lewis E. Platt
When HP's fortunes slowed in the late 1990s, HP's humble then-CEO made way for the flashy Fiorina. He is one of the 12 members of the Packard Foundation board who voted against the deal.

The Supporters

Richard A. Hackborn
The HP veteran, known for building the printing business from scratch, is just a notch below "Bill and Dave" in the HP pantheon. Now a board member, he is a crucial Fiorina ally through his staunch support for the Compaq deal.

Larry W. Sonsini
The chairman of law firm Wilson Sonsini Goodrich & Rosati has had a critical role in the Compaq feud. In August, he told Walter Hewlett that he could vote with HP's board to buy Compaq, even if he later chose to vote his shares against it.

Thomas J. Perkins
The 69-year-old founding partner of venture firm Kleiner Perkins Caufield & Byers sits on Compaq's board. He has become one of the merger's head cheerleaders and has voiced frustration with the HP infighting.

Michael D. Capellas
After taking over troubled Compaq in 1999, Capellas tried repeated restructurings that failed to reverse market share declines and mounting losses. He says the merger will beef up Compaq's key services and high-end computer businesses.

"ANALYZING AND ARGUING"

5   The stage was set for a soap opera of historic proportions. It pitted HP's top brass against the children of beloved founders William Hewlett and David Packard, who are so revered that to this day their offices are left open and look as they did when the founders were alive—from the funky linoleum floors to the loose change atop Hewlett's desk. The face-off is sure to strain past and present allegiances: The Packard Foundation's board includes former HP CEO Lewis E. Platt, who backed the hiring of Fiorina. Richard A. Hackborn, a highly respected HP board member and a former HP exec of 33 years, also is a member of the Hewlett Foundation. Hackborn says if the deal doesn't go through, he'll resign. "The board has held many, many meetings analyzing and arguing about this deal. We think it's the best thing for the company. If the shareholders feel that's not the case, then I'm out of ideas." All told, these players will wage one of the biggest proxy fights in

corporate history—one that could turn especially nasty. One HP executive hints at a possible lawsuit against Hewlett for improper corporate governance. Hewlett's attorney defends his client's actions. "What Walter is doing here is the highest example of a fiduciary trying to live up to his duties," says Stephen C. Neal, a partner in the law firm of Cooley Godward LLP.

6   Much hangs in the balance. If the deal is scotched, HP could fall into a dangerous limbo as an incoming CEO tries to figure out a fresh strategy. Compaq's future would be even more precarious. By throwing in its lot with HP, Compaq has signaled that it can't go it alone. That's already damaging sales. In the most recent quarter, Compaq's revenues fell 33%, compared with an 18% drop for HP and a 10% falloff for rival Dell Computer Corp. Compaq insiders say they remain committed to the merger, though they planned to discuss a backup plan at a Dec. 13 board meeting. Compaq board member Thomas J. Perkins says that if it looks as if investors are going to turn down the merger, the boards should dump the deal before it gets to a vote. He thinks the feud is about who will run HP—Fiorina or the families. "This is really a struggle for the soul of Hewlett-Packard," says Perkins. "Compaq is a bit in the crossfire. We can only cheer from the sidelines."

7   Fiorina has no doubts about who is running HP and that a merger with Compaq is the best thing for the venerable computer maker. She says that these are just the early days in her campaign to show shareholders just how smart the deal really is. Persuasive detail will be in a proxy statement due out early next year. There is at least one more quarter of financial results from both companies that could improve the picture. And as regulatory approval is obtained, execs will be freer to share the data they have on product road maps, synergies, and cost-savings. "It ain't over till it's over," says Fiorina.

8   When all this is added up, it shows the potential for a tech titan with clout in nearly every major market, says Fiorina. Compaq's huge storage business would vault HP ahead of EMC Corp. in the fast-growth business. Compaq's robust Himalaya servers are popular with corporate customers who want super-reliable gear. The deal could double the size of HP's computer-repair business, churning out roughly $1 billion in annual profits. And the pair could take better advantage of the powerful Itanium microprocessor developed by HP and Intel Corp. On top of it all are huge cost efficiencies—some $2.5 billion a year by 2004. As for the pitfalls of the PC business? Fiorina says cost savings there can turn this, too, into a profitable business. Some analysts agree. "There's enormous opportunity for synergies," says CS First Boston analyst George D. Elling, who thinks HP's shares will be worth $40 if the companies execute as planned.

9   That's a big "if." This merger would be the biggest in high-tech history. Operations in 160 countries would have to be melded together, thousands of redundant products discontinued, and some 15,000 people laid off. Any missteps could result in losses from the massive $27 billion PC business that could undercut synergies in other areas such as servers, storage, and consulting services.

TOO MUCH CHANGE?

10   Clearly, HP, the granddaddy of Silicon Valley, will never be the same. Its congenial, egalitarian culture will career headlong into Compaq's confrontational one. And the increased reliance on commodity hardware will alter "Bill's and Dave's" legendary formula for success. For decades, HP prospered by building the most innovative products—ones that carried the juiciest margins. Only then could they run the company according to the HP Way, a set of corporate values codified in 1957 that give as much authority and

EXHIBIT 2
Merger Pros
and Cons

The Positives

Cost Savings

HP and Compaq expect the merger to save them $2.5 billion in operating costs by 2004, largely because of layoffs that insiders say range between 15,000 and 30,000.

Financial Bulk

HP–Compaq would have revenues of $87 billion, putting them neck and neck with IBM for the title of the largest tech company. They would have plentiful cash flow from businesses such as computer repair services, which are expected to generate $1 billion in profits a year.

Cross-Selling

The companies will be able to sell their hot products to the other's existing customers. For example, HP could sell its printers to Compaq's longtime customers and HP could hawk Compaq's storage gear to HP customers.

Technology

The companies' technologies complement each other in key areas. HP would be able to build better "always on" Internet systems with Compaq's super-reliable Himalaya servers and its clustering software, which enables many servers to operate as a single entity.

The Negatives

Execution Challenges

Tech megamergers typically run into big problems. And the HP–Compaq deal is by far the biggest high-tech merger, involving 150,000 people in 160 countries. Bringing it off without losing momentum is a long shot.

PCs

The deal would make HP the king of the PC business, with 18% of the market. Problem is, the business is troubled, with negligible operating margins and no revenue growth. If it is not run well, losses could mount—and siphon investment dollars from other, more profitable parts of the company.

Competitive Position

The new HP would be tops in PCs, back-office computing gear, and printers—but for how long? While HP will keep dominating printers, it will be surrounded by rivals better positioned in other areas, including Dell in PCs and IBM in services.

Morale

Compaq has struggled for years with layoffs and poor performance. HP was struggling to adapt to Fiorina's management changes even before the downturn. Now, the prospect of massive layoffs could send the mood at both companies further south.

job security to employees as possible. This deal instead casts HP as the No. 1 player in the commodity PC business, which means low margins and low job security. "HP has a long tradition of product development and a long tradition of innovating for the future," Hewlett told *BusinessWeek* on Nov. 6. "We shouldn't try to purchase the past."

11   If Hewlett plays a leading role in this drama, the central character is Fiorina—a charismatic CEO, whose irrepressible, can-do spirit could turn out to be her best asset as well as her biggest liability. Experts say her willingness to take radical steps was just the tonic HP needed when its growth stalled during the economic boom. Brought in 28 months ago, Fiorina quickly set out to transform HP into a Web services powerhouse, providing all the gear that corporations would need to do business on the Internet. She collapsed 83 units into six centralized divisions, wiping out fiefdoms and creating a more effective selling organization. She scrapped HP's cushy profit-sharing plan in favor of bonuses tied

to company performance. And she goosed innovation by creating an incentive program that has doubled the number of patents HP filed this year. That same gutsy style, however, has worked against HP during the past year when the company was juggling too many disruptive changes while trying to grapple with an economic slowdown. The result was missed financial targets and some market-share slippage. "If the economy hadn't gone bad, Carly might be a hero by now," says one recent HP departee. "In the real world, there was just no way all these changes could work out."

12 And that may wind up being the ultimate irony of this saga. When all the details are spelled out, the merger may make sense. But it has gotten so bollixed up in squabbles with HP heirs and the ferment over changes within HP, that shareholders may shy away because it would mean even more disruption. And what of Fiorina, a self-described "change CEO"? She could become as successful as the master of change, Jack Welch, former CEO of General Electric Co., or she could flame out like Jacques A. Nasser, a CEO who failed to get buy-in for his overhaul at Ford Motor Co. How HP wound up in this place serves as a cautionary tale for any executive trying to push through big makeovers without first building crucial support. "An outsider making change has a lot harder time than someone inside because they have no constituency," says Welch. The GE chairman says he doesn't know whether an HP–Compaq merger makes sense. But, he says, for a board member to vote one way and then reverse that stand is "unpardonable, it's a sin. It's corporate governance at its worst." He says this type of reversal wreaks havoc as employees who hate change think "they can get things back to the good old days."

13 Brand-new days were just what Fiorina had in mind last spring after she had revamped HP's organizational structure and was casting about for how to supercharge growth. In May, she hired consulting firm McKinsey & Co. to look at strategic options. These included a go-it-alone plan, one that would split the company up, and one in which HP would buy tech-services companies. Some of the options called for potential acquisitions. "Any name you throw at me, we've looked at them," says Fiorina.

DISCOMFORT

14 HP insiders say Compaq jumped to the fore on June 22. That's when Fiorina visited CEO Michael D. Capellas to see if he would license HP software but wound up talking about a merger instead. From the start, say insiders, HP execs and board members began hashing out the potential pitfalls of the merger. At one Thursday meeting in July, the McKinsey team gave board members a thick document outlining the synergies of the two companies. Hewlett, however, was not there. Instead, he was playing the cello in a concert at the Bohemian Grove north of San Francisco—an annual event he had appeared in for the past three years. Hewlett assumed HP would accommodate him, as it had in the past, and save important topics for the board's Friday session, says his attorney Neal. But HP's board plowed ahead, believing Hewlett wouldn't miss such an important session, says an HP insider.

15 In August, McKinsey went to the next step, laying out how HP might defy conventional wisdom and make a tech merger work. After studying a slew of deals, they reached this conclusion: Most of the botched tech mergers involved companies that were trying to buy their way into new businesses they knew little about. This deal, on the other hand, could be more like successful mergers in other industries where similar companies combined, such as Exxon and Mobil. "There was a tremendous amount of deliberation," says Larry W. Sonsini, a partner with law firm Wilson Sonsini Goodrich & Rosati, who worked for HP during the negotiations.

16   And there was action. Two HP board members with experience doing huge mergers—Boeing CEO Philip M. Condit and Sam Ginn, who ran AirTouch Communications when it was sold to Vodafone Group in 1999—helped devise detailed integration plans. These included who would run each of the combined company's businesses and naming an integration office to merge the companies. Other board members developed cost reduction goals for each business. And the compensation committees of both boards worked up bonus plans to persuade key execs to stay on after the merger—to the tune of $55 million, should all the execs accept.

17   One issue the board did not successfully resolve was Hewlett's discomfort with the deal. "Walter was very vocal in the board meetings," says an HP insider. In an interview on Nov. 6, Hewlett said he was concerned that the acquisition would further expose HP to the PC business, diluting the earnings of its printing business. And one friend with ties to the Hewlett foundation says that Walter Hewlett feared the merger, combined with Fiorina's already radical reinvention of HP, would leave little of his father's company intact. Hewlett's vocal opposition should have been a warning in itself, say friends and colleagues of Hewlett's. They describe him as deliberate, analytical, and slow to make waves. Intensely private, he prefers playing chamber music and duck hunting to playing boardroom politics. "Walter is not the type to try to grab control of a board or twist arms to force his opinion," says former Bell Atlantic Corp. President James Cullen, who serves on the Agilent Technologies Inc. board with Hewlett.

18   HP did make Hewlett comfortable enough to approve the deal. After an August board meeting, Hewlett pulled aside Sonsini, HP's attorney, for advice. In a 10-minute discussion, Sonsini told Hewlett he could vote with the board to OK the merger and later vote his own shares as he saw fit without breaking his fiduciary duty to shareholders, says an HP insider. Hewlett never warned HP that he might publicly oppose the deal or declare a proxy fight, says the HP insider. Neal says Hewlett didn't explicitly say he would go public, but "no one had reason to believe he would come out quietly."

19   In hindsight, it's clear HP's board should have gone the extra mile to make sure Hewlett's misgivings wouldn't mushroom into a public showdown. At the time, advisors to the HP board debated among themselves whether to ask Hewlett to sign a document pledging his support for the deal, say HP insiders. In the end, they decided not to use such pressure tactics. "We didn't want in any way to embarrass the family," says an HP insider. "Instead, we decided to treat him like all other shareholders," and leave him free to vote as he wanted.

20   When the deal was announced, Hewlett's fears of an investor revolt came true. After the Sept. 4 merger announcement, HP shares plunged from $23.21 to $17.70 on Sept. 6, as investors slashed the value of the deal from $25 billion to $19 billion. Still, HP's brass didn't think Hewlett would break rank. Indeed, analyst John B. Jones Jr. of Salomon Smith Barney, Compaq's banker on the deal, sent a voice mail to top shareholders on Nov. 5 assuring them that the HP family still supported the deal. HP's execs also believed that. HP board member Hackborn, who sits on the Hewlett foundation, told Fiorina the foundation's stock committee did not plan to decide how to vote until January. By then, HP execs felt they would have swayed investor sentiment in their favor.

LITTLE WARNING

21   Unbeknown to HP, Hewlett was making his move. On Sept. 23, he visited the law offices of Cooley Godward in Palo Alto to make plans. His first step was to ask the stock committee of his parent's foundation to do their own financial analysis of the merger. The

committee—which includes no family members, nor general board members such as Hackborn—gave the job to foundation Chief Investment Officer Laurance R. Hoagland. If Hoagland, a former director of Stanford University's $10 billion investment and real estate arm, decided the merger was in the foundation's best interest, Hewlett probably wouldn't vote the family trust's shares against it.

22   Hewlett, however, accelerated his timetable. Hoagland had planned to make his recommendation in January. With the stock languishing at around $16, Hewlett told Hoagland he couldn't wait. Hewlett wanted to know quickly whether Hoagland was going to oppose the deal—so he could do the same. His reasoning: If it's a bad deal, better to get it over with sooner rather than later. In early October, Hewlett hired San Francisco investment firm Friedman Fleischer & Lowe to do an analysis of the merger. When the foundation's stock committee agreed to meet on the subject on Nov. 6, Hewlett asked Friedman Fleischer to have their findings ready that day.

23   Hoagland and Friedman Fleischer came back with their conclusions that day: The deal would be bad for HP. Having already hired a press-relations firm to help get the word out, Hewlett called Fiorina to let her know what he was about to do. Just a half hour later, he issued the press release. Why did he give Fiorina so little warning? Insiders close to Hewlett say he was advised not to give her time to get out a press release and frame the issue to HP's benefit. The next morning, David Woodley Packard—who had resigned both from the HP board and the board of the David & Lucile Packard Foundation in recent years—announced he would vote his 1.3% stake against the deal as well. He felt the massive layoffs that would be brought on by the merger were counter to the HP Way.

24   Inside HP, the Hewlett and Packard offspring had quickly become a rallying point for the employees who had lost faith in Fiorina's management. In an Internet posting entitled "Walter Hewlett Is My New Hero," one HP-er wrote on Nov. 11 that "he has given me a new energy simply by making his announcement. I pray that he gathers enough support to nix this deal, and hopefully, Carly can be swept under the rug along with it. Thank you, Walter, for standing up for what your Dad and Dave had created." While HP surveys done before Nov. 6 showed that 84% of employees supported the acquisition, that fell to 55% after Hewlett's bombshell. HP Vice-President for Human Resources Susan Bowick concedes that morale statistics are now "lower than we've ever seen them. Employees were really with us until Walter did what he did, but he opened up a flurry of doubt."

25   HP's brass fumed. Fiorina and board members had been frustrated with Hewlett's habit of missing parts of board meetings. Now they were angered about his going public, and about what they say was an unfair position paper prepared by Friedman Fleischer. "It's a misleading advocacy piece," says one HP executive. "Walter and David Woodley are acting without integrity in every conceivable way." Early next year, they vow they will refute Friedman Fleischer's findings in detail when they file their proxy statement.

GREAT EXPECTATIONS

26   To win over investors, Fiorina will have to convince them that the deal makes strategic sense and that she can implement it in a company already wracked by turmoil. Brought in as HP's first outside CEO, she quickly launched sweeping reforms that touched every facet of the company. The only problem is, it's unclear whether HP is better off for the changes. Indeed, some of the market share gains made in Fiorina's first year have begun to recede. While HP continues to dominate the inkjet and laser printer business with 41% share, its PC share has fallen from 7.8% to 6.9% over the past 12 months. Sales of HP's Windows servers have dropped from 10.6% to 8.2% in the same period. And while HP's

EXHIBIT 3
Key Shareholders That Will Decide

Source: Bloomberg Financial Markets.

Whether Hewlett-Packard ends up combining with Compaq depends on whether HP's institutional shareholders support the deal. Here's a look at the top 15 institutional shareholders in HP and also how much Compaq stock they hold.

	HP Stock	Compaq Stock
	Percent of Shares Outstanding	
Capital Research and Management	3.55%	2.84%
Barclays Bank	3.10	3.65
Bank of America	2.84	0.22
State Street	2.33	2.04
State Farm Mutual Automobile Insurance	2.14	NM
Putnam Investment Management	1.74	4.82
Vanguard Group	1.54	1.53
Davis Selected Advisors	1.44	NM
Wellington Management	1.21	1.00
Citigroup	1.18	0.53
Taunus	1.15	1.02
AXA Financial	1.10	0.47
Jennison Associates	1.03	NM
Mellon Bank	1.01	1.11
Fidelity Management & Research	0.88	1.01
Total	26.24%	20.24%

NM = not meaningful

share of the critical high-end Unix server business vaulted to 28% in the most recent quarter, up from 23.3% the year before, that puts HP back to where it was in early 2000, according to IDC. Meanwhile, HP remains an also-ran with single-digit share in software, storage, and consulting, says Technology Business Research Inc. analyst Robert Sutherland.

27   Worse, Fiorina was brought in by HP's board to find new sources of earnings growth, yet HP is more dependent than ever on its last gold mine: printer supplies such as ink cartridges and photo paper. This $9 billion business churned out $658 million in operating profit in HP's fourth quarter ended Oct. 31—the third consecutive quarter that it subsidized losses at the rest of the company, says Sanford Bernstein & Co. Fiorina says segments such as Unix servers and computer-repair services are making money. Still, "they're hanging on to profitability by a thread," says Sutherland.

28   How did this happen after such a promising start? Current and former employees say many of the problems stem from an organization reeling from too many changes. Out went the old system in which 83 product chiefs had their own research and development budgets, sales staffs, and profit-and-loss responsibility. Instead, there would be three "front-end" sales forces, for consumer products, corporate products, and consulting. These would market and sell products made by three "back-end" groups—printers, computers, and tech services and consulting.

29   At the same time, she cranked up expectations. Fiorina promised 15% revenue and earnings growth in the year ended Oct. 31, 2000. She delivered: Sales jumped 15.4% and earnings rose 15.8%. Such progress ended when tech buying started to drop in the fall of 2000. That November, HP missed the signs and continued to spend freely, while telling Wall Street it would make its numbers. It was only after the quarter had closed that Fiorina realized it was too late to hit the brakes. The result: HP's earnings of $922 million were 25% below Wall Street expectations. Even then, she didn't take her foot off the gas.

She again pledged revenue growth of at least 15% for 2001, and days later told *Business-Week* that talk of a free fall in spending by telecom providers was untrue. "Telcos always say that this time of year," said Fiorina, a former Lucent Technologies Inc. exec who had spent 20 years selling to these accounts.

30   That earnings slip triggered a cascade of problems. For starters, it caused a 14% drop in HP's stock—which put an end to Fiorina's $18 billion bid to buy the consulting arm of PricewaterhouseCoopers. While panned at the time, the deal would have been far less onerous than the Compaq merger. What's more, the miscalculation forced management to take cost-cutting actions that were like stomach punches to HP's pampered troops. In December, HP asked workers to take five days of vacation, put off pay hikes for three months, and in January announced it would lay off 1,700 people.

ANGRY WORKERS

31   Things got worse. When management announced it would need to lay off 6,000 workers in July—less than a month after 80,000 employees had willingly taken pay cuts—the mood of many turned mean toward Fiorina. Management had tried to ward this off by sending out memos, saying layoffs were coming and that volunteering for pay cuts was no guarantee of continued employment. Still, many employees felt duped. And when a staffer shut down an internal message board after the Fiorina-bashing peaked, workers took it as a sign of insensitivity by their well-paid leader. "Either she has gotten remarkably bad advice, or she's actively trying to anger people," says one employee in HP Labs. A Fiorina backer, he thinks she should have taken a $1-a-year salary a la Apple Computer Inc.'s Steven P. Jobs and Cisco Systems Inc.'s John T. Chambers, rather than her $2.9 million in salary and bonus for the year. Throw in the merger layoffs and "it's getting to be like Chainsaw Carly," gripes an HP veteran.

32   Fiorina's reforms fueled employee confusion. Take the front-back reorganization. On paper, it makes sense. HP's customers no longer have to deal with scores of different salespeople—and those that do call can sell the full suite of products. In reality, though, the new structure is riddled with problems, say more than a dozen current and former employees. For starters, managers accustomed to running their own show now lack the power to deliver on their goals. With no authority to set sales forecasts, back-end managers may not be able to allocate the R&D funds to stay ahead. At the same time, front-end sales reps may have trouble meeting their forecast if their back-end colleagues gin up the wrong products.

JUMP-START?

33   These kinds of problems are a key reason investors worry about Fiorina's ability to execute such a megamerger. "It comes down to whether you believe management can pull it off or not," says Kevin M. Rendino, portfolio manager of the Mercury Basic Value Fund, which owns two-plus million HP shares. "If IBM CEO Lou Gerstner said he wanted to buy Compaq, I'd give him the benefit of the doubt. But what has she done to make me think she can pull this off? There's not a long enough track record—or enough accomplishments."

34   Fiorina's supporters argue that it's too soon to judge her results, which she always said would take three years or more to pay off. Even Gerstner took five years to transform IBM from a lumbering dinosaur into a limber powerhouse—and he didn't have to deal with the economic downturn of the past year. HP supporters point out that only a handful of major tech companies have remained profitable throughout the slump, including Microsoft, Intel, IBM, Oracle, and HP. "Before she became CEO, I was seriously thinking of shorting the stock," says Allison Kent, an HP manager in Richmond, Va. "But I think she knows exactly what needs to be done."

35   The game plan for winning big investors centers on Institutional Shareholder Services, which makes recommendations on proxy voting to many top HP shareholders such as Barclays. HP management will meet with ISS by the end of the year, and ISS is expected to provide an opinion shortly after the proxy is issued early next year. If ISS votes in favor, HP will then have to win over less than 50% of other shareholders. One wildcard that may play in their favor: Many institutions own both HP and Compaq shares and may vote for the deal on the assumption it would lift Compaq shares more than it would hurt HP's.

36   The essence of her message to investors is simple. She says the computer industry will commoditize and consolidate faster than people think. To stay ahead of that curve, HP needs to do a deal now that will give it enough bulk to take advantage of volume sales. She says the two companies buy $65 billion worth of materials a year. Execs figure that by combining they can save 1% of that, but she says the number could well be higher—say, 3% or 4%. Executives also believe they can make their PC business more efficient by moving closer to a Dell-like model of selling direct and doing away with the middleman. Compaq is closer to that model and can help HP make the leap. Says Compaq former chairman, Ben Rosen: "[The deal] will jump-start both companies in their race for efficiency."

37   That's assuming the deal happens. Much will be put to the test between now and the shareholder vote—a merger, a chief executive, and the fate of one of America's great companies. Massive change is always difficult, and executives either fall on their faces, like Nasser, or become heroes, like Welch. Which one Fiorina becomes will serve as a lesson for decades to come.

Source: Adapted by Richard Robinson, University of South Carolina, based on "Peter Burrows, "Carly's Last Stand?" *BusinessWeek,* December 24, 2001.

Case 7

BusinessWeek

Compaq: If the HP Merger Falls Through

1   For three months, Compaq Computer Corp. CEO Michael D. Capellas has been so gung ho about the $23 billion Hewlett-Packard Co. deal that he has been telling his top lieutenants there's no need for a fallback scheme. "Plan B is see Plan A," Capellas has said.

2   Now, it's time for a real Plan B. With opposition to the deal coming from members of the HP founders' families, Compaq is preparing for the bleak prospect of going it alone in an industry that has been ravaged by price wars, slowing growth, and consolidation. In a Dec. 7 memo, Capellas told employees that Compaq's "responsibility is to maintain a pragmatic view of our business and a clear focus on the future," no matter what happens with HP. At a board meeting on Dec. 13 in Houston, Compaq's directors were to discuss how to help sell investors on the deal and hash out plans should there be no deal. "Obviously at this juncture, Compaq has a Plan B," says Thomas J. Perkins, a Compaq director.

3   If the deal collapses, the future looks shaky for Compaq. Perkins says the company will remain independent. But going it alone after signaling to the market it needed a partner will be difficult. Compaq will have to focus on its best-performing businesses, like Windows servers and storage devices—and shed such poor performers as home PCs and high-end computers that are heavy on technology but light on market share.

4   Compaq's woes only deepened after the HP deal was announced on Labor Day. The distraction of the merger, coupled with the effect of September 11 and Typhoon Nari's impact on Compaq's supply chain, pushed third-quarter sales down 33% from the quarter a year ago, to $7.5 billion. Desktop computer sales fell 42%, and PC server revenue tanked 44%. For the period, Compaq lost $499 million, including a charge for losses from its investment in the Internet company CMGI. By contrast, Dell finished its third quarter ended Nov. 2 with a profit of $429 million on $7.5 billion in sales, which were off only 10%.

5   Time isn't on Compaq's side. Analysts have slashed next year's profit targets by 76%, to $271 million. And sales, expected to fall 23% this year, are pegged to drop 6% more next year, to $30.7 billion, which would be the lowest in five years, says Merrill Lynch & Co. analyst Steven M. Fortuna. The company is losing market share in key areas such as PCs, servers, and handheld computers, as rivals sow doubts about its future. If the merger with HP falls apart, UBS Warburg analyst Don M. Young says Compaq shares, already at an anemic $9.79, could tumble to $5, below its $6.63 book value. "The only company that really needs to do this deal is Compaq," says Young. "HP has options. Compaq has problems."

6   One solution may be for Capellas to drop some businesses. Analysts say that if the merger with HP fails, Compaq will have to exit the cutthroat consumer PC business, which accounts for one-third of its $17 billion in PC revenue. Already, Compaq is evaluating "any and all options," even taking products off retailers' shelves in favor of in-store kiosks and Web sales, says one executive in Compaq's PC business. Capellas declined requests to be interviewed.

UNDER ATTACK

7   Falling PC profits drove Compaq into the cushier server business in the early 1990s. Today, that business is under attack as well. While PC servers make up one of Compaq's strongest product lines, they have been steadily losing profitability. Late last year, Dell started a price war and by the first quarter was storming ahead in North America, the largest market, with a 32% share according to researcher IDC Corp. Only by slashing prices has Compaq been able to stay close to Dell with a 30% share. But it paid a price: Revenue fell 16% in the third quarter, to $1.4 billion, even as unit sales held steady. Dell has no plans to call a truce. Says CEO Michael S. Dell: "That's the last place we're going to lighten up."

8   Capellas can't count on pricey high-end computers to make up the sales shortfall. In the third quarter, IBM's share of total server revenues soared seven percentage points, to 30%, while Compaq's share fell nearly two points, to 14%, according to Gartner Dataquest. One reason for the gap is that IBM and Sun Microsystems Inc. are bringing out new high-end servers, while Compaq is phasing out its lineup in favor of new designs from Intel Corp. The new machines won't hit the market until 2004. The move holds promise for Compaq, which has conquered Intel-based server markets before. But if revenue continues to slide, Compaq will have to dump older product lines, analysts say.

9   Capellas will likely return to his ambitious plan to turn Compaq into a services company a la IBM. On its own, though, Compaq has little chance of getting there. It lacks IBM's software prowess, a key to selling the large integrated solutions, as well as consulting and outsourcing skills that generate big revenues and steady profits. Compaq has a $7 billion services business, but 56% of its revenue comes from maintenance and support, which only grows as fast as computer sales.

10   For now, the Compaq board is backing the HP merger. The recent tussling over the deal does not spring from a change of heart on Compaq's part. "It's a deep flaw within Hewlett-Packard," says Perkins. Still, Capellas had better start fleshing out Plan B.

Source: Adapted by Richard Robinson, University of South Carolina, based on Andrew Park, "Can Compaq Survive Solo?" *BusinessWeek*, December 24, 2001.

Case 8

BusinessWeek

Telecom Meltdown

Profits are vanishing. Companies are going belly-up. And this industry's troubles just might flatten the economy.

1   Last year, Sycamore Networks Inc. was white-hot, with a soaring stock price and booming sales as telecom players scooped up its cutting-edge communications equipment. But on Apr. 5, CEO Daniel Smith told Wall Street analysts that his largest customer, Williams Communications Group Inc., and other telephone companies were slashing their spending. Smith said the company's sales for the current quarter would be only $50 million to $60 million, about $100 million less than analysts expected. "This is shaping up to be a very difficult and disappointing quarter," he said. The next day, the company's stock plummeted 20%, to $7.25—a far cry from its 52-week high of $172.50. Worse, Sycamore's troubles will trickle throughout its hometown of Chelmsford, Mass., about 25 miles northwest of Boston. The company will lay off 140 of its 1,100 employees, cut back its spending, and delay construction on a new corporate campus in nearby Tyngsboro.

2   Sycamore is just one example of how the meltdown in the telecom industry is rippling through the economy. Just five years ago, the opportunities for telephone companies looked limitless as deregulation in the U.S. and Europe opened up markets to competition and demand exploded for new Internet and wireless services. Established players began spending wildly on networks that would carry voice and data, while upstarts emerged, offering high-speed lines at low prices. Now, what once looked like the land of promise is quickly turning into a wasteland, as profits vanish, revenues slump, stocks plummet, and companies begin going belly-up.

3   As it turns out, too many players were chasing too little business. Brutal price competition set in, hammering profits, particularly at long-distance companies in the U.S. European phone companies went so far into hock for new wireless licenses that they're now scrambling to sell off assets to pay for them. Seven American upstarts have filed for bankruptcy, and dozens more are expected. And the industry's debt looks like a ticking time bomb: Telecom players in the U.S. and Europe have nearly $700 billion of it, and some analysts estimate that more than $100 billion in junk bonds will end up in default or restructured. Ultimately, the telecom meltdown could be almost as costly as the $150 billion taxpayer bailout of the savings and loan industry in the late 1980s. "It has been really ugly, and it could get a lot worse," says Austan D. Goolsbee, an associate professor of economics at the University of Chicago.

4   The fallout will be felt far beyond the borders of telecom, potentially crippling the U.S. and European economies. The telecom industry plays such a big role in economic growth that its troubles could wind up toppling other industries like dominoes. Already, fears about the health of communications-equipment makers have grown so thick that bankruptcy rumors swirl around Lucent Technologies Inc. and Motorola Inc. Both companies deny them. And that's just the start. Nearly every technology sector is linked with telecom: Phone companies buy networking equipment to route Internet traffic, computer servers to offer Web hosting, software to dish up services, and fiber-optic gear to transport bits of information. Last year, spending on communications gear in the U.S. totaled $124 billion, or 12% of business spending on equipment and software, according to the Commerce Dept.

Moreover, it accounted for one-quarter of the rise in business spending. Now, after boosting their spending 25% per year since 1996, U.S. telecom companies are slashing it.

5   The size of the spending cuts will affect the severity and length of the economic downturn, perhaps even causing a recession. Late last year, many Wall Street analysts were projecting that capital expenditures by U.S. players would be flat to down 5% in 2001, which would have triggered a mild, short-lived setback. Now, with the bankruptcies of some and the financial troubles of others, telecom companies are paring back more than expected. Spending is likely to drop 10% to 15% this year and stay flat in 2002. There's even a chance that expenditures will plunge as much as 25% this year. "This is how you get recessions," says David Wyss, chief economist at Standard & Poor's.

DOMINO EFFECT?

6   Compounding the problems, the health of some financial institutions could be threatened as telecom companies continue to default on their loans. At best, the banks, insurance companies, and mutual funds that are owed that money will see their profits clipped in the months ahead. Bank One Corp. warned on Mar. 27 that its commercial loan losses would double, to $1.2 billion, in part because of its telecom exposure. At worst, widespread defaults could wipe out financial institutions with large exposure, much the way the oil industry's collapse in the 1980s battered money-center banks and crushed dozens of banks in Texas. In a Mar. 21 report, the Federal Deposit Insurance Corp. wrote that "cash-hungry telecom firms may have difficulty obtaining financing" and there could be "a serious risk for banks with a significant exposure to telecom startups." The Bank of England, Britain's central bank, has warned twice that the rising debt of telecom companies worldwide may cause instability in the financial markets.

7   To be sure, the telecom sector is just one part of the economic picture. If spending by other businesses and consumers remains strong, the economy may be able to avoid the two quarters of decline that define a recession. But if the rest of the economy is weakened by other factors, telecom's troubles could flatten it. Already, some parts of the economy look shaky. Other industries are cutting back on spending, too. And the consumers who have kept the U.S. economy chugging along may start shelling out a lot less because of rising layoffs and steep losses in the stock market. "With the stock market having dropped off, they're going to have to slow their spending," predicts Peter Hooper, chief U.S. economist at Deutsche Bank.

8   The sorry state of the industry will have a profound impact on the landscape of telecom for years to come. In Europe, British Telecom, France Télécom, Deutsche Telekom, and KPN went so far into debt for new wireless licenses that they may need to find merger partners to be able to afford the construction costs of the new networks. In the U.S., AT&T, WorldCom, and Sprint are so weakened that they may soon become takeover targets. At a Mar. 28 Morgan Stanley & Co. conference, WorldCom Inc. CEO Bernard J. Ebbers joked that the top execs from the Big Three long-distance companies and from local carriers Verizon, SBC, and BellSouth should meet in one room and figure out who should merge with whom. "Let them pick partners," he said.

9   All this has regulators a bit queasy. With more consolidation among the giants and less capital available for newcomers, there will be far less competition in some segments of the industry. Business customers, for example, won't see as many companies pounding on their doors with offers of cheap local telephone service. Several experts worry that the Baby Bells, especially SBC Communications Inc. and Verizon Communications, could wind up controlling virtually all of the consumer market and the vast majority of the business mar-

ket. "God knows America is not getting the competition promised under the Telecom Act," says William Kennard, the former Federal Communications Commission chairman.

10 Telecom's troubles even threaten the spread of the Internet. Some upstart providers of broadband Net connections are so financially strapped that they can't expand as quickly as they had once hoped. Covad Communications Group, for one, is planning to deploy no more than 190,000 new high-speed Internet lines this year, compared with previous plans for 380,000. Without a mass audience tapped into the Net at broadband speeds, the entire food chain depending on the growth of the Web could be hurt. Content companies could backtrack, software developers flee, advertisers return to television, and individuals who may have been drawn to the Net with promises of TV-like experiences could leave disappointed and not return. "I am really concerned," says Alan Ramadan, chairman of Quokka Sports Inc., which provides online coverage of everything from mountain climbing to the Olympics. "Anything that slows down consumer adoption puts an industry in formation at risk."

SIMPLE MATH

11 Not all of telecom, however, is on the ropes. The local phone companies—SBC, Verizon, BellSouth, and Qwest—have continued to turn in steady financial results, in part because they face relatively little competition in their core markets. At the same time, they've been able to capitalize on some of the fast-growing segments of the industry, such as data and wireless services. Verizon thinks the communications business is promising enough that it's boosting its capital spending to $18 billion this year from $17.6 billion in 2000. "We're going through a period where the fittest and the best-financed will do well," says co-CEO Ivan Seidenberg.

12 To understand how telecom got into this jam, turn back the clock to 1996. The U.S. passed the landmark Telecom Reform Act that year to deregulate the industry. And European countries, led by Britain, were opening up their markets to competition. The stakes were huge. Telecom revenues on both continents totaled nearly $300 billion, and the markets were growing about 10% each year.

13 The model for how to make a fortune in the new world of telecom was set by one oft-forgotten telephone company: MFS Communications Co. Led by James Q. Crowe, MFS laid telephone lines around major cities that would allow long-distance companies to bypass the Baby Bells. By the time the Reform Act passed in 1996, MFS had networks in most of the big cities in the U.S., and WorldCom agreed to buy the company for a staggering $14 billion, only slightly less than what SBC had paid for Baby Bell Pacific Telesis Group earlier that year. What WorldCom was paying for was not an operating business but strategic assets that would save it hundreds of millions of dollars it otherwise would have paid the Bells to deliver calls. The figure that stuck out for every would-be telecom entrepreneur was that WorldCom paid more than six times the value of the assets MFS had put in the ground.

14 The math was simple. You didn't need to build a business. You just needed to raise money, put telephone lines in the ground, and you could make a bundle. Some giant would pay you a multiple of every dollar you invested. The MFS model seemed to work for the next couple of years. In 1997, WorldCom bought another competitive upstart called Brooks Fiber for about $7 billion, or nine times the company's assets in the ground—the property, plant, and equipment.

15 When Net mania hit in the late 1990s and data traffic started doubling every few months, the telecom buildout became a free-for-all. Companies such as XO Communications and Focal Communications sprang up to build local telephone networks throughout the U.S.

RSL Communications and Viatel Inc. started building telecom systems in Europe. Global Crossing, Flag Telecom, and others started stringing fiber-optic cables through the world's oceans to carry the booming data and voice traffic. At the same time, megacarriers were investing heavily: WorldCom, for example, was building its own metropolitan phone networks from Stockholm to Madrid. All told, telecom players worldwide have raised $650 billion in debt and equity since 1996, according to Thomson Financial Securities Data.

16   In their rush, many execs built less-than-steady foundations for their companies. Rather than sell stock, they found the quickest way to get capital was to issue junk bonds. "It was high-yield heroin," says Royce J. Holland, former president of MFS and now CEO of Allegiance Telecom Inc., which provides voice and data services to businesses. "You didn't need to do a road show with investors. You just had a conference call and you could get a few hundred million bucks." While having debt equal to a company's equity value is reasonably healthy, telecom upstarts took on debt that was 5, 10, or even 20 times their equity. They figured the more they could invest, the higher the price a giant would pay for their company.

17   Last year, the signs of trouble began. With so many networks being built on both sides of the Atlantic, prices started to tumble. Howard Jonas, CEO of international phone company IDT Corp., estimates that an STM-1—a phone line that can carry 576 conversations at once—between the U.S. and Britain costs $1.8 million today, down 85% from $12 million in 1999. "Prices have gone through the floor," says Jonas. Why? The economics of telecom are very similar to those for the railroad industry: Once you sink the money into the ground, it costs almost nothing to provide the service. "If there's a glut, it's going to be brutal," says the University of Chicago's Goolsbee.

18   Telecom just didn't turn out to be the fast-growth business executives had banked on. The number of bits transmitted and the number of minutes on the phone are rising rapidly, but severe price drops have meant overall revenue growth is modest. As U.S. telecom players boosted their capital spending by some 25%, their revenue growth was stuck at about 10%. That squashed profits. The return on equity dropped from 13.8% in 1996 to 5.9% last year, according to Lehman Bros Inc.

19   Company after company has missed its financial targets, stocks have plunged, and burned investors have slammed the capital markets shut. U.S. telecom players that pulled in an average of $2 billion a month in initial public offerings over the past two years raised a measly $76 million in IPOs in March. On Mar. 15, the highly leveraged wireless service provider Nextel Communications Inc. had to yank the IPO of its international arm. France Télécom had such a disappointing stock offering for its Orange wireless unit in February that it raised half of the $13 billion it had expected.

20   The troubles in telecom are being felt on both sides of the Atlantic. Wireless giant Motorola is cutting 22,000 jobs, and Sweden's phone maker Ericsson says it may lose as much as $500 million in the current quarter. Telecom-equipment makers Cisco Systems, Nortel Networks, and JDS Uniphase have missed their financial projections and started laying off workers. On Mar. 19, Solectron Corp. CEO Koichi Nishimura said the contract manufacturer of telecom gear had seen a "phenomenal downturn" in demand. He said revenues for the current quarter would fall sharply and that Solectron would cut 8,200 jobs, or 10% of its workforce.

21   It won't get better anytime soon. The closing of the capital markets has left dozens of half-built upstarts gasping for cash. They have huge debt loads, they can't get new financing, there's nobody to buy them out, and their businesses are generating less money than expected because of brutal price wars. Bear Stearns & Co. analyst James H. Henry predicts that half of the 50 publicly held upstarts will disappear through bankruptcy or merger over the next few years.

WEAKLINGS

22   Two dozen bankruptcies in an industry once safe enough for widows and orphans is no longer unthinkable. For example, PSINet Inc., one of the leading providers of Internet backbone services, has $3.4 billion in debt, annual interest expenses of more than $300 million, and a business that doesn't generate any cash. On Apr. 3, the company conceded it will probably have to file for bankruptcy protection. And remember Alex Mandl, the onetime heir apparent at AT&T? In 1997, he left AT&T to become CEO of Teligent Inc., which planned to provide local telecom services using innovative wireless technology. With revenues growing more slowly than expected and financing drying up, Teligent could end up in bankruptcy court. It has $1 billion in debt, more than $100 million in annual interest expense, and widening losses from operations. In its latest Securities & Exchange Commission filing, Teligent's auditors said the company may not be able to survive. Michael Kraft, senior vice-president at the company, says Teligent has cash to last through June and is trying to raise more.

23   The telecom giants aren't in such dire straits, but yesterday's powerhouses are weaklings today. Many experts think AT&T, WorldCom, or Sprint could be acquired in the next two years. "The only thing standing in the way are the regulators," says one telecom exec. That barrier may not last long: FCC Chairman Michael K. Powell has said he favors less government interference in markets.

24   Europe's goliaths could fall, too. Shareholders are clamoring for the resignations of the heads of the three biggest carriers—British Telecom, France Télécom, and Deutsche Telekom. BT is the most likely takeover candidate among the major players. With intense competition in its domestic market and heavy debt from wireless auctions, BT's market cap has dropped by more than 60% since the beginning of 2000, to about $50 billion. Its credit rating has been cut. And the British government is less likely to stand in the way of an acquisition by a foreign buyer than, say, the French government.

25   For the next year or two, bankruptcies and mergers will sweep the industry. The assets of bankrupt companies will be sold off for as little as 25 cents on the dollar to the few remaining strong players, including Verizon and SBC. Capital spending will fall, hurting the other tech companies that have grown dependent on steady increases in expenditures. The financial institutions holding telecom debt could face a crisis. And the economy could slip into its first telecom-driven recession.

26   Relief could come in 2002 or 2003, when the industry has a shot at becoming a profitable, growing business for the remaining players. "We're weeding out the weak," says Rick Ellenberger, chief executive of Broadwing Inc., which provides local phone service in Cincinnati and data services nationwide. "At the end of the day, this can be a good business." The end of the dark days of telecom, however, are still a long way off.

COMMENTARY: 8 LESSONS FROM THE TELECOM MESS

Deregulation simply isn't working. Here's a *BusinessWeek* plan to get the $700 billion industry back on track.

27   Celebrations broke out on Feb. 8, 1996, as the U.S. telecommunications markets were thrown open to competition. A mogul-studded audience in the grand rotunda of the Library of Congress watched a Webcast of comedian Lily Tomlin and local schoolchildren eager to have broadband Internet services. President Bill Clinton signed the Telecommunications Act of 1996 into law using the very pen President Dwight D. Eisenhower used in 1957 to authorize the interstate highways. "We will help to create an open marketplace where competition and innovation can move quick as light," Clinton vowed. Some public officials, however, suspected the plan was a mess. Shortly after the ceremony, one senator who backed the legislation took Federal Communications Commission Chairman Reed Hundt aside. "We gave one side everything they wanted, and then we gave the other side everything they wanted," the senator said, according to Hundt. "Good luck."

28   Five years later, the telecom industry is a mess. For the first time, industrywide revenues are contracting. Profits are disappearing as prices for service plummet. On July 26, JDS Uniphase Corp., which makes optical components for the telecom sector, reported a loss of $50.6 billion for its fiscal year, the largest loss ever reported. Such horrific news has investors fleeing the scene. At least a dozen upstarts, from PSINet Inc. to 360networks Inc., have filed for bankruptcy protection. Cash-starved companies have laid off 170,000 workers since January, more than any other sector of the economy, according to Challenger, Gray & Christmas and company announcements. And market forces are ripping apart industry giants AT&T, WorldCom, and Lucent Technologies. "Never before have you seen this kind of bust in telecom," says James Glen, a telecom economist with market researcher Economy.com.

29   And consumers? They're still waiting for the competition Clinton promised. The local telecom markets remain almost complete monopolies, with Baby Bell rivals controlling just 8.5% of all phone lines. That's one-third of the 25% AT&T's competitors had swiped in the long-distance business five years after the breakup of Ma Bell in 1984. New York has the most competition, with upstarts handling 20% of the local phone business, but most of the customers who have benefited are corporations, not residential customers. Broadband is still a distant dream for most Americans: Less than 5% of U.S. households have any type of speedy Internet hookup. Says Larry Irving, who was Clinton's top communications adviser: The state of the telecom industry is "the worst of all possible worlds."

Major Overhaul

30   As bad as it is, though, there is a way out. After the maelstrom of the past year, it's possible to pick through the wreckage and find crucial lessons about what went wrong—and what went right. After identifying the do's and the don'ts, we picked the brains of more than three dozen industry executives, telecom economists, and Washington policymakers. With all this in hand, *BusinessWeek* has come up with eight lessons and a series of steps that have the potential to not only stabilize the telecom industry but get it growing again. They also could help consumers get broadband Internet connections more quickly, more innovative wireless services, and better local phone service.

31   But brace yourself: This blueprint isn't about tweaking an industry. It's about making wrenching changes. Much of the overhaul will come from state and federal regulators, who must remain deeply involved in the industry even though the Telecom Act was touted as "deregulation." The key is to establish rules and regulations that will spur capital investment and spark innovation. In the local residential phone markets, for example, state regulators should slash subsidies and let the Bells raise prices for basic service so that competitors will have an incentive to battle for customers. In rural areas, the government should subsidize the rollout of broadband Net connections to make it profitable for the Bells, cable companies, and others to invest in more expansive networks. And in wireless, Washington should make more spectrum available to companies such as Verizon Wireless Inc. that are ready to invest billions to deliver new services.

32   The suggested steps are sure to spark controversy. For instance, 50 million consumers would have to let go of cherished telephone subsidies that have been in place for about

60 years. Politicians would have to raise phone rates for half of their constituents. And the laissez-faire Bush Administration would have to take an active role in a nationwide rollout of broadband service. Any chance of the entire plan being enacted? Probably not. But this blueprint for reform could make a big difference even if just a few steps are taken.

Crucial Link

33   Why go through such a major revamp? There's a lot riding on telecom's recovery. At $700 billion in annual revenues, the U.S. industry is so big that the economy's fortunes often rise and fall with its health. When telecom players boosted their capital spending by 25% per year from 1996 to 2000, to $124 billion, that helped drive torrid economic growth. What's more, telecom is a crucial link in the technology food chain: Not only do telecom companies purchase enormous amounts of high-tech products and services themselves, but their networks provide the foundation for entirely new industries, including Web hosting and online video. "Telecom is critical to getting the tech sector moving again, and telecom is critical for the U.S. economy as a whole," says William Taylor, senior vice-president at National Economic Research Associates, an economics think tank in Cambridge, Mass.

34   Even if all these steps are taken, it's unlikely that telecom growth will return to the scorching levels of the past few years. But the current contraction, in which capital spending is expected to fall 15% or more this year, need not last indefinitely. With the right incentives, telecom companies would begin to pour money back into the local residential market, broadband services, and wireless services. Telecom capital expenditures would rebound to low double-digit growth as soon as 2003, analysts say. That would add up to a rise in capital spending of at least $10 billion a year—hardly pocket change for the ailing communications-equipment makers.

35   If this plan were to be adopted, the telecom industry would look very different than it does today. The country would have cutting-edge communications services, but the companies providing them would not be the ones that were expected. The upstarts that were supposed to wrest power from the Bells would play only a minor role. The local phone giants would dominate the industry along with the cable operators. And the long-distance carriers with the big brand names—AT&T, Sprint Corp., and WorldCom Inc.—would probably be acquired, most likely by the Bells. It wouldn't be a dream world. However, it would be better than what we have today.

36   Here are the lessons from the telecom meltdown and the steps necessary to get the industry back on track.

37   1. **Unless big changes are made, most consumers will not see the benefits of competition in local phone service.** Five years after the Telecom Act was signed into law, the biggest disappointment is that most consumers still have only one option for local phone service. According to the FCC, the Bells still control 96% of the local residential phone lines. The reason is simple: The economics of the business as it's currently structured can't support competition. For starters, residential local phone service is less profitable than business service because it costs more to wire individual homes than it does to wire tightly clustered office buildings.

38   The real culprit is a 60-year-old subsidy system that's increasingly outdated. In the 1940s, AT&T agreed to provide cheap local phone service throughout the country to boost phone penetration, then at 40% of U.S. homes. To subsidize this "universal service," AT&T charged extra for long-distance, business lines, and other features. The pricing system has changed little since. About 70% of local residential phone lines are still subsidized, to the tune of $3 to $15 a month.

39   Since only incumbents typically can get the subsidies, competitive phone companies chase fat margins in the business market and largely ignore consumers. In New York, for example, basic residential local phone service is priced as low as $6.11 a month while a business next door pays $15.74 for the same service. The companies that have tried to move into the consumer market, including AT&T and WorldCom Inc., have found out that it's next to impossible to make money taking on Bells that often charge consumers less than their own cost. "One of the dirty little secrets in America is that most people pay less for local phone service than it costs to provide," says William E. Kennard, the former FCC chairman and now a managing director at Carlyle Group, a private equity investment firm in Washington, D.C. "You can't have a robustly competitive marketplace unless you have a rational pricing structure."

40   The solution is to remove most of the subsidies and let local phone companies raise their rates for basic phone service. Subsidies could be kept for the 10 million homes in high-cost regions, the 7 million people considered low-income by state governments, and a few other customers. All told, that's less than 20% of the U.S. population. Limiting subsidies to 20% of consumers, would cut the total subsidy amount in half or more from the current $25 billion to $30 billion a year.

Temporary Pain

41   Yes, that means higher rates for half the country's population. No doubt, consumers and politicians would scream bloody murder. But experience suggests that the rate hikes would be modest and that the higher prices would attract a flock of entrepreneurs with capital to invest. In a few years, consumers would have more choice and their telephone bills would be driven back down to the levels that existed during the subsidy days. What's more, consumers should get more for their money in the way of innovative new services and features. "Regulators are caught in this paradox: They want competition, but they don't want to raise the cost of basic telephone service," says Terry Barnich, the ex-chairman of the Illinois Commerce Commission and president of telecom consultant New Paradigm Resources Group. "You have to bite the bullet." National Economics Research Associates estimates that boosting below-cost local phone rates by 10% could lead to competitive phone companies taking 9% to 13% of the market.

42   The prime example is Massachusetts. State regulators have gradually raised the price that Verizon Communications charges for basic residential local phone service from $8 a month in 1990 to $21 a month today. It's now about $2 above the cost of providing the service. That has helped lure 161 competitors into the market, double the number two years ago. The residential market is one of the most competitive in the country, with rivals like AT&T and RCN Corp. grabbing 20% of the market, five times the national average.

43   Now Massachusetts residents are seeing real benefits from the competition. Their average local phone bill is about $32, on par with the rest of the country and the same as it was in 1990. Better yet, customers are getting a lot more for their money—including more local toll calls, goodies like caller ID and voice mail, and in about 20% of the homes, second phone lines. Here's how the math works: While the price of basic service has increased threefold, competition has helped push the price of local toll calls and other services such as caller ID down by as much as 75%. "By improving profit margins, more capital is committed to local phone competition," says Paul B. Vasington, a commissioner at Massachusetts' Telecom & Energy Dept.

44   **What to Do:** Eliminate subsidies for all but the truly needy, and let the Bells raise basic phone rates. That will encourage competitors to enter the market, bringing prices back down while improving phone service.

45   2. **The Bells are more effective at stomping out local competition than anyone expected.** The economics of the local residential communications market are inhospitable to newcomers, and the Bells have done everything in their power to make it worse. Because upstarts frequently use parts of the Bells' networks, they're dependent on the local phone giants to help provide the service they've sold to their customers. Any delay or quality problems by the Bells reflects badly on their rivals. AT&T alleges that 4% to 6% of its new customers in California lose service each month because of Pacific Bell errors. Internet service providers contend that Bells have cut off service to their customers and then tried to win the customers for themselves. "Folks really didn't understand how well-armed the Bells were for a long fight," says Clinton adviser Irving, who is a board member at DSL provider Covad Communications Group. The Bells deny they have engaged in anticompetitive behavior.

46   What few people outside telecom realize is how helpless regulators are against the Bells. Many state regulators don't have the authority to fine local phone companies. Even those states that can impose financial penalties often have very low limits on fines. For example, Maryland can fine Verizon just $10,000 for each incident of wrongdoing. "Our penalty is a joke," says Joan F. Stern, a state delegate. States need to give their regulators the means to impose substantial fines on the Bells or they will not change their ways. "We don't need the Wild West, we need the sheriff to come to town," says Robert C. Taylor Jr., CEO of the Chicago-based upstart Focal Communications Corp.

47   A handful of states are leading the charge. New York can penalize Verizon up to $270 million a year for anticompetitive behavior. In Illinois, Republican Governor George Ryan just signed legislation that raises fines for anticompetitive behavior to as much as $250,000 per offense. Since companies often are charged with multiple offenses, the penalties could reach several million dollars. Other states, such as Maryland, are looking at the legislation as a model for their own enforcement efforts.

48   If tougher financial penalties don't do the job, regulators may have to turn to a more radical alternative. They could push to split the Bells into separate retail and wholesale operations, something known as "structural separation." The retail company would retain the Bell's customers. The other would sell network access on a fair basis to all rivals. Not only would the network company be an impartial wholesaler, but it would have a huge incentive to upgrade its network with new technology so that it could accommodate more traffic. Stern plans to introduce legislation for the structural separation of Verizon in Maryland next year. "I think it's the quickest and most effective way to bring about competition," she says.

49   Structural separation has been a political nonstarter so far. Verizon defeated Pennsylvania regulators' efforts to split the company and forced Stern to delay her effort in Maryland for a year. "It would cost a lot of money to break these companies apart and build the new systems necessary for these companies to operate," says Thomas J. Tauke, senior vice-president for public policy at Verizon. "We estimate that just in Pennsylvania it would cost us $1 billion to have structural separation." AT&T and other rivals argue such costs are overblown, though they admit it could cost $100 million or more.

50   Despite the cost, the proposal may be necessary to spur competition, and it may become politically feasible in the next two or three years. If the Bells grow larger through acquisition, and if local competition fails to materialize, public sentiment may favor a breakup of the Bells. "Any time one company wears two hats—supplier and competitor—you don't have a clean relationship," says Dan Moffat, CEO of upstart New Edge Networks. "That's basically an untenable situation."

51 **What to Do:** Give regulators the tools they need to force the Bells to open their markets to competition.

52   3. **The rollout of broadband net connections is going to be slow, costly, and incomplete.** As things stand, many Americans will never have the chance to get broadband Internet service because certain regions of the country are too expensive to wire up. Some 20% to 25% of the population lives in areas that are too difficult to reach for most providers. Why should we care? Because widespread availability of speedy Net connections is good for the economy. Letting people work or shop from home boosts productivity. Consulting firm Eastern Management Group estimates that broadband could add 3.7 billion work-hours to the economy each year as people commute less and drive less to stores. "Like basic phone service, the gains to the U.S. economy are going to be huge," says Taylor of National Economic Research Associates.

53   The country should improve consumer broadband deployment by creating a fund for network construction in low-profit-margin areas. It could use some of the $10 billion to $15 billion saved by reducing local phone subsidies. If it collected $2 a month from each phone customer, it would have $2.5 billion a year for the fund. That should be plenty to fill out the network in the least profitable areas. Instead of giving all the money to the Bells, let local phone, cable, and satellite companies compete for the subsidies. After determining which regions require subsidies, the government should hold auctions, allowing companies to bid on how little cash they would need to provide service for a defined period of time.

54   Government-led broadband deployments are working elsewhere. South Korea spent $7.5 billion over five years laying the infrastructure for broadband. Now 42% of consumers have DSL service, adding about 1% to economic growth, say government officials. The U.S. government played a crucial role in the deployment of basic local phone service. It will have to play a role in the deployment of broadband, too.

55 **What to Do:** Take the money saved by eliminating residential phone subsidies to pay for a broadband rollout.

56   4. **The wireless industry is being handicapped by the shortage of spectrum.** What are U.S. wireless companies to do? They can't get their hands on the radio spectrum they need to deploy new voice and Internet services. Earlier this year, Verizon Wireless and others agreed to pay the FCC $17 billion for new spectrum only to find out in June that the commission didn't have the authority to auction it off. "There is a serious spectrum shortage," says Thomas E. Wheeler, CEO of the Cellular Telecommunications Industry Assn., an industry trade group. "We're at a competitive disadvantage compared with the rest of the world."

57   This is poor public policy. The solution? Politicians need to take spectrum away from some of the most politically connected interests in Washington. Start with the Defense Dept. It holds about 170 megahertz of radio spectrum, about seven times the amount of the average wireless company, and uses less than half of that, according to a wireless executive. Linton Wells II, acting Assistant Defense Secretary, testified before Congress in July that the department needs much of the spectrum to protect the country. "There can be no economic prosperity without national security," he said. But he left the door open to compromise by suggesting the department would give up spectrum if it could move its security operations to other radio bands.

58   Television broadcasters pulled off the biggest boondoggle. After receiving their original spectrum for free, they got Congress to give them a second slice of spectrum, also for nothing, to roll out high-definition television. Now they can hoard the original and new spectrum for pretty much as long as they want, even though they won't need both in the long haul. Kennard railed against this giveaway, but Congress never had the stomach to take on the companies that give them free airtime during elections. The National Association of Broadcasters says it needs extra time because of the slow adoption of HDTV.

59   Without spectrum, the wireless players are left sitting on their hands. They may not have enough capacity to offer voice service to all their potential customers. They certainly will be hamstrung in rolling out wireless Internet services. The one sector of the telecom industry that is willing to aggressively invest in new services is being stopped by misguided public policy.

60   **What to Do:** Slaughter the sacred cows. Take spectrum away from the Defense Dept., television broadcasters, and the satellite industry.

61   5. **Given the change, telecoms will litigate endlessly.** The country got a taste of what the Telecom Act was really about the day Clinton signed it into law, on Feb. 8, 1996. Several hours after the ceremony, the three big long-distance carriers filed a lawsuit against Ameritech Corp., now a part of SBC Communications Inc., arguing that the company was erecting roadblocks to keep rivals out of the local market. The litigation hasn't stopped since. The Bells have opposed matters of pricing, network interconnection, and even the fundamental rules of the Telecom Act itself. The effect of the endless litigation? Uncertainty and delay.

62   Here's how to get the process moving. For minor disputes, there should be a more effective arbitration process. Currently, the FCC is supposed to mediate disputes between the Bells and their rivals that involve federal issues—typically anything involving products or services that cross state borders. But the commission's enforcement bureau is understaffed, so it hasn't been able to arbitrate many issues. Some end up in court. Royce Holland, chairman and CEO of Allegiance Telecom Inc., has testified before Congress that the FCC should have 25 arbitration specialists who can resolve issues before they end up in litigation. "Rather than having a court try something that is very technical, you have experts in the field make those decisions," he says.

63   For weightier legal issues, a single federal court should be designated to oversee disputes. Take the breakup of AT&T in 1984 as a model. Judge Harold Greene of the U.S. District Court in Washington, D.C., handled the breakup and any appeals. That allowed consistent and speedy decision making. "Greene had extraordinary power, and everyone knew they couldn't get around him by finding a judge who knew nothing about the case," says former FCC Chief of Staff Blair Levin, now an analyst at Legg Mason Inc. A similar approach now would put a stop to the endless legal disputes and give the industry a dependable legal framework within which competition could flourish.

64   **What to Do:** Streamline decision making by regulators and courts, eliminating delays that have thwarted the Telecom Act.

65   6. **Telecom regulators are reviewing mergers using old-fashioned criteria.** Antitrust regulators evaluate proposed mergers and acquisitions with outdated measures. For example, when WorldCom launched its ill-fated attempt to buy Sprint, regulators were alarmed that the deal would put 80% of the long-distance market in the hands of two rivals, AT&T and WorldCom-Sprint. The merger was rejected. But the decision was made just as the long-distance market was starting to collapse. If WorldCom and Sprint Corp. had been allowed to combine, they might have been able to cut costs fast enough to keep pace with falling prices and revenue. Instead, they are likely to be acquired by other com-

panies during the next year or two, removing once-powerful rivals from the market. The decision ignored the fact that AT&T's biggest competitive threat in the long-distance market no longer came from WorldCom and Sprint. Rather, it came from Verizon, SBC, and the wireless industry. "It was a big mistake that the Justice Dept. shot down the WorldCom-Sprint merger," says telecom analyst Brian Adamik of Yankee Group. "Both companies are now struggling for survival."

66 What to do? Antitrust regulators should evaluate the proposed company's share of the total telecom market. For example, the combination of WorldCom and Sprint would have controlled only 22% of the U.S. telecom market. Already, AT&T and Verizon are both larger. Regulators could stop mergers that would result in 30% of the market in the hands of one company, such as the combinations of Verizon and SBC or Verizon and AT&T. But smaller competitors, such as WorldCom and Sprint or BellSouth and Sprint, should be able to merge to gain the scale to slug it out with the heavyweights.

67 **What to Do:** Regulators shouldn't worry about whether a merged company would dominate one niche, but instead consider its share of the total telecom market.

68 7. **Brand names and "one-stop shopping" are marketing myths.** The biggest mistake AT&T made was to assume that consumers would be confused by technology and that they would pay a premium for the services of a trusted company to guide them into the digital era. As it turns out, most people weren't as confused by technology as AT&T executives thought.

69 The lesson is that brands, even great ones such as AT&T, must constantly be reinvigorated by new products and services. Deutsche Telekom hit on the right strategy a few years ago in Germany. Faced with deadly competition in the residential phone market, DT slashed the price of phone service. Its margins fell apart, but it managed to hold on to its market share. Then it rolled out more lucrative services, such as high-speed ISDN. Now 19.3 million customers, or 38%, take ISDN service, one of the highest penetration rates in the world.

70 Most communications services, from long-distance to ISDN, eventually turn into commodities. That means companies must constantly develop unique products that can command higher prices. If telecom players fail to develop products at a sufficient pace, revenues across the board decline. The goal of deregulation is not so much to cut the average monthly telephone bill as it is to make sure that consumers and businesses get innovative new products. "Competition in Massachusetts has had a beneficial effect in terms of new services," says Vasington, the Massachusetts telecom commissioner. "The political structure always focuses on price above all else. That is entirely the wrong way to look at it."

71 The trouble these days is that telecom players tend to promise innovative services, then fail to deliver. Whatever happened to one single phone number for phone, office, and cell phones? What about single mailboxes for voice mail, e-mail, and faxes? If the industry wants to enjoy strong growth, it must stop trying to coast on the strength of its brands and start delivering services that are worthy of premium prices.

72 **What to Do:** If companies want to charge premium prices, they must develop premium products.

73 8. **Open internet standards really do encourage innovation and lower prices.** One way to speed the arrival of innovative products is for established telecom giants to give up their old proprietary technology. The local networks operated by the Bells and the other incumbents, which handle 91.5% of the nation's telecom traffic, tend to run on technology outdated by the Internet Age. Just try ordering a high-speed business data line from one of the Bells. That can take months, and a line that carries 45 megabits of traffic costs on average $6,400 a month—out of reach for most small and medium-size businesses. To make matters worse, customers can get a 45-megabit line or a 1.5-megabit line—and typically nothing in between.

74   Local phone networks would perform much better if they were redesigned using the open standards of the networking world. Consider the upstart Yipes Communications Inc. It sells lines that handle 45 megabits of traffic for $4,300 a month, and discounts can exceed 50%. The service can be scaled up or down to suit a customer's needs, from 1 megabit to 1 gigabit, in a matter of hours, not months. The key is that Yipes uses optical equipment based on ethernet, the networking standard of the data world. It's faster and cheaper to operate because it requires fewer pieces of equipment than the older, optical technologies used by the Bells. The local phone giants say they are installing billions in new technology each year, although a total shift to new optical technology is years away.

75   In the end, it really shouldn't be a surprise that telecom ended up in such a mess. The Telecom Act evolved from political compromise. As the senator admitted to Hunt, lawmakers avoided upsetting their contributors by giving everything to everybody. That may have worked well enough during the long era of telecom monopoly, but if the U.S. really expects to get the competitive market it was promised, it's going to have to make some tough decisions.

76   **What to Do:** Telecom-equipment makers and carriers must accelerate the deployment of new technologies based on Internet protocols and other open standards.

Source: Adapted by Richard Robinson, University of South Carolina, based on Peter Elstrom with Heather Timmons, "Telecom Meltdown," *BusinessWeek,* Asian Edition, April 23, 2001, and Steve Rosenbush and Peter Elstrom "8 Lessons from the Telecom Mess," *BusinessWeek,* August 13, 2001.

Case 9

Motorola

1   During the fall of 1999, Geoffrey Frost went to his boss, Motorola Inc. CEO Christopher B. Galvin, and recommended that he fire the advertising agency that was creating ads for its wireless phones. Frost, a marketing executive freshly recruited from Nike Inc., wanted one agency that could produce a killer campaign for the whole company, and he felt that McCann-Erickson Worldwide didn't have the creative juice. Galvin wasn't so sure. McCann was run by Galvin's close friend John Dooner, and Galvin wanted Frost to give McCann a chance to compete for the business. The agency put together a new campaign—and again failed to impress Motorola. Finally, last fall, Galvin agreed to dump McCann as the creative force behind Motorola's ads. Frost, though, had to deliver the bad news. "Chris has a huge sense of responsibility and commitment," says Frost of Galvin's hesitancy. "But McCann just didn't cut it."

2   Frost couldn't help but compare Galvin's actions with that of his former CEO, Nike's Philip H. Knight. At Nike, Frost had stalled for days before telling his boss that ad titan Weiden & Kennedy—run by a college buddy of Knight's—wasn't doing a good job. They needed to scale back the ad agency's contract. Finally, Frost gingerly broke the news. Knight's reaction? "What the f— took you so long!"

3   Since taking over at Motorola in January 1997, Chris Galvin has struggled mightily in the chief executive's seat. The biggest problems, analysts say, have been his Hamlet-like indecisiveness and his hands-off management style in a tech industry that increasingly demands speed and conviction. Galvin took years to put a crack executive in charge of his largest business, wireless phones. He sat by while execs let costs spin out of control and failed to deliver on promises to customers. He has allowed competitors to beat Motorola to market with everything from cell phones to the latest microprocessors. And when opportunities arose to sell or close poorly performing businesses, Galvin has moved methodically, losing money and dampening employee morale at the same time. "From 1997 until now, he has made every wrong bet," says James E. Schrager, clinical professor of entrepreneurship and strategy at the University of Chicago Graduate School of Business. "His radar screen is so bad."

4   By all accounts, Galvin is smart, gentlemanly, and—well, a really nice guy. But his genteel ways have taken a heavy toll on the company that his grandfather founded 73 years ago. Under Galvin, 51, Motorola has lost its lead in wireless phones, slipping to a 13% share of the market vs. Nokia Corp.'s 35%. Although his semiconductor unit is a leading seller of chips to the auto industry, that's a slow-growth business. Galvin has not managed to steal the spotlight from Intel Corp. and Texas Instruments in chips for PCs and wireless equipment. And he lost credibility, to say nothing of millions of dollars, by holding on too long to the company's ill-fated satellite venture, Iridium LLC.

NO CONFIDENCE?

5   Motorola's spotty performance since 1997 has worsened in the past 12 months. Since last May, the $37.6 billion electronics conglomerate has lost 72% of its market value as the stock dropped from $60 to $16.75. On Apr. 10, the company reported a quarterly loss of $206 million on sales of $7.8 billion—its first loss from operations in 16 years. Come July 11, it is expected to report an even deeper loss of $269 million, according to First

EXHIBIT 1 Grading Galvin

In his four years as CEO, Galvin has found success elusive. Save for a few months in early 2000, when Motorola's stock soared amid a seeming turnaround, his reign has been characterized by more missteps than accomplishments. Here's an assessment of his performance:

Vision: B
Galvin is more philosopher than operations chief. He relishes studying technology and economic trends. He defined Motorola's current mission: to tailor the wireless Internet for the person, the work team, the home, and the car. And he is the chief proponent of Motorola's research into biotech, a budding industry that Galvin suggests could produce Motorola's next great innovation.

Management: C
Galvin has taken months to make key decisions. For example, he let the ill-fated Iridium satellite network proceed for almost a year after his lieutenants warned him it was troubled. He's also struggled to find the right corporate organization, with three restructurings in four years. After costs spun out of control, he decided to cut 26,000 jobs and sell businesses to rein in expenses.

Products: C
Motorola has repeatedly misread what buyers want. In 1999 and 2000, Galvin's troops insisted on making expensive phones when buyers wanted stylish, sub-$100 phones. Motorola's share of the mobile-phone market has dropped from 26% in 1996 to 13% today. Galvin and Motorola listen better now: Galvin spends more than 30% of his time visiting customers.

Innovation: C
Motorola has a strong legacy of innovation. It designed the first portable two-way radio, and was a pioneer in TVs and car radios. Yet Motorola hasn't had a breakthrough product since the StarTAC, the clamshell mobile phone introduced in 1996. His biggest innovation is an Internet phone that will transmit data as fast as standard PC modems.

Shareholders: D
Motorola's stockholders have fared badly. Since the beginning of 1997 when Galvin became CEO, shareholders have lost 16% of their money. Over the same period, the Standard & Poor's 500 rose 76%. Nokia and Qualcomm, leaders in wireless, have given stockholders returns of 544% and 1,100%, respectively. Since May 2000, Motorola's stock is off 72%, to $16.75.

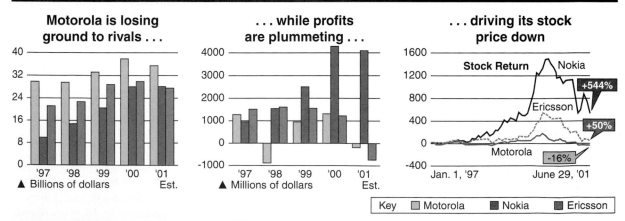

Motorola's Slide

Data: Bloomberg Financial Markets, , WIT Soundview Group © BW.

Call's consensus estimate of analysts. "Confidence in Galvin? I have none at all," says Jane A. Snorek, vice-president at Firstar Investment Research & Management Co., a Milwaukee investment house that owns shares in the company.

6   Certainly, Galvin is not to blame for all of Motorola's woes. Iridium was dreamed up in the 1980s and championed by his father, Robert Galvin. Motorola fell behind in the transition from analog mobile phones to digital phones under Galvin's predecessor, Gary Tooker. And now, Motorola's problems are exacerbated by a technology downturn that's slamming small fry and highflier alike—from Intel to Palm, from Nortel to Nokia. That's one reason Galvin's job is secure, says the company's board. "If Motorola were out there alone having trouble, that would be another issue," says Nicholas Negroponte, a board member and director of Massachusetts Institute of Technology's Media Laboratory. Many other companies "are having more trouble than we are. It would be a total mistake, in any way, to indicate that we don't have confidence in Chris."

7   Still, during Galvin's tenure, Motorola has underperformed its peers by a wide margin. Since the beginning of 1997, Motorola shareholders have lost 16% of their money, while the Standard & Poor's 500-stock index has increased 76%. Wireless rivals Nokia and Qualcomm Inc. have seen their stocks soar 544% and 1,100%, respectively. Even beleaguered Ericsson has recorded a respectable 50% return to shareholders. The only major telecom-equipment company with a track record worse than Motorola's since 1997? Lucent Technologies Inc., whose CEO, Richard A. McGinn, was booted out nine months ago.

8   Now, workers inside Motorola are questioning Galvin's leadership. Since his grandfather, Paul Galvin, founded Galvin Manufacturing in 1928, he is the third member of his family to head the company that has become Motorola. Under Paul Galvin and then Robert Galvin, Motorola developed a reputation for cutting-edge innovation by designing the first portable two-way FM radio and the first pagers. Robert Galvin's emphasis on product excellence helped Motorola win the famed Malcolm Baldrige Quality Award in 1988. But the latest Galvin chief, whose family now owns 2.5% of the company's stock, has been unable to lead Motorola to any sustainable glory.

9   Indeed, some current and former Motorola executives say Galvin should give up the CEO post and become a visionary chairman a la Ford Motor Co.'s William C. Ford Jr., great-grandson of Henry. Galvin is most inspired, and most inspiring, when he spins a vision of the future of technology. For example, he has been critical in focusing the company on the opportunities of the wireless Internet. That has made Motorola an early leader in telematics, technology that lets drivers surf the Net from their cars to find the nearest repair station or Starbucks. And he is the chief proponent of Motorola's research into biotech, a budding industry that Galvin says could produce the company's next great innovation. For instance, the company could use its wireless and chip technology to create a smart card with a person's genetic code to enable better health care. As chairman, Galvin could safeguard Motorola's values of integrity and share his passion and ideas for Motorola—while not being on the hot seat for preserving his family's legacy. "He's got the family fortune, his own reputation, plus the company's reputation to worry about," says Professor Schrager. "Phew, he's got too much on the table there."

TOO HANDS-OFF

10   Galvin is both introspective and resolute in the face of such criticism. While he acknowledges being too detached, he disagrees with the notion that he has been indecisive. He says few people understand the complexity of issues he must weigh as CEO of a global conglomerate. "When people bring high quality of thought on a proposal or an

investment and all the questions are answered, we make decisions in nanoseconds," he says. But if his managers don't have the answers, "I've had to send people back to sharpen their pencils," he says, and that takes time.

11   As for being too hands-off, he couldn't agree more and is on a mission to change that. He has spent his entire 28-year working career at Motorola and was brought up on his father's management style of delegating and trusting executives to execute smartly. He did what his father had done and focused on vision and strategy, only to find that some of his management team let him down. "I take full responsibility for what has occurred at Motorola," Galvin says. "But I get up every day saying, 'Don't focus on what happened yesterday. All you can do is take what you know today and put together a plan.'"

12   He vows not to give up the CEO post. "Been there. Done that," he says of his past tactics of handing off to others. "Why do you think we got into trouble? Until October of last year, I had created a chairman-like role for myself. Not any more. Today, in partnership with our new team, I'm running it. I will not move to a chairman-like role again until Motorola is performing preeminently."

13   He has an ambitious plan for restoring his grandfather's company to its former glory. Since January, he has dumped the nice-guy, hands-off approach that got him and Motorola into such hot water. He is delegating less and demanding more. The new Galvin meets weekly with the top execs from Motorola's main sectors—four times as often as in the past. They review the revenue flow over the phone for a couple of hours. Once a month, he holds a Customer Performance and Operations meeting, in which he stresses the importance of product quality and solid customer relations. And Galvin, who rarely used to work on weekends, now routinely calls managers on Saturday and Sunday mornings to discuss personnel moves or product reviews. "I began with a philosophy that we could create an environment where leaders felt empowered," Galvin explains. "Now, I'm not trusting in people so much."

14   All this is putting an end to his old 8 A.M. to 6 P.M. workday. Now he's in the office by 7 A.M. He wakes at 5 A.M. and rides his exercise bike for about 30 minutes while reading the morning papers and watching business news on TV. By 6:15, a Motorola security official picks Galvin up and drives him from his home in Winnetka, Ill., to the office. Galvin's workday begins in the backseat, where he makes calls to lieutenants in Europe and Asia or reviews memos and product research submitted by his reports.

GADGET GUY

15   At the office, Galvin starts off talking with Chief Operating Officer Robert Growney and other direct reports about the day's priorities. Afterward, he checks his list of appointments for the day: technology reviews, customer phone calls, scheduled meetings with employees in his office, calls to government officials and policymakers such as Michael Moskow, head of the Chicago Federal Reserve. Despite his impeccable attire for public appearances, most workdays Galvin is tieless, his shirt sleeves rolled up. He's a gadget guy, rarely without his black briefcase full of the latest Motorola phones, pagers, and radios. Comfortable with computers, Galvin wears a headset that allows him to send e-mail orally through voice-recognition software. Sometimes he'll send a "three-page" response, says marketing exec Frost. His weekly e-mail to staff used to focus on the balance between work and life. But starting this year, his messages are about the economy, its impact on the company, and how best to prioritize work to make it through rough times.

16   Is all this enough to retore Motorola's former luster? It will be a hard slog. Galvin's gentility and his tendency toward study instead of action are at odds with the hurly-burly,

EXHIBIT 2
Christopher Brian
Galvin's Résumé

Born
Mar. 21, 1950, in Chicago

Childhood
Acted like a grown-up even as a kid. While his three siblings hiked in the fields of their parents' farm, Galvin sold homemade butter door-to-door. When his brother and two sisters played in the snowfalls of their Skokie (Ill.) neighborhood, Galvin earned money by shoveling neighbors' driveways.

Education
Graduated from Cranwell, a Lenox (Mass.) prep school, in 1969. He was captain of his ski and lacrosse teams and senior-class president. He received a BA in political science from Northwestern University in 1973 and an MBA from Northwestern's J.L. Kellogg Graduate School of Management in 1977.

Career Highlights
Has spent his entire career at Motorola. Began as a college student, working summers selling two-way radios to police precincts in Chicago. In 1973, he joined Motorola's radio division. In 1984, he got a big boost—to general manager of U.S. operations for Tegal, a unit that made semiconductor components. He rose through the ranks to COO in 1993 and CEO in 1997.

Mentor
His father and former Motorola CEO, Robert. Chris has tried to emulate his dad's commitment to innovation and his management philosophy that lieutenants should run their own businesses.

Home Life
He usually leaves work by 6:30 P.M. to be with Cynthia, his wife of 22 years, and their teenage son. The couple has another son in college.

Hobbies
Fly-fishing with his sons and golf. Galvin, about a 12 handicapper, tries to squeeze in rounds at Pebble Beach when he's in Silicon Valley. Although his game needs work, he's intensely competitive, friends say. He gets anxious about short putts. "[He] hates losing the five bucks," says Scott McNealy, CEO of Sun Microsystems and an occasional golf mate.

combative world of technology. Insiders say the privilege of family ties has prevented him from taking the lumps most executives experience. "You need to experience failure to hone your success characteristics," says Frank Wapole, who was Galvin's boss in the two-way radio business and later a cellular executive before he retired. Insiders say what the company needs now is a hyperaggressive leader who can break down Motorola's bureaucratic ways and get innovation popping again. Even if Galvin retains the CEO title, he could hand off responsibility for day-to-day operations to a strong No. 2. Growney, the current chief operating officer, may retire soon because of health issues, say Motorola insiders. That would open the door for Galvin to promote someone else to COO—probably Edward D. Breen, a hard-charging exec who heads Motorola's broadband business.

17   No question, Motorola will need all the leadership it can muster in the coming year. In wireless network equipment, Ericsson has the lion's share of the market, with a 30% share, and will be tough to budge. And in the mobile-phone market, the company's market share has slid from 26% in 1996 to an estimated 13% this year, according to Bear

Stearns & Co. Galvin plans to stop the slide with a new batch of phones. One already selling in Europe can tap the Net at speeds as fast as today's computer modems, and several neon-colored phones will be introduced in the coming months, targeting the sub-$100 market where the company has been weak. "They do have products that are pretty cool," says Frank C. Boyer, a vice-president at Cingular Wireless. But "we are cautious. They need to execute on their plan better than they have in the past."

18   Galvin realized he needed to change his ways when Motorola missed the goal it had announced of selling 100 million mobile phones in 2000. Employees inside the cellular unit knew for months that they wouldn't make the target, but Merle Gilmore, head of the communications businesses, never let on to Galvin that there were problems—and Galvin never dug deep enough to find out. Once Galvin learned how bad it was, he fired Gilmore, a longtime friend, and vowed never to be blindsided again. "I saw a thickening of the skin," says Janiece Webb, a marketing exec in the mobile-phone division. He was "hurt, disillusioned, pissed, scared, and determined. He realized that his reputation and his father's company would come down on his watch." Gilmore declined to comment for this article.

19   The troubles began when Galvin started his CEO tenure by delegating responsibility to his top managers. Take the first few months of 1999, when Galvin sat in on meetings with the mobile-phone group. Back then, he rarely attended meetings held by the unit, and when he did visit the cramped 12-by-15-foot conference room in suburban Chicago, he usually listened without saying much.

20   Two and a half years ago, the group was working on a phone with the code name "Shark," a peanut-shaped design that was designed to steal share from market leader Nokia. Galvin's troops were trying to produce the new phone in three different technologies and target the all-important low end of the market—the fastest-growing segment. The version for Europe, rival Nokia's backyard, had to be exactly right. Galvin knew that Europeans preferred sleek, simple, cheap phones. Would consumers buy this curvy, 150-gram phone when competitors offered smaller ones at comparable prices? Those in the meeting remember Galvin turning to his marketing manager and asking: "Does the market data really support this?" Absolutely, the manager replied. Galvin didn't delve any deeper into the matter, letting his managers launch the product.

21   Pity. Once the phone hit the stores a year later, it bombed in Europe. Frugal, fashion-conscious consumers wouldn't pay for handsets bulkier than those from Nokia and Siemens. Rather than gaining ground in the wireless-phone war, the gaffe contributed to Motorola's loss of share. Galvin concedes that the Shark phone was one example where his hands-off approach failed. "In some cases, it worked well," he says. "In other cases, it didn't."

PONDEROUS

22   Galvin's measured ways have proved to be an even bigger liability. He is a deliberate man, from the crease in his slacks to his perfectly combed, gray-streaked hair. He weighs important decisions carefully—at times too carefully, co-workers say. "People get pissed off at him" because they think he sometimes doesn't act quickly, says Patrick Canavan, special assistant to the CEO. To Galvin, his methodical ways are simply smart business. "Depending on the complexity of the situation, you had better think through it, because you want to make sure that decision is a net-net positive," Galvin says. "Whether on acquisitions or dispositions in the business, most of the time decisions have been made in eight weeks. We're not ponderously studying them for eight months or eight quarters or eight years."

23   Yet it took 18 months, executives say, for the company to decide to sell its semiconductor-components business. Hector Ruiz, president of Motorola's semiconductor unit in 1998, came to Galvin early that year to propose that Motorola sell a portion of the division that made older-generation components. The move would help return the semiconductor unit, about 20% of overall sales, to profitability and would help it focus on core products. Still, it wasn't until the summer of 1999 that Galvin approved the sale.

24   Why? Galvin, executives say, wanted answers to countless questions—some were reasonable, others didn't matter: Would we ever see the acquirer as a competitor? Or, how is the sale going to be perceived by employees? "Chris is very worried about how he's perceived," says a top manager who recently left Motorola. "We would have to go back and lay out what the issues would be for employees and how we should manage them. That burns time, resources, and effort."

25   One example of Galvin's decision making involved Iridium, the go-anywhere portable-phone system that beamed signals down from 66 satellites orbiting the globe. By late 1999, some of Galvin's most trusted lieutenants were advising him to abandon the business, which had cost $5 billion. To them, it was clear that no viable market existed for the service and its $1,500 phones. Iridium had already filed for Chapter 11, its investors were frustrated, and last-ditch negotiations to sell the system were stalling. All the while, Gilmore—then head of Motorola's Communications Enterprise division—Wapole, and other top wireless execs tried to counsel Galvin to cut his losses and bail out of Iridium.

26   Although Iridium's phones were clunky and the service spotty, Galvin called the globe-girdling system "the eighth wonder of the world." He stood behind the money-losing satellite system until December 2000—a year after colleagues first advised Galvin to cut the cord. Executives close to the company say he told staffers that holding on was important to Motorola's image and that the company needed to stand behind the venture's investors.

"PARALYSIS"

27   All told, Motorola wrote off $2.6 billion on Iridium. Galvin says that Motorola bore most of the expenses up front and that any costs Motorola incurred over the year were minimal. He also says he couldn't dispose of the satellites until the courts gave Motorola the go-ahead. "If there was a way to save money and to have [dissolved] it faster, we would have done it," he says. Perhaps, but Motorola shelled out $50 million to $60 million a quarter in cash to maintain Iridium—some $200 million over the final year—for a service that was doomed, according to analysts at Bear Stearns.

28   Galvin's indecision was compounded by an organizational mistake he made two years ago. In 1998, COO Growney, Galvin, and his assistant Canavan realized that Motorola needed to break up the fiefdoms that had built up in the company over the years. Besides its six main divisions, Motorola had dozens of $100 million to $1 billion businesses, all with their own managers controlling profit and loss, marketing, and development. As technologies converged—pagers and cell phones morphed into one, computing and Web browsing went wireless, and semiconductors were needed for all of these—the myriad units caused confusion among customers. Galvin ordered them brought together under an umbrella called Communications Enterprise. But he left the controls in the hands of Gilmore, an engineer who many thought was headed for stardom at Motorola. Distanced in his CEO chair, Galvin didn't realize that the new organization created another

EXHIBIT 3
Q&A with Chris Galvin on the Record

With his company on the ropes, Motorola Inc. CEO Christopher B. Galvin scarcely has time for the media. But in a rare series of interviews—including one conducted while racing through the restricted back hallways of the Venetian Hotel in Las Vegas and another by phone from the backseat of a company car—Galvin talked with BusinessWeek correspondent Roger O. Crockett. Some excerpts:

On criticism that he takes too long to make decisions:
Most people don't know the complexity of the issues that get dealt with at the level of the CEO. When people look at another person's world from far away, it looks much simpler to them. When you're just involved with the law, you look at it from the legal standpoint. If you're just involved in finance, you look at it from a finance standpoint. When the buck stops here—when you're responsible for the ultimate shareholder value—you've got to take 10 or 30 or 100 variables into consideration. And those have to be thought through.

On criticism that he delegates too much:
Bob Galvin [his father and former Motorola chief executive] started the process of delegation, and it helped the company grow. When I came to the business, we were much bigger. I began with a philosophy of: Could we create an environment where five to seven or so managers felt empowered and energized around being their own CEO? In some cases it worked well; in other cases it didn't. When it didn't, we said: Let's put systems in that have more control and involvement by me, so that we're not trusting so much in people for follow-up mechanisms.

On whether he can change his hands-off style to a more aggressive management approach:
In managing activities throughout my career, I was very activist in all of those roles. In running paging and the Tegal (semiconductor-parts) business—whatever job it was. Motorola is a large multibusiness operation. When a company gets large, you have to find a balance between delegating and being involved. When not enough got accomplished in our Communications Enterprise (the division that makes mobile phones and other wireless equipment), then we said: Fine, that approach didn't work. If you don't like the results, you have to put yourself in the mix—which is what I did.

problem: bureaucracy run amok. "The last year I was there, you could get nothing accomplished," says Julie A. Shimer, a 3Com Corp. exec who had been a vice-president in Motorola's Internet unit. "The whole organization was in paralysis."

29　　The Communications Enterprise was a massive organization with some 500 executives across the nation overseeing cellular phones, infrastructure, and broadband devices. A dozen or so lieutenants reported to Gilmore, but many of the managers who once held profit-and-loss responsibility had been stripped of their autonomy. They were expected to channel key decisions—which circuit boards and software codes to embed in a line of phones, for example—up to Gilmore. That could take weeks. "You couldn't make a decision without needing 99 other people to make a decision," Shimer says. "It was horrible."

30　　Galvin was shielded from the frustration, getting regular reports from Gilmore but meeting with the communications unit just once a month. "Chris didn't screw it up," Shimer says. "He was asleep at the switch while some of his lieutenants screwed it up." Galvin acknowledges that the reorg was a mistake, and he restructured the company again this year to remove one layer of management and have the heads of Motorola's six main businesses report directly to him. "I hoped that it would work, but it didn't," he says.

EXHIBIT 3
(continued)

On why Motorola took hits from the economic slowdown before other technology companies:
I was willing to stand up and say: There is an Asian currency crisis, and it will affect us, and it will affect others. At the time, I took a lot of criticism by people saying it's not happening to any of us—and whoops! It did. The same thing has been true with what has been going on with today's economy. Very early on, because our business model is one where we're selling to almost every major industry in the world, we do get a sense for what's happening before other people see it. My interest is not to be popular but to lead—and that means sometimes you have to stand alone. I was willing to stand up and say the world is in more trouble from a recession standpoint than a lot of people cared to or wanted to believe.

On his job performance and security:
The board of directors is focusing on the same thing I'm focusing on. They understand the [economic] tornado that came in and disrupted the landscape. They know we're proven reducers of cost and capacity. No one likes the fact that we have another 1984–85 boom-bust cycle that's even faster than before. But how productive is it to blame everything on one person? I get up every day saying: Don't focus on what happened yesterday. All you can do is take what you know today and put together a plan.

On cost-cutting and layoffs:
We were way ahead of our competitors. You're now seeing them do what we started many quarters ago: reducing head count, reducing facilities, and curtailing our capital expenditures by trimming nonstrategic investments. We got after it faster than others. And by the way, I think we are pretty darn good at it. It's strategic. You don't want to take out all your capacity, just the capacity you don't need for the future. We want to take out a layer at a time, because the worst thing is to not be able to serve customers.

On the challenges of leadership:
You have to live with the downside. You can be subject to all sorts of criticism. But I understand that all problems are solvable, and there's no sense wasting energy worrying about it or fretting about it.

31   That's just one sign that Galvin is beginning to change his ways. Since January, he has become relentless about staying involved with his businesses. In addition to meeting with the heads of each sector weekly, he also huddles with top managers monthly about the progress of key corporate initiatives, say, in e-business. And a handful of times a year, Galvin convenes leadership-alignment meetings to ensure that everybody is operating under the new rules. In short, no special turf allowed, only cooperative teams.

32   Still, most Motorola employees rarely see Galvin. He is not like George M. C. Fisher, who held the top post at Motorola from 1988 to 1993. Fisher liked "walking the halls. And that made him seem more approachable than Chris," says Roberta Gutman, who as executive director of the Motorola Foundation has worked for both Fisher and Galvin.

33   Galvin is simply private, but people who know him say that he is certainly approachable and down to earth. For example, after a red-eye flight to Germany, all-day meetings with staff, and then a flight to Paris that arrived at 10 p.m., Galvin was asked by a company security official to have a drink. Galvin said: "What the heck," Canavan recalls. The three of them hung out drinking wine at a local bistro for a couple of hours before going to bed. The next morning, however, Galvin was in the hotel lobby by 6:45. "That shows stamina," Canavan says.

REFRESHING

34 If Galvin does decide to give up the CEO job, he need look no further for a successor than straight down his chain of command to Breen. Some current and former executives, as well as institutional investors, say Breen is getting top marks as the no-nonsense leader Motorola adopted when it acquired broadband-cable leader General Instruments in September 1999. Assigned the task of integrating GI and Motorola after the deal closed in January 2000, Breen was given six months to consolidate the staffs, their products, and resources, and come up with strategic plans. Never mind that he had about 15 to 20 committees working on various projects and combing hundreds of pages of legal issues related to the merger. By Feb. 1, the decisions were made. "His ability to decide which issues to firefight and which ones to bury is what Motorola would benefit from," says Wapole.

35 Galvin agrees that Breen is an asset. "Ed is one of the key members of a larger new team which we put in at the end of last year. We're building superb depth in our bench. We are making available to the company, and the long-term succession of the institution, a short list of people of which Ed is certainly a member."

36 Now Breen oversees not only the broadband-cable unit but also Motorola's entire network-systems business. His cut-to-the-chase style is a refreshing break from Motorola's bureaucratic culture. During a quarterly operations review in which wireless execs set forecasts for phones and options for plant expansions, Breen was quickly bored by what seemed like endless debate over a frivolous matter, executives in the meeting recall. Whenever discussion lingered, "his eyes opened wide, he looked around and said, 'For Christ's sake, why don't we make a decision? We don't have to talk it to death,'" Wapole remembers. "It became very obvious to folks that Breen's sort of leadership and decision making is what Motorola needs."

37 The idea of tacking Breen's name on the CEO's office is being whispered more and more around the company's water coolers. And what of Galvin? If he kicked himself up to chairman and "backed off on assuming sole leadership, he'd be revered," says one former manager. Galvin has no plan to do that. "My interest is not to be popular, but to lead," he says. Galvin doesn't intend to be Corporate America's Hamlet. He plans to turn forceful, decisive, ruthless even. That's what it may take to put the sheen back on Granddad's legacy.

Source: Adapted by Richard Robinson, University of South Carolina, based on Roger O. Crockett, "Motorola," *BusinessWeek,* July 16, 2001.

Case 10

Nokia

The Finnish wireless giant has "everything clicking," and most analysts think it's set to soar again.

1 Among CEOs, Jorma Ollila has a reputation for putting his money where his mouth is. So it was no surprise when he ascended the podium for a keynote speech at the COMDEX computer industry trade show on Nov. 12 and dropped a bombshell. Ollila offered to license the software that powers his red-hot Nokia cell phones and other personal communication devices to competing handset manufacturers.

2 More than that, the unflappable Finn said he was willing to show competitors his source code to help them develop products that are more compatible with Nokia phones. That's akin to Bill Gates agreeing to show the source code of the Windows operating system to archrivals Sun Microsystems and Oracle in the interest of promoting better interoperability in business software.

"BIGGER AND BETTER"

3 True, the bold move wasn't exactly a total leap of faith. Nokia had already thrown in with a group of 16 wireless players, including its chief competitors as well as mega-carriers such as Verizon and SBC, that had agreed to push for open standards and enhanced technological transparency in the wireless sector. Their unification aims to foster greater growth for the entire industry by making it easier to build systems that talk to each other.

4 Still, Nokia took that notion further than anyone else by agreeing to show its crown jewels to competitors. The Finnish phenom believes it can stay ahead of the pack, even if the pack has the latest blueprints from Helsinki. "It's not about us trying get our software on every handset. It's about trying to make the market bigger and better," says Paul Chellgren, vice-president for Nokia Mobile Phones.

5 Of course, as the market dominator with a 32% share of the global handset business, Nokia can afford to take some risks. The question is, will they pay off for this year, or will investors continue to feel skittish toward the stock, which is 49% off its 52-week high. Analysts overwhelmingly think Nokia is a solid investment play right now. And Ollila's bold move only bolsters their confidence. "I think these guys have everything clicking," says Paul Sagawa, a senior analyst at investment research firm Sanford C. Bernstein.

FOREBODING

6 The company comprises two primary business groups. Nokia Mobile Phones makes the handsets and most of the money. That unit, which sold 128 million handsets in 2000, accounted for 72% of Nokia's revenues that year, according to Standard & Poor's, which, like *BusinessWeek* Online, is a division of The McGraw-Hill Companies. The other big group is Nokia Networks, which builds a wide variety of equipment, including wireless infrastructure gear, digital subscriber line (DSL) networking equipment, and high-capacity Internet security appliances. Nokia Networks accounted for 25% of the company's 2000 revenues, according to S&P.

7   The remainder came from Nokia Ventures, a small part of the company, which focuses on bleeding-edge technologies for transporting data, plus software and content for mobile devices. Combined, the three groups produced revenues of $30.3 billion in 2000, a 34.4% increase over 1999's $19.9 billion. Net income also increased 34% that year, to $3.9 billion.

8   This year has been much more traumatic. In the first three quarters of 2001, overall sales growth slowed to only 6%. Worse, net profits plunged 36% for the nine-month period. And sales at Nokia Networks have suffered significantly as European cell-phone operators have slowed infrastructure build-outs partly because of financial troubles resulting from inflated prices they paid for spectrum licenses.

HARDLY STELLAR

9   The bad news came to a head in early July, when Nokia shocked investors by announcing that it could miss its 2001 earnings targets by as much as 25%. That set off a selling spree that dropped the stock by 23% in the first day of trading after the news and sliced $31 billion off Nokia's market cap. The stock hasn't yet recovered.

10   And third-quarter earnings, though they met analysts' expectations, were hardly stellar. The company posted a 14% decline in sales at Nokia Networks vs. the same quarter the year before, and operating profit fell 57% in the unit. Nokia Mobile Phones suffered a 3% decline in sales and a 6% decline in operating profit.

11   So why does the Street still love Nokia? Of the 29 analysts who track the stock, according to S&P, 12 have strong buy ratings on the stock and 14 have buy ratings. The other three rate it a hold. Nokia bulls figure the company has weathered tech downturn far better than most and looks set to soar again in the coming year. Says Bernstein's Sagawa: "They have economies of scale. They are willing to take chances. They are introducing brand-new products to the market, which has always meant share gain and margin expansion for the company."

BAILING OUT

12   With operating margins in its predominant handset business of 19%, Nokia trounces competitors Ericsson and Motorola in terms of profitability. In fact, neither of the other two are making any money on their cell-phone operations. Both have largely abandoned the idea of doing their own production, with Motorola looking at outsourcing all manufacturing to Siemens and Ericsson striking a deal with consumer electronics wizard Sony to build handsets jointly.

13   What's more, Nokia has managed to defy logic by keeping margins up in a business many experts say should be headed for the commodity dustbin. Its secret is that it controls both the software and the hardware. "They are like Dell and Microsoft rolled into one," enthuses Sagawa. Furthermore, handsets have succeeded in becoming a style accessory, while PCs have, with the exception of Apple's products, remained boring boxes devoid of sex appeal. And Nokia has proven the most adept at selling handsets customers love. That's why Sagawa believes that anyone who says Nokia will get caught in the commodity trap is "flat-out wrong."

14   As for Nokia Networks, it won the equivalent of the Powerball Jackpot in the last week of October. No. 2 U.S. wireless carrier Cingular signed up Nokia to provide infrastructure for a planned GSM (global system for mobile communications) network—

which allows for international roaming capability. This means Nokia, which also has built a network for No. 1 U.S. cell-phone provider AT&T Wireless, has a firm foothold in America with long-term cash cows in terms of service contracts and upgrades.

15   "They were a nonentity [in the wireless infrastructure sector] in the U.S. and Latin America. Now they are definitely a player," says David Berndt, the director of wireless research at consultancy the Yankee Group. "Over the next three years, as they support Cingular and AT&T Wireless, they will get a significant market share."

"MISSING LINK"

16   The U.S. beachhead also takes Nokia one step closer to its ultimate goal of becoming a vertically integrated business. That means selling complete wireless packages to carriers—including base stations, software management tools, and the latest handsets, all based on Nokia's GSM technology. That standard already dominates Europe and Asia, but not the U.S. "The missing link has been the critical mass in the U.S.," says Niklas Savander, Nokia's vice-president for mobile Internet applications. "Now we have that, as well."

17   Not that Nokia's rivals are rolling over. Motorola, the next-closest competitor in terms of global handset market share, has embarked on an aggressive cost-cutting plan that will include using fewer basic platform designs for its phones. "All the indications are that we are gaining share in the market over the last three quarters," says Leif Soderberg, a senior vice-president at Motorola. He also claims that a renewed focus on design, particularly for the company's trademark flip-phones, is winning over carriers and customers alike.

18   At the same time, a deal between Sony and Ericsson to work together on cell-phone design and production could pit Nokia's product engineers against the formidable Tokyo designers who have cornered the style market in everything from the Walkman to plasma TVs. In the Far East, Samsung, Kyocera, and others have also drawn a bead on Nokia. The Asian players have a reputation for brutal pricing tactics in consumer electronics, which could prove hazardous to Nokia's wealth.

19   Even so, the game is Nokia's to lose. As the world economy recovers and consumers develop a taste for new and expensive wireless services, Nokia, more than any other company, is positioned to gain from every level of sales in the cell-phone business. That's a nice place to call home, even if the winters are long and dark up around the Arctic Circle.

Source: Adapted by Richard Robinson, University of South Carolina, based on Alex Salkever, "Why the Street Keeps Calling on Nokia," *BusinessWeek* Online Extra, November 26, 2001.

Case 11

BusinessWeek

AT&T: Is This the Beginning of the End?

If the cable TV operations go, the telecom giant won't have much to sustain it.

1 Comcast President Brian L. Roberts couldn't have hoped for a more receptive audience. Stung by the AT&T board's rejection of his offer to acquire the telecom giant's cable assets, Roberts swept into New York on July 9 to present the $41.3 billion plan directly to AT&T investors. "We fit like a glove with AT&T," Roberts said to a room packed with 500 investors on the top floor of the St. Regis Hotel. The audience, along with some 1,500 others listening in via conference call, obviously agreed. AT&T's stock jumped 8% the following day. "The surprising thing about the meeting at the St. Regis was how much support Roberts had," said one AT&T investor who was there.

2 The question is whether Comcast Corp. can turn that support into victory. AT&T Chairman and CEO C. Michael Armstrong appears dead set against a deal—and for now, the board looks as if it backs him. Says Armstrong in his first extended interview since news of the bid broke: "We're under no obligation to sell Broadband." But if Comcast and Roberts prevail, as it looks as though it might, the upstart cable operator will in one swoop transform the dynamics of the fledgling broadband industry even as it deals a near-death blow to AT&T.

3 Already, AT&T's fast-growing wireless unit has been spun off. Without the future growth engine of cable to pull along the rest of its remaining empire, the telecom giant's core long-distance and business-services units would be left severely weakened—and right back where they started a decade ago. "The telephone business may be too small to survive on its own," says Jim Bitter, a telecom analyst at Wilmington Trust Corp, which holds about 500,000 shares. "Now, it looks like you could see the disappearance of this American icon very quickly."

4 "It's not just AT&T's future that's at stake. The embattled Armstrong looks increasingly vulnerable. He now runs the very real risk of losing control of his weakened empire. With the cable unit in play, rumors are swirling about possible bids by every industry player from AOL Time Warner Inc. to Paul Allen's Charter Communications. Sources say Walt Disney Co. is also considering a counteroffer with other content producers. And though Liberty Media has said it will not bid, industry insiders know never to count out John Malone. And with AT&T Broadband on the table, the opening has other opportunistic investors eyeing the rest of the once-mighty corporation.

5 Selling off AT&T bit by bit is a scenario Armstrong adamantly rejects. He insists that, with or without its cable assets, the company has a bright future. "Let's talk about the end of AT&T," says Armstrong. "You're not going to end something that has a strong and growing business. The brand will survive."

6 Outside the corridors of AT&T's Basking Ridge, N.J., headquarters, though, most people think the battle has clearly been joined. And if AT&T as we now know it fades away, its demise will likely be just the start of a wave of consolidation that could rip through the cable and telecom industries around the globe. In the U.S., relatively strong Baby Bells, such as SBC Communications or Verizon Communications, could snatch up troubled WorldCom as well as parts of AT&T. Remaining midsize cable operators, such as Charter and Atlanta-based Cox Communications Inc., could rush to embrace each other. In Europe, wounded giants Deutsche Telekom and British Telecommunications will likely be picked over for their broadband assets. Investors such as George Soros and Hicks, Muse, Tate & Furst Inc. have already started buying smaller distressed carriers at discount prices. "AT&T is just the beginning," says Francis McInerney, a partner at consultant and investment firm North River Ventures. "We'll see value investors pick up a large number of telecom assets around the world during the next 6 to 12 months."

PHILLY POWER

7   For Comcast, a successful deal would elevate a family-controlled business in Philadelphia to the top tier of media and communications giants. The new company would be nearly triple the size of the current Comcast. That would make it the country's largest provider of cable TV and cable-modem service by far. Its sheer bulk would give Comcast enormous influence over TV, media, and the Internet. It would be able to compete with AOL Time Warner and Microsoft Corp. for high-speed Internet-access customers. And it could use its expanded cable network as a platform for advanced digital TV services, such as e-commerce and instant messaging. "Everybody in cable and satellite now has to be asking themselves: 'Is this kind of dominant size necessary to be in this business?,'" says John B. Frelinghuysen, a media consultant at Booz, Allen & Hamilton Inc.

A LOWBALL OFFER

8   An AT&T-Comcast deal could provide a clear benefit for consumers by speeding the rollout of broadband services. With operating margins more than twice AT&T's anemic 19% margins, Comcast will be in a better position to subsidize efforts to offer telephone and broadband services. And the economies of scale generated by the new company would create cost savings that might help pay for speedier upgrades of homes. Moreover, by having a cable footprint in 8 of the top 10 markets where consumers have shown a willingness to pay for broadband services, a combined AT&T-Comcast would be able to focus sooner on creating an array of new services to go over the upgraded broadband lines.

9   For now, the Comcast bid is the only one on the table. But that could change quickly. Cox has hired Salomon Smith Barney to help assess an offer. Disney, concerned that consolidation of cable companies could block its programs from reaching TV audiences, is scrambling to put together a consortium of other programming companies to make a counterbid, sources say. Neither Disney nor Cox would comment. But whether it's Disney or some other company that steps forward, a counteroffer is clearly in Armstrong's interest. That may be the proud CEO's only chance of securing more than a token higher price—not to mention a face-saving exit strategy.

10   How much are AT&T's cable assets worth? Clearly, Comcast has lobbed a lowball offer—roughly $4,000 per subscriber. Sources say AT&T is unlikely to consider anything below $5,000 a person. That would add $13 billion to the purchase price, for a total of $67 billion, including debt. A key player in negotiations will be Liberty Media CEO John C. Malone, who stepped down from the AT&T board on July 10. Malone is still a force even off the board. He owns 25 million shares of the stock and quit the board with a letter to Armstrong calling Comcast's bid "inadequate." Other investors agree. The price should be about 20% higher, says Richard F. Lawson of Wallace R. Weitz & Co., which is among AT&T's largest investors, with 13.3 million shares.

11   Price aside, investors seem to want the Roberts family in the corner office. Most view Comcast as far better managed than AT&T's unit. "AT&T is in a very tough position if it wants to try and demonstrate that these assets would be worth more under AT&T management. It's a nonstarter," says fund manager William C. Nyregn of Harris lp Associates, one of AT&T's 20 largest shareholders, with 18 million shares. The fallout from the Comcast bid may include the job of AT&T Broadband CEO Dan Somers. When asked if he would consider changing management at Broadband, Armstrong replied: "No comment."

12   So how do things proceed from here? AT&T's board will consider the Comcast offer during a meeting on July 17–18 in Denver. AT&T says it may spend as much as several weeks reviewing it before making a decision; meanwhile, the board is clearly waiting for other bids to materialize. But if Comcast agrees to up the price and meet AT&T's other conditions, even Armstrong may have trouble opposing a deal. Aside from price, AT&T objects that there's no protection for investors if Comcast shares fall too low and that no cash is involved. Another stumbling block: Comcast would control 49% of the voting stock.

13   One way or another, it seems likely that AT&T Broadband will soon slip out of Armstrong's grasp. Where will that leave him—and what will be left of AT&T?

14   About the only upside of such a development would be that $13.5 billion of its crushing $47.5 billion in debt would shift to Comcast. But AT&T would be deprived of its best growth engine during an extremely weak market for telecommunications.

15   Still, Armstrong insists that AT&T has a bright future. He says sales of data and consulting services to businesses are growing an average 20% a year. Later this year, he expects revenue from these operations to exceed the sale of long-distance phone service to businesses. And even though the consumer long-distance unit is shrinking fast, its margins still exceed 30%. That may be, but it is a far, far cry from the brave new world Mike Armstrong wanted to build.

COMMENTARY: HOW THE "TURNAROUND CEO" FAILED TO DELIVER

16   It's hard to remember the euphoria that greeted C. Michael Armstrong when he was named chairman and chief executive of AT&T on Oct. 20, 1997. Back then, the long-distance giant had been floundering for years under his predecessor, Robert E. Allen. With a stellar track record from his days at IBM and Hughes Electronics Corp., Armstrong came in as the superman CEO who could fix the flagship of American telecom. The stock surged as rumors of Armstrong's appointment swirled—and jumped another 5%, to a split-adjusted $25, the day of the announcement. "This is great news," said analyst David Otto of Edward Jones at the time. "We have a turnaround CEO in a turnaround situation."

17   My, how things have changed for Mike Armstrong. Now, four years later, all the hype and outsized expectations have vanished right along with the stock market frenzy that helped propel those hopes. Armstrong laid out a grand vision to remake AT&T, overhauled his strategy amidst Wall Street complaints, and failed to deliver on both counts. "He may be a business-school case study of a successful CEO whose skills were not transferable," says Robert Frieden, a professor at Pennsylvania State University.

18   A series of execution problems at AT&T, compounded by the telecom industry meltdown, have left the company down and out. Its stock, which peaked at $49 adjusted for splits and the spin-off of AT&T Wireless back in 1999, had tumbled to $17.27 on July 6. When cable giant Comcast Corp. made a $55 billion bid for AT&T's cable operations on Sunday, July 8, investors seemed ready to replace their erstwhile savior. AT&T's stock spiked 20% over the next two days, to $20.64. "Shareholders are angry at AT&T and Armstrong," says Scott C. Cleland, an analyst with the Precursor Group. "They want someone who will create value at the helm, not someone who will destroy value."

19   "That's why Armstrong's days as head of AT&T—or whatever remains of it after the Comcast fight—seem numbered. Most analysts and investors think he will ultimately have to sell the cable unit. If that happens, the remaining telephone operations are likely to be scooped up by the Baby Bells or foreign acquirers. Armstrong had wanted to become the CEO of the cable business, known as AT&T Broadband, when it was spun off next year. Instead, he may have to settle for a short stint as head of AT&T's telecom operations before retirement.

Stubborn Culture

20   Why couldn't the super-CEO save AT&T from what looks to be an ugly demise? In reality, he may never have had much of a chance. The telephone giant was run as a monopoly for decades and, even after its breakup in 1984, continued to have the management, cost structure, and culture of its past. When the Telecom Act of 1996 laid the groundwork for the Baby Bells to get into long distance, AT&T's core business was doomed. Armstrong grabbed control, slashed costs, and then bet more than $100 billion buying the cable businesses that he could move into local telephone and broadband Net services. But neither he nor AT&T moved fast enough: The long-distance business collapsed before Armstrong developed the local phone and Net initiatives. "I don't think there are five people who could have turned AT&T around," says Ken McGee, an analyst at Gartner Group. "Mike was one of the possibilities, but he failed."

21   Armstrong made plenty of mistakes along the way. He fumbled the delivery of data services to business customers last year. His in-your-face leadership style alienated some top execs, leading to heavy turnover. And he misjudged how quickly the core telecom business would deteriorate. Last May, he conceded that the company was going to badly miss its financial targets for the year. AT&T's stock plunged 14% in a single day. Armstrong admits that he didn't foresee the troubles, but his rivals didn't, either. "This company missed it, our competitors missed it, the whole industry missed it," he insists.

22   All those gaffes pale in comparison to what will forever define Armstrong's tenure: his acquisitions of cable players Tele-Communications International Inc. and MediaOne Group. His concept of using the cable networks to move AT&T into local telephone and broadband services may have made sense, but Armstrong couldn't execute fast enough to satisfy shareholders. When the long-distance business hit the skids last summer, the new initiatives were suffering technical problems and were too small to make up the difference. "He promised the equivalent of the D-day invasion," says Cleland. "He was more vision than execution." By last October, under shareholder pressure, Armstrong said he would break AT&T up into four pieces, opening the door to Comcast.

23   Armstrong takes strong exception to the argument that he has failed to remake AT&T. For starters, he says, it's way too early to discuss his legacy, since he is still overseeing AT&T telephone and cable business. "Legacy is about what you've done; I'm so consumed with doing," he says. Aside from the cable business, he points out that he has invested tens of billions in AT&T Wireless, international networks, and in local operations

for business customers. "This is not the AT&T communications company that we started with," he says. "This is a powerful, state-of-the-art communications company." What's more, he says he won't sell the cable business to any company that will compromise his strategy. He wants to make sure that any acquirer continues to invest in the local telephone and broadband Net services.

24   But Armstrong may no longer control the unit's destiny. Investors will probably push him to sell to the highest bidder. And Comcast does not seem inclined to invest heavily in the local phone business. That would be a blow for AT&T's onetime savior. He will leave AT&T as something less than the superman in pinstripes that he once was.

Source: Adapted by Richard Robinson, University of South Carolina, based on Steve Rosenbush, with Tom Lowry, Ron Grover and Amy Barrett, "AT&T: Is This the Beginning of the End?," *BusinessWeek,* July 23, 2001, and Peter Elstrom, "Commentary: How the 'Turnaround CEO' Failed to Deliver," *BusinessWeek,* July 23, 2001.

Case 12

AOL Time Warner

Bob Pittman's job is to implement the biggest merger in U.S. history. That's a tall order.

1. It's a decade ago. Warner Communications and Time Inc. are merging, and wicked-smart CEO Steven J. Ross brings back his former protege, 36-year-old Robert W. Pittman, one of the creators of MTV, in a risky effort to fire up the combo's creative juices. Pittman's mission improbable: to launch a host of new businesses by exploiting synergies between the fiercely independent magazine, movie, and cable-TV units. If the division chieftains don't cooperate, Pittman has the green light to forge ahead without them. It's a dicey proposition, since the execs have "their knives out" for Pittman, says Henry R. Silverman, a Ross associate who now heads Cendant Corp.

2. Yet barely a drop of blood is shed while Pittman promotes one new venture after another—including the new cable channel Court TV, the hit TV sitcom *Fresh Prince of Bel Air,* and the revitalization of the Six Flags amusement parks. The biggest twist of all, though, is how Pittman manages it. By turns charming and steely, he convinces proud and powerful business-unit executives that they'll win more battles by playing ball than by balking. It doesn't hurt that he gives them much of the credit. "I try to be gracious to people," says Pittman.

3. Today, the 47-year-old son of a Mississippi preacher and his stone-simple management philosophy are being put to the ultimate test. His task is to help make a success of the $97 billion merger of Internet powerhouse America Online Inc. and old-line media kingpin Time Warner Inc. The deal is expected to close any day, after getting approval from the Federal Communications Commission. While AOL's Stephen M. Case will be chairman and Time Warner's Gerald M. Levin will be CEO, the two have turned to Pittman to exploit synergies between their diverse properties—from websites and e-commerce to movie studios and book publishers. As co-chief operating officer, Pittman now has the formidable task of melding the yin and the yang of Old and New Media, breaking down barriers and getting people to work together on everything from ad and subscription sales to online music.

4. The goal is to take full advantage of the Internet. In spite of the crash of the dot coms, Pittman believes the Net will ultimately transform business and social life every bit as profoundly as electricity did a century ago. "With all its copyrights, Time Warner is in a marvelous position to take advantage of the Net and not be frightened by it," he says. "AOL's mind-set, assets, and expertise help them in that path."

5. This is the long-awaited convergence of the analog present and the digital future. But, like two galaxies coming together, AOL's and Time Warner's brightest stars could be pulled into new orbits, releasing vast energies, or, if things go horribly wrong, they could be smashed in a collision. At a time when it appears that hybrids of old-line and Net-style companies have the best chance of thriving in a softening economy, all eyes are on this merger—and on Pittman.

6. Already, there are troubling signs. Early last year, the company predicted 12% to 15% annual revenue increases and $1 billion in combined cost savings and new revenues in the first year. Those targets seemed doable at the time, given AOL's 37% revenue growth last year and Time Warner's 6% growth over the same period. Now they're beginning to look like a stretch. On Dec. 18, Time Warner announced that it will have slower-than-expected fiscal year 2000 growth, caused primarily by the box-office flop of

Little Nicky and weakening cable-network ad sales. Those two factors could knock $100 million off the top line, says First Union Securities. Merrill Lynch & Co. analyst Henry Blodget figures the new company will pull in $41 billion in revenue this year, up just 11%, while losses could top $5 billion, thanks to merger write-offs.

7   Other analysts are more worried. "Any big deal is difficult, but it's particularly challenging against the backdrop of a slowing macroeconomic environment," says CIBC World Market analyst John Corcoran, who believes the company will have to cut its targets early this year. First hit will be advertising revenues. The company relies on ad sales for about 20% of its revenues, and according to media buying firm Universal McCann, overall advertising expenditures are expected to slow to a 6% growth rate this year, down from 10% last year. If AOL Time Warner is hard hit by this, it could slow revenue growth. Another potential trouble spot: Time Warner has traditionally used EBITA—operating income before amortization of intangible assets—when it sizes up its profitability. Investors may be less tolerant of that practice in a tougher economy.

8   Already, investors are skeptical—at least for the short run. Since the deal was announced last Jan. 10, AOL's stock has dropped from $73 a share to $37.50, down 48%. That's got some observers clucking their tongues at Levin for selling his company at a time when AOL stock was soaring—and not building in safeguards to adjust the price in the event of a stock market swoon. The premium to Time Warner shareholders the day the deal was announced last January was 70%. But with AOL's sagging stock price, the premium has evaporated. Sure, many Internet stocks have fallen even more: AOL rival Yahoo! has plummeted 89%, while e-tailer Amazon.com is down 87%. Of course, the Net upstarts don't boast the multibillion-dollar revenue streams that AOL Time Warner does—nor the management burden of blending two cultures. "The odds are against them," says John H. Bogush, a managing director at KPMG LLP. "The biggest challenge Pittman will have is to redefine the corporate culture." According to a November study by KPMG, 83% of the 700 largest corporate mergers from 1996 to 1998 failed to boost the stock price because of poor execution. And AOL Time Warner carries extra baggage: continual governmental antitrust oversight by a special monitor. To convince Wall Street that the deal is working, Pittman needs to deliver results that boost the stock to $90 within 18 months, says Blodget.

HOT SEAT

9   Pittman concedes he's on the hot seat. "The company must hit the numbers expected of it," he says. If not, "I'll be responsible." Despite concerns about doom and gloom, the company says it will stick to its financial targets and that its diversified revenue streams and opportunities for cost-cutting will keep it humming. "We're standing by those forecasts. There are lots of dials and levers in achieving our results," says Michael Kelly, the new company's CFO. Pittman argues that in bad times, advertisers will spend their money on the top ad venues, like AOL and Time Warner properties. Indeed, AOL Time Warner has some distinct advantages even over its top competitors. No other U.S. media powerhouse, such as Walt Disney Co., can boast as strong an Internet partner as the world's leading online service, AOL. And Net archrival Yahoo lacks a close partnership with an old-line media company and the broadband cable distribution that Time Warner will provide.

10   Pittman figures his ticket to success is creating valuable synergies between AOL and Time Warner. Over the next two years, he plans to dish up powerful new consumer services. First, the company will deliver AOL's Internet access and content to homes over Time Warner Cable wires—and to people wherever they may be through wireless mobile devices. In Year Two, expect liftoff of the company's online music business, where

subscriptions to music from Time Warner artists and others will be offered on the AOL site. Ditto interactive-TV services, perhaps offering such features as Warner Bros. and New Line Cinema videos to consumers, on demand, via AOL's websites. "Everything," says Pittman, "must be a series of interlocking teams."

11   While Pittman is a dedicated team player, he's also coolly calculating. He sizes up a situation, figures out the best way to proceed, and then carefully maneuvers like a sapper through a minefield. "He personifies Southern charm, but when it comes to business, he switches to a different DNA. He's cold-blooded," says *NBC Nightly News* Anchor Tom Brokaw, a Pittman pal. His detractors go even further. "He has found great parades and hopped in front," says a former colleague at AOL.

12   Anticipating that he'll persevere once again, Pittman's fans have anointed him the heir apparent when AOL Time Warner CEO Levin's contract expires in 2003. He's already clearly the first-among-equals with co-COO Richard D. Parsons, the former Time Warner president, who is a candidate for a job in the Bush Administration. Insiders say Pittman will take over Parsons' duties if he jumps ship.

13   The top brass won't commit to promoting Pittman to CEO some day, but they lavish him with praise. "Bob Pittman blends the realism of a top-flight executive with the creative vision of an entrepreneur," says Levin. While Levin and Case do best as visionaries up in the corner office, Pittman makes things happen down in the trenches. "Bob has an operational zeal," says Case.

14   Now that the merging begins in earnest, Pittman will need all of the *esprit de corps* he can muster. Even Time Warner execs who are in sync with the strategy say it won't be easy to get all of the new company's businesses marching in lockstep. "Managing Time Warner is like herding cats," says Time CEO Don Logan. Making matters worse, there's a huge cultural gap between AOL's twentysomethings and Time Warner's graybeards. When it comes to making deals or launching new ventures, they move at two speeds. It's "Let's do lunch" vs. "Let's skip lunch." "AOL would say we're as entrepreneurial as a couple of 90-year-olds," Logan says.

15   The trick is getting people to work together. While Pittman is known for his diplomatic skills, he also can be intimidating. Once, when he ran independent TV-production house Quantum Media Inc., he summarily fired Morton Downey Jr. after the loudmouth talk-show host asked for permission to tone down his on-air style. "His strength is he's unyielding, and his weakness is he's unyielding," says Downey, who was later rehired. At MTV, Pittman occasionally sent handwritten notes to the veejays critiquing their performances. "It was scary," says former veejay Alan Hunter. "He was saying, 'I'm watching you.'"

POWER SHARING

16   As AOL and Time Warner come together, Pittman's first task is mastering the intricacies of a power-sharing arrangement with Parsons. Pittman and Parsons say they have a collegial relationship. They had lunch together every six months or so after Pittman left Time Warner in 1995, and today they work together on many of the same charities, such as the Fresh Air Fund. So far, there's no sign that Parsons or other Time Warner execs are looking for a fight with Pittman. "We're all going to play nice in the sandbox," Parsons says.

17   The two men have set up housekeeping near Levin's office in Time Warner's Manhattan headquarters. Pittman oversees the company's advertising and subscription-based businesses. With their combined 128 million subscribers, AOL, Time Inc., Turner Broadcasting, Time Warner Cable, Home Box Office, and the The WB Television Network are expected to contribute 60% to 70% of total revenues in 2001 and to reap the first rewards

EXHIBIT 1
Can These Two
Make the Marriage
Work?

Source: *BusinessWeek,* First
Union Securities.

Co-Chief Operating Officer Bob Pittman's Portfolio

Estimated 2001 revenues: $30.2 billion

America Online Inc.
With 29 million subscribers, AOL dominates the consumer online access market. Now it's migrating the AOL service beyond the PC to TVs, cell phones, and mobile devices. It also aims to make AOL a top brand for interactive television.

Estimated 2001 revenues: $10.3 billion

Time Warner Cable
The second-largest U.S. cable operator is pushing digital services and broadband Web access to the 21% of U.S. households reached by its network. The plan is to offer interactive shopping and entertainment. AOL's own branded interactive-TV package will be pushed via cable.

Estimated 2001 revenues: $6.9 billion

Time Inc.
The publisher of 40 magazines has enjoyed 28 straight quarters of operating profit growth, fueled by the success of *Time, Sports Illustrated, People,* and *Fortune.* With the merger, it is promoting magazine subscriptions heavily on AOL.

Estimated 2001 revenues: $5 billion

Home Box office
The largest premium cable network, with 37 million subscribers, keeps raking in Emmy nominations for high-quality productions, such as *The Sopranos* and *Sex in the City*—and rolling in the dough.

Estimated 2001 revenues: $2.4 billion

Turner Broadcasting System, Inc.
With some of cable TV's top networks, such as CNN, TBS, and TNT, the Turner properties contribute significant ad revenues—though the slowing economy may dent that. Synergies already are at play here: CNN has a spot on AOL's high-traffic Netscape website.

Estimated 2001 revenues: $5.1 billion

WB Television Network
Ratings were down 23% last year, but the six-year-old network is now rebounding, led by a 14% increase in popularity among 18- to 49-year-olds. The network targets young viewers with hits such as *Felicity.*

Estimated 2001 revenues: $495 million

---

from the online revolution. Parsons will mind the studios at Warner Bros., New Line Cinema, and Warner Music Group. His businesses may take longer to find the right Internet model. Part of Pittman's mission is to build bridges between his units and Parsons'.

18   He has made a solid start. Using methods he honed as the president of AOL, he and Parsons have held meetings every two or three weeks since June with their division chiefs. It's the first attempt ever to gather the Time Warner bosses regularly. Together they have hammered out budgets and Web strategies and agreed on technologies. Since summer, Time Inc. magazines have sold 100,000 subscriptions a month via AOL. In turn, Time has promoted AOL by sending AOL disks with magazines reaching 40 million households. In late January, the company plans on launching a new personal-finance portal on AOL using content from Time Warner's CNNfn cable network and *Fortune* and *Money* magazines.

EXHIBIT 1
(continued)

Co-Chief Operating Officer Dick Parsons' Portfolio

Estimated 2001 revenues: $13.4 billion

Warner Bros.
Despite this summer's hit *The Perfect Storm,* it ranks third among movie studios with a 12% share and U.S. movie theater revenues of more than $420 million last year. Ultimately, movies will be delivered on demand through cable TV and over the Web.

Estimated 2001 revenues: $7.1 billion

New Line Cinema
The No. 9-ranked studio was once a maker of slasher movies but now produces more mainstream fare such as *Austin Powers.* Box-office flop *Little Nicky,* however, contributed to Time Warner's slower-than-expected fourth-quarter growth.

Estimated 2001 revenues: $1.6 billion

Warner Music Group
After calling off its merger with London-based EMI Music because of regulatory pressures, Warner must now find ways to grow its business solo. The AOL deal should speed up digital distribution of its music via the Net.

Estimated 2001 revenues: $4.4 billion

Time Warner Trade Publishing
The parent company of Warner Books and Little Brown has launched iPublish, an online publisher dedicated to e-books. In December, Warner Books released Brad Meltzer's *First Council* to Gemstar-TV Guide International for its e-book reader—a month ahead of the hardcover release.

Estimated 2001 revenues: $300 million

Note: First Union estimates total revenues of $42 billion in 2001. These business-unit estimates include internal transactions.

19   Pittman's methods are starting to cascade through AOL Time Warner. On Dec. 12 and 13, 50 top executives in charge of online stuff at all the divisions met at AOL's Netscape subsidiary offices in Mountain View, Calif., to carry out his mandate: creating an integrated Net strategy. The summit was the first time the entire group had met. Their coffee arrived late and the projector broke—but no matter. "What broke out was spontaneous collaboration," says Scott Davison, the AOL senior vice-president who called the meeting. They agreed to cross-promote their websites, hook consumers with AOL's instant messaging, and adopt the same technologies.

20   Pittman is pressing for more cross-pollination. He's heading the new company's so-called advertising council, which comes up with ways for making AOL, Time, and Turner ad sales forces work together more closely. That could bring in an extra $280 million next year from new ad sales, according to Merrill Lynch. For example, AOL Time Warner could sell Coca-Cola Co. a package of ads on cable TV and the AOL website, plus product placements in Warner Bros. movies. We "can look at opportunities together, instead of just pieces of the opportunity," says Pittman.

SKIRMISHES

21   So far, the conflicts between Time Warner's cats and AOL's dogs are minor skirmishes. Pittman persuaded Time Warner execs to trade in their e-mail system for AOL's. Then he put all employee-benefit processing online to save the company tens of millions of dollars

EXHIBIT 2
Pittman's Highest Hurdles

Show Wall Street the Money
Pittman must make good on AOL Time Warner's promises to grow 12% a year. First on the attack list: cross-selling AOL and Time Warner's subscriptions and advertising space.

Get Time Warner Operating on Internet Time
Pittman needs Time Warner's traditional media properties to carve out smart Web strategies. To do this, he has to inject AOL-style urgency into the Old Media company's relatively hidebound culture.

Break Down the Barriers between Businesses
Pittman must unite Time Warner's warring divisions if he's going to push new ventures such as interactive TV. He's giving division heads two tasks: overseeing their own units and watching out for the company's overall financial performance.

Keep Raking in the Ads
Already, the softening ad market has eaten into Turner Broadcasting's revenues in 2000. Pittman believes AOL Time Warner can maintain its 2001 targets of 12% to 15% annual revenue growth because advertisers are better off choosing blue-chip ad venues.

in paperwork. Both times, the Time Warner folks at first resisted—but gave in when Pittman explained the advantages for the company. They say serious infighting could still crop up, but for now, the open discussions help quell corporate intrigue. "The sunshine enables us to guess less" about each others' motives, says Turner President Steven J. Heyer. "It's about creating a safe environment of trust and an expected mode of behavior."

22   Pittman has pulled off this kind of management feat before. Consider AOL. The Dulles (Va.) company was in crisis when he arrived on Oct. 29, 1996. Investors were impatient with the company's fixation on growth at any cost. The stock had fallen to a low of $25, down from a high of $83 in February 1994. Pittman began refocusing AOL on the bottom line—slashing costs, and building ad and e-commerce revenues. He retooled the culture, forging a team among AOL's aggressive, individualistic senior execs by holding biweekly operating committee meetings and forcing them to use the same in-house marketing, engineering, and dealmaking teams. He encouraged vigorous debate, and got it. Execs even threw food at each other during these sessions. Chuckles Pittman: "It's more like Dodge City than polite society, but I try to maintain order."

23   There are lines, however, that can't be crossed. Pittman bars personal attacks. "He has zero tolerance for bad behavior," says Jan Brandt, president of AOL Marketing. Indeed, after he first arrived, Pittman chastised Brandt and others for name-calling. He is setting a similar tone now. And he applies the same rules to himself. "Just because I play the role of team leader doesn't give me the right to throw tantrums and rob people of their dignity," he says.

24   Pittman's greatest challenge at AOL may have been getting along with the boss. After running the company for 11 years, Case loosened his grip only gradually. "We had some differences," Case admits. Indeed, the pair clashed several times. In 1998, for instance, Case argued against Pittman's plan to raise AOL's monthly fee by 10%, to $21.95. Pittman prevailed, insisting that the brand would lose few customers. He was right. The April 1998, price increase boosted profits, and AOL's subscribers rocketed from 11 million then to 29 million today. Case gives Pittman much of the credit for AOL's success. "He legitimized the medium and AOL in particular," says Case.

25   Where does Pittman's drive come from? Since the day he lost his right eye in a fall off a horse at his grandparents' farm at age 6, he has been obsessed with overcoming hurdles.

As a kid, he learned to compensate for his lack of depth perception by mastering fly-fishing—casting repeatedly into a bucket. At 15, he talked his way into a disk-jockey job to pay for airplane flying lessons. And at 27, he turned the pop music world upside down when he helped launch MTV. "He triumphed over everything," says Pittman's cousin, Lanier Hurdle.

26   Becoming a leader in the digital world has taken Pittman a long way from his roots in small-town Mississippi. But the seeds for a media maven were planted in childhood. After his riding accident, he spent hours watching television—and has even said that TV shaped him more than his parents did. He believes TV changed his generation's method of processing information—an insight that helped him craft MTV. "TV babies sense impressions, mood, emotion, and images as a message," he says. "My parents were more focused on what the words said."

27   These years also shaped Pittman's diplomacy skills. The family led a nomadic life as the father moved from church to church in a succession of towns. That life taught the then undersize Pittman how to overcome being an outsider. "When you have one eye and you're the smallest kid in the class, you've got to figure out how to get along with people, as opposed to bludgeoning your way in," he says.

"HIPPIE FROM MISSISSIPPI"

28   The comfortable family in which Pittman grew up helped incubate his ambitions. His parents, Warren and Lanita, both University of Southern Mississippi graduates, instilled the value of education in their two sons, the elder Tom and the younger Bob. "In my household, there was no yelling, screaming, or pounding of fists. Just unconditional love," says the younger Pittman. Dinner-table conversation revolved around school-day activities and current events, such as the civil rights movement, which his family supported.

29   The Pittman boys had two distinct styles. Tom turned out to be the model eldest son, following in his father's footsteps to become an ordained Methodist minister. Now, however, he is a newspaper publisher in DeSoto, Miss. Bob was the family rebel. He listened to rock 'n' roll and grew his hair long: He was sent home from high school in Brookhaven, Miss., one day because his hair hung below his earlobes. "Fortunately, my dad backed me up," arguing that the school's dress code was irrelevant to the goals of education, says Pittman. He started getting A's only after his father began paying him 50 cents for each, according to brother Tom. Pittman was cocky, too. "He was one of these kids that drove his parents and teachers crazy because nobody else knew as much as he did," says W. L. Roach, Brookhaven High's retired principal. Pittman's explanation: He was just bored with small-town life.

30   That maverick streak ultimately drove Pittman out of Mississippi. He was ashamed of the way blacks were treated and, as a teen, vowed, "I'm getting the hell out of here," he recalls. At 15, Pittman found the exit by accident while looking for a job to pay for flying lessons. After being rejected by the local Piggly Wiggly supermarket for a bagging job, he took a post as a deejay at Brookhaven radio station WCHJ-AM.

31   After he was graduated from high school, he moved quickly from one radio station to another, hopping to Pittsburgh, Detroit, Chicago, and, finally, New York. He took a few college courses here and there but never graduated. Known in the industry as the "hippie from Mississippi," he wore a beard and long hair. While his brother has said Pittman's big ambition was always to be rich and famous, Pittman says: "What I really wanted to do was something fun. And if I could make money doing it, that would be great."

32   At first, Pittman was content to spin records, but he quickly switched to management. Turns out he was good at it. He was one of the pioneers of calling listeners to find out

their musical preferences. He had learned that lesson firsthand when, during his first deejay job, he had tried unsuccessfully to force his own taste—progressive rock—down the throats of rural listeners. That almost got him fired.

33   The young Pittman always had an edge. A practical jokester, "he liked to scare people a little," says Jim Ryan, who worked with Pittman at a rock station in Pittsburgh. He got a package in the mail when Pittman was wooing him to join WMAQ in Chicago. In the package were tapes of the station's music, along with a fake glass eye and a note: "You need to change your eye." The radio star wasn't above sticking his fake eye in other people's mashed potatoes either, recalls Charlie Lake, now operating manager at Infinity Broadcasting Co. in Columbus, Ohio. Says Pittman: "Having an extra eye in my pocket was always a lot of fun."

34   Mainly, though, he focused on his career. His big break came in 1979 with Warner AmEx Satellite Entertainment Co., a joint venture of Warner Communications and American Express set up to create programming for cable TV. Pittman persuaded skeptical Warner CEO Ross and Amex CEO James D. Robinson III to back the creation of an all-music-video cable channel. "People had grown up with rock 'n' roll and with TV, but the two had never been put together successfully," says Pittman, who launched MTV on Aug. 1, 1981.

35   It was a fateful day, but MTV was no overnight success. That took years of relentless preaching by Pittman to consumers, advertisers, and cable operators. The message: MTV would change the way TV was made and watched. "He would say it and say it until it actually happened," says Geraldine Laybourne, a former MTV Networks exec, now CEO of New York cable-and-Web startup Oxygen Media Inc.

36   Throughout his Time Warner career, Pittman got plenty of advice from Ross. His mentor, who died in 1992, viewed the younger man as a kindred visionary and risk taker. "Steve Ross had probably one of the greatest impacts on my life," says Pittman. "He was a father figure in the business and really took me under his wing." One memorable lesson: When Pittman told Ross that MTV was about to make its first profit ever, instead of congratulating him, Ross waxed on about the next deal MTV could make. The message was clear. "Every accomplishment was a stepping-stone to another accomplishment," says Pittman.

37   That approach has guided Pittman ever since. When Warner sold its investment in MTV to Viacom in 1985, he left to build his own production company, Quantum Media Inc., and introduced *The Morton Downey Jr. Show,* where Pittman broke TV's mold again with an in-your-face talk format.

38   Then came the tumultuous return to Time Warner. After his successes with Court TV and *Fresh Prince,* Pittman got Time Warner to buy Six Flags Entertainment—then as CEO turned around the underperforming amusement parks. After Time Warner sold a controlling stake in the parks, Pittman started looking for a new job.

39   The last stop before AOL was a one-year stint as CEO of Century 21 Real Estate Corp. While some people wondered why the media star would go to a real estate brokerage firm, Pittman says: "It's not media I'm interested in. It's the consumer. It fit my criteria of a consumer product or service." During that spell, Pittman joined the board of America Online. From there it was an easy step into the AOL executive suite.

"I'M SANE"

40   As his career soared, Pittman also remade his own image. During the height of MTV's success, Pittman and his glamorous first wife, Sandy, were dedicated social climbers—living the fast life in New York, Aspen, and St. Bart's with celebrities such as *Rolling Stone* publisher Jann Wenner, NBC's Brokaw, and musician Quincy Jones, who became godfather to their son, Bo. Jones recalls a big bash in the early 1990s on St. Bart's where

EXHIBIT 3
What They're Saying about Pittman

"He personifies Southern charm. But when it comes to business, he switches to a different DNA. He's cold-blooded."—Tom Brokaw, *NBC Nightly News* anchor and longtime friend

"He's my kind of people. We talk about vision and astounding ideas."—Quincy Jones, music producer and close friend

"He can drive 15 people who don't want to be led."—Jann Wenner, publisher of *Rolling Stone,* who accompanied Pittman on a group cross-country motorcycle trip

"His strength is he's unyielding, and his weakness is he's unyielding."—Morton Downey Jr., former TV talk-show host and Pittman employee

he, Pittman, and music producer John "Jellybean" Benitez dressed up as the Supremes. "We were the Supremes that looked like the O'Jays," says Jones. In 1992, Pittman led a dozen friends on a well-publicized cross-country Harley ride from Manhattan to San Francisco's Golden Gate Bridge. "He can drive 15 people who don't want to be led," says Wenner, who took the ride.

41   Today, however, Pittman is a family man. He and Sandy divorced in the summer of 1997. That fall, he married Veronique Choa, a former webpage designer. They have a 2-year-old son, Andrew, and a newborn daughter, Lucy. Pittman pilots his own jet, shuttling the family between homes in Manhattan, Great Falls, Va., Telluride, Colo., and Roundhill, Jamaica. He also flies himself to business meetings. And he hasn't forgotten Mississippi. At an Oct. 25 fund-raiser at his Virginia home, he raised $2.1 million to help connect the state's schools to the Web. Says Pittman of his more balanced lifestyle today: "It's more fun. I'm sane."

42   Given his full family life and a long career that started at 15, those who know Pittman are divided over whether he will stay around long enough to ascend to the top spot at AOL Time Warner. Some insiders say: "Don't count on it." After all, Levin may decide he wants to hang on for years, and in the past he has ousted executives who threatened his power. Pittman won't speculate on his future. "In my career, I have never planned what I do next," he says.

43   If Pittman does stick around, it could take a long time to make this deal pay off. It took Time Inc. and Warner Bros. five years to show the benefits of their 1990 merger. Because of the complexities of creating new online businesses with unproven business models, the merger of Time Warner and AOL could take even longer to bear fruit. Pittman says a lot of the newest stuff, such as interactive TV and video-on-demand, won't take hold for 7 to 10 years.

44   He seems to have the right skills for the long haul. Levin and Case had the guts to bet on new technologies they believe will transform consumers' lives, but Pittman is adept at delivering experiences consumers actually want. And he senses when a new business is set to take off. "He's got a great sniffer," says former HBO Chief Executive Michael Fuchs, now the chairman of Web startup MyTurn.com Inc. That instinct will be crucial if AOL and Time Warner are to deliver on their promise. But first, Pittman has to master the basics of making the two run like one.

THE MAN WHO MADE LEVIN LOOK GOOD

45   In the media business, where top executives are often afforded celebrity status, Time Warner Inc. President Richard D. Parsons is the anti-mogul. For six years, Parsons, 52, steadfastly served Chairman Gerald M. Levin in a stealthlike manner. Behind the scenes,

EXHIBIT 4
Robert Warren
Pittman's Résumé

Born
Dec. 28, 1953, Jackson, Miss.

Childhood
Son of a Methodist minister, he grew up in rural Mississippi towns. His most traumatic moment was losing his right eye when he fell off a horse at age 6. He has worn a glass eye since.

Early Musical Tastes
Jefferson Airplane, Doors, Iron Butterfly.

Education
Never graduated from college, though attended four while deejaying across the country, including stints at Millsaps College in Mississippi and the University of Pittsburgh.

Career Highlights
Starting at age 15, he worked at about a dozen radio stations until age 23. In 1981 he launched MTV. CEO of MTV Networks, 1983–86. The next three years he ran his own production company, Quantum Media Inc., where he produced *The Morton Downey Jr. Show.* CEO of Time Warner Enterprises, 1990–95. CEO of Century 21 Real Estate, 1995–96. President of Interactive Services, then president, America Online, 1996–2000. Soon, co-chief operating officer, AOL Time Warner.

Management Philosophy
"There's no rocket science to it. It's just a matter of rolling up your sleeves and doing it."

Hobbies
Pilots his own Falcon 20 jet or Bell helicopter to many of his business meetings. Rides his Big Dog, Harley Electric Slide, and Honda CBR 1000 motorcycle on long trips with friends. "When you do the kind of work that I do, your biggest problem is you're in the past with your regrets or in the future with your anxieties. When you're on the road, you're in the now," says Pittman.

Family
Married to second wife, Veronique, for three years; 2-year-old son, Andrew, newborn daughter, Lucy; 17-year-old son, Bo, from previous marriage.

Mississippi Longings
Fried okra and boiled peanuts. Gets back home about twice a year.

he has been a dealmaker and a peacemaker between fractious divisions. "He is the least visible presence in any major media company, but he is the one who has been enormously valuable," says a management consultant who has worked with Parsons through the years.

46   Given Parsons' style, it comes as no surprise that much of the focus on the AOL-Time Warner merger has been paid to media darling Bob Pittman, the high-profile president of America Online Inc. and, in an earlier life, one of the creators of MTV. The two men will share the title of co-chief operating officer, but all indications are that Pittman will be first among equals.

Irreplaceable

47   That's if Parsons hangs around. The longtime Republican is being mentioned as a candidate for a post in George W. Bush's administration, possibly the U.S. Trade Representative job. People who know Parsons say he believes public service is an important

EXHIBIT 5
Pittman's Co-Pilot

Here's what AOL Time Warner co-COO Richard Parsons did at Time Warner.

Debt Cutter
During his first year, Parsons oversaw the sale of $3.2 billion worth of assets, including a share of Six Flags Entertainment and a stake in Black Entertainment Television. The goal: to pay down company debt.

Fixer
Handled tumultuous transitions at Warner Music and Warner Bros. movie studio. After years of rapid executive turnover, he got the units running smoothly by appointing Roger Ames to head music and Barry Meyer to oversee movies.

Dealmaker
Engineered $20 billion proposed joint venture with London-based music company EMI, then negotiated directly with European regulators. (Time Warner and EMI terminated agreement amid heightened regulatory pressures.)

Peacemaker
Led a cross-divisional task force at Time Warner to help the company's staunchly independent divisions to work better together.

calling and that if offered the government position, he would consider it seriously. Time Warner would not comment on the matter, and Parsons did not grant an interview for this profile.

48   If Parsons were to leave the company now, it would present some ticklish challenges for those left behind. At 6 foot 4, with a scruffy beard and a paunch, Parsons is a teddy bear of a man who excels at bringing out the best in people and mediating among warring factions. His skills could prove vital during the first year after the merger when culture clashes seem inevitable. "He's not going to be replaceable," says John Utendahl, a long-time friend of Parsons and chairman and CEO of investment firm Utendahl Capital Corp.

49   If he stays, Parsons faces tough challenges at the divisions he oversees. In December, America Online and Time Warner officials lowered their revenue-growth estimates for 2000 because of softness in the movie and music businesses. The company was hurt when New Line Cinema's movie *Little Nicky,* starring Adam Sandler, flopped, and music sales were left stagnant by Warner Music's shortage of hot new artists. "These are hit-driven businesses," says analyst Scott B. Davis of First Union Securities Inc. Parsons must put the right people in place to sniff out those hits.

50   Even if he doesn't go into the Bush Administration, Parsons may decide that his diminished role at AOL Time Warner doesn't suit him, so he may move on. "He's a natural target. Dick Parsons is one of the up-and-coming CEO players," says Dennis C. Carey, vice-chairman of executive search firm Spencer Stuart. It may just be that after six years of nursing bruised egos, improving the balance sheet, and tackling corporate crises, Parsons will decide it's time to try something new.

AOL ABROAD: MILES TO GO

51   Boris Becker may be fearsome on the tennis court, but gosh, he sure looks confused by this Internet thing. Then the German sports idol gets America Online. A few clicks, and the familiar blue triangle pops onto his PC screen. "I'm in!" cries Becker in a German TV spot promoting the portal, which in Germany runs customized channels on topics like finance, travel, and sports, just as it does in the U.S.

EXHIBIT 6
A Global Report Card on AOL

Source: *BusinessWeek*

Eyeballs
Strong showing in Europe, where members like the content. Elsewhere, so-so.

Ranking
Faces stiff competition from the local telcos and ISPs, like Deutsche Telekom in Germany or Fujitsu's Nifty Corp. in Japan.

Innovation
Ambitious plans are afoot for wireless Net applications, especially in tandem with Japan's AOL.

52   The strategy of offering special content and easy access has boosted AOL subscriptions 60% in the past year, to 3.9 million, in Europe. Still, AOL subscriber numbers lag behind the big telecom companies. In Germany, for example, anyone who upgrades to Deutsche Telekom's high-speed digital phone service automatically gets a subscription to T-Online, the company's Internet access provider. Elsewhere in Japan and Latin America, AOL is still small potatoes. Yet AOL Time Warner boss Robert W. Pittman wants AOL to succeed overseas. When AOL memberships in the U.S. peak, growth has to come from somewhere.

53   So AOL is forging ahead. Company executives predict a boom as European countries finally move toward flat-rate local phone service. That will allow people to surf as long as they want without paying extra phone charges. In Britain, AOL usage doubled to an average of an hour a day with the introduction of flat rates, says Michael Lynton, president of AOL International. When rates drop, he says, "the Net becomes a mass-market product, where AOL succeeds."

Key Task

54   America Online Inc. needs to pile up foreign subscribers for its fixed-line service to prepare for the spread of the Internet from PCs to TVs, handheld computers, and—especially in Europe—mobile phones. If AOL can create a mobile online world as friendly as the one it created for PCs, it could finally bust ahead of competitors.

55   For AOL, the key will be to exploit its expertise in packaging content, which keeps its German subscribers, for example, online nearly four times as long as T-Online users. AOL is also lining up partners such as Carphone Warehouse Group PLC, the British-based mobile-phone retailer, and British Telecommunications PLC's Genie service, which provides mobile Internet access.

56   The biggest growth potential for mobile services is probably in Asia and Latin America. There, mobile phones offer cheap access to millions of people who can't afford PCs. Yet in Japan, AOL is a weak player, with only 400,000 fixed-line subscribers.

57   A key weapon may be AOL's alliance in Japan with mobile-phone operator NTT DoCoMo. The deal gives AOL a chance to learn from the only company that has helped create a mobile Internet with mass appeal, thanks to the DoCoMo i-mode service. AOL is also in talks with Dutch telecom company KPN Mobile, DoCoMo's European partner. That could give AOL important access in Germany, where KPN owns No. 3 mobile service provider E-Plus. "AOL has to develop services specifically for the wireless market, so it needs to get close to operators," says Kiyoyuki Tsujimura, DoCoMo's global strategist.

58   Tsujimura sees plenty in the deal for DoCoMo as well. DoCoMo hopes to tap Time Warner's music, movies, cartoons, and more. AOL can help DoCoMo deliver service too:

Japanese can reserve a plane ticket by visiting an AOL site from their desktop PCs, then be notified on their handsets when the tickets are ready to be picked up at the closest travel office. Already in Europe, an AOL service cuts between the fixed line and mobile world by letting people send short messages from AOL screens to mobile phones.

59   Yet AOL also faces competition from other content providers. Adversary No. 1 may be Bertelsmann, until earlier this year 50-50 partner in AOL Europe and still a provider of content to the American portal. Yet the Time-Warner union compelled Bertelsmann to sell its stake in AOL Europe, and AOL Europe chief Andreas Schmidt has bolted to Bertelsmann, where he plans to use the mobile Net to steer users to his company's online book and music shops.

60   AOL has to get its own house in order overseas: The company still hasn't replaced Schmidt. Lynton is running AOL Europe from New York, and insiders say the U.S. managers are too preoccupied to pay attention to international. Lynton denies there's any management drift. And AOL does have a great product, abroad as well as at home. But AOL's foreign adventure will need constant, loving attention to achieve its goals.

Source: Adapted by Richard Robinson, University of South Carolina, based on Catherine Yang, with Ronald Grover and Ann Therese Palmer, "Show Time for AOL Time Warner," *BusinessWeek,* January 15, 2001; and Jack Ewing and Catherine Yang, with Irene M. Kunii, "AOL Abroad: Miles to Go," *BusinessWeek,* International Edition, January 15, 2001.

Case 13

BusinessWeek

Rethinking the Internet

1   Everywhere we look, the once-limitless promise of the Internet appears to be fading. The dot-coms that were supposed to topple industry giants have mostly vanished. The last of the Net's bluest-chips are on the ropes. No. 1 e-tailer Amazon.com Inc. can't extract a profit from its $2.8 billion in sales, leading some to predict it will run out of money. And on Mar. 7, one of the few profitable Web companies, portal Yahoo! Inc., said it would badly miss sales projections for the first quarter. Internet stocks are in free fall, many of them lucky to top a buck a share—sending billions of dollars of investment up in smoke.

2   And the collapse isn't stopping at the dot-coms, as the once-untouchable makers of the networking and computer gear that serve as the Internet's foundation are also on the run. On Mar. 9, network equipment maker Cisco Systems Inc. jolted the market with its second warning of slower growth to come, announcing its first-ever widespread layoffs. That followed a warning of slowing sales in late February from Sun Microsystems Inc., whose servers run countless websites.

3   Now, the mounting woes of the Internet sector seem to be spreading to the rest of the economy. Just as the rollout of the Internet helped fuel the boom of the 1990s, the evaporation of Net euphoria is helping drag down consumer confidence and corporate capital spending, not to mention the stock market. Since the beginning of the year, the Standard & Poor's 500-stock index is down 12%, and the U.S. economy looks ready to slide into its first tech-triggered recession.

4   But look beyond the current economic and market plight, and a different picture emerges. As with any new technology, the early years of the Internet have been a learning process—and here's what we now know. First, the Internet was supposed to change everything. That's just plain wrong. The reality is, there was no way that a single technology could fulfill such an extravagant promise.

5   Instead, it turns out that the transformative power of the Internet is being felt unevenly. There are plenty of industries and situations where the Net has the potential to be revolutionary, as its most enthusiastic backers had predicted, and their number will

EXHIBIT 1

Source: Jupiter, Media Metrix Inc., Commerce Dept. Bureau of Labor Statistics © BW.

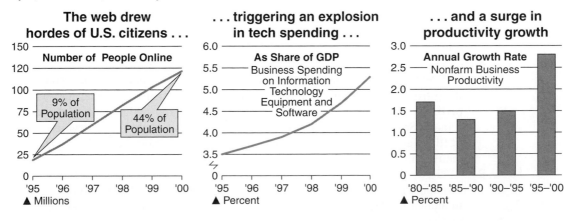

EXHIBIT 2

Source: Commerce Dept., Bloomberg Financial Markets © BW.

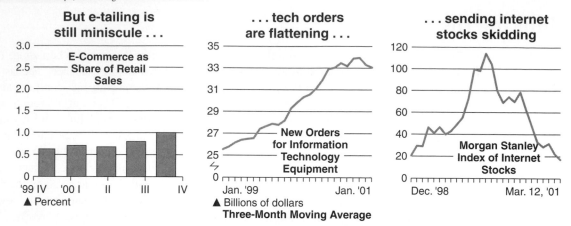

only widen as new technologies such as broadband come into widespread use. But clearly in much of the economy, the Internet offers incremental payoffs without substantially altering core businesses. And even in industries where the Net can effect profound change, institutional barriers and business inertia mean the big gains may not come for years.

6   Strip away the highfalutin talk, and at bottom, the Internet is a tool that dramatically lowers the cost of communication. That means it can radically alter any industry or activity that depends heavily on the flow of information. In areas such as financial services, the process is well under way. In other information-intensive industries, such as entertainment, health care, government, and education, the potential lies in the future. But it's there. Says Gary E. Rieschel, executive managing director at Softbank Venture Capital, one of the biggest backers of Internet ventures: "The Internet is about communications, and people have never at any time in history stopped wanting to communicate."

7   That means the Internet can dramatically reduce the cost of both consumer and business transactions. It also can improve coordination, both within and across companies, while giving them direct contact with consumers. "The reality is that e-business is a tremendous tool for cost reduction, it's a tremendous tool to help you get closer to your customer, it's a tremendous tool for what used to be called Old Economy companies to apply to our current processes," says Brian P. Kelley, vice-president of global consumer services at Ford Motor Co. and the architect of most of the auto maker's e-business initiatives.

8   Over the coming decade, the biggest gains will come from restructuring the way work is done within companies. The Net can become the communications backbone for everything from linking supply chains for speedy product turnarounds to storing employee expertise so that co-workers can tap into ready-made knowledge instead of starting from scratch. Says Massachusetts Institute of Technology economist Erik Brynjolfsson: "Most of [the Net's benefits] will come in changes to business practices and organization. What really matters is when companies and markets reorganize."

9   Given the crucial role of communication and information, the long-term impact on economic growth could be substantial. The Internet could add up to 0.4 percentage points to annual productivity growth over the next five years, according to new research from

EXHIBIT 3
Where the Internet
May Be
Revolutionary . . .

These information-intensive industries are good candidates to be transformed by the Web.

Financial Services
Most financial services can potentially be handled electronically. But so far, banks can't
even figure out a good way of letting people pay bills online.

Entertainment
Much of entertainment can easily be digitized. But no one knows how to make money
yet, and the technology is lagging.

Health Care
The benefits of shifting health-care transactions to the Web could be enormous. But so
are the institutional barriers.

Education
E-learning could cut the costs of education, but only at the price of making education
more impersonal.

Government
Delivering information to citizens electronically has enormous appeal, but requires massive
investments.

. . . and Where the Impact May Be Incremental

Industries where information plays a relatively small role.

Retailing
The glitzy websites got all the attention. But dot-com success turned more on who had
the best logistics.

Manufacturing
Web-enabled supply chains and intranets are important, but ultimately a manufacturer
lives or dies on the quality of its goods.

Travel
Online travel sites are popular, but the ultimate constraint on travel is the physical capacity
of the air and road systems.

Power
Online energy exchanges get the publicity, but power generation and transmission
capabilities will have the bigger economic impact.

the Brookings Institution. "We're looking at an improvement in income per person of
roughly $1,500 in 2010," says Robert E. Litan, director of economic studies at Brookings,
who led the study, along with Alice M. Rivlin, former vice-chairman of the Federal Reserve. And this estimate doesn't take into account the further gains that would come
should broadband be affordably piped into every home, making interaction with the Internet far richer.

10   If applied right, ultimately, the Internet could boost the rate of innovation by increasing the speed at which ideas spread between companies, within economies, and across
countries. With more information available, new ideas will get noticed and put into practice faster. "The Internet is the friend of companies making products that are truly unique
and different," says Gary Hamel, chairman of the San Francisco office of consulting firm
Strategos. "That means the premium for real innovation will go up."

TRUE GRIT

11   But the very strengths of the Internet are also its limitations. Just because communication is ubiquitous doesn't mean it's everything. The last five years have taught us that in industries such as retailing, manufacturing, and transportation, physical factors overpower the virtual. E-tailing turns out to be more about which company is best at moving boxes around rather than who has the glitziest website or the biggest virtual store on earth. Linking supply chains over the Net cuts costs and improves response times, but ultimately manufacturers succeed or fail if they develop good products and figure out how to produce them at low cost and high quality. Online airline reservation systems can improve customer convenience and boost the revenue yield per passenger, but they can't do anything about long delays caused by runaway congestion, too few loading gates, antiquated air traffic control systems, and mechanical difficulties on airplanes.

12   Even in areas where the Internet can play a central role, the big changes are not going to come overnight, as investors have found to their chagrin. Some of the information-intensive industries where the Internet could have its biggest effect are also the ones where institutional and regulatory barriers are the highest and vested interests are the strongest. In health care and education, for example, the possible benefits from widespread use of the Web are enormous, but it's going to happen in baby steps, over time. What's more, it's a difficult, painful, and slow process to restructure companies and markets. "We have cherry-picked some of the easy projects," says Andrew McAfee, a Harvard Business School professor who has studied how businesses use the Internet.

13   In the end, it turns out that the speed of Internet time has more to do with the capital markets than with the pace of technology adoption. The enormous amounts of venture capital available to startups drove companies to grow far faster in a few short years than the underlying infrastructure or consumer demand could support. In fact, the eventual benefits of the Web should be measured over a decade. "People had higher expectations for the next couple of years than are likely to be realized," says Jeffrey P. Bezos, CEO of Amazon.com. "And people have much lower expectations for the next couple of years than are likely to be realized over the next 10 years."

14   That may help explain the current confusion about the future of the Internet. On one hand, Internet usage continues to rise, and consumer e-commerce sales are up by 67% over a year earlier, according to the Census Bureau. "Our research doesn't show any downturn in consumer behavior," says Mary Modahl, vice-president of marketing at Forrester Research.

GOT WEB?

15   That's why Internet optimists are refusing to retreat. Analyst Mary Meeker of Morgan Stanley Dean Witter is urging Net leaders such as Amazon, Yahoo, and AOL Time Warner to band together in a Got Milk?-style marketing campaign promoting the idea that the Web is alive and well. Another group, led by Michael Tchong, CEO of technology consultant Iconocast Inc., has launched a Back the Net campaign to urge people to buy something online or 10 shares in a Net company on Apr. 3.

16   Such Webfests, however, aren't likely to change the minds of burned investors or restore the once-buoyant expectations for the Net. For instance, Merrill Lynch & Co. analyst Henry M. Blodget recently reduced his expectations for how much retail sales will go online to only 5% to 10%, down from 10% to 15% he envisioned just a few months ago. Even Bradford C. Koenig, head of the technology banking practice at Goldman, Sachs &

Co., which underwrote many of the hottest Net initial public offerings, has lost confidence in pure Internet companies: "The notion of an Internet company is no longer viable."

17   But that's too pessimistic. In fact, part of the problem was that much of the investment flowed into areas where the Internet is incremental rather than revolutionary. Take retailing. The hyped consumer dot-coms were supposed to blow away their brick-and-mortar counterparts. But it turns out that the importance of information and communication in retailing—the Internet's forte—is much smaller than the role of logistics. How much smaller? According to Softbank's Rieschel, it takes between $15 million and $25 million to build a top-of-the-line website. Yet it costs at least $150 million to build a warehouse and distribution system for a consumer Web operation. "The Internet only solved 10% of the process, the front-end purchase process," says Rieschel. "What we really needed to do was fund the back end."

18   All across retailing, the Internet is no longer seen as the 800-pound gorilla. For example, a year ago, the prevailing wisdom was that old-fashioned auto dealers were going to be passé. But so far, that hasn't turned out to be true. "There hasn't been the massive shift to buying cars online that we thought there would be 18 months ago," admits Mark T. Hogan, president of e-GM, the auto maker's online consumer unit.

19   And there's growing evidence that shoppers on the Net are supersensitive to price, according to Austan Goolsbee, an economist at the University of Chicago. The implication is that any profits e-tailers might make could be short-lived as competition drives prices down on the Web. "Now, retail once again looks like a brutal, low-margin business," says Goolsbee.

20   The Internet was also supposed to transform markets by wiping out the middlemen. Real estate agents, for example, were expected to dwindle away as buyers located homes on the Web while paying lower commissions. But the reverse turned out to be true, since the number of real estate agents has grown rather than fallen. "Studies have shown that people who use the Internet use Realtors more than those who don't," says Stuart Wolff, CEO of Homestore.com Inc., the largest home and real estate related site.

21   Perhaps the biggest surprise is the comparatively limited impact that the Internet may have on manufacturing. To be sure, there is no doubt that e-business has become an essential part of any manufacturer's toolkit. The use of the Internet can reduce inventories, take costs out of the supply chain, and eliminate unnecessary transactions. Collaboration can also speed up product development, e-marketplaces can lower the cost of components and other supplies, and detailed info on customers can help customize products to snag bigger orders or even help determine which customers aren't cost-effective. At Procter & Gamble Co., a Web-based information-sharing network makes it easier to collect and evaluate new product ideas from the company's far-flung workforce of 110,000 people.

22   Nevertheless, at the end of the day, manufacturers are still in the business of making things, not simply moving bits and bytes around. Wheels have to be bolted onto the car, circuit boards have to be installed in the router—and that has to be done physically.

23   To understand how this limits the impact of the Internet in manufacturing, look at the example of Cisco, the communications equipment maker that is universally regarded as the poster company for using the Web. Some 68% of Cisco's orders are placed and fulfilled over the Web and 70% of its service calls are resolved online. Cisco is in the process of linking all of its contract manufacturers and key suppliers into an advanced Web supply-chain management system, dubbed eHub. This speeds up the rate at which information about demand is distributed to suppliers.

24   According to Cisco's own calculations, its payoff from its use of the Internet amounts to $1.4 billion per year, or 7% of sales. If the rest of manufacturing could do even half as well as Cisco in using the Internet, that would cut an impressive $150 billion from annual

manufacturing costs. But these figures need to be put in perspective. A 7% reduction in costs is nothing to sneeze at, but it is not the radical reduction in costs that would signal a revolution.

SLOW AS MOLASSES

25   And while supply chains linked over the Net are more responsive than their predecessors, they have their limits, too. "The flexibility now being demanded by customers exceeds the physics of what the supply chain can actually deliver," says Kevin R. Burns, chief materials officer for contract manufacturer Solectron Corp., whose big customers include Cisco and IBM. Now that companies have switched to Web-based models, he notes, they expect to be able to ramp up or halt production of a product within weeks. But it still takes at least three months to get a specially designed chip made in a Taiwanese foundry and around 40 weeks to order an LCD screen.

26   And while the unprecedented communications capabilities of the Web should enable corporations and markets to be organized in new ways, it's going to take longer than proponents expected. "At the marketplace level, I haven't seen radical changes brought on by the Internet," says McAfee. "It's going to be a much more gradual process."

27   While the obstacles don't disappear, it's easier to see the far-reaching potential of the Internet in those industries that are primarily about moving information rather than truckloads of goods. Take financial services. In many ways, financial products are ideally suited to the Internet, since they deal only with information. Indeed, a recent Goldman Sachs survey reported that 63% of financial companies had sold their products through an e-marketplace or a website, the highest of any industry.

28   The Internet is already well on its way to transforming financial services. Online brokers such as E*Trade Group Inc. have completely changed how the retail brokerage business worked. And Internet services are now offered by nearly every U.S. bank and credit union. Bank of America says it's signing up 130,000 online customers a month, giving it more than 3 million Internet customers. Citigroup has 2.2 million, Wells Fargo & Co. more than 2.5 million. FleetBoston Financial Corp., the nation's seventh-largest bank, combined its online banking services with its online brokerage business, Quick & Reilly, and its online customer base jumped 50%, to more than 1 million customers, which is 35% of the total customer base.

29   But as in the case of entertainment, technological and institutional barriers are slowing down the eventual gains. Consider online bill-paying, widely anticipated to be the "sticky app" that drives traffic. The benefits of paying bills on the Net, for both consumers and businesses, could be enormous. But the technology has proven exceptionally complicated, and it has hit a wall trying to penetrate the banking industry. Among the problems: Banks and billers have been unable to agree on how bills should actually appear online. Still, Bank of America plans to launch a big ad campaign later this year to promote its bill-paying service.

30   And then there's health care. Despite the tangible nature of many medical services, health care has a very large information component that makes it a natural for Internet applications. Just shifting claims-processing to the Web could save $20 billion a year, according to the Brookings economists. At Merck-Medco Managed Care, the nation's leading provider of prescription drug care, it costs a matter of cents to handle a prescription order on the Internet, as opposed to more than $1 through other methods, notes Stephen J. Gold, senior vice-president.

BROADBAND'S PROMISE

31   But there are enormous institutional barriers. For one, privacy considerations may slow down the full shift of health-care records to the Web. Moreover, health-insurance companies, doctors, and hospitals are unwilling to give up control of patient records and insurance payments to a third party. This reluctance helped frustrate WebMD and Healtheon, which expected to lead a restructuring of health care by moving many claims, payment, and related processing services to the Net. WebMD's efforts to provide real-time payment capabilities were shunned by insurers and HMOs, who prefer the current cumbersome process that lets them hold money longer.

32   There's also the technology factor. In the long run, realizing the promise of the Net will depend on the widespread introduction of advanced technologies such as broadband to the home and high-speed wireless. With broadband connections over telephone or cable-television lines, consumers will be able to watch TV-quality video clips of the NCAA basketball tournament or download crystal-clear music files faster than ever before. What's more, they're more likely to use the Net because they'll always be connected and won't have to spend minutes dialing into the Net each time they want to visit a site.

33   The problem is that getting the new technologies in place may take longer than expected. Financially stressed telecom companies are slowing down the roll out of broadband. The failure of small telecom providers means that subscriber growth may slow down in second- or third-tier markets. And the prices for high-speed Internet access may rise. SBC Communications Inc. recently raised the price of its residential high-speed Internet service by 25%, or $10 per month, which is likely to slow its adoption. "Until the foundation of Internet infrastructure gets built out, we're not going to see any consumer Net companies emerging," says Michael Parekh, director of Internet research, GoldmanSachs.

34   In the end, the Internet seems likely to revolutionize mainly communications-intensive industries and activities. If that seems too limited, remember that almost every breakthrough technology over the last 200 years affected some areas of the economy more than others. The automobile transformed personal transportation and patterns of housing while little affecting manufacturing. Electricity radically altered manufacturing practices and any industry that was power-intensive, while not having an enormous effect on health care. The Internet deserves to be put in such august company.

E-BIZ: DOWN BUT HARDLY OUT

35   It's hard to ignore the economy when it comes up and slaps you hard across the face. Take General Motors Corp. Its sales of cars and trucks slipped 9% last month on top of a 5% drop in January and a rough fourth quarter last year. Now the company is cutting costs across the board—even shaving 10% off the budget at e-GM, its e-commerce unit that generates 1,000 sales leads per week for its dealers and incorporates Web technology in its cars. Its president, Mark T. Hogan, says the corporate parent remains a big believer in how the Internet will reshape the way it will do business, but those changes will happen more slowly. "We're pushing out some future stuff that we would have liked to have done quicker," says Hogan.

36   With the economy stalling, expect GM's brand of reluctant pragmatism to rule the day. The companies that have begun remaking their businesses by shifting operations

EXHIBIT 4

Source: Forrester Research Inc. © BW.

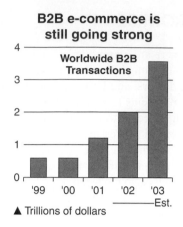

B2B e-commerce is still going strong

Worldwide B2B Transactions

'99 '00 '01 '02 '03
—Est.

▲ Trillions of dollars

onto the Internet still see the financial benefits in doing so. But the economic malaise is delaying their efforts. New tech orders slipped to $33.1 billion in January, down from $34 billion in November, according to the Commerce Dept. And in a February survey of 150 corporate chief information officers by Morgan Stanley & Co., 11% said they plan on spending less on technology because of the slowing economy. Another 27% said they're evaluating whether to cut back or delay purchases. "If you're scared, you wait, and a lot of people are scared," says analyst Charles E. Phillips of Morgan Stanley.

37   Not everyone, however. For companies that have tasted the early results of the Internet, there's a strong will to stay the course. According to interviews with dozens of corporations and surveys of hundreds more, many of the e-business pioneers are forging ahead even as the economy falters and dot-coms implode. From conglomerate General Electric Co. to office-products retailer Staples Inc., they're determined to get the most they can out of the Internet. And they warn others to back off at their own peril. When the stock-market bubble burst for Net companies, "it was like the pressure was off. I think that's going to lead to a significant reduction in efforts," says Jeffrey K. Skilling, chief executive of energy supplier Enron Corp. "We think that's a huge mistake. Incumbent companies have got to come to grips with this new technology because it is very, very powerful."

38   Selling stuff online is the least of it. What Skilling and others are doing is integrating the Internet into every nook and cranny of their businesses. Call it managing by Web. They're using the Net for everything from filing expense reports and calculating daily sales tallies to sharing employees' intellectual capital and communicating instantaneously with suppliers. The Web, for example, lets Cisco Systems Inc. connect directly with its suppliers so that when the maker of networking equipment gets an order, suppliers can start making parts right away. That puts inventories on a bread-and-water diet. The Net also can automate interactions with customers: About 40 of Dow Chemical Co.'s customers reorder chemicals without human intervention when sensors in their storage tanks signal they're running dry.

39   Corporate transformations like those being undertaken at Cisco and Dow Chemical represent the real potential of the Internet. Even considering the slowdown, market researcher Gartner Group expects business-to-business e-commerce to reach $3.6 trillion in 2003, compared with just $107 billion in consumer transactions. With a lure like that, companies that are holding off buying traditional computing gear are focusing their tech dollars on e-business. But not all e-business. Companies are focusing on areas that give the quickest results. According to a January survey of corporate execs by AMR Research, 87% will either sustain or increase their spending on Internet initiatives for sales growth

EXHIBIT 5
Hitting Pay Dirt in
the Virtual World

Even with the crash in Internet stocks, companies are investing heavily in online initiatives. Here's a look at where they're putting their money—and the payoff.

Electronic Commerce
Pegged to hit $6.8 trillion in 2004, with 90% of that coming from business-to-business sales, says Forrester Research. About 80% of Cisco Systems' orders are taken online, about $5 billion last quarter—saving the networking giant $760 million in annual operating costs.

E-Marketplaces
Transactions on e-marketplaces expected to reach $2.8 trillion in 2004, says AMR Research. Defense contractor United Technologies bought $450 million worth of metals, motors, and other products from an e-marketplace in 2000 and got prices about 15% less than what it usually pays.

Procurement
Businesses will buy $2.8 trillion in supplies over the Internet in 2004, excluding e-marketplace purchases, says AMR Research. Eastman Chemical is buying 19% of its supplies online now, up from almost nothing two years ago. That has helped boost productivity 9% per year.

Knowledge Management
Companies will spend $10.2 billion to store and share their employees' knowledge over the Net by 2004, says IDC. Electronics manufacturer Siemens has spent $7.8 million to create a website for employees to share expertise to help win contracts. The result: new sales of $122 million.

Customer Relationships
Corporations will invest $12.2 billion by 2004 on linking customers, sales, and marketing over the Web, says the META Group. Lands' End converts more than 10% of its Web visitors to buyers—compared with the average 4.9%—in part because it offers live chat and other customer-service extras.

and customer management, and 84% will hold firm or increase their budgets for taking purchasing online. Health maintenance organization Kaiser Permanente, for example, is investing heavily in moving its purchasing to the Net, and that will contribute to a 10% increase in its overall spending on e-commerce this year. "We're not abandoning our commitment to these investments because we think they're going to yield long-term benefits for us," says Richard Pettingill, president of Kaiser's California division.

"Whole Hog"

40   The pull of e-biz is obvious. Companies find that moving their operations to the Net means money in their pockets. After just over two years, Staples, the $10.7 billion office-supply retailer, boosted annual online sales to $512 million last year. And that's not robbing from store sales. The average yearly spending of small-business customers leaps from $600 to $2,800 when they shop online. Staples is slowing store openings to a trickle, but plans to spend $50 million on technology this year—the same as last. "We're still going whole hog," says CEO Thomas G. Stemberg. "The payoffs are just very high."

41   Still, many companies are more cautious about shifting their businesses to the Net these days. Dazzling promise has given way to more realistic expectations. For starters, the technology is expensive and complicated. At a large corporation, a big e-biz project can cost tens of millions of dollars and take a year or more to install properly. And, when things go wrong, it gets even pricier. On Feb. 26, Nike blamed its software suppliers when problems with a new supply-chain management system contributed to the loss of up to $100 million in sales and a profit shortfall. "So this is what we get for our $400 million!" thundered CEO Philip H. Knight in an earnings conference call. While analysts say it's unclear who deserves the blame, disasters like this are a black eye for e-business.

42   There are cultural hurdles to overcome, too. Just because technology is available to turn a company's business processes upside down doesn't mean the folk who work there welcome the shake-up. When chemical maker Buckman Laboratories International Inc. launched its companywide information sharing system, managers at first declined to participate. They figured knowledge is power and were reluctant to give it up. So the company had to come up with ways of rewarding participation and punishing those who held back. According to Gartner Group, a full 50% to 70% of the work it takes to make a knowledge-management initiative a success revolves around coaxing cultural changes.

43   Another hang-up: Suppliers and customers might not be ready to play along. A Mar. 4 report issued by Jupiter Research showed that 50% of the procurement agents surveyed see so little advantage in going online that they expect to do less than 20% of their purchasing over the Net for at least the next two years. The primary reason? Their existing suppliers aren't online yet, and they want to keep buying from suppliers they know.

44   Things get even dicier when it comes to public e-marketplaces where buyers and sellers gather to haggle. More than 1,500 e-marketplaces were launched in the past five years, and already 125 of them are either out of business or have been acquired. Corporations are nervous about handing over their purchasing processes to dinky outfits that might go dark next month. Then there's the trust issue. "Everybody believes their supply chain is a competitive advantage," says Douglas J. Grimm, senior vice-president for global strategic sourcing at auto parts maker Dana Corp. "Why would I want to share that with a competitor?"

45   All this means that the e-business revolution now looks like it will advance at an evolutionary pace rather than a gallop. Citing the economic slowdown and disarray among the e-marketplaces, Gartner Group on Mar. 13 issued a less aggressive forecast for the future of worldwide business-to-business e-commerce. Instead of hitting $7.3 trillion in 2004, Gartner now predicts a total of $6 trillion—less than 10% of all B2B transactions.

Window of Opportunity

46   For e-business believers, the key to getting started is leadership. Is the boss behind the Net? John F. Welch, CEO of GE, left no doubt in the minds of his 340,000 employees when he said during a Jan. 17 TV interview that GE wouldn't let up on its tech projects. In fact, tech spending is growing by 12%. "This is the moment to widen the gap as far as we're concerned," he said. On Mar. 13, GE said that it expects to save $1.6 billion from its tech projects in the next year and that Web sales will hit $15 billion. "GE won't slow down," says Adrian J. Slywotzky, a vice-president at Mercer Management Consulting Inc. and co-author of the book *How Digital Is Your Business?* "It depends on how many people think and behave like Jack Welch that will determine how long this slowdown lasts and how much productivity improvement happens in the next 12 months."

47   There seems to be a Welch-like impulse among some corporate leaders these days. In Forrester's survey, 35% of 1,000 large North American companies said they already are selling products online, either to consumers or businesses. An additional 30% said they're now rolling out such systems, and 16% said they're considering it.

48   E-business pioneers light the way. Tech companies such as Cisco have moved more than 80% of their sales online—and much of their purchasing, too. Cisco's Net systems haven't

EXHIBIT 6
How Companies Use
the Web

Source: Forrester Research and
AMR Research.

	Got It Already	Starting It Now	Considering	No Plans Yet
Company Intranets	65%	15%	4%	17%
Selling Online	35	30	16	19
Customer Service	21	34	28	18
Capturing Worker Knowledge	15	32	27	27

Percent of companies sticking to key e-business expansion plans

Sales and Customer Service	87%
Supply-Chain Management	84
Group Trading Exchanges	94

inoculated it from the sick economy, but when the company got hit with a sudden drop-off in orders in mid-December, just-in-time information let it immediately cut back on its parts ordering and set in motion a cost-cutting strategy that includes 8,000 job losses.

49   While tech companies have been e-business leaders, others are experimenting, too. In just two years, Eastman Chemical Co., a $5.1 billion chemical manufacturer in Kingsport, Tenn., has moved 15% of its sales and 19% of its purchasing online. To help transform the way the chemical industry operates, Eastman is entering joint ventures with other industry players—including a logistics website to coordinate shipping and storage. Next, it will be piloting a collaborative planning, forecasting, and replenishing system that links Eastman with its customers and suppliers. Thanks to the Net, Eastman has improved its revenues per employee—now at $340,000—by an average of 9% each year for the past five years.

Ford's Promise

50   Hard numbers are difficult to nail down, but it seems e-business is having a considerable impact on companies latching onto the Net. In a quarterly survey released on Mar. 8 of nearly 500 top executives, Pricewaterhouse-Coopers reported that those that used the Net aggressively last year scored productivity gains—measured by increases in revenues per employee—2.7 times greater than those of businesses who had not yet embraced the Net.

51   Consider Ford Motor Co. Engineers searching for ways to improve the fuel efficiency of its vehicles are using Web collaboration technology to share design changes and other information with engineers and suppliers scattered around several locations. That way, they can instantly analyze how a proposed design change would affect a vehicle's fuel economy. Analysis that might have taken three days can now be completed in less than a minute. That's important as Ford races to make good on a promise to boost the fuel economy of its sport-utility vehicles 25% by 2005. Just as significantly, the technology will shave $5 million to $15 million off a vehicle's development costs. While that's small change on a car that costs $2 billion to develop, the savings would be sizable if it were applied companywide, Ford says.

52   General Mills Inc. harnesses the Net to cut down on shipping expenses. Rather than do things the old-fashioned way and ship its products on scores of half-empty trucks, it now uses the Web to collaborate with 20 other companies from other industries that are shipping products on the same routes. General Mills, its partners, and their trucking companies can tap into the system from any Web browser and find somebody to help them fill up trucks on outbound trips and load empty trucks with goods on return journeys. On test routes, General Mills has saved 7% on shipping costs—or about $2 million in the first year.

EXHIBIT 7
Consumer Web
Unplugged

With the future of Yahoo! and Amazon.com growing dicier, BusinessWeek *offers these "bets" on business-to-consumer models that work:*

Niches Are Nice
E-tailers that focus on a niche will fare better. Profitable pet supplier Waggin' Tails specializes in high-margin products, unlike the defunct Pets.com, which tried to do it all.

Information Brokers
The No. 1 thing Netizens do online is look for information. Those that make it pay will win. Job-listing site Monster.com, which charges employers to post positions, makes money.

The Fence-Straddlers
Businesses in both the physical and virtual worlds reign. Merck-Medco, the nation's leading provider of prescription-drug care, racking up $460 million in online sales last year, has clobbered Net upstarts drugstore.com and PlanetRx.

A la Carte Models
Business models that boast multiple ways of making money have good odds. Real estate listing service Homestore.com, which sells technology and ads, will be profitable this year on projected revenues of $440 million.

What We'll Pay For

Internet Access
A few free, plain-vanilla dial-up services may persist, but nearly all will charge for a connection and technical support, especially for high-speed broadband access.

Analysis
Highly valued analyses of information, such as stock market prognostications or a city-by-city list of best doctors, will come with a fee.

Entertainment
Just as we pay for all-movie and music-video cable TV, we'll pay for video-on-demand and music on the Web, especially now that the courts have outlawed Napster's free file-sharing service.

Specialized Services
How about an online personal shopper? Or an advance peek at the Armani line for fall? An upscale e-tailer may offer paying club members such online extras.

What Will Remain Free

Commodity Data
Stuff that's widely available everywhere, such as stock quotes, weather, and news, will be Internet giveaways.

Shopping Information
The Web will remain a great place to comparison-shop and gather info on everything from car models to real estate.

Search Engines
They may cost a bundle to build, but the incremental cost of additional searches is minuscule, so they'll stay free and rely on advertising and licensing to companies.

Purchases
Surcharges would make e-shopping lose its competitive advantage over catalog retailers and in-store purchasing.

Fresh Paranoia

53 For such old-line companies as General Mills, braving the new world of e-business involves tearing up and replacing old systems. Young companies have the distinct advantage that they can get wired from the ground up. Look at Juniper Networks Inc. In just three years, it came out of nowhere to capture 35% of the market for high-end Internet routers. Juniper outsources 100% of its production to contract manufacturers. Juniper's customers, mainly big telecom service providers, order their equipment on Juniper's Web portal—but the orders go straight to the contract manufacturers. Sales have exploded from just $3.8 million in 1998 to $673 million in 2000. And, thanks to the Net, Juniper has $726,000 in annual revenues per employee, vs. $320,600 for older rival Nortel Networks, which handles considerably less of its sales online.

54 The first phase of the Net—when retailers worried about being Amazoned—may be over. But in the dawning e-business era, a new rallying cry will be heard: Don't get Junipered. This threat could turn out to be much more potent than the last.

Source: Adapted by Richard Robinson, University of South Carolina, based on Michael J. Mandel and Robert D. Hof, "Rethinking the Internet," *BusinessWeek,* March 26, 2001.

Case 14

BusinessWeek

Microsoft's Great Web Offensive

Undaunted by the dot-com downturn, Gates & Co. isn't hedging its bets on .Net. The goal: Dominate cyberspace as Windows does PCs.

1   When Microsoft announced its new software platform, called .Net, in June 2000, the response was lukewarm. Cynical reporters and software developers wondered whether hulking, old-school Microsoft could create new consumer and business software that would achieve the company's goal of dominating the free-spirited Internet.

2   In a column entitled, "Microsoft's .Net: Visionary or Vaporware?" Salon.com's Scott Rosenberg summed up what everyone was thinking: "Here they go again. . . . This is the classic language of vaporware: Software products that do not yet exist but that companies feel compelled to announce in an effort to cow competitors and wow investors." Adds Jamie Lewis, CEO of the Burton Group, a research firm that recently published a report titled *Deciphering Microsoft .Net:* "When [.Net] was announced, it certainly appeared to be 'market-techture'—lots of slides without much real architecture."

3   Nearly 18 months later, the doubters are fewer—or at least, less vocal. Microsoft is one of the few big players on the Web that has weathered the dot-com meltdown well. The company has already delivered the first product in its ambitious strategy—Windows XP, the new operating system for PCs, which launched on Oct. 25.

QUESTIONED COMMITMENT

4   With .Net as its roadmap, Microsoft is moving full-steam ahead with its plan to convert tens of millions of computer users to a subscription model, with Microsoft storing information and providing application software over the Internet—also managing the lion's share of each customer's online commercial transactions. With dot-com competitors of every variety falling by the wayside, the much-ridiculed .Net initiative could put Microsoft in the Internet's catbird seat.

5   You can't blame anyone for questioning Microsoft's commitment to a concept as sweeping as .Net—even when that strategy is mandated by Chairman Bill Gates. The risk involved in leaving behind the PC-centric world to embrace a new paradigm where every future Microsoft product would depend on the Net seemed wildly extreme.

6   Even the software king's employees appeared skeptical of its commitment, judging by how they voted with their feet: Through the summer of 2000, Microsoft, like other traditional tech companies, continued to lose key thinkers to dot-com startups at a furious pace. So numerous were the defections that Microsoft's sworn oath to "bet the company" on the Web began to seem suspiciously like a desperate and belated effort to catch the Internet wave.

BUILDING BLOCKS

7   Whatever its initial motivation, Microsoft seems to be following through. "The paradigm shift"—in which corporate customers would move an ever-increasing volume of business functions to the Web—"was going to happen with or without Microsoft," says Matt

Rosoff, an analyst at Seattle-based research firm Directions on Microsoft. "That's why they jumped in." And how: It's impossible to figure out the budget for .Net because it amounts to a realignment of the entire business of the Colossus of Redmond.

8   Microsoft's aim, as it was with Windows, is to define the basic activities that companies and consumers want to engage in on the Internet, then package those functions into components, says Mark Specker, an analyst with Soundview Technology Group in San Francisco. With Windows, the building blocks were word processing and spreadsheets. For .Net, the elements will include instant messaging via the Net, user authentication, improved security for popular applications such as e-mail and personal calendars, and commercial transactions for consumers.

9   "Businesses will typically gravitate to more prepackaged, functional blocks to do the things they want to do and move away from custom consulting projects," says Specker. "That has been the case in the big tech cycles, from mainframes to DOS"—Microsoft's original operating system, the software that controls the basic functions of a computer. And if corporate tech chieftains are reluctant to bite? "Software is three parts tech and two parts marketing," Specker adds. And no marketer can outspend a determined Microsoft.

MICROSOFT 2.0?

10   The first set of these iconic building blocks is already appearing for consumers. On Oct. 15, just before XP's debut, the company launched the latest version of its consumer Web service, MSN 7, which CEO Steve Ballmer called "the pillar on which we are building the next version of Microsoft." It includes functions such as .Net Alerts, a service that allows consumers to sign up for updates from their favorite websites. So that you don't have to check traffic news before heading out the door from work, .Net Alerts will send rush-hour reports directly to your e-mail, mobile phone, or handheld.

11   The idea is to make something that's useful more so, says Lisa Gurry, an MSN product manager: "The whole industry has gained a lot of knowledge from the dot-com bust. We benefited from watching different models and then supplementing that learning with Microsoft's big R&D budget to figure out what people want now—and five years from now." .Net Alerts are a modest first step. But Specker thinks it's a step in the right direction. "Microsoft is a pile-'em-high, sell-'em-cheap company," he says. "They are right to be betting on the next set of basic functionality that will predominate."

12   Creating those basic building blocks means roping in software developers and end-users simultaneously. For developers, Microsoft will provide a set of tools, based on open standards such as eXtensible Markup Language (XML) and Simple Object Access Protocol (SOAP), with which programmers can build new applications that will work with Microsoft products. Those apps, which could include anything from a shopping "bot" that scours the Net for the cheapest prices to fancy scheduling software, would in turn be sold to corporate customers or visitors to MSN or the sites of other Microsoft partners.

WOOING CONSUMERS

13   In essence, the idea is to create a Web equivalent of AOL's proprietary service—one in which a customer who has signed up can move seamlessly from Web browsing to online shopping and banking. On AOL, that navigation is transparent, but on the Web it can be clunky because each step requires entering a user name and password as well as other personal information, such as a credit-card number.

14 Microsoft won't totally control the code, as it now does with Windows. But the company hopes that as developers start using the platform—which is already available—the must-have services they'll design will become extensions of .Net. In theory, anyway, that will make .Net as irreplaceable for computer users as Windows is today, opening multiple new revenue opportunities for Microsoft and cementing its leadership role in the software business.

15 Still, creating a platform for something as uninhibited as the Internet won't be as easy as designing software for PCs. In fact, .Net's goals are so ambitious that some analysts wonder whether even Microsoft—with its $35 billion cash reserve—can pull it off. To link PCs with wireless devices and businesses with consumers—and provide everyone with a single password that works across all platforms—Microsoft will need to work with many different companies whose software must be altered to work with the coming .Net standard.

FIGHT TO THE FINISH?

16 Microsoft also must win the hearts and minds of consumers. To do this, the software giant will need to pay much more attention to security—an issue that has plagued it over the years and earned the animosity of programmers and consumers alike. Last summer, the CodeRed worm took advantage of flaws in the out-of-the-box Microsoft NT and 2000 Web server software to hijack home PCs and corporate networks. The worm also defaced Web pages and created a significant spike in bogus data traffic that slowed down the entire Internet.

17 In short, .Net is a good idea. But can it be done? That, more than the level of Microsoft's commitment, is what's really still up in the air. Even so, analysts overwhelmingly believe that Microsoft has the determination and cash to make .Net a reality. "As much as we like to pick on big companies, it's the big companies that have the resources, wherewithal, and clout to make something of this scale happen," says Burton Group's Lewis.

18 For proof, just look back over Microsoft's history. It took the company years and billions of dollars to successfully foster the migration of the world's computer users from DOS to Windows 95. Microsoft has now bet its future on .Net. Dot-com meltdown or not, it isn't likely to spare any effort in its bid to make sure that initiative succeeds.

BILL GATES IN YOUR LIVING ROOM

Can Microsoft control the digital home?

19 Meander through the corridors of Building 50 on Microsoft Corp.'s campus and you might, for just one mind-bending moment, feel as if you're in the bowels of consumer-electronics powerhouse Sony Corp. In one room, engineers are ginning up a way to record TV programs on a PC so they can be watched at any hour. Around the corner, workers are noodling over software that makes it a snap to edit home movies and copy them onto a DVD. Still others are figuring out better methods for managing thousands of digital music files. And in the main conference room, rather than the typical corporate white boards, there is a wall-size viewing screen and a sound system that would make the neighbors call the cops—if you dared to have one in your home.

20 Is Microsoft, the no-nonsense king of PC software, having a midlife crisis? Not at all. The software giant is trying on a new persona for a new environment. With PC sales

expected to decline for the second straight year as corporate spending withers, Microsoft is aiming its big guns on entertainment goodies for the home. It's spending more than $2 billion building and marketing its new Xbox game console. And it's sure to spend millions more on everything from its UltimateTV videorecording service to an online subscription music service to a handy wireless electronic tablet for the home, code-named Mira. On Jan. 7, at the Consumer Electronics Show in Las Vegas, Chairman William H. Gates III revealed Microsoft's next-generation technologies aimed at making the PC the electronic hub of the digital home. They'll route music, movies, TV programming, e-mail, and news between the Web and PCs, TV set-top boxes, gadgets, and stereo speakers. "Everything in the home will be connected," predicts Gates. And if he gets his way, most of the gizmos will use Microsoft software.

21   That's why Building 50, brand-spanking new, is the digs for the software maker's eHome division, a skunk works of more than 200 engineers responsible for turning Microsoft into the Sony of the 21st century. The digital home is the biggest market push by Microsoft since it launched its assault on server computing a decade ago, and the front-line troops are stoked. Says J. Allard, one of the architects of the company's Internet strategy and now the lead technologist on the Xbox: "This is a way to build a whole new Microsoft."

22   And perhaps a whole new industry. In the next half-decade, Microsoft hopes to spark a revolution in consumer technology that transforms people's home lives every bit as much as the PC has changed their work lives. The concept is far from new, but Gates and other tech execs say the timing is right now that the Internet has made many consumers more tech-savvy. Indeed, other computer companies are doing the same—from Seagate Technology, which is making storage devices for consumer electronics products, to Apple Computer Inc., which debuted its new iMac for the home on Jan. 7. Says Gates lieutenant Robert J. Bach, who oversees the Xbox group: "The technology revolution has changed the way people do business. The next 5 to 10 years will be the digital entertainment revolution."

23   Microsoft is banking on its consumer business, along with server sales, to help revive growth, which was stuck at about 10% for much of last year. Morgan Stanley Dean Witter & Co. estimates that Microsoft will earn $9.3 billion in the fiscal year that ends on June 30, on revenue of $28.8 billion. In fiscal 2003, it expects Microsoft's earnings to climb to $11.7 billion on sales of $32.7 billion. Much of that growth will be driven by consumer sales, which include the MSN online service, Xbox, and games. This year, sales from the consumer group will account for 12% of Microsoft's total business. In fiscal 2003, that will jump to 18%—just shy of the 21% that's expected from server products. That's one reason why Microsoft's stock is up more than 50% in the past year, to $70. "This is a large market," says CEO Steven A. Ballmer. "There's a great chance to add value. And anytime there's a great chance to add value, there's also a great chance to make money."

24   The consumer push comes at a time when the company seems to be coming out from under the cloud of its antitrust woes. Unless nine dissenting state attorneys general succeed in beefing up the remedies, a settlement with the Justice Dept. and nine other states will do little to prevent Microsoft from using the power of its Windows desktop monopoly to help it win new battles in the consumer realm.

25   For all of Microsoft's power and ambitions, though, the digital home may turn out to be the toughest market it has ever tried to crack. At best, Microsoft will be one of several top players, but it will never dominate digital entertainment the way it does PC software. Analysts expect the markets for video games, consumer online services, home networking, and interactive TV software to collectively top $63 billion in 2005. Microsoft could win in areas such as home networking, where its PC hegemony gives it an advantage. But it will lag in markets such as video game consoles and online services, where entrenched rivals rule.

26   Indeed, AOL Time Warner Inc. has a huge lead in the online service business with 33 million subscribers to Microsoft's 7 million. And Sony may be even harder to beat. The world's leading consumer-electronics brand, Sony makes every key piece of hardware—from PCs to set-top boxes to game consoles. Microsoft's focus is primarily the software that goes inside the machines, and so its success depends, in part, on the smarts of its hardware partners. "Ultimately, it's the hardware that provides the great consumer experience," says Sony President Kunitake Ando.

27   Moreover, Microsoft has been missing the consumer gene for years. All of its major consumer-electronics gambits so far have ended up as disappointments. Its WebTV Internet-access service stalled at 1 million subscribers, and its interactive-TV technologies have gone nowhere. The company's digital stereo speakers and PC-connected telephones were introduced in 1998 only to be abandoned a year later. And the gee-whiz technology in Gates's suburban Seattle mansion—which includes electronic pins that each person wears to signal a preference in digital art, music, and temperature—has required as many as 50 servers, not the stuff of a simple consumer experience. Says Minoru Arakawa, who retired on Jan. 8 as the president of Nintendo of America Inc.: "Microsoft is spending a lot of money, but they are beginners."

28   Even Microsoft's allies are tinkering with rival software, not convinced that Microsoft will be the end-all in the digital home. Microsoft buddy Intel Corp. has used non-Microsoft software in some of its Web appliances. "There will be a lot of experimentation," says Intel CEO Craig R. Barrett. While he thinks the PC can be a hub for home networking, in some cases it will be on the periphery. One alternative to the PC emerged on Jan. 7 when startup Moxi Digital Inc. debuted a system for managing home entertainment via a set-top box.

29   Microsoft is playing to win, though. It's going about this with the patient, war-of-attrition approach that has been so successful in the past. The seeds of this assault were planted in March 1999, when Microsoft execs gathered at a retreat on the shores of Puget Sound to ponder their strategy for the home. Gates, Ballmer, and Bach wondered if they could build a new generation of consumer devices based on PC technologies.

30   Around the same time, a handful of engineers deep inside the company wanted to build the hottest-ever game console. Nat Brown, one of the ringleaders, recruited Allard to get behind the project during a day they spent together playing video games at Allard's cabin in the Cascades. "The heart and soul of this thing came from the garage—5 to 10 dreamers who wanted to take Microsoft into a new space," says Allard.

31   Microsoft's brass decided to attack on all fronts. Microsoft seemed to turn the corner at the 2000 Consumer Electronics Show when it abandoned its tradition of setting up a series of booths to market its products. Instead, it created a model home on the showroom floor—complete with Jetson-like gadgets and a family of actors—to show people how digital technologies might shape their future. "That's when the whole company got the 'aha!'" says Microsoft consumer products strategist Craig J. Mundie.

32   Microsoft decided it would build off what it sees as its "three pillars" for the digital home: MSN, Xbox, and Windows XP, which includes home networking technology. That way the software giant can leverage its strengths into new home entertainment categories such as online music. The plan now is to create specialized products in a wide range of markets rather than try to build an *uber*-box that would handle every function

from gaming to spreadsheets. So, Microsoft teams are pursuing separate tacks on game consoles, consumer PCs, interactive TV, digital home appliances, handheld gizmos, and online services. "The way you get to our vision is by building individual products that are the best in their own categories," says Gates. "It's like Microsoft Office. We built that with Word being the best, Excel being the best. They all had to be the best before the whole integration thing came together."

33   Although Gates says no detailed plan exists for integrating all these home products, Windows and the PC are central to the strategy. That's why Windows XP, the newest version of the company's operating system, is so important. After years of producing crash-prone software, Microsoft finally delivered an operating system that is more like a consumer appliance. Launched on Oct. 25, XP seldom crashes and is easy to use. With XP, it's a snap to edit home movies or burn CDs, programs that are likely to greatly expand the use of the PC in the home. And Windows XP's home networking technology lets the PC automatically discover and connect such networked devices as digital audio receivers. "We're moving Windows to the living room," crows James E. Allchin, group vice-president in charge of Microsoft's operating systems.

34   Microsoft also is taking a page from its past playbook: It's creating an ecosystem in which hardware makers and software developers can create products based on Microsoft technology. "We have partners who are doing cameras and screens and lots of peripherals that will let you reach out to all the different things around the home," Gates says. Already signed up: Samsung, Hewlett-Packard, and NEC, all of which are developing media center PCs that use eHome technology.

35   Those PCs will use a Microsoft software code-named Freestyle. In addition to peripherals such as a mouse and keyboard, PCs loaded with Freestyle would include a TV tuner card to connect to a cable service and a remote control to navigate the system from a couch. That way, consumers could organize their music files or home movies while they're sitting at a desk and later, use the remote control to select tunes or videos from anywhere in the room. The first-generation, all-in-one Freestyle PCs will have all the functionality of a TV and a stereo. The target market: college students and apartment dwellers who might not have the space or budget for a PC, a TV, and a stereo. The second-generation Freestyle PCs will focus on the broad consumer market, selling boxes that sit next to TVs around the house and connect back to the main PC.

36   The first major connected-home product from Microsoft will be a gizmo code-named Mira. By next Christmas, consumers will be able to buy a flat-panel monitor that detaches from its stand and continues to connect wirelessly to the PC from anywhere in the house. With a stylus tapping icons or scrawling letters on a touch screen, Mom can check e-mail from the kitchen, the kids can chat with online buddies from the couch while watching MTV, and Dad can shop at Amazon.com from the back porch. ViewSonic Corp. and Wyse Technology Inc. will make the devices for as little as $500.

37   Microsoft is counting on Xbox to jump-start its digital home initiative. Already, Xbox sales are hitting the high end of analysts' expectations. Since the launch on Nov. 15, about 1.5 million consoles have been sold. That beats Nintendo's GameCube, which has sold 1.2 million units since its Nov. 18 launch. Meanwhile, Sony's PlayStation2, out since Oct. 25, 2000, rang up 2.5 million unit sales in North America this Christmas season.

38   Even the bookish Gates has been sucked in by Xbox. Although he was never much of a gamer before, he took a test version on his vacation in October. Each night, after putting their two children to bed, Gates and wife Melinda plopped down on the couch and found themselves absorbed by Fuzion Frenzy, a collection of 45 arcade-style games. "We played four hours straight the first day, since it was so cool," says Gates.

39   While Xbox is designed first and foremost to best PlayStation 2 and GameCube, the connected-home vision is a constant undercurrent. Microsoft built networking technology into the Xbox that will let gamers compete against one another from across the street or around the world. The company plans to launch its Xbox online gaming service by the middle of this year. Robert A. Kotick, chairman and CEO of Activision Inc., the No. 2 game publisher, believes online tournaments will be immensely popular. "It's a lot of fun to waste time playing video games. It would be a lot more fun wasting time playing video games and winning a trip to Hawaii as well," Kotick says.

40   For all the nifty technology, Xbox still needs killer games. And analysts don't count any sure blockbusters in the initial bunch of 20. "What's the must-have game that's going to get people to pay $300 to buy this console? I just haven't seen it," says analyst Edward Williams of Gerard Klauer Mattison & Co. He expects Xbox to capture about 10% of the game console market during the five-year life cycle of game consoles that's just beginning. So, while Xbox could become a sizable business for Microsoft, it's only a piece of the puzzle.

41   The companies that win biggest in the home will likely be the ones with the most direct ongoing relationships with customers. Right now, that's AOL Time Warner, which touches 46 million subscribers with its online and cable businesses. "The value is in the consumer relationships, not the technology. It's about subscriptions," says AOL Time Warner Co-Chief Operating Officer Robert W. Pittman. AOL is collecting $24 a month from most of the 33 million consumers who connect to its online service. And its Time Warner Cable unit gets another $54 per month, on average, from its 12.7 million homes. Microsoft can't touch that. It's lucky if it sells a home PC user a $90 operating-system upgrade every three or four years.

42   And when it comes to mastering consumer technology, Microsoft sucks Sony's exhaust. As cool as Microsoft's Freestyle sounds, Sony already has introduced its Vaio MX media center PC, which does everything that Freestyle aspires to. Microsoft's Mira is nearly a year away. But more than a year ago, Sony introduced its Airboard in Japan, a flat-panel screen that can be used to check e-mail, surf the Web, and play video games. And Sony is developing networking technology, dubbed Feel, that will make it easy to connect all of its devices to one home network.

43   Still, no company is better fixed than Microsoft to make long-term investments in the digital home. With $36 billion in cash, it can afford to invest heavily, experiment broadly, and wait patiently for the payoff. Microsoft's history is loaded with examples of perseverance. MSN foundered for years before Microsoft figured out how to turn it into one of the top destinations on the Web. For most of a decade, its server software was the laughingstock of corporate computing. This year, it's expected to claim 47% of the market.

44   So it's not surprising that Microsoft is confident it will win in the home. "A lot of this stuff isn't a question of, 'Will the dogs eat the dog food?' It's 'When?'" says Microsoft's Mundie. Maybe so, but competitors such as Sony have thrived by offering customers steak rather than dog chow. If Microsoft can't match Sony, it will end up on the outside of the digital home, looking in.

Source: Adapted by Richard Robinson, University of South Carolina, based on Jay Greene, with Steve Hamm, Catherine Yang, and Irene M. Kunii, "Bill Gates in Your Living Room," *BusinessWeek,* January 21, 2002; and Jane Black, "Microsoft's Great Web Offensive," *BusinessWeek,* November 14, 2001.

Case 15

BusinessWeek

Excite@Home

1 In August, Patti S. Hart made a last-ditch effort to save Excite@Home. The chief executive at the provider of speedy Internet connections set up a videoconference call with top executives from AT&T, which had a controlling stake in Excite@Home. She told AT&T CEO and Excite@Home board member C. Michael Armstrong and other AT&T officials that Excite@Home had $100 million less in cash than her execs had told her to expect just weeks earlier. She needed financial help from AT&T to avoid bankruptcy. Armstrong said a cash infusion was out of the question. Hart pleaded and tears welled up in her eyes, according to one former exec close to Hart. Armstrong was not swayed. "After that, it was over," says the former exec. "It was just a matter of who turns out the lights."

2 That flick of the switch could be just weeks away. After filing for bankruptcy protection on Sept. 28, the company is auctioning off its few remaining assets and plans to shut down on Feb. 28. Already, a bankruptcy judge in San Francisco has allowed Excite@Home to shut off service to 850,000 AT&T customers—in a high-stakes game the startup is playing to force the phone giant to cough up more money. AT&T is refusing payment, and few expect Excite@Home will be saved. When the judge's gavel falls again, the startup that was once worth $35 billion could go for about $350 million, 1% of its peak market cap.

3 Eighteen months after the Internet bubble burst, it's hard to muster sympathy for yet another Net flameout. But this was no ordinary Web startup. Unlike the thousands of fledglings with harebrained ideas, Excite@Home could have become a Net powerhouse. It held a trump card: the exclusive right to offer broadband Net connections over the cable-TV networks of most top cable companies. Today, it claims 4.2 million high-speed subscribers, more than any other company in the U.S. What's more, it possessed the Excite portal, one of the most popular gateways to the Internet—and a challenger to the gateways of Yahoo! Inc. and America Online Inc. To top it off, it had big-moneybag backers: AT&T, Cox, Comcast, and Silicon Valley's premier venture-capital firm, Kleiner Perkins Caufield & Byers. "It looked like a marriage made in heaven," says Ron Conway, a founding partner of venture firm Angel Investors, which has no financial stake in the company. "I thought it was brilliant."

EXHIBIT 1

Source: Bleomberg Financial Markets.

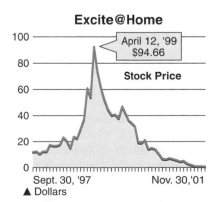

Excite@Home

April 12, '99
$94.66

Stock Price

▲ Dollars

SHARPIES

4   The company also boasted an all-star team. Kleiner Perkins' powerful venture capitalist L. John Doerr helped set up both Excite and @Home, then supported their merger in 1999. Cable mogul John C. Malone played a critical role in establishing @Home and was a longtime member of the board. So was AT&T's Armstrong. And the company's CEOs were sharpies: Thomas Jermoluk, who had run Silicon Graphics Inc. in its heyday, and George Bell, who brought his skills in documentary filmmaking and traditional magazines to the new-media world of the Net.

5   So why is Excite@Home in ruins? Blame it on a lethal combination of management missteps, clashing egos, and old-fashioned greed. In the end, the cable companies that backed Excite@Home and took more than $1 billion from investors to finance it decided to walk away, leaving public investors to pay the price. Cox Communications Inc. and Comcast Corp., which had pledged to keep all of their broadband customers on Excite@Home's network through June 2002, negotiated early exits so they could provide their own service.

6   The most serious questions, however, swirl around AT&T. The long-distance giant controlled the startup, thanks to its 74% voting stake and its 6 out of the 11 seats on the board. Several developments over the past year raise questions about whether those directors were looking out for Excite@Home and its shareholders or whether they pushed the company into bankruptcy so AT&T could buy its assets for very little. At minimum, AT&T pushed the company to spend heavily on its network earlier this year, refused to chip in more money when cash ran low, and then offered to buy Excite@Home's network for just $307 million—before withdrawing the bid just days ago. "There is a rightful concern that AT&T could have stepped up and supported the company in its time of need— or tried to pick up the assets on the cheap out of bankruptcy," says Andrew Watt, a debt analyst at Standard & Poor's.

7   AT&T says the idea that it drove Excite@Home into bankruptcy is ludicrous. After all, its execs point out, the long-distance giant paid $3.5 billion for its controlling stake in the company—then lost all its money. "We've always supported this company because we believed strongly in the broadband marketplace," says John Petrillo, AT&T's executive vice-president for corporate strategy and a former Excite@Home board member. What caused the company's demise, he says, were management mistakes, a steep slide in online advertising, and the persistent quality issues that alienated cable outfits. And AT&T was under no obligation to bail out the company with cash. "We didn't think it was a good application of AT&T shareholder money," he says. Armstrong, Jermoluk, and Hart declined to comment for this article.

8   Indeed, Excite@Home execs didn't do themselves any favors. Despite their strong reputations, former CEOs Jermoluk and Bell made loads of mistakes. Most damaging, they blew millions on investments and acquisitions—money that just might have saved the company. Example No. 1 is BlueMountain.com, an electronic greeting-card company that Bell bought in 1999—over the objections of several execs, including his chief financial officer, Kenneth A. Goldman. BlueMountain had become one of the most popular websites, so Excite@Home acquired it for a walloping $780 million, including $350 million in cash. There was just one problem: BlueMountain wasn't generating a dollar of revenue at that time and never became much of a business. It was sold in September for a paltry $35 million. "I was very vocal about it," says Goldman, now CFO at Siebel Systems Inc. "I didn't like the business model—since there wasn't one."

HURTING

9 The public investors are left holding the bag. Excite@Home raised $210 million by issuing stock and nearly $1 billion through debt issues. The company's stock is trading for 3 cents. Bondholders may get 10 cents on the dollar—or less—once the asset sales are completed. "We financed one of the great expansions of the Internet," says Michael Katto, a shareholder who has lost $188,000 and has joined a lawsuit seeking compensation from AT&T, Cox, Comcast, and Excite@Home.

10 Investors aren't the only ones to get hurt. The rollout of broadband Internet service throughout the country was supposed to bring a fundamental change in the way the U.S. economy works. With lightning-quick Internet links, people were going to be able to work from home, shop from home, and perform loads of other routine tasks more easily and quickly. The consulting firm Eastern Management Group Inc. estimates broadband may add 3.7 billion work hours to the economy each year.

11 Now that the biggest, highest-profile provider in the country is crashing, the promise of a broadband future is fading from sight. If the No. 1 broadband player, with so much money and corporate support behind it, cannot survive, which broadband player can? Local telephone companies and cable players will continue to roll out broadband service, but they're sure to move more slowly and charge customers more than upstarts such as Excite@Home. "It's very troubling," says William E. Kennard, former chairman of the Federal Communications Commission. "You're seeing a duopoly market develop. That's going to slow broadband down."

FAT PIPES

12 No one imagined such an end when @Home was launched in 1995 by Tele-Communications Inc. and Kleiner Perkins. At the time, the CEO was William R. Hearst III, grandson of newspaper kingpin William Randolph Hearst. Cox and Comcast joined the company the next year. Kleiner partner Doerr spun a magical vision of the company's potential. It would develop the technology to take advantage of the fat pipes that cable TV used, so that consumers could surf the Net at unheard-of speeds: 50 times as fast as the poky modems of the time. The cable players would market @Home's service to their customers, and the two sides would split the revenues. @Home got 35% of the typical $40 that customers paid each month, and the cable companies got the rest. The service was launched in September 1996, in Fremont, Calif., and became an instant hit. "People were flagging down our trucks to get the service," says ex-CFO Goldman. In 1997, @Home went public, raising $95 million, and quickly set out to build a national network.

13 In 1998, it became clear that such popularity had its price. As more customers signed up, the company's network often became overloaded, and quality deteriorated. Customers, particularly in Fremont and in Hartford, Conn., complained to local politicians. Since cable companies depend on local municipalities for their franchise, this was a grave problem. Execs at TCI and other cable outfits fretted that they could get their cable-TV licenses yanked. Screaming matches broke out during @Home board meetings, according to two former members. In one session at @Home's Redwood City (Calif.) headquarters, Leo J. Hindery Jr., then TCI's president, and Jermoluk traded expletives. "We're their customers," says Dallas Clement, Cox's senior vice-president for strategy and development. "And we never felt like they cared about their customers' needs."

14 @Home's move to acquire Excite in 1999 only added to the friction. Founded by six friends from Stanford University in 1993, Excite had grown into one of the Web's most popular portals, compiling news, stock quotes, and other information. By combining the two companies, @Home chief Jermoluk and Excite's Bell hoped to create an AOL on steroids. They would reap revenues from connecting users to the Web and from ads and e-commerce on the Excite site. Jermoluk boasted that Excite@Home would become "the new media network for the 21st century."

15   Meanwhile, AT&T was doing a deal of its own. It was in the midst of buying TCI, primarily so that it would have an alternative network for local phone service. It was only in May 1999, when Excite and @Home completed their merger, that AT&T and the other cable players fully realized the regulatory troubles it would cause them. AOL and others mounted a lobbying effort to force cable outfits to let other Net-access companies use their networks to provide broadband service. AOL's "open access" argument was this: The cable companies had been given monopolies in cable TV, so they had to let customers pick the Internet-access service they wanted—whether it was Excite or AOL. Excite@Home's cable investors found themselves spending time and money courting politicians, instead of building a business. "It opened up a Pandora's box of regulation," says Hindery.

16   It also created more conflicts in the boardroom. Hindery, the TCI president who continued to run the cable business after AT&T acquired it, hated the idea of Jermoluk's getting into the content business. In 1999, while Jermoluk was at an AT&T golf tournament in Pebble Beach, Hindery negotiated a tentative deal with Yahoo so that @Home customers could default to the Yahoo site instead of Excite. At a later board meeting, Jermoluk confronted Hindery and the deal was quashed. Cox and Comcast, however, supported the Excite deal, pulling Jermoluk in different directions. "That makes it difficult to execute," says Hearst.

SPEND, SPEND

17   More bad deals lay ahead. In the boom times of 1999, Jermoluk and Bell spent loads of cash. Over the summer of 1999, the company invested at least $60 million in startups, including Quokka Sports Inc., a website. Quokka is now defunct, and the other investments have dropped sharply in value. On Oct. 25, they cut the fateful deal for BlueMountain. Bell says the acquisition was a product of the times. "We had the mentality of scale," he says. "We thought scale mattered a lot, and we wanted to add to ours."

18   While Jermoluk and Bell were spending the company's cash, the stock market was beginning to turn against them. After hitting a high of $94.66 in April 1999, Excite@Home shares slid downward during the summer. Investors were concerned that if AOL won its "open access" battle, Excite@Home could lose its monopoly. When a newspaper reported in August that AT&T was negotiating a deal with AOL to give it access to AT&T's cable network, Excite@Home's stock dropped 11% in one day, to $38. Both AT&T and Excite@Home denied the report, but investors remained skittish. Its stock closed the year at $42.88.

19   The new year brought some measure of relief for the startup. On Jan. 10, AOL and Time Warner Inc. announced plans to merge. Once AOL planned to combine with a company that owned a cable network, it stopped pressing for open access. On Jan. 20, Bell took over the CEO post from Jermoluk, who stayed on as chairman. Jermoluk said he couldn't run the company properly because he was spending so much time soothing cable partners. The previous year was "the single most difficult and painful year of my life," Jermoluk said at the time. In May, he gave up the chairman's post and became a partner at Kleiner Perkins.

20   In March, Armstrong realized the huge potential for broadband and decided he wanted more control over Excite@Home. AT&T boosted its voting stake in Excite@Home to

74%, up from 56% when the startup gave Cox and Comcast the right to sell their 60 million shares to AT&T for $48 each. The way the change was announced, though, did not spell out all that it would mean. Jermoluk put out a statement saying: "We are delighted that our cable partners are committed to a long-term relationship that will provide consumers with a great broadband experience." In fact, the deal gave the cable companies an exit from Excite@Home they never had before. Starting in 2001, Cox and Comcast could give six months' notice and end their exclusive deals with Excite@Home. Before then, the cable companies could not offer any other broadband services through June 2002.

21   Excite@Home shareholders and bondholders point to that single change as erasing a big chunk of the company's value. Instead of keeping all their customers on the Excite@Home network through June 2002, Cox and Comcast could terminate exclusivity as much as a year earlier. "Who does that benefit? Not Excite@Home," says Don Morgan, a director at MacKay Shields, one of the company's largest bondholders. "AT&T got control, and what did Excite@Home get?" AT&T's Petrillo says that the upstart did benefit: Instead of having all the cable partners pulling in different directions, the company would finally have guidance from one company: AT&T.

QUASHED

22   With AT&T firmly at the helm, Bell laid out a new strategy. On Apr. 20, the CEO said the company was "doubling down on its bet on broadband." After adding 350,000 new subscribers in the first quarter and hitting 1.5 million subscribers total, Excite@Home was going to accelerate its rollout—to about 500,000 subscribers per quarter—so that it could reach 3 million subscribers by yearend. "We are committed to go big," said Bell. Bell admitted that this would result in at least $100 million in operating losses in 2000, vs. $24 million in 1999. But Bell and Daniel E. Somers, who had replaced Hindery as head of AT&T's cable operations, assured investors they would have enough cash to pull off the more aggressive strategy.

23   As the days of 2000 rolled on, that assurance became increasingly suspect. Technology stocks continued to drop precipitously throughout the summer. That quashed Bell's plan to raise more money through initial public offerings of its foreign operations. The result: The company was steadily burning through its money. Its cash and short-term investments fell from $502.3 million when Bell unveiled his "doubling down" strategy to $200.8 million at the end of the year. On Sept. 19, with the company's stock at $16, Bell announced he would resign the CEO post as soon as a replacement could be found. He said he would stay on as chairman through the end of 2001 at least, helping to manage the relationship with AT&T.

24   In January 2001, the lame-duck CEO made one of the most controversial decisions of his tenure. He brought in Hossein Eslambolchi, a networking veteran at the long-distance company, to improve the quality of Excite@Home's service. AT&T and Bell both say that AT&T requested that Bell hire Eslambolchi as president of Excite@Home, but Bell agreed to hire him only on a temporary basis. Eslambolchi improved Excite@Home's network—but at a tremendous cost. The company spent $54 million on equipment and other improvements, 29% more than the year before, according to Securities & Exchange Commission filings. That contributed to a 48% drop in the company's cash and short-term investments, to $104.5 million.

25   Excite@Home couldn't afford that kind of spending. On Apr. 17, Bell held a conference call with investors in which he admitted the company was in dire straits. It was going to miss its financial targets for the rest of the year and it needed to raise $75 million

EXHIBIT 2
Did AT&T Push
Excite@Home into
Bankruptcy?

Some shareholders and bondholders say it did.

Shareholders Contend that AT&T . . .

Was in Control
When AT&T (*T*) acquired Tele-Communications in 1999, it got a controlling stake in Excite@Home (*ATHMQ*). Later, AT&T execs gained a majority of the seats on the company's board. AT&T was critical in naming George Bell chief executive in 2000 and picking Patti S. Hart to replace him in 2001.

Urged to Splurge
AT&T urged the startup to spend big to sign up new customers, build out its network, and improve service. AT&T also persuaded Bell to hire Hossein Eslambolchi, an AT&T technical veteran, in January 2001, to work on Excite@Home's network. Eslambolchi invested heavily in equipment, just as the company was running short of cash—then returned to AT&T.

Held Down Revenues
Critics say conflicts of interest led AT&T execs on the startup's board to limit its revenues unfairly. When Excite@Home's cash started to dwindle, consultant PricewaterhouseCoopers recommended that the company raise the rates it charged AT&T and other cable companies for its broadband services. The board, with AT&T holding 6 of the 11 director seats, never approved it.

Didn't Force Others to Pay
Several cable companies stopped paying Excite@Home for as long as six months in 2000. The $50 million in lost cash was a key reason the company had to file for bankruptcy on Sept. 28. AT&T was current on its bills, but why didn't its execs force the other cable companies to cough up?

Turned Down Plea
Patti S. Hart asked AT&T CEO C. Michael Armstrong for more cash in August, and he turned her down. Experts say it would have cost AT&T as little as $100 million to have helped the company survive through 2002.

AT&T Replies . . .

Was in Control
AT&T says its control helped Excite@Home. When Cox and Comcast sat on its board, the upstart was pulled in too many directions.

Urged to Splurge
AT&T defends Eslambolchi's actions, saying he provided invaluable advice that helped correct Excite@Home's quality problems. AT&T also picked up the salaries of Eslambolchi and his assistants.

Held Down Revenues
AT&T argues that raising rates might have driven away Excite@Home's existing customers, forcing them to look for lower-cost alternatives.

Didn't Force Others to Pay
The phone giant says that collecting bills was the job of Excite@Home's execs, not its board members.

Turned Down Plea
AT&T says injecting more cash was not in the interest of AT&T's shareholders.

EXHIBIT 3
The Rise and Fall of Excite@Home

After the broadband Internet access provider @Home merged with portal Excite in 1999, its stock price soared to almost $95, and its market cap topped $40 billion. Today, the company is in ruins, and the shares are trading for 3 cents. Here's its sad saga:

March 1995
Tele-Communications Inc. and John Doerr of Kleiner Perkins establish @Home to provide broadband Net access over cable-TV networks. Cable companies Cox and Comcast become investors the next year.

September 1996
@Home launches its service in Fremont, Calif.

July 1997
@Home goes public, at a split-adjusted $5.25 a share.

January 19, 1999
@Home announces it will acquire Excite for $7 billion in stock.

March 9, 1999
AT&T closes its TCI acquisition, gaining a 58% voting stake in @Home.

April 12, 1999
The company's stock hits an all-time high of $94.66—as investors anticipate the combination of Excite's content and @Home's broadband service will create an America Online for the next generation of the Internet.

December 6, 1999
Excite@Home hits 1 million broadband subscribers, twice as many as the competing Road Runner service and 10 times as many as the largest telephone competitor.

January 20, 2000
Bell takes over as CEO from Jermoluk, who remains chairman.

September 19, 2000
With the company's shares dragged down to $16 in the tech-stock collapse, Bell announces plans to find a replacement CEO.

(continued)

to $80 million by June 30 to keep operating. AT&T's Petrillo says Eslambolchi's spending was necessary to boost the quality of Excite@Home's service. "Unless the quality improved, there was no argument to persuade Cox and Comcast to stay," he says. Petrillo and Bell say the key factor in the cash crunch was the steep drop in online advertising, which fell 41% in the first quarter to $45.1 million.

26   That set the stage for the entrance of Patti Hart on Apr. 23. The former Sprint Corp. executive was supposed to start as CEO before the Apr. 17 announcement, but she got wind of the bad news and insisted Bell take the heat. She also asked for the chairman position, so that she would have enough control to make some drastic changes.

27   It was a sign of the deteriorating times at Excite@Home. In June, Cox and Comcast gave six-month notice that they would discontinue marketing Excite@Home service

EXHIBIT 3
(continued)

January 2001
At AT&T's request, Bell hires Eslambolchi, an AT&T veteran who spends millions to improve the quality of Excite@Home's network.

April 17, 2001
The company announces that it will miss its financial targets for the rest of the year and that it needs to raise $75 million to $80 million by June 30 to continue funding its operations.

April 23, 2001
Patti S. Hart is named chairman and CEO. Bell resigns.

June 11, 2001
The company raises $100 million by issuing convertible debt to a group led by Promethean Capital Group.

June 19, 2001
The company raises $85 million from AT&T. Separately, Cox and Comcast say that, as of Dec. 4, they plan to stop using Excite@Home as the exclusive provider of their broadband Net service, a move that could eliminate 30% of the company's customers.

July 23, 2001
Excite@Home says it needs to raise even more money to survive through the end of the year.

August 20, 2001
In an SEC filing, auditor Ernst & Young says there is "substantial doubt" the company can continue as "a going concern."

September 28, 2001
The company files for Chapter 11 bankruptcy protection.

November 28, 2001
The bankruptcy court approves the sale of most of the assets of the Excite portal to InfoSpace for $10 million.

November 30, 2001
A bankruptcy judge rules that Excite@Home may cut off service to AT&T and other cable outfits.

exclusively. Still, Hart was able to raise twice as much money as Bell had said was necessary in April. On June 11, the company received $100 million from a group led by Promethean Capital Group. Eight days later, the company got an additional $85 million from AT&T by selling the long-distance company certain assets, which it then leased back.

28   Even that cash wasn't enough. On July 23, Hart told shell-shocked investors that the company needed still more money to survive the year. What happened? In an interview at the time, Hart explained that online ads had continued to plunge, that other companies planning to lease Excite@Home's office space had disappeared, and that suppliers were demanding cash up front. During the next few weeks, Hart made several appeals to AT&T for more cash, according to AT&T and others. On Sept. 28, the company filed for Chapter 11 bankruptcy protection.

DEADBEATS

29   That wasn't the end of the rancor. Once the company was in bankruptcy, bondholders found out that one factor contributing to the cash crunch was that several cable companies weren't paying their bills to Excite@Home—because of quality issues, they said. The total amount in arrears: about $50 million. "The liquidity problem was caused in large part by the cable companies withholding payments," says William P. Weintraub, a lawyer at Pachulski, Stang, Ziehl, Young & Jones who represents bondholders. AT&T was up to date on its bills, but Weintraub wonders why AT&T execs on Excite@Home's board didn't lean on other cable players. "Our guys made phone calls," says Petrillo. "[But] the management team had the responsibility to collect the money."

30   Is AT&T responsible for the demise of Excite@Home? Certainly, the company had only the upstart's best interests in mind at the beginning. Armstrong, perhaps more than anyone else involved, believed in the prospects for broadband Internet services. But at some point, Armstrong and AT&T decided they were not going to help Hart any more. Why? Ultimately, AT&T, like Cox and Comcast, decided that broadband was too important a business to leave in the hands of another company. "The business is so bad that every cable company wants to be in it," says Hearst. In the end, what sealed Excite@Home's fate was that it was the company that stood between the cable companies and that goal.

Source: Adapted by Richard Robinson, University of South Carolina, based on Peter Elstrom, "Excite@Home: A Saga of Tears, Greed, and Ego," *BusinessWeek,* December 17, 2001.

Case 16

BusinessWeek

Cisco

1   The questions are brutal and surprisingly frank. Each one is a challenge Cisco Systems CEO John T. Chambers would not have heard even a year ago. "What can I do to combat the increase in politics and empire-building inside Cisco?" wonders a female employee. "Will we see more layoffs?" inquires another. "Does the Internet now have negative connotations?" asks one man.

2   Such candid employee question-and-answer sessions have been a staple of Chambers' management approach since he became CEO of Cisco seven years ago. But on this cool November morning in San Jose, Calif., in an auditorium filled with more than 200 staffers, the inquiries betray a sagging morale and unease that until recently were unknown inside this high-tech stalwart.

3   Once one of the world's fastest-growing companies, Cisco is struggling to find its footing amid a severe economic downdraft. The company is in the red. Its sales are slumping, and its market valuation has fallen by some $430 billion, to $154 billion, since March 2000, one of the deepest losses of shareholder wealth in history. The decline puts many of Cisco's employee stock options under water and limits the company's ability to acquire new companies.

4   Yet even after this comeuppance, Chambers, 52, continues to insist in public and private that Cisco can still "change the world" and increase revenues as much as 30%-plus a year. Just as the spending boom of 1999 and early 2000 may have been overdone, he says, the dramatic shrinking of technology budgets in 2001 was also exaggerated—and temporary. He points to new markets, from voice-over-Internet systems and wireless networking gear to storage-networking devices and optical equipment, that he believes can fuel Cisco's next round of hypergrowth. "There is a confidence that if we execute right, we have a higher probability of winning now than ever before," says Chambers. "I believe the best years are in front of us."

5   But skeptics abound, starting inside the company auditorium where Chambers is getting the hard questions. Many are wondering if the ultimate Internet salesman of the 1990s is simply in denial. After all, the Cisco that dazzled investors and business observers at the height of the high-tech bubble now looks like a company that caught a spectacular wave. Its success and Chambers' own rise as a New Economy visionary were

EXHIBIT 1

Source: Bloomberg Financial Markets.

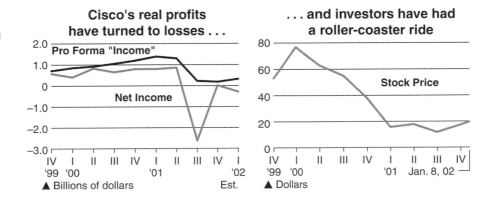

Cisco's real profits have turned to losses . . . . . . and investors have had a roller-coaster ride

a function of a near mania for tech stocks. In those heady days, all the stars seemed to align in Chambers' favor: a massive Internet buildout, a breathtaking stock price, and an era that allowed companies to push the boundaries of acceptable accounting. "Cisco was at the right place at the right time and exploited it very well," says Robertson Stephens senior technology analyst Paul Johnson. "Chances are they won't be able to do it again."

6   There has always been a good deal of myth-making where Cisco is concerned. At the height of the Internet frenzy, it was the very embodiment of the age. When it came to Cisco, everything seemed faster, bigger, and better. Its sales and earnings growth were second to none. It sold more sophisticated gear over the Internet than any other company as it raced to fill a demand that seemed unquenchable. It could close its books in a day, thanks to its powerful information systems. For 43 quarters in a row, Cisco met or beat Wall Street's hungry expectations for higher earnings. For one brief, heady moment, it became the most valuable corporation on the planet.

7   Now, in the cold light of the tech downturn, some of those myths are being exploded. As academics and other experts reassess the tech era, they are raising serious questions about how well Cisco and other highfliers actually performed, even at the height of the boom. They say that a history of aggressive accounting, from massive write-downs of assets to the use of now-banned "pooling of interest" accounting for acquisitions, makes it hard to gauge how much many of these companies actually earned from ongoing operations. These bold accounting techniques became standard operating procedure at many companies during the boom. But few applied them as deftly or with greater effect than the much-emulated Cisco.

8   To be sure, Chambers' company is hardly an Enron in the making. Cisco's accounting practices, while aggressive, are not illegal and have been certified without qualification by PricewaterhouseCoopers LLP, its independent auditor. With $19.1 billion in cash and equivalents, more than double that of competitors Alcatel, Lucent Technologies, and Nortel Networks combined, the company boasts a pristine balance sheet with zero debt. Plus, Cisco still holds a dominant share of the $15 billion market for corporate network gear and has recently boosted its market share in some key product categories, including routers. Long term, analysts believe the company can achieve 15% to 20% annual earnings growth.

9   But Cisco's core business of supplying Internet infrastructure, while solid, is nowhere near capable of generating the 70% growth rates of yesteryear. After all, the corporations and telecom carriers that lined up for Cisco's gear in the '90s are spending much less to expand networks. Many of the telecom players are laden with debt and overcapacity. Some analysts believe the current down cycle for overall corporate capital spending could last years, even when the recession ends. Meanwhile, those that do want to spend can pick up some bargains. For example, eBay Inc. lists more than 3,000 Cisco products that are being auctioned for much less than their initial prices. "The bubble companies that fueled Cisco's growth have largely been wiped off the face of the earth," says Scott C. Cleland, chief executive of the Precursor Group, a high-tech consultant that recently bought $27,000 worth of Cisco gear for $7,000 on eBay. "Chambers' core business has matured, and all the growth markets are speculative." Indeed, in many of the markets that Chambers points to as engines of future growth, Cisco faces large and entrenched competitors. In others, such as voice-over-Internet, it's becoming clear that the potential first envisioned will take much longer to materialize.

10   Yet while the bubble has burst elsewhere in techdom, Cisco continues to exist in its own separate universe. Legions of true believers still cling to the hope that Cisco will reemerge as the high-tech bellwether that will lead the sector out of its slump. Their continuing faith is why Cisco stock trades at a spectacular 95 times estimated 2002 earnings

EXHIBIT 2
How Cisco Tripped
Up the Sherlock
Holmes of
Accounting

Howard Schilit, a former American University accounting professor, has been dubbed "the Sherlock Holmes of accounting." As the director of the Maryland-based Center for Financial Research & Analysis, he and his team of forensic accountants attempt to unravel financial results for major investors. But Cisco's latest quarterly results confused even him. If the most prominent forensic accountant couldn't get it right, what chance do investors have?

November 5, 2001
In a conference call with analysts, Cisco reveals that its "normal reserves for accounts receivable and credit memos, as well as reserves for leases and structured loans" had declined in the quarter to 9% from 15% despite a worsening economy.

November 7
Schilit's Center releases an explosive report. It claims that Cisco's reduction in reserves was responsible for its reported 3.5% rise in quarter-to-quarter revenue. If Cisco had reserved at the previous quarter's level, it would have reported a revenue decline of 3.3%.

December 12
Cisco files its 10Q. The percentage breakdowns for these reserves are nowhere to be found. But on page 20, Cisco refers to "revenue adjustments" that include such things as "customer incentives and other discounts." The $409 million reduction in sales and $649 million for the previous quarter match the reserve percentages reported on Nov. 5.

December 21
Cisco vigorously disputes the center's analysis after a *BusinessWeek* inquiry. The company insists that the "revenue adjustment" in its 10Q was one of many and does not reflect its total adjustments. Cisco points to data to support its claim that bad debt reserves have in fact increased, but it declines to detail all the adjustments.

January 9, 2002
The center backs down from its analysis, but Schilit remains suspicious. "The fact that a company apparently said certain things in a conference call that don't jibe with its SEC filings obviously doesn't make one feel very comfortable," he says.

despite losing money in 2001. A new study by Robertson Stephens estimates that even if Cisco grew at 20% annually over the next 10 years, to $100 billion in sales, and sustained operating margins of 15%, an investor who bought the entire company at its current market value would earn a measly 3% return a year, based on projected cash flow. They'd be lucky to do so well. The chances of hitting that 20% growth target now seem a stretch.

11   For all the disquieting signs, an almost dreamlike view seems to prevail among the company's Wall Street supporters. In a 90-minute conference call between Wall Street analysts and Chambers on Nov. 5 to discuss first-quarter results, few analysts acknowledged that Cisco had posted a net loss of $268 million or that sales had plummeted 32%, to $4.4 billion. Nor did any of the analysts grill Chambers on the $290 million Cisco disclosed that it earned by selling "excess inventory" written off as worthless only seven months earlier. (At the time, critics wondered if the huge sum included some still-good equipment that could be sold later, inflating the bottom line. "We have no plans to use it, period," a company spokesman told *BusinessWeek* last spring.) Without the gain, Cisco's net losses would have been nearly half a billion dollars.

12   It's not just the numbers that deserve greater scrutiny. Part of the Cisco myth revolved around the company's super-sophisticated information systems. Cisco was supposedly using the Internet to bind together its suppliers and contract manufacturers into a seamless whole, pointing the way to the corporation of the future. In fact, Cisco's "network organization" did little to soften the impact of the downturn—or save Cisco from the disastrous inventory buildup.

13   Similarly, its vaunted acquisition strategy was supposed to make the world Cisco's lab, allowing it to pluck promising technology after someone else had borne the development risk. But many of the companies Cisco snapped up with its inflated stock came with steep price tags, reaching as high as $24 million per employee. Often, high-priced talent walked soon after the deals were done. Many of those companies have yet to deliver new products or markets or contribute to Cisco's bottom line.

14   Indeed, there are serious questions about how successful many of the high-tech companies were during their halcyon days. Michael Porter, a Harvard Business School professor, is now completing a major research project on the era's massive distortions in financial reporting. One astounding finding: He and his colleagues can't figure out how much money Cisco really made in the 1990s. After spending billions on buying companies, Cisco routinely wrote off massive amounts of acquisition-related charges—$5.4 billion in the past five years alone—making it nearly impossible to piece together how much Cisco actually invested or how much it earned on its capital. Says Porter: "When the historians actually plow through all the data, we will likely find that even during its so-called heyday, Cisco wasn't nearly as profitable in terms of return on invested capital as many believed."

15   Chambers and his top executives strongly defend the company's accounting practices. "I've got an extremely conservative chief financial officer, and we have been conservative all the way through," says Chambers. "We provide a tremendous amount of information. The more information we provide, the more questions it raises."

16   Trouble is, even the most sophisticated forensic accountants have had difficulty burrowing through the company's less-than-transparent financial reports. Only recently, for example, the Maryland-based Center for Financial Research & Analysis reported that a 3% growth in revenues from the previous quarter occurred only because Cisco reserved less for bad debts. The center used Cisco's own numbers released in its Nov. 5 conference call. Now, the center is backing away from its report because Cisco says it has actually been putting aside more money for uncollectible receivables, not less. However, not all of its offsetting "revenue adjustments" are broken out in its filings. Concedes Chambers: "We've got to be able to articulate [our numbers] better."

17   Chambers may be chastened, but he hasn't lost his confidence or charisma. In his upbeat, rat-a-tat style, Chambers moves through a standard stump speech. He says the company's customer focus, culture of empowerment, prowess with acquisitions, and dominant market share will allow it to overcome the odds. "Let's not kid ourselves," he says. "This market is coming to us. It is going to consolidate. Who in this industry is better at consolidation than Cisco? And who, by the way, has the assets that Cisco does?"

18   Even with questions about the company's past, no one doubts that Chambers can reestablish Cisco as a viable and solidly profitable company. But Cisco's current market valuation is largely based on Chambers' highly optimistic view of the company's growth potential and Wall Street's willingness to accept its more bullish unaudited, pro forma financials. Chambers thinks he can reach his lofty growth targets by taking greater share from rivals and conquering new markets. But the chances of finding another bonanza like network switching, which helped propel Cisco's fast-track growth in the '90s, are slim.

19   Cisco insiders acknowledge the difficulty of returning to the growth rates of its glory days. "When you're a really tiny company, you can jump into one new market and it can make you a lot bigger," says Michelangelo Volpi, Cisco senior vice-president in charge of Internet switches and services. "You can't do that at Cisco anymore. You can't take a $20 billion company and say one market is going to make us a $40 billion company. In each of those markets, there will be entrenched competitors. They'll know the business well, and they'll be tough."

20   It's a far cry from the '90s, when the company averaged 70% annual sales growth. But that torrid pace covered up a multitude of weaknesses. Cisco was famed for systems that were supposed to give its managers unparalleled access to real-time data. But when business weakened, those systems proved to be flawed.

21   Just how flawed became apparent shortly before midnight on Saturday, Jan. 27, last year, as the company prepared to close out its 2001 second-quarter numbers. Analysts were expecting a profit of 19 cents per share, but a slowdown in orders and shortages of certain parts would bring this quarter down to the wire in ways that would belie Cisco's reputation as a superefficient producer in the New Economy.

22   That night, at the company's main San Jose warehouse, employees scrambled to load as many boxed-up machines onto trucks as possible, thus enabling them to be counted as "sold" for accounting purposes before the quarter ran out at midnight. "We had guys running with parts, trying to run them up to the trucks," recalls Larry R. Carter, chief financial officer, who monitored the action from a computer terminal in the warehouse that tallied shipments in real time. One harried staffer, in his haste, fell headlong to the concrete floor in front of Carter. Ten minutes before midnight, Chambers called Carter's cell phone from Davos, Switzerland, where he was speaking at an economic summit. "Did we make it?" Chambers asked. After a few more minutes of watching the numbers come in, Carter had to pass along the bad news: Cisco would undershoot expectations by a penny per share, its first Wall Street miss in 11 years.

23   The news shaved 13% off the company's market value in one day, but there was worse to come. It turned out that Cisco's networked-manufacturing model was not nearly as accurate as Chambers had boasted. Only 40% of what Cisco sells is actually made by the company. Instead, a network of suppliers and contract manufacturers delivers an unusually large chunk of Cisco-branded merchandise direct to customers. This business model was supposed to keep fixed costs to a minimum, eliminate the need for inventory, and give management an instantaneous, real-time fix on orders, shipments, and demand.

24   The highly hyped systems, however, failed to account for the double and triple ordering by customers tired of long waits for shipments. So Cisco began to stockpile parts and finished products. "We made a conscious decision when our lead times were 12 to 13 weeks to build inventory, because we were leaving a sizable amount of revenues on the table every quarter," says Carter. Soon inventories were growing faster than sales. The result: When a weakening economy brought capital spending to a near halt, Chambers found himself stuck with billions of dollars of inventory he didn't expect to have. In April, he wrote off $2.2 billion of excess inventory and cut 18% of Cisco's staff, or 8,500 employees.

25   Despite the massive write-off, Cisco still holds surprisingly high levels of finished-goods inventory: 26 days of finished inventories in October, three days more than it had in April when it took its big bath of a write-down. It's just another question mark about demand for Cisco's products. Dennis Powell, vice-president for corporate finance, calls the change in finished-goods inventory "inconsequential" and points out that overall inventories have fallen to $1.3 billion from $2.5 billion in the past nine months.

26   To improve manufacturing and sales forecasting, Chambers says, Cisco has added new checks and balances. It now disseminates more information about demand and product backlog not only to contract manufacturers but increasingly to the hundreds of suppliers who provide the parts for contract manufacturers. The idea: to make sure everyone works off the same information, making it less likely Cisco will see any inventory surprises. In addition, Cisco has added new ways to gauge customer demand. For instance, not only does Cisco cull sales projections by region and business unit, it now double-checks this against monthly customer surveys of expected spending up to 180 days in the future.

27   The inventory debacle was the first major miss Cisco had. Indeed, there was good reason for its obsession with meeting Wall Street's expectations each quarter. The continual earnings gains kept Cisco's stock price high, which in turn allowed the company to make acquisitions and lure talent. That obsession explains the creative ways Cisco found to account for its purchases and tally its earnings. Among the $5.4 billion in acquisition-related charges it took in the past five years, for example, the lion's share—$3.8 billion—covered "in-process research and development." In some cases, these expenses nearly equaled the cost of the acquired companies. By taking these charges up front, a move that is supposed to reflect that the acquired research and development may prove worthless regardless of the sum paid for it, future earnings tend to look a lot rosier. The reason: If the technology ultimately pays off, the earnings are unencumbered by their true costs, which otherwise would have been amortized as goodwill.

28   Like many companies, Cisco's financials have long been boosted by the use of "pooling of interest" accounting for acquisitions. By employing this accounting, Cisco significantly reduced the impact of many acquisitions on its books and avoided potentially troublesome write-downs on the acquired assets in future years. When Cisco bought GeoTel Communications in 1999 for some $2 billion in stock, it recorded only $41 million for the deal on its books—roughly the amount of GeoTel's shareholders' equity. Abraham J. Briloff, professor emeritus at Baruch College, estimates that in the two fiscal years ended in July 2000, Cisco "suppressed a grand total of $18.2 billion in costs" by using this method of accounting. "It inflates their subsequent results to the extent that they avoid having to charge off everything from inventory, patents, licenses, plant, equipment, and goodwill," says Briloff. Cisco disputes Briloff's analysis, maintaining that the success of many of its acquisitions might not have led to write-offs and could just as easily have resulted in an increase, rather than a decrease, in goodwill.

29   One of Cisco's most frequent accounting tactics comes up every quarter when the company directs shareholders to its unaudited pro forma earnings numbers as the best gauge of profitability. In the first quarter of fiscal 2001, for example, Cisco reported pro forma earnings of $1.4 billion, nearly $600 million over its net income. It arrived at that tally by excluding such ordinary and important costs as acquisition expenses and payroll taxes on stock-option exercises. In the fourth quarter, Cisco's pro forma income of $163 million was 23 times its actual net earnings.

30   While liberal use of more malleable pro forma earnings is not a rarity, most high-tech stalwarts, from Microsoft to Oracle, do not report such unaudited numbers. The Securities & Exchange Commission recently cautioned companies and their investors about the potentially misleading metrics, warning companies that they could face civil-fraud lawsuits. "It's like students deciding the process of how they're graded so that they can always get an A from the teacher," says Howard Schilit, who directs the Center for Financial Research & Analysis. Cisco's Carter maintains that pro forma numbers more accurately portray the company's operating results because they exclude volatile charges, such as acquisition expenses. "The more information you give investors, the better," says Carter. "It's sort of like 'What do you like, vanilla or chocolate? We're going to give you both so you can choose.' "

31   Even the quality of Cisco's pro forma earnings is deteriorating. Well before Cisco's write-down in April, the company was relying on nonoperating income for a growing portion of its pro forma earnings. By the January quarter of 2001, for instance, interest and other nonoperating income had increased as a percentage of Cisco's pro forma results for each of the past five quarters, rising from just 8.8% to 14.9%. In the latest quarter, more than a third of Cisco's pro forma earnings come not from operations but from interest and other income.

EXHIBIT 3
Where Cisco Plans to Grow

Voice-Over-Internet Systems

Cisco's Spin: With more voice traffic over the Internet, Cisco believes this market can account for $10 billion in Cisco sales in five years.
Skeptics View: Cisco is well positioned, but its projections are overblown. Companies and carriers will likely stick with their existing networks for the foreseeable future because of the downturn in capital spending.

Wireless-Networking Gear

Cisco's Spin: Cisco already boasts about 20% of the office market, expected to grow to $3.2 billion from $1 billion by 2005. Cisco expects this business to be a billion-plus opportunity soon.
Skeptics View: Lots of entrenched competitors are already in the business, making it difficult if not impossible to dominate the market as Cisco does in other core areas.

Storage Area Networks

Cisco's Spin: Cisco believes it can grab a 10% to 30% share of this fast-growing market for data storage in coming years. Analysts say the current size of the market is $4 billion.
Skeptics View: Another billion-dollar business for Cisco? It's a stretch until the networking giant rounds out its still limited range of storage-networking products.

Optical Networking

Cisco's Spin: Cisco sold about $520 million in local fiber-optic networking gear in 2001, according to analysts, down from $740 million in 2000, but believes it is well positioned for an eventual upturn.
Skeptics View: Depressed telecom spending has badly crunched the business. It will take a long time to come back, and Cisco hasn't gained share.

32   Accounting issues aside, Chambers' real test will come in the next few quarters as Cisco attempts to wring greater profits out of existing products and step into new growth areas. Given the company's valuation and its current size, Cisco will have to dominate not one or even two but several of these new markets to meet its growth goals. That's no small feat given the slew of big-name competitors, from Nortel Networks to Nokia, going after these same markets. And as the corporate-networking market—Cisco's bread and butter—continues to mature, the pressure on Chambers to conquer new markets will only increase.

33   The most promising growth industry could be voice-over-Internet systems. By using Internet-based phones, or so-called IP phones, a company no longer has to invest in building and servicing a separate voice network. In addition, IP users can easily combine voice and Internet features—such as accessing e-mail via telephone—since they spring from the same network. About 7% of the new underlying phone-switching systems, or PBXes, sold to corporations are Internet-based, made by companies like Cisco. That's expected to jump to 19% of the $10 billion market by 2004, according to International Data Corp. "Voice alone could represent $10 billion [in revenues] a year for us," in the next five or six years, says Volpi. Reaching $10 billion so quickly may be more than a stretch goal. After all, the overall market is still tiny and Cisco's corporate customers have been slow to adopt this technology. "It's a slow road ahead," says International Data analyst Tom Valovic. The optical-networking market, pegged as another future growth engine, has much less potential. Cisco already trails a host of competitors, including Lucent, Alcatel, Nortel, Fujitsu, and Ciena. Although Cisco claims a strong position in the local rather than long-haul part of optical networking, even the local segment suffered its first-ever sequential decline in the third quarter of this year.

EXHIBIT 4
A Costly Acquisition
Strategy

Often lauded for its buyout successes, Cisco has purchased more than 70 companies in the past eight years. In 1999 alone, it paid $15 billion for 18 startups, many of which never delivered on their early promise. Here are the most noteworthy:

Company	Price	Status	Skinny
Cerent	$6.9 billion	Alive and well	Although Cerent has generated $1 billion in estimated sales for Cisco, two decades could be needed to recoup the steep price.
Pirelli Optical Systems	$2.2 billion	Alive but struggling	A disappointing attempt to bolster Cisco's long-haul optical networking. But Pirelli's technology still trails that of rivals.
Monterey Networks	$500 million	Dumped in April	This upstart optical company never produced a viable product, and Cisco cut its losses with a $108 million write-off in April.
Amteva	$170 million	Sold at a loss in July	Lackluster revenue forced Cisco to sell this unified-messaging business.
Maxcomm Technologies	$143 million	Part of their DSL strategy	Founders and key technologists walked out soon after the deal closed.

34 The wild card in Cisco's growth plans is its effort to woo telecom companies. These massive purchasers of networking gear have largely stayed loyal to traditional vendors such as Nortel and Lucent. Cisco, at its peak, was generating 40% of its business selling to telecoms, many of them upstarts challenging incumbents like Sprint Corp. and Verizon Communications. But as many of these outfits faltered, Cisco has become more dependent on established corporations. Upstarts, however, continue to haunt Cisco. El Paso Global Networks Co., for example, announced in October it was putting the brakes on a massive billion-dollar network, of which Cisco was slated to be the primary supplier. The reason? Just too much capacity in the market.

35 But Cisco's struggles with carriers have gone well beyond market conditions. To get back on track, Cisco is rethinking its approach to this market. First, it is aiming nearly all of its resources on the 50 biggest carriers. Second, it's trying to forge relationships beyond the executive suite with the networking and operations people who often influence which vendors are used.

36 Perhaps Chambers' biggest challenge is the switch from leading hypergrowth to grappling with issues of cost control and productivity that will restore the company to profitability. Some question whether the cheerleading CEO who has known only 50% growth since taking over the helm in 1995 can stomach an environment of disciplined cost cuts and layoffs. The decision to lay off 8,500 employees last March weighed so heavily on Chambers that he mulled over its consequences on his treadmill one night at 2:30 A.M. "He's

almost too nice to kick the asses that need to be kicked," says John Thibault, a former Cisco executive and colleague of Chambers' at Wang Laboratories during the late 1980s.

37   If Chambers is worried about the tough decisions ahead, he's not letting on. "Last year was tremendously humbling. It knocked us on our tail. But if we execute right, our future is very, very bright," he says. "Cisco is clearly positioned to break away." Investors buying up Cisco stock at 95 times earnings are banking on it. But Chambers will need much more than bold accounting and long-shot bets on fledgling markets to deliver.

Source: Adapted by Richard Robinson, University of South Carolina, based on John A. Byrne and Ben Elgin, "Cisco: Behind the Hype," *BusinessWeek,* January 21, 2002.

eBay

1   It seemed like a boffo idea to the brass at the Internet auction site eBay Inc.: By referring losing bidders to similar auctions by other eBay sellers, they'd keep bidders coming back. Within minutes of the program's debut in early June, though, all hell broke loose. Hundreds of angry sellers jammed eBay's online discussion boards, furious that their bidders were being siphoned away. One veteran seller of stamps and postcards, Bob Miller, auctioned a rare eBay jacket as an excuse to post a long screed slamming "eBay's new policy of screwing the folks who built them."

2   Even among the 7 million ongoing auctions, this one quickly caught the attention of Chief Executive Margaret C. Whitman and founder Pierre Omidyar. Within a week, they met with Miller in eBay's suburban Salt Lake City office near Miller's home. As they listened for 45 minutes, Whitman took four pages of notes. Two days later, they promised to switch course.

3   E-mails would first recommend the same seller's other auctions, or the seller could simply opt out. "No other large corporation listens nearly as well as they do," says Miller, who's now happily running several thousand auctions on eBay.

GOOD TIMES AND BAD

4   Meet the People's Company. Like a democracy, it can be a noisy and unruly place, where citizens sometimes think the folks in charge are numbskulls. But the people's passion prevails at eBay because the people are firmly in charge. Its customers—the 38 million buyers and sellers who trade on its site—wield the kind of influence over the online auction site that most consumers and businesses could never dream of exerting on conventional companies.

5   Oh, sure, eBay has a delicious business model that doesn't require carrying any inventory. And, yes, it's growing like a weed and minting juicy profits because bargain hunters, in good times and bad, flock to the auction site. But the real secret of eBay's unlikely success is this: It's a master at harnessing the awesome communications power of the Net—not just to let its customers sound off directly in the ears of the big brass, but to track their every movement so new products and services are tailored to just what customers want. Remember that famous tagline, "When E. F. Hutton speaks, people listen"? At eBay, it's the other way around: When people speak, eBay listens.

6   One month in late 1998, for instance, eBay managers noticed an uptick in listings in various miscellaneous categories, such as die-cast cars—suddenly, people were selling *real* cars. Now, eBay's the country's biggest car dealer, with $1 billion in sales of cars and car parts this year. In January, shortly after an eBay seller suggested speeding up auctions for impatient bidders, eBay debuted a Buy It Now feature that lets bidders end an auction at a set price. Now, 40% of listings use it, attracting more mainstream buyers and helping close auctions nearly a day faster on average than a year ago.

ALL IN ONE

7   In essence, customers are eBay's de facto product-development team, sales and marketing force, merchandising department, and security detail—all rolled into one. It's not just that they have catapulted eBay, in just three short years, from a funky little online garage

sale full of Beanie Babies and attic trash into a global marketplace for almost anything, from a $1 baseball card to a $4.9 million Gulfstream jet. eBay's customers also take it upon themselves to tell the world about eBay through word of mouth. They crowd eBay's online discussion boards, posting 100,000 messages a week to share tips, point out glitches, and lobby for changes. eBay's customers even police the site by rating each other, keeping fraud minimal.

8   By using the Net to tap into the talent and imagination of its customers, eBay has multiplied the brainpower of its executives by millions. Imagine a retailer trying to do this: It would have to interview every single person leaving every store, post a list of what each thought of the shopping experience, then ask them to write up a merchandising plan and call suppliers to arrange deliveries—and oh, by the way, could they keep an eye out for shoplifters? That's what eBay's customers voluntarily do each day. Says Whitman: "It is far better to have an army of a million than a command-and-control system."

9   The success of this let-'em-loose-and-listen strategy holds some potent lessons for Corporate America. By staying in close touch with customers, eBay can reinvent itself every day, since it knows precisely what its clientele wants. The trick is to keep up with what buyers and sellers want. "We've had to constantly change how we run," says Chief Operating Officer Brian Swette. "We start from the principle that if there's noise, you better listen."

10   And, because it set a firm corporate goal from the start—to create "global economic democracy"—it has managed to maintain focus even while growing at a crazy clip. First-time eBay buyers are often shocked at the intensely personal service they get from eBay merchants, from handwritten thank-you notes to free shipping. It's an example of how building a strong brand depends more on understanding that each and every transaction can create a personal, one-on-one relationship that will endure. Says eBay board member Howard Schultz, CEO of Starbucks Corp.: "The imprinting of the eBay brand was not based on 30-second ads, but the relationship with the users."

11   That's why neither the September 11 tragedy nor the recession has put a pall on eBay's prospects. Despite losing about $5 million in revenues from a drop in activity following the terror attacks, eBay beat third-quarter estimates. Sales rose 71%, to $194.4 million, surpassing expectations by 3%. It earned an $18 million profit, 15% above analysts' forecasts. eBay even raised its fourth-quarter sales forecast by 5%, to $200 million or more. Analysts now expect 2001 sales to jump at least 70%, to $736 million. Next year looks just as promising. Analysts figure sales will rise 40%, to $1 billion, and profit will be up 56%, to $150 million. Rivals are in awe: "These guys have done a killer job," admits Amazon.com Inc. Chief Financial Officer Warren C. Jenson.

SMARTS, MOXIE

12   Now, eBay appears poised to buck what looks to be a gloomy holiday season for almost every retailer, online and off. That's largely thanks to the smarts and the moxie of its customers, who—unlike big retailers—can switch gears instantly on what they sell or buy and at what price. This year, for instance, sales of discount products, from overstocked PCs to excess toasters and bedsheets, have rocketed. As the economy worsens, more and more corporations, from IBM to Walt Disney to Sears Roebuck, are turning to eBay as a place to unload mounting inventory. "The mix of products on the site changes by the minute as our highly entrepreneurial community of users adapts their own buying and selling strategies to trends in the economy," says Whitman.

13   eBay aims to press that advantage hard this season. It has just kicked off its first-ever holiday TV-ad campaign, which aims to show how shoppers can find almost anything on eBay. Produced by AOL Time Warner Inc., for which eBay is the exclusive auction part-

EXHIBIT 1

eBay Shines in a Dark Economy

eBay's revenues keep rocketing . . .

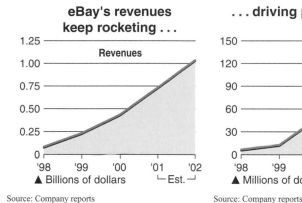

▲ Billions of dollars └ Est. ┘

Source: Company reports

*Morgan Stanley Dean Witter estimate.

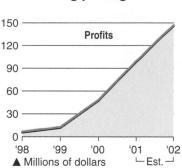
. . . driving profit growth . . .

▲ Millions of dollars └ Est. ┘

Source: Company reports

*Morgan Stanley Dean Witter estimate.

. . . but its stock remains pricey

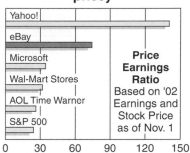

Price Earnings Ratio
Based on '02 Earnings and Stock Price as of Nov. 1

Source: Thomson Financial Network.

ner, the ads also promote how easy it is for AOL members to find the perfect gift on eBay. eBay also is sending out catalogs in newspapers nationwide on Dec. 2 and opening a "Great Gifts" shop on its site, highlighting auctions of everything from gold necklaces to digital cameras.

14 For all its nonstop success, though, eBay faces a lot of challenges. Its $60 stock price represents a nosebleed 2002 price-to-earnings ratio of 82, more than double Microsoft's premium ratio of 31. The tiniest slip—or even, say, a few more anthrax-laden packages—could whack billions off its value overnight and limit the expansion opportunities that have in turn buoyed the stock.

15 Indeed, eBay is increasingly a victim of its own success. As Whitman moves to make eBay more of a clean, well-lighted place that attracts greater numbers of mainstream merchants and shoppers, she has riled existing customers who don't want more rules—or more rivals. These moves also pit eBay much more directly against bigger and more consumer-savvy behemoths. AOL Time Warner, Microsoft, Amazon, and Yahoo! are all trying to create online malls where people can buy just about anything from anyone.

MOMENTUM

16 Still, eBay has the Big Mo' right now, thanks to the groundwork laid way back on Labor Day weekend in 1995, when Omidyar unveiled a bare-bones site called Auction Web. Even then, the programmer and entrepreneur had much more in mind than simply helping his girlfriend trade Pez dispensers. He aimed to create a Nasdaq-like market for a wide range of goods, but with a twist. "I wanted to give the power of the market back to individuals, not just large corporations," says Omidyar. "It was letting the users take responsibility for building the community—even the building of the website."

17 For instance, he would answer e-mails from buyers and sellers during the day, then rewrite the site's software that night to incorporate their suggestions, from fixing software bugs to creating new product categories. Says e-commerce expert John Hagel III, chief strategy officer with e-business incubator 12 Entrepreneuring Inc.: "It really helped give people a sense of ownership and participation." Likewise, Omidyar set up an online bulletin board for customers, whose volunteered help kept early support costs almost nil—and cemented their loyalty.

18   Omidyar's biggest breakthrough was the Feedback Forum, a rating system that allows buyers and sellers to grade each transaction positive, negative, or neutral. Amazingly, it works. More than 99% of feedbacks are positive (sample comment: "Great Bidder! AAAAA+++++ Highly Recommended!"). And eBay's rate of fraud remains below 0.01%. By contrast, credit card fraud runs at nine times that rate. And positive ratings, which translate to more sales, keep people from straying to other sites. Says Dwayne Rogers, who sells vintage fruit crate labels on eBay from his home in Chico, Calif.: "They just don't have any competition."

STRINGENT RULES

19   But as eBay grew from a small town into a city, urban problems erupted, such as contraband goods. Since early 1998, eBay has used more stringent rules to crack down on crime, and banned sales of firearms. Indeed, eBay has increasingly realized that, like government in a democracy, it can't leave absolutely everything to the people. Says Jeff Jordan, senior vice-president in charge of eBay's U.S. operations: "You can't govern a metropolis the same way you governed Mayberry."

20   eBay's key public-works project: its computer network. Until last year, it was plagued with outages—including one in June 1999, when eBay was completely shut down for 22 hours thanks to software problems and no backup systems. Former Gateway Inc. Chief Information Officer Maynard Webb, who joined as president of eBay's technology unit, has upgraded systems so eBay's site is down less than 42 minutes a month despite much higher traffic. Credit that partly to Whitman, who dived into the technology despite her lack of experience in it. Still, eBay's customers had a big part, too. Shortly after Webb joined, he recalls, eBay's discussion boards twice lit up with user complaints about site glitches. His techies claimed nothing was amiss—and both times were proved wrong. "They catch things we don't," Webb says of eBay's customers. "The community actually moves faster than we do.

21   "Sometimes, so do rivals. Yahoo and Amazon beat eBay on such features as online bill payment and uploading of product photos. Shmuel Gniwisch, CEO of online jewelry seller Ice.com, says Yahoo early on provided services more tailored to helping commercial companies. eBay admits it sometimes doesn't have the resources to do everything all its customers want—and, on occasion, just forgets to listen. Says Brian T. Burke, senior manager of community support: "Sometimes we're kind of slow."

22   As befits a corporate democracy, eBay's biggest challenges are political. Features good for buyers, such as those e-mail auction referrals, can hurt sellers. Lately, sellers are especially peeved at eBay's promotion of large commercial companies such as Disney, which rates a special area in the Disneyana category. Says David Steiner, an eBay seller who's also president of the online auction watchdog site AuctionBytes.com: "The general consensus of veteran sellers is that they've forsaken the people who built them in favor of corporate sellers." eBay argues that commercial sellers lend credibility to their categories, drawing more buyers to all the sellers—a point many merchants concede.

TOO BIG?

23   Yet others think eBay isn't listening as well as it once did to its core individual and small-business merchants. "They've gotten too big for their britches," fumes Ron Saxton, an Apple Creek (Ohio) seller of die-cast cars. eBay didn't consult its customers when it launched its Auction for America campaign a week after the September 11 attacks,

aiming to raise $100 million in 100 days for victims. And eBay's insistence that sellers use its billing system, rather than let them accept checks or use a more popular rival system called PayPal, rubbed many the wrong way. That may partly explain why the charity drive has raised less than $6 million halfway through—despite donations such as Jay Leno's celebrity-signed Harley-Davidson motorcycle, which sold for $360,200.

24   Few complaining sellers, however, stop or even reduce selling on eBay, or go anywhere else. Partly, that's because eBay commands more than 80% of the online person-to-person auction market. "The only way I'm leaving eBay is kicking and screaming," says longtime eBay collectibles seller Tina DeBarge. Sure, eBay's relationship with its customers can be messy, says eBay board member Scott Cook, chairman of financial software maker Intuit Inc., "but in the same way that democracy is messy compared with the straightforwardness of a dictatorship."

25   It doesn't hurt that Whitman, despite her traditional top-down marketing background at Disney, FTD.com, and Stride Rite, became a convert to the eBay way shortly after she joined as CEO in early 1998. Indeed, she's a top seller among the company's 2,500 employees, with a positive feedback rating in the hundreds. In May, she auctioned some $35,000 worth of furnishings in her ski condo in Colorado to understand the selling experience—and immediately required fellow execs to sell on eBay so they, too, can detect problems firsthand.

26   It's no surprise, then, that as eBay grew beyond its ability to address individual user concerns, Whitman has pushed it to devise a constant stream of new ways to tap the expertise of its customers en masse. Naturally, eBay harnesses the special qualities of the Internet to gather intelligence much deeper than most brick-and-mortar businesses can obtain. For instance, before eBay revamped its bread-and-butter collectibles categories earlier this year to make products easier to find, it first e-mailed 1.2 million customers asking them to check out the proposed structure. Of the 10,000 who responded, 95% of them had suggestions, and many were used.

CHANGES

27   Some of its most effective ways of getting user input, though, don't depend on the Net. Since early 1999, eBay has convened Voice of the Customer groups, flying in a new group of about 10 sellers and buyers from around the country to its San Jose (Calif.) headquarters every few months. Execs grill them on issues and ask for their views on new features and policies. "Some of the things we discussed led to changes," such as improving eBay's feedback policies, says Voices participant George Hawkins, who sells antiques and collectibles on eBay from Duncan, B.C.

28   The result: fewer problems with new features and policies, and fewer big blowups. Even when something does go wrong, eBay uses all that input to shift gears quickly. In the past three months, in fact, Whitman says eBay has deliberately started budgeting an extra 10% to new projects so it has the resources in place to make a quick turn. "They can essentially negotiate with 50,000 users at once and make it work," says Munjal Shah, CEO of the auction services firm Andale Inc.

29   Most of all, eBay simply watches—very carefully. Virtually all of its fastest-growing new categories, such as autos, grew out of its noticing seller activity and giving it a shove at the right moment. After noticing random car sales, eBay created a separate site called eBay Motors in 1999, with special features such as vehicle inspections and shipping. This year, eBay expects to gross some $1 billion worth of autos and parts—many of them sold by dealers. "It's the way of the future," says Bradley Bonifacius, Internet manager at Dean Stallings Ford Inc. of Oak Ridge, Tenn., which has sold 50 cars on eBay in the past year.

EXHIBIT 2
eBay: Of the People,
by the People, for
the People

From its start in September 1995, most of eBay's features were suggested by users or created as a direct result of their activity on the website. That has paid off for eBay in lower support and marketing costs, higher loyalty, and quick pushes into new markets.

Fall 1995
Let's Talk
Swamped by e-mails from people asking for help, founder Pierre Omidyar creates an online bulletin board for users to share tips. Since then, more than a dozen forums and chat rooms, with 100,000 posts a week, have sprouted up, creating a community of eBay loyalists.

February 1996
Rating One Another
After watching customers discuss ways to gauge the trustworthiness of other buyers and sellers, Omidyar sets up a way for people to give each other ratings on every transaction. Result: Sellers with good ratings stay on eBay, helping it keep its online auction share at 80%.

Spring 1996
Feedback Frenzy
Users constantly e-mail founder Omidyar with suggestions. During the day, he answers them. At night, he makes changes to the software to incorporate the suggestions. That makes users eager to offer advice—keeping support costs down.

February 1998
Safe Harbor
Following complaints about fraudulent buyers and sellers, the company sets up a Safe Harbor program that offers services such as fraud reimbursement and identity verification. Today, less than 0.01% of auctions involve fraud, vs. an average fraud rate of 0.09% for credit cards.

April 1999
Hearing Voices
eBay convenes its first "Voice of the Customer" group, flying 10 users from around the country to eBay's San Jose headquarters. Formed every few months, the gatherings serve as ongoing focus groups to help eBay improve the site.

NEW TERRITORY

30 Most intriguing, customers have been pushing eBay to move its e-commerce system outside the borders of its own website. Ritz Interactive, the online unit of Ritz Camera, for instance, is using the technology to run eBay auctions on its own site. Says Ritz CEO Fred H. Lerner: "eBay has very, very aggressive plans to create an e-commerce platform." Indeed, eBay is encouraging others to build software applications based on eBay technology—much as Microsoft does with its Windows operating system. A flourishing ecosystem of companies could enrich eBay's marketplace by providing support services such as listing tools, escrow, and bill payment. Essentially, says S. G. Cowen Securities Corp. analyst Scott Reamer, eBay aims to become the operating system for e-commerce: the preeminent place for people and businesses to sell online.

31   It's exciting new territory—and dangerous, too. For starters, a raft of rivals from Yahoo and AOL to Microsoft and Amazon aim to be the biggest places for e-commerce,

EXHIBIT 2
(continued)

August 1999
Motoring On
Noticing a one-month jump in several miscellaneous categories, eBay spots a surprising reason: auto sales. So it creates a category for sales of used cars and car parts. eBay Motors now accounts for 16% of the company's gross merchandise sales—an annual rate of $1 billion.

July 2000
Beyond Auctions
eBay acquires Half.com Inc., which hosts sales of books and CDs at half-price or less. It's a first step toward satisfying sellers who want to charge fixed prices to appeal to more buyers. eBay's fixed-price sales have shot up to 16% of gross merchandise sales, from almost zero a year ago.

August 2000
Back to School
After sellers clamor for training to improve their auctions, eBay offers classes. Called eBay University, the program has attracted more than 20,000 people in 19 cities. It's a great marketing tool as well: Within a month, these users double their activity on eBay.

August 2000
House Hunting
A few months after noticing that sellers were listing homes for auction, eBay creates a real estate category. Although it still accounts for under 1% of eBay's overall sales, about 25 properties a day sell on eBay.

January 2001
Buy It Now
Several months after a seller suggested giving buyers a way to end auctions faster, eBay tries out a Buy It Now feature that allows buyers to stop the auction with a bid at a set price. Today, 40% of listings feature Buy It Now. That has helped close auctions in an average 6.1 days today, vs. 6.9 days at the end of 2000, so eBay gets paid faster.

July 2001
Open for Business
After a year of requests, eBay allows sellers to open storefronts on the site. eBay hopes this will prevent sellers from using eBay simply to drive buyers to their own websites. Some 30,000 merchants have signed up. In January, they will begin paying $9.95 in monthly "rent."

too, and some are making fast progress. But there's a bigger question: Can eBay's values survive such grand ambitions? After all, trying to be the Microsoft of e-commerce doesn't sound, well, very eBaysian—which may be why Whitman frowns and demurs when people describe eBay's goal in such stark terms.

32   For his part, Omidyar frets that the growing participation of large commercial sellers could dilute eBay's unique culture. "If we lose that, we've pretty much lost everything," he says. eBay's people power made building a business a breeze compared with everything conventional companies must do. Keeping in touch with all those millions of customers from here on out won't be so easy.

Source: Adapted by Richard Robinson, University of South Carolina, based on Robert D. Hof, "The People's Company," *BusinessWeek,* December 3, 2001.

Case 18

Ford

1   Jacques A. Nasser was on top of the world. Striding the halls of the Detroit auto show in January 1999, the freshly minted CEO of Ford Motor Co. commanded attention. Just a few days into his new job, Nasser was being hailed as the industry's newest auto baron— who might at any moment pull off a huge merger with the likes of Honda, BMW, Volvo, or Nissan. Indeed, Nasser seemed to revel in the speculation about how Ford would spend its $23 billion cash hoard, cracking jokes about the media frenzy. Outside, enormous snowdrifts paralyzed the city. But inside, as he contemplated Ford's future, Nasser's mood couldn't have been sunnier.

2   Last month, Nasser, 53, once again found himself the center of attention. But this time, as he stepped in front of the cameras, the mood was starkly different. Haunted by safety concerns about the popular Ford Explorer in the wake of last year's Bridgestone/ Firestone Inc. tire recall, a somber Nasser announced that Ford would replace an additional 13 million Firestone tires on its pickups and sport-utility vehicles. The cost: a staggering $3 billion.

3   Nasser's latest announcement makes the Firestone debacle the biggest product recall in automotive history and he'll be back in front of Congress on June 19 to explain. But as devastating as it has been, the tire scandal is only the most public of an array of crises confronting Nasser. The company, widely regarded as the strongest and best-run U.S. auto maker, is suddenly on the defensive. Ford is suffering from a series of self-inflicted wounds, from embarrassing quality glitches and costly product delays to declining productivity. Those mistakes couldn't come at a worse time: The economy is slowing, and Ford's share of the U.S. truck market—its main source of profits—is dwindling.

FLOORING IT

4   Certainly, Ford's problems aren't all Nasser's doing. Many are the result of industry trends that have been in the making for years. Yet underlying many of Ford's troubles are the wrenching cultural changes mapped out by Nasser as part of his bold attempt to transform an Old Economy auto manufacturer into a nimble, Net-savvy, consumer power-house. Nasser is driving fast—too fast, for many in the company. In his 33-year career at Ford, he has often shown quick reflexes and sharp instincts. This time, though, the stakes are higher than ever. "Would we like to do better?" he says of the company's current woes. "Of course. But we'll take our lumps. We've been through much worse and we'll come through strong." If he's right, Jacques Nasser will go down in history as the man who brought Ford into the 21st century. If he isn't, he risks becoming a management lesson in how not to remake a company.

5   Almost as soon as he ascended to the corner office, Nasser began overhauling Ford, unveiling one initiative after another. He signed agreements to partner with Microsoft Corp. and Yahoo! Inc. on the Web. He pushed out Ford's Old Guard and brought in talented young stars from the auto industry and beyond. He flattened Ford's bureaucracy, giving more autonomy to regional executives, and shook up senior managers by tying their bonuses to gains in customer service. Gone were the days of automatic promotions and seniority. "You've got to earn a promotion" he thundered at young execs shortly after becoming CEO. "The days of entitlement at Ford Motor Co. are gone forever."

6   He also changed the face of Ford. He added Volvo and Land Rover. Then, convinced that Ford's commitment to consumers shouldn't end when they drive off the dealer's lot, Nasser also bought repair shops, a driving school, the Hertz car-rental agency—even a junkyard. For Nasser, it wasn't enough to be one of the best global automakers. His goal was to make Ford one of the best global companies, period. He wanted Ford—and himself—to one day be as revered as General Electric Co. and its much-admired CEO, Jack Welch.

7   But while Nasser has roared ahead, observers inside and outside Ford say the rest of the company hasn't always followed. As employees at all levels struggle to adapt to the host of sweeping changes Nasser has set in motion, many say Ford has lost of sight of its fundamental mission: building quality vehicles as efficiently and profitably as possible. "It's all these things being jammed down our throats," says John Wyrwas, 61, a power-train engineer who retired this month. "When we're working on all these things, who's working on the product?" It isn't just a rhetorical question. Harbour & Associates' annual ratings of auto-factory efficiency, released June 14, showed labor productivity at Ford falling 7% in 2000, while that of its rivals rose.

8   Now, there's a backlash against the pace and intensity of many Nasser initiatives. A new performance-review system for Ford's 18,000 managers has met with such hostility that 42 of them, including Wyrwas, have filed two class actions, charging that the system targets older workers and white males who are stereotyped as resistant to change. Nasser preaches relentlessly about the need to get closer to the Ford customer, but he has had to rebuild his marketing team after Vice-President James C. Schroer and other marketing execs fled to Chrysler in February. Nasser imported Six Sigma, the management technique popularized by Jack Welch, as a way to teach Ford managers to root out flaws, but in a ranking of quality among the seven largest carmakers this year, Ford came in last. With all the turmoil, it's no wonder Ford has given up 1.7 percentage points of market share in the first five months of the year.

9   As if Nasser didn't have enough problems, rumors have surfaced of a rift between him and Ford family scion William Clay Ford Jr., the company's chairman. Nasser was forced to respond publicly in early June, declaring that he has the full backing of Ford's board of directors. Those directors aren't talking, but sources close to them confirm that the CEO's job is safe. However, the board does feel that Nasser—with 16 direct reports and no clear No. 2—is overextended and needs help managing the company's operations. One rumor has Ford bringing the chairman of its European operations, Nick Scheele, back to the U.S. as president of Ford Automotive Operations. Nasser says only, "I think I've got the best team in the business. However, if we can make it even stronger for our customers and shareholders, we will."

10   Nasser may still have the board's support, but he has lost the goodwill of some Ford employees, the trust of many consumers, and the confidence of Wall Street. The missteps at Ford may even force him to give up one of his greatest dreams—that the company would soon overtake General Motors Corp. as the world's largest automaker. That seemed a foregone conclusion last year. Not anymore. Says Morgan Stanley Dean Witter & Co. analyst Stephen Girsky: "It's amazing to me how fast Ford has unraveled."

11   In Nasser's defense, many of the problems he's grappling with result from decisions made long before he took charge. "He gets nailed with the problems, but they're what he's trying to change," says Noel M. Tichy, a University of Michigan professor and close adviser to Nasser. Improving quality and business productivity across a $170 billion company takes time, argue Nasser's supporters, and initiatives begun two to three years ago, are just beginning to kick in. Nasser admits that Ford's record on quality has been spotty, but he points out that there are bright spots. Its Jaguar brand, for instance, was notorious

EXHIBIT 1
Nasser's
Management
Breakdown

Nasser's aggressive drive to shake up Ford has the company sputtering. Here are some of the problems:

Quality Decline
Ford now ranks last among the seven biggest carmakers in quality. Last year, recalls and delays cost it at least $1 billion, not counting the tire recalls. The redesigned Explorer, out since February, has already been recalled twice. Now, Ford is delaying new versions of its Expedition and Lincoln Navigator for extra testing.

Firestone Fiasco
Last August's recall of 6.5 million tires on the popular Explorer and Mercury Mountaineer SUVs cost Ford about $500 million. This year Ford will take a $2.1 billion aftertax charge to replace 13 million more Firestones. To cap it off, Explorer sales have plunged 21% this year through May.

Sagging Performance
With the huge hit from the Firestone tire recall, Ford has suspended $2.8 billion in stock buybacks. Company earnings are expected to sink by 65% this year, to $2.3 billion, while Ford's share of the U.S. market has fallen by 1.7 percentage points so far in 2001, to 23.1%. And last year, productivity sank by 7%, compared with an 8% gain for GM.

Plummeting Morale
Ford has suffered a number of high-level departures, including the defection of Global Marketing V-P James C. Schroer, who bailed in February for a job at Chrysler. Meanwhile, middle managers have filed two class actions alleging that a new employee-review system that pushes underachievers out the door is discriminatory.

for its lousy quality 10 years ago, and now is ranked second best in the industry. But Nasser emphatically rejects the notion that he's trying to force change too quickly on the carmaker. "If there are any regrets," he says, "it's that we're not moving fast enough."

12   Until recently, Ford was Detroit's Golden Child. When Nasser took over, archrival GM was a basket case, steadily losing market share even as industry sales soared. Chrysler was still reeling from its 1998 takeover by Daimler Benz. And Japanese automakers had only begun to attack the U.S. truck market. Ford, on the other hand, was in the fast lane. It dominated the enormously profitable market for pickups and sport-utility vehicles. Profits from North American truck sales made it easy for investors to overlook Ford's sagging car business, losses in Europe, and troubles in Ford's Asian and South American operations. Fueled by sales of its industry-leading trucks and SUVs, Ford's profits grew more than 60% to $7.2 billion from 1996 to 1999.

FULL TANKS

13   With a strong balance sheet, Ford was also able to keep shareholders happy with a variety of share buybacks and other maneuvers, such as the spin-off of parts maker Visteon Corp., that put more cash in investors' pockets. Ford was also busy cultivating a socially responsible image by promising to clean up the environment—a passion of Bill Ford's—with more fuel-efficient vehicles and by giving employees free personal computers and on-site child care.

14   So when industry pundits warned earlier this year that Detroit was going to get clobbered in an economic slowdown, Ford declared itself far better positioned than its

crosstown rivals to weather a slump. Even though profits in 2000 had dropped by more than half to $3.5 billion on sales of $170 billon, most Wall Street analysts agreed, recommending Ford's shares over GM's or DaimlerChrysler's.

15   Suddenly, Ford's outlook is much cloudier. Most analysts have downgraded the stock. It's clear that the financial hit from the Firestone crisis is brutal. Last year's tire recall cost Ford about $500 million. To pay for the latest recall, the company is suspending the remaining $2.8 billion of a $5 billion share buyback and will take a $2.1 billion aftertax charge in the second quarter. And that doesn't address Ford's potential liability from hundreds of pending lawsuits or lost sales as car buyers shun the troubled Explorer brand. So far this year, Explorer sales are down 21% despite an improved replacement model that debuted in February.

16   Even laying aside the costs of the Firestone mess, Ford told analysts recently that it will have difficulty meeting the profit targets it set at the beginning of the year. With competition intensifying, Ford's U.S. market share has fallen to 23.1% so far this year. Ford now says its goal of increasing revenues to $175 billion is a stretch. Net margins are getting squeezed, too. In the first quarter, they fell to 3.2% from 4.8% in 2000. And the pressure is only going to increase. GM, the sleeping giant, has come roaring back with a revamped truck lineup that includes the Chevrolet Tahoe and Silverado pickup and an aggressive pricing strategy that has already displaced Ford as the market leader in large pickups and SUVs. Japanese manufacturers, too, are going full throttle for the SUV market with new entrants such as Toyota Motor Corp.'s Highlander and Sequoia.

17   With so many new competitors gunning for Ford's rich truck franchise, the automaker's margins will come under increasing assault. As rivals jack up discounts and incentives to woo buyers, Ford has been forced to match them. Both Ford and GM are spending roughly $2,300 per vehicle to sell their large pickups and SUVs. Those incentives will further depress profits. Ford has warned analysts that even without the Firestone recall, it might not meet its 4% net-margin target for North America this year. Deutsche Bank analyst Rod Lache sees a repeat of what happened to Detroit automakers in the car business back in the 1980s: Profits vanished amid increased competition and overcapacity. "It's very possible that trucks will be just as unprofitable as cars in three to four years," warns Lache.

18   The threats to Ford don't all come from the outside. After all, it's not outsiders who have caused its embarrassing quality slipups. In a recent survey by J. D. Power & Associates Inc., Ford ranked worst of the top seven global auto companies in quality. The No. 2 automaker had 162 problems per 100 vehicles, compared with just 115 for Toyota. Such glitches led to a string of recalls. The Focus compact car, which debuted in 1999, had six recalls, and the Escape, a small SUV introduced a year later, had five. Even the 2002 Explorer, which was closely scrutinized by Ford engineers, was recalled twice—once to fix a loose bracket that could allow the rear window to shatter and again to check for gashes on the tires caused by Ford's own assembly line. In another humiliating blunder, Ford was forced to cancel the entire 2000 model year for its souped-up Mustang Cobra muscle car because the 1999 model's engine couldn't generate the 320 horsepower advertised. It took the company a year to fix the problem and get the Cobra back to dealer showrooms for 2001.

QUALITY'S COST

19   Shoddy vehicles have hurt Ford's bottom line in several ways. Quality problems and related production delays cost the company more than $1 billion in lost profits last year alone, according to Nasser. Obviously, sales suffer for a vehicle that is perceived as a

EXHIBIT 2

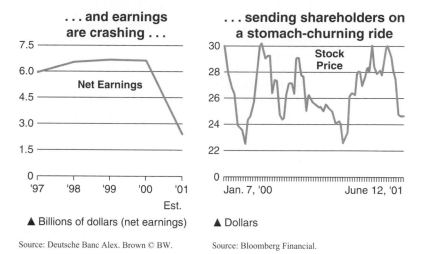

... and earnings are crashing ...

Net Earnings

▲ Billions of dollars (net earnings)

Source: Deutsche Banc Alex. Brown © BW.

... sending shareholders on a stomach-churning ride

Stock Price

Jan. 7, '00   June 12, '01

▲ Dollars

Source: Bloomberg Financial.

lemon. But lousy quality also means higher warranty costs. Deutsche Bank estimates Ford's average warranty cost per vehicle at $650, vs. $550 at GM and only $400 for Toyota. That puts Ford's annual warranty costs at about $2.6 billion. A car of mediocre quality also yields less at resale time, which affects lease-payment calculations. In order to keep the payments low, the automaker must subsidize the car's trade-in value. That helps explain why Ford's average incentive per vehicle is $2,122, on a par with GM's, while Toyota's, whose cars fetch more at trade-in time, is just $1,150, according to Deutsche Bank.

20   Add it all up and Ford has a huge cost disadvantage compared with the Japanese. A study by Deutsche Bank concludes that Toyota has an $1,800 per vehicle advantage over Ford because of its greater efficiency and ability to command higher prices. So to match Toyota on price and remain profitable, Ford has to find a way to cut annual costs by more than the $1 billion it had planned. As the company tightens its belt, it is also pushing back car launches. A new version of the F-Series pickup—its best-selling vehicle—has been delayed a year, while an updated Ranger pickup has been postponed indefinitely, say dealers and suppliers, allowing Ford to put off billions in capital spending.

21   GM has a similar cost disadvantage. But as the Harbour Report showed, GM has made big leaps in productivity, which means it's on a faster cost-cutting track than Ford. GM's productivity, as measured by the number of worker-hours needed to make a vehicle, increased 8%, while Ford's fell 7%. Ford maintains a slight edge overall, but GM has just about closed the gap. Nasser points out that Ford's productivity is excellent in plants where new lean manufacturing processes are taking root. Still, he vows improvement and says, "I take full responsibility. I don't walk away from anything."

22   So why can't Ford—a company that has been in the business of launching cars for nearly 100 years—get it right? Distractions caused by Nasser's cultural revolution, coupled with dramatic changes in how the industry operates, simply left too much room for error. Like other automakers, Ford is pressuring suppliers to take on more of the engineering while demanding ever-increasing price cuts. Some suppliers say the added pressure can lead to defects down the line. Speed is also a factor. A new car now takes about 28 months from drawing board to showroom, nearly half as long as it took a decade ago. In the rush to bring vehicles to market faster, Ford sometimes turns over its plans to suppliers before all the engineering and testing are completed, says the CEO of a major supplier. Last-minute design changes, he says, then put added pressure on suppliers, which can result in production screwups.

EXHIBIT 3
The Quality Thing at Ford

"Quality is Job 1." That boast was once widely used in Ford's advertising. But the automaker has recently been plagued by a spate of recalls. Ford hopes its embrace of Six Sigma will reduce defects in the future. Here are some recent recalls:

1999 Mustang Cobra
The engine in the SVT Mustang Cobra was unable to generate 320 horsepower, as advertised. About 4,000 were recalled, and the 2000 model year was scrapped entirely.

2000 Focus
This compact endured six recalls. One of them, covering 207,000 cars, concerned faulty hub nuts that could cause the wheel and brake-drum assembly to come off.

2001 Escape
This new model has had five recalls since its introduction. The last covered 51,000 vehicles. Problems included defective speed-control cables, leaking fuel lines, and missing rivets on windshield parts.

2002 Explorer
Some 52,000 SUVs were recalled to check for gashes in the tires, which occurred on the assembly line. The government said the defect could result in tire failure and crashes.

23   But Ford's internal strife is just as much to blame. "There has been so much emphasis on cost reductions, on task forces and new teams, that they lose sight of what's really important," says David E. Cole, director of the Center for Automotive Research in Ann Arbor, Mich. Over the past several years, Ford has lost many of its most experienced workers through buyouts and early retirements. That brain drain and the pressure to cut costs and move faster may explain errors like the one that caused the most recent Explorer recall. Despite extra quality checks to make sure the redesigned Explorer was free of defects, no one remembered during the planning stage to relocate a conveyor belt guide post on the assembly line to accommodate the 2.5-inch wider body. The result was a recall of 53,000 brand-new SUVs to check for gashes up to nine inches long in their tires.

24   Nasser believes that Six Sigma, the system for continuous improvement in quality and efficiency, will help Ford avoid similar mistakes in the future. Six Sigma relies on statistical analysis to get to the root of intractable problems. Ford began training managers in the technique a year ago and says the system has already produced results. Last year, for instance, one group tackled a nagging problem on the newly introduced Lincoln LS sedan: Why wouldn't the engine always start on the first try? Using Six Sigma, they reverse-engineered the vehicle and traced the problem to a screw that wasn't fully tightened. The true culprit? Workers were using the wrong power tool. Ford says Six Sigma saved it $52 million last year, and it expects to save another $300 million this year.

25   But if Six Sigma is so great, why isn't Ford's quality improving? Ford officials insist that it is—it just takes a while for the improvements to show up, they say. "We've had some very good results from Six Sigma projects so far, but there just aren't enough of them yet to affect broad-based results," says Richard Parry-Jones, group vice-president for global product development and quality.

26   Like quality, employee morale could also use a lift. Many Ford workers are upset that in a bid to shake up the culture, Nasser chose outsiders rather than Ford veterans for powerful management posts. He recruited J Mays, the hotshot designer of the redesigned Volkswagen Beetle, to head Ford's design studio, and plucked BMW's former president, Wolfgang Reitzle, to run Ford's beefed-up luxury-car business. Tichy sees the backlash

as the predictable response to change and the inevitable resistance of entrenched managers. "You need to bring in new blood. It's how you change your DNA," he says. "The Old Guard gets threatened and upset."

27   Perhaps nothing has been more upsetting to Ford's middle managers, however, than the employee-evaluation system introduced last year. The new policy requires supervisors to rank employees from best to worst along a curve: 10% get A's, 80% get B's, and 10% get C's. Getting a C means no bonus; two Cs in a row is grounds for demotion or dismissal. Instead of measuring an employee's performance against a set of objectives, the employee is measured against others with similar jobs—a radical change for a traditionally paternalistic company. The policy was intended to weed out underperformers and build a sense of teamwork. But employees say it has had the opposite effect. "If anything, this has caused extensive navel-gazing rather than staring out at the horizon at the consumer and the competition," says Pam Tucker, 48, a Ford manager and plaintiff in one of the class-action suits. "People are constantly looking over their shoulder."

28   Nasser says the new job-review process is fair. "This is a company that has always had a policy of inclusion, going all the way back to Henry Ford." But he adds that it's important for management to be candid with employees about their performance. "A system that doesn't encourage that dialog in a positive way is a very cruel system, because you end up with employees who are not motivated, and maybe in the wrong positions. Then, when reality dawns, it may be too late." Still, Nasser has heard the complaints and backed off some. Now only the bottom 5% of performers will get C grades.

29   Can Ford become the next GE? It's way too early to say. After all, Jack Welch spent the first decade of his tenure absorbing criticism for his relentless cost-cutting and layoffs. But Cole says the blueprint that eventually brought Welch great success may just be wrong for a company like Ford. With GE's diversified portfolio of businesses, it's easy to sell off the dogs. But a carmaker can't dump an underperforming marketing or design unit. "What Jac has tried to do is force-fit Ford into the GE model in a fashion that may not work," says Cole.

30   The uproar over Nasser's initiatives underscores the difficulty and risks of trying to remake a company's basic values in a relatively short time. Convinced that successful companies in the Internet Age must move at Net speed, Nasser plunged headlong into a dizzying array of initiatives designed to reshape the century-old automaker. CEOs at plenty of other Old Economy companies, from Procter & Gamble to Gillette to Xerox, were trying to do exactly the same thing when Nasser took the wheel at Ford: shake up the status quo and return their companies to their "former" greatness. But overhauling an entrenched culture is exceedingly difficult. Companies that have succeeded, such as Fannie Mae and Wells Fargo & Co., did so one step at a time, without making a lot of bold promises, says Jim Collins, author of the upcoming book, *Good to Great: Why Some Companies Make the Leap . . . And Others Don't,* due in October. "They weren't focused on changing the culture," he says. "They were focused on changing the results." He says that getting the rest of the company on board is the hardest challenge. "You have to focus on getting the right people on the bus and the wrong people off the bus, and the right people in the right seats." Nasser is trying to do just that. But with so much at stake, it's turning into a white-knuckle ride.

FORD PART 2: ENTER WILLIAM C. FORD, JR.

31   William C. Ford Jr. is tightening his grip on the automaker founded by his great-grandfather. Sources say Ford's chairman began consulting outside directors this spring about the company's deepening problems—worsening quality, productivity, profits, and market share—and the dearth of information flowing to him and the rest of the Ford board.

32   The board concluded that Ford CEO Jacques Nasser was spreading himself too thin. It voted on July 12 to beef up the responsibilities of his top managers. Then, on July 25, it created an office of the chairman and CEO. Nasser is now required to meet twice a month with Bill Ford, who is not involved in day-to-day operations.

33   Ford's expanded role makes him both a sounding board for Nasser and a conduit of information to the rest of the board. He's expected to join the CEO in deciding how to fix the company's biggest problems and deepen its management bench, as well as vetting the turnaround plans of new North American auto boss Nick Scheele.

FORD PART 3: BILL FORD TAKES THE WHEEL

34   For a brief, shining moment on the morning of Oct. 30, Ford Motor Co.'s Dearborn (Mich.) headquarters felt like Camelot. Cheering workers surged to their feet as William C. Ford Jr. introduced himself as the company's new chief executive officer at a hastily arranged press conference. Amid the gloom about worsening profits and quality, the ouster of CEO Jacques A. Nasser at the hands of founder Henry Ford's well-liked great-grandson was a tonic to battered morale. And the shift in mood was almost palpable. "It was like the old Ford again," says one company insider. "People were smiling again instead of staring at the ground."

35   Trouble is, it's not the old Ford. The company, hailed by Wall Street just last year as the best-managed of the Big Three, is in a tailspin. Its stock has tumbled 58% since May, 1999, its 10-year high. And it has slipped 32% this year—about twice as far as General Motors Corp. or DaimlerChrysler. The company lost more than $1.4 billion in the past two quarters, thanks to soaring costs, falling prices, big rebates, and the Firestone tire recall. With the popularity of such mainstay models as the F-150 pickups and the Explorer SUV waning, Ford has surrendered 1.5 points of market share this year alone, slipping to 22.8% of U.S. vehicle sales. All this in an economy that's heading south.

36   Toughest of all will be Ford's deepest problems—quality snafus, putting the Firestone debacle behind it, a lack of exciting vehicles in the pipeline, and a brain drain. Indeed, on Oct. 31, lawyers for Explorer owners alleged that Ford withheld knowledge that the vehicle was unstable. At best, it will take Bill Ford and his new team years to reverse the damage. They are already hammering out a broad restructuring plan that Ford promises to produce by early January. Whatever shape the plan takes, it will have to tackle a big question about the future: Should Ford shrink to become stronger, as Nasser argued, or plot a new strategy for growth? "Bill is the right leader," says one former Ford manager. "But he's got a crippled company to work with."

NO DREAM

37   The crippled company part is surely true. Far less clear is whether Bill Ford is really the right leader. The new CEO did spend 15 years in Ford management, before leaving to assume broader board responsibilities in 1995. But he has never run anything larger than Ford's minuscule Swiss operations. No one pretends he would be running the world's fourth-largest industrial company at age 44 if his last name weren't Ford. And no one on Wall Street sees this as a dream team. Shrugs veteran analyst Maryann Keller: "You go with the best you've got."

38   Nor is it clear whether Ford's No. 2, 57-year-old Chief Operating Officer Nick Scheele, has what it takes to fix so large and complex a mess. Just two years ago, Scheele was running Ford's prestigious but tiny Jaguar unit. He has since leapfrogged through

EXHIBIT 4
Bill Ford's Job List
2002

Restore Morale
He must boost spirits of Ford's unhappy salaried workforce—and rebuild relations with unions, dealers, suppliers, and investors.

Improve Quality
Among the big carmakers, Ford now ranks lowest in terms of quality. That has caused delays in the launch of products such as the T-Bird and has led to embarrassing recalls on its new Escape and Focus models.

Strengthen the Lineup
Longtime best-sellers such as the F-150 pickup series and the Explorer are fading. Ford needs fresh product to regain market share, raise revenues, and reduce the need for costly marketing incentives.

Cut Costs
To restore short-term profits, Ford will have to sell assets, squeeze suppliers, trim its workforce, and idle excess capacity. Eventually, Ford also needs to design lower-cost vehicles.

two big jobs, before becoming head of operations on Oct. 30. Meantime, board member Carl E. Reichardt, 70, the retired chairman of Wells Fargo & Co., who as new vice-chairman will oversee Ford's finances, is taking on a huge task. The job, he jokes, is akin to "a 45-year-old quarterback being asked to strap on the pads again."

EASY MANNERS

39   But don't write off this unlikely crew quite so fast. Any one of them on his own wouldn't be able to run the company. But Ford and team, among them, possess an impressive array of skills the carmaker will need. Bill Ford is no lightweight: He's a quick study who has run auto operations from climate control to commercial trucks and has had stints in sales, manufacturing, and labor relations. For six years, he headed the board's powerful finance committee. What's more, Ford enjoys a strong bond with the rank and file—at a company that prizes its ties to the Ford family. Ford's dealers, who bear the brunt of quality woes, also seem to have a soft spot for the new CEO. "You can't get mad at Bill Ford," says Lincoln-Mercury dealer Martin J. "Hoot" McInerney. "He's just too nice a guy."

40   Bill Ford's two henchmen bring their own assets. Scheele earned his stripes turning around Ford's quality-plagued Jaguar division in the 1990s. In early 2000, the 35-year Ford veteran took on the company's perennially troubled European operations, launching a $1 billion restructuring that slashed output by 17% and launched snazzy new products. The unit is expected to turn a profit in 2002. In just three months, Scheele has won a solid following among Ford's North American ranks for his candor and popular "back to basics" mantra that puts the focus squarely on making and selling cars and trucks. Signing on Reichardt, a top banker favored by investing whiz Warren E. Buffett, wowed Wall Street and gives Ford much-needed financial acumen. "It's a stroke of genius," says Keller.

41   Running Ford Motor is hardly a one-man job, as the new CEO hastens to point out. "I expect the three of us will have an easygoing partnership," he adds. That would be a big improvement over his strained power-sharing arrangement with Nasser, a talented but autocratic manager who hated to delegate and tried to keep his boss out of the loop. This time, Bill Ford has handpicked his team, choosing managers known for their willingness to be team players.

42   Indeed, just the absence of Nasser makes Bill Ford's job easier. The ex-CEO's willingness to squeeze suppliers, upset dealers, and shed experienced employees as he rushed to remake Ford as a consumer company made him a lightning rod. Several top Nasser confidants have also already gotten the ax, and others may follow. Ford really needed to see a new team to lead [it] out of the wilderness," says David E. Cole, director of the Center for Automotive Research in Ann Arbor, Mich.

43   The hard part is yet to come. The restructuring plan is expected to trim away $3 billion to $5 billion in costs. Shrinking the company to match its diminished market share would be the quickest way to repair Ford's finances. But insiders say Bill Ford will be less likely than Nasser to favor downsizing the company. Nor has the new team yet spelled out how it will deal with nagging problems such as quality. Last-minute glitches have delayed the launches of a series of products, most recently the eagerly awaited new Ford Thunderbird. But the choice of manufacturing boss James Padilla to replace Scheele as head of North America is seen as a step to bolster quality.

HAMSTRUNG

44   It will also be tough to get crowd-pleasing new cars and trucks into showrooms on a shoestring. Scheele says Ford has locked in future product plans, but insiders concede what's in the pipeline isn't exciting enough to rebuild sales. Scheele says he would like to add more car-based SUVs and other innovative crossover vehicles to the lineup, but that will take years. So will rebuilding Ford's depleted talent bank.

45   The most immediate challenge will be eliminating the cost of excess factory capacity. Analysts believe that Ford needs to close at least two or three assembly plants to stop its hemorrhaging. But the company is hamstrung by its 1999 contract with the United Auto Workers, in which Ford agrees not to close or sell any plants. "The contract's in cement," says UAW President Stephen P. Yokich. Still, Chrysler and the UAW worked together to devise a plan that eliminates work shifts and slows assembly line speeds at North American factories to cut output and minimize job losses. And with the good will that comes with his popularity and name, Bill Ford might be able to find some wiggle room to hatch a similar deal.

46   Where else could Ford economize? Analysts also suggest Ford might find it easier to unload some of the "downstream" auto-related ventures Nasser acquired now that he's gone: the British repair chain, Kwik-Fit; a junkyard business in Florida; and a slew of small e-business startups the company financed. Bill Ford will only say: "Everything is up for review—every asset, every piece of geography. We'll continue to review our mix of businesses."

47   Such cuts, no doubt, would provide the quickest path back to the basics, and that's exactly where the new team wants to take Ford. "It's not the Internet, junkyards, or auto parts," says Cole. "It's building cars and trucks." Now there's a novel idea.

Source: Adapted by Richard Robinson, University of South Carolina, based on Joann Muller with Kathleen Kerwin, David Welch, Pamela L. Moore and Diane Brady, "Ford: Why It's Worse Than You Think," *BusinessWeek,* June 25, 2001; Kathleen Kerwin, "Bill Ford: A Ford with Better Ideas?" *BusinessWeek,* August 13, 2001; and Kathleen Kerwin and Joann Muller, "Bill Ford Takes the Wheel," *BusinessWeek,* November 12, 2001.

Case 19

BusinessWeek

Volkswagen

1   Volkswagen CEO Ferdinand Piëch has every reason to feel satisfied. The Austrian engineer and scion of one of Europe's most noted automotive dynasties is less than a year from retirement as chief of the German carmaker. As he looks back, Piëch can boast of one of the great turnarounds in automotive history. Since taking the top job at the Wolfsburg headquarters in 1993, his engineering brilliance has helped resurrect Volkswagen quality and turn models such as the Golf and Passat into all-time best-sellers. Piëch's relaunch of the Beetle has cemented VW's hold in the U.S. market. Only VW has successfully revived a communist-era carmaker, Skoda of the Czech Republic. Even now, as the global car industry lurches through a stressful year, VW expects profits to grow: In 2000, they more than doubled, to $1.8 billion, on sales of $76 billion. And before Piëch steps down, VW will launch his pet project, the powerful D1 sedan, the company's first foray into the luxury market under the VW name. He even seems to have settled on his heir apparent—Bernd Pischetsrieder, the former boss of BMW and a supremely able executive in his own right.

2   Looks like a job well done. Piëch has already rewarded himself by buying a 102-foot yacht to sail around the world with his family. The boat is the talk of nautical circles. The gossip is that the $15 million yacht, being built by the top-notch Dutch shipyard Jongert, will be one of the most powerful, best designed private vessels ever launched, a fitting tribute to Piëch, who is passionate about superbly crafted objects.

RAIDERS?

3   And so another corporate chieftain prepares to sail off into the sunset. End of story? Hardly. In recent weeks, Piëch 64, has not acted like an exec who's winding down, a boss whose company is going from strength to strength. If anything, he's behaving like a CEO in the midst of a full-blown crisis, a corporate hero surrounded by dim-witted underlings and hostile outside forces. Piëch has publicly lambasted the management of VW's Audi luxury car division for timid product choices. He has discussed the potential value of spinning off Audi, a potentially huge transaction in the global auto industry. He has mused aloud that VW needs a major management realignment. Most amazing, he frets that VW could be a takeover candidate, "a tempting worm" to other companies on the prowl. VW officials have even named Ford Motor Co. as a potential suitor. Execs at beleaguered Ford, meanwhile, wonder what the Germans are smoking. "There's another agenda here," says a senior Ford of Europe manager.

4   If there is another agenda, it's Piëch's Discussing the likelihood of takeovers and restructurings is a classic way to talk up a company's stock price. Yet many investors are mystified by the idea of Piëch as the shareholder's friend. Historically, Piëch—who will not even reveal how much VW stock he owns, although it's believed to be negligible—has shown scant regard for boosting shareholder value. So wary investors and auto execs wonder whether his talk is a drive to bid up the price and leave in a blaze of glory, which in turn would allow Piëch to exert power after retirement.

5   How? After he steps down as boss, Piëch wants to be named chairman of VW's supervisory board, a position that must be approved by a majority of shareholders. If he can goose the stock, Piëch should be a shoo-in for chairman, a seat that gives him power to

influence management and executive appointments. That could create complications for his successor. "The new CEO will have a big handful of challenges," says one former board member. "But the one [challenge] that's make-or-break will be managing Piëch."

SQUELCH

6   Piëch, by the way, is not talking for this story. Most outsiders don't want to talk on the record about Piëch, either. But the question remains: Would the continued presence of Piëch be good for VW? Piëch the engineer has always excelled. "He is completely focused on the product. He lives, breathes, loves cars," says a former manager of VW's vast Wolfsburg assembly plant in Lower Saxony. The VW he has revived is in many ways the legacy of the best of the old Europe. It makes products that are the envy of rivals, employs thousands of workers for life, and enjoys the protection of the government: The state of Lower Saxony owns 18.6% of VW. Piëch is close to German Chancellor Gerhard Schröder, who as Prime Minister of Lower Saxony sat on VW's supervisory board. (The Chancellor's office now employs Audis in its fleet.)

7   But Piëch the executive will bequeath quite a number of problems to the company's next boss. VW, Europe's largest carmaker and the fourth-largest globally in terms of vehicle sales, has long struggled to improve profitability and productivity. The company's ambitious push to drive the brand upmarket risks hurting its existing premium marque, Audi. VW has far too many highly paid workers at its German plants. Yet politics prevents a radical restructuring. Many outside shareholders, who have seen the stock stagger back down to 1997 levels, distrust the numbers they're given by the company. Finally, some former execs say Piëch cows subordinates, squelching debate at VW's top levels.

8   All these issues loom just as uncertainty is mounting about what will happen next. The supervisory board, which oversees the management board in German companies, is not expected to announce a successor—probably Pischetsrieder—until November. Meanwhile, the industry picture is darkening. Sales are soft in the U.S., Europe, and South America. The last thing VW needs is a messy transfer of power at the moment it should be building on Piëch's gains.

9   Without question, those achievements have been considerable. Volkswagen's four main brands—VW, Audi, Seat, and Skoda—have taken 19% of the European auto market, a gain of some three points in eight years, mostly at the expense of General Motors Corp. and Ford. Not bad for a company that eight years ago suffered from quality problems and a paucity of hit models. In South America, VW vehicles account for one-quarter of car sales, and in China, one-half.

10   Piëch had a dynastic interest in seeing VW revive. His grandfather Ferdinand Porsche, founder of the sportscar maker, designed the first Beetle in the 1930s, and his father, Anton Piëch, ran the factories during the Third Reich. Anton's son, after working for Porsche, switched to Audi, which he eventually headed, and then moved on to VW itself. Ferdinand Piëch certainly doesn't need to work. His clan is worth about $4 billion, thanks to its Porsche businesses.

11   But Piëch is driven. Unlike many other auto chiefs, he calls the shots on product design and engineering. And if you work for Dr. Piëch, you had better get it right. In Wolfsburg, executives joke that PEP, the acronym for the product development process *(Produktentwicklungsprozess)* really stands for *Piëch entscheidet persönlich*—Piëch decides himself. And he can do it fast. He is said to have sketched out the Audi's all-wheel-drive system on the back of an envelope.

12   When Piëch isn't drawing up the plans, he's examining them with a gimlet eye. No screaming, of course: That's not the way for Piëch, an Austrian blueblood. One former transmission-plant manager said Piëch would tour the factory quietly, reviewing production data sheets and zeroing in instantly on any numbers suggesting something was amiss in the manufacturing process. "He's the only person whose very presence on the floor would make my stomach begin to hurt," says this manager.

13   Terrifying, yet inspiring. Under Piëch's tutelage, VW sweats the small stuff. Check this out, says one rival exec: On VW models, the gap between body panels—say between the front fender and wheel panel—has been cut to 1 millimeter. That puts them in a league with the industry's best.

14   Obsession with detail is one reason VW has succeeded so brilliantly in reviving its fortunes in the U.S., where the VW brand was road kill a decade ago. Last year, VW and Audi sales in the U.S. jumped 14%, to 437,000 units, for a combined 2.5% market share. That's up from a microscopic 0.5% in 1993. Although VW trails its Japanese rivals, it's the only European mass-market carmaker in the U.S.

15   The top VW brands in the U.S. are the Jetta, Passat, and the new Beetle, a remake of the humble bug so beloved of '60s youth. Part of VW success lies in its quirky features. At night, the dashboard instruments the driver looks at, such as the speedometer and clock, light up in red, while those the driver touches, such as the radio, are backlit in blue. "It gives the vehicle some soul, which many of VW's competitors lack horribly," says Wes Brown, a consultant at Nextrend Inc., a Thousand Oaks (Calif.) auto-research firm.

16   Delivering the soul stuff is good for prices. A well-equipped Passat can top $29,000 in the U.S., making it one of the most expensive cars in its segment. In Europe, meanwhile, the $15,300 Golf compact commands a premium of some 20% over other cars in its class. "Very wealthy people will buy a Golf. You never rub people the wrong way with a Golf," says Joachim Rebmann, the owner of Autohaus Rebmann, a VW and Audi dealership in Stuttgart.

EXHIBIT 1

Source: European Car Makers' Assn. (ACEA) © BW.

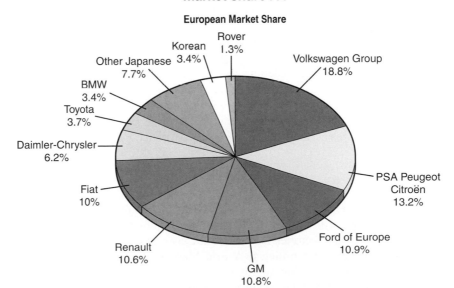

VW has strong market share . . .

European Market Share

PET PROJECT

17   Piëch wants to extend the VW magic—in several directions. On the drawing board is a 21st century remake of the old VW bus, the chariot of hippiedom in the 1960s. And in the power category, a $35,000 super Passat will soon be on the autobahn, equipped with an eight-cylinder, W-shaped engine that delivers super acceleration. "They've fit a huge engine into a medium-size bay," says Goldman, Sachs & Co. analyst Max Warburton.

18   Dear to Piëch's heart is the D1, which launches in Europe next spring. This is the first Volkswagen luxury car and the cornerstone of Piëch's efforts to move upmarket. Positioned to compete with the stately Mercedes S-Class in the $50,000-plus segment, the sleek D1 recalls the swooping lines of BMW sedans, while the interior is a rich mix of walnut and leather. Piëch took an obsessive interest in the D1's top engine, a direct-injection diesel-fueled V-10 monster. And the D1 is not the only new model for the ruling classes. Piëch, who bought the Bentley and Bugatti brands, is preparing a $700,000, 800-horsepower Bugatti able to go from 0 to 60 mph in four seconds.

19   This is impressive stuff. So why do many investors have such uneasy feelings about VW? "Shareholders are second-class citizens in this company," says Simon Waxley, a fund manager at Liverpool Ltd. Partnership, which owns just under 2% of VW's preferred shares. Strong language—and this from a guy who sees some value in VW.

20   To the frustration of Waxley and other investors, VW has shown little interest in giving them the data they hunger for. The company does not disclose operating profits, for example, and it's hard to figure out how VW calculates earnings. "It looks like their market dominance is paying off, but I see some investors who are still mistrustful as to whether these are real or pumped-up earnings because of Dr. Piëch's desire to depart on a high note," says John Lawson, chief car analyst at Schröder Salomon Smith Barney. He estimates VW's profit margin was 1.9% in 1999, rising to 3.6% in 2000. Other analysts think it's even thinner. Investors, meanwhile, are frustrated that VW is not able even to reach its own announced target of a 6.5% return on sales. Last year, its return on sales was 4.1%.

21   Investors have long harbored the suspicion that Piëch and his top managers care little for the margins. As a result, VW stock has one of the lowest price-earnings ratios in the European auto sector: Based on projected 2002 earnings, it's between 7 and 8, compared with industry averages of 13 to 14, according to Merrill Lynch. Even poor old DaimlerChrysler has a p-e of 16. VW's market capitalization of $17.6 billion is a fifth less than BMW's, even though Volkswagen generates more than twice as much revenue. In the second half of 2000, VW's shares rose about 40%, thanks to a $2 billion share buyback, but they have mostly drifted sideways this year. At $45, VW stock is about where it was in the spring of 1997. Rolf Drees, a financial analyst at Germany's third-largest fund, Union Investment, which owns a 1% stake in VW, says the return on VW stock in the three years to the end of 2000 was an average annual 5.2%, using dividends plus the change in the stock price. That's just a third of the 15.3% return on the blue-chip DAX index over the same period.

HARD SLOG

22   A swift boost to the stock is a hard feat to pull off. The government of Lower Saxony, the biggest investor, worries more about jobs than shareholder value. Five of VW's seven German factories are located in Lower Saxony, and they're among the least productive in Europe. According to World Markets Research Center in London, production at the Wolfsburg plant runs at 46 cars per worker per year, compared with 101 at Nissan Motor Co.'s British factory in Sunderland.

23   Piëch would love to change that. In 1993, to buy labor peace, he cut the workweek at VW's German plants from 35 hours to 28.8. That saved 30,000 jobs. But now VW workers can make upwards of $34 an hour. Piëch is trying to push through a plan to lower the base wages of new German workers and link them to output instead of hours. If this doesn't succeed, VW threatens to put new projects in places such as the Czech Republic, where wages are less than one-third German levels. Cutting such a deal is turning into a hard slog. The unions concede they need to be more flexible. But they are resisting management's demands to increase the workweek to more than 40 hours during peak production without paying overtime.

24   Profitability has remained an issue even though Piëch has worked hard to cut costs in other ways. Soon after he arrived, he decided to build all Skoda, Seat, VW, and Audi cars on four shared platforms, or chassis components. The Golf, Skoda Octavia, Beetle, and even the Audi TT roadster share platforms. The strategy has helped save up to $1.5 billion a year. Now, VW plans to share brakes, transmission, and other systems. "We can save billions of marks with these strategies," says Martin Winterkorn, VW's research and development chief.

25   Sharing the ingredients, however, may have harmed some of VW's own marques, as some consumers conclude that cars sharing platforms are sisters under the skin. Although hard to prove, it seems that some potential VW and Audi customers in Europe end up going for lower-priced Skodas and Seats. Since 1996, Skoda's share of the European market has more than doubled, to 1.5%, while the VW brand's share dipped slightly. "Skoda's image of 'value for money' is too close to VW's brand image, which hasn't been moved upmarket fast enough," says a German auto consultant.

26   VW also has gaps in its product lineup. It has nothing to offer in the category of compact minivans—the scaled-down versions of minivans that are popular in Europe. A sport-utility vehicle will not come out until 2002. "We're [also] missing some niche models—sports car, roadster, another convertible," says Jürgen Lehmann, manager of the Autohaus Moltke dealership in Stuttgart. VW has to sort out these issues while the competition gets tougher. According to market researchers J. D. Power & Associates, Renault, Peugeot, and Ford of Europe have closed the quality gap with VW. What's more, luxury auto makers are venturing downmarket. Mercedes is expanding the $18,000 A-Class, while BMW has rolled out a $14,000 Mini and has a compact in the works.

27   With the markets weakening, VW's next CEO will find it hard to keep boosting profits, especially if VW produces too many cars this year. According to Merrill Lynch & Co.

EXHIBIT 2

Source: Volkswagen, Bloomberg Financial Markets, Schroder Salomon Smith Barney, ICF Group © BW.

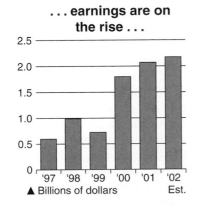

. . . earnings are on the rise . . .

▲ Billions of dollars   Est.

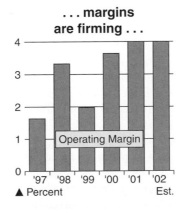

. . . margins are firming . . .

Operating Margin

▲ Percent   Est.

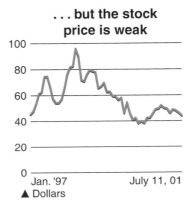

. . . but the stock price is weak

Jan. '97   July 11, 01

▲ Dollars

VW's factory sales to dealers rose by 4.6%, whereas dealers' sales to customers nudged up only 0.7% in the first quarter. And production jumped 13.4%, Merrill Lynch reports. "There's a big disparity between what they're producing and what they're selling," says analyst Zee Tull. Higher sales to dealers boost short-term profits, and the first-quarter results were impressive, surging 57%, to $330 million. But "payback can be brutal" if production must be slashed later, according to the Merrill report. VW says the gap between production and sales narrowed in April and May, and the company predicts its half-year results will show production and sales in closer alignment.

28   Piëch has vowed to cut costs by about $1 billion this year. He has not specified how. A less-than-premium stock performance is not an immediate threat to the company. But if VW ever wants to use its stock to acquire another carmaker or expand further into the truck business, it needs a high share price. Also, the European Union is scrutinizing a German law that specifically bars any VW shareholder from voting more than 20% of the stock. If the law is repealed, VW could be vulnerable to outside pressure. For the time being, Lower Saxony's clout and the voting limits shield VW's management. "If you look at the supervisory board, you see all the union and local state people . . . it's not sufficiently profit-oriented," says Union Investment's Drees.

29   It all spells a big headache for Piëch's successor. While speculation lingers that Pischetsrieder might be upstaged at the last minute, the bigger issue is whether he or any new CEO will be able to set his own strategy and unleash more of VW's earnings potential. At the least, Piëch's presence in the background will complicate the succession.

30   Pischetsrieder has sterling qualifications. He played an important role in revamping BMW's factories into models of flexibility and efficiency. Piëch hired him last July and named him head of Seat, VW's Spanish brand, and put him in charge of group quality. That was after Pischetsrieder lost his job at BMW, taking the fall for the acquisition of Rover, the floundering British carmaker.

31   Critics say Pischetsrieder was dominated by BMW's supervisory board chairman, Eberhard von Kuenheim, who had been CEO for 23 years and fully backed the Rover acquisition. As the deal soured, detractors dubbed Pischetsrieder "*der Zauderer*"—the ditherer. Former colleagues say Pischetsrieder is very much his own man, but there's some doubt whether he will be able to stand up to Piëch. In a long year as heir apparent, Pischetsrieder has discreetly withstood the glare of publicity. That's probably smart. But the uncertainty about VW's next boss adds to the doubts surrounding the future of one of Europe's great companies.

VW AND THE U.S. MARKET: ANOTHER TRIP DOWN MEMORY LANE?

32   Is Volkswagen about to tap into America's '60s nostalgia again? Its first retro-hit, the new Beetle, has paid off handsomely for the German company. A wonderfully detailed variation of the sturdy little classic—with frills such as a dashboard bud vase—the new Beetle is VW's third-best-selling car in the U.S., after the Jetta and Passat.

33   Inspired by the bug's success, Volkswagen has created a 21st century update of its old VW bus, which was launched in 1950 but didn't enter the public consciousness until a decade or more later. If you're over 40, you remember the bus as the archetypal vehicle for hippie road trips—you know, guitar in the back, Jefferson Airplane on the AM radio, the distinctive rattling sound of an air-cooled engine as the bus tools down Highway 1 in California.

34   That's the nostalgia inspiring the remake. So far, the Microbus, conceived by VW's design studio in Simi Valley, Calif., is only a show vehicle. But chances look good that the studio will develop a Microbus for the market. VW expects to reach a decision before the end of the year. "We've had a very positive reaction," says marketing chief Robert Büchelhofer.

EXHIBIT 3
Challenges Facing VW's Next Boss

- A slowdown in the U.S. and European car markets
- Nimble archrivals in Europe—PSA Peugeot Citroën, Ford of Europe, and Renault—are closing the quality gap
- Fierce competition for the Chinese market
- Luxury auto makers such as BMW and Mercedes are moving downmarket into VW's core segments
- Icy relations with investors
- Possible interference from retiring CEO Ferdinand Piëch, who will probably chair the supervisory board

SUV Fatigue

35   It's no coincidence VW unveiled the Microbus in Detroit at the January car show. "The U.S. is its target audience," says Goldman, Sachs & Co. analyst Max Warburton. The Microbus, which is roughly the same size as the current Eurovan, about 15 feet long, is expected to be priced at about $35,000, the premium end of the minivan market. The company also hopes to benefit from drivers who are showing signs of SUV-fatigue. Sport-utility sales are down 7.5% in the U.S. so far this year. "It's going to come down to how they position it," says Wes Brown, a consultant at Nextrend Inc., an auto-research firm in Thousand Oaks, Calif.

36   The Microbus' exterior is quite faithful to the old, oblong-shaped VW bus, which was a popular family hauler in the U.S. as well as a flower-power mobile. But the interior has been transformed to resemble the inside of a space vehicle. That's important, since the cutting-edge features inside the bus are likely to appeal to Europeans, who look back less than fondly on their austere postwar landscape. Although VW sells seven times as many vehicles in Europe as it does in the U.S., Americans buy twice as many Beetles as Europeans.

37   Selling nostalgia certainly does not mean selling old technology. The Microbus would utilize new safety systems, for example, to help prevent rollovers. The show bus features rotating, removable seats with video screens in the seat backs and a table that folds out of one of the middle seats with a monitor for DVD movies, games, or Web surfing. A seven-inch screen in the front provides an extensive view of what's happening on the road behind the Microbus, all captured by a camera. A clever touch, for those who want to look back.

VW & CHINA: THE PEOPLE'S CARMAKER IN CHINA, FOR NOW

38   Zhen Zhijun is ready to buy his first car, and the 34-year-old financial adviser at Shanghai's Jubo Investment Co. likes the slick look of Volkswagen's $29,000 Passat. On a salary of $1,200 a month, the price is steep. But Zhen plans to get a 5.9% car loan, which local banks are pushing as a way to boost domestic consumption. Zhen isn't interested in any brand but VW, which goes by the name of Dazhong, or "the masses," in Chinese. "I know I'll get good after-sales service with Volkswagen, and besides, the European design looks cool," he says.

39   Hot models. Reliable service. VW has worked out a winning formula in China. It got in early and now has a 53% share of a rapidly growing market. Last year, car sales rose 8%, to 628,659; they are projected to increase 14.5% this year. Competition is heating up, of course, and VW probably won't hold on to that huge share. Ford is moving into Chongqing to turn out a budget car, and Toyota will start turning out a compact in Tianjin. But with the market expanding, VW should still get its share of the booty.

Revved up

40   It didn't have to turn out this way. VW was the first foreign carmaker to set up a joint venture in China back in 1985, in Shanghai. But getting in first in China has often proved

EXHIBIT 4
Sisters under
the Skin?

By building more than 60 models on four main platforms, or chassis components, Volkswagen saves up to $1.5 billion a year. That's great—as long as the customer can't tell. Here are four top VW sellers that share the same platform, even though they occupy different market segments.

Skoda's New Octavia offers great value for money under VW's Czech badge. Problem: The Octavia's sales may be eating into the Golf's customer base.
U.S.: Not Available
Europe: $11,600

VW'S Golf, now in its fourth generation, is Europe's best-selling car despite a sticker price 20% higher than rivals in its class. The challenge is to keep it fresh and prevent lower-priced rivals from grabbing market share.
U.S.: $15,600
Europe: $15,300

The VW Beetle, a robust update of VW's original sedan, has registered a so-so performance in Europe. But its clever design and marketing have been a hit in the U.S.
U.S.: $16,450
Europe: $16,200

The Musclebound Audi TT has been so successful that it has inspired a new car that mimics the TT's styling, the Lexus SC430 coupe.
U.S.: $33,775
Europe: $26,700

foolish: Many early joint ventures were ill-advised partnerships between overconfident foreigners and inexperienced, often greedy locals.

41   VW, however, played its cards right—and enjoyed a bit of luck. It hooked up with powerful local partners at a time when there was little competition but a surging demand for cars. Better yet, the government in Shanghai shielded VW from central government meddling and gave the joint venture quite a bit of business at a time when most cars were bought by institutions rather than individuals. Now, for 2001, VW's two joint ventures will turn out more than 400,000 Audis, Jettas, Passats, Santanas, and Polos. "Everybody in China knows Volkswagen," says Credit Suisse First Boston analyst Catherine Zhu.

42   VW can expect to remain the market leader in China for a few more years. Other carmakers will find it hard to beat VW's prices, kept lower by the fact that 90% of its cars' parts are locally produced. Competitor General Motors Corp.'s new $44,000 Buick GS sedan has only 60% of its components made in China, and its sales have been disappointing.

43   But imports of cheaper parts and even cheaper cars are likely to rise, which will blunt VW's edge. "With China's WTO entry, the pressure from imported cars will grow," admits Johannes Wyrwoll, executive director of finance at SAIC-Volkswagen Sales Co. Customs duties make imports cost 70% to 80% more than cars built in China, but if China enters the World Trade Organization, lower duties will boost the cost by only 25%.

44   To keep its advantage, VW will probably have to cut prices and offer even better after-sales service. It might even consider bringing the lower-priced Skoda brand to China. "It's imperative to strengthen our position and bring in new products," says VW board member Robert Buchelhofer. Image-conscious consumers like Mr. Zhen are waiting.

Source: Adapted by Richard Robinson, University of South Carolina, based on Alysha Webb with Michael Shari, "Volkswagen," *BusinessWeek*, July 23, 2001.

Case 20

BusinessWeek

Hyundai Gets Hot

1   When Chung Mong Koo became CEO of Hyundai Motor Co. in March 1999, the industry yawned. Chung, the eldest living son of Chung Ju Yung, Hyundai's late founder, was widely deemed a colorless executive who would promote the status quo: cranking out cheap knockoffs of Japanese cars and flooding the market with them. Chung, 63, had spent much of his career running Hyundai's after-sales service division, a post that required no overarching vision or boardroom combat. Was this the man to breathe new life into a company on the brink? True, Hyundai Motor dominated the car market at home, but in crucial overseas markets, it had a reputation for poor quality—doors that didn't fit properly, frames that rattled, engines that delivered puny acceleration—and it was losing money.

2   Chung has proved the skeptics wrong. Turns out the socially awkward CEO had a real agenda, and he was prepared to use unconventional means—at least for a Hyundai exec—to ensure its success. Days after he took over, Chung visited Hyundai's sprawling plant at Ulsan on the southeastern tip of the Korean peninsula. To the shock of his employees, who had rarely set eyes on a CEO, Chung strode onto the factory floor and demanded a peek under the hood of a Sonata sedan. He didn't like what he saw: loose wires, tangled hoses, bolts painted four different colors—the kind of sloppiness you'd never see in a Japanese car. On the spot, he instructed the plant chief to paint all bolts and screws black and ordered workers not to release any car unless all was orderly under the hood. The plant chief recalls Chung fuming: "You've got to go back to basics. The only way we can survive is to raise our quality to Toyota's level."

3   Today, Chung is well on his way. Thanks to improved quality and design—and brisk sales in the U.S.—Hyundai sold 1.34 million vehicles in the first 10 months of this year, an increase of 8% over the same period in 2000. Much of the improvement was in the U.S., where, by the end of November, sales had hit 322,000, up 42% from 2000. Net profit for 2001 is projected to reach $860 million on revenues of $13.2 billion, up 65% year-on-year. And the U.S. was responsible for 40% of that. The stellar results have prompted Chung to authorize the opening of Hyundai's first U.S. plant, though no date is set. And increasingly, he is moving the design process to America, too, including a planned test track in the Mojave Desert.

EXHIBIT 1

Source: Hyundai Motor Co.,
Ward's Automotive Report,
BusinessWeek.

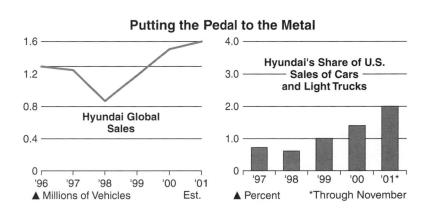

Putting the Pedal to the Metal

4   Along the way, Hyundai has become emblematic of the changes sweeping Korea's economy. "Not all companies have taken advantage of the Asian crisis to strengthen their market positions at home and abroad, but Hyundai Motor is one of them," says Chu Wu Jin, professor of motor-industry economics at Seoul National University. "More significantly, it has a chance to make another leap forward."

5   The encounter at Ulsan was the opening salvo in Chung's battle to turn the Korean auto maker into a global player. Within months, Chung had established a quality-control unit. He shuffled management, promoted a pair of top U.S. designers, and wrested control of Hyundai Motor from parent Hyundai Group, which has a history of using profitable units to prop up weak ones. Last year, Chung sold 10% of Hyundai Motor to Daimler-Chrysler with the aim of building a strategic alliance. The partnership has yet to bear fruit, but it could give Hyundai access to technology down the road.

6   At the same time, Chung's team used the 1998 acquisition of Kia Motors Co.—bought at the depth of the Asian crisis for the fire-sale price of $910 million—to boost both companies' market pull. "The combined operation gave us not only bargaining power but important leverage to play parts suppliers against each other, making them compete for quality," says Han Sang Joon, chief engineer of the Ulsan plant.

7   After these initial restructuring moves, Chung could have reverted to type and used Hyundai's new quality controls and economies of scale to flood the world with more cheap Korean cars. Instead, he decided to change Hyundai more profoundly. Chung poured money into research and development—$1.4 billion this year, up 20% from 2000—to build cars that not only compete on price but also deliver on quality. He chose to make the U.S. the key battleground.

8   That required a radical shift in corporate mindset: For the first time, Korean execs were ordered to act on key recommendations made by their American colleagues. At the same time, Chung was determined to build cars that would appeal to U.S. drivers. To that end, he handed his California design team unprecedented control over the company's first sport-utility vehicle.

9   The result: the Santa Fe, which has developed an almost evangelical following in the U.S. Leonard Guest, a 57-year-old retired school teacher from East Aurora, N.Y., bought a Santa Fe last February after exhaustively researching the small SUV segment. "I love the styling," he says. "To me, it's aggressive but pleasing." Guest has put 24,000 km on the odometer and says the quality is "exceedingly high." His assessment is echoed by J. D. Power & Associates, the U.S. arbiter of auto excellence. The firm reports that Hyundai's quality has jumped 28% over the past four years. That compares with 14% for the industry as a whole. Says Brian Walters, J. D. Power's director for product research: "Hyundai has done a tremendous job."

10   The key was creating the post of quality-control czar, something Hyundai never had before. Chung turned to Kim Sang Kwon, a veteran who developed the latest model of the Sonata sedan. Kim's first job: coming up with a quality-control bible. After studying manuals of U.S. and Japanese auto makers, he and his 100-strong team produced their own. It makes clear who's responsible for each manufacturing step, what outcome is required, and who checks and confirms performance levels. To drive home the message, Kim held a ceremony in which all 380 Hyundai and Kia section heads vowed to uphold the manual.

11   With the quality-control issue on its way to resolution, Chung focused on producing hits. "We needed attention-grabbing models to improve our image," he says. In 1991, Hyundai had opened a design studio in Fountain Valley, Calif., and hired Andrew Kort, formerly of Chrysler and Mercedes-Benz, and Derek S. Sancer, who had worked at ASHA Corp., a small component designer in Santa Barbara, Calif. Kort and Sancer were recruited to design concept cars for the auto-show circuit. In 1995, Hyundai execs told Sancer and Kort the company needed an SUV. Midway through devising a concept car based on the Ducati motorcycle, the designers transferred the theme, with its distinctive exoskeleton, to what is now the Santa Fe.

12   As the designers were tinkering with clay models, Toyota Motor Corp. and Honda Motor Co. rolled out the RAV4 and CR-V, auto-chassis SUVs of the same kind Hyundai was developing. Hyundai bought several of each and tore them apart to analyze them and devise features that would set the Santa Fe apart. "We looked at every interior and exterior component to find a way to improve on it," Sancer recalls. Innovations ranged from a cupholder sufficiently capacious to hold a liter soft-drink bottle to extra power points for cell phones.

13   Hyundai needed to make sure the Santa Fe stood out on the highway, too. Hence the decision to widen and lengthen it—a shrewd move because the RAV4 and CR-V were often criticized for being too small. Sancer and Kort also gave the truck muscular curves on the hood and door panels—a design flair since echoed by Toyota, Nissan Motor Co., and others. Back in Korea, Park Jong Suh, a 54-year-old design chief, recalls battling company conservatives—they felt the Santa Fe looked crumpled—to preserve Kort and Sancer's vision. "People have a strong opinion about it," says Kort. "Some may not like it, but at least they can see the difference."

14   One of Hyundai's most important moves was the decision to feed the American driver's hunger for horsepower. The RAV4 and CR-V came equipped only with two-liter, four-cylinder engines. The Santa Fe offers a 2.7-liter, V-6 engine. "It turned out to be a winning factor," says Lee Hyoung Keun, who runs global marketing. Indeed, the Santa Fe was a bona fide hit when it debuted in the autumn of 2000. "The Santa Fe was well-received right out of the blocks," says George H. Glassman, a Hyundai dealer in Southfield, Mich. "It's not just the price, it's about styling, value, and warranty." Not that the impact of price should be underestimated: The Santa Fe sells for an average of $21,000. When a friend asked him why he bought one, Arnie Goodman, a roofing-company manager in Southfield, said: "When I drive down the street, I've got leather, a CD player, four-wheel drive, and anti-lock brakes. The only thing missing is the $42,000 price tag."

15   Encouraged, Hyundai's next step is to cement its place in the biggest car segment: the family sedan. Through next summer, Hyundai is focusing its marketing efforts on the Sonata, which competes with the top-selling Honda Accord and Toyota Camry. After giving the Sonata a facelift and a new engine, Hyundai moved 5,923 units in November versus 2,881 a year earlier. One reason for the robust sales is that the V-6 Sonata, at about $20,000, costs about the same as four-cylinder versions of the Accord and Camry. The current model was designed in Korea, but the next will be dreamed up in the U.S.

IMAGE SHIFT

16   So far, so good: Chung & Co. have rescued Hyundai's image and designed cars that people want. The next question is whether customers will stick with Hyundai when they decide to buy another vehicle. "They started like the Japanese, selling inexpensive cars. Over time, the Japanese were able to convince the consumers to pay more," says a U.S.-based auto executive. "So, can Hyundai move the transaction price up?" Indeed, the Hyundai name continues to turn some people off. When the company conducted a blind test for the Santa Fe, customers who liked the car said they would expect to pay $5,000 to $10,000 less because it was a Hyundai.

17   Another question is the role of Hyundai's famous 10-year drive-train warranty in the U.S. A brilliant stroke, it convinced Americans that they should give Hyundai cars one more chance. At some point, though, the company will have to pull the plug because the warranty will be too costly to maintain. Finbarr O'Neill, president and CEO of Hyundai Motor America, says the warranty will continue through the 2005 model year. Will sales plunge once it's withdrawn? Not likely, says O'Neill. "The warranty allowed us to get on people's shopping lists," he says. "But warranties don't sell cars."

18   Despite all the progress made under his stewardship, Chung still has his critics. Many expressed doubts when he replaced respected Hyundai Motor President Lee Kye Ahn in July with his close associate Kim Dong Jin, who negotiated the DaimlerChrysler alliance. "I think he is surrounding himself with yes-men," says Lee Jeong Ja, a strategist for HSBC Securities Inc. in Seoul. Another concern is that Chung's ambitious expansion plans could prompt Hyundai to put market share before profits—in the hoary *chaebol* tradition. Indeed, Chung aims to boost the combined capacity of Hyundai and Kia this decade to about 5 million units a year from some 3 million now. Hyundai argues that it must make 1 million vehicles per platform to survive bruising competition. But that strategy could leave the auto maker with a lot of unsold cars.

19   Still, there's no denying that Chung has made an enormous difference to Hyundai Motor's international stature. That can be seen in the kind of people buying the company's cars. Traditionally, Hyundai customers were budget shoppers who often had bad credit. O'Neill says the people who now shop for Hyundais also look at Hondas, Nissans, and Toyotas. And dealer Glassman says he even gets Lincolns and Mercedes as trade-ins. "Our customer," says O'Neill, "is now more educated and has a higher income than five years ago—than one year ago."

20   Back in Korea, Chung exudes confidence. "Our prospects are good as long as we offer value for money," he says. Chung aims to make Hyundai one of the top five carmakers on the planet before 2010. To do so, he will have to resist the temptation to overreach—the fatal mistake of many a Korean executive. For an example of what can go awry, Chung need look no further than his father, the man who founded Korea's top conglomerate—only to see it crumble under a mountain of debt.

THE KOREAN MOUSE THAT ROARED

21   A disaster in the making: That's what analysts and investors saw when Hyundai Motor Co. announced in 1998 its intention to acquire insolvent Kia Motors Corp. After all, the Asian crisis was raging. At the same time, Hyundai Motor's parent, Hyundai Group, was so weighed down by deadbeat units that it seemed incapable of digesting Kia.

22   Today, Kia is a company transformed. Its pretax profit in the first nine months of 2001 was $368 million, up 180% from a year earlier. Kia, long associated with cars that are cheap and cheerful, is making steady inroads in the U.S. with models such as the Spectra, featured in irreverent TV ads aimed at the college set. Says Song Byoung Jun, an analyst at the Korean Institute for Industrial Economics & Trade: "Kia is a pleasant surprise. No one expected such a swift makeover."

"A Miracle"

23   At first, Hyundai Chairman Chung Mong Koo's turnaround blueprint looked preposterous. When senior execs drew up a plan to cut Kia's loss to $855 million in the first year, Chung ordered them to double the sales target for the year, to 800,000 vehicles—

and make a profit. "It looked like a goal you couldn't pull off without a miracle," recalls Yang Sung Joon, Kia's executive vice-president in charge of planning. "But then Kia made it."

24   What Hyundai brought to the table was speedy decision making—something new for Kia. The first thing Hyundai did was cut the number of models from 30 to 20. In the process, it eliminated several me-too vehicles competing in the crowded, midsize car and minitruck segments. Over the next 2 1/2 years, Hyundai more than tripled production of the Carnival minivan while cutting back on car output.

25   Next, Hyundai began looking for synergies. To boost Kia's lineup, the larger auto maker shared the platform of its popular Sonata sedan with Kia's new midsize Optima while making a minivan and minicar on behalf of Kia. Kia also shed about one-third of its workforce, going from 44,000 workers to 29,000 while merging Hyundai and Kia's research and development, after-sales services, and procurement departments. Projected savings from sharing parts, purchasing, and platforms between 1999 and 2004: $5.7 billion.

26   Now, Kia is cashing in on the craze for minivans and sport utilities at home and in the U.S. The new Sedona, a small van with a V-6 engine, is already selling well in America, and Kia aims to penetrate the midsize-SUV niche next year. "We've only plugged the holes so far," says Lee Ji Won, Kia's marketing chief. Still, that's not bad for a company left for dead three years ago.

Source: Adapted by Richard Robinson, University of South Carolina, based on Moon Ihlwan with Larry Armstrong and Katie Kerwin, "Hyundai Gets Hot," *BusinessWeek,* International Edition, December 17, 2001.

Case 21

GM-Daewoo Deal

1   Drive through most Asian cities and you'll encounter few vehicles built by General Motors Corp. Despite its vow in 1994 to become a leading player in a region long dominated by the Japanese, the world's No. 1 auto maker remains an also-ran. Of every 100 cars sold in Asia, just four bear the GM marque.

2   Now, GM seems poised to change that. On Sept. 21, it agreed to buy control of Korea's Daewoo Motor Co. through a joint venture with at least one of GM's Japanese partners—Isuzu Motors, Fuji Heavy Industries, and Suzuki Motors. Before it was declared insolvent in 1999, Daewoo controlled a third of Korea's 1.2 million car market. It has been shopping for a buyer ever since. Under the deal, GM gets two factories in Korea, smaller plants in Egypt and Vietnam, and a chain of service centers it can use to support its own cars. Daewoo is a good fit because GM owned half of the Korean company from 1972 to 1992 and most Daewoo cars are still built on its platforms. Says Alan Perriton, GM's executive in charge of business development in Asia: "This gives us high-quality, low-cost products for the rest of Asia."

3   Moreover, by most accounts, GM is getting a steal. The company was able to strike a hard bargain because it was the only bidder; Ford Motor Co. backed out of a deal for Daewoo last year. GM will invest some $300 million to acquire Daewoo assets valued at $1.2 billion. GM and its partners will put $400 million into a joint venture that takes control of the Daewoo assets. Daewoo's creditors, meanwhile, will take a stake as well and receive $1.2 billion in preferred stock, paying 3.5%, in the new company. People close to the deal say GM has the option of buying back those preferred shares sometime after 2011. And there's more: The new company would assume just $830 million of Daewoo Motors' $17 billion in debt. All of this is a major comedown for a Korean government that had once hoped to get as much as $6 billion for Daewoo.

LABOR PACT

4   GM also made sure Daewoo's unions wouldn't be a problem. To appease them, GM agreed to sell cars built at Daewoo's oldest, least efficient plant, outside Seoul, on a contract basis for six years. While GM wouldn't actually take over the factory, its 5,000 workers would keep their jobs, paid by—who else?—the creditors, who will also absorb the losses if the cars don't sell.

5   Now for the hard part: Restoring the tarnished Daewoo brand will take time and money. Perriton says sales have been hit badly because Koreans weren't sure if Daewoo would survive. "We have to let customers know that the company is back in business and stands behind its products," he says. In 1998, Daewoo had 33% of Korea's passenger-vehicle market. Today, it has less than half that. GM Asia Pacific President Rudolf A. Schlais Jr. says: "We need to get back to 25% within two years."

6   To pull that off, the new Daewoo venture will have to roll out new models. Style-conscious Koreans are shunning dated Daewoos for flashier cars made by Hyundai and Kia Motors. Moreover, the two plants GM aims to take over specialize in small cars, with 1.5 liter or smaller engines. Perriton says a Daewoo sport utility built with GM know how and diesel engines designed by Fiat, GM's Italian partner, are a possibility.

EXHIBIT 1
The Daewoo Saga

Source: *BusinessWeek.*

July 1999 Daewoo Motor collapses

August Creditors agree to put the auto maker into a workout program

January 2000 Creditors decide to sell Daewoo

February GM, Ford, and Daimler express interest in acquiring the carmaker

June Ford is named preferred suitor after submitting a nonbinding $5.9 billion bid

September Ford abandons its bid

October GM and its partners announce their intention to buy Daewoo Motor

November Daewoo Motor is officially bankrupt

May 2001 GM delivers a formal proposal

September GM agrees to buy the Korean auto maker's best assets for $1.2 billion

7   Longer term, GM aims to use Daewoo as an Asian beachhead. Until now, the company has relied on its Europe-based Adam Opel subsidiary to develop small cars for emerging markets. But with that business struggling, GM would like to use Daewoo's small-vehicle expertise to create an Asia-based business. Schlais sees China, India, and Thailand, in addition to Korea, as key markets for the next 10 years.

8   GM has a lot at stake. If its game plan works out, the new Daewoo venture, for which it projects annual sales of $5 billion within a couple of years, could help GM put more distance between it and the No. 2 auto maker, Ford, which has been narrowing the gap. But first, GM must whip Daewoo into shape—and build cars people want to drive.

Source: Adapted by Richard Robinson, University of South Carolina, based on Moon Ihlwan and David Welch, "GM May Have Landed a Dandy Daewoo Deal," *BusinessWeek,* International Edition, October 8, 2001.

Case 22

BusinessWeek

Tyco (A)

1   On a summery afternoon in early May, Tyco International chief executive L. Dennis Kozlowski strode into the New Jersey board room of his latest prey, CIT Group Inc., the nation's largest independent commercial finance company. Technically, CIT was not yet in Kozlowski's grip: Tyco's $9.2 billion offer wouldn't come up for a shareholder vote for another three weeks, and the deal wasn't expected to close until June 1. But as he huddled with CIT CEO Albert R. Gamper Jr., Kozlowski made clear he was already impatient for Gamper to get with the Tyco program. "It is crucial that we push growth coming out of the box," Kozlowski said, pressing for dramatic action that CIT could take as soon as the deal closed. "I want people to say, 'Wow, this is a real step up.'"

2   Kozlowski stunned investors and executives with his bid for CIT—an outfit that, ironically, once rejected him for a low-level auditing job. Skeptics question what an industrial conglomerate specializing in such mundane products as valves and garbage bags can possibly bring to the competitive world of commercial finance. It's a field that has proven to be a veritable graveyard for expansion-minded CEOs. "Kozlowski is putting his toe [into an area] that ostensibly he doesn't know anything about," says former AlliedSignal CEO Larry Bossidy. And he's doing it at a time when even Gamper warns that a softening economy is producing "a credit world that is tougher today than a year ago." But Kozlowski is undaunted. He predicts that under Tyco, CIT will double in size within a few years and achieve earnings growth of 15% a year. Says Kozlowski: "I think CIT will be one of the best deals we've ever done."

3   Coming from most CEOs, such talk would be dismissed as hubris or worse. But Kozlowski has made a career of confounding the critics. Since taking the reigns at Tyco in mid-1992, the son of a Newark detective has become one of the most aggressive CEOs in the land—spending some $53 billion on 120 major acquisitions, most of which have been folded seamlessly into Tyco's hyperefficient operations. That plus a willingness to test the limits of acceptable accounting and tax strategies have transformed the $3 billion also-ran outfit he inherited into a colossus that will ring up $38.5 billion in sales in the

EXHIBIT 1

Source: Tyco International Ltd., Merrill Lynch & Co. Bloomberg Financial Markets © BW.

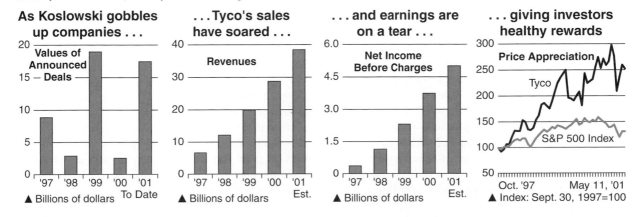

As Koslowski gobbles up companies . . .
Values of Announced Deals
▲ Billions of dollars To Date

. . . Tyco's sales have soared . . .
Revenues
▲ Billions of dollars Est.

. . . and earnings are on a tear . . .
Net Income Before Charges
▲ Billions of dollars Est.

. . . giving investors healthy rewards
Price Appreciation
Tyco
S&P 500 Index
Oct. '97   May 11, '01
▲ Index: Sept. 30, 1997=100

fiscal year ending Sept. 30, including a quarter of CIT's sales. With earnings rising even faster, Tyco recently vaulted to the top of the *BusinessWeek* 50 ranking of top-performing companies.

4   Kozlowski, who relaxes by piloting his 130-foot J-class sloop, *Endeavour,* in international regattas, so far has managed to sail smoothly through the economic slowdown. In the first quarter, the worst in a decade for U.S. corporate profits, Tyco's earnings soared 33% on a 26% jump in sales. As a result, Tyco, with its decidedly unglamorous product lineup, is now worth roughly $93 billion, more than Ford Motor Co. and General Motors Corp. combined. And the scary thing is, at 54, Kozlowski seems to be just getting started. "Dennis has more fire in his belly today than the day he became CEO," says Joshua M. Berman, Tyco's former outside counsel and a board member since 1967.

5   Kozlowski's ambitions stretch far beyond his audacious five-year plan of adding another $50 billion of acquisitions and reaching $100 billion in sales while maintaining 25%-plus annual earnings growth. He aspires to nothing less than guru status, the sort of peer recognition that would once and for all put behind him an army of short-sellers and other critics. He isn't modest in stating his goals. "Hopefully, we can become the next General Electric," Kozlowski muses in his Exeter (N.H.) office as his helicopter waits outside to whisk him to yet another dealmaking session. He wants to be remembered as "some combination of what Jack Welch put together at GE . . . and Warren Buffett's very practical ideas on how you go about creating return for shareholders."

THE SIZE BARRIER

6   To attain that summit, Kozlowski must surmount some formidable challenges. First is his business model, which anticipates ever more acquisitions. "To keep up this tremendous growth, they'll have to do bigger and bigger deals that entail bigger and bigger risks," warns Harvard Business School Professor Robert Kennedy, who has written a case study of the unusual home-grown culture behind Tyco's success. Looming over Kozlowski's strategy is the simple fact that sooner or later, virtually every U.S. conglomerate that's aspired to these heights has imploded. "ITT and AT&T are great exemplars of companies who've been forced to break up," cautions Michael Useem, professor of management at Wharton. "GE is the exception to the rule that conglomerates in the American market have not worked well."

7   That's one reason Tyco is such a fat target for skeptics. But Kozlowski also faces more pointed questions about Tyco's financial credibility. As 1999 ended, he was on the ropes over accusations that he had used accounting tricks to pump up Tyco's results. The charges, first leveled by short-seller and accounting analyst David W. Tice of David W. Tice & Associates, cut Tyco's stock in half and prompted a Securities & Exchange Commission inquiry. The SEC ended its investigation last July without taking any action, but the lingering taint is one reason Tyco's stock garners such a low price-earnings multiple. At $53 a share, it's selling at just 18 times this year's expected earnings. That compares with GE's p-e of 38, and is only 0.8 times Tyco's expected five-year growth rate—half the 1.7 ratio for the much slower-growing Standard & Poor's 500-stock index. "That is very unusual," says Charles L. Hill, director of research at First Call Corp., "and it raises the question of why?" Kozlowski's answer: "It will take more quarters of pounding out good earnings and cash flow" to convince investors to pay up for Tyco.

8   Tyco's obscurity doesn't help the stock price either. Despite its dramatic growth, it remains less well known than companies like Boeing, Hewlett-Packard, or Merrill Lynch, all of which have lower market capitalizations. Even Gamper concedes that while he had

been expecting takeover overtures for CIT, "never in my wildest dreams had I thought of the name Tyco." Once Kozlowski approached him, Gamper asked KPMG and Credit Suisse First Boston to give Tyco a thorough review. Gamper says he came away impressed—and he isn't alone. "He's made dramatic progress in building a major industrial conglomerate," says Bossidy. That's high praise coming from a man whose 1998 bid for AMP Inc., the world's leading maker of electronic components, was trumped by Kozlowski's $11.3 billion offer. "He is aggressive," Bossidy says. "But so what? I don't find that offensive."

9   Recently, Kozlowski also has sought to nurture an image as a leader among peers. He is chairman of the M&A Group, a recently formed club of about 60 CEOs that sees itself as a more useful alternative to such traditional CEO gatherings as the Business Roundtable. Says Robert Monks, an institutional-shareholder activist who served on the Tyco board: "I don't think there's a better CEO in America."

10   Kozlowski's signature contribution to management theory is his highly systematized method for identifying, assimilating, and wringing growth out of acquisition targets. He relies on a hand-picked team of six in-house M&A specialists that moves with blinding speed and uses outside investment banks sparingly. "Investment bankers will tell you it takes six months to do a deal; we often get them done in two weeks," says Irving Gutin, a senior vice-president who until recently headed the team. Tyco screens more than 1,000 potential targets a year, most of which filter up from its operations executives. It doesn't do hostile takeovers, since that would keep it from getting a thorough look inside. Once it has a confidentiality agreement with the target company's CEO, Tyco's team pores over the books and tours operations, looking closely at what—and who—is worth keeping. That almost always means lopping off the incumbent CEO. (Gamper would be an exception: He's been offered a three-year contract.) Only deals that add immediately to Tyco's bottom line go on to completion. Says Gutin: "Dennis doesn't want to buy dreams."

NOT A GAME

11   Typical is his 1994 purchase of Kendall, a maker of low-tech medical supplies. Kozlowski stunned the industry by offering $1 billion for the financially troubled company. "Everyone was asking, 'Who is Tyco?' " recalls Richard J. Meelia, a Kendall executive who has since risen to president of Tyco Healthcare Group. "The first response was, the toy company"—that is, Tyco Toys, maker of Tickle Me Elmo.

12   No wonder. At the time, Tyco's minuscule medical business had perhaps $50 million in sales, vs. $600 million for Kendall. Kendall execs were even more aghast when Kozlowski said he wanted to build Kendall to $3 billion in three years. It was an insane target for an old-line company that had managed to buy only two companies with $50 million in sales in two years. But after gobbling up such medical-products giants as U.S. Surgical, Sherwood, and Mallinckrodt, Tyco Healthcare will ring up $7 billion in sales this year, predicts Merrill Lynch & Co. analyst Phua Young. It is now compared with the likes of Johnson & Johnson. "They've done a terrific job of consolidating certain segments of the medical market," says John Strong, CEO of Consorta Inc., a hospital purchasing cooperative.

13   At a time when at least half of all U.S. mergers founder, one reason Tyco so rarely stumbles is that it develops a detailed game plan for integrating each acquisition before the deal even closes. With AMP, that plan was hammered out in a secret meeting in Germany with Jürgen W. Gromer, then AMP's head of sales, whom Kozlowski had tapped to take charge. CEO Robert Ripp, who left AMP once the deal closed, wasn't invited. In the first

EXHIBIT 2
Tyco, The Stealth Conglomerate

Source: Tyco International, Merrill Lynch.

One reason for Tyco's low profile is its decidedly unglamorous but fast-growing roster of businesses. Here's what the mix will look like after Tyco's deal to buy CIT Group goes through:

Electronics: $13 billion sales
Components, including connectors, switches, and sensors

Health Care: $9 billion sales
Syringes and wound-care products; includes plastics unit that makes garbage bags and sheeting

Fire, Security Systems: $8 billion sales
Fire protection and electronic security, including ADT

TyCom: $3 billion sales
Makes and installs undersea communications systems for the telecom industry, building a global network

CIT Group: $6 billion sales*
Third-largest commercial-finance company in the U.S.

Flow Control: $4 billion sales
Industrial valves and controls

Total 2001 Sales†: $38.5 billion

* CIT sales estimate for 12 months.
† Sales are estimates for fiscal year ending Sept. 30, assuming ownership of CIT for one quarter.

two days after the contracts were signed in April 1999, Gromer reorganized the struggling company, firing 60 of 66 vice-presidents and unveiling plans to cut $1 billion in costs in 18 months. Now highly profitable, AMP has been gobbling up weaker players such as Lucent Power Systems. "They've done quite a job turning around AMP," marvels Fred Krehbiel, co-chairman and co-CEO of Molex Inc., Tyco's largest competitor in connectors.

14   With CIT, Kozlowski has once again climbed onto the high wire. If it turns out the operation doesn't smoothly fit into Tyco's industrial mix, Kozlowski's growth machine could sputter. Tyco is just the latest of a long line of industrial companies—from Westinghouse Electric to AT&T, ITT, and Textron—that have been lured into costly forays in financial services. "You just need to look back in history and see how all those other companies did," warns one senior financial-services industry executive. "Most have failed because they took on too much risk . . . and didn't understand the business."

15   Yet as Tyco's board mulled CIT, that sorry history was eclipsed by one stunning exception: General Electric Capital Services Inc. Kozlowski says the Tyco board had been looking to add a finance arm for nearly four years. "But there had always been a fatal flaw" with possible targets, he says. Then late last year, director Frank E. Walsh Jr. suggested that CIT's Gamper—whom he's long known—might be ready to deal. In December, Walsh arranged a private lunch to introduce the two CEOs.

DOWN, NOT OUT

16   Like many of Tyco's targets, CIT was a fundamentally solid company going through a rocky period. Under Gamper, who's been in charge since 1987, it built a reputation as a blue-chip lender financing everything from the rag trade to planes, trains, and the big earth-moving equipment known as yellow iron. With $54 billion in assets, it ranks behind only GE Capital and Citigroup Inc. in commercial finance. It's also the largest U.S. factor,

or purchaser of receivables from textile and apparel makers, which means it is knee-deep in a slow-growth business. But in 1999, CIT busted out of its conservative mold by acquiring an aggressive Canadian upstart, Newcourt Credit Group of Toronto. Overnight, CIT doubled in size but was soon choking on unfamiliar businesses such as international lending and tech financing. CIT's shares fell to a low of $13 last fall, half the price at which it had gone public in 1997. Little wonder Gamper leapt at Tyco's offer of $35 a share.

17   Kozlowski has a three-pronged plan to Tyco-ize CIT. For starters, he's pressing Gamper to swiftly sell or liquidate more than $4 billion in underperforming loans. Meanwhile, CIT, sidelined since it bought Newcourt, will aggressively hunt for acquisitions in its still-fragmented industry. And he's appointed J. Brad McGee—a former Marine and one of his most trusted lieutenants—to help CIT finance Tyco's customers. After some two dozen meetings between CIT and Tyco business units, McGee argues CIT could finance everything from $75 million wastewater treatment plants built by Tyco to monthly lease plans for customers of its ADT home-security unit. In all, he figures such financing could boost Tyco's sales by $4 billion to $6 billion a year.

18   But in the conservative world of commercial lending, such a go-go approach could backfire. True, the auto industry has long financed its customers. But other captive finance companies have "often [been] a recipe for disaster," warns banking consultant Bert Ely of Ely & Co. in Alexandria, Va., especially if they become a lender of last resort. Loans to customers turbo-charged growth during boom times for Lucent Technologies Inc., for instance, but burned it when the slowdown hit. Ely notes that GE Capital finances just 2% of its parent's industrial sales: "GE Capital has done as well as it has because it's had a much higher degree of financial independence."

19   Kozlowski says he's well aware of the dangers and vows to maintain CIT's A+ rating from Standard & Poor's. "I give him the benefit of the doubt, based on his track record," says Keith DeVore, an analyst at American Express Financial Advisers Inc., one of Tyco's largest shareholders. But Kozlowski will have to tread carefully. "If they stick to their knitting and let Gamper run it, they'll be fine," says a senior finance executive who has competed with CIT for years. "But Kozlowski doesn't seem to be a very patient guy."

20   That's an understatement. The CIT gamble comes hot on the heels of Kozlowski's biggest crisis, the controversy over Tyco's liberal use of merger-related charges. In an October 1999 report, analyst Tice suggested Tyco might be creating "cookie jar" reserves that could be used to inflate profits. Although Kozlowski vehemently denied any wrongdoing, proving that to investors was almost impossible because Tyco's financial statements are so devilishly complex. Says Harvard's Kennedy: "I think Tyco got an incredibly bad rap but then handled it about as well as they could." By the time the SEC showed up in December 1999, Kozlowski knew that a regulatory review might be his best option. Tyco was clearly a top priority for then–SEC Chairman Arthur Levitt Jr., who was crusading against accounting abuses. But last July, after seven months of digging, the SEC dropped its investigation without taking any action beyond its earlier demand that Tyco change the timing of certain charges. SEC officials don't dispute Tyco's statement that the matter is closed.

21   Kozlowski's nonstop dealmaking has also raised questions about how dependent Tyco's growth is on acquisitions. But he maintains that internal growth alone is increasing earnings by better than 20% a year. The businesses may not be exciting, but they're nearly all in fragmented fields with solid growth. Revenues in the health care and electronics industries are growing around 8% annually; in security, it's 11% to 12%. And though Tyco ranks first or second in virtually all of its businesses, it still has enormous room to expand.

22   Tyco managers have become ruthless at stealing market share. Take plastic garbage bags. When Tyco acquired the maker of Ruffies in 1996, it was a lethargic No. 3 brand, earning minimal margins of about 5%. Tyco moved swiftly to cut costs, boost customer service, and introduce new products, such as a baking soda bag to limit odors. The result? Ruffies is now No. 1, having vaulted past Glad and Hefty Bags, and has tripled margins to 16%.

TAX MASTER

23   Kozlowski is just as aggressive in pursuing financial advantages. When Tyco snapped up Bermuda-based ADT, he structured the deal as a reverse merger, moving Tyco's headquarters to an island haven where the corporate tax rate is zero. The deal initially ignited a firestorm among shareholders, who had to pay capital-gains taxes on the transaction. But it has become a gold mine for the company. Because of its Bermuda base, Tyco no longer pays U.S. taxes on its growing overseas income. Tyco also has set up a Luxembourg-based subsidiary to finance most of Tyco's debt. In a process known as income-stripping, the Luxembourg subsidiary makes loans to Tyco units in the U.S. and elsewhere, which then deduct the interest payments from their taxable income. Together, these ploys sliced Tyco's effective tax rate to 25% last year, from 36% the year before the ADT deal. That saved $500 million-plus in taxes last year alone, or more than Whirlpool Corp. earned. "There is no question about the legality of this," says Louis Feldman, an expert on cross-border taxation at Credit Suisse First Boston, though he says Tyco is probably the largest outfit to go offshore.

24   Legal, it may be, but it doesn't look very good for a guy who aspires to the Jack Welch mantle. "Tyco is the equivalent of the Benedict Arnold billionaires who have moved offshore," fumes Bill Allison, senior editor at the Washington-based Center for Public Integrity. "They're turning their backs on the American people." Tyco says that it pays far more in U.S. taxes today than before its merger with ADT.

25   As Tyco's low p-e proves, many skeptics still doubt that Kozlowski, even with such gimmicks, can keep growing at a breakneck pace. "There will be a stumble, and it's coming soon," predicts analyst Tice. He and others are alarmed that Tyco's debt soared to $18.3 billion on Mar. 31, up from less than $1 billion in 1996, pushing its debt-to-total-capital ratio to 47%, from 25%. "What concerns me is the absolute levels of debt and the possibility there will be poor integration of a large acquisition," says George A. Meyers, an analyst at Moody's Investors Service. But he says that is offset by rising free cash flow, expected to top $4 billion this year. The mostly stock-financed purchase of CIT will actually reduce Tyco's leverage. As a result, both Moody's and Standard & Poor's have Tyco on credit watch for an upgrade.

26   Kozlowski has been in a hurry ever since growing up in a six-family apartment building in a blue-collar, ethnic neighborhood in Newark's inner city. Since his father, a police detective, couldn't afford to send him to college, Kozlowski lived at home and worked 30 hours a week to pay the tuition at Seton Hall University. His main source of income: playing guitar in a band whose gigs ranged from Polish weddings to stints on the Jersey Shore. While majoring in accounting, Kozlowski found time to take flying lessons and now logs 250 hours a year piloting Tyco's helicopter and his personal plane.

27   After graduating in 1968, Kozlowski headed to New York as an auditor in the M&A department of SCM Corp., a conglomerate snapping up everything in sight. Itching for more responsibility, he jumped to more senior finance jobs at chemicals company Cabot Corp. and office-products marketer Nashua Corp. Kozlowski came away convinced that

he could do a far better job. He got his chance in 1975 when a recruiter lured the 28-year-old to a meeting with Joe Gaziano, CEO of Tyco, then a diversified manufacturer with just $15 million in sales. But Gaziano, a bear of a man who shaved his head daily, told Kozlowski he wanted to build it to $1 billion through purchases. Kozlowski's job: cleaning up Tyco's troubled acquisitions. That included Grinnell, a money-losing fire-protection company that Tyco bought from ITT. Grinnell epitomized ITT's bureaucratic culture. Field managers spent one week a month in meetings at headquarters. In his first week, Kozlowski scrapped the meetings and shrank the corporate staff to 30 from 200.

28   It was the precursor to what today may qualify as the leanest operation in Corporate America. Kozlowski oversees his 205,000-employee empire with a corporate staff of just 140. He still operates out of the modest, two-story wooden building in Exeter, N.H., that Tyco built when it had $100 million in sales, even though the company is officially based in Bermuda. "If you build an elaborate headquarters, people are tempted to spend a lot of time there and it becomes really unproductive," Kozlowski reasons. And perks such as country-club memberships and executive dining rooms are taboo. Kozlowski himself keeps a low social profile. His primary residence remains a 3,500-square-foot house on the coast in Rye, N.H., that he bought 15 years ago, although he now keeps a summer home in Nantucket and a place in Boca Raton, Fla.

29   In Tyco's entrepreneurial culture, managers have enormous autonomy. Kozlowski relies on a computerized reporting system that gives him a detailed snapshot of how each business is performing. It's updated several times a week with information including sales, profit margins, and order backlog sliced by geography and product area. If he spots a problem, Kozlowski invariably uses the phone rather than e-mail. "If you're on forecast, there's no need to talk with me," he tells managers. "But if there is any bad news at all, find me wherever I am, so we can figure out what actions to take." He doesn't have a quick temper, but those who don't deliver don't last.

30   Kozlowski seeks out managers cast from the same mold as himself: someone who is "smart, poor, and wants to be rich." He keeps them motivated with a demanding compensation plan. Tyco executives don't receive bonuses unless they come close to meeting the aggressive earnings targets set by Kozlowski: typically about 15%. If they hit the target, they'll get a bonus at least equal to their salary. And if they blow past the target, the sky's the limit. Last year, Gromer received a base salary of $625,000. But after he nearly tripled Tyco Electronics' operating income on 62% higher sales, he pocketed a $13 million bonus. Kozlowski, with a $1.35 million salary, took home $125.3 million in total compensation—more than GE's Welch.

31   Kozlowski's adept handling of Tyco's toughest assignments made him the obvious replacement when CEO John F. Fort retired in 1992. With Tyco reeling from a downturn in spending on valves and other construction equipment, he set out to expand into recession-resistant businesses. That was the rationale behind the Kendall deal, and his $5.6 billion 1997 bid for ADT Ltd., which instantly made Tyco the world leader in home security.

CRUNCH TIME

32   Now, with the economy slowing again, that strategy is being put to its first real test. Tyco's largest business, the $13 billion electronics unit, is suffering a spectacular slowdown. Kozlowski says electronic sales will be flat on a sequential basis in the second and third quarters. But sales growth is holding up in Tyco's other units, he says. Jack L. Kelly, an analyst at Goldman, Sachs & Co., figures fiscal 2001 earnings will rise 26% on a per-share basis. That's an achievement these days, but down from last year's 42% rate.

And not all of Kozlowski's bets are clear winners. Tyco entered the undersea cable business in 1997 when it bought an AT&T unit. TyCom Ltd. has since more than doubled sales, to $2.5 billion last year, but a $5 billion investment in its own global cable network could drag down future results. "There is a glut of undersea capacity," warns Qwest Communications International Inc. CEO Joseph P. Nacchio. TyCom's stock, sold publicly last year to help finance the network, is 64% off its high.

33   Even many of Kozlowski's fans concede people might feel more comfortable if he would just slow down so they could get a better handle on his fast-evolving empire. But after nearly a decade at the top, Kozlowski clearly relishes a pace that keeps him on the road 70% of the time. Kozlowski admits the pace helped trigger his divorce five years ago. But he still has energy to ski and fly on weekends and during the three weeks of vacation he takes each year. His favorite escape, though, is *Endeavour*. With more than 9,000 square feet of sail and a 63-foot boom, the vessel invariably draws attention as it pulls into ports from Nantucket to the Caribbean.

34   And there are always more deals on the horizon. Even as he was scrambling to map out his plan for CIT, he confided: "I've spent the last couple of days looking at three or four different opportunities in each of our business segments." There's no doubt he likes this market. "Things are a lot less expensive than they were a year ago," he says. So when Kozlowski is asked if it's time to slow down, he just laughs, and says: "I'm just starting to figure out this job."

Source: Adapted by Richard Robinson, University of South Carolina, based on William C. Symonds with Pamela L. Moore, "The Most Aggressive CEO," *BusinessWeek,* May 28, 2001.

Case 23

BusinessWeek

Tyco (B): Tyco's About-Face

1   The sudden about-face of L. Dennis Kozlowski, chief executive of Tyco International Ltd., is striking evidence of how radically the business landscape has shifted since Enron Corp.'s collapse. Only last May, as he was putting the finishing touches on his $10 billion takeover of CIT Group, Kozlowski said that he was just getting started. He figured he would easily do another $50 billion worth of deals in the coming five years. Ultimately, he told *BusinessWeek,* he hoped Tyco would "become the next General Electric."

2   But on Jan. 22, Corporate America's most aggressive dealmaker announced a shocker, laying out plans to dismantle the empire he built over the past decade with $62 billion worth of deals. By yearend, Kozlowski, 55, hopes to sell Tyco's plastics business to reduce debt, while splitting the rest of his $36 billion conglomerate into four separate, midsize companies.

3   Why quit now? The short answer is that Tyco's gunslinger has run out of ammunition. His stock has tumbled nearly 25% since the end of last year and now trades at just 12 times this year's expected earnings—a huge 50% discount to the multiple accorded the Standard & Poor's 500-stock index. So, Kozlowski would have found it hard to keep forking over paper for new purchases, making it difficult to meet his growth targets. "A company like Tyco makes sense when the market is willing to pay a premium over the underlying asset value, since that gives you a cheap currency for acquisitions," says Robert Monks, the famed shareholder activist who once served on Tyco's board of directors.

4   For years, it didn't matter to most investors whether they could figure out how Kozlowski was squeezing out double-digit growth from such mundane products as syringes and fire sprinklers. "Kozlowski, like [former General Electric CEO] Jack Welch, was defying gravity," says Michael Useem, professor of management at the Wharton School. Indeed, Kozlowski knit together such multibillion-dollar pieces as CIT, the nation's largest independent commercial finance company; AMP, a leader in electronic connectors; and ADT, the world leader in home security.

5   But with all the additions, it became nearly impossible to get an apples-to-apples comparison of Tyco's results over time. And now, post-Enron, investors aren't willing to

EXHIBIT 1

Source: Bloomberg Financial Markets.

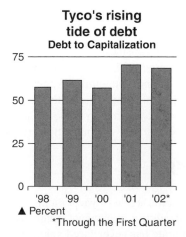

Tyco's rising tide of debt
Debt to Capitalization

▲ Percent
*Through the First Quarter

stomach stocks that seem based on faith. Kozlowski may have built a GE-like conglomerate, but he never won the kind of credibility enjoyed by Welch. True, he beat back critics after an analyst set off a storm of stock-selling in October 1999, with allegations that Kozlowski had pumped up earnings with accounting gimmicks. In mid-2000, the Securities & Exchange Commission ended an intense review without taking significant action. Tyco's shares quickly regained the ground they had lost and Kozlowski resumed his dealmaking. But Tyco's books remained a maze for all but the most persistent investors.

6   When Enron turned out to be hiding massive debt off its books, investors panicked and looked for other dominoes. They zeroed in on Tyco. "They're playing games" with their numbers, charges Albert T. Meyer, forensic accountant at David W. Tice & Associates Inc., the analytical firm that first raised serious questions about Tyco's accounting. The recent run on the stock was remarkably reminiscent of late 1999. But this time, Kozlowski found that it was nearly impossible to combat rumors—regardless of whether the charges had any merit. Sources close to the SEC took the unusual step of denying a report that the agency was launching a fresh probe of Tyco. It didn't matter. "When you don't fully understand something, you get a little worried," explains Charles L. Hill, director of research at First Call Corp. "And you get even more worried when you've just had the biggest bankruptcy in history."

7   Tyco's own statements were also raising new questions of whether it could maintain its pace. For the quarter ended Dec. 31, Tyco had to make a huge restatement of earnings because of an accounting-rule change that required the company to amortize earnings from sales of its security systems over time, rather than at the time of sale. That resulted in a cumulative downward adjustment of $654 million in earnings through Oct. 1, 2000.

8   Kozlowski was smart enough to realize the game was up. Still, a breakup seems unlikely to unleash the "50% upside" that he sees in Tyco's stock. It rose a paltry 2.4%, to $47.55, on the day of the announcement, and fell anew by 5% on Jan. 23. "I would not expect smooth sailing to successful execution" of Kozlowski's spin-off plan, warns Carol Levenson, an analyst at Gimme Credit, a bond-research firm based in Chicago. A key problem is that the managers who were named to run two of the Tyco spin-offs—health care and fire protection and flow control—are almost unknown. That raises doubts about whether the company can raise enough money from the initial public offerings to meet its goal of retiring $11 billion in debt. Critics also point out that partial IPOs will effectively dilute Tyco's shares. Kozlowski might fare better if he just sells some of the businesses to other companies.

9   Ironically, Tyco should be relatively easy to break up. It is highly decentralized, and each of the individual businesses is more than capable of prospering on its own. CIT, the first to be spun off, was a public company until last June. In fire protection, Tyco is the dominant player worldwide, and it is the world's second-largest maker of medical devices. And Kozlowksi will remain as CEO of the most troubled unit, the security and electronics business.

10   But even if Kozlowski sticks around, the Jan. 22 announcement marks a winding down of one of the most extraordinary corporate strategies of the past 10 years. He built an industrial conglomerate that grew like a high-tech star. In the new post-Enron environment, it may be a long while before we see another empire builder on this scale. Investors today are not only demanding performance—they also want to know what's behind it.

TWO WEEKS LATER

11   In the elite world of yacht racing, Tyco International CEO L. Dennis Kozlowski is known for his ability to navigate rough seas. But the captain of America's most ambitious conglomerate has never faced gale-force winds like these. Just two weeks after he unveiled a

EXHIBIT 2
Kozlowski's Plan
for Carving Up Tyco

Source: Tyco International, Ltd.

Security and Electronics

Sells home and business security services and electronic components
CEO: Dennis Kozlowski
Revenues: $17.6 billion
Earnings: $4.2 billion

Financial Services

Provides financing for vendors, consumers, factors, and equipment deals
CEO: Al Gamper
Revenues*: $5.4 billion
Earnings*: $1.2 billion

Fire Protection and Flow Control

Sells automatic sprinkler systems, and specialized valves
CEO: Jerry Boggess
Revenues: $7.6 billion
Earnings: $1.3 billion

Health Care

Makes syringes and other disposable equipment, wound-closure products, and imaging devices
CEO: Rich Meelia
Revenues: $7.1 billion
Earnings: $1.7 billion

*All financials are pro-forma company estimates for 2001.

surprise plan to break up Tyco into four midsize companies, investors and bondholders alike were jumping ship in sheer panic. The move was sparked by fears of an impending cash crunch, after Tyco and its finance arm, CIT, announced they would swap all their $13 billion in commercial paper for more expensive bank debt. Both had been effectively shut out of the commercial paper market—leaving even big fund companies saying "let's shoot first and ask questions later," says an analyst at one institutional holder.

12 The question now is whether Kozlowski can regain control in time to salvage Tyco's underlying value. He took a small step in that direction on Feb. 6, announcing that rather than waiting for a public offering, Tyco will spin off CIT to shareholders within 8 to 12 weeks. And it will move even sooner if it gets a better offer from one of its potential bidders, possibly General Electric Co. That news boosted the stock $2.83, to $25.93— finally ending a slide that sent shares down from $59 on Dec. 31. Fears about Tyco's opaque accounting had branded it "the next Enron," vaporizing more than $60 billion in market value.

13 A successful spin-off or sale of CIT is needed to head off a potential cash squeeze at Tyco's finance arm. The company has $12.5 billion in commercial paper and other debt obligations coming due just through June. CIT says that between an $8.5 billion bank line it tapped and about $5 billion more in securitization facilities, it is covered for five months or so. But the company, which was the nation's largest independent commercial-finance outfit before Tyco bought it, has enormous financing needs. "There is less confidence in us, and that poses terrific issues," says CIT CEO Al Gamper Jr.

14 Even without CIT, Kozlowski still must deal with a mountain of debt left over from the $63 billion acquisition binge he has indulged in since 1995. As of Dec. 31, Tyco's industrial companies had $28.3 billion in debt, according to Standard & Poor's, up from just $20 billion last March. The swap to bank credit should cover Tyco's debt obligations for the next year. But combined with CIT's similar move, it also will cut earnings up to $300 million this year, due to higher interest costs, Kozlowski admits. Worse, it signals that the debt clock is ticking. "They have diminished financial flexibility," even as they have more than $9 billion of debt still coming due next year, says Cynthia M. Werneth, an analyst at S&P, which cut Tyco's debt rating three notches, to BBB, on Feb. 4.

15   Kozlowski has long argued that he has plenty of cash coming in to meet Tyco's ongoing financial needs. "There is a crisis of confidence, but there is no cash crisis," he insisted in the Feb. 6 conference call. But Tyco likes to use an unusually generous definition of cash flow. In the fiscal year ended Sept. 30, it reported $4.75 billion in "free cash flow." But that didn't count more than $2 billion it spent to build the massive Tycom undersea global-telecom network. Subtract that, and Tyco had just $2.5 billion in cash flow, figures S&P's Werneth. Nor did it count some $900 million spent on "purchase accounting liabilities," or acquisition-related costs such as layoffs. Subtract those, and free cash drops to just $1.6 billion, argues Albert J. Meyer, an analyst at David W. Tice & Associates Inc., a frequent critic of Tyco's accounting.

16   Meyer is equally skeptical of Kozlowski's claim that Tyco will generate $4 billion in cash flow this year. Kozlowski brandished the same number a month ago, while predicting Tyco would earn $3.70 a share this year. Yet now he admits earnings could come in 45 cents—or some $900 million—lower, due to higher interest costs and new weakness in its depressed electronics unit.

17   With Tyco unable to tap equity or debt markets, Kozlowski has little choice but to sell off his businesses. After CIT, the next to go will likely be Tyco's plastics units, which make everything from garbage bags to coat hangers. "There's an awful lot of interest" in those businesses, says Kozlowski, who hopes to announce a deal by spring. Problem is, Tyco is in no position to run an orderly auction. And given the bull-market prices it paid for many acquisitions, it could book losses on many of the sales. That's particularly true of CIT, for which it paid $10 billion last June, warns Barry B. Bannister, a Legg Mason Inc. analyst. Another investment banker says Tyco "won't come close" to fetching the $3 billion Kozlowski wants for plastics. "We think it's more likely a fire sale" will occur now, he adds. Tyco is adrift in a steadily pounding sea, with little letup in sight.

Source: Adapted by Richard Robinson, University of South Carolina, based on William C. Symonds with Emily Thornton, "Is Tyco Looking at a Fire Sale?" *BusinessWeek,* February 18, 2002.

Case 24

Pearson PLC

1   Marjorie Scardino isn't the table-pounding type. Unlike many media moguls, she relies to a surprising degree on gentle humor to do her persuading. But that doesn't mean she's easily satisfied. Olivier Fleurot, the suave Gallic head of the *Financial Times* newspapers, discovered as much when he made his first presentation to the CEO of Pearson PLC in July 1999. Fleurot was feeling pretty confident when he promised her that by 2005 he would push the pink business papers' global circulation to 750,000—an increase of almost 90%. Scardino's response: "I am disappointed, Olivier," she said with a smile. "I thought you were going to say 1 million." That taught Fleurot something about his boss: "One of Marjorie's great qualities is that she is pushy," he says.

2   That's putting it mildly. Four years after she left the *Economist* magazine to take charge of its part owner, the 53-year-old native of Texarkana, Tex., is making a splash on both sides of the Atlantic with her moves to remake stodgy Pearson into a media and education juggernaut. She has inked 120 deals, selling off a haphazard collection of businesses that included the Tussaud's Group of wax museums and Pearson's share of the Lazard Freres investment-banking group.

3   In their place, Scardino engineered a gutsy $4.6 billion purchase of Simon & Schuster Inc.'s education business in May 1998. That instantly transformed Pearson from an afterthought in educational publishing to the industry leader, with 27% of the key U.S. school and college market.

4   But Simon & Schuster was just the biggest ticket in Scardino's $7.5 billion cash spending spree for a collection of education and publishing assets. She bought British children's and illustrated book publisher Dorling Kindersley Holdings PLC for $466 million in March. And her most controversial move came in July when she paid a hefty $2.5 billion for National Computer Systems (NCS), a little-known Eden Prairie (Minn.) educational-testing company. Scardino contends that she's building a 21st century learning company, capable of delivering its products and services to any audience, on paper or online. "People are going to school longer, and people are reeducating themselves professionally," Scardino explains. "This is a huge potential opportunity."

5   That whirl of dealmaking put a spotlight on the charismatic Texan. Scardino jolted London on her arrival at Pearson in 1997, becoming the first woman to head a top British company. An unlikely career climb—she once ran a muckraking weekly newspaper—guaranteed rapt attention in the British press for her every move.

BIG PUSH

6   Scardino gets credit for imposing a bold vision on what many have seen as a plodding industry. By building up education, which contributed more than half of Pearson's operating profits last year, she has provided a stabilizing element to the company's cyclical newspapers. Her recent acquisitions place Pearson atop a Big Five of education publishers, including McGraw-Hill (which publishes *BusinessWeek*), Houghton Mifflin, Reed Elsevier (which is buying Harcourt General for $4.5 billion), and Thomson. Scardino is pushing her troops hard to transfer their content to digital formats. Says Greg Dyke, who ran Pearson's television unit before becoming director general of the BBC last year: "During the dot-com craze, she convinced the press that we were a

dot-com without overcommitting the company. I was quite hostile to her appointment, but I was wrong."

7   Now, Scardino finds herself at a critical juncture. Most of the easy work is done. As a swashbuckling outsider, she was able to sell off Pearson's sacred cows. Scardino also got lucky: Her cleanup coincided with a booming world economy. She dove right into the business she knew best, news publishing, and parlayed a rising stock price to buy up goodies. But can Scardino nail a much more demanding second act?

8   That will be tough, considering the prices she paid—particularly in the case of NCS, for which she coughed up a 31% premium to the stock price. A recent report by Morgan Stanley Dean Witter notes that Pearson also paid 29% more for Simon & Schuster on a multiple-of-earnings basis than Reed Elsevier is paying for Harcourt General's education assets. Matthew Owen, an analyst at Morgan Stanley in London, estimates that Pearson Education's profits will fall short of its 7.7% aftertax cost of capital in all but one of the next five years. Owen credits Scardino with "the most coherent strategy in publishing," but worries that her drive to introduce online technology to schools will be slowed by the bureaucratic and conservative nature of the education Establishment. Terry Smith, an analyst at London broker Collins Stewart, is blunter: "What I disagree with is the cult of personality. When I get outside of all that and analyze the businesses . . . they've bought lots of things with very low returns."

9   Some competitors are especially skeptical of Scardino's digital investments, saying it might take decades for her to build a powerhouse in electronic learning—if she's able to pull it off at all. And huge questions remain about how she will integrate the many new assets. If Scardino stumbles, she will lose the halo effect generated by her early cleanup efforts. It may already be fading: Pearson's stock has returned 137% since Scardino took over, compared with a 69% return for the FTSE 100. But the shares are sharply off their high of $36 last March, to about $24 today.

10   While much of the attention these days is on Scardino's digital dreams, Pearson's foundation is built on three solid, cash-generating businesses: the Financial Times Group; Pearson Education, now the world's leading purveyor of textbooks; and Penguin Group, which includes Penguin, Putnam, Viking, and other imprints and offers a stable of best-selling authors, such as Tom Clancy and Patricia Cornwell. Morgan Stanley's Owen expects the company to report 2000 sales of $5.93 billion, up 19% from 1999. Operating profits, before Internet expenses, goodwill, and exceptional items, should rise 16%, to $1 billion. However, if some $300 million in Internet spending is included, Owen points out, Pearson's profits would fall 19%.

11   When Scardino was hired four years ago, Pearson was a hodgepodge of blue-chip assets down on their luck. Management was lambasted for a disastrous $405 million loss from an investment in Mindscape, an electronic-games maker. The FT newsroom was close to rebellion, thanks to fear of staff cuts and rumors that the paper—which is the bible of the City, London's Wall Street—might be put on the block.

12   Scardino had been running the Economist Group in London for four years, during which time she made a name as an aggressive yet collegial manager. Still, she wasn't on the Pearson board's initial short list. That changed after a lunch in fall of 1996 with Dennis Stevenson, a politically well-connected business consultant. Unbeknown to Scardino, Stevenson had been tapped as Pearson's nonexecutive chairman. He had read the latest Economist Group annual report—the company is half owned by Pearson—and came away impressed by its eloquent enthusiasm. During their meal, a lightbulb went on in his head: "Why shouldn't it be her?" Stevenson thought. The appointment was announced in October 1996.

SHARE THE WEALTH

13 The new CEO's first priority was to change Pearson's dawdling mind-set. Its managers weren't pushed very hard to perform or to work with other parts of the group. Annual earnings growth of 3% was OK. That didn't last long. "The company had not had a performance culture," Scardino says today. "So we said we were going to produce double-digit earnings growth because that was a simple idea and easy to communicate." Some well-placed performance incentives worked wonders. This year, for instance, even the lowest-level FT staffers will likely get $3,000 individual payouts for producing margins above 28%. "When you have such goals, you tend to make them," says Stephen Hill, CEO of Pearson's Financial Times Group, which includes the newspapers and various Internet and financial-data ventures. Scardino also extended stock options far down the ranks. When she started, about 300 employees were included. Now, some 4,000 are, out of 28,000 total.

14 Scardino's tireless cheerleading and readiness to back others' projects with serious money infused Pearson with an American-style entrepreneurial esprit de corps. "She has real courage of her convictions," says Michael Lynton, who ran Penguin Books and now heads AOL International. "She is willing to try things and fail and try again. And she encourages her managers to do the same." Pearson's CEO has become known for her folksy "Dear Everyone" motivational memos. Soon after arriving, she ended one with: "I've found a lot I like here. I think I'll stay. There's plenty for us all to work on together." Scardino also is relentless about sharing credit. She rarely agrees to be photographed without finance director John Makinson, who has negotiated most of Pearson's deals, at her side.

15 Her refreshing informality can be traced to growing up in a small, hardscrabble city on the Texas-Arkansas border. Scardino enjoyed a real Texas girlhood, riding in rodeos with her father, Robert Morris, an engineer in a local defense plant. Her mother, Beth Morris, remembers a girl who was "never frivolous" but always fun. Scardino's maternal grandfather, H. L. Lamb, a school principal, helped raise her sights beyond small-town Texas. He introduced her to Representative Wright Patman of Texas, who employed her in his office during a college summer and sent her to Europe on business.

16 Scardino took a meandering route to the executive suite. Upon graduating from Baylor University in Houston in 1969, she started law school, then dropped out. She later finished law school at the University of San Francisco. Moving in 1970 to Charleston, W.Va., Scardino worked as an editor at the Associated Press. There she met the man she would marry, Albert J. Scardino, who was a young reporter at the wire agency. They still joke about their first encounter—she spiked a story he had written about "John Henry: The Steel Driving Man." Not newsy enough, she said. Later, another editor transmitted it anyway.

DREAM TEAM

17 By all accounts, theirs has been a stimulating union, with Marjorie playing the role of breadwinner and often supporting Albert's creative projects. Albert is said to be a great cook, while Marjorie avoids the kitchen. And, as her business career flourished, Albert has taken more and more responsibility for their children: Adelaide, 22, William, 21, and Hal, 16. That includes managing Hal's acting career—he has appeared in several films, including the starring role in *The Indian in the Cupboard.* "She had the babies. Albert raised them. He's the nurturer," says Elaine Longwater, a family friend in Savannah, Ga., Albert's hometown.

18   It was around Savannah that the pair embarked on several formative ventures in the '70s. Albert briefly owned a shrimp boat, and the couple made a TV documentary about Georgia's barrier islands. Marjorie practiced at Savannah law firm Brannen, Wessels & Searcy, eventually becoming a managing partner. With money they borrowed from friends, family, and a bank, the couple threw themselves into launching a progressive weekly paper, *The Georgia Gazette.* It tackled "investigative stories that nobody else in town did," recalls Charles H. Morris, president of Savannah-based Morris Newspaper Corp. That included an exposé of improprieties at the state Labor Department and reporting on the kidnapping of the son of a prominent local family, which upset some residents, who thought the stories endangered the victim.

19   The *Gazette,* circulation 4,000, was more of a crusade than a business, say acquaintances. Albert did much of the writing and editing. As the paper struggled, Marjorie took over the business side, working as a lawyer by day and as publisher nights and weekends. "The *Gazette* was an act of love," says William T. Daniel Jr., a colleague at the law firm. "Albert had the journalistic talent. Marjorie fought the day-to-day battle of keeping the paper going." Their efforts paid off in 1984 when Albert won the Pulitzer Prize for his crusading editorials. But it couldn't keep the paper afloat. After the county moved its legal ads to a competitor, the *Gazette* closed in 1985. Albert landed a job at *The New York Times,* later becoming press secretary to Mayor David Dinkins. Marjorie decided to go into business.

20   In 1985, the *Economist* was looking for a U.S. chief to boost its low profile in America. John Evans, then publisher of the *Village Voice,* recommended Scardino, a recent acquaintance. "The headhunters were very reluctant because of her track record of failure," recalls David Gordon, then CEO of the *Economist.* But Gordon, a journalist-turned-manager himself, was a believer in unconventional career paths. While that choice may seem reckless now, in 1985, the *Economist* was relatively obscure in the U.S. Its North American circulation was just 108,000. By 1993, when Scardino succeeded Gordon as CEO of the overall group, circulation had climbed to 243,000 through aggressive marketing.

21   Scardino was hardly in the door at Pearson before she started disposing of businesses. The Tussaud's Group was sold for $528 million in 1998. Pearson's 18% stake in the Lazard investment banks went to Lazard boss Michel David-Weill in 1999, for $615 million. And last spring, Scardino merged Pearson TV, a producer of soap operas and game shows, with the broadcasting interests of Germany's Bertelsmann and Belgian investor Albert Frere. Pearson got a 22% stake in the combined RTL Group, worth $2.6 billion.

IMPRESSIVE GAINS

22   At the same time, she lavished funds on the FT, which was a big name with a small circulation. In March 1997, Pearson announced that it would put up as much as $150 million, most of it to expand in the U.S. The resulting gains have been impressive—U.S. circulation for the FT rose from just 36,000 at the end of 1996 to 120,000 today. The makeover of Pearson's traditional businesses helped boost its stock price, which fueled the subsequent buying binge.

23   Scardino's challenge is to show that she can deliver on her boldest move, into education. She is convinced that it represents a vast opportunity of untapped growth. Demographic trends and political pressure to upgrade teaching have boosted spending growth at an 8% annual clip in the U.S. and about 10% worldwide. At the same time, she believes that schools and local governments see the potential of using new technologies to improve teaching.

24 When she arrived, Scardino found that Pearson, then ranked fifth, was ill equipped to take advantage of those trends. "We had management that wasn't up to doing all that much more," she says. So she lured away Peter Jovanovich, head of the education unit at The McGraw-Hill Companies, in August 1997, promising him the resources to make Pearson Education the global leader. With the purchase of Simon & Schuster's education unit, Pearson became the U.S. leader in college texts and a close rival to McGraw-Hill in schoolbooks. The deal "was a once-in-a-lifetime opportunity," says Jovanovich. But competitors say the Pearson juggernaut has had problems hanging on to market share, particularly in elementary school texts. Pearson stumbled in a recent $200 million round of textbook adoptions in Texas, one of the bellwether states. It finished a disappointing third behind Harcourt and McGraw-Hill, according to Simba Information Inc. in Stamford, Conn.

25 Jovanovich acknowledges that the company probably didn't gain any market share in U.S. school publishing last year, after picking up 1% to 2% in 1999. Still, Pearson says its schoolbook revenues grew by high single digits. "I have been in the business for 29 years, and this market is the best I have ever seen," Jovanovich says. "I worry about a lot of things, but not about Marjorie's and my bets paying off."

26 If the bulk of Pearson's education sales and profits are still in old-fashioned textbooks, its most high-profile effort is in the online arena. Scardino is a huge fan of the Web, which she views as a tool that can tap into all of Pearson's content offerings and deliver them to a broad audience. Pearson already has some 2,500 websites, mostly for textbooks that come with online access. Such products brought in sales of about $660 million last year, up 20% over 1999. Scardino, who describes her own children as having "variable learning styles," says educators are excited about the Web's potential to enrich and customize education: "We have a chance to find solutions, and it will be a good business for our shareholders."

27 She plans to draw not only on traditional textbooks but also on other Pearson products, such as Penguin's mammoth library of classics and reference books. Scardino was looking for more such content when she bought Dorling Kindersley. She thinks the publisher's distinctive illustrated pages and 2 million digitalized images can be sprinkled into other Pearson products, from history texts to educational games.

28 Pearson isn't alone in this vision. All book publishers are speedily making the transition to digital, believing that students will increasingly dial up for study materials. "You will go to your room and study from your computer," says Nader F. Darehshori, CEO of Boston-based Houghton Mifflin Co. Houghton Mifflin just announced a deal with netLibrary—a leading producer of e-books—to create electronic versions of its texts. McGraw-Hill also is moving fast, with ventures that include Primis Online, which enables professors to design custom online texts.

29 Scardino seems to boast the most aggressive online effort, though. She's spending big money on a portfolio of distribution channels. Last June, Pearson shelled out $129 million to acquire 87% of Family Education Network, a leading supplier of education content on the Internet. That became the core of Pearson's Learning Network, a portal that offers everything from homework help for kids to teacher aids to training programs for professionals. The network currently generates revenues of about only $10 million a year from product sales and advertising. But Jovanovich figures Pearson can also interest school districts in sharing ad revenues. It is already talking with the Denver school system about setting up a portal.

30 Scardino's main bet for penetrating the online school market, though, is NCS Pearson. The unit's $2.5 billion price tag, 35 times its operating income of $70 million, raised eyebrows. Pearson defends that by pointing out that income has grown at a 24% annual clip. NCS makes much of its money from scoring tests but also supplies software to 40% of

U.S. and Canadian schools to manage payrolls, send out report cards, and keep track of attendance and discipline records. It also sells nifty electronic wares for teachers, such as online lesson plans and tests.

SCHOOL TIES

31   Scardino plans to use NCS as a platform to wire America's 2.5 million teachers—the last large group of professionals who don't widely use the Web. She wants to distribute reams of educational content from Pearson and others for a fee. And a new product called NCS 4 School, still in development, will allow students and parents to interact with the school. At a cost of $25 per pupil per year, students could check grades and teachers' comments and download recommended materials.

32   Some school administrators are excited about the technology. Says Don Hooper, superintendent of the Fort Bend school district, outside Houston: "The Web-based approach will ultimately be the best way for districts to go." But others in the industry are skeptical that Pearson can execute its plan. NCS's strength is in accounting and other management software for school back offices, they say, and it's a stretch to think that such systems can be upgraded to serve classrooms. "The systems those guys have are low-end and can in no way be used to deliver content," asserts one publishing insider. Another exec says Pearson isn't factoring in the resistance that a revolutionary system is likely to encounter from the education bureaucracy. Even if it works, it could take years. "Schools are not like Internet companies," he says. "They are bureaucracies. This will be like turning a battleship around."

33   If an advertising recession hits the FT, it will only put more pressure on Scardino to make her vision in education pay off. "She has a lot of ingredients in a huge pot," says Jeffrey T. Leeds of Leeds Weld & Co., which invests in education companies. "But when it is all cooked, does it wind up a delicious bouillabaisse or just dead fish?" If dead fish is the answer, Scardino will quickly come under fire from the markets. But if she's worried now, she isn't letting it show.

EXHIBIT 1
Pearson's Growing Empire

Source: Morgan Stanley Dean Witter.

In each of its segments, the company posted healthy growth rates this year.

Total Sales*: $5.93 billion (+19%)
Operating Profits*: $1.0 billion (16%)

Pearson Education
(Publishers Scott Foresman, Prentice Hall, Addison-Wesley Longman; National Computer Systems, and Learning Network)

Sales: $3.3 billion (+26% from 1999)
Operating Profits: $504 million (+31%)

Financial Times Group
(*Financial Times,* French business paper *Les Echos,* Spanish paper group Recoletos, online financial-data business)

Sales: $1.3 billion (+21%)
Operating Profits: $285 million (+25%)

Penguin Group
(Penguin, Putnam, Dorling Kindersley, and Viking imprints)

Sales: $1.1 billion (+35%)
Operating Profits: $112 million (+15%)

---

* For 2000, excludes Internet, goodwill, and exceptionals.

EXHIBIT 2
Scardino the
Dealmaker

In four years as CEO, she has completed deals worth at least $11 billion to tighten Pearson's focus.

Quirky Businesses Are History

- Sold Tussaud's Group of wax museums and other attractions to Charterhouse Development Capital, a private equity firm, for $528 million in October 1998.
- Sold an 18% stake in Lazard investment banks to Gaz et Eaux holding company, which is controlled by Michel David-Weill and associates, for $615 million in June 1999.

While Media Holdings Grow

- Bought Simon & Schuster's education business for $4.6 billion from Viacom in May 1998.
- Acquired British children's and illustrated book publisher Dorling Kindersley Holdings PLC for $466 million in March 2000.
- Bought National Computer Systems, an educational testing company, for $2.5 billion in July 2000.
- Merged Pearson Television with the broadcasting assets of Germany's Bertelsmann and Belgium's Albert Frere to form RTL Group in April 2000. Pearson holds a 22% stake, now worth $2.6 billion.

Source: Adapted by Richard Robinson, University of South Carolina, based on Stanley Reed with Aixa M. Pascual and William C. Symonds, "Chapter 2 at Pearson PLC," *BusinessWeek,* January 22, 2001.

Case 25

BusinessWeek

MTV Goes Global

Mando-Pop. Mexican Hip Hop. Russian Rap. It's all fueling the biggest global channel.

EXHIBIT 1

Source: Viacom, Merrill
Lynch & Co.

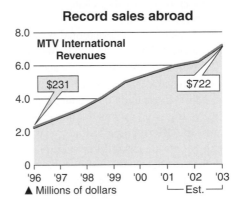

Record sales abroad

MTV International Revenues — $231 (1996) ... $722 (2003 Est.)
Millions of dollars

1   It's the Suit vs. the Tattoo Set. Foggy Bottom and the Hip Hop Crowd. The General and the Veejay. It's, it's . . . well, it's another weird but fascinating cultural moment on MTV, the Viacom-owned music network that supplements its core mission of delivering 150–decibel music to the world's teens with straight-talking programs on issues such as AIDS, drugs, and racism. On Feb. 14, U.S. Secretary of State Colin L. Powell will lead *Be Heard,* a no-holds-barred talk show on MTV Networks, where he will field questions on the crisis in Afghanistan from teens from Boston to Berlin to Bombay. The program will air on MTV's 33 channels worldwide and reach almost 375 million households. MTV's video jockeys—the ones who usually deliver wall-to-wall Hindi film music, German hard rock, Mando-pop, and Mexican hip hop to local viewers—will moderate the meeting, and translators will be on hand to turn questions into English. It will be, in other words, an Event.

2   Powell's appearance is a media moment that only MTV could pull off. Media moguls can babble on about the global village, on how CNN or BBC can reach out and touch the world. But those news shows are bush league operations compared with MTV's global clout. Thanks to the roaring success of its subsidiary, MTV Networks International, the music channel and its sister operations, VH1 and Nickelodeon, reach 1 billion people in 18 different languages in 164 countries. Eight out of ten MTV viewers live outside the U.S. CNN International reaches an international audience less than half the size of MTV's. Its impressive global reach has earned MTV membership in that tiny elite of such globally transcendent brands as Coke and Levi's.

3   MTV seems not to have missed a beat as turmoil roils the executive ranks at parent Viacom, whose board in late January called upon CEO Sumner Redstone and Chief Operating Officer Mel Karmazin to cease feuding. The stock is down almost 20% since early January, but analysts say the strife should have no impact on operating units like MTV. MTV Networks International makes buckets of money year after year from a potent combination of cable subscriber fees, advertising, and increasingly, new media. Very few other transnational media operations can claim to make profits at all. But revenues at

MTV Networks International increased 19% in 2001, to $600 million, while operating profits grew a hefty 50%, to $135 million. They are expected to more than double by 2004, according to Merrill Lynch & Co. media analyst Jessica Reif Cohen. In the past three years, the growth of MTV Networks International has outpaced the domestic network, accounting for 16% of MTV Networks' overall revenues, says co-founder and Chairman Tom Freston. He aims to increase that to 40% within five years, as MTV in the U.S. begins to plateau. MTV's international success is attracting a host of imitators, one of them spawned by the relentless Rupert Murdoch. But for now, MTV's version of globalization really rocks.

4   MTV Networks International owes its success to a lot of factors. First, demographics: There were 2.7 billion people between the ages of 10 and 34 in 2000. By 2010, there will be 2.8 billion. Increasingly, this age group is acquiring the bucks to buy CDs, jeans, acne cream—whatever brands are hot in each country. That means advertisers increasingly love MTV International. Second, music: All that stuff about music being a universal language is true, and rock is the universal language for Planet Teen. What MTV does is customize the offering in a brilliant way. Third, television: The number of sets in the world's living rooms—especially in such places as China, Brazil, Russia, and India—is exploding. So are the globe's cable networks. "Everyone who has a TV knows there's something called MTV," says Chantara Kapahi, a 17–year-old student at Jai Hind College in Bombay. The fourth reason is Bill Roedy.

5   Roedy, a 53-year-old West Point grad, is president of MTV Networks International and, theoretically, is based in London. Theoretically, since his real office is more of a semiperpetual airborne state involving him, his trademark army green pen and paper, and a business-class round-trip ticket to wherever. To give kids their dose of rock, he has breakfasted with former Israeli Prime Minister Shimon Peres, dined with Singapore founder Lee Kuan Yew, and chewed the fat for five hours with Chinese leader Jiang Zemin. Roedy even met with El Caudillo himself—Cuban leader Fidel Castro, who commended Roedy for his educational efforts on AIDS and wondered if MTV could teach Cuban kids English. Says Roedy: "We've had very little resistance once we explain that we're not in the business of exporting American culture."

6   Roedy & Co. are shrewd enough to realize that while the world's teens want American music, they really want the local stuff, too. So, MTV's producers and veejays scour their local markets for the top talent. The result is an endless stream of overnight sensations that keep MTV's global offerings fresh. Just over a year ago, for example, Lena Katina and Yulia Volkova were no different than most Moscow schoolgirls. Today, Katina, 16, and Volkova, 15, form Tatu, one of the hottest rock groups ever to come out of Russia. Tatu has won a cult following among local teens since their debut single, *Ya Soshla s Uma (I've Gone Crazy),* first aired on MTV Russia 15 months ago. Universal even plans to promote Tatu's next recordings in the U.S. "Our producers could have signed a contract with Sony or Warner, too. We had offers from all of them," says Katina.

7   Tatu is just one of a slew of emerging local music groups gaining international exposure through MTV and a wider audience in the U.S., too. Colombian rock singer Shakira, unknown outside Latin America until she recorded an MTV Unplugged CD—the acoustic live concerts recorded by MTV—in 1999, is now the winner of one U.S. Grammy and two Latin Grammy awards. Her CD has gone platinum, selling more than 2 million copies worldwide. After releasing four CDs in just three years, Taiwanese pop star Jolin Tsai, 21, is gaining popularity in mainland China thanks to heavy airplay on MTV. More unusual is Pakistani-born pop singer Adnan Sami. He's a cross-border phenom, too—only this border is bristling with guns. After appearances on MTV India last year, Sami's first album, *Kabhi to Nazar Milao (Look at Me Sometimes)* has sold 2 million copies there.

8   Viacom is now counting on MTV to be one of its biggest growth drivers in the next decade. There's plenty of room to launch new channels on cable and satellite outside the U.S., where penetration, at 38%, is about where the American market was in 1983. As digital television takes off in Europe, MTV plans to introduce more music channels, such as the seven it has in Britain that focus on such genres as rhythm-and-blues and dance. Another part of the strategy: make MTV "a vehicle to develop business [for other Viacom brands]," says Viacom COO Karmazin. "Let's face it, the way people know Viacom is through MTV." Viacom can parlay growth abroad for its lesser-known VH1, Nickelodeon, and TV Land brands "off MTV's reputation."

9   MTV also is betting heavily on emerging technologies. Last November, MTV UK created interactive applications for digital TV that enable viewers to buy CDs, get information on gigs, and vote for nominees in MTV's European Music Awards. Now available on Sky Digital, the applications will be rolled out across Europe this year. Another premier, this time in Scandinavia, was MTV Live, which goes to homes with broadband cable. Viewers can play virtual games, such as *Trash Your Hotel Room,* where users get the chance to be a rock star and wreak virtual havoc.

10   Meanwhile, in July 2000, MTV Asia launched LiLi, a virtual animated veejay who interacts with viewers on air and online in five Asian languages. An actor behind the image controls LiLi's responses, letting her interview artists and offer viewers tips on pop culture in real time. LiLi is now so popular with Asian teens that Ericsson has launched a line of LiLi mobile phones. In Japan, an MTV wireless Internet service lets users download entertainment news, vote for their favorite veejays, or choose music. MTV "tries to make a lot of noise off the channel," says Nigel Robbins, CEO of MTV Group Japan.

11   MTV's early international expansion—it got into Moscow in 1993, for example—puts it ahead of the competition in nearly every market. Hong Kong-based Channel V's 24-hour music channel, owned by Rupert Murdoch's Star TV, reaches nearly 47 million homes but has yet to make a profit. VIVA—owned 45.9% by AOL Time Warner, EMI, and Vivendi Universal—is MTV's biggest rival in Europe. It reported a net loss of $9.4 million on sales of $40 million in the first nine months of 2001 but expects to be in the black in 2002. "The market is big enough for both of us," says VIVA CEO Dieter Gorny.

12   The music channel also faces some risks in a handful of countries, such as Italy and Brazil, where MTV operates its channels in partnership with a local player. "It's really a question of whether they can maintain distribution on outlets they don't own," says Sanford C. Bernstein & Co. media analyst Tom Wolzien. Wolzien says News Corp. and Vivendi have much stronger relations with local regulators, giving them an edge in launching music channels they can control.

13   MTV's best response to these threats is to make its programming as strong as possible. Its policy of 70% local content has resulted in some of the network's most creative shows, such as MTV Brasil's monthlong *Rockgol,* a soccer championship that pits Brazilian musicians against record industry executives. In Russia, the locally produced *Twelve Angry Viewers* was voted one of Russia's top three talk programs. In a colorful studio amid bright blue steps and large green cushions, a dozen teens watch and discuss the latest videos. Periodically, they break into spontaneous dance or pop one another over the head with inflatable lollipops. OK, it's not Chekhov. But Russian groups beg to be featured on it. Says producer Piotr Sheksheyev: "MTV trusts that we Russians know best what works."

14   Ceding so much control to local channels does result in the occasional misstep. While watching MTV in Taiwan, Roedy was aghast to see nude wrestling. That was one time we had to "intervene," he recalls. When MTV first entered the Indian market in 1996, Hindi film music—the romantic, colorful soundtracks of Bollywood films—was wildly popular, but the channel's locally hired programmers disdained it as uncool. Viewers abandoned the channel, forcing it to air Bollywood music, and ratings are up 700%.

15   India is one of the giant markets that MTV is determined to dominate. The other big-country play is China. Analysts believe it is likely to be some time before the government grants 24–hour broadcasting licenses to foreigners on a nationwide basis. Still, in 2001, MTV's ad revenue in China almost doubled—even though the network airs only a maximum of six hours daily through Chinese cable systems.

16   Roedy has spent the past decade cultivating relationships in China. At one long dinner with Chinese cable operators, he desperately attempted to hold his own through countless toasts and karaoke songs. While his Chinese counterparts sang Chinese opera arias, Roedy sang a few songs from *Madame Butterfly,* while MTV Chairman Freston belted out *House of the Rising Sun,* the bluesy ballad about a New Orleans whorehouse. They must have been in tune: MTV Mandarin is seen in 60 million homes in China via 40 Chinese cable systems. Last year, more than 10,000 teens came from all over China to audition to become the next veejay on MTV Mandarin. One finalist, who had traveled 18 hours to Beijing, was so distraught at losing that MTV offered to let her veejay for a day. Anything to keep a viewer.

EXHIBIT 2
MTV on the Move

Source: Viacom Inc.

Europe	
Households Reached	124.1 million
Channels	15
Websites	9
Languages	7
Hottest Market Revenue Growth	Russia/80%
Artist to Watch	Alsou
North America	
Households Reached	84.6 million
Channels	6
Websites	2
Languages	2
Hottest Market/Revenue Growth	United States/5%
Artist to Watch	Jennifer Lopez
Asia/Pacific	
Households Reached	137.9 million
Channels	8
Websites	6
Languages	8
Hottest Market/Revenue Growth	China/80%
Artist to Watch	Na Ying
Latin America	
Households Reached	28.1 million
Channels	4
Web sites	2
Languages	2
Hottest Market/Revenue Growth	Mexico/27%
Artist to Watch	Alejandro Sanz

Source: Adapted by Richard Robinson, University of South Carolina, based on Kerry Capell with Catherine Belton, Tom Lowry, Manjeet Kripalani, Brian Bremner, and Dexter Roberts, "MTV's World," *BusinessWeek,* February 18, 2002.

B Traditional Cases

Toys "R" Us (A) in the Online Toy Business

1 "How do I explain to my son that Santa is giving him a gift a week late?" said Michele Read on December 24, 1999 as she worried how to explain to her 4-year-old son Tyler that the Leap Frog Learning toy she had ordered from Toysrus.com was not going to be under the Christmas tree the next day.[1]

2 "This does nothing to appease a child on Christmas morning when he doesn't find his present," said Kevin Davitt, a customer who was still waiting for an order from Toysrus.com on December 23, 1999. "A 6-year-old doesn't want a gift certificate, he wants his Nintendo or his Pokemon," said Davitt, who is a publicist from Glen Rock, N.J., had ordered two video games for his 6-year-old son on December 13, 1999, and agreed to pay $19.90 for express shipping so that the gift would arrive within five days.

3 Michael Kinney, a customer from South Pasadena, California who is the manager of a local taxi service, ordered a Chickaboom game for his son and was promised delivery within two weeks. After seven weeks, Kinney declared, "I'll never shop Toysrus.com again."

4 During Christmas 1999 Toysrus.com employees faced a real siege. The company's "Black Sunday" came on Sunday, November 6, 1999 as 62 million advertising circulars were placed in local newspapers around the U.S. offering free shipping on Christmas toy orders placed over the Internet. When Toysrus.com was unable to fulfill orders in time for Christmas, the firm received numerous consumer complaints and negative publicity from newspaper and magazine articles and TV news reports about the firm's problems. Toys "R" Us had the toys available in its warehouses, but was unable to pick, pack, and ship customer orders in a timely manner. Many employees worked for 49 straight days to fill orders, with some employees reported to pull sleeping bags out from under their desks to rest during the round-the-clock operation.[2] Despite the heroic efforts, customers were still displeased. "I have never been exposed to fouler language," explained Joel Anderson, a Toysrus.com vice president, as he described the angry e-mails from unhappy customers.

5 In January 2000 John Eyler became the fourth CEO of the 53-year-old Toys "R" Us toy chain and parent of Toysrus.com. He came from being president of much smaller FAO Schwarz toy chain and entered on the heels of the 18-month tenure of the previous CEO. He was immediately faced with the aftermath of the Christmas 1999 crisis and less than twelve months to fix things for Christmas 2000.

[1] James T. Madore, "Toys "R" Late, Some Parents Fume," *Newsday,* December 24, 1999, p. A39.
[2] Mark Albright, "Toysrus.com Learned Difficult Christmas Lesson," *New York Times,* January 30, 2000, p. 1H.

Case prepared by Alan B. Eisner, Lubin School of Business, Pace University, Jerome C. Kuperman, Minnesota State University, Moorhead, Department of Business Administration, Robert F. Dennehy and John P. Dory, Lubin School of Business, Pace University. These cases are under review at the *Business Case Journal.* This case is solely based upon library research. Special thanks to Margaret Ann deSouza-Lawrence for research assistance on this project. Previous versions of this case were presented at the 2001 NACRA meeting and 2001 EAM/CASE meeting.

EXHIBIT 1
Breakdown of Stores
by Divisions by Year

Source: Toys "R" Us, Inc.,
10-K report.

Number of Stores	2001	2000	1999	1998	1997	1996	1995	1994	1993	1992
Toys "R "Us, U.S.	710	710	704	700	682	653	618	581	540	497
Toys "R" Us, International	491	462	452	441	396	337	293	234	167	126
Kids "R" Us, U.S.	198	205	212	215	212	213	204	217	211	189
Babies "R" Us, U.S.	145	131	113	98	82	—	—	—	—	—
Imaginarium	37	40	—	—	—	—	—	—	—	—
Total Stores	1,581	1,548	1,481	1,454	1,372	1,203	1,115	1,032	918	812

TOYS "R" US TODAY

6 Toys "R" Us stores carried everything from Crazy Bones at $1.99 to Sony PlayStation at $129.99. Toys "R" Us, Inc., headquartered in Paramus, N.J., is one of the largest toy store chains in the U.S. with sales of $11,332 million reported in the fiscal year 2000. The merchandise mix included both children's and adult's toys and games, bicycles, sporting goods, small pools, infant and juvenile furniture, infant and toddler apparel, and children's books. An electronics section, which featured video games, electronic handheld toys, videotapes, audio CDs, computer software, along with a smattering of small TVs, shelf-stereos and radios, generated about $2 billion in sales in 1998.[3] Most Toys "R" Us stores conformed to a traditional big-box format, with stores averaging about 46,000 square feet. Stores in smaller markets ranged between 20,000 and 30,000 square feet. In 1999, the company began converting stores to a new layout named the "C3" (customer driven, cost-effective concept) format store intended to make the Toys "R" Us stores easier to shop with wider aisles, more feature opportunities and end-caps, more shops, and logical category layouts.

7 In addition to the traditional brick-and-mortar locations, Toys "R" Us Direct was organized in 1999 and consolidated both selling via the Internet (www.toysrus.com) and through mail-order catalogs. The website opened in June 1998 with about 2,000 products representing over 200 vendors. Two catalogs were introduced in 1998, "Differently Abled" and "Holiday Toys," which were also posted on the website. The company marketed several catalogs in 1999 branching into the juvenile and collectible markets. In May 1999 they made an effort to join the online market with the introduction of Toysrus.com. In July 1999, Toys "R" Us, with an interest in the educational and learning toy segment, announced the purchase of Imaginarium, the number 37 player ranked by sales. Existing stand-alone Imaginarium stores continued, and Toys "R" Us incorporated in-store Imaginarium World sections in 10 to 20 of its C3 format stores in time for Christmas 1999.

8 In February 2001 the company had a total of 1,581 stores worldwide. Toys "R" Us strived to be the "Worldwide Authority on Kids, Families and Fun" with 6 divisions: Toys "R" Us USA, Toys "R" Us International, Kids "R" Us, Babies "R" Us, Toysrus.com, and the newest division, Imaginarium. See Exhibit 1 for store types and see Exhibit 2 for company vision.

---

[3] "Playthings Top 50: A List of the Nation's Largest Toy Retailers," *Playthings* 97, no. 9 (September 1999), pp. 36+.

EXHIBIT 2
Vision, Mission,
and Goals

Source: Toys "R" Us, Inc. 2000
Annual Report.

Vision: Put joy in kids' hearts and smiles on parents' faces.

Mission: A commitment to making each and every customer happy.

Goal: To be the "Worldwide Authority on Kids, Families and Fun."

EXHIBIT 3
Consolidated
Statements
of Earnings

Consolidated Statements of Earnings: Toys "R" Us, Inc. and subsidiaries

(In millions except per share data)

	Feb. 2001	Jan. 2000	Jan. 1999	Jan. 1998
Net sales	11,332	11,862	11,170	11,038
Cost of Sales	7,815	8,321	8,191	7,710
Gross Profit	**3,517**	**3,541**	**2,979**	**3,328**
Selling general and administrative expenses	2,832	2,743	2,443	2,231
Depreciation, amortization, and asset write-offs	290	278	255	253
Restructuring			294	
Equity in net earnings Japan	(31)			
Total Operating Expenses	**3,091**	**3,021**	**2,992**	**2,484**
Operating Income/Loss	426	520	(13)	844
Gain from IPO Japan	315			
Interest expense	(127)	91	102	85
Interest and other income	23	(11)	(9)	(13)
Interest Expense Net		80	93	72
Earnings/Loss before Income taxes	**637**	**440**	**(106)**	**772**
Income Taxes	233	161	26	282
Net Earnings/Loss	**404**	**279**	**(132)**	**490**
Basic earnings/loss per share	1.92	1.14	(0.50)	1.72
Diluted earnings/loss per share	1.88	1.14	(0.50)	1.70

Background

9   Charles Lazarus started Toys "R" Us in 1948 in Washington, D.C. Lazarus started out in business with a baby furniture store. However, as customers requested toys too, he gradually moved into the toy business. In 1957 Charles opened the first toy supermarket. Specialty retailing and off-price positioning were revolutionary concepts in those premall, prediscount store days. With the success of these stores, Toys "R" Us became a public company in the late 1970s. Lazarus pioneered the toy supermarket concept and led Toys "R" Us to dominate the industry. The company has evolved into an $11 billion business with over 1,581 stores worldwide. See Exhibit 3—it contains company performance data.

THE TOY INDUSTRY

Brick and Mortar

10   The $29.4 billion traditional toy industry had undergone significant changes during the 1990s (see Exhibit 4 for industry growth). General mass merchandise retailers had grown, as had their toy departments. Mall retailers like KB Toys managed to channel a great deal of money into shopping malls with the introduction of their small mall-based toyshops. Exhibit 5 shows the changing market share among retailer types. The Toys "R" Us chain suffered and saw its market share drop from 25% in 1990 to 18% in 1997 and 16.5% in

EXHIBIT 4
U.S. Toy
Industry Sales

Sources: Toy Manufacturers of
America, Inc., New York and
NPD Group, New York.

Industry Segments	1993	1994	1995	1996	1997	1998	1999	2000
Total Industry (with Video Games)	18.7	20.1	20.8	22.7	25.6	27.2	29.9	29.4
Traditional Toys	14.8	17.0	17.7	19.1	20.6	21.0	23.0	23.0
Video Games	3.9	3.1	3.1	3.6	5.0	6.2	6.9	6.4

Note: Stated in billions of dollars

EXHIBIT 5
Distribution of Sales
by Retailer Type

Sources: Toy Manufacturers of
America, Inc., New York and
NPD Group, New York.

Type	Dollar Share (%)					
	1995	1996	1997	1998	1999	2000
Discount Stores	41.2	40.7	41.6	41.5	40.0	41.8
National Toy Stores	23.6	23.6	23.2	21.7	20.8	21.0
All Other Outlets	13.8	13.4	12.9	12.8	13.8	11.9
Mail Order	4.4	4.8	4.6	5.3	5.0	5.1
Card/Gift/Stationery	0.9	1.2	1.9	3.1	4.2	2.2
All Other Toy Stores	3.6	4.3	3.9	3.7	3.9	3.4
Food/Drug Stores	3.4	3.4	3.5	3.6	3.4	2.9
Department Stores	4.1	3.8	3.4	4.1	3.3	4.0
E-Tailers*	—	—	—	—	1.2	2.1
Hobby/Craft Stores	2.9	3.1	3.2	2.7	2.8	3.5
Variety Stores	2.1	1.7	1.8	1.5	1.7	2.1

* New category

1998.[4] Toys "R" Us had been the leader for over a decade, however, in 1998 the scenario changed as Wal-Mart ousted Toys "R" Us and became the top toy retailer in the U.S. as indicated in Exhibit 6.

Online

11   The online toy industry that exploded in 1999 was estimated at $300 million and was expected to reach $1.8 billion by 2003 according to Forrester Research.[5] Between 1999 and 2002 the share of the toy market held by Internet retailers was expected to grow 10 times according to Deutsche Bank's Alex Brown,[6] which would amount to 2.2% of the market. However, even that small percentage of the market was likely to influence the industry profoundly. One major way Internet retailers competed in the toy market was based upon price. For online retailers the object was quite simple—sell the greatest volumes of toys since profit margins were quite slim. Participants in the toy war on the Web besides Toys "R" Us included eToys, Amazon.com, Smarterkids.com, Target.com, and Toysmart.com. The year 2000 brought approximately 28+ million shoppers online and $793 million in total online toys sales, compared to $650 million in online sales in 1999.[7] In 1998

[4] Laura Liebeck, "TRU Follows a New Leader," *Discount Store News* 38, no. 8 (1999), pp. 1, 92.
[5] Forrester Research.
[6] "Net Gains Take Precedence over Bricks and Mortar: Toys "R" Us," *Financial Times,* London Edition, August 28, 1999, p. 19.
[7] NPD Group, Inc., New York.

EXHIBIT 6   Percent of Annual Industry Sales, Top Toy Sellers

Sources: NPD Group, New York and Toy Manufacturers of America, Inc., New York.

Retailer	1991	1992	1993	1994	1995	1996	1997	1998	1999	2000
Wal-Mart	10.2	10.4	13.4	14.1	14.6	15.3	16.3	17.4	17.4	19.0
Toys "R" Us	19.1	20.6	19.7	21.0	19.2	18.9	18.3	16.8	15.6	16.5
Kmart	6.9	6.9	7.6	7.4	8.5	8.3	8.2	8.0	7.2	7.4
Target	4.9	5.6	5.2	5.6	6.1	6.4	7.1	6.9	6.8	7.2
KB Toys/Toy Works	5.0	4.6	3.9	4.3	4.3	4.3	4.9	4.9	5.1	4.7
Ames			—	1.0	1.2	1.2	1.1	1.3	1.6	1.9
J.C. Penney	1.3	1.4	2.1	2.2	1.5	1.7	1.5	1.6	1.2	1.4
Hallmark								1.0	1.1	0.9
Meijer						1.0	1.1	1.2	1.0	0.9
Shopko								0.9	0.8	0.8
Lionel Leisure	1.7	1.4*								
Child World	3.1	1.4*								
Service Merchandise	1.8	2.1	1.8	1.9	1.8	1.6	1.1			
Sears	2.4	2.0*								
Hills			1.2	1.4	1.6	1.3	1.2	1.1		

* Exit the toy business.

EXHIBIT 7
**1999 Online
Toy Sales**

Source: *USA Today* research.

Company	Online Toy Sales (millions)	Percentage of Total Toy Revenue
eToys.com	$151	100%
Amazon.com	95	100
Toys "R" Us	50	0.4
KB Toys	26	1.5

EXHIBIT 8
**Overall Consumer
Experience Scores**

Source: Scorecard for Top
Internet Toy Stores for Fall
2000, Gómez.com

Firm	Score*	Firm	Score*
1. eToys.com	8.17	6. Wal-Mart Stores, Inc.	6.33
2. Amazon.com/Toys "R" Us	8.02	7. NuttyPutty.com	6.30
3. SmarterKids.com	7.99	8. J.C. Penney Co., Inc.	5.73
4. ZanyBrainy.com	7.33	9. Target	5.61
5. KBkids.com	7.06	10. FAO Schwarz	5.56

*10 is the highest possible score, see www.gomezpro.com for scorecard methodology.

eToys.com was the number one online toy merchant, stunning industry watchers—and complacent offline retailers—by selling $23 million in toys and related products during the holiday season. In 1999 eToys.com topped the market again with $151 million in sales. Analysts attributed the Etoys.com win to the company's ability to help shoppers find items easily and quickly.[8] Exhibit 7 shows the selected sales and percentages of toy revenues derived from online sales by the top players in 1999. See Exhibit 8 for consumer experience rankings of the major competitors.

[8] Connie Guglielmo, "Online Toys Get Serious," *Upside,* December 1999.

SELECTED ONLINE COMPETITOR PROFILES

eToys.com

12 Launched in October of 1997, eToys.com was a leading online retailer exclusively focused on children's products. This online only store offered an extensive selection of products from well-known and specialty toy brands. In addition to toys, the company offered over 100,000 carefully chosen items including children's video games, software, videos, books, and music. The eToys.com corporate vision was to create the premier family-oriented destination on the Internet. In fact, in July 2000, eToys.com was named the best Internet toy store by Gómez Advisors, with the highest overall score for the fourth consecutive quarter. Net sales for the fiscal year ended March 31, 2000 reached $151 million, up fivefold compared with $30 million in the prior year. Cumulative customer accounts over that same period also grew fivefold from 365,000 to about 2 million. By June 2000 the scenario had changed drastically, a venture into the European market was a disaster and the company took heavy losses. eToys.com stock traded at $86 in October 1999 and was down to $6 in June 2000 as investors were disillusioned and wary. Further the company faced stiff competition and was quickly burning away cash reserves to keep up. In June 2000 they were forced to raise $100 million through the sale of preferred stock to a group of private investors. The stock carries a 7% dividend yield payable in cash or eToys.com common stock.

13 **The Website.** The user-friendly website combined detailed product information, helpful shopping services, and innovative merchandising strategies, along with the convenience and flexibility of shopping 24 hours a day, 7 days a week. The site's advanced search technology made it easy for customers to locate products by any combination of age, toy category, keyword, or price. In addition, eToys.com provided regularly updated product recommendations through the site's favorites by age, bestsellers, birthday gifts, and under $20 sections of the online store. eToys.com also highlighted award-winning products from prominent parenting and family publications.

14 By enhancing the current product offerings and expanding into additional categories, eToys.com aim was to be the primary resource for consumers of children's products. Many of the store's brand name and specialty products were carefully selected and personally tested to provide customers with the highest quality. This level of product evaluation enabled eToys.com to deliver valuable, personalized product information to shoppers. eToys.com gift services supplied gift recommendations by age, relationship, and price specification, child-appropriate gift-wrapping, personalized message cards to accompany the gifts, and electronic gift certificates. The gift services also provided a birthday reminder service, through which shoppers could be notified of a child's birthday three weeks in advance via e-mail with age-appropriate gift ideas. Through a wish list service, parents and children could e-mail family and friends a list of gifts wanted.

SmarterKids.com

15 SmarterKids.com sold toys, but the company wanted to supply parents with many tools not just toys—to help their children learn. "We consider ourselves an educational destination a whole lot more than a store," said Al Noyes, the company's executive vice president of sales and marketing. "We're a combination Sylvan Learning Center and eToys."

16 This online company made $4.3 million in revenue during the last quarter of 1999, far outpacing the $22,000 recorded for the same period in 1998. The fourth-quarter total also accounted for the biggest chunk of $5.4 million in yearly revenue, but even that respectable increase was overshadowed by eToys.com, which had sales of nearly $107 million during the quarter, up 366% from 1998. On a typical day, 35,000 unique visitors stopped by SmarterKids, adding up to about 1 million a month, although those figures inflate during the holiday season—2 million visitors came to the site in December 1999. Of those visitors, anywhere from 2 to 10% were converted from browsers to buyers, according to CEO Al Noyes.[9] Although SmarterKids had a clear niche and offered more content and customization than competitors, Pain Stubing, a retail analyst with Ernst & Young, was skeptical it could survive the cutthroat online toy market.

> The site is charming, but I don't think it's absolutely essential. Big players such as Wal-Mart, eToys, and Toys "R" Us could easily roll over SmarterKids if they branch into educational toys.

Stubing suggested that SmarterKids could partner with a big bricks-and-mortar toy seller or else tie in with all the mom-and-pop toy retailers out there and set up a purchasing co-op, transforming itself from a retailer to a wholesaler.

17   **The Website.** At first glance, the website did not differ much from eToys.com or Toysrus.com. Shoppers could search for merchandise based on age and grade, by keyword, by themes like construction and pretend play, by brand, or by character, such as Barney.[10] Nonparents stumped over finding an age-appropriate gift could head for the gift center or the online registry for help. But a closer look showed that the site's huge selection of learning toys was also searchable by skill and subject, such as alphabet, counting, and writing. SmarterKids was packed with educational content. The "parents center" was a hub for news, activities, links to other sites, articles and columns to help moms and dads inspire their children to turn learning into a fun, ongoing pastime, not a classroom-only event. In fact, Gómez Advisors chose SmarterKids as the top educational toy site on its Internet Toy Scorecard. The site's free specialty centers, housed within the parents' section, gave information on talented and gifted children as well as those with special needs. For kids in the latter category, the offerings included fact sheets on autism, visual impairment, learning disabilities, and attention-deficit disorder, along with recommendations for toys that nurture children with those needs. A step-by-step guide helped parents determine whether their child fits into one of the special needs categories. Similarly, the gifted and talented center features resources, toy recommendations and tools for building aptitude in math, science, written and oral communication, and the arts. Both sections included "ask our teacher," a feature that allowed parents to query a resident educator. The preschool category broke out children's skills into social, emotional, language, motor, and cognitive. Clicking on any of those categories took you to a list of skills for that subset, and a button that brought up a roster of suitable products.

18   A particularly useful feature was "MySmarterKids" and its patent-pending "Smart-Picks" system, which allowed parents to customize their shopping and content browsing. After parents set up learning profiles for each child, the site matched learning needs, goals, and styles with merchandise tested and approved by teachers on staff. This feature was unique, but wasn't showcased as well as it could be, since the site didn't use technology to identify those who had previously set up a custom page. Instead, visitors who had used the feature saw the same home page as everyone else, rather than a tailored one that took them directly to their profile and product picks. Also, the home page was busy looking, and the design didn't telegraph the relative importance of each section.

---

[9] Janet Kalbhen, "SmarterKids Gives Toy Buyers an Education. But Will Kids Love Puzzles as Much as Pokemon," *Internet Retailer* 66 (May 2000).
[10] Barney is a purple dinosaur character from a popular public television show geared towards toddlers.

KBkid.com

19   Formed in June 1999, the KBkid.com was owned 80% by Consolidated Stores Corporation. A leading value retailer, Consolidated operated approximately 1,309 toy stores nationwide. KBkid.com, as a part of it, was one of the fastest growing online retailers with an exclusive focus on children's products. During 1999, this toy seller was ranked number one for online customer confidence and overall cost by Gómez Advisors, among the top e-commerce transaction gainers by Next Card, and was named one of the "Ten Best Online Software Stores" of 1999. KBkid.com hoped to do for the toy industry what Amazon.com did for the staid world of selling books.

20   However, as Consolidated's losses widened during 2000, management sought a buyer for their toy division, which included the KBkid.com online. In March 2000 Consolidated changed its name to Big Lots, Inc. to emphasize the firm's focus on the closeout retail business. By the end of the second quarter of 2000 Consolidated reported a net loss of $62.7 million, or 68 cents a share compared with a net loss of $4.4 million, or 7 cents a share, in the same period of 1999. In December 2000 Big Lots sold the KB toy division to Bain Capital, a private investment firm.

21   **The Website.** The KBkid.com website was sleek, innovative with customer-friendly features, functionality, and an emphasis on great prices and strong merchandising. Toys could be found via a search engine or customers could shop by category: Toys, Videos, Games, Software, DVD & Video, Collectibles and Specialty Toys. Categories were broken down on the left frame and items were displayed in the right frame, making it easy for customers to find what they wanted. The site's search capabilities were also impressive; customers could easily comb through some 10,000 products. The product lists from which a customer searches were displayed with the product title, a thumbnail photo of the item, recommended age bracket, toy category, price, a short description, and a link to more details. Design expert and reviewers attributed the site's success to a clean interface, smooth search function, good use of graphics, and easy-to-use shopping-cart and checkout functions.

22   The KBkids.com was good enough to beat click-and-mortar rivals like Toys "R" Us but could not match the pure Internet plays for website style and function. Shortcomings included a lack of order tracking or real-time inventory information. Unlucky customers were notified via e-mail if their shipment would be late.

Amazon.com

23   Amazon.com opened its virtual doors on the World Wide Web in July 1995. Amazon's mission was to use the Internet to transform book buying into the fastest, easiest, and most enjoyable shopping experience possible. Amazon.com sought to be the world's most customer-centric company, where customers could find anything they wanted to buy online.

24   The Amazon.com net sales for the second quarter of 2000 were $578 million; an increase of 84% over the net sales of $314 million for the same period in 1999 (net sales for the entire year were only $511,000 in 1995). The company also reported significant increases in sales outside the U.S. Amazon.co.uk (United Kingdom) and Amazon.de (Germany) sales were $73 million, up 134% from $31 million for the second quarter of 1999. The two sites added 500,000 new customer accounts in the second quarter of 2000, bringing their total customer accounts to more than 3 million, up from about 800,000 as of June 1999.

25   The bad news for Amazon started in the beginning of 2000. Wall Street showed disenchantment with its former Internet darling. Top tech-fund managers began to reduce or

even eliminate Amazon.com from their portfolios. Ravi Suria, Lehman Brother Incorporated analyst, argued: "The only triple-digit that mattered is Amazon's cash-flow losses."[11] 2000 marked the end of Amazon's fairytale honeymoon of unlimited prospects with Wall Street.

26   **The Website.** The site offered millions of distinct items separated in different categories. The site was proud to have Earth's Biggest Selection™, along with online auction and free electronic greeting cards. Amazon.com listed more than 18 million items that could be found under books, CDs, toys, electronics, videos, DVDs, tools and hardware, lawn and patio items, kitchen products, software, and video games. Through Amazon's zShop, any business or individual could virtually sell anything to Amazon's more than 23 million customers. The site offered the customers superior shopping experience by product value through selection, low prices, product information and intense focus on customer service. Proven as a technology leader, Amazon.com had developed electronic commerce innovations such as 1-click technology, personalized shopping services, easy-to-use search and browse features, secure payment protections and wireless access to the stores.

THE NEW TOYS "R" US STRATEGY

27   Customers complained that the stores were ugly and untidy, shopping was difficult, and that there were not enough sales personnel. To help it regain its number one place from Wal-Mart, Toys "R" Us developed a new corporate strategy and marketing plan. Toys "R" Us hired a new Marketing VP, Warren Kornblum, who immediately overhauled their whole marketing operation. In the past Toys "R" Us had joined in small vendor promotions and managed scattered marketing efforts. Kornblum changed that around, deciding to do fewer but bigger promotions. The company teamed with Major League Baseball as a sponsor for the Diamond Skills Program, a youth skill competition. Then the firm helped a champion women's soccer team travel to 12 U.S. cities with a tie-in from SFX Entertainment to create the Toys "R" Us Victory Tour. Toys "R" Us also did a promotional deal with Fox Kids Network and Walt Disney for the feature film *Toy Story 2*. As a result of these marketing efforts, sales increased from $11.2 billion in 1998 to $11.9 billion in 1999.[12] For 2000–01, the company restructured its budget to allocate more money towards marketing. Toys "R" Us planned to continue with sports and movie entertainment themes for promotions.

28   Warren Kornblum's strategy seemed to work. He set up a "Scan and Win" promotion where shoppers held up UPC game pieces to scanners to see if they had won a prize. More than a million consumers were scanned in with this promotion, making this one of the company's most successful store traffic improvement programs. The mountains of sweepstakes entries and packed venues, however, began causing inventory shortages in the all-important holiday period of 1999. Inventory mishaps were the main reason why fourth-quarter 1999 sales stayed at a flat $5 billion.

29   When John Eyler came in as the new CEO of Toys "R" Us in January 2000, he slashed expenses across the board, started efforts to provide better customer service, increased the number of employees in stores, and expanded store operating hours. All of the marketing activities were aimed at bringing customers into the chain's new store

[11] Robert Hof, Debra Sparks, and Ellen Neuborne, with Wendy Zellner, "Can Amazon Make It," *BusinessWeek,* July 2000.
[12] "The Real Toy Story," *Promo* XIII, no. 5 (April 2000).

EXHIBIT 9
Toys "R" Us
Merchandise Worlds

Source: Toys "R" Us, Inc.

World	Description
R Zone	Video, electronics, computer software, and related products
Action and Adventure	Action figures, die-cast cars, etc.
Girls	Dolls, collectibles, accessories, lifestyle products
Outdoor Fun	Bikes, sports, play sets
Preschool	Toys, accessories
Seasonal	Christmas, Halloween, Summer, etc.
Juvenile	Baby products and apparel
Learning Center	Educational and developmental products
Family Fun	Games and puzzles

design and layout concept, C3: customer driven, cost-effective concept. This easier to shop C3 format allowed for 18% more selling space, wider aisles and were to be installed in 75% of the stores by the end of 2000. Toys "R" Us hoped this new strategy would take market share back from Wal-Mart, Kmart, Target, and KB Toys.

30   To make the stores more shopper-friendly and better able to compete with the more intimate specialty retailers, Toys "R" Us also introduced the merchandise "world" in 1999. See Exhibit 9 for a list of the "worlds" developed.

Toysrus.com

31   Toys "R" Us arrived late to the e-business world with Toysrus.com in 1998 losing critical early battles to eToys.com and ceding some of the market to Amazon.com and KBkids.com. The development, launch, and operation of Toysrus.com turned out to be both a corporate and public relations headache for almost a year. Things fell apart just as quickly as they came together. The investment deal they made with Benchmark Capital to fund their venture crumbled a few months after it was made as neither party could agree to the shares they would have. This reportedly prompted the resignation of Toys "R" Us CEO, Robert Nakasone. Bob Moog, who was hired to run Toysrus.com, backed out of his employment deal in July 1999, three months after agreeing to come onboard. With Christmas 1999 approaching, Toys "R" Us scrambled to put its Internet venture together. Hasbro executive John Barbour was hired as the new CEO for Toysrus.com in August 1999. He quickly developed a new plan, redesigned the site, and prepared for a holiday traffic onslaught. The company began promoting online offers in its off-line marketing efforts, the most ambitious of which dangled a $10 discount for online purchases in the nationally distributed Toys "R" Us "holiday big book" coupon circulars. Toysrus.com also offered free shipping for the holiday season.

32   The free shipping and "big book" coupon strategy worked, but a little too well for the logistics department of the company. Traffic exploded, and the site drowned in an avalanche of orders "beyond our most optimistic forecasts," said John Barbour. The site quadrupled its servers, but even the hardware improvements were no match for a tenfold increase in consumer traffic. The company was finally forced to announce that 5% of all online orders would not be fulfilled in time for Christmas. Embarrassed, Toys "R" Us issued a formal apology and issued $100 gift certificates to Web customers whose orders didn't make it under the tree.

33   Toysrus.com declared revenues of $49 million in 1999, $39 million of which came during the holiday season. The Web operation remained relatively quiet in the first quarter of 2000, as executives focused on upgrades. New marketing efforts were to break in

the second half of 2000 in readiness for the holiday season that would be "seamlessly" integrated with bricks-and-mortar promotions. In February 2000, Toysrus.com got a $57 million investment from Softbank Venture Capital to help improve the firm's operational readiness for the Christmas 2000 season.

Distribution Center Operations and Order Fulfillment

34 Learning from the fiasco of Christmas 1999 where Toysrus.com failed to deliver goods in time, the company decided to improve its distribution system. In April 2000, Toysrus.com announced plans to triple its fulfillment capacity, to 1.9 million square feet, by opening distribution centers in Mira Loma, California and Chambersburg, Pennsylvania in addition to upgrading the existing Memphis, Tennessee, facility. Toysrus.com's Memphis-based distribution center was designed to fill direct-to-consumer orders quickly and with great accuracy. The distribution center was able to hold very deep inventory in the most popular toy lines. It was also engineered to handle high-volume, small quantity orders, which are the staple of the e-commerce world. The facility was driven by piece movement and designed for enormous flexibility. The company could go from hockey sticks, to golf bags to shirts to Barbie dolls very easily. Not many pick and pack operations systems had this high level of product variability. The highlight of the system was a two-tiered cross-belt sorter (the only one of its kind in the nation).[13] The unit could perform 16,000 sorts per hour. The center's Memphis location also gave direct access to Federal Express's home hub for fast overnight shipping. Orders received by 9:00 P.M. CST could be processed and in the customer's home by the next morning. Many customer-specific services, such as personalization and gift-wrapping, were also performed at the facility. Toys "R" Us was banking on all these centers to add up to a successful online shopping experience.

Winter 2000 Approaches

35 John Eyler and his direct report John Barbour (president of the Toysrus.com division) still faced uncertain times ahead. The firm had placed orders earlier this year with suppliers and was more confident about sales forecasts and demand levels than they had been in the previous year. Toys "R" Us had placed 78% of its Christmas orders by April 2000, up 40% from 1999.[14] Eyler had also announced plans to beef up warehousing and logistics for both retail and online sales. He had aggressively continued efforts to refit the brick-and-mortar retail stores to the C3 layout. How would the firm weather the winter? Could Eyler avoid repeating Christmas past?

---

[13] Rapiston Systems (www.rapistan.com).
[14] Nanatte Byrnes, "Old Stores, New Rivals, and Changing Trends Have Hammered . . ." *Business Week*, December 4, 2000, pp. 128–40.

Toys "R" Us (B) Forms an Online Alliance

36   In August 2000, Toys "R" Us signed a 10-year contract with Amazon.com agreeing on a 10-year partnership to develop a cobranded toy and video game store website in the fall and baby products website the following year, 2001. Toysrus.com was to buy and manage inventory and Amazon would oversee site development, order fulfillment, and customer service.

37   Amazon was widely recognized as having one of the better CRM (customer relationship management) systems among online companies. "This showcases [Amazon.com's] ability to turn online transactions into reality," said Vernon Keenan,[15] senior analyst at Keenan Vision, in San Francisco, noting that Toysrus.com failed in this arena at Christmas 1999. Amazon, on the other hand, had been criticized for its expensive real-world warehousing infrastructure. In Amazon's favor, this deal may allow it to rationalize that cost, according to David Cooperstein, research director at Forrester Research, in Cambridge, Mass.

38   While Toys "R" Us brought the toy business expertise to the table, this deal solved the problem that many brick-and-mortar companies were having at the time. Toys "R" Us, among others, had not figured how to go from receiving an online order to getting products to the doorstep as well as Amazon. At the same, the deal showed that Amazon no longer believed it could single-handedly be a global online shopping center. The Toysrus.com and Amazon.com deal was structured as follows. Toysrus.com would identify, buy, and manage inventory. Amazon.com would create a cobranded site for toys and video games and a site for baby products. Amazon would do order fulfillment and customer service and house inventory. Toysrus.com will make fixed periodic payments to Amazon, per-unit payments, and a single-digit percentage of revenue.[16] This would allow Toys "R" Us to keep most of the profits. Yet, Amazon expected to make a profit on each sale from the venture. In addition, Amazon would receive warrants to acquire 5% of Toysrus.com. Both firms expected the site to be profitable by the fourth quarter of 2001. For the venture to be profitable, sales would have to triple or quadruple by 2002 according to John Eyler, CEO of Toys "R" Us.[2] The plan by Amazon.com and Toys "R" Us to create a joint toy sales website would likely make them much more formidable changing all the numbers around.

---

[15] Ephraim Schwartz, "Amazon, Toys "R" Us in E-commerce Tie-up, *InfoWorld,* August 14, 2000.
[16] Deborah Kong, "Amazon, Toys "R" Us Team for Online Toy Store. Complementary Skills Unite Rivals," *USA Today,* August 11, 2000.

Case 27

Wal-Mart Stores, Inc.:
Strategies for Dominance in the New Millennium

1   David Glass had recently announced that he was stepping down from his role as president and chief executive officer (CEO) at Wal-Mart Stores, Inc. He stepped to the podium in early 2000 at a Kansas City convention of the company's store managers to introduce Wal-Mart's new CEO, Lee Scott, 51, to a crowd of cheering executives. "I'm not going anywhere; I'll be around to give everyone more help than they probably would like," Glass suggested. At 64 years old, he would remain chairman of the firm's Executive Committee.

2   Lee Scott was only the third CEO in the entire history of Wal-Mart. Sam Walton had built the company from the ground up. During the 12 years that David Glass held the position, sales grew from $16 billion to $165 billion. Lee Scott had been personally recruited by David Glass 21 years before from a Springdale, Arkansas, trucking company to come to Wal-Mart as a manager of the truck fleet. In his years at Wal-Mart he had established himself as a leader, innovator, and team player. Over the last four years he served as chief operating officer (COO) and vice chairman of the company. He was aware that there were tremendous opportunities to serve new markets with the company's stores. His management mandate was to drive the company to a new level of success in domestic and international markets.

A MATURING ORGANIZATION

3   In 2000, Wal-Mart Stores, Inc., Bentonville, Arkansas, operated mass merchandising retail stores under a variety of names and retail formats including: Wal-Mart discount department stores; Sam's Wholesale Clubs, wholesale/retail membership warehouses; and Wal-Mart Supercenters, large combination grocery and general merchandise stores in all 50 states. In the International Division, it operated stores in Canada, Mexico, Argentina, Brazil, Germany, South Korea, United Kingdom, and Puerto Rico, and stores through joint ventures in China. It was not only the nation's largest discount department store chain, but had surpassed the retail division of Sears, Roebuck & Co. in sales volume as the largest retail firm in the United States. It was also considered the largest retailer in the world, with sales of $165 billion in 1999. The McLane Company, Inc., a Wal-Mart subsidiary, sold a wide variety of grocery and nongrocery products to a variety of retailers including selected Wal-Marts, Sam's Clubs, and Supercenters. In 1999, *Discount Store News* honored Wal-Mart as "Retailer of the Century" with a commemorative issue of the periodical.

4   A financial summary of Wal-Mart Stores, Inc. for the fiscal years ended January 31, 1999 and January 31, 2000 is shown in Appendix A. An 11-year financial summary for the fiscal years January 31, 1990 to January 31, 2000 is shown in Appendix C. Appendix B lists the Wal-Mart Board of Directors and Executive Officers on January 31, 2000.

THE SAM WALTON SPIRIT

5   Much of the success of Wal-Mart was attributed to the entrepreneurial spirit of its founder and Chairman of the Board, Samuel Moore Walton (1918–1992). Many considered him one of the most influential retailers of the century.

6   Sam Walton or "Mr. Sam" as some referred to him traced his down-to-earth, old-fashioned, home-spun, evangelical ways to growing up in rural Oklahoma, Missouri, and Arkansas. Although he was remarkably blase about his roots, some suggested that it was the simple belief in hard work and ambition that had "unlocked countless doors and showered upon him, his customers, and his employees . . . , the fruits of . . . years of labor in building [this] highly successful company."

7   "Our goal has always been in our business to be the very best," Sam Walton said in an interview, "and, along with that, we believe that in order to do that, you've got to make a good situation and put the interests of your associates first. If we really do that consistently, they in turn will cause . . . our business to be successful, which is what we've talked about and espoused and practiced." "The reason for our success," he said, "is our people and the way that they're treated and the way they feel about their company." Many have suggested it was this "people first" philosophy, which guided the company through the challenges and setbacks of its early years, and allowed the company to maintain its consistent record of growth and expansion in later years.

8   There was little about Sam Walton's background that reflected his amazing success. He was born in Kingfisher, Oklahoma, on March 29, 1918, to Thomas and Nancy Walton. Thomas Walton was a banker at the time and later entered the farm mortgage business and moved to Missouri. Sam Walton, growing up in rural Missouri in the depths of the Great Depression, discovered early that he "had a fair amount of ambition and enjoyed working," he once noted. He completed high school at Columbia, Missouri, and received a Bachelor of Arts Degree in Economics from the University of Missouri in 1940. "I really had no idea what I would be," he once said. "At one point in time," adding as an afterthought, "I thought I wanted to become president of the United States."

9   A unique, enthusiastic, and positive individual, Sam Walton was "just your basic home-spun billionaire," a columnist once suggested. "Mr. Sam is a life-long small-town resident who didn't change much as he got richer than his neighbors," he noted. Walton had tremendous energy, enjoyed bird hunting with his dogs and flew a corporate plane. When the company was much smaller he could boast that he personally visited every Wal-Mart store at least once a year. A store visit usually included Walton leading Wal-Mart cheers that began, "Give me a W, give me an A . . . " To many employees he had the air of a fiery Baptist preacher." Paul R. Carter, a Wal-Mart executive vice-president, was quoted as saying, "Mr. Walton has a calling." He became the richest man in America, and by 1991 had created a personal fortune for his family in excess of $21 billion. In 1999, despite a division of wealth, five family members were still ranked among the richest individuals in the United States.

10   Sam Walton's success was widely chronicled. He was selected by the investment publication, *Financial World* in 1989 as the "CEO of the Decade." He had honorary degrees from the University of the Ozarks, the University of Arkansas, and the University of Missouri. He also received many of the most distinguished professional awards of the industry like "Man of the Year," "Discounter of the Year," "Chief Executive Officer of the Year," and was the second retailer to be inducted into the Discounting Hall of Fame. He was recipient of the Horatio Alger Award in 1984 and acknowledged by *Discount Stores News* as "Retailer of the Decade" in December of 1989. "Walton does a remarkable job of instilling near-religious fervor in his people," said analyst Robert Buchanan of A. G. Edwards. "I think that speaks to the heart of his success." In late 1989 Sam Walton was diagnosed to have multiple myeloma, or cancer of the bone marrow. He planned to remain active in the firm as Chairman of the Board of Directors until his death in 1992.

THE MARKETING CONCEPT

Genesis of an Idea

11   Sam Walton started his retail career in 1940 as a management trainee with the J.C. Penney Co. in Des Moines, Iowa. He was impressed with the Penney method of doing business and later modeled the Wal-Mart chain on "The Penney Idea" as reviewed in Exhibit 1. The Penney Company found strength in calling employees "associates" rather than clerks. Penney's, founded in Kemerer, Wyoming, in 1902, located stores on the main streets of small towns and cities throughout the United States. Early Walton 5 & 10s were on main streets and served rural areas.

12   Following service in the U.S. Army during World War II, Sam Walton acquired a Ben Franklin variety store franchise in Newport, Arkansas. He operated this store successfully with his brother, James L. "Bud" Walton (1921–1995), until losing the lease in 1950. When Wal-Mart was incorporated in 1962, the firm was operating a chain of 15 stores. Bud Walton became a senior vice president of the firm and concentrated on finding suitable store locations, acquiring real estate, and directing store construction.

13   The early retail stores owned by Sam Walton in Newport and Bentonville, Arkansas, and later in other small towns in adjoining southern states, were variety store operations. They were relatively small operations of 6,000 square feet, were located on "main streets" and displayed merchandise on plain wooden tables and counters. Operated under the Ben Franklin name and supplied by Butler Brothers of Chicago and St. Louis, they were characterized by a limited price line, low gross margins, high merchandise turnover and concentration on return on investment. The firm, operating under the Walton five-and-dime name, was the largest Ben Franklin franchisee in the country in 1962. The variety stores were phased out by 1976 to allow the company to concentrate on the growth of Wal-Mart discount department stores.

Foundations of Growth

14   The original Wal-Mart discount concept was not a unique idea. Sam Walton became convinced in the late 1950s that discounting would transform retailing. He traveled extensively in New England, the cradle of "off-pricing." After he had visited just about every discounter in the United States, he tried to interest Butler Brothers executives in Chicago in the discount store concept. The first Kmart, as a "conveniently located one-stop shopping unit where customers could buy a wide variety of quality merchandise at discount prices" had just opened in Garden City, Michigan. Walton's theory was to operate a

EXHIBIT 1
The Penney Idea: 1913

Source: Vance H. Trimble, *Sam Walton: The Inside Story of America's Richest Man* (New York: Dutton), 1990.

1. To serve the public, as nearly as we can, to its complete satisfaction.
2. To expect for the service we render a fair remuneration and not all the profit the traffic will bear.
3. To do all in our power to pack the customer's dollar full of value, quality, and satisfaction.
4. To continue to train ourselves and our associates so that the service we give will be more and more intelligently performed.
5. To improve constantly the human factor in our business.
6. To reward men and women in our organization through participation in what the business produces.
7. To test our every policy, method, and act in this wise: "Does it square with what is right and just?"

similar discount store in a small community and in that setting, he would offer name brand merchandise at low prices and would add friendly service. Butler Brothers executives rejected the idea. The first "Wal-Mart Discount City" opened in late 1962 in Rogers, Arkansas.

15   Wal-Mart stores would sell nationally advertised, well-known brand merchandise at low prices in austere surroundings. As corporate policy, they would cheerfully give refunds, credits, and rain checks. Management conceived the firm as a "discount department store chain offering a wide variety of general merchandise to the customer." Early emphasis was placed upon opportunistic purchases of merchandise from whatever sources were available. Heavy emphasis was placed upon health and beauty aids (H&BA) in the product line and "stacking it high" in a manner of merchandise presentation. By the end of 1979, there were 276 Wal-Mart stores located in 11 states.

16   The firm developed an aggressive expansion strategy. New stores were located primarily in communities of 5,000 to 25,000 in population. The stores' sizes ranged from 30,000 to 60,000 square feet with 45,000 being the average. The firm also expanded by locating stores in contiguous geographic areas. When its discount operations came to dominate a market area, it moved to an adjoining area. While other retailers built warehouses to serve existing outlets, Wal-Mart built the distribution center first and then spotted stores all around it, pooling advertising and distribution overhead. Most stores were less than a six-hour drive from one of the company's warehouses. The first major distribution center, a 390,000 square-foot facility, opened in Searcy, Arkansas, outside Bentonville in 1978.

National Perspectives

17   At the beginning of 1991, the firm had 1,573 Wal-Mart stores in 35 states with expansion planned for adjacent states. Wal-Mart became the largest retailer and the largest discount department store in the United States.

18   As a national discount department store chain, Wal-Mart Stores, Inc. offered a wide variety of general merchandise to the customer. The stores were designed to offer one-stop shopping in 36 departments that included family apparel, health and beauty aids, household needs, electronics, toys, fabric and crafts, automotive supplies, lawn and patio, jewelry, and shoes. In addition, at certain store locations, a pharmacy, automotive supply and service center, garden center, or snack bar were also operated. The firm operated its stores with "everyday low prices" as opposed to putting heavy emphasis on special promotions, which called for multiple newspaper advertising circulars. Stores were expected to "provide the customer with a clean, pleasant, and friendly shopping experience."

19   Although Wal-Mart carried much the same merchandise, offered similar prices and operated stores that looked much like the competition, there were many differences. In the typical Wal-Mart store, employees wore blue vests to identify themselves, aisles were wide, apparel departments were carpeted in warm colors, a store employee followed customers to their cars to pick up their shopping carts, and the customer was welcomed at the door by a "people greeter" who gave directions and struck up conversations. In some cases, merchandise was bagged in brown paper sacks rather plastic bags because customers seemed to prefer them. A simple Wal-Mart logo in white letters on a brown background on the front of the store served to identify the firm. Yellow smiley faces were used on in-store displays. In consumer studies it was determined that the chain was particularly adept at striking the delicate balance needed to convince customers its prices were low without making people feel that its stores were too cheap. In many ways, competitors like Kmart sought to emulate Wal-Mart by introducing people greeters, by upgrading interiors, by developing new logos and signage, and by introducing new inventory response systems.

20 A "Satisfaction Guaranteed" refund and exchange policy was introduced to allow customers to be confident of Wal-Mart's merchandise and quality. Technological advancements like scanner cash registers, handheld computers for ordering of merchandise, and computer linkages of stores with the general office and distribution centers improved communications and merchandise replenishment. Each store was encouraged to initiate programs that would make it an integral part of the community in which it operated. Associates were encouraged to "maintain the highest standards of honesty, morality, and business ethics in dealing with the public."

THE EXTERNAL ENVIRONMENT

21 Industry analysts labeled the 1980s and early 1990s as eras of economic uncertainty for retailers. Many retailers were negatively affected by increased competitive pressures, sluggish consumer spending, slower-than-anticipated economic growth in North America, and recessions abroad. In 1995 Wal-Mart management felt the high consumer debt level caused many shoppers to reduce or defer spending on anything other than essentials. Management also felt that the lack of exciting new products or apparel trends reduced discretionary spending. Fierce competition resulted in lower margins and the lack of inflation stalled productivity increases. By 1998 the country had returned to prosperity. Unemployment was low, total income was relatively high, and interest rates were stable. Combined with a low inflation rate, buying power was perceived to be high and consumers were generally willing to buy. At the beginning of the year 2000, the United States had experienced one of the longest periods of economic expansion in its history.

22 Many retail enterprises confronted heavy competitive pressure by restructuring. Sears, Roebuck & Company, based in Chicago, became a more focused retailer by divesting itself of Allstate Insurance Company and its real estate subsidiaries. In 1993 the company announced it would close 118 unprofitable stores and discontinue the unprofitable Sears general merchandise catalog. It eliminated 50,000 jobs and began a $4 billion, five-year remodeling plan for its remaining multiline department stores. After unsuccessfully experimenting with an "everyday low-price strategy, management chose to realign its merchandise strategy to meet the needs of middle market customers, who were primarily women, by focusing on product lines in apparel, home, and automotive. The new focus on apparel was supported with the advertising campaign, "The Softer Side of Sears." A later companywide campaign broadened the appeal: "The many sides of Sears fit the many sides of your life." Sears completed its return to its retailing roots by selling off its ownership in Dean Witter Financial Services, Discovery Card, Coldwell Banker Real Estate, and Sears mortgage banking operations. In 1999 Sears refocused its marketing strategy with a new program designed to communicate a stronger wholehouse and event message. A new advertising campaign was introduced with the slogan "The good life at a great price. Guaranteed." In 2000 a new store format was introduced that concentrated on five focal areas: Appliances, Home Fashions, Tools, Kids, and Electronics. Other departments including men's and women's apparel assumed a support role in these stores.

23 The discount department store industry by the early 1990s had changed in a number of ways and was thought by many analysts to have reached maturity. Several formerly successful firms like E. J. Korvette, W. T. Grant, Atlantic Mills, Arlans, Federals, Zayre, Heck's, and Ames had declared bankruptcy and as a result either liquidated or reorganized. Venture announced liquidation in early 1998. Firms like Target Stores and Shopko

Stores began carrying more fashionable merchandise in more attractive facilities and shifted their emphasis to more national markets. Specialty retailers such as Toys "R" Us, Pier 1 Imports and Oshmans had matured and were no longer making big inroads in toys, home furnishing, and sporting goods. The "superstores" of drug and food chains were rapidly discounting increasing amounts of general merchandise. Some firms like May Department Stores Company with Caldor and Venture and Woolworth Corporation with Woolco had withdrawn from the field by either selling their discount divisions or closing them down entirely. Woolworth's remaining 122 Woolco stores in Canada were sold to Wal-Mart in 1994. All remaining Woolworth variety stores in the United States were closed in 1997.

24   Several new retail formats had emerged in the marketplace to challenge the traditional discount department store format. The superstore, a 100,000–300,000-square-foot operation, combined a large supermarket with a discount general-merchandise store. Originally a European retailing concept, these outlets where known as "malls without walls." Kmart's Super Kmart, American Fare and Wal-Mart's Supercenter Store were examples of this trend toward large operations. Warehouse retailing, which involved some combination of warehouse and showroom facilities, used warehouse principles to reduce operating expenses and thereby offer discount prices as a primary customer appeal. Home Depot combined the traditional hardware store and lumberyard with a self-service home improvement center to become the largest home center operator in the nation.

25   Some retailers responded to changes in the marketplace by selling goods at price levels (20 to 60 percent) below regular retail prices. These off-price operations appeared as two general types: (1) factory outlet stores like Burlington Coat Factory Warehouse, Bass Shoes, and Manhattan's Brand Name Fashion Outlet, and (2) independents like Loehmann's, T.J. Maxx, Marshall's, and Clothestime which bought seconds, overages, closeouts or leftover goods from manufacturers and other retailers. Other retailers chose to dominate a product classification. Some super specialists like Sock Appeal, Little Piggie, Ltd, and Sock Market, offered a single narrowly defined classification of merchandise with an extensive assortment of brands, colors, and sizes. Others, as niche specialists, like Kids Mart, a division of Venator (Woolworth) Corporation, targeted an identified market with carefully selected merchandise and appropriately designed stores. Some retailers like Silk Greenhouse (silk plants and flowers), Office Club (office supplies and equipment, and Toys "R" Us (toys) were called "category killers" because they had achieved merchandise dominance in their respective product categories. Stores like The Limited, Limited Express, Victoria's Secret, and Banana Republic became mini-department specialists by showcasing new lines and accessories alongside traditional merchandise lines.

26   Kmart Corporation, headquartered in Troy, Michigan, became the industry's third largest retailer after Sears, Roebuck & Co. and second largest discount department store chain in the United States in 1990. Kmart had 2,171 stores and $35,925 million in sales at the beginning of 2000. The firm was perceived by many industry analysts and consumers in several independent studies as a laggard. It had been the industry sales leader for a number of years and had recently announced a turnaround in profitability. In the same studies, Wal-Mart was perceived as the industry leader even though according to the *Wall Street Journal,* "they carry much the same merchandise, offer prices that are pennies apart and operate stores that look almost exactly alike." "Even their names are similar," noted the newspaper. The original Kmart concept of a "conveniently located, one-stop shopping unit where customers could buy a wide variety of quality merchandise at discount prices" had lost its competitive edge in a changing market. As one analyst noted in an industry newsletter: "They had done so well for the past 20 years without paying

EXHIBIT 2
Competitive Sales &
Store Comparison
(1990–1999)*

| Year | Kmart | | Wal-Mart | |
	Sales (000)	Stores	Sales (000)	Stores
1999	$35,925,000	2,171	$165,013,000	3,989
1998	33,674,000	2,161	137,634,000	3,999
1997	32,183,000	2,136	117,958,000	3,406
1996	31,437,000	2,261	104,859,000	3,054
1995	34,389,000	2,161	93,627,000	2,943
1994	34,025,000	2,481	82,494,000	2,684
1993	34,156,000	2,486	67,344,000	2,400
1992	37,724,000	2,435	55,484,000	2,136
1991	34,580,000	2,391	43,886,900	1,928
1990	32,070,000	2,350	32,601,594	1,721

*Number of general merchandise stores.

attention to market changes, now they have to." Kmart acquired a new president and chief executive officer in 2000. Wal-Mart and Kmart sales growth over the period 1990–1999 is reviewed in Exhibit 2. A competitive analysis is shown of four major retail firms in Exhibit 3.

27   Some retailers like Kmart had initially focused on appealing to professional, middle class consumers who lived in suburban areas and who were likely to be price sensitive. Other firms like Target, which had adopted the discount concept early, attempted to go generally after an upscale consumer. Some firms such as Fleet Farm and Pamida served the rural consumer, while firms like Value City and Ames Discount Department Stores chose to serve the urban consumer.

28   In rural communities Wal-Mart success often came at the expense of established local merchants and units of regional discount store chains. Hardware stores, family department stores, building supply outlets, and stores featuring fabrics, sporting goods and shoes were among the first to either close or relocate elsewhere. Regional discount retailers in the Sunbelt states like Roses, Howard's, T.G.& Y. and Duckwall-ALCO, who once enjoyed solid sales and earnings, were forced to reposition themselves by renovating stores, opening bigger and more modern units, re-merchandising assortments and offering lower prices. In many cases, stores like Coast-to-Coast and Ben Franklin closed upon a Wal-Mart announcement that it was planning to build in a specific community. "Just the word that Wal-Mart was coming made some stores close up," indicated one local newspaper editor.

DOMESTIC CORPORATE STRATEGIES

29   The corporate and marketing strategies that emerged at Wal-Mart were based upon a set of two main objectives that had guided the firm through its growth years. In the first objective the customer was featured, "customers would be provided what they want, when they want it, all at a value." In the second objective the team spirit was emphasized, "treating each other as we would hope to be treated, acknowledging our total dependency on our Associate-partners to sustain our success." The approach included: aggressive plans for new store openings; expansion to additional states; upgrading, relocation, refurbishing and remodeling of existing stores; and opening new distribution

EXHIBIT 3
An Industry
Comparative
Analysis (1999)

Source: Corporate Annual
Reports

	WAL-MART	SEARS	K MART	TARGET
Sales (Millions)	$165,013	$41,071	$35,925	$33,702
Net Income (Thousands)	5,377	1,453	403	1,144
Net Income Per Share	1.21	3.83	1.29	2.45
Dividends Per Share	.14	n/a	na	.40
% Sales Change	20.0%	2.7%	6.6%	9.9%

Number of Stores:

Wal-Mart United States
    Discount Stores - 1,801
    SAM'S Clubs - 463
    Supercenters - 721
Wal-Mart International
    Discount Stores - 572
    SAM'S Clubs - 49
    Supercenters - 383
Sears Roebuck & Company (all divisions)
    Sears Merchandise Group
        Full-line Department Stores - 858
        Hardware Stores - 267
        Sears Dealer Stores - 738
        Sears Auto Centers Stores - 798
        NTB National Tire & Battery Stores - 310
    Kmart Corporation
        Big Kmart - 1,860
        Traditional Kmart - 206
        Super Kmart - 105
    Target Corporation
        Target - 912
        Mervyn's - 267
        Department Stores - 64

centers. For Wal-Mart management, the 1990s were considered an era in which the firm grew to become a truly nationwide retailer which operated in all 50 states. At the beginning of 2000, Wal-Mart management predicted that over the next five years, 60–70% of sales and earnings growth would come from domestic markets with Wal-Mart stores and Supercenters, and another 10–15% from SAM'S Club and McLane. The remaining 20% of the growth would come from planned growth in international markets. As David Glass once noted, "We'll be fine as long as we never lose our responsiveness to the customer."

30   In the 1980s, Wal-Mart developed a number of new retail formats. The first SAM'S Club opened in Oklahoma City, Oklahoma, in 1983. The wholesale club was an idea which had been developed by other firms earlier but which found its greatest success and growth in acceptability at Wal-Mart. SAM'S Clubs featured a vast array of product categories with limited selection of brand and model; cash-and-carry business with limited hours; large (100,000 square foot), bare-bones facilities; rock bottom wholesale prices; and minimal promotion. The limited membership plan permitted wholesale members who bought membership and others who usually paid a percentage above the ticket price of the merchandise. A revision in merchandising strategy resulted in fewer items in the inventory mix with more emphasis on lower prices. A later acquisition of

100 Pace warehouse clubs, which were converted into SAM'S Clubs, increased that division's units by more than a third. At the beginning of 2000, there were 463 SAM'S Clubs in operation.

31   Wal-Mart Supercenters were large combination stores. They were first opened in 1988 as Hypermarket*USA, a 222,000-square-foot superstore that combined a discount store with a large grocery store, a food court of restaurants and other service businesses such as banks or video tape rental stores. A scaled down version of Hypermarket*USA was called the Wal-Mart Supercenter, similar in merchandise offerings, but with about 180,000 to 200,000 square feet of space. These expanded store concepts also included convenience stores and gasoline distribution outlets to "enhance shopping convenience." The company proceeded slowly with these plans and later suspended its plans for building any more hypermarkets in favor of the Supercenter concept. At the beginning of 2000, Wal-Mart operated 721 Supercenters. The name, Hypermarket*USA, was no longer used to identify these large stores.

32   Wal-mart also tested a new concept called the Neighborhood Market in a number of locations in Arkansas. Identified by the company as "small-marts," these green-and-white stores were stocked with fresh fruits and vegetables, a drive-up pharmacy, a 24-hour photo shop and a selection of classic Wal-Mart hard goods. Management elected to move slowly on this concept, planning to open no more than 10 a year. The goal was to ring the Superstores with these smaller stores to attract customers who were in hurry and wanted only a few items.

33   The McLane Company, Inc., a provider of retail and grocery distribution services for retail stores, was acquired in 1991. It was not considered a major segment of the total Wal-Mart operation.

34   Several programs were launched in Wal-Mart stores to "highlight" popular social causes. The "Buy American" program was a Wal-Mart retail program initiated in 1985. The theme was "Bring It Home to the USA" and its purpose was to communicate Wal-Mart's support for American manufacturing. In the program, the firm directed substantial influence to encourage manufacturers to produce goods in the United States rather than import them from other countries. Vendors were attracted into the program by encouraging manufacturers to initiate the process by contacting the company directly with proposals to sell goods that were made in the United States. Buyers also targeted specific import items in their assortments on a state-by-state basis to encourage domestic manufacturing. According to Haim Dabah, president of Gitano Group, Inc., a maker of fashion discount clothing which imported 95% of its clothing and now makes about 20% of its products here: "Wal-Mart let it be known loud and clear that if you're going to grow with them, you sure better have some products made in the U.S.A." Farris Fashion, Inc. (flannel shirts); Roadmaster Corporation (exercise bicycles); Flanders Industries, Inc. (lawn chairs); and Magic Chef (microwave ovens) were examples of vendors that chose to participate in the program.

35   From the Wal-Mart standpoint the "Buy American" program centered around value—producing and selling quality merchandise at a competitive price. The promotion included television advertisements featuring factory workers, a soaring American eagle, and the slogan: "We buy American whenever we can, so you can too." Prominent in-store signage and store circulars were also included. One store poster read: "Success Stories—These items formerly imported are now being purchased by Wal-Mart in the U.S.A."

36   Wal-Mart was one of the first retailers to embrace the concept of "green" marketing. The program offered shoppers the option of purchasing products that were better for the environment in three respects: manufacturing, use, and disposal. It was introduced through full-page advertisements in the *Wall Street Journal* and *USA Today*. In-store signage identified those products that were environmentally safe. As Wal-Mart executives saw it, "customers are concerned about the quality of land, air, and water, and would like the opportunity to do something positive." To initiate the program, 7,000 vendors were notified that Wal-Mart had a corporate concern for the environment and asked for their support in a variety of ways. Wal-Mart television advertising showed children on swings, fields of grain blowing in the wind, and roses. Green-and-white store signs, printed on recycled paper, marked products or packaging that had been developed or redesigned to be more environmentally sound.

37   The Wal-Mart private brand program began with the "Ol' Roy" brand, the private label dog food named for Sam Walton's favorite hunting companion. Introduced to Wal-Mart stores in 1982 as a low-price alterative to national brands, Ol' Roy became the biggest seller of all dog-food brands in the United States. "We are a (national) brand-oriented company first," noted Bob Connolly, Executive Vice President of merchandising of Wal-Mart. "But we also use private label to fill value or pricing void that, for whatever reason, the brands left behind. Wal-Mart's private label program included thousands of products that had brand names such as Sam's Choice, Great Value, Equate, and Spring Valley.

38   Wal-Mart had become the channel commander in the distribution of many brand name items. As the nation's largest retailer and in many geographic areas the dominant distributor, it exerted considerable influence in negotiation for the best price, delivery terms, promotion allowances, and continuity of supply. Many of these benefits could be passed on to consumers in the form of quality name brand items available at lower than competitive prices. As a matter of corporate policy, management often insisted on doing business only with producer's top sales executives rather than going through a manufacturer's representative. Wal-Mart had been accused of threatening to buy from other producers if firms refused to sell directly to it. In the ensuing power struggle, Wal-Mart executives refused to talk about the controversial policy or admit that it existed. As a representative of an industry association representing a group of sales agencies representatives suggested, "In the Southwest, Wal-Mart's the only show in town." An industry analyst added, "They're extremely aggressive. Their approach has always been to give the customer the benefit of a corporate saving. That builds up customer loyalty and market share."

39   Another key factor in the mix was an inventory control system that was recognized as the most sophisticated in retailing. A high-speed computer system linked virtually all the stores to headquarters and the company's distribution centers. It electronically logged every item sold at the checkout counter, automatically kept the warehouses informed of merchandise to be ordered and directed the flow of goods to the stores and even to the proper shelves. Most important for management, it helped detect sales trends quickly and speeded up market reaction time substantially. According to Bob Connolly, Executive Vice President of Merchandising, "Wal-Mart has used the data gathered by technology to make more inventory available in the key items that customers want most, while reducing inventories overall."

40   At the beginning of 2000, Wal-Mart set up a separate company for its website with plans to go public. Wal-Mart.com Inc., based in Palo Alto, California, was jointly owned by Wal-Mart and Accel Partners, a Silicon Valley venture-capital firm. The site included a wide range of products and services that ranged from shampoo to clothing to lawn mowers as well as airline, hotel and rental car bookings. After launching and then closing a SAM'S Club website, Wal-Mart had plans to reopen the site in mid-June 2000 with an emphasis on upscale items such as jewelry, housewares and electronics and full product lines for small business owners. SamsClub.com would be run by Wal-Mart from the company's Bentonville, Arkansas, headquarters.

INTERNATIONAL CORPORATE STRATEGIES

41 In 1994, Wal-Mart entered the Canadian market with the acquisition of 122 Woolco discount stores from Woolworth Corporation. When acquired, the Woolco stores were losing millions of dollars annually, but operations became profitable within three years. At the end of 1999, the company had 166 Wal-Mart discount stores in Canada and planned to open 17 new stores in fiscal 2000. The company's operations in Canada were considered a model for Wal-Mart's expansion into other international markets. With 35% of the Canadian discount and department store market Wal-Mart was the largest retailer in that country.

42 With a tender offer for shares and mergers of joint ventures in Mexico, the company in 1997 acquired a controlling interest in Cifra, Mexico's largest retailer. Cifra, later identified as Wal-Mart de Mexico, operated stores with a variety of concepts in every region of Mexico, ranging from the nation's largest chain of sit-down restaurants to a softline department store. Retail analysts noted that the initial venture involved many costly mistakes. Time after time it sold the wrong products, including tennis balls that wouldn't bounce in high-altitude Mexico City. Large parking lots at some stores made access difficult as many people arrived by bus. In 2000, Wal-Mart operated 397 Cifra outlets in Mexico, in addition to 27 Wal-Mart Supercenters and 34 SAM'S Club Stores.

43 When Wal-Mart entered Argentina in 1995, it also initially faced challenges adapting its U.S.-based retail mix and store layouts to the local culture. Although globalization and American cultural influences had swept through the country in the early 1990s, the Argentine market did not accept American cuts of meat, bright colored cosmetics and jewelry that gave prominent placement to emeralds, sapphires, and diamonds even though most Argentine women preferred wearing gold and silver. The first stores even had hardware departments full of tools wired for 110-volt electric power, the standard throughout Argentina was 220. Compounding the challenges was store layout that featured narrow aisles; stores appeared crowded and dirty.

44 Wal-Mart management concluded that Brazil offered great opportunities for Wal-Mart, with the fifth largest population in the world and a population that had a tendency to follow U.S. cultural cues. Although financial data was not broken out on South American operations, retail analysts cited the accounts of Wal-Mart's Brazilian partner, Lojas Americanas SA, to suggest that Wal-Mart lost $100 million in start-up costs of the initial 16 stores. Customer acceptance of Wal-Mart stores was mixed. In Canada and Mexico, many customers were familiar with the company from cross-border shopping trips. Many Brazilian customers were not familiar with the Wal-Mart name. In addition, local Brazilian markets were already dominated by savvy local and foreign competitors such as Grupo Pao de Acucar SA of Brazil and Carrefour SA of France. And Wal-Mart's insistence on doing things "the Wal-Mart way" initially alienated many local suppliers and employees. The country's continuing economic problems also presented a challenge. In 2000, Wal-Mart planned to expand its presence by opening three more SAM'S Clubs in Brazil.

45 Because of stubborn local regulations, management felt it would be easier for Wal-Mart to buy existing stores in Europe than to build new ones. The acquisition of 21 "hypermarkets" in Germany at the end of 1997 marked the company's first entry into Europe, which management considered "one of the best consumer markets in the world." These large stores offered one-stop shopping facilities similar to Wal-Mart Supercenters. In early 1999 the firm also purchased 74 Interspar hypermarket stores. All of these German stores were identified with the Wal-Mart name and restocked with a new and revamped selection of merchandise. In a response to local laws that forced early store closings and forbade Sunday sales, the company simply opened stores earlier to allow shopping to begin at 7 A.M.

46   Wal-Mart acquired ASDA, Britain's third largest supermarket group, for $10.8 billion in July 1999. With its own price rollbacks, people greeter, "permanently low prices" and even "Smiley" faces, ASDA had emulated Wal-Mart's store culture for many years. Based in Leeds, England, the firm had 232 stores in England, Scotland, and Wales. While the culture and pricing strategies of the two companies were nearly identical, there were differences, primarily the size and product mix of the stores. The average Wal-Mart Supercenter in 1999 was 180,000 square feet in size and had about 30% of its sales in groceries. In contrast, the average ASDA store had only 65,000 square feet and did 60% of sales in grocery items.

47   The response in Europe to Wal-Mart was immediate and dramatic. Competitors scrambled to match Wal-Mart's low prices, long hours and friendly service. Some firms combined to strengthen their operations. For example, France's Carrefour SA chain of hypermarkets combined forces with competitor, Promodes, in a $16.5 billion deal. In 1999, Carrefour dominated the European market with 9,089 locations. It was also one of the world's largest retailers with market dominance not only in Europe, but in Latin America and Asia as well.

48   Wal-Mart's initial effort to enter China fell apart in 1996, when Wal-Mart and Thailand's Charoen Pokphand Group terminated an 18-month-old joint venture because of management differences. Wal-Mart decided to consolidate its operations with five stores in the Hong Kong border city of Shenzhen, one in Dalian and another in Kumming. Although management had plans to open 10 additional stores in China by the end of 2000, analysts concluded that the company was taking a low profile approach because of possible competitive response and government restrictions. Beijing restricted the operations of foreign retailers in China, requiring them, for instance, to have government-backed partners. In Shenzhen, it limited the number of stores Wal-Mart could open. Planned expansion in the China market came as China prepared to enter the World Trade Organization and its economy showed signs of accelerating. At the beginning of 2000, Wal-Mart also operated five Supercenters in South Korea.

49   The international expansion accelerated management's plans for the development of Wal-Mart as a global brand along the lines of Coca-Cola, Disney, and McDonald's. "We are a global brand name," said Bobby Martin, an early president of the International Division of Wal-Mart. "To customers everywhere it means low cost, best value, greatest selection of quality merchandise and highest standards of customer service," he noted. Some changes were mandated in Wal-Mart's international operations to meet local tastes and intense competitive conditions. "We're building companies out there," said Martin. "That's like starting Wal-Mart all over again in South America or Indonesia or China." Although stores in different international markets would coordinate purchasing to gain leverage with suppliers, developing new technology and planning overall strategy would be done from Wal-Mart headquarters in Bentonville, Arkansas. At the beginning of 2000, the International Division of Wal-Mart operated 572 discount stores, 383 Supercenters and 49 SAM'S Clubs. Wal-Mart's international unit accounted for $22.7 billion in sales in 1999. Exhibit 4 shows the countries in which stores were operated and the number of units in each country.

DECISION MAKING IN A MARKET-ORIENTATED FIRM

50   One principle that distinguished Wal-Mart was the unusual depth of employee involvement in company affairs. Corporate strategies put emphasis on human resource management. Employees of Wal-Mart became "associates," a name borrowed from Sam Wal-

EXHIBIT 4
Wal-Mart International Division (1999)

Source: Wal-Mart, Hoover's Online.

Country	Stores
Mexico	460
United Kingdom	236
Canada	166
Germany	95
Brazil	16
Puerto Rico	15
Argentina	10
China	8
South Korea	5

ton's early association with the J C Penney Co. Input was encouraged at meetings at the store and corporate level. The firm hired employees locally, provided training programs, and through a "Letter to the President" program, management encouraged employees to ask questions, and made words like "we," "us," and "our" a part of the corporate language. A number of special award programs recognized individual, department, and division achievement. Stock ownership and profit-sharing programs were introduced as part of a "partnership" concept.

51   The corporate culture was recognized by the editors of the trade publication, *Mass Market Retailers,* when it recognized all 275,000 associates collectively as the "Mass Market Retailers of the Year." "The Wal-Mart associate," the editors noted, "in this decade that term has come to symbolize all that is right with the American worker, particularly in the retailing environment and most particularly at Wal-Mart." The "store within a store" concept, as a Wal-Mart corporate policy, trained individuals to be merchants by being responsible for the performance of their own departments as if they were running their own businesses. Seminars and training programs afforded them opportunities to grow within the company. "People development, not just a good 'program' for any growing company but a must to secure our future" is how Suzanne Allford, Vice President of the Wal-Mart People Division explained the firm's decentralized approach to retail management development.

52   "The Wal-Mart Way" was a phase that was used by management to summarize the firm's unconventional approach to business and the development of the corporate culture. As noted in a report referring to a recent development program: "We stepped outside our retailing world to examine the best managed companies in the United States in an effort to determine the fundamentals of their success and to 'benchmark' our own performances." The name "Total Quality Management" (TQM) was used to identify this vehicle for proliferating the very best things we do while incorporating the new ideas our people have that will assure our future." In 1999 *Discount Store News* honored Wal-Mart Stores, Inc. as "Retailer of the Century" with a commemorative 200-page issue of the magazine.

THE GROWTH CHALLENGE

53   H. Lee Scott, Jr. indicated that he would never forget his first meeting with Sam Walton. "How old are you?" Walton asked the then 30-year-old Scott, who had just taken a job overseeing Wal-Mart trucking fleet. "Do you think you can do this job?" asked Walton. When Scott said yes, Walton agreed and said "I reckon you can." More than 20 years later as Wal-Mart's new CEO, Scott was facing his toughest challenge yet: keeping the world's biggest retailer on its phenomenal roll and delivering the huge sales and earnings

increases that investors had come to expect from Wal-Mart over the years. Analysts had correctly projected that Wal-Mart would surpass General Motors to be ranked No. 1 in revenue on the *Fortune 500* list in 2000. The combination of growth and acquisition had caused revenue to make huge leaps every year. In 1999 it went up 20%, from $139 billion in 1998 to $165 billion. Earnings also increased in 1999 by 21%, to nearly $5.4 billion. Industry analysts noted that this growth was on top of an 18% compound annual growth rate over the past decade.

54   Wal-Mart Stores, Inc. revolutionized American retailing with focus on low costs, high customer service, and everyday low pricing to drive sales. Although the company had suffered through some years of lagging performance, it had experienced big gains from its move into the grocery business with one-stop supercenters and in international markets with acquisition and new ventures. To keep it all going and growing was a major challenge. As the largest retailer in the world, the company and its leadership was challenged to find new areas to continue to grow sales and profits into the future. Lee Scott knew that an ambitious expansion program was called for to allow the company to meet these objectives.

This case was prepared by James W. Camerius of Northern Michigan University and is intended to be used as a basis for class discussion rather than to illustrate either effective or ineffective handling of an administrative situation. All rights reserved to the author. Copyright © 2000 by James W. Camerius.

APPENDIX A

Wal-Mart Stores, Inc. Consolidated Balance Sheets and Operating Statements 1998–99

Consolidated Statements of Income
(Amounts in millions except per share data)

Fiscal years ended January 31,	2000	1999	1998
Revenues:			
Net sales	$ 165,013	$ 137,634	$ 117,958
Other income-net	1,796	1,574	1,341
	166,809	139,208	119,299
Costs and Expenses:			
Cost of sales	129,664	108,725	93,438
Operating, selling and general and administrative expenses	27,040	22,363	19,358
Interest Costs:			
Debt	756	529	555
Capital leases	266	268	229
	157,726	131,885	113,580
Income Before Income Taxes, Minority Interest, Equity in Unconsolidated Subsidiaries and Cumulative Effect of Accounting Change	9,083	7,323	5,719
Provision for Income Taxes			
Current	3,476	3,380	2,095
Deferred	(138)	(640)	20
	3,338	2,740	2,115
Income Before Minority Interest, Equity in Unconsolidated Subsidiaries and Cumulative Effect of Accounting Change	5,745	4,583	3,604
Minority Interest and Equity in Unconsolidated Subsidiaries	(170)	(153)	(78)
Income Before Cumulative Effect of Accounting Change	5,575	4,430	3,526
Cumulative Effect of Accounting Change, net of tax benefit of $119	(198)	-	-
Net Income	$ 5,377	$ 4,430	$ 3,526
Net Income Per Common Share:			
Basic Net Income Per Common Share:			
Income before cumulative effect of accounting change	$ 1.25	$ 0.99	$ 0.78
Cumulative effect of accounting change, net of tax	(0.04)	-	-
Net Income Per Common Share	$ 1.21	$ 0.99	$ 0.78
Average number of Common Shares	4,451	4,464	4,516
Diluted Net Income Per Common Share:			
Income before cumulative effect of accounting change	$ 1.25	$ 0.99	$ 0.78
Cummulative effect of accounting change, net of tax	(0.04)	0.00	0.00
Net Income Per Common Share	$ 1.20	$ 0.99	$ 0.78
Average number of Common Shares	4,474	4,485	4,533
Pro forma amounts assuming accounting change had been in effect in fiscal 2000, 1999 and 1998:			
Net Income	$ 5,575	$ 4,393	$ 3,517
Net income per common share, basic and diluted	$ 1.25	$ 0.96	$ 0.78

(continued)

Consolidated Balance Sheets
(Amounts in millions)

January 31,	2000	1999
Assets		
Current Assets:		
Cash and cash equivalents	$ 1,856	$ 1,879
Receivables	1,341	1,118
Inventories		
At replacement cost	20,171	17,549
Less LIFO reserve	378	473
Inventories at LIFO cost	19,793	17,076
Prepaid expenses and other	1,366	1,059
Total Current Assets	24,356	21,132
Property, Plant and Equipment, at Cost:		
Land	8,785	5,219
Building and improvements	21,169	16,061
Fixtures and equipment	10,362	9,296
Transportation equipment	747	553
	41,063	31,129
Less accumulated depreciation	8,224	7,455
Net property, plant and equipment	32,839	23,674
Property Under Capital Lease:		
Property under capital lease	4,285	3,335
Less accumulated amortization	1,155	1,036
Net property under capital leases	3,130	2,299
Other Assets and Deferred Charges:		
Net goodwill and other acquired intangible assets	9,392	2,538
Other assets and deferred charges	632	353
Total Assets	$ 70,349	$ 49,996
Liabilities and Shareholders' Equity		
Current Liabilities:		
Commercial paper	$ 3,323	$ —
Accounts payable	13,105	10,257
Accrued liabilities	6,161	4,998
Accrued income taxes	1,129	501
Long-term debt due within one year	1,964	900
Obligations under capital leases due within one year	121	106
Total Current Liabilities	25,803	16,762
Long-Term Debt	13,672	6,908
Long-Term Obligations Under Capital Leases	3,002	2,699
Deferred Income Taxes and Other	759	716
Minority Interest	1,279	1,799
Shareholders' Equity		
Preferred stock ($.10 par value; 100 shares authorized, none issued)		
Common stock ($.10 par value; 5,500 shares authorized, 4,457 and 4,448 issued and outstanding in 2000 and 1999, respectively)	446	445
Capital in excess of par value	714	435
Retained earnings	25,129	20,741
Other accumulated comprehensive income	(455)	(509)
Total Shareholders' Equity	25,834	21,112
Total Liabilities and Shareholders' Equity	$ 70,349	$ 49,996

APPENDIX B

Wal-Mart Stores, Inc. Board of Directors and Executive Officers January 31, 2000

DIRECTORS

John A. Cooper, Jr.	H. Lee Scott
Stephen Friedman	Jack C. Shewmaker
Stanley C. Gault	Donald G. Soderquist
David D. Glass	Dr. Paula Stern
Roland Hernandez	Jose Villarreal
Dr. Frederick S. Humphries	John T. Walton
E. Stanley Kroenke	S. Robson Walton
Elizabeth A. Sanders	

OFFICERS

S. Robson Walton
Chairman of the Board

H. Lee Scott
President & CEO

David D. Glass
Chairman, Executive Committee of the Board

Donald G. Soderquist
Senior Vice Chairman

Paul R. Carter
Executive V.P. & Vice President, Wal-Mart Realty

Bob Connolly
Executive Vice President Merchandise

Thomas M. Coughlin
Executive Vice President & President & CEO,
Wal-Mart Stores Division

David Dible
Executive Vice President, Speciality Division

Michael Duke
Executive Vice President, Logistics

Thomas Grimm
Executive Vice President & President & CEO,
SAM'S Club

Don Harris
Executive Vice President, Operations

John B. Menzer
Executive Vice President & President & CEO
International Division

Coleman Peterson
Executive Vice President, People Division

Thomas M. Schoewe
Executive Vice President & Chief Financial Officer

Robert K. Rhoads
Senior Vice President, General Counsel & Secretary

J.J. Fitzsimmons
Senior Vice President, Finance & Treasurer

Source: Wal-Mart Stores, Inc., 2000 Annual Report.

APPENDIX C

Wal-Mart Stores, Inc. Financial Summary 1990–2000

11-Year Financial Summary
(Dollar amounts in millions except per share data)

	2000	1999	1998
Net sales	$ 165,013	$ 137,634	$ 117,958
Net sales increase	20%	17%	12%
Comparative store sales increase	8%	9%	6%
Other income-net	1,796	1,574	1,341
Cost of sales	129,664	108,725	93,438
Operating, selling and general and administrative expenses	27,040	22,363	19,358
Interest costs:			
Debt	756	529	555
Capital leases	266	268	229
Provision for income taxes	3,338	2,740	2,115
Minority interest and equity in unconsolidated subsidiaries	(170)	(153)	(78)
Cumulative effect of accounting change, net of tax	(198)	—	—
Net income	5,377	4,430	3,526
Per share of common stock:			
Basic net income	1.21	0.99	0.78
Diluted net income	1.20	0.99	0.78
Dividends	0.20	0.16	0.14
Financial Position			
Current assets	$ 24,356	$ 21,132	$ 19,352
Inventories at replacement cost	20,171	17,549	16,845
Less LIFO reserve	378	473	348
Inventories at LIFO cost	19,793	17,076	16,497
Net property, plant and equipment and capital leases	35,969	25,973	23,606
Total assets	70,349	49,996	45,384
Current liabilities	25,803	16,762	14,460
Long-term debt	13,672	6,908	7,191
Long-term obligation under capital leases	3,002	2,699	2,483
Shareholders' equity	25,834	21,112	18,503
Financial Ratios			
Current ratio	.9	1.3	1.3
Inventories/working capital	(13.7)	3.9	3.4
Return on assets*	9.8%***	9.6%	8.5%
Return on shareholders' equity**	22.9%	22.4%	19.8%
Other Year-End Data			
Number of domestic Wal-Mart stores	1,801	1,869	1,921
Number of domestic Supercenters	721	564	441
Number of domestic SAM'S Club units	463	451	443
International units	1,004	715	601
Number of Associates	1,140,000	910,000	825,000
Number of Shareholders	341,000	261,000	246,000

*Net income before minority interest, equity in unconsolidated subsidiaries and cumulative effect of accounting change/average assets
**Net income/average shareholders' equity
***Calculated without giving effect to the amount by which a lawsuit settlement exceeded established reserves. See Management's Discussion and Analysis.

1997	1996	1995	1994	1993	1992	1991	1990
$ 104,859	$ 93,627	$ 82,494	$ 67,344	$ 55,484	$ 43,887	$ 32,602	$ 25,811
12%	13%	22%	21%	26%	35%	26%	25%
5%	4%	7%	6%	11%	10%	10%	11%
1,319	1,146	914	645	497	404	262	175
83,510	74,505	65,586	53,444	44,175	34,786	25,500	20,070
16,946	15,021	12,858	10,333	8,321	6,684	5,152	4,070
629	692	520	331	143	113	43	20
216	196	186	186	180	153	126	118
1,794	1,606	1,581	1,358	1,171	945	752	632
(27)	(13)	4	(4)	4	(1)	—	—
—	—	—	—	—	—	—	—
3,056	2,740	2,681	2,333	1,995	1,609	1,291	1,076
0.67	0.60	0.59	0.51	0.44	0.35	0.28	0.24
0.67	0.60	0.59	0.51	0.44	0.35	0.28	0.24
0.11	0.10	0.09	0.07	0.05	0.04	0.04	0.03
$ 17,993	$ 17,331	$ 15,338	$ 12,114	$ 10,198	$ 8,575	$ 6,415	$ 4,713
16,193	16,300	14,415	11,483	9,780	7,857	6,207	4,751
296	311	351	469	512	473	399	323
15,897	15,989	14,064	11,014	9,268	7,384	5,808	4,428
20,324	18,894	15,874	13,176	9,793	6,434	4,712	3,430
39,604	37,541	32,819	26,441	20,565	15,443	11,389	8,198
10,957	11,454	9,973	7,406	6,754	5,004	3,990	2,845
7,709	8,508	7,871	6,156	3,073	1,722	740	185
2,307	2,092	1,838	1,804	1,772	1,556	1,159	1,087
17,143	14,756	12,726	10,753	8,759	6,990	5,366	3,966
1.6	1.5	1.5	1.6	1.5	1.7	1.6	1.7
2.3	2.7	2.6	2.3	2.7	2.1	2.4	2.4
7.9%	7.8%	9.0%	9.9%	11.1%	12.0%	13.2%	14.8%
19.2%	19.9%	22.8%	23.9%	25.3%	26.0%	27.7%	30.9%
1,960	1,995	1,985	1,950	1,848	1,714	1,568	1,399
344	239	147	72	34	10	9	6
436	433	426	417	256	208	148	123
314	276	226	24	10	—	—	—
728,000	675,000	622,000	528,000	434,000	371,000	328,000	271,000
257,000	244,000	259,000	258,000	181,000	150,000	122,000	80,000

The effects of the change in accounting method for SAM'S Club membership revenue recognition would not have a material impact on this summary prior to 1998. Therefore, pro forma information as if the accounting change had been in effect for all years presented has not been provided. See Management's Discussion and Analysis for discussion of the impact of the accounting change in fiscal 2000, 1999 and 1998.

The acquisition of the ASDA Group PLC and the Company's related debt issuance had a significant impact on the fiscal 2000 amounts in the summary. See Notes 3 and 6 to the Consolidated Financial Statements.

Case 28

Kmart Corporation (A): Seeking Customer Acceptance and Preference

1   On June 1, 2000, the search for the new chairman and chief executive officer of Kmart Corporation was over. Charles C. Conaway, a 39-year-old drugstore chain executive, was selected to fill the position. His appointment meant that the strategic direction of Kmart would come from a man who was previously unknown outside of the drugstore industry. He would have to provide an answer to a crucial question: How can Kmart respond to the challenges of industry leader Wal-Mart Stores, Inc. in the extremely competitive arena of discount retailing?

2   As president and chief operating officer of CVS Corporation, Mr. Conaway was the No. 2 executive at the nation's largest drugstore chain, whose annual sales were about half those of Kmart's annual revenue of $36 billion. By all accounts, Mr. Conaway had made a sizable contribution in sales, earnings and market value at CVS, Inc., headquartered in Woonsocket, R.I. CVS had 1999 sales of $18 billion with 4,100 stores. Mr. Conaway, who became president and chief operating officer of CVS in 1998, was responsible for merchandising, advertising, store operations, and logistics. After joining the firm in 1992, he helped engineer the restructuring of the then parent Melville Corporation, a diversified retailer, into a successful drugstore chain. Mr. Conaway said in an interview upon assuming his new position with Kmart that his primary task would be to improve customer service, productivity of resources, and address problems with out-of-stock merchandise. Setting the stage for a new direction, Mr. Conaway said, "Customer service is going to be at the top. We're going to measure it and we're going to tie incentives around it," he noted.

3   Floyd Hall, the previous chairman, president, and chief executive officer of Kmart since June of 1995, appeared pleased with the appointment. He had announced two years earlier that he had wanted to retire, and now he would be able to do so. Mr. Hall in the last five years had restored Kmart profitability and made improvements in store appearance and merchandise selection. Analysts had noted, however, that the firm was without a definable niche in discount retailing. Studies had shown that No. 1 ranked Wal-Mart, originally a rural retailer, had continued to be known for lower prices. Target Corporation, No. 3 in sales, had staked out a niche as a merchandiser of discounted upscale products. Kmart was left without a feature that would give it competitive distinction in the marketplace.

4   Kmart's financial results reported in the fiscal first quarter of 2000 noted that net income fell 61% to $22 million. The decline ended a string of 15 consecutive quarters of profit increases that Floyd Hall felt had signaled a turnaround at the discount chain. Hall, however, was very optimistic about the company's future. The financial information over the previous periods had convinced him that a new corporate strategy that he introduced would revitalize Kmart's core business, its 2,171 discount stores, and put the company on the road to recovery. Industry analysts had noted that Kmart, once an industry leader, had posted 11 straight quarters of disappointing earnings prior to 1998 and had been dogged by persistent bankruptcy rumors. Analysts cautioned that much of Kmart's recent growth reflected the strength of the consumer economy and that uncertainty continued to exist about the company's future in a period of slower economic growth.

5   Kmart Corporation was one of the world's largest mass merchandise retailers. After several years of restructuring, it was composed largely of general merchandise businesses in the form of traditional Kmart discount department stores and Big Kmart (general merchandise and convenience items) stores as well as Super Kmart Centers (food and general merchandise). It operated in all 50 of the United States and in Puerto Rico, Guam, and the U.S. Virgin Islands. It also had equity interests in Meldisco subsidiaries of Footstar, Inc. that operated Kmart footwear departments. Measured in sales volume, it was the third largest retailer and the second largest discount department store chain in the United States.

6   The discount department store industry was perceived by many to have reached maturity. Kmart, as part of that industry, had a retail management strategy that was developed in the late 1950s and revised in the early 1990s. The firm was in a dilemma in the terms of corporate strategy. The problem was how to lay a foundation to provide a new direction that would reposition the firm in a fiercely competitive environment.

THE EARLY YEARS

7   Kmart was the outgrowth of an organization founded in 1899 in Detroit by Sebastian S. Kresge. The first S. S. Kresge store represented a new type of retailing that featured low-priced merchandise for cash in low-budget, relatively small (4,000 to 6,000 square ft.) buildings with sparse furnishings. The adoption of the "5¢ and 10¢" or "variety store" concept, pioneered by F. W. Woolworth Company in 1879, led to rapid and profitable development of what was then the S. S. Kresge Company.

8   Kresge believed it could substantially increase its retail business through centralized buying and control, developing standardized store operating procedures, and expanding with new stores in heavy traffic areas. In 1912, the firm was incorporated in Delaware. It had 85 stores with sales of $10,325,000, and, next to Woolworth's, was the largest variety chain in the world. In 1916 it was reincorporated in Michigan. Over the next 40 years, the firm experimented with mail order catalogues, full-line department stores, self-service, a number of price lines, and the opening of stores in planned shopping centers. It continued its emphasis, however, on variety stores.

9   By 1957, corporate management became aware that the development of supermarkets and the expansion of drug store chains into general merchandise lines had made inroads into market categories previously dominated by variety stores. It also became clear that a new form of store with a discount merchandising strategy was emerging.

THE CUNNINGHAM CONNECTION

10   In 1957, in an effort to regain competitiveness and possibly save the company, Frank Williams, then president of Kresge, nominated Harry B. Cunningham as general vice president. This maneuver was undertaken to free Mr. Cunningham, who had worked his way up the ranks in the organization, from operating responsibility. He was being groomed for the presidency and was given the assignment to study existing retailing businesses and recommend marketing changes.

11   In his visits to Kresge stores, and those of the competition, Cunningham became interested in discounting—particularly a new operation in Garden City, Long Island. Eugene Ferkauf had recently opened large discount department stores called E. J. Korvette. The stores had a discount mass-merchandising emphasis that featured low prices and margins, high turnover, large freestanding departmentalized units, ample parking space, and a location typically in the suburbs.

12 Cunningham was impressed with the discount concept, but he knew he had to first convince the Kresge Board of Directors, whose support would be necessary for any new strategy to succeed. He studied the company for two years and presented it with the following recommendation:

> We can't beat the discounters operating under the physical constraints and the self-imposed merchandise limitations of variety stores. We can join them—and not only join them, but with our people, procedures, and organization, we can become a leader in the discount industry.

In a speech delivered at the University of Michigan, Cunningham made his management approach clear by concluding with an admonition from the British author Sir Hugh Walpole: "Don't play for safety, it's the most dangerous game in the world."

13 The Board of Directors had a difficult job. Change is never easy, especially when the company has established procedures in place and a proud heritage. Before the first presentation to the Board could be made, rumors were circulating that one shocked senior executive had said:

> We have been in the variety business for 60 years—we know everything there is to know about it, and we're not doing very well in that, and you want to get us into a business we don't know anything about.

The Board of Directors accepted H. B. Cunningham's recommendations. When President Frank Williams retired, Cunningham became the new President and Chief Executive Officer and was directed to proceed with his recommendations.

THE BIRTH OF KMART

14 Management conceived the original Kmart as a conveniently located one-stop shopping unit where customers could buy a wide variety of quality merchandise at discount prices. The typical Kmart had 75,000 square feet, all on one floor. It generally stood by itself in a high-traffic, suburban area, with plenty of parking space. All stores had a similar floor plan.

15 The firm made an $80 million commitment in leases and merchandise for 33 stores before the first Kmart opened in 1962 in Garden City, Michigan. As part of this strategy, management decided to rely on the strengths and abilities of its own people to make decisions rather than employing outside experts for advice.

16 The original Kresge 5 & 10 variety store operation was characterized by low gross margins, high turnover, and concentration on return on investment. The main difference in the Kmart strategy would be the offering of a much wider merchandise mix.

17 The company had the knowledge and ability to merchandise 50% of the departments in the planned Kmart merchandise mix, and contracted for operation of the remaining departments. In the following years, Kmart took over most of those departments originally contracted to licensees. Eventually all departments, except shoes, were operated by Kmart.

18 By 1987, the 25th anniversary year of the opening of the first Kmart store in America, sales and earnings of Kmart Corporation were at all-time highs. The company was the world's largest discount retailer with sales of $25,627 million and operated 3,934 general merchandise and specialty stores.

19 On April 6, 1987, Kmart Corporation announced that it agreed to sell most of its remaining Kresge variety stores in the United States to McCrory Corporation, a unit of the closely held Rapid American Corporation of New York.

THE NATURE OF THE COMPETITIVE ENVIRONMENT

A Changing Marketplace

20   The retail sector of the United States economy went through a number of dramatic and turbulent changes during the 1980s and early 1990s. Retail analysts concluded that many retail firms were negatively affected by increased competitive pressures, sluggish consumer spending, slower-than-anticipated economic growth in North America, and recessions abroad. As one retail consultant noted:

> The structure of distribution in advanced economies is currently undergoing a series of changes that are as profound in their impact and as pervasive in their influence as those that occurred in manufacturing during the 19th century.

21   This changing environment affected the discount department store industry. Nearly a dozen firms like E. J. Korvette, W. T. Grant, Arlans, Atlantic Mills, and Ames passed into bankruptcy or reorganization. Some firms like Woolworth (Woolco Division) had withdrawn from the field entirely after years of disappointment. St. Louis-based May Department Stores sold its Caldor and Venture discount divisions, each with annual sales of more than $1 billion. Venture announced liquidation in early 1998.

22   Senior management at Kmart felt that most of the firms that had difficulty in the industry faced the same situation. First, they were very successful five or ten years ago but had not changed and, therefore, had become somewhat dated. Management that had a historically successful formula, particularly in retailing, was perceived as having difficulty adapting to change, especially at the peak of success. Management would wait too long when faced with a threat in the environment and then would have to scramble to regain competitiveness.

23   Wal-Mart Stores, Inc., based in Bentonville, Arkansas, was an exception. It was especially growth-oriented and had emerged in 1991 and continued in that position through 2000 as the nation's largest retailer as well as largest discount department store chain in sales volume. Operating under a variety of names and formats, nationally and internationally, it included Wal-Mart stores, Wal-Mart Supercenters, and SAM'S Warehouse Clubs. The firm found early strength in cultivating rural markets, merchandise restocking programs, "everyday low-pricing," and the control of operations through companywide computer programs that linked cash registers to corporate headquarters.

24   Sears, Roebuck & Co., in a state of stagnated growth for several years, completed a return to its retailing roots by spinning off to shareholders its $9 billion controlling stake in its Allstate Corporation insurance unit and the divestment of financial services. After unsuccessfully experimenting with an "everyday low-price" strategy, management chose to refine its merchandising program to meet the needs of middle market customers, who were primarily women, by focusing on product lines in apparel, home, and automotive.

25   Many retailers such as Target Corporation (formerly Dayton Hudson), which adopted the discount concept, attempted to go generally after an upscale customer. The upscale customer tended to have a household income of $25,000 to $44,000 annually. Other segments of the population were served by firms like Ames Department Stores, Rocky Hill, Connecticut, which appealed to outsize, older, and lower income workers, and by Shopko Stores, Inc., Green Bay, Wisconsin, which attempted to serve the upscale rural consumer.

26   Kmart executives found that discount department stores were being challenged by several other retail formats. Some retailers were assortment-oriented, with a much greater depth of assortment within a given product category. To illustrate, Toys "R" Us was an example of a firm that operated 20,000-square-foot toy supermarkets. Toys "R" Us prices were very competitive within an industry that was very competitive. When the consumers entered a Toys "R" Us facility, there was usually no doubt in their minds if the product wasn't there, no one else had it. In the late 1990s, however, Toys "R" Us was challenged by Wal-Mart and other firms that offered higher service levels, more aggressive pricing practices, and more focused merchandise selections.

27   Some retailers were experimenting with the "off-price" apparel concept where name brands and designer goods were sold at 20 to 70% discounts. Others, such as Home Depot and Menards, operated home improvement centers that were warehouse-style stores with a wide range of hard-line merchandise for both do-it-yourselfers and professionals. Still others opened drug supermarkets that offered a wide variety of high turnover merchandise in a convenient location. In these cases, competition was becoming more risk-oriented by putting three or four million dollars in merchandise at retail value in an 80,000 square-foot facility and offering genuinely low prices. Jewel-Osco stores in the Midwest, Rite Aid, CVS, and a series of independents were examples of organizations employing the entirely new concept of the drug supermarket.

28   Competition was offering something that was new and different in terms of depth of assortment, competitive price image, and format. Kmart management perceived this as a threat because these were viable businesses and hindered the firm in its ability to improve and maintain share of market in specific merchandise categories. An industry competitive analysis is shown in Exhibit 1.

EXHIBIT 1
An Industry Competitive Analysis (1999)

Source: Company annual reports.

	Kmart	Wal-Mart	Sears	Target
Sales (millions)	$35,925	$165,013	$41,071	$33,702
Net Income (millions)	403	5,575	1,453	1,144
Sales growth	6.6%	20%	2.7%	10%
Profit margin	1.1%	3.4%	2.8%	3.4%
Sales/sq.ft.	233	374	318	242
Return/equity	6.4%	22.9%	23%	19.5%
Number of Stores:				
Kmart Corporation				
Kmart Traditional Discount Stores - 202				
Big Kmart - 1,860				
Super Kmart Centers - 105				
Wal-Mart Stores, Inc. (includes international)				
Wal-Mart Discount Stores - 2,373				
Supercenters - 1,104				
SAM'S Clubs - 512				
Sears, Roebuck & Company				
Full-Line Stores - 858				
Hardware Stores - 267				
Sears Dealer Stores - 738				
Sears Automotive Stores:				
Sears Auto Centers - 798				
National Tire & Battery stores - 310				
Contract Sales				
The Great Indoors (Prototype decorating) - 2				
Target Corporation				
Target - 912				
Mervyn's - 267				
Department Store Division - 64				

EXPANSION AND CONTRACTION

29   When Joseph E. Antonini was appointed chairman of Kmart Corporation in October 1987 he was charged with the responsibility of maintaining and eventually accelerating the chain's record of growth, despite a mature retail marketplace. He moved to string experimental formats into profitable chains. As he noted:

> Our vision calls for the constant and never-ceasing exploration of new modes of retailing, so that our core business of U.S. Kmart stores can be constantly renewed and reinvigorated by what we learn from our other businesses.

30   In the mid-1970s and throughout the 1980s, Kmart became involved in the acquisition or development of several smaller new operations. Kmart Insurance Services, Inc., acquired as Planned Marketing Associates in 1974, offered a full line of life, health, and accident insurance centers located in 27 Kmart stores primarily in the South and Southwest.

31   In 1982, Kmart initiated its own off-price specialty apparel concept called Designer Depot. A total of 28 Designer Depot stores were opened in 1982, to appeal to customers who wanted quality upscale clothing at a budget price. A variation of this concept, called Garment Rack, was opened to sell apparel that normally would not be sold in Designer Depot. A distribution center was added in 1983, to supplement them. Neither venture was successful.

32   Kmart also attempted an unsuccessful joint venture with the Hechinger Company of Washington, D.C., a warehouse home center retailer. However, after much deliberation, Kmart chose instead to acquire, in 1984, Home Centers of America of San Antonio, Texas, which operated 80,000 square-foot warehouse home centers. The new division, renamed Builders Square, had grown to 167 units by 1996. It capitalized on Kmart's real estate, construction, and management expertise and Home Centers of America's merchandising expertise. Builders Square was sold in 1997 to the Hechinger Company. On June 11, 1999, Hechinger filed for Chapter 11 bankruptcy protection. As a result, Kmart recorded a noncash charge of $354 million that reflected the impact of lease obligations for former Builders Square locations that were guaranteed by Kmart.

33   Waldenbooks, a chain of 877 bookstores, was acquired from Carter, Hawley, Hale, Inc. in 1984. It was part of a strategy to capture a greater share of the market with a product category that Kmart already had in its stores. Kmart management had been interested in the book business for some time and took advantage of an opportunity in the marketplace to build on its common knowledge base. Borders Books and Music, an operator of 50 large format superstores, became part of Kmart in 1992 to form the "Borders Group," a division that would include Waldenbooks. The Borders Group, Inc. was sold during 1995.

34   The Bruno's Inc., joint venture in 1987 formed a partnership to develop large combination grocery and general merchandise stores or "hypermarkets" called American Fare. The giant, one-stop-shopping facilities of 225,000 square feet traded on the grocery expertise of Bruno's and the general merchandise of Kmart to offer a wide selection of products and services at discount prices. A similar venture, called Super Kmart Center, represented later thinking on combination stores with a smaller size and format. In 2000, Kmart operated 105 Super Kmart Centers, all in the United States.

35   In 1988, the company acquired a controlling interest in Makro Inc., a Cincinnati-based operator of warehouse "club" stores. Makro, with annual sales of about $300 million operated "member only" stores that were stocked with low-priced fresh and frozen groceries, apparel and durable goods in suburbs of Atlanta, Cincinnati, Washington, and Philadelphia. PACE Membership Warehouse, Inc., a similar operation, was acquired in 1989. The "club" stores were sold in 1994.

36 PayLess Drug Stores, a chain that operated super drug stores in a number of western states was sold in 1994 to Thrifty PayLess Holdings, Inc., an entity in which Kmart maintained a significant investment. Interests in The Sport Authority, an operator of large-format sporting goods stores, which Kmart acquired in 1990, were disposed of during 1995.

37 On the international level, an interest in Coles Myer, Ltd., Australia's largest retailer was sold in November 1994. Interests in 13 Kmart general merchandise stores in the Czech and Slovak Republics were sold to Tesco PLC at the beginning of 1996, one of the United Kingdom's largest retailers. In February 1998, Kmart stores in Canada were sold to Hudson's Bay Co., a Canadian chain of historic full-service department stores. The interest in Kmart Mexico, S.A.de C.V. was disposed of in FY 1997.

38 Founded in 1988, OfficeMax with 328 stores was one of the largest operators of high-volume, deep discount office products superstores in the United States. It became a greater than 90% owned Kmart unit in 1991. Kmart's interest in OfficeMax was sold during 1995. In November 1995, Kmart also sold its auto service center business to a new corporation controlled by Penske Corporation. In connection with the sale, Kmart and Penske entered into a sublease arrangement concerning the operation of Penske Auto Service Centers.

39 During 1999, Kmart signed agreements with SUPERVALU, Inc. and Fleming Companies, Inc. under which they would assume responsibility for the distribution and replenishment of grocery-related products to all of Kmart stores. Kmart also maintained an equity interest in Meldisco subsidiaries of Footstar, Inc., operators of footwear departments in Kmart stores.

THE MATURATION OF KMART

40 Early corporate research revealed that on the basis of convenience, Kmart served 80% of the population. One study concluded that one out of every two adults in the United States shopped at a Kmart at least once a month. Despite this popular appeal, strategies that had allowed the firm to have something for everybody were no longer felt to be appropriate for the new millennium. Kmart found that it had a broad customer base because it operated on a national basis. Its early strategies had assumed the firm was serving everyone in the markets where it was established.

41 Kmart was often perceived as aiming at the low-income consumer. The financial community believed the Kmart original customer was blue collar, low income, and upper lower class. The market served, however, was more professional and middle class because Kmart stores were initially in suburban communities where that population lived.

42 Although Kmart had made a major commitment in more recent years to secondary or rural markets, these were areas that had previously not been cultivated. The firm, in its initial strategies, perceived the rural consumer as different from the urban or suburban customer. In re-addressing the situation, it discovered that its assortments in rural areas were too limited and there were too many preconceived notions regarding what the Nebraska farmer really wanted. The firm discovered that the rural consumer didn't always shop for bib overalls and shovels but shopped for microwave ovens and the same things everyone else did.

43 One goal was not to attract more customers but to get the customer coming in the door to spend more. Once in the store the customer was thought to demonstrate more divergent tastes. The upper-income consumer would buy more health and beauty aids, cameras, and sporting goods. The lower-income consumer would buy toys and clothing.

44   In the process of trying to capture a larger share of the market and get people to spend more, the firm began to recognize a market that was more upscale. When consumer research was conducted and management examined the profile of the trade area and the profile of the person who shopped at Kmart in the past month, they were found to be identical. Kmart was predominately serving the suburban consumer in suburban locations. In 1997 Kmart's primary target customers were women, between the ages of 25 and 45 years old, with children at home and with household incomes between $20,000 and $50,000 per year. The core Kmart shopper averaged 4.3 visits to a Kmart store per month. The purchase amount per visit was $40. The purchase rate was 95% during a store visit. The firm estimated that 180 million people shopped at Kmart in an average year.

45   In "lifestyle" research in markets served by the firm, Kmart determined there were more two-income families, families were having fewer children, there were more working wives, and customers tended to be homeowners. Customers were very careful how they spent their money and were perceived as wanting quality. This was a distinct contrast to the 1960s and early 1970s, which tended to have the orientation of a "throw away" society. The customer had said, "What we want is products that will last longer. We'll have to pay more for them but will still want them and at the lowest price possible." Customers wanted better quality products but still demanded competitive prices. According to a Kmart Annual Report, "Consumers today are well-educated and informed. They want good value and they know it when they see it. Price remains a key consideration, but the consumers' new definition of value includes quality as well as price."

46   Corporate management at Kmart considered the discount department store to be a mature idea. Although maturity was sometimes looked on with disfavor, Kmart executives felt that this did not mean a lack of profitability or lack of opportunity to increase sales. The industry was perceived as being "reborn." It was in this context, in the 1990s, that a series of new retailing strategies, designed to upgrade the Kmart image, were developed.

THE 1990 RENEWAL PROGRAM

47   The strategies that emerged to confront a changing environment were the result of an overall reexamination of existing corporate strategies. This program included: accelerated store expansion and refurbishing, capitalizing on dominant lifestyle departments, centralized merchandising, more capital investment in retail automation, an aggressive and focused advertising program, and continued growth through new specialty retail formats.

48   The initial 1990, five-year, $2.3 billion program involved virtually all Kmart discount stores. There would be approximately 250 new full-size Kmart stores, 620 enlargements, 280 relocations, and 30 closings. In addition 1,260 stores would be refurbished to bring their layout and fixtures up to new store standards. Another program, introduced in 1996, resulted in an additional $1.1 billion being spent to upgrade Kmart stores. By year-end 1999, 1,860 new "Big Kmart" stores offered more pleasant shopping experiences thanks to the updated and easy-to-shop departmental adjacencies, better signing, lighting, wider aisles, and more attractive in-store presentation.

49   One area receiving initial attention was improvement in the way products were displayed. The traditional Kmart layout was by product category. Often these locations for departments were holdovers from the variety store. Many departments would not give up prime locations. As part of the new marketing strategy, the shop concept was introduced. Management recognized that it had a sizable "do-it-yourself" store. As planning management discussed the issue, "nobody was aware of the opportunity. The hardware department was right smack in the center of the store because it was always there. The paint

department was over here and the electrical department was over there." "All we had to do," management contended, "was put them all in one spot and everyone could see that we had a very respectable 'do-it-yourself' department." The concept resulted in a variety of new departments such as "Soft Goods for the Home," "Kitchen Korners," and "Home Electronic Centers." The goal behind each department was to sell an entire lifestyle-orientated concept to consumers, making goods complementary so shoppers would want to buy several interrelated products rather than just one item.

50   Name brands were added in soft and hard goods as management recognized that the customer transferred the product quality of branded goods to perceptions of private label merchandise. In the eyes of Kmart management, "if you sell Wrangler, there is good quality. Then the private label must be good quality." The company increased its emphasis on trusted national brands such as Rubbermaid, Procter & Gamble, and Kodak, and put emphasis on major strategic vendor relationships. In addition it began to enhance its private label brands such as Kathy Ireland, Jaclyn Smith, Route 66, and Sesame Street in apparel. Additional private label merchandise included K Gro in home gardening, American Fare in grocery and consumables, White-Westinghouse in appliances, and Penske Auto Centers in automotive services. Some private labels were discontinued following review.

51   Kmart hired Martha Stewart, an upscale Connecticut author of lavish best-selling books on cooking and home entertaining, as its "lifestyle spokesperson and consultant." Martha Stewart was featured as a corporate symbol for housewares and associated products in advertising and in store displays. Management visualized her as the next Betty Crocker, a fictional character created some years ago by General Mills. Inc., and a representative of its interest in "lifestyle" trends. The "Martha Stewart Everyday" home fashion product line was introduced in 1995 and expanded in 1996 and 1997. A separate division was established to manage strategy for all Martha Stewart label goods and programs. Merchandise was featured in the redesigned once-a-week Kmart newspaper circular that carried the advertising theme "The quality you need, the price you want."

52   Several thousand prices were reduced to maintain "price leadership across America." As management noted, "it is absolutely essential that we provide our customers with good value—quality products at low prices." Although lowering of prices hurt margins and contributed importantly to an earnings decline, management felt that unit turnover of items with lowered prices increased significantly to "enable Kmart to maintain its pricing leadership that will have a most positive impact on our business in the years ahead."

53   A "centralized merchandising system" was introduced to improve communication. A computerized, highly automated replenishment system tracked how quickly merchandise sold and, just as quickly, put fast-moving items back on the shelves. Satellite capability and a Point-of-Sale (POS) scanning system were introduced as part of the program. Regular, live satellite communication from Kmart headquarters to the stores would allow senior management to communicate with store managers and allow for questions and answers. The POS scanning system allowed a record of every sale and transmission of the data to headquarters. This enabled Kmart to respond quickly to what's new, what's in demand, and what would keep customers coming back.

54   The company opened its first Super Kmart Center in 1992. The format combined general merchandise and food with emphasis upon customer service and convenience and ranged in size from 135,000 to 190,000 square feet with more than 40,000 grocery items. The typical Super Kmart operated 7 days a week, 24 hours a day and generated high traffic and sales volume. The centers also featured wider shopping aisles, appealing displays and pleasant lighting to enrich the shopping experience. Super Kmarts featured in-house bakeries, USDA fresh meats, fresh seafood, delicatessens, cookie kiosks, cappuccino bars, in-store eateries and food courts, and fresh carry-out salad bars.

55   In many locations, the center provided customer services like video rental, dry cleaning, shoe repair, beauty salons, optical shops, express shipping services, as well as a full line of traditional Kmart merchandise. To enhance the appeal of the merchandise assortment, emphasis was placed on "cross merchandising." For example, toasters were featured above the fresh baked breads, kitchen gadgets were positioned across the aisle from produce and baby centers featured everything from baby food to toys. At the end of 1999, the company operated 105 Super Kmart stores.

THE PLANNING FUNCTION

56   Corporate planning at Kmart was the result of executives, primarily the senior executive, recognizing change. The role played by the senior executive was to get others to recognize that nothing is good forever. "Good planning" was perceived as the result of those who recognized that at some point they would have to get involved. "Poor Planning," was done by those who didn't recognize the need for it. When they did, it was too late to survive. Good planning, if done on a regular and timely basis, was assumed to result in improved performance. Kmart's Michael Wellman, then Director of Planning and Research, contended, "planning, as we like to stress, is making decisions now to improve performance tomorrow. Everyone looks at what may happen tomorrow, but the planners are the ones who make decisions today. That's where I think too many firms go wrong. They think they are planning because they are writing reports and are aware of changes. They don't say, 'because of this, we must decide today to spend this money to do this to accomplish this goal in the future.'"

57   Kmart management believed that the firm had been very successful in the area of strategic planning. "When it became necessary to make significant changes in the way we were doing business" Michael Wellman suggested, "that was accomplished on a fairly timely basis." When the organization made the change in the 1960s, it recognized there was a very powerful investment opportunity and capitalized on it—far beyond what anyone else would have done. "We just opened stores," he continued, "at a great, great pace. Management, when confronted with a crisis, would state, 'It's the economy, or it's this, or that, but it's not the essential way we are doing business.'" He noted, "Suddenly management would recognize that the economy may stay like this forever. We need to improve the situation and then do it." Strategic planning was thought to arise out of some difficult times for the organization.

58   Kmart had a reasonably formal planning organization that involved a constant evaluation of what was happening in the marketplace, what competition was doing, and what kinds of opportunities were available. Management felt a need to diversify because it would not be a viable company unless it was growing. Management felt it was not going to grow with the Kmart format forever. It needed growth and opportunity, particularly for a company that was able to open 200 stores on a regular basis. Michael Wellman, Director of Planning and Research, felt that, "Given a 'corporate culture' that was accustomed to challenges, management would have to find ways to expend that energy. A corporation that is successful," he argued, "has to continue to be successful. It has to have a basic understanding of corporate needs and be augmented by a much more rigorous effort to be aware of what's going on in the external environment."

59   A planning group at Kmart represented a number of functional areas of the organization. Management described it as an "in-house consulting group" with some independence. It was made up of (1) financial planning, (2) economic and consumer analysis, and (3) operations research. The chief executive officer (CEO) was identified as the primary planner of the organization.

REORGANIZATION AND RESTRUCTURING

60 Kmart financial performance for 1993 was clearly disappointing. The company announced a loss of $974 million on sales of $34,156,000 for the fiscal year ended January 26, 1994. Chairman Antonini, noting the deficit, felt it occurred primarily because of lower margins in the U.S. Kmart stores division. "Margin erosion," he said, "stemmed in part from intense industrywide pricing pressure throughout 1993." He was confident, however, that Kmart was on track with its renewal program to make the more than 2,350 U.S. Kmart stores more "competitive, on-trend, and cutting merchandisers." Tactical Retail Solutions, Inc., estimated that during Mr. Antonini's seven-year tenure with the company, Kmart's market share in the discount arena fell to 23% from 35%. Other retail experts suggested that because the company had struggled for so long to have the right merchandise in the stores at the right time, it had lost customers to competitors. An aging customer base was also cited.

61 In early 1995, following the posting of its eighth consecutive quarter of disappointing earnings, Kmart's Board of Directors announced that Joseph Antonini would be replaced as chairman. It named Donald S. Perkins, former chairman of Jewel Companies, Inc. and a Kmart director, to the position. Mr. Antonini relinquished his position as president and chief executive officer in March. After a nationwide search, Floyd Hall, 57, and former chairman and CEO of the Target discount store division of the Dayton-Hudson Corporation, was appointed chairman, president and chief executive officer of Kmart in June of 1995.

62 The company concluded the disposition of many noncore assets in 1996, including the sale of the Borders group, OfficeMax, the Sports Authority, and Coles Myer. During the 1990s, it also closed a large number of underperforming stores in the United States, and cleared out $700 million in aged and discontinued inventory in the remaining stores.

63 In 1996, Kmart converted 152 of its traditional stores to feature a new design that was referred to as the high-frequency format. These stores were named Big Kmart. The stores emphasized those departments that were deemed most important to core customers and offered an increased mix of high frequency, everyday basics and consumables in the pantry area located at the front of each store. These items were typically priced at a one to three percentage differential from the leading competitors in each market and served to increase inventory turnover and gross margin dollars. In an addition to the pantry area, Big Kmart stores featured improved lighting, new signage that was easier to see and read, and adjacencies that created a smoother traffic flow. In 1999, 588 stores were converted to the new Big Kmart format bringing the total to 1,860. Other smaller stores would be updated to a "best of Big Kmart" prototype.

64 Kmart launched its first e-commerce site in 1998. The initial Kmart.com offered a few products and was not considered a successful venture. In 1999, it partnered with SOFT-BANK Venture Capital, who provided technical expertise, experienced personnel and initial capital to create an Internet site 60% owned by Kmart. BlueLight.com increased the number of Kmart products it offered online to about 65,000 from 1,250. It planned to boost the number to 100,000 by year-end 2000 and possibly to millions of items in the future.

65 Major changes were made to the management team. In total, 23 of the company's 37 corporate officers were new to the company's team since 1995. The most dramatic restructuring had taken place in the merchandising organization where all four of the general merchandise managers responsible for buying organizations joined Kmart since 1995. In addition, 15 new divisional vice presidents joined Kmart during 1997. Significant changes also were made to the Board of Directors with 9 of 15 directors new to the company since 1995. A list of the Board of Directors and corporate officers at the beginning of 2000 is shown in Appendix D.

66   At the end of his tenure, Floyd Hall announced that the company mandate in the year and century ahead was to create sustained growth that would profitably leverage all of the core strengths of the firm. The corporate mission in 2000 was "to become the discount store of choice for low- and middle-income households by satisfying their routine and seasonal shopping needs as well as or better than the competition." Management believed that the actions taken by Charles Conaway, the new president, would have a dramatic impact on how customers perceived Kmart, how frequently they shopped in the stores, and how much they would buy on each visit. Increasing customer's frequency and the amount they purchased each visit were seen as having a dramatic impact on the company's efforts to increase its profitability.

This case was prepared by James W. Camerius, Northern Michigan University, and is intended to be used as a basis for class discussion rather than to illustrate either effective or ineffective handling of an administrative situation. All rights reserved to the author. Copyright © 2000 by James W. Camerius.

APPENDIX A

Kmart Corporation
Consolidated Balance Sheets and Operating Statements 1998–99

Years Ended January 26, 2000, January 27, 1999 and January 28, 1998	1999	1998	1997
Sales	$ 35,925	$ 33,674	$32,183
Cost of sales, buying and occupancy	28,102	26,319	25,152
Gross margin	7,823	7,355	7,031
Selling, general and administrative expenses	6,523	6,245	6,136
Voluntary early retirement programs	—	19	114
Continuing income before interest, income taxes and dividends on convertible preferred securities of subsidiary trust	1,300	1,091	781
Interest expense, net	280	293	363
Income tax provision	337	230	120
Dividends on convertible preferred securities of subsidiary trust, net of income taxes of $27, $27 and $26	50	50	49
Net income from continuing operations	633	518	249
Discontinued operations, net of income taxes of $(124)	(230)	—	—
Net income	$ 403	$ 518	$ 249
Basic earnings per common share			
Net income from continuing operations	$ 1.29	$ 1.05	$ .51
Discontinued operations	(.47)	—	—
Net income	$ .82	$ 1.05	$ .51
Diluted earnings per common share			
Net income from continuing operations	$ 1.22	$ 1.01	$ .51
Discontinued operations	(.41)	—	—
Net income	$ .81	$ 1.01	$ .51
Basic weighted average shares (millions)	491.7	492.1	487.1
Diluted weighted average shares (millions)	561.7	564.9	491.7

As of January 26, 2000 and January 27, 1999	1999	1998
Current Assets		
Cash and cash equivalents	$ 344	$ 710
Merchandise inventories	7,101	6,536
Other current assets	715	584
Total current assets	8,160	7,830
Property and equipment, net	6,410	5,914
Other assets and deferred charges	534	422
Total Assets	$15,104	$14,166
Current Liabilities		
Long-term debt due within one year	$ 66	$ 77
Trade accounts payable	2,204	2,047
Accrued payroll and other liabilities	1,574	1,359
Taxes other than income taxes	232	208
Total current liabilities	4,076	3,691
Long-term debt and notes payable	1,759	1,538
Capital lease obligations	1,014	1,091
Other long-term liabilities	965	883
Company obligated mandatorily redeemable convertible preferred securities of a subsidiary trust holding solely 7-3/4% convertible junior subordinated debentures of Kmart (redemption value of $1,000)	986	984
Common stock, $1 par value, 1,500,000,000 shares authorized; 481,383,569 and 493,358,504 shares issued, respectively	481	493
Capital in excess of par value	1,555	1,667
Retained earnings	4,268	3,819
Total Liabilities and Shareholders' Equity	$15,104	$14,166

APPENDIX B

Kmart Corporation
Financial Performance 1990–1999

Year	Sales (000)	Assets (000)	Net Income (000)	Net Worth (000)
1990	$32,070,000	$13,899,000	$756,000	$5,384,000
1991	34,580,000	15,999,000	859,000	6,891,000
1992	37,724,000	18,931,000	941,000	7,536,000
1993	34,156,000	17,504,000	(974,000)	6,093,000
1994	34,025,000	17,029,000	296,000	6,032,000
1995	31,713,000	15,033,000	(571,000)	5,280,000
1996	31,437,000	14,286,000	(220,000)	6,146,000
1997	32,183,000	13,558,000	249,000	6,445,000
1998	33,674,000	14,166,000	518,000	6,963,000
1999	35,925,000	15,104,000	403,000	7,290,000

Source: *Fortune* financial analysis and Kmart Annual Reports.

Note: After taxes and extraordinary credit or charges. Data from 1995, 1996 and 1997 reflects disposition of subsidiaries.

APPENDIX C

Financial Performance
Wal-Mart Stores, Inc. 1990–1999

Year	Sales (000)	Assets (000)	Net Income (000)	Net Worth (000)
1990	$32,601,594	$11,388,915	$1,291,024	$ 5,365,524
1991	43,886,900	15,443,400	1,608,500	6,989,700
1992	55,484,000	20,565,000	1,995,000	8,759,000
1993	67,344,000	26,441,000	2,333,000	10,753,000
1994	82,494,000	32,819,000	2,681,000	12,726,000
1995	93,627,000	37,541,000	2,740,000	14,756,000
1996	104,859,000	39,604,000	3,056,000	17,143,000
1997	117,958,000	45,384,000	3,526,000	18,503,000
1998	137,634,000	49,996,000	4,393,000	21,112,000
1999	165,013,000	70,349,000	5,575,000	25,834,000

Source: Wal-Mart annual reports/*Fortune* financial analysis.

APPENDIX D

Corporate Officers
Kmart Corporation March 27, 2000

Board of Directors

James B. Adamson, [1*]
Chairman, President and Chief
Executive Officer, Advantica
Restaurant Group

Lilyan N. Affinito [1,3,5]
Former Vice Chairman of the
Board, Maxxam Group Inc.

Stephen F. Bollenbach [4*]
President and Chief Executive
Officer, Hilton Hotels Corporation

Joseph A. Califano, Jr. [4]
Chairman and President, The
National Center on Addiction and
Substance Abuse at Columbia
University

Richard G. Cline [2,3,5]
Chairman, Hawthorne
Investors, Inc., Chairman,
Hussmann International, Inc.

Willie D. Davis [2]
President, All Pro Broadcasting, Inc.

Joseph P. Flannery [3,4,5]
Chairman of the Board, President
and Chief Executive Officer,
Uniroyal Holding, Inc.

Floyd Hall [3*]
Chairman of the Board, President
and Chief Executive Officer,
Kmart Corporation

Robert D. Kennedy [2*]
Former Chairman of the Board and
Chief Executive Officer, Union
Carbide Corporation

J. Richard Munro [3,4,5]
Former Co-Chairman of the Board
and Co-Chief Executive Officer,
Time Warner Inc.

Robin B. Smith [1,5*]
Chairman and Chief Executive
Officer, Publishers Clearing House

Thomas Stallkamp [4]
Vice Chairman and Chief Executive
Officer, MSX International

James O. Welch, Jr. [2]
Former Vice Chairman, RJR
Nabisco Inc. and Chairman,
Nabisco Brands, Inc.

Committees:
1 = Audit
2 = Compensation & Incentives
3 = Executive
4 = Finance
5 = Directors and Corporate
Governance
* = Committee Chair

Corporate Officers (as of March 27, 2000)

Floyd Hall
Chairman of the Board, President,
Chief Executive Officer

Michael Bozic
Vice Chairman

Andrew A. Giancamilli
President and General
Merchandise Manager, U.S. Kmart

Donald W. Keeble
President, Store Operations, U.S.
Kmart

Warren F. Cooper
Executive Vice President, Human
Resources and Administration

Ernest L. Heether
Senior Vice President, Merchandise
Planning and Replenishment

Paul J. Hueber
Senior Vice President, Store
Operations

Cecil B. Kearse
Senior Vice President, General
Merchandise Manager - Home

Larry E. Carlson
Vice President, Real Estate Market
Strategy

Ronald J. Chomiuk
Vice President, General Merchandise
Manager -
Pharmacy/HBC/Cosmetics/Photo
Finishing

Timothy M. Crow
Vice President, Compensation,
Benefits, Workers Compensation
and HRIS

Larry C. Davis
Vice President, Advertising

David R. Fielding
Vice President, Northwest Region

Larry J. Foster
Vice President, Training and
Organizational Development

G. William Gryson, Jr.
Vice President, Special Projects

Walter E. Holbrook
Vice President, Southeast Region

Shawn M. Kahle
Vice President, Corporate Affairs

Harry Meeth, III
Vice President, Design and
Construction

Douglas M. Meissner
Vice President, Northeast Region

James L. Misplon
Vice President, Taxes

Ann A. Morgan
Vice President, Field Human
Resources

Lorna E. Nagler
Vice President, General Merchandise
Manager - Kidsworld and
Menswear

Gary J. Ruffing
Vice President, Merchandise
Presentation and Communication

Lucinda C. Sapienza
Vice President, General Merchandise
Manager - Ladieswear, Fashion
Accessories and Lingerie

David L. Schuvie
Vice President, Electronic Sales and
Services

Brent C. Scott
Vice President, Grocery Operations

Jerome J. Kuske
Senior Vice President, General
Merchandise Manager - Hardlines

James P. Mixon
Senior Vice President, Logistics

Joseph A. Osbourn
Senior Vice President and Chief
Information Officer

E. Jackson Smailes
Senior Vice President, General
Merchandise Manager - Apparel

Martin E. Welch III
Senior Vice President and Chief
Financial Officer

Lorrence T. Kellar
Vice President, Real Estate

Nancie W. LuDuke
Vice President and Secretary

Ronald Lulla
Vice President, Merchandise
Controller

Thomas W. Lemke
Vice President, Data Base Marketing

Michael P. Lynch
Vice President, Southwest Region

Michael T. Macik
Vice President, Human Resources
and Labor and Associate Relations

Lee L. Maniago
Vice President, Mideast Region

David R. Marsico
Vice President, Store Operations

Stephen E. Sear
Vice President, Facilities
Management and Corporate
Purchasing

Stephen W. St. John
Vice President, Great Lakes Region

E. Anthony Vaal
Vice President, Global Operations,
Corporate Brands and Quality
Assurance

John S. Valenti
Vice President, Southern Region

Leland M. Viliborghi
Vice President, Central Region

Michael J. Viola
Vice President and Treasurer

Francis J. Yanak
Vice President, General Merchandise
Manager - Food and Consumables

Kmart (B): Bankruptcy 2002

67   Directors of the Troy (Mich.) discount giant hoped the Jan. 17, 2002 firing of its president and chief operating officer, along with the appointment of a respected board member as chairman, would keep the vultures away long enough for it to secure a much-needed line of credit.

68   In the face of intense market speculation that the company was headed for bankruptcy, Kmart named director James B. Adamson, former chairman and CEO of Advantica Restaurant Group, as its chairman, stripping CEO Charles C. Conaway of that title. The company also dismissed Mark S. Schwartz, a former Wal-Mart executive, as president and chief operating officer. "Kmart's board continues to have confidence in Mr. Conaway's ability to lead the company as its CEO," said spokesman Jack Ferry. Even so, Conaway, 41, was on thin ice. Despite an ambitious turnaround plan he began in autumn 2000, Kmart fell further behind discount rivals Wal-Mart Stores and Target. After a dismal 2001 holiday shopping season, Kmart went back to the drawing board to revise its business plan. Analysts predicted a major restructuring, including the closing of hundreds of underperforming stores. Even the night before news of the management changes was made public, company executives began contacting major suppliers to enlist their support for a financial restructuring outside of bankruptcy court. Kmart desperately needed their cooperation to ensure that its stores remain fully stocked while it rethinks its stalled turnaround strategy.

69   The board's goal in announcing the management shakeup, say sources close to the company, was to persuade suppliers, banks, and investors that Kmart intends to work through its cash difficulties without seeking bankruptcy protection. "We're trying to do everything we can to avoid it," said one insider. Instead, industry sources say Kmart is asking a group of banks, led by J. P. Morgan Chase, for as much as $3 billion in loans secured by Kmart inventory.

70   The decision to try to avert a bankruptcy filing was a reflection of the board's confidence in Adamson, the former head of the Burger King and Denny's restaurant chains. His role in helping lead turnarounds at Denny's and the Revco drugstore chain gives him the credibility on Wall Street that Conaway lacks. Besides his expertise in managing troubled companies, he also has much-needed marketing and merchandising experience from his earlier days at Revco and at Kmart's discount rival, Target.

71   Putting Adamson in charge was "a brilliant move by the board," according to Burt Flickinger, managing director of Reach Marketing, a strategic consulting firm that works with retailers and major consumer products companies. "Jim Adamson is one of the great turnaround specialists in the history of modern retailing."

72   The dismissal of Schwartz as chief operating officer was no surprise. The 16-year Wal-Mart veteran who managed the rapid growth of that company's grocery supercenters in the early 90s is widely considered the architect of Kmart's ill-conceived strategy to engage Wal-Mart in a price war in 2001.

73   "Schwartz started the food fight with Wal-Mart and a price war that was unwinnable," said Flickinger. Schwartz, as chief operating officer, was also blamed for Kmart's bloated inventories. He purchased too much merchandise in anticipation of sales growth that didn't materialize, said one insider. Schwartz couldn't be reached for comment.

74   Industry insiders agree that if the company is going to save itself, it must radically alter its turnaround strategy. Instead of attacking main competitor Wal-Mart Stores head-on, Kmart must carve out a less competitive niche for itself. And, they say, the retailer must quickly shutter underperforming stores. "It's a nail-biter," says Sanford Bernstein analyst Emme Kozloff.

75   Although he put in a successful stint as president of CVS before joining Kmart in June 2000, Conaway has had trouble making headway at the retailer. Early moves to improve inventory control and customer service proved smart, but Conaway also has made costly mistakes. His initial strategy was to get more shoppers into stores by lowering prices to match Wal-Mart on more than 30,000 basic items such as toothpaste and diapers. The move backfired when Wal-Mart responded by dropping its own prices even further.

76   Meanwhile, Conaway cut the size of Kmart's advertising inserts in Sunday newspapers: He viewed them as costly and inefficient. But with advertising down, Kmart attracted even fewer shoppers as the economy worsened.

77   The sorry result: In the quarter ended Oct. 31, 2001 Kmart lost $224 million, as sales fell 2.2%. Worse, in the crucial December 2001 month, its sales fell 1% as Wal-Mart's surged 8% and Target's rose 0.6%.

78   How can Conaway reverse Kmart's slide? One no-brainer: He could dump unprofitable stores instead of trying to fix them. Kmart has identified a group of 250 poor-performing outlets. While some estimate that closing them would cost about $1 billion, such a move would let the company direct resources toward more promising urban stores catering to Latino and African American consumers.

79   That move will take time, but the company also plans to quickly redouble efforts to promote its private-label brands Martha Stewart Everyday, Sesame Street, and Route 66 clothing. Martha Stewart sales alone grew 25% last year, to $1.5 billion. And with a new seven-year contract that provides increased royalties and minimum sales guarantees, Stewart's company seems solidly behind Conaway's turnaround effort. Says Sharon Patrick, president of Martha Stewart Living Omnimedia: "You have to credit him with taking on the monster."

ONE WEEK LATER . . .

80   Does America need Kmart? That's what really matters in the wake of the giant discount chain's bankruptcy filing on Jan. 22, 2002. Certainly, the opportunity for a swift financial makeover is a plus. By keeping creditors at bay, Kmart is free to close underperforming stores, walk away from bad leases, and trim debt. But what then? Unless Kmart Corp. can give consumers a good reason to shop at its stores, the once-mighty retailer will slide into oblivion.

81   There's little doubt that Kmart, based in Troy, Mich., will survive the largest-ever retail bankruptcy—at least for a while. But to thrive in the long run, it has to face some uncomfortable truths. First, it has to accept the reality that it has long since lost the battle with Wal-Mart Stores Inc. Its bigger competitor is both ubiquitous and light-years more efficient. Trying to compete on price last year was a colossal error. However much Kmart cuts prices, Wal-Mart can cut more. Kmart has to be more than a Wal-Mart wannabe if it wants to survive.

82   Second, a healthy Kmart very likely means a smaller Kmart. The discounter should close at least 250 of its 2,114 stores. Five hundred would be even better. Then it needs to carve out a niche between Wal-Mart and Target Corp., the purveyor of cheap chic. Most of all it has to capitalize on its urban locations.

83   CEO Charles C. Conaway laid out his vision for Kmart soon after arriving in June 2000. His plan: to make Kmart "the authority for moms, home, and kids." But grappling with Kmart's myriad operational problems, from logistics to technology, has left precious little time for bonding with moms. To make his fuzzy description of the new Kmart mean something, Conaway must pump new life into tired apparel lines, such as the Jaclyn Smith and Kathy Ireland labels, and add more exclusive brands like Martha Stewart Everyday.

EXHIBIT 1
Four Corner Stones Experts Say a Bankrupt Kmart's Strategy Must Include

- Add full-line groceries to core urban stores
- Develop more unique brands like Martha Stewart
- Fix nagging supply chain problems
- Improve marketing, to give consumers a reason to shop

84   Kmart's best hope for survival lies in a core group of several hundred stores in urban areas, far from any Wal-Mart and Target outlets. "Their urban locations provide a level of convenience that's potentially unmatched," says Sanford C. Bernstein & Co. analyst Emme P. Kozloff. "Wal-Mart and Target won't go into those areas." Plus, she adds, Kmart has very low-cost, long-term leases on those stores. Kmart hopes to dramatically boost sales and profits at its urban stores by adding a full assortment of groceries—including fresh meat, produce, and bakery products—tailored to each community's ethnic mix. If Kmart executes this play correctly, it stands a good chance of success.

85   But that's a big if. Kmart has been experimenting with food for a decade but has lacked the resources and the focus to make it work. Today it has just 124 supercenters, compared with 1,060 Wal-Mart supercenters. That's one reason Wal-Mart zoomed past Kmart in sales. Shoppers visit supercenters two or three times a week, compared with three times a month for a typical discount store.

86   Here again, Kmart has to avoid the temptation to try to out-Wal-Mart Wal-Mart. In a hopeful sign, Kmart is dusting off a strategy cooked up four years ago that it never implemented. Instead of rolling out 140,000-square-foot grocery-discount-store combos, it is converting smaller stores to the Super Kmart format. The strategy makes sense for urban stores where real estate prices are high. At $2.5 million to $5 million per store, the conversion is a bargain, compared with the cost of building a giant new outlet.

87   But it's a balancing act. To shoehorn a full grocery into an existing Kmart, the company has to pare back on general merchandise. The trick is doing it so customers don't notice anything is missing. Done correctly, sales can actually increase, says James Funk, a district manager in Michigan for Super Kmart. At one store in Bloomfield Hills, for instance, Funk cut the electronics department by more than 15%—and sales grew nearly threefold.

88   In neighborhoods starved for decent grocery stores, Kmart's urban supercenters could be a hit. But their success depends on flawless execution, something Kmart has not been known for. And it still has the rest of its stores to fix up. Clearly, Kmart has lots of work ahead before investors have something to feast on.

Created by Richard Robinson, University of South Carolina, based on "One More Strategy Shift for Kmart," *BusinessWeek,* January 18, 2002; and "Kmart: Find a Niche," *BusinessWeek,* February 4, 2002.

Kmart Financials Through 2001

Revenue

Revenue bar chart (Millions of Dollars):
- '97: $31,437 ▼9%
- '98: $32,183 ▲2%
- '99: $33,674 ▲5%
- '00: $35,925 ▲7%
- '01: $37,028 ▲3%

▲ Millions of Dollars

Net Income

Net Income bar chart (Millions of Dollars):
- '97: ($220) ▲58%
- '98: $249 ▲213%
- '99: $518 ▲108%
- '00: $403 ▼22%
- '01: ($244) ▼161%

▲ Millions of Dollars

Profit Margin

Profit Margin chart:
- '97: (0.7%)
- '98: 0.8%
- '99: 1.5%
- '00: 1.1%
- '01: (0.7%)

▲ Profit margin is net income divided by revenue.

Return on Equity

Return on Equity chart:
- '97: ne
- '98: 4.6%
- '99: 8.7%
- '00: 6.4%
- '01: ne

▲ Return on equity is net income divided by shareholders equity.

Valuation

Source: MGFS

For valuation purposes, this table compares Kmart with its Industry (Discount, Variety Stores) as well as with over 7,000 other companies in the Media General Market Index (Market).

Relative Size	KM	Industry	
Revenue *2001, Million $*	$37,028	$354,579	
Net Income *2001, Million $*	($244)	$8,243	

Price Multiples	KM	Industry	Market
Current Price *02/25/02*	$1.14	$47.10	$24.82
Current Price / Earnings			
Fiscal Year *2001*	nm	45.3×	26.7×
Last 4 Quarters	nm	45.3×	26.7×
Current Price / 2001 Book Value	0.1×	6.4×	5.3×
Current Price / 2001 Cash Flow	nm	26.2×	11.2×

Return Ratios	KM	Industry	Market
Profit Margin *L4Q*	(0.3%)	2.3%	4.2%
Return on Equity *2001*	ne	14.2%	8.3%
Return on Investment *2001*	(2.7%)	9.4%	4.2%
Return on Assets *2001*	(1.7%)	5.7%	1.6%
Sales Per Employee *2001*	$146,936	$158,750	$261,175

5 Yr. Annual Growth Rate	KM	Industry	Market
Revenue *1997–2001*	3%	10%	11%
Net Income *1997–2001*	na	4%	(5%)
Dividends *1997–2001*	na	6%	(12%)

Capitalization Ratios	KM	Industry	Market
Debt to Equity *2001*	51%	64%	131%
Interest Coverage *2001*	nm	6.9¥	2.0¥
Interest / Debt *2001*	9%	7%	11%

Price Movement	KM	Industry	Market
Last Month	(23%)	(0%)	10%
Since Jan 1, 2001	(79%)	4%	7%
Last Twelve Months	(88%)	20%	11%

Per Share Data	KM	Industry	Market
Earnings	Per Share		
Fiscal Year *2001*	($0.48)	$1.04	$0.93
Last 4 Quarters	($0.17)	$1.04	$0.93
Book Value Per Share *2001*	$12.50	$7.37	$4.70
Cash Flow Per Share *2001*	na	$1.80	$2.22

Balance Sheet Data

Source: MGFS

$ In Millions	Fiscal Year End: Jan 31	
	2001	**2000**
Current Assets	7,624	8,160
Non-Current Assets	7,006	6,944
Total Assets	**14,630**	**15,104**
Current Liabilities	3,799	4,076
Non-Current Liabilities	4,748	4,724
Total Liabilities	**8,547**	**8,800**
Shareholder's Equity	6,083	6,304
Total Liab. & Equity	**14,630**	**15,104**
Debt / Equity	51%	45%
Curr. Liabilities / Curr. Assets	0.5	0.5

Case 29

Moss Adams, LLP

1   In early January 2001, Jeff Gutsch, senior manager at Moss Adams LLP, an accounting firm located in Santa Rosa, California, met with his team to discuss the progress of a new initiative for developing the firm's accounting practice to serve clients in the Northern California wine industry. At the meeting, Gutsch and his wine niche team reviewed the strategic plan for the coming year. (See Exhibit 1, 2001 Wine Niche Strategic Plan.)

EXHIBIT 1
Moss Adams's Wine Niche Strategic Plan, 2001

Moss Adams LLP
Santa Rosa Office
Wine Industry Advisors
2001 Strategic Plan

Mission Statement

Our goal is to become the dominant accounting and business consulting firm serving the wine industry by providing superior, value-added services tailored to the needs of Northern California vineyards and wineries, as well as becoming experts in the industry.
• We expect to achieve this goal by December 31, 2004.

Five-Year Vision

We are recognized as the premier wine industry accounting and business consulting firm in Sonoma, Mendocino, and Napa counties. We are leaders in the Moss Adams firm wide wine industry group, helping to establish Moss Adams as the dominant firm in the Washington and Oregon wine regions. We have trained and developed recognized industry experts in tax, accounting, and business consulting. Our staff is enthusiastic and devoted to the niche.

The Market

• A firmwide objective is to increase the average size of our business client. We expect to manage the wine niche with that objective in mind. However, during the first two to three years, we intend to pursue vineyards and wineries smaller than the firm's more mature niches would. When this niche is more mature we will increase our minimum prospect size. This strategy will help us gain experience, and build confidence in Moss Adams in the industry, as it is an industry that tends to seek firms that are well established in the Wine Industry.
• There are approximately 122 wineries in Sonoma County, 168 in Napa County and 25 in Mendocino County. Of these approximately 55% have sales over $1 million, and up to one-third have sales in excess of $10 million. In addition to these, there are over 450 vineyards within the same three counties.
• The wine industry appears to be extremely provincial. That combined with the fact that most of our stronger competitors (see "Competition" below) are in Napa County, we consider Sonoma County to be our primary geographic market. However, Mendocino County has a growing wine industry, and we certainly will not pass up opportunities in Napa and other nearby counties in 2001.

Our Strengths

The strengths Moss Adams has in competing in this industry are:
• We are large enough to provide the specific services demanded by this industry.
• Our firm's emphasis is on serving middle-market businesses, while the "Big 5" firms are continually increasing their minimum client size. The majority of the wine industry is made up of middle-market companies. This "Big 5" trend increases our market each year.

(continued)

EXHIBIT 1
(continued)

- We do not try to be all things to all people. We focus our efforts in specialized industries/niches, with the goal of ultimately becoming dominant in those industries.
- We emphasize value-added services, which create more client satisfaction, loyalty, and name recognition.
- We have offices located throughout the West Coast wine regions.
- We have individuals within the firm with significant wine industry experience, including tax, accounting and consulting. We also have experts in closely related industries such as orchards, beverage and food manufacturing.
- Within California, we have some high profile wine industry clients.
- The majority of our niche members have roots in Sonoma County, which is important to Sonoma County wineries and grape growers.
- Our group is committed to being successful in and ultimately dominating the industry in Sonoma, Napa, and Mendocino counties.

Challenges

- Our experience and credibility in the wine industry are low compared to other firms.
- There has been a perception in the Sonoma County area that we are not local to the area. As we continue to grow and become better known, this should be less of an issue.

If we can minimize our weaknesses by emphasizing our strengths, we will be successful in marketing to the wine industry, allowing us to achieve our ultimate goal of being dominant in the industry.

Competition

There are several CPA firms in Northern California that service vineyards and wineries. The "Big 5" firms are generally considered our biggest competitors in many of the industries we serve, and some have several winery clients. But as noted earlier, their focus seems to be on larger clients, which has decreased their ability to compete in this industry. Of the firms with significant wine industry practices, the following firms appear to be our most significant competitors:

- Motto Kryla & Fisher. This firm is a well-established wine industry leader, with the majority of their client base located in Napa County, although they have many Sonoma County clients. They are moving away from the traditional accounting and tax compliance services, concentrating their efforts on consulting and research projects. We can take advantage of this, along with the perception of many in the industry that they are becoming too much of an insider, and gain additional market share.
- Dal Pagetto & Company. This firm was a split off from Deloitte & Touche several years ago. They are located in Santa Rosa, and have several vineyard and winery clients. At this time, they are probably our biggest Sonoma County competitor. However, they may be too small to compete once our momentum builds.
- Other firms that have significant wine industry practices that we will compete against include G & J Seiberlich & Co., Brotemarkle Davis & Co., Zainer Reinhart & Clarke, Pisenti & Brinker, Deloitte & Touche, and PriceWaterhouseCoopers. The first two are wine industry specialists headquartered in Napa County, and although very competitive there, they each do not appear to have a large Sonoma County client base. The next two are general practice firms with several wine industry clients. However, each of these firms has struggled to hold themselves together in recent years, and they do not appear to have well coordinated wine industry practices. The last two firms listed above are "Big 5" firms that, as noted earlier, focus mostly on the largest wineries.

EXHIBIT 1
(continued)

Annual Marketing Plan

Our marketing strategy will build on the foundation we laid during the prior two years. We have established the following as our marketing plan:

- Increase and develop industry knowledge and expertise:
  1. Work with other Moss Adams offices, particularly Stockton, to gain knowledge and experience from their experienced staff. Additionally, work with Stockton to have Santa Rosa Wine Niche staff assigned to two of their winery audits.
  2. Continue to attend industry CPE, including the Vineyard Symposium, the Wine Industry Symposium, the California State Society of CPAs–sponsored wine industry conferences in Napa and San Luis Obispo, and selected Sonoma State University and UC Davis courses. We would like eight hours of wine industry specific CPE for each Senior Level and above committed member of the Wine Niche. Jeff will have final approval on who will attend which classes.
  3. Continue to build our relationship with Sonoma State University (SSU). Our wine niche has agreed to be the subject of a SSU case study on the development of a CPA firm wine industry practice. We feel this case study will help us gain additional insight into what it will take to be competitive, as well as give us increased exposure both at SSU and in the industry. We will also seek to become more involved in SSU's wine industry educational program by providing classroom guest speakers twice a year.
  4. Attract and hire staff with wine industry experience. We should strongly consider candidates who have attained a degree through the SSU Wine Business Program. We should also work to recruit staff within the office that have an interest in the industry.
- Continue to form alliances with industry experts both inside and outside the firm. We are building relationships with Ray Blatt of the Moss Adams Los Angeles office who has expertise in wine industry excise and property tax issues. Cheryl Mead of the Santa Rosa office has developed as a Cost Segregation specialist with significant winery experience.
- Develop and use relationships with industry referral sources:
  1. Bankers and attorneys that specialize in the wine industry. From these bankers and attorneys, we would like to see three new leads per year.
  2. Partner with other CPA firms in the industry. Smaller firms may need to enlist the services of a larger firm with a broader range of services, while the "Big 5" firms may want to use a smaller firm to assist with projects that are below their minimum billing size for the project type. We will obtain at least two projects per year using this approach.
  3. Leverage the relationships we have to obtain five referrals and introductions to other wine industry prospects per year.
  4. We will maintain a matrix of Sonoma, Mendocino, and Napa County wineries and vineyards, including addresses, controller or top financial officer, current CPA, and banking relationship. This matrix will be updated as new information becomes available. From this matrix, we will send at least one mailing per quarter.
- Increase our involvement in the following industry trade associations by attending regular meetings and getting to know association members. In one of the following associations, each committed niche member will seek to obtain an office or board position:
  1. Sonoma County Wineries Association
  2. Sonoma County Grape Growers Association
  3. Sonoma State University Wine Business Program
  4. Zinfandel Advocates and Producers

(continued)

EXHIBIT 1
(continued)

   5. Women for Winesense
   6. California Association of Winegrape Growers
   7. Wine Institute
- Establish an environment within the niche that promotes and practices the PILLAR concept. Encourage staff in the niche to be creative and strive to be the best. Provide interesting projects and events for the niche to make participation more interesting.
- Use the existing services that Moss Adams offers to market the firm which include:
   1. BOSS
   2. Business Valuations
   3. Cost Segregation
   4. SCORE!
   5. SALT
   6. Business Assurance Services
   7. Income Tax Compliance Services
- Make use of Firm Resources
   1. Use Moss Adams' Info Edge (document management system) to share and refer to industry related proposals and marketing materials.
      a. All Wine Niche Proposals will be entered into and updated in InfoEdge as completed.
      b. All Wine Niche Marketing letters will be entered into InfoEdge as created.
- Continue to have monthly wine industry niche meetings. We will review the progress on this plan at our March, April and September niche meetings. Within our niche, we should focus our marketing efforts on Sonoma County, concentrating on smaller prospects that we can grow with, which will enable us to increase our prospect size over time. We would like to be in position to attract the largest wineries in the industry by 2004.
- Establish a Quarterly CFO/Controller roundtable group, with the Moss Adams Wine Industry Group working as facilitator. We will have the Group established and have our first meeting in the summer.
- Quarterly, at our niche meetings, monitor progress on the quantifiable goals in this strategic plan.

Summary

In 2001, one of our goals is to add a minimum of three winery clients to our client base. We feel this is a reasonable goal as long as we continue to implement our plan as written.

We believe we can make the wine industry niche a strong niche in the Santa Rosa office. The firm defines niche dominance as having a minimum of $500,000 in billings, a 20% market share, and having 40% of the services provided be in value-added service codes. We expect to become the dominant industry force in Sonoma, Mendocino, and Napa counties by 2004.

We are also willing to assist other offices within the firm to establish wine industry niches, eventually leading to a mature niche within the firm. We believe with the proper effort we can accomplish each of these goals.

2   The meeting took place just before the height of the busy tax and audit season. Gutsch, 39, had been concentrating on the firm's clients in its construction industry niche. He had not made as much headway developing new business with wine industry clients as he had hoped and opened the meeting by saying:

> I think the issue we are all struggling with is how to break into a well-established mature niche. Do we discount fees? If so, is that our desired position in servicing the wine industry? Do we advertise? Seems like a big commitment for something that we can't be sure will produce results. Do we just get on every panel we can and shake as many hands as we can? I'm still trying to find the right formula.

3   Chris Pritchard, an accounting manager who had worked with Gutsch for two years to develop the wine niche, said:

> Sorry, Jeff, but I've been too busy working in health care. Health care is taking off, so my time is limited on the wine side. There's something missing, sort of a spark in this niche. There's not as much of a hunger to close, to go out and actually close a deal, or at least go out and meet with somebody. I think that's what's lacking for our success right now. I think we have all of the tools we need. But we don't have an aggressive nature to go out and start shaking hands and asking for business. We're doing everything else except asking for the business. We don't follow up.

4   Neysa Sloan, a senior accountant, nodded in assent:

> I personally do not see us making our objectives of gathering 20% of the market share in the regional wine industry over the next 3–5 years. Our marketing tactics are not up to the challenge. We need to seriously look at what we have done in the last year or two, what we are currently doing, and what we are proposing to do in regards to marketing. If we looked at this objectively, we would see that we have not gained much ground in the past using our current tactics—why would it work now? If you allowed more individuals to market and be involved, we might get somewhere.

5   Cheryl Mead, a senior manager whose specialty was conducting cost segregation (Cost segregation is a process of breaking a large asset into its smaller components so that depreciation may be taken on an accelerated basis.) studies, commented:

> Growing wineries are looking for help. We need to focus on wineries that are expanding their facilities, and then grow with their growing businesses. Value-added services like cost segregation could represent as much as 40% of our wine industry practice. If we want to get in, we've got to do much more networking, marketing, and presentations. The challenge for us here in Santa Rosa is how to manage our resources. Career choices are changing; you can't be a generalist anymore. We need both people-related and technical skills, but those don't usually go hand-in-hand. We need someone who is famous in the field, a "who's who" in the wine accounting industry.

6   Claire Calderon, also a senior tax manager, said to the team:

> This is a hard niche to break into, Jeff. It takes a long time to develop relationships in specific industries. It could take a couple of years. First you find forums to meet people, get to know people, get people to trust you and then you get an opportunity to work on a project and you do a good job. It takes a while. Our goal is to become a trusted advisor and that doesn't happen overnight.

7   Gutsch replied:

> While consolidation is happening in the wine industry, many of the wineries we are targeting are still privately owned. When you're dealing with privately owned businesses it's much more personal than with public companies.

8   Calderon added:

> That might explain part of it, Jeff, but the reality is that there are two other fledgling niches that are doing well and going like gangbusters. This niche is off to a slow start!

9   Barbara Korte, a senior accountant, reassured him:

> Jeff, you have been very focused, very enthusiastic about this project. You've put a lot of time into it. As a leader, I think you are a real good manager.

10   At stake was the opportunity to generate significant incremental client fee revenues. More than 600 wine producers and vineyards (grape growers) were in business in the premium Northern California wine-growing region encompassing Napa, Sonoma, and Mendocino counties. According to the Summer 2000 issue of *Marketplace,* there were 168 wine producers and 228 vineyards in Napa; 122 wine producers and 196 vineyards in Sonoma; and 25 wine producers and 61 vineyards in Mendocino. Few of these operations were large, according to *Marketplace.* Napa and Sonoma each had 14 wine producers reporting over $10 million in sales, and Mendocino, only one.

COMPANY BACKGROUND

11   Moss Adams was a regional accounting firm. It had four regional hubs within the firm: Southern California, Northern California, Washington, and Oregon. By late 2000, Moss Adams had become one of the 15 largest accounting firms in the United States, with 150 partners, 740 CPAs, and 1,200 employees. Founded in 1913 and headquartered in Seattle, the full-service firm specialized in middle-market companies, those with annual revenues of $10–$200 million.

12   Each office had a managing partner. Art King was the managing partner of the Santa Rosa office. (See Exhibit 2 for The Santa Rosa office organization chart.) The firm was

EXHIBIT 2
Moss Adams's Organizational Chart

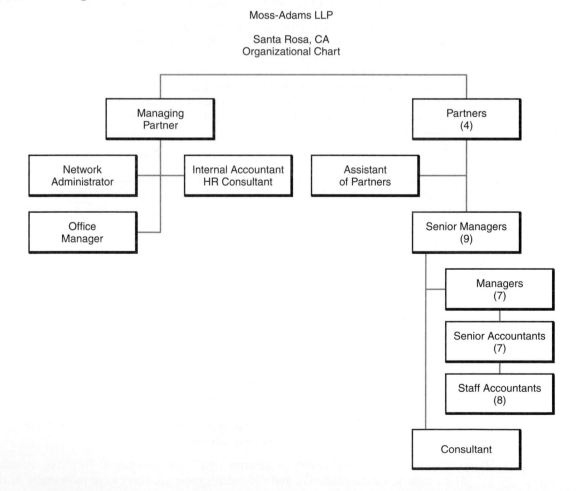

considered mid-size and its client base tended to mirror that size. King reflected on Moss Adams's advantages of size and location:

> . . . it is an advantage to be a regional firm with a strong local presence. For one thing, there just aren't that many regional firms, especially out here on the West Coast. In fact, I think we're the only true West Coast regional firm. That gives us access to a tremendous number of resources that the larger firms have. We have the added advantage of being a big part of Sonoma County. Sonoma County companies want the same kind of services they can get from the Big Five operating out of places like San Francisco, but they also like to deal with local firms that are active in the community. Our staff is active in Rotary, 20–30, the local chambers of commerce, and so on, and that means a lot to the businesspeople in the area. Sonoma County companies will go to San Francisco for professional services, but only if they have to, so we offer the best of both worlds.

13   Each office within the firm was differentiated. An office like Santa Rosa had the ability to be strong in more niches because it was one of the dominant firms in the area. Moss Adams did not have to directly compete with the Big Five accounting firms as they are not interested in providing services to small to mid-size business. Since it was a regional firm, Moss Adams was able to offer a depth of services that most local firms were not able to match. This gave Moss Adams a competitive advantage when selling services to the middle market company segment.

14   Moss Adams provided services in four main areas of expertise: business assurance (auditing), tax, international, and consulting. Auditing comprised approximately 35%–40% of Moss Adams's practice, the remainder being divided among tax work in corporate, partnerships, trusts and estates, and individual taxation. In its Santa Rosa office, Moss Adams serviced corporate business and high-wealth individuals.

15   On the international side, Moss Adams was a member of Moores Rowland International, a worldwide association of accounting firms. Moss Adams primarily worked with local companies that did business overseas or that wanted to set up a foreign location. It also did a lot of work with local companies that had parent firms located overseas.

16   On the consulting side, Moss Adams had about 80 full-time consultants, and this line of business represented probably 15%–20% of the total practice. A large part of the consulting work performed by Moss Adams was in mergers and acquisitions. Its M&A division helped middle-market companies, which formed the bulk of its clientele, develop a coherent, consistent strategy, whether they were planning on selling the business and needed to find an appropriate buyer or were looking for a good acquisition target.

17   The Big Six (now Big Five) accounting firms had developed niche strategies in the 80s, and Moss Adams had been one of the first mid-level accounting firms in the nation to identify niches as a strategy. Adopting a niche strategy had allowed Moss Adams to target a basket of services to a particular industry of regional importance. As each practice developed a niche, it also identified the "famous people" in that niche. These people became the "go-to persons," the leaders of that niche.

18   The high technology sector represented one of the fastest-growing parts of Moss Adams's business. According to King:

> It's big in the Seattle area (where Moss Adams has its headquarters), and with the development of Telecom Valley, it's certainly becoming big in Sonoma County. We're finding that a great deal of our work is coming from companies that are offshoots of other large high-tech companies in the area. Financial institutions represent another client group that's growing rapidly, as is health care. With all of the changes in the health care and medical fields, there's been a good deal of turmoil. We have a lot of expertise in the health care and medical areas, so that's a big market for us. Have I seen a drop-off? No, not really.

The interesting thing about the accounting industry is that even when the economy slows down, there's still a lot of work for a CPA firm. There might not be as many large, special projects as when the economy is really rolling, but the work doesn't slow down.

THE INDUSTRY AND THE MARKET

19 Accounting was a large and relatively stable service industry, according to *The Journal of Accountancy,* the industry's most widely read trade publication. The Big Five accounting firms (Andersen Worldwide, PriceWaterhouseCoopers, Ernst & Young, Deloitte & Touche, and KPMG) dominated the global market in 1998 with combined global revenue exceeding $58 billion, well over half the industry's total revenue. All of the Big Five firms reported double-digit growth rates in 1998. However, some of the most spectacular growth was achieved by firms outside the top 10, some of which registered increases of nearly 60% over 1997 revenues. Ninety of the top 100 firms had revenue increases, and 58 of them had achieved double-digit gains.

20 In 1999, accounting industry receipts in the U.S. exceeded $65 billion. The industry now employed more than 632,000 people. However, the industry was expected to post more modest growth in revenues and employment into the 21st century. Finding niche markets, diversifying services, and catering to global markets were key growth strategies for companies in the industry. Large international firms, including the Big Five, had branched out into management consulting services in the late 1980s and early 1990s.

21 Accounting firms and certified public accountants (CPAs) nationwide began offering a wide array of services in addition to traditional accounting, auditing, and bookkeeping services. This trend was partially a response to clients' demand for "one-stop shopping" for all their professional services needs. Another cause was the relatively flat growth in demand for traditional accounting and auditing services over the past 10 years, as well as the desire of CPAs to develop more value-added services. The addition of management consulting, legal, and other professional services to the practice mix of large national accounting networks was transforming the industry.

22 Many firms began offering technology consulting because of growing client demand for Internet and e-commerce services. *Accounting Today*'s 1999 survey of CPA clients indicated that keeping up with technology was *the* strategic issue of greatest concern, followed by recruiting and retaining staff, competing with larger companies, planning for executive succession, and maximizing productivity.

23 However, according to *The CPA Journal,* the attractive consulting fees may have led many firms to ignore potential conflicts of interest in serving as an auditor and as a management consultant to the same client. The profession's standards could be jeopardized by the entrance of non-CPA partners and owners in influential accounting firms. Many companies facing these problems had split their accounting and management consulting operations. In January 2001, Arthur Andersen had spun off its consulting division and renamed it "Accenture" to avoid accusations of impropriety.

24 Still, CPA firms could be expected to continue to develop their capabilities and/or strategic alliances to meet clients' demands. Some other areas of expansion among accounting firms included administrative services, financial and investment planning services, general management services, government administration, human resources, international operations, information technology and computer systems consulting, litigation support, manufacturing administration, marketing, and research and development. Many small and medium-size independent firms were merging or forming alliances with large service companies such as American Express, H&R Block, and Century Business Services.

25   By the late 1990s, a trend toward consolidation got under way in the accounting industry. Several factors were fueling the drive toward consolidation. Large increases in revenue among the top 100 accounting firms between 1997 and 1998 may have been partially attributable to this trend toward consolidation. Consolidators wanted access to the large volume of business currently being done by independent CPAs. The trust that small businesses and individuals had in their CPAs was considered very valuable, and consolidators wanted to leverage the potential of an individual firm's integrity to expand their own businesses. Consolidation caused a decline in the number of independent accounting firms that offered only tax and accounting services. The New York State Society of CPAs estimated that there was a strong possibility that up to 50 of the largest accounting firms in the United States would dissolve or merge with other entities by the end of the year 2000. In the San Francisco Bay Area, for example, the Big Five dominated the industry. (See Exhibit 3, Top 20 Accounting Firms in the SF Bay Area.)

THE WINE INDUSTRY NICHE

26   The wine industry practice was a new niche for the Santa Rosa office, as well as Moss Adams in general. Moss Adams allowed any employee to propose a niche. All accounting firms bill at fairly standard rates so the more business that is generated the greater the profit. Moss Adams felt it was in their long-term best interest to allow employees to focus on areas in which they were interested. The firm would benefit from revenues generated, but, more important, employees would likely stay with a firm that allowed a degree of personal freedom and promoted professional growth.

27   Gutsch and Pritchard had begun this niche in mid-1998 for several reasons. First, both had an interest in the industry. Second, Sonoma and Napa counties had over 200 wineries and numerous vineyard operations. Third, Moss Adams had expertise in related or similar business lines such as orchards, as well as significant related experience in providing services to the manufacturing sector. Finally, the wine industry had been historically serviced by either large firms that considered the typical winery a small client, or by smaller firms that were not able to offer the range of services that Moss Adams could provide.

28   Sara Rogers, a senior accountant and member of the wine niche team, recalled:

> It first started with Jeff Gutsch and Chris Pritchard and another senior manager, who was in our office until November 1999. Anyway, I think it was their motivation that really started the group. The three of them were doing everything in building the niche. When the senior manager left, it sort of fell flat on its face for a little while. I think it got stagnant. Pretty much nobody said anything about it until last summer, when Jeff started the organization of it again and brought in more people, and then he approached people that he wanted to work with.

29   Gutsch felt that Moss Adams was in position to move forward to make the wine industry niche a strong niche both in the Santa Rosa office, and eventually the firm as a whole. He was committed to that goal and expected to achieve it within five years. Gutsch saw this niche as his door to future partnership. Moss Adams's marketing strategy included the following:

1. Develop industry marketing materials that communicate Moss Adams's strengths and commitment.

2. Develop a distinctive logo for use in the industry.

3. Create an industry brochure similar to that of the firm's construction industry group.

EXHIBIT 3   **Top 20 Accounting Firms in SF Bay Area, Ranked by Number of Bay Area CPAs, June**

Sources: Viva Chan, *San Francisco Business Times*, 14 i46, June 16, 2000, p. 28; Strafford Publications, *Public Accounting Reports*, vol. XXIV, June 2000.

Rank	1999 Rank	Company	No. Bay Area CPAs	No. Company CPAs	No. Bay Area Employees	1999 Billings Bay Area	No. Partners in Bay Area	No. Company Partners	FYE	US Net Revenue ($mil)	% Chg. Vs. Prev. Yr.
1	2	Deloitte & Touche LLP	439	8,380	1,437	NR	172	2,066	May 99	$5,336.00	24.2
2	1	PricewaterhouseCoopers LLP	430	430	2,000	NR	138	9,000	Sep. 99	6,956.00	18.7
3	3	KPMG Peat Marwick LLP	316	NR	1,778	NR	157	6,800	Jun. 99	4,112.00	21.5
4	4	Arthur Andersen**	312	6,161	821	NR	63	3,059	Aug. 99	3,300.00	17.9
5	5	Ernst & Young LLP	300	NR	850	NR	77	2,465	Sep. 99	6,100.00	10.0
6	6	BDO Seldman LLP	72	1,650	122	NR	15	360	Jun. 00	408.00	36.9
7	14	Seiler & Co. LLP	44	44	110	NR	12	12	NR	NR	NR
8	7	Frank, Runerman & Co. LLP	43	51	76	NR	12	13	May 99	17.23	9.2
9	9	Hood & Strong LLP	42	42	89	NR	12	12	NR	NR	NR
10*	10	Harb, Levy & Weiland LLP	38	38	80	NR	13	13	NR	NR	NR
10*	13	Ireland San Filippo LLP	38	38	81	12.7M	13	17	Apr. 00	12.71	15.8
12	15	Burr, Pilger & Mayer	35	35	110	NR	10	10	NR	NR	NR
13	11	Armanino McKenna LLP	34	34	87	NR	13	13	NR	NR	NR
14	14	Novogradac & Co. LLP	31	36	80	NR	6	8	NR	NR	NR
15	12	RINA Accountancy Corp.	26	29	59	7.3M	13	14	NR	NR	NR
16*	16	Grant Thornton LLP	25	1,300	90	NR	10	300	Jul. 00	416.00	10.9
16*	18	Shea Labagh Dobberstein	25	25	35	NR	3	3	NR	NR	NR
18	18	Moss Adams LLP	24	800	39	NR	7	144	Dec. 99	109.00	31.3
19	16	Lindquist, von Husen & Joyce	23	23	47	NR	5	5	NR	NR	NR
20	21	Lautze & Lautze	21	28	39	NR	9	11	NR	NR	NR

NR = Not reported
* Indicates tie in ranking.
** Excludes consulting.

4. Develop industry service information flyers such as the business lifecycle, R&E (Research & Exploration) credit, excise tax compliance and BOSS (Business Ownership Succession Services).

5. Develop relationships with industry referral sources (e.g., bankers and attorneys that specialized in the wine industry or current clients who served or had contacts in the industry).

6. Join and become active in industry trade associations.

7. Use existing relationships with industry contacts to obtain leads into prospective wineries and vineyards.

8. Use the existing services that Moss Adams offered to market the firm, particularly in Cost Segregation.

9. Focus efforts on Sonoma County, as well as adjacent wine-growing regions, which would enable Moss Adams to increase its prospect size over time.

30   Pritchard reflected on those early days:

> The first thing we did was to develop a database of regional wineries and send out an introduction letter. The other thing we did was to develop marketing materials. Jeff developed a logo. We used a top-down approach pyramid for an introduction letter, starting out general and then with an action step at the end to call us. So, we used that at first. Usually with that we'd get about 2% response which is good out of 300 letters or whatever we sent out.

31   However, according to King, the major issue in growing the wine industry practice was selling:

> The thing about selling in public accounting is that you have to have a lot of confidence in what you do and what you can do for the client. You have to have confidence that you know something about the industry. If you go into a marketing meeting, or a proposal meeting and you're saying, "Well, we do a couple of wineries but we really want to do more and get better at it," you're not going to get the work. You gain confidence by knowing how to talk the language, knowing the buzzwords, knowing some of the players in the industry. You go into a meeting, all of a sudden you're on an equal footing with them. From a confidence standpoint, that's huge. You can't sell public accounting services unless you're confident about you and your firm and the people that are going to do the work. Over the last two years, Jeff has gone to the classes, gone to the meetings and his confidence level is much higher than it was a year ago. When he goes into these meetings he's going to be at a level where he doesn't have to make excuses for not having a lot of winery clients, because we have a lot of activity in the wine and the beverage processing industries. So, I think that's going to help a lot. That's where he's going to have more success because we're getting the at bats, we just need to get some hits.

32   One of the roles of the managing partner was to mentor potential partners and help them attain the role of partner. The training process included marketing and helping them build a practice, according to King:

> When we're talking with senior managers, I explain to them what they need to do to get to that next level. I had this conversation with Jeff because his primary focus when he came was, "I need to build a big practice, nothing else matters." He trusts the system now. He's transferred some clients to others and received some clients. You have to work well with people, you have to train people, you have to have some responsibilities, and you have to get along with your peers.

33   The firm's philosophy was to encourage people to really enjoy what they did. Anyone was allowed to propose a niche, *even* a senior manager. Pritchard explained:

> Well, part of the way our firm works is, there is a "four-bucket" tier to make partner. One of the buckets is to become a famous person and the fastest way of doing that is through the niche base; within a niche you get the experience and the reputation faster than you would as a generalist. Jeff is a senior manager, so now he's trying to figure out a way to become partner. I work on Bonny Doon Winery. I have a grower client in Kenwood, so I do have some experience with that. I also like wine because I make wine. It's an untapped market in Sonoma County for our firm. So we both got together—I had the entrepreneurial spirit to start and Jeff had the need.

34   King described in detail the "four bucket" evaluation system at Moss Adams:

> We have four criteria that get evaluated by the partner and the compensation committee on a scale of one-to-ten. All of these are weighted equally, 25%, with a possibility of 40 points. The first is financial. We take a look at the potential partner's financial responsibilities, what their billings are, what their fee adjustments are, what their charge hours are. I've transferred many clients to people in the office. That's one way I help others grow their practices. I'm still responsible for some of those clients, because I'm the one who brought them in and I'm still the primary contact. My billing numbers may be this, but my overall financial responsibility may be bigger. That's an objective measure because we look at the numbers, we look at the trends.
>
>   The second is responsibility. Managing partner of a big office gets more points than the managing partner of a smaller office does, who in turn gets more points than a person in charge of a niche, who in turn gets more points than a line partner. Somebody who is a partner and is responsible for the tax department, let's say, might get an extra point or half a point, whereas someone in charge of a niche might get an extra point. If they're in charge of an office they get more points.
>
>   The third is personnel. Personnel is a very big initiative within Moss Adams. Upstream and downstream evaluations are conducted by our HR person for each office and measures staff retention and the quality of our mentoring program. Each partner is also evaluated up or down from an overall office rating score. For example, our office may get a "seven," but I may get an "eight" because I'm really good with people. Somebody who's really hard on people would get a lower rating.
>
>   The fourth and final "bucket" is peer evaluation. We have three other partners evaluate each partner. They evaluate the partner for training, mentoring, marketing, and involvement in their community. Then, evaluations are used by the Compensation Committee to review individual partner compensation. They are also used for partner counseling sessions.

35   King also assured a "soft landing" to the participants of the niche teams. This meant that if a niche didn't work out, he would assure the individuals that another niche in the firm would be found for them. This, it was hoped, fostered entrepreneurial behaviors that had their potential upsides and downsides. According to King:

> A high level of practice responsibility for a partner would be $1 million in this office. The range is anywhere from $600,000 to $1 million in billings a year. The overall picture is, where we try to get people involved in at least two niches in the office, until a niche becomes large enough that you can spend full-time in it. The upside potentially of the wine niche would be a practice of from $500,000 to $1,000,000 based on Sonoma and maybe some Napa County wineries. So, the upside is a very mature, profitable niche that fits right into our model of our other niches of middle market companies that have the need, not only for client services, but also our value added services.
>
>   If for some reason the wine niche didn't take off, Jeff would become more involved in the manufacturing niche—well, wine is manufacturing anyway, but it's just a subset of

manufacturing. It might slow his rate to partner. It could also turn out that—all of a sudden—Jeff gets four great referrals in the manufacturing niche this year, he builds this great big practice in manufacturing, and as a result he has less time for the wine niche. The downside is we've spent some money on marketing, and Jeff has spent some time on marketing when he could have been doing something else. Then, we abandon the project. If that happens, then Jeff's time becomes available and the money becomes available to go after some other initiative or something we're already doing or some new initiative. Nobody is going to lose his/her job over it. We haven't lost a lot of money over it.

THE AFTERMATH

36   After the January 2001 meeting, Gutsch pondered how he should proceed to overcome some major roadblocks to building his team. King took Gutsch aside for counseling:

> . . . target the $10 million to under $20 million winery for which we can provide a full range of services. There's nobody else with our range of services that's really doing a good job in that area. There's an under-served market for those middle-market companies. When you started, I knew it would take 2 or 3 years to really get the ball rolling. This is really going to be your year, Jeff. If it isn't, well, we'll re-evaluate at the end of the year. Our overall marketing budget is probably in the area of 1.5% to 2% of total client billings. In 1999, the first year for the wineries, we probably spent somewhere in the neighborhood of $5,000 to $8,000, which wasn't a lot but you joined some organizations and you did some training. Last year we probably spent $10,000 to $12,000. Now, Jeff, I know that some of our other offices spend a lot more on marketing than we do. We'll have to decide: is this the best use of your time? Is this the best use of our resources to try to go after an industry where we just tried for three years and haven't made any inroads?

37   The decision to develop a niche had been based upon a gut feeling. Moss Adams did not use any litmus test or hurdle rate of return to screen possible niches. This was because, with the exception of nonprofits, most clients had similar fee realization rates. Moss Adams looked at the potential volume of business and determined whether it could handle that volume. Yet Moss Adams remained unknown in the wine industry. Time was running out.

This case study was prepared by Professors Armand Gilinsky, Jr. and Sherri Anderson at Sonoma State University as a basis for class discussion rather than to illustrate either effective or ineffective handling of an administrative situation. This case was originally presented at the 2001 meeting of the North American Case Research Association in Memphis, Tenn. The authors gratefully acknowledge the support of Moss Adams PLC and the Wine Business Program at Sonoma State University for assistance in preparation of this case.

Case 30

Napster and MP3: Redefining the Music Industry[1]

1   In the summer of 2000, the Recording Industry Association of America (RIAA) was awarded an interim injunction against the Internet's largest facilitator of MP3 file exchanges, Napster Inc. (Napster), forcing it to shut down its system. However, less than a week after the injunction was issued, Napster successfully appealed and the injunction was lifted. The RIAA argued that Napster distributed allegedly "pirated" music (i.e., music that the user uploaded or mounted on their computer for distribution as an MP3 file, thereby allowing people free access to the MP3 files in clear violation of copyright by the user). Although they fought in court, the RIAA and Napster were both members of the Secure Digital Music Initiative (SDMI). The SDMI, established in December 1998, was a forum for the music industry to develop a voluntary open framework for playing, storing, and distributing digital music, while at the same time enabling the new market to emerge.[2] The essence of SDMI was to develop a new paradigm in the digital music industry such that alternatives to the current "in the box" thinking regarding the eradication of music piracy could be explored through mutual agreement and understanding coupled with technological innovation. However, as the Napster/RIAA lawsuit demonstrated, membership did not mean that the fight for a competitive advantage in the industry would end.

THE MUSIC INDUSTRY

2   In 1999, the recorded music industry in the United States alone was estimated by the RIAA to be worth close to US$15 billion. The stakes were high as was the competition. Although there was a seemingly endless source of music from established and new artists, the industry was in a constant search for the newest trend and potential star. The costs of finding the newest superstar were high and the odds of success were low. Record companies could spend between US$150,000 and US$500,000 to sign a new artist, and nearly the same amount to promote them.[3] Exhibit 1 presents a diagram depicting the steps through which recorded music reached the end consumer. The left side of the diagram depicts the value-added stages as artists provide music and lyrics to record companies who record, combine, and market music through a variety of distribution channels. The right side depicts the value-added processes involved in the manufacturing and distribution of the technology to play the music. Exhibit 2 presents a breakdown of how the revenues from the sale of a CD are distributed.

Richard Ivey School of Business
The University of Western Ontario

Case prepared by Trevor Hunter and Tammy Smith under the supervision of Professors Mary Crossan, Margaret Ann Wilkinson and Mark Perry solely to provide material for class discussion. The authors do not intend to illustrate either effective or ineffective handling of a managerial situation. The authors may have disguised certain names and other identifying information to protect confidentiality. Ivey Management Services prohibits any form of reproduction, storage or transmittal without its written permission. This material is not covered under authorization from CanCopy or any reproduction rights organization. To order copies or request permission to reproduce materials, contact Ivey Publishing. Ivey Management Services, c/o Richard Ivey School of Business, The University of Western Ontario, London, Ontario, Canada, N6A 3K7; phone (519) 661-3208; fax (519) 661-3882; e-mail cases@ivey.uwo.ca. Copyright © 2000, Ivey Management Services. Version: (A) 2001-06-28. *One-time permission to reproduce granted by Ivey Management Services on March 1, 2002.*

EXHIBIT 1
Distribution Chain for the Consumption of Recorded Music

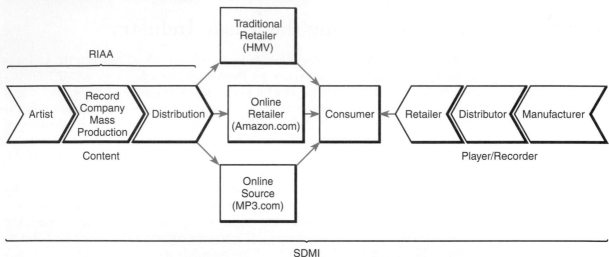

EXHIBIT 2
Breakdown of Revenue Distribution from the Sale of One CD*

Assume Retail Selling Price of US$16.98	
Where the money goes	
Co-op advertising and discounts to retailers	.85
Pressing album and printing booklet	.75
Profit to label	.59
Retail markup	6.23
Company overhead, distribution and shipping	3.34
Marketing and promotion	2.15
Royalties to artist and songwriter	1.99
Signing act and producing record	1.08
	16.98

*Jeffry Scott, "Will Federal Pact Slash CD Costs?" *Atlanta Journal and Constitution,* May 12, 2000.

3   As a new channel of distribution, the Internet enabled artists to deal directly with customers, and enabled one customer to access another in order to exchange music. It was the development of MP3 format and player technology that enabled the distribution of music over the Internet.

The MP3 Format

4   The traditional means of music distribution was for recording artists to use a music publisher that would market compact discs (CDs).

> The typical five-minute track on a CD is a digital file that [contains] around 50 megabytes (MB) of data . . . By using file compression technologies such as MP3, it was possible to reduce the file size to around one-twelfth of that of the CD version, whilst achieving good quality for reproduction.[4]

5   Developed by the Fraunhofer Institute in Germany in 1992, MP3 was a format similar in nature to jpg. It was used to transfer and store digital music over the Internet.[5] What

EXHIBIT 3
A Sample
Comparison of MP3
Players*

Product Name	Price (USD)	Storage Capacity
Audiovox MP-1000	$ 180	32MB
Casio MP3 Wrist Audio Player	249	16MB
Creative Labs Nomad II	330	64MB
HanGo Remote Solution Personal Jukebox	749	4.86GB
I2Go Ego	269	64MB
I-Jam	220	32MB
RCA Lyra Player	199	32MB
Samsung Yepp	229	64MB
Sensory Science RaveMP 2100	269	64MB
Sony Memory Stick Walkman	400	64MB

*This information was selected from a list published in *PC World,* July 2000, pp. 126–127.

made it so pervasive was that the file, while significantly compressed, retained near CD-quality sound. This reduced size made the exchange, transfer and storage of digital music far more convenient than ever before. Hundreds of songs, even entire albums could be stored on a computer hard drive and downloaded with relative ease.

6   MP3 files were routinely exchanged through the Internet. With the advent of digital recording, it became relatively simple and inexpensive to record a CD full of copyrighted material, and further, to upload it onto a computer. Once uploaded, the files could be converted to the MP3 format and made available to anyone in the world having unhindered access to the Internet. Numerous websites sprung up, making available MP3 files to download for free. Examples of these sites include the more infamous Napster, MP3.com, Freenet, and Gnutella. Also some users set up file transfer protocol (FTP) sites, allowing other users access to files on their computer. This list is by no means an exhaustive survey of the varied and numerous ways to exchange digitized data.

MP3 Players

7   Initially a limiting factor to MP3 popularity was the lack of a device to play MP3 files aside from a computer. This changed when Diamond Multimedia introduced its Rio 300 MP3 player.[6] However, the system was relatively expensive at the time and had such limited storage capacity that only a few songs could be stored.

8   In a relatively short period of time, the number of producers increased dramatically. The door opened to a new industry that quickly filled with competitors who added functions and storage capacity to their models, while at the same time lowering prices to the consumer. By mid-2000, there were numerous models on the market produced by large, established multinationals like Sony and Samsung, as well as new start-ups. (Exhibit 3 presents a list of MP3 players). The machines could store about one hour of music. When consumers wanted to change the music they listened to, they would have to erase what was stored and upload new files onto the player. Depending on the player, this could be a time consuming and confusing process. Although the functionality and ease of use was not at the level of more established competing products (like personal cassette or CD players), the manufacturers continued to innovate. The confluence of the MP3 format, player technology and the Internet greatly simplified the access, transfer, copy and playing of music. In doing so, the issues surrounding copyright became more prevalent. However, challenges to copyright were not new.

COPYRIGHT: HISTORICAL PERSPECTIVE

9   Copyright, itself a legal solution to the challenges of the changes wrought by the industrial and print revolutions, had traditionally been created in works of four kinds: literary, artistic, dramatic, and musical. Over time, technology had required the courts and legislatures of various jurisdictions to examine and re-examine the balance created by their copyright legislative regimes.

10   For example, there was a technological and social challenge to the notion of copyright, particularly in musical works, with the widespread adoption of sound recording technology earlier in the 20th century. Canada early on created a limited right for the producer of the sound recording itself, which existed independent of the copyrights already created for the literary or musical works that might be recorded on the sound recording.

11   Then, the jukebox, which played the sound recordings of popular copyrighted musical works at the drop of a coin, became a popular addition to restaurants and other gathering places.

12   Technically, the patrons of these establishments could have been considered to be "performing a work in public" when they dropped the coin in and caused the songs to play to the other restaurant patrons and employees. To do this legally, they would have been required to obtain the prior permission of the copyright holders of the musical works and the permission of those who held the rights in the sound recordings. It would then have been within the copyright holders rights to require payment for these playings.

13   The Canadian Parliament decided, however, that this situation was unworkable in light of the technical limitations of the new technology and the social demands of Canadians. The *Copyright Act* had therefore been amended to provide that the Copyright Appeal Board, a federal administrative agency, was to provide in advance for the collection of fees from the radio broadcasting stations or the gramophone manufacturers to compensate the rightsholders for the anticipated playing of their works and recordings which would occur through jukeboxes. These moneys would be payable to the Canadian Performing Rights Society and would then be distributed among its members (the rightsholders). It was anticipated that these costs would then be passed through to the ultimate consumers of the music by way of pricing mechanisms—the cost to the restaurants of having jukeboxes installed and maintained, or the cost per song for the paying customer.

14   Although the legislation provided for this administrative mechanism administered by the Copyright Appeal Board, by 1940, it had not yet come into existence. The Canadian Performing Rights Society was not actually getting any recompense for its members from the playing of members' songs on jukeboxes. A case involving this impasse reached the Privy Council (which was then the highest court in Canada) on appeal from the Supreme Court of Canada.[7]

15   The Court held that the right of "public performance," reserved to copyright holders under the copyright regime, did include those performances whereby music is played on a jukebox. However, said the Court, Parliament had expressly removed that right from among those for which the rightsholders were to be compensated in its legislation. This removal operated even though the federal government had failed to implement the alternative administrative scheme they had legislated, which was supposed to have replaced the rightsholders' former statutory rights. The court held that "no charge of any kind is to be collected from the owner or user of the radio receiving

set or gramophone."[8] Essentially, the Privy Council exonerated both owners and users of jukeboxes from "all payments in respect of public performances of musical compositions"[9] to the holders of the rights conferred by the *Copyright Act.*

16   These reactions to earlier music technology illustrated several points about the law relating to copyright. The rights were created through actions of the appropriate legislative bodies. Governments could change the legislation in response to changing social and economic conditions as the political process dictated. They could reallocate rights. They could create new classes of rightsholders. The role of the courts was to apply the law to the individual disputes between users and rightsholders who came before them (or, in criminal proceedings, between the state and the individuals accused), according to the provisions of the legislation as it existed at the time the disputes arose. In periods of technological change, the courts were often faced with disputes in technological environments that were not clearly covered by the legislation and, in these situations, would still need to resolve the disputes between the litigants before them.

THE RECORDING INDUSTRY ASSOCIATION OF AMERICA (RIAA)

17   Working to protect the interests of the industry players on the left side of the chain in Exhibit 1 was the RIAA. The RIAA was the main champion of intellectual property rights in the American recorded music industry. As a lobbying organization, it was influential and proactive both in the United States and around the world in trying to protect the copyrights of its hundreds of members. Its mission was simple.

> The Recording Industry Association of America is the trade group that represents the U.S. recording industry. Our mission is to foster a business and legal climate that supports and promotes our members' creative and financial vitality. Our members are the record companies that comprise the most vibrant national music industry in the world. RIAA members create, manufacture, and/or distribute approximately 90 percent of all legitimate sound recordings produced and sold in the United States.
>
> In support of our mission, we work to protect intellectual property rights worldwide and the First Amendment rights of artists; conduct consumer, industry and technical research; and monitor and review . . . state and federal laws, regulations and policies.[10]

18   The main thrust of the RIAA activities was in helping members to achieve value from their intellectual property in music in the form of copyright. As an intellectual property right, copyright is that bundle of rights that arises on the creation of original works, including musical works. These rights include the right to control the reproduction and distribution of such works. Copying of musical works without the permission of the copyright holder, either the creator or successor to ownership of the right, was actionable in the courts. However, there was provided in the copyright legislation of most jurisdictions a limited exception to the rights of the copyright holder that permitted copying of musical works for personal use.

19   As the MP3 technology that enabled the replications and distribution of musical works became increasingly widespread, the RIAA became increasingly proactive in protecting the rights of its members. As part of its strategy, the RIAA became one of the more important groups in championing the creation of SDMI and pushing for focus and standardization of formats in the music industry.

20   The RIAA was not the only such recording industry association around the world. In Canada, the Canadian Recording Industry Association (CRIA) protected Canadian

recording artists, while the British Phonographic Industry (BPI) did the same in the United Kingdom. Interestingly, although both the CRIA and BPI had nearly identical mandates to that of their U.S. counterpart, neither was a member of the SDMI.[11]

SDMI

21   Although it was founded in 1998, plans for an initiative such as the SDMI dated back to the mid-1990s. SDMI was an organization of what the administration referred to as "technology" companies. Exhibit 4 presents a list of the SDMI participants. As Cary Sherman, senior vice-president and general counsel of the RIAA put it,

> [SDMI] includes information technology (IT) companies, and consumer electronic (CE) companies, and telecommunications companies, and Internet companies, and vendors of security technologies and everyone else whose technology products and services are critical to the distribution of digital music, in all formats and through all channels.[12]

22   Together, their aim was to

> attempt to create an open architecture and specification that [would] make it possible for consumers and content providers to find common ground on the terms on which music can be accessed and used . . . a specification for how music can be marked at the source, identified and labelled with rights-management information that is embedded in the music or carried with it in such a way that it remains with that piece of music no matter what system, network or device it passes through . . . any device in which it is recorded, stored or played on will know how and where to look for and act upon that data.[13]

23   The mission was at once both reactive and proactive to the MP3 phenomenon, since the members were trying to curb the existing piracy of copyrighted material and develop a strategy by which all members could gain from an innovative technology. As Sherman stated, this technology offered new business models for gaining a competitive advantage in the music industry. The MP3 format provided an easy and efficient format, the Internet provided a pervasive and efficient medium for distribution, and the playing technology provided a new method of listening to music. Under the leadership of Dr. Leonardo Chiariglione, one of the creators of the MPEG format for audio and video exchange through the Internet, SDMI was well connected within the worldwide music industry. What was needed was a way to secure the content to capture the economic gains the SDMI foresaw.

24   From its inception, the SDMI was intended to be a forum involved in the development of a secure method of transferring and distributing digital music. As a result, it needed to involve content producers, digital music distributors of all sorts (from record labels to Internet sites), and finally, current or potential producers of digital music players and recorders. In February 1999, a meeting with representatives from over 100 different companies was held to announce the plans for the SDMI. Within weeks, more meetings were held and documents were drafted that would establish the ground rules for SDMI. The organization would institute its plan in two phases.

25   Phase 1 was a solicitation for designs for SDMI-compliant MP3 devices to be available to the market by December 1999. These devices would "accept any content, regardless of format, whether secure or insecure, whether legitimate or illegitimate."[14] The purpose for this "open" device was to gain market share for its members before implementing Phase 2. Additionally, and more importantly, within these players there would be a mechanism that would read digitally "watermarked" SDMI-compliant content and eventually filter out content that was illegally obtained. By August 1999, ARIS Technologies had been selected to provide the watermark encryption systems.

EXHIBIT 4
SDMI Participant
List as of July 5, 2000

Source:www.sdmi.org,
June 2000.

Adaptec
AegiSoft Corp
AEI Music/Playmedia
Aiwa Limited
Am. Federation of TV and Radio Artists
    (AFTRA)
Am. Soc of Composers, Authors &
    Publishers (ASCAP)
American Federation of Musicians
AMP3.com/JVWeb
Amplified.com
AOL
ARM Limited
AT&T/a2b
Audible, Inc.
Audio Explosion/Mjuice
Audio Matrix
Audiohighway.com
AudioSoft
AudioTrack
Aureal Semiconductor
Be Inc.
Beatnik, Inc.
Blue Spike, Inc.
BMG Entertainment
BreakerTech
Broadcast Music, Inc. (BMI)
Broadcom HomeNetworking, Inc
Bureau International
    des Sociétés Gérant les
Droit d'Enregistrement et de Reproduction
    Méchanique (BIEM)
Canal Plus
Casio Computer
CDDB, Inc.
Cductive.com
CDWorld
Cinram International
Cirrus Logic
Cognicity, Inc.
Compaq Corp.
Comverse Technology
Confédération Internationale des Sociétés
    (d'Auteurs et Compositeurs (CISAC)
Creative Technology Ltd
Dataplay.com, Inc
Dentsu
Deutsche Telekom AG
DigiMarc
Digital Media on Demand
Digital On-Demand/RedDotNet

Digital Theater Systems (DTS)
Digitalway Co. Ltd.
DiscoverMusic (formally Enso Audio
    Imaging)
DnC Tech, Inc.
Dolby Laboratories
e.Digital Corp.
Earjam, Inc.
EMDES Systems Company LTD.
EMI Capitol Music
Emusic
Encoding.com/Loudeye Technology
Entrust
Ericcson
Federation of Music Producers Japan (FMPJ)
4C Entity, LLC
Fraunhofer Institute
Full Audio Corporation
Funai Corp.
Geidankyo (Japan Council of Performers
    Rights Admin.)
Gemplus
General Instruments
Grundig Digital Systems
Guillemot
Harry Fox Agency
Hewlett-Packard
Hilomusical (Telefonica)
Hitachi
Hithive Inc.
HMV Media Group
12GO.COM
Infineon (formerly Siemens Semiconductor)
Intel Corporation
International Federation of Phonographic
    Industries (IFPI)
InterTrust
InterVideo, Inc
Intervu
Iomega
J.River
JASRAC
JVC Victor
Kenwood Corp.
Lexar Media
LG Electronics
Liquid Audio
Lucent Technologies
M.Ken
Macrovision
MAGEX (formerly NatWest)

(continued)

EXHIBIT 4
(continued)

MarkAny	Reciprocal
MARS (Multimedia Archive and Retrieval System)	Recording Industry Association of America (RIAA)
Matsushita	Recording Industry Association of Japan (RIAJ)
MCY Music	Rowe International
Media Fair, Inc	RPK SecureMedia, Inc.
Media Tag Limited	S3/Diamond Multimedia
Mediamatics	Samsung Electronics
Memory Corporation	SanDisk
Midbar Tech Ltd	Sanyo
MHS SA	SealTronic Technology
Micronas Intermetall	Sharp Electronics
Microsoft	Softlock
MIDI Manufacturers Association (MMA)	Sonic Foundry
Mitsubishi	Sonic Solutions
Mitsubishi Electric Corp.	Digital World Services (Sonopress/BMG Storage Media)
MODE (Music-on-Demand)	Sony Electronics
Motorola	Sony Music
MPMan.com (formerly Saehan Information Systems)	Spectra.Net/Throttlebox
Music Copyright Operational Services (MCOS)	Sphere Multimedia
Music Producers Guild (MPG)	ST Microelectronics
Music.co.jp	Sun Microsystems
Musicmaker	Sunhawk.com Corp.
MusicMarc, Inc.	Supertracks
MusicMatch	TDK Electronics
Napster	Telecom System International
National Association of Recording Merchandisers (NARM)	Telian
National Music Publishers Association (NMPA)	Texas Instruments
NetActive	Thomson Consumer Electronics
News Corp (NDS Technologies)	Tokyo Electron Device
Nielsen Media Research	Tornado Group, Inc.
Nokia	Toshiba
NTT	Touchtunes Digital Jukebox
NTT DoCoMo	Unitech Electronics
Oak Technology, Inc.	Universal Music
Oberthur Card System Analog Devices	URocket, Inc. (formerly Packard Bell NEC)
Perception Digital, Ltd.	Vedalabs
Philips	Verance Corporation
Pioneer	Voquette, Inc.
PortalPlayer, Inc.	Warner Music
Preview Systems	Wave Systems
PricewaterhouseCoopers	Waveless Radio Consortium (WLR)
QDesign	Wavo
QPASS	World Theater, Inc.
QPICT	Xerox
Real Networks	Yamaha
	ZipLabs

26   Phase 2 was the heart of what SDMI stood for, which was the protection of copyrighted material. Phase 2 was to be implemented by late 2000 or early 2001 and involved the digital "watermark." Phase 2 was described by SDMI as follows:

> The transition from first- to second-generation portable devices would be handled by having Phase 1 and Phase 2 computer applications supporting the devices.
>
> The computer application supporting the device will include a mechanism, or trigger, to prompt the user to upgrade to Phase 2 technology, once such technology is available, in order to play or copy Phase 2 content. The mechanism will be triggered by data incorporated in new, SDMI-compliant music that is released after the Phase 2 technology is available.
>
> The transition mechanism [*Phase 2 technology that is embedded in the device*] will not cut off any function of the Phase 1 application or portable device. However, consumers who want to be able to play or copy new, SDMI-compliant music through an SDMI-compliant computer application will have to upgrade their application to Phase 2 technology. The owner of a Phase 1 device and supporting application may choose not to do so, but that person will not be able to use it for new, SDMI-compliant music. The trigger mechanism will not automatically upgrade the computer application; the individual user will have to choose the upgrade.
>
> The Phase 2 computer application supporting portable devices will enable consumers to "rip" CDs, as they do now, but only for personal use on their own computers or portable devices. That application will not allow the user to make those copies available on pirate sites on the Internet. Moreover, the Phase 2 application will be able to recognize pirated music—i.e., music that has not been authorized to be distributed in insecure, compressed form—and it will refuse to accept a download of that pirated music from the Internet. The application will not reject authorized distributions, such as where an artist or record company chooses to make music available on the Internet for free distribution.
>
> Finally, computer and consumer electronics devices will be able to accommodate both SDMI-compliant and non-SDMI-compliant formats (e.g., MP3) in the same application. The only music files that will be rejected in Phase 2 applications are those that are identified as "pirated."[15]

27   Essentially, Phase 2 of the SDMI would limit the number of times a user could copy a CD or MP3 file to one, for their own personal use. While this limited the extent of the "personal exemption" granted in copyright, such a limitation would be legal since the personal use was an exemption, not a right. As well, Phase 2 applications would not allow a user to copy or download and play an illegally copied CD or file that had been made in the past.

28   Critics of the SDMI suggested that the organization was designed to limit competition and control the industry. Exhibit 5 presents the position SDMI took against accusations of antitrust violations.

29   Critics also suggested that the SDMI would not be the secure system it proposed to be. To counteract such criticism, the SDMI looked to a group that they felt would be the best at developing a secure system for help hackers themselves. In September of 2000, the SDMI launched its "crack SDMI" contest where hackers were given the opportunity to hack into the system and potentially win US$10,000 for their innovativeness. Exhibit 6 presents the open letters on the SDMI website explaining the contest, and the following quote presents their rationale.

The Challenge[16]

Several proposals are currently being considered for the Phase Two screening technology. Some are digital watermarking technologies; others use a different technology to provide the screening functionality. The challenge is to defeat the screening technology. For example,

EXHIBIT 5
Antitrust Statement on the Secure Digital Music Initiative*

Two points of antitrust law govern the SDMI process:

First, many of the companies in this process are competitors of other participants. SDMI is not intended to be, and cannot take the form of, an agreement that limits competition.

Second, the antitrust laws permit, indeed under appropriate circumstances encourage, the creation of neutral standards that benefit the affected industry and consumers.

The SDMI specification is such a standard. Record companies have identified the lack of an open and interoperable standard for security as the single greatest impediment to the growth of legitimate markets for electronic distribution of copyrighted music. Likewise, technology companies developing computer software, hardware and consumer electronics devices that will handle new forms of digital music have realized that an important part of these devices is the presence (or absence) of adequate security for electronic music. The SDMI specification will reflect both the legitimate needs of the record labels for security of digital music and the technical constraints and realistic needs of technology companies. By supporting a wide variety of agreements between rights owners and consumers, such as specification will enable multiple new and flexible business models to emerge in the marketplace.

Technology companies can reasonably conclude that an SDMI-compliant product will meet the security needs of record companies and that consumers purchasing such devices will have broad, legitimate access to music. Moreover, the SDMI process has the potential for facilitating broad interoperability between compliant software and electronic devices. Both results create value of consumers.

The result of the process however, will be a specification, not a agreement. Each music company, and indeed each participant, will make its own decisions as to the degree the security it finds acceptable in light of marketplace conditions and each technology company will decide whether and the extent to which it incorporates the SDMI specifications in its designs.

*SDMI Portable Device Specification, Part 1, Version 1.0, Los Angeles, July 8, 1999, Document Number pdwg99070802, p. 5.

where the proposed technology is a watermark, the challenge is to remove or alter the watermark while not significantly degrading the quality of a digital music sample. Marked samples and files may be downloaded from this site. If you believe you have successfully defeated the security technology you may upload the attacked sample or file to this website. We will evaluate your submission. Under certain conditions, challengers may be able to receive compensation for describing and providing to SDMI their successful attack.

30   Some felt this was an innovative method for the SDMI to deal with a major problem for the protected industry it was trying to create. Others were not as optimistic.

As things stand, however, SDMI is more likely to be sunk by the forces in the marketplace than by clever hacking. It has been overtaken by events following the rise of Napster. Some of its members of the SDMI consortium are already selling proprietary systems of their own. Most damming of all is the fact that any software-based music-protection system can be attacked by analysing the software player itself—as was shown when the system that protects DVDs was compromised last year. In other words, whatever happens over the next few weeks, SDMI is certain to be cracked sooner or later. So even if nobody defeats the security mechanisms and claims the $10,000, SDMI's triumph will probably be hollow. Worse, if the protection software is cracked straightaway, it could deal a fatal blow to what is already an ailing standard.[17]

EXHIBIT 6
An Open Letter to the Digital Community

Source: SDMI website, July 2000.

Here's an invitation to show off your skills, make some money, and help shape the future of the online digital music economy.

The Secure Digital Music Initiative is a multi-industry initiative working to develop a secure framework for the digital distribution of music. SDMI-protected content will be embedded with an inaudible, robust watermark or use other technology that is designed to prevent the unauthorized copying, sharing, and use of digital music.

We are now in the process of testing the technologies that will allow these protections. The proposed technologies must pass several stringent tests: they must be inaudible, robust, and run efficiently on various platforms, including PCs. They should also be tested by *you*.

So here's the invitation: Attack the proposed technologies. Crack them.

By successfully breaking the SDMI-protected content, you will play a role in determining what technology SDMI will adopt. And there is something more in it for you, too. If you can remove the watermark or defeat the other technology on our proposed copyright protection system, you may earn up to $10,000.

To participate, just go to the website at www.hacksdmi.org after September 15, 2000 and read the public challenge agreement. If you agree to the terms, you will have until at least October 7, 2000 to do your best.

SDMI is a body that includes 200+ companies and organizations from start-ups to global enterprises, and from around the world. Participants include leading consumer electronics, information technology, music, and wireless telecom companies. (More information can be found at www.sdmi.org)

Here's your chance to shape the future of digital music.

Sincerely,
Leonardo Chiariglione
Executive Director, SDMI
September 6, 2000

(continued)

31   In some ways the music industry was similar to the computer software industry in that the digital format facilitated easy copying of the original product and mass distribution. As personal computers first became widespread, there were fears that mass pirating of computer software would destroy the legitimate software market. Indeed there was pirating of many programs, but the majority of the software used around the world was purchased legally and the software industry was one of the strongest in the world.

32   In practice, SDMI appeared to focus solely on the MP3 market.

> Although MP3 files are the most prevalent on the Internet, there are many other audio compression formats in use or under development that achieve better compression and/or quality. A competitor to the portable MP3 player, for example, is the MiniDisc that uses higher quality ATRAC compression though only achieving a reduction of 5:1 in file size.[18]

It is therefore conceivable that all of SDMI's proverbial eggs were in one basket.

ATTEMPTING TO CONTROL THE INDUSTRY

33   Prior to the formation of the SDMI, the RIAA had been fighting legal battles to preserve the existing industry order. The introduction of an MP3 player to the market sparked the RIAA to sue the manufacturer for violating the 1992 Audio Home Recording Act

EXHIBIT 6
(continued)

SDMI welcomes this opportunity to correct a few misconceptions that have surfaced since the public challenge was announced (see www.hacksdmi.org for details about the challenge).
To be clear, with SDMI:

- You will be able to make personal copies of your music. The SDMI specification allows people to make an unlimited number of personal copies of their CDs if in possession of the original CD. Nothing SDMI is doing will conflict with journalists' and educators' use. What will be affected is the ability to make large numbers of perfect digital copies of music, and distribute them instantaneously on the Internet without any compensation to the creator or copying holder.
- SDMI-compliant players will play music already in your library, as well as new unprotected music, and new SDMI-protected music that has been legitimately acquired.
- You will be able to access more music. SDMI-complaint devices will permit consumers to access more music than they currently can over the Internet, because copyright holders will be able to distribute music online without fear that it will be distributed instantaneously worldwide on the Internet.
- You will be able to play the music you already own. The CDs and MP3s you already have will be able to play on any SDMI-compliant device.

SDMI will enhance your ability to put music online, whether you are affiliated with a record label or not. Prior to the inception of SDMI, an artist who wanted to distribute his or her music over the Internet could not be assured of retaining control of it. With SDMI, a person will be able to choose SDMI protection if he or she wants. In fact, SDMI is taking pains to be sure its protections are available to all who want them, affiliated or independent, large or small, famous or undiscovered.

SDMI has engaged in dialogue with critics of the SDMI effort. Movements such as open source software and groups such as the Electronic Frontier Foundation play a valuable role in bringing attention to important policy issues as technology advances and new business models emerge. We have had extensive dialogue with EFF and with representatives of the open source community since the public challenge was announced. While we have agreed to disagree on certain details. SDMI has always welcomed and continues to welcome dialogue on this effort. I hope this answers some misconceptions and unfounded fears that have recently emerged.

Sincerely,

Leonardo Chiariglione
Executive Director, SDMI

because "it does not employ a Serial Copyright Management System ("SCMS") that sends, receives, and acts upon information about the generation and copyright status of the files that it plays."[19] The suit was lost and appealed. The appeal was denied on the ground that while the memory cards that the Rio player used to store music could be viewed as a recording device, the player itself was not a recording device and therefore not subject to the stipulations of the Act. The player was termed a "space-shifting" device that allowed the owner to shift materials from one format to another for their own, non-commercial purposes.

> The Rio's operation is entirely consistent with the Act's main purpose—the facilitation of personal use. As the Senate Report explains, "[t]he purpose of [the Act] is to ensure the right of the consumers to make analog or digital audio recordings of copyrighted music for their private, noncommercial use." The Act does so through its home taping exemption which

"protects all noncommercial copying by consumers of digital and analogue musical recordings." The Rio merely makes copies in order to render portable, or "space-shift," those files that already reside on a user's hard drive.[20]

34   The RIAA also attacked the new business models, such as the MP3.com website, that did not pay royalties for the music being made available to the public, arguing that they robbed the artists and the record companies of their due revenue. The RIAA sued MP3.com for copyright infringement. Although MP3.com argued that it was merely a "listening post" for subscribers to listen to the songs and then purchase those they liked, the court ruled that the service MP3.com provided was in fact a service that allowed the copying of copyrighted material for commercial use, not for a consumer's personal use, and therefore was done in violation of copyright. As the judge in the case observed,

> The defendant purchased tens of thousands of popular CDs in which the plaintiffs held the copyrights, and, without authorization, copied their recordings onto its computer servers so as to be able to replay the recordings for its subscribers.[21]

35   Other types of MP3 file sharing sites known as "peer-to-peer" systems allowed members to utilize software that connected their computers to other members on the network, allowing all members to search for and access music files.

> The technology, popularized by Napster, [was] that of allowing users to share their MP3 file collection by logging on to a common server. The system allow[ed] users to search and download files from a distributed system that often [had] over 750 GB of files available. There [were] other similar systems online that [used] a centralized server system such as CuteMX and iMesh, which offer[ed] other types of media in addition to MP3 files. A recent potential addition to the menu of online offerings for file sharing called Gnutella, from Nullsoft, [had] for the moment been nipped in the bud by its parent company, America Online.[22]

36   The service provided by these websites operated in a legal gray area. It appeared legal for the owners of a CD to copy it, store it onto their computer hard drives and further upload it onto their MP3 player so long as it was for private use.[23] Private use, by definition, does not indicate that users exchange these copies with others through a computer network. The legality of the above-mentioned file-swapping facilitators was also questionable. It was unclear if it was legal to directly or indirectly make money from the provision of this service. These sites defended their actions as being merely facilitators for Internet users, as opposed to being actual distributors of copied materials in violation of copyright laws. It was this defense that Napster used against the injunction brought against it by the RIAA.

37   Although the majority of the MP3 files found on the Internet infringed copyright, it was possible to obtain noninfringing MP3 files. In fact, the availability of MP3 files on some websites had become a new marketing tool to increase record sales. Often, record companies or established artists would post files containing newly released songs that were free to the public in order to create publicity for an upcoming release, in the hope that such interest would generate additional sales of the album. For example, a 1999 study by Warner music indicated that "following the release of a Tom Petty track in MP3 format on the Internet prior to the album's street release . . . first week sales (of the new album) were considerably higher than the first week for Petty's previous album."[24]

38   Although this study suggested that the sharing of MP3 files increased CD sales, it was criticized as being focused on the music-buying public in general, not the specific demographic who were most likely to use Napster. Another study presented by the plaintiffs in the case against Napster suggested that among college students (who constituted a large majority of Napster users at the time), "the more songs Napster users have downloaded, the more likely they are to admit or imply that such has reduced their music purchases," and that "sales at stores near colleges or universities declined." Ultimately, the judge in the case concluded that "Napster use is likely to reduce CD purchases by college students, whom defendant admits constitute a key demographic."[25]

39   Occasionally, established artists, themselves, would release entire albums in MP3 format onto the Internet. This occurred under their own label to gain more control over their music and earn more revenue than they would if they were tied to a record company.[26] Additionally, some MP3 sites would pay licensing fees to the record companies and charge consumers for downloading files. For artists who were not established or did not have a recording contract, MP3 files and the Internet were tools to spread their music and hopefully generate sales. There were thousands of MP3 music files available from unknown groups looking to be discovered.

40   Industry observers thought there was a real opportunity for content providers and MP3 distributors to work together and reap huge revenues. By paying or collecting licensing fees to the record companies and then charging their users a nominal fee, MP3 file distributors or search networks like Napster (who had around 20 million users in July 2000) could make millions. As one analyst noted, "[t]he idea is to sell record companies a minority stake in Napster and split subscription, sponsorship, and advertising revenues. If 20 million users pay $100 a year for subscriptions, that's $2 billion."[27] However, many of the MP3 distribution sites on the Internet and their users were staunchly anticommercial. There was a strong culture of free exchange of ideas and information over the Net, and often the word "free" meant "no-fee" as well as open. The differing philosophies made relations between the two players somewhat adversarial.

41   Listen.com was launched in August 1999 as a "comprehensive" Web directory for legal downloadable music, garnering unprecedented investments from all five of the major record labels (BMG, EMI, Sony, Universal, Warner). The company hired an editorial staff of about 50 to find, review, and categorize hundreds of thousands of music files in genres ranging from "hip-hop" to "cuddlecore."[28]

NAPSTER AND THE SDMI: NEXT STEPS

42   With the 11th-hour removal of the injunction against them, Napster was free to resume business as usual; however, they were not cleared of any wrongdoing. Although they were allowed to remain in operations until a final decision, they were still being sued for copyright infringement. A final decision would come sometime in September 2000.

43   The decision would have a number of important ramifications for the industry as well as for the SDMI. The various stakeholders watched with great interest, particularly the SDMI. By early fall 2000, Phase 2 was moving along on schedule, but the infighting between two important members of the initiative posed a major threat to the entire organization.

44   While Napster was contemplating its next moves, the SDMI was assessing whether its attempts to control the industry would prevail. It needed to assess whether the legal framework within which the industry operated would offer sufficient control, or whether additional efforts to control the technology, as was progressing in Phase 2, were required. Napster realized that while it may be able to succeed with the current players, the global nature of the industry left open the possibility for noncompliant technology and modes of operation.

1. This case has been written on the basis of published sources only. Consequently, the interpretation and perspectives presented in this case are not necessarily those of Napster, Inc. or any of its employees.

2. www.sdmi.org/who_we_are.htm.

3. Richard Henderson, Music & Money: The Billboard Spotlight—How Much Is That Deal in the Window?" *Billboard Magazine,* April 29, 2000.

4. Mark Perry, "Audio-files: Good Sounds on Trial," *1 Technology Law Forum,* September 2000, p. 5.

5. *PC World Magazine,* July 2000, p. 127.

6. *A&M Records, Inc. et al.* v. *Napster Inc.,* Case Nos. C99-5183 MHP (ADR), C00-0074 MHP (ADR) United States District Court, Northern California District, San Francisco Division, July 26, 2000, p. 23.

7. *Vigneux et al.* v. *Canadian Performing Rights Society,* [1945] 2 D.L.R. 1, reversing [1943] 3 D.L.R. 369, affirming [1942] 3 D.L.R. 449 [hereinafter Vigneux].

8. Ibid. at 10.

9. Ibid.

10. www.riaa.org/About-Who.cfm.

11. Both CRIA and BPI are members of the International Federation of the Phonographic Industry (IFPI). Also members of the IFPI are the recording industry associations of: Argentina, Australia, Austria, Belgium, Brazil, Bulgaria, Chile, Colombia, Czech Republic, Denmark, Egypt, Finland, France, Germany, Ghana, Greece, Hong Kong, Hungary, Iceland, India, Ireland, Israel, Italy, Japan, Kenya, Lebanon, Malaysia, Mexico, the Netherlands, New Zealand, Nigeria, Norway, Poland, Portugal, Singapore, Slovak Republic, South Africa, Spain, Sweden, Switzerland, Taiwan, Thailand, Turkey, United States and Venezuela. The IFPI is a member of the SDMI. As such, the IFPI members are represented in the SDMI process. Because of the size of the RIAA relative to the industry associations of the other member countries, it is feasible that the RIAA maintains an independent membership in the SDMI.

12. Presentation to the SDMI Organizing Plenary, Feb. 26, 1999. www.sdmi.org/present.org.plenary.htm.

13. Ibid.

14. SDMI Update: Statement from the Executive Director and Portable Working Group Chair, May 25, 1999, www.sdmi.org/statement_May_25_1999.htm.

15. SDMI Update: Statement from the Executive Director and Portable Working Group Chair, May 25, 1999, www.sdmi.org/statement_May_25_1999.htm.

16. SDMI website www.hacksdmi.org.

17. *The Economist,* September 23, 2000, p. 96.

18. Supra note 3 at 2.

19. *Recording Industry Association of America* v. *Diamond Multimedia Systems Inc.,* No. 98-56727 (9th Cir. 06/15/1999), p. 3.

20. Ibid. p. 7.

21. *RIAA* v. *MP3.com, Inc.* United States District Court, Southern District of New York, 00 Civ. 472 (JSR). May 4, 2000, p. 2.

22. Supra note 3 at 4–5.

23. *Copyright Act,* R.S.C. 1985, c-42 at s.81.

24. *A&M Records, Inc. et al.* v. *Napster Inc.,* Case Nos. C99-5183 MHP (ADR), C00-0074 MHP (ADR) United States District Court, Northern California District, San Francisco Division, July 26, 2000, p. 23.

25. *A&M Records, Inc. et al.* v. *Napster Inc.,* Case Nos. C99-5183 MHP (ADR), C00-0074 MHP (ADR) United States District Court, Northern California District, August 10, 2000.

26. Some artists released newly recorded music online prior to release by their label because they were rebelling against the control extended over their music by their label (i.e., Offspring, Smashing Pumpkins).

27. Steven V. Brull, Dennis K. Berman, and Mike France, "Inside Napster," *Business Week,* August 14, 2000, p. 120.

28. H. C. Lee, "Listen.com chimes in on the layoff trend," *The Standards,* January 3, 2001.

Case 31

Colorado Creative Music

> *. . . I was a good musician, so I thought, what better thing to start than a music company?*

1   Darren Skanson, lead artist and CEO of Colorado Creative Music (CCM) settled into his flight on Friday, March 9, 2001. He was heading to New Smyrna Beach, Florida, where he would perform at the *Images* arts festival. As lead artist, Darren had been traveling all over the country performing light classical guitar and selling his line of CDs. As CCM's biggest money machine, Darren was performing 40 2–3-day weekends a year. As CEO, Darren's concerns were increasing. He was being pulled in too many directions. He realized that he couldn't continue to travel and perform as much as he had been and still manage the growth of his record label. While he waited for the plane to take off, he thought about how to turn the nightmare that his company had become into the dream that he believed it could be.

DARREN CURTIS SKANSON

> I've always been a performer; music was in our household from very early on. When I first saw what a musical group, a band, can do to an audience—just the excitement and the adulation that they received—that moment changed my life. I said, "I want to do that."

2   Darren Curtis Skanson was born and raised on a farm seven miles outside of Fertile, a small town of about 800 people in the northwest part of Minnesota. Darren's father was an elementary school teacher, and his mother was a piano teacher and a teacher's aid. Darren was the oldest of four boys.

3   Darren's passion for music began at an early age. Some of his earliest memories were of singing with his brother Brant in church at the age of four. Darren traced his dream of being a rock star to watching the crowd respond to a high school band performance.

> I was in seventh or eighth grade and one of my best friends, a tenth-grader, was playing with a bunch of seniors. They played a pep rally for a sporting event, and the school all comes down and gets together. Everyone came out of the bleachers and went up to the stage and, you know, it was a pretty strong experience. . . . The first night that I ever played live with a band on stage and got a similar response just reinforced it.

4   With the encouragement of his parents, Darren went to Moorhead State University, graduating with a BA in music in 1989. This education helped him discover the intellectual and emotional aspects of music. Darren had originally intended to get a Music Industry degree, which required a minor in business. But during his senior year, the music took over, and he ended up without enough business courses to fulfill the minor. Darren regretted that now, "but you know when you are 22 years old you don't really foresee the future very well. You see the ideals and not the practicalities."

5   Just out of college, Darren began performing as lead guitarist in a heavy metal band called Mata Hari. The band toured the U.S. playing in small venues and opening for bigger bands in larger venues. After four years Darren was frustrated. The band had produced only one CD, and the band members did not want to move to a place that was more conducive to making a break in heavy metal. They had been living and performing out of

Fargo, North Dakota, which was not a hotbed for performing artists. When Jack, the lead singer, left the band to get married, Darren was ready to call it quits and break up the band.

6   In March of 1993, Mata Hari's last stretch of a tour put the group in Denver. Darren liked Denver and looked for an excuse to stay. He found an ad in the newspaper soliciting a guitarist for a Classical-New Age duo called "Watson and Company." Darren's classical training gave him the courage he needed to call and set up an audition. He got the job, which turned out to be a major turning point in his musical career.

7   Malcolm Watson was a classical violinist, who was making his living by performing at art festivals around Colorado and selling his CDs. Darren and Malcolm produced Watson and Company's third CD. Darren's college friend, Jennifer, was hired to serve as Watson and Company's booking agent. She began booking the duo nationwide, and within a year Watson and Company's sales increased from $100,000 a year to a quarter of a million dollars.

8   Darren believed that there were ways to capitalize on the knowledge the team had about the art festivals. He saw art festivals as a strong distribution venue that could be tapped. Darren's vision was to sign on other artists in a way that kept them tied in so that they could not just absorb the knowledge and leave. Discouraged that Malcolm wanted to move more slowly, Darren and Jennifer decided to end their relationship with Watson.

9   Jennifer began booking other artists, taking a percentage of their sales. Darren wanted to move beyond booking artists to forming a company that would manage and promote artists. His vision was to record, produce, and sell his own music as well as the music of a cohesive group of artists that would comprise a unique record label and distribution company. Jennifer was helpful as a booking agent, but Darren's vision of a viable business venture differed from hers. Jennifer was not the person Darren was looking for in a business partner.

COLORADO CREATIVE MUSIC

I've always been a very driven person, and I got tired of waiting or depending on other people to get things done. I was always the spearhead in getting stuff done in every other organization or business relationship I was in.

10   Darren started Colorado Creative Music in January of 1995. Working solo, Darren produced two CDs and sold them at the art festivals that Jennifer booked for him. He did this on his own for two and a half years, and as sales grew and doing business got more complicated he began seeing a need for bringing others onboard.

11   In June of 1997, Darren's cousin Ted, a business school student at St. Cloud State University in Minnesota, contacted him about doing a business internship. Darren and Ted began writing down everything about how the business was run. "We started transferring the knowledge to my cousin, and then into processes." At the end of Ted's internship, Darren tried to find someone who could continue the work Ted had begun, with hopes of fine-tuning them into a workable set of operational systems. In early 1998, Darren hired Ryan, a young musician who was familiar with the music industry, to continue documenting processes and also to help with equipment repairs and recordings. By summer, CCM was so busy that Darren started to look for someone to take over some of the day-to-day operations, like filling and mailing orders, and handling the bookkeeping. In late fall he hired Andy Harling, a classical guitarist, to help with the day-to-day office work and the maintenance of instruments and equipment. When Ryan left CCM to go back to school to finish his music degree, Andy inherited the task of examining the day-to-day processes to make CCM operate more efficiently.

12   Soon after Andy was hired, Jennifer, who had continued to act as Darren's booking agent, had openings for two shows that had been left vacant by a musician who had cancelled at the last minute. Darren was already booked for other gigs, but felt it was important to find another artist to do the shows. Darren quickly recorded a CD of Andy's repertoir, duplicated it in-house, and sent Andy out to do the two gigs. To Darren's excitement, Andy was successful. But now that Andy had actually gone out and done an art festival under Darren's direction, Andy had valuable knowledge of how to capitalize on art festivals. Darren felt there was a risk that Andy could leave and become his competitor. Recognizing this as an opportunity, Darren signed Andy for a recording contract. Andy's first full CD with CCM was launched as Andrew Thomas Harling.

13   As Andy's responsibilities expanded into more and more performing, CCM needed someone else to help answer telephones and fill orders. Amy was hired in August 2000 as Andy's assistant.

14   Darren's growing company required more space, so Darren moved CCM from his one-bedroom office and recording studio to a large rental house. A large laundry room in the basement was transformed into a well-organized mailroom; a spare bedroom served as an office. Darren built a workbench for repairing equipment and turned another room in the basement into a nearly soundproof recording studio. The garage served as a warehouse, with all inventory and equipment neatly organized on labeled shelves and workbenches.

THE PERFORMANCE MUSIC RECORDING INDUSTRY AND THE DIGITAL REVOLUTION

> What used to be a quarter of a million dollar piece of gear ten years ago, say in the late 80s, you can get now for five thousand dollars, and the quality is just as good, maybe even better.

15   Traditionally, the record industry was the exclusive domain of 5 or 6 major record labels. These major labels had large staffs, big budgets, and huge distribution. The cost of recording and pressing vinyl was very high. In the early 1980s, a professional recording studio could cost several million dollars. Although most performances were recorded on tape, editing was virtually nonexistent. Music was typically recorded onto a multimaster track. This was then mixed down to a ½-inch tape called the master. The master was then transferred to vinyl. In order to cut anything, the ½-inch tape had to be physically spliced with a razor. Because of the high cost of recording and of pressing in vinyl, a company had to produce a minimum of about five thousand copies of any given album just to cover fixed expenses. The costs and difficulty of building a major record label kept industry competition in the hands of a few established companies.

16   With the digital revolution came the compact disc. The cost of digitally recording and burning a CD was significantly less expensive than creating copies from a vinyl or tape master. In 2000, a professional recording studio could be assembled for about $5,000. In addition, the hardware and computers used to edit music were affordable, even for the spare-room hobbyist. The ability to edit music and manipulate it via computer became far more comprehensive than in the past. Not only was digital recording and editing cheap, CDs were cheap to duplicate, even in small quantities. Kashif (1996) estimated that 500 CDs cost between $1.90 and $3.63 per CD to duplicate. A production run of 2,000 CDs would bring the cost down to under $1 per unit.

17   Unlike vinyl or tape masters, digital recordings could be duplicated without deterioration of the master disc. A musician could create a master CD on his own home computer, design and print attractive labels, and duplicate 500–1,000 without investing in expensive

EXHIBIT 1   Record Label Company Categories

Major Labels Over 100 artists	Independent Labels 10–100 artists	Micro-Labels 2–10 artists	Vanity Labels 1 artist
Sony	Soundings of the Planet (Inspirational/Healing)	Etherian (meditative)	Bob Culbertson
Columbia	Narada (New Age)	Evol Egg Nart (rock/pop)	Lisa Lynn Franco
BMG	Higher Octave Metal (New Age)	Cuneiform Records (progressive jazz)	Watson & Company
EMI	Metal Blade Records (Heavy Metal)	CCM (light acoustic)	Lao Tizer
Giant Records	Rhino Records (Compilations)		Esteban Ramirez
Warner Brothers	W.A.R. (Punk, Rock, & Reggae)		
Elektra Records	Windham Hill (light classical & easy listening)		
Atlantic Records			

Note: Hustwit lists over 1000 major and independent labels. This table illustrates CCM's perceived competitor and/or partner labels. (Hustwit, Gary (1998) *Releasing an Independent Record*, Rockpress Publishing Company.)

equipment or contracting with a professional studio. The size and weight of compact discs made storage and shipping cheap and convenient, thus opening the music recording and distribution industry to an uncountable number of players in even remote locations.

18   Production costs represented only part of the total cost picture to launch a recording. Major recording labels invested heavily in marketing, promotion, distribution, royalties and "image" building, often exceeding one million dollars. On the other end of the spectrum, "anyone with talent and a business perspective can start their own virtual reality or vanity label . . ." (Wacholtz, 2001).

19   With the availability of cheap production equipment and easy access to internet marketing and distribution, the industry became fragmented and distinct segments appeared. Music production companies, or labels, generally fell into four categories, or levels. Exhibit 1 gives some examples of the labels within these categories.

20   The "first tier companies" consisted of the major labels such as Columbia, BMG, EMI, and Sony Music. These labels had national, or even international, distribution. Typically, they had more than 100 artists under contract, representing a broad array of musical styles. They did not tend to focus on just one genre. CCM did not really compete with major labels, and Darren Curtis Skanson didn't want to position himself to compete directly with classical guitarists such as Christopher Parkening and John Williams, whose music was produced by Sony's Classical Division.

21   Independent labels were the next largest segment of the industry. Many of these companies were managed by a musician/artist, but larger Independents were run by professional managers. Independent labels had anywhere from 10–100 artists under contract. Some of these labels may have been comparable in size to some of the major labels, but independents tended to focus on one or two genres of music. Narada, whose focus was New Age music, was a typical example of a successful independent label. Another producer of New Age music was Higher Octave. Metal Blade Records was an independent label that focused on heavy metal. Rhino Records focused on re-releasing compilations. Soundings of the Planet produced several easy-listening and classical offerings that directly competed with CCM. Some of the larger independent labels had national distribution, but most were regional or specialty distributors.

22   The next tier of recording companies were known as the "micro-labels." These labels typically had fewer than ten artists under contract, and tended to be more tightly focused than the independent labels. The micro-labels had small staffs, and the owner/manager was often the lead artist. Micro-labels seldom had formal distribution systems, relying on direct sales to fans and wholesale to clubs and specialty retailers. Because of the size of these labels and the small distribution networks they commanded, they existed only because of the low costs involved in digital recording. Etherian was an established micro-label that competed directly with Colorado Creative Music.

23   The most specialized segment of the music industry consisted of the vanity labels. These labels were created by independent artists who wanted to record and sell their own music. They were usually one-person operations with no formal distribution. These artists relied on direct sales to concertgoers and loyal fans. Musicians such as Bob Culbertson, Lisa Franco, Watson & Company, Peruvian Bands, and Lao Tizer are examples of artists on vanity labels that had been successful at direct selling at art festivals.

24   While it was fairly common for a vanity label to move up to micro-label status, it was quite uncommon for a micro-label to move up to the independent label level. Soundings of the Planet was one example of a record label that was able to do this. It was virtually unheard of for an independent to compete at the major label level, although some independent labels had been acquired by major label companies.

MARKETING AND PROMOTION

25   A key element in recorded-music sales was getting music heard. In general people didn't want to buy music they had not heard. The major labels used their established relationships with prominent radio stations for tremendous leverage in getting new music played on prime-time programs. Command of distributors and capital to produce in large quantities allowed major record labels to offer new recordings for sale at the same time that radio stations gave the music airplay. Music was a fashionable business, and sales were heavily correlated to good timing.

26   The radio stations' primary relationship was with the major labels, so independents, micro, and vanity labels had to rely on other means of getting their music heard. Many bands on these smaller labels relied on touring and performing. Big Head Todd and the Monsters (Giant Records), Phish (Warner Brothers), and Widespread Panic (Capricorn Records) found their fame through the college circuit, performing and selling their music all over the country. Musicians who recorded their music on vanity labels often played small local venues, such as bars, coffee houses, and bookstores.

27   Because getting music heard was so essential, there were promotional companies that specialized in getting music airplay. These companies called stations to negotiate airplay, promotional giveaways, and interviews. While many independent labels might have had the funding for this, smaller labels could rarely afford such extensive promotional campaigns.

DISTRIBUTION

28   Most recorded music was distributed through major distributors and "one-stops" (see Exhibit 2) Major distributors contracted with large chain stores like Tower Records, Sam Goody, Barnes and Noble, and Borders Books and Music. It was very difficult for small record labels to use a major distributor because of the large requirements and risky payment policies that had become standard for the industry. These distributors generally

EXHIBIT 2
**The Recording
Industry
Distribution Chain**

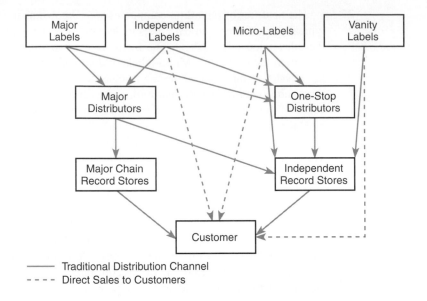

operated on a 60–90-day turnaround with full return. This meant that if a CD sold, the producer would typically be paid two or three months later. In addition, all those CDs that didn't sell were returned to the label or producer. Major distributors also wanted large quantities of inventory. A label might have to front the money for 40,000 CDs, which required a large amount of working capital, with no guarantee that the CDs would sell.

29   One-stops started out mainly to service independent music stores like Joe's Records on the corner. These one-stops allowed stores to buy in smaller quantities than from a major distributor. One-stops would sometimes carry music from major labels, but were similar to an independent label in that they tended to specialize in one type of music.

FROM MUSICIAN TO ENTREPRENEUR

I started this business because I was a good guitar player, so I thought a music company is perfect. But what you need to start a business—to be an entrepreneur—is different than being a guitar player. So I had to learn not to concentrate so much on the musical end of things, and instead to concentrate on the entrepreneurial things. That was a huge shift that started with Acoustitherapy. That is really where that whole process began, when I said I don't need to make guitar music, I can make any kind of music, I just have to look at it as a businessman not a musician.

30   Darren Skanson soon realized that the physical work involved in setting up a studio was much easier than building and managing a business. His music degree did not prepare him for the tasks of marketing and promoting his music, nor did it provide a framework for creating a workable system of operations and control.

31   When Darren began Colorado Creative Music out of his bedroom in 1995, he did everything himself. He was his own accountant, desktop publisher, database manager, newsletter editor, website designer, and copywriter. Early on, he started transferring his stack of art festival contacts from 3 × 5 notecards to a computerized database. By 1997, he switched to a computerized accounting system.

32   Using only his own savings to finance the company, Darren was concerned about keeping overhead low and expense down (see Exhibit 3 for Income Statement

EXHIBIT 3 CCM Income Statements

Year ending	2000	1999	1998	1997
Income				
GIG sales	$181,451.92	$148,839.76	$145,721.78	$129,445.25
Wholesale	12,238.83	19,556.04	17,587.02	10,887.02
Mail & phone orders	11,442.24	2,928.72	3,148.00	included with wholesale
Website sales	6,419.35	760.50	0.00	0.00
other	1,758.79	1,417.89	3,714.98	1,259.59
Total Sales	213,311.13	173,502.91	170,171.78	141,591.86
other income	3,302.92	2,750.09	4,329.00	1,527.28
Total Income	216,614.05	176,253.00	174,500.78	143,119.14
cost of good sold	22,034.33	23,311.38	36,468.62	36,226.52
Gross Profit	$194,579.72	$152,941.62	$138,032.16	$106,892.62
Expenses				
Advertising Expense	$ 10,422.83	$ 4,388.71	$ 11,432.35	$ 4,110.43
Automobile Expense	0.00	2,279.01	1,644.83	4,016.88
Bad Check Expense	156.00	583.14	416.99	1,072.50
Bank Service Charges	5,320.39	4,790.75	3,070.60	2,509.47
Commissions	32,861.14	31,333.92	30,283.59	27,828.66
Dues and Subscriptions	10.00	0.00	0.00	397.45
Depreciation Expense	0.00	5,820.00	0.00	0.00
Equipment Rental	491.14	0.00	0.00	0.00
Furniture and Fixtures	0.00	0.00	329.95	656.84
Insurance	2,344.79	2,655.51	2,109.19	1,173.00
Interest Expense	631.96	0.00	0.00	0.00
Licenses and Permits	0.00	0.00	218.00	327.09
Miscellaneous	580.37	1,077.27	1,462.62	2,282.64
Parking Expense	308.75	661.00	348.00	258.00
Payroll	15,515.76	6,660.29	5,150.64	0.00
Payroll expenses/taxes	3,143.38	11,671.74	0.00	0.00
Postage and Delivery	6,432.22	2,321.22	1,626.06	2,150.97
Printing and Reproduction	4,691.82	1,818.19	4,414.28	7,409.34
Professional Fees*	29,719.26	2,242.50	217.10	1,145.00
Rent and storage fees	14,080.45	13,368.07	9,973.29	2,174.75
Repairs and Maintenance	2,531.25	1,863.00	3,217.77	2,229.01
Royalties	17,283.39	8,848.99	1,776.91	746.57
Shipping	3,776.97	3,257.89	2,804.05	2,345.05
Subscriptions	80.95	443.18	472.76	0.00
Supplies	13,142.81	7,343.05	5,343.78	8,247.67
Taxes	4,744.94	4,678.58	7,961.01	6,796.28
Telephone	4,399.22	5,269.83	4,860.00	4,754.38
Travel & Entertainment	16,156.64	23,889.21	17,759.91	19,092.13
Utilities	1,461.29	1,262.04	511.78	244.92
Total Expense	$190,287.72	$148,527.09	$117,405.46	$101,969.03
Net Income	$ 4,292.00	$ 4,414.53	$ 20,626.70	$ 4,923.59

*Note: This includes payments to backup musicians at live performances and an independent music consultant to direct the production of the "Classica" and "A Christmas Story" CDs.

Summaries). To save on time, Darren would purchase rolls of stamps and postage packages according to their weight. This sometimes resulted in over-postaging some packages. Stamps and address labels were affixed by hand, since CCM didn't have enough mail orders to warrant purchasing an automated postage system. As mail order demand grew, the wastefulness of the system became significant.

33   Promotion was most effective at art festivals, but Darren understood the need for retail distribution to increase sales. He approached some retailers himself, but found that it was an onerous and time-consuming task.

> I tried to take care of it myself, going out there trying to get CDs into stores, but it's too big a job for me. I have too many things pulling me into too many other directions. I actually hired a sales guy in the summer of '98, and he turned out to be worthless. He basically didn't do anything; he took the money and didn't do anything—the employer's nightmare. Then I tried friends who wanted to do it part time, but that didn't work out either.
>
> Then we hooked up with one of the "one-stops" here in Colorado. Basically what a one-stop does is they have a huge catalog of stuff. If the demand is there, the stores will ask the one-stop, "Do you have any Darren Curtis Skanson CDs?" The thing we ran into with that is we had some Barnes & Noble stores calling the one-stop to get our stuff, but the one-stop put such a mark-up on the CDs that B&N didn't want to buy from them. He's got to make money too, that I understand, but B&N would call us wanting to get more CDs and we'd tell them, "That's great, but we're doing business with John over there at USA One-stop. Just give him a call and he'll set you up." Then they call us back, and tell us that John is charging them a ridiculous amount for the CDs wholesale, and they say, "We don't want to deal with John, we want to deal with you." And you're back to where you started from.

34   In 1999, feeling overwhelmed with the tasks of running a business, Darren outsourced the accounting function and made a list of tasks and systems that needed to be codified (Exhibit 4). He also began reading books on entrepreneurship, searching for a way to organize Colorado Creative Music and to make it more profitable.

CREATING A SUSTAINABLE ENTERPRISE

35   Darren wanted Colorado Creative Music and Darren Curtis Skanson to become identifiable names, with enough demand to make distribution through large book and record stores feasible. He envisioned a promotional spot on the evening news, with thousands of people watching, and then heading out to buy his CD in a store. He wanted someone browsing the shelves to see a Darren Curtis Skanson CD, recognize him from the newscast, and buy it.

> I think you always start with a vision, and of course that vision was to record, produce, and sell my own music. And that of course still is a major part of CCM. Your vision always changes. I'm amazed at how much your vision changes as you learn and grow as a business person.

36   Darren's early success in selling his and Andy's recordings led him to realize the potential for profitability and growth that the digital revolution had opened up. He knew enough about the music industry to be wary of labeling himself "new age" or "classical" or "folk," competing with established artists. He decided to call his own music "light classical," and position CCM as a company that handled a portfolio of artists, each with a distinctive light acoustic style.

37   The first step in "branding" CCM was a promotional catalog that could be handed out to people who approached his sales table at art festivals and shopping malls. He enclosed the catalog with every sale and offered it for free on CCM's website.

EXHIBIT 4   Colorado Creative Music Task List

Research and Development

Musical
1. Song Writing
2. Arranging
3. Pre-production
4. Recording, Producing, Engineering
5. Mastering

Books to Read:
Zen and the Art of Motorcycle Maintenance, Persig

Market
1. CCM R + D Worksheet
2. Artwork

Books to Read:
Positioning: the Battle for Your Mind, Reis/Trout
22 Immutable Laws of Branding, Reis
The New Positioning, Trout
Guerilla Marketing, Levinson
Kottler on Marketing, Kottler

Operations

Accounting

Fulfillment

Maintenance
1. Instruments and Gear
2. Office Equipment

Gear Preparation for Shows

Duplication

Inventory Management

Database Management

Design
Books to Read:
The E-Myth, Gerber
Software to Know:
Quickbooks 2000 Pro
Microsoft Access
Microsoft Works
Microsoft Word 2000

Brand Marketing

Live Performance
1. Malls
2. Art Festivals
3. Concerts

Website

Essential elements
Books to Read:
Front-Page 2000 for Dummies
Software to Know:
Front-Page 2000

Publicity
1. Airplay: Radio, TV, Internet Radio
2. Live Interviews: Radio, TV
3. Print Press: Reviews, Features, Events listings

Promotions
1. In store
2. Contests
3. Sponsoring
4. Give-away

E-Mail

Monthly Newsletter
Books to Read:
Guerilla Marketing, Levinson
Software to Know:
Aureate Group Mail

Sales

Direct
1. Live performance
2. 800 #
3. Website
4. Mail order catalog
5. After sale
Thank you letter
Direct letters from database
Direct response

Books to Read: Guerilla Marketing, Levinson

Indirect

Traditional
1. Chain music stores
2. Chain book stores
3. Independent music stores

Nontraditional
1. Retail chains
2. Catalogs
3. Gift stores
4. Independent book stores
5. Health, Massage, Yoga, Thai Chi, Day care
6. Christian: chains and independents

---

38   CCM's first catalog was a small brochure. With the addition of new CCM offerings, Darren felt the need for an upgrade that would portray a high quality image. He was able to reproduce an attractive catalog for about 12 cents apiece. He was pleased with the appearance of catalogs, but he wasn't sure how to manage them as inventory or how to decide how many to produce at one time. He didn't want a box of 1,000 old catalogs on hand when he needed to add a new product to the order form. The company was adding two new titles a year, which made sales and inventory increasingly difficult to manage.

39   By December of 2000, CCM had four product lines, and a total of eleven different records. The four product lines (or brand names) were Darren Curtis Skanson, Acoustitherapy, Andrew Thomas Harling, and Music for Candles.

40   **Darren Curtis Skanson.** Darren described this line of music as "Light Classical Guitar." This product line was marketed as a more gentle and intimate approach to classical music, positioned against more purist classical guitarists such as John Williams and

Christopher Parkening. Darren has released five titles under this brand name. "Peace, Earth, and Guitars" was released in September of 1995. Due to the success of this title, CCM released "Peace, Earth, and Guitars, Volume II" in January 1997. Darren's next title was a Christmas album "Angels, Guitars, and Joy" released in October 1996. "Classica" was released in May 2000; "A Christmas Story" was released in November 2000. These last two releases featured a cello backup to Darren's solo guitar, in an effort to broaden Darren's audience appeal.

41   **Acoustitherapy.** This line of records was Darren's response to what many customers wanted from instrumental music. Customers specifically wanted acoustic instrumental music that was slow, soft, and soothing. Darren collected music from various artists who wrote original music and performed on a variety of acoustic instruments. "Relaxation" and "Regeneration" were released in September of 1997. "Gentle Passion" was released in October of 1998, and in July of 2000 "World Meditations" was released. Acoustitherapy was marketed as soft and soothing music for the mind, body, heart, and soul.

42   **Andrew Thomas Harling.** Andy's debut CD "The Road to the Soul" was a combination of traditional melodies and new compositions written by modern classical guitarists. A second CD was in the making, to be released by August of 2001.

43   **Music for Candles.** CCM engineered and produced a CD called "Starry Night," for the vanity label "Music for Candles." In 2001, CCM carried this product in its catalog under a distribution contract with the Music for Candles artists. Darren hoped to produce and distribute CDs for other labels to expand CCM's catalog offerings and promote CCM's name recognition.

PUSHING THE PRODUCTS

44   Darren knew that he needed to understand his customers and cater to their tastes. He had noticed that the people who approached him at the art festivals and shopping malls where he sold his CDs were generally white, middle-class adults, mostly mid-40s to 60-year-old women whose children were grown. These people expressed their delight in meeting Darren personally, and often asked for his autograph. Phone orders appeared to be coming from a similar demographic, with callers enthusiastic about talking with Darren personally when they placed an order for one of his recordings. Darren was careful to keep this personal touch and sent regular e-mails to his growing list of fans.

45   Darren understood quickly that these people were not classical music enthusiasts, but rather drawn to his music for its blend of soft acoustic sounds and familiar classical tunes. He chose his music offerings carefully, trying to maintain a distinction between himself and other artists. He knew that his company would need to offer a variety of titles to gain the sales volume he needed to compete for retail space.

46   Darren had an easy time selling his CDs in local music and book stores, but had not been able to set up distribution beyond his home state. Out of town, Darren relied on live performances to sell his recordings. For these shows (art festivals, shopping malls, and concerts), he set up a pricing structure that he hoped would encourage the purchase of more than one CD (see Exhibit 5). Darren wanted to encourage an impulse buy with customers that were harder to reach on a regular basis.

47   With regular appearances at two local upscale malls, Darren's pricing structure appeared to create some saturation. Many customers were returning fans who already had all his CDs. For this reason he changed the price at local mall performances to $17 per CD. Darren's rationale was clear, "if we are going to be playing at these places over and

EXHIBIT 5
CCM Pricing Structure for Recorded Compact Discs

At live shows	Mail, e-mail, and 800 number orders
1 CD $17.00	$16.00 per CD
2 CDs $28.00	_1.75_ shipping and handling per CD
3 CDs $38.00	$17.75 Total per CD
4 CDs $47.00	
5 CDs $55.00	(no mail-order discount for multiples)
6 CDs $62.00	
7 CDs $68.00	

over again, we can't be shooting ourselves in the foot by selling five CDs at a great price, then when the customer comes back, he or she has everything. We might even be too late on that. We may have shot ourselves in the foot already."

48   Darren was also concerned that Jennifer was not finding many new venues for him, preferring to book him at the regular shows and festivals where he already had a strong presence. Traveling around the country gave him exposure to a wider customer base, but he was afraid that bookings at the same shows year after year limited his ability to reach a broader market. As he brought more musicians on board, Darren believed that he could produce music that would appeal to a broader audience. By rotating artists, each performer would be able to do different festivals each year, minimizing the saturation problem.

49   In addition to festival and shopping mall distribution, Darren wanted to be able to offer his CDs in retail outlets nationwide. He knew he couldn't compete with the major labels, but he did not know how to break into the traditional industry distribution networks. From some of his reading on entrepreneurship, Darren concluded that it was important to think in terms of company "saleability" as a measure of business success, even though selling CCM to a major label was not his ultimate goal. He felt he could build a stronger, more focused business if he thought of CCM in terms of its attractiveness as a potential acquisition or investment. That meant that he needed to build enough volume for CCM products to be sold nationally through traditional distribution channels. Major labels expected sales of 15,000 copies of a recording in one year before they would consider offering a contract. This was the benchmark that Darren set for himself.

DARREN'S DILEMMA

The major dilemma is that we have built the backbone of our company on direct sales, whether it is at the gig, in the mall, or in the back end (800 number, website, mail order). That has been a very profitable thing for us, but as I discovered this last Christmas, I only have so many hours of performance in me to be out there direct selling—which is the engine that drives all of the other back end sales.

50   Darren realized that he had a long way to go in getting national distribution. By the end of 2000, Colorado Creative Music had sold over 30,000 "Darren Curtis Skanson" CDs, but that number included all five Darren Curtis Skanson titles over six years. Over a seven-month period, CCM sold 4,100 units of his CD "Classica" that was released in May 2000. Most of these were from direct sales, stemming from Darren's tireless efforts as performer, publicity agent, promoter, and salesman.

51   Darren started to list his goals and think about his options:

1. To create a profitable record label with a complementary range of artists.

2. To position Darren Curtis Skanson to compete with artists on a recording label on par with Sony Classical. This required selling records in stores through traditional distribution methods.

3. To create a product line, such as Acoustitherapy, that was saleable, and use the funds to work towards accomplishing goals 1 and 2.

52   Feeling strongly that something was missing in his efforts to make CCM and his music more successful, Darren began researching and reading books about marketing and positioning. He was searching for a way to position Acoustitherapy and Darren Curtis Skanson against the competition.

> One of the better books I found was *The E-Myth* by Michael Gerber. He talks about thinking about a business as a franchise. You can be successful if you can define everything in your business, like a franchise does, like McDonald's does. They say, cook these fries for 3 minutes at × number of degrees and plop them out there and leave them in the drainer for 30 seconds. It's the same thing with me. The thing I need to concentrate on now is my promotion and publicity processes. How do you promote a record? It should be a fairly simple process, but I should have a process for it.

53   When Darren began thinking of CCM as a franchise, he thought in terms of having a system into which he could plug other artists. He felt that by putting Andy into the systems that he had tried and tested, he was franchising the company. As he fine-tuned these processes, Darren started seeking out other artists that he felt would fit well into the system. Darren wanted to train each artist to sell in a way that would allow them to focus their energies on performing without having to worry about the business end of things. Darren had already compiled a procedures manual that included checklists for equipment necessary to take to a show, settings for the soundboard and speakers, and even a script for making sales. Darren saw his main weakness in the area of marketing.

> I had always thought that the better quality product always wins. So I had to be a better guitar player, I had to be faster and all those things. When I read those books I realized that quality matters, but it is not near as important as the position that you own in the mind of whomever. If you say classical guitar to someone, most people would say "Andre Segovia," and then they'd say "John Williams" or "Christopher Parkening." There's an implicit ranking, a product ladder in people's minds. There is no way that I will compete—EVER compete—with those people. It doesn't really matter if I'm a better musician. The reality or the truth makes no difference. In people's minds, truth and perception become melded. So I need to work on the image, the perception in people's minds, of the CCM label and the artists it employs.

54   Having been bitten by this marketing mind set, Darren became driven in his pursuit of product positioning and image creation. He began formulating a worksheet for positioning CCM products and documenting a process for publicity. He created a system for writing press releases that included information on the timing and frequency of sending press releases. Darren purchased a nationwide publicity database to help prepare in advance for every trip.

55   Even with all of these new ideas being put into action, Darren was still traveling about 40 weekends a year to perform at art festivals and shopping malls where the largest portion of direct sales could be made. Most phone, mail, and e-mail orders were still directly related to Darren's art festival appearances. Although website (Internet) sales increased threefold in 2000, this was still a small portion of overall direct sales.

56   In December 2000, when Darren was playing a ten-day stint at a shopping mall in Denver, the reality of Darren's limitations began to set in. He began feeling the pains of tendonitis in his left elbow, and soon after Christmas he realized he had a significant problem. His plan to put out two new Darren Curtis Skanson CDs in order to ride a wave of recent publicity would have to be put on hold.

57   With the harsh realization that Darren could not continue to perform at his previous level, he knew he needed to find other musicians to drive sales. In January of 2001, he began to formulate some ideas for growing the label that would take some of the pressure for performance off him.

58   First he decided to produce only one new Darren Curtis Skanson CD, and instead produce a second Andrew Thomas Harling CD. Darren felt that if Andy had another CD he would be in a better position to take over some of the bigger art festivals that Darren had been doing himself.

59   To compensate for the fact that CCM would produce only one Darren Curtis Skanson CD (which might not be released until November), Darren knew he had to do something different to attract a bigger crowd of listeners. He decided to look for violists or violinists to play with him when he played larger Colorado festivals, capitalizing on the success of the cello-enhanced "Classica." He transcribed the cello harmonies from the "Classica" CD into a score for viola and violin and auditioned musicians who would make a commitment to do a certain number of shows. He found musicians, set up rehearsals, and sold more CDs at their first show together than Darren had sold alone the previous year with the initial release of "Classica."

60   Darren also began actively searching for other artists who would fit well with the CCM label. He began negotiations with a pianist and a violinist, but both eventually broke down. The pianist wanted 50% ownership of CCM, which made Darren nervous.

THE NEXT STEP

In order for us to get legitimate, and our product lines to be legitimate in the "standard music industry," we have to have distribution through retail stores. It's just how the music business machine works. That's the distribution dilemma. Of course personally, I would like Darren Curtis Skanson the brand name to be courted by Sony Classical because we've sold 15,000 of my next CD through established chains. And they'd be calling and asking who Darren Curtis Skanson is, saying that they want to sign him. And we could say "well, CCM has his contract and we would let him go for × number of dollars," or whatever deal you negotiate.

I guess in a nutshell the dilemma is this, in order to (a) grow the company or (b) sell the product lines to an entity larger than CCM, those entities want to see your sales in traditional outlets. But in order to get it into those outlets, you either have to commit to a huge product run, or be satisfied with pounding away at it, or just incrementally working your sales up. I would love to get bigger distribution because bigger distribution means bigger sales, but I can't handle huge distribution without a bigger base of performers and a bigger push for publicity. In the short term, making direct sales is good for cash flow, it's good for the bottom line, it's good for the business, but in the long term, in order to turn any one of our product lines into something bigger than just making direct sales, you have to make a significant amount of sales through the established music business machine, which is record stores.

I think ultimately one-stops and distributors is the way you have to go, that's the way the whole industry works, but I don't believe that I can do that myself. That is going to have to be someone's job. If it means hiring a guy part time to start, it's just going to have to be his responsibility—that is, all he does is chase that down.

61   Darren was caught in a chicken-and-egg dilemma. He knew that CCM needed more sales to be attractive to the retail distributors, and he needed retail distribution to increase sales. Unless he could produce more CDs, Darren's festival performances would not yield the sales volume he needed to keep CCM profitable. Even if he produced another Darren Curtis Skanson CD, he was not sure that it would sell if he could not actively promote it himself. Until his elbow healed, his performance schedule would have to be curtailed.

62   As CCM's lead performer, Darren had hoped to turn over the sales and managerial functions to others. Now he was forced to rethink his role. Darren knew that he still wanted to perform, but it was clear that he could not keep up his current performance schedule. Should he work harder to get other musicians on board to tour and publicize the CCM name while he acted as master manager and coach? Should he hire a sales manager or focus his energies on getting CCM's products into retail outlets himself? Should he concentrate on recording-studio activities to increase CCM's product offerings and try to push the catalog sales, which had higher profit margins? Would hiring an experienced marketing manager help Darren uncover new arenas for growth? Could a new salesperson free Darren up to explore alternative performance venues? Or were his talents best directed at refining the CCM "system" and managing the recording studio?

63   Darren felt that his company was at a crossroads. His first love was music, and he loved to perform, but he knew that his personal satisfaction hinged on building a profitable company. He understood that growth and profitability were directly tied to maintaining and building CCM's customer base. As the plane started its descent into the Orlando airport, Darren tried to ready himself for the performance weekend ahead. But visions of CCM as a sought-after label were not far from his mind. He wished he could build a business as easily as he could serenade a crowd.

Hustwit, G. (1998) *Releasing an Independent Record,* sixth ed., San Diego, California: Rockpress Publishing Company.

Kashif (1996). *Everything You'd Better Know About the Record Industry,* Venice, California: Brooklyn Boy Books.

Wacholtz, L.E. (2001). "The New Music Business: Internet Entrepreneurial Opportunities in the Performing Arts," *Proceedings of the 2001 USASBE/SBIDA National Conference,* Orlando, Florida, August 2001.

Copyright © 2001 by Rachel Deane Canetta and Joan Winn of the University of Denver. Partial funding for preparation of this case was provided by the John E. and Jeanne T. Hughes Charitable Foundation Entrepreneurship Education and Awareness Grant. This case is intended to stimulate class discussion rather than to illustrate the effective or ineffective handling of a managerial situation. *All events and individuals in this case are real, but some names may have been disguised.* Do not reproduce or distribute without permission. December 12, 2001.

Case 32

Green Mountain Coffee Roasters

1 In comparing the growing strength of the competitor Starbucks brand, Bob Britt, Green Mountain Coffee's vice president and CFO, questioned whether Green Mountain was missing the window of opportunity by not moving faster to expand. Growth was imminent for Green Mountain but competition was fierce in retail with the Goliaths Dunkin' Donuts and Starbucks. As Britt sipped his cup of Rain Forrest Nut coffee, his thoughts turned to distribution.

2 To accelerate distribution of their coffee brand in the grocery channel, Starbucks selected a long-term licensing agreement with Kraft. In contrast, Green Mountain Coffee Roasters (GMCR) relies on its own distribution and sales force to grow the Green Mountain brand in the grocery channel. According to Britt, the Starbucks-Kraft venture is believed to generate sales of 20–40 pounds of coffee per store per week on average. In comparison, GMCR averages 100 pounds of coffee per store per week in the grocery channel. Primarily generated through the retail and office coffee channel, consumer demand pulls specialty coffee through the grocery channel.

BACKGROUND

3 In 1981, Green Mountain Coffee Roasters (GMCR) hung its shingle on the front of a small café in Waitsfield, Vermont. The company roasted and served premium coffee on the premises. The demand for high-quality, freshly roasted coffee soon grew beyond the café's walls. Restaurants and inns in the area asked for coffee and equipment. Green Mountain Coffee Roasters was soon in the wholesale business. Before long, skiers asked if the café could send Green Mountain Coffee to their homes in New York, Connecticut, Pennsylvania, and Florida. This demand was filled by the birth of the company's mail-order business. Today, Green Mountain is one of the leading specialty coffee companies in its established markets. See Exhibit 1 for established markets.

4 Green Mountain Coffee roasts over 25 high-quality Arabica beans to produce over 60 varieties of finished coffee products, which it sells through a coordinated multichannel distribution network in its wholesale and direct mail operations.

5 The majority of Green Mountain's revenue is derived from over 7,000 wholesale customer accounts located primarily in the northeastern United States. The wholesale operation serves supermarkets, specialty food store, convenience store, food service, hotel, restaurant, university, travel and office coffee service customers. Wholesale customers resell the coffee in whole bean or ground form for home consumption and/or brew and sell coffee beverages at their places of business. Green Mountain offers single-origin, estate, certified organic, Fair Trade, flavored and proprietary blends of coffee. The company roasts its coffee in small batches to ensure consistency. Green Mountain utilizes state-of-the-art roasting software that enables it to more exactly duplicate specific roasts, ensuring Green Mountain's ability to offer consistent taste profiles.

6 Green Mountain uses convection air roasters, offering a higher degree of flexibility than other commercially available roasters. In addition, the company has developed

EXHIBIT 1   Wholesale Coffee Pounds by Geographic Region (as a % of Total Wholesale Coffee lbs Sold)

Source: Green Mountain Coffee, Inc. 2000 Annual Report.

Region	53 wks ended 9/30/00	52 wks ended 9/25/99	Full Year Y/Y lb. Increase	Full Year % Y/Y lb. Increase
Northern New England (ME, NH & VT)	33.2%	36.4%	338,000	10.7%
Southern New England (MA, CT & RI)	24.5	24.2	478,000	22.7
Mid-Atlantic (NY, NJ & PA)	21.8	20.8	488,000	27.0
South Atlantic	6.9	5.3	257,000	55.2
Midwest	2.5	1.9	101,000	60.5
South Central & West	2.1	1.4	102,000	81.6
Multi-Regional	7.9	9.2	29,000	3.6
International	1.1	0.8	39,000	54.2
Totals	**10,546,000**	**8,714,000**	**1,832,000**	**21%**

specific roasting programs for each bean type to establish a Green Mountain "signature" for that bean type, which the company calls its "appropriate roast." Green Mountain believes that this process distinguishes it from other specialty coffee companies and has resulted in strong customer brand loyalty.

7   Green Mountain nitrogen flushes its packaged coffee and employs one-way valve bag packaging technology that provides a minimum shelf life of six months for the company's coffees. This technology enables Green Mountain to expand its distribution while maintaining its high standards for high quality and freshness.

8   In October 2001, *Forbes* magazine recognized Green Mountain Coffee, Inc. as one of the "200 best small companies in America." The company was ranked 16 based upon factors including return on equity and sales and earnings growth over the past five years.

Retail Operations

9   In fiscal 1997, Green Mountain Coffee Roasters was operating 12 company-owned stores in Vermont, Connecticut, Illinois, Maine, Massachusetts, New Hampshire, and New York, which made up approximately 10% of total revenues. However, by April of 1998, sales had fallen to 6% of total net sales. Reasons for the decrease included the elimination of the Plattsburgh, New York store (for which the lease had expired), the temporary closing of two stores due to relocation, as well as overall flat sales in the other company-owned retail stores. Furthermore, the stores did not generate positive cash flows, nor did they contribute positively to the company's net income. Since 1981, the company-owned stores had been an important part of the company's strategy of getting consumers to sample Green Mountain Coffee by the cup (see Exhibit 2 for financial data).

Socially Responsible Business Practices

10   Green Mountain is committed to conducting its business in a socially responsible manner. The company believes that doing well financially can go hand in hand with giving back to the community and protecting the environment. In fiscal 2000, the company contributed over 5% of its pretax income to various coffee farms, cooperatives, and nonprofit organizations in the U.S. and in coffee-producing countries. Domestically based organizations benefiting from cash or coffee product donations in 2000 included Conservation International, Rainforest Alliance, Coffee Kids, and the United Way.

EXHIBIT 2   **Green Mountain Financial Data**

Source: Green Mountain Coffee, Inc. 2000 Annual Report.

Fiscal Year Ended	Sept. 30, 2000	Sept. 25, 1999	Sept. 26, 1998	Sept. 27, 1997	Sept. 28, 1996
			(In thousands, except per share data)		
Coffee pounds sold	10,871	9,004	7.739	6,239	5,108
Net sales from continuing operations (1)	$84,001	$64,881	$55,825	$42,908	$33,377
Income from continuing operations (1)	$4,153	$2,247	$340	$1,539	$1,429
Income per share from continuing operations, diluted	$1.19	$0.64	$0.10	$0.44	$0.42
Total assets	$27,174	$23,878	$24,563	$23,544	$17,243

11   The company is committed to improving the quality of life in coffee-producing countries, and therefore supports projects that foster self-sufficiency, which it believes, yields the best results. In the Aceh region of Indonesia, for example, Green Mountain provided seed funding to Gayo Organic Coffee Farmer's Association (GOCFA), which now produces the company's Organic Sumatran Reserve coffee. This project was started in partnership with ForesTrade, a Vermont-based supplier of organic oils and spices. In addition to local quality of life improvements, these programs help ensure that a stable supply of quality organic coffees will be available to Green Mountain Coffee to satisfy growing consumer demand.

THE COFFEE INDUSTRY

12   The U.S. coffee market is flat today, even with the success of the specialty sector. The dynamism it once displayed has moved on to Europe and Asia (particularly Japan). The U.S., responsible for up to 80% of world coffee consumption during World War II, now accounts for only 20%. While part of this decline results from a stagnant U.S. market, much of it has been due to growth in coffee drinking elsewhere. Consumption has grown in traditional and new coffee drinking countries in Europe and Asia, and also in producing countries, to the extent that Brazil is now the second-largest consumer after the U.S. In 1997 absolute worldwide consumption was more than double what it had been at the end of World War II.

13   According to marketing consultants Adrian Slywotzky and Kevin Mundt, "What occurred was value migration . . . The majors' business designs—their customer selection, resource allocation, and growth strategies—were marred by an overly categorical definition of products and benefits, a limited field of competitive vision, and an obsolete view of the customer. A new innovator implemented business designs that anticipated shifts in customer priorities ahead of the established three.

14   Value migration occurred rapidly. The three majors held nearly 90% of the multibillion-dollar retail market in 1987. Within six years, the gourmet, whole-bean roasters, Starbucks, and other regional cafes had collectively created nearly $1 billion in shareholder value, and together obtained 22% of the coffee market share. By the end of 1993, the approximate market value of the majors was $4 billion, down $1 billion from 1988. The

EXHIBIT 3

Procter & Gamble

35% of U.S. coffee market
4% of revenue from coffee sales
$1.5 billion revenue from coffee in 1996
Brands—Folgers, High Point, Millstone

Philip Morris/Kraft

30% of the U.S. coffee market
2% of revenue from coffee
$1.2 billion revenue from coffee in 1996
Brands—Maxim, Maxwell House, Brim, Gevalia, Sanka, General Foods International Coffee, Chase & Sanborn

Nestlé SA

10% of the U.S. coffee market
.9% of revenue from U.S. coffee sales
$400 million revenue from U.S. coffee sales
LARGEST BRAND IN THE WORLD
Brands—Hills Bros, MJB, Nescafe, Taster's Choice

majors failed to create a new design for their coffee business to respond to the trend. Instead, they reverted to price-cutting and coupons.[1]

15   During the 1980s and 1990s, the large corporations paid scant attention to the new specialty roasters. Industry executives spent millions on advertising to maintain share in the shrinking market. Discounting and millions of coupons did nothing to raise brand prestige. Despite constant price promotion, coffee was a supermarket loss leader.

16   The Big Three (P&G, Philip Morris/Kraft, Nestlé) did not feel threatened by the growing host of regional whole-bean roasters who were marketing their premium brands in supermarkets and specialty stores (see Exhibit 3). Although these start-ups were experiencing double-digit growth rates, to the majors their total sales seemed miniscule. It was difficult for the majors to measure or even imagine the momentum of such tiny numbers relative to a $5 billion industry. Having made several failed attempts at marketing gourmet coffee, the brand leaders falsely assumed that gourmet coffee was a fad.[2]

17   In the U.S., and increasingly abroad, the specialty coffee industry continues to grow. In 1998, industry sources estimated that total retail sales of specialty coffee would reach $5 billion in 2000 from $1.5 billion in 1990. According to the Specialty Coffee Association of America (SCAA), sales of brewed, whole bean and ground specialty coffee totaled approximately $7.5 billion in 1999. This new U.S. industry now consumes 5% of the world's coffee output—diverting some fine coffees from European markets that were accustomed to high-quality beans.

18   An important aspect of the specialty coffee industry is its relative de-commoditization of coffee. Where the conglomerates had been concerned only with price and consistency, this new industry considers origin, quality, processing, and cultivation methods as relevant qualities of the bean. It also extends the option of choosing roasts, grinds, and so on, to the consumer, thus creating a much richer, personal coffee landscape.

---

[1] Adrian J. Slwotzky and Kevin Mundt, "Hold the Sugar; Starbucks Corp.'s Business Success." *Across the Board* 33 (8), September 1996, p. 39.
[2] Ibid.

19   The next step in this industry's development is now taking place, as specialty coffee continues to grow and develop major presences; it has begun to consolidate into a few major corporate brands. Many regional companies are looking to expand. Everyone's looking to see who is going to be number two to Starbucks.[3]

20   The traditional coffee sector has finally taken notice of this boom. The majors have launched their own specialty coffee brands, such as Philip Morris' Gevalia (the world's largest mail-order coffee business, with annual revenues of more than $100 million), Procter & Gamble's Millstone brand—a gourmet whole bean supermarket entry, and Chock Full O'Nuts short-lived cafes and their Quickava drive-throughs. The majors created the poor coffee image prior to the development of the specialty coffee industry. The idea of a Maxwell House or Nescafe gourmet coffee is contradictory —their French roast and espresso roast is undermined by the fact that it is vacuum packed in cans or instant. The most effective entry strategy for the majors could be an acquisition of an independent specialty coffee roaster.

21   Developing during a time of uncertain affluence, specialty coffee has been part of a larger trend that includes such developments as micro-brewed beer, specialty bread, single malt scotches, and organic vegetables. In each case, a consumer product has been recast as something more authentic, more traditional, diverse, flavorful, and healthful than the mass-produced product it supplants. In each case, the new "specialty" product is hyped as the original, traditional item that had been debased by mass production and corporatism.

THE "SPECIALTY COFFEE" INDUSTRY

22   Specialty coffee is coffee roasted using mainly high-quality Arabica beans. The Arabica bean is widely considered superior to its counterpart, the Robusta, which is used mainly in nonspecialty coffee. High-quality Arabica beans usually grow at high elevations, absorb little moisture and mature slowly. These factors result in beans with a mild aroma and a bright, pleasing flavor that is suitable for specialty coffee.

23   The specialty coffee industry consists of two distinct business segments: whole bean, including ground, coffee sales (for home, office, and restaurant consumption) and coffee beverage sales. One major thrust behind the specialty coffee growth is the increase in the number of specialty coffeehouses, which grew from 500 units in 1991 to over 12,000 in 2000, as reported by the SCAA.

24   The specialty industry has tapped into an unrequited desire for diversity and quality among existing, affluent coffee drinkers. It has stopped the slide in overall coffee consumption and produced an increase for the first time in a third of a century. In 1998 five million more Americans reported drinking coffee than in 1997, and almost half of all Americans reported drinking a specialty coffee drink in that year. While the overall coffee market is stagnant, the specialty industry grew by 8% annually in the U.S. in the decade to 1998.

25   In its diversity and focus on quality and distinctiveness, the specialty coffee industry is singularly profitable. Specialty beans that retail for $12 per pound are initially purchased (green) for about $2 per pound.

26   Consumers have a strong interest in purchasing whole bean specialty coffee for home consumption. The sale of whole bean coffee has grown in popularity because the increasingly sophisticated consumer grinds the beans at home and brews the freshly ground

[3] Carl Peel, "Los Angeles, a Microcosm of the Country." *Tea and Coffee Trade Journal* 169 (4), April 1997, pp. 16–28

coffee. The result of this domestic grinding of specialty coffee is a brew palatable for even coffee connoisseurs. According to the 1999 Gallup Survey on Coffee Consumption, nearly 36% of all coffee drinkers purchased specialty whole bean coffee for home consumption over the past three-month period. In the same survey, consumers stated that 33% of those whole bean purchases were made at a retail price per pound of over $7.00, reflecting the interest in high quality, premium priced coffee.

27   Consumers favor the supermarket or grocery store for the purchase of whole bean specialty coffee. According to the 1999 Gallup Survey, 61% of those consumers who had purchased such products did so most frequently in a supermarket or grocery store. Other important purchase locations included specialty coffee stores (14%), mail-order catalogs or clubs (4%), and gourmet food stores (2%).

28   The whole bean specialty coffee category is highly fragmented. Green Mountain's primary competitors in whole bean specialty coffee sales include Gevalia, Illy Café, Millstone, Peet's Coffee & Tea, Seattle's Best, and Starbucks. There are an estimated 500 smaller and regional brands that also compete in this category. In addition, Green Mountain competes indirectly against all other coffee brands on the market.

29   Competition in the specialty coffee market is becoming increasingly intense as relatively low barriers to entry encourage new competitors to enter the specialty coffee market.

GREEN MOUNTAIN COFFEE'S GROWTH STRATEGY

30   Green Mountain Coffee is focused on building its brand and profitably growing its business. Management believes it can continue to grow sales over the next few years at a rate similar to its historical five-year growth rate (18–25%), by increasing market share in existing markets and expanding into new geographic markets.

31   In recent years, the primary growth in the coffee industry has come from the specialty coffee category, driven by the wider availability of high-quality coffee, the emergence of upscale coffee shops throughout the country, and the general level of consumer education. Green Mountain has benefited from this trend in ways that may generate distinctive advantages over its competition.

32   Green Mountain coffee is available in various distribution channels and customer categories in its primary geographic area. This multichannel strategy provides widespread exposure to the brand in a variety of settings, ease of access to the products, and many tasting opportunities for consumer trial. Green Mountain coffee is widely available throughout the day: at home in the morning, in hotels, on airplanes and trains, at convenience stores on the way to work, at the office, in restaurants, in supermarkets, and at the movie theatre. See Exhibit 4 for sales distribution by channel.

33   The company believes that its coffee's convenient availability for consumer trial through convenience stores, office coffee services and food service establishments is a significant advantage and a key component of its growth strategy. It has been the company's experience that consumer trial of Green Mountain coffee at one level of distribution often leads to a subsequent purchase at another level of distribution.

34   As brand awareness increases through trial by consumers of the company's coffee by the cup, demand for whole bean sales of the company's coffee for home consumption also increases. The National Coffee Association of USA, Inc. in its National Coffee Drinking Trends through 2000 study states, "over 75% of coffee drinkers drink coffee at home." As brand equity is built, wholesale expansion typically continues through customers such as supermarkets and specialty food stores, who in turn, sell the company's whole bean coffee to consumers. This expansion process capitalizes upon this cup/whole

EXHIBIT 4 Coffee Pounds Sold (Whole Bean and Ground) in Fiscal 2000 and Fiscal 1999, Broken Down by Sales Channel

Source: Green Mountain Coffee, Inc. 10-K Report.

Sales Channel	53 wks ended 9/30/00	52 wks ended 9/25/99	Full Year Y/Y lbs. Increase	Full Year % Y/Y lb. Increase
Convenience Stores	26.8%	26.6%	520,000	21.7%
Supermarkets	24.9	28.0	186,000	7.4
Office Coffee Service Distributors	23.8	17.6	1,003,000	63.4
Restaurants	11.2	13.3	20,000	1.7
Other Food Service	8.1	8.7	95,000	12.1
Other Retail	2.2	2.6	8,000	3.4
Direct Mail, including Internet Sales	3.0	3.2	35,000	12.1
Totals	**10,871,000**	**9,004,000**	**1,867,000**	**20.70%**

EXHIBIT 5 Green Mountain Notable Wholesale Accounts

Source: Green Mountain Coffee, Inc. 10-K Report.

Convenience Stores

RL Vallee Inc. dba Maplefields
Unimarts
Marabito Fuel Group dba Quickway

Restaurants

Aureole Restaurant, NYC
Culinary Institute of America
New England Culinary Institute
The Harvard Club, NYC

Supermarkets

Hannaford Bros. - 132 stores
Kash 'n Karry - 135 stores
Price Chopper - 27 stores
Roche Brothers - 13 stores
Stop & Shop - 231 stores
(primarily coffee by the cup)
Shaw's - 107 stores

Office Coffee Services

Bostonbean Coffee Company
Coffee Pause Company
Corporate Coffee Systems
Crystal Rock Water/Vermont
 Pure Springs Company
Perrier's Poland Springs
U.S. Coffee

Other Food Services

Amtrak - Northeast corridor
American Skiing Company
Delta Express and Delta Shuttle
Columbia University
New Jersey State Aquarium
Stowe Mountain Resort

bean interrelationship. The strategy is designed to further increase Green Mountain's market share in geographic areas in which it already operates in order to increase sales density and drive operational and brand-equity efficiencies. "Flagship" customers, such as Amtrak, Delta Express, Delta Shuttle and American Skiing Company, are key to the Company's geographic expansion strategy, as they provide great visibility and sampling opportunities. See Exhibit 5 for Notable Wholesale accounts including "Flagship" customers.

COMPETITOR ANALYSIS: STARBUCKS

35 Starbucks had record sales of $2.2 billion in fiscal 2000. At fiscal year end (10/1/00), Starbucks had 2,619 company-operated stores in 34 states, the five Canadian provinces

(238), the United Kingdom (156), Thailand (15), and Australia (2). All Starbucks stores are located in leased premises.

36 Starbucks strategy for expanding its specialty operations is to reach customers where they work, travel, shop, and dine by establishing relationships with prominent third parties who share Starbucks values. These relationships take various forms, including retail store licensing agreements, wholesale accounts, grocery channel licensing agreements, and joint ventures. Specialty sales exceeded $345 million in fiscal year 2000. Starbucks sells whole bean and ground coffee to several types of wholesale accounts, including office coffee distributors and institutional food service management companies that service business, industry, education and healthcare accounts, and hotels, airlines and restaurants. In 1995, Starbucks became the coffee supplier to the 20 million passengers flying United Airlines each year. Starbucks mail-order sales division accounted for roughly 2% of total revenue. Starbucks management believes that its direct-response marketing effort helped pave the way for retail expansion into new markets and reinforced brand recognition in existing markets.

37 In 1998, Starbucks entered into a long-term licensing agreement with Kraft Foods, Inc. (Kraft) to accelerate growth of the Starbucks brand into the grocery channel in the U.S. Pursuant to this agreement, Kraft manages all distribution, marketing, advertising and promotion for Starbucks Coffee in grocery, warehouse club, and mass merchandise stores. By 2000, Starbucks Coffee was available in 16,000 supermarkets throughout the U.S. Starbucks coffee sold in supermarkets featured distinctive, elegant packaging; prominent positions in grocery aisles; and the same premium quality as that sold in its stores.

38 Starbucks has spent very little money on advertising, preferring instead to build the brand cup by cup with customers and depending on word-of-mouth and the appeal of storefronts. The company is, however, engaged in a growing effort to extend the Starbucks brand and penetrate new markets, including a joint venture with Dreyer's for a branded ice cream and a joint venture with Pepsi to distribute bottled Frappuccino, licensee partners, mail order and specialty sales, and international expansion.

39 By the end of fiscal year 2000, Starbucks had more than 3,500 locations worldwide, serving more than 12 million customers per week in 17 countries. In their 2000 annual report Letter to Stockholders, Starbucks stated they believed that in the past they dramatically underestimated the size of the global market and the power of the Starbucks brand. Starbucks management believes they have the potential to have 20,000 locations worldwide, with 10,000 locations in international markets.

40 Industry analysts see Starbucks becoming the Nike or Coca-Cola of the specialty coffee segment. It is the only company with near national market coverage. Starbucks vision is to become the most recognized and respected brand of coffee in the world. The company's efforts to increase its sphere of strategic interest via its joint venture with Pepsi and Dreyer's and its move to sell coffee in supermarkets represents an ongoing drive on Schultz's part to continually reinvent the way Starbucks does business. To sustain the company's growth and make Starbucks a strong global brand, Schultz believes the company must challenge the status quo, be innovative, take risks, and alter its vision of who it is, what it does, and where it is headed.

The Future of Green Mountain Coffee

41 The company's partnership with Keurig, Inc. developed into an important growth driver in fiscal 2000, as the unique Keurig one-cup brewing system gained momentum in the marketplace. Sales of K-cups made up 15.7% of total company sales in fiscal 2000. In fiscal 2000, coffee pounds sold to distributors through the office coffee service channel grew 63.4% over the previous year and Keurig coffee pounds accounted for 76.4% of that growth. In September 1999, the company introduced a new line of frozen granita and hot cappuccino beverages, two high-growth areas of the specialty beverage market. These products, which are marketed under the Monte Verde brand, complement the traditional line of specialty coffees and make Green Mountain a full-service provider to certain channels, such as convenience stores.

42   An important task in global marketing is learning to recognize the extent to which marketing plans and programs can be extended worldwide, as well as the extent to which they must be adapted. Green Mountain cannot afford to replicate Nestlé's marketing blunder. Nestlé sought to transfer its great success with a four-coffee line from Europe to the United States. Nestlé's U.S. competitors were delighted because the transfer led to a decline of 1 percent in Nestlé's U.S. market share.[4]

43   Green Mountain is focused on the wholesale channel in the gourmet coffee niche. Green Mountain has made trade-offs, divesting their retail store operations to focus on wholesale.

44   The question for Bob Britt and Kevin McBride, vice president of marketing at Green Mountain Coffee Roasters, remains what strategic paths GMCR should pursue to achieve its objective of becoming the most recognized and respected brand of coffee in the world. Brand awareness could provide a host of competitive advantages for Green Mountain Coffee.

---

[4] Warren J. Keegan, *Global Marketing Management*. Interview with Raymond Viault, vice chairman of General Mills, Inc., p. 7.

Keith F. Moody and Alan B. Eisner, Ph.D., Lubin School of Business, Pace University. Copyright © 2001 Moody and Eisner. All rights reserved.

Case 33

The Web's Favorite Airline

The safest way to become a millionaire is to start as a billionaire and invest in the airline industry.

Richard Branson, Founder, the Virgin Group

1 "If you create the right expectations and you meet or exceed those expectations, then you will have happy customers," proclaimed Stelios Haji-Ioannou, the 32-year-old founder and CEO of easyJet airlines. Since its launch in November 1995, easyJet had become one of Europe's leading low-cost airlines by adopting an efficiency-driven operational model, creating brand awareness, and maintaining high levels of customer satisfaction.

2 Stelios, who preferred to be addressed by his first name only, considered himself a serial entrepreneur. Although he gained international fame as a pioneer in the airline industry, he first achieved business success at the age of 25 when he created Stelmar, a specialized tanker company. Anxious to replicate his past successes, Stelios aggressively pursued any business opportunity that he believed he could operate profitably.

3 Despite its early success, easyJet airlines still faced internal challenges that were typical of many start-up companies. Growing competition from other small, low-cost carriers, as well as threats from Europe's major carriers, required much of the company's attention and resources. Undeterred, Stelios relished the challenge and moved ahead in his mission "to offer low-cost airline service to the masses."

4 Stelios believed that in order to be successful, it was important to be first to market and to saturate the geographic market. "You don't need to conquer the world in order to be profitable," he argued. His strategy for market entry had been successful in the airline industry, but many wondered if he could transfer his low-cost business model to Internet cafés, rental cars, and Internet banking, three ventures he considered in 1999.

COMPANY BACKGROUND

5 Stelios first became interested in the idea of a European low-cost airline in May 1994, after being asked to invest in a Virgin Atlantic Airlines franchisee. Although he refused, soon thereafter, he flew on Southwest Airlines, a successful low-cost carrier in the U.S. That experience became the catalyst in his decision to create easyJet. Stelios asked his father, Lukas Haji-Ioannou, a Greek shipping tycoon, to invest in his startup airline. In November 1995, after receiving £5 million from his father, Stelios began operating easyJet with two leased aircraft and a staff primarily comprised of teenagers who served as reservation agents. Although London's Heathrow and Gatwick were major international airports with higher passenger traffic, Stelios chose Luton because it offered lower labor costs and close proximity to downtown London, and charged lower airport fees.

Copyright © 2000 by IMD—International Institute for Management Development, Lausanne, Switzerland. All rights reserved. Not to be used or reproduced without written permission directly from IMD, Lausanne, Switzerland.

6   The first easyJet flight, from London to Glasgow, was advertised for a one-way fare of £29. The flight was completely full, in large part because Stelios had launched an extensive public relations and advertising campaign with the slogan, "Fly to Scotland for the price of a pair of jeans!" Increasing demand soon led to flight service to Edinburgh and Aberdeen. Over the next two years, Stelios raised an additional £50 million in debt and equity to finance the purchase of four additional aircraft and to speed expansion. By early 1998, easyJet owned a fleet of six Boeing 737-300s and flew 12 routes in five countries. However, by November 1999 easyJet owned and/or leased 18 Boeing 737-300s, and flew 27 routes in Europe.

7   Stelios modeled easyJet after Southwest Airlines. He researched Southwest intensively and even met with the airline's CEO, Herb Kelleher, before launching easyJet. Stelios deeply admired the concept behind Southwest Airlines: one type of aircraft, point-to-point short-haul travel, no in-flight meals, rapid turnaround time and very high aircraft utilization. However, Stelios added his own twist to the Southwest concept: he completely avoided travel agents, issued no tickets, encouraged direct sales over the Internet, and flew brand new Boeing 737s using the maximum seat capacity of 149 seats. Moreover, he decided not to offer free drinks or peanuts; everything would be for sale. Stelios championed the idea of no-frills travel; the only free item on board an easyJet flight was easyRider, the airline's in-flight magazine. He argued, "When someone is on a bus, he doesn't expect any free lunch. I couldn't see why we cannot educate our customers to expect no frills on board." (Refer to Exhibit 1 to view items available from the easyKiosk.)

8   The company's headquarters, referred to as "easyLand," was located at London's Luton airport. Just like the airline, easyLand was no-frills. Employees were instructed to dress casually, and Stelios sat in the same open-plan office as everyone else. He had no personal secretary, maintained a paperless office, and expected everybody else to do the same.

9   In 1996–97 easyJet suffered pretax losses of £3.3 million (£1 = US$1.60). However, in 1998 the company announced annual pretax profits of £2.3 million, the first time the airline had posted a profit in its brief history. (Refer to Exhibit 2 to review easyJet's financial performance.)

Deregulation of the European Airline Industry

10   Until the early 1990s the European airline industry had been highly regulated, in large part because individual countries wanted to protect their own national carriers, commonly referred to as "flag carriers." However, in December 1992 the European Union passed legislation that deregulated the airline industry. Similar to the deregulation of the U.S. airline industry in the 1980s, the new directive meant that any European carrier could fly to any destination and demand landing slots.

11   The proliferation of airlines offering highly competitive fares after December 1992 revolutionized European air travel, especially from the United Kingdom. New airlines were created, and travelers could fly from most airports in the U.K. to almost anywhere in the world for very low prices. This prompted one commentator to reply, "You can now fly from one end of Europe to the other for the cost of two hardback books." Richard Wright of the Civil Aviation Authority, which regulated British aviation, postulated that many new carriers set up operations from the U.K., rather than other European countries, because the British, along with the Germans, traveled most often.

12   Deregulation in Europe, however, spawned fewer new competitors than in the U.S. In 1999, only 3% to 5% of passengers in Europe flew on a low-cost carrier, compared to 24% in the U.S. On some routes in Europe, high-speed rail service competed directly with airlines. Furthermore, industry experts believed that the cost of running an airline in Europe was, on average, 40% higher than in the U.S.

EXHIBIT 1
Food Selections from the easyKiosk

Source: easyJet.

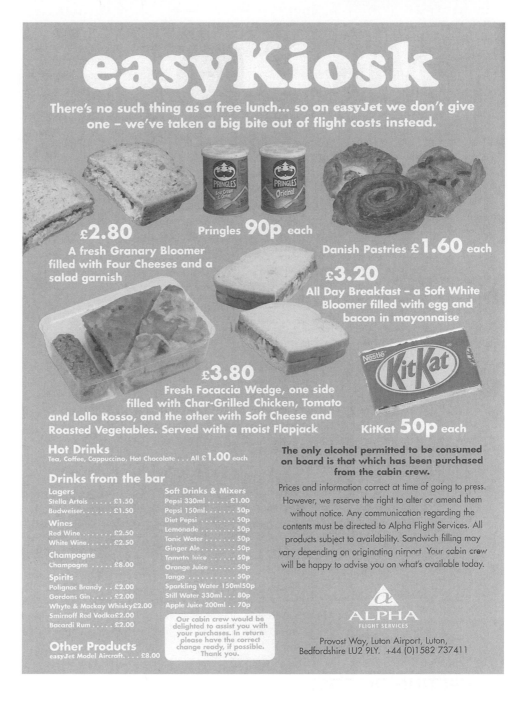

EXHIBIT 2
Financial
Performance,
1997–1998

Source: Directors' report and
financial statements, September
30, 1998.

easyJet Airline Company Limited	1997	1998
PROFIT AND LOSS ACCOUNT	**£**	**£**
Turnover	**46,034,549**	**77,000,035**
Cost of Sales	(38,963,150)	(61,525,257)
Gross Profit	**7,071,399**	**15,474,778**
Distribution and marketing	(6,324,068)	(7,748,225)
Administrative expenses	(4,491,338)	(6,260,124)
Operating Profit/(Loss)	**(3,744,007)**	**1,466,429**
Other interest receivable and similar income	607,392	978,268
Interest payable and similar charges	(135,250)	(125,759)
Profit/(Loss) on Ordinary Activities before Taxation	**(3,271,865)**	**2,318,938**
Tax on profit on ordinary activities		
Retained Profit/(Loss) for the Year	**(3,271,865)**	**2,318,938**
Retained loss brought forward	(5,872,621)	(9,144,486)
Retained Loss Carried Forward	**(9,144,486)**	**(6,825,548)**

easyJet Airline Company Limited	1997	1998
BALANCE SHEET	**£**	**£**
Fixed assets		
Tangible assets	**1,529,161**	**2,601,184**
Current assets		
Restricted deposits	343,476	1,416,457
Debtors	3,888,546	10,887,761
Cash at bank and in hand	16,877,623	12,506,665
Creditors	(17,783,292)	(20,237,615)
Net current assets	**3,326,353**	**4,573,268**
Net assets	**4,855,514**	**7,174,452**
Capital and reserves		
Called up share capital	14,000,000	14,000,000
Profit and loss account	(9,144,486)	(6,825,548)
Equity shareholders' funds	**4,855,514**	**7,174,452**

13   Understandably, few low-cost carriers enjoyed the same success as easyJet. Of the 80 carriers that had begun operations after 1992, 60 had already gone bankrupt by 1996. Still, analysts predicted that the European low-cost market could grow by as much as 300% by 2004.

COMPETING ON COST

14   Because easyJet offered low fares, it sought to minimize costs where possible. For example, easyJet saved £14 per passenger by not offering meal service, and estimated that by flying into London's Luton Airport instead of Gatwick, it saved £10 per passenger. The airline also shaved costs by not offering business class seating, thus allowing for more overall seating capacity. (Refer to Exhibit 3 to view a comparison of the costs of easyJet and other carriers.)

EXHIBIT 3
Cost Comparison

Source: easyRider magazine,
July 1999.

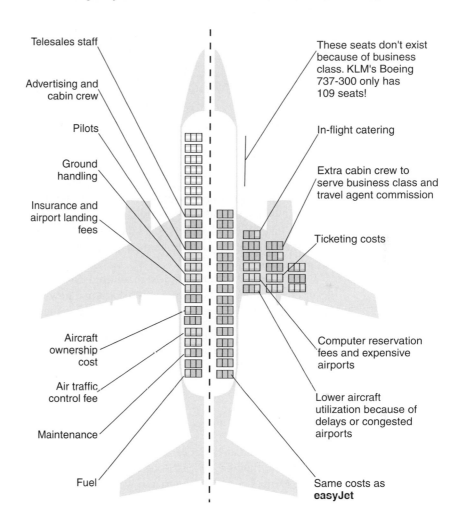

The lefthand side of the diagram shows the costs incurred by all airlines including **easyJet**.

The righthand side of the diagram shows the additional costs incurred by big airlines, but NOT by **easyJet**.

Telesales staff

Advertising and cabin crew

Pilots

Ground handling

Insurance and airport landing fees

Aircraft ownership cost

Air traffic control fee

Maintenance

Fuel

These seats don't exist because of business class. KLM's Boeing 737-300 only has 109 seats!

In-flight catering

Extra cabin crew to serve business class and travel agent commission

Ticketing costs

Computer reservation fees and expensive airports

Lower aircraft utilization because of delays or congested airports

Same costs as **easyJet**

15   Moreover, easyJet encouraged Internet sales. In March 1999, Internet sales accounted for 15% of revenues; however, by October 1999, Internet sales had soared to 60% of revenues. Stelios offered discounted fares to customers who purchased over the Internet because such sales reduced the need to hire additional reservation agents. He avoided computer reservation systems and travel agents because he believed that they added 25% to total operating costs.

Illustration: Saying No to Travel Agents

In 1998, Stelios enraged travel agents in Greece by selling cheap daily flights to Athens and flaunting his commission-free service by advertising to "forget your travel agent." Travel agents there took him to court. He won and then immediately thumbed his nose at his foes by plastering "say no to travel agents" in bright orange letters across the first plane to fly from London to Athens, earning him huge amounts of press.

EXHIBIT 4
Cost of an easyJet
flight from London
to Geneva

Source: easyJet.

Cost Item	£	%
Airport charges	600	15%
Aircraft ownership	560	14
Air traffic control	480	12
Crew	400	10
Marketing/sales	400	10
Fuel	400	10
Maintenance	400	10
Overhead	400	10
Ground handling	360	9
Total Costs	**£4000**	**100%**

Assumptions: The table approximates easyJet's costs for a one-way trip. All costs are fixed.

16   The airline also turned its airplanes around faster, flying planes 11.5 hours per day, instead of 6 hours, the industry average. Because easyJet flew its planes more hours, Stelios claimed that he could fly just 2 planes, and do the work of 3. Although easyJet had achieved profitability in 1999, margins were quite small; the airline earned £1.50 profit per passenger.

17   Even though easyJet carefully monitored costs, Stelios emphasized that safety was never compromised. The airline only flew brand new Boeing 737s, and only hired experienced pilots who were paid market rates. Stelios commented:

> If you advertise a very cheap price, people expect an old airplane. But when they come on board and see a brand new plane, they are impressed. Likewise, many customers expect an unhappy staff because they believe they are not paid well, but they come on board and see the staff is smiling!

COMPETING ON SERVICE

18   One of the distinguishing characteristics of easyJet was its approach to customer satisfaction. Stelios flew on at least four flights per week, and enjoyed interacting with customers. He had even been known to work the phones selling tickets. Stelios was wary of market research, preferring to cull information directly from passengers. He also read and replied to many of the e-mails he received from customers. He considered himself a man of the people and worked hard to cultivate this image. (Refer to Exhibit 5 to view an example of his communication with customers.)

19   All of easyJet's fares were one-way fares and had the same restrictions. The cost to change a flight was £10 plus the difference between the two fares. Only 4% of customers failed to show up for their flights, and easyJet offered no reimbursement for missed flights.

20   To book a flight, customers either purchased their tickets over the Internet or they called a local number and were connected to one of easyJet's reservation agents in easy-Land. Because easyJet was a 100% direct-sell operation, the marketing department knew the relative effectiveness of different media and could react quickly. Oftentimes, the company placed different phone numbers on different types of advertisements to measure consumer response precisely.

21   Customers were required to pay by credit card, after which they received a six-character booking reference number. This reference number was the only information passengers needed to board the plane. Reservation agents were paid on a commission basis, at a rate of £0.80 per seat sold, and could sell 60 to 90 seats during an average eight-hour shift.

EXHIBIT 5
Message from Stelios

Source: easyJet, November 1999.

We have arrived! (Well, sort of.) The ultimate magazine for fat cat business travelers did a poll of its readers, and we were voted the best low-cost airline. What pleases me more than anything is that we beat the low-cost clone by British Airways (BA). It's not bad if you think that they lost £22m in the first year alone trying to break into our market.

So we must be doing something right. With our fleet of 18 Boeing 737-300s, one of the youngest in the world, and a far better punctuality record than BA and other so-called flag carriers, we are flying fuller than ever before. We now have 27 routes, and not only will we fly more frequently on our existing routes, but we are also planning new ones later in the year 2000, when the next 15 brand new 737-700s start arriving.

On other fronts, my Internet shops are doing very well and I will expand easyEverything in all the cities that easyJet flies as soon as I can. At the time of publishing this message on the web site, we have signed for five in London with a total of 2300 seats (yes - the biggest has 630 seats!), and have already signed for sites in Edinburgh and Amsterdam.

My easyRentacar.com project is on track for being up and running by April 2000, and you should be able to rent an 'orange car' over the Internet for £9/day.

As you can see, the common theme for all my ventures is the heavy use of the Internet. Take my word for it, all the best deals on the airline will be available on the Net from now on. So, if you don't get online you might lose out. Remember you can always use an easyEverything Internet shop to book your flight or car, coming to a place near you soon!

On another subject, we continue our battle against Swissair. As you may remember, in July we were blocked from operating a scheduled service between Geneva and Barcelona, due to political pressure from Swissair who wanted to preserve their monopoly on this route. So, to get round this, I set up easyJet Tours, a charter operation which offers passengers return flights, transfers, and accommodation (even though this is only a tent!). This service has proved very popular (I mean the flights, not the tents), and we will continue to fly this route throughout the winter. In the meantime, we will carry on lobbying the Swiss government to make changes to the law. I am encouraged by the fact that a large number of Swiss MPs have signed a motion supporting this cause, even before it is debated in Parliament.

Thank you for visiting our web site.

Stelios

EXHIBIT 6
easyJet Mission Statement

Source: easyJet.

To provide our customers with safe, low-cost, good value, point-to-point air services. To offer a consistent and reliable product at fares appealing to leisure and business markets from our bases to a range of domestic and European destinations. To achieve this we will develop our people and establish lasting partnerships with our suppliers.

EXHIBIT 7
Destinations Served from London's Luton Airport

Source: easyJet,
November 1999.

22   The airline did not offer any pre-assigned seating, but instead utilized a priority boarding procedure. Passengers were given a number based on the time they checked in, and those passengers who arrived late for check-in had to sit in whatever seats remained.

23   Generally speaking, easyJet defined its target customers as "people who pay for travel from their own pockets." The target group consisted of travelers visiting relatives, leisure travelers making brief trips, as well as entrepreneurs and managers working for small firms. While easyJet typically ignored the large market of business travelers, on some routes, such as London-Glasgow, London-Edinburgh, and London-Amsterdam, business travelers represented 50% of the passengers. Stelios argued that larger airlines ripped off traveling business customers who usually did not want to stay over a Saturday night or who wanted complete flexibility to change their travel plans.

24   Using yield management, easyJet tried to fill as many seats as possible. Seats were sold in what could be considered a lottery system; the more people demanded a particular flight, the higher the fare. Put differently, if the load factor (percentage of seats sold) was higher than normal, prices automatically increased. This system worked well for easyJet because it helped avoid selling out popular flights months in advance.

25   Yield management also served another purpose: it drew potential customers who were in search of cheap fares. Once they found there were no more cheap seats, they usually bought a ticket anyway, since the next highest fare was still cheaper than easyJet's competitors. Stelios defended his policy vigorously: "We decided that people who are willing to give us their money early should get a better price, and those who want the flexibility of booking late should pay a bit more." (Refer to Exhibit 9 to view a report on availability of fares.)

EXHIBIT 8
Destinations Served from Geneva

Source: easyJet, November 1999.

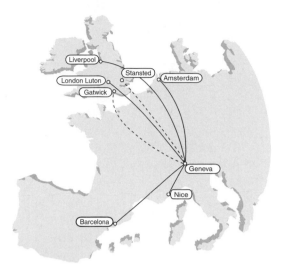

EXHIBIT 9

A *Sunday Times* Reporter Investigates Availability of easyJet's Low Fares

Source: "Fare Play." *Sunday Times,* October 18, 1998.

Four weeks before travel date

I had to wait 10 minutes before speaking to Richard, a sales assistant. I asked for the cheapest fare to Barcelona, leaving Saturday, September 26 and staying two nights. Richard said that a ticket for the 8:10 PM flight would cost £49 one way (an earlier flight would be much more expensive). The return would cost £99 for the 4:45 PM flight, or £69 for the 6:50 AM flight. So the cheapest fare was £118 including tax. Richard warned me that the 4:45 PM flight was filling up fast and prices would only go up.

Three weeks before travel date

Prices were the same, but there were then only six seats for the return leg. I felt pressured to book, so I did. There was no charge for using my credit card and no hard sell to take easyJet insurance. I was given a reference number and told I won't be issued a ticket. Confirmation of my flight was faxed through about an hour later; the paperwork arrived in the post a week later, with a discount voucher for train travel.

Two weeks before travel date

The prices had risen by £10 for the outward flight; the 4:45 PM flight was sold out.

One week before travel date

My outward flight was £64; there were only two seats left. Interestingly, seven seats were available again on the return flight at £129.

One day before travel date

The outward flight cost £69, and the return flight cost £139.

26   Punctuality at easyJet was important. Because customer satisfaction was linked so closely to punctuality, responding adequately to the needs of customers was very important to Stelios. If a flight arrived more than four hours late, Stelios instructed his staff to write a letter of apology with his signature and to issue a full refund. Because the airline had many repeat customers, Stelios was confident that customer satisfaction was high. (Refer to Exhibit 10 to view additional data on punctuality.)

EXHIBIT 10
Airline Punctuality Comparisons for the Period Ending August 1999: Arrivals and Departures

Source: U.K. Civil Aviation Authority.

		Percentage of Flights Late				
		Early to 15 minutes	16 to 30 minutes	31 to 60 minutes	1 to 3 hours	3 to 6 hours
easyJet	London-Glasgow	90%	8%	2%	0%	0%
	London-Zurich	52%	33%	11%	4%	0%
	London-Mallorca	79%	13%	6%	2%	0%
go	London-Malaga	64%	18%	9%	6%	3%
	London-Mallorca	53%	8%	25%	14%	0%
RYANAIR THE LOW FARES AIRLINE	London-Dublin	63%	20%	10%	7%	0%
Virgin Express	London-Malaga	70%	0%	10%	20%	0%
	London-Mallorca	78%	11%	11%	0%	0%
swissair	London-Zurich	43%	31%	18%	8%	0%
BRITISH AIRWAYS	London-Glasgow	88%	6%	3%	3%	0%
	London-Zurich	69%	23%	6%	2%	0%

EXHIBIT 11
Destinations Served from Liverpool

Source: easyJet, November 1999.

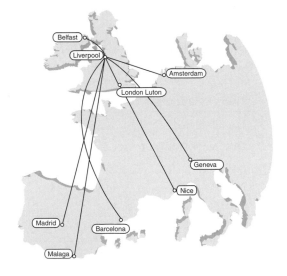

Outsourcing

27   Initially, Stelios had outsourced many of the airline's operations because it lowered costs and increased efficiency. Typically, the airline provided the planes, pilots, cabin crew, marketing and sales people. Subcontractors handled all other responsibilities, from check-in to the on-site customer information desk.

28   By early 1998, however, easyJet had acquired its own operating certificate and reached a scale where it would have been possible to bring certain operations in-house. Nevertheless, Stelios still maintained that it made more sense to continue working with subcontractors. The airline's ability to remain ticketless, meet its goal of a 20-minute turnaround at the gate, and maintain its safety depended on subcontractors.

29   To improve its relationships with these outside vendors, easyJet often led workshops, role-reversal exercises, and simulations to explain its objectives and expectations. The company evaluated subcontractors not only on quantitative criteria, such as percentage of on-time flights, but also on qualitative criteria, such as understanding of the easyJet concept.

CREATING BRAND AWARENESS

30   Because Stelios felt that brand awareness was critical to the success of the airline, approximately 10% of easyJet's revenues were spent on newspaper, magazine, and radio advertising. Because of its marketing approach, easyJet's top management believed that easyJet was able to differentiate itself from its competitors. Management was also of the opinion that its efforts had been rewarded through a significant growth in sales and through the company's high level of brand awareness. A 1998 industry poll indicated that the easyJet brand had a recognition rate of 88% in London; in Geneva, brand awareness was 82%.

31   Stelios also generated publicity for easyJet through highly publicized, and often full-scale attacks on his competitors. According to Philippe Vignon, marketing director, "Whenever there is an opportunity to make some news, we do it!" (Refer to Exhibits 12 and 13 to view examples of easyJet's attacking ads.)

CORPORATE CULTURE

32   Stelios wanted to build a strong, inclusive employee-culture at easyJet, which led to the creation of the easyJet Culture Committee. The committee, an elected group drawn from company staff, was responsible for establishing company policy on the working environment, communications between management and staff, and social events such as staff parties for the airline's 1,000 employees. Every Friday at Luton, easyJet held a company-sponsored barbecue that the staff used to get to know one another better.

33   Stelios believed in complete transparency, and all documents had to be scanned and placed on the computer system, so that anyone in the company could access them. This included mail, internal memos, press cuttings, business plans, and sales data (the only confidential information was payroll-related).

34   Stelios stressed that culture was not something leaders can create overnight. As he put it, "You build your legend slowly, bit by bit, battle by battle. You talk about it, and then you get together and have fun. I believe that work should be fun."

EXHIBIT 12   Ad Attacking British Airways

Source: easyJet.

It's time BA came out of the closet!

On 25 May 1999, British Airways announced their 1998/99 results, but they still refuse to disclose how much of the £25 million they put in their low-cost airline has been lost over that period. Last year **easyJet** convinced a High Court Judge that any cross subsidy between BA and its subsidiary could be illegal. The case is still pending, and BA is doing everything it can to avoid disclosure of the facts.

We are so convinced that BA's low-cost airline has made a substantial loss in their first year that we are having a competition over the Internet to guess the total amount lost in its first year of trading.

The 50 entrants nearest the correct figure will win themselves a pair of **easyJet** flights anywhere on the **easyJet** network! If there are more than 50 correct answers a tie-breaker will apply. The competition will close as soon as the results are released. In due course they will have to file them with Companies House. So if you want the chance to win a prize sooner, why not e-mail Bob Ayling at BA and persuade him to release the results.

COMPETITION
50 pairs of **easyJet** flights up for grabs!

Entries will ONLY be accepted over the Internet at

www.**easyJet**.com
the web's favourite airline

EXHIBIT 13

Stelios' Pet Hates

Source: easyJet.

Stelios' pet hates

Air Miles = Air Bribes

Air Miles is a bribery scheme invented by British Airways and designed to induce business travellers to waste their companies' money by travelling business class and then collecting the reward for their personal benefit. (Usually lavish holidays in the Caribbean frequently in the company of their secretaries)!

Those Chief Executives with the best interest of the company and its shareholders at heart must ban the collection of air miles by their staff while travelling on business. It's not going to be a popular decision, which goes to prove the degree of corruption!

In addition, the taxman has done British Airways a huge favour by miraculously not including air miles as a taxable perk, in the same way that company cars are taxed.

Write to your MP about the great Government rip-off!

The last Tory Chancellor increased airport tax (officially called Air Passenger Duty or APD) from £5 to £10. Zurich, outside the EU, has an even higher tax at £20. Contrary to popular belief this money does not contribute to the improvement of airports, but ends up in the pocket of the taxman. This tax is totally unfair to **easyJet** customers as on some occasions the tax has been more than our one-way air fare (Yes, we have sold seats for £8.50). Please write to your MP expressing your dissatisfaction and suggesting that APD should be a percentage of the fare, just like VAT.

www.**easyJet**.com

EXHIBIT 14
The Barcelona Controversy

Source: easyJet.

In early 1999, easyJet advertised for months that the airline was planning to offer service to Barcelona (from Geneva), and had even sold 7,000 seats. However, this new service was contingent upon approval from the Swiss authorities. Swissair, which had a monopoly over the Barcelona-Geneva route, fought against easyJet's entry into the market. The Swiss government ruled in favor of Swissair, stating that easyJet could not fly scheduled flights between the two cities. On the inaugural flight to Barcelona, Stelios appeared and personally issued refunds to passengers, in essence, giving them a free trip to Barcelona. He even emblazoned the words, "Say no to Swissair monopoly" in bright orange letters across the fuselage of the plane. During the flight, he asked for a donation from passengers in order to "protect consumers against the Swissair monopoly." Surprisingly, 50% to 60% of the money he refunded was donated back to easyJet. Undeterred, easyJet found a loophole. The company set up a new company, called easyJet Tours, which offered chartered service to Barcelona as part of a package that included the flight, a bus ticket, and the right to stay in a tent on a campsite near the city. (Staying in the tent was not a requirement.) Stelios believed such acts created affinity. In addition to building brand loyalty, the extra media attention helped easyJet gain widespread support in Switzerland for its willingness to stand its ground against Swissair.

EXHIBIT 15
The Fight with Go

Source: easyJet.

In 1996, Bob Ayling, British Airways' chief, approached Stelios in what appeared to be an offer to buy easyJet. Instead, after a three-month courtship, British Airways abandoned the deal, and one year later, launched Go, its own budget airline. Still angry over the incident, Stelios got his revenge by buying several rows of seats on Go's first flight. He commanded his staff to don orange boiler jackets, and they all boarded the flight like a group of merry pranksters, offering free flights on easyJet to Go's passengers. Barbara Cassani, chief executive of Go airlines, was on the inaugural flight to welcome new passengers. When she saw what was occurring, she lapsed into stunned silence. The publicity stunt paid off for easyJet. Go Airlines announced losses of £22 million in 1999. However, Stelios was wounded yet again when British Airways hired away easyJet's lawyer at an estimated annual salary of £500,000.

35   Stelios strongly believed that being the underdog in such a highly competitive industry strengthened his team and brought them closer together. He recalled:

> I noticed how much more motivated the staff was when British Airways launched the Go airline and when the whole country was talking about us and we were on television every night. All of these things created a sense of pride for the company. The same thing happened in Switzerland. People at TEA, a Swiss charter airline, were no longer motivated, so we bought the company and turned it around. As soon as we had the run-in with Swissair, morale really picked up. We were the underdogs. Our employees would go home and their neighbors had heard about the company they work for, which gave them the courage to stay and fight.

36   Because of the airline's high-profile battles, Stelios had become famous and people began to recognize him when he was out in public. When asked about his increasing popularity, he replied:

> It is nice to be considered as sort of a Robin Hood, and have people stop you in the street and say, "Thank you for flying to London. Now I can go and see my family." My father was a very successful shipper, but no one ever stopped him in the street and said, "Thank you for transporting oil to my house." It is very satisfying to be recognized and to be appreciated.

COMPETITION

Ryanair

37 Ryanair, based in Ireland, was established in 1985. Initially, Ryanair was a full-service, traditional airline with two classes of seating, but in the early 1990s, the airline changed its focus to become a no-frills carrier. Unlike easyJet, Ryanair used travel agents, issued tickets, and participated in the global distribution system. Utilizing a fleet of 20 Boeing 737s and servicing 26 destinations, the airline had more than 100 scheduled flights per day in late 1999, and planned to expand both its route base and the size of its fleet. (Refer to Exhibits 16 and 17 for additional information on easyJet's competitors.)

38 In 1999, Ryanair experienced its ninth straight year of strong growth. For the six month period ending June 30, 1999, Ryanair had sales of IR£66.2 million (IR£ 1.00 = US$1.30) and the operating profit margin was 28%.

Go

39 Go was established by British Airways in May 1998 as a no-frills airline to compete in the low-cost segment of the European market. Financed with £25 million from British Airways, Go was founded in large part to defend British Airway's market share, since easyJet was stealing its passengers. In 1999 the company suffered financial losses, although Go's CEO, Barbara Cassani, expected to achieve profitability by 2001. For the period ending March 31, 1999, Go had sales of £31.6 million, and operating losses of £22 million. Before Go announced that the airline was losing money, Stelios set up a contest offering free easyJet flights to whoever came closest to guessing the amount of Go's losses.

40 Go's flights were based out of London's Stansted Airport instead of London's Heathrow Airport, where British Airways was headquartered. Stelios considered Go a copycat of easyJet, and believed that Go was heavily influenced by parent company British Airways in the way it structured its fares. Stelios also suspected that British Airways unfairly subsidized Go; therefore, he filed a lawsuit alleging that British Airways violated Article 86 of the Treaty of Rome, which says that dominant players in a market should not operate at below the cost of production.

Virgin Express

41 Virgin Express Holdings plc, headquartered in Belgium, was set up in 1996 when the Virgin Group acquired a controlling stake in EuroBelgian Airlines. Virgin Express Holdings plc was principally engaged as a low-fare carrier, and provided short to medium-haul jet service to markets principally within continental Europe from the company's base in Brussels. For the fiscal year ending December 31, 1998, Virgin Express had sales of BEF 10.5 billion (BEF 40 = US $1.00).

42 Virgin Express differentiated itself from other low-cost carriers in that it had formed an alliance with Sabena Airlines, the flag carrier in Belgium. This relationship provided Virgin Express with a steady stream of contractual revenue, since Sabena bought seats on Virgin Express in order to offer better connections to destinations throughout Europe.

Buzz

43 In September 1999 KLM announced that it would enter the low-cost segment of the market with Buzz airlines. From its base at London's Stansted airport, Buzz planned to offer service to Berlin, Dusseldorf, Frankfurt, Milan, Vienna, Paris, and Lyon. KLM already had one brand in place at London Stansted, KLM UK.

To avoid confusion, management stated that KLM flights would go to Amsterdam, while Buzz would fly to all other destinations.

EXHIBIT 16   Airlines Routes of Competing Low-Cost Carriers

Sources: www.easyJet.com; www.Go-Fly.com; www.Ryanair.com; www.Virgin-Express.com.

	easyJet	**go**	**RYANAIR** THE LOW FARES AIRLINE	**Virgin Express**
Belgium			Brussels	Brussels*
Czech Republic		Prague		
Denmark		Copenhagen	Arhus	Copenhagen
France	Nice	Lyon	Biarritz, Carcassonne, Dinnard, Lyon, Paris, St. Etienne, Toulouse	Nice
Germany		Munich	Frankfurt	
Greece	Athens			
Ireland	Belfast		Cork, Derry, Dublin,* Kerry, Knock	Shannon
Italy		Bologna, Milan, Rome, Venice	Ancona, Genoa, Pisa, Rimini, Turin, Venice	Milan, Rome
The Netherlands	Amsterdam			Rotterdam
Norway			Oslo	
Portugal		Faro, Lisbon		
Scotland	Aberdeen, Edinburgh, Glasgow, Inverness	Edinburgh	Glasgow*	
Spain	Barcelona, Madrid, Malaga, Mallorca	Alicante, Barcelona, Bilbao, Madrid, Malaga, Mallorca		Barcelona, Madrid, Malaga, Mallorca
Sweden			Kristianstad, Malmö, Stockholm	
Switzerland	Geneva,* Zurich	Zurich		
United Kingdom	Liverpool,* London*	London*	Birmingham, Bournemouth, Bristol, Cardiff, Leeds Bradford, Liverpool, London,* Manchester, Teesside	London

*Represents a hub.

CHALLENGES

44   Stelios faced several challenges at easyJet. In November 1999, he struggled with the decision of whether to take his privately held company public. On one hand, he believed he could better motivate his staff by offering them shares in the company. On the other hand, however, his team of advisors feared his management style was too entrepreneurial. Regarding the decision to refund passengers who had already paid for the Geneva-Barcelona flight during the battle with Swissair, he remarked, "Do you think the finance director of a public company would say, 'Refund every customer on the Geneva flight' like I did? My finance director was pulling his hair out!" Although plans were underway to float the company on the London Stock Exchange and NASDAQ in early 2000, Stelios

EXHIBIT 17 **Comparative Financial and Operational Statistics for Selected Airlines**

Source: Company Annual Reports, Reuters Business Briefing.

	easyJet[1]	Go[2]	Ryanair[3]	Virgin Express[4]	Southwest[5]	British Airways[6]	Swissair[7]
				(US$ million)			
Revenue	123	51	303	262	4,164	14,264	7,290
Operating expenses	121	83	233	261	3,480	13,557	6,897
Operating profit/(loss)	2	(32)	70	1	684	806	452
Net profit/(loss)	4	(22)	59	(3)	433	330	233
Market Capitalization	n/a	n/a	1,794	95	8,197	6,504	2,439
Pre-tax Profit Margin	3.0	(63)	25.6	0.5	16.9	2.5	4.9
Return on Assets	32.3	(57)	18.8	(2.8)	9.7	1.6	2.6
Return on Equity	16.6	(177)	31.6	(6.6)	19.7	6.1	13.0
Debt/Equity	1.4	n/a	59.3	140.3	96.7	282.2	385.2
Sales to Assets	10.7	91.1	96.9	292.0	92.9	69.5	82.5
Price-Earnings Ratio	n/a	n/a	21.7	170.8	20.4	21.4	10.0
Capacity ('000) - ASKM[a]	2,801,000	2,052,000	3,000,000[b]	2,657,814	76,069,624	161,291,000	40,560,000
Load Factor	75%	53%	71%	75%	66%	71%	72%
Passengers per year	1,714,761	2,000,000	4,900,000	2,600,000	52,586,400	45,049,000	12,199,000
Number of Aircraft	8	13	20	20	280	278	129
Employees	394	500	1094	639	25,844	63,779	43,696

[1]For the period ending Sept. 30, 1998
[4,5,7]For the period ending Dec. 31, 1998
[2,3,6]For the period ending Mar. 31, 1999
[a]ASKM = Available Seat Kilometers;
[b]This figure is an estimate.

frequently asked himself and others around him if the market would trust him to run the company the way he felt was best.

45   Second, the airline had a history of using subcontractors, but found that at times, the outsourcing of vital functions posed certain problems. For example, at some airports that were not frequently serviced, easyJet hired external ground handlers. Because the handlers were not easyJet employees, they did not attend to customers' needs in a manner that satisfied Stelios. He commented:

> Making sure that these subcontractors meet the quality standards we have set is very difficult. The weakest link in the chain is in Mallorca. There, we have people who maybe work on an easyJet flight once a day or once a week, and therefore don't know the company very well. I've been telling my staff, "If I hear another ground handler refer to easyJet in the third person, I will sack him!" There is nothing worse for a customer to go to a check-in desk and say, "When is the flight?" and the person responds, "easyJet is an hour late." When the customer asks why, the person responds, "Ask easyJet!"

46   Third, Stelios believed that easyJet needed to become more corporate in its processes. In his opinion, it took certain skills to start a company from scratch, and people who were good at starting companies were not necessarily good at running big companies. In late 1999, the company was recruiting 3 or 4 senior managers.

47   A fourth challenge at easyJet was the relative youth and inexperience of some employees. Although it was not unusual to find a 24-year-old handling a monthly budget of £500,000, the airline nonetheless had high rates of absenteeism among phone operators.

48   Recognizing that easyJet was in a phase where it needed to stabilize itself internally, Stelios decided not to enter any new markets in the short-term. He felt that he needed to consolidate and do more in the countries where they had already set up operations. He asked, "What's wrong with flying 10 times a day between London and Geneva?" He added, "One of the biggest mistakes that airlines make is spreading themselves too thin."

49   When asked how many low-cost carriers could survive in Europe, Stelios replied:

> The market is bigger than most people think, although availability of slots at airports is a problem. London is getting a bit crowded, but then again, London is a big place and just about any city out of London can work as a destination. Start looking around Europe, and there aren't many other low-cost carriers. [. . .] The big prize in Europe is Paris. There is no low-cost flying in and out of Paris whatsoever. Any city with 3 or 4 million people should be capable of sustaining a low-cost airline.

FROM EASYJET TO EASYEVERYTHING

50   Pleased with his success in the airline industry, Stelios was ready to try his hand at other businesses in 1999. Among his pet projects was the creation of a cybercafé business called easyEverything café. The idea behind easyEverything was "to offer the Internet to the masses" and "to be the cheapest way to access the Web." Charging £1 per hour of Web access, Stelios stated that surfing the Internet at easyEverything was less than the cost of a phone call in London. He hoped that customers would come to the café not only to surf the Internet, but also to send e-mails and do their online shopping. Stelios joked, "If flying people to Scotland for £29 is crazy, this is crazier!"

51   The first easyEverything café debuted in London on June 21, 1999 near Victoria Station and was open nonstop 24 hours per day. It was quickly considered one of the hot spots in London, and there was often a queue to get inside, even at 3 A.M. Customers could purchase coffee and snacks or rent the services of a tutor, who showed them how to use the Internet to access online bargains.

52   In June 1999, Stelios signed four more leases for bigger locations in London. The key to success for the café was thought to be size; the first café contained 400 terminals. Another perceived advantage was the use of state-of-the-art hardware, including flat screens and fiber-optic communication lines, which offered much faster connection and downloading than most home systems.

53   Not content to stop with cybercafés, Stelios also considered entering the rental car business and starting up an Internet-based bank. He wondered if he could successfully apply the concept behind easyJet to these new businesses. Given that Stelios was known to be rather risk-averse, the decision would not be an easy one.

Research Associate Brian Rogers prepared this case under the supervision of Professor Nirmalya Kumar as a basis for class discussion rather than to illustrate either effective or ineffective handling of a business situation.

The case was written using interviews and materials provided by the company. Among the materials provided were a case study from the February 1999 issue of the European Management Journal written by Don Sull, and an article on easyJet from the November 1999 issue of Bilan magazine written by Giuseppe Melillo, which we would like to gratefully acknowledge.

Case 34

The North Face, Inc. (A)

1 On July 6, 1998, James Fifield, recently appointed president and CEO of The North Face, Inc. ("TNFI" or "the Company"), proudly announced that TNFI would be moving its corporate headquarters to a 36-acre parcel of land in Carbondale, Colorado. Starting in August 1998, the Company's corporate headquarters would be located in temporary buildings on the new property while the future executive offices were being constructed. During the transition, Fifield claimed that the Company would relocate a portion of its executive offices to Carbondale while maintaining its current facility in San Leandro, California. Fifield stated that the Company's Marketing, Research Design and Development, Product Acquisition, and most of the Company's Executive Team would be moved to the Carbondale site by year-end.

2 Fifield acknowledged that the Carbondale facility was within a half hour of his Aspen home, but he believed that the move was important to TNFI for two reasons. First, Fifield believed that some "weaker" employees were expected to refuse the move and leave the Company, and Fifield believed that he could recruit "better managers" to the new location as "the mountainous surroundings in Colorado will improve the Company's image and attract top management talent." Second, Fifield believed that the new location would strengthen the North Face brand by "projecting a technical, extreme and authentic image that appealed to professionals and serious outdoor athletes as well as to broader segments of the population."

3 After two years on the Board of Directors, James Fifield became CEO on TNFI on May 15, 1998. During his career, especially during the last year, when, as CEO of EMI Music, James G. Fifield was one of the highest paid European-company executives, Fifield was known as "Lucky Jim." Fifield joined EMI Music in May 1988 as President and COO and was appointed President and CEO in April 1989. Before joining EMI Music, Fifield served for three years as the President and CEO of CBS/Fox Video and held a number of executive positions with General Mills during a career spanning 20 years. Current Vice-Chairman William N. Simon, North Face's former CEO, and Marsden S. Cason, its current chairman both hoped that Fifield could use his luck to bring the North Face brand to a higher level of sales and profitability. Fifield tried to underscore his own personal faith in the brand and his ability with a $14 million investment in newly issued TNFI shares concurrently with his appointment as CEO.

4 By mid-1998, The North Face had evolved into one of the world's premiere brands of high-performance outdoor apparel and equipment. The Company designed and distributed (but did not manufacture) technical outerwear, skiwear, sportswear, equipment, and outdoor accessories under The North Face brand name. The Company distributed its products in the United States, Canada, Europe, and Asia through approximately 1,500 high quality specialty dealers representing more than 2,200 storefronts worldwide. The Company also owned nine retail stores and three outlet stores in the United States.

5 The North Face offered a broad range of high-performance, technically oriented products in the following categories: (1) outerwear; (2) functional synthetic sportswear ("Tekwear"); (3) equipment (sleeping bags, backpacks, and tents); (4) snow sports wear (ski and snowboard apparel); (5) Ascentials (gloves, hats, daypacks, adventure travel accessories); and, (6) footwear (The North Face brand scheduled for Spring 1999 introduction) but at the time only under the La Sportiva brand name. Exhibit 1 shows relative sales by major product lines.

EXHIBIT 1
Segment Sales

Source: The North Face, Inc.

Sales as a % of net sales	1995	1996	1997
Outerwear	50%	52%	48%
Equipment	25%	25%	22%
Skiwear	14%	12%	10%
Other products	11%	4%	4%
Tekwear	—	7%	12%
Ascentials	—	—	4%
Net Sales ($mil.)	$121.50	$158.20	$208.40

6   The Company's outerwear products were organized into two categories, Expedition System Outerwear and Technical Outerwear. The Company's outerwear was designed to provide protection from various combinations of cold, wet, and windy conditions and to accommodate the range of motion required for the most extreme outdoor activities. In addition, many of the Company's outerwear products were designed to adapt to varying conditions and situations, taking into account the unpredictability of the weather and the fact that some outdoor activities alternate between periods of extreme exertion and total rest, requiring a proper balance between ventilation and insulation. In a May 1998 *Backpacker Magazine* survey, the North Face was ranked as a leading brand in the outerwear category by 64% of the respondents, significantly more than any other brand.

7   Tekware represented the Company's entry into the broader casual sportswear market with a line of high-performance functional sportswear. Tekware was offered in three lines: (1) Bouldering/Climbing; (2) Trail Running/Performance; and (3) Trekking/Adventure Travel. Each line offered styles for men and women and featured a collection of pants, shorts, shirts, pullovers, fleece garments, wind jackets, vests, tank tops, and tights. The synthetic fabrics from which the Company's Tekware products are made offered significant advantages such as rapid drying and resistance to shrinking, tearing, fading, staining, mildewing, and wrinkling. Tekware was designed for serious outdoor pursuits but was also functional for everyday use.

8   Ascentials was comprised of the Company's line of technical apparel and equipment accessories, including a range of lumbar packs, cargo bags, T-shirts, high-performance thermal underwear, hats and gloves/mittens, which were tested extensively in extreme conditions by the Company's team of elite athletes.

9   The Company entered into the rugged footwear market in spring 1999 with the North Face branded products in two key categories: Trail Running and Trekking. The Trekking category was the largest category of the rugged footwear business, while the Trail Running category was the fastest growing segment.

10   TNFI was engaged primarily in a two-season business, spring and fall. Sales were seasonal, with approximately 34% of annual sales recorded during the January through June period and the 66% balance being booked between July and December.

11   International operations as shown in the table below were becoming increasingly more important for the Company. Canadian and European subsidiaries were wholly owned, while products were sold through a licensee, Mitsui & Co., in Hong Kong and Macao. In Japan and Korea, Kabushiki Kaisha Goldwin ("Goldwin"), a leading manufacturer and distributor of high-end sports and outdoor apparel and equipment, owned virtually all of the Company's trademarks and the two worked closely with regard to product design, sourcing, and brand imaging.

12   The Company believed that it was well positioned in Europe to take advantage of the same industry trends that were occurring in the United States. The Company's European

EXHIBIT 2
Regional Sales

Source: The North Face, Inc.

Sales by Geographic Region ($ millions)			
Market:	**1995**	**1996**	**1997**
Europe	20.3	28.7	39.8
United States	96.1	120.0	156.0
Canada	5.1	9.5	12.7
Total	121.5	158.2	208.4

operations were headquartered in Scotland. The Company distributed its products directly to approximately 650 wholesale customers representing an estimated 950 storefronts throughout Europe. Its primary markets were the United Kingdom, Germany, Italy, France, Spain, Sweden, Denmark, and the Netherlands. Both Company and independent sales representatives reporting to the Company's sales director were responsible for sales in each country.

13   The Company sourced most of its products through approximately 50 unaffiliated manufacturers that were located in North America, Asia, and Europe. Ten of those manufacturers produced approximately 75% of the Company products during 1997. Approximately 60% of the merchandise was imported from contract manufacturers located outside of the United States, primarily in the Far East, which included Bangladesh, Thailand, Philippines, Korea, Hong Kong, China, and Indonesia.

14   In order to maintain high product quality standards, the Company managed all key aspects of the production process. Quality control specialists from the Company conducted on-site inspections of the mills where the materials used for their products were manufactured, and at the plants during the different stages of the product manufacturing process, in addition to inspecting the finished product before it was shipped to the Company.

15   Between 1991 and 1996 the U.S retail market for outdoor apparel grew 18% to $10.4 billion from $8.8 billion. The increased sales of outdoor apparel had resulted, in large part, from the growth in popularity of outdoor activities. According to the National Sporting Goods Association, between 1994 and 1996 the number of people who participated in snowboarding increased 76%, climbing 39%, in-line skating 31%, mountain biking 27% and backpacking 17%. The growth in the popularity of outdoor activities also spurred an increase in sales of active outdoor apparel to consumers who did not participate in these activities. Even individuals who did not participate in outdoor activities or require the functionality of a high performance product increasingly wore outdoor or rugged apparel as casual clothing.

16   Sales of sportswear and rugged footwear also increased in recent years. From 1995 to 1996 sales of sportswear and rugged footwear in the U.S. increased 6.6% and 4.3%, respectively, and the Company expected the growth in these markets to continue as the number of products designed to suit a variety of outdoor activities and conditions expanded. The trekking category was the largest category of the rugged footwear business with over 49% market share. The trail running category accounted for over 10.2% of the rugged footwear business and was the fastest growing segment. TNFI was well positioned to benefit from these trends as their equipment and products, including footwear, focused on these fast growing segments.

17   The trend towards more active lifestyles was demonstrated by increased participation in a variety of outdoor activities such as camping, hiking, and backpacking. These positive trends translated into excellent sales dollars for outdoor equipment manufacturers. Exhibit 3 illustrates growth trends for the markets the Company catered to.

EXHIBIT 3
Equipment Sales
(in millions)

Source : National Sporting
Goods Association

Sport Activity	1994	1995	1996	1997	1998	CAGR
Baseball	295	251	287	293	329	2.2%
Football	85	77	77	78	84	(0.2%)
Camping	1,017	1,205	1,122	1,156	1,264	4.4%
Skiing, Alpine	609	567	706	763	647	1.2%
Skiing, Cross Country	43	84	60	62	42	(0.5%)
Total	16,676	17,442	17,618	18,064	19,639	3.3%

CAGR = Compound Annual Growth Rate

EXHIBIT 4
Key Financial Data

Source: Bloomberg and
Company SEC filings.

Total Sales (000)s	1995	1996	1997	1998
Marker	$ 84.0	$ 87.1	$ 83.0	$ 81.4
Timberland	655.1	690.0	796.5	862.2
Columbia Sportswear	303.8	299.0	353.5	427.3
North Face	121.5	158.2	208.4	262.6

Total Sales Growth	1995	1996	1997	1998
Marker	1.7%	4.6%	(4.7%)	(1.9%)
Timberland	2.7	5.3	15.4	8.3
Columbia Sportswear	18.5	(1.6)	18.2	20.8
North Face	36.3	30.2	31.7	25.9

Gross Profit Margin	1995	1996	1997	1998
Marker	41.8%	40.2%	39.3%	33.1%
Timberland	31.0	36.5	39.2	39.8
Columbia	39.8	40.8	43.7	43.7
North Face	45.3	44.3	45.6	45.3

Operating Profit Margin*	1995	1996	1997	1998
Marker	10.6%	6.6%	5.6%	2.1%
Timberland	(1.1)	7.4	10.5	28.8
Columbia	12.7	8.9	12.5	13.0
North Face	8.7	8.6	7.9	4.3

*Operating Profit Margin equals net operating profit before interest and taxes divided by net sales.

18   The wholesale market for the outdoor and equipment and apparel was highly fragmented. Major competitors included private entities such as Patagonia and Mountain Hardware, and publicly owned companies such as Marker (ski), Timberland (boots/apparel), and Columbia Sportswear. A financial comparison follows in Exhibit 4.

19   Given the various product lines, the components of sales vary greatly between companies. For example, Timberland product mix is 75%/25% footwear/apparel while Columbia generates over 60% of sales from outerwear. The North Face commands the highest gross margin levels among the peer group. Timberland, which is the only player in the above group with significant in-house manufacturing, has a lower gross and EBITDA margin compared to the other companies, which outsource most of their manufacturing. Columbia outsources over 85% of their product. The North Face outsources approximately 60%.

BACKGROUND

20   The North Face was founded in 1965 and was synonymous with high performance climbing and backpacking equipment. The North Face name was selected because, in the Northern Hemisphere, the north face of the mountain is generally the coldest, iciest, and most formidable to climb. In 1968, the Company began to manufacture and wholesale backpacking equipment. In the early 1970s the Company began to offer outerwear and, in the early 1980s, added extreme skiwear to its product offerings. However by the late 1980s the Company's financial performance deteriorated for a variety of reasons.

21   In May 1988, and in serious financial difficulty, Odyssey Holding, Inc., acquired TNFI. In addition to TNFI, Odyssey owned, directly or indirectly, approximately 30 other businesses in the outdoor and brand name apparel industries, including Marmot, Head Sports Wear, Apex One, and Sierra Designs. In January 1993, Odyssey filed for protection in the United States under Chapter 11 of the U.S. Bankruptcy Code.

22   In June 1994, Marsden Cason, William Simon, and William McFarlane purchased TNFI out of the Odyssey bankruptcy for $62.1 million. The debt incurred to purchase the Company was subsequently paid down with the proceeds from an initial public offering and secondary offering in July and November 1996, respectively.

23   As a public company, TNFI attracted its share of analyst coverage. In March of 1998, when the stock was priced at $24.38, Alexandra DalPan of BancAmerica Robertson Stephens initiated coverage on TNFI with a rating of long-term attractive. She felt that there was potential long-term strength in earnings due to:

- Improvements in sales productivity from continued rollout of Summit Shops, the in-store concept.
- Broader and deeper penetration of the Tekware line of functional casual wear.
- Sustained healthy trends in the Company's retail stores.
- Continued growth in the automatic replenishment business.
- Improved leverage of fixed expenses from higher levels of sales.

24   Later in March of 1998, TNFI announced the addition of James Reilly as chief operating officer. Wall Street was generally pleased with the appointment as noted by DalPan of BancAmerica Robertson Stephens; "Mr. Reilly brings the company several years of experience in the athletic apparel industry. His background includes the position of chief operating officer of Adidas America, where he was instrumental in effecting a sales reorganization and operational turnaround."

25   During the summer of 1998, TNFI brought two new executives into its senior management team. First, the Company promoted Christopher Crawford to chief financial officer. Second, the Company named James Fifield as president and CEO. Fifield replaced William Simon, who remained vice chairman of the Board, as CEO. Wall Street generally approved of the additions with an analyst noting that "we believe that (Fifield) is very familiar with the Company and the North Face strategy. As such, we do not expect any major strategic changes; we would expect a continuation of the company's efforts to extend the brand's reach through broader distribution and new product initiatives, including the recently announced footwear line." Chris Crawford was appointed General Manager of California Operations on July 6, 1998 and was appointed CFO of the Company on Aug. 29, 1997. From March 1992 through May 1997, Mr. Crawford served as the vice president of Business Development and Strategic Planning for CFM Majestic, Inc. and as CFO for its subsidiary, Vermont Castings, Inc. CFM Majestic was a manufacturer and marketer of premium health products. Mr. Crawford is both a CPA and a member of the Oregon Bar.

BRAND MANAGEMENT

26 The new management team sought to aggressively grow the Company. By August of 1998, the new team released its three-year business plan. Management targeted at least a 25% annual increase in sales, and a 30% increase in net income. (See Exhibits 7, 8, 9 for financial statements.) Highlights from the Company's presentation of its business plan include brand reinforcement, brand management, expanding retail presence, category management, distribution, and strengthening margins.

Brand Reinforcement

27 The North Face was committed to functional apparel and equipment for the extreme sports enthusiast. TNFI's goal was to design and market the most recognized and respected brand of high performance, technically oriented outerwear, outdoor equipment and functional sportswear in the world. Key elements of the strategy were to:

1. *Offer Technically Superior Products.* Many of the Company's product lines featured technically superior, high-performance products designed to be used in remote, mountainous polar environments and to withstand the harshest conditions. To reinforce The North Face's image of quality and reliability, the Company's products carried a lifetime warranty.

2. *Design Innovative Products.* More than 85% of the products offered by TNFI in 1998 were new products or had been updated since 1993. In designing and developing new product styles and features the Company's team of world-class climbers, explorers, and extreme skiers contributed design ideas and tested new products.

3. *Promote Its Extreme Brand Image.* The Company devoted significant resources to strengthening the North Face brand by projecting a technical, extreme and authentic image that appealed to professionals and serious outdoor athletes as well as to broader segments of the population. The Company provided equipment and outerwear for expeditions and other high profile outdoor activities and promoted the North Face's products through its teams of world-class climbers, explorers, and extreme skiers. The Company planned to have athletes play a greater, more active role in the Company's new marketing and product development programs. In addition, the North Face planned to develop a more "event marketing" driven program with increased sponsorship of highly visible (televised) sporting events. The Company planned to increase the marketing budget as a percentage of sales, with additional new marketing initiatives including product specific advertisements and increased partnerships with retailers.

4. *Pursue International Opportunities.* In 1998 the North Face had established a regional headquarters in Europe, and combined its domestic and international product development, sourcing and marketing functions to improve efficiencies and develop an integrated effort designed to increase its global focus.

Brand Management

28 TNFI had realized significant growth through an expansion into complementary product lines. These products, while still best of class, carried a relatively high price point within each category, and created significant incremental sales for the Company. The introduction of Tekwear in 1996 proved to be one of the most successful product launches in Company history. The formalization of the Ascentials line of accessories and travel bags,

including daypacks, again provided a means to reach a broader consumer audience. These products, at much lower average price points than the core apparel categories, brought many consumers within reach of the North Face.

29 The Company intended to continue to introduce products in more moderate price-point segments, so as to access a broader consumer base. In order to increase market penetration, the Company planned to expand its distribution beyond its specialty retail base and into the department store channels. While the sales dynamics (sales dilution, chargebacks) were clearly different in department stores, TNFI believed that its high gross profit margin would offset any losses caused by sales dilution.

Expanding Retail Presence

30 The Company continued to focus on Summit Shop (a TNFI store within a store such as Paragon Sporting Goods, see below) growth to increase the North Face presence at retail. Summit Shop expansion plans remained unchanged at 375 new shops in 1998 with a goal of 800 shops by 2001. The Company indicated that increased square footage would come from increased penetration within existing customers, and through the acquisition of new customers.

Category Management

31 As part of the Company's overall efforts to enhance execution, the Company created a less centralized decision-making structure, which was planned to lead to more efficient decision making among mid-level managers.

Distribution

32 At fiscal year end 1998, the Company distributed its products in the U.S. through a 250,000 square foot facility in Vacaville, California, and in Europe through a 77,000 square foot facility in Port Glascow, Scotland. In an effort to reduce the number of TNFI employees and improve distribution, the Company plans to close its Vacaville facility and contract their distribution to a third party distribution center in Missouri. The transition should take place during the late summer of 1999.

Strengthening Margins

33 The Company plans to improve operating profitability by 50% over the next three years, with initiatives including increased outsourcing of distribution and more focused investments in equipment. In addition, the Company plans on reducing the number of styles it offers by 30% over the next three years.

OPERATIONS

34 Starting in May 1998, TNFI took steps to improve shareholder value by restructuring some operations. Since Fifield and Crawford took over active management, the Company had executed the following:

- In May of 1998, TNFI announced plans to close its only owned production facility and to consolidate its Canadian unit into a combined North American operation. The outdated plant was located in Scotland, and the charge to earnings related to the closing was $1.1 million. Another $400 million was allocated to the Canadian consolidation.

- Also in May of 1998, TNFI announced that it would design and manufacture a line of outdoor performance footwear, scheduled to launch in 1999.

- In July of 1998, the Company acquired 100% of the outstanding shares of La Sportiva for 133,335 shares of TNFI Common Stock. La Sportiva was a North American distributor of specialty outdoor footwear based in Boulder, Colo. The Company also acquired a 20% interest in La Sportiva S.r.l. of Italy with a commitment to purchase another 31% over the next two to five years. The total cost was projected to be $6.6 million. The Italian company was known as a premier manufacturer and distributor of specialty outdoor footwear based in Ziano di Fiemme, Italy.

- In July of 1998, the Board of Directors approved an antitakeover provision known as the "Rights Agreement." The Board of Directors declared a dividend of one right to purchase one one-thousandth of a share of the Company's Series A Participating Preferred Stock, $1.00 par value per share, for each outstanding share of Common Stock, $0.0025 par value per share, of the Company. Each Right entitled the registered holder to purchase from the Company one one-thousandth of a share of Series A Preferred at an exercise price of $140.00, subject to adjustment.

35   The introduction of the footwear line was well received. Alexandra DalPan of BancAmerica Robertson Stephens noted that there was considerable upside to the new business since "The Company has built management expertise . . . notably with the March 1998 appointment of James Reilly, . . . and Patrick Seehafer, formerly global product director of footwear research of Nike's ACG line." However, the new plans were not implemented with universal consensus, and not all of the moves were embraced by Wall Street.

36   For example, the move of the headquarters from San Leandro to Carbondale was greeted with a 17% drop in stock price on the day the plan was announced. Said Marcia Aaron of BT Alex. Brown at the time, "We can't help but be somewhat concerned about the soft costs. We believe that most, but clearly not all of the key employees will move. Additionally, we believe that employees will be distracted and managers will not be challenged to keep their groups focused. The effect and impact likely will not be known or seen for a period of time." Furthermore, an unnamed analyst quoted in *The San Francisco Chronicle* complained, "These things don't look good. Not only are people concerned about the self-interests at work here, but (North Face is) also splitting up the company, which raises some risk."

37   In addition, the departure of COO James Reilly was greeted with similar share price declines. On August 26, 1998 Bloomberg News reported "North Face shares fell 13% on concern that the departure of its chief operating officer will cause disruption at the maker of outdoor clothing and gear, analysts said." Analyst James Palczynski of Ladenburg Thalmann & Co. explained, "The perception is that there is management turmoil. That said, I think the price reaction is overdone."

38   By mid-January of 1999, TNFI's executive offices were located in a modular building on a $7 million parcel of land in Carbondale, Colo. and the operating offices were located in San Leandro, Calif. Crawford's team, which included the day-to-day operating staff, was slowly making the move to Carbondale. Fifield, not long removed from his role at EMI Records, made a habit of making grand pronouncements from Carbondale without consulting the rest of senior management. A prime example was the business strategy set forth by Fifield only 90 days after Fifield was hired as CEO. The strategy called for increased sales of moderately priced new products into the department store channel, while at the same time calling for a reduction in overall products. Besides Fifield, only Crawford was fully aware of the strategic shift. Neither man had a plan to achieve the goal.

39   At the same time, TNFI was also preparing to close down its leased distribution center in Vacaville, Calif. at the end of the lease, and outsource the distribution to Caliber Corporation, a subsidiary of Federal Express. The new distribution center was located in Lenexa, Mo., and was expected to be ready to begin shipping for the holiday 1999 sea-

son. With the lease expiring on July 31, 1999, product flow was expected to begin in Missouri on the same date. The Company did not plan on moving any of the Vacaville employees to Lenexa.

40   Since TNFI designed its products in the United States and then contracted for their completion with Asian firms, the distribution center in Vacaville received all finished goods after clearing U.S. Customs. In most cases the goods were unpacked and then stored in the warehouse until an order delivery date approached. At that time, TNFI would "pull" or "pick" selected styles based on a retailer's order, "tag" the styles with store specific tags if necessary, and "pack" the styles for shipping.

41   The Vacaville distribution center was adequate for the current sales volume and was current in terms of technology. However, order flow was somewhat erratic. The Company would, on occasion, overship or undership some of the smaller retailers. Rumors had persisted through most of 1997 that TNFI would routinely ship more product to a retailer than ordered, a practice known as "stuffing the channel." While the financial press was unable to get a single retailer to go on the record, it was rumored that this practice was widespread and intentional. As an example: A retailer would order 1,000 Mountain Light jackets and receive 1,500. The incentive for TNFI would be that the items would be classified as sales when they ship, allowing TNFI to meet its public growth targets. The small retailer needed the North Face name in its stores, and would not be able to force North Face to take goods back for fear of being eliminated as a North Face retailer altogether. In certain instances, TNFI would offer extended payment terms to the retailer if the retailer received too much inventory. The Company believed that the technology available at the new Lenexa distribution center would help them better manage customer orders.

42   The Company's distribution strategy was based on a strategy that categorized its customers as either "regional" or "major." The regional customers were those that historically had been identified as the Company's core customer base. These specialty outdoor retailers generally had an identity with the elite athlete and his companions. These retailers may have had only one store location and most did not have more than two. Customers classified as "major" customers included the Company's largest customers REI and Eastern Mountain Sports ("EMS") had been buying and selling North Face products since the early 1980s. This category also included customers that had only recently been buying in volume from the Company, but had quickly become major customers (Galyans, Finish Line, Gart's, Dick's, and The Colorado Stores). In the future, with a more aggressive strategy, the Company expected to realize significant sales from new major customers such as Eddie Bauer, Footlocker, Track & Trail, Oshman's, Sports Authority, Nordstrom's, J.C. Penney, and others.

MARKETING

43 In the regional channel, the Company sold its products to a select group of specialty mountaineering, backpacking and skiing retailers, and premium sporting goods retailers. Major customers included major outdoor specialty retail chains, national general sporting goods chains, and department stores. The Company sold its products in the United States to approximately 840 wholesale customers, representing an estimated 1,350 storefronts. In Canada, the Company sold its products to approximately 260 wholesale customers, representing an estimated 290 storefronts, and in Europe, it sold to approximately 650 wholesale customers, representing an estimated 950 storefronts.

44   Summit Shops were year-round concept shops introduced in 1996 dedicated to North Face products, which were located within certain of its wholesale customers' stores.

Summit Shops were intended to increase sales at existing specialty retailers by offering an attractively designed, professionally merchandised, dedicated selling space featuring an array of North Face products.

45   The Company provided merchandising support for the Summit Shops as well as fixtures and signage (approximately $35,000 per store average, four-year life) while the specialty retailer provided the customer service, sales personnel, floor space, and operational guidelines and maintained minimum inventory levels. Summit Shops were intended to increase sales at existing specialty retailers by offering an attractively designed, professionally merchandised, dedicated selling space featuring an array of North Face products. In order to provide consistent product flow to both the Summit Shops and its other wholesale customers, the Company adopted a new core inventory replenishment program, which inventories certain popular core products for quick reorder delivery. The Company believed that Summit Shops provided many of the same benefits as its Company-operated retail stores and that the substantially reduced operational and financial commitments associated with Summit Shops would result in a higher return on investment.

46   These shops allowed retailers and consumers the benefit of Head to Toe merchandising; that is, one stop shopping. They also allowed a retailer to stock a greater volume of the Company's products generating higher sales per square foot and greater inventory turn. The shop was designed to present most, if not all, of the product line in a setting consistent with the brand's image. For example, Nautica's products were designed with an active outdoor image and its in-store shops supported this through fixturing, which was contemporary, and signage that was sporty and outdoor oriented. According to Goldman Sachs, sales per square foot in a Nautica or Tommy Hilfiger Shops averaged $545 and $690 respectively, compared with a typical department store average of $230. The North Face believed its concept shops increased sales by displaying a complete selection of merchandise and promoting cross-merchandising opportunities on a year-round basis. Columbia Sportswear, for example expected to have 328 concept shops and 1,000 "in-store brand enhancement systems" by the end of FYE 98.

47   In the major channel, TNFI management planned to introduce the North Face brand at the department store level of distribution, in addition to their smaller regional retail partner. TNFI was fully aware that they would cede some leverage to the department store retailer when compared with their traditional retail partners. Requiring that an apparel company share in any markdowns of prices on the retail floor to clear retail inventories was common practice at the department store level. Most department store retailers required that any product sold on their floor must produce at least a 40% gross margin for the retailer.

YEAR END

48   Initially, the Company seemed to achieve success in its new strategy. On January 29, 1999, James Fifield announced the fiscal year end 1998 results and proudly commented, "Our financial success in 1998 is a strong indication that the North Face brand has never been stronger and I am very excited about our market opportunity as we enter 1999. Throughout the past year, we maintained our focus on enhancing our premier brand while we continued to implement our broader distribution strategy. Internally, our focus has been on improving the efficiency and service of our business management practices. These key initiatives helped drive our success in 1998 and will continue to drive growth in the coming years."

EXHIBIT 5
Selected Income
Statement Data

Source: The North Face, Inc.
press release dated January 29,
1999.

The North Face, Inc. (000)s omitted	FYE95	FYE96	FYE97	FYE98
Revenues	121,534	158,220	208,403	262,557
Sales Growth	36.3%	30.2%	31.7%	25.9%
Gross Profit Margin	45.3	44.3	45.6	45.1
Operating Profit	11.7%	11.1%	12.3%	11.8%
Net Profit	3,485	5,664	11,107	10,787

Note: The chart above presents FYE earnings before any restatements.

EXHIBIT 6
The North Face, Inc.
Share Price
Performance

Following are the high and low closing prices for the Company's Common Stock for each of the four quarters of 1998 and 1997 and for the third and fourth quarters of 1996:

Year Ended December 31, 1998	HIGH	LOW
First Quarter	$28.38	$20.75
Second Quarter	$26.13	$20.50
Third Quarter	$24.25	$ 9.50
Fourth Quarter	$14.38	$ 9.50

Year Ended December 31, 1997	HIGH	LOW
First Quarter	$21.75	$16.00
Second Quarter	$19.50	$13.63
Third Quarter	$26.88	$18.50
Fourth Quarter	$27.63	$18.75

Year Ended December 31, 1996	HIGH	LOW
Third Quarter	$32.00(1)	$15.25(1)
Fourth Quarter	$29.75	$19.25

49 For the 12 months ended December 31, 1998, TNFI reported record growth (see Exhibits 5–9). Sales increased 26% to $263.3 million compared with $208.3 million for the 12 months ended December 31, 1997. Net income increased 24% to $13.8 million, or $1.11 per share, from $11.1 million or $0.96 per share, in the comparable period of 1997.

50 Operating cash flow or EBITDA for the year was $35.3 million as compared to $25.6 million for 1997, an increase of 37.8%, excluding one-time charges. TNFI's growth had caught the eye of Wall Street (see Exhibit 6). In mid-1996 TNFI completed an initial public offering at $14 per share. In February of 1998, the shares had traded as high as $27.88. As of January 29, 1999, TNFI's shares were trading at $15.00, with a valuation slightly lower than the average branded apparel company. Shawn Milne of Hambrecht and Quist, LLC felt that "a small portion of the discount was due to recent changes in management (and location)." However, he expected that the price would improve as the strategy was fully implemented.

51 With the product designs for fall 1999 complete in January, TNFI began contracting Asian manufacturers for the production of its fall 1999 lines in January 1999. Since James Reilly left the Company in August 1998, all of the operating responsibility had fallen to Chris Crawford in San Leandro. Therefore, in addition to his existing responsibilities as CFO, Crawford had the task of implementing the corporate strategy publicly announced by Fifield.

EXHIBIT 7
The North Face, Inc.
Audited Financial
Statements (Income
Statement) from
Form 10-K dated
May 7, 1999

Financial Statements and Supplementary Data
The North Face, Inc.
Consolidated Statements of Operations
(In thousands, except per share amounts)

	For the Years Ended December 31,		
	1998	**1997**	**1996**
Net sales	$247,096	$203,247	$158,226
Cost of sales	135,134	110,764	88,195
Gross profit	111,962	92,483	70,031
Operating expenses	93,897	76,350	56,487
Other operating expenses (Note 4)	7,379	—	—
Operating income	10,686	16,133	13,544
Interest expense	(4,907)	(2,238)	(4,625)
Other income (expense), net	64	(749)	356
Income before provision for income taxes and extraordinary items	5,843	13,146	9,275
Provision for income taxes	2,251	5,191	3,611
Income before extraordinary items	3,592	7,955	5,664
Extraordinary items—losses on extinguishments of debt, net of income taxes of $575	—	—	(863)
Net income	$ 3,592	$ 7,955	$ 4,801
Income per share before extraordinary items:			
Basic	$ 0.30	$0.70	$0.84(1)
Diluted	$ 0.29	$0.69	$0.62
Net income per share:			
Basic	$ 0.30	$0.70	$ 0.71(1)
Diluted	$ 0.29	$0.69	$0.52
Weighted average shares outstanding:			
Basic	12,121	11,297	6,742
Diluted	12,485	11,578	9,183

52   Many securities analysts covering TNFI had questions regarding the implementation of the strategy, but roundly applauded Fifield's goal to build TNFI's sales level to $500 million by 2002. As Fifield said at the time, "There is a big change in lifestyle towards outdoor leisure, and we are perfectly positioned."

53   Morgan Stanley securities analyst David Griffith responded, "They have the potential to be the dominant high-end equipment and apparel brand, but there is a risk of diluting their franchise."

54   "You don't do that using the same business practices that you have been using," Fifield said. "The risks get bigger when the numbers get bigger. I've had experience over the years growing businesses. And, in doing so rapidly."

EXHIBIT 8
The North Face, Inc.
Audited Financial
Statements (Balance
Sheet) from Form
10-K dated May 7,
1999

The North Face, Inc.
Consolidated Balance Sheets
(In thousands, except share and per share amounts)

| | December 31, | |
	1998	**1997**
ASSETS		
Current assets:		
Cash and cash equivalents	$ 13,452	$ 4,511
Trade accounts receivable, net	71,460	48,745
Other receivables	10,069	6,112
Inventories	57,457	46,682
Deferred taxes	3,661	2,865
Other current assets	8,820	9,046
Total current assets	164,919	117,961
Property and equipment, net	25,916	17,524
Trademarks and intangibles, net	33,975	29,066
Debt issuance costs, net	1,730	27
Other assets	6,104	2,871
Total assets	$232,644	$167,449
LIABILITIES AND STOCKHOLDERS' EQUITY		
Current liabilities:		
Accounts payable	$ 22,773	$ 18,113
Accrued employee expenses	5,063	2,917
Short-term borrowings and current portion		
of long-term debt and capital lease obligations	55,910	25,734
Income taxes payable	1,508	2,077
Other current liabilities	11,119	7,125
Total current liabilities	96,373	55,966
Long-term debt and capital lease obligations	5,360	5,177
Other long-term liabilities	7,000	6,165
Total liabilities	108,733	67,308
Minority interest	701	—
Commitments and contingencies (Notes 11, 12 and 15)	—	—
Stockholders' equity:		
Preferred stock, $1.00 par value-shares		
authorized 4,000,000; none issued and outstanding	—	—
Common stock, $.0025 par value-shares		
authorized 50,000,000; issued and outstanding		
12,494,000 and 11,502,000, respectively	31	29
Additional paid-in capital	101,049	81,727
Retained earnings	21,660	18,068
Accumulated other comprehensive income –		
cumulative translation adjustments	470	317
Total stockholders' equity	123,210	100,141
Total liabilities and stockholders' equity	$232,644	$167,449

EXHIBIT 9

The North Face, Inc.
Audited Financial
Statements
(Statement of Cash
Flows) from Form
10-K dated May 7,
1999

The North Face, Inc. Consolidated Statements of Cash Flows (In thousands)			
	For the Years Ended December 31,		
	1998	**1997**	**1996**
CASH FLOWS FROM OPERATING ACTIVITIES:			
Net income	$ 3,592	$ 7,955	$ 4,801
Adjustments to reconcile net income to cash used in operating activities:			
Depreciation and amortization	7,728	5,130	3,595
Loss on disposal of property and equipment	2,235	2,869	—
Adjustment to warranty accrual	(90)	(895)	—
Deferred income taxes	(796)	(375)	(260)
Extraordinary items—losses on extinguishment of debt	—	—	863
Provision for doubtful accounts	799	278	427
Tax benefit of exercise of stock options	1,285	4,803	3,595
Other	(43)	—	—
Changes in operating assets and liabilities (net of effects of acquisition):			
Accounts receivable	(22,849)	(27,618)	(7,994)
Inventories	(9,717)	(15,207)	(10,427)
Income tax receivable	(671)	—	—
Other assets	(5,279)	(11,714)	(2,054)
Accounts payable, accrued liabilities and other liabilities	9,272	13,435	1,290
NET CASH USED IN OPERATING ACTIVITIES	(14,534)	(21,339)	(6,164)
CASH FLOWS FROM INVESTING ACTIVITIES:			
Cash acquired as a result of the purchase of La Sportiva USA	235	—	—
Investment in La Sportiva, S.r.l.	(3,086)	—	—
Purchases of property and equipment	(17,236)	(13,935)	(4,621)
Other	43		
NET CASH USED IN INVESTING ACTIVITIES	(20,044)	(13,935)	(4,621)
CASH FLOWS FROM FINANCING ACTIVITIES:			
Long-term debt proceeds	—	6,826	2,825
Repayments of long-term debt	(348)	(546)	(32,009)
Proceeds from revolver, net	30,707	24,400	(11,812)
Payment of debt issuance costs	(1,915)	(94)	(262)
Collection of note receivable	6,549	—	—
Proceeds from issuance of stock	8,373	889	56,884
NET CASH PROVIDED BY FINANCING ACTIVITIES	43,366	31,475	15,626
Effect of foreign currency fluctuations on cash	153	(5)	651
INCREASE (DECREASE) IN CASH AND CASH EQUIVALENTS	8,941	(3,804)	5,492
CASH AND CASH EQUIVALENTS, BEGINNING OF YEAR	4,511	8,315	2,823
CASH AND CASH EQUIVALENTS, END OF YEAR	$13,452	$ 4,511	$ 8,315

EXHIBIT 9
(continued)

	1998	1997	1996
NONCASH INVESTING ACTIVITY—ISSUANCE OF COMMON STOCK FOR THE ACQUISITION OF LA SPORTIVA USA:			
Purchase of working capital	$ (798)	$ —	$ —
Purchase of property and equipment	(28)	—	—
Purchase of other long-term assets	(34)	—	—
Assumption of other long-term liabilities	702	—	—
Excess purchase price over the fair value of net assets acquired	(3,835)	—	—
Redeemable preferred stock	876		
TOTAL ISSUANCE OF COMMON STOCK FOR THE ACQUISITION OF LA SPORTIVA USA	$(3,117)	$ —	$ —
SUPPLEMENTAL CASH FLOW INFORMATION:			
Cash paid for:			
Interest	$ 3,934	$ 2,136	$ 4,859
Income taxes	$ 4,398	$ 4,488	$ 1,302
Noncash financing activities:			
Conversion of preferred stock into common stock	$ —	$ —	$15,075
Issuance of common stock for note receivable	$ 6,549	$ —	$ —

The North Face, Inc. (B)

55   In late 1998 and early 1999, Linda Patterson (Names have been changed at the request of those interviewed.) was managing the portfolios of high net worth individuals. A number of her clients had read about the success of The North Face, Inc. ("TNFI" or "the Company"). The Company's brand, The North Face, had brand recognition that placed them in the top 20 of the Fairchild 100 brand ranking, and its performance gear was a must have for outdoor enthusiasts and hip urban teenagers as well. With the Company's CEO, James Fifield, recently proclaiming that he sought to increase sales to $500 million by 2002, the future trends continued to look good. Based on the financial statements and the industry, Linda felt that the Company presented an acceptable risk. She began buying the stock for her clients in mid-February 1999.

56   Naturally, with strong operating results under their wings, and a mid-range stock price, TNFI attracted many potential inventors and business partners. Therefore it was no surprise that on March 1, 1999, a respected firm made a buyout offer. Leonard Green & Partners, L.P. and The North Face, Inc. agreed to a buyout offer in which Leonard Green would make a tender offer for all shares of the Company at $17.00 per share in cash. Fifield was part of the Leonard Green investor group and excused himself from the board vote. The Board of TNFI voted unanimously to accept the offer. As is commonplace with insider lead buyouts, individual shareholders who declared that the price was too low immediately filed several lawsuits. However the $17.00 per share price represented a gain for Linda and her clients.

57   Surprise did follow six days later when the tender offer was withdrawn on March 5, 1999 following a disclosure that TNFI was experiencing unexpected delays in preparing its audited fiscal year end 1998 financial statements. Several days later, the buyout offer was reinstated even though several accounting issues were under intensive review by the auditors, Deloitte & Touche, as well as Leonard Green. The first issue was the consolidation of La Sportiva into TNFI's income statement (see Exhibits 1–3). Under the original 1998 La Sportiva acquisition agreement, TNFI would acquire majority interest of La Sportiva over the next two to five years. The purpose of this structure was to allow the Company to argue that La Sportiva income consolidation was appropriate even though TNFI's actual ownership was lower than GAAP required.

58   The second issue involved the company's treatment of a licensing agreement that the brand entered into with China and Nepal. Management had pushed the company's auditors (Deloitte & Touche) to record the revenue from the deal in the third quarter of 1998 (Deloitte refused), and then during the fourth quarter. Since the Company did not have full compliance on both ends of the agreement, the auditors refused to allow TNFI to recognize the funds as revenue. The fiscal year end 1998 press release numbers included this revenue in the fourth quarter.

59   A third accounting issue under review centered on bartering agreements made during Q4 1997 ($5.2 million in barter revenues) and Q1 1998 ($2.4 million in barter revenues). TNFI claimed that they "routinely traded excess product for goods and services" (i.e., advertising). However, GAAP required that barter sales be recognized in the same period that barter credits are used. TNFI apparently recognized all of the barter sales when the transaction was initiated.

60   The delay in producing TNFI's 1998 statement 10-K caused significant uncertainty in the financial markets. As the March 31, 1999 10-K filing deadline passed with little new public information, the NASDAQ market briefly halted trading in the Company's shares in an effort to open the flow of information. Following some brief public comments by

EXHIBIT 1
Balance Sheet

The North Face, Inc. Condensed Consolidated Balance Sheets (In thousands, except share and per share amounts) (unaudited)			
	June 30, 1999	**December 31, 1998**	**June 30, 1998**
ASSETS			
Current assets:			
Cash and cash equivalents	$ 5,946	$ 13,452	$ 5,303
Trade accounts receivable, net	57,408	71,460	49,791
Other receivables	7,108	10,069	6,445
Inventories	71,839	57,457	64,852
Tax benefit receivable	13,926	6,470	6,581
Deferred taxes	3,666	3,661	2,865
Other current assets	6,830	4,692	4,061
Total current assets	166,723	167,261	139,898
Property and equipment, net	32,387	25,916	20,072
Trademarks and intangibles, net	33,516	33,975	28,405
Other assets	4,742	5,492	6,274
Total assets	$237,368	$232,644	$194,649
LIABILITIES AND STOCKHOLDERS' EQUITY			
Current liabilities:			
Accounts payable, accrued expenses and other current liabilities	$ 35,524	$ 40,463	$ 30,428
Short-term borrowings and current portion of long-term debt and capital lease obligations	68,432	55,910	40,985
Total current liabilities	103,956	96,373	71,413
Long-term debt and obligations under capital leases	13,651	5,360	4,435
Other long-term liabilities	7,023	7,000	6,045
Total liabilities	124,630	108,733	81,893
Minority Interest	642	701	—
Commitments and contingencies	—	—	—
Stockholders' equity:			
Common stock, $.0025 par value— shares authorized 50,000,000; issued and outstanding: 12,726,000 at June 30, 1999, 12,494,000 at December 31, 1998 and 12,337,000 at June 30, 1998	32	31	31
Additional paid-in capital	103,809	101,049	97,761
Retained earnings	8,584	21,660	14,647
Accumulated other comprehensive income—cumulative translation adjustments	(329)	470	317
Total stockholders' equity	112,096	123,210	112,756
Total liabilities & stockholders' equity	$237,368	$232,644	$194,649

EXHIBIT 2   Income Statement

The North Face, Inc. Condensed Consolidated Statements of Operations (In thousands, except per share amounts) (unaudited)				
	Three Months Ended June 30,		Six Months Ended June 30,	
	1999	**1998**	**1999**	**1998**
Net sales	$54,596	$43,171	$105,852	$88,875
Cost of sales	30,681	24,261	58,590	50,040
Gross profit	23,915	18,910	47,262	38,835
Operating expenses	31,692	21,253	59,389	41,578
Other operating expenses	2,837	1,518	4,440	1,518
Operating loss	(10,614)	(3,861)	(16,567)	(4,261)
Interest expense	(1,467)	(848)	(2,788)	(1,522)
Other income (expense), net	(353)	517	(2,081)	220
Loss before income tax benefit	(12,434)	(4,192)	(21,436)	(5,563)
Income tax benefit	(4,849)	(1,613)	(8,360)	(2,141)
Net loss	$ (7,585)	$ (2,579)	$ (13,076)	$ (3,422)
Net loss per share:				
Basic	$ (.60)	$ (0.22)	$ (1.03)	$ (0.29)
Diluted	$ (.60)	$ (0.22)	$ (1.03)	$ (0.29)
Weighted average shares outstanding:				
Basic	12,726	11,968	12,707	11,752
Diluted	12,726	11,968	12,707	11,752

Crawford, NASDAQ allowed trading to resume, but soon halted trading again after rumors began to swirl. The second trading suspension lasted for three weeks and was lifted only after the Company filed its form 10-K with the Securities and Exchange Commission.

61   On May 7, 1999 TNFI announced that it would require a restatement of earnings for the years ended 1997 and 1998. The Company's 1998 financial statements reflected a reduction in revenue from $263.3 million to $247.1 million, a reduction in net income from $9.5 million to $3.6 million, and a reduction of earnings per share from $0.76 cents to $0.29 cents from the results announced in the Company's 1998 earnings release issued on January 29, 1999. Excluding charges for facility closure, relocation and realignment, 1998 net income was reduced from $13.8 million to $8.1 million, and earnings per share was reduced from $1.11 cents to $0.65 cents. The Company's restated 1997 financial statements reflected a reduction in revenue from $208.4 million to $203.2 million, a reduction in net income from $11.1 million to $8.0 million, and a reduction of earnings per share from $0.96 cents to $0.69 cents from the results reported in the Company's 1997 10-K filed with the SEC on March 6, 1998.

62   The restatements for each of the periods reflected three primary categories of adjustments affecting the income statement: (1) the reversal of revenues previously recognized which were associated with sales to two distributors because sales accounting was not consistent with certain terms of those transactions (channel stuffing) which were designed to avoid distribution into inappropriate channels and preserve The North Face

EXHIBIT 3
Cash Flow Statement

The North Face, Inc.
Condensed Consolidated Statements of Cash Flows
(In thousands) (unaudited)

	Six Months Ended June 30,	
	1999	**1998**
CASH FLOWS FROM OPERATING ACTIVITIES:		
Net loss	$(13,076)	$ (3,422)
Adjustments to reconcile net loss to cash used in operating activities:		
Depreciation and amortization	6,686	3,073
Loss from the disposal of property and equipment	—	912
Provision for doubtful accounts	2,660	220
Tax benefit of exercise of stock options	131	1,306
Other	(5)	(43)
Effect of changes in:		
Accounts receivable	11,391	(1,266)
Inventories	(14,350)	(18,171)
Income tax receivable	(7,456)	(782)
Other assets	1,344	(1,816)
Accounts payable, accrued expenses and other current liab.	(4,947)	76
NET CASH USED IN OPERATING ACTIVITIES	(17,622)	(19,913)
CASH FLOWS FROM INVESTING ACTIVITIES:		
Deposit for investment in La Sportiva S.r.l.	—	(2,488)
Purchases of property and equipment	(8,855)	(6,090)
Proceeds from the sale of property and equipment	—	43
NET CASH USED IN INVESTING ACTIVITIES	(8,855)	(8,535)
CASH FLOWS FROM FINANCING ACTIVITIES:		
Borrowings on long-term debt	10,000	—
Repayments of long-term debt	(592)	(624)
Proceeds from revolver, net	10,291	15,134
Collection of note receivable	—	6,549
Proceeds from issuance of stock	130	8,181
Redemption of LaSportiva USA preferred stock	(59)	—
NET CASH PROVIDED BY FINANCING ACTIVITIES	19,770	29,240
Effect of foreign currency fluctuations on cash	(799)	—
(DECREASE) INCREASE IN CASH AND CASH EQUIVALENTS	(7,506)	792
CASH AND CASH EQUIVALENTS, BEGINNING OF PERIOD	13,452	4,511
CASH AND CASH EQUIVALENTS, END OF PERIOD	$ 5,946	$ 5,303
SUPPLEMENTAL CASH FLOW INFORMATION:		
Cash paid for:		
Interest	$ 2,538	$ 1,354
Income Taxes	423	20
Noncash financing activities:		
Issuance of common stock for note receivable	—	6,549
Issuance of common stock for land	2,500	—
Acquisition of property and equipment through capital leases	1,114	—

brand. The reversal of this revenue lowered pretax earnings by $3.1 million in 1997 and $6.0 million in 1998; (2) the write-off of capitalized and previously incurred costs to expense in order to more appropriately reflect the future value of those costs. These write-offs lowered pretax earnings by $1.8 million in 1997 and $1.0 million in 1998; and (3) increases in accrued expenses, which reduced pretax earnings in 1997 by $0.3 million and $2.7 million in 1998.

63   The aggressive recognition of revenue left management with little credibility in the financial markets and even less leverage with its buyout partner. Worse yet, the buyout group had to decide by July 31 whether to go ahead with its plans to take the company private with Fifield at the helm. If Leonard Green elected to pass on the opportunity, North Face could owe as much as $7.0 million in breakup fees to Leonard Green.

64   While TNFI, Deloitte & Touche, the SEC, and Leonard Green were sorting out the accounting for 1997 and 1998, the Company was still proceeding with its previously announced move from Vacaville, Calif. to Carbondale, Colo. As expected, some managers left the company, but were not immediately replaced as executive management struggled with past accounting issues. Also on track were the changes in distribution centers from Vacaville, Calif. to Lenexa, Mo. scheduled for July 31, 1999 and the expansion of TNFI's distribution channel.

65   By mid-July of 1999, the CFO, Chris Crawford, left the Company. Roxanna Prasher, financial consultant and former CFO prior to 1997, was named as acting CFO. However, it was clear that she had no intention on staying with the Company for any extended period of time.

66   As the company continued to implement its marketing strategy of entering more mainstream retailers like the Foot Locker and J.C. Penney, sales continued to climb. However, the sales came at the price of lower profit margins and increased returns of goods. The returns came from retailers like J.C. Penney as it found that the retail price exceeded its customer's allotted funds for outerwear purchases thereby stifling demand, and from REI and Eastern Mountain Sports who revolted when they found identical products in J.C. Penney's selling for 30% less than in their own stores.

67   Perhaps the largest issue was the change of distribution centers. The Company planned to "flip the switch" from the old distribution center to the Lenexa distribution center on July 31, 1999 with no back-up plan in place at the beginning of the busiest shipping season of the year. Not one TNFI employee was transferred from Vacaville to Lenexa. Several securities analysts questioned the wisdom of the decision, but the Company repeatedly cited the excellent track record of the contracted distribution center manager, Caliber, a subsidiary of Federal Express, at start-up distribution centers.

68   By late September of 1999, the Company should have been shipping between $1 million and $1.5 million a day. However, only $500,000 to $800,000 in shipments were leaving the distribution center each day. As of September 14, the back up in the distribution center was approximately $12 million. The Company communicated the problem to customers, telling them that the entire inventory was in the U.S. but that they were having trouble getting it out of the distribution center. Several orders were canceled or prices were renegotiated to virtually eliminate all projected profits for the last four months of 1999.

69   The delays were squarely blamed on Caliber, but clearly Fifield and Crawford bore some responsibility. TNFI leased a warehouse in Lenexa and Caliber was contracted to manage the distribution center and TNFI's inventory. Therefore, Caliber needed to hire employees for 190 line and supervisory positions. Overlooked by Caliber and TNFI is the fact that the metropolitan Kansas City area had a sub 1% unemployment rate at the time, so staffing was difficult. Bill Simon (vice chairman TNFI) stated that 400 employees had cycled through the 190 positions in the first six weeks of operation. In addition to the employee retention problem, TNFI and Caliber computer systems apparently were not communicating properly in the first few weeks requiring manual workaround procedures.

70   By September 2, 1999, James Fifield resigned as president and CEO, and current Board Audit Committee member Robert Bunje was named to succeed him. However, by this time, TNFI was $30 million off sales plan for its North American Wholesale business and well over plan on expenses and capital spending. With working capital stretched due to increased slow moving inventory, the Company reached a cash flow crunch by the end of September and was in default of its loan agreements with its banks. The Leonard Green buyout deal, which had been extended earlier in the year, was withdrawn.

71   However, at this time, management (acting CEO, CFO, and COO) was projecting a breakeven 1999 with EBITDA of $21.9 million versus an original plan of $52.7 million. This new plan did not include the Leonard Green breakup fee or the cost of the crisis management consultant forced on the Board by the bankers.

72   With financial managers inside the company, and a crisis consulting team on board, a strong brand, and the biggest selling season of the year in front of the Company, Linda was faced with an uncomfortable decision: buy more TNFI to average down, sell, or hold.

Case prepared by Stephen M. Leavenworth and Alan B. Eisner, Ph.D., Lubin School of Business, Pace University. Copyright © 2001 Leavenworth and Eisner, all rights reserved.

Case 35

Swatch and the Global Watch Industry

1   In early June 1999, the management of the Swatch Group could be satisfied with the company's accomplishments over the last 15 years. Thanks to its 14 brands and unusual approach to marketing, and with 116 million finished watches and movements produced in 1997, the Swatch Group had helped resuscitate the Swiss watch industry and become, in value terms, the world's largest watch manufacturer. Despite an enviable track record, there was a growing sense of anxiety over the future of the company in an industry that seemed to be in a perpetual state of change.

EARLY HISTORY

2   Until 1957, all watches were mechanical. The aesthetics of the exterior visible elements (dials, hands, and case) as well as the reliability and accuracy of a traditional timepiece depended on the meticulous care and precision that had been dedicated to its manufacturing and assembling processes. Mechanical watches consisted of between 100 and 130 components that were to be fitted together in the ébauche (winding stem, gear train) and regulating parts (mainspring, escapement, balance wheel). Most expensive watches contained at least 15 jewels (very hard stones such as synthetic sapphires or rubies that had been drilled, chamfered and polished), which were inserted in places that were most subject to metal wear. The tiny dimensions of a watch case did not leave much room for approximation, and watchmakers were required to have a great deal of micro-mechanical engineering expertise, craftsmanship spirit, patience, experience, and ingenuity.

3   By most accounts, the first reliable pocket watch was invented in 1510 by Peter Henlein, a locksmith from Nuremburg, but the promising art of watchmaking in Germany was rapidly killed by the Thirty Years' War (1618 to 1648). Starting in the late 1500s, the development of the watchmaking industry in Europe traced its roots to the flight of Protestant Huguenots who were driven out of France by a series of religious persecutions. The Huguenots found refuge in Geneva, bringing with them skills in numerous handicrafts. For centuries, Geneva had been a center of ornate jewelry making, but it was left with little industry after John Calvin's famous *Sittenmandate* edicts against luxury and pleasure had progressively put an end to the goldsmiths' activities in the city. Looking for a new source of income, and with their knowledge of metals, skills in jewelry making and artistic flair, many Genevan goldsmiths embraced the watchmakers' profession.

Richard Ivey School of Business
The University of Western Ontario

Cyril Bouquet prepared this case under the supervision of Associate Professor Allen Morrison solely to provide material for class discussion. The authors do not intend to illustrate either effective or ineffective handling of a managerial situation. The authors may have disguised certain names and other identifying information to protect confidentiality.

Ivey Management Services prohibits any form of reproduction, storage, or transmittal without its written permission. This material is not covered under authorization from CanCopy or any reproduction rights organization. To order copies or request permission to reproduce materials, contact Ivey Publishing, Ivey Management Services, c/o Richard Ivey School of Business, The University of Western Ontario, London, Ontario, Canada, N6A 3K7; phone (519) 661-3208; fax (519) 661-3882; e-mail cases@ivey.uwo.ca. Copyright © 1999, Ivey Management Services. Version: (A) 1999-09-23. One time permission to reproduce granted by Ivey Management Services on March 1, 2002.

EXHIBIT 1
**Watch Production
in Switzerland**

Source: FH, Federation of the
Swiss Watch Industry.

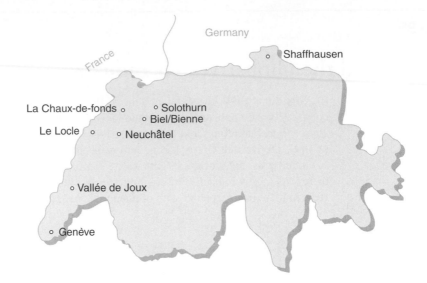

4   As they were becoming more and more numerous, watchmakers decided to regulate their activities, and incorporated into a guild in 1601. The development of the industry in Geneva and the surrounding Jura Mountains was rapid. By 1686, there were 100 masters in Geneva; 165 in 1716; and 800 in 1766 employing some 3,000 people. By 1790, Geneva exported more than 60,000 watches throughout Europe. Many of the Genevese moved north along the French frontier in the Vallée de Joux, Neuchatel and La Chaux-de-Fonds (see Exhibit 1).

5   The emergence of the watch industry in Switzerland was a blessing for the local farmers who could extract only modest agricultural revenues from their mountainous terrain. In fact, many families—who had been educated through a close-knit system of community schools—were looking for an additional source of income, particularly during the long and snow-filled winters. Thanks to advances in new machine-powered watchmaking tools, individual Swiss families began to specialize, some in the production of single components, others in assembly. The small size of watches and watch components allowed for relatively easy transportation from mountain farms and villages to commercial centers.

6   Swiss watches were sold exclusively through jewelry and upscale department stores, which were also fully responsible for repair and aftersales services. Watches were purchased as lifetime investments and were often handed down from generation to generation. Swiss watches found ready acceptance throughout Europe and later in the U.S., in part because of their promotion by jewellers who saw them as a source of ongoing revenues through their repair services.

7   In the 18th and 19th centuries, English competitors were a constant challenge for the Swiss who undertook serious efforts to overcome early British supremacy. First, the Swiss invested in education and training, establishing several watchmaking academies at home and watch-repair schools in major foreign markets. Second, and to strengthen their image internationally, they created a "Swiss made" label, which would become by 1920, an important symbol of quality, style, and prestige. Third, the Swiss significantly improved process technology, setting up the world's first mechanized watch factory in 1839. British watchmakers made no attempt to mass manufacture watches until much later. Seeing mass production techniques as a threat to their craft, they persuaded Parliament to pass a law barring the use of specialty production tools in the British watch industry, and devoted themselves to the production of very expensive marine chronometers. As a result, the British watch industry steadily declined during the 19th century, while the

Swiss industry was on its way to achieving world dominance, thanks to significant advances in design, features, standardization, interchangeability of parts and productivity. In 1842, Adrien Philippe introduced complicated watches featuring perpetual calendars, fly-back hands and/or chronographs. Other early Swiss names included Beaume & Mercier (1830), Longines (1832), Piaget (1874), Omega (1848), Movado (1881) and Rolex (1908).

8   The U.S. watch industry appeared in the middle of the 19th century. Local production consisted of high-volume, standardized products manufactured in machine-driven factories. U.S. watches—such as the US$1 *Turnip* pocket watch introduced under the Ingersoll brand name by the Waterbury Clock Company—were cheap but also of very poor quality. Anyone who wanted a "real" watch bought Swiss.

9   In the early 20th century, the hard economic times (collapsing sales and soaring unemployment) following the First World War, led to a profound reorganization of the Swiss watch industry. Almost 2,500 distinct watchmaking firms grouped together into three associations, namely, the Federation of the Swiss Watch Industry (FH) in 1924, the Ebauches SA in 1926, and the group Union des Branches Annexes de l'Horlogerie (UBAH) in 1926. The associations agreed to coordinate activities (for example, watch components had to be bought from members of the associations only) and maintain high prices. The Swiss Laboratory for Watchmaking Research (CEH) was also founded in 1924, with the objective of strengthening the country's technological advantage. Finally, and in response to the world depression at the time, the Swiss government pushed several important watch assembly firms to form a holding company, ASUAG, in 1931.

POSTWAR COMPETITIVE CHANGES (1945–1970)

10   By 1945, the Swiss accounted for 80% of the world's total watch production, and 99% of all U.S. watch imports. Swiss watch production was divided among nearly 2,500 distinct companies, 90% of which employed fewer than 50 people. Despite the 200-year dominance of Swiss watchmaking companies, much would change in a short period of time.

U.S. Competitors

11   The main source of competition for the Swiss arose from two American watchmakers, Timex and Bulova. Using a combination of automation, precision tooling and simpler design than that of higher-priced Swiss watches, U.S. Time Corporation introduced in 1951 a line of inexpensive (US$6.95 to US$7.95), disposable, yet stylized and highly durable Timex watches, whose movements had new hard alloy bearings instead of traditional and more expensive jewels. Hard alloy metals allowed for the creation of durable watches at lower costs than jewelled lever timepieces. They also allowed U.S. Time to more effectively automate its production lines, further lowering costs.

12   Traditional jewellers were very reluctant to carry the brand for a variety of reasons. Its prices and margins were slim compared to those offered by the Swiss, while the watches' riveted cases could not be opened, thereby eliminating the possibility for jewellers to generate aftersales repair revenues. Locked out of jewelry stores, Timex had no choice but to innovate in its marketing and distribution strategy. Its first extensive worldwide advertising campaign on television, "Took a licking and kept on ticking," was to become a legend in marketing history. Consumer demand soared after John Cameron Swazey, a famous news U.S. commentator, was featured in live "torture tests" commercials emphasizing the watch's low cost and incredible durability. The disposable aspect of Timex watches (no local repair involved) pushed the company to develop new distribution channels, including drugstores, discount houses, department stores, catalogue showrooms, military bases and

sporting goods outlets. By 1970, Timex (having changed its name from U.S. Time) had established a manufacturing and/or marketing presence in over 30 countries and become the world's largest watch manufacturer in terms of units sold.

13   Bulova was the leading U.S. manufacturer of quality, jewelled-lever watches. Integrating the highly accurate tuning fork technology bought from a Swiss engineer in 1959, after the main Swiss companies had turned down the technology, Bulova introduced *Accutron* in 1962. Five years later, *Accutron* was the best-selling watch over $100 in the U.S. Bulova also formed a partnership with Japan's Citizen Watch Company to produce the movements for the *Caravelle* line, designated to meet the low-cost/high-quality challenge imposed by Timex. By 1970, Bulova had expanded its international presence all around the world, and become the largest seller of watches, in revenue terms, in both the United States and the world overall.

Japanese Competitors

14   Like the U.S. industry, the Japanese watch industry was highly concentrated. In 1950, three main competitors, K. Hattori (which marketed the Seiko brand), Citizen and Orient accounted for 50%, 30%, and 20% of the Japanese market respectively. Their positions were protected by the 70% tariff and tax sales imposed on all imported watches by the Japanese government.

15   As the Japanese market became saturated in the 1960s, Hattori and Citizen moved aggressively into other Asia Pacific countries. After first exporting from Japan, Hattori and Citizen established component and assembly operations in low-cost Hong Kong, Singapore and Malaysia. With hundreds of millions of unserved consumers, the region was also a highly attractive market. From a position of strength in Asia, the Japanese watch companies began in earnest to push into Europe and North America.

16   The Swiss response to the growing power of U.S. and Japanese competitors was limited. In 1962, the Swiss FH and ASUAG created a research organization, the Centre Electronique Horloger (CEH) to develop a competitive alternative to the tuning fork technology patented by Bulova. These efforts were unsuccessful, in part because of only lukewarm support from member companies. A rising worldwide demand for watches did little to slow the steady decline in the Swiss share of the world market (from 80% in 1946 to 42% in 1970).

CHANGING TECHNOLOGIES (1970–1990)

17   The advent of light-emitting diodes (LED) and liquid crystal display (LCD) watches constituted a true revolution in the world of watchmaking, as they allowed the digital display of time. In 1970, Hattori, Seiko became the first to develop and commercialize a quartz watch named *Astron,* based on LED technology.

18   Despite their novelty, LED watches had many flaws. A button had to be pushed to activate the display of LED watches, a process that consumed a lot of electrical energy and wore out batteries quickly. Additionally, most people felt that LEDs were distracting and inconvenient to use. In 1973, Seiko introduced the world's first LCD quartz watch with six-digit display and by the late 1970s, LCDs dominated the digital segment. However, digital watches remained largely plagued by quality problems, and consumers never fully embraced the style. Quartz analogue watches, which involved a more delicate manufacturing, and conserved—with their hands and gear train—the traditional appearance of mechanical timepieces, increasingly gained consumers' acceptance. By 1984, over 75% of all watches sold around the world were based on quartz technology, versus only 3% in 1975. The large majority of quartz watches were analogue.

19   Quartz watches used an integrated circuit, made up of numerous electronic components grouped together on the basis of a few square millimeters. Extremely accurate, thanks to their high frequency of vibrations (32 kHz), they were accurate to less than one second per day. Generally more sophisticated—in terms of functions—than their mechanical counterparts, they were also far less expensive to manufacture. The average production cost of a standard quartz watch fell from US$200 in 1972 to about US$50 in 1984, the cost of components being constantly driven down by the main U.S. chipmakers such as National Semiconductor and Texas Instruments.

20   Faced with soaring international competition, the Swiss abolished all internal regulations in 1981, and the industry began to consolidate. Many firms merged in an attempt to leverage their marketing and/or manufacturing capabilities. The largest operation resulted in the creation of the Société Suisse pour L'Industrie Horlogèrc (SSIH), which controlled brands such as Omega and Tissot, among others.

THE JAPANESE INDUSTRY

21   Convinced that technologically sophisticated watches could allow Swiss prices at Timex costs, Hattori Seiko and Citizen made important efforts to promote the new quartz technology. Large investments were made in plant and equipment for fully automated high-volume production of integrated circuits, batteries, and LCD panels. Hattori's production lines were designed to produce up to 1,000,000 watches per year per product line. Manufacturing/assembly facilities were set up all around the world (Japan, the United States, western Europe, Australia, Brazil, Hong Kong, Korea, Mexico). To ease the transition, employees were retrained, relations with distributors were reinforced, and advertising budgets were increased.

22   By 1979, Hattori produced about 22 million watches annually and became the world's largest watch company in terms of revenues, with sales approaching US$1.2 billion, versus only US$503 million for the Swiss ASUAG. Citizen launched the world's first wristwatch movement with a thickness of less than one millimeter in 1978, and became the global leader in both movement and finished wristwatch production volumes in 1986.

23   Casio entered the watch market in 1974 with a digital model priced at US$39.95. Its subsequent low-cost, multifunction digital plastic watches were rapidly fitted with gadgetry such as timers and calculators. By 1980, the company had captured 10% of the Japanese digital watch market, and became the world's second most important player in the under US$50 world watch market, behind Timex.

24   Hattori, Casio, and Citizen were largely integrated companies. Most operations, from the production of movements and components to the assembly and distribution of finished watches, were carried out through wholly owned subsidiaries and/or majority joint ventures. In 1980, Japan produced about 67.5 million watches, up from 12.2 million in 1970.

THE U.S. INDUSTRY

25   U.S. competitors were relatively slow to get on the electronic bandwagon. Neither Bulova's nor Timex's facilities easily allowed the production of quartz crystal or integrated circuits. In fact, they were rapidly becoming obsolete in light of those new technologies sweeping the industry. In addition, Timex was struggling with management problems as Mr. Lehmkuhl—who had run the business for almost 30 years with no clear successor—fell ill and could no longer work. Nevertheless, both companies finally entered the quartz watch market in the mid-1970s, sourcing their quartz components from a variety of suppliers and backing their product lines with full-scale advertising

and promotion campaigns. The Timex model was priced at US$125, which was 60% below Seiko's least expensive watch on the market at that time.

26   About 100 semiconductor firms such as National Semiconductor, Texas Instruments (TI), and Litronix, were also attracted to the promising market for digital watches and circuits for electronic movements in the mid-1970s. Most started as suppliers of quartz movements and components, then invested in high-volume, fully automated watch-manufacturing plants. The belief was that their huge existing distribution channels for consumer electronics products would give them a strong competitive advantage. Watches were introduced at very aggressive prices (TI's retailed at $19.95 in 1976 and $9.99 in 1977). In 1978, TI's digital watch sales reached $100 million, for a pretax profit of US$28 million. However, stagnant demand coupled with continuous price wars and numerous distribution problems led all semiconductor firms to exit the market one by one. In the end, most customers felt uncomfortable buying watches in electronic stores where the semiconductor firms had a distribution advantage.

27   The price wars following the arrival of these semiconductor firms were also largely detrimental to the main U.S. watchmaking companies. Although it was constantly underpriced by Texas Instruments, Timex turned down a number of propositions to form manufacturing partnerships with several chipmakers. Some observers argued that Timex was probably too proud to accept the idea of cooperation. Timex lost US$10 million in 1980, being surpassed by Seiko as the world's largest watch manufacturer company (both in units and total sales), while its share of the U.S. market fell to under 33%. The two other U.S. players remaining in the industry were not in a much better situation. Bulova experienced three years of significant losses before being purchased by Loews Corporation; Hamilton lost $15 million in 1970 and went bankrupt in 1978: the Pulsar rights were bought by Seiko and the remaining assets purchased by SSIH.

WATCHMAKING ACTIVITIES IN HONG KONG AND KOREA

28   By the end of the 1970s, Hong Kong had become the highest volume producer of timepieces in the world. Japanese, American, and European watchmakers had all established assembly plants (mechanical, digital, and quartz analogue watches) in the city to take advantage of highly skilled, cheap labor and favorable tax conditions. Numerous local semiconductor firms had also engaged in the production of low-cost digital quartz watches that were then distributed through local retail chains and department stores, or exported, mainly towards mainland China.

29   The timepiece industry in Korea also experienced considerable growth in the 1970s. By 1988, the country's total watch exports amounted to US$39 million, along with a rising reputation in the eyes of the world for quality assembling capabilities.

30   The Hong Kong and Korean watch industries benefited from their flexible manufacturing systems, capable of handling small quantity orders in different styles. However, downward pressures on prices and low profit margins discouraged local watch producers from investing in technology and branding.

THE SWISS INDUSTRY RESPONDS SLOWLY

31   Although the Swiss pioneered quartz technology, they were particularly reluctant to adopt the new technology. Contrary to the Japanese, their industry structure was very fragmented and, therefore, not adapted to high-volume mass production procedures. Besides, electronic watches were regarded as being unreliable, unsophisticated, and not up to

EXHIBIT 2
Exchange Rate to the U.S. Dollar (Annual Average)

	1950–1970	1971	1972	1974	1976	1978	1980
Swiss Franc	4.37	4.15	4.15	3.58	2.89	2.24	2.18

Source: *International Monetary Fund Yearbook of Statistics.*

Swiss quality standards. Consequently, digital and analogue quartz watches were regarded as just a passing fad, and in 1974, accounted for only 1.7% of the 84.4 million watches exported from Switzerland. Instead, the Swiss focused on the high-end, mechanical segment of the industry, where traditional craftsmanship remained the deciding factor.

32   As SSIH and ASUAG regularly increased prices to maintain profitability, foreign competition rapidly established a strong foothold in the low and middle price ranges where the Swiss were forced to abandon their leadership, virtually without a fight. Compounding the problems faced by the Swiss, the U.S. dollar more than halved its value against the Swiss franc during the 1970s. The appreciating Swiss franc effectively raised the export prices of Swiss watches (see Exhibit 2).

33   The Swiss industry experienced a severe crisis in the late 1970s and early 1980s. Its exports of watches and movements decreased from 94 million in 1974 to 43 million in 1983, while its world market share slid from 43% to less than 15% during that same period. Employment fell from 90,000 (1970) to 47,000 (1980) to 34,000 (1984) and bankruptcies reduced the number of firms from 1,618 to 860 to 630, respectively. These competitive changes resulted mainly from the seeming inability of the Swiss to adapt to the raid emergence of new watch technologies.

Near Death Experience

34   In the early 1980s, Swiss watch production hit an all-time low. SSIH and ASUAG faced liquidation and a profound restructuring of the Swiss industry became necessary. The Swiss government provided financial assistance and initiated the "electronic watch" program in 1978 to promote new technologies as well as the production of electronic watch components in Switzerland. But this initiative was not sufficient, and in 1981 SSIH reported a loss of SFr142 million, giving the company a negative net worth of SFr27.4 million. The Swiss creditor banks—which had just taken over the country's two largest watchmaking groups—were getting ready to sell prestigious brand names, such as Omega, Tissot, or Longines to the Japanese. But Nicolas Hayek, the already well-known founder and CEO of Hayek Engineering, a consulting firm based in Zurich, was convinced he could revive the Swiss industry and regain lost market share, primarily in the lower-end segment. He invested $102 million—mostly his own money—and led a group of 16 investors in buying back the two groups, before orchestrating their merger in 1983.

SMH and Swatch

35   Hayek teamed with Dr. Ernst Thomke to head the new group, Société Micromécanique et Horlogère (SMH). After the merger, SMH owned many of the country's famous watchmaking names, such as Omega, Tissot, Longines, and Rado. Five years later, the group had become the world's largest watchmaking company. Its first product initiative, Swatch, was to become an enormous commercial success, as well as the main instrument behind the revitalization of the entire Swiss industry.

36   The Swatch mania marked the 1980s for the Swiss industry. The Swatch (contraction of "Swiss" and "watch") was conceived as an inexpensive, SFr50 (US$40), yet good quality watch, with quartz accuracy, water and shock resistance, as well as a one-year

guarantee. The concept was challenging. Particular efforts were needed to reduce production costs down to Asian levels. Watch engineers slashed the number of individual parts required in the production of a watch from 91 to 51, and housed them in a standardized plastic case that could be produced on a fully automated assembly line. For the first time ever, it became possible to produce cheap watches in high cost Switzerland. By 1985, production costs were decreased to under SFr10 per unit, and only 130 people were needed to assemble the first eight million Swatch models. By comparison, 350 people were still required to assemble 700,000 Omega watches.

37   Swatch was an immediate success. Within two years of its 1983 launch, sales were averaging 100,000 units a month, for a cumulative total of 13 million sold. In 1985, Swatch accounted for over 80 of SMH's total unit sales, and by 1989, just six years after its debut, the company had placed 70 million Swatches on customers' wrists.

38   Marketing was key to the watch's success. Franz Sprecher, an independent consultant, and Max Imgrüth, a graduate of New York's Fashion Institute of Technology, helped SMH position the watch as a lifestyle symbol and fashion accessory, not as a traditional timekeeping instrument. With their trendy and colorful designs, models were created for every occasion.

39   Initially, the media appeared to be mesmerized by Hayek's charismatic style and unusual approach to marketing. This resulted in lots of free media coverage and publicity. The company also spent liberally on special events and public relation activities. SMH budgeted about SFr5 million per Swatch product line per year in promotional money, and used celebrity endorsements extensively. Swatches were sold through nonconventional channels of distribution such as discount houses and department stores, where variety and low prices constituted the main selling points. Swatch made a few attempts to diversify, but its line of accessories (casual clothing and footwear, umbrellas, sunglasses, and cigarette lighters) experienced mixed success and was discontinued in 1988.

COMPETING IN REAL TIME (1990s)

40   Global watch production grew steadily in the 1990s, at a rate of about 4% per annum, and reached 1.3 billion watches in 1998, equivalent to 22% of the world's population (see Exhibit 3). The production of mechanical watches (and to a lesser extent, that of digital watches) gradually decreased over the years, while that of analogue quartz watches rose 11% per year on average. In 1998, quartz watches—digital and analogue—accounted for about 97% of the worldwide industry production in volume. On average, annual watch purchases were about one unit per person in North America, and 0.6 unit per person in Europe and Japan. Together these three regions—which accounted for 14% of the world's population—generated about 56% of global watch demand (see Exhibit 4).

Industry Restructuring

41   The global watch industry experienced downward profit pressures in the 1990s, as many watchmakers incessantly cut prices—driven in part by a push for economies of scale. Overcapacity and tough head-to-head competition led prices of basic watch movements to be slashed by over 30% in 1998 alone. By the end of the decade, consolidation had reduced the number of watch movement manufacturers form 30 to just three (the Swatch Group—having changed its name from SMH—as well as Seiko and Citizen). The achievement of a critical mass was becoming a necessity to compete globally in all segments of the industry.

42   Several types of internal reorganizations allowed companies to realize economies of scale and/or maintain profitability. These included:

EXHIBIT 3
Global Watch Production; 1984 to 1998

Source: FH, Federation of the Swiss Watch Industry, and Japan Clock and Watch Association.

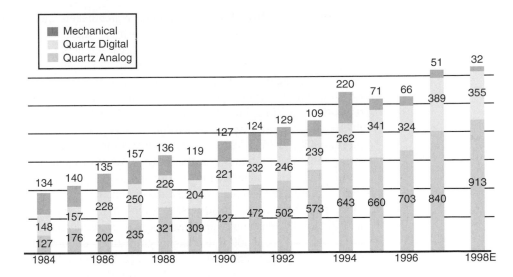

EXHIBIT 4
Per Capita GNP and Annual Watch Purchases, by Region

Source: Japan Clock and Watch Association, *United Nations Demographic Yearbook,* The World Bank.

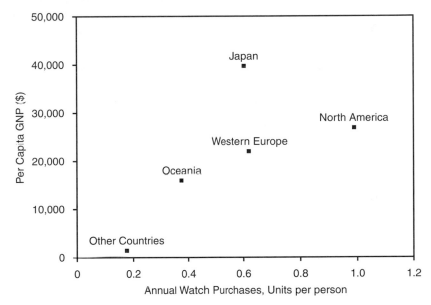

43   **Restructuring Initiatives.** Many watchmaking companies reacted to declining prices in their core business by increasing productivity and shifting manufacturing overseas. With the exception of the Swatch Group, most watch companies manufactured in Southeast Asia exclusively.

44   **Pursuing Acquisitions.** In tune with its strategy to reinforce its position in the luxury or prestige brands, the Swatch Group acquired Blancpain in 1992, thereby also taking control of Frederic Piguet, a company admired for its complex, high-quality mechanical movements. In January 1999, the Swatch Group purchased the total shares of Favre and Perret, the highly reputed producer of quality Swiss watchcases. As another example, Gucci, the luxury Italian company, acquired Severin Montres, its 23-year Swiss watch manufacturer, for $150 million in November 1997. The following year, Gucci's watch sales increased by 160% to $60.1 million. "There is no question that Gucci is destined to become more than a shoe and bag business," said De Boisgelin, an equity analyst with Merrill Lynch in London.[1]

[1] *Women's Wear Daily,* March 20, 1998.

45   **Accessing New Distribution Channels.** Watchmakers traditionally used independent agents to sell products around the world. However, increasing difficulties controlling the merchandising and pricing policies used by local retailers led many of them to alter their strategies. In 1997, the Swatch Group opened 61 new free-standing Swatch stores (mostly operated as franchisees), bringing the total to 120 (including five megastores) in more than 20 countries. Despite the risks involved, the strategy was promising: sales at New York's Swatch Time Shop boutiques approached 100,000 units in 1998, up 32% over 1997. By taking over 85% of its distribution network, Tag Heuer increased its gross margins from 45% to 65%, which more than offset the cost of running local subsidiaries. According to CEO Christian Viros, the move allowed "greater control of our destiny, better control of the implementation of our marketing programs, better understanding of local issues, and greater reactiveness to new developments."[2]

46   **Creating New Niche Products.** Despite ongoing consolidation, there was a viable place for niche companies with clearly defined brands and images. By the late 1990s, Switzerland had about 600 watchmaking companies, employing 34,000 employees, in addition to the big four (The Swatch Group, The Vendôme Luxury Group, Rolex, and Tag Heuer), which together accounted for 75% to 80% of Swiss industry turnover. As examples of niche players, St. John Timepieces entered the industry in 1997 with a collection of Swiss watches specifically designed for sophisticated women, retailing from $450 to $18,000. Breitling scarcely deviated from the aerial image it established in 1884. In 1999, it equipped Breitling Orbiter 3's pilots, Bertrand Piccard and Brian Jones, with wristwatches for their successful, first nonstop 26,602-mile balloon flight around the world.

47   **Increasing Advertising.** The overabundance of supply in the industry implied that watchmakers had to find ways to distinguish their offerings from those of their competitors. Advertising expenditures reached unprecedented levels. In the 1990s, 40% of the value of all Swiss advertisements in international media promoted wristwatches, not banking institutions. Seiko's 1998 *Electricity* campaign was backed with a 60% increase in media spending, while Timex allocated about US$8 million in 1999 to market its *Turn 'n' Pull* Alarm watches.

48   Huge advertising budgets were not, per se, a guarantee of success. The campaigns also needed to be creative in order to get consumers' attention. Companies turned down conservative ads in favor of eye-popping, humorous, and thought-provoking messages that obtained an emotional reaction from viewers. For example, Bulgari formed a one-year partnership with Alitalia, Italy's national airline, to have a personalized Boeing 747 fly around the world with a three-dimensional image of its latest cutting-edge aluminum timepiece painted on the fuselage. Audemars Piguet's ad crusade, "Who is behind an Audemars Piguet Watch?" featured mysterious men and women showing off their watch faces while their own faces remain obscured. Other watchmakers tried to get exposure in action-packed movies such as *Men in Black* and *Lethal Weapon 4* (Hamilton), James Bond (Omega), or *Armageddon* (Tag Heuer). Strong marketing muscle was also put behind sports partnerships. For example, Tag Heuer and Hugo Boss had long been associated with Formula One auto racing, and Spanish-based Festina with cycling events such as the Tour de France.

49   **Emphasizing Quality.** Faced with strong competition from independent, low-cost Asian producers, many European and U.S. watchmakers chose to gradually reposition their brands in the upper market, and proposed increasingly expensive and sophisticated watches. According to the Federation of the Swiss Watch Industry, the average price of a Swiss wristwatch, taking account of all materials, rose from US$132 in 1996 to US$157

[2] *Chief Executive,* 1998.

in 1997. A growing number of customers were becoming aware of quality and increasingly wanted a watch with lasting value.

50 **Emphasizing Technology.** The end of the 1990s looked promising in terms of technological breakthroughs. Bulova's *Vibra Alarm* watch featured dual sound and vibrating alarms. In Seiko's *Kinetic,* an oscillating weight was set in motion by the slightest movements of the wearer's arm ("If you're going to create electricity, use it!"). Timex's *DataLink* pioneered the utilization of wristwatches as wearable information devices. Following Timex's lead, various watch manufacturers introduced multifunctional watches that could be interfaced with personal computers. Other manufacturers designed watches with built-in global positioning systems (Casio, Timex), or offered fast, customized and reliable access to Internet services.

51 **Accentuating Fashion.** Another noticeable trend was the entry of fashion house designers. By 1999, and partly thanks to the Swatch revolution, people increasingly believed that they were judged by what they wore on their wrists. Fashion designers strove to create new watch brands to meet every one of their possible fashion needs. Some decided to put their signatures on stylized watches produced in cooperation with major specialist manufacturers. Examples included Emporio Armani (Fossil), Calvin Klein (The Swatch Group), Guess (Timex), and Yves St Laurent (Citizen). Others, such as Bulgari, Hermes, and Dior set up their own in-house manufacturing operations. "We have very high expectations for this side of the business," said Guillaume de Seynes, director of Hermes Montres. "Watches are already our fourth biggest product in sales terms after leather, silk, and ready-to-wear. We've made a significant investment in the new factory because we expect even faster growth in the future."[3]

DEVELOPMENTS IN THE HONG KONG AND JAPANESE INDUSTRIES

52 In the late 1990s, Hong Kong was the world's dominant center for watch assembly. In 1998, about 80% of all watches produced worldwide were assembled in the city (see Exhibit 5).

53 Japanese watch manufacturers saw their combined domestic and overseas watch production rise about 14% per year in the 1990s. Particularly strong in the sports watch segment, the Japanese offered an impressive range of multifunction chronographs for virtually any type of outdoor activity, including diving, mountain climbing, and flying. However, sales and profitability deteriorated between 1993 and 1996 due to a rapid appreciation of the yen. In addition, the average unit price of analogue quartz movements fell by nearly 50% to ¥234 in the first half of the decade, and by over 30% in 1998, as major companies boosted production. This collapse severely shook the industry, and many manufacturers, such as Orient Watch, had to exit the market. Throughout the last half of the 1990s, Seiko and Citizen began cutting production in order to hold prices firm.

54 Citizen maintained its world's volume leadership with 2,500 new models released every year and 311 million timepieces produced in 1997 (about 25% of the world's total and 36% of the global market for analogue quartz watches). Sales were mainly dependent upon Japan (38%), Asia (32%), America (15%), and Europe (14%). Two new collections—the light-powered *Eco-Drive* watches and the affordable luxury *Elegance Signature* dress watches—marked the company's desire to move from traditional sports watches towards more sophisticated or expensive timepieces.

[3] *Financial Times,* April 24/25, 1999.

EXHIBIT 5
**World Production
of Finished Watches:
500 Million Pieces
(1997)**

Source: Federation of the Swiss
Watch Industry.

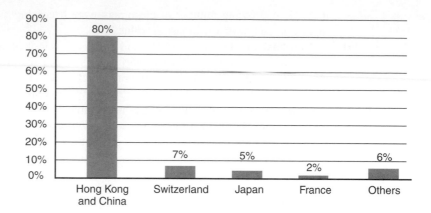

55   Seiko introduced a few technological marvels in the early 1990s, such as the *Perpetual Calendar* watch, with the first built-in millennium plus (1,100 years) calendar, *the Scubamaster,* with the first integrated computerized dive table, and the *Receptor MessageWatch,* with paging functions and built-in antenna that allowed access to specialized information services and incoming alphanumeric messages. In 1995, Seiko introduced the *Kinetic* series, backed with a $20 million advertising campaign. The futuristic line became the driving force behind the company's growth in the late 1990s, accounting for 25% of Seiko's $3 billion global sales. Great hopes were also placed on *Kinetic*'s lower-cost cousin, the $200 *Pulsar* solar-powered quartz watch, which was launched at the end of 1996.

56   Casio enjoyed a significant expansion of its wristwatch division, thanks to the successful launches of the *G-shock* and *Baby-G* product lines. The company was particularly strong in the U.S. (second largest market share after Timex), but also heavily dependent on domestic Japanese sales, which made up two-thirds of total *G-shock* and *Baby-G* sales. A depressed Japanese economy in the late 1990s had a profound negative effect on the company's profits, which were estimated to drop from ¥38 billion in 1998 to ¥19 billion in 1999.[4]

THE U.S. INDUSTRY

57   The biggest single watch market in the world was also the one with the largest trade deficit. In 1991, exports amounted to $73.4 million compared to an import total of $1.84 billion. Thanks to a factory in Little Rock, Arkansas, Timex was the only U.S. watch company with any domestic production in the late 1990s.

Timex

58   From sports watches and classic styles to watches featuring *Star Trek* and Walt Disney characters, Timex offerings strove to address a variety of consumer trends in the 1990s. The production of watches for Guess, Timberland, Nautica, and Reebok further emphasized Timex's willingness to reach a mass audience. Two innovations distinguished the company. The first was the durable, multifunction *Ironman Triathlon* watch, named after the gruelling annual Hawaiian sports event. Initially positioned as an instrument for serious athletes, the watch rapidly appealed to a wider audience of pedestrian customers. By the late 1990s, it

[4] In June 1999 US$1 = ¥119.

EXHIBIT 6
Share of Purchasers by Brand in the U.S. Market—1999

Source: Euromonitor.

Timex	30.6%	Gitano	2.0%
Casio	7.8%	Gucci	1.9%
Seiko	7.4%	Swatch	1.6%
Guess (Timex)	5.0%	Rolex	1.1%
Armitron (Gluck)	4.5%	Movado	1.0%
Citizen	4.0%	Tag Heuer	0.8%
Fossil	3.5%	Hamilton (Swatch)	0.7%
Pulsar (Seiko)	3.1%	Tissot (Swatch)	0.7%
Lorus (Seiko)	2.5%	Omega (Swatch)	0.5%
Bulova	2.2%	Rado (Swatch)	0.2%

was the world's best-selling sports watch with more than 25 million units sold since its 1986 introduction. The second was *Indiglo,* a patented luminescent dial technology launched in 1992, and credited with more than doubling the company's sales by 1994. *Indiglo* received considerable attention in 1993 after a group of people trapped in the World Trade Center bombing had been led to safety by an *Indiglo* owner, who guided them down 34 flights of pitch-black stairs through the glow of his Timex watch. Other technological innovations rapidly followed, with Timex *DataLink,* a $139 wristwatch allowing wireless transfer to and from a desktop PC, and *Beepwear,* a $160-alphanumeric pager wristwatch developed and commercialized in partnership with Motorola.

59   Timex's annual sales exceeded $600 million in the late 1990s, one-quarter of which came from the U.S. market where the company remained the top-selling watch company, far ahead of its main competitors. By 1999, with a 30% market share in its hands, Timex had sold more watches in the U.S. than the next five competitors combined (see Exhibit 6). However, the huge majority of these watches were manufactured in Asia.

NEW ENTRANTS IN THE 1990s

60   By the early 1990s, mainland China and India had emerged among the fastest growing watch markets in the world. With a combined population of 2.1 billion people, these markets could not be ignored, especially after a series of government decisions to liberalize trade and investment in those countries. A number of reputable watchmaking companies had established a presence in India and mainland China, despite the threat of counterfeiting (about 50% of wristwatches sold in those markets were either counterfeited or smuggled in). Most came in via the trading route, appointing local distributors such as Dream Time Watches in India. This strategy was ideal for the Swiss, who could capitalize on the well-appreciated label "Swiss made." Others such as Timex, Seiko and Citizen established their own production facilities, often in cooperation with key local partners.

61   Titan Industries was probably one of the most remarkable industry success stories of the 1990s. The group was established in 1987, with a greenfield investment of $130 million from giant Indian conglomerate Tata Group and the government of Tamil Nadu state, where Titan built one of the world's biggest integrated watch factories, near India's technological center, Bangalore. Constantly scanning the world for best practices, Titan sourced designs and technology from France, Switzerland, and Germany, watchstraps from Austria, and cases from Japan. This world-class strategy created a remarkably successful company. During its first year of operation, 750,000 high-quality finished timepieces were produced and, in 1997, the company enjoyed a

dominant 60% share of the organized Indian watch market, with pretax profits amounting to US$7.5 million on turnover of US$96 million. Titan's management believed the company had little choice but to internationalize, partly to defend its own domestic position. Mr. Desai, Titan's vice-chairman and managing director, commented on the need to globalize: "India is being globalized and the whole world is now turning up in India. So the kind of protection we've enjoyed will go. It's going to get very crowded."[5] By 1997, the company exported over 600,000 watches annually and had established offices in Dubai, London, New York, and Singapore. However, by the end of the 1990s and despite the company's recent $20 million advertising campaign, it was difficult to predict international success. Seducing consumers into buying $120 to $700 Indian-made wristwatches was challenging given the country's poor reputation for the quality of its exports.

THE SWISS INDUSTRY IN THE LATE 1990s

62   In the late 1990s, watch production in Switzerland was the country's third most important industry behind the chemical-pharmaceutical and electronic industries. In 1998, 34 million timepieces were produced in Switzerland for a total value of SFr8.2 billion.[6] Of those, 90% were exported, positioning the country as the world's leading exporter—in value—of finished watches (see Exhibit 7).

63   The Swiss industry had the ability to provide consumers with a comprehensive choice of products in all market segments. Whatever their needs and preferences (mechanical versus quartz technologies; diamond set watch of precious metals versus stainless steel, plastic or ceramic; classic appearance versus trendy design), consumers could always find a "Swiss made" solution when shopping for their wristwatches. Of course, the Swiss industry stood apart in the upper market range where its watches had gained an unequalled reputation for quality, styling, reliability, and accuracy. In 1998, the average price of watches exported by Switzerland was SFr235, four times higher than the average of the world industry (see Exhibits 8 and 9). The "Swiss made" label remained one of the oldest examples of a registered and fiercely protected national branding name, which could be used only on watches and clocks containing at least 50% Swiss-manufactured components by value.

64   The Vendôme Luxury Group accounted for about 20% of Swiss industry turnover, privately held Rolex for 15% and Tag Heuer—which sold over 673,000 units in 1997, for 7%. The Swatch Group was the main player with a third of industry turnover. Thanks to

EXHIBIT 7
World Production of Finished Watches in Value Terms: 16 Billion Swiss Francs (1997)

Source: Federation of the Swiss Watch Industry.

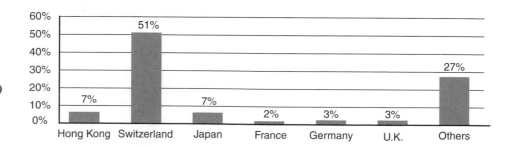

[5] *Financial Times* London Edition, September 10, 1997, p. 43.
[6] In June 1999, SFr = US$0.66.

its 14 brands (Blancpain, Omega, Rado, Longines, Tissot, Calvin Klein, Certina, Mido, Hamilton, Pierre Balmain, Swatch, Flick Flack, Lanco, and Endura), the group had gained a presence in all price and market categories.

65   Swiss watches were sold all around the world. Exports to the United States increased by more than 10% in 1998 for the third consecutive year. Sales in Europe were also on the rise, especially in Spain (+41.3%), Italy (+18%) and France (+16%). In Asia, the on-going economic crisis depressed demand and put downward pressures on prices (the demand in Hong Kong, Singapore, Thailand, and Taiwan dropped by 23% or SFr500 million in 1998). In 1997, Tag Heuer saw Asian sales drop by 21.4% from SFr130 million to SFr102.9 million, accounting for the brand's overall 5.4% decrease.

The Swatch Group

66   In value terms, the Swatch Group was the world's leading manufacturer of watches (14% share of the world market). In 1998, the Swatch Group increased its gross sales and net profits by 7.1% and 7.5% respectively. With a growth averaging 15% to 25% per year, Omega had been a major profit driver for the group (see Exhibit 12 on p. 35-18), thanks to a successful repositioning strategy initiated in the early 1990s. To rejuvenate the brand, cheaper, silver-plated gold was used to replace more expensively metals (platinum, titanium, solid gold, and special steel alloys). The company also streamlined its models from 2,500 to 130 representing four distinct product lines. Other major initiatives consisted of integrating distribution and launching a new advertising campaign (with Cindy Crawford, Michael Schumacher, Martina Hingis, and Pierce Brosnan as high-profile "ambassadors"). The strategy was quite successful and with an average price point 50% lower than its main competitior, Rolex, Omega seemed to have plenty of room to grow.

EXHIBIT 8
Luxury, Prestige and Top Range: Global Market Players (1998)

Source: Bank Leu estimates, Vendôme Group Data.

	Turnover in SFr. Million	Market Share (%)
Rolex	2,200	28%
Vendôme*	1,540	20
Swatch Group**	1,000–1,100	14
Gucci	620	8
TAG Heuer	470	6
Patek Philippe	250	3
Bulgari	215	3
Chopard	195	3
Jaeger LeCoultre	180	2
Audemars Piguet	120	2
Other (Ebel, IWC, Breguet . . .)	910	12
Total	7,750	100%

*(Cartier, Piaget, Vacheron and Constantin, Beaume & Mecier)
** (Blancpain, Omega, Rado, Longines)

EXHIBIT 9
Average Price of Watches in 1998 (In Swiss francs)

Source: Federation of the Swiss Watch Industry.

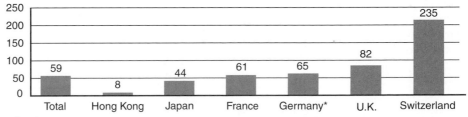

* estimate

67   Despite the success of the Omega brand, the Swatch Group was facing seveal issues. Management problems were plaguing the organization. Key figures such as Klaus Schwab, a professor at the University of Geneva and founder of the World Economic Forum in Davos, Drs. Stephan Schmidheiny, Pierre Arnold, and Walter Frehner all stepped down from the board of directors in the mid-1990s. Several managing directors also left the group in the last two years. Hayek's management style was resulting in growing criticism in the company. Dr. Ernst Thomke, a former partner, had less-than-flattering comments about Hayek: "He has to be the big boss alone, and can never share opinions. He was a consultant all his life and he wanted to become a marketer and product developer. But he never learned that job."[7]

68   The Swatch Group was also experiencing persistent difficulties in establishing a strong foothold in the U.S. market, where it faced stiff competition from Timex, Casio, Seiko, and Citizen. Even the Swatch Group's role as the official timekeeper of the 1996 Summer Olympic Games in Atlanta failed to significantly boost interest in the company's offerings. Although the group generated about 19% of its sales in the U.S., its market share in the basic and middle-priced segments was particularly weak (see Exhibits 6 and 10). Finally, its highly successful and emblematic Swatch brand appeared to be at a crucial crossroads.

69   The brand had sold a total of 200 million watches since its introduction in 1983. A Collectors' Club (100,000 members worldwide) was founded in 1990 to create an international link between fans around the world. Limited edition watches, special events, and the quarterly *Swatch World* journal also contributed to reinforce the value of the brand. Demand rapidly exceeded supply for a number of special launches and collectors started to compare the rarity of their collections, to trade and to speculate around Swatches during auction sales. In the early 1990s, it looked as if Swatch's expansion had no limit. So great was management's confidence that the group even decided to actively contribute to the development and market introduction of the small ecological smart car.

70   Despite the growing interest of many, Swatch sales had plateaued at 18 million to 20 million units a year. In 1998, sales and profit margins were well below the levels acheived in the early 1990s as Swatch was facing increased competition from the likes of Fossil and Guess. One concern was whether there were too many Swatch products on the market. Another concern centered on the product mix. Many young Swatch fans of the past wanted more expensive and sophisticated watches as their incomes increased. A proliferation of products also led to a growing problem with Swatch distributors. Many retailers were dropping Swatch from their shelves. The number of stores selling the trendy watch decreased from 3,000 in the early 1990s to 1,200 in 1998. For Steven Rosdal, co-owner of Hyde Park Jewelers, expressed the views of some retailers: "Swatch came out with more products than the market could bear, and the consumers seemed to back off. I guess if you use the word 'fad' for anything, it could be used for Swatch."[8]

71   The group was undertaking several steps to revamp and differentiate the brand. First, Swatch was trying to reposition itself from a low-margin, high-volume business involved

EXHIBIT 10
U.S. Market and Swatch Group's Market Share—1999

Source: Dresdner Kleinwort Benson estimates.

	Units	%	Value	%	Swatch market share
Mass (under $50)	124,653	78%	2,056	34%	9%
Middle market ($50–299)	31,840	20%	2,219	37%	4
Upper/Luxury ($300)	2,705	2%	1,771	29%	21
Total	159,198	100%	6,046	100%	11%

[7] *Time,* March 28, 1994.
[8] *Jewellers' Circular-Keystone,* December 1998.

in day-to-day fashion watches to a high-margin, high-volume enterprise focusing on watches fitted with state-of-the-art electronic gadgetry. As an example of its repositioning efforts, it launched the *Access* watch in 1995, which could be programmed to function as a pass to access ski lifts, hotel chains, public transport and numerous other applications. Although the watch had yet to achieve its commercial potential, there were promising signals: Swatch equipped the Lisbon universal exhibition with one million units and about 200 ski resorts in some 17 countries. Also, with assistance from German electronics giant Siemens, Swatch developed *Swatch Talk,* a Dick Tracy type wristwatch with an integrated mobile telephone. Finally, Swatch created the *Swatch Beat,* as a completely new global concept of time, as well as a whole new area of market potential. With *Swatch Beat,* time was the same all over the world "No Time Zones, No Geographical Borders." People using the same clock could agree to a phone call at "500," without time zone arithmetic required. The day was divided into 1,000 units (each one being the equivalent of one minute and 26.4 seconds) with a new BMT meridian created in Bienne, home of the Swatch Group.

72   As a second initiative, Swatch launched a new advertising campaign ("Time is what you make of it") designed to reinforce the brand's primary message ("Innovation, provocation, fun. Forever.") Sponsorship was primarily focused on new and youth-oriented sports or events with an offbeat lifestyle, such as snowboarding, mountain-biking, bungee jumping, and rock climbing.

73   However, in October 1998, Swatch sold its minority 19% shareholding of Micro Compact Car, the vehicle producer, to manufacturing partner Daimler-Benz. Although the group was still looking for key partners to develop the hybrid electric *Swatchmobile,* management made it clear that its core business remained the watch industry and microelectronics.

STRATEGIC DECISIONS

74 In early June 1999, Hayek was under growing pressure to clarify the company's strategy. Many observers and shareholders were wondering whether the original management philosophy that shaped the company's success remained viable.

75   Conventional wisdom suggested that all watch companies should locate manufacturing activities in countries that offered low-cost production solutions. The Swatch Group had always remained committed to its Swiss home base, leaving the bulk of its technology, people and manufacturing in the isolated villages surrounding the Jura Mountains. Those places possessed hundreds of years of experience in the art of watchmaking. Employees had spent generations in the factories controlled by the Swatch Group, where they developed a special feel and touch for this business along with a true sense of organizational commitment. However, the company's junior secretaries in Switzerland earned more than senior engineers at competitors in Thailand, Malaysia, China or India. Maybe it was time to move on and stop building watches in one of the most expensive countries in the world. But which, if any, of the value-added chain activities should be moved (see Exhibit 11)?

76   With its huge domestic demand and low-cost labor, India offered interesting sourcing opportunities. Many industry analysts believed that Titan Industries was looking for key foreign partners, after the demise of an early alliance with Timex. Would a partnership with a company like Titan make sense, or if and when the company were to move, should it go it alone?

77   Another trend management had to address was the movement of many watch companies into ever more narrow or differentiated market niches. The Swatch Group was present in all market segments and price categories, but its performance depended mainly on four brand names, Omega, Swatch, Tissot and Rado, which together accounted for 82% of total

EXHIBIT 11
Watch Production and Value Added Chain

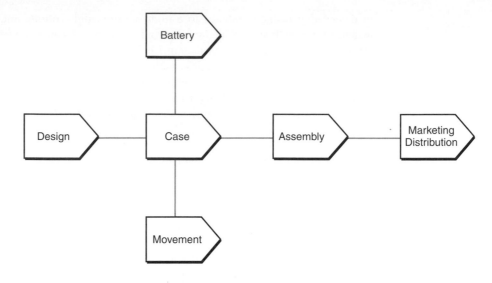

EXHIBIT 12   The Swatch Group's Turnover and Margin Estimates for 1998

Source: Bank Leu estimates.

	Units in thou.	Average price in SFr*	Turnover in SFr. million	% of total	EBIT in SFr. million	% total	Margin in %
Omega	550	1,200	670	28%	147	47%	22%
Swatch	26,000	36	925	38	79	25	9
Tissot	1,600	100–150	210	9	20	6	10
Rado	300	570	170	7	31	10	18
Longines	550	270	150	6	23	7	15
Calvin Klein	600	130	75	3	4	1	5
Blancpain	10	6,500	65	3	6	2	9
Other	1,500	80	145	6	3	1	2
Total	31,110	80	2,410	100%	312	100%	13.0%

*Factory gate price

sales and 88% of operating profit in 1998 (see Exhibit 12). Perhaps it was time to reorganize the company's portfolio. Advertising budgets had already been reallocated towards the luxury and high-tech markets, where the company was also constantly looking for key partners and acquisition targets. However, for many industry observers, this product market strategy (luxury–high tech and/or globalization) was becoming too complex for the company's internal capabilities, as indicated in the failure of the smart car project.

This case has been written on the basis of published sources only. Consequently, the interpretation and perspectives presented in this case are not necessarily those of the Swatch Group or any of its employees.

Case 36

The Wall Street Journal: Print versus Interactive

1 In early January 1999, Peter Kann, chief executive officer of Dow Jones & Company, pondered the future of one of the company's most valuable brands and products, *The Wall Street Journal.* A meeting with Kann's top management team had been called for the following month to discuss the future of this brand, primarily focusing on the relative positioning and performance of the print and Interactive Journal.

2 *The Wall Street Journal* had enjoyed an unrivaled position as the top daily business newspaper in the United States for over 109 years. The *Journal* was the largest circulation newspaper in the United States with approximately 1.8 million subscribers, reached five million worldwide readers daily, and enjoyed tremendous loyalty among readers. However, the newspaper industry was facing a future of little to no growth and mounting competition from other forms of news delivery, most recently and saliently, the Internet.

3 Internet news providers threatened the typical newspaper's core product and service of timely, current news reporting and delivery. The threat to *The Wall Street Journal* was felt not only from competitors on the Web, such as CNN and CBS MarketWatch who operated free sites, but from its own Interactive Journal. The Interactive Journal was introduced in 1996 and within a year became the largest paid subscription site on the Internet. But what would the rising demand for instant, Web-based news do to the company's mainstay business of the print edition? Would the Interactive Journal serve as a complement or a substitute for print? Given this, Peter Kann wondered how the two products should be positioned, priced, and promoted in order to maximize revenue for both. The answers to these questions would fundamentally shift the industry as well as Dow Jones & Company.

DOW JONES & COMPANY

4 Dow Jones & Company was a global provider of business news and information. Its primary operations were in three business segments: print publishing, electronic publishing, and general-interest community newspapers.

5 The print publishing segment included *The Wall Street Journal, Barron's, National Business and Employment Weekly, The Asian Wall Street Journal, The Wall Street Journal Europe, Far Eastern Economic Review* and *SmartMoney Magazine.* The electronic publishing segment included The Wall Street Journal Interactive Edition, Dow Jones Newswires, Dow Jones Interactive and the Dow Jones Indexes.

IVEY

Richard Ivey School of Business
The University of Western Ontario

Amy Hillman prepared this case solely to provide material for class discussion. The author does not intend to illustrate either effective or ineffective handling of a managerial situation. The author may have disguised certain names and other identifying information to protect confidentiality.

Ivey Management Services prohibits any form of reproduction, storage or transmittal without its written permission. This material is not covered under authorization from CanCopy or any reproduction rights organization. To order copies or request permission to reproduce materials, contact Ivey Publishing, Ivey Management Services, c/o Richard Ivey School of Business, The University of Western Ontario, London, Ontario, Canada, N6A 3K7, phone (519) 661-3208; fax (519) 661-3882; e-mail cases@ivey.uwo.ca. Copyright © 1999, Ivey Management Services. Version: (A) 2001-10-02. One time permission to reproduce granted by Ivey Management Services on March 1, 2002.

The Wall Street Journal Print Edition

6   *The Wall Street Journal* (WSJ), Dow Jones' flagship publication, was long considered the most respected source of business and financial news in the United States. By 1999, *The Wall Street Journal* was one of the most recognized brands in the world with a subscription renewal rate of 80%. Its circulation rate of approximately 1.8 million subscribers remained relatively stable in the 1990s.

7   Over 600 reporters and editors—who also support other Dow Jones products—contributed to an outstanding record of journalistic excellence. In 1997, the company received its 19th Pulitzer Prize, an award also given to its chief executive officer in 1972. Each of the print editions of *The Wall Street Journal* drew heavily upon *The Wall Street Journal*'s worldwide news staff. *The Wall Street Journal* Europe, headquartered in Brussels, had an average circulation in 1998 of 71,000 and sold on day of publication in continental Europe, the United Kingdom, the Middle East, and North Africa. *The Asian Wall Street Journal,* headquartered in Hong Kong, had an average circulation of 62,000 in 1998 and was printed in Hong Kong, Singapore, Japan. Thailand, Malaysia, Korea, and Taiwan. In addition, the company distributed special editions of Wall Street Journal news within 30 newspapers in 26 countries, published in 10 languages with a combined circulation of four million.

8   Despite its long-standing traditional front page format without full paper-width headlines, six columns, dot print photos, and the "What's News" summaries, the *Journal* innovated many new formats in the 1990s. Starting in 1993, the *Journal* expanded its business and economic trend regional coverage to select parts of the United States, including Texas, Florida, California, New England, the Northwest, and the Southeast. These *Journal* editions consisted of a four-page weekly section included in papers distributed in those regions. Four-color advertising, introduced in 1995, saw increased revenue of 60% in 1997, contributing to overall advertising linage up 13%, on top of a 14% growth in 1996, 1997 saw the addition of a daily page of international business news and 1998, a two-page technology section. *Weekend Journal,* introduced in 1998, expanded typical content to include lifestyle issues such as personal finance, food and wine, sports, travel, and residential real estate, as well as other new editorial features appealing to new advertisers and readers.

9   However, these new innovations in the *Journal* served as supplements rather than substitutes to the three traditional sections of the five-day-a-week paper. Kann explains, "Visually, the *Journal* has a unique trademark quality. It's a uniquely recognizable page. But the main reason we haven't changed it is it's a very useful format." Section A included the front page and business and political news. Section B, "Marketplace," focused more on lifestyle and marketing issues, including regional editions, and the technology section. Finally, Section C, "Money & Investing," centered on financial news, daily stock and bond quotes and other financial information. Dow Jones also announced plans to spend US$230 million between 1999 and 2002 to expand the number of color pages and total page capacity. This investment would increase the color page capacity from eight to 24 and the total page capacity from 80 to 96.

Economics of Print Publishing

10   Within the relevant range (circulation and advertising within 15%), most print WSJ expenses were fixed. Variable components (including newsprint, ink, plates, production and delivery overtime) account for approximately 15% of costs. Print WSJ revenues came from two primary sources: sales/subscriptions and advertising. Advertising rate growth was dependent upon at least roughly preserving the circulation level. Hence, if circulation dropped 10%, ad revenue could fall 10% or more.

11   The paper was printed in 17 company-owned U.S. and 13 overseas plants, 12 of which were leased. Company employees (through the company's National Delivery Service, Inc. subsidiary) delivered 75% of U.S. subscriber copies by 6:00 A.M. daily. This system provided delivery earlier and more reliably than the postal service. Company plants were unionized, operated one shift daily, six days a week, and were important to maintaining the *Journal*'s traditional size, which was larger than typical print newspapers. This size format was believed to be more appealing to advertisers and to readers alike.

The Print Newspaper Industry

12   Wall Street had long found newspaper stocks appealing and therefore priced them at a premium to the rest of the market. Exhibit 1 includes stock data for Dow Jones & Company. However, newspapers faced increasing media competition in the 1990s, making advertising sales a harder pitch. Local newspapers in general turned to supplemental advertising flyers and catalogues placed between the pages of daily and Sunday papers in order to provide more dependable cash flow. In addition, growth of classified ads was strong due to the general expansion of the economy resulting in strong real estate, automobile and job markets. Classified volume typically contributed 15 to 25% of total newspaper linage sales and was the industry's most profitable ad category on a per-line basis in the 1990s. However, classified ads also faced increased competition from online offerings. Overall, newspapers benefited from the robust economy in 1998 by encouraging more advertisers to buy more linage at increased rates. The total advertising market in the United States for print medium was US$72 billion in 1999, up from US$55 billion in 1995, and projected to exceed US$83 billion by 2001.

EXHIBIT 1
Stock Performance for Dow Jones & Company

Source: Interactive Chart—dowjones.htm; October 4, 1999.

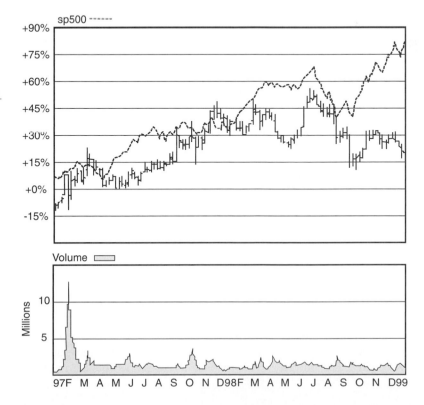

13   Despite relatively stable cash flows in the past, newspaper circulation was in a general downward trend from 1987 through late 1996, although there was some stability starting in 1997. Local distribution of newspapers, both home and newsstands, was increasingly contracted out to third parties.

14   *The Wall Street Journal* was the first national daily paper in the United States and enjoyed status as the only national daily until the advent of *USA Today* in 1985. In the late 1990s, *The New York Times* and *Los Angeles Times* also nominally entered into the nationally distributed sector of the industry. However, their entry into the nationally distributed sector did not indicate a shift towards nationally focused news; *The New York Times* and *Los Angeles Times* still concentrated on a fairly targeted geographic region in terms of subscribers and content. In addition, the business-versus-general-interest focus of *The Wall Street Journal* kept it relatively immune from direct competitors until the expansion of U.K.-based *Financial Times* in 1998. While the *Financial Times*'s focus was primarily business news, its exposure in the U.S. market was dwarfed by that of *The Wall Street Journal,* with the circulation level of the *Journal* around 35 times that of the *Financial Times.*

The Wall Street Journal Interactive Edition

15 *The Wall Street Journal* Interactive Edition (wsj.com), introduced in April 1996, was another innovation for Dow Jones as well as for the publishing industry. While initially a free site, subscribers were first asked to pay in August of 1996. Subscribers totaled over 100,000 within the first year of launch, and reached over 266,000 subscribers by the end of 1998. While many competitors were delivering news on the Web for free, *The Wall Street Journal* Interactive Edition became the largest paid subscription site on the World Wide Web. Around 1% of the content at the website was free access, with the remaining 99% accessible only to subscribers. "Our proprietary information has value, and we have the guts to charge," said Peter Kann.

16   *U.S. News & World Report* called the Interactive Journal "the best single financial site on the Internet." The Interactive Journal offered continuously updated news and market information, access to the international editions, in-depth background reports on over 20,000 companies and pay-per-view access to the Dow Jones Publication library. In addition, the Interactive Journal included proprietary information and coverage not found in the print editions. Within each story in the Interactive Journal were links to stock quotes and other information about the companies discussed.

17   Careers.wsj.com was a free site, launched in 1997 and linked to the Interactive Journal, that offered a searchable database of employment listings and content from the National Business and Employment Weekly.

18   Advertising sales were relatively stable in 1998, coming off two relatively strong years of growth. Subscription renewal rates were approximately 75% to 80%. Further comparison of subscribers, subscriber revenue and acquisition costs for both the print and Interactive editions is given in Exhibits 2 and 3.

Economics of Electronic Publishing

19 Typically for Web-based publishing, most costs were fixed or step-function fixed, except for subscriber acquisition and advertising selling expenses.

20   For free sites, primary revenue came from advertising, with the number of people visiting the site largely determining the fees charged to advertisers. For subscription sites, however, revenue came from both advertising and subscriptions, similar to print publishing. A third category of revenue also became possible in electronic publishing: transac-

EXHIBIT 2
Per-Subscriber
Revenue and
Acquisition Costs

	Print WSJ	Electronic WSJ
One-Year Subscription Nonprint Subscriber	N/A	$59
One-Year Subscription Print Subscriber	$175	$29
Advertising Revenue Per Year Per Subscriber	$500	$40
Average Acquisition Cost New Subscriber	$160	$40
Average Renewal Cost	$5	$5
Renewal Rate	80%	75%

EXHIBIT 3
*The Wall Street
Journal*
Print/Electronic
Interaction

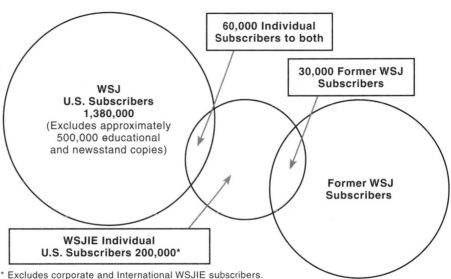

60,000 Individual Subscribers to both

30,000 Former WSJ Subscribers

WSJ
U.S. Subscribers
1,380,000
(Excludes approximately
500,000 educational
and newsstand copies)

Former WSJ
Subscribers

WSJIE Individual
U.S. Subscribers 200,000*

* Excludes corporate and International WSJIE subscribers.

tion fees. Forrester Research predicted that online revenue from subscriptions, advertising and transaction fees would grow from just over US$520 million in 1997 to US$8.5 billion within five years.

21   The total advertising market for Internet medium was approximately US$2 billion in 1999 and was projected to exceed US$5 billion in 2001. As a quarterly comparison, the first quarter of 1996 saw total U.S. Internet advertising spending at US$29.9 million. By the first quarter of 1998, this number had grown to US$351.3 million and second quarter of 1998 to US$423.0 million. Unlike television, radio or print advertising, an almost unlimited supply of advertising and a concurrent glut of it accompanied the advent of the Internet. As a result, advertising rates plummeted in 1998 due to the lack of target viewers. However, this trend did not apply to websites that could offer advertisers access to more targeted demographics.

22   A 1998 GVU Internet survey indicated the attitudes about pay versus free sites on the Internet. Of those individuals who refused to pay for information on the Internet, 44.5% did so because the information was available elsewhere for free, while 32.7% would not pay for Internet information because they were already paying to gain access to the Internet itself.

EXHIBIT 4
Print Publishing
Primarily *The Wall
Street Journal*
($ Millions)

	1997	1998
Revenue:		
Advertising	$ 790	$ 777
Circ. & Other	353	360
Total	$ 1,143	$ 1,137
Operating Expenses	$ 896	$ 931
Operating Income	$ 247	$ 174

EXHIBIT 5
Electronic Products,
Dow Jones
Interactive, Dow
Jones Newswires, *The
Wall Street Journal*
Interactive Edition
($ Millions)

	1997	1998
Revenue:		
Dow Jones Newswires/Indexes	$ 204	$ 220
Interactive Publishing	159	172
Total	$ 363	$ 393
Operating Expenses	$ 302	$ 315
Operating Income	$ 61	$ 78

Other reasons given for the resistance to pay for site access included excessive cost and poor site quality. Similarly, a survey conducted by the BBDO advertising agency found that 60% of respondents replied negatively when asked if they would be willing to pay for an online subscription edition of their favorite print publication. Of those that answered "yes," 89% indicated they would not be willing to pay more than the newsstand price for an online version.

23   Unlike print publishing, editorial and news skills for a near–real time environment became necessary skills for electronic publishing. With continual news updates, reliability and quality of journalism reports became subject to increased time pressure. Accuracy, the elimination of bias, clarity and comprehensiveness in the face of a flood of information became critical for electronic publishing. In addition, new skills of technology, ease of website navigation, effective layout for a computer screen, etc., became necessary for Web publishing.

24   *The Wall Street Journal* Interactive Edition was expected to attain its break-even point in 1999. Forrester Research estimated the average annual operating costs of content Internet sites of US$893,000 and of transactional sites at US$2.8 million in 1998. For Income Statement information for both Print and Electronic products, see Exhibits 4 and 5. Companywide financial information is provided in Exhibits 6 and 7.

25   The electronic publishing division, which included Dow Jones Interactive, provided subscribers with a news library of over 5,000 publications, including a full-text archive of *The Wall Street Journal* and Dow Jones Newswires as well as roughly 1,200 non-U.S. news sources, and the 50 largest U.S. newspapers and business magazines.

The Internet/Web Publishing Market

26   Growth in the use of the Internet exploded in the 1990s. It was estimated that in 1998, the number of worldwide Internet users was over 147 million with over 57 million in the United States alone. The number of U.S. households joining the Internet was estimated at 760 per hour in 1999 with nearly 38% of households being reached by the Internet. Nearly 90% of Internet users gathered news and information from the Web's news, information and entertainment sites. In 1996, Pew Research Center estimated that only 4% of Americans got their news online. This number jumped to nearly 20% in 1999.

EXHIBIT 6
Financial Highlights

Income Statement Results

(in thousands except per share amounts)	1998	1997	% Increase (Decrease)
CONSOLIDATED			
Revenues	$2,158,106	$2,572,518	(16.1)
Operating Income (Loss)	218,573	(741,974)	—
EBITDA[1]	437,127	510,023	(14.3)
Net Income (Loss)	8,362	(802,132)	—
Net Income (Loss) Per Share—Diluted	.09	(8.36)	—
EXCLUDING SPECIAL ITEMS[2]			
Revenues	1,872,204	1,776,238	5.4
Operating Income	327,915	335,955	(2.4)
EBITDA	416,456	454,071	(8.3)
Net Income	185,039	185,707	(0.4)
Net Income Per Share—Diluted	1.92	1.92	

Financial Position and Cash Flows

(in thousands except per share amounts)	1998	1997	% Increase (Decrease)
Long-Term Debt, Including Current Portion	$149,889	$234,124	(36.0)
Stockholders' Equity	509,340	780,822	(34.8)
Capital Expenditures	225,834	347,797	(35.1)
Cash From Operations	306,226	459,763	(33.4)
Purchase of Treasury Stock, Net of Put Premiums	291,215		—

Revenues and Operating Income (Loss) by Segment

(in thousands except per share amounts)	1998	1997	% Increase (Decrease)
REVENUES			
Print Publishing	$1,161,939	$1,143,395	1.6
Electronic Publishing[3]	393,178	363,232	8.2
Community Newspapers	317,087	300,611	5.5
Segment Revenues	1,872,204	1,807,238	3.6
Divested/Joint Ventured Operations:			
Print Television Operations		21,091	—
Telerate	285,902	744,189	(61.6)
Consolidated Revenues	$2,158,106	$2,572,518	(16.1)
OPERATING INCOME (LOSS)[4]			
Print Publishing	$ 173,582	$ 247,191	(29.8)
Electronic Publishing	56,060	61,089	(8.2)
Community Newspapers	44,760	50,584	(11.5)
Corporate	(22,602)	(18,189)	(24.3)
Segment Operating Income	251,800	340,675	(26.1)
Divested/Joint Ventured Operations:			
Print and Televisions Operations		(18.239)	—
Telerate	(33,227)	(1,064,410)	96.9
Consolidated Operating Income (Loss)	$ 218,573	$ (741,974)	—

[1] EBITDA is computed as operating income (loss) excluding depreciation and amortization and restructuring costs.
[2] Consolidated excluding Telerate operations and loss on its sale, and other special charges/gains.
[3] 1997 revenue includes $31 million of one-time index licensing fees.
[4] excluding restructuring charges, segment operating income would have been as follows (000's):

	1998	1997
Print Publishing	$223,496	$251,903
Electronic Publishing	65,921	78,138
Community Newspapers	61,100	50,584
Corporate	(22,602)	(18,189)
	$327,915	$362,436

EXHIBIT 7   Five-Year Financial Summary

(in thousands except per share amounts)	1998	1997	1996	1995	1994
REVENUES					
Advertising	$1,031,210	$1,011,864	$ 896,981	$ 771,779	$ 724,990
Information Services	670,441	1,101,696	1,125,625	1,092,002	976,800
Circulation and Other	456,455	458,958	458,986	419,980	389,187
TOTAL Revenues	2,158,106	2,572,518	2,481,592	2,283,761	2,090,977
EXPENSES					
News, Operations and Development	677,381	899,868	820,564	748,945	642,184
Selling, Administrative and General	762,803	895,707	831,270	764,161	681,244
Newsprint	163,146	152,478	164,766	157,047	107,178
Second Class Postage and Carrier Delivery	117,649	114,442	110,256	103,497	96,751
Depreciation and Amortization	142,439	250,734	217,756	206,070	205,303
Restructuring	76,115	1,001,263			
Operating Expenses	1,939,533	3,314,492	2,144,612	1,979,720	1,732,660
Operating Income (Loss)	218,573	(714,974)	336,980	304,041	358,317
OTHER INCOME (DEDUCTIONS)					
Investment Income	12,266	3,473	4,249	5,379	4,884
Interest Expense	(7,193)	(19,367)	(18,755)	(18,345)	(16,858)
Equity in Losses of Associated Companies	(21,653)	(49,311)	(5,408)	14,193	(5,434)
(Loss) Gain on Disposition of Businesses & Investments	(126,085)	52,595	14,315	13,557	3,097
Other, Net	(4,250)	(9,300)	(121)	4,075	(5,981)
Income (Loss) Before Income Taxes & Minority Interests	71,658	(763,884)	331,260	322,900	338,025
Income Taxes	63,083	37,796	147,728	139,878	157,632
Income (Loss) Before Minority Interests	8,575	(801,680)	183,532	183,022	180,393
Minority Interests in (Earnings) Losses of Subsidiaries	(213)	(452)	6,437	6,550	787
Income (Loss) Before Cumulative Effect of Accounting Changes	8,362	(802,132)	189,969	189,572	181,180
Cumulative Effect of Accounting Changes					(3,007)
NET INCOME (LOSS)	$ 8,362	$ (802,132)	$ 189,969	189,572	178,173
PER SHARE Basic					
Income (Loss) Before Cumulative Effect of Accounting Changes	$ .09	$ (8.36)	$ 1.96	$ 1.96	$ 1.83
Net Income (Loss)	.09	(8.36)	1.96	1.96	1.80
PER SHARE Diluted					
Income (Loss) Before Cumulative Effect of Accounting Changes	.09	(8.36)	1.95	1.94	1.82
Net Income (Loss)	.09	(8.36)	1.96	1.94	1.79
Weighted-Average Shares Outstanding (000's):					
Basic	95,180	95,993	96,703	96,907	99,002
Diluted	96,404	95,993	97,371	97,675	99,662
Dividends	$ .96	$ .96	$ .96	$ .92	$ 84
OTHER DATA					
Long-term debt, including Current Portion, as a % of Total Capital	22.7%	23.1%	17.0%	13.9%	16.9%
Newsprint Consumption (Metric Tons)	278,000	270,000	252,000	224,000	221,000
Number of Full Time Employees at Year End	8,253	12,309	11,844	11,232	10,265
Cash From Operations	306,226	459,763	405,157	371,887	403,142
Capital Expenditures	225,834	347,797	232,178	218,765	222,434
Cash Dividends	91,662	92,116	92,969	89,131	83,360
Total Assets	1,491,322	1,919,734	2,759,631	2,598,700	2,445,766
Long-term Debt, Including Current Portion	149,889	234,124	337,618	259,253	300,870
Stockholders' Equity	509,340	780,822	1,643,993	1,601,751	1,481,611

27   It was projected that by 2003, over 55 million professionals, managers and executives would be using the Internet at work. In 1999, over 17% of the online population preferred to receive their financial news online.

28   Internet penetration by age was concentrated in younger generations by the end of 1998. Fifty-nine percent of 12- to 17-year-olds used the Internet, with the percentage dropping with each higher age group to 27% of the population aged 55 to 64, and only 14% of the population over age 65. In 1996 the male to female ratio of Internet use was 57 to 43 but by 1998, this ratio had changed to 51 to 49.

29   The Interactive Journal competed with a variety of business news sources on the Internet, including sites maintained by traditional print competitors such as *BusinessWeek, Fortune, The New York Times,* and the *Financial Times.* In addition, it faced competition from non-print competitors such as CNNfn, Bloomberg, online brokerage firms, CBS MarketWatch, TheStreet.com, and Yahoo and others who received their news from Reuters. Many of these competitors provided news and information on their website for free (for example, CNNfn, Yahoo, Bloomberg, and *The New York Times*). Still others provided limited free information for nonprint subscribers and free online access to print subscribers (e.g. *Fortune* and *BusinessWeek*). Due to the ease of entry into Web publishing, as opposed to print publishing, competition was growing and fluid. One important difference between print competitors and purely online competitors had to do with branding. Companies with established brand names outside of the Internet had a cost advantage over competitors that were Internet-born (e.g., Yahoo and Amazon) due to the high costs of marketing new brands.

Print versus Interactive Customers

30   Since its introduction, the Interactive Journal was not aggressively promoted to current print subscribers of *The Wall Street Journal.* Partially, this was a result of the difference in customer profiles for the two products.

31   Print WSJ customers had a higher average age than Interactive Journal customers and were more likely to be retired. Print customers tended to use the Internet more at work than at home, to have a higher total value of investments, were more likely to have a home office, and were more likely to live in the eastern United States. Interactive Journal customers, on the other hand, were more likely to have children at home, to use the Internet at home than at work, to have a lower total value of investments, to use online brokers and other online information, and to travel internationally for business.

32   Simmons Market Research Bureau reported that of WSJ print readers, 9.3% had completed high school, 8.3% had some college education, 33.57% had graduated from a four-year college or university, and 30.68% had attended graduate school. The subscription base of WSJ was characterized by an average age of 52 with an average household income of US$75,000. The majority of print readers were 35 years old or older (75.7%), with only 24.3% within the 18 to 34 age group. Most print subscribers were male with a male to female ratio of 75 to 25. Nearly 74% of WSJ print subscribers read the paper every day, spending on average 50 minutes per issue. As of 1999, 40% of Interactive Journal subscribers read the edition on a daily basis and 36% reported using the edition a few times a week.

Current Pricing, Promotion, and Positioning

33   Currently, the Interactive Journal is positioned as a supplement, not a substitute for the print edition and is priced accordingly. Nonprint subscribers pay $59 per year while print subscribers pay $29 per year. The print edition is priced at $175 per year with newsstand copies for 75 cents each. The print pricing compares with other print competitors as follows. *BusinessWeek*—US$42.95 for 51 issues; *Fortune*—US$54.55 for 26 issues; *Forbes*—US$23.97 for 17 issues; *USA Today*—US$119/year; *New York Times*—US$208/year for weekly editions only; and *Financial Times*—US$175/year (This price is the effective price after taking into consideration widespread discounting.), although most magazine competitors did offer discount subscription rates.

The Challenge

34 The challenge ahead of Peter Kann was a serious one, but he was no stranger to tensions. His Pulitzer Prize was awarded for coverage of the Indian-Pakistan war. As he looked towards the next month's meeting, which would largely shape the direction of the future for *The Wall Street Journal* print and interactive, Kann wondered: Would the future mean prosperous co-existence of the two formats or a battle with but one format as the victor?

Case 37

USA *Today*: The Nation's Newspaper and the World's Online News Source

1   *USA Today,* subtitled "The Nation's Newspaper," debuted in 1982 as America's first national general-interest daily newspaper. The paper was the brainchild of Allen H. Neuharth, who until 1989 was Chairman of Gannett Co., Inc., a diversified international $5.3 billion news, information, and communications company that publishes newspapers, operates broadcast television stations, and is engaged in marketing, commercial printing, a newswire service, data services, and news programming. Gannett is currently the largest U.S. newspaper group in terms of circulation, with seventy-four daily newspapers having a combined daily paid circulation of 6.6 million and a daily readership of over 5.4 million. Gannett publications include *USA Today,* the nation's largest-selling daily newspaper, with a circulation of approximately 2.3 million, and *USA Weekend,* a weekly newspaper magazine, as well as a number of nondaily publications. Online properties have also exploded in recent years, with Gannett generating about $40 million in revenue in 1999 from Internet activities, with minimal loss.

PRELAUNCH SITUATION ANALYSIS

2   In February 1980, Allen Neuharth met with "Project NN" task force members to discuss his vision for producing and marketing a unique nationally distributed daily newspaper. Satellite technology had recently solved the problem of limited geographical distribution. Neuharth was ready to take advantage of two seemingly disparate trends among the reading public—an increasingly short attention span in a generation nurtured on television rather than print, coupled with a growing hunger for more information. Neuharth believed that readers face a time crunch in a world where so much information is available but where there is so little time to absorb it. *USA Today*'s primary mission would be to provide more news about more subjects in less time. Task force members were enthusiastic about the concept.

3   Research suggested that *USA Today* should target primarily achievement-oriented men in professional and managerial positions, who are heavy newspaper readers and frequent travelers. Whereas the *New York Times* is targeted at the nation's intellectual elite, its thinkers and policymakers, and *The Wall Street Journal* is aimed at business leaders, *USA Today* would be edited for what has been called Middle America—young, well-educated Americans who are on the move and care about what is going on.

4   By early 1982, a team of news, advertising, and production personnel from the staffs of Gannett's daily newspapers developed, edited, published, and tested several different prototypes. Gannett sent three different forty-page prototype versions of *USA Today* to almost 5,000 professional people. Along with each prototype, they sent readers a response card that asked what they liked best and least about the proposed paper, whether or not they would buy it, as well as whether they would give it approval. While the content of each prototype was similar, what differed were the layout and graphics. For example, one prototype included a section called "Agenda" that included comics and a calendar of meetings to be held by various professional organizations. According to marketplace feedback, readers liked the prototypes. The Gannett Board of Directors unanimously approved the

paper's launch, and so, on April 20, 1982, Gannett announced that the first copies of *USA Today* would soon be available in the Washington/Baltimore era.

PRODUCT LAUNCH

5 On September 15, 1982, 155,000 copies of the newspaper's first edition hit the newsstands. On page 1, founder Neuharth wrote a short summary of *USA Today*'s mission statement, explaining that he wanted to make *USA Today* enlightening and enjoyable to the public, informative to national leaders, and attractive to advertisers. The first issue sold out. A little over a month following the debut, *USA Today*'s circulation hit 362,879, double the original year-end projection. In April 1983, just seven months after its introduction, the newspaper's circulation topped the 1 million mark. The typical reader turned out to be a professional, usually a manager, about forty years old, well educated, with an income of about $60,000 a year (in 1997 dollars). He or she is often a news and sports junkie. As one company official put it, "When he wakes up in the morning his first thought is: 'What city am I in?' The local newspaper doesn't mean a thing to him."

6 For a newspaper, *USA Today* was truly unique. It was a paper created for the TV generation, an idea reflected in its distinctive coin box, designed to look like a television set. News was layered for easy access and quick comprehension by time-pressed readers. Among examples of this format were extensive use of briefs columns, secondary headlines, subheads, breakouts, at-a-glance boxes, and informational graphics. These techniques capture the most salient points of a story and present them in a format that readers appreciate. Gannett's research had shown that readers get most of their information from such snippets in a newspaper.

7 Because *USA Today* was nontraditional, the critics were all over it. In their view, it was loaded with "gimmicks"—tight, short stories; no jumps from page to page, except for the "cover story" (stories that jump to another page are one of newspaper readers' major complaints); splashy, colorful graphics everywhere; a distinctive, casual writing style; a colorful national weather map; a roundup of news items from each state, one paragraph each; summary boxes; little charts and statistics-laden sports coverage; and a focus on celebrity and sports, with more detailed sports stories than almost any other paper in the nation. There was no foreign staff and little interest in the world outside the United States. It was quickly labeled "McPaper"—junk-food journalism—the fast food of the newspaper business—due to its terse, brash writing style and its short coverage of complex issues. It was not considered serious. Even within Gannett, Neuharth met with bitter resistance from certain senior executives. "Brought new depth to the meaning of the word *shallow*," quipped John Quinn, its editor. Nevertheless, readers admired the paper for its focus on brevity and clarity—short sentences and short words.

8 Each issue presented four sections, labeled News, Money, Life, and Sports. The paper's motto was: "An economy of words. A wealth of information." Page 1 included a bulletin board announcing what is inside. Each issue featured a box for top sports news in the upper left corner of page 1, a box for top entertainment news in the upper right corner, and a news summary running down the left side of the page, like a table of contents. A prospective reader could grasp the top news of the world on the top of page 1 while viewing it in the coin box.

9 Gannett did not plan a grand nationwide debut. In order to monitor results carefully and modify the paper and its marketing as needed, Gannett implemented a regional rollout distribution strategy. Produced at facilities in Arlington, Virginia, *USA Today* was transmitted via satellite to printing plants across the country. The newspaper's marketers

divided the country into 15 geographical market segments. *USA Today* was available within a 200-mile radius of these 15 major markets, making the paper accessible to 42% of U.S. households. Significantly, these markets contained 23 million of the 35 million adults who read two or more newspapers daily.

10 Gannett's focus group research indicated that many readers were bringing the paper into their homes rather than reading it on their commute or at work. Consequently, Gannett launched a home delivery subscription service in 1984. Home delivery caused problems at first, because the in-house computer technology could not handle subscription mailing lists efficiently, and the postal service did not always deliver the paper on its publication day. Nevertheless, subscriptions grew, and by 1991 nearly half of *USA Today*'s distribution was via home and office delivery.

11 Clearly, the paper filled a gap in the market, satisfying several unmet needs and wants. *USA Today*'s success came from listening to its readers and giving them what they wanted. The paper communicates with readers on a personal level very quickly (many of the short, fact-filled stories are under 250 words), clearly, and directly, in an upbeat and positive way. The color is riveting and gives the paper a contemporary look. The space-defying number of stories, factoids, larger-than-usual pictures, bar graphs, and charts that are squeezed onto each page never seem crowded. Instead of confusion, readers get neatness and order. The paper's dependably consistent organization enables readers to go directly to any one of *USA Today*'s major sections. It takes an average of only 25 minutes for a reader to peruse the paper.

12 *USA Today* strives to be a balanced newspaper, reporting positive stories along with negative ones and reflecting America's diversity. The editorial page always presents the main editorial, called "Our View." Directly beneath it there is usually an editorial labeled "Opposing View." This approach earned the paper a reputation for fairness. *USA Today*'s own editorial position on most major social, economic, and political issues can be described as middle-of-the-road, a position its staff believes is in tune with the general public. The newspaper's intent is to allow readers to get the information and opinions they need to form their own views, rather than pushing an overtly liberal or conservative agenda. Fair and balanced reporting appeals to readers, some of whom become very angry and look for another newspaper when they think the reporting isn't fair.

MARKETING MIX CHANGES

13 Despite the media's early criticism, circulation surpassed 1.4 million by late 1985 as the paper expanded to 56 pages in length. The cover price of the paper had also increased to 50 cents, double its original price. By this time, *USA Today* had become the second-largest paper in the country, with a circulation topped only by the *Wall Street Journal.* Although Neuharth's early predictions were that *USA Today* would turn a profit within a few years of launch, that proved to be overly optimistic. It took about five years to move from the red to the black, but by 1993 profits were approximately $5 million and the following year they doubled to about $10 million.

14 Although *USA Today* competes more directly with news weeklies and business newspapers than with local papers, many papers, including its previous detractors, began to adopt some of *USA Today*'s style. Old-line newspapers, even the "gray lady," the *New York Times,* began adding more colorful looks, shorter, more tightly written stories, and beefed-up circulation campaigns to compete with "The Nation's Newspaper." In the face of this competition, as well as an awareness of changing reader needs, by the late 1980s it was time for *USA Today* to respond to those needs and evolve.

Product Innovation

15   To stay ahead of the imitative competition, *USA Today* had to continue to innovate. Long identified with short stories, infotainment, bright colors, and its weather map, Gannett's national daily decided to become a more serious newspaper with improved journalism. The shift from primarily soft news to mainly hard news began with the space shuttle Challenger disaster in 1986, when the paper played that news story big and circulation skyrocketed as a result. By 1991, editors began focusing much more sharply on hard news rather than soft features, and by 1994, under president and publisher Tom Curley, there was a massive drive to upgrade the product to be a more serious, more responsible news-oriented product.

16   Beginning in the late '80s, Gannett began incorporating less traditional value-added features to keep readers interested. The paper added 1-800 and 1-900 "hot-line" numbers that readers could call for expert information on financial planning, college admissions, minority business development, taxes, and other subjects. By 1989, over 3 million readers had called the hot-line numbers, with over half of them calling for up-to-the-minute information on sports, weather, stocks, and lottery numbers. Thousands of readers responded to reader-opinion polls and write-in surveys on political and current event issues. In 1991, the editorial pages were also redesigned to provide more room for guest columnists and to encourage debate. The change was popular: The volume of letters to the editor increased by over 500 percent. Gannett also initiated a high school "Academic All Star" program that it later expanded to include colleges and universities. In its continuing quest to upgrade product quality, in 2000 *USA Today* asked sources in a special survey if the paper accurately reported their data, quotes, and other newsworthy information. The year-long survey was devised to counter growing reader complaints of declining credibility and accuracy in many daily publications.

17   The increasing ubiquity of the Internet in the late 1990s also resulted in some changes in content. For instance, the Money section began to focus more on technology issues and to look at business through an "e-lens," that is, a filter for the electronic revolution in the economy. For example, a stock index, the Internet 100, was added to traditional stock indexes. The Life section incorporated a daily e-world feature, covered just as aggressively as entertainment and TV.

18   The year 2000 saw the first major redesign in *USA Today*'s history as the paper moved from a 54-inch to a 50-inch web width. This was aimed at making the paper easier to read and cleaner in look. The slimmer pages were easier to handle, especially in tight spaces like airplanes, trains, buses, and subways, and they fit more readily into briefcases, as Gannett had learned was desirable from focus groups.

Promotional Innovation

19   *USA Today* has also innovated over the years in its promotional activities. Historically, the paper limited its promotions mostly to outdoor advertising and television. However, in the late 1980s Neuharth undertook a "BusCapade" promotion tour, traveling to all fifty states and talking with all kinds of people, including the governor of each state. Neuharth succeeded in raising public awareness of his paper, allowing *USA Today* to make money for the first time. Encouraged by his success, Neuharth forged ahead with a "JetCapade" promotion in which he and a small news team traveled to thirty countries in seven months, stimulating global demand for the paper. During a visit to the troops of Operation Desert Storm in the Persian Gulf in 1991, General Norman Schwarzkopf expressed a need for news from home. *USA Today* arranged for delivery of 18,000 copies per day. The overseas success of *USA Today* led to the publication of *USA Today International*, which is available in more than ninety countries in Western Europe, the Middle East, North Africa, and Asia.

20   The paper continued to drum up demand among advertisers by adding marketing enhancements. Selling space to Madison Avenue advertisers presented a challenge to *USA Today,* because those agencies weren't convinced that it would pay to advertise in the paper. Gannett's first strategy for enlisting advertisers, called the Partnership Plan, provided six months of free space to those who purchased six months of paid advertising. In 1987 *USA Today* also began to accept regional advertising across a wide variety of categories, such as regional travel, retail, tourism, and economic development. Color advertisements could arrive as late as 6 P.M. the day before publication, giving local advertisers increased flexibility. The paper also moved aggressively into "blue-chip circulation," where bulk quantities of *USA Today* are sold at discounted prices to hotels, airlines, and restaurants and are provided free of charge to customers. Today, over 500,000 copies of *USA Today* are distributed through blue-chip circulation every day.

21   In 1998 *USA Today* became a delivery vehicle for product samples, thanks to Maverick Media's AD/IMPAC, through which an advertiser can contract for production of product samples and associated advertising, which then may be distributed in *USA Today* either nationwide or regionally. Samples are inserted right in the centerfold. Initial customers included America Online and Prodigy, which distributed diskettes in a limited run in the Washington, D.C., area, and AT&T, which distributed samples of its One Rate calling card nationwide in May of that year. Gannett has plans to work on specific promotions for specific days, such as Alka-Seltzer on Thanksgiving Day and gambling chips when a new casino opens.

22   *USA Today* pulled off another promotional first in 1999 when they broke one of the most sacred practices of most daily newspapers and began offering display advertising space on page one, with one-inch strips across the entire width of the bottom of the front page, a position that the paper had previously used to promote itself. This front-page bottom color bar position was sold through one-year contracts for $1 million to $1.2 million each, with each advertiser taking one day a week.

23   Given the success of *USA Today,* advertisers are obviously quite attracted to the paper's large volume of readers. To help cope with advertiser demand, in the mid-1990s the paper implemented the necessary technology to allow advertisers to transmit advertising copy electronically twenty-four hours a day. As has been true for so many of *USA Today's* innovations, critics were quick to criticize this move, claiming that the paper had "besmirched" its front page with advertising.

Distribution Innovation

24   Fast delivery has always been important to *USA Today.* By the mid-1990s the paper was earning kudos for its ability to deliver timely news, thanks to its late deadlines. For instance, in many parts of the country *USA Today* prints later sports scores than local or regional papers. In hard news, *USA Today* was able to offer more up-to-date coverage by rolling the presses over four hours earlier than the *Wall Street Journal* and almost three hours later than the *New York Times.*

25   To speed distribution, the paper has added print sites around the world, with the tally in 2000 being thirty-six. An innovative readership program brought *USA Today* to 160 college campuses in 1999, with more to be added in 2000. Technological advances in 1999 allowed production of *USA Today* to be totally digital. Arriving in 2000 was computer-to-plate technology that provides newsrooms with later deadlines and readers with earlier delivery times.

SPIN-OFF ACTIVITIES

26   A decade after *USA Today*'s launch, Gannett found itself in the enviable position of owning one of America's most successful newspapers. *USA Today* was the most widely read newspaper in the country, with daily readership of over 6.5 million. In an era when nearly all major national media were suffering declines in readership or viewing audience, *USA Today* continued to grow. Rising distribution and promotion costs, however, were beginning to make the newspaper slightly unprofitable.

27   To reverse this trend, *USA Today* created several spin-offs, including its first special-interest publication, *Baseball Weekly*. During its first month of operation, *Baseball Weekly*'s circulation reached 250,000 copies. Today, the *Weekly*'s circulation is roughly 425,000.

28   Venturing into news media, *USA Today* joined with Cable News Network to produce a football TV program, and launched SkyRadio to provide live radio on commercial airline flights. In 2000, Gannett launched a new broadcast and Internet initiative known as *USA Today Live* to provide information to Gannett television stations. *USA Today Live* produced prepackaged segments based on *USA Today* content and made them available for use by Gannett television stations in their news reports, with *USA Today* reporters also being available for live interviews.

USA TODAY ONLINE

29   The major spin-off, however, was *USA Today Online,* which the company introduced in 1995. Five of the reasons Al Neuharth gave for starting *USA Today,* as outlined in the October 1982 Bulletin of the American Society of Newspaper Editors, were equally applicable for the paper's expansion from print to online news delivery. They are as follows.

1. *The information age:* Neuharth recognized that the "explosion of new and/or improved information sources has stimulated, rather than satisfied, the American people's appetite for still more news and information when they want it, where they want it, and how they want it." The World Wide Web led to an even greater explosion of news and information sources, creating an even bigger craving for knowledge.

2. *Satellite technology:* Neuharth observed that "along with instant global communications, the space age brought the feasibility and flexibility to deliver a daily newspaper across the United States." Likewise, the global communications network of the Internet brought the feasibility of delivering a daily online newspaper across the world.

3. *Changing lifestyles:* "America is a nation on the move—physically, geographically, intellectually, and sentimentally," noted Neuharth back in 1982, suggesting the rationale behind creating a daily national newspaper, so that anyone traveling anywhere could find some news from his or her own hometown. With the development of niche information services on the Internet, people want to be able to find deep and rich resources on very narrow geographic or lifestyle interests.

4. *Stability:* "With the excitement of mobility comes the grasp for stability." Neuharth wanted *USA Today* to provide that stability, that common look and easy access that a comfortable and familiar publication gives readers. Likewise, this became the goal of most online newspapers too.

5. *The need to know:* "This Information Age generation is looking for more—more local emphasis in the hometown newspaper, more detailed news on radio and TV, more frequent news broadcasts." This "need to know," coupled with "give me more," is the compelling reason that news organizations ventured into Web publishing. Online news allows the breadth and depth of coverage plus the frequency of updating that Neuharth saw as being of interest to news consumers.

30   The *USA Today* venture into online products began on April 17, 1995. The online version was seen as a natural companion to the print version of *USA Today,* given the paper's worldwide distribution. The first version was available through CompuServe's Mosaic browser and required special software, A CompuServe Network connection, and a monthly subscription of $14.95 plus $3.95 per hour. By June of 1995, they unveiled the World Wide Web version, which worked with any Web browser and Internet provider service, and it was free.

31   Like its print sister, the website (www.usatoday.com) is bright, upbeat, and full of nugget-sized news stories. The online version allows readers to receive up-to-the-moment news that incorporates colorful visuals and crisp audio. It provides one of the most extensive sites on the World Wide Web, featuring over 140,000 pages of up-to-the-minute news, sports, business and technology news, five-day weather forecasts, and travel information, available twenty-four hours a day, seven days a week.

32   The website's design features brightly colored buttons in the banner that invite you to go to News, Sports, Money, Life, or Weather. The left-hand column has choices of places to go: world, politics, stocks, scores, etc. Story links off the home page offer other directions to take. However, the home page, with its links to the next layers, has a cluttered, crowded look. Nonetheless, the bright blue of the banner and the clean white background of each page help the eye when trying to make choices from all the options available. At the bottom of the page is a navigation bar with links to the main sections of the website: Front Page, News, Sports, Money, Life, Weather, and Marketplace.

33   The price since migrating to the Web has been free, although Gannett leaves open the option to charge site users sometime in the future. It is primarily advertising that provides revenue streams. Ad revenues increased as new advertisers were attracted to the online format and the potentially huge worldwide reach, and by the dawn of the new millennium *USA Today* led all major publications in paid dot-com advertising. Thus, while the consumer's monetary cost is free, the intangible cost is the consumer's time and attention, which is then sold to advertisers.

34   Another revenue generator, launched in response to frequent reader requests for archived material, was the pay-per-view archives service (archives.usatoday.com) launched in 1998. The *USA Today* Archives section allows readers to do a free, unlimited search of the paper's articles that ran since April 1987. Articles may be downloaded for $1 per story, with payments handled by credit card.

35   Given the surge in Internet subscribers, *USA Today* made a strategic decision to link their online news with popular Internet providers' websites. These Internet providers agreed to incorporate *USA Today Online* as their default news source. This strategy allowed *USA Today* to increase its readership substantially while also increasing its name recognition.

36   Like its print cousin, *USA Today Online* has evolved to meet consumers' changing desires. In 1987 the Web site launched an online classifieds area and twenty-four marketplace partnerships, giving readers the capability to buy the goods and services of 24 companies found in 6 marketplaces: classifieds, travel, financial, technology, entertainment,

and flowers and gifts. Partners in this venture include AutoWeb Homebuyer's Fair, The Monster Board, and The National Association of Realtors' Realtor.com.

37   In another effort at quality improvement, since its inception this Web site has studied its server logs to make decisions about editorial content, transfer and addition of staff, and even budgetary expenditures. In 1998 it adopted custom software developed by Intelligent Environments, a leading provider of Web development software and services, to create a real-time system to survey online readers. It was incorporated into the Web site as "Quick Question," an area devoted to gauging the opinions of *USA Today Online* readers on newsworthy events and issues. Not only does this survey system capture and tally votes in real time, it even recognizes if someone tries to vote more than once.

LOOKING AHEAD

38   In looking at the total national newspaper market, *USA Today* has been quite successful. It has seen 17 years of continuous circulation growth. By 2000, over 5.4 million consumers were reading *USA Today* on a daily basis and approximately 2.3 million people were subscribing to the paper. This success had occurred during a time when newspaper readership overall was declining. Of all the national daily papers in the United States, only *USA Today,* the *Los Angeles Times,* and the *Denver Post* were experiencing large gains in circulation.

39   In 1999, advertising revenues grew 17% as several of the paper's largest ad categories experienced double-digit growth. Dot-com advertising added to the boom: *USA Today* led all major print publications in the share of paid dot-com advertising pages. *USA Today Online* was one of the few moneymakers on the Web. *USA Today Online* was the world's most visited Web site, according to Media Metrix, with 15 million different people per month clicking on the site by the end of 1999, a 79 percent increase over 1998. The number of domestic newspaper websites grew to sixty by the end of 1999, and Gannett more than doubled the products offered online to 480+, including news sites, rich classified verticals, community-oriented sites, and numerous specialty sites based on the unique characteristics of the individual markets.

40   At the corporate level, earnings for 1999 advanced 13% to approximately $886 million, fueled by strong advertising demand at all the papers and lower newsprint prices. For 2000, the corporation intended to add more products and launch the remainder of the small-market newspaper sites.

41   Because newspapers are often subjected to high newsprint costs, most newspaper firms, just like *USA Today,* have added online news as a means to increase readership and cut distribution expenses. Whether online news poses a major threat to *USA Today* and other newspaper firms is debatable. Some experts suggest that approximately 14% of readers will switch from newspaper to online news, effectively cannibalizing the readership of printed news. However, Tom Curley, the publisher of *USA Today,* said he is not worried about the Internet and the other media competitors that are pushing into traditional newspaper markets because newspapers have unique strengths that competitors can't rival. He confidently told the 1998 Coronado convention of the California Newspaper Publishers Association: "This era is about massive data transfer, and nobody is in a better position to analyze it, put it in context, and shape it than newspapers. And we still have the ability to connect with people in ways that other media can't." However, at this same meeting other speakers sounded dire warnings about the inroads the Internet and other media are making into newspaper advertising and readership. The current editor, Karen Jurgensen, is nonetheless upbeat, telling *Advertising Age,* "One question I am often asked is whether there is a future for newspapers in the era of the Internet. The answer is obvious: Of course there is. . . . If we are able to deliver a daily report that is insightful, informative, and even entertaining, then they will continue to make time for papers. And *USA Today*—and the advertisers in its pages—will continue to thrive."

42 But despite the enormous potential of online news, many companies have yet to turn a profit on their online ventures. In 1998, *USA Today Online* for the first time only broke even, even though it earned over $4 million from online ad revenues. Still, the Gannett Letter to Shareholders in the 1999 Gannett Annual Report viewed the Internet as an opportunity, not a threat: "The Internet is a challenge and an exciting opportunity for our community newspapers to extend their brand, generate revenue and, ultimately, profits. Our newspapers will continue to use the Internet to leverage those important local brands, and enhance the strong relationships we already enjoy with our readers and advertisers in the communities we serve. And our websites are attracting visitors who are not readers and are generating subscriptions for our print products."

43 To remain competitive, *USA Today* has moved to increase the value-added components of both its print and online versions. In the print version, in the late 1990s *USA Today* split its Friday Life section into two separate sections: Weekend Life and Destinations & Diversions. This format change, the first major change in the history of *USA Today,* allows the paper to devote more space to weekend entertainment and travel news. This entertainment and travel focus has been mirrored in the online version of *USA Today* in its Travel Marketplace. *USA Today* in the late 1990s signed up six travel partners that will offer online travel services via the *USA Today* Web site.

44 In 2000, the print version planned to expand from fifty-six to sixty-four pages per issue. Despite cost pressures, the publisher sees holding the price at 50 cents as priority 1. Another priority is to continue to update both products to make sure they are breaking stories and providing a complete read that people can trust. A third priority is to push the technology so the print product can be later with sports scores and news. Adopting a value-added strategy can help *USA Today* differentiate itself from other national news providers. In the future, the key will be to ensure that both the print and online versions of *USA Today* provide readers with content they cannot find anywhere else.

This case was prepared by Geoffrey Lantos, Stonehill College, for classroom discussion rather than to illustrate either effective or ineffective handling of an administrative situation. Cheryl Anne Molchan, Stonehill College, and James G. Maxham, University of Virginia, provided research assistance on earlier versions.
Sources: These facts are from "Baseball Weekly Hits Record Circulation," *PR Newswire,* April 13, 1998, 413; "Circulation Slide for Newspapers," *Editor & Publisher,* May 10, 1997, 3; R. Cook, "Gannett Hits Heights in Print but Falls Short of TV Stardom," *Campaign,* January 17, 1997, 24; R. Curtis, "Introducing Your New *USA Today," USA Today,* April 3, 2000, 27A; J. Duscha, "Satisfying Advertiser Position Demands Now Easier," *NewsInc,* September 13, 1999; Gannett Company, Inc., 1997 Annual Report; Gannett Company, Inc., Gannett Company, Inc., 1999 Annual Report; Gannett Company, Inc., 1996 Form 10-K (on file with the Securities and Exchange Commission); "Giving Samples Made Easy Through *USA Today* from Shampoo to CDs," *NewsInc,* June 22, 1998; K. Jurgensen, "Quick Response; Paper Chase: *USA Today* Editor Sees Shifts in How Information Is Generated and Delivered to Readers," *Advertising Age,* February 14, 2000, S6; K. Jurgensen, "*USA Today's* New Look Designed for Readers," *USA Today,* April 3, 2000, 1A; A. M. Kerwin, "Daily Paper's Circulation Woes Persist into '97," *Advertising Age,* May 12, 1997, 26; P. Long, "After Long Career, *USA* Today Founder Al Neuharth Is Ready for More," *Knight-Rider/Tribune Business News,* April 28, 1999; J. McCartney, "*USA Today* Grows

Up," *American Journalism Review,* September 1997, 19; B. Miller, "*USA Today,* Gannett to Launch *USA Today Live,*" *Television & Cable,* February 8, 2000; T. Noah, "At Least It's Free, Right?" *U.S. News & World Report,* December 2, 1996, 60; N. Paul, "McWeb Site: *USA Today Online,*" *Searcher,* May 1997, 58; M. L. Stein, "Don't Sweat the Internet Says *USA Today*'s Curley," *Editor & Publisher,* August 22, 199??, 40; M. Stone, "*USA Today Online* Listens to Its Logs," *Editor & Publisher,* August 7, 1999, 66; J. Strupp, "Accuracy Is the Aim," *Editor & Publisher,* May 1, 2000, 9; J. Strupp, "*USA Today* Ads Go Page One," *Editor & Publisher,* May 8, 1999, 40; Sullivan, "Where Are Newspapers Headed?" *Editor & Publisher,* June 28, 1997; R. Tedesco, "Internet Profit Sites Elusive," *Broadcasting & Cable,* November 17, 1997, 74; "*USA Today:* A Case Study," prepared by M. Condry, R. Dailey, F. Gasquet, M. Holladay, A. Johnson, S. Menzer, and J. Miller, University of Memphis, 1997; "*USA Today* Launches New Life Section Friday Format," *PR Newswire,* March 16, 1998, 316; "*USA Today* Launches Online Classifieds Area and 17 new Marketplace Partnerships," *Business Wire,* April 15, 1997; "*USA Today* Launches Pay-per-View Archives Service," *Business Wire,* January 5, 1998; "*USA Today Online* Launches Real Time Survey System," *Business Wire,* February 18, 1998; *USA Today* Press Kit, 1997, Gannett Company, Inc.; "*USA Today* Sells Page One Advertising Space," *PR Newswire,* May 5, 1999, 3517; and I. Wada, "*USA Today* Marketplace Signs Up Six for Online Services," *Travel Weekly,* April 28, 1997, 44.

Case 38

DoubleClick, Inc.

1 DoubleClick, Inc., is an information-revolution phenomenon. What started out as an outgrowth of self-proclaimed computer "geeks" and savvy advertising agency executives has grown into a high-tech heavyweight providing advertising services and information about Internet users for advertisers, website operators, and other companies. The nature of its business has also put DoubleClick in the center of a brewing digital storm. At the core of this controversy is the issue of a person's right to privacy on the Internet. DoubleClick, which contends that it is committed to protecting the privacy of all Internet users, views its role as important in maintaining the Internet as a free medium driven by highly targeted advertising. Consumer groups, however, see it differently, noting that Double-Click's actions loom larger than its words regarding access to personal information. Opponents, which include Michigan Attorney General Jennifer Granholm, regard DoubleClick's business practices as little more than a "secret, cyber-wiretap." To understand how DoubleClick found itself in this uncomfortable position, it is helpful to examine the firm's history, key strategic business units, and the issue of Internet privacy.

MERGE ONTO SILICON ALLEY

2 Like many entrepreneurs in recent years, Kevin O'Connor and Dwight Merriman, two Atlanta-based engineers, saw an opportunity to cash in on the growing popularity of the Internet. O'Connor and Merriman had observed the challenges faced by niche-driven, subscription-based content websites attempting to compete with America Online's growing mass audience. They reasoned that they could capitalize on this situation by creating a single network to bring together numerous online publications to create a critical mass of information. With the idea of multiple publications forming a larger online network, it became crucial to address a significant issue for each of the various publications: advertising. After substantial research, O'Connor and Merriman decided to move forward with a network concept. However, after careful research, they decided that the advertising industry, rather than the publishing industry, could be better served with such a network. Thus, they founded the DoubleClick Network in January 1996.

3 Although O'Connor and Merriman's engineering backgrounds helped them tremendously with the technology issues associated with their concept, their engineering experience provided little insight into the world of sophisticated advertising. To resolve this issue, the software-based start-up formally merged with a division of ad agency Poppe Tyson. O'Connor believed the marriage of nerd and Madison Avenue cultures was possible because of a common bond—the love of the Internet. However, as O'Connor admitted, "The two cultures are completely ignorant of each other's ways." The "offspring" of this union set up shop in the heart of Silicon Alley in New York City—the same location, coincidentally, where some of New York's first advertising agencies sprang up a century ago.

4 Like traditional advertising agencies, DoubleClick's focus is to get the right advertisement to the right person at the right time. The difference between DoubleClick and offline ad agencies is the use of technology to track Web-surfing activities more directly as opposed to older media such as magazines. A magazine publisher, for instance, can detail the number of subscribers as well as the number of issues sold at newsstands.

Unfortunately, the publisher does not have a very clear picture as to which articles in a magazine issue have been read, by whom, and when. Online, however, technology developed by DoubleClick can track traffic to a given customer's Web site and identify specific articles selected. Moreover, DoubleClick can trail traffic to and from the website to establish a surfing portfolio of site visitors. This breadth and depth of information quickly made DoubleClick a valuable service provider to online advertisers trying to make advertising work on the Internet.

THROWING DARTS

5   The heart of DoubleClick's technology is its DART—Dynamic Advertising Reporting and Targeting—system. DART works by reading twenty-two criteria about Web site visitors' actions, such as their cyberlocation and time of visit. This technology also leaves, often without the user's knowledge, a "cookie" on his or her computer. Cookies are simply bits of information sent to a Web browser to be saved on the user's hard drive. Cookies are helpful for Internet users because they can contain important information like login information and user preferences that make return visits to subscription-based websites more manageable. Cookies are also useful for website operators because they can include additional information such as evidence of repeat visits and advertisements viewed. The information provided by the cookie about a website visitor's activities and interests helps DoubleClick tailor advertisements to specific users. It should be noted, however, that cookies do not collect personally identifiable information, such as user's name, mailing address, telephone number, or e-mail address, so individual profiles are essentially anonymous. Instead of tracking an identifiable individual, cookies track user's digital footsteps.

6   With the wealth of information DoubleClick can provide for its network members, customers continue to join. By the end of its first year of business, DoubleClick had secured the business of 25 websites. Today, the company places banner advertisements on more than 11,500 websites. As Andy Jacobson, regional vice president for sales, says "We set a goal: sell $500,000 of advertising in a week, and we'll buy lunch for everyone in the room." With 2000 revenues of almost $507 million—an average of nearly $10 million a week—DoubleClick is buying a lot of lunches these days (see Exhibit 1). The company is buying a lot of cookies, too—the eatable kind. After the company achieved the milestone of 500 million advertisements placed in one day, company executives had cookies delivered to the technical engineers who manage the DART system.

7   This growth and increasing volume have allowed DoubleClick to command fees of 35–50% of advertising expenditures compared to the 15% fee structure charged by more traditional offline advertising agencies. Consider as well that the DoubleClick network has the capability to add hundreds of thousands of anonymous consumer profiles per day. Thus, it becomes clear that its technological capabilities make it an increasingly attractive ad-servicing option.

8   Despite the phenomenal sales growth DoubleClick has achieved, executives believe there is further potential available from the DART system. In fact, the expectation is for DART technologies alone to account for 50% of future revenues. However, those revenue expectations are not limited just to the DoubleClick network. The company is intent on servicing clients outside of its own network and growing complementary businesses in the projected $11.3 billion (by 2003) ad-servicing business. Like traditional companies, DoubleClick has used its expanding clout to develop and acquire important worldwide subsidiaries both on and offline.

EXHIBIT 1
DoubleClick, Inc., Financial Performance (in millions except per-share amounts) during Four Fiscal Years Ended December 31, 2000

Source: MSN MoneyCentral, moneycentral.msn.com/investor.

	2000	1999	1998	1997
Net Sales	$505.60	$258.30	$80.20	$30.60
Cost of Sales	$228.10	$90.40	$51.10	$19.70
Selling, General & Admin. Expenses	$284.40	$168.30	$47.20	$18.40
Net Income (Loss) ($8.40)	($156.00)	($55.80)	($18.20)	
Earnings per Share ($0.20)	($1.29)	($0.51)	($0.29)	

KEY SUBSIDIARIES

9 Despite the prevalence of high technology today, targeting remains surprisingly low-tech. According to Jim Nail, a Forrester research analyst:

> To get advertisers to continue to pay the big premiums, DoubleClick will have to tell advertisers more than just where you are and the kind of site you visit. It might have to tell them whether your are married or single, what your income is, and whether or not you have kids. What it needs to do above all is predict, with greater accuracy, how likely you are to buy an advertised product.

10 To that end, DoubleClick acquired offline catalog database company Abacus Direct shortly after buying NetGravity, Inc., a direct competitor. The idea behind the Abacus acquisition was the potential to merge that company's database of personally identifiable offline buying habits with DoubleClick's database of nonpersonally identifiable online habits to provide even greater depths of information to current and future clients. The trend toward collecting more personally identifiable information continued with Double-Click's development of Flashbase, an automation tool that allows DoubleClick clients a means of collecting personal information by running contests and sweepstakes online. Additionally, DoubleClick websites such as www.NetDeals.com and www.IAF.net collect personally identifiable information online. However, DoubleClick contends that it provides ways for consumers to limit communication only to prize or deal-specific information. In other words, consumers have the ability to "opt out" of future communications not specific to the instance when and where they entered their personal data.

THE CONTROVERSY

11 The only problem with these developments and acquisitions is that their intended use signaled a significant philosophical shift in the way DoubleClick had always done business. Specifically, it created a drastic change in the company's consumer privacy position, a fact that consumer privacy groups and the Federal Trade Commission (FTC) did not take long to notice. According to Jason Catlett of Junkbusters, an Internet privacy activist, "Thousands of sites are ratting on you, so as soon as one gives you away, you're exposed on all of them. For years, [DoubleClick] has said (their services) don't identify you personally, and now they're admitting they are going to identify you."

12 In the face of growing public concern, Kevin O'Connor defended the company's plans: "The merger with Abacus Direct, along with the recent closing of the Net-Gravity merger, will allow us to offer publishers and advertisers the most effective means of

EXHIBIT 2

DoubleClick, Inc., Stock Valuation during Three Years since the Initial Public Offering (Symbol = DCLK)

Source: MSN MoneyCentral, moneycentral.man.com/investor.

	2000	1999	1998
January	$98.81	$24.06	N/A
February	$88.81	$22.47	N/A
March	$93.63	$45.52	N/A
April	$75.88	$69.91	$10.42
May	$42.25	$48.72	$8.66
June	$38.13	$45.88	$12.42
July	$35.94	$40.50	$11.00
August	$40.69	$49.94	$5.97
September	$32.00	$59.56	$5.97
October	$16.25	$70.00	$8.25
November	$14.19	$80.03	$10.13
December	$10.38	$126.53	$11.13

advertising online and offline." Kevin Ryan, DoubleClick's CEO, took it a step further: "What we continue to hear from consumers is that they'd like to be in a position to have better content, greater access for everyone in the United States, and they would love it all to be free and advertising-served." Ryan pointed out that the Internet is driven by advertising and that advertising companies need to know their substantial investments are being spent in the best way possible—that is, targeted to the right audience or individual. Without more accurate information, Ryan asserted, much of the gratis content on the Internet would no longer be free.

13   Initially, the merger announcements were well received as shares of DoubleClick traded as high as $179.00 per share in early December 1999. Unfortunately, the comments of O'Connor and Ryan failed to stem the stock's decline after privacy concerns were voiced by Junkbusters and others in the aftermath of the Abacus Direct merger (see Exhibit 2).

14   DoubleClick's posted privacy policy states that online users are given *notice* about the data collection and the *choice* not to participate or to opt out. However, Internet users must read carefully to understand that granting permission, or failing to deny permission, at even one DoubleClick or Abacus-serviced website allows the company to select personal information across all sites. Consequently, the Center for Democracy and Technology (CDT), a Washington-based watchdog organization, launched a hard-line campaign against DoubleClick. The focus of the campaign centered on a "Website" under the slogan, "I Will Not Be Targeted," where users can opt out of DoubleClick's profiling acitivities. According to Deirdre Mulligan, CDT's staff counsel, "You may have already been doublecrossed by DoubleClick or you may be next in line. In either case, if you care about your privacy and want to surf the Web without your every move being recorded in a giant database connected to your name, it's time to opt out."

15   The CDT campaign was just one of the challenges DoubleClick faced as public concerns about Internet privacy escalated. A California woman brought a lawsuit against DoubleClick, alleging the company had unlawfully obtained and sold her private personal information. Media critics labeled DoubleClick an online "Big Brother" that passed information about employees' Internet surfing behavior on to their employers. Attorneys general in Michigan and New York launched investigations into DoubleClick's business practices. One of the most publicized challenges was the Electronic Privacy Information Center (EPIC) complaint filed with the FTC regarding DoubleClick's profiling practices. The complaint led to a full-scale investigation of DoubleClick's business practices by the

federal watchdog. EPIC and similar privacy groups prefer an opt-in mechanism as opposed to DoubleClick's current opt-out platform. EPIC Executive Director Marc Rotenberg said, "Several years ago, DoubleClick said it would not collect personally identifiable information and keep anonymous profiles. Privacy experts applauded that approach." But as a result of the Abacus merger, "DoubleClick has changed its mind and they're trying to convince users they should accept that [new] model."

16   DoubleClick attempted to defuse the growing controversy (and reverse the plummet of the stock price) by announcing a program to protect consumers it tracks online. The program included a major newspaper campaign, 50 million banner ads directing consumers to the privacy rights information and education site PrivacyChoices (www.privacychoices.org), the appointment of a chief privacy officer, the hiring of an external accounting firm to conduct privacy audits, and the establishment of an advisory board. The board, in particular, was less than well received. Calling the board a "facade," Jeffrey Chester, executive director of the Center of Media Education, said, "This is a public relations ploy to ward off federal and state scrutiny." Chester and other privacy organizations expressed dismay that the advisory board included no true privacy advocates and worse, it included a DoubleClick customer. Moreover, that customer advocated technologies called "Web bugs" or "clear-gifs" that some consider even more intrusive than cookies. These sentiments prompted O'Connor to state, "It is clear from these discussions that I made a mistake by planning to merge names with anonymous user activity across websites in the absence of government and industry privacy standards."

17   Another attempt to regain consumer goodwill is DoubleClick's participation in the Responsible Electronic Communication Alliance (RECA) along with fifteen of the nation's leading online marketers. The purpose of the RECA is to give consumers greater choice and notice regarding their online activities. To identify companies that subscribe to the RECA's proposed standards, the alliance is developing a "seal of approval" program in the spirit of *Good Housekeeping.* According to Christopher Wolf, RECA President, "Our ultimate goal is to phase in a set of firm standards on privacy, notice, access, and choice."

A NEW ERA

18   On January 22, 2001, the Federal Trade Commission announced that it had completed its investigation of DoubleClick. In a letter to the company, the commission said, "It appears to staff that DoubleClick never used or disclosed consumers' PII [personally identifiable information] for purposes other than those disclosed in its privacy policy." On news of the announcement, the company's stock price jumped 13%, although it remained well below the company's historic high. However, the FTC also warned that its decision "is not to be construed as a determination that a violation may not have occurred" and reserved the right to take further action. Needless to say, the privacy advocates were not happy with the announcement. EPIC, for example, contends that the FTC never addressed its allegations. CEO Kevin Ryan, however, feels DoubleClick has been vindicated: "We felt from the beginning that our privacy policy and practices are solid. We never felt there was any substantial problem with them." Although it seems that the storm has quieted for now, Internet consumers, privacy advocates, and government officials will be watching DoubleClick closely, and the issue of Internet privacy will almost certainly continue.

19   Even DoubleClick was not able to escape what the market terms a dot-com fallout. In early 2001, DoubleClick laid off 150 employees, approximately 7% of their 2001 workforce. According to an article published in *eCompany,* however, DoubleClick is expected to rise from its ashes and flourish as an e-business. Currently it has a stock price of $10.55 and a three- to five-year estimated EPS growth rate of 46.91% DoubleClick has also made a change to their current business model. They have left the pay-for-performance approach and are trying an upfront fee. At present they are selling 1,000 impressions for $2.00, well below past fees in the market of $20.00 per 1,000 impressions. This switch will have a large impact on competitors, for DoubleClick's fee will depress ad rates for the entire market, and other media companies typically sell only one-quarter of their available space. The ride has been wild for DoubleClick, but if they can persevere, as suggested by *eCompany,* they will continue to change the advertising market forever.

20   DoubleClick should continue to monitor feedback regarding privacy policy issues. The company can be successful both eternally and externally if they can find a way to regain consumer trust. Many consumers enjoy and examine advertising on the Internet in order to learn about interesting products. As long as they feel their personal information is being used in an appropriate, unthreatening manner, they will continue to click through the ads. DoubleClick is on the right track with the announcement of a recent alliance with NetScore. NetScore enables the tracking of Internet use at home, work, and schools as well as international Internet use. Perhaps along with this alliance, DoubleClick should change their opt-out option to an opt-in option. Allowing the customer to choose whether or not to make personal information available would probably be welcome more than leaving the consumer with the responsibility of requesting their information not be recorded.

21   DoubleClick may consider reevaluating their growth strategy. The company started, as all do, small and unrecognized. They proceeded by building brand equity while simultaneously growing. Now that they have had to downsize some, they should take advantage of that by concentrating on rebuilding their name and making their service more customer friendly without trying to expand. Currently, they have a wide enough customer base to sustain the business. Once they have established a stronger reputation and a service that accommodates privacy issues, they can focus on growth.

22   All in all, DoubleClick is still in a position to revolutionize marketing. In early 2001, they reached a milestone by achieving the one-trillionth-ad mark. If they play their cards right, they could be the leading player in this industry.

This case was prepared by Tracy A. Suter, Oklahoma State University, for classroom discussion rather than to illustrate either effective or ineffective handling of an administrative situation.
Sources: These facts are from Eryn Brown, "The Silicon Alley Heart of Internet Advertising," *Fortune,* December 6, 1999, 166–167; Lynn Burke, "A DoubleClick Smokescreen?" *WiredNews,* May 23, 2000,

http://www.wirednews.com/news/print/ 0,1294,36404,00.html; "Company Briefing Book," *Wall Street Journal Interactive,* http://interactive.wsj.com, accessed January 29, 2001; Tom Conroy and Rob Sheffield, "Hot Marketing Geek," *Rolling Stone,* August 20, 1998, 80; "Crisis Control: DoubleClick," *Privacy Times,* February 18, 2000, http://www.privacytimes.com/New Webstories/doubleclick_priv_2_23 .htm; "DoubleClick Accused of Double-Dealing Double-Cross," *News Bytes News Network,* February 2, 2000, http:// www.newsbytes.com; "DoubleClick Completes $1.8 Bil Abacus Direct Buyout," *News Bytes News Network,* November 30, 1999, http://www.newsbytes.com; "DoubleClick Outlines Five-step Privacy Initiative," *News Bytes News Network,* February 15, 2000, http://www.newsbytes.com; "DoubleClick Tracks Online Movements," *News Bytes News Network,* January 26, 2000, http://www.newsbytes.com (originally reported by *USA Today,* http://www.usatoday.com); Jane Hodges, "DoubleClick Takes Standalone Route for Targeting Tools," *Advertising Age,* December 16, 1996, 32; "I Will Not Be Targeted," Center for Democracy and Technology, http://www.cdt.org/action/doubleclick.shtml; Chris Oakes, "DoubleClick Plan Falls Short," *WiredNews,* February 14, 2000, www.wirednews.com/news/print/ 0,1294,34337,00.html; Chris O'Brien, "DoubleClick Sets Off Privacy Firestorm," *San Jose Mercury News,* February 26, 2000, http://www.mercurycenter.com/ business/top/042517.htm; "Online Marketing Coalition Announces Proposals for Internet Privacy Guidelines," *MSN MoneyCentral,* September 25, 2000, http://news.moneycentral.msn.com/; "Privacy Choices," DoubleClick, Inc., http://www.privacychoices.org/; "Privacy Policy," DoubleClick, Inc., http://www.doubleclick.net/; "Privacy Standards Proposed," *MSNBC,* September 25, 2000, www.msnbc.com/news/467212.asp; Randall Rothenberg, "An Advertising Power, but Just What Does DoubleClick Do?" *New York Times: E-Commerce Special Section,* 1999, http://www.nytimes.com/ library/tech/99/09/biztech/technology/ 22roth.html; Allen Wan and William Spain, "FTC Ends DoubleClick Investigation," CBC MarketWatch.com, January 23, 2001, http://www.aolpf.marketwatch.com/pf/archive/20010123/news/ current/dclk.asp; "DoubleClick's Reprieve," *Marketing News,* February 16, 2001, 48; "eCompany 40," *eCompany,* April 2001, 147; and "DoubleClick Rolls Out Better Method for Ad Tracking," http://news.moneycentral.msn.com/ (March 5, 2001).

Case 39

Avid Technology, Inc.

1 "I think that any company that is very successful can be a victim of its own success," proclaimed David Krall in the fall of 2000 as he pondered Avid Technology's past performance. He was Avid's third CEO in almost as many years. Poor financial performance led the board to replace a company founder in 1996 with a successful outside executive from a large, high-tech company to turn Avid around. However, results were slow in coming, causing the board to replace him three years later with Krall, one of the company's divisional chief operating officers.

2 The burden of a second attempt at a turnaround was squarely placed on the shoulders of the 39-year-old Krall, a relatively young man with only four year's experience in one of the company's divisions. Krall had a history as an innovator. He won the Harvard Business School entrepreneur of the year award for one of his inventions: a backup battery for laptop computers for which he received a patent, and he navigated Digidesign, a division of Avid, to strong performance while the overall company suffered poor results. Avid's board was counting on the entrepreneurial Krall to orchestrate the strategic renewal the company desperately needed.

3 Avid Technology, Inc. was the quintessential high-tech success story. Sales grew rapidly following the company's first product shipment in late 1989. Avid achieved high growth rates and accolades from customers and industry analysts by applying digital technology to processes used to manipulate pictures, graphics, and sound in the creation of movie films, television programming, and news broadcasts. In effect, Avid built "a better mouse trap" in the way moving pictures, graphics, and sound were captured, edited, and then reproduced for an audience's viewing and listening pleasure.

4 However, by 1995 sales growth began to slow. New management was brought in by the end of 1996 to turn Avid's fortunes around and place the company, once again, on a profitable growth path. The return to Avid's stellar past, though, was a tumultuous one. The new management team, which had been in place for three years, made several strategic decisions to turn the company around. However, their efforts failed to achieve sustainable results, and they soon lost the confidence of the company's board. Their departure was indicative of Avid's failure to find the strategic prescription to the problems that plagued the company.

5 By decisively replacing top management for a second time, the board sent a strong signal to the company's newest management team that nothing short of Avid's immediate turnaround was expected. Understanding what had happened to Avid over the past few years was the urgent task now facing Krall. The new CEO had to determine what the prior two CEOs had done, or not done, that turned Avid's fortunes so quickly. And, more important, Krall had to determine a new course of action to return the company to its glorious past.

COMPANY OVERVIEW AND HISTORY

6 Located within the high-tech metropolitan area of Boston, Massachusetts, Avid Technology produced systems to digitally capture, edit, and distribute media in the forms of movie films, television programming, and news broadcasts. The company was an

industry leader in several markets. This was accomplished by providing products that improved the productivity of film editors. Traditional analog technology required the capturing of moving pictures, graphics, and sound on magnetic tape, the cutting and splicing of this tape to edit picture sequences, and the duplication of this tape for distribution. Digital technology captured moving pictures, graphics, and sound in the form of binary codes recognizable by computers. Editing these digitized pictures, graphics, and sound sequences therefore became a process similar to editing a word processing file (which consists of digitized text)—a mouse is used to cut and paste the pictures, graphics, and sound into the desired sequence on the computer. The resulting movie film, for example, is a computer file of digitized pictures, graphics, and sound. Digital technology enabled editors to manipulate moving pictures, graphics, and sound in a faster, more creative, and less costly manner than that of traditional analog, tape-based systems. It also provided editors with greater capabilities for creating special effects. Editing and creating the special effects in the new *Star Wars* series, as an example, was accomplished through the use of Avid products. Similarly, Avid systems were employed by producers to achieve the visualization of Gary Sinise (Lieutenant Dan Taylor) as a double amputee in the movie *Forrest Gump.* Moreover, unlike analog film that shows wear and tear after 15–25 showings, no quality is lost in digital films.

7   Avid also developed computer systems for digital-editing in news rooms, which helped create content for television news programs. Additionally, the company developed digital audio systems for professional use. Avid's products were used worldwide in film studios; network, affiliate, independent, and cable television stations; recording studios; advertising agencies; government and educational institutions; and corporate video departments. Corporate uses included video applications by real estate firms to display property listings and by professional sports teams, such as the Green Bay Packers, to analyze game plays.

8   Avid was founded in 1987 by William Warner, who left his position at Apollo Computer, Inc., a manufacturer of computer systems, to pursue his revolutionary idea of digitizing moving pictures and sound onto computer disk to enhance the ability to edit stored images and sounds. In 1988, Curt Rawley, former president of Racal Design Services, a designer of printed circuit boards, and Eric Peters, former engineer at Apollo Computer and Digital Equipment Corporation (now Compaq Computers), joined Warner in his vision.

9   The three entrepreneurs developed Media Composer, the product upon which the new company was launched. Product shipment began in the fourth quarter of 1989. Sales grew rapidly, rising from $1 million in 1989 to $7 million, $20 million, and $52 million in 1990, 1991, and 1992, respectively.

10   To finance the company's growth, Avid went public in 1993 (NASDAQ: AVID), generating additional capital of $53 million. In the same year, sales more than doubled to $113 million. The company rose to the fifth position in *Inc.* magazine's list of "100 Fastest Growing Small Public U.S. Companies" and ranked ninth on *Fortune*'s list of "100 Fastest Growing American Companies." Rapid growth continued, with Avid recording revenues of $204 million in 1994 and $407 million in 1995, an 81% and 100% increase over the prior year, respectively. Through 1995, Avid was achieving its objectives to quickly gain market share and develop a leadership position in its markets. However, sales growth following 1995 slowed, with revenues increasing only 5% to $429 million in 1996, 10% to $471 million in 1997, and 2% to $482 million in 1998. In 1999, revenues decreased for the first time in the company's history, dropping 6% to $453 million. Exhibit 1 provides a consolidated statement of operations and Exhibit 2 a consolidated balance sheet for the company. Avid grew to about 1,700 employees by the end of 1999.

EXHIBIT 1   Avid Technology, Inc. Consolidated Statement of Operations for the Periods Ending 1989–2000

Source: Avid annual reports/10Ks 1993–2000.

Financial Data in $millions (except per share data)												
	1989	**1990**	**1991**	**1992**	**1993**	**1994**	**1995**	**1996**	**1997**	**1998**	**1999**	**2000**
Net Revenues	0.9	7.4	20.1	51.9	112.9	203.7	406.6	429.0	471.3	482.4	452.6	476.0
Cost of Sales	0.5	3.4	9.6	23.7	54.1	99.9	198.8	238.8	221.5	190.2	205.9	234.4
Gross Profit	0.4	4.0	10.5	28.2	58.8	103.8	207.8	190.2	249.8	292.2	246.7	241.6
Operating Expenses	2.1	6.3	10.5	24.7	55.7	87.0	185.2	220.5	219.7	242.6	246.9	229.8
Nonrecurring Costs	0	0.6	1.0	0.9	0	0	5.5	.29	0	28.4	14.5	0
Amort. of Acquired Assets	0	0	0	0	0	0	0	0	0	34.2	79.9	66.9
Other Inc. (Expense)	0	0.1	0.1	0	1.5	1.0	1.4	3.4	8.1	8.6	3.5	3.7
Income Taxes	0	0	0	1.2	0.9	4.8	8.6	−17.9	11.8	−0.8	46.4	5.0
Net Income (Loss)	−1.7	−2.8	−0.9	1.4	5.5	13	15.4	−38	26.4	−3.6	−137.5	−56.4
Net Income (Loss) Per Common Share	−0.57	−0.84	−0.27	0.29	0.38	1.1	0.77	−1.8	1.08	−0.15	−5.75	−2.28
Common Stock Value												
High	n/a	n/a	n/a	n/a	27.16	43.50	48.75	25.88	38.00	47.75	34.25	24.50
Low	n/a	n/a	n/a	n/a	16.00	20.50	16.75	10.13	9.00	11.06	10.00	9.38

Note: Nonrecurring costs primarily relate to writeoffs resulting from restructurings and/or acquisitions. Amortization of acquired assets relates to the Softimage acquisition.

EXHIBIT 2
Avid Technology, Inc. Consolidated Balance Sheet for the Years Ending 1998–2000

Source: Avid annual reports/10Ks 1998–2000.

Financial Data in $millions			
	1998	**1999**	**2000**
Assets			
Cash & marketable securities	111.8	72.8	83.2
Accounts receivable, net	89.8	76.2	90.0
Inventories	11.1	15.0	21.1
Other current assets	29.0	12.6	11.7
Total Current Assets	241.7	176.4	206.1
Property, plant and equipment, net	35.4	32.7	26.1
Other assets	209.6	102.9	34.2
Total Assets	486.7	312.0	266.4
Liabilities & Stockholders' Equity			
Accounts payable	24.3	24.0	28.8
Other accrued charges	75.4	61.8	56.2
Deferred revenues	22.9	20.3	24.5
Total Current Liabilities	122.6	106.1	109.5
Long-term debt	13.3	14.2	13.4
Other	60.5	23.8	5.7
Stockholders' equity			
Common stock	0.3	0.3	0.3
Additional paid-in-capital	349.3	366.6	359.1
Retained earnings	14.3	−128.1	−197.8
Treasury stock	−68.0	−66.5	−15.6
Deferred compensation	−3.8	−1.9	−4.8
Cumulative translation adjustment	−1.8	−2.5	−3.4
Total Stockholders' Equity	290.3	167.9	137.8
Total Liabilities and Stockholders' Equity	486.7	312.0	266.4

11   A key factor in Avid's rapid sales growth was its ability to establish a channel for international sales during its earliest days. Avid established sales offices in seven different countries by 1993, and by 1999 it had offices in 20 different countries. Sales outside North America quickly grew from 11% of revenues in 1990, to 42% in 1992 and 51% by 1999, with Avid selling to over 75 foreign markets. European sales showed the most promise, representing approximately 87% of total international sales. Sales from the Asian region were disappointing, but were expected to generally improve as the economy of the region, especially that in Japan, came out of recession.

AVID'S MARKETS

12   Avid served three markets. Avid's primary market as a source of company revenues was the film, television, and related industries. The film and television industries came to recognize digital technology as state-of-the-art, and Avid Technology as the leader in this technology. Exhibit 3 provides a sample listing of films and television programs that were created using Avid products. The estimated $1 billion film industry was a rapid adopter of new technology and thus quickly migrated from analog to digital products, giving Avid more than an 80% share of the market segments it served in this industry.

13   On the other hand, the $2 billion television industry was still predominantly tape-based, as was the $900 million audio industry. These industries represented a significant growth opportunity for the company. The $985 million corporate and institutional video industry was also predominantly tape-based, with Avid holding the leadership position in the digital segment (Avid's total industry share was 13%, versus all other digital-based competitors who comprised 27%). Thus, the company saw an opportunity for significant growth in this industry as well.

14   Avid's secondary market as a source of company revenues was the $350 million news broadcast industry. Although the company had focused on this market since 1993, its efforts to gain a strong foothold in the news broadcast industry were less successful than its efforts in the film and television industries. A key factor was the cost of the large, integrated systems these customers required, which ran into the millions of dollars. Additionally, Avid did not offer products that could perform all the functions required in the highly complex process of news broadcast creation. To satisfy the diverse needs of news broadcast customers, the company's products required bundling with digital or analog products made by other vendors.

15   Further, this industry was still predominantly analog-based. Its migration from an analog to a digital format was significantly influenced by the high switching costs involving capital outlays and personnel training, as well as the perceived risks associated with systems that may have an unwieldy mix of both analog and digital devices. However, news

EXHIBIT 3
Films and Television Programs Created Using Avid Products (Sample Listing Only)

Source: Avid Technology, Inc. public document; *The Boston Globe,* April 30, 2001.

Films	Television Programs
Lethal Weapon 4	Ally McBeal
Lost in Space	Frasier
Perfect Storm	Friends
Star Trek: Insurrection	Just Shoot Me
Titanic	Survivor II
The X-Files Fight the Future	Veronica's Closet

Note: 85% of films made in the U.S. in 2000 were edited on Avid systems,
95% of prime time television programs in 2000 were edited on Avid systems.

broadcast firms were expected to more readily make the transition to digital technology as their expensive analog equipment reached replacement age.

16   Other factors limiting Avid's performance in this industry were the company's relative size and experience compared to competitors such as Sony. When making high-cost investments reaching and exceeding one million dollars in highly critical areas of their operations, news broadcast firms relied heavily on suppliers with financial stability, past performance, and long-lasting relationships. As a result, Avid, a small high-tech company (i.e., less than $500 million in sales) and a relative newcomer to the industry, realized that establishing a strong presence in this market would take time.

17   Avid's tertiary market as a source of company revenues was the retail consumer market. The company entered this market in 1994. The retail consumer includes individuals who, for example, edit home videos or photos on their personal computers. Several firms were producing products to serve the home market, yet no one firm had yet emerged as the market leader.

18   Avid competed in this market with its Avid Cinema product. Avid Cinema was created by the company as an easy-to-use video software package for the retail consumer. Individuals with video tapes of school plays, sporting events, weddings, birthdays, and family get-togethers, for example, could use Avid Cinema to add special effects, songs from favorite CDs, and professional-looking titles to these tapes, turning them into entertaining movies. Avid Cinema had received strong industry reviews. It was named finalist in 1999 for best digital video product by the editors of *Popular Photography Magazine* and *DigitalFocus,* the leading digital imaging newsletter publishers, and, in 1998, it was nominated for Best of Comdex Fall 1998 and won "best new product" at Retail Xchange n8 (both industry trade shows).

19   Because this market was still in its infancy, sales to retail consumers were expected to remain modest over the next few years. However, Avid realized that the retail consumer market had great sales potential once the individual gained an understanding of and appreciation for digital editing technology as a standard home-computer application. More excitement was being generated by this market as the cost for high-quality digital cameras (a product that enhanced the utility of Avid Cinema) fell under $500, and computer retailers such as Best Buy and CompUSA began reporting that digital cameras were one of their fastest moving electronic/computer accessories.

PRODUCT DEVELOPMENT

20   Avid's first product, Media Composer, was designed specifically for the film and television industries. Indeed, the company's rapid growth was largely attributed to the market's acceptance of this initial product. Although Avid offered other products to the film and television industry, Media Composer remained its key product offering by contributing the most to both revenues and company profits.

21   Avid was dedicated to new product development. The company maintained a consistent level of R&D activity approximating 17% of sales, which mirrored its industry average. In addition, Avid engaged in several acquisitions to purchase leading technology in the form of existing products and capabilities that the company believed complemented its existing in-house technology. Exhibit 4 identifies Avid acquisitions that provided the company product diversification and sales growth. As a result of these acquisitions, Avid was able to develop a presence in the news broadcast industry (with systems installations at CBS, NBC, CNN, CNBC, and the BBC, for example), as well as the audio and special effects markets. Avid also formed alliances with other firms to help develop new technologies (see strategic alliances section).

EXHIBIT 4 Avid Acquisitions**** ($ in millions)

Source: Avid annual reports, public documents, and on-site interview with company representative; *Computer Reseller News* (10/31/94), Newsbytes News Network (3/31/95), *The Boston Herald* (10/22/98 and 6/30/00), CCN Disclosure (9/10/00).

Year	Company	Revenues	Cost	Description
1993	Digital Video Applications Corp.	n/a	$4.6	Developed video editing and presentation software products targeted for sale to nonprofessional video editors.
1994	Basys Automation Systems (newsroom division)	$26***	$5***	Developed newsroom automation systems.
1994	Softech Systems			Developed newsroom automation software.
1995	Digidesign, Inc.	$39	$205	Leading provider of computer-based, digital audio production systems for the professional music, film, broadcast, multimedia, and home recording markets.
1995	Elastic Reality	$12**	$45**	Developed digital image manipulation software.
1995	Parallax Software			Developed paint and compositing software.
1998	Softimage	$37	$248	Leading developer of 3D animation, video production, 2D cel animation, compositing software.
2000	The Motion Factory	n/a*	$2.3*	Developed 3D media for games and the Web.
	Pluto Technologies International			Developed newsroom storage and networking products.

****Represents significant acquisitions from 1993 to 2000.
***Combined totals for Basys Automation Systems and Softech Systems acquisitions.
**Combined totals for Elastic Reality and Parallax Software acquisitions.
*Combined totals for The Motion Factory and Pluto Technologies International acquisitions.
n/a data not available.

Notes:
1. Digital Video Applications Corp. was acquired to give Avid a presence in the nonprofessional video market as well as enhance its existing market capabilities.
2. Basys Automation Systems (newsroom division) and Softech Systems were acquired to provide Avid access to the news broadcast industry.
3. Digidesign, Inc. was acquired to give Avid a leadership position in the digital audio market.
4. Elastic Reality and Parallax Software were acquired to form Avid's graphics and effects group; the companies developed a range of image manipulation products that allow users in the video and film postproduction and broadcast markets to create graphics and special effects for use in feature films, television programs and advertising, and news programs. The Softimage acquisition significantly strengthened Avid's capabilities and market presence in these areas.
5. The Motion Picture Factory was acquired to enhance Avid's gaming and Web capabilities.
6. Pluto Technologies International was acquired to diversify its product offerings for the news broadcast industry.

22   Avid's products could be classified into six general categories: video and film editing products, audio products, digital news gathering systems, newsroom computer systems, graphics and special effects products, and storage systems. The company offered numerous products that ranged widely in cost and target market. For example, Avid Symphony, a sophisticated film editing system, cost $150,000 and was designed for professional editors. On the other hand, Avid Cinema cost $139 and was marketed to nonprofessionals—retail consumers using personal computers.

ESTABLISHING INDUSTRY STANDARDS

23   As a pioneer in digital technology, Avid took the lead in developing and promoting open industry standards. The company released into the public domain the platform of basic digital technology it developed and applied to specific product creations. This platform, or basic standards observed in the creation of digital media products, became known as Open Media Framework (OMF). OMF grew into a cooperative effort involving more

than 150 leading manufacturers of digital products. Products based on OMF standards were compatible with other OMF-based media products (whether graphics, video, audio, animation, or text), allowing different products from different vendors to be used simultaneously during the production process.

24   Avid understood the advantages of releasing its basic digital technology to firms providing competing as well as complementary products. These open standards resulted in increased development of innovative digital media technology and products, with more firms producing complementary as well as competing products. This increased the speed at which industries migrated from analog to digital technology. Additionally, by establishing industry standards, Avid ensured that its products would be compatible with complementary products of other firms. This increased the utility of Avid products. However, by making its basic digital technology available to other firms, Avid lost the ability to distinguish itself in this respect from competitors.

STRATEGIC ALLIANCES

25   To enhance its competitiveness, Avid engaged in several alliances with other technology firms. They included both horizontal and vertical alliances and were designed to address specific needs of the company. For example, Avid products were originally designed to operate solely on Apple computers. However, during the 1990s personal computer (PC) manufacturers began to erode product performance differences between Apple and IBM-compatible computers. As a result, Apple's market share dropped, causing some industry experts to question the continued viability of Apple. Avid realized the risk of being dependent on Apple technology to run its software and thus entered into a vertical alliance with Intel to develop the technology necessary to migrate the company's software to PC-based systems. This pact also included Intel taking a subsequent 6.75% ownership stake in Avid in 1997, providing the company $14.7 million in cash to help fund the process. By 1994, Avid began shipping comparable products on both Apple and PC platforms and continued to migrate and develop additional products to and for PC-based systems. Consequently, Avid reduced the uncertainty connected with being dependent on Apple, while at the same time making its products available to a wider market of both Apple and PC users.

26   Another partnership formed by Avid was the 1993 vertical alliance with filmmaker George Lucas and his Lucas Film and Lucas Digital groups. This agreement allowed for cooperation on the development of an extended line of special-effects products for the film industry. Avid provided software and hardware, and Lucas provided design specifications. Avid also entered into a partnership with Ikegami Tsushinki Co., Ltd. in 1994 to develop the world's first full-motion, digital-based camera.

27   More recent arrangements included Avid's 1998 acquisition of Softimage, a Canadian company located in Montreal. Although criticized by some industry analysts for not meeting product development deadlines and maintaining product quality, Softimage was recognized as a leader in 3D software designed to generate special effects in movies and advertisements using Microsoft operating systems. Softimage was formerly a division of Microsoft and was considered a fringe competitor of Avid. As part of the $248 million acquisition that included $128 million in goodwill, Microsoft took a 9.1% ownership stake in Avid. Changing the relationship with Microsoft from competitor to part-owner effectively aligned Avid with one of the most powerful firms in the technology industry.

28   In 1998, Avid also entered into a horizontal strategic alliance with Tektronix. This agreement resulted in a joint venture between the two competitors. Avid and Tektronix were able to identify mutual needs in responding to competition in the news broadcast

market. Tektronix, a diversified organization with revenues of $2 billion, had advantages in the areas of digital storage technology as well as in its network of news-broadcast-industry customers. Although Avid produced digital storage devices, it conceded that the storage devices produced by Tektronix were more widely accepted by the industry. In addition, being relatively new to the news broadcast industry, Avid had yet to develop its customer network on par with that of Tektronix. Further, the market would perceive Avid to have greater financial stability if it partnered its operations with those of a larger firm. At the same time, Tektronix conceded that Avid's digital editing products were superior to its own.

29   The joint venture was called Avstar. Each partner took a 50% ownership position in the venture and, in 1999, each contributed an initial $2 million in cash and assets. Through Avstar, Avid and Tektronix planned to combine their competencies in both digital editing and storage technology, while further enhancing innovation and product development in the news broadcast market. Together, they expected to more quickly grow market share in this industry, while reducing the risk each would face if it sought to develop the market on its own.

AVID MANAGEMENT

30   From its founding in 1989 through 1995, Avid co-founders held the position of CEO. Initially, William Warner held the position until 1991, before leaving to start another, noncompeting company. Subsequently, Curt Rawley held the position until 1995. They both answered to a board of directors chaired by the general partner of Greylock Management Corporation, a venture capital firm that played a significant role in the company's initial equity funding. These co-founders led Avid through a period of remarkable growth and success.

31   However, Avid's initial objectives to gain market share and develop a position of industry leadership eventually took their toll on company profitability. Lack of strong controls to monitor growth resulted in large write-downs in 1996 of various assets, including obsolete inventories and uncollectable receivables. At the same time, sales growth slowed, thus exacerbating the impact of insufficient controls on the company's bottom line.

32   Slowing sales and decreasing profits during this period led Avid's board of directors to recognize the need for a new management team that could institute the functional competencies necessary to halt the company's deteriorating financial performance. As a consequence, emphasis shifted from being a market-share driven firm to one seeking balanced growth with increased profitability. The board decided that an "outside" individual with proven experience running a large technology firm in a highly competitive environment was needed to provide the leadership necessary to guide Avid through these trying times.

33   In 1996, Bill Miller, 53, a seasoned executive in the technology industry, was hired to turn the fortunes of Avid around. As former chair and CEO of Quantum Computers, Miller had proven his ability to direct a large technology company in a highly competitive industry—the computer hard-drive industry. Under Miller's leadership, Quantum grew from $1.1 billion in revenues to $3.4 billion in five years.

34   Miller's responsibilities as Avid's new CEO included implementing the controls necessary to reduce the company's cost structure and reestablishing Avid as a profitable growth company. Understanding the need for Avid's quick turnaround, the board provided Miller with a high level of authority. He was granted CEO-duality status by being appointed to the positions of both CEO and chair of the board. The remaining eight board members were all non-executive directors.

AVID ATTEMPTS A TURNAROUND

35   Miller was excited about Avid's prospects and competitive staying power, saying that "in a world in which media can be used for virtually any message and delivered across the airwaves, a cable, or a computer network, we intend to continue to provide the tools that people use to tell their story." The proliferation of television channels alone signaled to Miller future potential for Avid, as he exclaimed, "the average cable household will soon have 90 channels, and with the fast spread of digital signals, that number may increase very quickly. More channels mean more programming to edit with software like Avid's."

36   However, Miller also recognized that Avid had outgrown the capabilities of its management, and that market leadership had to be paired with superior profitability. As a result, he began his tenure by building a new management team. This included hiring a new CFO to establish necessary financial control systems to decrease costs. Inventories and accounts receivables were significantly reduced, from $63.4 million and $107.9 million in 1995, respectively, to $9.8 million and $79.8 million in 1997, respectively. These efforts improved the company's cash flow, while reducing risks associated with inventory obsolescence and the collectibility of receivables. The turnaround entailed streamlining the organization, staffing reductions of approximately 70 positions, and discontinuance of development and sale of certain products. The total one-time cost to the company was $15.8 million.

37   In addition to shaping a new management team, Miller began to make significant changes in operations in an effort to boost company growth and profitability. One such change involved the company's product distribution channels. During Miller's tenure, Avid developed stronger relationships with firms that could distribute its products to a broad base of commercial and retail customers. As this channel grew, Avid was able to reduce its direct sales (in-house) activities to only key accounts that required a significant amount of time during the sales and postsales process. Avid was thus able to take advantage of its indirect channel members' (independent distributors, value-added re-sellers, and dealers) well-developed networks to commercial and retail accounts, while reducing overall operating expenses relating to in-house sales and marketing activities. Sales through indirect channel members (as opposed to the direct, in-house sales function) grew from 50% of total annual sales in 1996 to 85% in 1999.

38   The company also focused on its customer support function, by expanding resources and restructuring the function to increase customer satisfaction. For example, Miller increased training for his support staff, which helped improve its ability to fix a problem on the first service call from under 50% to over 90%, while reducing the period of time customers waited for technical help to about two minutes (*Forbes,* 1998).

39   Under Miller's leadership, Avid worked toward realizing its mission statement of becoming the leading provider of powerful digital content creation tools used to "entertain and inform the world." The company sought to focus on and expand its presence in its existing digital media markets. The company also targeted new markets and continued to drive and support open industry standards.

40   However, the benefits of Miller's restructuring were short lived. The Softimage acquisition, Miller's most significant strategic action while running Avid, and perhaps the most important single transaction in the company's history, was more difficult for the company to digest than originally expected. Additionally, sales growth and profits three years into Miller's tenure as Avid's chief executive remained elusive. In 1999, Avid recorded revenues of $452.6 million, a 6% decrease from 1998, and a net loss of $137.5 million—the company's worst performance in its 10-year history. Further, from 1998 to 1999, cash and marketable securities decreased from $111.8 million to $72.8 million; the current ratio decreased from 2:1 to 1.7:1, and long-term debt as a percentage of equity increased from 4.6% to 8.5% (see Exhibit 1 for consolidated statement of operations and Exhibit 2 for consolidated balance sheet).

41   This resulted in the board of directors once again taking action by replacing top management. In late 1999, Bill Miller, CEO and chair of the board, and Clifford Jenks, president, both resigned. A few months later in early 2000, William Flaherty, CFO under Miller, resigned. The company stated that its business plan was no longer achievable given rapid changes in the market. As a result, the board determined that another thorough restructuring was necessary to position the company for future growth and profitability.

42   Krall, who was COO of Avid's Digidesign division, was appointed to the position of CEO in April 2000. The Digidesign division had been a bright spot for Avid, as it achieved record sales and operating income while the company as a whole was underperforming expectations. In making these changes, though, the board eliminated the company's CEO-duality status. The board chair position (also held by Miller during his rein) was filled by Robert Halperin, a non-executive board member. Krall was the only executive on the now six-member board. The restructuring also entailed an 11% reduction in staff. About 200 jobs were terminated at a $10 million cost to the company. Avid expected the restructuring to reduce forward costs by $20 million annually. The company also announced that it would discontinue the development and sale of a limited number of existing products. The recent Softimage acquisition was, for the most part, spared of any significant restructuring and allowed to continue operating as a relatively autonomous division of the company.

THE COMPETITIVE LANDSCAPE

43   Avid benefited from introducing digital technology to the film and television industries. The company's success was achieved by providing superior digital products as a substitute for traditional analog products. The new digital technology was originally developed and marketed by small, innovative firms, many of which had since failed or been acquired by Avid or other firms in an attempt to establish industry leadership.

44   However, competition was intensifying. As digital technology became more firmly established, competition was expected from some of the big, well-entrenched analog firms that were beginning (or expected to begin) to produce their own digital products. These firms, such as Sony and Panasonic, were much larger than Avid and had significantly greater financial, technical, distribution, support, and marketing resources to bear on any strategic decision designed to take away the leadership position Avid held in digital technology. Avid also expected to face competition in one or more of its markets from computer manufacturers, such as IBM, Compaq, and Hewlett-Packard, and software vendors, such as Oracle and Sybase. All of these firms had announced their intentions to enter some or all of the company's target markets, specifically the broadcast news and special effects markets. Exhibit 5 provides further information on key competitors.

KRALL'S DILEMMA

45   "We revolutionized the digital content industry," said Krall. "We build the best content creation tools in video, film, 3D, and audio; 85% of films made in the U.S. actually utilize Avid tools." Additionally, Avid equipment is used to edit 95% of prime time television programs. The company had established a leadership position in several markets by applying

EXHIBIT 5
Key Competitors*
(excluding music
production markets)

Source: Avid annual reports,
public documents, and onsite
interview with company
representative; individual
company 10K/10F filings.

Company Name	Sales F/Y 2000 ($ millions)
Digital (direct competition)	
Adobe	$ 1,266
Alias/Wavefront (subsidiary of Silicon Graphics)	2,331**
BTS (subsidiary of Philips Electronics)	35,253**
Discreet Logic (subsidiary of Autodesk)	936**
Kinetix (subsidiary of Autodesk)	936**
Lightworks USA (subsidiary of Tektronix)	1,103**
Media 100	73
Panasonic (subsidiary of Matsushita)	63,470**
The Grass Valley Group (subsidiary of Tektronix)	1,103**
Analog (indirect competition)	
Sony	63,607
Matsushita	63,470
Tektronix	1,103***

*Includes video and film production and postproduction markets, broadcast news market, and graphics and special effects market; does not include the music production and postproduction markets.
**Annual sales represent that of the parent company's total operations; most subsidiaries represent acquisitions by larger firms as a means to enter Avid's markets.
***Tektronix annual sales at the time of the 1998 joint venture with Avid were $2.1 billion. The decrease from 1998 to 2000 is due to divestitures of certain businesses in 1999 and 2000.

new technology in a timely fashion to meet emerging customer needs. However, for Avid to remain a leader, it was necessary to maintain an accurate understanding of customer needs, technological advancements, and competitive dynamics in the markets it served.

46   Krall and the new management team he needed to build faced many challenges. Concern existed over the slowed rate of growth in company revenues and the staggering losses. Some industry analysts viewed the purchase of Softimage as a signal for investors to "wait and see," wondering whether the sheer magnitude of Avid's first cross-border acquisition was too much for the company to manage. Krall acknowledged that "it's easy for expenses to get ahead of revenues," and indicated that "the company's first goal was to bring expenses back in line (with company revenues)." He also noted that the company's "second goal was to lay the foundation for growth in the future." Meanwhile, Avid risked competition from major international firms, such as Sony and Panasonic, that were attracted to opportunities offered by digital technologies the company pioneered. Avid's ability to compete effectively against these well-established firms would be severely tested.

47   Krall had nearly four years' experience working for Avid prior to his appointment as CEO, first as the Digidesign division's director of program management and then later as the division's vice president of engineering and, eventually, COO. His strong technical background, with BS and MS degrees from MIT and an MBA from Harvard, as well as his company and industry knowledge, would all come to bear on the strategic decisions he would have to make to turn Avid around.

48   During his first year as CEO, the proactive Krall announced a new focus on Internet-related editing products and once again set Avid on an acquisition track. In 2000, Avid purchased Pluto Technologies International Inc. and The Motion Factory Inc. for an aggregate $2.3 million. Pluto Technologies specialized in storage and networking products for the news broadcast industry, and The Motion Factory specialized in interactive games for the Web. These are Avid's first acquisitions since its 1998 acquisition of Softimage. Krall also oversaw an alliance with Intel and Microsoft to develop products for creating interactive digital television.

49   Krall finished his first year with Avid on a modestly successful note. Avid's 2000 revenues were up 5% from 1999, and, although the company incurred a net loss of $56 million, it was significantly less than the $137 million loss incurred in 1999.

50   As Avid's now experienced CEO entered 2001, he had to reevaluate his first-year decisions and determine what new strategic actions, if any, should be made to ensure Avid's successful turnaround. With competition intensifying, Krall knew he had to act fast. His strategic decisions to further diversify the company into the Internet, gaming, and digital television markets as well as make further commitments to the news broadcast market would have to be weighed against the company's performance in 2000. Krall had to assess whether he had addressed the causes of the company's past performance problems. Another downturn in Avid's financial performance would not only result in further turmoil within the company and investment community, but even jeopardize the company's ability to survive as an independent entity. In a keen sense of humor, the youthful Krall stated, "If you look at Avid's history, it has roughly had a new CEO every three years. One could guess that perhaps I've got two years left on my clock."

A case study prepared by Philip K. Goulet and Alan Bauerschmidt, both of the Moore School of Business, University of South Carolina.
Avid 10K Reports, 1998–2000.
Avid 10Q Reports, 3/31/98, 6/30/98, 9/30/98, 3/31/01.
Avid Annual Reports, 1993–2000.
Avid Business Overview, Prudential Securities Technology Conference, Fall 1998.
Avid on-site interview with company official, 12/29/98.
Avid: Leadership & Vision, 1998.

Avid: NAB '98 Avid Teaser, 1998.

Avid Prospectus, 3/1/93.

Avid Prospectus, 9/21/95.

Avid: The Corporate Overview, 8/14/98.

Avid web page, www.avid.com, various press releases 1998–2001.

Broadcasting & Cable, Glen Dickson. Avid makes new friends in Las Vegas: Forms alliances with Hewlett-Packard and Panasonic, 4/17/96, volume 126, number 17, p. 12.

Broadcasting & Cable, Glen Dickson. Avid's turnaround man; No matter how good the technology, Krall sees execution as key, 10/9/00, p. 81.

Business Wire. Softimage enters agreement with Microsoft to develop tools and middleware for Xbox, 5/15/01.

CCN Disclosure. Avid acquires Pluto, expanding its broadcast and post-production product line-up, 9/10/00.

CNBC on air interview with Bill Griffith, 10/20/00.

Computer Reseller News, Avid Technology to acquire Digidesign in a stock-swap merger worth about $205 million, 10/31/94, number 602, p. 231.

DTV Business. Avid, Microsoft, Intel alliance, 4/17/00, vol. 14, no. 8.

Film + Television, first quarter 1998, volume 2, issue 1.

Forbes, Anne Linsmayer. The customer knows best, 8/24/98, pp. 92–93.

Newsbytes News Network, Avid Technology acquired two software companies, Elastic Reality and The Parallax Software Group, for $45 million, 3/31/95.

The Boston Globe, Anthony Shadid. Technology & Innovation: Fast forward; there's no firm more avid for digital film technology, 4/30/01, p. C2.

The Boston Herald. Avid acquires The Motion Picture Factory, 6/30/00, p. 30.

The Boston Herald. Avid's acquisition posted losses, 10/22/98.

The Wall Street Journal. Avid agrees to buy Softimage unit from Microsoft, 6/16/98, Sec. B, p. 7.

The Wall Street Journal. Avid Technology Inc. staff to be trimmed 11% under restructuring plan, 11/11/99, Sec. B., p. 23.

The Wall Street Journal. Best Buy Co.: December sales rose 21% on strong DVD purchasing, 1/7/99.

The Wall Street Journal. Computers: Cheaper PCs start to attract new customers, 1/26/98, Sec. B., p. 1.

The Wall Street Journal. The Internet; advancing the film: For those who want to beam photos over the internet, digital cameras may be the way to go, 3/22/99, Sec. R., p. 6.

The Wall Street Journal. Technology: CompUSA net rises 44% as revenue jumps 22% to $1.46 Billion, 1/29/98, Sec. A., p. 10.

The Wall Street Journal. Who's news: Avid Technology Inc., 4/27/00.

The Wall Street Transcript. CEO interviews, 47(12), 12/29/97.

TV Technology, Jay Ankeney. A summertime trip to Avid, 6/27/98.

Case 40

ZAP and the Electric Vehicle Industry

1   Soon after Kevin Spacey won the 2000 Oscar for Best Actor, the actor made his appearance onstage the "Late Show with David Letterman" by riding a Zappy electric scooter. It was at that moment that Gary Starr, the CEO and co-founder of ZAP Corporation ("ZAP"), felt that his efforts at creating electric vehicles ("EVs") for the masses had reached a milestone. ZAP designed, manufactured, and marketed electric bicycles, scooters, motorcycles, and other short-range, electric transportation products. Following a recent return in popularity of nonpowered, "kick" scooters, ZAP had experienced a rise in sales of its electric-powered Zappy scooter. As sales figures approached record levels, ZAP was poised to take a leadership position in the emerging alternative short-range transportation industry, an industry that Starr predicted could grow to $5 billion by 2005.

2   The appearance of the Zappy on the Late Show was a high point in a marketing campaign that had included associated tie-ins with Old Navy, Sprite, and the 2000 Olympics in Sydney. Yet the unplanned appearance of ZAP's flagship product also left Starr with several unanswered questions. Should his company ramp-up production to meet a sudden spike in demand, or follow a more carefully controlled growth path? Would demand be sustained, or was the resurgence of scooters a fad? What position could ZAP's electrically powered bicycles and scooters occupy in an evolving market for alternative transportation?

3   By 2001, Starr and his management team were considering ways to match ZAP's internal resources and capabilities with external market demand. An internal debate raged over how to allocate ZAP's resources between its flagship scooter products and the remaining product line in order to put the company on a path to profitability. In the company's early years, Starr had often relied on "gut" feelings to forecast demand. As ZAP had matured as a business, however, Starr felt that proper demand forecasting by his team was necessary to assemble the needed capital, manufacturing facilities, marketing, and staff to take the company to the next level. An onslaught of new, lower cost competitors had recently entered the EV market. Starr knew that he needed to act quickly to assemble a critical mass of resources in order to protect ZAP's early market leadership.

COMPANY HISTORY

4   James McGreen and Gary Starr founded ZAP Power Systems in Sebastopol, California in 1994. Sebastopol, a town of 7,750, was located 56 miles north of San Francisco in the heart of the Sonoma County wine grape and apple-growing region. ZAP, an acronym for Zero Air Pollution, arose out of McGreen and Starr's residual interests in U.S. Electricar, a now defunct organization that made a run at producing electric automobiles. Having spent their careers designing electric vehicles, McGreen and Starr had been encouraged by the growing public attention on curbing fossil fuel emissions.

5   In 1996, ZAP began to sell its electrically powered bikes through auto dealerships and started offering products through catalogs. The company's business began to improve in 1997, when ZAP and electric scooter maker Motivity formed ZAP Europa to cross-distribute products. The company also signed manufacturing and distribution agreements that year with Dantroh Japan, XtraMOBIL of Switzerland, and Forever Bicycle Co. in Shanghai, China.

6   ZAP began selling its stock directly to the public via the Internet in 1997, the first Internet IPO in history. It then opened an outlet store in San Francisco. A year later it introduced the Zappy scooter, which boosted sales. The company changed its name to Zapworld.com just prior to the Internet frenzy that was to follow shortly thereafter. Although the Internet represented a significant marketing tool and sales outlet, the name was changed back to ZAP in April of 2001 following an industrywide shakeout in which hundreds of dot-com companies went out of business.

7   In November 1999, an agreement was reached with ZEV Technologies of Syracuse, N.Y. for the exclusive right to distribute its electric Pedicab, a three-wheeled vehicle capable of carrying a rider and one or two passengers. In December of 1999, an agreement was reached to purchase EV maker emPower, a developer of advanced electric scooters founded by MIT engineers. ZAP then acquired emPower in an exchange for 525,000 shares of common stock. In that same month, a second company-owned EV store was also opened in Key West, Florida.

8   In February 2000, ZAP bought EV Systems, an EV company based in Los Altos, Calif. EV Systems produced a two-wheeled vehicle designed to tow skaters and skateboarders. EV Systems was obtained for 25,000 shares of common stock. Looking to further broaden ZAP's product lines, in May 2000 Starr introduced a new generation of non-powered scooter called the Kick™ that used inline skate technology. This compact scooter could be folded to fit into a backpack. In the same month ZAP also acquired Aquatic Propulsion Technology, Inc., a company that developed a product called a sea scooter, in that it pulled scuba divers, snorkelers, and other swimmers through water. This deal was secured in exchange for 120,000 shares of common stock.

9   In August 2000, ZAP formed a joint venture agreement with Nongbo Topp Industrial Co. Ltd. of China to manufacture and distribute EVs in China. This joint venture purchased key components from ZAP and assembled and distributed the Zappy scooter in China and paid royalties on each electric scooter sold in China. ZAP also received a share of the profits from the joint venture.

10   *Automotive News* recognized Starr as one of the ten most influential EV authorities in September 2000. In October 2000, at the 17th International EV Symposium in Montreal, Quebec, Starr spoke to a plenary session:

> Light EVs don't require the development of sophisticated hybrid or fuel cell technologies to bring them to market. With nearly 20 different models of EVs now available, ZAP is already delivering thousands of EVs to consumers. This industry [segment] has already surpassed the market for all other electric transportation.

11   Later that month, ZAP purchased Electric Motorbike Inc., a firm that developed electric scooters, motorbikes, and motorcycles. As with most of the other acquisitions, under the terms of this purchase agreement, ZAP acquired all assets, technology, engineering capabilities, and customer contacts including the components and designs for the Lectra motorcycle and its proprietary VR24 drive system. The Lectra motorcycle was capable of reaching speeds of over 50 mph and at the time was the world's only electric motorcycle in production.

12   An exclusive distribution contract with Oxygen S.p.A. of Italy was signed in October 2000 to sell the Zappy folding electric scooter and other ZAP EVs in Italy and three other

European countries. In February of 2001, this agreement was expanded to allow ZAP to distribute the Lepton in North America. The Lepton was a moped-class, sit-on scooter built by Oxygen S.p.A.

13 Internal product development efforts also aided Starr's efforts to expand his product base. In 2001, five new personal electric transportation products were unveiled at the industry Super Show in Las Vegas, NV. These products included the Zappy Jr., a smaller version of the Zappy targeted at younger riders, and the Zappy Turbo, an improved version of the popular Zappy electric scooter. The Zappy and Kick lines of products accounted for approximately 85% of total sales in 2000, and product expansions and improvements were necessary to secure ZAP's market position in the face of increasing competition. Other products under development included an electrically powered tricycle specifically designed for golf courses called the Golfcycle™. This single passenger golf vehicle was equipped with a hybrid human-electric propulsion system and room to carry a set of golf clubs, and was offered as an alternative to the ubiquitous golf cart. Also scheduled for release in 2001 was a new electric motor device called ZapAdapt™ that attached to manual wheelchairs. This device provided an affordable, convenient means of power-assistance without the need to purchase a fully powered wheelchair.

14 The string of acquisitions and marketing agreements, along with ongoing internal product development efforts, resulted in a product line of personal EVs consisting of offerings in over ten different product categories. (See Exhibit 1 for a list of ZAP's most popular products.) Accessories for these products also contributed to increasing sales. The promotional publicity garnered by ZAP's products created a source of momentum for the entire product line and contributed to a doubling of revenues for the small company for the year 2000 versus 1999. (Financial statements for the company are provided in Exhibit 2 and Exhibit 3.)

MARKETING

15 After the most recent acquisitions and product development efforts, ZAP's electrically powered product offerings included scooters, bicycles, power skis, patrol bikes, tricycles, sit-down scooters (similar to a moped), motorbikes, pedicabs, underwater propulsion devices, and neighborhood cars. ZAP also offered the ZAP Power System™ to address the market of the do-it-yourselfer who preferred to transform his or her own bicycle into an electric bike.

16 Through internal development and acquisition, ZAP had procured 14 patents associated with EV design implementation. This strong patent portfolio was secured as a means to protect the company's interests in light of increasing competition. Although the patent position represented a significant investment for ZAP, Starr conceded in a recent interview that patents simply gave companies the right to sue and that in a competitive environment, litigation could become burdensome and costly. Nonetheless, he was forced to hire legal counsel in early 2001 in an attempt to stop patent infringers from stealing ZAP's technology.

17 The increasing popularity of electrically powered vehicles, coupled with increasing political and social activity favoring environmentally friendly transportation, resulted in other unplanned exposure for ZAP. Twelve electric bikes were used at the 2000 Olympics in Sydney for regular patrols of the Olympic Village. Other unsolicited product

EXHIBIT 1
ZAP's Product Line
(Most Popular Iems)

ZAPPY™

The ZAPPY™ folding electric scooter is what the Company calls a "destination vehicle." Folded, the ZAPPY™ is just over three feet long and stores easily almost anywhere. Lightweight at only 36 pounds, the ZAPPY can be carried or rolled like luggage, and an optional tote bag makes transporting the ZAPPY even easier. Due to its small size when folded, the ZAPPY can be transported via a number of means including car, train, bus, and commercial airlines. When they're ready to roll users simply pop up the ZAPPY's handlebar, stand up, and push off. The powerful electric drive system propels the ZAPPY at speeds up to 13mph for a fast, safe and fun trip, without poisoning the environment. Line extensions include the Zappy Turbo (higher performance model capable of 19mph), Zappy Stap fighter (a Star Wars promotional model), the Zappy Mobility (a model with an added seat), the Skootr-X (a less expensive alternative to the Zappy capable of 12mph), and the Zappy Junior (classified as a toy with maximum speed of 8mph).

KICK™

The Kick™ weighs only nine pounds, and folds to the size of a tennis racquet. No assembly is required. The Kick™ is easier to ride than a skateboard with its lightweight design. Inline style wheels provide a smooth ride. This foot powered scooter is built with high tensile steel and can handle bumps, jumps and other obstacles and includes a convenient rear compression foot brake. It has an adjustable handlebar and the unit folds small enough to fit in a locker or backpack. The heavy-duty steel construction and rigid, braced frame design provide riders with an extremely quiet and effortless ride, while competitive models have been found to produce annoying buzzes and rattles.

PowerBike®

Introduced in 1995, the PowerBike is one of the original electric bikes in America. The PowerBike combines a rugged mountain bike-style frame with the world-record-breaking ZAP Power System. The PowerBike is designed for long rides out on the open road, with an easy "ZAP" boost for passing, assist on hills or a short rest on the fly. With the electric "power-assist" benefits of the PowerBike, riders are able to enjoy the outdoor environment without polluting it. The PowerBike unit includes a tough, high-tensile strength mountain bike frame, 18-speed index shifting, and the revolutionary ZAP Power System. PowerBike also features front suspension, V-style brakes, spring saddle, and is offered with a choice of power systems tailored to the budget and power preferences of the consumer.

ElectriCruizer

The ElectriCruizer brings back the "Retro" look of older bicycle styles with a futuristic ZAP power system. The new ElectriCruizer is the ultimate way to cruise any neighborhood. Designed for trips around town, commuting, errands, and just plain old fun, the eye-catching frame style uses rugged, high-tensile steel, equipped with high-quality, 6-speed grip shifting and front and rear cantilever brakes. Wide, semislick, white wall, road tires and a springy contour saddle help smooth out even the bumpiest roads and the curved handlebars make for an even more comfortable upright riding position. Equipped with the ZAP Power System, the ElectriCruizer has the power to climb virtually any hill. Accessories for this ElectriCruizer include front and rear fenders, baskets, rear racks, lights, and horns. The ZAP ElectriCruizer SX (for "Single Speed") is equipped with a single-motor system, and although the top speed is less than the DX

EXHIBIT 1
(continued)

standard, its range is greater. After being pedaled to start, the ElectriCruizer SX reaches approximately 14mph, and has a range of up to 20 miles. The DX (for "Dual Speed") offers a more powerful motor with a higher top-speed.

ZAP Patrol Bike™

ZAP's police bike looks and pedals like a normal bicycle. But, with the flip of a switch, the bike leaps forward with a silent burst of speed, working in conjunction with leg power to help peace officers arrive on the scene faster and in better physical condition to handle the situation. The ZAP Patrol Bike™ is designed to maneuver through busy city traffic with an available ZAP of acceleration for sticky situations. Silent electric power gives officers stealth when approaching areas of suspected criminal activity, and the Quick Release Battery system allows for around-the-clock operation. The ZAP Patrol law enforcement bicycle is identifiable with decals (Police, Sheriff, EMT etc.), front suspension, 24-speed index shifting, front and rear V-brakes, heavy duty Continental Goliath tires, rear rack, and the NiteRider Pursuit Kit. The kit includes dual red and white or blue and white headlamps with night and flashing pursuit settings, 115-decibel siren, rear rack with taillight and the ZAP Power System.

ZAP Trike™

The ZapTrike™ was designed for those who have trouble pedaling heavy three-wheelers. The burden of pedaling is taken away with the on-board ZAP Power System. This vehicle is popular among seniors and can be an inexpensive alternative for commercial use. The unit includes a sturdy high-tensile steel frame, wide semislick road tires, front side-pull and coaster brakes, comfortable extra-wide contour saddle and large rear basket. The ZAP Trike Power System includes a 2-speed, dual motor with long range (33ah) battery.

ZAP Kits

ZAP provides everything needed to turn virtually any bicycle into a quiet, nonpolluting, fun electric vehicle. A complete conversion kit includes a motor, a maintenance-free battery, a heavy-duty battery bag, controller, automatic portable charger (either 110 or 220v), on/off switch, wiring and mounting hardware. The system is so light at 22 pounds that it is barely noticeable, yet it is powerful enough to provide extra bursts for passing or climbing hills. The patented Auto Engagement Feature allows the bike to be pedaled normally with the system off. The typical range of bicycles utilizing a ZAP kit varies from 5–20 miles per charge, depending on model, user input and riding conditions

ZAP kits come in four varieties: DX, SX, Step Thru and Trike. The DX motor is a dual motor assembly and is designed for higher speeds. People who want the most power to supplement their pedaling for short bursts of turbo power for hills, like the police, find the DX most appropriate. The DX also features a Regenerative Mode, which recharges the battery by coasting the bike down a big hill. The "Regen" (one of the only electric bikes with regenerative braking) feature turns the system's motors into generators, helping to recharge some of the lost electricity. The SX is a single motor system, and is designed for greater range. The Step-Thru systems are designed for a "woman's" style bike frame, and have the battery mounted on a rear rack rather than in the frame. The Trike kit is great for seniors or people with disabilities.

(continued)

EXHIBIT 1
(continued)

ElectriCycle™

The ElectriCycle™ is powered by two 12V batteries and a 24V DC motor. This vehicle is very similar in performance to a standard 50cc gas scooter without the fumes and noise. It has a range of up to 20 miles and can top out at up to 25 mph, going from 0 to 18 mph in 6 seconds. The ElectriCycle™ features front and rear drum brakes, a power indicator, a speedometer, and an on-board charger that charges the battery in 2–8 hours.

Lectra™ Motorbike

Lectra developed one of the world's only electric motorcycles and also represents a world-class application of the most advanced technologies available in electric energy storage, display, and delivery. The Lectra offers superior acceleration, braking, and handling, and the advanced electric drive system is accurately controlled from the fingertips. The antilock electrically assisted regenerating rear brake and floating caliper front disk brake provide smooth, powerful braking. Also featured are the convenience of on-board, fully automatic charging and a maintenance-free energy storage system.

Electric Pedicab

Developed with the support of the New York State Energy Research and Development Authority, the ZAP Pedicab is an all-new three-wheeled electric bicycle capable of carrying a rider and two passengers. Operating at 24 volts DC, the Pedicab has a top speed of 15mph and has a 20-mile range. Each ZAP Pedicab is equipped with an onboard 120-volt charging system that will completely recharge the vehicle in less than three hours from any standard power outlet. A convenient state-of-charge meter provides the operator with current information about the vehicle's remaining range and the amount of energy it consumes. The ZAP Pedicab is capable of navigating through spaces that are inaccessible to cars and buses. As a result, for-hire pedicabs can be found in many cities around the world, including several in the U.S.

PowerSki®

The PowerSki is a radical new form of personal transportation that creates a downhill skating or skiing environment on flat ground. Much like a water-skier, an in-line or roller skater holds onto poles as the PowerSki tows them along at speeds of up to 15mph. The PowerSkier has complete control of the trigger switch and speed. A single battery charge lasts up to seven miles, and the PowerSki has enough torque to pull an average man up just about any hill, taking PowerSkiers practically anywhere their feet can take them, including on the street, over rough terrain, and up and down hills. This powerful design gives skaters a new form of transportation, exercise and pure skating fun.

Swimmy/Sea Scooter

The SWIMMY is a fun new water sport device for the whole family. Whether you're snorkeling in a tropical paradise or swimming in your backyard pool, the SWIMMY offers a totally new underwater experience. This "sea scooter" pulls the swimmer through the water, providing more enjoyment in swimming pools and less exertion in reaching coral reefs and other underwater sights.

EXHIBIT 1
(continued)

Neighborhood Cars

Neighborhood EVs (NEVs) are engineered like an automobile for dependable performance on both street and turf. Standard features include: rear brake light and backup alarm, anchored seatbelts, windshield wiper and safety glass windshield, auto-style headlights, rear-view mirror, and turn-signals.

EXHIBIT 2   ZAP's Consolidated Statement of Operations, 1995–2000

ZAP Financial Results Fiscal Years 1995–2000 Condensed Statement of Operations (Thousands, except per share amounts)						
	Year ended December 31					
	2000	**1999**	**1998**	**1997**	**1996**	**1995**
Net Sales	$12,443	6,437	3,519	1,640	1,171	651
Cost of Goods Sold	7,860	4,446	2,391	1,275	863	465
Gross Profit	$ 4,583	1,991	1,127	366	308	215
Operating Expenses:						
Selling	2,204	1,187	968	633	477	90
General and administrative	3,824	1,945	979	820	555	282
Research and development	699	365	203	246	100	75
Total Operating Expenses	6,727	3,497	2,150	1,700	1,132	447
Loss from Operations	(2,144)	(1,506)	(1,022)	(1,334)	(824)	(232)
Other Income (Expense):						
Interest Expense	(21)	(267)	(100)	(85)	(11)	(3)
Interest Income						
Miscellaneous	269	81	14	11	20	222*
Total Other Income	248	186	(86)	(74)	8	219
	(1,896)	(1,693)	(1,109)	(1,408)	(817)	(13)
Provision for Inc. Taxes	1	1	1	2	2	4
Net Loss	(1,897)	(1,694)	(1,109)	(1,409)	(817)	(16)
Net Loss Attributable to Shares:						
Net Loss	(1,897)	(1,694)	(1,109)	(1,409)	(817)	(16)
Preferred Dividend	(2,649)	—	—	—	—	—
Total	(4,546)	(1,694)	(1,109)	(1,409)	(817)	(16)
Net Income/(Loss) per Common Share, Basic and Diluted	(0.85)	(0.43)	(0.42)	(0.62)	(0.45)	(0.01)
Weighted Average of Common Shares Outstanding	5,361,905	3,927,633	2,614,563	2,289,165	1,805,317	1,582,656

*Includes $210,000 in royalty income and $20,000 in grant income.

EXHIBIT 3   ZAP's Balance Sheets, 1995–2000

ZAP Financial Results
Consolidated Balance Sheets
Years Ending December 31, 1995–2000
(Thousands, except per share amounts)

	Year 2000	1999	1998	1997	1996	1995
Assets						
Cash	$3,543	$3,184	$475	$691	$162	$22
Accounts Receivable	1,613	353	284	122	61	31
Inventories	2,898	1,725	634	267	247	58
Prepaid expenses and other assets	696	323	98	66	116	—
Total Current Assets	8,750	5,585	1,491	1,145	585	111
Property and Equipment-Net	510	350	177	163	100	66
Other Assets						
Patents and trademarks, less accum. amort.	1,432	1,176				
Goodwill, less accumulated amortization	2,023	112				
Advance to retail stores & technology companies		479				
Intangibles, net of accumulated amort.			80	20	7	8
Deposits and other	112	25	12	14	78	6
Total Other Assets	3,567	1,792	92	34	85	14
Total Assets	$12,827	$7,727	$1,760	$1,342	$770	$191
Liabilities and Stockholder's Equity						
Current Liabilities						
Accounts Payable	$398	742	334	162	301	94
Accrued liabilities and customer deposits	1,167	368	151	189	67	13
Notes payable, current maturities of LT debt	99	15	867	52	249	22
Current maturities of obligations under capital leases	32	9	10	16	13	—
Income taxes payable						3
Total Current Liabilities	1,696	1,134	1,362	418	629	131
Other Liabilities						
Long-term debt, less current maturities	95	24	11	60	5	
Obligations under current leases, less current	31	14	1	11	24	
Total Other liabilities	126	38	12	71	28	
Total Liabilities	1,822	1,172	1,374	489	657	131
Stockholder"s Equity						
Pref'd stk, authorized 10M sh. issued and outstanding	1,812					
Com. stk, authorized 20M sh. issued and outstanding	19,117	12,053	3,732	3,169	1,019	150
Accumulated deficit	(9,664)	(5,118)	(3,346)	(2,316)	(907)	(90)
Unearned compensation	(42)	(96)				
Less: notes receivable from shareholders	(218)	(285)				
Total Stockholder's Equity	11,005	6,555	386	853	112	60
Total Liabilities and Stockholder's Equity	$12,827	$7,727	$1,760	$1,342	$770	$191

exposure included Zappy appearances on popular television sitcoms such as the "Drew Carey Show" and "Just Shoot Me" and in television commercials with the popular Blue Man Group for Intel Corporation. The Swimmy sea scooter was selected as a finalist for the NASDAQ Sports Product of the Year. The PowerSki product was featured in a segment of the popular morning talk program, "The Today Show," as Matt Lauer demonstrated his prowess with the device on the streets of New York City. Other ZAP products were also slated to appear in four big screen movie productions to be released in the summer of 2001.

18   Increasing demand coupled with increasing competition prompted Starr to shift production of high volume products to Taiwan to trim costs and to allow the company to focus its efforts on improving distribution. Although Starr strongly believed that ZAP must continue its efforts at product development, competitive pressures required that ZAP begin to shift more of its resources on finding ways to reach the customer. In early 2001, a new "Zapworld" retail store and test track for customers was opened in a shopping mall in Santa Rosa, California. Planning was underway to open similarly configured retail outlets around the country to improve distribution and to build name recognition. The number of independent retail outlets that carried ZAP products in the U.S. also continued to grow and had exceeded 100 by this time.

19   Although Starr and his team had expended much effort in creating a broad range of offerings, he also knew that he needed to find new ways to reach consumers. By mid-year 2001, after shifting much of ZAP's manufacturing operations overseas, Starr announced that he and his management team were "undertaking a significant repositioning of ZAP from an electric scooter-only company to an overall provider of premier EV products."

20   Under the plan, ZAP would be positioned as a distributor of high-margin, foreign manufactured products, with a primary focus on aggressive sales activity. ZAP would continue to place an emphasis on the research and development of new EV products, although acquisition plans remained a significant part of the new plan, allowing the company to diversify its product line more rapidly.

21   With regards to ZAP's developments and repositioning plans, Starr commented:

> ZAP took a bold step to introduce electric bicycles and scooters during the 90s when electric cars seemed to be the center stage. Today, we have proven to the world there is a market for low-speed EVs, but we need to continue to be a pioneer and a leader in this industry, introducing new products and opening up new markets. We must draw on all of our talents to design superior vehicles, manufacture those products at competitive prices, and market them with utmost creativity. We believe we have the entrepreneurial team to accomplish all of the above, backing our mission to make ZAP the name in clean transportation.

MANAGEMENT

22   Starr assembled a Board of Directors that included ZAP's former President, John Dabels. Dabels had come to ZAP after having served as CFO and member of the Board of EV Global Motors, an electric bicycle company founded and chaired by Lee Iacocca, the former CEO of Chrysler. Starr felt that the Dabels' experience provided a necessary element for managing the growth of ZAP. In early 2001, however, Dabels left ZAP to spend more time with his family. Dabels' departure left a considerable vacancy on the Board for Starr to fill and put added pressure on the other Board members to guide the organization. (Biographies of the current Board members and management team for ZAP are provided in Exhibit 4.)

EXHIBIT 4
Biographies of ZAP's Board and Management Team

 Gary Starr (45), CEO of ZAP, has been a director and executive officer since 1994, and Chief Executive Officer since September 1999. Mr. Starr founded U.S. Electricar's EV operation in 1983 and has been building, designing, and driving electric cars for more than 25 years. He has overseen the marketing of more than 50,000 electric bicycles and other EVs and has invented several solar electric products and conservation devices. Mr. Starr was named one of the ten most influential electric car authorities by *Automotive News* and has appeared on numerous radio, television talk, and news shows, and is a published author of articles and books on energy efficiency and electric vehicles. He has received several recognition awards for his contributions towards clean air, including the American Lung Association of San Francisco, Calstart, and U.S. Senator Barbara Boxer. He holds a BS in Environmental Consulting and Advocacy from the University of California, Davis.

Robert E. Swanson (53), Chairman of the Board of ZAP since 1999, is Chairman of the Board, sole director and sole stockholder of Ridgewood Capital Corporation. Mr. Swanson is also Chairman of the Board of the Fund and President, registered principal and sole stockholder of Ridgewood Securities Corporation. In addition, Mr. Swanson is President and sole shareholder of Ridgewood Energy, Ridgewood Power and Ridgewood Power Management Corporation. Ridgewood Power is a managing shareholder of each of the prior Programs and Mr. Swanson is the president of each prior Program. Since 1982, Mr. Swanson, through a number of entities, has sponsored and been a principal of more than 47 investment programs involved in oil and gas exploration and development, which programs have raised approximately $200 million from the sale of investment units. Mr. Swanson was also a tax partner at the former New York and Los Angeles law firm of Fulop & Hardee and an officer in the Investment Division of Morgan Guaranty Trust Company. His specialty was in personal tax and financial planning, including income, estate and gift tax. Mr. Swanson is a member of the New York State and New Jersey bars. He is a graduate of Amherst College and Fordham University Law School. Mr. Swanson and his wife, Barbara Mardinly Swanson are the authors of *Tax Shelters, A Guide for Investors and Their Advisors* published by Dow Jones-Irwin in 1982 and published in revised editions in 1984 and 1985.

Douglas R. Wilson (40), Director of ZAP, is Vice President Acquisitions of RCC and the Ridgewood Fund. He was a principal of Monhegan Partners, Inc., which provided acquisition and financial advisory for Ridgewood Power and the Prior Programs, from October 1996 until September 1998, when he joined Ridgewood Power an RCC as Vice-President of Acquisitions. He has over 14 years of capital markets experience, including specialization in complex lease and project financings and in energy-related businesses. He has a Bachelor of Business Administration from the University of Texas and Master's degree in Business Administration from the Wharton School of the University of Pennsylvania.

Lee Sannella, M.D. (84), Director of ZAP, has been an active researcher in the fields of alternative transportation, energy and medicine for more than 25 years. Dr. Sannella has been a founding shareholder in many start-up high-tech companies. Dr. Sannella is a best-selling author. He has served on advisory boards of the City of Petaluma, California, on the Board of Directors of the San Andreas Health Council of Palo Alto, the Veritas Foundation of San Francisco, and the AESOP Institute. He is a graduate of Yale Medical School.

William D. Evers (73), Director of ZAP, is one of the leading SEC attorneys in California with extensive experience in start-up and emerging companies, specializing for a number of years in private placements, Section 25102(n) offerings, Small Corporate Offering Registration, Regulation A exemptions and Small Business Registrations. He has handled numerous mergers and acquisitions. Mr. Evers heads the Evers and Hendrickson Internet Law Group with its emphasis on Internet relationships. Mr. Evers has also had extensive experience in franchising and has been the CEO or President of various business ventures. He holds a BA from Yale University and a JD from University of California, Berkeley.

EXHIBIT 4
(continued)

Harry Kraatz (51), became a director of ZAP on December 7, 2000. Since investing in ZAP in 1998, he has provided franchise consulting and certain financial services. Beginning in June 1986, Mr. Kraatz has been the sole officer and director of The Embarcadero Group II, and T.E.G. Inc., a franchise management and financial consulting company located in San Francisco, California. Working with those companies he has provided consulting services to numerous finance and franchising companies including Montgomery Medical Ventures, Commonwealth Associates, Westminster Capital and World Wide Wireless Communications, Inc. He received a degree from SMSU in 1971.

Andrew Hutchins (40), Mr. Hutchins was appointed Vice President for Operations in October 1999. He joined the company in December 1996 and since June 1997 has been General Manager. Successful as an entrepreneur, Mr. Hutchins started, developed and managed a retail bicycle business for 11 years prior to selling it for several times his initial investment. In 1982, Mr. Hutchins received a Bachelor of Arts degree with a double major in Business Economics and Communication Studies from the University of California at Santa Barbara.

Scott Cronk (35), Mr. Cronk was the founder of Electric MotorBike, Inc. and served as its President from 1995 to 1999. Previously, as Director of Business Development & International Programs, he led strategic venturing activities for U.S. Electricar, Inc. Mr. Cronk was appointed Vice President of Business Development of ZAP in December 1999 shortly after ZAP acquired Electric Motorbike, Inc. Mr. Cronk has a Bachelor of Science degree in Electrical Engineering from GMI Engineering & Management Institute (now Kettering University) and a Master's of Business Administration degree from the City University of London, England.

EXHIBIT 5   ZAP's Organization in 2001

Source: Company records.

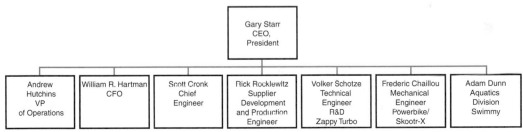

23   Starr oversaw day-to-day operations at ZAP. (See the organization chart in Exhibit 5.) Andrew Hutchins, VP of Operations, oversaw production of the various products that ZAP manufactured, such as the Zappy line of scooters. One of Hutchins' primary responsibilities in early 2001 was to ensure a smooth transition of the Zappy manufacturing operation to Taiwan. Rick Rocklewitz filled in as Supplier Development and Production Engineer in Taiwan to assist in the transition. Product development at ZAP was split into specific product categories. Volker Schotze handled development of extensions of the Zappy scooter line. Frederic Chaillou oversaw the PowerBike line. Adam Dunn was in charge of the Aquatics Division. Starr was looking to each of these individuals to identify and fill market niches with extensions of existing products or development of new products. Their charge was to build upon the technology base that had been developed internally at ZAP and via acquisition.

THE EV INDUSTRY

24   The overall electric vehicle industry was very broad in scope. Vehicles in production ranged in size and sophistication from military tanks and large transport vehicles used in airports at the high end, to plastic toys for toddlers at the low end. Included within this wide range of cost and complexity were golf carts, personal transport vehicles for disabled persons, and electric automobiles.

25   In 2000, Peter Harrop, a consultant to the EV industry, estimated that industry sales would exceed $6B in 2000 and $26B by 2010. (Harrop's ten-year estimates of unit sales volumes and value by individual market segments for the EV industry are provided in Exhibit 6 and Exhibit 7.) Harrop described the market forces driving growth in the EV industry:

> Contrary to popular opinion, pollution control is not often the primary reason why EVs are bought today or will be bought in future. Even those solely concerned with pollution would do well to make their vehicles more acceptable by featuring other, more compelling attributes. Blockbuster EVs usually capture the imagination, make something new possible, replace human effort, and/or save cost over the life of the product. Even where they save cost over life it is not necessarily against a vehicle powered by an internal combustion engine (ICE). For example, an EV access platform replaces scaffolding and ladders and the attendant high labor costs. EVs usually create new markets with EV bicycles and 3/4 wheel, single-seat vehicles for the slightly infirm being recent examples. Home robots are likely to emerge in this category next.

26   Harrop also described the growth factors driving several EV market segments:

Heavy industrial vehicles

Heavy industrial vehicles, such as the archetypal forklift, are increasingly used to replace human effort in enclosed factories and warehouses and laws increasingly call for them to be used in orchards. Most growth in heavy industrial EV sales derives from the demands of the Fast Moving Consumer Goods (FMCG) logistic chain and from the industrialization of third world countries.

It is increasingly accepted that there is about 30% reduction in cost-over-life versus ICE anyway, so penetration will also rise steadily, encouraged by increased use of hybrids and later fuel cell EVs for the high energy, long-range applications.

Two-wheel vehicles (bikes, scooters, etc.)

Projected growth is very substantial for this sector because there are many strong influences. This is the only sector where prices have halved in three years and where fashion, and draconian new pollution laws are brought to bear together.

This is, and will remain, most true in East Asia where most of the world's conventional bicycles and scooters reside anyway. China banning further purchases of ICE two wheelers in several major cities will continue to provide a large boost to output of 2-wheel EVs as will the promotion of the EV industry in China as a whole. However, most usually they replace human effort and not ICE vehicles.

Increasing success of 2-wheel scooters and later motorcycles increases the average selling price of the 2-wheel sector but volume production and severe competition causing price erosion with bicycles is more than an offset.

The market drivers are likely to be performance and pollution issues. Motorcycle EVs and their derivatives are barely selling at all in 2001 but they will become popular within five years. Improved batteries and hybrids, rather than fuel cells, are key to the larger 2-wheel EVs selling strongly in the next few years. There is a real possibility that tens of millions of 2-wheel EVs will be sold in 2010.

EXHIBIT 6
Forecasted Volume
of EVs Worldwide
Sales, 2000–2010,
by Market Segment
(units in 000s)

	2000	2001	2002	2003	2005	2010
Heavy industrial	230	240	250	255	260	350
Light industrial/commercial	64	100	120	150	250	400
Disabled	420	470	530	590	740	1,300
2-wheel	500	700	1,000	1,300	3,000	6,000
Golf car and caddy	256	265	280	300	320	330
Cars	60	100	150	200	500	1,250
Military	2	2	2	3	6	10
Mining	2	2	3	3	4	6
Mobile robots	10	30	300	400	1,000	2,800
Others	15	14	17	20	25	30
Total Market	**1,559**	**1,923**	**2,652**	**3,221**	**6,105**	**12,476**

Source: Peter Harrop, "EV Markets, Players, Forecasts," www.footnoteanalysis.com.

EXHIBIT 7
Forecasted Value
of EVs Worldwide
Sales, 2000–2010,
by Sector ($ billions)

	2000	2001	2002	2003	2005	2010
Heavy industrial	2.80	2.90	3.07	3.26	3.35	3.35
Light industrial/commercial	0.55	0.65	0.80	1.00	1.60	2.50
Disabled	0.42	0.47	0.53	0.59	0.74	1.30
2-wheel	0.40	0.54	0.71	0.94	1.50	3.00
Golf car and caddy	0.51	0.53	0.55	0.56	0.60	0.60
Cars	0.60	1.01	2.00	3.00	4.50	10.00
Military	0.18	0.21	0.24	0.30	0.60	1.00
Mobile robots (except toys)	0.08	0.10	0.90	1.12	2.50	2.80
Mining	0.44	0.46	0.50	0.67	1.00	1.50
Other (mainly marine)	0.23	0.28	0.25	0.40	0.50	0.60
Total Market	**6.21**	**6.68**	**9.55**	**11.84**	**16.89**	**26.65**
% Growth yearly	15%	11%	43%	24%	19%	11%

Source: Peter Harrop, "EV Markets, Players, Forecasts," www.footnoteanalysis.com

Golf carts and caddies

Market growth for golf carts and motorized golf caddies has slowed because golf course construction in the U.S. has slowed and the rest of the world is not compensating. There is some growth from the expansion of leisure activities globally and from changes in local bylaws that increasingly permit golf carts on public roads in Europe and North America.

There is also some growth from the cost saving over the life of the product being accepted as an argument by most golf clubs worldwide. Current 60–70% penetration of electric vehicles may slowly rise to 90% or so but most are leased to golf clubs, keeping prices down despite the small number of suppliers.

Vehicles for the disabled

The EV market segment for the disabled can be divided into wheelchairs for supervised severely disabled people, where increased concern and funding is creating market growth, and the larger market for mobility aids for unsupervised, less-disadvantaged people such as those who are pregnant, temporarily injured, or old rather than registered disabled. These same products may start to appear in locations such as airports for those with a lot to carry.

Such people have increasing disposable income and will purchase on impulse from the expanding variety of single-rider EVs being made available to them such as ones for the home, for country paths, for the obese, or for folding into a car trunk. More countries are enjoying these products and an increasing number are on free loan in large buildings, supermarkets, town centers, and leisure parks having been bought by local government or large companies. A fairly strong growth rate is anticipated in this market segment.

Special EV applications

Emerging types of EVs include special models for mining, marine, police, military, research and leisure beyond golf cars and two wheelers. That covers everything from silent airships to disposable handheld $1,000 military surveillance aircraft, "pigs" in pipelines and leisure boats for silent surface trolling or wildlife study. Pure EV leisure submarines, power assistance for scuba divers, and remote-controlled undersea search robots are also in this category.

Noise, air, and water pollution are all relevant in some of the new EV markets. This sector is rife with innovation and includes thousands of mobile robots sold for the first time in Japan in 1999 and in the West in 2000. These robots variously perform multiple tasks such as vacuum cleaning, fetching and carrying, and some monitor the elderly. They are not toys, however, in the sense of small remote-controlled or pre-programmed boats, cars, dogs, and cats. Mobile robots save human effort and make new things possible. These products have little or nothing to do with reduction in pollution.

Most of the serious new products make possible something new, creating markets from thin air. Looking at the preparation of yet other new EV products in universities and elsewhere, explosive growth will occur. Initially this growth will occur through the adoption of military EVs, home robots, and marine EVs.

A remarkable variety of new concepts is being proven every year giving great optimism about the future. Robots searching for earthquake survivors or doing the gardening will come, as will seagoing hybrid electric ships and much more. Trials are being carried out today. This is not science fiction.

27   Like Harrop, some industry observers predicted that the short-range EV industry was poised to experience record global growth in the foreseeable future. The industry was offering various alternatives for urban commuters and a direct means for lessening pollution. Between bicycles and automobiles lay a broad range of short-range vehicles that fell into the category of individual transportation vehicles. Unlike the maturing bicycle market, which had achieved a high level of market penetration with over 1.4 billion bicycles in service worldwide by 2000, the individual electric transportation market was considered to have greater opportunity for growth.

28   The unexpected boom in popularity of nonpowered scooters in recent years provided an indication of the strength of demand for alternatives in this market and the potential for growth. Although kick scooters had been introduced over 50 years ago, their resurgence in 2000 suggested that there was unmet demand for alternatives to the bicycle and other recreational short-range modes of transportation such as inline skates and skateboards. With almost no demand for scooters in 1999, sales of nonpowered scooters were estimated at between 2–5 million units in 2000 for models priced in the range of $50–$120. (See Exhibit 8.) The preliminary expectations for the nonpowered "kick" scooter market, based on sluggish sales since the 2000 Christmas buying season, were that sales for 2001 would be significantly lower than the previous year. It was not yet clear whether the forecasted decline in sales was due to rapid market saturation or if it was an indication that the nonpowered scooter was a short-lived fad.

29   The largest segment of the individual transportation industry belonged to the bicycle industry, which had experienced a resurgence of its own since the introduction of the mountain bike in 1981. Year 2000 sales volumes in the U.S. bicycle market reached lev-

EXHIBIT 8
Units Shipped
and Sales Volume
of Nonpowered
Scooters, 1998–2000

	No. Units Shipped	Industry Sales Volume
1999	—	$5–10 million
2000	2–5 million	$100–600 million
2001	1–2.5 million	$50–300 million

Source: Rita Haberman, "Wheels of Fortune or Passing Fad?," www.redchip.com, August 25, 2000.

EXHIBIT 9
Bicycles Sold in the
U.S. Market, by Size
of Bike, 1973–2000

	20" and Up Wheel Sizes (Millions)	All Wheel Sizes (Millions)
2000	11.9*	18.1*
1999	11.6*	17.5*
1998	11.1*	15.8*
1997	11.0*	15.2*
1996	10.9	15.4
1995	12.0	16.1
1994	12.5	16.7
1993	13.0	16.8
1992	11.6	15.3
1991	11.6	
1990	10.8	
1989	10.7	
1988	9.9	
1987	12.6	
1986	12.3	
1985	11.4	
1984	10.1	
1983	9.0	
1982	6.8	
1981	8.9	
. . . 1973	15.2 (record high)	

Source: Bicycle Manufacturers Association. *Indicates projections from The Bicycle Council based on a compilation from numerous sources. Available at www.nbda.com/statpak.htm. (Note: The Bicycle Manufacturers Association no longer exists.)

els in excess of 16 million units with revenues of over $5 billion. The worldwide bicycle market exceeded 60 million units in 2000. (See Exhibit 9 and Exhibit 10.) In the 1990s, bicycle manufacturing in the U.S. was, for the most part, left to manufacturers of high-end specialty bikes. By the end of the decade, most bicycles targeted for the mass market in the U.S. were made in Taiwan. Exhibit 10 shows the reduction in U.S. domestic production for bicycles and the associated increase in imports for the years 1991 to 1998. In 1998, U.S. domestic production had fallen to 2.3 million units from its 1993 peak of 9.9 million units. The corresponding retail sales values for each year are also provided in Exhibit 10. Bicycles were sold as a means of transportation and for recreational purposes. Of these, only about 5% of bicycles sold were used as commuter vehicles, the primary market for alternatives such as electric vehicles. In Exhibit 11, a breakdown of U.S. retail sales in 1999 and 2000 by market segment for nonpowered bicycles is shown along with the average selling price for each segment.

EXHIBIT 10
U.S. Bike Market,
1991–1998

	Total (millions)	Imports (millions)	Domestic (millions)	Market Value ($billions)
1990				3.6
1991	15.1	6.5	8.6	4.0
1992	15.4	6.3	9.0	4.5
1993	17.0	7.1	9.9	4.3
1994	16.7	7.0	9.7	5.0
1995	16.0	7.2	8.8	5.2
1996	15.5	7.5	8.0	5.2
1997	15.8	9.8	6.0	5.4
1998	16.1	13.9	2.3	5.6

Source: "Bicycle Retailer and Industry News," www.nbda.com/statpak.htm.

EXHIBIT 11
Specialty Bike Sales
Distribution for Top
13 Brands

Category	2000	1999	Avg. Price
Mountain	43.10%	46.40%	$449
Youth	25.10%	27.50%	$206
Comfort	13.50%	8.70%	$338
Hybrid	11.50%	11.80%	$368
Road	3.85%	2.60%	$1,109
Cruiser	2.60%	2.60%	$297
Tandem	0.13%	0.12%	$1,069

Source: National Bicycle Dealers Association Retail Data Capture Program. www.nbda.com/statpak.htm.

30   Electric power-assist add-ons to enable conversion of almost any nonpowered bicycle were developed and introduced by a number of manufacturers and were targeted for the 1.4 billion nonpowered bikes that had already been sold. These add-ons ranged in price and complexity of installation.

31   Sales of EVs were expected to grow not just because of their appeal to recreational riders, but also because they cut across many other market segments. Aging baby boomers were finding it increasingly difficult to get outdoors and exercise and the lack of short-range vehicle alternatives put their independent lifestyles in jeopardy. Seniors were turning to electrically powered vehicles as a way to extend their present habits and preferences. Electric bicycles were thoroughly practical, both for personal transit and transporting moderate loads. Improved battery technology, worsening traffic congestion, and new community infrastructure (bike lanes, bike racks, secure parking, etc.) were also thought to be major attractions to prospective consumers of electric bikes.

32   Police and law enforcement agencies were also discovering the benefits of EVs. Officers on local patrols could respond more quickly than their bicycle-pedaling colleagues and were not as susceptible to the traffic snarls experienced by patrol cars. These officers also required less training to handle an electrically powered bike or scooter than those trained to ride a motorcycle or horse. In Florida, electrically powered bike sales began to experience significant growth, due to law enforcement agencies' purchases of those vehicles for use in resort areas.

33   Short-range EVs were also becoming popular in a range of industrial applications, on golf courses, in parks, at airports, and other environments in which the traditional automobile proved inconvenient. Commuters, frustrated with traffic congestion and parking limitations, also found EVs to be a practical transportation choice.

EXHIBIT 12

Major Electric
Bicycle
Manufacturers
in 2000

Brand or Manufacturer	Final Assembly	Qty. Sold
EV Rider	Taiwan	62,000
Currie Technologies	Taiwan/Thailand	39,000
ZAP	USA/Taiwan	33,000
Giant Bicycle Co.	Taiwan	20,000
EV Global	Taiwan	17,000
Master Shine	China	15,000
ETC	Taiwan	10,000
JD Components	Taiwan	6,000
Sunpex	Taiwan	3,500
Merida	Taiwan	3,000
Bikit	China	2,500
HCF	Taiwan	2,500
Schwinn	Taiwan	800
Badsey	USA	500
Trek	USA	500
Heinzmann	Germany	400
SRAM	Germany	300
Th!nk Mobility	Taiwan	250
Denali	USA	200
Diamond Firefly	China	200
Mercedes	Germany	165
Moterrad	Germany	100
Electricbike factory	USA	100

Note: Sales volumes include totals of electric bikes and electric scooters where applicable.

Source: Personal communication with Ed Benjamin.

COMPETITIVE FORCES

34 By 2000, competition in manufacturing, developing, and marketing EVs had increased in expectation of sustained industry growth rates. Major manufacturers mainly sold products to Japan and Europe. Smaller manufacturers sold products in the U.S., European, and Asian markets. Prices for e-bikes typically fell within the range of $500 to $1,000 for a typical bicycle with an electric power-assist, add-on package. High-end electric bikes with integrated drive trains, such as those offered by EV Global, ranged from $1,000 for the base model to $2,000 for the high-end model. (A list of the top 23 electric bike manufacturers is provided in Exhibit 12.) Most EV manufacturers had their roots entirely in the electric bicycle industry. As shown in Exhibit 12, Taiwanese manufacturers dominated offshore production of EVs.

35 Many short-range EVs were marketed as alternatives to existing gasoline-powered vehicles. Stand-up scooters with small gas-powered engines, although relative newcomers to the marketplace, offered consumers the ability to refuel in a matter of minutes as opposed to the time it took to recharge a battery. A relatively noisy two-stroke engine, however, accompanied this convenience.

36 The potential for two-wheeled EVs induced large established automakers and manufacturers of nonpowered bicycles to introduce models under new brand names. Th!nk was an enterprise of Ford Motor Company that designed and marketed electric bicycles. Mercedes Benz introduced its own version of the electric bicycle. Trek, Schwinn, and Murray, three of the largest nonpowered bicycle sellers in the U.S., also introduced electrically powered

EXHIBIT 13
Estimated Sales
Volume for Electric
Bicycles in Four
Largest Markets

	Japan	China	Europe	U.S.	Total
1998	270,000	40,000	35,000	25,000	370,000
1999	200,000	200,000	40,000	25,000	465,000
2000	200,000	250,000	55,000	30,000	535,000

Source: Personal communication with Ed Benjamin.

EXHIBIT 14
Electric Bicycle
Market Sales in Four
Largest Markets
($ Millions)

	Japan	China	Europe	U.S.	Total
1998	175.5	12.0	26.3	17.5	231.9
1999	130.0	60.0	30.0	17.5	251.0
2000	130.0	75.0	41.3	21.0	267.3

Source: Personal communication with Ed Benjamin.

EXHIBIT 15
Estimated
Worldwide Sales
of Electric Bicycles
and Electric Scooters,
1993–2003
(Units Sold)

Year	Annual	Cumulative
1993	36,000	36,000
1994	60,000	96,000
1995	116,000	212,000
1996	133,000	345,000
1997	285,000	630,000
1998	400,000	1,030,000
1999	470,000	1,500,000
Projected		
2000	800,000	2,300,000
2001	1,000,000	3,300,000
2002	1,200,000	4,500,000
2003	1,500,000	6,000,000

Source: personal communication with Ed Benjamin.

bicycles, as did a number of large foreign bicycle companies, such as Giant, a China-based manufacturer. (A breakdown of the estimated sales volumes for the four largest geographic markets is provided in Exhibit 13. Estimates of the total sales in U.S. dollars for these markets are provided in Exhibit 14. Data for the adoption rate of electric bicycles worldwide since 1993 are shown in Exhibit 15 along with projected sales volumes to 2003. Several key players in the electric-powered scooter industry are listed in Exhibit 16. Estimated sales volumes for electric scooters in 2000 and projected sales volumes for 2001 in the U.S., the primary market for these vehicles, are provided in Exhibit 17.)

37   Differentiation in the electric scooter market began to emerge as manufacturers raced to identify new niche markets. Some manufacturers focused on stand-up scooters (rider stands while driving), others produced scooters with attachable seats, scooters with built-in seats, and mopedlike scooters. Higher performance (i.e., faster than 15mph) stand-up scooters were also under development, ahead of legislation that would permit their usage on public roadways. Top speed and expected mileage between charges were considered performance benchmarks for these high-end models.

EXHIBIT 16

Top Electric Scooter
Manufacturers
in the U.S. Market

E-Scooter Manufacturer	Products	Est. Price Range
ZAP	SkootrX, Zappy	$200–$700
Currie Technologies	Phat Phantom, Phat Flyer	$570–$700
Badsey	Hot Scoot, Cruiser, Racer	$1,000–$3,000
Go-Ped	Hoverboard	$800
BatteryBikes	CityBug, Citibug e^2	$500–$600
Nova Cruz Products	Xootr, eX3	$269–$1,100

Source: Prices and product offerings compiled from a survey of numerous retail websites.

EXHIBIT 17

Estimated U.S. Sales
Volume for Electric
Scooters in 2000 and
Projections for 2001

Year	Sales volume
2000 (estimated)	80,000
2001 (projected)	500,000

Source: Personal communication with Ed Benjamin.

38   Advances in battery technology were also driving the rise in interest and investment in the short-range EV market. Batteries were now much safer, more compact, and more affordable than ever before and could be charged more quickly and easily. Significant short-term innovations in battery technology were expected to arrive in the marketplace with increasing global utilization of electric-powered vehicles. Future advances in battery technology were also expected to continue to invigorate the EV industry, as creative individuals discovered new and exciting ways to attach the latest batteries to new and existing modes of transportation.

39   Rapidly rising gasoline prices and an electric power crisis in California during 2000 and early 2001 contributed to the level of uncertainty in the external environment for EVs. Global environmental pressures, higher oil prices, population pressures, and urban traffic congestion were expected to contribute to rising demand for short-range transportation solutions. Increasing energy costs translated into higher operating costs and a potential backlash from consumers. Electricity had historically been an inexpensive source of power with a typical charge on an electric bicycle costing a few cents. Higher electric energy costs had the potential of altering this perception in the minds of consumers.

40   The legal environment for short-range EVs was also changing. The failure of the automobile industry to provide nonpolluting alternatives to the internal combustion engine resulted in a series of extensions for automobile manufacturers to meet a mandate initiated by the State of California, the largest U.S. market for automobiles and the market with the highest antipollution standards. Initiated by the California Air Resources Board in the early 1990s, the mandate required that 4% of all vehicles sold in the state by 2003 fall into the category of zero emission vehicles. Other states, including New York, Vermont, and Massachusetts, had adopted similar legislation. In California and elsewhere, extensions had been necessary to provide automobile manufacturers with more time to develop automobiles that could compete in price and reliability against vehicles based on internal combustion engines. Industry analysts suggested that gas-electric hybrids such as the Toyota Prius and the Honda Insight were an interim alternative until further improvements in battery technology made electric automobiles more practical to produce. Missed deadlines nevertheless stirred concern among hardcore environmentalists, who increased their pressure on lawmakers to pass legislation expediting development of nonpolluting alternatives.

41 As of early 2001, light EVs in most states and countries did not generally require an operating license, insurance, or registration. New legislation was on the docket in many states to provide reclassification of EVs to broaden their acceptance in the marketplace and to remove potential legal barriers to widespread acceptance. Pressure on lawmakers in California, for example, resulted in the adoption of legislation in 2000 legalizing roadway usage of electric scooters that traveled at top speeds of up to 15 mph. Prior to January 1, 2000, these vehicles had not been permitted on California roads.

42 A 2000 study by the National Renewable Energy Laboratory noted that 45 million automobiles in the United States drove less than 20 miles per day, within the range of many EVs then on the market. Investments in new short-range transportation infrastructure at federal, state, and local levels began emerging as a means to provide equal access for alternatives to the automobile and to provide open space for recreational purposes. Programs such as Rails-to-Trails were initiated to convert unused railway right-of-ways to bicycle trails. As of September 2000, over 11,000 miles of old railways in the U.S. had been converted for bicycle usage. Similar projects to improve access and safety for short-range transportation vehicles included bike lanes and limited access areas for gas-powered vehicles in urban centers. Continued investment in these programs was expected to play a major role in the market acceptance for EVs.

ZAP'S CHALLENGES

43 At the same time that ZAP was transferring its manufacturing overseas, it was attempting to reposition itself as "an overall provider of premier EV products with a primary focus on aggressive sales activity." In the U.S. market, ZAP's primary market for electric bicycle and electric scooter sales, a combined estimated total of 120,000 units had been sold in 2000, with scooter sales leading bicycle sales by a ratio of approximately 7:1. This breakdown implied that electric scooter sales had reached approximately 105,000 units and electric bicycle sales approximately 15,000 units for the year. In the future, more sizeable markets for EV products were expected to emerge abroad.

44 In early 2001, widespread advertising by competitors for a new electric scooter priced at under $200 had resulted in increased sales in mass-market channels. These channels included Target, Toys "R" Us, and other "big box" chain stores. Competitors had created a new price point that ZAP was then forced to meet by developing a low-end version of the Zappy, called the Skootr-X.

45 In light of these trends, Starr called a meeting of his product launch team in May 2001 to develop a long-range product strategy. Starr led the product-launch team, which included Hutchins, Cronk, Rocklewitz, Schotze, and Chaillou. The team was charged with creating a forecast of the expected demand for scooters and electric bicycles, ZAP's two best-selling product lines. Starr argued that forecasting the sales of the Zappy electric scooter and ZAP PowerBike had to be made within the context of similar recreational products, such as the bicycle. Other team members felt strongly that sales forecasts could only be obtained after careful study of market demographics and environmental variables to arrive at a projected adoption rate that could be used to project future sales.

46 The team also debated ZAP's generic strategy to stake out a position in an industry that was still in its infancy. Starr made the case for the benefits of a "market penetration strategy," meaning higher volume sales at lower prices. Lower pricing had the potential of increasing demand and limiting future opportunity for lower priced competitors that were already driving down the average selling price for electrically powered scooters and bicycles. Other team members argued for a "skimming strategy," that is, restricting demand by maintaining a high price. Higher pricing might provide for enhanced profit margins and allow ZAP's products, which had become benchmarks of quality and performance, to maintain a position of superiority in the industry. Regardless of which approach the ZAP team ultimately chose, the probable reactions of competitors were expected to have a major impact on the success or failure of ZAP's long-range strategy.

This case study was prepared by Armand Gilinsky, Jr., Associate Professor of Business at Sonoma State University, and Robert Ditizio, MBA student, as a basis for class discussion rather than to illustrate either effective or ineffective handling of an administrative situation. This case was originally presented at the 2001 meeting of the North American Case Research Association in Memphis Tenn.
Bicycle Retailer and Industry News website, www.bicycleretailer.com/public_pages/pubstats.html.
Donner Corporation International, Analyst Report on Zapworld.com, September 5, 2000, www.donnercorp.com.
Donner Corporation International, Analyst Report on Zapworld.com, June 12, 2000, www.donnercorp.com.
Ed Benjamin, Electric Bicycle Market Information Report.
Ed Benjamin, *Is There an Electric Bike in Your Future?*, prepared for the Earth Options Institute.
Haberman, Rita, Redchip.com website, *Wheels of Fortune or Passing Fad?* www.redchip.com. August 25, 2000.
www.electric-bikes.com.
International Bicycle Fund website, www.ibike.org/statistics.htm.
National Bike Dealers Association website, 2000 NBDA Statpak, www.nbda.com/statpak.htm.
Personal Communication with Peter Harrop.
Personal Communication with Ed Benjamin.
Peter Harrop, "EV Markets, Players, Forecasts," www.footnoteanalysis.com.
Union Atlantic Corporation L.C., Research report on Zapworld.com, November 13, 2000.
Zapworld.com press release, *ZAP Previews Italian Electric Scooter to Motorcycle Industry at Indianapolis Dealer Expo,* www.zapworld.com, February 16, 2001.
Zapworld.com press release, *ZAP CEO Gary Starr Predicts $5 Billion Industry for Light Electric Transportation by 2005,* www.zapworld.com, October 18, 2000.
Zapworld website, www.zapworld.com.
Zapworld.com 1996–2000 10-KSB filings.

Case 41

Battle in the Air: Intrinsic and China's Wireless Industry

> Wu Jun, a Shanghai native, exemplifies the best Chinese entrepreneurs in his accomplishments and his ambitions . . . his company, Intrinsic Technology Ltd., a wireless technology company, is just over a year old and already, at least conceptually, he has outgrown the Chinese market.
>
> *The Asian Wall Street Journal*

1 The last decade of the 20th century witnessed the upsurge of two revolutionary innovations. The first of these technologies was the Internet, which has completely altered information dissemination, commerce and virtually every other facet of society. The other innovation, wireless communication, was the key that unlocked the full potential of the Internet. These twin technologies have converged to create an exciting new consumption spotlight—wireless Internet—which has allowed people to view messages, send and receive e-mails, order tickets and buy or sell stocks through their mobile handset.

2 According to the statistics of the Ministry of Information Industry (MII), by the end of 2000, China had more than 60 million mobile phone users, thus making it the second largest mobile telecommunication market in the world. Given the fact that this figure was continuing to expand at a rate of three million users per month, various domestic and overseas players scrambled to capture this opportunity to expand their business by showcasing new technologies. Shanghai-based Intrinsic Technology Ltd., founded in 1999, became an early player in China's budding wireless Internet industry with its effort to develop software and Web services specifically for mobile phone users. However, with the approach of the entry into the World Trade Organization (WTO), the market in China was full of uncertainty and volatility. Intrinsic needed to adjust its strategy continually to take full advantage of the market opportunity.

UNIQUE MARKET STRUCTURE AND UNCERTAINTY IN CHINA

3 In the late 1970s, China adopted a policy of "reform and opening up." Since then, China's economy grew at an average rate of close to 9% and the number of foreign firms doing business in or with China since the early 1970s grew exponentially. According to

IVEY

Richard Ivey School of Business
The University of Western Ontario

Professor Wei Lu, Shen Zhang and Wu Wanlin prepared this case solely to provide material for class discussion. The authors do not intend to illustrate either effective or ineffective handling of a managerial situation. The authors may have disguised certain names and other identifying information to protect confidentiality. Ivey Management Services prohibits any form of reproduction, storage or transmittal without its written permission. This material is not covered under authorization from CanCopy or any reproduction rights organization. To order copies or request permission to reproduce materials, contact Ivey Publishing, Ivey Management Services, c/o Richard Ivey School of Business, The University of Western Ontario, London, Ontario, Canada, N6A 3K7; phone (519) 661-3208; fax (519) 661-3882, e-mail cases@ivey.uwo.ca. Copyright © 2001, Ivey Management Services. Version: (A) 2001-09-05. *One-time permission to reproduce granted by Ivey Management Services on March 1, 2002.*

EXHIBIT 1
Sector Contribution to Gross Domestic Product in China and Most Advanced Countries

Source: National Accounts of OECD Countries, OECD, *China National Statistics Bureau,* Paris, 2000.

	Agriculture %		Industry %		Services %	
	1988	1998	1988	1998	1988	1998
United States	1.8	1.7	29.7	26.1	68.4	72.2
France	3.8	3.2	30.7	26.1	65.5	70.8
United Kingdom	2.0	1.3	36.4	28.8	61.7	69.9
Germany	1.5	1.3	37.9	32.1	60.7	66.6
Japan	2.7	1.7	40.7	37.2	56.6	61.1
China	25.7	18.4	44.1	48.7	30.2	32.9

Chinese government statistics, foreign firms (including Hong Kong, Macao, and Taiwan) have invested about US$200 billion in China—90% of it between 1990 and 2000. But China continued to be only a medium-sized market with vast potential. It was still striding from agro-economy toward industrialization.

4   The nascent services sector was still emerging in China. Advertising, retailing, computer services were growing faster than China's healthy GDP. The Internet and the telecommunication industry were growing even faster, at an explosive annual rate of 50%. And as its entry to the WTO approached, China started to open service sectors to foreign providers. But not surprisingly, many obstacles still existed as China's economy continued its evolution from a centrally controlled command economy to a market economy.

5   Over-regulation, opaque and inconsistent rules and outright protectionism were still major obstacles in many sectors, including the insurance, Internet, financial and telecommunication sectors. Prohibitions to foreign firms distributing foreign-made consumer products stymied development in this sector. However, China would, between 2000 and 2010, be forced by its membership in the WTO to bring its commercial law and trading system closer to conformity with world standards.

WTO TO CHINA: OPPORTUNITY OR CHALLENGE?

6   China's selection for entry into the WTO was yet another acknowledgment that, with every passing day, this once-sheltered nation was becoming more integrated into the world economy. According to the bilateral agreement with United States, Europe and other WTO members, China was prepared to take important concessions in traditional merchandise trade in order to gain entry into the WTO. But as was often the case, China and the Western world were not quite on the same wavelength. Western countries such as the United States were interested in service trade, where they had an advantage, as well as commodity trade, where China had a cost advantage. This discrepancy derived partly from the fact that in the advanced economies, services made up over 60% of the GDP, whereas in China, the corresponding percentage was around 30% (see Exhibit 1).

7   Indeed, the potential effects of WTO membership on China were far from being clear. Although China's markets would be more open to multinationals, whether and how they could defeat state-owned companies and nimble mid-size firms remained an open question. Some industries, such as banking and insurance, would be altered fundamentally. Yet others, such as consumer products and electronics, were already highly competitive and open to global competition and thus would see little real change (see Exhibit 2).

EXHIBIT 2
Changes for China's Industry upon Entry to WTO

Source: United States–China Business Council.

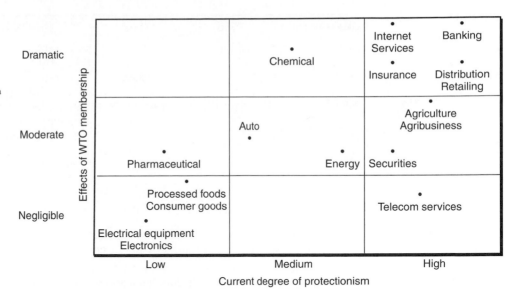

DEVELOPMENT OF TELECOM AND INTERNET INDUSTRY

8   In recent years, inexpensive and ubiquitous telecommunication through voice, data and image communication have changed the world. The ease of accessing information and people anywhere at anytime on the globe has had a major impact on society, business and finance. These changes and impacts have continued to increase and expand, due to constant and rapid advances in telecommunication technology.

9   Two major trends have occurred in telecommunications technology. The first trend has been the incredible increase in the processing power of digital computers, namely, dramatic decreases in physical size, along with equally dramatic increases in complexity, speed and capacity. The second trend has been the explosive growth in transmission capacity through the widespread use of fiber optics across continents and under oceans. These two trends have had, and will continue to have, impressive long-term consequences for telecommunication in the world.

Technology Progress in the Mobile Telecommunication Industry

10   Three generations of mobile phones have emerged so far, each successive generation more reliable and flexible than the last:

- Analog cellular could be easily used to make voice calls, typically only within one country.

- Digital mobile phone systems added fax, data and messaging capabilities as well as voice telephone service in many countries.

- Multimedia services added high-speed data transfer to mobile devices, allowing new video, audio and other applications through mobile phones—allowing music, television and the Internet to be accessed through a mobile terminal.

11   With each new generation of technology, the services that can be deployed on them have become more and more wide-ranging and truly limited only by imagination.

EXHIBIT 3
The Evolution
of Mobile
Communication
Technology

Source: Intrinsic Technology.

Generation	Type	Time	Description
First	Analog	1980s	Voice centric, multiple standards (NMT, TACS, etc.)
Second	Digital	1990s	Voice centric, multiple standards (GSM, CDMA, TDMA)
2.5	Higher Rate Data	Late 1990s	Introduction of new higher-speed data services to bridge the gap between the second and third generation, including services such as General Packet Radio Service (GPRS) and Enhanced Data Rates for Global Evolution (EDGE)
Third	Digital Multimedia	2000s	Voice and data centric, single standard with multiple modes

12 The third generation of mobile communications systems would soon be implemented. Following on the heels of analog and digital technology, the third generation will be digital mobile multimedia offering broadband mobile communications with voice, video, graphics, audio and other information. This transition is shown in Exhibit 3.

Internet Industry

13 The Internet has changed greatly since the 1970s when it came into existence. It was conceived in the era of time-sharing, but has survived into the era of personal computers, client-server and peer-to-peer computing, and the network computer. It was designed before local area networks (LANs) existed, but has accommodated new network technology, as well as the more recent ATM and frame-switched services. It was envisioned as supporting a range of functions from file sharing and remote login to resource sharing and collaboration, and has spawned electronic mail and, more recently, the World Wide Web. But most important, it started as the creation of a small band of dedicated researchers, and has grown to be a commercial success, spawning billions of dollars of annual investment.

Background of Wireless Internet Industry

14 The days when mobile phones were "just phones" were quickly coming to an end. People in the industry were looking towards closer integration with the Internet, which was expected to bring personalized applications such as games, chat and news as the next big things.

15 Since 1999, industry participants, such as mobile operators, phone manufacturers, and enablers (i.e., application software developers, systems integrators and content aggregators), all declared that WAP-based (Wireless Application Protocol, see Exhibit 4) m-commerce (mobile commerce) would be their newest revenue source. All mobile phones, produced by infrastructure providers/handset manufacturers like Ericsson and Siemens would be equipped with a WAP browser. It was expected that by the end of 2002, consumers would have access to over 100 million mobile phones possessing wireless Internet capabilities (see Exhibit 5). Additionally, the number of WAP-capable mobile phones used to access the Internet worldwide is expected to exceed one billion by 2003, according to Internet Data Corporation (IDC). Motorola even predicted that wireless Net use would overtake fixed-line access by 2005.

EXHIBIT 4
What Is WAP?

Source: Intrinsic Technology.

WAP is a worldwide standard for providing Internet communications and advanced telephony services on digital mobile phones, pagers, personal digital assistants, and other wireless terminals.

It has been developed by the WAP forum with the objective of establishing a defined common data interface, now known as the Wireless Application Protocol (WAP), for the delivery of Internet content on mobile terminals and other wireless devices across different network standards.

The WAP architecture is essentially based on a set of languages and specifications that enable mobile terminals to load and display information. It comprises three key components: the WAP client premise equipment (CPE), the WAP gateway, and the WAP Web server. The CPE refers mainly to handsets or other wireless access devices. The WAP gateway acts as the interface between the CPE and the WAP Web server. The WAP Web server stores the actual content at its site and performs the same function as the conventional Web server.

EXHIBIT 5
Predicted Mobile Internet User Growth

Source: Mobile Internet Applications Primer, UBS Warburg.

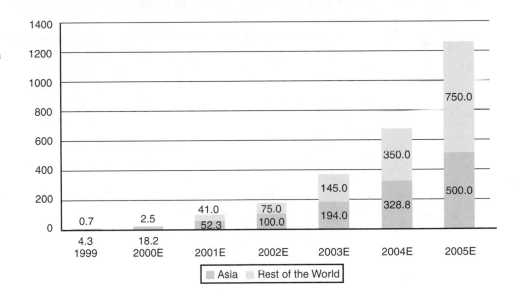

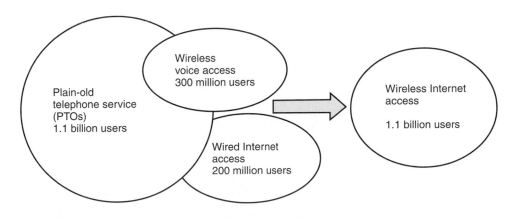

16   As a wide-ranging set of WAP-based technical and commercial developments are deployed over the next several years, mobile Internet user momentum is expected to build rapidly, driving wireless data usage to ubiquity.

INTRINSIC: BATTLE IN CHINA'S WIRELESS INTERNET INDUSTRY

China's Wireless Communication Industry

17   The number of mobile phone subscribers in China has grown to over 65 million users, up 35 million from the 1999 year-end figure. Every day about 100,000 new mobile customers sign up for service. China's average annual growth rate of mobile telephony was 135% in the 1991 to 2000 period (see Exhibit 6).

18   China has rapidly become the second largest mobile telecommunication network in the world after the United States. Experts expect it to move into first place and become the largest mobile telephone market in the near future. China mobile telephone growth has offset, to a large extent, the impact of the Asian economic crisis on mobile equipment vendors.

19   Despite the large absolute numbers of mobile phone subscribers, nationwide cellular penetration remained low at about 5%. Opportunities for cellular equipment vendors were abundant and newspapers reported almost daily on new telecommunications contracts. The main equipment purchasers for cellular infrastructure were China Mobile Communications Corporation (CMCC) and China United Telecommunications Corporation (China Unicom). For handsets, the key end-users included businesspeople and young individuals in their 20s and 30s.

20   Leading players in the international market included Motorola of the United States, Ericsson of Sweden, Nokia of Finland, and Siemens of Germany. Each of these companies set up either wholly owned factories or joint ventures with local Chinese partners to manufacture handsets, mobile exchanges and base station equipment. Others have sold their handsets and base station equipment in the Chinese market through agents and distributors. About 75% of cellular equipment was imported and local production, outside of joint ventures, has been limited.

21   China's rapid expansion of the cellular phone network has mainly been due to its underdeveloped fixed line infrastructure, inadequate service and a high telephone price. The

EXHIBIT 6
Mobile Telephone Subscribers in China

Source: Ministry of Information Industry of China.

Year	Users Added	Total	Increase (%)
1988	3,000	3,000	N/A
1989	6,800	9,800	227
1990	8,200	18,000	84
1991	29,500	47,500	164
1992	129,500	177,000	259
1993	461,000	638,000	260
1994	930,000	1,600,000	146
1995	2,100,000	3,000,000	132
1996	3,300,000	6,800,000	90
1997	6,400,000	13,200,000	93
1998	8,000,000	21,200,000	60
1999	8,800,000	30,000,000	41
2000	35,000,000	65,000,000	117

latter was created by China having a monopoly operator, China Telecom, owned by the former Ministry of Posts and Telecommunications (MPT). Even China's competitor, China Unicom, was state-mandated and placed under the former Ministry of Electronic Industry (MEI). The two ministries were combined to form Ministry of Information Industry (MII) in 1998. Aggressive foreign cellular sales and an initial lack of overly restrictive Chinese government regulations assisted in the cellular expansion.

22 However, Chinese authorities increasingly emphasized mobile phone technology transfer and production localization and are currently reviewing telecom investment methods used by Unicom with an eye to limiting foreign equity influence in telecom projects. The centralization of telecommunications regulatory power into MII in March 2000 may actually result in raising the boom for access to China's cellular phone market.

China: Wireless Data in the Air

23 Two main factors have driven the growth of the wireless Internet in China: a mobile infrastructure that was more developed than its fixed-line counterpart, and the greater affordability of mobile telephones as compared with personal computers (PCs).

24 China's fixed-line Internet users amounted to 22.5 million by the end of 2000 (see Exhibit 7), a figure lagging far behind that of mobile phone users. The favorable demographics of Chinese mobile-phone users—indicating that they were much more attractive commercial prospects than typical fixed-line Internet users—would also play an important role in driving the growth of wireless Internet services. As many as 92% of mobile-phone subscribers have been documented as being upwards of 25 years old, compared with 58% of fixed-line Internet users (see Exhibit 8). Mobile-phone subscribers were also

EXHIBIT 7
Fixed-Line Internet Users in China

Source: China Internet Network Information Center (CNNIC).

Report Date	1997–10	1998–07	1999–01	1999–07	2000–01	2000–07	2001–01
Fixed-line Internet users (million)	0.62	1.18	2.1	4	8.9	16.9	22.5

EXHIBIT 8
Mobile Users Have More Buying Power

Source: China Internet Network Information Center (CNNIC).

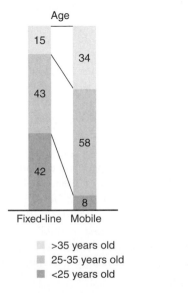
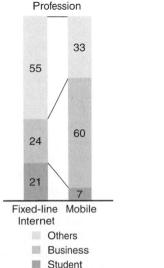
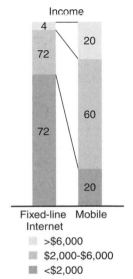

shown to have much greater earning power: 80% made more than US$2,000 a year, compared with only 28% of fixed-line Internet users.

25   Moreover, half of the fixed-line users were college students with family incomes under Yuan2,000 (US$241) a month. Most did not even have their own computers, using PCs at school instead. Mobile phones, by contrast, were shown to be a link to China's richest consumers.

26   With the potential opportunity being so large, competition to dominate the wireless Internet market was intensifying. Chinese operators, besides upgrading their networks, were orchestrating a variety of WAP trials with equipment manufacturers in China's major provinces. On May 17, 2000, China Mobile declared that most cities in China already had the ability to utilize the Wireless Internet using WAP technologies. The services—featuring news, travel information and reservations, stock quotations, e-mail, and entertainment—resembled those being introduced in markets outside China.

27   But building the systems necessary to run wireless Internet applications was a formidable technical task, one that could create a bonanza for third-party providers. Intrinsic, a Shanghai-based wireless software developer, aimed to dominate that niche in China.

Intrinsic Technology Ltd. (Intrinsic)

28   Intrinsic was a Shanghai-based wireless Internet software provider, founded by industry veteran Wu Jun. Before returning to China, Wu had been the instrumental force in building Sendit, a Stockholm-based leader in wireless data and Internet technology that was eventually acquired and renamed the Microsoft Mobile Internet Division. As Sendit and Microsoft, Wu served as chief designer of the company's Internet Circuit Service Application (ICSA) system which has been deployed by two cellular operators throughout the world. He was also a principal architect of Sendit's Protocol for Internet Circuit Entity (SPICE) protocol, one of the competing standards that were a precursor to WAP.

29   Viewing the intense penetration rate of mobile phones in China, Wu foresaw a burgeoning marketing opportunity in China. He then founded Intrinsic alongside Joseph Lee, a technology specialist who had founded and ran his own consultancy company in London called Palmtree Assoc., Derek Sulger, who had worked at Goldman Sachs for seven years; and Patrick Benzie, who had served previously at Nomura and D.E. Shaw.

30   Wu believed that the days when mobile phones were "just phones" were quickly coming to an end. People in the industry were looking towards closer integration with the Internet, which was expected to bring personalized applications such as games, chat and news into the foreground. Under this assumption, Intrinsic aimed to develop carrier-class mobile platform facilitating advanced messaging functionality ranging from Instant message, e-mail alerts, e-mail to short message service (SMS), SMS to e-mail to entertainment services (dating services, electronic pets, and icon downloads, etc.), mobile commerce, and information distribution.

31   Eyeing the huge market in China, Intrinsic aimed to make a "leap of faith" and develop WAP services before the demand actually existed. The first step was to get people comfortable with mobile (phone) e-mail, messaging systems and other functions. Then Intrinsic could move to e-commerce, through which people's cell phones would become a virtual wallet. "You are potentially talking about 50 million people walking around with this device in their pocket—and it's always turned on," said Derek Sulger, CFO of Intrinsic.

32   Most Chinese observers saw China's wireless Internet market potential as nothing less than fabulous. Some estimates even put the number of WAP users in China at one million by the end of 2000. Intrinsic was not so optimistic, but expected the country would have at least one million WAP-enabled phones in use by that time. Intrinsic hoped to play a major role on the crest of that wave.

33   In March 2000, Intrinsic, together with its newly established WAP portal Linktone, began running trials with several networks and found the response to be more enthusiastic than expected. At its office in Shanghai, Intrinsic received so many calls from WAP phone owners on how to configure their phones that the company had to set up a separate customer help line. Mobile phone makers also benefited from this enthusiasm, with the sales of Nokia's WAP-enabled 7110 model at up to 100,000 units in a single month.

Linktone

34   To capture the large market of mobile consumers, Intrinsic funded and launched a company called Linktone to operate a wireless portal. Linktone was a consumer-targeted mobile information service that allowed Intrinsic to market its products. Linktone worked on both mobile devices and traditional PCs, which demonstrated the new paradigm of the anytime, anyplace Internet (www.linktone.com, wap.linktone.com). Linktone selectively drew its architecture and applications from Intrinsic Technology's product bank. The portal's aim was to attract other content providers, using its technology as a carrot. Intrinsic utilized Linktone to showcase its newly developed products. But Intrinsic did not want to be labeled a "dot.com." According to Derek Sulger, Intrinsic was "more telecom focused than Internet focused." Success in the wireless Internet world required both a deep understanding of mobile phone networks and close connections with mobile operators. The average dot.com company was neither of these things.

35   Acting as a middleman for the anticipated e-commerce transactions provided a revenue stream for Linktone. Selling or licensing those products—mainly wireless applications—would be another revenue stream. Linktone estimated that it would hit the break-even point when there were about 500,000 users signed up for its services.

Market Structure

36   In June 1997, the WAP forum was founded through an alliance forged by Motorola, Nokia, Ericsson and Phone.com. As of September 2000, more than 500 companies had joined this organization. Members included terminal and infrastructure manufacturers, operators/carriers/service providers, software houses, content providers, and service/application providers. Many of these members built and marketed their own portals.

37   **Manufacturers.** Most mobile phone manufacturers regarded the WAP phone as a totally new product line that would provide a golden opportunity to gain market share. They spent large amounts of research and development (R&D) dollars on the development and implementation of mobile data solutions. For instance, Motorola declared that until 2002, all of its m-phones would be equipped with wireless browsers. Trying to become the standard of the wireless Internet industry in China, the company launched an information campaign called "Wireless net, Wireless life." Other manufacturers, including Nokia, Ericsson, and Siemens, poured money and marketing efforts into this new field. Besides new product lines, most of them developed applications by partnering with application providers. Examples of these include the Nokia-Sohu alliance and, the Siemens-Linktone alliance.

38   **Operators.** One of the key differences between e-commerce and m-commerce was the presence of the mobile operator between the end-user and content/service provider. Only partners of the operator could link to its portal and bill through the operator. Therefore, the coming wireless Internet would provide operators with a new revenue stream.

39   Upon China's entrance into the WTO, traditional Chinese operators would be forced to compete with highly commercial foreign telecom giants. Industry leaders such as CMCC were seeking innovative solutions to this problem to maintain a commensurate share of the market. In order to differentiate themselves and improve their image to the consumer, operators had chosen to build their own portals with support from wireless solution and application providers such as Intrinsic.

40　　**Traditional ICPs.** After the declaration by CMCC that China would be allowed to have its own WAP portals, key Internet Content Provider (ICP) players like Sina.com and Sohu.com announced that they would expand their business scope by stepping into the wireless Internet space. Many of them had already developed their WAP portals. However, as wireless applications involved many new, complex mark-up languages and technologies, ICPs had a difficult time assimilating into the new market.

41　　**WAP Portals.** Some of the most successful applications being developed for wireless Internet actually came from niche startups that had a unique understanding of particular consumer or industry segments. Already, more than 100 companies asserted that they were wireless Internet businesses. However, most of these companies were located in smaller Chinese cities and therefore had a difficult time gaining market share, influence, and expertise. In Beijing and Shanghai, however, China's two largest cities, wap.linktone.com and wap.byair.com solidified their leadership in their own particular wireless markets.

42　　**wap.byair.com.** Founded in Santa Clara, California, in 1994, Byair services had been in operation since 1997. Byair's comprehensive range of wireless services delivered instant Internet access to searches, shopping services, banking, trading, as well as key location sensitive applications such as store locators. The portal viewed stock trading as a lucrative area with large market potential and was collaborating with China Unicom in this area. They joined efforts to establish a new wapsite called wap.yestock.com. The wapsite provided information and instruction about stock trading. In late 2000, the supporting website side of the wap.yestock.com wireless portal merged with Chinese Legend Computer Co. Ltd. As a Beijing-based portal, it started expanding its business in more than 50 cities.

43　　**Linktone.** With a strong technical background and tremendous experience in the mobile industry, Linktone expanded its successful operation in Shanghai and aimed to be a market leader in both China and (eventually) Europe.

Content Selection

44　In terms of content development, Linktone chose to emphasize entertainment applications. As key competitors dedicated many resources to developing stock-trading capabilities, they were forced to deal with the government-run stock market. Linktone, however, did not focus entirely on stocks, and therefore avoided this problem. The company believed that entertainment-related services such as games and music would be some of the most widely used data applications of the mobile phone.

45　In Japan, NTT DoCoMo had become a role model for the rest of the wireless industry through its successful operating portal, called I-Mode. In 2000, 50% of I-mode's data being used was entertainment-related, with paid ringing tone downloads being the most popular of I-mode services (300 Japanese yen for 10 downloads per month). While lack of speed and poor graphics limited the popularity of sophisticated WAP-based games, both device and network capabilities were expected to improve significantly. However, when the already savvy younger generation increased its phone usage, entertainment applications would still be used.

46　Using I-mode as a successful business model, Linktone decided to focus its services on cutting-edge mobile-oriented applications, particularly messaging and entertainment. Its content was offered in four distinct modules including messaging, entertainment, m-commerce, and information platforms.

Collaboration with Different Participants

47 **Operators.** In the early growth stages of the wireless Internet industry, Intrinsic provided Chinese operators with wireless applications and consulting services. This helped to build long-lasting partnerships with these extremely important clients and improved future revenue opportunities. Intrinsic assisted in constructing portals for China Mobile Communication Corporation (CMCC), Zhe Jiang Mobile Communication Corporation (ZMCC), Guang Dong Mobile Communication Corporation (GMCC) and Shen Zhen Mobile Communication Corporation (SMCC).

48 Aside from the possibility of revenue sharing with operators, Intrinsic's applications allowed consumers to familiarize and associate their wireless experience with Intrinsic's unique, personalized services. As Linktone used this same style, consumers readily identified and adopted the Linktone portal.

49 In addition, Intrinsic began to make some inroads into Europe. It exported its technology to European service providers and corporations and provided portal players with SMS services, technology solutions and consulting.

50 **Manufacturers.** From early 2000, top mobile vendors like Motorola, Nokia, Ericsson, and Siemens decided the development of the wireless Internet was their top priority. Having established strategic partnerships with Ericsson and Siemens, Intrinsic was now poised to forge other essential alliances with content providers, applications service providers, and infrastructure providers throughout China and Asia. By raising Intrinsic's corporate profile and, similarly, the profile of the consumer-driven Linktone through mediums such as advertising, media coverage and aggressive Linktone "roadshows" in key Chinese cities, Intrinsic and Linktone hoped to spread the good word regarding their products and expertise, and in turn establish new, exciting partnerships.

51 **Alliance with ICPs.** Keeping an eye on the developing e-commerce market, Linktone cooperated with ICPs by traditional means such as exchanging banners, icons, or by advertisement. In addition, Linktone developed the Linktone Alliance, a platform for several traditional Chinese ICPs including Dang Dang, Ctrip, China Byte, Stock2000 and Eachnet. This allowed people to acquire a wide variety of products and services, such as books, mobile phones, traveling info, online booking and stock services.

Current Market Situation

52 At the end of 2000, in China, Internet user penetration was only 1.7% of its total population. Obviously, the true potential for Internet penetration had yet to be realized.

53 With the rise of Wireless Application Protocol (WAP), consumers finally realized that wireless devices were the way to get connected to the Internet. However, the bandwidth and technological constraints of the existing GSM/RDMA network infrastructure hampered the quick growth of WAP services. For instance, consumers were frustrated by low data downloading speed. Over time, this was expected to change as new wireless standards were introduced, bringing faster speeds and more robust data outputs.

54 The limited availability of data applications had been another major factor holding up widespread wireless data adoption. WAP had not lived up to user expectations because WAP services and available content had proven to be scant and uninspiring.

55 Users would switch to WAP technology when there was richer content and higher transmission speeds. However, application developers had not yet devoted their full resources towards creating top-notch applications since the user base was not large enough. Thus, as transmission speeds increased, so would the number of innovative and technologically advanced applications, and, logically, users.

A Strategic Turning Point

56 Initially, Intrinsic focused on the development of WAP for its technology in China with little success. China's consumers showed little interest in using their mobile phones for anything other than making voice calls. No more than about 300,000 WAP-enabled phones had been sold in China since the devices were put on the market in March 2000. Although China Mobile, the nation's dominant mobile-phone operator, started charging for the service, most experts doubted that the number of consumers who had actually used a WAP phone to connect to the Internet exceeded 50,000.

57 Recognizing that revenue from WAP user take-up would be difficult, Linktone did not expect a significant market expansion in WAP services in the short term. But strategies for future wireless revenues needed to be implemented. China Mobile, the most powerful operator in China, was facing the restructuring of its economic environment in which it was essential to employ effective solutions to withstand competition from budding domestic mobile operators such as China Unicom and from potential international competitors upon China's entrance into WTO.

SMS

58 SMS (Short Messaging Service) was originally intended as a simple information tool built on mobile operating platforms to take advantage of unused bandwidth. It had become an important form of data transmission through which information could be "pushed" to users. This revolutionized the wireless industry and made mobile commerce possible by providing complete access to mobile users. The SMS "push" functionality had been instrumental in the success of Japan's wildly popular NTT DoCoMo i-mode service. In China, mobile operators, until the end of 2000, only made SMS available to its users, and the response has been very enthusiastic. Mobile phone users could send and receive Chinese language SMS messages by inputting characters from their keypad.

59 SMS changed and simplified the concept of wireless services for many current and potential industry participants. No longer did the success of the wireless industry hinge upon WAP. SMS had shown that wireless services could exist in many forms and that its appeal was very different from that of the Internet. Compared to conventional information media, SMS services were more personalized. People could send and/or choose to receive information through different channels according to their own needs. The target audience was easier to identify because every new mobile phone user was included automatically in the database.

60 Unlike the poorly offered and poorly operated WAP service, short messaging services had become a proven, global phenomenon. Considering the massive growth of Chinese mobile phone users and people's keen need for information, Linktone believed that SMS could work as a transitionary technology and a testing ground for the evolution of wireless data in China. From a business standpoint, China's 65 million mobile handset users provided Linktone with a large customer base to access its m-commerce platform.

61 A strong relationship forged with China Mobile and its provincial subsidiaries provided Linktone with instant brand recognition as the number 1 featured site on CMCC's WAP portal. This strategic collaboration between Linktone and CMCC reflected a new revenue-building model for wireless Internet companies in China, and the model had many facets. One such effect is advertising revenue. Users of CMCC's WAP portal would encounter a highly targeted advertising campaign that would promote brand icons and consumer products. China Mobile also considered SMS an important strategic aspect of its revenue model, charging a small per message fee and also gathering data with the intention of providing a user database service and a new revenue stream.

62   The concept of SMS (as the new media versus conventional media such as the newspaper, TV and, to a certain extent, the Internet) could be seen through the business opportunities that stem from it.

63   Intrinsic expected three revenue models to dominate an SMS platform in the future:

- With cooperation between CMCC and Linktone, Linktone could realize revenue by charging information fees from consumers.

- As a new media, SMS could provide different companies with another communication channel to end-users. Advertisement through SMS could be a new profitable medium to access a customer-base and Linktone could charge for these ads.

- As an information platform, Linktone could also charge fees from business organizations by issuing information from a proprietary database.

64   All of this way very exciting to Linktone, who had become an important part of the business model along with WAP service.

65   For example, the Sydney Olympic games provided Linktone with a great opportunity. Linktone decided the popularity and excitement of the Olympic games was the ideal showcase to launch its SMS plan.

66   On August 31, 2000, China Mobile and Linktone announced their plans to deliver minute-by-minute Olympic updates to mobile phone users during the Sydney games, using SMS. China Mobile's 50 million subscribers would be allowed to receive live, personalized wireless updates during the world's top sporting event. They would be able to choose from a list of Linktone SMS channels that include Olympic history, event updates, medal rankings, daily schedules, Chinese-athlete updates and trivia sweepstakes.

67   At Linktone, the marketing team developed a range of promotional materials designed to attract the attention of and excite mobile users. These marketing materials needed: (1) Olympic sign-up leaflets to be distributed through different channels, like phone bills, from China Mobile and m-phone retail stores; (2) Collaborative promotional advertising with partners, such as operators and retail channels, to be spread out in various major Chinese cities; (3) Promotional stimuli to consumers, such as the attractive gold medal sweepstakes.

68   Through the above efforts, Linktone believed that mobile-phone users would gradually learn about the new, personalized wireless media. Furthermore, Linktone brand awareness should increase significantly as a result.

69   SMS would be provided free of charge in many regions to promote the Linktone Olympic Update project and generate interest in SMS. But as a key revenue stream, Linktone would need further solutions to retain mobile-phone users, as will Linktone's regular SMS customers.

Intrinsic's Strategic Transition

70   As it entered into the second year since the 2000 announcement of WAP trial services by CMCC, WAP service continued to be a hot topic. New WAP sites were continually being established and new WAP specifications were continually being developed. The mobile Internet was still in the infant stage of its growth process, while Intrinsic and Linktone were preparing and strategizing to maintain industry leadership throughout the wireless evolution.

71   Recognizing that a lack of favorable application service had become a bottleneck to explosive development of WAP service in China, Intrinsic decided to focus on licensing its enabling technology to mobile Web content providers. According to Intrinsic, software was essential for building a robust service, and was something Intrinsic expected to continue development over the next 12 to 18 months while the infrastructure was groomed for greater wireless Internet use.

72　　In October 2000, Intrinsic would pitch iDAP.CN[1] applications, to China Mobile, hoping to become a "preferred partner" of the nation's dominant mobile communications company. As of early 2001, Intrinsic landed Shanghai Mobile and Tianjin Mobile as clients for this system. It also deployed a system in Morocco through its fledgling European division. That sale gave evidence of the company's international ambitions, but most of its energy was still concentrated in China. Though CEO Wu Jun held a British passport, and Intrinsic was legally a wholly foreign-owned enterprise, for most interests and purposes, Intrinsic was considered to be a Chinese company: apart from being headquartered in Shanghai, it boasted 79 Chinese staff members out of a total of 84.

73　　Apart from iDAP.CN, Intrinsic planned to launch Intrinsic Data Application Protocol for Service Provider (iDAP.SP) in the coming months. This would allow wireless Internet users to preset customized applications and services without wading through unwanted page connections or links. This customization tool also incorporated a navigation functionality that would let users easily move to other Linktone services.

74　　Intrinsic felt that providing different services for different end users was critical to the success of the wireless Internet. From this point of view, iDAP.SP would be the next step in wireless personalization and wireless convenience.

75　　On the consumer side, in succession to the launch of Sydney Olympic SMS service, Linktone again partnered with China Mobile to provide "Century Blessing" SMS service at the end of 2000. With this service, companies and people could send best wishes via SMS to their relatives, friends and colleagues. About 100,000 mobile phone users applied for Linktone's service, a figure higher than its main competitors Sina, Sohu and wap168.

76　　Meanwhile, during the WAP forum in Hong Kong, Intrinsic released a comprehensive forecast and overview of China's rapidly growing wireless telecom sector. The Intrinsic Wireless Handbook for China went beyond the estimates provided by other institutions, breaking down total cellular revenues, average revenue per user, and wireless data-related revenue over the next five years (see Exhibit 9).

EXHIBIT 9
Instrinsic's Prediction for China's Mobile Internet

Source: Intrinsic Technology.

	2000	2001	2002	2003	2004	2005
Number of Cellular Subscribers (millions)	65.2	105.6	155.3	209.8	228.2	254.1
Cellular Revenues (US$ millions per year)	$22,689	$32,472	$56,728	$73,446	$79,495	$87,969
Average Revenue per User (US$ millions per month)	$30.10	$29.85	$29.75	$29.24	$29.03	$28.85
Wireless Internet Users (millions)	0.3	3.7	22.4	55.6	65.9	79.3
Wireless Internet Penetration	0.50%	3.5%	14.4%	26.5%	28.9%	31.2%
Data-Related Revenue (US$ millions per year)	$2.6	$151.3	$1,181	$2,625	$3,759	$5,844

[1] Intrinsic Data Application Platform for Cellular Network operating system.

INTRINSIC, WHERE TO GO?

77   Fireworks, dumpling, lantern . . . the 2001 Chinese lunar year was rapidly approaching. Standing on the terrace of Harbour Ring Plaza, headquarters of Intrinsic located in the downtown area of Shanghai, Wu Jun pictured the smoke of fireworks in the air. The smoke, however, was no longer limited to that from fireworks. Another intangible smoke was derived from the intensifying battle in China's wireless Internet market. What should Intrinsic's next step be to consolidate its existing technological base and customer base and enhance its reputation as the solution provider to China's wireless Internet? Wu eyed the vehicles shuttling back and forth on the street below him lost in contemplation.

Case 42

Robin Hood

1   It was in the spring of the second year of his insurrection against the High Sheriff of Nottingham that Robin Hood took a walk in Sherwood Forest. As he walked he pondered the progress of the campaign, the disposition of his forces, the Sheriff's recent moves, and the options that confronted him.

2   The revolt against the Sheriff had begun as a personal crusade. It erupted out of Robin's conflict with the Sheriff and his administration. However, alone Robin Hood could do little. He therefore sought allies, men with grievances and a deep sense of justice. Later he welcomed all who came, asking few questions and demanding only a willingness to serve. Strength, he believed, lay in numbers.

3   He spent the first year forging the group into a disciplined band, united in enmity against the Sheriff and willing to live outside the law. The band's organization was simple. Robin ruled supreme, making all important decisions. He delegated specific tasks to his lieutenants. Will Scarlett was in charge of intelligence and scouting. His main job was to shadow the Sheriff and his men, always alert to their next move. He also collected information on the travel plans of rich merchants and tax collectors. Little John kept discipline among the men and saw to it that their archery was at the high peak that their profession demanded. Scarlock took care of the finances, converting loot to cash, paying shares of the take, and finding suitable hiding places for the surplus. Finally, Much the Miller's son had the difficult task of provisioning the ever-increasing band of Merrymen.

4   The increasing size of the band was a source of satisfaction for Robin, but also a source of concern. The fame of his Merrymen was spreading, and new recruits were pouring in from every corner of England. As the band grew larger, their small bivouac became a major encampment. Between raids the men milled about, talking and playing games. Vigilance was in decline, and discipline was becoming harder to enforce. "Why," Robin reflected, "I don't know half the men I run into these days."

5   The growing band was also beginning to exceed the food capacity of the forest. Game was becoming scarce, and supplies had to be obtained from outlying villages. The cost of buying food was beginning to drain the band's financial reserves at the very moment when revenues were in decline. Travelers, especially those with the most to lose, were now giving the forest a wide berth. This was costly and inconvenient to them, but it was preferable to having all their goods confiscated.

6   Robin believed that the time had come for the Merrymen to change their policy of outright confiscation of goods to one of a fixed transit tax. His lieutenants strongly resisted this idea. They were proud of the Merrymen's famous motto: "Rob the rich and give to the poor." "The farmers and the townspeople," they argued, "are our most important allies. How can we tax them, and still hope for their help in our fight against the Sheriff?"

7   Robin wondered how long the Merrymen could keep to the ways and methods of their early days. The Sheriff was growing stronger and becoming better organized. He now had the money and the men and was beginning to harass the band, probing for its weaknesses. The tide of events was beginning to turn against the Merrymen. Robin felt that the campaign must be decisively concluded before the Sheriff had a chance to deliver a mortal blow. "But how," he wondered, "could this be done?"

8   Robin had often entertained the possibility of killing the Sheriff, but the chances for this seemed increasingly remote. Besides, killing the Sheriff might satisfy his personal thirst for revenge, but it would not improve the situation. Robin had hoped that the perpetual state of unrest, and the Sheriff's failure to collect taxes, would lead to his removal from office. Instead, the Sheriff used his political connections to obtain reinforcement. He had powerful friends at court and was well regarded by the regent, Prince John.

9   Prince John was vicious and volatile. He was consumed by his unpopularity among the people, who wanted the imprisoned King Richard back. He also lived in constant fear of the barons, who had first given him the regency but were now beginning to dispute his claim to the throne. Several of these barons had set out to collect the ransom that would release King Richard the Lionheart from his jail in Austria. Robin was invited to join the conspiracy in return for future amnesty. It was a dangerous proposition. Provincial banditry was one thing, court intrigue another. Prince John had spies everywhere, and he was known for his vindictiveness. If the conspirators' plan failed, the pursuit would be relentless, and retributions swift.

10   The sound of the supper horn startled Robin from his thoughts. There was the smell of roasting venison in the air. Nothing was resolved or settled. Robin headed for camp promising himself that he would give these problems his utmost attention after tomorrow's raid.

Prepared by Joseph Lampel, New York University. Copyright © 2001, by Joseph Lampel.

Case 43

The Kimpton Hotel & Restaurant Group

> When your strategy is deep and far reaching,
>
> then what you gain by your calculations is much,
>
> so you can win before you even fight. When your
>
> strategic thinking is shallow and nearsighted, then what you
>
> gain by your calculations is little, so you lose before
>
> you do battle. Therefore it is said that victorious warriors
>
> win first and then go to war, while defeated warriors
>
> go to war first and then seek to win.
>
> *Sun Tzu, "The Art of War"*

1   At 8:30 A.M. on June 3, 1999, Steve Marx, vice president hotels, of the Kimpton Hotel and Restaurant Group, Inc. ("KG"), left the office of Thomas La Tour, president of Kimpton. The hour-long breakfast meeting in the company's San Francisco headquarters had been bittersweet. On the previous day, Marx had accepted an "irresistible" offer from Jonathan Tisch, president of Loews Hotels, to manage its hotel operations based in New York City. Marx had wrestled with the decision, but recognized that professionally, he almost *had* to accept the offer from Loews. La Tour understood the dilemma and, with regret, accepted Marx's resignation and two-week notice. The two men anticipated a continuation of the friendship that had characterized their relationship from the beginning. The personal aspect of the decision was as difficult for Marx as the professional component had been. He and his wife and 10-year-old son loved living in the San Francisco Bay area and were not thrilled about the prospect of relocating to the New York metropolitan area.

2   Over the past six years, Marx and La Tour had built the ninth-largest hotel management company in the U.S., with Group-wide revenues per available room or RevPAR approaching $125 per night and occupancy rates an estimated 85%, placing it in the top tier of all U.S. hotel management companies. (RevPAR is a key industry benchmark that really indicates how one makes money in the hotel industry. The term RevPAR refers to the average revenue per available hotel room.) Since its formation in 1981, KG had, by 1999, grown into a $250 million hotel company with 5,308 rooms and 5,325 employees, among whom 40 staff managed its hotel division alone. In early 1998, La Tour had said publicly that he expected the growth pattern of opening three new hotel properties a year to continue "indefinitely." Whereas seed investment capital had originally come from some 200 loyal investors contributing $100,000 apiece, more recently, a partnership with the Crow family in Texas provided a $300 million development fund to acquire new hotel properties. The company was privately held.

3   At 51 and now in his 26th year in the industry, Marx had previously worked his way up at Hilton to become a manager of several hotels. He then left Hilton in the late 1980s for London to manage Trusthouse Forte's hotel properties in the United Kingdom. Just before their son was born, Marx and his wife relocated to Monterey, Calif., where he managed a Doubletree hotel for three years before being headhunted by KG in 1992.

4   Prior to his 3:00 P.M., June 3, 1999 meeting with his two senior direct reports, David Martin, director of Operations and Jeff Senior, vice president, hotel sales and marketing,

Marx had reflected upon the several key strategic issues that he thought the senior management team would need to address in the near future. Among the strategic choices that he thought would require attention were: 1) determining the feasibility of acquiring new properties in new markets in the East Coast and South; 2) evaluating the near term potential to gain additional revenue by developing and adding new services such as Internet connectivity and related products; 3) the pros and cons of developing product branding to increase market identification, using perhaps the "Hotel Monaco" as the flagship brand. Additionally, Marx would encourage the senior managers to consider how much longer Kimpton could continue to capitalize on the benefits of the rapidly closing "window" in the real estate market. Historically, Kimpton has prospered by purchasing and renovating buildings at a discount in strategic nationwide locations that matched Kimpton's niche segment. Aggressive national growth could potentially create a strong base of resources and core competencies to support an eventual long-term growth strategy of diversification and globalization. In the short-term, maybe some forms of value-added services could be added to the marketing mix to win the battle for more discriminating customers in a highly competitive marketplace. The hotel industry in general had been slow to enter the boutique niche and Kimpton currently enjoyed a substantial edge in experience in developing higher value-added services for guests. Another potential strategic choice could have the Kimpton team focus on the individual brand equity of each hotel and embrace the entry of new boutique competitors into the competitive set, since they would help grow/create the category, in essence giving the "boutique category" the credibility necessary to generate long-term profitability and growth.

5   Marx would caution Senior and Martin that any future strategy would have to be guided by founder Bill Kimpton's original formula for acquiring undervalued assets:

> We are proud of our value engineering, construction, and design. We make very few mistakes. Kimpton doesn't build hotels from the ground-up. We buy buildings and renovate them, primarily undervalued assets in downtown, urban locations. We try to outperform other hotels in our particular segment and create value for our owners.

6   Equally important, Marx would remind his executive team, is that the important strategic decisions that must be made must also uphold the company's mission of "Getting and keeping guests, keeping and developing employees." He felt personally responsible for having developed an organization and management style to attract professional managers from other hotel chains to Kimpton. Martin and Senior were part of his recruited talent and will now be expected to take increasingly more highly visible roles in determining the company's destiny after Marx's departure.

7   As the meeting began, Marx reflected upon the Kimpton Group's (KG) rapid growth and strategic positioning within the hotel industry:

> Five or six years ago we made a conscious decision to grow. Life is growth; you can't ever stay where you are. Our investors see us as the future of the industry, as we have created a category and become a dominant player in that category. We offer personal, intimate service to our guests, people who live in an increasingly impersonal world. We provide five-star service at a four-star price. We need to become the most unique 'four-diamond' hotel in each market we serve. That's our niche, and we welcome imitators because they validate what we're doing.

8   Since Marx joined the company, KG had grown from 14 hotels and restaurants in San Francisco to 23 boutique hotels and 24 upscale and popular restaurants in major cities such as San Francisco, Portland (OR), Seattle/Tacoma, Chicago, Denver, and Salt Lake City. Two new properties, Serrano Hotel and Hotel Palomar, were scheduled to be opened in San Francisco in summer 1999. A list of KG's leading hotel and restaurant properties is provided in Exhibit 1.

EXHIBIT 1
Kimpton Group
Operated Hotels
and Restaurants
as of June 1999

Source: The Kimpton Group.

	Date Opened	No. of Rooms	No. of Seats
San Francisco			
Clarion Bedford Hotel at Union Square	4/81	144	
Hotel Vintage Court/Masa's	4/83	107	100
Galleria Park Hotel/Perry's Downtown	6/84	177	133
Juliana Hotel	9/85	106	
Villa Florence Hotel/Kuleto's Italian Restaurant	5/86	180	176
Monticello Inn	10/87	91	
Puccini & Pinetti	6/95		160
Prescott Hotel/ Postrio	4/89	158	150
Carlton Hotel	6/89	165	
Splendido	11/89		150
Cartwright Hotel	1/90	114	
Tuscan Inn/Café Pescatore	7/90	221	
Harbor Court Hotel/ Harry Denton's	4/91	131	176
Hotel Triton	10/91	140	
Kuleto's Trattoria	9/93		200
Sir Francis Drake Hotel	4/94	417	
Scala's Bistro	1/95		200
Hotel Monaco/Grand Café	6/95	201	260
Serrano Hotel	6/99	236	
Hotel Palomar/Fifth Floor	8/99	198	75
Portland			
Hotel Vintage Plaza/ Pazzo Ristorante	5/92	107	200
Fifth Avenue Suites Hotel/Red Star Tavern & Roast House	5/96	221	200
Seattle/Tacoma			
Alexis Hotel	9/82	109	
The Painted Table	5/92		100
Hotel Vintage Park/Tulio	8/92	127	156
Hotel Monaco Seattle/Sazerac	8/97	189	185
Sheraton Tacoma Hotel/Broadway Grill	5/84	319	170
Chicago			
Hotel Allegro/312 Chicago	3/98	489	244
Hotel Monaco Chicago/Mossant	11/98	193	174
Denver			
Hotel Monaco Denver/ Panzano	10/98	189	244
Salt Lake City			
Hotel Monaco Salt Lake	7/99		

THE U.S. HOTEL INDUSTRY

9   Global issues, changing industry fundamentals, increasing volatility in the capital markets, and a general unease with the direction of the economy created opportunities for Kimpton to aggressively expand nationally while its competitors were scrambling to refocus. For hotels, managing supply and demand was a top priority for decision-makers.

Since the hotel industry's recovery from the recession of the early 1990s, it had changed from the high growth and fragmented state that dominated the 1980s to the fierce competitive environment of the late '90s. As the industry approached the millennium, demand for hotel rooms increased by 3.1% in 1997–1998 over 2.5% in 1996–1997, while RevPARs also grew by 5.3% and 3.5%, respectively, during the corresponding periods, according to Smith Travel Research. Exhibit 2 provides a summary of the generally upward trends of occupancy rates and RevPARs for the 1994–1998 period. Exhibit 3 provides time series data on occupancy and average daily revenue trends in the U.S. lodging industry.

10   The American Hotel and Motel Association has forecasted that both business and tourist travel would increase during the early 21st century, and that more than one billion people would be traveling worldwide by 2006, when international tourism dollars were projected to total more than $7.1 trillion. The U.S. would continue to be the first choice for tourists, attracting almost 50 million for 1999 alone. Employment was also expected to rise, with estimates of 1.89 million working in the tourism industry by 2005, according to the U.S. Department of Commerce's *1998 Census of Service Industries.*

11   KG's competition in the full-service hotel segment included many well-known brand names such as Hilton, Hyatt, Marriott, Promus (Doubletree), and Starwood (Sheraton and Westin brands). For the year ending December 1998, revenues rose at Hilton by 35%, Promus by 25% and Marriott by 20%. In 1998 RevPARs at these hotels demonstrated the continued strong recovery of the industry from the recession of the early 90s, rising by 8% at Hilton, 6% at Promus, and 6% at Marriott. This upsurge in business made its way to the bottom line. Hilton's earnings before taxes and other nonoperating income rose by 75%; Promus's corresponding earnings rose 25% and Marriott's by 18%, according to *Moody's Industry Review* on January 22, 1999. Operating profit margins for some of the more profitable companies reached a high of 35% in 1997, according to *Moody's.* Selected 1998 operating results for the top ten publicly traded U.S. hotel corporations are presented in Exhibits 4 and 5. A brief overview of the strategies and competitive tactics of the three largest competitors are shown in Exhibit 6.

EXHIBIT 2

U.S. Lodging Industry Supply and Demand, 1994–1998

Source: Bear Stearns & Co., Smith Travel Associates Research, Coopers & Lybrand L.L.P.

	All Hotels in the U.S.									
	% Change in Supply					% Change in Demand				
	1994	**1995**	**1996**	**1997**	**1998**	**1994**	**1995**	**1996**	**1997**	**1998**
	1.0	1.5	2.8	3.4	4.0	3.0	1.7	2.3	2.5	3.1

EXHIBIT 3

U.S. Lodging Industry Occupancy and Average Daily Rates (ADR), 1991–1999

Source: Bear Stearns & Co., Smith Travel Associates Research, Coopers & Lybrand L.L.P.

	1991	**1992**	**1993**	**1994**	**1995**	**1996**	**1997**	**1998**	**1999 (1st quarter)**
Occupancy %	61.8	62.6	63.5	64.7	65.0	65.1	64.5	64.0	59.4%
% Change	(1.7)	0.8	0.9	1.2	0.3	0.1	(0.6)	(0.5)	(4.6)%
ADR $	58.10	58.90	60.50	62.80	65.80	69.90	75.20	78.60	$81.90
% Change	0.2	1.4	2.8	3.8	4.7	6.2	5.3	3.5	3.3%

EXHIBIT 4
U.S. Lodging
Industry Rankings
by Revenues,
Fiscal Year 1998
($ millions)

Source: "Hotels and Motels,"
Moody's Industry Review,
January 22, 1999.

Company Name	Latest Revenues
Sodexno Marriott Services, Inc.	$12,034
Hilton Hotels Corp.	5,316
Starwood Hotels & Resorts	4,700
Trump Hotels and Casino Resorts	1,399
Host Marriott Corp.	1,147
Promus Hotel Corp.	1,038
MGM Grand, Inc.	828
Red Roof Inns, Inc.	351
Prime Hospitality Corp.	341
Sunterra Corp.	338

EXHIBIT 5
Financial Ratio Data
for Top Ten Hotel
Chains (ranked by
FY 1998 revenues)

Source: "Hotels and Motels,"
Moody's Industry Review,
January 22, 1999.

Company Name	Return on Capital %	Return on Assets %	Current Ratio (x)	Operating Profit Margin %	$ Rev's per Employee
Sodexno Marriott, Inc.	10.13	5.30	.88	6.03	$ 61,713
Hilton Hotels Corp.	3.73	3.19	1.07	11.21	87,147
Starwood Hotels & Resorts	12.40	7.70	.50	7.62	36,154
Trump Hotels	nmf	nmf	1.55	10.23	12,580
Host Marriott Corp.	0.80	0.72	10.43	35.05	n/a
Promus Hotel Corp.	4.52	4.01	.55	17.72	25,317
MGM Grand, Inc.	9.47	8.24	.94	23.08	126,219
Red Roof Inns, Inc.	2.91	13.15	.71	25.05	60,517
Prime Hospitality Corp.	2.36	2.16	.76	26.64	50,147
Sunterra Corp.	3.23	2.83	4.67	15.89	81,445
Marcus Corp.	5.32	4.68	.43	17.16	48,000
Industry averages	4.00%	5.90%	1.00·	2.99%	$ 62,343

nmf = not meaningful figure

n/a = not available

EXHIBIT 6
Major Lodging
Companies'
Strategies

Source: www.mariott.com,
www.hilton.com,
www.prnewswire.com,
accessed May 12, 1999.

Marriott	Hilton	Promus
• Price segmentation • Customer segmentation • Global presence • Time-share segments • Senior care—bought senior living Forum Group-now largest operators of senior housing • Brand management • Selling non-industry-related businesses • Selling hotels which do not match strategy • Acquisitions in mid-priced segment • Acquisition of small hotel companies	• Price segmentation • Customer segmentation • Global presence • All-suites segment • Gaming—now industry leader in facilities • Brand management • Acquisition of full-service hotels • Global expansion in mid-priced segment • Electronic marketplace • Employee training in quality improvement	• Price segmentation • Customer segmentation • Global presence • Time-share segments • All-suites segments • Merger with other large hotel leader • Brand management • Partnership with food producer (Dole) • Sponsorship of sporting events • Restructuring of management in early 1999

12   Some industry observers commented that the hotel industry's future outlook remained uncertain. Joseph Tardiff, an analyst writing in *U.S. Industry Profiles, 1998,* reported that across the nation, room supply grew by about 4% in 1998 after 3.5% growth in 1997. In the July 1998 edition of *Lodging,* a leading industry trade publication, Smith Travel Research forecasted that demand growth would average 2.4% through the year 2000. Analysts also cautioned that room supply growth would average 3.2%, raising fears of oversupply, declines in occupancy rates, and probable diminution of growth rates in RevPAR as well as industrywide profitability. Industrywide profits had risen 20.5% from 1997 to a record $17.6 billion in 1998, and were forecasted by Smith Travel Research to increase to $19.2 billion in 1999 and $21 billion in 2000, respectively. To partially offset the prospect of oversupply in the industry, some hotel companies (e.g., Marriott) were said to be pursuing diversification into retirement facilities and time-share programs, according to Bill Scatchard, publisher of *Hoteliers' Infosource.*

13   Ted Mandigo, an industry observer quoted in *Hotel & Motel Management,* felt that location was the key to success. "Finding a good location in a commercial district is an excellent way to enter a market. Many such opportunities have already been exploited. The operator looking for undervalued assets that can be turned into boutique hotels will need a sharp pencil to avoid buying bargain properties that do not create a situation of oversupply." Other critical success factors appeared to determine a firm's ability to remain competitive in the hotel industry. At the basic level, hotel owners strove to create a level of service that attracted and retained customers. The "experience" of staying at a particular hotel facility was intended to have a lasting and memorable effect if a hotel was to be distinguished from the competition.

14   The trend noted in the *1994 Atlas of the American Economy,* toward hotel property and management consolidation, posed several threats for owners of small and midsized hotel chains. As the larger firms continued to grow and expand their operations, it became easy to expand beyond economies of scale factors and create an oversupply, driving down room rates. This threat was heightened during economic downturns and could significantly affect the overall occupancy rate in the industry and similarly negatively impact profitability. In the early 1990s there was a notable and steady increase in the number of establishments, according to Smith Travel Associates (Exhibit 7). The result was a surplus of rooms and low occupancy rates. High operating expenses diminished profit margins considerably in years with low occupancy rates, especially given that hotels had to keep room rates down in such years as well. The predictable outcome was that record losses were experienced by the industry during a period of oversupply (e.g., full-service hotels with significant departmental expenses particularly experienced this loss history). The occupancy rates for

EXHIBIT 7
Hotel Industry Growth, 1990–1998

Source: Smith Travel Associates Research.

Year	No. of Hotels	% Growth	No. of Rooms	% Growth
1990	30,114		3,206,454	
1991	30,384	0.9%	3,234,673	0.8%
1992	30,516	0.4%	3,249,699	0.5%
1993	30,727	0.7%	3,270,864	0.6%
1994	31,152	1.4%	3,306,304	1.1%
1995	31,808	2.1%	3,354,970	1.5%
1996	32,851	3.3%	3,455,087	2.9%
1997	34,225	4.2%	3,588,072	3.8%
1998	35,013	2.3%	3,662,524	2.1%

limited-service hotels were not significantly different from that of full-service hotels, according to Smith Travel Associates. This suggests why some large corporate hotel operators in the late 90s were emphasizing a more limited-service facility that had lower operating costs yet retained good customer traffic and operating gross margins. Exhibit 8 presents 1995 data on hotel real estate selling prices and estimated costs of replacement per room.

15 Perhaps the most profound change in hotel industry strategy arose from the dramatic shift of hotel properties from private to public ownership. The volume of investment dollars for the hotel industry was significantly greater in the late 90s than it had been historically. Banks, insurance companies, finance companies, equity investors and Real Estate Investment Trusts (REITs) entered the hotel industry with aggressive parameters as they perceived that the market oversupply had begun to dissipate. The latter instrument, REITs, which emerged in 1991, had become a major source of low-cost capital that fueled growth and construction in the hotel industry. Starwood Lodging had used REITs as a vehicle to acquire Westin Hotels and Sheraton Hotels from IT&T. The availability of low-cost capital became an especially important factor for the larger players in the industry, who moved increasingly towards consolidation via acquisition of other chains, according to Smith Travel Associates. However, the lowering of barriers to entry allowed disproportionate levels of new supply in the industry.

16 Aging of the "baby boomers" also emerged as a significant demographic factor. Seventy million Americans were moving into their midlives (over 50) and were expected to seek greater comfort and choose service over price in their choice of hotels. In the late 90s, other emerging trends in the hotel industry included: 1) the introduction of limited-services suites; 2) additional emphasis on higher value-added business-related amenities such as data ports for laptops and interactive Web TV sets in rooms; 3) automation of labor-intensive functions via information technology; 4) development of extended-stay or "residence-style" hotels and time-share projects; 5) reduction in marketing expenses and long-term operating costs via standardization and branding of properties.

17 In spite of the many changes in the hotel industry, comments made by Kimpton executives, suggest the essential several factors in addition to location that are generally considered to be critical to success in the hotel industry still include:

- Low-cost purchases of land or buildings

- Greater latitude in product/service offerings at comparable profit margins

- Customer service

- Effective utilization of technology

- Brand loyalty

- Employee training and development

EXHIBIT 8
Hotel Real Estate Selling Prices and Estimated Costs of Replacement, 1995

Source: National Hotel Realty Advisor.

Lodging Segment	Average Selling Price per Room ($)	Estimated Cost of Replacement per Room ($)
Budget	11,804	25,000–30,000
Economy, Limited Service	20,538	30,000–30,000
Economy, Full Service	19,239	35,000–50,000
Mid-market, Limited Service	42,244	35,000–50,000
Mid-market, Full Service	42,117	45,000–70,000
Luxury, Limited Service	65,174	80,000–150,000

- Complementary services

- Revenue management systems

- Clean and comfortable lodging

- Strategic alliances

- Convenience in making reservations

- Access to growth capital

- Value-added services

THE BOUTIQUE HOTEL NICHE

18   As the millennium approached, the emerging boutique or small luxury hotel niche began attracting new entrants both large and small. For example, Starwood Hotels & Resorts announced in late 1998 that it was launching a new "W" line of boutique hotels with fewer than 400 rooms in an attempt to replicate the Kimpton formula for success.

19   Based in White Plains, New York, Starwood Hotels & Resorts managed, owned, and operated such branded properties as St. Regis and The Luxury Collection (luxury hotels), Westin (upscale full-service), Sheraton (full-service), W (boutique full-service hotels for business travelers), and Caesars World (which it sold in early 1999). Starwood's meteoric yet troubled rise had been guided by Chairman Barry Sternlicht (German for "starlight"), an aggressive dealmaker who snatched ITT from Hilton Hotels. Sternlicht owned about 5% of the firm. In 1999 the company abandoned its paired-share real estate investment trust (REIT) structure for a standard corporate structure with a property-owning REIT subsidiary; Starwood Hotels & Resorts Worldwide managed the operation of the properties. A 21-story W Hotel opened across from the Moscone Convention Center in San Francisco in April 1999. Despite heavy debt and the high costs of integrating operations acquired during the whirlwind buying spree that preceded the change in its structure, in mid-1999 Starwood announced that it planned to expand into Latin America.

20   The other national player in the boutique hotel category, according to a July 1999 story in the *San Francisco Examiner,* was New York hotelier Ian Schrager (formerly co-owner of the Studio 54 disco). Schrager ran the Royalton in New York, the Mondrian in Los Angeles, and had purchased the Clift Hotel in San Francisco for $80 million in June 1999. The Clift was undergoing a $25 million facelift prior to its reopening in October 1999.

21   Boutique hotels accounted for about 15% of San Francisco's estimated 31,000 rooms. In San Francisco, KG was the recognized market leader, with 67% of the city's boutique hotels, according to analyst Anwar Elgonomy of PKF Consulting. Chip Conley's Joie de Vivre Hotels enjoyed 20% of the San Francisco market, and Yvonne Lembi-Detert's Personality Hotels on Union Square, with four properties, had 12% of the market. Other operators split the remaining 1%. "It's a very specific group of people [boutique hoteliers] are going after: well-educated professionals," Elgonomy said recently in an interview in the *San Francisco Examiner,* "people who don't like generic activities. People who don't like Starbucks."

22   Chip Conley, president of Joie de Vivre, a $40 million chain of 14 boutique hotels and motels in the San Francisco Bay Area, commented on the boutique lodging niche in an April 1999 interview with Neal Templin in the *Contra Costa Times:*

> The question is whether the big boys will have the agility to handle the boutique market. We look for aging hotels with "good bones"—good elevators, plumbing and electrical systems—and bad images. We spend our money on things that get a lot of bang for the buck. Our

strategy is to make our Hotel del Sol a national brand by buying a portfolio of motels around the country and converting them to the same concept. There's a huge collection of 1950s and 1960s hotels waiting to be fixed up. Our next project to open will be a boutique camping resort south of San Francisco where guests will rough it in tents but still be able to order up café lattés after their hikes in the woods. It is aimed at the sort of people who buy sport-utility vehicles even though they rarely drive off-road. They can feel like they're connected with nature while not getting their hands dirty.

23   One reason San Francisco spawned so many boutique hotels is that it had had a big in-ventory of older hotels that could be cheaply acquired and converted. Analyst C. Jay Scott, of Scott Hospitality Services in San Francisco, noted, "Boutique hotels don't work everywhere. They work only in downtowns that are still vibrant relative to business and leisure travel markets. It's a concept that has been well-received by the marketplace. Why try to continually reinvent yourself when you have a concept that works?"

24   As property values in San Francisco soared, KG's competitors were increasingly building all-new developments, which, in the opinion of Kimpton executives, were both more risky and less profitable than conversions. By contrast, most of the KG's hotels were converted buildings that had been built for other purposes. In the words of Jeff Se-nior, the Group's director of marketing:

> Our lowered asset investment requires a lesser average rate to be successful. In other words, it costs us less, so we can charge less and still be as much or more profitable than our competitors. In reality, any full service hotel in markets we compete within is a competitor, including Sheraton, Westin, Hyatt, Starwood, etc. Other competitors include other boutique providers.

25   According to Bill Scatchard, publisher of *Hoteliers' Infosource,* the baby boomer gen-eration was attracted to the boutique style hotel that Kimpton Group pioneered. The brightly trimmed decor with a hint of European luxury appeared to capture the taste of this lucrative segment. In general, the market appeared to favor properties that offered a fun at-mosphere in an intimate surrounding. One hotel manager at the Kimpton Group suggested that his organization was one of two or three companies that had responded to this bou-tique hotel niche very well. This general manager, keenly aware of Kimpton's prominent in the San Francisco market, took a more globally perspective. He emphasized the relative smallness of the company's presence overall and described the Kimpton Group niche in the hotel industry colorfully: "We're like a pimple on the ass of an elephant."

THE KIMPTON ORGANIZATION

26   The Kimpton Hotel and Restaurant Group consisted of a family of 23 boutique-style ho-tels and 24 unique and often independently successful restaurants. Its hotels ranged in size from 91 rooms to 483 rooms, and a typical hotel had between 100–200 rooms. KG's destination restaurants, each with its own local following, were located in the same build-ings as the hotels.

27   Founder William (Bill) Kimpton, now 63, bought his first hotel in 1981. Kimpton was born in Kansas City, Missouri, and in his schoolboy days was hampered by what he now believes was dyslexia. He has noted that he did not learn to read until he reached high school. He struggled academically but was encouraged by his family to continue school-ing. Kimpton earned a Bachelor of Science in Economics from Northwestern University and was a graduate of the renowned University of Chicago Lab School. Prior to starting the Kimpton Group in 1981, Kimpton served for three-and-a-half years as director and vice president of Lepercq de Neuflize, an international investment banking firm. During his stint at Lepercq, Kimpton participated in negotiating, structuring, and overseeing the projects of Lepercq de Neuflize. Preceding Lepercq, Kimpton was a partner in Shuman, Agnew & Co., Inc., in Belvedere, Calif., where he was responsible for project finance. Other experiences which helped shape his acumen for project financing included almost four years as a manager with Lehman Brothers (now Shearson–Lehman Brothers American Express, Inc.) in their San Francisco office. This assignment in San Francisco followed his three years as an associate for Lehman Brothers in their Chicago office.

28 Bill Kimpton's approach to the hotel industry was based on his prior career as an investment banker. Kimpton began his foray into the hotel industry by structuring a highly creative investment strategy for the Helmsley Hotel organization. He worked with Harry Helmsley (now probably best known for the exploits of his controversial wife, Leona Helmsley, the "Queen of Mean") to raise seed money for the $23 million renovation of the New York Palace Hotel. Kimpton's role in that project became legendary for his imaginative approach to raising investment capital. Kimpton also handled the financing for the exclusive Kapalua Bay resort in Maui and brought in the Rockefeller family's RockResorts to manage the property.

29 Bill Kimpton recalled that he wanted to get into a business "that sells sleep, because sleep has high [profit] margins." He combined his bottom-line focus with a unique feel for offering value and comfort with a "personality" in all the Kimpton Group properties. He imprinted a flair for being different yet profitable upon his hotel and restaurant management team. "My theory is, no matter how much money people have to spend on big, fancy hotels, they are intimidated," Kimpton said recently. "The psychology of how you build restaurants and hotels is very important. You put a fireplace in the lobby and create a warm, friendly restaurant and the guest will feel safe."

30 Bill Kimpton, by 1999, had served as chairman and chief executive of KG since its inception. Although he was by then no longer intimately involved in day-to-day management, Kimpton's entrepreneurial style was still very visible in the organization. His style was very personal, and he practiced a decentralized approach to decision making since the early days of the corporation. Following his entrepreneurial flair, each property emphasized guestroom comfort rather than high overhead amenities such as fancy water fountains, ornate lobbies and excessive brass and glass.

31 Guestrooms were tastefully decorated in cheerful colors with elegant bedspreads and thick carpeting, perhaps reflecting Bill Kimpton's trademark multicolor sweaters. Each room was meant to feel like a comfortable guest room in a friend's luxury home and was complete with good lighting, stocked honor bar/refrigerator, direct dial phones with extra long cords to reach the bed, the desk and other parts of the room. Hotel lobbies were furnished with the emphasis on comfort, not on waiting, and each had a cozy fireplace.

32 KG's strategy was to create each hotel as a stand-alone "personality" that appealed to its own unique customer group. The hotels shared a common upscale theme and appearance but priced the rooms below the full-service hotels such as Marriott or Hilton. A European-style was visible in almost every KG property. Kimpton's aggressive expansion in San Francisco made it very difficult for other chains to find low-cost property in commercial locations that could compete on both price and amenities found at the KG properties.

33 A high degree of personalized service and numerous complementary amenities were also the hallmark of KG's hotels. Some KG hotels were testing a system to provide arriving guests with "desk-less" check-in via use of cellular and digital communications technology. Doormen were equipped with headsets and could escort new guests directly to their rooms without the usual paperwork and waiting around, considered to be some of the most "unwelcoming" experiences of tired travelers who just want to get into their rooms. Most hotels featured some or all of the following complementary services: limousines to the financial district, wine served in the lobby each evening, continental breakfast, and coffee and tea availability throughout the day. Most hotels also offered same-day valet and laundry service, room service and express checkout with on-site parking. According to Kimpton executives, all of these services were provided at room rates that averaged 25% to 30% lower than comparable hotels in the same markets. Indicative of the success of KG's strategy was its annual occupancy rates, which averaged 85% over the Group, compared to the industry average, which hovered between 68% and 75%, depending on the geographical market segment served.

HUMAN RESOURCES

34 Hotel general managers were strongly encouraged to innovate and provide their specific property with a personality that separated it from the other properties in KG's portfolio. Senior management practiced reciprocal communication and was very reluctant to impose anything other than customer-related service standards on each property.

35 Nanci Sherman, general manager of the Hotel Monaco in San Francisco, confirmed this approach.

> Most of our general managers have a hotel background, but like me are refugees from patriarchal companies like Hilton, Disney, and Ritz-Carlton. People come to Kimpton because they see there's another way. Why is it that in 200,000 hotels around the world that the staff meet every Tuesday and Friday for two hours but no changes ever take place? We built our business around the 2% that rarely occurs, not on the 98% that happens regularly. We really want to look good. Very rarely do we (as industry people) want to take risks. Building a Group culture starts with who we are as people: giving, teamwork, friendship, and confidence. People who get rewarded and promoted here are team players. But you can't run a highly bureaucratic, top-down management style anymore, even in a conservative industry like the hotel industry. That's a major reason why our staff turnover rate has been 18–21% over the past two years, far below the average rate of 50% in the industry. Low turnover rates are absolutely essential to us, because the hotels with the lowest turnover rates have the highest financial performance, particularly in the tight labor markets that we are experiencing now.

36 Each hotel manager and line staff member attended "Kimpton University," a program of in-house classes on front desk service, housekeeping, finance and recordkeeping, and corporate wellness. In keeping with KG's philosophy of the "gracious host," general managers poured wine for guests at the cocktail hour each night. It was on these occasions that feedback on amenities and service was most readily obtained on a first-hand basis. Feedback from guests was systematically gathered via comment cards in guestrooms. Some of its hotels were experimenting with using interactive TV in guestrooms to obtain comments at check-out. The company also had hired Pannell Kerr Foster (PKF), a San Francisco–based consulting firm, to obtain quality control information using "phantom guests." Executives were also considering the use of focus groups to obtain feedback about the efficacy of current and planned future service offerings. KG observed a "sundown rule," in that each general manager must respond to a guest's comments on their stay by the end of the business day.

37 KG hired people whose "light had been hidden under a bushel," according to Jim McPartlin, general manager of the Prescott Hotel in San Francisco and the citywide manager for KG's San Francisco Hotels. "We encouraged the operating managers to 'be different' and think 'outside-of-the-box,'" said McPartlin. "The incentives are there, as we can earn up to 25% bonus on our salaries, paid out quarterly. Our typical wage percentage of sales is about 22%, of which 70% is 'raw' wages and 30% are benefits. We also have a 'Circle of

Stars,' an employee luncheon once a month, where employees who are recognized by guests for outstanding service can win prizes in a 'Wheel-of-Fortune-type game,' " he added.

38   KG did not have a formal organization chart. According to David Martin, the director of hotel operations:

> Perhaps this is because we try to create an entrepreneurial atmosphere. We hire managers who have the guts to make decisions. Internal competition—creativity—that we label as entrepreneurial is healthy, as long as it's in the customer's best interests. We must meet minimum customer standards. There's sort of a Maslow's hierarchy almost. We gotta be clean, personable, and offer quick service.
>
> We have a "fireside chat" once a quarter, where we put Steve [Marx] on the firing line with the hotel general managers. He gets people to express their needs. We've challenged Steve on many occasions. We talk about real issues that are important to managers.

"MONGOOSE" STRATEGY

39   Since its inception in 1981, KG had followed a so-called "mongoose strategy"—named after the ferretlike animal that successfully kills poisonous animals by circling them until they tire, at which point it dives in quickly and finishes them off. Before the company successfully bought its Bellevue property, Kimpton bid $10 million and was outbid by investors who paid $15 million, according to the *New York Times* on January 16, 1994. The company watched the property for seven years until it was able to pick up that property from those owners for $5 million. Similarly, the firm bought the Sir Francis Drake property for $19.5 million, although the property had been on the market eight years earlier for $60 million. If a property possessed the three attributes of uniqueness in character, location, and design potential, it became a target for the patient capital of the KG and its co-investors. Each new property was typically financed by 60% equity and 40% debt, considered low leverage in the hotel industry.

40   In the San Francisco market, which by 1999 included 15 semiluxury hotels and 16 destination restaurants, KG began with the Bedford Hotel in 1981, which was followed by the Vintage Court, the Galleria Park, and the Juliana and so on until the firm controlled some two thousand rooms in its home market. As a point of reference, the Hilton, which towered in the skyline of San Francisco, had almost as many rooms as the entire collection of KG properties in that city. Other properties were located in Seattle, Tacoma, Portland, Denver, Chicago, and the soon-to-be opened Hotel Monaco in Salt Lake City.

41   By mid-1999, KG was considering expansion to the East Coast and had begun looking at properties in New York, Boston, and Washington, D.C. "It's time to start looking outside the West Coast," Bill Kimpton recently told the *San Francisco Examiner,* "it's difficult to find a building that hasn't already been worked over. We'd love to be in New York. We'd like to be in San Diego. We're going into Vancouver (in Spring 2000)."

CUSTOMER TARGETS

42   The KG avoided targeting the 10% of customers that wanted absolute luxury. Nor was it after the backpacking student. Rather, KG had sought to serve the 50–60% of the market that was looking for "comfort and value." In 1994, Bill Kimpton summarized his approach quite succinctly in *The New York Times.* "We sell sleep, while corporation lodging (full-service hotels) is in the entertainment business because of all the extras it has to offer." Guests at those other hotel facilities paid for the meeting rooms, the ornate lobbies, the fabulous water fountains, the unused restaurants and other services that most

would never use. A hotel, according to KG's philosophy, should relieve a traveler of his or her loneliness. It should make you feel "warm and cozy," Bill Kimpton told the *Chicago Tribune* in 1998. This vision shaped the organization's approach to the hotel industry in general and to its markets in particular.

43 In discussing KG's success, Steve Marx spoke of a "customer intimacy" that gave "personality" to each one of its properties. This focus on service details resembled the attention to cost details that characterized the property acquisition process for which the KG had become noted.

44 According to Jeff Senior:

> How do we build brand equity? Classic brand management. We need to rely on the power of the individual hotel brands, a core premise in our niche/boutique hotel segment. We need to focus on the product positioning, ensuring uniqueness and legitimate competitive advantage; product and service delivery consistency with the positioning; distribution focus against the highest yielding channels for our target; and performance management to ensure desired results are achieved, appropriate corrective action taken, and strategic revisions evaluated in an ongoing manner. We compete within the deluxe category in urban markets . . . both reflecting much higher barrier to entry.

45 The target customer for KG included both business and tourist travelers who were looking for a unique, intimate and personal hotel experience. International guests represented about 11% of KG's total. The amenities offered by KG properties bordered on luxury but provided each guest with a clearly recognized bargain compared with the upscale chains such as Hilton or Marriott.

RESTAURANT OPERATIONS

46 Each of the restaurants that KG operated had a separate entrance and a separate identity from its hotel location. The company took pains to avoid its restaurants being perceived as "hotel restaurants." Niki Leondakis, vice president of restaurant operations for the KG, and six-year veteran of the organization, said that hotel restaurants were the antithesis of what her company did best. "The minute that we become a hotel-restaurant," Leondakis added, "that's death. A hotel-restaurant has a stigma: over priced [and] poor service." KG strove to offer dining patrons a "handcrafted" experience—something that gave character and personality. "[We] want our guests to feel they're getting something they can't get anywhere else," commented Leondakis.

47 Jeff Senior commented:

> When I came to Kimpton less than a year ago, we were already structured with a separate restaurant division. While the downside is a duplication of resources to support the respective businesses, the upside is a focus on the core competencies of each business and the key drivers of profitability. The result: we have profitable restaurants and profitable hotels.

Following this strategy, each KG restaurant was custom-made for each property and market location. Each restaurant was allowed to run as an independent and exist with renowned chefs including Julian Serrano at Masa's, Wolfgang Puck (at the Postrio), and Gionvanni Perticone (at the Splendido). According to KG's San Francisco city manager Jim McPartlin, "We create free-standing restaurants that actually make an operating profit, around 5–15%, versus the breakeven margins at typical hotel restaurants."

48 In December 1998, the Smith Travel Associates Report on the U.S. lodging industry noted that, on average, 73% of a hotel's revenue came from rooms, 20.6% from food and beverage and 6.4% from minor operations such as telecommunications, space rentals and other miscellaneous sources. KG depended on its restaurants to deliver extra-perceived value to customers, much as the full-service hotel with much higher room rates would. The most obvious cross-marketing between the restaurant and hotel operations occurred when restaurant customers visited the restroom and they inevitably had to walk through the lobby of the hotel. Diners would hopefully spread the word about the little boutique hotel that they had "discovered" while having a terrific dinner.

49   Thus, KG helped pioneer the strategy of a stand-alone restaurant as a lure to get word-of-mouth advertising for its hotels. However, other chains such as Fairfield Inns by Marriott, Hilton Garden Inn and Microtel were known to be operating some of their properties under a strategy very similar to the Kimptom Group's approach of attracting travelers by being closely associated with a world-class restaurant. A potential concern for all using this strategy is that there is a limited pool of quality chefs willing to work within the structure of a corporation, especially when the strong suit of the corporation is the hotel division.

50   Each of the KG-managed restaurants was individually themed and offered a variety of food styles, price ranges, and ambiences. Many of the restaurants featured exhibition kitchens and counter seating that made them user-friendly for single guests who wished to dine alone. " Our restaurants are run by restaurateurs," said Leondakis. "We provide service to the hotel, but our restaurants are more than a food and beverage outlet. We are a profitable, independent and separate business."

THE FUTURE

51   As with most business situations, past success could turn out to be a double-edged sword for KG. A recent collaboration with the Trammel-Crow investment group made funds more or less readily available for property acquisition and rapid growth. Yet, it was not clear that KG's strategy could be easily transferred to other markets. KG needed to decide on its desired growth rate and how it could manage growth without losing the uniqueness and decentralized culture that its senior management held in high regard.

52   According to PKF, the San Francisco-based hotel and real estate research firm, the projected profitability of the industry could, by the year 2000, reach the highest in at least a half-century. Gross margins could exceed 30%, fattening returns on investment and permitting aggressive expansion by KG into untapped markets.

53   Still, KG has insisted that the organization does not do deals just to do deals. By 1999, the Group was managing almost 4,000 rooms in increasingly far-flung locations. Although privately held, KG executives revealed that revenues had grown by an estimated 15–20% per year in the past six years. The organization had been generating a consistent 15–20% return for its investment partners, all high net worth individuals including movie stars Paul Newman and Harrison Ford, as well as members of the Getty family. The level of return also exceeds the 13% ROI target set by the Crow family.

54   In order to continue to differentiate itself from the competition, in 1999 KG added new amenities in its guest rooms such as telephones that easily accommodated laptop computers, easy chairs and desks with large work surfaces and improved lighting. Technological trends that may affect the competitive landscape of the hotel industry included the emerging use of "smart cards" to replace cash and capture unique preferences of the hotel guest. Technology similarly made hotel-specific websites and bargain-hunting at sites like www.priceline.com almost ubiquitous within the industry.

55   According to Jeff Senior, KG was experiencing difficulty entering the Internet age:

> Fear of technology and systems is serious around here. The infrastructure does not exist. We have only one MIS person in this entire organization. We're not using e-mail. Our high technology is voicemail.

56   Also in 1999, KG began to emphasize on-site revenue management systems. This information would help general managers decide what each part of their operation contributed to profitability, which, in turn, would help senior executives at the Group level to understand the potential for increasing internal efficiencies. Additionally, information access improvements were expected to give each property general manager a sense of decentralized decision making in spite of living under a corporate umbrella.

STRATEGIC MEETING AT KG: AFTERTHOUGHTS

57   Before the 3:00 P.M. meeting with David Martin and Jeff Senior ended, Marx had an opportunity to explore with them the range of strategic choices that he thought were critical to the continued success of the KG. Looking back after that meeting, Marx noted:

> There are people in integral positions in this organization who remain "small thinkers" and who are afraid to step up to the plate. Our greatest fault is that we're sometimes not ready to put our money where our mouth is. That's a real danger. From the top, you've got to send a signal that it's okay to take risks, that it's (sort of) okay to fail. Mind you, we have made very few mistakes. Still, we have to be more careful about seducing ourselves that every market is the right place for our hotels. The problem is the fragility of the tourism economies in other cities, making it difficult to expand into new markets.
>
>   We're sort of disorganized; I know we like to kid ourselves about how "seat-of-the-pants" we are, and we say we're strategic but we're really very tactical. This is typical of the hotel industry. We are trying to be strategic in what really is a tactical industry. We need to decide where we're going in the future. You can't have two sides of an organization in conflict. We have tension that is unnecessary, sort of a push-pull between those managers that advocate returning to what we used to be and those that advocate changing into what we're going to become. Even Bill (Kimpton, the founder and Chairman of the Kimptom Group) is torn. We need to preserve our philosophy to enable a general manager to imprint their personality on an individual hotel. We need to continue to go to great lengths to attract and nurture people who believe that their success is also the success of the company. Always stay in touch with line employees. I actually want to hear bad news. Be unreasonable. Set unreasonable expectations. And always be really hands-on with our owners. These are hallmarks of what we do.

58   After the afternoon meeting with Martin and Senior, Marx wondered to what extent his successor(s) could cope with the changing dynamics in the hotel industry and at the same time continue the open management philosophy and participatory decision-making style that had served KG so well during his tenure. The strategic choices to be made now fell— at least, temporarily—on Martin and Senior's watch. He wondered in what direction they would take KG and which issues they would make their priorities.

This case study was prepared by Armand Gilinsky, Jr., Associate Professor of Business at Sonoma State University, and Richard L. McCline, Assistant Professor of Business at San Francisco State University, as a basis for class discussion rather than to illustrate either effective or ineffective handling of an administrative situation. Copyright © 2000 by Armand Gilinsky, Jr. and Richard L. McCline. All rights reserved.

Allen, J. L. (1998) "San Franciscan making more room at inns," *Chicago Tribune,*
    March 18.

Anderson, R. (1994) *Atlas of the American Economy,* Washington, D.C.: Congressional Quarterly.

Anon. (1999) "Motels and hotels." *Moody's Industry Review,* 22 January.

Anon. (1998) "Front desk," *Lodging,* July, p. 16.

Anon. (1998) "Ratings of hotels and motels," *Consumer Reports,* July, p. 17.

Armstrong, D. (1999) "Keeping hotels hot," *San Francisco Examiner,* July 18, B1.

Garfinkel, P. (1994) "Bed & breakfast? No, bed and dinner," *The New York Times,* January 16.

Higley, J. (1998) "Kimpton Group broadens its horizon," *Hotel & Motel Management* 213:13, July 20.

Scatchard, B. (1999) "Occupancy was down last year. . . ." *Hoteliers' Infosource* 7:1, January.

Smith, R. A. (1999) "Lodging outlook survey for the year ending December 1998," Smith Travel
    Associates Research, www.hotel-online.com, May 16, 1999.

Tardiff, J. C. (1998) *U.S. Industry Profiles,* New York: Gale Research.

Templin, N. (1999) "Eccentric sells: S.F. firm finds a profitable niche with boutique hotels," *Contra Costa
    Times,* April 17, pp. C1–C2.

U.S. Department of Commerce (1998). *Census of Service Industries.*

Case 44

R. David Thomas, Entrepreneur: The WENDY'S Story

1   Wendy's International grew from one store to over 1,800 company-owned and franchised outlets in 10 short years. Between 1974 and 1979, Wendy's growth was explosive with sales, including company-owned and franchised units, growing 4,200% ($24 million to $1 billion). Net income increased 2,091% in this period from $1.1 million to $23 million. Earnings per share made substantial gains from $.12 in 1974 to $1.54 in 1979, a 1,283% rise. Wendy's grew to a position of being the third-largest fast-food hamburger restaurant chain in the United States, ranking behind Burger King and McDonald's, the leading U.S. hamburger chain.

2   Wendy's entry and amazing growth in the hamburger segment of the fast-food industry shocked the industry and forced competitors within it to realize that their market positions were potentially vulnerable. Wendy's flourished in the face of adversities plaguing the industry. Throughout the 1970s, experts said the fast-food industry was rapidly maturing. Analysts for *The Wall Street Journal,* citing a "competitively saturated fast-food hamburger industry," predicted in the early 1970s that the Wendy's venture would not succeed. As they saw it, market saturation, rising commodity prices, fuel costs, and labor costs were already plaguing the fast-food industry.

3   Clearly unconcerned about such commentary, R. David Thomas pushed Wendy's relentlessly. It opened an average of one restaurant every two days during its first 10 years, becoming the first restaurant chain in history to top $1 billion in sales in its first 10 years.

HISTORY

4   R. David Thomas had an idea. He knew Americans love hamburgers. If he could develop a hamburger better than those currently offered, he believed he could use it to establish a leadership position in the competitive fast-food hamburger market. A high school dropout found success as an Army cook, R. David Thomas loved to cook fresh hamburgers. But he detoured into chicken after the Army, where one of his early jobs was helping Mr. Harland Sanders sell chicken recipes and utensils to restaurants in the Southeast. Not long after teaming with Kentucky's John Y. Brown, Mr. Sanders became "Colonel Sanders" and KFC was born. R. David Thomas returned to Columbus, Ohio, where he became a successful KFC franchisee in the 1960s.

5   In November 1969, Thomas, by now an experienced restaurant operator and veteran Kentucky Fried Chicken franchisee, began to put his idea into reality when he opened Wendy's first unit in downtown Columbus. A year later, in November 1970, Wendy's opened its second unit in Columbus, this one with a drive-through pickup window. In August 1972, Wendy's sold L. S. Hartzog the franchise for the Indianapolis, Indiana, market, kicking off Wendy's rapid expansion into the chain hamburger business. Later the same year, Wendy's Management Institute was formed to develop management skills in managers, supervisors, area directors, and franchise owners. After five years, company revenues exceeded $13 million with net income in excess of $1 million. Sales for both company-owned and franchised units topped $24 million for the same period. In June 1975, the 100th Wendy's opened in Louisville, Kentucky. Three months later, Wendy's went public. December 1976 saw Wendy's 500th open in Toronto, Canada. In 1977, Wendy's went national with its first network television commercial, making it the first restaurant chain with less than 1,000 units to mount a national advertising campaign. Eleven months later, Wendy's broke yet another record by opening its 1,000th restaurant in Springfield, Tennessee, within 100 months of opening the first Wendy's in Columbus. In 1979, Wendy's signed franchise agreements for eight European countries and Japan and opened the first European restaurant, company-owned, in Munich, West Germany. Also 1979 saw test marketing of a limited breakfast menu, a children's menu, and salad bars.

R. DAVID THOMAS'S VISION OF A PROFITABLE OPPORTUNITY: THE WENDY'S CONCEPT

The Menu

6   Thomas knew from experience that a limited menu could be a key factor contributing to Wendy's success. The idea was to concentrate on doing only a few things, but to do them better than anyone else. As a result, the aim was to provide the customer with a "Cadillac" hamburger that could be custom-made to meet individual preferences.

7   The basic menu item was the quarter-pound hamburger made of only fresh, 100% beef hamburger meat converted into patties daily. This kept Wendy's out of head-on competition with McDonald's and Burger King's 1/10th pound hamburger. If people desired a bigger hamburger, they could order a double (two patties on a bun) or a triple (three patties on a bun). Besides having just one basic menu item, the hamburger, Wendy's also decided to differentiate itself by changing their hamburger's design. Instead of the traditional round patty found in competing fast-food outlets, Wendy's patty was square and sized so its edges would stick out over the edge of the round bun. The unique design alleviated the frequent complaint by most people that they were eating a breadburger. It also made more efficient use of refrigeration space, saving store operators money in the process. Other menu decisions included the following:

- To offer different condiments to the customers—cheese, tomato, catsup, onion, lettuce, mustard, mayonnaise, and relish.

- To provide a unique dairy product, the frosty—a cross between chocolate and vanilla flavors that borders between soft ice cream and a thick milk shake.

- To serve a product that was unique in the fast-food market—chili.

- To sell french fries because the public expected a hamburger outlet to offer them.

8   Chili was an unusually clever menu item. First, it was an adult-oriented item not found on other fast-food menus. So an adult could have a hamburger one day and return for something different, chili, the next. Second, chili was made overnight—a slow cooking process—using the cooked hamburger meat that was not sold during the day and would otherwise have been thrown out or sold to hog farmers. Since meat costs were the largest single part of Wendy's [or any chain's] cost of goods sold, using otherwise wasted meat in chili to generate additional revenue provided a "double whammy"—it reduced costs and increased revenue. All fast-food restaurants face a sizable problem with wasted food—burgers in heated racks not sold within 10–15 minutes are typically thrown out or sold at a minimal charge to local hog farmers. And since most hamburger chains use precooked, frozen, round hamburger patties, they cannot recycle it into chili like Wendy's,

which uses larger patties of fresh meat cooked on site. The bottomline, then, is that Wendy's chili created a strategic cost advantage/margin-increasing advantage in addition to adding a unique, adult-oriented product that other competitors could not easily add without disrupting their current operations and concept.

Facilities

9 Under Thomas's direction, the exterior style and interior decor of all Wendy's restaurants conformed to company specifications. The typical outlet was a freestanding one-story brick building constructed on a 25,000-square-foot site that provided parking for 35 to 45 cars (see Exhibit 1). There were some downtown storefront-type restaurants, which generally adhered to the standard red, yellow, and white decor and design. Most of the freestanding restaurants contained 2,100 square feet, had a cooking area, dining room capacity for 92 persons, and a pickup window for drive-in service (see Exhibit 2). The interior decor featured table tops printed with reproductions of 19th century advertising, Tiffany-styled lamps, bentwood chairs, colorful beads, and carpeting.

10 Generally, the strategy was to build a functionally modern building that would reflect the old-fashioned theme. Another plus for their building design was its flexibility. With only minor changes, they could sell almost any type of food in the building. It would also be possible to change from the Gay 90s theme to any other theme in just a matter of days. But the setting was to be a bit upscale and adult-oriented among fast-food outlets.

11 The most unique feature in their building design was the addition of the pickup window, and Wendy's was the first major restaurant chain to successfully implement the use of one. Here, Wendy's was able to gain an advantage because their units could be smaller and at the same time handle the larger amount of business volume generated by using the pickup window. The logic for implementing the use of the pickup window was that people in their cars don't fill up tables or take up a parking space. The result showed that on a square-foot basis, Wendy's units did more business than any other chain.

12 The building design also contributed to what Michael J. Esposito, an investments analyst for Oppenheimer & Company, has called the most impressive part of the company's operation: the delivery system. In a report recommending Wendy's as an investment, Esposito wrote:

> In our judgment, the transaction time (time elapsed from when order is placed to its delivery to the customer) is the lowest in the industry, generally averaging about one minute. Utilizing a grill system where a constant flow of hamburgers is cooked at a relatively low temperature, a worker takes the hamburger off the grill, places it on a bun, adds the condiments ordered by the customer, assembles and wraps the sandwich. Another crew member supplies chili, french fries, beverage, and a frosty dessert, and another reviews the order and releases it to the customer.

The Marketing Strategy

13 In their book *The Chain-Restaurant Industry,* Earl Sasser and Daryl Wycoff stated:

> The Wendy's strategy was described by one analyst as "selling better hamburgers than McDonald's or Burger King at a cheaper price per ounce." As he commented, it takes no more labor to prepare a large hamburger at a higher price.

14 To support the higher-priced hamburger, Wendy's marketing strategy has been to stress the freshness and quality of their product. The objective of this strategy is to target Wendy's for the world's fastest-growing market segment. By offering a freshly ground, made-to-order hamburger as well as stylish, comfortable decor, Wendy's was aiming squarely at a key segment of the population: young adults with a taste for better food. With the

EXHIBIT 1
Wendy's Typical Site 1–Typical Lot Layout for Freestanding Unit

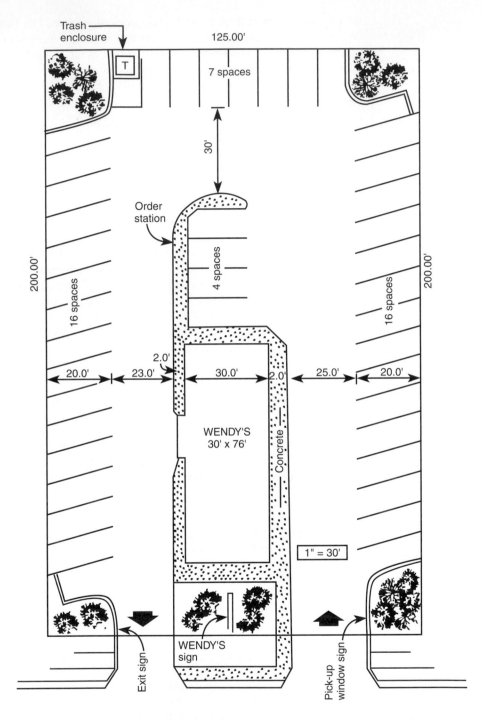

Lot area, 25,000 square feet; building, 2,310 square feet; parking spaces, 43.

EXHIBIT 2 Restaurant Interior Layout

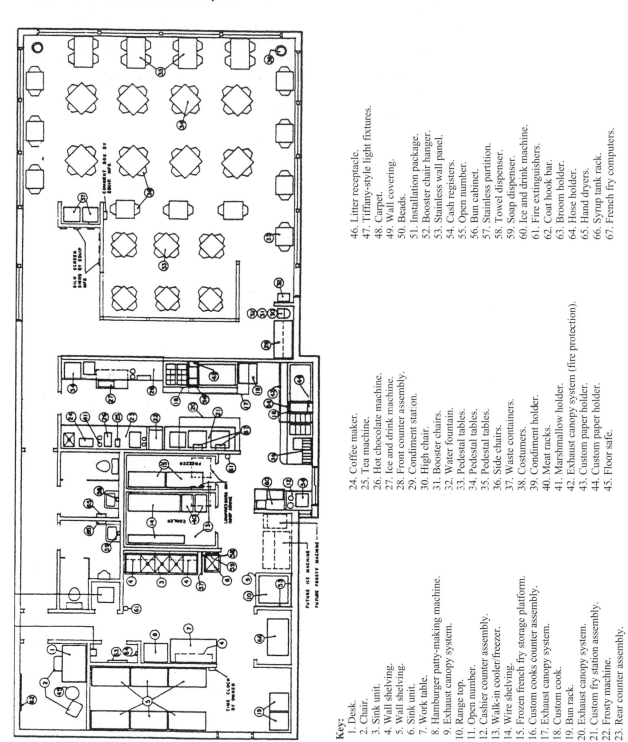

Key:
1. Desk.
2. Chair.
3. Sink unit.
4. Wall shelving.
5. Wall shelving.
6. Sink unit.
7. Work table.
8. Hamburger patty-making machine.
9. Exhaust canopy system.
10. Range top.
11. Open number.
12. Cashier counter assembly.
13. Walk-in cooler/freezer.
14. Wire shelving.
15. Frozen french fry storage platform.
16. Custom cooks counter assembly.
17. Exhaust canopy system.
18. Custom cook.
19. Bun rack.
20. Exhaust canopy system.
21. Custom fry station assembly.
22. Frosty machine.
23. Rear counter assembly.
24. Coffee maker.
25. Tea machine.
26. Hot chocolate machine.
27. Ice and drink machine.
28. Front counter assembly.
29. Condiment station.
30. High chair.
31. Booster chairs.
32. Water fountain.
33. Pedestal tables.
34. Pedestal tables.
35. Pedestal tables.
36. Side chairs.
37. Waste containers.
38. Costumers.
39. Condiment holder.
40. Meat racks.
41. Marshmallow holder.
42. Exhaust canopy system (fire protection).
43. Custom paper holder.
44. Custom paper holder.
45. Floor safe.
46. Litter receptacle.
47. Tiffany-style light fixtures.
48. Carpet.
49. Wall covering.
50. Beads.
51. Installation package.
52. Booster chair hanger.
53. Stainless wall panel.
54. Cash registers.
55. Open number.
56. Bun cabinet.
57. Stainless partition.
58. Towel dispenser.
59. Soap dispenser.
60. Ice and drink machine.
61. Fire extinguishers.
62. Coat hook bar.
63. Broom holder.
64. Hose holder.
65. Hand dryers.
66. Syrup tank rack.
67. French fry computers.

post-World War II babies reaching their 20s and 30s, those young adults have been expanding faster than any other age group. As a result, it is thought that Wendy's success is coming not so much at the expense of the other burger chains but from having selected a special niche in the otherwise crowded market. Most agree that Wendy's basically expanded the market, and statistics from customer surveys bear out the claim. Fully 82% of all Wendy's business comes from customers over 25, an unusually old market for any fast-food chain. By contrast, McDonald's generated 35% of its revenues from youngsters under 19.

15   Wendy's advertising efforts have emphasized nationwide television advertising to attract this young adult market. Since 1974, Wendy's "Hot 'N Juicy" advertising theme has been central to this effort. In the late 1970s, with its position established, Wendy's national advertising started focusing on new market segments like dinner after 4 P.M. after family meals on weekends.[1] Wendy's early "Where's the beef" campaign became an advertising classic which forever distinguished Wendy's from the "bread burger." Since the 1980s, R. David Thomas [Dave] has increasingly been a key, cost-effective figure in Wendy's advertising.

Franchising

16   In 1972, Wendy's management made the decision to become a national chain as quickly as possible, which meant growing through franchising. The franchises were awarded on an area basis, rather than single-store franchises. While McDonald's awarded franchises on a site-by-site basis, Wendy's sold whole states or large areas as franchise territories. As a result, Wendy's 10 largest franchise owners operated a total of 406 restaurants by 1979. The franchise agreements were among the most straightforward in the restaurant industry and are deliberately designed to establish a fair business relationship. They specify the number of units to be opened within a certain time frame, the area to be developed, a technical assistance fee, and a royalty of 4% of gross sales. They also stipulate that 4% of gross sales be spent for local and national advertising. Wendy's operated no commissaries and sold no food, fixtures, or supplies to franchise owners.

17   To support their growing network of franchised restaurants, Wendy's franchise operations department maintained a staff of 50 franchise area supervisors who are the company's operations advisers to the franchise owners. They are charged with ensuring that Wendy's quality standards are met throughout the entire franchise network.

18   Wendy's also provided the following services to their franchisees:

- Site approval procedures for locations.

- On-site inspection and evaluation by staff representative.

- Counseling in business planning.

- Drawings and specifications for buildings.

- Training for franchisees at Wendy's headquarters.

- Advice on supplies from suppliers selected by Wendy's and assistance in establishing quality-control standards and procedures for supplies.

- Staff representatives to help in the opening of each restaurant.

- Assistance in planning opening promotion and continuing advertising, public relations, and promotion.

- Operations manual with information necessary to operate a Wendy's restaurant.

- Research and development in production and methods of operations.

- Information on policies, developments, and activities by means of bulletins, brochures, reports, and visits of Wendy's representatives.

- Paper-goods standards.

- National and regional meetings.

19   The criteria used by Wendy's for franchise selection is basically simple but strictly adhered to. They look for good proven business ability. The applicant must demonstrate that he or she is interested in making profits and does not mind getting involved. Wendy's did not make their profits by selling goods and services to their franchisees. Their income came from the restaurants' sales volume. Therefore, the franchisee must be able to build sales. While well known national franchises (e.g., McDonald's, Holiday Inn) discouraged or prohibited franchises owning competing brands (e.g., if McDonalds, then no KFC; if Holiday Inn, then no Days Inn), R. David Thomas rejected these industry norms. He reasoned, to create rapid growth via franchising, that he should choose the most experienced restaurant chain builders that he could. He wanted them to have good local supplier contacts, a strong financial capability, ideally to have access to good restaurant operating people, and to understand how franchising worked—the role of franchisor and franchisee, the importance of national advertising, the dependence of each franchise location on another to build and maintain a quality image. Thomas's answer: seek Wendy's franchises among proven, successful builders of other food franchises (e.g., KFC franchises). As his new "entrepreneurial team" in any given territory, they brought restaurant expertise, local area expertise, and a capacity to understand the many strengths of Thomas's Wendy's concept if it was developed quickly.

20   Wendy's operates company-owned restaurants in 26 markets around the following cities:

Columbus, Ohio	33	Indianapolis, Indiana	15
Cincinnati, Ohio	20	Dallas/Ft. Worth, Texas	26
Dayton, Ohio	26	Houston, Texas	25
Toledo, Ohio	12	Oklahoma City, Oklahoma	12
Atlanta, Georgia	35	Tulsa, Oklahoma	12
Tampa, Sarasota	22	Memphis, Tennessee	13
St. Petersburg	15	Louisville, Kentucky	14
Clearwater, Florida	4	Syracuse, New York	10
Jacksonville, Florida	20	Harrisburg, Pennsylvania	22
Daytona Beach, Florida	10	Philadelphia, Pennsylvania	20
Detroit, Michigan	6	Virginia Beach, Virginia	15
Portland, Oregon	10	Charleston, West Virginia	14
Reno, Nevada	6	Parkersburg, West Virginia	20
Greensboro, North Carolina	10	Munich, West Germany	2

Other than Detroit, no franchises exist in these markets.

21   At the end of 1979, there were 1,385 franchised restaurants operated by 161 franchise owners in 47 states and 3 foreign countries.

22   In a report to the Securities and Exchange Commission, Wendy's discussed the current state of its franchise program and described the franchise owners' relationship with the company:

> Although franchised areas exist in all states except three, areas of some states remain unfranchised. In addition, most franchise owners have the right to build more units in their

franchised areas than had been constructed at December 31, 1979. At that date, no franchise owner had more than 88 stores in operation. Several franchise owners operate restaurants in more than one state.

The rights and franchise offered by the company are contained in two basic documents. A franchise owner first executes a development agreement. This document gives the franchise owner the exclusive right to select proposed sites on which to construct Wendy's Old Fashioned Hamburgers restaurants within a certain geographic area (the franchised area), requires the submission of sites to the company for its acceptance, and, upon acceptance of a proposed site by the company, provides for the execution of a unit franchise agreement with the company to enable the franchise owner to construct, own, and operate a Wendy's Old Fashioned Hamburgers restaurant upon the site. The development agreement provides for the construction and opening of a fixed number of restaurants within the franchised area in accordance with a development or performance schedule. Both the number of restaurants and the development and performance schedules are agreed upon by the franchise owner and the company prior to the execution of the development agreement. The development agreement also grants a right of first refusal to the franchise owner with respect to the construction of any additional restaurants in the franchised area beyond the initially agreed-to number.

The development agreement requires that the franchise owner pay the company a technical assistance fee. The technical assistance fee required by newly executed development agreement is currently $15,000 for each franchise restaurant which the franchise owner has agreed to construct. Under earlier forms of the development agreement or franchise agreements, this fee was either $5,000, $7,500, or $10,000. However, approximately 12 existing franchise owners have the right under certain circumstances to receive additional franchise areas on the basis of the earlier $10,000 fee.

The technical assistance fee is used to defray the cost to the company of providing to its franchise owners site selection assistance; standard construction plans, specifications, and layouts; company review of specific restaurant site plans; initial training in the company's restaurant systems; and such bulletins, brochures, and reports as are from time to time published regarding the company's plans, policies, research, and other business activities.

23   From time to time, during its early years, Wendy's reacquired selective franchised operations. In 1979, the company adopted a rather aggressive approach to franchise acquisition. Of 145 new company-owned operations in 1979 (representing a 50% increase during the year), 84 were acquired from franchisees. This major shift to company-owned restaurant growth away from franchised growth reflects the concern for systemwide control of quality as well as the increasing competition for available locations. Granting large territorial franchises rather than single-outlet franchises was similarly practiced by Burger King in its formative stages. At Burger King, this led to franchise empires that were bigger than parent-company operations. Wendy's emphasis on company-owned growth was intended to avoid the problem that led to Burger King's decline in the late 1960s. At the same time, selling area franchises rather than single sites accelerated Wendy's growth and its ability to attract large, financially strong franchises with proven success in other restaurant concepts.

Finances

24   Wendy's revenues (see Exhibit 3) increased steadily between 1975 and 1980. Net income dropped in 1979 compared to 1978, but Thomas explained:

> During 1979, we were informed by the U.S. Department of Labor that a review of company labor for a three-year period indicated that certain company policies had not been uniformly adhered to, and, as a result, the company was not in full compliance with the Fair Labor Standards Act.
>
> Based on this review and the company's own investigation, we have determined that $3,800,000 should be accrued and charged against 1979 pretax income. Had this charge not

EXHIBIT 3 Wendy's International, Incorporated Consolidated Statement of Income for the Years Ended
December 31, 1975–1979

Source: Wendy's International, Form 10-K, 1979.

	1979	1978	1977	1976	1975
Revenue:					
Retail operations	$237,753,097	$198,529,130	$130,667,377	$ 71,336,626	$ 35,340,665
Royalties	30,564,613	23,396,211	11,810,277	4,655,432	1,567,008
Technical assistance fees	2,822,500	3,540,000	2,510,000	1,560,000	622,500
Other, principally interest	2,903,261	2,685,909	1,802,691	965,521	246,901
Total revenues	274,043,471	228,151,250	146,790,345	78,517,579	37,777,074
Costs and expenses:					
Cost of sales	146,346,806	113,812,874	72,482,010	40,509,285	19,629,179
Company restaurant operating costs	51,193,050	43,289,285	28,088,460	14,348,150	7,292,391
Department of Labor compliance review	3,800,000				
Salaries, travel, and associated expenses of franchise personnel	4,187,399	3,148,532	1,936,877	1,156,493	622,879
General and administrative expenses	15,741,592	13,292,845	8,191,394	4,137,226	2,581,166
Depreciation and amortization of property and equipment	7,355,818	5,444,092	3,767,259	2,240,215	799,876
Interest	4,357,973	3,771,878	3,215,432	2,583,876	995,410
Total expenses	232,982,638	182,759,506	117,681,432	64,975,245	31,920,901
Income before income taxes	41,060,833	45,391,744	29,108,913	13,542,334	5,856,173
Income taxes:					
Federal:					
Current	15,583,700	18,324,600	12,052,200	5,784,600	2,926,700
Deferred	1,303,200	1,020,800	323,700	(19,600)	(501,900)
	16,886,900	19,345,400	12,375,900	5,765,000	2,424,800
State and local taxes	1,077,500	1,559,700	1,296,200	694,400	298,800
Total income taxes	17,964,400	20,905,100	13,672,100	6,459,400	2,723,600
Net income	$ 23,096,433	$ 24,486,644	$ 15,436,813	$ 7,082,934	$ 3,132,373
Net income per share	$1.54	$1.63	$1.04	$.57	$.29
Weighted average number of common shares outstanding	14,970,526	15,017,708	14,855,503	12,525,294	10,645,694
Dividends per common share	$0.40	$0.14	$0.125	$0.004	$0.001

been made, 1979 net income would have been $25,096,000, an increase of 8% over the
$23,215,000 originally reported a year earlier. We believe company labor practices now
comply with both company policy and the act, and, in addition, future compliance will not
materially affect net income in 1980 and ensuing years.

25   Whether the cost of labor compliance was the only cause of the abrupt slowdown in
Wendy's steady increase in revenue and profit is questionable. Several factors suggest
that Wendy's, after a decade of rapid growth, was reaching the limits of its current
capabilities.

EXHIBIT 4
Yearly Average Meat Price per Pound for Company-Owned Stores

1969	$0.59	1975	$0.69
1970	0.62	1976	0.72
1971	0.64	1977	0.72
1972	0.67	1978	1.02
1973	0.90	1979	1.29
1974	0.74		

EXHIBIT 5
Percentage Price Increases for Hamburgers

1/1/77	0.6%	10/22/78	0.15%
3/1/77	0.3	10/29/78	0.10
12/10/77	6.0	12/17/78	3.40
3/19/78	3.0	1/14/79	3.06
4/16/78	2.5	2/25/79	3.60
5/21/78	1.8	4/8/79	0.10
7/23/78	1.2	4/15/79	0.03
10/1/78	1.7	12/16/79	4.45

EXHIBIT 6
Average Sales per Restaurant

	1979		1978	
	Amount	Percent Change*	Amount	Percent Change*
Company	$624,000	(2.9)%	$624,900	14.3%
Franchise	618,800	(12.4)	706,000	11.7
Systemwide	620,000	(10.0)	688,800	13.0

*Percent increase (or decrease) over the same figure for the previous year.

26   The heart of Wendy's success has been its streamlined, limited menu with primary emphasis on a quality hamburger. Since 1977, beef prices have soared, as shown in Exhibit 4. And while Wendy's has responded with tighter controls and a series of price increases just under 15% for 1979 alone (see Exhibit 5), this has still contributed to a decline in profitability.

27   Further evidence suggests that Wendy's may have been reaching a pleteau in its historical pattern of growth. The average sales per restaurant, which climbed steadily from $230,000 in 1970 to $688,800 in 1978, declined significantly in 1979 at both company-owned and franchised restaurants, as shown in Exhibit 6. The impact on the parent company was felt in every revenue category, as shown in Exhibit 7. Wendy's continued to experience increased retail revenue (company-owned stores) and royalties (from franchises based on a percent of sales) but at a drastically slower rate. And for the first time, Wendy's experienced a decrease in technical assistance (franchise) fees.

28   Other evidence of a slowdown in Wendy's growth can be seen in the rate of new store openings. For the first time in its history, Wendy's experienced a decline in the rate of new store openings, as shown in Exhibit 8.

29   While revenue and profitability growth slowed in 1979, Thomas was confident this was only temporary. Feeling strongly that Wendy's was in a good position to finance continued growth, Thomas offered the following observation:

> While construction money is more difficult to obtain than in the last few years, lines of credit already arranged guarantee financing of 1980 company plans to open 60 or more restaurants. We also anticipate exploring avenues of long-term debt to finance our growth beyond 1980.

EXHIBIT 7
Changes in Revenue
from 1978 to 1979

	1979		1978	
	Amount*	Percent†	Amount	Percent
Retail operations	$39,224,000	19.8%	$67,862,000	51.9
Royalties	7,168,000	30.6	11,586,000	98.1
Technical assistance fees	(718,000)	(20.3)	1,030,000	41.0
Other, principally interest	(217,000)	(8.1)	883,000	49.0

*Absolute dollar increase (or decrease) over the previous year.
†Percent increase (or decrease) over the previous year.

EXHIBIT 8
New Restaurant
Openings: 1979
versus 1978

	Company*		Franchise		Systemwide	
	1979	1978	1979	1978	1979	1978
Open at beginning of year	348	271	1,059	634	1,407	905
Opened during the year	71	77	340	425	411	502
Purchased from franchise owners	14	—	(14)	—	—	—
Total open at end of year	433	348	1,385	1,059	1,818	1,407
Average open during year	381	309	1,235	828	1,616	1,137

*Restaurants acquired from franchise owners in poolings of interest have been included since date of opening.

We believe that with $25 million of long-term debt, exclusive of capitalized lease obligations, and over $100 million in shareholders' equity, we have substantial untapped borrowing power.

Exhibit 9 summarizes Wendy's balance sheet for 1978 and 1979.

WENDY'S FUTURE

30 Addressing Wendy's stockholders in early 1980, R. David Thomas offered the following thoughts about Wendy's first 10 years:

We are proud to be marking the 10th anniversary of Wendy's International, Inc. Just 10 years ago, in November 1969, we opened the first Wendy's Old Fashioned Hamburgers restaurant in downtown Columbus, Ohio. Now, after a decade of explosive growth, there are 1,818 Wendy restaurants in 49 states and in Canada, Puerto Rico, Germany, Switzerland and agreements for development of Japan, France, Belgium, Luxembourg, the Netherlands, Switzerland, Spain, Germany, and the United Kingdom. In 1979, our industry was faced with major challenges, such as inflation and energy problems. Higher labor costs and rising beef prices affected Wendy's profitability and depressed profits for our entire industry. The minimum wage, which affects 90 percent of our employees, increased in January 1979 and January 1980. Ground beef prices increased to an average of $1.29 per pound in 1979, 79 percent higher than the 1977 average price. During 1979, we minimized our retail price increases, with the goal of increasing our market share. This strategy, coupled with more aggressive marketing, helped rebuild customer traffic in the latter part of the year. Although holding back on price increases affected our margins, we believe it was appropriate and that margins benefited by our cost efficiencies, especially in purchasing and distribution.

During 1979, we remained flexible and open to changing customer needs and attitudes, and we continued to take the steps necessary to achieve and support future growth and profitability as we—

- Tested and implemented a highly successful salad bar concept.
- Tested a breakfast concept and other menu items.

EXHIBIT 9

Wendy's
International,
Incorporated
Consolidated Balance
Sheets for the Years
Ended December 31,
1978, and 1979

Source: Wendy's International,
Form 10-K, 1979.

	1979	1978
Assets		
Current assets:		
Cash	$ 2,285,180	$ 1,021,957
Short-term investments, at cost, which		
approximates market, including accrued interest	12,656,352	27,664,531
Accounts receivable	4,902,746	3,248,789
Inventories and other	2,581,528	1,855,313
Total current assets	22,425,806	33,790,590
Property and equipment, at cost Schedule 5:		
Land	30,916,049	23,906,365
Buildings	40,784,581	30,049,552
Leasehold improvements	16,581,947	8,954,392
Restaurant equipment	34,052,952	24,461,860
Other equipment	9,722,666	8,413,363
Construction in progress	1,751,788	2,027,570
Capitalized leases	21,865,829	18,246,427
Total property and equipment before depreciation	155,675,812	116,059,529
Less: Accumulated depreciation and amortization	(20,961,702)	(13,543,473)
Total property and equipment	134,714,110	102,516,056
Cost in excess of net assets acquired, less		
amortization of $699,410 and $481,162, respectively	8,408,788	5,207,942
Other assets	7,152,131	2,377,648
Total cost over net assets and other assets	15,560,919	7,585,590
Total assets	$172,700,835	$143,892,236
Liabilities and Shareholders' Equity		
Current liabilities:		
Accounts payable, trade	$ 10,174,980	$11,666,272
Federal, state, and local income taxes		7,839,586
Accrued expenses:		
Administrative fee		664,770
Salaries and wages	2,368,244	1,970,977
Interest	433,540	369,603
Taxes	1,932,192	1,498,521
Department of Labor compliance review	3,800,000	
Other	1,576,851	739,588
Current portion, term debt, and capitalized lease obligations	3,891,247	2,781,671
Total current liabilities	24,177,054	27,530,988
Term debt, net of current portion	25,097,688	15,308,276
Capital lease obligations, net of current portion	18,707,838	15,130,617
	43,805,526	30,438,893
Deferred technical assistance fees	1,995,000	2,117,500
Deferred federal income taxes	2,027,604	664,300
Shareholders' equity:		
Common stock, $.10 stated value; authorized:		
40,000,000 shares; issued and outstanding:		
14,882,614 and 14,861,877 shares, respectively	1,488,261	1,486,188
Capital in excess of stated value	34,113,173	33,962,916
Retained earnings	65,094,217	47,691,451
Total shareholders' equity	100,695,651	83,140,555
Total liabilities and shareholders' equity	$172,700,835	$143,892,236

- Began development of the European and Japanese markets.
- Initiated a new marketing program designed to increase dinner and weekend business.
- Prepared to open another 250 to 300 Wendy's restaurants systemwide annually.

31   And, setting the tone for Wendy's in the 1980s, Thomas said:

> We are aware, as we enter our second decade, that we have achieved a unique position in a highly competitive industry. It was no less difficult and competitive 10 years ago than it is today, we believe, than it will be 10 years from now. We intend to build further on our achievement of being recognized as a chain of high-quality, quick-service restaurants. We will continue to produce fresh, appealing, high-quality food; price it competitively; and serve it in a clean, attractive setting with employees who are carefully selected, well trained, and responsive to our customers.

32   Similar to the way they questioned R. David Thomas's venture into the hamburger jungle, several business writers once again began to question Wendy's future. Illustrative of this is the following article, which appeared in *The Wall Street Journal:*

> Wendy's International, Inc., is making changes it once considered unthinkable.
>
> Wendy's faced the choice confronting many companies when the initial burst of entrepreneurial brilliance dims: Should it stick with the original concept and be content with a niche in a bigger market, or should it change and attempt to keep growing? Wendy's chose to revamp its operations. It is adding salad bars, chicken and fish sandwiches, and a children's meal to its menu, adopting a new advertising strategy, and considering whether to alter the appearance of its restaurants.
>
> Some observers predict Wendy's will regret the quick changes. "This is a company that was able to convince a certain segment of the country it had a different taste in hamburgers," says Carl De Biase, an analyst with Sanford C. Bernstein & Co. in New York. "They've achieved their mandate, and anything they do now is just going to screw up the concept."
>
> But Robert Barney, Wendy's president and chief executive officer, says the company is "in some very difficult times right now." Among the problems: discontented franchise holders and the likelihood that beef prices will rise sharply again in the second half. Barney says Wendy's doesn't even "have the luxury of waiting to see" how each change works before moving to the next one.
>
> This spring, shortly after the changes began, Thomas resigned as chief executive, saying he wanted more time for public relations work and community affairs. Thomas, who is 47 years old and will continue as chairman, had been closely identified with the old ad campaign and with company resistance to broadening the menu.
>
> The company has been doing a little better so far this year, and franchisees say they're much more optimistic. The menu changes, they say, were long overdue. "It had been suggested to everyone in the company," says Raymond Schoenbaum, who operates 33 Wendy's outlets in Alabama and Georgia. "But the mentality wouldn't allow menu diversification before. It had to be forced on them."
>
> Barney concedes that prior to last year "we never did a lot of planning." But that has been remedied, he says, partly with a "research and development department" that will examine new menu prospects.
>
> Not everyone believes that tinkering with the menu will bring back customers and profits. Edward H. Schmitt, president of McDonald's, predicts an image problem for Wendy's and maintains that the company will lose the labor advantage it held over other fast-food outlets. He adds that McDonald's tried and abandoned salad bars. "It's practically a no-profit item," he says, "and it's a high-waste item."
>
> Some franchisees complain that the new children's meal, called Fun Feast, will draw the company into a can't-win competition with McDonald's and Burger King for the children's market, which Wendy's has avoided so far. "Every survey we have says we shouldn't go after that market," a franchisee reports. "Our chairs aren't designed for kids to climb on, and our carpet isn't designed for kids to spill ketchup on."

But Barney insists that Fun Feast isn't intended to attract children. He says Wendy's is trying to remove the adults' reason for not coming to the restaurant. "Where we tested it," he says, "we didn't sell so many of them but we did see an increase in adult traffic."

Wendy's may evolve from a sandwich shop into a more generalized quick-service restaurant that doesn't compete as directly with McDonald's and Burger King. "We're going to be between" McDonald's and quick-service steakhouses, says Schoenbaum, the Georgia and Alabama franchise holder.

To this end, Schoenbaum says, Wendy's will reduce the abundance of plastic fixtures in its restaurants and perhaps cut down on the amount of glass. He says the glass makes Wendy's a pleasant, brightly lit lunch spot but doesn't create a good atmosphere for dinner.

Wendy's officials confirm that they are considering altering the appearance of their restaurants, but they aren't specific. And as for whom Wendy's competes with, Barney says: "We're in competition with anywhere food is served, including the home."[2]

SEARCHING FOR A NEW IDENTITY: 1980–1990

33   Focusing on a long-term growth strategy of continued U.S. penetration, international growth, and concentric diversification into the chicken segment, Wendy's management team reached 4,000 Wendy's restaurants by 1990. Several things have happened, including numerous changes at Wendy's, since 1979. This section provides 29 observations to help you see what happened at Wendy's between 1979 and 1989.

Product/Market Developments

34   The R&D department has helped develop quality products that will help Wendy's growing in the future. The department develops new products within these guidelines:

Any product additions must reinforce their quality image.

They must be profitable.

They must expand a market base.

They must increase frequency of visits.

They must merge easily into their system of operations.

They must help reduce vulnerability to beef price.

35   Wendy's developed and introduced in the 1980s the following products:

The "Garden Spot" Salad Bar and Baked Potatoes for weight-conscious people.

The Chicken Breast Sandwich to respond to high beef price and to provide variety.

The Wendy's Kids' Fun Pack for families with children.

Breakfast to attack McDonald's lack of variety.

36   The core of the strategic role of R&D is to increase sales up to $1 million a year per restaurant. In 1989, the average net sales per domestic restaurant was $789,000, representing a 28% increase in 10 years.

Financial

37   Wendy's revenues result primarily from sales by company-operated restaurants. Royalties and technical-assistance fees from franchisees make up the other major source of revenues. In 1989, 91% of the $1.07 billion revenues came from retail sales, 7% from royalties, and 2% from others.

38   With the exception of the buns sold by New Bakery Company of Ohio, Inc., Wendy's does not sell food or supplies to the franchise owners. The New Bakery Company of Ohio, Inc., was acquired by Wendy's in 1981 and now supplies about 1,000 restaurants with buns.

39   Revenues went up to reach a peak in 1986 with $1.15 billion, then decreased to $1.06 billion in 1987 and 1988, and gained 1% in 1989 to reach $1.07 billion. After 1979, net income increased steadily until 1985, when it reached $76 million. Wendy's suffered from a loss of $4.6 million the next year, but its profits became positive and increasing again the following years. In 1989, net income was $30.4 million. The dip in net income of 1986 is reflected in the lower pretax profit margin, which dropped from 11.9% to 1.3% in one year.

40   Out of the capital expenditures in the beginning of the 80s, about 50% were for new domestic restaurants, 25% for the new subsidiary Sisters and international restaurants, and 25% for costs associated with the image-enhancement program, restaurant refurbishing, and computerized registers. After reaching a peak in 1985, with $222 million capital expenditures, Wendy's decreased gradually its investments to $39 million in 1989. In this last year, Wendy's spent $24 million for improvements to existing restaurants and $15 million to others' additions. Exhibit 10 contains additional financial information summarizing Wendy's 1980–1990 results.

Operations

41 Wendy's marketing strategy has been to target the high-quality end of the quick-service market with primary appeal among young middle-age adults, and its philosophy of quality, service, cleanliness, and value was aimed at this key segment of the population.

42   The population of the baby boomers matures. The age range of this segment will be from 35 to 54 years old from 1980 to 1995. Also, currently 50% of Wendy's orders are eaten away from the restaurant. Therefore, the maturing population and the increasing demand for convenience and portability will shape Wendy's products in the future.

43   Wendy's is moving its exterior image further away from the brightly colored, plastic fast-food atmosphere with a new, upgraded image, which features copper-colored roof panels and decorative awnings and lightings. The company spent $18 million on remodeling restaurants in 1989.

44   Advertising spending has been increased. Franchise owners, in addition to spending 3% of their gross receipts for local advertising and promotions, have increased their contribution to Wendy's National Advertising Program (WNAP) from 1% in 1980 to 1.5% in 1985, and to 2% in 1989. This same year, WNAP spent $55 million on advertising and promotion expenses, a 4% increase over 1988 spending levels.

45   Advertising in the fast-food burger chain industry has become more fierce since Burger King launched its now-famous comparative advertising campaign.

46   In the second half of 1985 and into 1986, the company's efforts and advertising were focused on implementing the breakfast program systemwide. During that period, Wendy's major competitors also began to more aggressively advertise their hamburger products. Wendy's began to see some sales erosion in its products and dayparts. As a result, the challenges Wendy's faced were intensified.

47   Management took decisive action in response to these issues. The breakfast program was made optional for franchise owners and retained by the company only where economically viable. Also, the company launched a realignment program in mid-1986,

EXHIBIT 10 Selected Financial Data

Wendy's International, Inc. & Subsidiaries

	1990	1989	1988	1987	1986	1985	1984	1983	1982	1981	1980
Operations (in millions)											
Systemwide Wendy's sales	$3,070.3	3,036.1	2,901.6	2,868.9	2,747.2	2,694.8	2,423.0	1,922.9	1,632.4	1,424.2	1,209.3
Retail sales	$ 922.2	973.1	976.6	987.2	1,039.3	1,033.0	877.3	671.6	565.4	450.9	310.1
Revenues	$1,010.9	1,069.7	1,062.6	1,059.8	1,149.7	1,128.6	946.7	728.7	613.1	492.8	348.4
Company restaurant operating profit	$ 115.5	84.1	107.1	81.8	136.6	176.8	166.4	129.6	104.3	76.8	54.4
Income (loss) before income taxes	$ 60.7	36.9	43.8	(11.6)	14.9	134.7	128.4	101.4	80.7	64.7	54.7
Net income (loss)*	$ 39.3	30.4	28.5	4.5	(4.9)	76.2	68.7	55.2	44.1	36.9	30.1
Capital expenditures	$ 41.7	38.9	56.0	73.9	120.3	221.9	153.5	87.4	81.6	74.9	52.6
Financial Position (in millions)											
Total assets	$ 757.9	779.6	777.0	786.2	814.2	853.3	656.1	542.5	485.0	387.4	220.3
Property and equipment, net	$ 569.6	579.6	593.1	610.2	643.8	704.9	518.2	405.4	348.3	291.9	175.6
Long-term obligations	$ 168.1	178.9	192.6	195.4	223.2	235.5	139.0	115.7	128.2	105.6	43.1
Shareholders' equity	$ 446.8	428.9	419.6	412.2	424.7	443.5	364.5	308.3	264.7	201.7	125.6
Per Share Data											
Net income (loss)*	$ .41	.32	.30	.05	(.05)	.82	.75	.61	.51	.46	.40
Dividends	$ .24	.24	.24	.24	.21	.17	.15	.12	.09	.08	.08
Shareholders' equity	$ 4.61	4.44	4.36	4.29	4.45	4.65	3.98	3.40	2.92	2.37	1.68
Market price at year-end	$ 6.38	4.63	5.75	5.63	10.25	13.38	10.00	9.38	6.63	4.25	2.88
Ratios											
Company restaurant operating profit margin	% 12.5	8.6	11.0	8.3	13.1	17.1	19.0	19.3	18.4	17.0	17.5
Pretax profit margin	% 6.0	3.4	4.1	—	1.3	11.9	13.6	13.9	13.2	13.1	15.7
Return on average assets†	% 10.8	7.9	8.5	2.1	4.8	21.7	24.7	23.5	22.7	24.9	31.1
Return on average equity	% 9.0	7.2	6.9	1.1	—	19.3	20.4	19.3	19.5	22.0	26.6
Current	.90	.95	1.00	.75	.81	.44	.56	.69	.81	.61	.54
Debt to equity	% 38	42	46	47	53	53	38	38	48	52	34
Debt to total capitalization	% 27	29	31	32	34	35	28	27	33	34	26

EXHIBIT 10

Wendy's International, Inc. & Subsidiaries

	1990	1989	1988	1987	1986	1985	1984	1983	1982	1981	1980
Restaurant Data											
Domestic Wendy's open at year-end											
Company	**982**	1,031	1,076	1,114	1,206	1,135	1,014	887	802	734	502
Franchise	**2,454**	2,459	2,445	2,468	2,290	2,106	1,801	1,633	1,503	1,386	1,450
International Wendy's open at year-end											
Company	**88**	87	97	115	129	122	43	35	25	14	4
Franchise	**203**	178	144	119	102	79	134	118	100	95	78
Total Wendy's	**3,727**	3,775	3,762	3,816	3,727	3,442	2,992	2,673	2,430	2,229	2,034
Average net sales per domestic Wendy's restaurant (in thousands)											
Company	**$ 832**	808	793	786	765	850	874	749	687	679	650
Franchise	**$ 803**	781	744	721	748	846	870	769	712	670	634
Total domestic	**$ 811**	789	759	741	754	847	871	762	704	672	638
Other Data											
Weighted average shares outstanding (in thousands)	**96,707**	96,378	96,168	95,783	95,879	92,828	91,903	91,168	87,034	80,990	75,702
Shareholders of record at year-end	**53,000**	55,000	58,000	52,000	48,000	41,000	31,000	25,000	20,000	19,000	18,000
Number of employees at year-end	**35,000**	39,000	42,000	45,000	50,000	48,000	43,000	36,000	29,000	26,000	18,000

*1990, 1989, and 1987 reflect a $696,000, $1.6 million, $.02 per share; $1 million, $.01 per share extraordinary gain on early extinguishment of debt, respectively; net income in 1989 includes the cumulative effect of change in accounting for income taxes of $5.2 million, $.05 per share.

†Return on average assets is computed using income before income taxes and interest charges.

intended to substantially improve its operating and financial performance. The major portion of the plan involved the disposition of all marginal or unprofitable company-operated restaurants, including international restaurants and Sisters as well as domestic restaurants. The company intends to franchise the majority of the domestic restaurants, and the remaining restaurants have been closed.

Franchising

48   Two main thrusts appear to characterize Wendy's franchising emphasis for the 1980s: (1) enhanced operational control and support of domestic franchises and (2) expansion through international locations.

49   The systemwide number of restaurants reached 3,755 in 1989. But as a result of the realignment program, the number of company-owned restaurants kept decreasing from 1986 to 1989, while the number of franchises increased during the same period. However, Wendy's continues to buy franchises from time to time.

50   To stimulate growth, the company announced a unit franchise strategy in the early 1980s. This concept enabled individuals who could not develop a multiunit franchise to join the Wendy's family. To avoid the problem that led Burger King to a decline in the 1960s, Wendy's spends an increasing time in assessing and selecting the franchised locations and managers and also provides the personnel an increasing amount of training. This reflects the concern for systemwide control of quality.

International

51   Wendy's established an international division in 1979, and, by 1989, there were 265 restaurants in foreign countries—87 of them were company-owned. The top 5 international markets and number of restaurants were Canada (131 restaurants), Japan (26), Spain (17), Korea (14), and the Philippines (13).

52   Of the fast-food industry, McDonald's is the best established internationally, with approximately 1,500 units in 32 countries (data of 1983). They are heavily concentrated in Canada, Japan, Australia, and various parts of Europe. It is expecting to develop this international market at a rate of 150 additional units a year. Burger King had in 1983 about 300 units abroad.

53   There are numerous pitfalls and high risks to overseas expansion since, for instance, European per capita spending on "fast-food" is only $3.50 a year, compared to approximately $150 for each American in 1982. Also capital investment—land and buildings—and labor consume a large part of revenues in some countries, such as West Germany. As a matter of fact, after having opened about 30 restaurants in West Germany, Wendy's decided to terminate those operations in 1987.

54   Wendy's strategy in the international market is to be flexible in order to be successful in the face of differing eating habits and tastes. It consistently opens new international restaurants but it does not hesitate to terminate any unprofitable operations.

Sisters' Development

55   Thinking that the fast-food burger industry might be oversaturated, Wendy's decided to apply the principles that built its success to other segments of the industry, particularly to the chicken restaurant industry.

56   Wendy's initially owned 20% of Sisters International and, in 1981, exercised its option to purchase the remaining 80%. The Sisters' concept, to combine the self-service of the quick-food industry with the full menu and warmth of comfortable dining facilities of the traditional family restaurant, is designed to appeal specifically to the maturing, value-conscious consumer.

57 There were 79 Sisters open at the end of 1985. The company operated 38 of these. However, in 1987, as a result of the realignment program Wendy's sold its subsidiary to SIS CORP, Sisters' largest franchisee, for $14.5 million in cash and notes.

Management Reorganization

58 For the first 10 years of its history, Wendy's was guided by an entrepreneurial spirit that gave the company the fastest growth record in the history of this industry. However, with the pressure of soaring beef prices, inflation, and recession, founder and former chairman R. David Thomas, who served as senior chairman of the board, took the first step in 1980, when he recommended to the board that president Robert L. Barney be named chief executive officer. Barney implemented the remainder of the management reorganization program.

59 In 1989, James W. Near assumed the functions of CEO, president, and chief operating officer. He replaced Ronald Faye, president from 1980 to 1986, and Barney, former CEO and chairman of the board, who retired in 1989. A new regional structure was also instituted for the Company Operations and Franchising Department, along with the Franchise Advisory Council, in order to increase communication and cooperation between company management and franchisees.

60 The company had 50,000 employees in 1986, but, as part of the realignment program, this number decreased to 35,000 people by 1990.

Wendy's (B): Returning to Its Entrepreneurial Roots?

61 Throughout the 1980s, Wendy's appeared to explore numerous ways to continue growth. Some felt it began to lose focus over the course of these events. By the end of the decade Dave Thomas and the Wendy's management team felt these observations had validity. Perhaps Wendy's had lost its focus. They sought, in a sense, to return Wendy's to its "entrepreneurial roots." This [B] case describes Wendy's strategic program in preparation for the 21st century. Chairman and CEO Gordon Teter gave an overview of Wendy's search for a new entrepreneurial focus when he recently reflected on those deliberations:

> Seven years ago we decided the Wendy's strategic plan would be to refocus on four key strategies and to be consistent, yet flexible, in achieving our goals. The validity of our resolve has been borne out by marked success since that time.
>
> Staying focused on our strategic goals hasn't always been easy. Our fiercely competitive environment became cluttered with discount schemes. Despite the temptation to emulate someone else's game plan, we kept ourselves on our playing field with a strong, balanced strategic plan. Thus far, our steady focus on our long-term goals has proven to be a winner.
>
> Our average domestic company unit volumes have increased for nine consecutive years. Mainly that is a reflection of consumer satisfaction with our program. It is gratifying to know that they continue to tell us that in the world of quick service, Wendy's is their favorite restaurant, number one in the quality and variety of food on our menu, first in overall satisfaction, and tops in other more specific attributes, such as nutrition.
>
> When customers visit Wendy's we want to be predictable and familiar yet strive to exceed their expectations. We believe, too, that when customers and employees alike are treated with respect, it creates a strong performance-driven culture and a solid base of people throughout the system.
>
> Our strategic plan also calls for stepped up Wendy's activity in international markets. We have spent several years strengthening our franchise system as well as restructuring and staffing Wendy's international operations. That work is virtually complete, giving us a strong, dedicated development team. Among their first tasks will be to complete an exciting joint venture in Argentina—a large, local quick-service restaurant chain will join forces with Wendy's to penetrate the Argentine market.
>
> Argentina could well serve as a gateway to other South American countries, particularly Chile.
>
> Asia continues to be our strongest overseas market, led by Japan, where our franchisee opened its 50th Wendy's restaurant in 1995.
>
> The global strategy is exciting and holds tremendous promise. While the Wendy's domestic operation is still the engine that powers the entire system, our goal is for our International Division to become a strong driver of growth.
>
> No matter what the setting, we are confident we have a strong brand, an equally strong people base, and the focused strategies to build on our success.

WENDY'S CORE (DOMESTIC) STRATEGY: FOCUS ON FOUR BASIC THEMES

62 Since Dave Thomas served his first hamburger thirty years ago, Wendy's has enjoyed a reputation for quality. It is a reputation well earned and justly recognized. For 20 years, surveys by *Restaurants & Institutions* magazines named Wendy's America's favorite (highest quality) quick-service hamburger chain. In addition to being the consumer's restaurant of choice, Wendy's has set its sights on being the "franchisor of choice" and the "employer of choice." Its four-part strategy, which Wendy's initiated around 1990, is designed to help their domestic operation achieve and maintain a vision of Wendy's as a quality leader providing fresh food, fast, in convenient, adult-friendly locations.

63 The first part of Wendy's strategy is to strive to operate its restaurants in a manner that exceeds customer expectations on each visit. They see the key to this being to never underestimate the importance of operational excellence. To achieve this, Wendy's approach to management includes such characteristics as relatively narrow spans of control, heavy investment in training, exacting standards, and incentive compensation systems.

64 Having modern, efficient restaurants also is important in exceeding customer expectations, so Wendy's is making some major changes in its properties. To improve speed of service and convenience for its customers, for example, Wendy's has been adding a second pick-up window for drive-through service. By the end of the decade, virtually all of Wendy's restaurants will have been retrofitted to have two pick-up windows, significantly improving service.

65 In addition, Wendy's is adding drive-through "WenView," an electronic menu board. It has been well received by Wendy's customers because it visually displays what was ordered and the total price, which, Wendy's believes, improves accuracy.

66 Wendy's second theme is to accelerate new store development while strengthening the quality of each Wendy's location. Bottomline, Wendy's seeks to eliminate weaker existing locations or turn around those with higher performance potential. Two examples illustrate this: 1) Wendy's acquisition of a New York competitor and 2) Wendy's franchise "simultaneous equation" program.

- Wendy's aggressively looks for competitor restaurant sites that might be available to buy and convert to Wendy's. In 1995, for example, Wendy's acquired 45 restaurants belonging to a competitor in the New York market. After their conversion to Wendy's, its presence in that market increased by approximately one-third.

- Wendy's aggressively buys back franchisee stores, usually weak performers, then refurbishes and otherwise "fixes" each store. It then resells the store(s) to other franchisees or new franchisees—what Wendy's calls its "simultaneous equation" program—which Wendy's feels has been successful in boosting the health of the system through the buying and selling of restaurants between Wendy's and the franchise community. Where necessary, purchased stores have been remodeled and improved and, in some cases, refranchised. The results of this program in 1991–1997 are summarized in Exhibit 11.

67 The third key element of Wendy's domestic strategy is to aggressively increase market penetration by adding new units or what Wendy's call "special sites"—locations such as retail centers, hospitals and gasoline outlets.

EXHIBIT 11

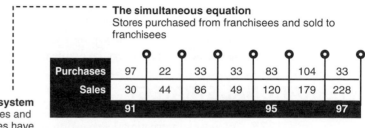

The simultaneous equation
Stores purchased from franchisees and sold to franchisees

Purchases	97	22	33	33	83	104	33
Sales	30	44	86	49	120	179	228
	91			95			97

Growing a healthy system
Restaurant purchases and sales with our franchisees have helped us to build a stronger Wendy's system

68   Wendy's is particularly focusing on truck stops which will give way to "travel centers" that are as inviting to families as they are to truckers. Exxon, BP, Texaco, Shell, Pilot Oil, and Petro are among the oil companies that are working with Wendy's to develop these locations. Wendy's seeks to establish 25–50 Wendy's restaurants each year in concert with a service station or "travel center." And Wendy's will also add airport sites on a selective basis.

69   The fourth element of Wendy's new millennium strategy is a marketing strategy of leveraging Wendy's strong quality perception with promotional items positioned at the upper end of the price-quality spectrum. Examples include: Fresh Stuff Pitas, Smoky Bacon Cheeseburger, Monterey Ranch Chicken, Chicken Cordon Blue, and the extremely popular Spicy Chicken Sandwich, which appeared for the third time, doing better each time.

70   Wendy's seeks to balance these check building tactics with a daily, low-price approach to providing economical options to its customers through the Super Value menu, combination meals, and a $1.99 Kids' Meal. This approach, Wendy's believes, enables it to compete in an environment in which their competitors have heavily discounted their flagship products. Discounting tends to erode profits and brand equity. Wendy's prefers to avoid discounting and rather to offer value in ways consistent with building the strength of its brand.

71   Wendy's believes that one of its greatest assets is the equity in the "Wendy's" brand. Another is Dave Thomas. Wendy's thoughts about Dave:

> He represents everything that is good about our brand. Consumers can easily identify with Dave Thomas because he is very likable, approachable, very honest, has real integrity, and he is a genuine human being. In our advertising, people can see that and identify with him. Dave Thomas will continue to be our advertising spokesman. Our total advertising awareness ratings approach or surpass those of our two major competitors, both of whom dramatically outspend us in terms of media dollars. This speaks to both the effectiveness of the Dave Thomas advertising campaign as well as to the efficiency with which we spend our advertising dollars.

Wendy's Domestic Franchising

72   Wendy's expects 25 to 30 new franchisees each year, with a significant number being minority operators. Of the new franchisees entering the system in the late 1990s, approximately one-third were minority operators. Approximately one in four stores were minority-owned by 1998, which is increasing at 16% annually. Wendy's believes this trend is further strengthening and diversifying the system.

73   Wendy's believes it provides a very attractive program for franchisees. Each year Wendy's gets approximately 10,000 inquiries from individuals interested in joining the Wendy's franchise system.

74   To help its franchisees expand with new stores, Wendy's maintains relationships with nine financial institutions that provide financing for new stores, remodeling and other needs. It also has a new program that enables both new and existing franchisees to finance new stores at very favorable rates.

INTERNATIONAL STRATEGY

75   Wendy's international expansion in the 1980s was sporadic and largely unsuccessful. The "catch-22" for Wendy's is the realization that the international arena is perhaps its most untapped growth opportunity. So Wendy's has sought to reconsider its international strategy and improve it for the next century. Wendy's sought to do this via two key initiatives:

1. Put a solid international development team into place, and

2. Enter Canada via a major acquisition of a compatible chain, Tim Hortons coffee/bakery shops.

Building an International Development Team

76 In 1995 Wendy's began building the foundation of its growth strategies by ensuring that it had the support structure required for growth. Wendy's hired several qualified management with food service or international experience, and the obstacles it faced earlier in the 90's began to disappear. Wendy's now has what it believes to be a strong organization in the field, with a vice president heading up each of four regional offices: in Honolulu for the Pacific region; in Miami for Latin American operations; in London for the European-Middle East region; and in Toronto for Canadian operations.

77 Each of the regional organizations has marketing, purchasing, operations, engineering, and other key support staff. In addition, training has been shifted to within each region, with satellite training centers in individual locales as needed.

78 Exhibit 12 summarizes Wendy's international growth plans. Canada was Wendy's largest region, with 245 Wendy's in 1998.

79 There's little question that Asia, Wendy's largest region, will be the immediate growth engine for international. It started 1998 with 235 sites. Japan, Indonesia, and the Philippines all have large populations and strong or emerging middle classes, and thus give Wendy's confidence that it can support expansion in those areas. These nations are its prime Asian targets. Of all new units planned for Asia, three-fourths of them will be in these three countries. On average, a restaurant approved for development internationally will open a year and a half later. In Japan, however, units open very quickly, so Wendy's expects this market to grow the fastest in number of stores.

EXHIBIT 12   **International Growth Plan**

Latin America/Caribbean	Canada	Europe/Middle East	Asia/Pacific
Status			
• Solid presence in the Caribbean • South America entry under way • 100% franchised and joint ventures	• Strongest penetration of a single country • Potential to more than double penetration • 50% franchised	• United Kingdom stores primarily company operated	• Solid presence in most major markets • Largest opportunity • 100% franchised and joint ventures
Priorities			
• Argentina, Puerto Rico, Venezuela, Brazil, Mexico	• Ontario, British Columbia, Alberta	• United Kingdom, Greece, Turkey	• Japan, Indonesia, Philippines
Strategy			
• Joint venture in new countries • Grow with existing franchisees in the Caribbean and Central America	• Grow with company and franchised stores • Continue development of combination units with Tim Hortons	• Expand franchising in the United Kingdom • Grow with existing franchisees	• Grow with existing franchisees

80   Latin American development will begin with Argentina, the fourth largest country in the region with a population of more than 33 million and a gross national product that ranks third in South America. Wendy's recently signed an agreement with the owners of an established restaurant chain in the Republic of Argentina for the development of Wendy's restaurants. This arrangement leverages the strength of both entities. Wendy's provides capital for development while its partner provides real estate, local market knowledge and restaurant operating skills.

Tim Hortons—Canada

81   Apart from the scarlet tunics of the Royal Canadian Mounted Police, nothing signifies quality, integrity, and service to Canadian consumers more than the bright, cardinal-red Tim Hortons signs throughout the northern nation. Founded in 1964, it is far and away Canada's largest quick-service restaurant chain offering primarily coffee and fresh baked goods. It is also Canada's overall second largest quick-service restaurant chain. At the end of 1997 there were 1,578 Tim Hortons restaurants, all but 38 of which were franchise operations, and systemwide sales were $771 million.

82   Wendy's and Tim Hortons completed a merger in late 1995. Wendy's agreed to issue 16.45 million common shares in exchange for all of the outstanding shares of Tim Hortons' Canadian parent company. The transaction was treated as a pooling of interests. Wendy's also assumed about $105 million in debt in connection with the transaction.

83   Wendy's and Tim Hortons began working together in 1992 when the first Wendy's/Tim Hortons combination restaurant opened June 1 in the Niagara peninsula at Beamsville, Ontario. A day later, it seemed as though the entire town of Montague, P.E.I., turned out to celebrate the grand opening of a second combination unit.

84   At the close of 1997, Wendy's crimson signs had joined Tim Hortons' in 48 successful Wendy's/Tim Hortons combination restaurants including the first in the United States in the Minneapolis suburb of Hopkins, Minnesota.

EXHIBIT 13
A Wendy's Milestone

50th Wendy's Opens in Japan

As Wendy's Senior Chairman and Founder Dave Thomas walked into the restaurant on a busy Tokyo street, he noticed an employee polishing the Wendy's sign outside. It sparkled in the bright sun.

Inside he was greeted, as are all customers, with a chorus of "Irasshaymase!" (Welcome!) by the team of well-groomed, smiling young managers and crew people. He looked around; the store was spotless. For Dave Thomas, the 50th Wendy's in Japan was nirvana—the perfect Wendy's.

The restaurant, at 1-27-12 Hamamatsu-cho, is operated by franchisee Wenco Japan, a subsidiary of the Daiei, Inc., one of the world's largest retailers. Wenco opened its first store in Tokyo in 1980 and the 50th, October 2, 1995.

During the opening ceremonies, the store manager personally pledged to his crew and to Wenco President Toshihiko Taniguchi "that we will put all our effort into providing the highest quality, made-to-order, juicy hamburgers and other incomparable food, supplied faster than anybody, thus ensuring our Number One position in the Hamamatsu area."

There's little question the manager felt challenged. Some Wenco Wendy's have the highest sales averages in the system. One Tokyo store averages $94,600 a week, or more than $4.5 million a year.

"This is just a beginning," said Mr. Taniguchi, who expects to have twice as many units open by 1997.

85   Fresh baked products prepared twice a day are vital to the chain's successful marketing mix. Freshness is the key, and it is achieved through "producing stores" equipped with bakeries.

86   The standard Tim Hortons units being built today are primarily freestanding "producing stores" totaling 3,000 square feet. Each includes a bakery capable of supplying fresh baked goods every 12 hours to several satellite Tim Hortons within a defined area. Most of the new stores also have drive-through windows.

87   In addition, Tim Hortons has had considerable success with prefabricated, 500 square foot, drive-through-only units. Satellite units and drive-through only units receive their baked goods from a "producing store" nearby. This concept leverages the capital invested in the kitchens of the larger restaurants.

88   Tim Hortons is proud to say, "We fit in anywhere," pointing out the versatility of the concept, from the Wendy's/Tim Hortons combination stores to the mobile cart that requires only 36 square feet in which to do business. In between are larger kiosks and full-service carts that can easily be placed in high traffic areas. Many of the smaller, modular Tim Hortons adapt well to special sites, such as airport terminals, hospitals and universities. At the University of Western Ontario in London, Ontario, for example, there are 14 Tim Hortons sites of different sizes. At the Calgary International Airport there are six outlets—one "producing store" and five satellites.

89   The largest of the freestanding units, of course, are the Wendy's/Tim Hortons combination restaurants, which average 5,000 square feet. Wendy's and Tim Hortons share a common dining room seating 104, but each has its own food preparation and storage areas and most have a pick-up window for each restaurant. The combination works because approximately 85% of Tim Hortons traffic takes place before Wendy's opens or during the afternoon snack hours when Wendy's is less busy. At midday and again at the dinner hour, the heaviest traffic is Wendy's.

90   Throughout the Tim Hortons system, approximately 71% of the restaurants are leased or subleased by Tim Hortons to the franchisees. The senior management of Tim Hortons actively participates in the selection of all new restaurant locations.

91   Over 40% of Tim Hortons' sales volume is in coffee—13 million pounds of its special blend last year. Every million pounds of coffee represents about 50 million 7-ounce

EXHIBIT 14
**A Combination
That Works**

A Canadian franchisee of both Wendy's and Tim Hortons, Danny Murphy found it a natural and successful step to also operate a pair of Wendy's/Tim Hortons combination units in his home province of Prince Edward Island. According to Murphy, "Sales at both Wendy's and Tim Hortons benefit from cross-marketing. Regular customers of one concept are introduced to the other concept at the combination units. Our 5,000 square-foot Canadian combination units feature separate kitchens for Wendy's and Tim Hortons, a shared 104 seat dining area, and drive-through windows for both concepts."

Development cost is generally lower for a combination unit than for separate Wendy's and Tim Hortons restaurants. Less land is required, and it is cheaper to build one combined larger building. This means that both concepts can enter areas together that might otherwise be impossible because of high land costs. Also, investment returns can be higher.

Yet another benefit realized at the Wendy's/Tim Hortons combination units is greater employee efficiency and stability. Murphy says he is able to offer eight-hour shifts instead of four, with some employees splitting their shift between Wendy's and Tim Hortons, changing uniforms in between.

The synergy is outstanding considering that more than 60% of Tim Hortons' average daily sales occur before 10:30 A.M., when the Wendy's side of the restaurant opens.

cups. Ground coffee is also sold in a 13-ounce can at the restaurants as well as in select supermarkets. Coffee is to Tim Hortons what beef is to Wendy's, so coffee price fluctuations are closely watched. After hitting highs in the fall of 1994, prices have declined dramatically.

92   Coffee and other nonperishable goods are distributed from six warehouse distribution centers in Moncton, New Brunswick; Calgary, Alberta; Debert, Nova Scotia; Langley, British Columbia; Kingston, Ontario; and Oakville, Ontario, Tim Hortons' corporate headquarters. The award-winning graphic design, featuring the coffee and a selection of freshly baked products, makes Tim Hortons' trucks rolling billboards on Canadian highways.

93   In the United States donut shops represent only 1.8% of traffic share among quick-service restaurants. The category's share is 11 times greater in the Canadian market. The result is that despite a population that is 10% of the United States, the donut category is larger in Canada. In 1995 revenues among Canada's donut shops totaled $987.4 million; in the U.S. revenues were almost $192 million less.

94   Tim Hortons leads the coffee and donut segment with 45.1% market share. Among all categories of quick-service restaurants, Tim Hortons enjoys the second-largest share of customer traffic with about 7.3% of the Canadian market.

95   Tim Hortons enjoys extraordinary loyalty. So devoted are its customers, who are primarily between 25 and 54 years of age, that it is not uncommon for some to visit the restaurant two or more times a day. Tim Hortons is a way of life for many customers, a meeting place, 24 hours a day. Often the staff will spot a "regular" coming in, knowing that customer wants a medium coffee black and an Apple Fritter, and have the order ready by the time the customer reaches the counter.

96   Tim Hortons' systemwide sales growth has averaged more than 20% annually in recent years. Buoyed by an annual national television and print advertising budget of more than $25 million, a minimum of 2,000 units in Canada was projected by the year 2000.

97   There is ample room for further development. For example, studies indicate metropolitan Toronto could absorb 100 to 150 Tim Hortons and twice that many in the province of Ontario, which already boasts more than 500 units.

DIVERSITY

98   Wendy's has developed a number of relationships with culturally and ethnically diverse entities, such as the National Minority Supplier Development Council, the Urban League, U.S. Hispanic Chamber of Commerce, and the NAACP. Wendy's has also had outstanding experiences. *Black Enterprise* Magazine and the Women's Foodservice Forum named Gordon Teter "Trailblazer of the Year" for building a diverse organization at Wendy's with women and minorities. In 1997 Wendy's increased purchases of goods and services from minority and female-owned businesses by 15%—its sixth consecutive year of increases. By 1999 over 25% of Wendy's franchisees were minority or female and minorities and females make up 75% of Wendy's workforce and 56.8% of its management.

SUPPLIER DIVERSITY

99   An example of Wendy's efforts to build a diverse group of partners is the founder and president of its sandwich wrap vendor, Wolf Packaging. Robert Ontiveros founded his company more than 20 years ago and has been an outstanding partner for over three

years. Today, Ontiveros' company is Wendy's exclusive sandwich wrap supplier throughout the U.S. and his company ranks 72nd in sales among the nations's top 500 Hispanic-owned businesses. Among his honors, Ontiveros was named Midwest Business Man of the Year in 1991, an award that recognizes business people of Hispanic descent who have achieved outstanding growth for their company, annual sales expansion, and civic involvement.

COMMUNITY INVOLVEMENT

100 Wendy's has a diverse community involvement program. For example, Wendy's sponsored the *Black Enterprise* "Kidpreneur Konference" in 1996 and 1997. Children ages four to 17 attended the conference and other events to learn about building a successful business. The older children also learned about writing a business plan, managing finances, and advertising while participating with a franchisee in the Orlando, Fla., market.

THE DAVE THOMAS FOUNDATION FOR ADOPTION

101 Started in 1992, the foundation continues to focus on making the adoption process easier and more affordable while creating awareness and educating the public about the thousands of children waiting to be adopted. Last year it celebrated the passage of landmark legislation and funding for some of the premier adoption projects in the country—all bringing the issue of adoption to national attention. But most gratifying to the trustees of the foundation and Dave was to see how the Wendy's family embraced the adoption cause in 1997. By developing relationships with local adoption agencies, Wendy's restaurants throughout the U.S. and Canada are supporting the foundation with wonderful programs. Company employees and franchisees have created dozens of programs and local public service announcements to bring prospective parents in touch with local agencies to help find children loving, permanent homes. In-store canister programs and other charity events have raised money for adoption organizations and awareness of the adoption cause. In Florida, a statewide in-store canister program generated more than $100,000 last year while thousands of restaurants displayed posters and tray liners during National Adoption Month in November featuring children waiting to be adopted along with the 1-800-TO-ADOPT phone number.

WENDY'S LOSES DAVE THOMAS

102 In early 2002, Wendy's beloved founder, Dave Thomas, died of liver cancer at age 69. Ronald McDonald aside, Mr. Thomas was the most familiar face in the fast-food industry for both insiders and consumers.

103 It wasn't ego that pushed Thomas to appear in almost 1,000 Wendy's commercials. It was necessity. Nothing else sold fast-food consumers on Wendy's like Dave. Although in reality day-to-day control of Wendy's had since 1989 been out of his hands, consumers still seemed to believe Thomas was somewhere in the back of the restaurant with an apron around his waist cooking the customized burger they had just ordered.

104 Now Wendy's is blessed to be linked with a lovable icon, and cursed with the reality that the man whose kind face sold more burgers than any single person on earth is gone. Said their CEO: "Dave was the messenger, not the message. We've been working on a seamless transition for three years."

105   Not so easy say others. $1.5 billion was spent over 12 years to create and broadcast ads featuring Thomas. The underlying message of every Wendy's ad: How could you NOT trust THIS guy when he says his food's good? "He's everybody's nice uncle," says one prominent advertiser, "you simply can't walk away from him as a character."

106   What are some options? Expert Della Famina suggests:

1. Wait six months. Then bring back his illustrious image much as KFC did with Colonel Sanders in the early 1980s after his death.

2. Consider his daughter, Wendy, the chain's namesake. After Orville Redenbacher died in 1995, he was quickly replaced by a look-alike grandson, Gary, whose accent and trademark glasses were similar to his grandfather's. But daughter Wendy was historically a reluctant representative and hasn't been used since she was a young child.

3. Link Wendy's to Dave's legacy as a pioneer in the industry and an undying advocate for adoption. A tireless advocate for adoption, Thomas was universally admired for his untiring commitment to the idea that every child deserves a permanent, loving home.

107   Thomas nearly died of a massive heart attack in 1997. But just three months after his bypass surgery, he was back making ads. Not without his humor, Thomas handed out T-shirts to the filming crew that said on the back, "Dave's Back!" On the front of each T-shirt was the proclamation, "Dave's Front!"

108   Nonetheless, the transition with Dave as pitchman had begun. Instead of being the single star in ads, Thomas increasingly became an icon who appeared only at the end of each ad—usually with a catchy punch line. About three years prior to his death, company executives began planning a succession campaign, said Don Calhoon, executive VP of marketing at Wendy's. Thomas's health was slowly failing, and he had noticeably lost weight. Although Thomas was aware that a so-called succession campaign was in the planning stage, he stayed out of it.

109   That was his way. Back in 1997, while recovering from heart surgery, Thomas spent the better part of two days taping several Wendy's ads. Speaking to a *USA Today* reporter during breaks in the shooting, Thomas said, "it's important not to be a big shot." He continued, "each of us are fragile human beings. We don't know when we're going. Or where. But in the end, we all have to go."

EXHIBIT 15 Ten-Year Selected Financial Data

Source: Wendy's Intrernational, Inc. 2000 Summary Annual Report.

Operations (in millions)		2000[1]	2000	1999	1998[2,3]	1997[3]	1996	1995[2]	1994[3]	1993[5]	1992[2,3]	1991[3]
Systemwide sales												
Wendy's	$	6,412	6,412	5,994	5,528	5,202	4,760	4,469	4,203	3,890	3,591	3,200
Tim Hortons	$	1,287	1,287	1,080	895	772	646	541	440	377	341	308
Retail sales	$	1,808	1,808	1,666	1,580	1,646	1,560	1,455	1,359	1,282	1,196	1,028
Revenues	$	2,237	2,237	2,067	1,942	2,031	1,890	1,739	1,585	1,475	1,370	1,176
Income before income taxes	$	290	271	269	208	219	255	165	150	118	104	79
Net income	$	181	170	167	123	130	156	110	97	81	66	52
Capital expenditures	$	276	276	248	242	295	307	218	172	137	140	86
Financial Position (in millions)												
Total assets	$	1,973	1,958	1,884	1,838	1,942	1,781	1,509	1,215	1,100	1,013	966
Property and equipment, net	$	1,504	1,497	1,389	1,281	1,266	1,208	1,007	865	787	745	682
Long-term obligations	$	248	248	249	246	250	242	337	145	201	234	240
Shareholders' equity	$	1,138	1,126	1,065	1,068	1,184	1,057	819	702	624	553	504
Per Share Data												
Net income—diluted	$	1.53	1.44	1.32	.95	.97	1.19	.88	.79	.67	.56	.45
Dividends	$	.24	.24	.24	.24	.24	.24	.24	.24	.24	.24	.24
Shareholders' equity	$	9.96	9.86	9.01	8.61	8.95	8.16	6.81	5.94	5.33	4.80	4.43
Market price at year-end	$	26.25	26.25	20.81	21.81	22.88	20.88	21.25	14.38	17.38	12.63	9.25
Ratios												
Domestic Wendy's company operating profit margin	%	16.5	16.5	16.7	15.7	14.9	13.4	15.2	15.8	15.0	14.3	13.5
Pretax profit margin	%	13.0	12.1	13.0	10.7	10.8	13.5	9.5	9.5	8.0	7.6	6.7
Return on average assets[4]	%	17.2	16.2	16.2	12.8	13.4	17.6	13.6	15.0	13.4	13.1	11.6
Return on average equity	%	16.9	15.9	15.4	11.0	11.5	16.6	14.5	14.7	13.8	12.7	10.7
Long-term debt to equity[5]	%	22	22	23	23	21	23	41	21	32	42	48
Debt to total capitalization[3]	%	18	18	19	19	17	19	29	17	24	30	32
Price to earnings[6]		17	18	16	23	24	18	24	18	26	23	21
Restaurant Data												
Domestic Wendy's open at year-end												
Company			1,034	982	928	1,073	1,191	1,200	1,168	1,132	1,117	1,080
Franchise			4,061	3,886	3,748	3,502	3,178	2,997	2,826	2,657	2,490	2,408
International Wendy's open at year-end												
Company			119	130	108	129	124	111	96	92	91	82
Franchise			578	529	549	503	440	359	321	287	264	234
Total Wendy's			5,792	5,527	5,333	5,207	4,933	4,667	4,411	4,168	3,962	3,804
Tim Hortons			1,980	1,817	1,667	1,578	1,384	1,197	943	721	628	546
Total Units			7,772	7,344	7,000	6,785	6,317	5,864	5,354	4,889	4,590	4,350
Average net sales per domestic Wendy's restaurant (in thousands)												
Company	$		1,314	1,284	1,174	1,111	1,049	1,014	1,001	978	924	874
Franchise	$		1,130	1,102	1,031	1,017	978	974	982	960	907	843
Total domestic	$		1,167	1,138	1,062	1,042	998	986	988	966	912	852
Average sales per Canadian Tim Hortons standard restaurant (in thousands of Canadian dollars)	$		1,354	1,216	1,091	986	908	878	854	769	734	714
Other Data												
Diluted shares (in thousands)			122,483	131,039	137,089	140,738	133,684	130,164	128,718	127,377	125,994	115,836
Registered shareholders at year-end			82,000	87,000	92,000	92,000	82,000	63,000	57,000	56,000	56,000	53,000
Number of employees at year-end			44,000	40,000	39,000	47,000	49,000	47,000	45,000	44,000	43,000	40,000

(1) Before the international charge of $18.4 million pretax ($11.5 million after tax)
(2) Fiscal year includes 53 weeks.
(3) Includes pretax charges of $33.9 million ($25.3 million after tax) and $72.7 million ($50.0 million after tax) for 1998 and 1997, respectively. Includes special pretax charges of $49.7 million, $28.9 million, $23.3 million, $17.7 million and $17.8 million, for 1995, 1994, 1993, 1992, and 1991, respectively, primarily all related to special profit sharing contributions made at Tim Hortons.

(4) Return on average assets is compared using income before income taxes and interest charges.
(5) Excludes company-obligated mandatorily redeemable preferred securities.
(6) Price to earnings is computed using the year-end stock price divided by the net income for the year.

EXHIBIT 16
The Impact of Dave Thomas's Commercials Since 1990, and a Snapshot of His Life

Source:*USA Today,* January 22, 2002.

Thomas' commercials helped revive Wendy's
Humorous commercials featuring Wendy's founder Dave Thomas—as well as Thomas's return to the company in 1989 after retiring seven years earlier—are given much credit for reviving the restaurant's sagging sales and share price. Monthly stock closings since 1984:

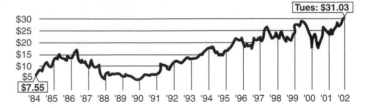

Wendy's International
Founded: 1969
Rank in fast-food sales: No. 3, behind McDonald's, Burger King
Sales: $7.7 billion[1]
Employees: 44,000
Restaurants: 6,000 worldwide
Went public: 1976
Also owns: Tim Hortons, Canadian coffee and baked goods chain
NYSE ticker: WEN
[1] for 2000

Fast-food hamburger market share

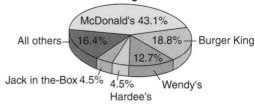

About Dave Thomas
Born: July 2, 1932, in Atlantic City, to parents he never knew.
Adopted: At 6 weeks by Rex and Auleva Thomas of Kalamazoo, Mich. His adoptive mother died five years later. Thomas' father, looking for work, took him from state to state.
Best childhood memories: Summers spent with his grandmother, Minnie Sinclair.
First job: Delivering groceries in Knoxville, Tenn., at age 12. Later was soda jerk at a Walgreens, but was fired when the boss found out he wasn't 16.
Dropped out: After moving to Fort Wayne, Ind., he dropped out of high school—a decision he later regretted—at age 15 to work full time.
In uniform: Joined Army at age 18 and managed an enlisted men's club. Returned to Fort Wayne.
Greatest influence: Met Kentucky Fried Chicken founder Harland Sanders in 1956.
First million: Took over four failing KFC restaurants in Columbus, Ohio, in 1962, revived them and sold them back to KFC for $1.5 million in 1968.
First Wendy's: Opened Nov. 15, 1969, in Columbus, Ohio. It was named after his 8-year-old daughter, Melinda Lou—nicknamed Wendy.
Retired: In 1982. Came back to work in 1989.
Cause: Headed White House Initiative on Adoption in 1990 and supported adoption groups.
Back to school: Returned to high school in 1993, about 45 years later. Earned GED from Coconut Creek High School in Fort Lauderdale. Named Most Likely to Succeed by graduating class.
Books: *Dave's Way* (1991), *Well Done!* (1994), *Franchising for Dummies* (2000).
Ad record: More than 800 ads are Guinness record for longest TV campaign by company founder.
Favorite Wendy's meal: Single with cheese, mustard, pickle, onion; fries; chili; Frosty; Diet Coke.
Family: Lorraine, wife of 47 years; five children; 16 grandchildren.

Copyright © 2002, Richard Robinson, University of South Carolina.
[1]An article in *The Wall Street Journal* (July 8, 1980, p. 29) offered another explanation: "Wendy's ads showed diners biting into its hot and juicy hamburgers and then mopping juice from their chins. But some people thought the image projected by the ad was hot and greasy. Many franchises quit advertising, in effect voting no confidence in the company's marketing plan."
[2]"Its Vigor Lost, Wendy's Seeks a New Niche," *The Wall Street Journal,* July 8, 1980, p. 29.

Case 45

Frisbie Tool & Die

FRIDAY JANUARY 11, 2002

"Alex, I haven't heard from you and I was beginning to get worried."

"Don't worry Max, I told you that I would let you know before I did anything."

"It's Friday, Alex, and you said that you would make your decision no later than Monday."

"That's right, you will have your decision by Monday."

"You can't go to work for UCANB2, it would be like giving up your identity."

"Max, I told you I have looked at all the options."

"Alex, we can do great things together. I look forward to hearing from you on Monday."

1   Alex sat back in his chair and thought about how to make a decision in three days on something that had taken him 23 years to build. Max Decker had been his friend and competitor in the tool & die business for over 20 years, but could they work together as partners? How would he like being an employee again if he took UCANB2's offer? Did he want to keep running his own business? Was closing the business a real option?

FRISBIE TOOL & DIE BACKGROUND

2   Three years ago the decision would have been easy. Because of rapid growth in the stock market, Alex's retirement account increased in value by 107% between 1994 and 1998. Now three years later the value of his retirement fund had declined by 46% from its peak value. The money he had counted on to provide an easy retirement was gone. Based on his estimated expenses, as shown in Exhibit 1, he could barely get by without touching the principal of his retirement account. Early retirement would have to be postponed.

3   Alex Frisbie owned a tool and die company called Frisbie Tool & Die. Alex had started the company in 1978 after getting frustrated while working for one of his competitors. Alex had the gift of gab like many salesmen. Alex also had the technical and hands-on skills that made it possible for him to repair or replace almost any piece of fitting or equipment. Many of his earliest customers came to him not because of his prices or products, but because they wanted him available if anything broke.

4   During the first ten years of business, Frisbie Tool & Die had seen dramatic growth in both sales and in income. At its peak Frisbie Tool & Die had three outside and two inside salespeople. Sales in 1991 reached a high of $3.7 million. In 2001 sales were less than $1.3 million.

5   During the recession of 1990–91, margins in the industry began to shrink. During the same period, foreign producers flooded the market with inexpensive parts. The foreign producers primarily sold mass produced, low margins parts. The quality of the imported

parts was good. Many customers began to purchase imported parts when they found out there was little or no difference in quality between domestic and imported parts. Buyers also liked the fact that the imported parts were cheaper.

6   Tool and die companies were caught in a very difficult situation. Many customers wanted to deal only with companies that could provide them with a full line of products and services. The same customers felt no obligation to purchase from a company if they could get a similar product someplace else at a better price.

7   Since 1991, there has been a steady decline in the number of companies in the tool and die business. The survivors tend to be very large companies, sales in excess of $30 million annually, or small specialty companies with sales less than $2 million annually. Alex Frisbie and Max Decker are two of the small specialty survivors.

8   The respect that is given to Alex for his expertise and technical skill in solving a difficult problem is a source of great pride. Customers ask Alex to outline a strategy of how to solve a problem they are facing with regards to repairing or replacing equipment. If they agree with the strategy, most customers then use Frisbie Tool & Die to make the necessary repairs or purchase new equipment.

9   Recently, the use of the expert advice he provides certain customers has become a source of frustration. A number of companies have taken the plans put together by Alex and "shopped them around" to get the best price on each of the items involved. Frisbie

EXHIBIT 1
Personal Financial Statement Prepared for Alex and Emily Decker as of December 31, 2000

Assets	
Checking Account	15,511
Savings Account	34,076
Investment Accounts	136,589
Retirement Accounts	517,233
Cash Value of Life Insurance	17,566
Automobiles	51,067
Clothing & Furniture	64,751
Personal Residence	455,000
Equity in Frisbie Tool & Die	627,615
Total Assets	1,919,408
Liabilities	
Credit Cards	14,078
Loans on Automobiles	41,236
Mortgage	236,417
Total Liabilities	291,731
Net Worth	1,627,677
Monthly Expenditures (Based on 2000 expenses)	
Mortgage Payment	2,231
Automobile Payments	1,205
Health Insurance	741
Food	843
Utilities	485
Entertainment	1,833
Automobile Insurance	135
Country Club	345
Clothing	462
Miscellaneous	1,416
Total	9,696

Tool & Die would only get a small part of the business and only on those parts where their prices were the lowest. Most times the profits on the items sold did not justify the value of Alex's time.

10   In order to survive the last 10 years, Frisbie Tool & Die has cut down on the number of product lines they carry, eliminated salespeople, offered more hands-on service and controlled costs. Currently there is one outside salesperson, Alex Frisbie, and one inside salesperson, his wife Emily Frisbie.

11   Alex Frisbie is 57 years old and his wife Emily is 55. They met while they were in college and have been married for 32 years. Emily has worked with her husband for the past 11 years after the last of their three children went off to college. Their children admire their parents' efforts in running the business, but have no interest in either working in the business or taking it over.

THE UCANB2 OFFER

12   Six weeks ago, the UCANB2 company approached Alex about coming to work for them. In the past Alex had been approached by several other companies, but this time it was different. UCANB2 not only wanted Alex to come to work for them, but they also wanted to hire Emily to work in their inside sales division.

13   Emily liked the idea for the simple reason that it lifted a burden from their lives. Alex was willing to listen, but only if it could be shown that it would be more profitable for him in the long run. Alex also liked the idea that he was not being hired as a salesperson but rather as a technical expert to support the sales team. The terms of the potential agreement are shown in Exhibit 2.

14   UCANB2 has grown dramatically over the last 10 years by systematically picking up the pieces of companies that were either too small, inefficient, or undercapitalized to survive. The acquisition philosophy was simple. Because of changes in the industry, most markets were served by too many suppliers. There was no need to pursue all or even a significant number of the companies in a specific market but to identify an "ideal target" in a market.

EXHIBIT 2
Terms of Acquisition of Frisbie Tool & Die by the UCANB2 Corporation

UCANB2 will sell the inventory of Frisbie Tool & Die through its normal sales process and will pay Frisbie Tool & Die the proceeds when the inventory is completely liquidated. (Alex anticipates he will receive approximately 95% of his carrying value when the inventory is sold.)

UCANB2 will purchase all equipment owned by Frisbie Tool & Die for fair market value. (Alex anticipates this will equal approximately 65% of book value.)

Alex Frisbie will receive an annual salary of $85,000 with a bonus of 2% of sales in excess of 1.5 million dollars annually. (Alex anticipates the bonus will be approximately $10,000 annually.)

Emily Frisbie will receive an annual salary of $35,000.

As employees of UCANB2 Alex and Emily will be eligible for all employee benefits, including health care coverage for themselves free of charge, participation in the 401K plan and paid sick leave and vacation.

Because Alex and his wife are part of a company that is being acquired rather than new hires, they would be vested into the company's retirement system for the number of years they worked for Frisbie Tool & Die. The retirement plan pays out a benefit of 1.5% per year worked for the first $40,000 an employee earns as an average of their highest five years of earnings and 2.25% of salaries and bonuses earned in excess of $40,000 as an average of their highest five years of earnings.

15   The identification of an "ideal target" was based on two factors, presence and vulnerability. An "ideal target" had a strong market presence including both name recognition and market penetration. The company was one of the first mentioned when you spoke to anyone in that market. The company had also established "goodwill" within their operating market.

16   The "ideal target" was also vulnerable. Vulnerability most often existed because of financial weakness, but also occurred because of the potential retirement of the owner with no visible plan of succession. The company could also be vulnerable because of losing key personnel that could not be easily replaced. Because of the nature of the market, many long-time companies were faced with the possibility of losing their "intellectual capital" as long-time employees retired.

17   The amount paid to acquire these companies varied greatly based on the percent of market penetration, operating margin, financial status and the number of employees that would be retained. The offering price for a company declined when it would be necessary to replace and/or retrain a significant portion of the employees. The closest estimate on a purchase price would be a multiple of no greater than five times gross operating margin.

18   The owners of the companies felt that the prices being offered did not represent the true potential value of their companies; however, they recognized that in liquidation or bankruptcy they would get only about 40 cents on the dollar for inventory and less for any equipment that could be sold. Many times, because the decline had occurred over a period of years, the company would be paid only enough money to pay off their creditors.

19   Alex's company was an "ideal target." What was different about Frisbie Tool & Die was that UCANB2 had no real interest in continuing to operate the company, but wanted Alex Frisbie. The terms they offered Alex represented the clear recognition that he was the primary asset of his company. They structured a deal, the terms of which are listed in Exhibit 2, that allowed them to basically allow Frisbie Tool & Die to cease operations, without having to sell inventory and equipment at fire sale prices. To sweeten the deal UCANB2 also offered a job to Emily Frisbie.

MAX DECKER MAKES AN OFFER

20   As part of the decision process, Alex discussed the proposal with his longtime friend Max Decker. Four days later, Max came to Alex with a proposal that they form a partnership. Max said it "would give us the best of both worlds" by allowing us to retain our independence and increase our margins by eliminating certain duplicated costs. Alex liked the idea of staying in the business and felt that he and Max would make a good team.

21   Max felt that by combining forces they could increase their gross margin to 35% and could cut administrative and operating expenses between 20 and 30%. The company would be set up as an equal partnership. Max offered to make Alex the lead partner and chief operating officer.

22   During the first year, sales would most likely be flat. The feeling was that even with combined efforts, a certain number of customers would be lost due to the merger. During the next five years, it was anticipated that sales would increase by approximately 10% annually. The gross margin would stay the same for the first year and would probably increase to 35% by the end of year five.

23   Because of redundancies, it would be possible to reduce inventory by approximately 20%. The reduction in inventory could be achieved mainly by decreasing orders for the next six months and meeting customer demand out of inventory on hand. Much of the equipment used in operations of the two companies was similar. If any equipment was found to be unnecessary, and was subsequently sold, the proceeds would be split equally.

24   Because Max already had in place an inside salesperson, Emily could stop working if she wanted to. Alex felt that if Emily did not work, the anticipated decrease in operating expenses could be as much as 25%. Emily liked the idea, but was also not certain whether she wanted to stop working.

25   The downside to the potential merger was obvious, both companies were small players in a consolidating market. If the merger was to be successful over the long run, it would be necessary to institute a long-term plan. The plan would have to include objectives, projected financial statements, and a marketing plan. The new company would have to find a way to differentiate itself from competitors and identify their market niche. Alex's key concern was how Max would react to all the changes that would be necessary.

MAX DECKER AND DECKER T&D BACKGROUND

26   Max Decker owned Decker T&D, a company he started almost 25 years ago. Max Decker was 60 years old. Max's daughter Cheryl works for him as office manager. It is likely that when Max decides to retire, Cheryl will take over the business.

27   Cheryl Decker Booco is 35 years old. She is married and has three children. For the past 10 years she has worked full time for Decker T&D. Cheryl represents the future of the tool and die business. She has integrated automated inventory control and other management software into the operations of Decker T&D.

28   Like most companies in the tool and die business Decker T&D has experienced declining margins and sales. Sales for the year 2000 were slightly less than $2 million. Increased costs for advertising, telephone, and salaries relating to establishing an Internet website reduced income by almost $20,000 in the year 2000. These costs will not increase as rapidly in the future.

29   Decker T&D is similar to Frisbie Tool & Die in most respects but is very different in its use of the Internet and in customer focus. Decker T&D has developed and is operating a website. The number of customers using the website has been slowly increasing. Still, few orders, other than standing monthly orders, are being made through the website. Recently, a number of customers have started using the website to verify price and availability of products before they call in and place their orders.

30   Decker T&D is also different in the services they offer customers. Decker provides limited technical support for their customers. Typically, if a customer is experiencing difficulty, they are directed to the manufacturer. Decker T&D has developed its customers based on price and speed of delivery.

STAY THE COURSE

31   With the opportunities available to him, Alex felt that he could not overlook the most obvious, staying the course. Alex and Emily had worked hard over the last decade to keep their business running and it appeared that maybe they could see the light at the end of the tunnel.

32   The decision to continue running Frisbie Tool & Die would require that Alex and Emily make a commitment to stay in the business at least another five years. The sales for the company would have to increase by at least 25% over that period. Cost-cutting measures that had been put in place could not be relaxed. It would be unlikely that any additional personnel could be hired during the next five years.

33   If they were to continue in operation it would be necessary for Alex to reevaluate several decisions that he had made regarding which lines to carry. In the past Alex has

attempted to carry mainly domestic lines. Imports have been used to fill out the lines when a high quality, reasonably priced domestic product could not be found. This might have to change.

34   Recently a manufacturer, based in Southeast Asia, has approached Alex about carrying their line of products. Because much of what the company offered he already carried, Alex initially was inclined to reject the offer. The manufacture being aware of the reputation of Frisbie Tool & Die for quality and service offered Alex a special deal.

35   The company offered to sell Frisbie Tool & Die all inventory on a consignment basis, meaning that no monies would be paid to the manufacturer until Frisbie Tool & Die had sold the inventory. Unsold inventory could be returned to the manufacturer within six months of delivery. Inventory that was retained by Frisbie Tool & Die for more than six months was not returnable, but was not considered sold until it was purchased by a customer.

36   Frisbie Tool & Die would be responsible for all shipping and handling charges. The cost of inventory damaged while on the premises of Frisbie Tool & Die was its responsibility.

37   The manufacturer made parts that could replace approximately 60% of Frisbie Tool & Die's inventory. This would free up a significant amount of cash and would diminish the amount of inventory written off on an annual basis by 50%.

38   The margins on the new parts would be higher than those on many of the domestic parts Frisbie Tool & Die currently carried. It would be likely that the gross margin could be expected to increase by 15%.

39   Technology would have to be integrated into the company. Automated ordering, inventory control and accounting packages would have to be evaluated. Frisbie Tool & Die would also need to evaluate its presence on the Internet. Currently it is not even connected to the Internet at the office.

40   The downside of this route was that it represented a complete change of direction. Many of Frisbie Tool & Die's customers were familiar with the lines it carried. The process of educating customers about the advantages and disadvantages of the new line would be time consuming. Alex estimated that in the first year overall sales could potentially drop by 5%. The estimate for the following five years would be for slow growth of around 5% annually.

THE DECISION

41   Alex wants to make the decision in a logical manner. The decision must take into account not only the numbers, but also the people involved. All of the alternatives have strengths and weaknesses. None of the alternatives represents a perfect solution.

42   As part of the decision-making process, Alex must put together a strategy that outlines how to proceed over the next five years. The strategy should include sales projections, marketing plans, inventory and cost controls together with any other pertinent information.

Pat De Mouy, University of South Carolina, 2001.

Case 46

ABB in the New Millennium: New Leadership, New Strategy, New Organization

> Extrapolation is a besetting sin of economists and engineers. [. . .] Instead, we must take a more creative approach, basing our actions not on what *was,* but on what *could be.*
>
> *Göran Lindahl, Chief Executive Officer, ABB Asea Brown Boveri Ltd.*

1 At the start of 1997 Göran Lindahl became CEO of ABB Asea Brown Boveri, one of the world's largest electrical engineering companies. He succeeded Percy Barnevik, ABB's first CEO. ABB had been formed in 1987 after the merger between Sweden's ASEA and Switzerland's Brown Boveri. Under Lindahl's predecessor, ABB had more than doubled its revenues to $34 billion in 1996 through more than 160 acquisitions worldwide, and implemented a matrix organization with 4 global business segments and over 5,000 profit centers in 140 countries. During this radical transformation ABB had become one of the world's most admired companies. In early 1997 Lindahl set a revenue goal of $50 billion by 2001, targeting emerging markets such as Southeast Asia, where ABB had massively transferred manufacturing capacity from Western Europe and the U.S.

2 However, by the end of 1997, Asia was in disarray. A currency crisis in Thailand had precipitated unprecedented financial turmoil in the whole region, which most experts predicted would take years to resolve. As a result, projects such as Malaysia's $5 billion Bakun dam project—the largest in ABB's history—were "indefinitely postponed." In early 1998 Lindahl admitted that ABB was unlikely to meet its 2001 revenue target. Moreover, profound changes in other key competitive factors suggested that a much deeper transformation might be required in ABB's strategy and organization if the company was to maintain its competitive edge in the new millennium.

A DIFFICULT END OF THE MILLENNIUM FOR ABB

3 One of these changes concerned the very core business of ABB. During the 1988 to 1996 period, Barnevik had clearly focused the company's efforts on electrical power generation and transmission. To those who, already in 1988, had argued that increasing deregulation would swiftly turn these areas into mature, commoditized businesses, Barnevik typically responded:

> Remember: (1) You do not have to be in high-growth business to make big money (sometimes a reverse correlation), (2) you can achieve good/high growth in worldwide mature business (product and country niches, competitors disappearing, etc.), (3) to go against the mainstream is often profitable, and (4) with the right strategy and properly implemented, a lot of money is to be made in the electrotechnical industry.[1]

Professor Piero Morosini prepared this case as a basis for class discussion rather than to illustrate either effective or ineffective handling of an administrative situation. Copyright © 2000 by IMD (International Institute for Management Development), Lausanne, Switzerland. All rights reserved. Not to be used or reproduced without written permission directly from IMD, Lausanne, Switzerland.

4   Based on these considerations, Barnevik had spent most of his time closing excess capacity in ABB's core electrical power business, building a global managerial and financial structure and expanding the company's reach outside Western Europe. Between 1991 and 1996 ABB cut 59,000 jobs in Europe and the U.S. but simultaneously created 56,000 new jobs in Asia and Eastern Europe. During the same period, Asia had represented over 50% of new orders of electrical power plants and equipment.

5   However, by the end of 1996 ABB's revenue growth had abruptly come to a standstill, particularly affected by the financial crises in Asia and other emerging economies. At the same time, deregulation of electricity markets continued to increase its pace in the European Union and the U.S. creating new customers and market opportunities as traditional state-owned utilities were privatized around the world.

6   Nevertheless, in early 1997 ABB still favored some conventional customer segments. For example, in large markets such as Germany, ABB was involved in the district heating-technology business which, as demonstrated in 1996, could unexpectedly become a source of trouble for the company. That year, ABB was accused of forming a cartel together with other companies in the German district heating-market. As a result of these allegations, the European Union imposed a fine of close to $100 million on ABB, one of the largest ever.

Sweeping Technological Changes

7   By 1997, radical technological advances were also creating new markets where ABB had not been seen as focusing enough effort during the 1988 to 1996 period. One example was the growing area of industrial automation processes. Electrical engineering companies such as Siemens, General Electric (GE), or ASEA had historically been involved in automating industrial processes for large customers that built energy intensive plants, such as chemical or paper producers. However, starting in the late 1970s and following continuous developments in software, the traditional electrical and mechanical approaches to automation were radically improved, which created growing business opportunities.

8   In addition, market liberalization allowed for the introduction and rapid development of technologies that country regulators had previously frowned on across the European Union and the U.S. One of these technologies was "distributed generation." An ABB senior executive observed in 1998:

> Distributed generation is one of the most exciting developments (in the electrical power industry). It consists of technology that allows the generation of electricity from small units, no larger than a kitchen table, fueled by gas and working at up to 10 megawatt in power. These units can be comfortably placed in the basement of hotels, factories, hospitals, and other similar electrical power consumers. But the big advantage here is that this technology allows the consumer to entirely do away with transportation and distribution costs. At current (early 1998) electricity prices, this gives consumers savings of up to 50% vis-à-vis the conventional power generation, transmission and distribution technologies.

Organizational Drawbacks

9   In 1997 the drawbacks of ABB's "multidomestic" structure, introduced by Barnevik in 1988, were becoming increasingly apparent. The much-admired matrix organization, under which three regional chief executives shared responsibilities with the heads of ABB's four core business segments, had been designed to promote decentralized, consensual and team-based management. However, over time, local business managers found themselves reporting to two bosses, with important decisions often being dragged into political conflicts, or into "unfocused and mediocre compromise"—as one former ABB employee described it.[2]

10   At the same time, ABB had maintained some poor-performing units throughout its 1988 to 1996 corporate transformation. Paramount amongst these was Adtranz, a 50/50 joint venture with Daimler-Benz AG[3] to manufacture railway equipment. In the overcrowded railway manufacturing industry, Adtranz had lost $239 million on revenues of $3.74 billion in 1997. More disturbingly, Adtranz had failed to produce profits for years and, according to most financial analysts, its prospects of changing that pattern looked bleak in the medium term.

Faltering Performance

11   All these factors rapidly took a toll on ABB performance. Although the company's share price had risen at an annual rate of 23% between 1988 and 1996, it substantially underperformed the market in 1997. Sweden's Wallenberg and Switzerland's Schmidheiny families, which had traditionally been the two largest investors in ABB, started to reduce their protective stakes in 1997. A main beneficiary was Martin Ebner, one of Switzerland's better-known raiders, who at that time became one of ABB's largest shareholders.

UNPRECEDENTED CHANGES IN ABB'S COMPETITIVE ARENA

12   Lindahl knew that the electrical power industry would never be the same after 1999. In February of that year, European Union (EU) directives were expected to fully liberalize the distribution of electricity to industrial consumers. In preparation for this, most EU countries had privatized and massively deregulated their former state-owned electricity suppliers. The U.S. electrical power industry had experienced similar developments since the mid-1980s.

13   Following deregulation, electricity markets were typically rationalized into three separate businesses: generation, transmission and distribution, each of which underwent distinct competitive developments. Power generation faced substantial overcapacity and had experienced technological developments that favored relatively small, flexible entrants. Power transmission had been concentrated and restructured, largely remaining in government hands in countries such as the U.K. The distribution of electrical power had been massively privatized, and the new competitors had embarked on aggressive investment plans to gain share in their domestic markets as well as abroad, upgrade technology and increase operational efficiency and productivity.

14   At the same time, technological developments were making possible a convergence of telephony, data networking, and cable TV over a single platform, which could be transported directly to the customers' homes via power lines. This could potentially allow electrical utilities to compete directly against telephone companies, that is, in Internet access or long-distance services. Companies such as Siemens were very actively pursuing developments around this technology during the late 1990s.

15   Another area where power equipment suppliers had been traditionally involved was industrial automation. During the 1990s manufacturers of robots and related automation equipment had seen significant increases in volume and price reductions at the same time. Their traditional customers—industries such as chemicals or pulp and paper—were increasingly demanding software platforms that could integrate automated manufacturing processes into management information systems. Leading providers of these software platforms, such as Germany's SAP, were experiencing dramatic growth in revenue and profitability.

IS MORE CONSOLIDATION OF POWER EQUIPMENT SUPPLIERS ENOUGH?

16   As might be expected, the fortunes of the power equipment industry have traditionally followed those of the power industry. In most cases, the former were originally organized as national champions to supply a country's electrical power monopolies. During the late 1980s, significant overcapacity, as well as economies of scale in R&D, marketing and manufacturing, had brought a first wave of restructuring in the U.S. and Europe. In 1987 Sweden's ASEA and Switzerland's Brown Boveri merged to form ABB. GEC Alstom was created in 1989 by merging U.K.'s General Electric Company (no relation to U.S.-based GE) power generation equipment unit with France's Alstom. In the U.S., during the early 1990s, Westinghouse dismantled most of its electrical power activities—largely turning itself into a broadcasting operation, while GE undertook a massive restructuring of its power equipment and engineering businesses.

17   A decade later the economic crisis in Asia prompted another wave of consolidations, aggravated by sudden financial turmoil in Russia. As mentioned, during the late 1980s and early 1990s, Asia had accounted for more than half of the new orders of electrical power plants and related equipment. During 1997 ABB had started to significantly reduce capacity, closing 13 factories and obtaining one of the industry's highest capacity utilization rates. As a result, there were 12,000 job cuts in Europe and the U.S. The company announced a massive investment plan in Asia in spite of the looming financial crisis. Also in 1997 Siemens, a power equipment manufacturer heavily focused on the German market, bought the remaining power generation divisions of U.S.-based Westinghouse for $1.5 billion. During early 1998, Alstom, a relatively strong competitor in the European power transmission and distribution equipment market, had only half the sales of ABB, the world's largest company in that sector.

18   ABB's main areas of activity were undergoing unprecedented change after the mid-1990s, and company analysts and investors were increasingly impatient to see Lindahl's strategic responses to these challenges. With sales and share prices tumbling in 1997, many company observers took the opportunity to highlight the "excessive" risks of ABB's strategy of rapid expansion in Asia and Eastern Europe during the first half of the 1990s, as well as its having put too much emphasis on mature manufacturing business, while global deregulation was rapidly tilting the scales in favor of more "value-added" and service-based offerings to electrical utilities.

ABB'S "BIG BANG" AT THE TURN OF THE MILLENNIUM

19   However, Göran Lindahl was about to carry out the most dramatic transformation in the company's history. In just over two years, ABB turned itself into the world's largest process-automation player, by combining its internal automation businesses and carrying out large acquisitions abroad. It also divested its noncore transportation businesses and restructured its mature power generation businesses through a 50/50 joint venture with Alstom. ABB also invested heavily in creating "solutions" businesses in automation and electrical power distribution, hiring over 15,000 software engineers and targeting large industrial customers and newly privatized electrical utilities. ABB simultaneously embarked on a major internal reorganization, strengthening key global processes such as financial services, information technology and knowledge management, while maintaining its global network of 5,000 profit centers. By early 2000 ABB was again showing strong sales growth, record profitability and double-digit earnings growth, nearly doubling its stock market capitalization during 1999.

20   The results of ABB's radical transformation could already be seen during early 1999. Speaking at a press conference in Zurich in early March 1999, Lindahl released the company's 1998 results. ABB had exceeded most analysts' expectations with an 11% rise in net income to US$1.3 billion. "The worst is behind in Asia and we expect it to grow," he said.

21   Lindahl added:

> We moved decisively in 1998 towards our [strategic] goal of creating a faster, more knowledge- and service-based global company. We acquired several major players in the promising automation field, the largest being Elsag Bailey, and we divested our interest in Adtranz [the 50/50 railway equipment manufacturing joint venture between ABB and Daimler-Benz]. We achieved a 17% higher operating cash flow, and net income margins increased from 3.8% to 4.2%. With this momentum, I am confident that net income will continue to grow in 1999.

22   In response to a question, he noted, "We have spelled out a growth strategy based on acquisitions." Indeed, only a few weeks after this press conference, on March 24, it was announced that ABB was combining its power generation business with Alstom's, in an $11 billion joint venture. The deal created the world's largest power generation player by revenue size, which would be based in Brussels, report in euros and employ 54,000 people. As part of the deal, Alstom paid ABB $1.5 billion in cash to compensate for the difference in size between the two companies, allowing for a 50/50 joint venture. Following this deal, Siemens of Germany, U.S.-based General Electric and ABB Alstom would control about 80% of the world demand for steam- or gas-driven turbines for new power stations. (In 1997 orders for all new power stations amounted to $60 billion.)

23   The ABB-Alstom deal provided ABB with $1.5 billion in cash resources. This added to the $472 million ABB had obtained as a result of divesting its 50% share of Adtranz, which was acquired by DaimlerChrysler AG. Earlier on, ABB had announced that it was also pulling out of the district heating-technology business. All these operations provided fresh financial resources that ABB could invest in other areas, such as the fast-growing oil, gas, and petrochemicals sector, where the company was spending an increasing share of its $2.5 billion total R&D budget in 1998.

24   The $1.5 billion acquisition of Amsterdam-based Elsag Bailey from Italy's Finmeccanica in October 1998 made ABB the world leader in the high margin process-control automation market. Prior to the acquisition, ABB had a small presence in the U.S. automation market. Elsag Bailey had 33% of its annual $1.5 billion turnover in the Americas, giving ABB a strong U.S. presence and creating a formidable challenge to players such as Emerson. The German company Siemens was also expected to come under increasing pressure from ABB in this area, as Elsag Bailey generated 23% of its sales in Germany, where ABB had had a limited presence before the acquisition. "We are expanding into businesses where we can be leaders and leaving businesses where we can't," Lindahl was reported as saying, highlighting ABB's shift from slow-growth, capital intensive businesses into fast-growing high technology areas.

25   In October 1998 ABB announced a reorganization of the matrix structure it had had in place since 1993 but had grown too difficult to manage. Instead, Lindahl scrapped the regional structures and reorganized the global segments into seven product areas: power generation, power transmission, power distribution, automation, oil and gas, products and contracting and financial services. The simplified structure maintained the 5,000 profit centers network but placed it under a stronger global management. ABB's group of

500 global managers, responsible for coordinating the company's global resources across countries, was reduced to 400, of which a total of about 140 were newly appointed individuals. A number of global processes, that is, financial and administrative, IT infrastructure and procurement, were standardized and strengthened under central control.

26   ABB had also chosen its March 1999 press conference to announce that it was creating a unified, single-class ABB share. This change aimed at simplifying its ownership structure by replacing four types of securities with a single ABB share, which would clear the way for an eventual U.S. stock exchange listing. The new single-share structure, heralded by Lindahl as the "final step in fully integrating ABB," was well received by shareholders because it appeared to improve ABB's appeal to foreign investment, especially minority investors. By January 1999 Switzerland's Martin Ebner had accumulated a larger shareholding in ABB Sverige (ABB Sweden) than the Wallenberg family, the company's traditionally dominant shareholders. Following approval at the March 1999 annual shareholders meeting, Ebner became a board member of ABB.

Implementing the "Big Bang" (1): ABB Distribution Solutions

27   Following ABB's October 1998 reorganization, a new business area (BA) was created inside the newly formed power distribution product area. This new BA was called "distribution solutions" (or ABB DDS), and placed under the responsibility of Kurt Håkansson, a veteran executive in the former ABB transmission and distribution segment. ABB DDS's initial offerings included electrical substations, automated feeder systems, airport systems and rural electrification networks. In 1999 ABB DDS had a total of 2,359 employees and received orders for approximately $800 million. Håkansson explained:

> The regulated environment was a world of fixed technical specs, competitive bidding, few customers and technical support which had not changed in 100 years. [But in late 1998, following deregulation,] Scottish Power set up a "pre-qualifying" process to choose one supplier of [electrical power] distribution solutions. They asked all of us to look at an [electrical] distribution network they had in Liverpool, and come up with our thoughts, ideas and capabilities to help them. We understood that they didn't want to hear about products, but about optimization: how to save money running the network—at the same time increasing reliability and efficiency. We teamed up with [ABB] experts from Germany, Switzerland, the U.S. and the U.K., and made a two-hour presentation. On a scale of zero to ten we got ten plus. But our closest competitor, Siemens, got two plus something. They [Siemens] had only talked about products, and had only lined up their U.K. people to present to Scottish Power.

28   Experiences such as the Scottish Power tender convinced the senior executive team at ABB DDS that there was a real opportunity in "helping customers create competitive advantages through systems and solutions." Håkansson explained:

> Systems and solutions reflects our division of the market into classical and new businesses. Systems are defined as the traditional projects business where the customer requires an optimal integration of products into a working system. This business is relatively standard, of high volume and low unit value. Solutions are defined as risk-sharing business models that improve customer competitiveness through innovative integration of products, systems and services. This is a new, low-volume and high-value business, requiring substantial initial definition. In our industry, growth is driven today by these new customers, who everybody talks about these days. Our target is to grow our business there, double our revenues to $1.6 billion in two years. That is why we are offering 'solutions' to these new customers.

29   After the major lines of ABB DDS's strategy had been agreed upon, Håkansson concentrated his attention on implementing the new business vision. There were significant challenges ahead for ABB DDS as it entered the new millennium:

Focusing on systems and solutions can easily stretch any company's organizational skills. You require 'solutions salesmen' with an intimate understanding of customers' needs and business objectives; a world-class business portfolio of products, systems and services; fast processes to determine system requirements; business cases to quickly evaluate projects based on the customers' functional specifications; and global capabilities to manage and implement complete system and solution projects. In 1998, when we started with this whole thing, we had very few of these things in place. You could find most of these elements here and there inside ABB, but how can you bring them to the customer as part of an integrated offering?

PREPARING FOR THE KNOWLEDGE REVOLUTION AT ABB

30 During 1999 ABB entered new businesses, such as EnergyPact, a joint venture between ABB and U.S.-based PacifiCorp, designed to help utilities and energy companies increase their competitiveness in a deregulated electrical industry. Another example was Digital Plant Technologies AB, a joint venture between ABB and Sweden's Prosolvia to develop and provide software products and consulting services focused on flexible industrial automation. Between 1996 and 1999 ABB was reported to have recruited well over 15,000 software engineers, mostly in Europe.

31 Some of these engineers set to work in areas which had not traditionally been regarded as ABB's "core businesses." In November 1999 ABB launched EuropeLoan.com, an Internet-based mortgage services company, in alliance with a number of Belgian and Dutch service companies. Lindahl strongly supported this, and other similar ventures, under the code-name Project Alpha, a high-profile initiative encompassing ABB's main forays into knowledge-based industries.

32 In a March 2000 press release, ABB announced the launch of "b-business partners," a new, €1 billion venture company that would invest in and develop business-to-business e-commerce companies across Europe, aimed at forging closer links between "new economy" and traditional enterprises. Lindahl observed:

> At ABB, we are embracing the new economy with its greater emphasis on IT, knowledge and services. Across the whole spectrum of our businesses [. . .] we add intelligence through IT as the route to success. The launch of 'b-business partners' underlines our determination to explore the great opportunities offered by combining the entrepreneurial spirit and new skills of the business-to-business e-commerce world with the business skills of the industrial sphere.

Implementing the "Big Bang" (2): ABB's Global IS Group

33 In October 1999 the ABB executive committee approved the creation of a global information systems (IS) organization as proposed by a select team of IS executives/experts from the corporate, country and business functions lead by the CIO. This global IS organization, called GP-IS, integrated the previously fragmented IS functions into one global IS unit that consisted of some 4,500 people worldwide. Jim Barrington, a former VP from a leading U.S.-based electrodomestics multinational, was recruited and named ABB's CIO in mid-1999 with direct responsibility for the entire global IS organization in ABB. In Lindahl's words:

> [The global] IS [group] in ABB shall be a key enabler to drive change, increase business performance and help transform ABB into an IT company.

34 IS was defined as one of the global processes in ABB (each process was sponsored by a member of the ABB executive committee). IS was thus part of the global process organization (GP). Lindahl became the sponsor of the IS process, and each of the business segments (as well as their business areas) was assigned an IS manager reporting to GP-IS as well as to his business management. This created a link between business and IS. An IS council chaired by the CIO, including his direct reports (thus also including the segment IS managers), became the top forum for driving IS development and service delivery in the ABB group. Jim Barrington remarked:

> IT penetrates every [ABB] process, regardless of where it takes place, or in which business. Therefore global IS, as a group, will be key to globalizing ABB. We want to move from capital-intensive and heavy engineering products to knowledge- and service-based businesses and high-tech, integrated solutions. We want to become a wholly customer-focused organization. We want to become faster at penetrating new markets, and more flexible at always adapting to customer demands. We want to maximize the value of our acquisitions and global capabilities through common, standard processes. So, global IS is partly about standardizing IT infrastructure and support to make us more efficient and cost effective. But, perhaps more importantly, it is primarily about helping ABB's businesses change fast to become leading players in the so-called new economy.

35   During early 2000 Barrington decided to organize an eight-week IS executive program spread over two years at a well-known international business school in Lausanne for ABB's top 50 IS managers. The program would combine the building of a global IS team for driving the change into a global effective IS organization with the creation of IS plans for the business segments and business areas, and would thus make IS a natural part of the business plans and strategies. At the first session, held in March 2000, there was an open exchange among the participants, and various questions were raised, ranging from how to turn ABB into the "new" knowledge- and service-based company, to the long way it took to implement global processes and establish a single face to the customer. Participants also raised issues about how to offer solutions rather than products, how to balance the local and global groups and constituencies inside ABB, how to combat the lack of involvement of the global IS group in the business planning, how to address the need to change people's mindsets, how to attract and retain the best professionals, etc. One participant captured the feeling in the room:

> I believe we all agree on the vision that we should change radically in order to become more knowledge- and service-based. But the question is: How do we go about it?

36   Another participant remarked:

> We need to start by changing inside our own [global IS] group first. This is important in attracting, coaching and retaining the right people who will help us move from the 'old' to the 'new' economy. And simultaneously, we have to establish the right relationship with the business segments and areas to help them change. With the creation of one global IS organization we should now have a much better opportunity to support the global business requirements of the new connected economy.

The "New" ABB

37   The results of all these initiatives were clearly visible as ABB entered the new millennium. In early 2000 the company reported a 24% increase in net income to $1.6 billion, and a 4% increase in revenues to $24.7 billion in 1999. Company analysts unanimously regarded the company's perspectives as outstanding. "ABB is no longer a cost story. It is a growth story," one such company analyst observed.

38   In April 2000 ABB sold its 50% of Alstom Power—the jointly held global power generation venture between ABB and Alstom—to Alstom for €1.25 billion ($1.19 billion).

EXHIBIT 1
ABB Revenues by Business Segment (in $ million)

Source: CSFB.

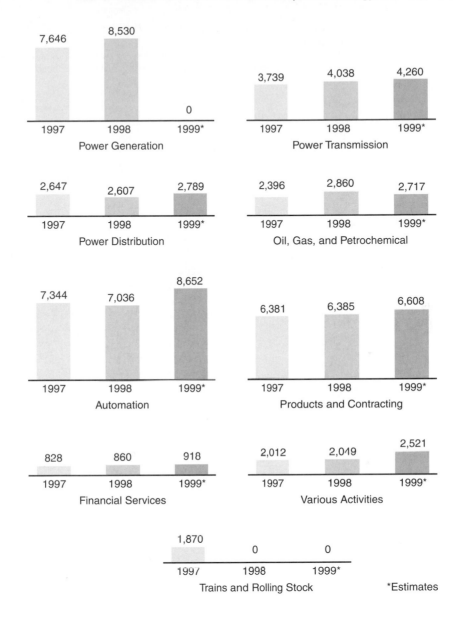

Two months later, ABB announced an alliance with PaperLoop.com, an online paper-industry marketplace, aimed at creating a new category of Web portal. The new portal would go beyond conventional transaction- or marketing-only sites by putting technical information databases online, offering consulting services via the Web and providing industrial software that customers could download or use directly online. Such developments were seen as emblematic of ABB's goals of moving from capital-intensive to more knowledge-based businesses.

39   Nevertheless, the company's transformation was far from complete in early 2000. "We are about halfway. It will take another couple of years to complete the platform," Lindahl remarked in a December 1999 public interview. And added: "We have to make change the natural state of this company." As the new millennium unfolded, Lindahl's frenetic pace gave no signs of relenting, a reflection of both the swift market changes and the inherent difficulties in turning an engineering company into a high-technology concern.

1. Hugo Uyterhoeven, *ABB Deutschland (A) (Extended)*. HBS Case No. 392-065. Boston: Harvard Business School Publishing, p. 14.
2. William Hall, "All the Power but None of the Glory," *Financial Times,* August 24, 1998.
3. Daimler-Benz AG merged with Chrysler Corporation in May 1998, becoming DaimlerChrysler AG.

Case 47

Hewlett-Packard's Home Products Division in Europe (1996–2000)

> Making money in the [home PC] business is like landing a man on the moon.[1]
>
> *Webb McKinney, General Manager, Home Products Division*

1 By November 2000, Hewlett-Packard's (HP) Home Products Division in Europe (HPD-E) had been selling HP's Pavilion line of personal computers in Europe for almost five years. During that time, HPD-E had entered and exited Germany, fought for a 13.5% and 5.2% market share in France and in the United Kingdom, respectively, and had significantly reorganized its European operations twice.[2] Some felt that the European operation had now become everything HP aspired to be. Others wondered why Europe had been so hard and whether the model of "operational excellence"[3] adopted by HPD-E to compete there was adequate for a very fast changing market.

FIRST LESSONS FROM EUROPE—1996

2 In September 1996, *BusinessWeek* reported that even though "[HP] had made an impressive leap to Number 4 in the U.S. market in just 16 months, the business ha[d] barely broken even."[4] HP was nevertheless intent on sticking with home PCs and turning the business into a moneymaker. HPD's strategy was to straddle the gap between the price-conscious Parkard Bell and the more technologically sophisticated Compaq Computers. Webb McKinney, HPD's general manager, was striving for 25% annual growth in sales, but, as a senior HP manager noted, "just because [the Pavilion] was successful in the United States [did] not mean that it [would] be successful elsewhere. . . . We [knew we had] to be careful to balance that business with our return on investment."[5]

3 The first HPD products launched in Europe were priced at parity or better with Compaq and IBM on like-for-like features. HPD's prices and features placed them at the higher end of the market. "One of the fundamental things we did not realize about the European market," McKinney recalled, "is that prices were lower than expected." In the United States the $2,000 price point had become almost standard, buying evermore capability (processor speeds, amount of memory)[6] "We assumed that whatever technology we developed in the U.S. was fine for Europe." McKinney explained.

Professor David J. Arnold and Caren-Isabel Knoop, Executive Director, Global Research Group, prepared this case as the basis for class discussion rather than to illustrate either effective or ineffective handling of an administrative situation. This case contains information from two supplements, Hewlett-Packard's Home Products Division in Europe (C): Lessons from Europe, HBS case no. 399–060 and Hewlett-Packard's Home Products Division in Europe (D): The Matrix Model, HBS case no. 500-063. The two supplements can be used instead of the case. Copyright © 2000 by the President and Fellows of Harvard College. To order copies or request permission to reproduce materials, call 1-800-545-7685, write Harvard Business School Publishing, Boston, MA 02163, or go to www.hbsp.harvard.edu. No part of this publication may be reproduced, stored in a retrieval system, used in a spreadsheet, or transmitted in any form or by any means—electronic, mechanical, photocopying, recording, or otherwise—without the permission of Harvard Business School.

Although we customized our products for Europe, they were basically assembled from a menu of technology developed in the United States. With the price points we selected, we could only expect to reach the top third of the market. In the United States these price points cover 80% of the market. In the portion of the market we reached in Europe we did well, but did not go down far enough. We basically screwed up.

4 In addition, while HPD's four-tiered product line changed seasonally, its German competitor's six-week product cycles enabled them to adjust price and product. Explained Fay Barrow, the HPD-E marketing manager who had taken over from Amanda Barker:

They manage a lot of SKUs[7] and do not come to market with five products that last six months [as manufacturers such as HP and Compaq typically had]. They bring new products to market every few months. To cope, we need to have flexible manufacturing and this will require complete reengineering. We are geared to bringing a product line with a fixed number of SKUs to market in each country.

5 Moreover, the selling window in Europe was compressed to two weeks, particularly during rapid-turnover seasons such as Christmas. "It only takes two weeks for the entire business to collapse unless you manage inventory and price movement well," Barrow explained. "The challenge is getting the data from retail chains [that is imperative to] price accurately and responding fast to any price movements by major competitors, especially in peak selling season."

THINKING THINGS THROUGH—1997

6 Barrow decided that to compete in Europe, HPD needed to do things differently. In January 1997, the European division undertook a major strategy review. Recalled Barrow:

We said, "let's take a clean sheet of paper and see whether we need a different business model in Europe than the one we have today." A different business model could be a different channel, different products, anything. We gathered everything we knew about the marketplace and consumers, country by country. That led us to explore three classic business models: operational excellence, product innovation, and customer intimacy. We evaluated the models by cross-referencing them with all of the marketplace scenarios we could imagine.

7 HPD decided to focus on operational excellence, broadly defined as tightly matching supply and demand. Product innovation would cost too much in R&D to enable HPD to succeed in Europe. Moreover, Barrow believed direct marketing, although successful in some European countries such as the United Kingdom, was not widely enough accepted in Europe in 1997 to warrant investment in the customer intimacy model.

8 HPD undertook two projects to implement operational excellence. The first was to review customer behavior in six European markets. Barrow explained, "We really did not understand the purchasing behavior of consumers." The second was to analyze those six markets through a simulation exercise. Barrow asked:

How do you compare one country against another when you are not in that country? We took the product lines we were about to launch in the U.K. and France and asked retailers what we would have to price them at today if we were going to launch them in their country in the coming summer. We also asked them how many they thought they could sell over six months, through which channels and at what margins. This gave us a notion of a price point. This way we figured out whether our current structure for manufacturing was appropriate or out of range. The aim was to simulate the revenue and profit size with the existing product lines. The financial model told us what exactly we had to do to build a profitable operation.

The evaluation revealed that some smaller countries would be too unprofitable to consider (e.g., Switzerland, in part because of its several language groups).

NEXT PRODUCT, NEXT APPROACH—1998

9   By summer 1997, the Pavilion's respective market shares in the United Kingdom and France were 2.2% and 6.4%, well below HPD-E's 15% target. Difficult market conditions and lack of experience with channels in their existing markets had forced Barrow and her team to set aside plans to enter new markets such as Spain and the Netherlands. In July 1997, HP was no. 3 in the United States, three years ahead of HPD's plan. The $300 billion PC industry was booming. HP managers felt that the secret to HP's success in the United States was not technological advantage (HP's traditional strength), but the company's brand, excellent relationships with major chains created by HP's dominant position in printers and fax machines, and "perfect" supply and demand management.

10   In September 1997, HPD-E launched a back-to-school product in France and the United Kingdom to address these issues. Armed with customer and market information, the division worked with retailers to set a price point for particular product specifications. The team added margins to manufacturing costs and then production cost to matched target pricing. It then tendered the work to four OEM manufacturers and suppliers in addition to HP. HP responded surprisingly well to the unusual step (for HP) of taking product to an OEM. Barrow felt this reflected an understanding that HPD was "doing what it takes to be successful in this business."

11   Although the initial launch was a success (earning HP the no. 3 position in France, no. 7 in the United Kingdom), "we made a few mistakes," Barrow conceded:

> We did a good job of selling to the channel, but were not good enough at managing sellout and watching our competitors as carefully as we should have. In addition, when a major competitor cut the price of its products by 17%, we were slow to react. Inventory built up in the channel extremely quickly and the technology became obsolete. We had to pay a huge price protection bill in France and the U.K.

12   At the same time the team had to contend with a fundamental shift caused by an aggressive low-price-point market attack by French hypermarkets. By summer 1998, hypermarkets accounted for 60% of industry sales in France. Barrow explained:

> Hypermarket chains contributed in a major way to price decline as well as volume increase. We did not really understand this channel and therefore did not know how to manage it as well as we should. We had to build the relationship and go through wholesalers to reach hypermarket chains. This is where the information bottleneck is. We started to negotiate a direct contract with them. We have also reduced the number of retail chains we sell to and built share in each retailer to match demand with supply in a perfect manner.

TWIN OBJECTIVES—1999

13   These events led to a change in strategy for the European operation and a decision in October 1998 to temporarily forego expansion for profitability in France and the United Kingdom and build market share there through improved supply chain management ("operational excellence"). According to Barrow, expansion was on hold "until we learn to execute well in a very challenging market like France and take the learning elsewhere." HPD also reorganized its local management team and created a European P&L.

14   Some at HP believed that operational excellence in the traditional retail arena was precisely the wrong focus at a time when the industry was being revolutionized by direct sales. Industry analysts were also surprised by HPD's decision.[8] HPD managers nevertheless felt that the strategy would prove successful for the 1998 back-to-school season and allow HPD to gain back market share in France and the United Kingdom. Barrow summarized:

> We backed into really managing the business to profitability and not to growth. It was a total reversal. We realized that to make money in this industry we had to drive all the costs out of the system; that is, manage the entire value chain from manufacturing to the final sales at retail very tightly. This forced us to focus on every aspect of internal operation.

15   Didier Chenneveau, HPD-E's general manager Europe, was transferred from California to Grenoble, France, to head up the European organization as it implemented this strategy. He felt that HP had to reassess the way it was approaching the European market:

> We are still following what is basically an American model, based on tackling relatively static markets one by one and focusing resources on within-market battles for dominance. The European market is too volatile for this to work. I [suggested] more of a matrix model, where we attack either regional segments or emerging business models which are better suited to our own and which offer some form of first-mover advantage.

16   This meant redefining HPD's business by channel rather than by country, marking a departure from the country priority matrix approach.[9] According to him, "market entry [was] not the major barrier to profitability, but maintenance of margins once in the market." He estimated that the fixed costs of entry into a new market were approximately $1 million, to cover market research, some localization of keyboard and software (particularly help files), and packaging. Margins were lower than in the United States because of more price-sensitive market conditions, higher retailer margins, and also because of structural factors such as higher sales taxes and less efficient transportation and supply chain systems. The net unit contribution to HP could be $50 to $100 lower in Europe than in the United States, depending upon the price level and distribution channel.

17   Two strategic options to boost profitability were considered: (1) enter the region's less developed markets to gain pioneer market share advantage; and (2) develop new marketing models. Spain provided a test case for the first option. Traditionally a specialty retail market, a number of franchised chains offered the chance for HPD to experiment with the configure-to-order model. In addition, Nordic countries (especially Sweden and Norway) and the Netherlands appeared less price-sensitive than other markets and were apparently open to new business models such as employee purchase program and Internet sales.

18   The second option was using new marketing models and approaches with which HP, like other major computer brands, was experimenting (often through marketing partnerships). These included selling hardware at a reduced price in combination with a contract which generated revenues via a subscription to online services;[10] and preinstalling a portal on the PC, accessed by a single clearly labeled key, in return for a royalty from the portal owner every time the user used the key. Such new integrated business models were in line with the strategy for HP being articulated by new CEO Carly Fiorina—putting HP at "the intersection of e-services wrapped around products, appliances, and infrastructure."[11]

19   By mid-1999, substantial market share gains had been achieved in France, where Pavilion was third in the market with a 12% market share. Progress in the United Kingdom had been slower, although HPD was the top-selling brand in two retailers. See Exhibit 1 for brand positions in 1999.

EXHIBIT 1
**European Home
Computer Market
1999—Brand
Positions**

Source: HP.

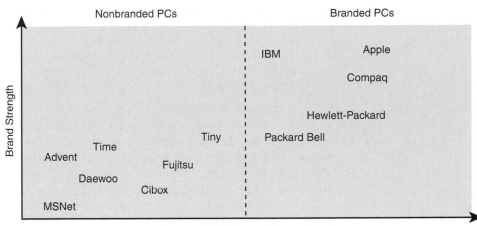

Note: Vobis was not measured.

GETTING IT RIGHT—2000

20 In September 2000, HPD managers felt that they "finally got it right [in Europe]." Much had changed. Emilio Ghilardi took over from Chenneveau on January 1, 2000. The concept of regional organization, which HPD-E had pioneered, was now being adopted across the company.[12] In mid-2000 HP was organized in four sectors, two product-facing organizations (all computer products and all imagining products) and two customer-facing ones (Business and Consumer). In 2000, HPD and the Pavilion were subsumed into a larger organization called Consumer Computing & Appliances, which also included the palmtop, the calculator business, personal storage appliances, CD writers, and Internet services. Ghilardi was its general manager for Europe, Middle East and Africa. The worldwide organization made product available and let regional organizations decide on the combination of technology and marketing strategy local markets warranted. Regional organizations had their own P & L. Noted Ghilardi:

> The regional organization takes care of product marketing, finance, business development, etc., all the standard things you would expect a regional organization to do—local people speak the same language and have the same culture as the customers and the people in the channels. That helps. Our support group devises and implements plans to support products everywhere in Europe. It is hoped that the new organization will increase speed and accountability. Sometimes speed is more important than cost.

21 Ghilardi felt that it was also "sometimes more important to be quick than right" and that the new organization would correct for past mistakes:

> At the outset HPD was given total autonomy. So they focused on making the best business model for the retail market in the U.S. That made it harder to internationalize. We thought we could make worldwide business decisions centrally and that proved difficult. Counterparts do not see us as being able to move fast. The fundamental point is that in Europe the market is dominated by local players, so the answer is coming from asking yourself the following question—why should people buy an HP instead of a no-brand home PC? Technology? No. Faster machine? No. What we have inside? No. So why would a customer value HP instead of somebody else? The first is look and feel in the product sense—quality and good value for what I am buying. The second is customer care, HP is

known for excellence in dealing with customers. Third, the product is optimized to give the best possible Internet experience. We want people to go through the Internet experience; in many cases we are still the first computer people buy. These are three areas we can add value that are consistent with HP values that echo with customers. People who make the rest their core competencies should do all the rest. For example, why were we doing the physical repair of breaks? The physical manufacturing? We can let other people focus on that.

22   On the strength of this realization, HPD was planning to relaunch in Germany on October 13 and moving into pretty much every country in Western Europe in the next 12 months. "We will be using blended channels—we will be where customers want to buy; retail is still by far the dominant place where people buy." Ghilardi was expecting to sell 150,000 to 200,000 units in Germany in the next 12 months. "We are aiming at 10% plus market share in two years in a market of 3 million units by 2002," Ghilardi explained.

EUROPEAN MARKET STRUCTURE

23   The European home PC market meanwhile was still growing at 15%–16% per year, though without predictable seasonality for most manufacturers. Competition remained strong and volatile across Europe (see Exhibits 2A and 2B and 3). Price points continued to fall. HPD's prices decreased in line with the overall market. "The delta in price between

EXHIBIT 2A   **Year-on-Year Top 10 Units for Consumer Desktop in Selected European Countries**

Vendor	1999, Q2	% Share	2000, Q2	% Share	Growth
Western Europe					
Fujitsu Siemens	174,123	13.1%	239,258	14.3%	37.4%
Compaq	105,423	7.9	200,614	12.0	90.3
NEC CI	98,642	7.4	192,495	11.5	95.1
Apple	44,853	3.4	86,136	5.2	92.0
IBM	57,562	4.3	72,305	4.3	25.6
Tiny Computers/Opus	55,952	4.2	70,415	4.2	25.8
Hewlett-Packard	33,124	2.5	62,304	3.7	88.1
Dell	49,847	3.8	60,030	3.6	20.4
Vobis	95,587	7.2	57,619	3.4	−39.7
Gateway	19,575	1.5	37,480	2.2	91.5
Others	593,057	44.7	593,387	35.5	−0.1
Total	**1,327,745**	**100%**	**1,671,043**	**100%**	**25.9%**
Austria					
Fujitsu Siemens	6,487	26.9%	24,491	40.9%	277.5%
Compaq	2,069	8.6	13,728	22.9	563.5
IBM	369	1.5	5,105	8.5	1,283.5
NEC CI	374	1.6	3,249	5.4	768.7
Birg	1,893	7.8	2,400	4.0	26.8
Maxdata	0	0.0	1,650	2.8	0.0
Vobis	3,822	15.8	1,260	2.1	−67.0
Apple	758	3.1	1,082	1.8	42.7
Actebis	1,985	8.2	703	1.2	−64.6
Acer	176	0.7	590	1.0	235.2
Others	6,196	25.7	5,563	9.3	−10.2
Total	**24,129**	**100%**	**59,821**	**100%**	**147.9%**

EXHIBIT 2A *(continued)*

Vendor	1999, Q2	% Share	2000, Q2	% Share	Growth
Belgium					
NEC CI	6,054	24.7%	12,711	34.1%	110.0%
Compaq	3,688	15.1	9,932	26.6	169.3
Apple	1,271	5.2	3,200	8.6	151.8
Vobis	2,822	11.5	2,203	5.9	−21.9
Fujitsu Siemens	2,121	8.7	2,015	5.4	−5.0
Dell	1,333	5.4	826	2.2	−38.0
IBM	1,087	4.4	306	0.8	−71.8
Actebis	0	0.0	138	0.4	0.0
Gateway	95	0.4	100	0.3	5.3
Laser	789	3.2	97	0.3	−87.7
Others	5,210	21.3	5,748	15.4	10.3
Total	**24,470**	**100%**	**37,276**	**100%**	**52.3**
Denmark					
Fujitsu Siemens	2,076	8.8%	6,210	19.4%	199.1%
Compaq	4,884	20.8	4,171	13.1	−14.6
IBM	2,850	12.1	3,996	12.5	40.2
Amitech	2,617	11.2	3,485	10.9	33.2
Newtech	4,275	18.2	2,264	7.1	−47.0
Apple	1,184	5.0	1,739	5.4	46.9
Actebis	0	0.0	1,599	5.0	0.0
Dell	1,084	4.6	1,447	4.5	33.5
Zitech	900	3.8	1,409	4.4	56.6
NEC CI	648	2.8	1,145	3.6	76.7
Others	2,951	12.6	4,485	14.0	52.0
Total	**23,469**	**100%**	**31,950**	**100%**	**36.1%**
Finland					
Fujitsu Siemens	3,390	14.1%	4,522	18.0%	33.4%
IBM	1,720	7.2	3,277	13.0	90.5
Compaq	1,308	5.5	2,528	10.0	93.3
DGC	1,302	5.4	1,771	7.0	36.0
DTK	755	3.2	1,617	6.4	114.2
Osborne	2,110	8.8	1,034	4.1	−51.0
ARC	701	2.9	870	3.5	24.1
Wings	1,116	4.7	762	3.0	−31.7
Apple	751	3.1	716	2.8	−4.7
Hewlett-Packard	1,004	4.2	706	2.8	−29.7
Others	9,811	40.9	7,364	29.3	−24.9
Total	**23,968**	**100%**	**25,167**	**100%**	**5.0%**
France					
NEC CI	21,360	11.4%	37,430	16.8%	75.2%
IBM	10,054	5.4	36,135	16.2	259.4
Hewlett-Packard	9,147	4.9	30,062	13.5	228.7
Apple	14,361	7.7	16,142	7.2	12.4
Fujitsu Siemens	10,370	5.5	15,816	7.1	52.5

(continued)

EXHIBIT 2A *(continued)*

Vendor	1999, Q2	% Share	2000, Q2	% Share	Growth
France *(continued)*					
Unika	10,710	5.7	9,680	4.3	−9.6
Cibox	16,965	9.0	9,294	4.2	−45.2
Compaq	6,279	3.3	7,872	3.5	25.4
Gateway	1,744	0.9	6,424	2.9	268.3
Acer	7,253	3.9	6,137	2.7	−15.4
Others	79,349	42.3	48,181	21.6	−39.3
Total	**187,592**	**100%**	**223,173**	**100%**	**19.0%**
Germany					
Fujitsu Siemens	93,947	25.5%	127,755	26.7%	36.0%
Compaq	15,168	4.1	93,779	19.6	518.3
Medion	16,317	4.4	26,851	5.6	64.6
Vobis	55,428	15.0	25,388	5.3	−54.2
Actebis	15,097	4.1	22,667	4.7	50.1
Peacock	0	0.0	22,609	4.7	0.0
PC Spezialist	12,062	3.3	22,456	4.7	86.2
Maxdata	0	0.0	20,168	4.2	0.0
Apple	8,877	2.4	16,155	3.4	82.0
Comtech	13,831	3.8	15,000	3.1	8.5
Others	138,028	37.4	86,262	18.0	−37.5
Total	**368,755**	**100%**	**479,090**	**100%**	**29.9%**
Greece					
Quest	860	9.9%	2,180	18.7%	153.5%
Altec	1,080	12.4	2,115	18.2	95.8
ICE	1,320	15.2	1,890	16.2	43.2
NEC CI	188	2.2	1,180	10.1	527.7
Compaq	297	3.4	984	8.5	231.3
Toshiba	0	0.0	544	4.7	0.0
Apple	276	3.2	317	2.7	14.9
Hewlett-Packard	104	1.2	147	1.3	41.3
Fujitsu Siemens	417	4.8	132	1.1	−68.3
Dell	3	0.0	118	1.0	3,833.3
Others	4,163	47.8	2,035	17.5	−51.1
Total	**8,708**	**100%**	**11,642**	**100%**	**33.7%**
Ireland					
NEC CI	3,016	20.1%	3,463	15.7%	14.8%
Gateway	1,822	12.1	3,125	14.2	71.5
Dell	1,974	13.1	3,066	13.9	55.3
Fujitsu Siemens	1,751	11.6	3,028	13.7	72.9
Compaq	2,443	16.3	2,832	12.8	15.9
Apple	309	2.1	969	4.4	213.6
PC Pro	0	0.0	397	1.8	0.0
Computer City	0	0.0	327	1.5	0.0
Acer	741	4.9	169	0.8	−77.2
IBM	694	4.6	134	0.6	−80.7
Others	2,282	15.2	4,563	20.7	100.0
Total	**15,032**	**100%**	**22,073**	**100%**	**46.8%**

EXHIBIT 2A   *(continued)*

Vendor	1999, Q2	% Share	2000, Q2	% Share	Growth
Italy					
Compaq	8,176	9.4%	17,429	15.8%	113.2%
CDC	20,365	23.5	16,722	15.1	−17.9
Vobis	11,259	13.0	10,978	9.9	−2.5
NEC CI	5,666	6.5	10,398	9.4	83.5
Olidata	7,837	9.1	9,391	8.5	19.8
Apple	2,743	3.2	8,565	7.8	212.2
Acer	3,367	3.9	7,321	6.6	117.4
Fujitsu Siemens	6,750	7.8	6,760	6.1	0.1
IBM	2,491	2.9	5,861	5.3	135.3
Dell	2,458	2.8	3,083	2.8	25.4
Others	15,425	17.8	13,973	12.6	−9.4
Total	**86,537**	**100%**	**110,481**	**100%**	**27.7%**
Netherlands					
NEC CI	11,911	17.3%	23,776	28.6%	99.6%
Compaq	15,567	22.6	14,277	17.2	−8.3
Vobis	9,769	14.2	9,616	11.6	−1.6
Fujitsu Siemens	11,994	17.4	8,441	10.2	−29.6
Gateway	1,303	1.9	6,475	7.8	396.9
Apple	3,269	4.7	4,141	5.0	26.7
Laser	2,334	3.4	3,978	4.8	70.4
Shitec	3,075	4.5	2,836	3.4	−7.8
Acer	1,194	1.7	1,724	2.1	44.4
Dell	2,430	3.5	1,679	2.0	−30.9
Others	5,981	8.7	6,128	7.4	2.5
Total	**68,827**	**100%**	**83.071**	**100%**	**20.7%**
Norway					
Fujitsu Siemens	1,831	5.9	4,013	14.7%	119.2%
Compaq	9,376	30.2	3,586	13.1	−61.8
Actebis	965	3.1	2,533	9.3	162.5
IBM	7,124	23.0	2,154	7.9	−69.8
Dell	2,049	6.6	1,563	5.7	−23.7
NEC CI	503	1.6	1,359	5.0	170.2
Apple	916	3.0	1,251	4.6	36.6
Evercom	1,334	4.3	1,224	4.5	−8.2
Hyundai	1,925	6.2	990	3.6	−48.6
REC	906	2.9	973	3.6	7.4
Others	4,068	13.1	7,676	28.1	88.7
Total	**30,997**	**100%**	**27,322**	**100%**	**−11.9%**
Portugal					
Compaq	3,746	18.7%	3,222	12.9%	−14.0%
Solbi/Citydesk	2,515	12.6	2,199	8.8	−12.6
Fujitsu Siemens	1,124	5.6	1,815	7.3	61.5
Triudus	1,107	5.5	1,705	6.8	54.0
Shine	1,346	6.7	981	3.9	−27.1
Vobis	483	2.4	919	3.7	90.3

(continued)

EXHIBIT 2A *(continued)*

Vendor	1999, Q2	% Share	2000, Q2	% Share	Growth
Portugal *(continued)*					
Tsunami	315	1.6	816	3.3	159.0
Apple	111	0.6	560	2.2	404.5
Acer	20	0.1	179	0.7	795.0
Dell	624	3.1	160	0.6	−74.4
Others	8,603	43.0	12,381	49.6	43.9
Total	**19,994**	**100%**	**24,937**	**100%**	**24.7%**
Spain					
Fujitsu Siemens	3,021	7.5%	10,532	17.9%	248.6%
NEC CI	3,955	9.8	7,472	12.7	88.9
Hewlett-Packard	3,476	8.6	7,044	12.0	102.6
Jump	4,856	12.1	5,192	8.8	6.9
El System	0	0.0	4,846	8.2	0.0
Inves	4,564	11.3	4,736	8.1	3.8
Compaq	3,505	8.7	3,899	6.6	11.2
Apple	2,394	6.0	2,938	5.0	22.7
KM Computers	1,820	4.5	1,950	3.3	7.1
Toshiba	0	0.0	1,655	2.8	0.0
Others	12,638	31.4	8,496	14.5	−32.8
Total	**40,229**	**100%**	**58,760**	**100%**	**46.1%**
Sweden					
Fujitsu Siemens	2,734	7.3%	8,054	25.3%	194.6%
Dell	4,455	11.9	4,258	13.4	−4.4
Compaq	7,164	19.1	4,096	12.9	−42.8
Apple	816	2.2	3,499	11.0	328.8
NEC CI	1,241	3.3	1,787	5.6	44.0
Network	475	1.3	1,361	4.3	186.5
Hewlett-Packard	1,693	4.5	1,139	3.6	−32.7
Acer	304	0.8	761	2.4	150.3
DGC	355	0.9	696	2.2	96.1
IBM	7,554	20.1	672	2.1	−91.1
Others	10,729	28.6	5,485	17.2	−48.9
Total	**37,520**	**100%**	**31,808**	**100%**	**−15.2%**
Switzerland					
Fujitsu Siemens	7,711	17.8%	9,923	18.6%	28.7%
Vobis	10,783	24.9	6,555	12.3	−39.2
Apple	2,046	4.7	6,385	12.0	212.1
Compaq	6,257	14.5	6,124	11.5	−2.1
Maxdata	0	0.0	5,379	10.1	0.0
Mandax	2,568	5.9	2,592	4.9	0.9
Dell	2,788	6.4	2,585	4.9	−7.3
Microspot	1,136	2.6	2,483	4.7	118.6
Athena	1,660	3.8	2,066	3.9	24.5
Actebis	121	0.3	1,074	2.0	787.6
Others	8,182	18.9	8,015	15.2	−0.9
Total	**43,252**	**100%**	**53,271**	**100%**	**23.2**

EXHIBIT 2A   *(continued)*

Vendor	1999, Q2	% Share	2000, Q2	% Share	Growth
United Kingdom					
NEC CI	39,444	12.2%	75,489	19.3%	91.4%
Tiny Computers/Opus	55,952	17.3	70,415	18.0	25.8
Granville/Time Computer	23,395	7.8	32,324	8.3	27.3
Dell	19,997	6.2	28,391	7.3	42.0
Hewlett-Packard	8,549	2.6	20,292	5.2	137.4
Viglen	21,844	6.7	19,348	4.9	−11.4
Apple	4,771	1.5	18,475	4.7	287.2
Gateway	11,217	3.5	17,595	4.5	56.9
Compaq	15,497	4.8	12,155	3.1	−21.6
Fujitsu Siemens	18,399	5.7	5,751	1.5	−68.7
Others	103,202	31.8	90,966	23.3	−11.9
Total	**324,267**	**100%**	**391,201**	**100%**	**20.6%**

Source: Company documents.

the branded and nonbranded PCs, or 'white boxes,' has shrunk dramatically in the past two years," Chenneveau noted. "There are HP and competitive branded products at FF4,990,[13] along with clones and white boxes. This was unheard of two years ago" (see Exhibit 4). He continued:

> The European market remains a tough one for major international brands. Compared to the United States, it's much less brand sensitive and more volatile. In most markets there are local competitors who are aggressive and very flexible, sourcing locally from whichever supplier can provide the right product fastest. By contrast, the international players, with globally integrated supply chains and supplier certification programs, can seem slow and expensive.

24   In Germany, the growth of the previously dominant vertically integrated manufacturer/distributors, Vobis and Escom, had stalled. The main beneficiary was the Japanese manufacturer Fujitsu, with its aggressive marketing of a limited range of relatively unsophisticated and low-priced PCs ("the simple box model," as Chenneveau described it). Following Escom's bankruptcy in 1997, Vobis had lost momentum during a period when it changed ownership and outsourced many of its procurement and operational functions.[14] While still present in Germany in late 2000, Vobis, too, had run into financial difficulties.

25   In France, HPD had overtaken IBM for third rank in unit market share in late 1999. Chenneveau attributed this gain to operational excellence in serving major retailers and the traditional strength of the HP brand in France, long the company's largest European operational base. "We have a strong salesforce here who have good relations with the very powerful mass merchants, such as Carrefour, Auchan, and Casino," explained Chenneveau. The strength of the brand made France the best cross-selling market for HP. HPD managers reported that the Pavilion was very strong in France, present in all retails channels as well as e-channels and HP's "shopping village." In late 2000, HP was fighting it out with Packard-Bell who remained the leader in France. IBM had exited retail and Fujitsu was a shadow of its former self, having lost its entire management team in France. In FY00, the Pavilion was expected to be a $120 million business, up 195% from FY99.

26   In the United Kingdom, HPD was represented only in small retail chains and had been unable to win space in the dominant outlets of PC World. Tiny, a fast-growing local

EXHIBIT 2B
Western European
PC Market Shares by
Manufacturers,
Year-End 1999

Source: Company documents.

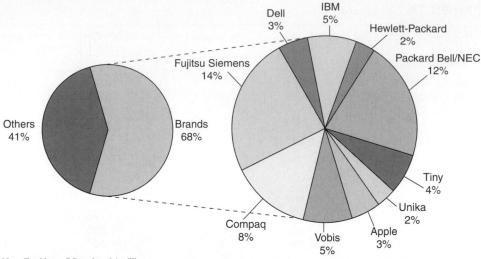

Note: Total home PC market: 6.4 million.

Europe Country
Share, Year-End
1999

Source: Company documents.

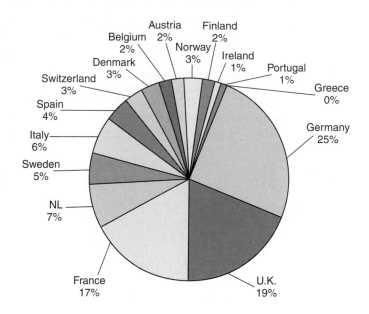

player, was pioneering inventory-less store formats, in which consumers looked at sample machines and placed orders for product which was later home-delivered from a central warehouse. The United Kingdom was also the fastest-growing market in Europe for direct sales by telephone and the Internet (the format growing fastest in the United States).[15] It, too, had been good to the Pavilion, expecting to register a FY00 300% increase in sales (in dollar terms) on FY99, despite the strong dollar that had increased the average sales price and HPD's underestimating of the back-to-school demand.

EXHIBIT 3
**HP Pavilion Sales vs.
Market in France,
July 1999–August
2000**

Source: Company documents.

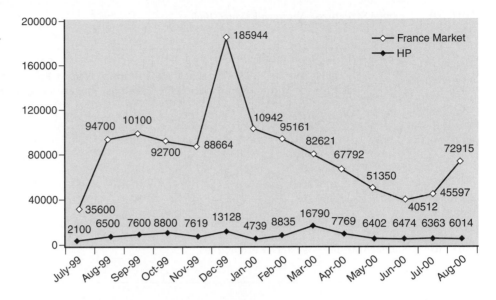

EXHIBIT 4
**HP Price Point
versus Competition
in France**

Source: Company documents.

France	Nov. '98–Feb. '99	Jan. '99–Apr. '99
Apple	8,780	8,506
Compaq	7,474	6,974
Fujitsu	7,268	7,319
Hewlett-Packard	7,399	5,358
IBM	7,711	8,400
Packard-Bell	7,371	7,152
Total Market	6,591	6,411

EVOLVING BUSINESS MODELS

27   At the same time, a range of business models had evolved (see Exhibits 5A and 5B). *Mainstream retail* was still the dominant model, but within this channel there were a number of alternative models in operation. *Line-up* described the conventional format, in which retailers carried a range of brands in inventory. This model had proven difficult to manage in both North America and Europe, principally because of rapid product obsolescence resulting from product range relaunch every two or three months. *Deal-based* business was when retailers placed large orders for single product types with configuration or branding often exclusive to the deal. Mass merchants frequently placed such orders because of the volumes they turned over, and this model was also employed by retailers who would otherwise not sell computers, such as the Conforama furniture hypermarket chain in France. Profitability was a challenge in these types of deals, despite the volumes involved—for example, the German discount chain Aldi could place orders for 30,000 units or more which it then used as loss-leaders to generate store traffic. The emerging retail format was *configure-to-order* (CTO), in which consumers visited a store to place an order for a PC built to their own specifications. This model, which Gateway was experimenting with in the United States, was proving successful in the United Kingdom for Tiny and Time Computer. Gateway had also opened up stores in France and the United Kingdom, but Chenneveau noted that the jury was still out about their success. It could deliver gross margins of up to 15%, compared with the 5% typical of line-up retail. In

EXHIBIT 5A Channel Structure—Western Europe, 2000

Source: Company documents.

Country	-Consumer Elec -Mass Merch -Computer Shore	Direct Retail	Local Shops	Fax/Phone Catalog	Web based	Employee Purchase Programs	-Bank Promos -Education -Trade Orgs
United Kingdom	46%	9%	10%	31%	2%	2%	0%
France	54%	3%	30%	5%	3%	5%	0%
Germany	46%	44%	5%	2%	1%	2%	0%
Spain	29%	46%	18%	6%	0%	0%	1%
Italy	48%	25%	22%	4%	0%	1%	0%
Nordics	47%	6%	10%	10%	2%	25%	0%
Netherlands	37%	25%	7%	9%	1%	21%	0%
Switzerland	45%	25%	20%	8%	1%	1%	0%

EXHIBIT 5B Channel Margins—Western Europe, 2000

Source: Company documents.

	Traditional Retail	Direct Retail	Kiosk order mgt	Fax/Phone Catalog	Web based	Corporate deals	Tax Advantage deals	Local Dealers
United Kingdom	28%	\	\	\	8%	8%	\	20%
France	22%	\	\	\	8%	8%	\	15%
Germany	20%	\	10%	\	8%	\	\	15%
Spain	18%	\	10%	\	10%	\	\	15%
Italy	20%	\	10%	\	\	8%	\	15%
Nordics	25%	\	\	\	\	\	7%	20%
Netherlands	25%	\	\	\	\	\	7%	20%
Switzerland	18%	\	\	\	\	8%	\	15%

2000, HPD ran a couple of experiments of kiosks within retail that did not prove to be as successful as expected. Average selling prices were up but unit sales were low and the experiments stopped. By contrast to these models, the *specialty retail* model relied on the economics of low-volume and high-margin business. Service in these outlets was personalized, with knowledgeable staff advising customers on the right computer for their needs, and even in some cases assembling the machine before delivery and installing it in the customer's home. This model was followed by both "mom-'n'-pop" outlets serving first-time buyers, and highly sophisticated boutique stores serving computer aficionados.

28   *Direct sales* offered three additional variants. *Internet sales,* relatively rare in Europe compared to North America, showed signs of growth particularly in the United Kingdom and Nordic countries. This model was also more profitable than retail (except retail CTO) because of the higher prevailing prices, a situation Chenneveau attributed to the fact that consumers typically undertook less brand comparison than when shopping in a retail environment. By contrast, *"direct direct,"* which consisted of telephone or catalog direct mail, was an established business model but one which showed little growth; HP was not represented in this channel in Europe. In 2000, HP opened HP.com e-stores in Germany and France in addition to the United Kingdom and Sweden.

29   Finally, an *employee purchase program* (EPP) model had emerged in certain high-tax countries, notably Sweden, where home computers were increasingly purchased through the consumer's employer to benefit from significantly more favorable tax treatment. EPP

EXHIBIT 6

HPD-E Historical Profitability

Source: Company documents.

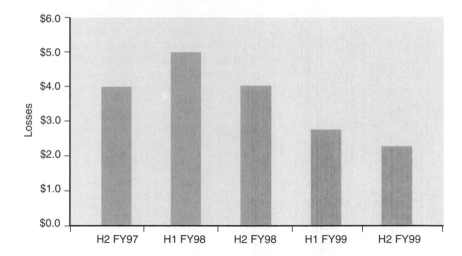

EXHIBIT 7

HPD-E Breakeven

Source: Company documents.

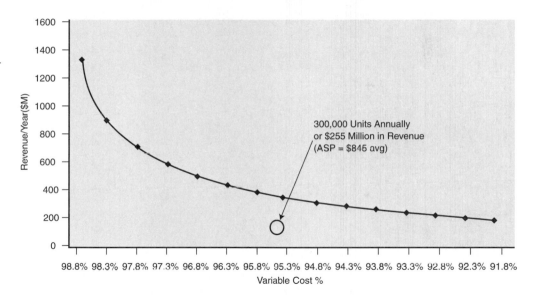

opportunities had been fueled by the publicity around some major deals with U.S. corporations, such as Ford. Ford's European competitors as well as large European MNCs were eager to replicate the formula. HP had won a lion share of this business worldwide and was at the forefront in Europe either implementing the European portion of worldwide deals (Ford, Intel, etc.) or in discussions with European MNCs.

30   In three years, HPD managers forecast, retail would still represent over 70% of the market, direct sales might be 15% in some countries, and EPP was increasingly popular and might reach 15% of sales in some countries. And within retail, Ghilardi noted, "the big boys are gaining momentum."

LESSONS FOR 2001

31   In November 2000, despite the division's economics (see Exhibits 6 and 7), Chenneveau remained convinced that operational excellence was "the strategic way [for HPD] to win" in Europe:

Right products at the right place at the right time is key. Inventory anywhere in the supply chain is evil. Suppliers price negotiation is crucial, a few dollars can make or break profitability. You cannot run your European consumer PC business from Palo Alto or from Austin. Beyond-the-box revenue (add-ons, e-services, etc.) are essential to improve profitability of an otherwise commoditized PC business. Despite all the talk of convergence with TV or handheld, PCs remain the platform of choice for consumer personal computing needs.

[1] Peter Burrows in "The Printer King Invades Homes PCs," *BusinessWeek,* August 21, 1995, p. 74.

[2] Some of the data in the case have been disguised.

[3] Broadly defined as tightly matching supply and demand.

[4] Burrows, ibid., p. 74.

[5] Jennifer Lien, "HP Cautious over Home PC Push into Asia-Pacific Market," *Business Times,* September 23, 1996, p. 12.

[6] "The Worldwide Web," *WorldTraveler,* December 1996, p. 136.

[7] Stockkeeping units.

[8] "HP Breaks through UK 1K Barrier with Premium II PCs," *Newsbytes,* February 20, 1998.

[9] See HBS case no. 397–001, "Hewlett-Packard Co.'s Home Products Division (A): Top Three in the Home PC Market by 1997."

[10] For example, a recent program in France offered consumers a FF2,000 discount off a PC retailing at FF4,900 in return for a two-year subscription to an Internet Service Provider (ISP) at FF124 per month. This program was offered via telephone sales.

[11] Speech delivered at the COMDEX trade show, Las Vegas, November 15, 1999.

[12] HP used to manage its business as a combination of product centric businesses with people with worldwide responsibility for managing different P & Ls.

[13] In September 1999, US$1 = FF6.4.

[14] In mid-1998, U.S.-based CHS Electronics acquired Vobis. Other major European computer distributors were bought by larger U.S. multinationals.

[15] HP had established its own online sales operation in the United Kingdom in 1998.

Case 48

Philip Condit and the Boeing 777: From Design and Development to Production and Sales

1 Following his promotion to Boeing CEO in 1988, Frank Shrontz looked for ways to stretch and upgrade the Boeing 767—an eight-year-old wide-body twin jet—in order to meet Airbus competition. Airbus had just launched two new 300-seat wide-body models, the two-engine A330 and the four-engine A340. Boeing had no 300-seat jetliner in service, nor did the company plan to develop such a jet.

2 To find out whether Boeing's customers were interested in a double-decker 767, Philip Condit, Boeing executive vice president and future CEO (1996) met with United Airlines Vice President Jim Guyette. Guyette rejected the idea outright, claiming that an upgraded 767 was no match to Airbus's new model transports. Instead, Guyette urged Boeing to develop a brand new commercial jet, the most advanced airplane of its generation. Shrontz had heard similar suggestions from other airline carriers. He reconsidered Boeing's options, and decided to abandon the 767 idea in favor of a new aircraft program. In December 1989, accordingly, he announced the 777 project and put Philip Condit in charge of its management. Boeing had launched the 777 in 1990, delivered the first jet in 1995, and by February 2001, 325 B-777s were flying in the services of the major international and U.S. airlines.

3 Condit faced a significant challenge in managing the 777 project. He wanted to create an airplane that was preferred by the airlines at a price that was truly competitive. He sought to attract airline customers as well as cut production costs, and he did so by introducing several innovations—both technological and managerial—in aircraft design, manufacturing, and assembly. He looked for ways to revitalize Boeing's outmoded engineering production system, and update Boeing's manufacturing strategies. And to achieve these goals, Condit made continual efforts to spread the 777 program innovations companywide.

4 Looking back at the 777 program, this case focuses on Condit's efforts. Was the 777 project successful and was it cost-effective? Would the development of the 777 allow Boeing to diffuse the innovations in airplane design and production beyond the 777 program? Would the development of the 777s permit Boeing to revamp and modernize its aircraft manufacturing system? Would the making and selling of the 777 enhance Boeing's competitive position relative to Airbus, its only remaining rival?

THE AIRCRAFT INDUSTRY

5 Commercial aircraft manufacturing was an industry of enormous risks where failure was the norm, not the exception. The number of large commercial jet makers had been reduced from four in the early 1980s—Boeing, McDonnell Douglas, Airbus, and Lockheed—to two in the late 1990s, turning the industry into a duopoly and pitting the two survivors—Boeing and Airbus—one against the other. One reason why aircraft manufacturers so often failed was the huge cost of product development.

Isaac Cohen, San Jose State University. The case was presented at the North American Case Research Association at San Antonio, Texas. Copyright Isaac Cohen, 2001.

6   Developing a new jetliner required an up-front investment of up to $15 billion (2001 dollars), a lead time of five to six years from launch to first delivery, and the ability to sustain a negative cash flow throughout the development phase. Typically, to break even on an entirely new jetliner, aircraft manufacturers needed to sell a minimum of 300 to 400 planes and at least 50 planes per year. Only a few commercial airplane programs had ever made money.

7   The price of an aircraft reflected its high development costs. New model prices were based on the average cost of producing 300 to 400 planes, not a single plane. Aircraft pricing embodied the principle of learning by doing, the so-called "learning curve": workers steadily improved their skills during the assembly process, and as a result, labor cost fell as the number of planes produced rose.

8   The high and increasing cost of product development prompted aircraft manufacturers to utilize subcontracting as a risk-sharing strategy. For the 747, the 767, and the 777, the Boeing Company required subcontractors to share a substantial part of the airplane's developed costs. Airbus did the same with its own latest models. Risk-sharing subcontractors performed detailed design work and assembled major subsections of the new plane while airframe integrators (i.e., aircraft manufacturers) designed the aircraft, integrated its systems and equipment, assembled the entire plane, marketed it, and provided customer support for 20 to 30 years. Both the airframe integrators and their subcontractors were supplied by thousands of domestic and foreign aircraft components manufacturers.

9   Neither Boeing nor Airbus nor any other postwar commercial aircraft manufacturer produced jet engines. A risky and costly venture, engine building had become a highly specialized business. Aircraft manufacturers worked closely with engine makers—General Electric, Pratt and Whitney, and Rolls Royce—to set engine performance standards. In most cases, new airplanes were offered with a choice of engines. Over time, the technology of engine building had become so complex and demanding that it took longer to develop an engine than an aircraft. During the life of a jetliner, the price of the engines and their replacement parts was equal to the entire price of the airplane.

10   A new model aircraft was normally designed around an engine, not the other way around. As engine performance improved, airframes were redesigned to exploit the engine's new capabilities. The most practical way to do so was to stretch the fuselage and add more seats in the cabin. Aircraft manufacturers deliberately designed flexibility into the airplane so that future engine improvements could facilitate later stretching. Hence the importance of the "family concept" in aircraft design, and hence the reason why aircraft manufacturers introduced families of planes made up of derivative jetliners built around a basic model, not single, standardized models.

11   The commercial aircraft industry, finally, gained from technological innovations in two other industries. More than any other manufacturing industry, aircraft construction benefited from advances in material applications and electronics. The development of metallic and nonmetallic composite materials played a key role in improving airframe and engine performance. On the one hand, composite materials that combined light weight and great strength were utilized by aircraft manufacturers; on the other, heat-resisting alloys that could tolerate temperatures of up to 3,000 degrees were used by engine makers. Similarly, advances in electronics revolutionized avionics. The increasing use of semiconductors by aircraft manufacturers facilitated the miniaturization of cockpit instruments, and more important, it enhanced the use of computers for aircraft communication, navigation, instrumentation, and testing. The use of computers contributed, in addition, to the design, manufacture, and assembly of new model aircraft.

THE BOEING COMPANY

12 The history of the Boeing Company may be divided into two distinct periods: the piston era and the jet age. Throughout the piston era, Boeing was essentially a military contractor producing fighter aircraft in the 1920s and 1930s, and bombers during World War II. During the jet age, beginning in the 1950s, Boeing had become the world's largest manufacturer of commercial aircraft, deriving most of its revenues from selling jetliners.

13 Boeing's first jet was the 707. The introduction of the 707 in 1958 represented a major breakthrough in the history of commercial aviation; it allowed Boeing to gain a critical technological lead over the Douglas Aircraft Company, its closer competitor. To benefit from government assistance in developing the 707, Boeing produced the first jet in two versions: a military tanker for the Air Force (k-135) and a commercial aircraft for the airlines (707-120). The company, however, did not recoup its own investment until 1964, six years after it delivered the first 707, and 12 years after it had launched the program. In the end, the 707 was quite profitable, selling 25% above its average cost. Boeing retained the essential design of the 707 for all its subsequent narrow-body single-aisle models (the 727, 737, and 757), introducing incremental design improvements, one at a time. One reason why Boeing used shared design for future models was the constant pressure experienced by the company to move down the learning curve and reduce overall development costs.

14 Boeing introduced the 747 in 1970. The development of the 747 represented another breakthrough; the 747 wide-body design was one of a kind; it had no real competition anywhere in the industry. Boeing bet the entire company on the success of the 747, spending on the project almost as much as the company's total net worth in 1965, the year the project started. In the short run, the outcome was disastrous. As Boeing began delivering its 747s, the company was struggling to avoid bankruptcy. Cutbacks in orders as a result of a deep recession, coupled with production inefficiencies and escalating costs, created a severe cash shortage that pushed the company to the brink. As sales dropped, the 747's break-even point moved further and further into the future.

15 Yet, in the long run, the 747 program was a triumph. The Jumbo Jet had become Boeing's most profitable aircraft and the industry's most efficient jetliner. The new plane helped Boeing solidify its position as the industry leader for years to come, leaving McDonnell Douglas far behind, and forcing the Lockheed Corporation to exit the market. The new plane, furthermore, contributed to Boeing's manufacturing strategy in two ways. First, as Boeing increased its reliance on outsourcing, six major subcontractors fabricated 70% of the value of the 747 airplane, thereby helping Boeing reduce the project's risks. Second, for the first time, Boeing applied the family concept in aircraft design to a wide-body jet, building the 747 with wings large enough to support a stretched fuselage with bigger engines, and offering a variety of other modifications in the 747's basic design. The 747-400 (1989) is a case in point. In 1997, Boeing sold the stretched and upgraded 747-400 in three versions, a standard jet, a freighter, and a "combi" (a jetliner whose main cabin was divided between passenger and cargo compartments).

16 Boeing developed other successful models. In 1969, Boeing introduced the 737, the company's narrow-body flagship, and in 1982 Boeing put into service two additional jetliners, the 757 (narrow-body) and the 767 (wide-body). By the early 1990s, the 737, 757, and 767 were all selling profitably. Following the introduction of the 777 in 1995, Boeing's families of planes included the 737 for short-range travel, the 757 and 767 for medium-range travel, and the 747 and 777 for medium- to long-range travel (Exhibit 1).

EXHIBIT 1

Total Number of Commercial Jetliners Delivered by the Boeing Company, 1958–2/2001*

Sources: Boeing Commercial Airplane Group, *Announced Orders and Deliveries as of 12/31/97; The Boeing Company 1998 Annual Report* p. 35; "Commercial Airplanes: Order and Delivery Summary," www.Boeing. com/commercial/ orders/index.html. Retrieved online, March 20, 2001.

Model	No. Delivered	First Delivery
B-707	1,010 (retired)	1958
B-727	1,831 (retired)	1963
B-737	3,901	1967
B-747	1,264	1970
B-757	953	1982
B-767	825	1982
B-777	325	1995
B-717	49	2000
Total	10,158	

*McDonell Douglas commercial jetliners (the MD-11, MD-80, and MD-90) are excluded.

EXHIBIT 2

Market Share of Shipments of Commercial Aircraft, Boeing, McDonnell Douglas (MD), Airbus, 1992–2000

Sources: *Aerospace Facts and Figures, 1997–98,* p. 34; *Wall Street Journal,* December 3, 1998, and January 12, 1999; *The Boeing Company 1997 Annual Report,* p. 19; Data supplied by Mark Luginbill, Airbus Communication Director, November 16, 1998, February 1, 2000, and March 20, 2001.

	1992	1993	1994	1995	1996	1997	1998	1999	2000
Boeing	61%	61%	63%	54%	55%	67%	71%	68%	61%
MD	17	14	9	13	13				
Airbus	22	25	28	33	32	33	29	32	39

17   In addition to building jetliners, Boeing also expanded its defense, space and information businesses. In 1997, the Boeing Company took a strategic gamble, buying the McDonnell Douglas Company in a $14 billion stock deal. As a result of the merger, Boeing had become the world's largest manufacturer of military aircraft, NASA's largest supplier, and the Pentagon's second largest contractor (after Lockheed). Nevertheless, despite the growth in its defense and space businesses, Boeing still derived most of its revenues from selling jetliners. Commercial aircraft revenues accounted for 59% of Boeing's $49 billion sales in 1997 and 63% of Boeing's $56 billion sales in 1998.

18   Following its merger with McDonnell, Boeing had one remaining rival: Airbus Industrie. In 1997, Airbus booked 45% of the worldwide orders for commercial jetliners and delivered close to 1/3 of the worldwide industry output. In 2000, Airbus shipped nearly 2/5 of the worldwide industry output (Exhibit 2).

19   Airbus's success was based on a strategy that combined cost leadership with technological leadership. First, Airbus distinguished itself from Boeing by incorporating the most advanced technologies into its planes. Second, Airbus managed to cut costs by utilizing a flexible, lean production manufacturing system that stood in a stark contrast to Boeing's mass production system.

20   As Airbus prospered, the Boeing Company was struggling with rising costs, declining productivity, delays in deliveries, and production inefficiencies. Boeing Commercial Aircraft Group lost $1.8 billion in 1997 and barely generated any profits in 1998. All through the 1990s, the Boeing Company looked for ways to revitalize its outdated production manufacturing system, on the one hand, and to introduce leading-edge technologies into its jetliners, on the other. The development and production of the 777, first conceived of in 1989, was an early step undertaken by Boeing managers to address both problems.

THE 777 PROGRAM

21   The 777 program was Boeing's single largest project since the completion of the 747. The total development cost of the 777 was estimated at $6.3 billion and the total number of employees assigned to the project peaked at nearly 10,000. The 777's twin engines were the largest and most powerful ever built (the diameter of the 777's engine equaled the 737's fuselage), the 777's construction required 132,000 uniquely engineered parts (compared to 70,000 for the 767), the 777's seat capacity was identical to that of the first 747 that had gone into service in 1970, and its manufacturer empty weight was 57% greater than the 767's. Building the 777 alongside the 747 and 767 at its Everett plant near Seattle, Washington, Boeing enlarged the plant to cover an area of 76 football fields.

22   Boeing's financial position in 1990 was unusually strong. With a 21% rate of return on stockholder equity, a long-term debt of just 15% of capitalization, and a cash surplus of $3.6 billion, Boeing could gamble comfortably. There was no need to bet the company on the new project as had been the case with the 747, or to borrow heavily, as had been the case with the 767. Still, the decision to develop the 777 was definitely risky; a failure of the new jet might have triggered an irreversible decline of the Boeing Company and threatened its future survival.

23   The decision to develop the 777 was based on market assessment—the estimated future needs of the airlines. During the 14-year period, 1991–2005, Boeing market analysts forecasted an +100% increase in the number of passenger miles traveled worldwide, and a need for about 9,000 new commercial jets. Of the total value of the jetliners needed in 1991–2005, Boeing analysts forecasted a $260 billion market for wide-body jets smaller than the 747. An increasing number of these wide-body jets were expected to be larger than the 767.

A Consumer Driven Product

24   To manage the risk of developing a new jetliner, aircraft manufacturers had first sought to obtain a minimum number of firm orders from interested carriers, and only then commit to the project. Boeing CEO Frank Shrontz had expected to obtain 100 initial orders of the 777 before asking the Boeing board to launch the project, but as a result of Boeing's financial strength, on the one hand, and the increasing competitiveness of Airbus, on the other, Schrontz decided to seek the board's approval earlier. He did so after securing only one customer: United Airlines. On October 12, 1990, United had placed an order for 34 777s and an option for an additional 34 aircraft, and two weeks later, Boeing's board of directors approved the project.

25   Negotiating the sale, Boeing and United drafted a handwritten agreement (signed by Philip Condit and Richard Albrecht, Boeing's executive vice presidents, and Jim Guyette, United's executive vice president) that granted United a larger role in designing the 777 than the role played by any airline before. The two companies pledged to cooperate closely in developing an aircraft with the "best dispatch reliability in the industry" and the "greatest customer appeal in the industry." "We will endeavor to do it right the first time with the highest degree of professionalism" and with "candor, honesty, and respect" [the agreement read]. Asked to comment on the agreement, Philip Condit said: "We are going to listen to our customers and understand what they want. Everybody on the program has that attitude." Gordon McKinzie, United's 777 program director, agreed: "In the past we'd get brochures on a new airplane and its options . . . wait four years for delivery, and hope we'd get what we ordered. This time Boeing really listened to us".

26   Condit invited other airline carriers to participate in the design and development phase of the 777. Altogether, eight carriers from around the world (United, Delta, American, British Airways, Qantas, Japan Airlines, All Nippon Airways, and Japan Air System) sent full-time representatives to Seattle; British Airways alone assigned 75 people at one time. To facilitate interaction between its design engineers and representatives of the eight carriers, Boeing introduced an initiative called "Working Together." "If we have a problem," a British Airways production manager explained, "we go to the source—design engineers on the IPT [Integrated Product Teams], not service engineer(s). One of the frustrations on the 747 was that we rarely got to talk to the engineers who were doing the work."

27   "We have definitely influenced the design of the aircraft," a United 777 manager said, mentioning changes in the design of the wing panels that made it easier for airline mechanics to access the slats (slats, like flaps, increased lift on takeoffs and landings), and new features in the cabin that made the plane more attractive to passengers. Of the 1,500 design features examined by representatives of the airlines, Boeing engineers modified 300. Among changes made by Boeing was a redesigned overhead bin that left more stand-up headroom for passengers (allowing a six-foot-three tall passenger to walk from aisle to aisle), "flattened" side walls that provided the occupant of the window seat with more room, overhead bin doors that opened down and made it possible for shorter passengers to lift baggage into the overhead compartment, a redesigned reading lamp that enabled flight attendants to replace light bulbs, a task formerly performed by mechanics, and a computerized flight deck management system that adjusted cabin temperature, controlled the volume of the public address system, and monitored food and drink inventories.

28   More important were changes in the interior configuration (layout plan) of the aircraft. To be able to reconfigure the plane quickly for different markets of varying travel ranges and passengers loads, Boeing's customers sought a flexible plan of the interior. On a standard commercial jet, kitchen galleys, closets, lavatories, and bars were all removable in the past but were limited to fixed positions where the interior floor structure was reinforced to accommodate the "wet" load. On the 777, by contrast, such components as galleys and lavatories could be positioned anywhere within several "flexible zones" designed into the cabin by the joint efforts of Boeing engineers and representatives of the eight airlines. Similarly, the flexible design of the 777's seat tracks made it possible for carriers to increase the number of seat combinations as well as reconfigure the seating arrangement quickly. Flexible configuration resulted, in turn, in significant cost savings; airlines no longer needed to take the aircraft out of service for an extended period of time in order to reconfigure the interior.

29   The airline carriers also influenced the way in which Boeing designed the 777 cockpit. During the program definition phase, representatives of United Airlines, British Airways and Quantas—three of Boeing's clients whose fleets included a large number of 747-400s—asked Boeing engineers to model the 777 cockpit on the 747-400's. In response to these requests, Boeing introduced a shared 747/777 cockpit design that enabled its airline customers to use a single pool of pilots for both aircraft types at a significant cost savings.

30   Additionally, the airline carriers urged Boeing to increase its use of avionics for in-flight entertainment. The 777, as a consequence, was equipped with a fully computerized cabin. Facing each seat on the 777, and placed on the back of the seat in front, was a combined computer and video monitor that featured movies, video programs, and interactive computer games. Passengers were also provided with a digital sound system comparable to the most advanced home stereo available, and a telephone. About 40% of the 777's total computer capacity was reserved for passengers in the cabin.

EXHIBIT 3 The 777: Selected Design Features Proposed by Boeing Airline Customers and Adapted by The Boeing Company

Source: The Boeing Company.

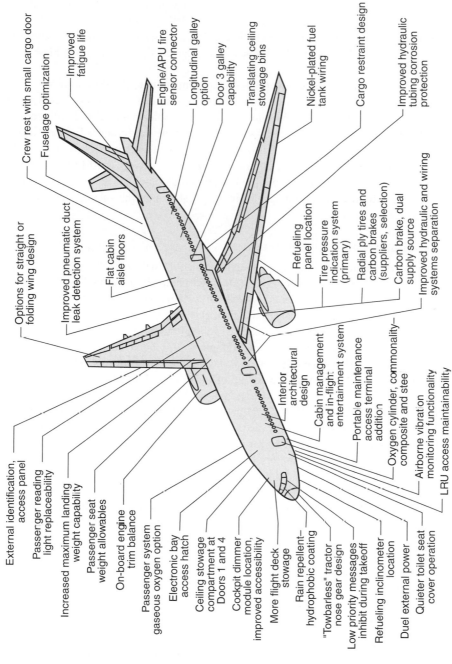

Crew rest with small cargo door
Improved fatigue life
Engine/APU fire sensor connector
Longitudinal galley option
Door 3 galley capability
Translating ceiling stowage bins
Nickel-plated fuel tank wiring
Cargo restraint design
Improved hydraulic tubing corrosion protection
Fuselage optimization
Options for straight or folding wing design
Improved pneumatic duct leak detection system
Flat cabin aisle floors
Refueling panel location
Tire pressure indication system (primary)
Radial ply tires and carbon brakes (suppliers, selection)
Carbon brake, dual supply source
Improved hydraulic and wiring systems separation
External identification, access panel
Passenger reading light replaceability
Increased maximum landing weight capability
Passenger seat weight allowables
On-board engine trim balance
Passenger system gaseous oxygen option
Electronic bay access hatch
Ceiling stowage compartment at Doors 1 and 4
Cockpit dimmer module location, improved accessibility
More flight deck stowage
Rain repellent–hydrophobic coating
"Towbarless" tractor nose gear design
Low priority messages inhibit during takeoff
Refueling inclinometer location
Duel external power
Quieter toilet seat cover operation
Interior architectural design
Cabin management and in-flight entertainment system
Portable maintenance access terminal addition
Oxygen cylinder, commonality—composite and stee
Airborne vibration monitoring functionality
LRU access maintainability

31   The 777 was Boeing's first fly by wire (FBW) aircraft, an aircraft controlled by a pilot transmitting commands to the moveable surfaces (rudder, flaps, etc.) electrically, not mechanically. Boeing installed a state-of-the-art FBW system on the 777 partly to satisfy its airline customers, and partly to challenge Airbus's leadership in flight control technology, a position Airbus had held since it introduced the world's first FBW aircraft, the A-320, in 1988.

32   Lastly, Boeing customers were invited to contribute to the design of the 777's engine. Both United Airlines and All Nippon Airways assigned service engineers to work with representatives of Pratt and Whitney (P&W) on problems associated with engine maintenance. P&W held three specially scheduled "airline conferences." At each conference, some 40 airline representatives clustered around a full-scale mock-up of the 777 engine and showed Pratt and Whitney engineers gaps in the design, hard-to-reach points, visible but inaccessible parts, and accessible but invisible components. At the initial conference, Pratt and Whitney picked up 150 airline suggestions, at the second, 50, and at the third, 10 more suggestions.

A Globally Manufactured Product

33   Twelve international companies located in 10 countries, and 18 more U.S. companies located in 12 states, were contracted by Boeing to help manufacture the 777. Together, they supplied structural components as well as systems and equipment. Among the foreign suppliers were companies based in Japan, Britain, Australia, Italy, Korea, Brazil, Singapore, and Ireland; among the major U.S. subcontractors were the Grumman Corporation, Rockwell (later merged with Boeing), Honeywell, United Technologies, Bendix, and the Sunstrand Corporation (Exhibits 4 and 5). Of all foreign participants, the Japanese played the largest role. A consortium made up of Fuji Heavy Industries, Kawasaki Heavy Industries, and Mitsubishi Heavy Industries had worked with Boeing on its wide-body models since the early days of the 747. Together, the three Japanese subcontractors produced 20% of the value of the 777's airframe (up from 15% of the 767's). A group of 250 Japanese engineers had spent a year in Seattle working on the 777 alongside Boeing engineers before most of its members went back home to begin production. The fuselage was built in sections in Japan and then shipped to Boeing's huge plant at Everett, Washington, for assembly.

34   Boeing used global subcontracting as a marketing tool as well. Sharing design work and production with overseas firms, Boeing required overseas carriers to buy the new aircraft. Again, Japan is a case in point. In return for the contract signed with the Mitsubishi, Fuji, and Kawasaki consortium—which was heavily subsidized by the Japanese government—Boeing sold 46 777 jetliners to three Japanese air carriers: All Nippon Airways, Japan Airlines, and Japan Air System.

A Family of Planes

35   From the outset, the design of the 777 was flexible enough to accommodate derivative jetliners. Because all derivatives of a given model shared maintenance, training, and operating procedures, as well as replacement parts and components, and because such derivatives enabled carriers to serve different markets at lower costs, Boeing's clients were seeking a family of planes built around a basic model, not a single 777. Condit and his management team, accordingly, urged Boeing's engineers to incorporate the maximum flexibility into the design of the 777.

EXHIBIT 4   777 Supplier Contracts

Source: James Woolsey, "777: Boeing's New Large Twinjet," *Air Transport World,* April 1994, p. 24.

U.S. Suppliers of Structural Components

Astech/MCI	Santa Ana, Calif.	Primary exhaust cowl assembly (plug and nozzle)
Grumman Aerospace	Bethpage, N.Y.	Spoilers, inboard flaps
Kaman	Bloomfield, Conn.	Fixed training edge
Rockwell	Tulsa, Okla.	Floor beams, wing leading edge slats

International Suppliers of Structural Components

Alenia	Italy	Wing outboard flaps, radome
AeroSpace Technologies of Australia	Australia	Rudder
Embraer-Empresa Brasiera de Aeronautica	Brazil	Dorsal fin, wingtip assembly
Hawker de Havilland	Australia	Elevators
*Mitsubishi Heavy Industries, Kawasaki Heavy Industries and Fuji Heavy Industries	Japan	Fuselage panels and doors, wing center section, wing-to-body fairing, and wing in-spar ribs
Korean Air	Korea	Flap support fairings, wingtip assembly
Menasco Aerospace/Messier-Bugatti	Canada/France	Main and nose landing gears
Short Brothers	Ireland	Nose landing gear doors
Singapore Aerospace Manufacturing	Singapore	Nose landing gear doors

U.S. Suppliers of Systems and Equipment

AlliedSignal Aerospace Company, AiResearch Divisions	Torrance, Calif.	Cabin pressure control system, air supply control system, integrated system controller, ram air turbine
Bendix Wheels and Brakes Division	South Bend. Ind.	Wheel and brakes
Garrett Divisions	Phoenix/Tempe, Ariz.	Auxilliary power unit (APU), air-driven unit
BFGoodrich	Troy,Ohio	Wheel and breaks
Dowty Aerospace	Los Angeles, Calif.	Thrust reverser actuator system
Eldec	Lynnwood, Wash.	Power supply electronics
E-Systems, Montek Division	Salt Lake City, Utah	Stabilizer trim control module, secondary hydraulic break, optional folding wingtip system
Honeywell	Phoenix, Ariz, Coon Rapids, Minn.	Airplane information management system (AIMS), air data/inertial reference system (ADIRS)
Rockwell, Collins Division	Cedar Rapids, Iowa	Autopilot flight director system, electronic library system (ELS) displays
Sundstrand Corporation	Rockford, Ill.	Primary and backup electrical power systems
Teijin Seiki America	Redmond, Wash.	Power control units, actuator control electronics
United Technologies, Hamilton Standard Division	Windsor Locks, Conn.	Cabin air-conditioning and temperature control system, ice protection system

International Suppliers of Systems and Equipment

General Electric Company (GEC) Avionics	United Kingdom	Primary flight computers
Smiths Industries	United Kingdom	Integrated electrical load management system (ELMS), throttle control system actuator, fuel quantity indicating system (FQIS)

*Program partners.

EXHIBIT 5

Source: Jeremy Main, "Corporate Performance: Betting on the 21st Century Jet," *Fortune* April, 20, 1992, p. 104.

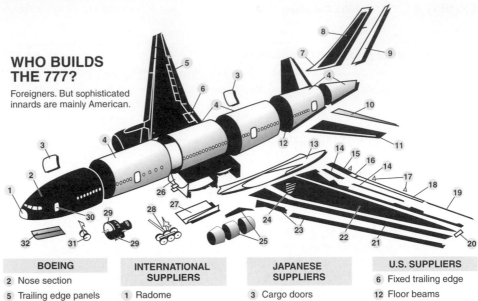

WHO BUILDS THE 777?

Foreigners. But sophisticated innards are mainly American.

BOEING		INTERNATIONAL SUPPLIERS		JAPANESE SUPPLIERS		U.S. SUPPLIERS	
2	Nose section	1	Radome	3	Cargo doors	6	Fixed trailing edge
5	Trailing edge panels	7	Dorsal fin	4	Fuselage panels	12	Floor beams
8	Vertical fin	9	Rudder	13	Wing-to-body fairing	14	Spoilers
11	Horizontal stabilizer	10	Elevator	24	In-spar ribs	15	Inboard flaps
21	Fixed leading edge	16	Flaperon	26	Wing center section	23	Leading edge slats
22	Wing box	17	Flap support fairings	27	Main landing gear doors	29	Engine
25	Nocelles,struts, and fairings	18	Outboard flap	30	Passenger doors		
		19	Aileron				
		20	Wing tip assembly				
		28	Main landing gear				
		29	Engine				
		31	Nose landing gear				
		32	Nose landing gear doors				

36　　The 777's design flexibility helped Boeing manage the project's risks. Offering a family of planes based on a single design to accommodate future changes in customers' preferences, Boeing spread the 777 project's risks among a number of models all belonging to the same family.

37　　The key to the 777's design efficiency was the wing. The 777 wings, exceptionally long and thin, were strong enough to support vastly enlarged models. The first model to go into service, the 777-200, had a 209-foot-long fuselage, was designed to carry 305 passengers in three class configurations, and had a travel range of 5,900 miles in its original version (1995), and up to 8,900 miles in its extended version (1997). The second model to be introduced (1998), the 777-300, had a stretched fuselage of 242 feet (10 feet longer than the 747), was configured for 379 passengers (3-class), and flew to destinations of up to 6,800 miles away. In all-tourist class configuration, the stretched 777-300 could carry as many as 550 passengers.

Digital Design

38　　The 777 was the first Boeing jetliner designed entirely by computers. Historically, Boeing had designed new planes in two ways: paper drawings and full-size models called mock-ups. Paper drawings were two dimensional and therefore insufficient to account for the complex construction of the three-dimensional airplane. Full scale mock-ups served as a backup to drawings.

39   Boeing engineers used three classes of mock-ups. Made up of plywood or foam, class 1 mock-ups were used to construct the plane's large components in three dimensions, refine the design of these components by carving into the wood or foam, and feed the results back into the drawings. Made partly of metal, class 2 mock-ups addressed more complex problems such as the wiring and tubing of the airframe, and the design of the machine tools necessary to cut and shape the large components. Class 3 mock-ups gave the engineers one final opportunity to refine the model and thereby reduce the need to keep on changing the design during the actual assembly process or after delivery.

40   Despite the engineers' efforts, many parts and components did not fit together on the final assembly line but rather "interfered" with each other, that is, overlapped in space. The problem was both pervasive and costly; Boeing engineers needed to rework and realign all overlapping parts in order to join them together.

41   A partial solution to the problem was provided by the computer. In the last quarter of the 20th century, computer-aided design was used successfully in car manufacture, building construction, machine production and several other industries; its application to commercial aircraft manufacturing came later, both in the United States and in Europe. Speaking of the 777, Dick Johnson, Boeing chief engineer for digital design, noted the "tremendous advantage" of computer application:

> With mock-ups, the " . . . engineer had three opportunities at three levels of detail to check his parts, and nothing in between. With Catia [computer-aided, three-dimensional, interactive application] he can do it day in and day out over the whole development of the airplane."

42   Catia was a sophisticated computer program that Boeing bought from Dassault Aviation, a French fighter planes builder. IBM enhanced the program to improve image manipulation, supplied Boeing with eight of its largest mainframe computers, and connected the mainframes to 2,200 computer terminals that Boeing distributed among its 777 design teams. The software program showed on a screen exactly how parts and components fit together before the actual manufacturing process took place.

43   A digital design system, Catia had five distinctive advantages. First, it provided the engineers with 100% visualization, allowing them to rotate, zoom, and "interrogate" parts geometrically in order to spotlight interferences. Second, Catia assigned a numerical value to each drawing on the screen and thereby helped engineers locate related drawings of parts and components, merge them together, and check for incompatibilities. Third, to help Boeing's customers service the 777, the digital design system created a computer simulated human—a Catia figure playing the role of the service mechanic—who climbed into the three-dimensional images and showed the engineers whether parts were serviceable and entry accessible. Fourth, the use of Catia by all 777 design teams in the U.S., Japan, Europe, and elsewhere facilitated instantaneous communication between Boeing and its subcontractors and ensured the frequent updating of the design. And fifth, Catia provided the 777 assembly line workers with graphics that enhanced the narrative work instructions they received, showing explicitly on a screen how a given task should be performed.

Design-Build Teams (DBT)

44   Teaming was another feature of the 777 program. About 30 integrated-level teams at the top and more than 230 design-build teams at the bottom worked together on the 777. All

EXHIBIT 6

The 10 DBTs ("little companies") Responsible for the Wing's Trailing Edge

Source: Karl Sabbagh, *21st Century Jet: The Making and Marketing of the Boeing 777* (New York: Scribner, 1996), p. 73.

Flap Supports Team
Inboard Flap Team
Outboard Flap Team
Outboard Fixed Wing Team
Flaperon* Team
Aileron* Team
Inboard Fixed Wing and Gear Support Team
Main Landing Gear Doors Team
Spoilers** Team
Fairings*** Team

* The Flaperon and Aileron were moveable hinged sections of the trailing edge that helped the plane roll in flight. The Flaperon was used at high speed, the Aileron at low speed.
** The spoilers were the flat surfaces that lay on top of the trailing edge and extended during landing to slow down the plane.
*** The fairings were the smooth parts attached to the outline of the wing's trailing edge. They helped reduce drag.

team members were connected by Catia. The integrated-level teams were organized around large sections of the aircraft; the DBTs around small parts and components. In both cases, teams were cross-functional, as Philip Condit observed:

> If you go back . . . to earlier planes that Boeing built, the factory was on the bottom floor, and Engineering was on the upper floor. Both Manufacturing and Engineering went back and forth. When there was a problem in the factory, the engineer went down and looked at it. . . .
>
> With ten thousand people [working on the 777], that turns out to be really hard. So you start devising other tools to allow you to achieve that—the design-build team. You break the airplane down and bring Manufacturing, Tooling, Planning, Engineering, Finance, and Materials all together [in small teams].

45   Under the design-build approach, many of the design decisions were driven by manufacturing concerns. As manufacturing specialists worked alongside engineers, engineers were less likely to design parts that were difficult to produce and needed to be redesigned. Similarly, under the design-build approach, customers' expectations as well as safety and weight considerations were all incorporated into the design of the aircraft; engineers no longer needed to "chain saw" structural components and systems in order to replace parts that did not meet customers' expectations, were unsafe, or were too heavy.

46   The design of the 777's wing provides an example. The wing was divided into two integration-level teams, the "leading edge" (the forward part of the wing) and the "trailing edge" (the back of the wing) team. Next, the trailing edge team was further divided into 10 design-build teams, each named after a piece of the wing's trailing edge (Exhibit 6). Membership in these DBTs extended to two groups of outsiders: representatives of the customer airlines and engineers employed by the foreign subcontractors. Made up of up to 20 members, each DBT decided its own mix of insiders and outsiders, and each was led by a team leader. Each DBT included representatives from six functional disciplines: engineering, manufacturing, material, customer support, finance, and quality assurance. The DBTs met twice a week for two hours to hear reports from team members, discuss immediate goals and plans, divide responsibilities, set time lines, and take specific notes of all decisions taken. Described by a Boeing official as "little companies," the DBTs enjoyed a high degree of autonomy from man-

agement supervision; team members designed their own tools, developed their own manufacturing plans, and wrote their own contracts with the program management, specifying deliverables, resources, and schedules. John Monroe, a Boeing 777 senior project manager, remarked:

> The team is totally responsible. We give them a lump of money to go and do th[eir] job.
> They decide whether to hire a lot of inexpensive people or to trade numbers for resources.
> It's unprecedented. We have some $100 million plus activities led by nonmanagers.

Employees' Empowerment and Culture

47 An additional aspect of the 777 program was the empowering of assembly line workers. Boeing managers encouraged factory workers at all levels to speak up, offer suggestions, and participate in decision making. Boeing managers also paid attention to a variety of "human relations" problems faced by workers, problems ranging from child care and parking to occupational hazards and safety concerns.

48 All employees entering the 777 program—managers, engineers, assembly line workers, and others—were expected to attend a special orientation session devoted to the themes of teamwork and quality control. Once a quarter, the entire "777 team" of up to 10,000 employees met off-site to hear briefings in the aircraft status. Dressed casually, the employees were urged to raise questions, voice complaints, and propose improvements. Under the 777 program, managers met frequently to discuss ways to promote communication with workers. Managers, for example, "fire fought" problems by bringing workers together and empowering them to offer solutions. In a typical "firefight" session, Boeing 777 project managers learned from assembly line workers how to improve the process of wiring and tubing the airframe's interior: "staffing" fuselage sections with wires, ducts, tubs, and insolation materials before joining the sections together was easier than installing the interior parts all at once in a preassembled fuselage.

49 Under the 777 program, in addition, Boeing assembly line workers also were empowered to appeal management decisions. In a case involving middle managers, a group of Boeing machinists sought to replace a nonretractable jig (a large device used to hold parts) with a retractable one in order to ease and simplify their jobs. Otherwise they had to carry heavy equipment loads up and down stairs. Again and again, their supervisors refused to implement the change. When the machinists eventually approached a factory manager, he inspected the jig personally, and immediately ordered the change.

50 Under the 777 program, work on the shop floor was ruled by the "Bar Chart." A large display panel placed at different work areas, the Bar Chart listed the name of each worker, his or her daily job description, and the time available to complete specific tasks. Boeing had utilized the Bar Chart system as a "management visibility system" in the past, but only under the 777 program was the system fully computerized. The chart showed whether assembly line workers were meeting or missing their production goals. Boeing industrial engineers estimated the time it took to complete a given task and fed the information back to the system's computer. Workers ran a scanner across their ID badges and supplied the computer with the data necessary to log their job progress. Each employee "sold" his/her completed job to an inspector, and no job was declared acceptable unless "bought" by an inspector.

Leadership and Management Style

51 The team in charge of the 777 program was led by a group of five vice presidents, headed by Philip Condit, a gifted engineer who was described by one Wall Street analyst as "a cross between a grizzly bear and a teddy bear. Good people skills, but furious in the market-place." Each of the five vice presidents rose through the ranks, and each had 25–30 years' experience with Boeing. All were men.

52   During the 777 design phase, the five VPs met regularly every Tuesday morning in a small conference room at Boeing's headquarters in Seattle in what was called the "Muffin Meeting." There was no agenda drafted, no minutes drawn, no overhead projectors used, and no votes taken. The homemade muffins, served during the meeting, symbolized the informal tone of the forum. Few people outside the circle of five had ever attended these weekly sessions. Acting as an informal chair, Condit led a free-wheeling discussion of the 777 project, asking each VP to say anything he had on his mind.

53   The weekly session reflected Boeing's sweeping new approach to management. Traditionally, Boeing had been a highly structured company governed by engineers. Its culture was secretive, formal, and stiff. Managers seldom interacted, sharing was rare, divisions kept to themselves, and engineers competed with each other. Under the 777 program, Boeing made serious efforts to abandon its secretive management style. Condit firmly believed that open communication among top executives, middle managers, and assembly line workers was indispensable for improving morale and raising productivity. He urged employees to talk to each other and share information, and he used a variety of management tools to do so: information sheets, orientation sessions, question and answer sessions, leadership meetings, regular meetings with workers, as well as middle managers, Condit introduced a three-way performance review procedure whereby managers were evaluated by their supervisors, their peers, and their subordinates. Most important, Condit made teamwork the hallmark of the 777 project. In an address entitled "Working Together: The 777 Story" and delivered in December 1992 to members of the Royal Aeronautics Society in London, Condit summed up his team approach:

> [T]eam building is . . . very difficult to do well but when it works the results are dramatic. Teaming fosters the excitement of a shared endeavor and creates an atmosphere that stimulates creativity and problem solving.
>
> But building team[s] . . . is hard work. It doesn't come naturally. Most of us are taught from an early age to compete and excel as individuals. Performance in school and performance on the job are usually measured by individual achievement. Sharing your ideas with others, or helping others to enhance their performance, is often viewed as contrary to one's self-interest.
>
> This individualistic mentality has its place, but . . . it is no longer the most useful attitude for a workplace to possess in today's world. To create a high performance organization, you need employees who can work together in a way that promotes continual learning and the free flow of ideas and information.

THE RESULTS OF THE 777 PROJECT

54   The 777 entered revenue service in June 1995. Since many of the features incorporated into the 777's design reflected suggestions made by the airline carriers, pilots, mechanics, and flight attendants were quite enthusiastic about the new jet. Three achievements of the program, in airplane interior, aircraft design, and aircraft manufacturing, stood out.

Configuration Flexibility

55 The 777 offered carriers enhanced configuration flexibility. A typical configuration change took only 72 hours on the 777 compared to three weeks in competing aircraft. In 1992, the Industrial Design Society of America granted Boeing its Excellence Award for building the 777 passenger cabin, honoring an airplane interior for the first time.

Digital Design

56 The original goal of the program was to reduce "change, error, and rework" by 50%, but engineers building the first three 777s managed to reduce such modification by 60% to 90%. Catia helped engineers identify more than 10,000 interferences that would have otherwise remained undetected until assembly, or until after delivery. The first 777 was only 0.023-inch short of perfect alignment, compared to as much as 0.5-inch on previous programs. Assembly line workers confirmed the beneficial effects of the digital design system. "The parts snap together like Lego blocks," said one mechanic. Reducing the need for reengineering, replanning, retooling, and retrofitting, Boeing's innovative efforts were recognized yet again. In 1993, the Smithsonian Institution honored the Boeing 777 division with its Annual Computerworld Award for the manufacturing category.

Empowerment

57 Boeing 777 assembly line workers expressed a high level of job satisfaction under the new program. "It's a whole new world," a 14-year Boeing veteran mechanic said, "I even like going to work. It's bubbly. It's clean. Everyone has confidence." "We never used to speak up," said another employee, "didn't dare. Now factory workers are treated better and are encouraged to offer ideas." Although the Bar Chart system required Boeing 777 mechanics to work harder and faster as they moved down the learning curve, their principal union organization, the International Association of Machinists, was pleased with Boeing's new approach to labor-management relations. A union spokesman reported that under the 777 program, managers were more likely to treat problems as opportunities from which to learn rather than mistakes for which to blame. Under the 777 program, the union representative added, managers were more respectful of workers' rights under the collective bargaining agreement.

Unresolved Problems and Lessons Learned

58 Notwithstanding Boeing's success with the 777 project, the cost of the program was very high. Boeing did not publish figures pertaining to the total cost of Catia. But a company official reported that under the 777 program, the 3D digital design process required 60% more engineering resources than the older, 2D drawing-based design process. One reason for the high cost of using digital design was slow computing tools: Catia's response time often lasted minutes. Another was the need to update the design software repeatedly. Boeing revised Catia's design software four times between 1990 and 1996, making the system easier to learn and use. Still, Catia continued to experience frequent software problems. Moreover, several of Boeing's outside suppliers were unable to utilize Catia's digital data in their manufacturing process.

59   Boeing faced training problems as well. One challenging problem, according to Ron Ostrowski, director of 777 engineering, was "to convert people's thinking from 2D to 3D. It took more time than we thought it would. I came from a paper world and now I am managing a digital program." Converting people's thinking required what another manager called an "unending communication" coupled with training and retraining. Under the 777 program, Ostrowski recalled, "engineers had to learn to interact. Some couldn't, and they left. The young ones caught on" and stayed.

60   Learning to work together was a challenge to managers too. Some managers were reluctant to embrace Condit's open management style, fearing a decline in their authority. Others were reluctant to share their mistakes with their superiors, fearing reprisals. Some other managers, realizing that the new approach would end many managerial jobs, resisted change when they could, and did not pursue it wholeheartedly when they could not. Even top executives were sometimes uncomfortable with Boeing's open management style, believing that sharing information with emloyees was likely to help Boeing's competitors obtain confidential 777 data.

61   Teamwork was another problem area. Working under pressure, some team members did not function well within teams and had to be moved. Others took advantage of their newborn freedom to offer suggestions, but were disillusioned and frustrated when management either ignored these suggestions or did not act upon them. Managers experienced different team-related problems. In several cases, managers kept on meeting with their team members repeatedly until they arrived at a solution desired by their bosses. They were unwilling to challenge senior executives, nor did they trust Boeing's new approach to teaming. In other cases, managers distrusted the new digital technology. One engineering manager instructed his team members to draft paper drawings alongside Catia's digital designs. When Catia experienced a problem, he followed the drawing, ignoring the computerized design and causing unnecessary and costly delays in his team's part of the project.

Extending the 777 Revolution

62   Boeing's learning pains played a key role in the company's decision not to implement the 777 program companywide. Boeing officials recognized the importance of teamwork and Catia in reducing change, error, and rework, but they also realized that teaming required frequent training, continuous reinforcement, and ongoing monitoring, and that the use of Catia was still too expensive, though its cost was going down (in 1997, Catia's "penalty" was down to 10%). Three of Boeing's derivative programs, the 737 Next Generation, the 757-300, and the 767-400, had the option of implementing the 777's program innovations, and only one, the 737, did so, adopting a modified version of the 777's cross-functional teams.

63   Yet the 777's culture was spreading in other ways. Senior executives took broader roles as the 777 entered service, and their impact was felt through the company. Larry Olson, director of information systems for the 747/767/777 division, was a former 777 manager who believed that Boeing 777 employees "won't tolerate going back to the old ways." He expected to fill new positions on Boeing's next program—the 747X—with former 777 employees in their 40s. Philip Condit, Boeing CEO, implemented several of his own 777's innovations, intensifying the use of meeting among Boeing's managers, and promoting the free flow of ideas throughout the company. Under Condit's leadership, all midlevel managers assigned to Boeing Commercial Airplane Group, about 60 people, met once a week to discuss costs, revenues, and production

EXHIBIT 7
Total Number of MD11, A330, A340, and 777 Airplanes Delivered during 1995–2001

Sources: For Airbus, Mark Luginbill Airbus Communication Director, February 1, 2000, and March 11, 2002. For Boeing, *The Boeing Company Annual Report,* 1997, p. 35, 1998, p. 35; "Commercial Airplanes: Order and Delivery, Summary," www.boeing.com/commercial/order/index.html. Retrieved online, February 2, 2000 and March 9, 2002.

	1995	1996	1997	1998	1999	2000	2001
McDonnell Douglas/ Boeing MD11	18	15	12	12	8	4	2
Airbus A330	30	10	14	23	44	43	35
Airbus A340	19	28	33	24	20	19	22
Boeing 777	13	32	59	74	83	55	61

schedules, product by product. By the end of the meeting—which sometimes ran into the evening—each manager had to draft a detailed plan of action dealing with problems in his/her department. Under Condit's leadership, more important, Boeing developed a new "vision" that grew out of the 777 project. Articulating the company's vision for the next two decades (1996–2016), Condit singled out "Customer satisfaction," "Team leadership," and "A participatory workplace" as Boeing's core corporate values.

CONCLUSION: BOEING, AIRBUS, AND THE 777

64   Looking back at the 777 program 12 years after the launch and seven years after first delivery, it is now (2002) clear that Boeing produced the most successful commercial jetliner of its kind. Airbus launched the A330 and A340 in 1987, and McDonnell Douglas launched a new 300-seat wide-body jet in the mid-1980s, the three-engine MD11. Coming late to market, the Boeing 777 soon outsold both models. The 777 had entered service in 1995, and within a year Boeing delivered more than twice as many 777s as the number of MD11s delivered by McDonnell Douglas. In 1997, 1998, 1999, and 2001, Boeing delivered a larger number of 777s than the combined number of A330s and A340s delivered by Airbus (Exhibit 7). A survey of nearly 6,000 European airline passengers who had flown both the 777 and the A330/A340 found that the 777 was preferred by more than three out of four passengers. In the end, a key element in the 777's triumph was its popularity with the traveling public.

APPENDIX A: SELECTED FEATURES OF THE 777

Aerodynamic Efficiency

Aircraft operating efficiency depended, in part, on aerodynamics: the smoother the surface of the plane and the more aerodynamic the shape of the plane, the less power was needed to overcome drag during flight. To reduce aerodynamic drag, Boeing engineers sought to discover the optimal shape of the plane's major components, namely, the wings, fuselage, nose, tails, and nacelles (engine protective containers). Speaking of the 777's "airfoil," the shape of the wing, Alan Mulally, the 777's director of engineering (he later succeeded Condit as the project manager), explained:

> The 777 airfoil is a significant advance in airfoil design over . . . past airplanes . . . We arrived at this shape by extensive analysis in wind tunnel. . . . [W]e learned new things by

EXHIBIT 8
The Choice of Engines: Boeing 777's Largest Customers

Source: Boeing Commercial Airplane Group, 777 Announced Order and Delivery Summary . . . as of 9/30/99.

Air France	GE
All Nippon Airways	P&W
American Airlines	RR
British Airways	GE
Cathay Pacific Airways	RR
Continental Airlines	GE
Delta Airlines	RR
International Lease Finance Corp.	GE
Japan Air System	P&W
Japan Airlines	P&W
Korea Airlines	P&W
Malaysia Airlines	RR
Saudi Airlines	GE
Singapore Airlines	RR
Thai Airways International	RR
United Airlines	P&W

testing the airfoil at . . . near flight conditions as far as temperature . . . pressures, and air distribution are concerned. And . . . we've ended up with an airfoil that is a new standard at maximizing lift versus drag.

The 777's advanced wing enhanced its ability to climb quickly and cruise at high altitudes. It also enabled the airplane to carry full passenger payloads out of many high elevation airfields served by Boeing customers. Boeing engineers estimated that the design of the 777 lowered its aerodynamic drag by 5–10% compared to other advanced jetliners.

A Service Ready Aircraft

A two-engine plane needed special permission from the Federal Aviation Administration (FAA) to fly long over water routes. Ordinarily, the FAA first certified a twin-jet for one hour of flight away from an airport, then two hours, and only after two years in service, three hours across water anywhere in the world. For the 767, Boeing attained the three hours certification, known as ETOPS (extended range twin-engine operations) approval, after two years in service. For the 777, Boeing customers sought to obtain an ETOPS approval right away, from day one of revenue operations. Boeing 777 costumers also expected the new jet to deliver a high level of schedule reliability from the start (Boeing 767 customers experienced frequent mechanical and computer problems as the 767 entered service in 1982).

To receive an early ETOPS approval, as well as minimize service disruptions, Boeing engineers made special efforts to produce a "service ready" plane. Using advanced computer technology, Boeing tested the 777 twice as much as the 767, improved and streamlined the testing procedure, and checked all systems under simulated flight conditions in a new $370 million high-tech lab called Integrated Aircraft System Laboratory. The Boeing Company, in addition, conducted flight tests for an extended period of time, using United pilots as test pilots. Following a long validation process that included taking off, flying, and landing on one engine, the FAA certified the 777 in May 1995.

The 777 proved highly reliable. During the first three months of its revenue service, United Airlines experienced a schedule reliability of 98%, a level the 767 took 18 months to reach. British Airways' first 777 was in service five days after delivery, a company record for a new aircraft. The next three 777s to join British Airways fleet went into service a day after they arrived at Heathrow.

The Use of Composite Materials

Advanced composite materials accounted for 9% of the 777's total weight; the comparable figure for Boeing's other jetliners was 3%. Improved Alcoa aluminum alloys that saved weight and reduced corrosion and fatigue were used for the construction of the 777's upper-wing skin; other nonmetallic composites were used for the 777's rudder, fins, and the tails. To help reduce corrosion around the lavatories and galleys, Boeing pioneered the use of composite materials for the construction of the floor beam structure. Boeing made a larger use of titanium alloys on the 777 than on any previous aircraft. Substituting steel with titanium cut weight by half, and space by one quarter; titanium was also 40% less dense than steel, yet of equal strength. The use of heat-resisting titanium in the 777's engine nacelle saved Boeing 180 pounds per engine, or 360 pounds per plane; the use of titanium rather than steel for building the 777's landing gear saved Boeing 600 pounds per plane. Although titanium was more expensive than steel or aluminum, the choice of its application was driven by economics: for each pound of empty weight Boeing engineers squeezed out of the 777, Boeing airline customers saved hundreds of dollars' worth of fuel during the lifetime of the plane.

APPENDIX B: THE 777'S CHOICE OF ENGINES

Pratt and Whitney (P&W), General Electric (GE), and Rolls Royce (RR) had all developed the 777 jet engine, each offering its own make. Boeing required an engine that was more powerful, more efficient, and quieter than any jet engine in existence; the 777 engine was designed to generate close to 80,000 pounds of thrust (the forward force produced by the gases escaping backward from the engine) or 40% more power than the 767's.

All three engine makers had been selected by Boeing airline customers (Exhibit 8). United Airlines chose the Pratt and Whitney engine. Partly because P&W supplied engines to United 747 and 767 fleets, and also because the design of the 777 engine was an extension of the 747's and 767's design, United management sought to retain P&W as its primary engine supplier. British Airways, on the other hand, selected the GE engine. A major consideration in British Airways' choice was aircraft efficiency: fuel consumption of the GE engine was 5% lower than that of the two competing engines. Other carriers selected the RR engine for their reasons pertaining to their own needs and interests.

EXHIBIT 9
Selected Financial
Data

Source: *The Boeing Company
2000 Annual Report*, pp. 8, 98.

(Dollars in millions except per share data)	2000	1999	1998	1997	1996
Operation					
Sales and Revenues					
Commercial Airplanes	$31,171	38,475	36,998	27,479	19,916
Defense and Space*	20,236	19,051	19,879	18,125	14,934
Other	758	771	612	746	603
Accounting Differences	(844)	(304)	(1,335)	(550)	
Total	$51,321	57,993	56,154	45,800	35,453
Net Earnings (Loss)	$2,128	2,309	1,120	(178)	1,818
Earnings (Loss) per share	2.48	2.52	1.16	(0.18)	1.88
Cash dividends	$504	537	564	557	480
Per Share	0.59	0.56	0.56	0.56	0.55
Other income (interest)	386	585	283	428	388
Research and Development	1,441	1,341	1,895	1,924	1,633
Capital expenditure	932	1,236	1,665	1,391	971
Depreciation	1,159	1,330	1,386	1,266	1,132
Employee salaries and wages	11,614	11,019	12,074	11,287	9,225
Year-end workforce	198,000	197,000	231,000	238,000	211,000
Financial Position at 12/31					
Total assets	$42,028	36,147	37,024	38,293	37,880
Working Capital	(2,425)	2,056	2,836	5,111	7,783
Plant and Equipment	8,814	8,245	8,589	8,391	8,266
Cash and Short-term Investments	1,010	3,454	2,462	5,149	6,352
Total debt	8,799	6,732	6,972	6,854	7,489
Customer and commercial financing assets	6,959	6,004	5,711	4,600	3,888
Shareholders' equity	11,020	11,462	12,316	12,953	13,502
Per share	13.18	13.16	13.13	13.31	13.96
Contractual Backlog					
Commercial airplanes	$89,780	72,972	86,057	93,788	86,151
Defense and Space*	30,820	26,276	26,839	27,852	28,022
Total	$120,600	99,248	112,896	121,640	114,173

*Including Information

Note: For additional financial data, as reported in the company's annual reports and other financial documents, check out Boeing Web address at www.boeing.com.

Eugene Rodgers, *Flying High: The Story of Boeing* (New York: Atlantic Monthly Press, 1996), pp. 423–15; Michael Dornheim, "777 Twinjet will Grow to Replace 747-200," *Aviation Week and Space Technology,* June 3, 1991, p. 43.

"Commercial Airplanes: Order and Delivery, Summary," http//www.boeing.com/commercial/orders/index.html. Retrieved from Web, February 2, 2000.

J. P. Donlon, "Boeing's Big Bet" (an interview with CEO Frank Shrontz), *Chief Executive,* November/December 1994, p. 42; Michael Dertouzos, Richard Lester, and Robert Solow, *Made in America: Regaining the Productive Edge* (New York: Harper Perennial, 1990), p. 203.

John Newhouse, *The Sporty Game* (New York: Alfred Knopf, 1982), p. 21, but see also pp. 10–20.

David C. Mowery and Nathan Rosenberg, "The Commercial Aircraft Industry," in Richard R. Nelson, ed., *Government and Technological Progress: A Cross Industry Analysis* (New York: Pergamon Press, 1982), p. 116; Dertouzos et al, *Made in America,* p. 200.

Dertouzos, et al., *Made in America,* p. 203.

Newhouse, *Sporty Game,* p. 188. Mowery and Rosenberg, "The Commercial Aircraft Industry," pp. 124–125.

Mowery and Rosenberg, "The Commercial Aircraft Industry," pp. 102–103, 126–128.

John B. Rae, *Climb to Greatness: The American Aircraft Industry, 1920–1960* (Cambridge, Mass.: MIT Press, 1968), pp. 206–207; Rodgers, *Flying High,* pp. 197–198.

Frank Spadaro, "A Transatlantic Perspective," *Design Quarterly,* Winter 1992, p. 23.

Rodgers, *Flying High,* p. 279; Newhouse, *Sporty Game,* Ch. 7.

M. S. Hochmuth, "Aerospace," in Raymond Vernon, ed., *Big Business and the State* (Cambridge: Harvard University Press, 1974), p. 149

Boeing Commercial Airplane Group, *Announced Orders and Deliveries as of 12/31/97,* Section A 1.

The Boeing Company 1998 Annual Report, p. 76.

Formed in 1970 by several European aerospace firms, the Airbus Consortium had received generous assistance from the French, British, German, and Spanish governments for a period of over two decades. In 1992, Airbus had signed an agreement with Boeing that limited the amount of government funds each aircraft manufacturer could receive, and in 1995, at long last, Airbus had become profitable. "Airbus 25 Years Old," *Le Figaro,* October 1997 (reprinted in English by Airbus Industrie); Rodgers, *Flying High,* Ch. 12; *BusinessWeek,* December 30, 1996, p. 40.

Charles Goldsmith, "Re-Engineering, After Trailing Boeing for Years, Airbus Aims for 50% of the Market," *Wall Street Journal,* March 16, 1998.

"Hubris at Airbus, Boeing Rebuild," *Economist,* November 28, 1998.

The Boeing Company 1997 Annual Report, p. 19; *The Boeing Company 1998 Annual Report,* p. 51.

Donlon, "Boeing's Big Bet," p. 40; John Mintz, "Betting It All on 777," *Washington Post,* March 26, 1995; James Woolsey, "777: A Program of New Concepts," *Air Transport World,* April 1991, p. 62; Jeremy Main, "Corporate Performance: Betting on the 21st Century Jet," *Fortune,* April 20, 1992, p. 104; James Woolsey, "Crossing New Transport Frontiers," *Air Transport World,* March 1991, p. 21; James Woolsey, "777: Boeing's New Large Twinjet," *Air Transport World,* April 1994, p. 23; Michael Dornheim, "Computerized Design System Allows Boeing to Skip Building 777 Mockup," *Aviation Week and Space Technology,* June 3, 1991, p. 51; Richard O'Lone, "Final Assembly of 777 Nears," *Aviation Week and Space Technology,* October 2, 1992, p. 48.

Rodgers, *Flying High,* p. 42.

Air Transport World, March 1991, p. 20; *Fortune,* April 20, 1992, p. 102–103.

Rodgers, *Flying High,* pp. 416, 420–24.

Richard O'Lone and James McKenna, "Quality Assurance Role Was Factor in United's 777 Launch Order," *Aviation Week and Space Technology,* October 29, 1990, pp. 28–29; *Air Transport World,* March 1991, p. 20.

Quoted in the *Washington Post,* March 25, 1995.

Quoted in Bill Sweetman, "As Smooth as Silk: 777 Customers Applaud the Aircraft's First 12 Months in Service," *Air Transport World,* August 1996, p. 71, but see also *Air Transport World,* April 1994, pp. 24, 27.

Quoted in *Fortune,* April 20, 1992, p. 112.

Rodgers, *Flying High,* p. 426; *Design Quarterly,* Winter 1992, p. 22; Polly Lane, "Boeing Used 777 to Make Production Changes," *Seattle Times,* May 7, 1995.

Design Quarterly, Winter 1992, p. 22; The Boeing Company, *Backgrounder: Pace Setting Design Value-Added Features Boost Boeing 777 Family,* May 15, 1998.

Boeing, *Backgrounder,* May 15, 1998; Sabbagh, *21st Century Jet,* p. 49.

Karl Sabbagh, *21st Century Jet: The Making and Marketing of the Boeing 777* (New York: Scribner, 1996), pp. 264, 266.

Sabbagh, *21st Century Jet,* pp. 131–132.

Air Transport World, April 1994, p. 23; *Fortune,* April 20, 1992, p. 116.

Washington Post, March 26, 1995; Boeing Commercial Airplane Group, 777 Announced Order and Delivery Summary . . . as of 9/30/99.

Rodgers, *Flying High,* pp. 420–426; *Air Transport World,* April 1994, pp. 27, 31; "Leading Families of Passenger Jet Airplanes," Boeing Commercial Airplane Group, 1998.

Sabbagh, *21st Century Jet,* p. 58.

Quoted in Sabbagh, *21st Century Jet,* p. 63.

Aviation Week and Space Technology, June 3, 1991, p. 50, October 12, 1992, p. 49; Sabbagh *21st Century Jet,* p. 62.

George Taninecz, "Blue Sky Meets Blue Sky," *Industry Week,* December 18, 1995, pp. 49–52; Paul Proctor, "Boeing Rolls Out 777 to Tentative Market," *Aviation Week and Space Technology,* October 12, 1992, p. 49.

Aviation Week and Space Technology, April 11, 1994, p. 37, and June 3, 1991, p. 35.

Quoted in Sabbagh, *21st Century Jet,* pp. 68–69.

This was the phrase used by Boeing project managers working on the 777. See Sabbagh, *21st Century Jet,* Ch. 4.

Fortune April 20, 1992, p. 116; Sabbagh, *21st Century Jet,* pp. 69–73; Wolf L. Glende, "The Boeing 777: A Look Back," The Boeing Company, 1997. p. 4.

Quoted in *Air Transport World,* August 1996, p. 78.

Richard O'Lone, "777 Revolutionizes Boeing Aircraft Development Process," *Aviation Week and Space Technology,* June 3, 1992, p. 34.

O. Casey Corr, "Boeing"s Future on the Line: Company's Betting Its Fortunes Not Just on a New Jet, But on a New Way of Making Jets," *Seattle Times,* August 29, 1993, Polly Lane, "Boeing Used 777 to Make Production Changes, Meet Desires of Its Customers," *Seattle Times,* May 7, 1995; *Aviation Week and Space Technology,* June 3, 1991, p. 34.

Seattle Times, August 29, 1993.

Seattle Times, May 7, 1995, and August 29, 1993.

Quoted in Rodgers, *Flying High,* pp. 419–420.

Sabbagh, *21st Century Jet,* p. 33.

Sabbagh, *21st Century Jet,* p. 99.

Dori Jones Young, "When the Going Gets Tough, Boeing Gets Touchy-Feely," *Business Week,* January 17, 1994. pp. 65–67; *Fortune,* April 20, 1992, p. 117.

Reprinted by The Boeing Company, Executive Communications, 1992.

Boeing, *Backgrounder,* May 15, 1998.

Industry Week, December 18, 1995, pp. 50–51; *Air Transport World,* April 1994, p. 24.

Aviation Week and Space Technology, April 11, 1994, p. 37.

Boeing, *Backgrounder,* "Computing & Design/Build Process Help Develop the 777." Undated.

Seattle Times, August 29, 1993.

Seattle Times, May 7, 1995.

Seattle Times, August 29, 1993.

Glende, "The Boeing 777: A Look Back," 1997, p. 10; *Air Transport World,* August 1996, p. 78.

Air Transport World, April 1994, p. 23.

Washington Post, March 26, 1995.

Seattle Times, May 7, 1995; Rodgers, *Flying High,* p. 441.

Seattle Times, May 7, 1995; Rodgers, *Flying High,* pp. 441–442.

Glende, "The Boeing 777: A Look Back," 1997, p. 10.

Air Transport World, August 1996, p. 78.

"A New Kind of Boeing," *Economist,* January 22, 2000, p. 63.

"Vision 2016," The Boeing Company, 1997.

"Study: Passengers Voice Overwhelming Preference for Boeing 777,"
   http/www.boeing.com/news/releases/1999. Retrieved from Web, 11/23/99.

Quoted in Sabbagh, *21st Century Jet,* pp. 46–47.

Boeing *Backgrounder,* May 25, 1998; Michael Dornmeim, "777 Twinjet Will Grow to Replace 747–200,"
   Aviation Week and Space Technology, June 3, 1991, p. 43; *Sabbagh 21st Century Jet,* pp. 286–87.

Air Transport World, April 1994, p. 27; *Fortune,* April 20, 1992, p. 117; Sabbagh, *21st Century Jet,*
   pp. 139–140.

Industry Week, December 18, 1995, p. 52; *Aviation Week and Space Technology,* April 11, 1994,
   p. 39; *Seattle Times,* May 7, 1995; Boeing, *Backgrounder,* May 15, 1998; Sabbagh, *21st Century Jet,*
   Ch. 24.

Industry Week, December 18, 1995, p. 52; *Air Transport World,* August 1996, p. 71.

Steven Ashley, "Boeing 777 Gets a Boost from Titanium," *Mechanical Engineering,* July 1993, pp. 61,
   64–65; *Aviation Week and Space Technology,* June 3, 1991, p. 49; Boeing, *Backgrounder,* May 15,
   1998; *Air Transport World,* March 1991, pp. 23–24.

Boeing, *Backgrounder,* May 15, 1998.

Sabbagh, *21st Century Jet,* pp. 12–122.

Arthur Reed, "GE90 Lives Up to Promises," *Air Transport World,* August 1996, p. 72.

Case 49

The Comeback of Caterpillar, 1985–2001

1   For three consecutive years, 1982, 1983, and 1984, the Caterpillar Company lost $1 million a day. Caterpillar's major competitor was a formidable Japanese company called Komatsu. Facing a tough global challenge, the collapse of its international markets, and an overvalued dollar, Caterpillar had no choice. It had to reinvent itself, or die.

2   Caterpillar managed to come back as a high-tech, globally competitive, growth company. Over a period of 15 years, and throughout the tenure of two CEOs—George Schaefer (1985–1990) and Donald Fites (1990–1999)—Caterpillar had transformed itself. George Schaefer introduced cost-cutting measures and employee involvement programs, outsourced machines, parts, and components, and began modernizing Caterpillar's plants. Donald Fites diversified Caterpillar's product line and reorganized the company structurally. He also completed Caterpillar's plant modernization program, revitalized Caterpillar's dealership network, and altered radically Caterpillar's approach to labor relations.

3   As Donald Fites retired in February 1999, Glen Barton was elected CEO. Barton was in an enviable position. The world's largest manufacturer of construction and mining equipment, and a Fortune 100 company, Caterpillar generated $21 billion in revenues in 1998, the sixth consecutive record year. Leading its industry while competing globally, Caterpillar recorded a $1.5 billion profit in 1998, the second best ever.

4   Notwithstanding Caterpillar's dramatic comeback, Barton could not count on the continual prosperity of the company because the U.S. construction industry was moving into a grinding economic downturn. At the time Barton completed his first year as CEO, on February 1, 2000, the company announced its 1999 result: sales declined by 6% and earnings by 37%. In March 2000, Caterpillar's share price was trading close to its 52-week low ($36 against a high of $66) and one industry analyst declared: "The stock for the foreseeable future is dead money."

5   What should Barton do? Should Barton follow the strategies implemented by Schaefer and Fites to enhance Caterpillar's competitive position relative to its principal rivals, Komatsu, John Deere, and CNH Global (CNH was the product of a 2000 merger between the Case Corp. and New Hollad)? Should he, instead, reverse some of the policies introduced by his predecessors? Or should he, rather, undertake whole new strategies altogether?

6   To assess Barton's strategic choices in improving Caterpillar's results, the case looks back at the experience of his two predecessors. How precisely did both Schaefer and Fites manage to turn Caterpillar around?

THE HEAVY CONSTRUCTION EQUIPMENT INDUSTRY

7   The heavy construction equipment industry supplied engineering firms, construction companies, and mine operators. The industry's typical product line included earthmovers (bulldozers, loaders, and excavators), road building machines (pavers, motor graders, and mixers), mining-related equipment (off-highway trucks, mining shovels), and large cranes. Most machines were offered in a broad range of sizes, and a few were available with a choice of wheels or crawler tracks. Most were used for the construction of buildings, power plants, manufacturing plants, and infrastructure projects such as roads,

Isaac Cohen, San Jose State University. This case was presented at the North American Case Research Association in Memphis, Tennessee. Copyright Isaac Cohen, 2001.

EXHIBIT 1
Global Demand of
Heavy Construction
Equipment by Major
Categories,
1985–2005.

Source: Andrew Gross and
David Weiss, "Industry Corner:
The Global Demand for Heavy
Construction Equipment,"
Business Economics, July 1996,
p. 56.

Item	1985	1994	2000	2005*
Earthmoving Equipment	50%	49%	49%	49%
Off-Highway Trucks	8%	7%	7%	7%
Construction Cranes	9%	11%	10%	10%
Mixers, Pavers, and Related Equipment	6%	6%	7%	7%
Parts and Attachments	27%	27%	27%	26%
Total Demand (billions)	$38	$56	$72	$90

* Percentages do not add up to 100 because of rounding.

airports, bridges, tunnels, dams, sewage systems, and water lines. On a global basis, earthmoving equipment accounted for about half of the industry's total sales in the 1990s (Exhibit 1). Among earthmovers, hydraulic excavators accounted for 45% of the sales. Excavators were more productive, more versatile, and easier to use in tight spaces than either bulldozers or loaders. Off-highway trucks that hauled minerals, rocks, and dirt, were another category of fast-selling equipment.

8   Global demand for heavy construction machinery grew at a steady rate of 4.5% in the 1990s. The rate of growth, however, was faster among the developing nations of Asia, Africa, and Latin America than among the developed nations. In the early 2000s, North America and Europe were each expected to account for 25% of the industry's sales, Japan for 20%, and the developing nations for the remaining 30%.

9   The distinction between original equipment and replacement parts was an essential feature of the industry. Replacement parts and "attachments" (work tools) made up together over a quarter of the total revenues of the heavy construction equipment industry (Exhibit 1), but accounted for a substantially larger share of the industry's earnings for two reasons: first, the sale of replacement parts was more profitable than that of whole machines; and second, the market for replacement parts was less cyclical than that for original equipment. As a rule of thumb, the economic life of a heavy construction machine was 10 to 12 years, but in many cases, especially in developing countries, equipment users kept their machines in service much longer, perhaps 20 to 30 years, thus creating an ongoing stream of revenues for parts, components, and related services.

10   Another characteristics of the industry was the need to achieve economies of scale. According to industry observers, the optimal scale of operation was about 90,000 units annually, in other words, up to a production level of 90,000 units a year, average equipment unit cost declined as output increased, and therefore capturing a large market share was critical for benefiting from economies of scale. The relatively low volume of global sales—200,000 to 300,000 earthmoving equipment units per year (1996)—further intensified competition over market share among the industry's leading firms.

11   Successful marketing also played an important role in gaining competitive advantage. A widespread distribution and service network had always been essential for competing in the heavy construction equipment industry because "downtime" resulting from the inability to operate the equipment at a construction site was very costly. Typically, manufacturers used a worldwide network of dealerships to sell machines, provide support, and offer after-sales service. Dealerships were independent, company-owned, or both, and were normally organized on an exclusive territorial basis. Since heavy construction machines operated in a tough and inhospitable environment, equipment wore out and broke down frequently, parts needed to be rebuilt or replaced often, and therefore manufacturers placed dealers in close proximity to equipment users, building a global service network that spread all over the world.

12   Manufacturers built alliances as well. Intense competition over market share drove the industry's top firms to form three types of cooperative agreements. The first were full-scale joint ventures to share production. Caterpillar's joint venture with Mitsubishi Heavy Industries was a notable case in point. The second were technology-sharing agreements between equipment manufacturers and engine makers to ensure access to the latest engine technology. The joint venture between Komatsu and Cummins Engine, on the one hand, and the Case Corporation and Cummins, on the other, provided two examples. The third type of agreements was technology-sharing alliances between major global firms and local manufacturers whereby the former gained access to new markets, and in return, supplied the latter with advanced technology. Caterpillar utilized such an arrangement with Shanghai Diesel in China, and Komatsu did so with the BEML company in India.

HISTORY OF CATERPILLAR

13   At the turn of the century, farmers in California faced a serious problem. Using steam tractors to plow the fine delta land of the San Joaquin valley, California farmers fitted their tractors with large drive wheels to provide support on the moist soil; nevertheless, despite their efforts, the steamer's huge wheels—measuring up to 9 feet high—sank deeply into the soil. In 1904, Benjamin Holt, a combine maker from Stockton, California, solved the problem by replacing the wheels with a track, thereby distributing the tractor's weight on a broader surface. Holt, in addition, replaced the heavy steam engine with a gasoline engine, thus improving the tractor's mobility further by reducing its weight (a steam tractor weighed up to 20 tons). He nicknamed the tractor "Caterpillar," acquired the "Caterpillar" trade mark, and applied it to several crawler-type machines that his company manufactured and sold. By 1915 Holt tractors were sold in 20 countries.

14   Outside agriculture, crawler tractors were first used by the military. In 1915, the British military invented the armor tank, modeling it after Holt's machine, and during World War I, the United States and its allies in Europe utilized Holt's track-type tractors to haul artillery and supply wagons. In 1925, the Holt Company merged with another California firm, the Best Tractor Company, to form Caterpillar (Cat). Shortly thereafter, Caterpillar moved its corporate headquarters and manufacturing plants to Peoria, Illinois. The first company to introduce a diesel engine on a moving vehicle (1931), Caterpillar discontinued its combine manufacturing during the 1930s and focused instead on the production of road-building, construction, logging, and pipelaying equipment. During World War II, Caterpillar served as the primary supplier of bulldozers to the U.S. Army; its sales volume more than tripled between 1941 and 1944 to include motor graders, diesel engines, and electric generators, apart from tractors and wagons.

15   Demand for Caterpillar products exploded in the early postwar years. Cat's equipment was used to reconstruct Europe, build the U.S. interstate highway system, erect the giant dams of the Third World, and lay out the major airports of the world. The company managed to differentiate itself from its competitors by producing reliable, durable, and high-quality equipment, offering a quick after-sales service, and providing a speedy delivery of replacement parts. As a result, during the 1950s and 1960s, Caterpillar had emerged as the uncontested leader of the heavy construction equipment industry, far ahead of any rival. By 1965, Caterpillar had established foreign manufacturing subsidiaries—either wholly owned or joint ventures—in Britain, Canada, Australia, Brazil, France, Mexico, Belgium, India, and Japan. Caterpillar's 50/50 joint venture with Mitsubishi in Japan, established in 1963, had become one of the most successful, stable, and enduring alliances among all American-Japanese joint ventures.

16   Caterpillar's distribution and dealership network also contributed to the company's worldwide success. From the outset, the company's marketing organization rested on a dense network of independent dealers who sold and serviced Cat equipment. Strategically located throughout the world, these dealers were self-sustaining entrepreneurs who invested their own capital in their business, derived close to 100% of their revenues from selling and supporting Cat equipment, and cultivated close relationships with Caterpillar customers. On average, a Caterpillar dealership had remained in the hands of the same family—or company—for over 50 years. Indeed, some dealerships, including several located overseas, predated the 1925 merger that gave birth to Caterpillar. In 1981, on the eve of the impending crisis, the combined net worth of Cat dealers equaled that of the company itself, the total number of employees working for Cat dealers was slightly lower than the company's own workforce.

THE CRISIS OF THE EARLY 1980s

17   Facing weak competition both at home and abroad, Caterpillar charged premium prices for its high-quality products, paid its production workers union-scale wages, offered its shareholders high rates of return on their equity, and enjoyed superior profits. Then, in 1982, following a record year of sales and profits, Caterpillar suddenly plunged into three successive years of rising losses totaling nearly $1 billion. "Quite frankly, our long years of success made us complacent, even arrogant," Pierre Guerindon, an executive vice president at Cat, conceded.

18   The crisis of 1982–84 stemmed from three sources: a global recession, a costly strike, and unfavorable currency exchange rates. First, the steady growth in demand for construction machinery, dating back to 1945, came to an end in 1980, as highway construction in the U.S. slowed down to a halt while declining oil prices depressed the worldwide market for mining, logging, and pipelaying equipment. Second, Caterpillar's efforts to freeze wages and reduce overall labor cost triggered a seven-month strike (1982–83) among its U.S. employees. Led by the United Auto Workers (UAW) union, the strike accounted for a sizable portion of the company's three-year loss. The third element in Caterpillar's crisis was a steep rise in the value of the dollar (relative to the yen and other currencies) that made U.S. exports more expensive abroad and U.S. imports (shipped by Caterpillar's competitors) cheaper at home. "The strong dollar is a prime factor in Caterpillar's reduced sales and earning . . . [and] is undermining manufacturing industries in the United States," said Cat's annual reports for 1982 and 1984.

19   Taking advantage of the expensive dollar, Komatsu Limited had emerged as Caterpillar's principal rival. Komatsu ("little pine tree" in Japanese) had initially produced construction machinery for the Japanese and Asian markets, then sought to challenge Caterpillar's dominance in the markets of Latin America and Europe, and eventually penetrated the United States to rival Caterpillar in its domestic market. Attacking Caterpillar head-on, Komatsu issued a battle cry, "Maru C," meaning "encircle Cat." Launching a massive drive to improve quality while reducing costs, Komatsu achieved a 50% labor productivity advantage over Caterpillar and, in turn, underpriced Caterpillar's products by as much as 30%. The outcome was a dramatic change in market share. Between 1979 and 1984 Komatsu global market share more than doubled to 25% while Caterpillar's fell by almost a quarter to 43%.

TURNAROUND: GEORGE SCHAEFER'S CATERPILLAR, 1985–1990

20   Competition with Komatsu and the crisis of 1982–84 forced Caterpillar to reexamine its past activities. Caterpillar's new CEO (1985), George Schaefer, was a congenial manager who encouraged Cat executives to openly admit the company's past mistakes. "We have experienced a fundamental change in our business—it will never again be what it was," Schaefer said as he became CEO. "We have no choice but to respond, and respond vigorously, to the new world in which we find ourselves." Under Schaefer's direction, Caterpillar devised and implemented a series of strategies that touched upon every important function of the company, including purchasing, manufacturing, marketing, personnel, and labor relations.

Global Outsourcing

21 Traditionally, Caterpillar functioned as a vertically integrated company that relied heavily on in-house production. To ensure product quality as well as an uninterrupted supply of parts, Cat self-produced two-thirds of its parts and components, and assembled practically all of its finished machines. Under the new policy of "shopping around the world," Caterpillar sought to purchase parts and components from low-cost suppliers who maintained high-quality standards. Working closely with its suppliers, Caterpillar moved towards the goal of outsourcing 80% of its parts and components.

22 An additional goal of the policy was branding, that is, the purchase of final products for resale. Through its branding program, Caterpillar sold outsourced machines under its own brand name, taking advantage of its superior marketing organization and keeping production costs down. Beginning in the mid-1980s, Cat contracted to buy lift trucks from a Norwegian company, hydraulic excavators from a West German manufacturer, paving machines from an Oklahoma corporation, off-highway trucks from a British firm, and logging equipment from a Canadian company, and resell them all under the Cat nameplate. Ordinarily, Caterpillar outsourced product manufacturing but not product design. By keeping control over the design of many of its outsourced products, Caterpillar managed to retain in-house design capability, and ensure quality control.

Broader Product Line

23 For nearly a decade, the DC10 bulldozer had served as Caterpillar's signature item. It stood 15 feet tall, weighed 73 tons, and sold for more than $500,000 (1988). It had no competitors. But as demand for highway construction projects dwindled, Caterpillar needed to reevaluate its product mix because heavy equipment was no longer selling well. Sales of light construction equipment, on the other hand, were fast increasing. Between 1984 and 1987, accordingly, Caterpillar doubled its product line from 150 to 300 models of equipment, introducing many small machines that ranged from farm tractors to backhoe loaders (multipurpose light bulldozers), and diversified its customer base. Rather than focusing solely on large clients, that is, multinational engineering and construction firms like the Bechtel corporation—a typical user of heavy bulldozers—Cat began marketing its lightweight machines to a new category of customers: small-scale owner operators and emerging contractors. Still, the shift in Cat's product mix had a clear impact on the company's bottom line. Unlike the heavy equipment market where profit margins were wide, intense competitions in the market for light products kept margins slim and pitted Caterpillar against John Deere and the Case Corporation, the light equipment market leaders.

Labor Relations

24 To compete successfully, Caterpillar also needed to repair its relationship with the union. In 1979, following the expiration of its collective bargaining agreement, Caterpillar experienced an 80-day strike, and three years later, in 1982, contract negotiations erupted in a 205-day strike, the longest companywide work stoppage in UAW history. Named CEO in 1985, George Schaefer led the next two rounds of contract negotiations.

25   Schaefer's leadership style was consensual. By contrast to the autocratic style of his predecessors, Schaefer advocated the free flow of ideas between officers, managers, and production workers, and promoted open communication at all levels of the company. A low-key CEO who often answered his own phone, Schaefer possessed exceptional people skills. Asked to evaluate Schaefer's performance, John Stark, editor of *Off Highway Ledger,* a trade journal, said: "Schaefer is probably the best manager the construction machinery industry has ever had."

26   Schaefer's social skills led to a significant improvement in Cat's relations with the UAW. Not a single strike broke out over contract negotiations during Schaefer's tenure; on the contrary, each cycle of bargaining was settled peacefully. Under Schaefer's direction, furthermore, the union agreed to reduce the number of labor grades and job classifications, and to streamline seniority provisions; a move that enhanced management flexibility in job assignment and facilitated the cross-utilization of employees. More important, improved labor relations contributed to the success of two programs that played a critical role in Caterpillar's turnaround strategy, namely, an employee involvement plan based on teamwork and a reengineering effort of plant modernization and automation.

Employee Involvement

27   An industrywide union famous for its cooperative labor-management efforts at the Saturn corporation, the NUMMI plant (a GM-Toyota joint-venture in Fremont, California), and elsewhere, the UAW lent its support to Caterpillar's employee involvement program. Called the Employee Satisfaction Process (ESP) and launched by Schaefer in 1986, the program was voluntary. ESP members were organized in work teams, met weekly with management, and offered suggestions that pertained to many critical aspects of the manufacturing process, including production management, workplace layout, and quality enhancement. Implemented in a growing number of U.S. plants, the program resulted (1990) in productivity gains, quality improvements, and increased employee satisfaction. At the Cat plant in Aurora, Illinois, for example, the local ESP chairman recalled: the ESP program "changed everything: the worker had some say over his job . . . . [and t]op management was very receptive. We zeroed in on quality, anything to make the customer happy." Management credited the ESP teams at Aurora with a steep fall in the rate of absenteeism, a sharp decline in the number of union grievances filed, and cost savings totaling $10 million. At another ESP plant, a Cat assembly-line worker told a *Fortune* reporter in 1988: "Five years ago the foreman wouldn't even listen to you, never mind the general foreman or plant supervisor. . . . Now everyone will listen." Caterpillar applied the ESP program to outside suppliers as well. Typically, ESP teams made up of Caterpillar machinists visited suppliers' plants to check and certify equipment quality. The certified vendors received preferential treatment, mostly in the form of reduced inspection, counting, and other controls. Only 0.6% of the parts delivered by certified suppliers were rejected by Caterpillar compared to a reject rate of 2.8% for noncertified suppliers.

Plant with a Future

28   Caterpillar's employee involvement plan went hand in hand with a $1.8 billion plant modernization program launched by Schaefer in 1986. Dubbed "Plant with a Future" (PWAF), the modernization program combined just-in-time inventory techniques, a factory automation scheme, a network of computerized machine tools, and a flexible manufacturing system. Several of these innovations were pioneered by Komatsu late in the 1970s. The industry's technological leader, Komatsu had been the first construction equipment manufacturer to introduce both the just-in-time inventory system and the "quick changeover tooling," technique, a flexible tooling method designed to produce a large variety of equipment models in a single plant.

29   To challenge Komatsu, top executives at Caterpillar did not seek to merely imitate the Japanese. This was not enough. They studied, instead, the modernization efforts of several manufacturing companies and arrived at two important conclusions: it was necessary (1) to change the layout of an entire plant, not just selected departments within a plant; and (2) to implement the program companywide, that is, on a global basis both at home and abroad. Implementing such a comprehensive program took longer than expected, however, lasting seven years: four under Schaefer's direction, and three more under the direction of his successor, Donald Fites.

30   The traditional manufacturing process at Caterpillar, known as "batch" production, was common among U.S. assembly plants in a number of industries. Under batch production, subassembly lines produced components (radiators, hydraulic tanks, etc.) in small lots. Final assembly lines put together complete models, and the entire production system required large inventories of parts and components owing to the high level of "work in process" (models being built at any one time). Under batch production, furthermore, assembly tasks were highly specialized, work was monotonous and dull, and workers grew lax and made mistakes. Correcting assembly mistakes, it should be noted, took more time than the assembly process itself because workers needed to disassemble components in order to access problem areas. Parts delivery was also problematic. Occasionally, delays in delivery of parts to the assembly areas forced workers to leave the line in order to locate a missing part. Occasionally, the early arrival of parts before they were needed created its own inefficiencies.

31   To solve these problems, Caterpillar reconfigured the layout of its manufacturing plants into flexible work "cells." Grouped in cells, workers used computerized machine tools to perform several manufacturing steps in sequence, processing components from start to finish and sending them "just-in-time" to an assembly area, as the following example suggests. To manufacture steel tractor-tread under the batch production layout, Cat workers were required to cut, drill, and heat-treat steel beams on three distinct assembly lines. Under cellular manufacturing, by contrast, all three operations were carried out automatically in single tractor-tread cells linked together by computers.

32   Caterpillar, in addition, reduced material handling by means of an automated electrified monorail that delivered parts to storage and assembly areas, traveling on a long aluminum track throughout the modernized plant. When parts arrived at the delivery point, a flash light alerted the assembly line workers, semiautomatic gates (operated by infrared remote control) opened, and a lift lowered the components directly onto an assembly. Don Western, a manufacturing manager at Cat Aurora plant, observed: "Materials now [1990] arrive at the assembly point only when required—and in the order required. At most, we hold about a 4-hour supply of large parts and components on the line."

33   Caterpillar, finally, improved product quality. Formerly, components moved down the assembly line continuously, not intermittently, and therefore workers were unable to respond quickly to quality problems. Managers alone controlled the speed of the line. Under the new assembly plan, on the other hand, components moved automatically between work areas and remained stationary during the actual assembly operation. More important, under the PWAF plan, managers empowered production workers to change the speed of the assembly line at will, granting them the flexibility necessary to resolve quality and safety problems.

34   The PWAF program resulted in productivity and quality gains across the board in many of Caterpillar plants. At the Aurora plant in Illinois, for instance, factory workers

EXHIBIT 2
George Schaefer's
Caterpillar,
Highlights of
Financial Data:
Caterpillar versus
Komatsu.

Source: For Caterpillar,
*Hoover's Handbook of
American Business, 1995,*
p. 329; for Komatsu, *Hoover's
Handbook of World Business,
1995–96,* p. 291.

	Cat		Komatsu	
	Sales ($ bil.)	Income as % of Sales	Sales ($ bil.)	Income as % of Sales
1985	$6.7	2.9%	—*	1.8%
1986	$7.3	1.0%	—*	2.8%
1987	$8.2	3.9%	$5.1	1.3%
1988	$10.4	5.9%	$6.2	0.4%
1989	$11.1	4.5%	$6.0	2.6%

*Sales are available only in yen: 1985, 796 billion yen; 1986, 789 billion yen.

managed to reduce the assembly process time fourfold, building and shipping a customer order in four rather than 16 days, and cutting product defects by one-half in four years (1986–1990). At the Cat plant in Grenoble, France, to mention another case, workers slashed the time it took to assemble machinery parts from 20 to 8 days in three years (1986–1989). Companywide changes were equally impressive: collectively, Caterpillar's 30 worldwide plants cut inventory levels by 50% and manufacturing space by 21% in three years.

35   Looking back at Schaefer's five-year-long tenure, Caterpillar had reemerged as globally competitive company, lean, flexible, and technologically advanced. Caterpillar's world market share rebounded from 43% to 50% (1984–1990), revenues increased by 66% (1985–1989), and the company was profitable once again. As Caterpillar prospered, Komatsu was retrenching. In 1989, Caterpillar's sales totaled over $11 billion or nearly twice the sales reported by Komatsu, Caterpillar's profit margins exceeded Komatsu's, and the gap between the two companies—in terms of both market share and income on sales—was growing (Exhibit 2).

THE TRANSFORMATION CONTINUED: DONALD FITES'S CATERPILLAR, 1990–1999

36   Notwithstanding Schaefer's achievements, the transformation of Caterpillar was far from over. For one thing, the company stock lagged far behind its earnings; Cat shares underperformed the S&P 500 index by over 50% for five years (1987–1992). For another, Caterpillar was facing an industrywide downturn in both its domestic and international markets. Partly as a result of the cyclical nature of the construction equipment industry, and also as a result of an increase in the value of the dollar (a weak dollar in the late 1980s helped Caterpillar's foreign sales), Caterpillar revenues and profits fell. During the two years following Schaefer's retirement, the company actually lost money (Exhibit 6).

37   Replacing Schaefer in the winter of 1990, Donald Fites viewed Caterpillar's financial troubles as an opportunity to introduce change: "I certainly didn't count on . . . [a] recession . . . but [the recession] made it easier to accept the fact that we needed to change." "It's hard to change an organization when you're making record profits."

Leadership

38   Fites leadership style stood in a stark contrast to Schaefer's. "George was . . . a consensus builder" while "[Don] expects people to challenge him forcefully," one Cat executive said, and another (former Cat CEO Lee Morgan) described Fites as "one of the most determined men I've ever met." Fites was a hard-line executive, feared by his subordinates,

respected by his peers, and cheered by Wall Street. An imposing man standing six-feet-five, Fites led by explicit command rather than persuasion, asserted the company's "right to manage" in face of mounting union opposition, and did not hesitate to cut thousands of management and production jobs at a stroke.

39　　The son of a subsistence corn farmer, Fites had joined Caterpillar in 1956, rising through the ranks, and spending 16 years overseas. A career marketeer, he worked for Cat in South Africa, Germany, Switzerland, Brazil, Japan, and other countries. In 1971, Fites had earned an MBA from MIT, writing a thesis titled "Japan Inc.: Can U.S. Industry Compete?" and soon thereafter, he received an assignment in Japan, serving nearly five years as the marketing director of Caterpillar-Mitsubishi joint venture. Fites' Japanese experience resonated throughout the remainder of his career. He was impressed, first of all, by the ways in which the Japanese trained their managers, rotating executives through functional departments in order to educate them in all aspects of the business. Returning from Japan to Peoria in the mid-1970s, Fites revamped Cat's product development process, utilizing an integrated approach based on Japanese-style functional teams. He also admired Japanese labor relations. Historically, American unions had been organized on an industrywide basis and therefore labor relations in the United States were often adversarial. Trade unions in Japan, by contrast, were company-based organizations, loyal, cooperative, and in Fites's words, "deeply dedicated to the success of the [firm]." Leading Caterpillar in the 1990s, Fites sought to bring Caterpillar's labor relations closer to the Japanese model.

Reorganization

40　A marketing manager, Fites was convinced that Caterpillar did not pay sufficient attention to customer needs because global pricing decisions were made at the company's headquarters in Peoria with little knowledge of the local market conditions around the world. In 1985, as he took charge of Cat's worldwide marketing organization, Fites delegated district offices the authority to set prices, thereby pushing responsibility down the chain of command to the lowest possible level. Promoted to president in 1989, Fites applied the same principle to Caterpillar's entire structure, developing a companywide reorganization plan under Schaefer's direction.

41　　Caterpillar's old organizational structure was archaic. It was a functional structure suitable for a small company that operated just a few plants, all located within the United States. A centralized body with only four primary functions— engineering, manufacturing, marketing, and finance—the old structure served Caterpillar well until World War II, but as the company expanded globally in subsequent decades, the limitations of such a structure had become apparent. First, decisions were made at the top of each functional unit, and executives were reluctant to delegate authority to mid-level or low-level managers. Second, each functional unit tended to focus on its own goal rather than the enterprise's objectives (marketing was preoccupied with market share, engineering with product safety, manufacturing with assembly problems, etc.), making it difficult for top management to coordinate functional goals. And third, the bureaucratization of the decision-making process impaired effective communication. Under the old structure, Fites recalled, the flow of information upwards was "so filtered with various prejudices— particularly functional prejudice[s]— that you didn't know whether you were really looking at the facts or looking at someone's opinion."

42　　To equip Caterpillar with the flexibility, speed, and agility necessary to operate in the global economy, Fites broke the company into 17 semiautonomous divisions or "profit centers," 13 responsible for products (tractors, engines, etc.), and four for services. He then required each division to post a 15% rate of return on assets, and threatened to penalize any division that fell behind. He stood by his words. When Caterpillar's forklift

EXHIBIT 3
Donald Fites's
Caterpillar:
Employment
and Sales

Source: For 1990–1997:
*Hoover's Handbook of
American Business,* 1999,
p. 329; for 1998, *Caterpillar
Inc. 1999 Annual Report,* p. 1.

	Number of Employees	Sales ($bil.)
1990	60,000	11.4
1991	56,000	10.2
1992	52,000	10.2
1993	50,000	11.6
1994	54,000	14.3
1995	54,000	16.1
1996	57,000	16.5
1997	60,000	18.9
1998	64,000	21.0

division failed to improve its return on assets in 1992, Fites transferred it into an 80%–20% joint venture controlled by Mitsubishi.

43   Caterpillar's new divisional structure facilitated downsizing. Under the new structure, Caterpillar cut 10,000 jobs in three years, 1990–1993 (Exhibit 3). Of the 7,500 employees who lost their jobs between January 1990 and August 1992, 2,000 were salaried managers and 5,500 hourly workers. As Caterpillar's sales grew from $10 billion to $15 billion in the first half of the 1990s, the number of managers employed by the company fell by 20%. In addition, the move from a functional into a divisional structure, coupled with the drive for profit making, brought about a change in the methods of managerial compensation. Traditionally, Cat managers were paid in proportion to the size of the budget they controlled or the number of employees they supervised. Under the new plan, Caterpillar based all its incentive compensation schemes on return on assets. Lastly, Caterpillar decentralized its research and development activities. With each division controlling its own product development programs and funding, R&D activities under the new plan were more customer-driven than at any other period in the past.

Marketing and Dealerships

44   Caterpillar's reorganization plan affected the company's distribution network as well. Under the new structure, dealers seeking assistance could contact any of the 17 product and service profit centers directly, saving time and money; they no longer needed to call the General Office in their search for assistance within the company. The new structure also facilitated a more frequent interaction between Caterpillar's managers and dealers, a development which resulted in "[v]irtually everyone from the youngest design engineer to the CEO" having "contact with somebody in [a] dealer organization [wrote Fites]." Ordinarily, low-level managers at Caterpillar communicated daily with their counterparts at Cat dealerships; senior corporate executives, several times a week.

45   Caterpillar's network of dealerships was extensive. In 1999, 207 independent dealers served Caterpillar, 63 of whom were stationed in the U.S. and 144 abroad. The number of employees working for Cat dealers exceeded the company's own workforce (67,000) by nearly one third; the combined net worth of Cat dealers surpassed Caterpillar's stockholders' equity ($5.5 billion) by nearly one quarter (Exhibit 4). Many of Caterpillar's dealerships were privately owned, a few were public companies. On average, the annual sales of a Caterpillar dealership amounted to $150 million (1996); several of the large dealerships, however, generated annual revenues of up to $1 billion.

46   To Caterpillar, the informal relationships between the company and its dealers were far more important than the formal contractual relations. Dealership agreements ran only a few pages, had no expiration date, and allowed each party to terminate the contract at will, following a 90-day notice. Notwithstanding the open-ended nature of the contract,

EXHIBIT 4
Caterpillar
Dealerships, 1999

Source: *Caterpillar Inc. 1999
Annual Report,* p. 43.

	Inside U.S.	Outside U.S.	Worldwide
Dealers	63	144	207
Branch Stores	382	1,122	1,504
Employees	34,338	54,370	88,709
Service Bays	6,638	5,529	12,167
Estimated Net Worth	$3.22 bil.	$3.54 bil.	$6.77 bil.

turnover among Cat dealerships was extremely low. Caterpillar actively encouraged its dealers to keep the business in their families, running seminars on tax issues and succession plans for dealers, holding regular conferences in Peoria for the sons and daughters of "dealer Principals" (dealership owners), and taking concrete steps to encourage a proper succession from one generation to another.

47   While Caterpillar had always protected its dealers against failure, under Fites's direction, Caterpillar did so more aggressively than before, assisting individual dealers who were subjected to intense price competition by rival manufacturers. To help a dealer, Caterpillar sometimes offered discounted prices, sometimes helped reduce the dealer's costs, and occassionally launched a promotion campaign in the dealer's service territory, emphasizing the lower lifetime cost of a Cat machine relative to a competitor's. Caterpillar also protected dealers during recessions. Despite the company's losses during the industry slump of 1991–92, Fites's Caterpillar helped vulnerable Cat dealers survive the downturn, stay in the business, and order equipment in advance of the 1993 upturn. Caterpillar's competitors, in contrast, saw several of their dealers go out of business during the recession.

48   Fites's Caterpillar cooperated with dealers in other ways. During the 1990s, Caterpillar worked together with its dealers to conduct surveys among customers in order to improve customer service and parts delivery. Sending out 90,000 survey forms annually, Cat received a response rate of nearly 40%. Through its "Partners in Quality" program, Caterpillar involved dealers in quality control discussions, linking personnel at Cat plants and dealerships and sponsoring quarterly meetings. Periodically, Caterpillar invited its entire body of independent dealers to a weeklong conference in Peoria to review corporate strategy, manufacturing plants, and marketing policies. A firm believer in strong personal business ties, Fites explained:

> Dealers can call me or any senior corporate officer at any time, and they do. Virtually any dealer in the world is free to walk in my door. I'll know how much money he made last year and his market position. And I'll know what is happening in his family. I consider the majority of dealers personal friends. Of course, one reason I know the dealers so well is that I rose through our distribution organization.

49   Caterpillar's worldwide distribution system, according to Fites, was the company's single greatest advantage over its competitors. It was a strategic asset whose importance was expected to grow in the future: "[u]ntil about 2010," Fites predicted, "distribution"— that is, after-sales support, product application, and service information— "will be what separates the winners from the losers in the global economy." Contrasting American and Japanese manufacturing firms, Fites elaborated:

> Although many Japanese companies had the early advantage in manufacturing excellence, U.S. companies may have the edge this time around. . . . [T]hey know more about distribution than anyone else. . . . Quite frankly, distribution traditionally has not been a strength of Japanese companies. Marketing people and salespeople historically have been looked down upon in Japanese society.

Information Technology

50   Fites's Caterpillar invested generously in expanding and upgrading Caterpillar's worldwide computer network—a system linking together factories, distribution centers, dealers, and large customers. By 1996, the network connected 1,000 locations in 160 countries across 23 time zones, providing Caterpillar with the most comprehensive and fastest part delivery system in the industry. Although Caterpillar had long guaranteed a 48-hour delivery of parts anywhere in the world, by 1996, Cat dealers supplied 80% of the parts a customer needed at once; the remaining 20%—not stocked by the dealers—were shipped by the company on the same day the parts were ordered. With 22 distribution centers spread all around the world, Caterpillar serviced a total of 500,000 different parts, keeping over 300,000 in stock and manufacturing the remainder on demand.

51   A critical element in Caterpillar's drive for technological leadership was an electronic alert information system the company was developing under Fites. The new system was designed to monitor machines remotely, identify parts that needed to be replaced, and replace them before they failed. Once fully operational in the early 2000s, the new IT system was expected, first, to help dealers repair machines before they broke down, thereby reducing machine downtime, on the one hand, and saving repair costs, on the other; and, second, provide Caterpillar and its dealers with the opportunity to slash their inventory costs. In 1995, the value of the combined inventories held by Caterpillar and its dealers amounted to $2 billion worth of parts.

Diversification

52   Fites's Caterpillar expanded its sales into farm equipment, forest products, and compact construction machines, introducing new lines of products, one at a time. Between 1991 and 1999, Caterpillar entered a total of 38 mergers and joint venture agreements, many of which contributed to the company's efforts to diversify.

53   The growth in Caterpillar's engine sales was the company's largest. Caterpillar had traditionally produced engines for internal use only, installing them on Cat machines, but beginning in the mid-1980s, as the company was recovering from its most severe crisis, Cat embarked on a strategy of producing engines for sale to other companies. In 1999, engine sales accounted for 35% of Cat's revenues, up from 21% in 1990, and Cat engines powered about one-third of the big trucks in the United States. Apart from trucking companies, Caterpillar produced engines for a variety of other customers including petroleum firms, electric utility companies, and shipbuilding concerns (Exhibit 6). Only 10% of the diesel engines manufactured by Caterpillar in 1999 were installed on the company's own equipment.

54   Two important acquisitions by Caterpillar helped the company compete in the engine market. In 1996, Donald Fites purchased the MaK Company—a German maker of engines for power generation. Partly because governments of developing countries were reluctant to build large power plants, and partly because the utility industry in the United States deregulated and new electrical suppliers entered the market, worldwide demand for generators was fast increasing. The rise in demand helped Caterpillar increase its sales of power generators by 20% annually between 1995 and 1999.

55   Similarly, in 1998, Fites bought Britain's Perkins Engines, a manufacturer of engines for compact construction machinery, for $1.3 billion. The new acquisition contributed to Caterpillar's efforts to increase its share in the small equipment market, which was growing at a rate of 10% a year. Perkins' best-selling engine powered the skid steer loader. A compact wheel tractor operated by one person and capable of maneuvering in tight spaces, the skid dug ditches, moved dirt, broke up asphalt, and performed a wide variety of other tasks.

Labor Relations

56   Perhaps no other areas of management had received more attention than Caterpillar's labor relations under Fites. For nearly seven years, 1991–1998, Fites fought the UAW in what had become the longest U.S. labor dispute in the 1990s. On the one side, a union official described the UAW relationship with Fites as "the single most contentious . . . in the history of the union"; on the other, a Wall Street analyst called Fites "the guy who broke the union, pure and simple."

57   In part, Fites's opposition to the UAW was ideological: it "is not so much a battle about economics as it is a battle about who's going to run the company." Yet economics did matter, and Fites was determined to ensure Caterpillar's global competitiveness by cutting the company's labor cost. His principal target was a UAW "pattern" agreement, a collective bargaining contract modeled on agreements signed by the UAW and Caterpillar's domestic competitors, John Deere, the Case Corporation, and others (a pattern agreement tied separate labor contracts together so that changes in one led to similar changes in others within the same industry). Fites rejected pattern bargaining because Caterpillar was heavily dependent on the export of domestically manufactured products, selling over 50% of its American-made equipment in foreign markets, and thus competing head-to-head with foreign-based, global companies like Komatsu. Cat's U.S.-based competitors, by contract, exported a far smaller proportion of their domestically made goods. Because Cat's global competitors paid lower wages overseas than the wages paid by Cat's American-based competitors at home, Fites argued, Caterpillar could not afford paying the UAW pattern of wages.

58   The first Caterpillar strike erupted in 1991, at a time Caterpillar's 17,000 unionized employees were working under a contract. The contract was set to expire on September 30, and Fites was prepared. He had built up enough inventory to supply customers for six months, giving Cat dealers special incentives to buy and stock parts and equipment in case a strike shut down the company's U.S. plants. Caterpillar's contract offer included three principal demands: no pattern on wages, flexible work schedules, and a two-tier wage system. The union rejected the offer outright and staged a strike. About 50% of the strikers were within six years of retirement, and as the strike prolonged, 30% of the strikers crossed the picket line. Five months into the strike, Fites threatened to replace the strikers permanently if they did not return to work within a week. Shortly thereafter, the union called off the strike, the strikers went back to work "unconditionally," and Cat's unionized employees continued working without a contract under the terms of the rejected offer.

59   One casualty of the 1991–1992 strike was Caterpillar's Employee Satisfaction Process. The strike effectively put an end to Cat's ESP program that George Schaefer had launched in 1986 and strove so painstakingly to preserve. As the climate of labor relations at Caterpillar deteriorated, the number of unresolved grievances increased. At the Aurora plant at Illinois, the number of grievances at the final stage before arbitration rose from less than 20 prior to the strike to over 300 in the year following the end of the strike. When Cat employees began wearing their own ESP buttons to read "Employee Stop Participating," Caterpillar terminated the program altogether.

60   During 1992–94, Caterpillar's unionized employees continued to resist Fites's hardline stand against the UAW. They organized shopfloor disruptions ("informational picketing"), slowdowns ("work to rule"), wildcat strikes in selected plants, and picket lines at Cat's dealerships. Fites, in the meantime, trained managers and office workers to operate factory machinery and reassigned many of them to the shopfloor of plants undergoing short-term work-stoppages. Once again, he was fully prepared for a long strike. The 1994–95 strike broke out in June 1994, lasted 17 months, was bitterly fought by the

Source: *Hoover's Handbook for American Business*, 1999, p. 329.

EXHIBIT 5
Caterpillar's
Financial Results
during the Labor
Disputes of the 1990s

	Sales ($mil.)	Net Income ($mil.)	Income as % of Sales	Stock Price FY Close
1991	10,182	(404)	—	10.97
1992	10,194	(2,435)	—	13.41
1993	11,615	652	5.6%	22.25
1994	14,328	955	6.7%	27.56
1995	16,072	1,136	7.1%	29.38
1996	16,522	1,361	8.2%	37.63
1997	18,925	1,665	8.8%	48.50

striking unionists, and came to an abrupt end when the UAW ordered its members to return to work "immediately and unconditionally" in order to save their jobs. During the strike, Caterpillar supplemented its workforce with 5,000 reassigned white-collar employees, 3,700 full-time and part-time new hires, 4,000 union members who crossed the picket line, and skilled workers borrowed from its dealerships. The company, furthermore, shifted work to nonunion plants in the South. Additionally, Caterpillar supplied the U.S. market with equipment imported from its plants in Europe, Japan, and Brazil. Operating effectively all through the strike, Caterpillar avoided massive customer defection, and managed to keep up production, expand sales, increase profits, and drive up the company stock price. In 1995, the company earned record profits for the second year in a row (Exhibit 5). During the two years following the end of the strike, the shopfloor struggle between Cat management and the union resumed. Caterpillar issued strict rules of workplace conduct, limiting employees' behavior as well as speech. Union activists, in response, launched a work-to-rule campaign in Cat's unionized plants. The UAW, in addition, filed numerous charges with the National Labor Relations Board (NLRB), alleging that the company committed unfair labor practices. Accepting many of these charges, the NLRB issued formal complaints. Meanwhile, in 1997, Caterpillar racked up record profits for the fourth year in a row (Exhibit 5).

61   In February 1998, at long last, Caterpillar and the union reached an agreement. The terms of the 1998 agreement clearly favored Caterpillar. First and most important, the contract allowed Caterpillar to break away from the long-standing practice of pattern bargaining. Second, the contract allowed Caterpillar to introduce a two-tier wage system and pay new employees 70% of the starting union scale. A third clause of the contract provided for a more flexible work schedule, allowing management to keep employees on the job longer than eight hours a day and during weekends (without paying overtime). The contract also granted management the right to hire temporary employees at certain plants without the union's approval, and reduce the number of union jobs a certain level. Running for six years rather than the typical three years, the contract was expected to secure Caterpillar with a relatively long period of industrial peace.

62   Several provisions of the contract were favorable to the union. The contract's key economic provisions included an immediate wage increase of 2–4% and future increases of 3% in 1999, 2001, and 2003; cost of living allowances; and substantial gains in pension benefits (the average tenure of the 1994–95 strikers was 24 years). Another provision favorable to the UAW was a moratorium on most plant closings. But perhaps the most significant union gain was simply achieving a contract, as AFL-CIO Secretary Treasurer Rich Trumka observed: "The message to corporate America is this: Here's one of the biggest companies, and they couldn't walk away from the union." Why, then was Fites

willing to sign a contract? Why did a company which operated profitably year after year without a contract, and operated effectively during strikes, suddenly sought to reach an agreement with the UAW?

63   Fites's decision was influenced by two developments. First, Caterpillar's record revenues and profits during 1993–97 came to an end in 1998–99, as the industry was sliding into a recession. Revenues and profits were declining as a result of a strong dollar coupled with a weak demand for Cat products. Caterpillar, therefore, needed a flexible wage agreement, stable employment relations, and a more cooperative workforce in order to smooth its ride during the impending downturn. Another reason why Fites sought accommodation with the union was the need to settle some 400 unfair labor practice charges filed by the NLRB against the company during the dispute. These charges were not only costly to adjudicate but could have resulted in huge penalties that the company had to pay in cases where the NLRB ruled in favor of the UAW. One of Caterpillar's principal demands in the 1998 settlement—to which the UAW agreed—was dropping these unfair labor practice charges.

THE FUTURE: GLEN BARTON'S CATERPILLAR, 1999–

64   As Fites retired in February 1999, Glen Barton, a 39-year Cat veteran, assumed the company's leadership. During his first year in office, Barton lost two potential allies on the Cat Board of Directors, George Schaefer and Donald Fites. In January 2000, Caterpillar's Board of Directors revised the company's corporate governance guidelines to prohibit retired Cat employees from sitting on the board. The move was intended to safeguard the interests of stockholders and prevent the company's inside directors from opposing swift actions proposed by the board's outside members.

65   Barton faced other difficulties. In 1999, Caterpillar's profits fell 37% to $946 million, the worst results since 1993, and its North American market, which accounted for half of Cat's sales and nearly 2/3 of its profits, was in a slump.

66   Barton believed that the downturn in the U.S. construction market could be offset by an upturn in the international market. He thought that Caterpillar could take advantage of global positioning to cushion the U.S. decline by increasing sales in Asia and Latin America whose economies were rebounding. But being cautious, Barton also realized that he needed to ensure the future of Caterpillar in the long run. He therefore embarked on four growth strategies: the expansion into new markets; diversification; the development of a new distribution channel; and the buildup of alliances with global competitors.

New Markets

67   In 1999, 80% of the world's population lived in developing countries, and Caterpillar's sales to developing nations accounted for only 23% of the total company's sales. Developing countries had limited access to water, electricity, and transportation, and therefore needed to invest in building highways, bridges, dams, and waterways. Under Barton's leadership, increased sales of Caterpillar's equipment to the developing nations of Asia, Latin America, Eastern Europe, and the Commonwealth of Independent States (the former Soviet Union) was a top strategic priority.

Diversification

68   Just as globalization protected Caterpillar from the cyclical movements of boom and bust, so did diversification. Cat's expansion into the engine business is a case in point. In 1999, Caterpillar's overall sales fell by 6%, yet its engine sales rose by 5%. Cat's engine

EXHIBIT 6
Cat Engine Sales to End Users, 1999, 2000

Source: *Caterpillar Inc. 1999 Annual Report,* p. 24; and 2000 Annual Report.

	1999	2000
Trucks	34%	27%
Electric Power Generators	26%	33%
Oil Drilling Equipment	20%	19%
Industrial Equipment	11%	13%
Ships and Boats	9%	8%

EXHIBIT 7
Caterpillar's Sales of Power Generators

Source: David Barboza, "Cashing in on the World's Energy Hunger," *New York Times,* May 22, 2001.

	Power Generators Sales (billions)	Power Generators Sales as % of Total Revenues
1996	$1.2	7.3%
1997	$1.3	6.9%
1998	$1.6	7.6%
2000	$1.8	9.1%
2001	$2.3	11.4%

business itself was further diversified, with truck-engine sales making up just over one-third of all Cat's engine sales in 1999 (Exhibit 6). Such a diversification, according to Barton, ensured the company that any future decline in truck engine sales could be offset, at least in part, by an increase in sales of nontruck engines. By 2010, Caterpillar's total engine sales were expected to double to nearly $14 billion.

69   Of all Cat engine sales, the growth in sales of electric diesel generators—20% a year since 1996—had been the fastest (Exhibit 7). Caterpillar's energy business clearly benefited from the energy crisis. Large corporations, manufacturing facilities, Internet server centers, and utility companies had installed back-up diesel generators for standby or emergency use; in the nine months ending May 2001, Cat sales of mobile power modules (trailer equipped with a generator) quadrupled.

70   The world's largest manufacturer of diesel generators, Caterpillar nevertheless faced a serious challenge in its efforts to transform itself into an ET (energy technology) company: diesel generators produced far more pollution than other sources of power. To address this problem, Barton's Caterpillar accelerated its shift towards cleaner micro power. In 2001, only 10% of Caterpillar's generators were powered by natural gas; in 2011, the corresponding figure was expected to climb to 50%.

71   To diversify the company in still another way, Barton planned to double its farm equipment sales in five years (1999–2004). In the agricultural equipment market, caterpillar needed to compete head-to-head with the John Deere Co. and the CNH Corporation (former Case Corp. and New Holland), the leading U.S. manufacturers.

A New Distribution Channel

72   Under Barton's direction, Caterpillar expanded its rental equipment business, reaching a new category of customers both at home and abroad. Formerly, Caterpillar sold or rented equipment to rental centers, and these centers, in turn, re-rented the equipment

EXHIBIT 8
Caterpillar: Five-Year Financial Summary

Source: *Caterpillar Inc. 2000 Annual Report*, p. 39.

(Dollars in million except per share data)	2000	1999	1998	1997	1996
Sales and Revenues	$20,175	19,702	20,977	18,925	16,522
Profits	$1,053	946	1,513	1,665	1,361
As % of Sales and Rev.	5.2%	4.8%	7.2%	8.8%	8.2%
Profits per Share	$3.04	2.66	4.17	4.44	3.54
Dividends per Share	$1.345	1,275	1.150	0.950	0.775
Return on Equity	19.0%	17.9%	30.9%	37.9%	36.3%
Capital Expenditures, Net	$723	790	925	824	506
R&D Expenses	$854	814	838	700	570
As % of Sales and Rev.	4.2%	4.1%	4.0%	3.7%	3.4%
Wage, Salaries and Employee Benefits	$4,029	4,044	4,146	3,773	3,437
Number of Employees	67,200	66,225	64,441	58,366	54,968
Total assets					
Consolidated	28,464	26,711	25,128	20,756	18,728
Machinery and Engines	16,554	16,158	15,619	14,188	13,066
Financial Products	14,618	12,951	11,648	7,806	6,681
Long-term debt					
Consolidated debt	11,334	9,928	9,404	6,942	5,087
Machinery and Engines	2,854	3,099	2,993	2,367	2,018
Financial Products	8,480	6,829	6,411	4,575	3,069
Total debt					
Consolidated	15,067	13,802	12,452	8,568	7,459
Machinery and Engines	3,427	3,317	3,102	2,474	2,176
Financial Products	11,957	10,796	9,562	6,338	5,433

Note: For additional financial data, as reported in the company's annual reports and other financial documents, check out Caterpillar's Web address at www.caterpillar.com.

to end-users. Rarely did Caterpillar rent directly to customers. Now Barton was making aggressive efforts to help Cat dealers diversify into rentals. Nearly half of all Cat's machines sold in North America in 2000 entered the market through the rental distribution channel, and the fastest growing segment of the business was short-term rentals. Implemented by Barton in 1999–2000, the Cat Rental Store Program was designed to assist dealers in operating a one-stop rental shop that offered a complete line of rental equipment from heavy bulldozers and tractors, to light towers, work platforms, and hydraulic tools.

Joint Ventures

73 Increasingly, Caterpillar had used joint ventures to expand into new markets and diversify into new products. In November 2000, Barton's Caterpillar announced a plan to form two joint ventures with DaimlerChrysler, the world's leading manufacturer of commercial vehicles. One was for building medium-duty engines, the other was for manufacturing fuel systems. The combined share of the two companies in the medium-duty engine market was only 10%, yet the medium-duty engine market generated worldwide sales of $10 billion annually. The sales of fuel systems were even more promising. Fuel systems were designed to increase the efficiency of diesel

engines and thereby reduce diesel emissions. Participating in the two joint ventures were Cat and DaimlerChrysler plants in four U.S. states (South Carolina, Georgia, Illinois, and Michigan) and at least five other countries.

Future Prospects

74 Notwithstanding their initial prospects, Barton's strategic initiatives failed to address adequately two major concerns that could have affected the company's future. One had to do with the state of labor relations, particularly Cat's Employee Satisfaction Program that Schaefer had introduced and Fites terminated. Implemented effectively by Schaefer, ESP, we have seen, contributed to increased labor productivity, improved product quality, enhanced employee satisfaction, and reduced employee absenteeism. Should Barton, then, re-introduce Cat's Employee Satisfaction Program and thereby improve the climate of labor relations at the company's U.S. plants? Would Barton be able to cooperate closely with the local union leadership to persuade shopfloor employees to join the program?

75 Another challenge Barton faced pertained to the impact of e-commerce. How could Caterpillar take advantage of the opportunities offered by e-commerce without undermining its distribution system? How, in other words, could Caterpillar benefit from utilizing the Internet for the marketing, distribution, and service of its products without weakening its strong dealers' networks?

76 Barton wondered, "What should I do next?"

The Caterpillar Company 1999 Annual Report, p. 39

Michael Arndt, "This Cat Isn't so Nimble," *BusinessWeek,* February 21, 2000, Start p. 148. Online. Lexis-Nexis. Academic Universe; Mark Tatge, "Caterpillar's Truck-Engine Sales May Hit Some Breaking," *Wall Street Journal,* March 13, 2000.

Andrew Gross and David Weiss, "Industry Corner: The Global Demand for Heavy Construction Equipment," *Business Economics,* 31:3 (July 1996), pp. 54–55.

Gross and Weiss, "Industry Corner," p. 54.

Gross and Weiss, "Industry Corner," p. 55.

Donald Fites, "Making Your Dealers Your Partners," *Harvard Business Review,* March–April 1996, p. 85.

U. Srinivasa Rangan, "Caterpillar Tractor Co.," in Christopher Bartlett and Sumantra Ghoshal, *Transatlantic Management: Text, Cases, and Readings in Cross Border Management* (Homewood IL.: Irwin, 1992), p. 296.

Fites, "Making Your Dealers Your Partners," p. 85.

Gross and Weiss, "Industry Corner," p. 58.

William L. Naumann, *The Story of Caterpillar Tractor Co.* (New York: The Newcomen Society, 1977), pp. 7–9.

"Caterpillar Inc.," *Hoover's Handbook of American Business 1999* (Austin: Hoover Business Press, 1999), p. 328; "The Story of Caterpillar." Online. Caterpillar.com. Retrieved March 9, 2000.

Michael Yoshino and U. Srinivasa Rangan, *Strategic Alliances: An Entrepreneurial Approach to Globalization* (Boston: Harvard Business School Press, 1995), p. 93; Naumann, *"Story of Caterpillar,"* pp. 12–14; William Haycraft, *Yellow Power: The Story of the Earthmoving Equipment Industry* (Urbana: University of Illinois Press, 2000), pp. 118–122, 159–167, 196–203.

Fites, "Making Your Dealers Your Partners," p. 94.

Rangan, "Caterpillar Tractor Co.," p. 304; James Risen, "Caterpillar: A Test of U.S. Trade Policy," *Los Angeles Times,* June 8, 1986. Online. Lexis-Nexis. Academic Universe.

Cited in Kathleen Deveny, "For Caterpillar, the Metamorphosis Isn't Over," *BusinessWeek,* August 31, 1987, p. 72.

Cited in Dexter Hutchins, "Caterpillar's Triple Whammy," *Fortune,* October 27, 1986, p. 91. See also Robert Eckley, "Caterpillar's Ordeal: Foreign Competition in Capital Goods," *Business Horizons,* March–April 1989, pp. 81–83.

James Abegglen and George Stalk, *Kaisha, the Japanese Corporation* (New York: Basic Books, 1985), pp. 62, 117–118; Yoshino and Rangan, *Strategic Alliances,* pp. 94–95; "Komatsu Ltd.," *Hoover's Handbook of World Business,* 1999, p. 320.

Quoted in Yoshino and Rangan, *Strategic Alliances,* p. 96.

Yoshino and Rangan, *Strategic Alliances,* p. 97; Eckley, "Caterpillar's Ordeal," p. 84.

Eckley, "Caterpillar's Ordeal," p. 84; *BusinessWeek,* August 31, 1987, p. 73; Yoshino and Rangan, *Strategic Alliances,* p. 97.

Ronald Henkoff, "This Cat Is Acting like a Tiger," *Fortune,* December 19, 1988, pp. 67, 72, 76; *BusinessWeek,* August 31, 1987, p. 73.

Eckley. "Caterpillar Ordeal," pp. 81, 83.

Quoted in *Fortune,* December 19, 1988, p. 76.

Eckley, "Caterpillar Ordeal," p. 84, *Fortune,* December 19, 1988, p. 76; Alex Kotlowitz, "Caterpillar Faces Shutdown with UAW," *Wall Street Journal,* March 5, 1986. Online. ABI data base.

Barry Bearak, "The Inside Strategy: Less Work and More Play at Cat," *Los Angeles Times,* May 16, 1995. Online. Lexis-Nexis. Academic Universe.

Fortune, December 19, 1988, p. 76.

Brian Bremner, "Can Caterpillar Inch Its Way Back to Heftier Profits?" *BusinessWeek,* September 25, 1989, p. 75.

Abegglen and Stalk, *Kaisha,* p. 118.

Fortune, December 19, 1988, pp. 72, 74; *BusinessWeek,* September 25, 1989, p. 75.

Karen Auguston, "Caterpillar Slashes Lead Times from Weeks to Days," *Modern Materials Handling,* February 1990, p. 49.

Barbara Dutton, "Cat Climbs High with FMS," *Manufacturing Systems,* November 1989, pp. 16–22; *BusinessWeek,* August 31, 1987, p. 73, September 25, 1989, p. 75.

Quoted in Auguston, "Caterpillar Slashes Lead Times," p. 49.

Auguston, "Caterpillar Slashes Lead Times," pp. 50–51.

Auguston, "Caterpillar Slashes Lead Times," pp. 49, 51.

BusinessWeek, September 25, 1989, p. 75.

Yoshino and Rangan, *Strategic Alliances,* p. 98.

Jennifer Reingold, "CEO of the Year," *Financial World,* March 28, 1995, p. 68.

Quoted in "An Interview with Caterpillar Inc. Chairman and CEO Donald V. Fites," *Inter-Business Issues,* December 1992, p. 32.

Quoted in Tracy Benson, "Caterpillar Wakes Up," *Industry Week,* May 20, 1991, p. 36.

Quoted in Reingold, "CEO of the Year," p. 74.

Quoted in Kevin Kelly, "Caterpillar's Don Fites: Why He Didn't Blink," *BusinessWeek,* August 10, 1992, p. 56.

Quoted in *BusinessWeek,* August 10, 1992, pp. 56–57.

BusinessWeek, August 10, 1992, p. 57.

Quoted in Benson, "Caterpillar Wakes Up," p. 32.

"An Interview with Fites," *Inter Business Issues,* p. 32.

Benson, "Caterpillar Wakes Up," p. 33.

BusinessWeek, August 10, 1992, p. 56.

J. P. Donlon, "Heavy Metal," *Chief Executive,* September 1995, p. 50.

Andrew Zadoks, "Managing Technology at Caterpillar," *Research Technology Management,* January 1997, pp. 49–51. Online. Lexis-Nexis. Academic Universe.

BusinessWeek, August 10, 1992, p. 56.

Donlon, "Heavy Metal," p. 50.

Benson, "Caterpillar Wakes Up," p. 36.

Fites, "Make Your Dealers Your Partners," p. 93.

Caterpillar Inc. 1999 Annual Report, p. 34.

Fites, "Make Your Dealers Your Partners." pp. 89, 91–92, 94.

Fites, "Make Your Dealers Your Partners," pp. 92–93.

Quoted in Fites, "Make Your Dealers Your Partners," p. 94, but see also pp. 90, 93.

Quoted in Donlon. "Heavy Metals," p. 50.

Quoted in Fites, "Make Your Dealers Your Partners," p. 86.

Myron Magnet, "The Productivity Payoff Arrives," *Fortune,* June 27, 1994, pp. 82–83; Benson "Caterpillar Wakes Up," p. 36; Fites, "Making Your Dealers Your Partners," pp. 88–89.

Quoted in Steven Prokesch, "Making Global Connections in Caterpillar," *Harvard Business Review,* March–April 1996, p. 89, but see also p. 88, and Donlon, "Heavy Metals," p. 50.

"Caterpillar's Growth Strategies," Copyright 1999. Online. Caterpillar.com

The Wall Street Journal, March 13, 2000; David Barboza, "Aiming for Greener Pastures," *New York Times,* August 4, 1999.

De'Ann Weimer, "A New Cat on the Hot Seat," *BusinessWeek,* March 9, 1998, p. 61, *The Wall Street Journal,* March 13, 2000.

BusinessWeek, March 9, 1998; *The Wall Street Journal,* March 13, 2000.

The quotations, in order, are from Reingold, "CEO of the Year," p. 72; Carl Quintanilla, "Caterpillar Chairman Fites to Retire," *The Wall Street Journal,* October 15, 1998. Online. ABI data base.

Quoted in Reingold, "CEO of the Year," p. 72.

"An Interview with Fites," *Inter Business Issues,* pp. 34–35; "What's Good for Caterpillar," *Forbes,* December 7, 1992. Online. ABI data base.

Michael Cimini, "Caterpillar's Prolonged Dispute Ends," *Compensation and Working Conditions,* Fall 1998, pp. 5–6; Kevin Kelly, "Cat May Be Trying to Bulldoze the Immovable," *BusinessWeek,* December 2, 1991, p. 116, "Cat vs. Labor: Hardhats, Anyone?" *BusinessWeek,* August 26, 1991, Start p. 48. Lexis-Nexis. Academic Universe.

Michael Verespej, "Bulldozing Labor Peace at Caterpillar," *Industry Week,* February 15, 1993, start p. 19. Online. ABI data base.

"Caterpillar: Union Bull," *Economist,* January 9, 1993, start p. 61. Online. Lexis-Nexis. Academic Universe; Cimini, "Caterpillar's Prolonged Dispute Ends," pp. 7–9.

Cimini, "Caterpillar's Prolonged Dispute Ends," p. 9; Robert Rose, "Caterpillar Contract with UAW May Be Tough to Sell to Workers," *The Wall Street Journal,* February 17, 1998. Online. ABI data base; Reingold, "CEO of the Year," p. 72.

Cimini, "Caterpillar's Prolonged Dispute Ends," pp. 8–9.

Cimini, "Caterpillar's Prolonged Dispute Ends," pp. 9–10.

Carl Quintanilla, "Caterpillar Touts Its Gains as UAW Battle Ends," *The Wall Street Journal,* March 24, 1998; Dirk Johnson, "Auto Union Backs Tentative Accord with Caterpillar," *New York Times,* February 14, 1998.

Quoted in Philip Dine, "Gulf Remains Wide in Caterpillar's Home," *St. Louis Post Dispatch,* March 29, 1998. Online. Lexis-Nexis. Academic Universe. See also Cimini, "Caterpillar's Prolonged Dispute Ends," p. 11.

"The Caterpillar Strike: Not Over Till It's Over," *Economist,* February 28, 1998.

BusinessWeek, February 21, 2000, start p. 148.

BusinessWeek, February 21, 2000, start p. 148.

"Growth Strategies." Caterpillar.com, p. 2.

The Wall Street Journal, March 13, 2000.

David Barboza, "Cashing In on the World's Energy Hunger," *New York Times,* May 22, 2001.

New York Times, May 22, 2001; "Energy Technology: Beyond the Bubble," *Economist,* April 21, 2001.

Heather Landy, "Putting More Cats Down on the Farm," *Chicago Sun Times,* March 28, 1999. Online. Lexis-Nexis. Academic Universe.

Michael Roth, "Seeing the Light," *Rental Equipment Register,* January 2000. Online. Lexis-Nexis. Academic Universe; Nikki Tait, "Cat Sharpens Claws to Pounce Again," *Financial Times,* November 8, 2000. Online. Lexis-Nexis. Academic Universe.

Joseph Hallinan, "Caterpillar, DaimlerChrysler Team Up," *The Wall Street Journal,* November 23, 2000.

Case 50

Kikkoman Corporation: Market Maturity, Diversification, and Globalization

1   In early 1996, Yuzaburo Mogi, president of Kikkoman Corporation, faced a number of challenges. Analysis indicated concern with Kikkoman's slow sales growth and noted that the company's stock had underperformed on the Nikkei Exchange in relation to the market and to its peers for several years. Throughout the world, ongoing changes in taste preferences and dietary needs presented threats to the company's traditional food lines. The company marketed its branded products in 94 countries and had to consider which products and markets to emphasize as well as which new markets to enter. As Mr. Mogi described the company's focus, ". . . we are now concentrating on further enhancing our ability to serve consumers in Japan and overseas. The basic keynotes of this effort are expansion of soy sauce markets, diversification, and globalization."

2   In Japan, Kikkoman had long dominated the soy sauce market, and its mid-1990s market share position of 27% was well beyond the 10% of its next closest competitor. However, its share of the soy sauce market had continued to decline from its high of 33% in 1983, falling from 28% in 1993 to 27.2% in 1994. Further, although the company's worldwide sales had increased slightly overall from 1994 to 1995, sales of soy sauce in Japan had decreased over 1% during that period.

3   The U.S. market had provided significant opportunity in the post-World War II period. However, the company's U.S. market share for soy and other company products was essentially flat. In addition, three competitors had built plants in the United States beginning in the late 1980s. Mr. Mogi was aware that Kikkoman's choices in the U.S. market would provide an important model for addressing higher income mature markets.

4   With a market capitalization of nearly ¥160 billion,[1] Kikkoman Corporation was the world's largest soy sauce producer, Japan's nineteenth largest food company, and also Japan's leading soy sauce manufacturer. The company was the oldest continuous enterprise among the 200 largest industrials in Japan. The company began brewing shoyu, or naturally fermented soy sauce, in the seventeenth century and had dominated the Japanese soy industry for at least a century. The company held 50% of the U.S. soy sauce market and 30% of the world market. Kikkoman had 13 manufacturing facilities in Japan and one each in the United States, Singapore, and Taiwan. The company was one

Case prepared by Norihito Tanaka, Kanagawa University; Marilyn L. Taylor, University of Missouri at Kansas City; Joyce A. Claterbos, University of Kansas. Paid-in-full members of NACRA are encouraged to reproduce any case for distribution to their students without charge or written permission. All other rights reserved jointly to the authors and the North American Case Research Association (NACRA).

    Copyright © 2001 by the *Case Research Journal* and Norihito Tanaka, Marilyn L. Taylor, and Joyce A. Claterbos.

    The authors express deep appreciation to Kikkoman Corporation, which provided encouragement to this study, including access to the U.S. manufacturing and marketing facilities in addition to time in the corporate offices in Japan. The authors also gracefully acknowledge the support for this study provided by the Japanese Department of Education and the Institute for Training and Development in Tokyo. Quotes and data in this case study were drawn from a variety of personal interviews in the United States and Japan, company documents, and public sources. Documents and public sources appear in the list of references at the conclusion of the case.

EXHIBIT 1 **Locations of Principle Subsidiaries**

Source: *"Flavors That Bring People Together,"* Kikkoman Corporation Brochure, 1994.

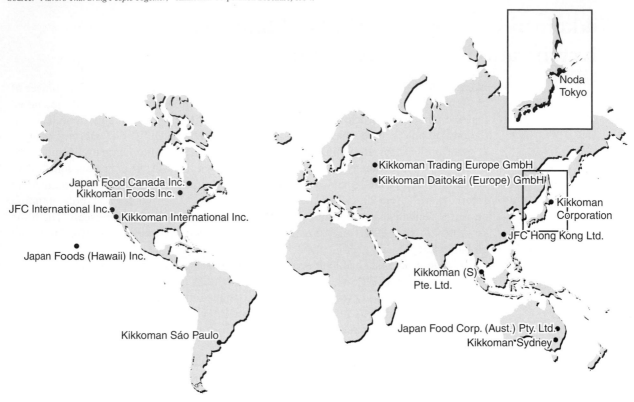

of the few traditional manufacturers to successfully establish a presence worldwide. (Exhibits 1 and 2 have the locations of and information on the company's principal subsidiaries. Exhibits 3 and 4 list the consolidated financial statements.)

KIKKOMAN IN JAPAN

The Beginnings in Noda

5   In 1615, the widow of a slain samurai warrior fled 300 miles from Osaka to the village of Noda near Edo (now called Tokyo). With her five children, the widow Mogi embarked upon rice farming and subsequently began brewing shoyu, or soy sauce. The quality of the Mogi family's shoyu was exceptional almost from its beginnings. At the time, households produced shoyu for their own use, or local farmers made and sold excess shoyu as a side enterprise to farming. As more people moved to the urban areas in the seventeenth and eighteenth centuries, there was increased demand for nonhome production. Households developed preferences for the product of a particular brewer. (See Appendix A: The Making of Soy Sauce.)

6   Shoyu had come to Japan with the arrival of Buddhism in the sixth century. The teachings of Buddhism prohibited eating meat and fish. Residents of the Japanese islands turned from meat-based to vegetable-based flavorings. One of the favorites became a flavorful seasoning made from fermented soy beans. A Japanese Zen Buddist priest who

EXHIBIT 2
Consolidated
Subsidiaries
as of FY 1995

Source: Table 4: Consolidated
Subsidiaries, UBS Securities
Limited, May 28, 1996, as
reported by *Investext*.

Subsidiary	Country	Paid-in-Capital ((Y)m/$m)	Kikkoman Equity (%)
Japan Del Monte	Japan	900	99.7
Mann's Wine	Japan	900	100
Pacific Trading	Japan	72	66.7
Morishin	Japan	30	66.7
Kikkoman Foods, Inc.	U.S.	US$6	100
Kikkoman International	U.S.	US$3.5	92.6
JFC International	U.S.	US$1.2	98
Kikkoman Trading Europe	Germany	DM1.5	75
Kikkoman Pte	Singapore	S$7.5	100
Kikkoman Trading Pte	Singapore	S$.4	100
Tokyo Food Processing	U.S.	US$.02	100
Hapi Products	U.S.	US$.05	100
Rex Pacific	U.S.	US$1.5	100

EXHIBIT 3   Consolidated Profit and Loss Statement ((Y) m)

Sources: Table 9: UBS Securities Limited, May 28, 1996; *The World Almanac*, 1998 (original source: IMF).

	1989	1990	1991	1992	1993	1994	1995
Sales	195,851	196,925	206,861	211,671	203,491	200,976	203,286
COGS	117,062	118,808	122,872	124,882	118,504	117,809	119,656
Gross Profit	78,789	78,117	83,989	86,789	84,987	83,167	83,629
Gross Profit Margin (%)	40.2	39.7	40.6	41	41.8	41.4	41.1
SG&A Expenses	71,227	71,876	74,181	76,019	74,320	72,689	72,836
SG&A Exp. (%)	36.4	36.5	35.9	35.9	36.5	36.2	35.8
Operating Profit	7,562	6,240	9,807	10,769	10,666	10,477	10,792
Operating Margin (%)	3.9	3.2	4.7	5.1	5.2	5.2	5.3
Net Non-Op. Income	−572	−1,042	−1,564	−1,895	−2,282	−2,197	−2,305
Recurring Profit	6,990	5,197	8,243	8,873	8,384	8,280	8,487
Recurring Margin (%)	3.6	2.6	4	4.2	4.1	4.1	4.2
Net Extraordinary Income	181	1,165	1,317	59	108	1,434	−1,177
Pretax Profit	7,170	6,363	9,559	8,932	8,493	9,714	7,310
Tax	3,327	3,299	4,726	5,178	4,597	4,157	3,569
Tax Rate (%)	46.4	50.7	49.4	58	54.1	42.8	48.8
Minority Interest	56	78	37	34	1	−52	46
Amortization of Consol. Dif.	0	0	−35	1	5	0	−314
Equity in Earnings	1,097	1,464	1,188	1,245	887	1,002	996
Net Profit	4,697	4,694	6,166	4,928	4,688	6,614	4,447
Shares Outstanding (m)	169.08	169.71	169.97	178.61	187.62	187.77	197.2
EPS	27.8	27.7	31.3	25	23.8	33.5	22.6
EPS Change (%_)	80	−0.4	13.3	−20.2	−4.9	41	−32.8
Cash Flow per Share	20.8	46.5	48	41.9	44.4	58.5	46.8
Average Exchange Rate (yen/USD)	137.96	144.79	134.71	126.65	111.20	102.21	94.06

EXHIBIT 4   Consolidated Balance Sheet ((Y) m)

Source: Nikkei Needs as reported in Table 12: Consolidated Balance Sheet, UBS Securities Limited, May 28, 1996.

	1990	**1991**	**1992**	**1993**	**1994**	**1995**
Current Assets	81,611	88,092	89,705	103,152	105,220	107,339
Cash and Deposits	13,254	17,570	18,261	28,826	36,381	37,366
Accounts Receivable	43,579	44,661	44,503	46,009	44,246	44,439
Securities	315	1,012	1,316	3,310	3,306	3,307
Inventories	21,769	21,300	22,484	21,469	18,579	19,258
Fixed Assets	94,631	97,999	105,231	113,940	112,183	119,411
Tangible Assets	52,087	53,254	59,276	67,649	65,795	72,684
Land	11,768	12,011	11,910	15,156	15,613	11,540
Investments	26,371	29,597	31,771	33,051	34,083	35,006
Total Assets	177,583	187,316	195,955	218,561	218,805	228,308
Liabilities and Owner's Equity						
Current Liabilities	48,040	52,626	54,014	50,272	46,663	63,400
Short-Term Borrowings	18,846	18,908	19,046	17,462	14,838	15,741
Fixed Liabilities	58,374	58,850	62,351	85,532	85,143	71,710
Long-Term Borrowings	4,457	4,549	4,723	3,274	3,091	2,312
Bonds and CBs[a]	26,565	26,346	26,231	46,170	44,776	29,921
Minority Interest	1,223	1,166	1,157	1,103	1,024	427
Total Liabilities	107,638	112,643	117,522	136,909	132,832	135,538
Shareholders' Equity	69,945	74,673	78,434	81,651	85,973	92,770
Total Liabilities and Equity	177,583	187,316	195,955	218,561	218,805	228,308

[a]There were two CBs issued Jan. 90 exercisable at (Y) 1,522. The other two were issued July 93 and were exercisable at (Y) 969. With the share price at approximately (Y) 100, the total dilution factor was about 18 percent, with 80 percent of that dependent on the two CBs exercisable at (Y) 969. Of 228 ((Y) m) in 1995, about 170 belonged to the parent (i.e., Japan corporation) company.

had studied in China brought the recipe to Japan. The Japanese discovered that adding wheat gave the sauce a richer, more mellow flavor.

7   Over the eighteenth century, Noda became a major center for shoyu manufacturing in Japan. Shoyu's major ingredients, soybeans and wheat, grew readily in the rich agricultural Kanto plain that surrounded Noda. The trip to the major market of Edo took only one day on the Edo River. The various shoyu-producing families in the Noda area actively shared their knowledge of fermentation. The Mogi family and another Noda area family, the Takanashi family, were especially active in the industry. By the late eighteenth century, the two families had become interrelated through marriage. Their various enterprises made considerable investment in breweries, and family members began ancillary enterprises such as grain brokering, keg manufacture, and transportation.

Japan's Shoyu Distribution System and Industry Structure

8   Japan's neophyte and fragmented shoyu industry had two distribution systems during this time. In the rural areas, the shoyu breweries sold their products directly to households. In the cities, urban wholesales distributed shoyu, vinegar, and sake. The wholesalers purchased bulk shoyu and established their own brands. The wholesalers controlled pricing, inventory, distribution, and marketing knowledge. They would distribute branded shoyu only on consignment. During the 1800s, the wholesalers formed alliances that gave them near monopolistic power over the Tokyo market. As the shoyu manufacturers became

more efficient, they found it impossible to lower prices or make other adjustments to increase their market share.

9   The Mogi and Takanashi families took several steps to counteract the wholesalers' dominance. The Takanashi family had diversified into wholesaling some years prior and were part of the wholesalers' alliance. One Mogi family intermarried with a wholesaler's family—a traditional strategy in Japan for cementing strategic alliances. In addition, the Mogi and Takanashi families worked to increase brand recognition and dominance. In 1838, Mogi Saheiji applied for and received the shogunate's recognition of his family's premier brand, named Kikkoman. He aggressively promoted the brand by sponsoring professional storytellers and sumo wrestlers, embossing paper lanterns and umbrellas with the Kikkoman trademark, and putting ornate gold labels from Paris on his Kikkoman shoyu kegs. In the latter part of the nineteenth century, Kikkoman shoyu won recognition in several world's fairs.

10   In reaction to depressed market prices and fluctuating costs of inputs, a number of the Noda shoyu brewers formed the Noda Shoyu Brewers' Association in 1887. The association purchased raw materials, standardized wages, and regulated output quality. The members' combined efforts resulted in the largest market share at the time, 5 to 10% of the Tokyo market, and widespread recognition of the high quality of Noda shoyu.

11   Noda brewers, and especially the Mogi and Takanashi families, began research and development activities early. The Japanese government encouraged the Noda shoyu brewers to conduct research in the recovery and processing of the two by-products of shoyu manufacture, shoyu oil and shoyu cake. In the early 1900s, the association began to fund a joint research and development laboratory.

The Shoyu Industry in the Twentieth Century

12   In 1910, there were still 14,000 known makers of shoyu in Japan. However, a number of changes led to consolidation. Manufacturing shifted from a small-batch, brewmaster-controlled production process to a large-batch, technology-controlled process. Mogi families in Noda invested in modernized plants, and a fifth-grade Japanese geography reader featured a state-of-the-art Kikkoman facility. A national market also developed, thanks to the development of a railway system throughout most of the country. In addition, consumer tastes shifted to the Tokyo-style shoyu produced by eastern manufacturers such as the Noda Shoyu Brewers' Association.

13   Consumers also began to purchase shoyu in smaller glass bottles rather than in the traditional large wooden barrels that sometimes leaked and were expensive to build and difficult to store. Raw materials also became more expensive as the brewers increasingly sought higher quality imported soybeans (from Manchuria, China, and Korea) and salt (from England, Germany, and China). The association members controlled costs by purchasing in bulk and demanding high-quality materials from suppliers.

The Noda Shoyu Company: 1918–1945—A Family Zaibatsu[2]

14   In 1918, seven Mogi families and a related Takanashi family combined their various enterprises into a joint stock holding company called the Noda Shoyu Company. The merger was in reaction to the market upheaval caused by World War I. The new company was a small zaibatsu with nearly a dozen companies in manufacturing fermented grain-based products, transportation, and finance. Unlike early shoyu manufacturing where ownership, management, and operations were clearly separated, the Mogi and Takanashi families owned, managed, and operated their firm. Initially, the family produced 34 different brands of shoyu at various price points. The Kikkoman brand had a history of heavy promotion for over 40 years, greater Tokyo market share, and a higher margin than the company's other brands.

The Kikkoman brand became the company's flagship brand. The new corporation continued its long-standing emphasis on research and development and aggressively pursued new manufacturing processes, increased integration, and acquisition of other shoyu companies.

15   After the Mogi Takanashi coalition, the company aggressively pursued a strong nationwide sole agent system and direct distribution. The combined company also continued Kikkoman's well-known advertising activities. Kikkoman had carried out the first newspaper advertising in 1878. In 1922, the company carried out the firm's first advertising on the movie screen.

16   During the 1920s, the company aggressively modernized with machines such as hydraulic presses, boilers, conveyors, and elevators. The company's modernization efforts were emulated by competitors, and the results were increased supply and heightened industry competition. The changes brought about by increased automation led to severe labor unrest. One particularly long strike against the Kikkoman company in the late 1920s almost destroyed the participating labor union. After the strike ended, Kikkoman rehired about a third of the striking employees. The company centralized and reorganized the work processes to accommodate improved technology, restructured work practices, and established methods to monitor and reward workers for their performance. However, the company also established efforts to improve the identity of the workers with the company. Internal communications carried the message that all employees were members of one family, or ikka, united in a common purpose, i.e., the production of shoyu. The Noda Shoyu Company was also heavily involved in the city of Noda and supported many of its cultural and charitable activities as well as the local railroad, bank, town hall, cultural center, library, fire station, elementary school, hospital, recreation facilities and association, and much of the city's water system.

Kikkoman's International Activities

17 Kikkoman's initial export activities began in the late seventeenth century with Dutch and Chinese traders. The Dutch began to export shoyu to Holland and the rest of Europe, while the Chinese served the southeast Asian markets. The shoyu brewers relied on agents for these early export transactions. During the nineteenth century, one Mogi patriarch opened a factory in Inchon, Korea. Demand for the increasing export, marketing, and direct investment continued to come primarily from Japanese and other peoples living abroad whose traditional cuisines called for shoyu. In 1910, the Noda city brewers' international activities were recognized when the Japanese government selected Noda shoyu to appear in a public relations publication introducing Japan's industries overseas.

18   Noda Shoyu Company continued to expand internationally between World War I and World War II. Acquisition of raw materials from abroad continued. The company added a manufacturing facility for shoyu and miso in Manchuria and two shoyu factories in North America. Other facilities in Japan were expanded or updated to support increasing international sales.

19   The company established sales offices in China and Korea to market shoyu, miso, and sake. By the late 1930s, the company exported 10 percent of its output, about half to the Asian region—especially Korea, China, and Indonesia—and half to Hawaii and California. Almost all of the exports were the Kikkoman brand and were sold through food import/export firms to the company's traditional customers.

Post–World War II Kikkoman in Japan

20 At the end of World War II, Kikkoman operated only in Japan. Activities elsewhere had been closed. To meet the need for capital, Kikkoman issued publicly traded stock in 1946, reducing family ownership markedly. (Exhibit 5 shows the changes in ownership

EXHIBIT 5
Noda Shoyu
Company and
Kikkoman
Corporation
Ownership

Sources: W. Mark Fruin,
*Kikkoman—Company, Clan,
and Community* (Cambridge,
MA, Harvard, University Press,
1983), pp. 98, 121, 249, Japan
Company Handbook, Toyo
Keizai, Inc., 1993, p. 207.

Shareholder Name	Holdings (% of total shares or assets)			
	1917	1925	1955	1993
Mogi-Takanashi-Horikiri Brewing Families	100%[a]	34.6%	15.0%[b]	2.3%
Senshusha Holding Company		62.0%	3.1%	3.4%
Insurance and Banking companies			9.9%[c]	20.5%[c]
All Others		3.6%	71.1%	73.6%

[a]Eight holdings ranging from 1.4 percent to 29.3 percent.
[b]Five holdings ranging from 1.5 percent to 4.4 percent.
[c]In 1955 and 1993, including Meiji Mutual Insurance Co, Mitsubishi Trust Bank; in 1955, including Kofukan Foundation and Noda Institute of Industrial Science; in 1993, including, Nitsuit Trust Bank, Nippon Life Insurance, Sumitomo Trust, and Yasuda Trust.

EXHIBIT 6
**National Output and
Company Market
Share of Shoyu (in
kiloliters)**[a]

Source: W. Mark Fruin,
*Kikkoman—Company, Clan,
and Community* (Cambridge,
MA, Harvard University Press,
1983), pp. 40–41.

Year	National Output (Japan)	Noda Shoyu Share
1893	230,360	3.5%
1903	317,500	4.5%
1913	430,435	6.1%
1923	624,764	5.1%
1933	576,026	10.1%
1943	680,955	12.0%
1953	822,179	14.1%
1963	1,051,730	21.4%
1973	1,277,887	31.4%
1983	n.a.	33.0%
1993	n.a.	28.0%[c]
1994	1,323,529[b]	27.2%[c]

[a]1 kiloliter = 264 gallons.
[b]Derived from Kikkoman's production of 360,000 kl and its 27.2% market share. Residents of Japan consumed about 2.6 gallons of soy sauce per capita yearly. In contrast, U.S. citizens consumed about 10 tablespoons.
[c]As reported by UBS Securities Limited, May 28, 1996, in *Investext*. This source also reported that demand for soy sauce was flat in Japan and production between 1984 and 1994 had declined about 5.1%.

from 1917 to 1993.) The post–World War II period brought a number of social changes to Japanese society. Japanese families began the change to nuclear rather than extended-family formation. Food tastes changed leading, among other trends, to a decline in per capita consumption of shoyu. Compared with other industries, demand for soy sauce grew very slowly. In 1942, demand for soy sauce in Japan was 1.7 times greater than in 1918. Demand in the 1960s was expected to be 2.2 times greater than that in 1918. However, modernization led to increased output.

21   Kikkoman had received considerable recognition for its advertising efforts prior to World War II. After the war, the company began to market even more aggressively in Japan. These efforts included establishing the company's strong nationwide distribution system throughout Japan; mounting aggressive activities in marketing research, advertising, and consumer education; and changing to a new and more Western image. As a result of Kikkoman's marketing efforts, the company's market share rose sharply. (Exhibit 6 shows the national output of shoyu and the company's market share from 1893 to 1994.) By 1964, the company officially changed its name to Kikkoman Shoyu and in 1980 became Kikkoman Corporation. The word *Kikkoman* is a combination of "kikko" (the shell of a tortoise) and "man" (10,000). It was taken from an old Japanese saying, "A crane lives a thousand years and a tortoise 10,000 years." (Implying, in other words, "May you live as long!") In essence, the Kikkoman brand cannotes a long-lasting living

EXHIBIT 7   Kikkoman Corporation Products and Product Lines

Sources: W. Mark Fruin, *Kikkoman—Company, Clan, and Community* (Cambridge, MA, Harvard University Press, 1983), pp. 275–276; "Flavors That Bring People Together," Kikkoman Corporation Brochure, 1994.

1949	1981	1994
Kikkoman Brand soy sauce, sauce, memmi and tsuyu (soup bases)	**Kikkoman Brand** soy sauce, mild soy sauce (lower salt, 8%), light color soy sauce (usu-kuchi), teriyaki barbecue marinade and sauce, Worcestershire sauce, tonkatsu sauce, memmi and tsuyu (soup bases), sukiyaki sauce, instant soy soup mix, instant osumono (clear broth soup mix)	**Kikkoman Brand** soy sauce, mild soy sauce (lower salt, 8%), light color soy sauce (usu-kuchi), teriyaki sauce, Worcestershire sauce, tonkatsu sauce, memmi (soup base), sukiyaki sauce, sashimi soy sauce, lemon falvored soy sauce, mirin (sweet rice wine), Aji-Mirin, plum wine, instant miso (soybean pasta) soups, egg flower soup mixes, rice crackers, tofu, neo-genmai (puffed brown rice), genmai soups, oolong tea, tsuyudakono (soup base), ponzu soy sauce, soy sauce dressing, oyster sauce, bonito stock
Manjo Brand mirin (sweet rice wine), sake, shochu, whiskey	**Manjo Brand** mirin (sweet rice wine), shochu, plum wine	**Manjo Brand** triangle, komaki
	Yomonoharu Brand sake	**Yomonoharu Brand**
	Del Monte Brand tomato ketchup, juice, puree, paste, chili sauce, Mandarin orange juice	**Del Monte Brand** tomato ketchup, juice, fruit drinks, Mandarin orange juice
	Disney Brand fruit juice (orange, pineapple, grape), nectar (peach, orange)	
	Mann's Brand^a — wine and sparkling wine, brandy	**Mann's Brand** koshu, koshu (vintage), zenkoji, blush, brandy
	Higeta Brand shoyu, tsuyu, Worcestershire sauce	
	Ragu Brand spaghetti sauces	
	Kikko's Brand tomato ketchup	**Beyoung** protein powder, wheat germ
	Monet Brand cognac	**Imported wines** aujoux, chateau tatour, borie-manoux, franz reh and sohn, pol roger

*Marketed, not manufactured, by Kikkoman.
^aThe company established its Mann Wine subsidiary in 1964.

thing. Kikkoman had become well known for its advertising skill in Japan and had found that the word *Kikkoman* was easy for Americans to pronounce.

22   The company also diversified its product line using its expertise in shoyu manufacture, fermentation, brewing, and foods marketing. This diversification included a 1963 venture to market Del Monte products in Japan. In 1990, the company bought the Del Monte assets and marketing rights for the Del Monte brand name in the Asia-Pacific region. (Exhibit 7 shows Kikkoman Corporation's product lists as of 1949, 1981, and 1993). Kikkoman's R&D expertise led to activities in biotechnology and products such as enzymes,

EXHIBIT 8
Parent Company Revenues by Product Line ((Y m)

Source: Table 5: UBS Securities Limited, May 28, 1996, as available on *Investext*.

	1994	1995	Percent Change	1996E	Percent Change
Soy Sauce	74,666	73,843	−1.1	75,000	1.6
Food	15,091	16,310	8.1	18,500	13.4
Del Monte	24,692	19,857	−19.6	19,000	−4.3
Alcohol	24,993	25,925	3.7	27,000	4.1
Others	4,159	4,285	3	4,500	5
Total	143,601	140,220	−2.4	144,000	2.7

EXHIBIT 9
Parent Company Balance Sheet ((Y) m)

Source: UBS Securities Limited, May 28, 1996. Table 11 as reported by *Investext*.

	1993	1994	1995
Current Assets	78,463	81,805	80,749
Fixed Assets	88,007	86,029	89,599
Total	166,802	168,000	170,348
Short-Term Liabilities	33,469	32,033	46,762
Long-Term Liabilities	79,898	79,527	66,567
Equity	53,434	56,440	57,019
Total Liabilities and Equity	166,802	168,000	170,348

diagnostic reagents, and other biologically active substances used to test for microorganisms in water samples in hospitals, food processing factories, and semiconductor plants. The company also developed a number of patents at home and overseas. The company became involved in both the import and export of wines. It also undertook activities in food processing machinery. In spite of the diversification, Kikkoman's domestic sales were still about 55% soy-sauce related.

23   In the 1990s, soy sauce continued as a perennial favorite in Japan's cuisine, although demand was essentially flat. Among the remaining 3,000 shoyu companies in Japan, Kikkoman produced 360,000 kl in Japan, or about 27% of the country's output. (Exhibit 6.) The company faced price pressures especially on its base product of soy sauce, mainly due to the competitive pressures at the retail level in Japan and the aggressive introduction of private brands. Sales in the Del Monte line also decreased in the early 1990s. To improve performance, Kikkoman began to reduce its product line from a high of 5,000 items to an expected eventual 2,500. One bright spot was the growth in wines and spirits. In addition, Kikkoman also introduced successful new soy-sauce related products in 1993, 1994, and 1995 in the form of two soup stocks and Steak Soy Sauce. Profit increases in the early 1990s came primarily from higher priced luxury products. (Exhibits 8 and 9 display the parent company financial statements.) The company recognized that continuing successs in its mature domestic market would depend on continuous development of new applications and variations of its older products as well as development of new products.

KIKKOMAN IN THE UNITED STATES IN THE POST–WORLD WAR II ERA

U.S. Market Potential

24   The various Mogi family branches and Noda Shoyu Company had expanded company efforts beyond Japan since the early 1800s. By the end of World War II, the various family enterprises and the Noda Shoyu Company had ended all activities outside Japan. Japanese expatriates living in various countries and other peoples whose traditional

cuisine used shoyu comprised the company's primary pre–World War II markets. In 1949, Kikkoman started to export soy sauce, mainly to the United States. In the 1950s, consumption of soy sauce began to decline in Japan. Noda Shoyu Company made the decision to invest heavily in expanding the international sales of Kikkoman brand shoyu to overseas markets. Prior to World War II, Noda Shoyu's major overseas markets were Asia and Hawaii. After the war, the company decided to focus on the mainland United States because (1) political and economic conditions in Asia were very unstable, (2) the Japanese community in Hawaii had relearned shoyu brewing during World War II, and there were many small Hawaiian shoyu breweries that would have made competition intense in that market, and (3) the United States had a healthy and rapidly growing economy.

25   Several changes in the U.S. market made that market attractive to Noda Shoyu Company. First, Americans who had been in Asia during or just after World War II developed a taste for Japanese goods, including food. Second, the company expected that as Asians in the United States became more Americanized, their consumption of traditional foods including soy sauce would decline. Third, American eating habits were shifting to more natural foods and to food that could be prepared quickly. Noda Shoyu Company moved to target both Asians and non-Asians in its marketing efforts.

26   During the 1956 U.S. presidential elections, Noda Shoyu bought air time to advertise Kikkoman brand products. Yuzaburo Mogi, son of the head of the company's planning department, urged this move to U.S. television advertising.

U.S. Distribution Activities

27   During the years immediately after World War II, Japanese companies in general relied on a small group of internationalized and entrepreneurial Japanese and Japanese-American individuals. Sale of food products in the United States involved a complex distribution system with heavy reliance on food brokers as promoters to local wholesalers and retailers. Food brokers required careful training by a knowledgeable sales team in how to use the product, especially where the product was unusual or unfamiliar to consumers. Food brokers marketed the product to wholesalers and large retailers, took orders for the product, and relayed the orders to the manufacturer or, in the case of foreign manufacturers, the manufacturer's agent. The manufacturer or agent then made delivery of the product to the wholesaler or retailer and handled all billing and accounts, paying the broker a commission for his/her marketing representation. The food broker was an important link between the manufacturer and the wholesaler or retailer. Food brokers were evaluated based on their ability to persuade retailers and wholesalers to carry products and to feature them prominently.

28   In 1957, the company formed Kikkoman International, Inc. (KII), a joint venture between Noda Shoyu Company in Japan and Pacific Trading of California. KII was incorporated in San Francisco to serve as the marketing and distribution center for Kikkoman products in the United States. Most of the products were produced by Noda Shoyu Company, but some were purchased from other manufacturers and sold under the Kikkoman label.

29   Over the next 10 years, sales grew 20 to 30% a year. In 1960, the Safeway grocery store chain agreed to have some of its stores carry Kikkoman Soy Sauce. Noda Shoyu opened regional sales offices for KII in Los Angeles (1958), New York City (1960), Chicago (1965), and Atlanta (1977). Retail marketing activities included in-store demonstrations, advertising campaigns in women's magazines that emphasized soy sauce use in American cuisine, and limited television commercials. The company used brokers as

their distribution channels to supermarkets and wholesalers for the small oriental retail stores. The company encouraged food brokers through contests and training. For the food service and industrial market segments, the company carried out industrial magazine ad campaigns and special educational programs. The company also formed partnerships with the American Veal Manufacturers' Association and the Avocado Association to feature Kikkoman Soy Sauce in their product advertisements.

30   Other major international companies had to modify their products for the United States. However, Kikkoman marketed the same soy sauce in the United States as in Japan. The company's experience in its campaign to "westernize" soy sauce for the Japanese market applied to the campaign in the United States. In the United States, Kikkoman provided traditional, low-sodium preservative-free, and dehydrated soy sauce. The company also marketed tailor-made sauces, other food extracts, and agents.

Exploration of Potential U.S. Manufacturing Capacity

31   As early as 1965, Kikkoman Corporation began to explore the possibility of manufacturing in the United States. However, the company determined that sales in North America were insufficient to support the economies of scale required for a minimum efficient scale production facility. Instead, in 1968 Kikkoman Corporation contracted with a subsidiary of Leslie Salt Company of Oakland, California, to bottle the Kikkoman soy sauce shipped in bulk from Japan and to blend and bottle teriyaki sauce, a major ingredient of which was soy sauce. These bottling efforts constituted Kikkoman's first post–World War II manufacturing efforts in the United States. Bottling in the United States reduced customs and tariff costs. However, moving goods back and forth from the United States and Japan added considerably to the company's costs. In the mid-1980s, Japan imported 95% and 88% of its soybeans and wheat, respectively. The United States was Japan's major source of supply. Transportation of raw materials (e.g., soybeans and wheat) to Japan was between 5 and 20% of preproduction costs; transportation costs of brewed soy sauce from Japan to the United States was 25% of production costs. Various import/ export restrictions and tariffs increased the risk and expense of importing raw materials to Japan and exporting finished goods to the United States.

32   The North American market was potentially much larger than the Japanese market, and Kikkoman had a greater share of the North American market than the company had in Japan. Yuzaburo Mogi hired a Columbia University classmate as a consultant, and the company formed a team to work with him to consider a U.S. plant. By 1970, the analyses, in spite of higher U.S. labor costs, favored construction of a U.S. manufacturing facility. As Yuzaburo Mogi put the company's motivation, "We made a decision to go after the American consumer."

Selection of Walworth, Wisconsin

33   The team considered over 60 potential sites in the East, West, and Midwest. The team chose the Midwest because of its central location and crop production. Ultimately, the team selected a 200-acre dairy farm site in Walworth, Wisconsin. Walworth provided the best fit with the five criteria established by the company: (1) access to markets (proximity to Milwaukee and Chicago, as well as the geographic convenience of a midway point between the East and West Coasts made shipping relatively efficient); (2) ample supplies of wheat and soybeans (soybeans came from Wisconsin, wheat from North Dakota, and salt from Canada); (3) a dedicated workforce; (4) a strong community spirit; (5) an impeccable supply of water. Kikkoman also appreciated Wisconsin's emphasis on a clean environment.

34 Walworth, Wisconsin, was situated about 2 hours northwest of Chicago and about 1 hour west of Milwaukee. A community of about 1,100, Walworth was surrounded by some of the most productive farmland in the United States. The area included a number of other smaller communities whose economies depended primarily on farming and summer vacation home residences. The company hired a local consultant, lawyer Milton Neshek, who ultimately became general counsel of Kikkoman Foods, Inc. Mr. Neshek described the original reaction to Kikkoman's purchase of prime farmland as mixed, "with a small faction on the town board opposed to the company coming in." Yuzaburo Mogi described the opposition as strong. Residents of the small, rural, close-knit farming community expressed concerns about the impact of a large, especially foreign, corporation in a small community, potential inflation of land values, and the possibility of industrial pollution.

35 One of Neshek's partners, Thomas Godfrey, visited Kikkoman facilities in Noda City, Japan. "When Kikkoman called me in 1971," said Godfrey, "and asked me to create a Wisconsin corporation for them so they could make soy sauce, I didn't even know what the hell soy sauce was. Nobody else around here did either." Walworth's plant manager, Bill Wenger, recalled his introduction to the company. In 1972, he was stationed with the U.S. Marines in Hawaii. His mother sent a newspaper clipping about the soy sauce plant, suggesting that it might be a good place to begin his return to civilian life. Wenger and his wife didn't know what soy sauce was either, but his wife went to the local grocery store and bought a bottle. As Wenger described it, the purchase was " . . . some horrible local Hawaiian brand. She brought it home and opened it. We looked at one another and said, '*@& . . . , this stuff is terrible.'" Another of the three American production managers employed at the plant had a similar tale. The production manager said, "The first year I worked here, we never had any soy sauce in my home. My wife wouldn't buy it, wouldn't even allow it in the house. I finally brought home a bottle and put it on some meatloaf. Now we use it on just about everything. I put it on peaches. And we even have a local minister who puts it on his ice cream . . . I do too. It's good."

36 No other Japanese-owned manufacturing facility had been constructed in the United States at the time. Neshek's partner, Godfrey, visited Noda because as he put it, "I had to see for myself what it was they were talking about. I had to make sure the factory wasn't going to pollute the air and water and stink up the place." Local Kikkoman representatives met with organizations such as the local Grange, Farm Bureau groups, church groups, Rotary, and ladies' clubs. Wisconsin's governor, Patrick Lucey, came to one of the seven town meetings held to discuss the plant and explain the state's role and position. Yuzaburo Mogi described the process as "removing the fears of the local people and local council about the building of the new factory." The company was able to convince area residents that Kikkoman would not pollute the environment and would use local labor and other resources. The final vote of the country zoning board was 53 for, 13 against. The town board declined to oppose the zoning board's action. Among other issues, Kikkoman put a great deal of effort into reducing potential pollution. In talking about this process of "nemawashi," or root tending, Mr. Mogi emphasized the importance of a prosperous coexistence between the company and the local community. He said, "We've been doing business in Noda for 360 years. We learned a long time ago that to survive you need to coexist with the surrounding community."

Opening the New Plant

37 In January 1971, Kikkoman executives along with Japanese, Walworth, and Wisconsin officials held a ceremonial groundbreaking on the 200-acre site. A Cleveland, Ohio, design and construction firm built the plant. Other American companies, many located in the region, built many of the critical components. The initial investment in the 10,000-

kiloliter facility was $8 million, and the plant was finished just in time to avoid the 1973 American embargo on the sale of soybeans to Japan. Kikkoman's Walworth plant was the first Japanese investment in production capacity in the United States in the post–World War II period and the first plant Kikkoman built outside Japan after World War II. Opening ceremonies included dignitaries and officials from Wisconsin, Kikkoman, Japan, and the United States. The 700 invited guests heard the texts of telegrams from the Japanese prime minister and President Richard Nixon. President Nixon referred to the plant as a " . . . visionary step (that) will mean meaningful trade relations and balance of trade and will enhance further friendships between our two countries."

38   From its opening in 1972 through the mid-1990s, the company expanded the Walworth facility eight times to 500,000 square feet. Kikkoman invested in facilities or equipment every year with production increasing 8 to 10% per year. Originally, the plant produced two products, soy sauce and teriyaki sauce. In the mid-1990s, the plant produced 18 products, including regular and light soy sauce, teriyaki steak sauce, sweet and sour sauce, and tempura dip. All but one used a soy base. The company had been very careful about pollution, treating its wastewater carefully so that there was no threat to nearby popular Geneva Lake. The Walworth town clerk said, "There's no noise, no pollution. I live about three-quarters of a mile from them, and once a day, I get a whiff of something that's like a sweet chocolate odor. It's no problem." The company marketed the plant's output in all 50 states plus Canada and Mexico. Soy sauce was shipped in many varieties, including bottles ranging from 5 to 40 ounces, 1- to 5-gallon pails, and sometimes in stainless steel tank trucks for large customers. McDonald's, for example, used soy sauce in one of the Chicken McNuggets condiments.

Management of the Walworth Plant

39   The company maintained a state-of-the-art laboratory at the Walworth facilities. However, plant management pointed out that the most accurate test during production was the human nose. "Our people have worked with the product for so long, a whiff can tell them something is not quite right," said one Kikkoman director. The venture was described as "a prime example of the best combination of Japanese and American business and industrial savvy." As the plant's general manager, Michitaro Nagasawa, a Ph.D. in biochemistry from the University of Wisconsin, put it, "The productivity of this plant is the highest of all our plants. . . . It's an exceptional case in Kikkoman history. We took the sons and daughters of farmers, trained them and caught them about total quality management. They were raw recruits with no experience in making soy sauce. People with farm backgrounds are very diligent workers. They will work 7 days a week, 24 hours a day if necessary. They understand what hard work is."

40   The plant opened with 50 employees. Originally, 14 Japanese Kikkoman employees and their families came to Walworth to train employees and get the plant functioning. The Japanese families scattered in groups of two or three to settle in Walworth and various nearby communities. Local women's community organizations "adopted" the Japanese wives, formed one-to-one friendships, and helped the Japanese wives become acclimated to the communities, including learning to drive, using the local supermarkets, and hiring baby-sitters for their children. The Japanese husbands joined local service clubs. "That helped achieve an understanding between the Americans and Japanese and helped them to assimilate faster. It exposed Japanese people to a farming town that had had no Asian people before," noted Bill Nelson, Kikkoman Foods vice president. Kikkoman established the practice of rotating its Japanese employees back to Japan after an average of 5 years in the United States. In the mid-1990s, only seven Japanese families remained in the Walworth area, still spread throughout the local communities.

Community Contributions

41 Kikkoman Foods, Inc., was an active and contributing member of the community. The company donated time and funds on three levels. At the local level, the company established Kikkoman Foods Foundation in 1993. The foundation, which was to be ultimately funded at the $3 million level, was formed to support area charitable activities. The company supported as many as 30 local projects a year, including college scholarships for area students, local hospital activities, a vocational program that assisted people in developing employment-related skills, and a nearby facility that preserved circus-related items. As Walworth's town clerk put it, "They sponsor just about everything—Community Chest (an organization similar to the United Way), Boy Scouts, Girls Scouts, all the way down the line. They're very good neighbors." The clerk treasurer from a nearby town said, "You see their name in the paper almost every week, helping out some organization."

42 At the state level, Kikkoman Foods, Inc., supported the University of Wisconsin educational system, established up to four Beloit College scholarships to honor Governor Lucey at his alma matter, and funded a Mogi Keizaburo scholarship at the Milwaukee School of Engineering. Members of the board of directors served on several public service boards and commissions. At the national level, Kikkoman Corporation, through its U.S. subsidiary Kikkoman Foods, Inc., supported Youth for Understanding exchange programs. At the fifth anniversary celebration, Kikkoman's chairman reported that the plant had developed better than had been anticipated. At the tenth anniversary celebration of the Kikkoman plant, the local Walworth paper reported, "In the 10 years that Kikkoman Foods, Inc., has been located here, it has become an integrated part of the community. The company has truly become a part of the Walworth community, and not only in a business sense." In 1987, reflecting Kikkoman's contributions, Wisconsin's govenor appointed Yuzaburo Mogi as Wisconsin's honorary ambassador to Japan.

Kikkoman's Japanese–American Management in the United States

43 In the mid-1990s, Kikkoman operated its U.S. activities through two subsidiaries, Kikkoman Foods, Inc. (KFI), and Kikkoman International, Inc. (KII). KFI owned and operated the Walworth manufacturing plant. KII in San Francisco, California, undertook marketing responsibilities, including wholesaler and distributor activities throughout the United States. The boards of directors for both subsidiaries had several members from the parent corporation but were primarily Americans from among local operations officers or local Walworth citizens (for KFI) or the broader U.S. community (for KII). The KFI board met as a whole once a year and rotated the site of its annual stockholders' meeting between Japan and Wisconsin. An executive committee met monthly to consider operational decisions. The executive committee included Yuzaburo Mogi, who attended two to three meetings in the United States every year, and the head of Kikkoman Corporation's International Division. The remaining members of the executive committee included American and Japanese officers from the U.S. corporation. The KII board operated in a similar manner but met only in the United States.

44 Yuzaburo Mogi believed that a long-term commitment was essential for international success. A 1961 alumnus of Columbia University's Graduate School of Business, Mr. Mogi was the first Japanese to graduate from a U.S. university with an MBA degree. In the years following graduation, he worked in various departments in Kikkoman, including accounting, finance, computers, long-range planning, and new product development. In time, he took on other roles, including member of Kikkoman's board of directors (1979), managing director of the company (1982), executive management director (1989), and executive vice president (1994). The seventeenth generation of his family to brew soy sauce, Mr. Mogi had become Kikkoman's president in early 1995. He explained his view regarding the necessity of a long-term perspective: "We should do business from a longer range viewpoint. It will be very difficult to expect fruitful results in the short run under different and difficult circumstances. Failure will be inevitable in foreign countries if one proceeds with a short-range view. In fact, it took Kikkoman 16 years to become established in the United States."

45   Of the five senior managers at the Walworth facility, three were Japanese and two were American. The plant manager, the finance manager, and the laboratory manager were Japanese. It was expected that these three positions would continue to be Japanese appointments. One American manager described the situation: "We know we will only attain a certain level, but that's OK, though. I can accept that. Soy sauce has been made in Japan for centuries. It's their product, their technology. They have the history, the research."

46   The general manager, i.e., plant manager, was the most senior person in authority at the plant and was responsible directly to headquarters in Japan. The appointment would be a person who had been with the company for many years. The finance manager's position required someone who was familiar with Japanese accounting systems and who was steeped in the Japanese emphasis on long-range profits. Japanese corporate headquarters controlled their foreign branches through their accounting and finance sections.

47   Mr. Mogi explained the Japanese appointment to the position of laboratory manager: "The production of soy sauce is very sophisticated. Normally, we recruit graduates with a master's degree in Japan who have gone to universities that have specialized programs in soy sauce production. In America, there is no university that teaches soy sauce production techniques, so it is difficult to promote Americans into general manager positions." As Dr. Magasawa, general manager at the Walworth plant, put it in explaining the discriminating tastes the Japanese have developed since childhood, "The sensory system, passion, feeling, or sensitivity can't transfer. That is based on just experience. Our vice president is a kind of god in this plant because he recognizes (even) a slight difference . . . I don't have that. That's why I can't be manufacturing vice president. I am a general manager—nothing special. I am a biochemist (with) 39 years in Kikkoman, mostly in research."

48   Decisions at the Walworth plant, when possible, were made by consensus. KFI vice president Bill Nelson described the plant management as American in content and Japanese in style, with decisions arrived at from the bottom up and most matters of importance needing a consensus of employees. "It's hard, really, to get at because of the fact that nothing . . . here should run in an American style or a Japanese style or what have you. It was just simply—let's see what happens when you have both parties participate," he said. Nelson gave the example of an idea for changing summer working hours to start at 7 A.M. instead of 8 A.M. so that workers could leave earlier and enjoy more daylight. It was, Nelson, pointed out, unusual for a company to even entertain the idea. Nelson explained the process: "Instead of simply exploring it on a management level, here we started the process by asking individual employees what personal inconvenience would be experienced if the hours were changed."

49   Milton Neshek observed that Japanese management and the middle management at the Walworth plant worked well together with long-range budgeting and strategic planning carried out by the Japanese executive team. He described the situation: "Our 30 employees feel like part of our family. That makes management more responsive to employees. Decisions, whenever possible, are made by consensus." The fact that the plant has no labor union was no surprise to Nelson. As he put it, a union "has never been an issue here."

50   Yuzaburo Mogi summarized Kikkoman's approach to its U.S. operations and, in particular, its Walworth plant as a five-point approach:

> Kikkoman has been successful doing business in the United States by adapting to American laws, customers, and most importantly, its culture . . . (An) important matter to consider, especially when establishing a manufacturing plant in a foreign country, is the maintenance of what has come to be called "harmony" with society and the local community. A foreign concern should try to prosper together with society and the local community. . . . It is important to try to localize the operation. . . . (Our) . . . first commitment is the employment of as many local people as possible. Second we try to participate in local activities . . . trying to be a good corporate citizen (in Wisconsin) and contributing to society through our business activities. Third, we have been trying to avoid the so-called "Japanese-village" . . . by advising our people from Japan not to live together in one single community, but to spread out and live in several separate communities in order to become more families with the local people. Fourth, we try to do business with American companies. The fifth commitments is our practice of delegating most authority to local management in order to better reflect local circumstances. Through this process we are better able to make the most responsible decision. If we have an opinion, for example, we discuss it with other members at a local meeting in our American plant before reaching a decision. Kikkoman attempts to avoid a remote-control situation with letters or telephone calls from Japan. . . . If we have an opinion, we discuss it with other members at a local meeting in our American plant before reaching a decision.

51   The plant did encounter intercultural issues, however. For example, plant manager Bill Wenger pointed out, "Communication can be a problem sometimes. The language barrier is one reason. Then there's the problem of saving face. If a mistake is made, the Japanese tend to cover up for one another so the person who made the mistakes doesn't lose face."

52   The company was a popular local employer in Walworth. Local unemployment was phenomenally low at 2%, but the Walworth plant had over 1,000 active applications on file for the plant's total 136 positions. However, turnover among plant employees was negligible. "No one quits unless it is a move by a spouse. Our absenteeism is minimal and as for tardiness—we just don't have it. We offer competitive wages and good benefits . . . employees feel like part of our family," said general counsel Neshek. Company officials stated that they paid about 10% more than the state average of $9.71 per hour, and employees did not have to contribute to the cost of their health insurance. As the company's vice president Shin Ichi Sugiyama put it, "In management, our primary concern is always the employee." The employees reported, "We feel like they listen to us. Our opinion counts, and we have the ability to make change, to better the company."

53   Mr. Sugiyama pointed out that the Walworth plant's productivity and quality had been about equal to that of Japanese plants. Productivity improved following the plant opening and by 1993 was actually the best of all the company's plants.

THE U.S. MARKET IN THE 1990s[3]

U.S. Demand in the 1990s

54   After the opening of the Walworth plant, Kikkoman's U.S. sales growth slowed somewhat. However, Ken Saito, Kikkoman's brand manager for the Midwest, summarized the company's hopes: "Americans are more adventurous than Japanese when it comes to trying new foods. That's why we have developed some products only for the American market. But most Americans still are not familiar with how to use soy sauce." Thus, the com-

EXHIBIT 10
U.S. Oriental Food
Sales ($000,000)

Year	1992	1993	1994
Sales	$275	$305	$301

Source: Information Resources,
Inc., Chicago, IL.

pany developed a number of non-oriental recipes that call for soy sauce and other Kikkoman products, for example, teriyaki chicken wings and Pacific Rim pizza with sweet and sour sauce, beef and chicken fajitas, and grilled salmon with confetti salsa flavored with "lite" soy sauce. Kikkoman clearly expected Americans to increasingly use soy sauce for applications beyond oriental foods and expected significant growth in the company's base product in the United States. According to Saito, "We figure the market in the United States will increase 100 times in the next decade." Kikkoman marketing coordinator, Trisha MacLeod, articulated the goal as ". . . to get consumers to realize soy sauce is the oldest man-made condiment, and that it can also be used in meatloaf, barbecue—across the spectrum."

55 MacLeod pointed out, "Americans eat a lot more soy sauce than they realize." However, America's per capita consumption was barely 10 tablespoons, translating into $300 million in North American sales. In contrast, Japanese per capita consumption was about 10.5 quarts per person, which translated into about $1.4 billion in annual in Japan.

56 The population of Asian immigrants and families of Asian descent was projected to grow significantly in the United States. The California population increased 127% to 2.8 million during the 1980s. The total population of Asian-Americans in the United States was estimated at 7.3 million in 1990, up 108% over the 1980s. Asian peoples represented the traditional mainstay market for oriental foods. Asians had higher income and educational levels than any other ethnic groups in the United States. However, each country represented a different cuisine, and the different Asian ethnic groups required different marketing approaches. Asian populations had spread throughout many parts of the United States, and retail outlets were learning how to highlight and display oriental foods to spur sales. Restaurants greatly influenced American food-buying habits. One industry executive observed that almost all U.S. restaurant kitches in the 1990s had soy sauce. A 1996 National Restaurant Association study indicated that ethnic foods were increasing in popularity. Thus, oriental food manufacturers and distributors expected that oriental food sales would increase sharply.

57 Some information in the mid-1990s suggested strong and increasing popularity for oriental foods. U.S. sales of oriental foods had slowed considerably. The most recent aggregate information regarding the demand for oriental food in the United States in the mid-1990s in shown in Exhibit 10.

58 By the late 1980s, consumers began to indicate dissatisfaction with canned entrees, at $81 million in sales the second largest subcategory of oriental foods. Sales of this subcategory had declined as much as 10% (1991 to 1992) and showed no signs of abating. Competition was intense, with a third of all products sold on the basis of feature, price, and/or display promotion.

U.S. Major Competitors

59 Kikkoman's two major competitors in the United States were Chun King and La Choy. Both companies made soy sauce by hydrolyzing vegetable protein. This European derived method was faster and less expensive than the six-month fermentation process Kikkoman used. By 1971, Kikkoman had surpassed Chun King in supermarket sales of soy sauce, becoming #2 in the American marketplace. In 1976, Kikkoman outsold

La Choy brand soy sauce and became the #1 retailer of soy sauce in the United States, a position it continued to hold in the mid-1990s. However, the company faced strong competitors in the oriented foods category and in the sauces and condiments subcategory.

60   The new consumer focus was on oriental food ingredients that individuals could add to home-cooked dishes. "People are cooking more oriental foods at home," said Chun King's vice president of marketing, "Over 40% of U.S. households stir-fry at least once a month. Sauces are an opportunity to get away from the canned image." Indeed, sauces were the only growth area on the oriental food category, with 1992 sales rising 11% over the previous year. Rivals Chun King and La Choy were flooding the oriental foods aisle in American supermarkets with new products. La Choy had about 40% of the shelf products in oriental foods, and Chun King had about 20%.

61   However, there were more changes than just new products. In the early 1990s, La Choy and Chun King had revved up their marketing efforts under new ownership. La Choy was owned by ConAgra's Hunt-Wesson division. Among other initiatives, ConAgra, a major U.S. food company, hired a new advertising firm for La Choy.

62   A Singapore-based firm purchased Chun King in 1989 and brought in a new management team. As one observer put it, "The brand had really been neglected as part of Nabisco (its previous owner). It was just a small piece of a big pie." The new management team introduced a line of seasoned chow mein noodles and another of hot soy sauces. The firm's marketing plan included consumer promotions and a print ad campaign in women's magazines. Chun King's 1992 oriental food sales were estimated at $30 million. In mid-1995, ConAgra purchased Chun King from the Singapore company and added the brand to its Hunt-Wesson division. Con-Agra was no stranger to the Chun King brand. The large U.S. competitor had purchased Chun King's frozen food line in 1986 from Del Monte. It was expected that Hunt-Wesson would eventually consolidate manufacturing but continue to aggressively advertise the two brands separately. As a Hunt-Wesson executive put it, "They're both established leaders in their field, and they both have brand strength."

63   La Choy advertised itself as "the world's largest producer of oriental foods created for American tastes." The company led the oriental foods category with sales (excluding frozen) of $87 million in 1992 and $104.4 million in 1994. Its products included chow mein noodles, bamboo shoots, sauces, and miscellaneous foods. About $28 million of the 1992 sales came from sauce and marinade sales. La Choy's manager of corporate communications indicated that the Chicago-based firm planned no increase in marketing spending in reaction to the new Chun King initiatives. However, the company did plan to advertise two new lines—Noodle Entrees and Stir-Fry Vegetables 'N Sauce. The company expected to expend most of its marketing support for the latter product line, a set of vegetables in four sauces formulated for consumers to stir-fry with their choice of meat.

Kikkoman and Other Competitors

64   Kikkoman remained the one bright sport in the oriental food category of sauces and marinades. Kikkoman controlled $63 million of the $160 million sauces/marinades segment and supported its position with a moderate amount of advertising—$3.2 million in 1992, about the same as 1991. In its major product lines, Kikkoman controlled about two-thirds of the California market and had about one-third market share in other major U.S. sales regions. The company was test-marketing a new line of sauces for addition to the consumer's own vegetables and meat.

65   Kikkoman also had to consider recent moves by several other competitors. Yamasa Shoyu Co., Ltd., Japan's second-largest soy sauce maker, had announced plans to build a factory in Oregon in mid-1994. This multigenerational company was founded in 1645 in Choshi City, Japan. Estimates on the cost of the Oregon factory ranged from $15 million to $20 million, and the plant was expected to eventually employ 50 workers. Yamasa intended to produce soy sauce for the U.S. market by using soybeans shipped from the Midwest. It took Yamasa 4 years to select the final site for its new plant. The company produced a number of products in addition to soy sauce, including other food and drugs made from biological raw materials such as soybean protein and wheat starch.

66   Hong Kong-based Lee Kum Kee was a producer and importer of Chinese-oriented sauces and condiments. Lee Kum Kee had opened a sauce manufacturing plant in Los Angeles in 1991 to keep up with rising U.S. demand and to reduce dependence on imports, thus avoiding payment of import duties, which could be as high as 20 percent. The company was a Hong Kong subsidiary of one of Japan's leading soy sauce brewers. Lee Kum Kee retailed its sauces in big supermarket chains in all 50 states. Historically, the company imported its soy sauce through an independent U.S.-based importer of the same name. The U.S. importer also imported about 40 other food products, mostly marinades, curries, and sauces from the East. Lee Kum Kee found its sales propelled by the population doubling of Americans of Asian or Pacific Island descent.

67   Competitor San-J International of the San-Jirushi Corporation of Kuwana, Japan, built a soy sauce plant in Richmond, Virginia, in 1988. Hawaiian competitor Noh Foods of Hawaii innovated a line of oriental dried seasonings and powdered mixes. In reaction, other manufacturers, including Kikkoman, produced copycat products. Noh Foods distributed its products in the United States, Europe, and Australia through distibutors and trade show activities.

KIKKOMAN'S INTERNATIONAL POSITION

The Kikkoman Vision

68   In the mid-1990s, Kikkoman manufactured in four countries and marketed its brand products in over 90 countries. (Exhibit 11 shows the comparison of domestic and non-Japan sales and operating profits.) Of the company's 3,200 employees, over 1,000 were in international subsidiaries, and only 5 percent of those were Japanese. The company saw at least part of its mission as contributing to international cultural exchange. Yuzaburo Mogi explained:

> Kikkoman believes that soy sauce marketing is the promotion of the international exchange of food culture. In order to create a friendlier world, I believe we need many types of cultural exchanges. Among these, there is one that is most closely related to our daily lives—the eating of food. Soy sauce is one of the most important food cultures in Japan. Hence, the overseas marketing of soy sauce means the propagation of Japanese food culture throughout the world.

69   As one U.S. scholar who had studied the company extensively in the 1980s put it, "There is an evident willingness on the part of Kikkoman to experiment with new products, production techniques, management styles, and operational forms in the international arena." Yuzaburo Mogi put it similarly when he said, "It should be understood that adjustment to different laws, customs, and regulations is imperative, instead of complaining about those differences."

EXHIBIT 11
Consolidated Results
FY 1995 ((Y)m)

Source: UBS Securities
Limited, May 28, 1996. Table 7
as reported by *Investext*.

	Domestic	Non-Japan
Sales	162,426	40,860
Operating Profit	6,640	4,152
Operating Margin	4.0	10.1

Kikkoman in Europe

70 Kikkoman began its marketing activities in Europe in 1972. Kikkoman found Europeans more conservative and slower to try new tastes than Americans. The firm found Germany the least conservative and opened restaurants there in 1973. By the early 1990s, the company had opened six Japanese steak houses in Germany. The restaurants gave their customers, over 90 percent of whom were non-Asian, the opportunity to try new cuisine. The Kikkoman trading subsidiary in Germany was the company's European marketing arm. Said the managing director for Kikkoman's European marketing subsidiary located in Germany, "Germany and Holland are big business for us, as both countries are very much into interesting sauces and marinades." Kikkoman's managing director of Europe made it clear that he had aggressive plans to grow sales both by increasing the sales of soy sauce as well as extending the markets in which the company operated. The massive ready-made meal business in both the United States and Europe had huge potential for Kikkoman. The firm would need to market to end consumers at the retail level as well as to food manufacturers.

71 The company established its second overseas manufacturing facility in 1983. This facility supplied soy sauce to Australian and European markets. By the early 1990s, Kikkoman had about 50% of the Australian soy sauce market. The United Kingdom brand debut occurred in 1986, and the 1992 U.K. market was estimated at 1 billion pounds. In 1993, the firm opened a 25,000-square-foot warehouse in London. With $1.66 billion (U.S.) in sales, Kikkoman had come a long way with "just" soy sauce. Overall, analysts noted that the United States had experienced about 10 percent annual growth in soy sauce demand and expected Europe to expand similarly.

Kikkoman in Asia

72 In Asia, the company opened a production facility in Singapore in 1983 and incorporated a trading company in 1990. Industry observers expected the company to enter the soy sauce market in China in the near future. In addition, other Asian countries offered various opportunities in sauces, condiments, and foods.

Kikkoman—The Challenges

73 The company the Mogi family had headed for nearly 400 years confronted a number of challenges on the global stage in the latter part of the 1990s. Kikkoman executives realized that the company's future could depend primarily on its mature domestic market. The multigeneration family firm would have to change its image as a maker of a mature product. As Mr. Mogi stated, "We . . . take pride in our ability to contribute to the exchange of cultures by using some of the world's most familiar flavors. We are now concentrating on further enhancing our ability to serve consumers in Japan and overseas. Kikkoman continues as a company that is proud of its heritage, but nevertheless willing and able to adapt to the constantly evolving requirements of our customers and markets."

1. In early 1996, the exchange rate was about 95 yen per U.S. dollar. Thus, in U.S. dollar. Thus, in U.S. dollars, Kikkoman's market value was about $1.7 billion. Sales at year end 1995 for the consolidated company were 203 billion yen, or slightly less than $2 billion (See Exhibits 2 and 3 for consolidated financial data and Exhibits 8, 9, and 11 for parent company and domestic versus non-Japan revenues plus other selected financial information.)

2. *Zaibatsu:* Industrial and financial combines dissolved by occupation fiat after World War II, but which have reemerged as somewhat weaker entities. Some of these *zaibatsu* have developed into large conglomerates such as Mitsubishi. However, they should be distinguished from *keiretsu* (of which Mitsubishi is also one of largest). *Keiretsu* are informal enterprise group-based associations of banks, industrials, and so forth.

3. Information on the market and competitors was drawn primarily from InfoScan.

Allen, Sara Clark. "Kikkoman, a Good Neighbor in Wisconsin," *Business,* June 11, 1996.

Bergsman, Steve. "Patience and Perseverance in Japan," *Global Trade,* Vol. 109, Issue 8 (August 1989), pp. 10, 12.

Campbell, Dee Ann. "Del Monte Foods to See European Foods Business," *Business Wire,* April 17, 1990.

Demestrakakes, Pan. "Quality for the Ages," *Food Processing,* Vol. 70, No. 6 (September 1996).

"Fireflies Help Kill Germs," *Times Net Asia,* January 1, 1996.

Forbish, Lynn. "Grand Oriental Celebration Held for Opening of Kikkoman Foods," *Janesville Gazette,* June 18, 1973.

Forrest, Tracy. "Kikkoman: A Way of Life," *Super Marketing,* January 28, 1994.

Fruin, W. Mark. *Kikkoman: Company, Clan, and Community* (Cambridge, Massachusetts: Harvard University Press, 1983).

Hewitt, Lynda. "Liquid Spice," *Food Manufacture,* February, 1993, p. 23.

Hostveldt, John. "Japan's Kikkoman Corp. Brews Success Story in Walworth," *Business Dateline: The Business Journal—Milwaukee,* Vol. 3, No. 31, Sec. 3 (May 19, 1986), p. 17.

"In-Store: Happy New Year's Feast" (Article on Kikkoman's In-Store Promotion), *Brandsweek,* Vol. 37 (January 1, 1996), pp. 14–15.

Jansen, Leah. "Kikkoman Spices Up Walworth's Quality of Life," *Janesville Gazette,* January 21, 1984.

Jensen, Debra. "Kikkoman Executive Lauds Wisconsin, Lucey," *Gazette,* January 13, 1989, p. 1B.

Jensen, Don. "A Stainless Success Story," *Kenosha News,* Business Section, August 1, 1993.

"The Joy of Soy: How a Japanese Sauce Company Found a Happy Home in Walworth, Wisc.," *Chicago Tribune Magazine,* January 31, 1993, p. 13.

Kikkoman Corporation: Flavors That Bring People Together (Company Brochure, 1994).

Kinugasa, Dean. "Kikkoman Corporation," 1979 (Private Translation by Norihito Tanaka and Marilyn Taylor, 1994).

La Choy's Homepage (www.hunt-wesson.com/lachoy/main/mission/).

LaGrange, Maria L. "RJR Sells Del Monte Operations for $1.4 Billion," *Los Angeles Times,* Vol. 108, Issue 297, September 26, 1989, p. 2.

Mogi, Yuzaburo. *"Masatsunaki Kokusai Senryaku,"* (Tokyo, Japan: Selnate Publishing Co., Ltd., 1988—in English Translation).

Mogi, Yuzaburo. "The Conduct of International Business: One Company's Credo—Kikkoman, Soy Sauce and the U.S. Market," (Available from Company).

Ostrander, Kathleen. "Kikkoman's Success Tied to Proper Blend," *Business Datelines (Wisconsin State Journal),* March 1, 1992, p. 29.

Plett, Edith. "Kikkoman Foods Marks Fifth Year," *Janesville Gazette,* January 26, 1979.

Redman, Russell. "Hunt-Wesson Acquires Chun King," *Supermarket News,* Vol. 45, No. 19 (May 8, 1995), p. 101.

SBA Homepage, Wisconsin Gallery.

Schoenburg, Lorraine. "Governor Supports Kikkoman," *Janesville Gazette,* September 14, 1989

Shima, Takeshi. "Kikkoman's Thousand-Year History," *Business JAPAN,* January 1989, p. 65.

Wilkins, Mira. "Japanese Multinational in the United States: Continuity and Change, 1879–1990," *Business History Review,* Vol. 64, Issue 4 (Winter 1990), pp. 585–629.

Yates, Ronald E. "Wisconsin's Other Brew," *Chicago Tribune Magazine,* January 31, 1993, p. 14.

In addition to personal interviews in Tokyo, Walworth, Wisconsin, and San Francisco, information and quotation were also drawn from these references. This list is part of a much broader set of sources that the authors consulted.

APPENDIX A: THE MAKING OF SOY SAUCE

The Chinese began making jiang, a precursor of soy sauce, about 2,500 years ago. The most likely story of soy sauce's origins relates how Kakushin, a Japanese Zen priest who studied in China, returned to Japan in the middle of the thirteenth century and began preparing a type of miso, or soybean paste produced through fermentation, that became a specialty of the area. By the end of the thirteenth century, the liquid was called *tamari* and sold commercially along with the miso. Experimentation with the raw ingredients and methods of fermentation began. Vegetarianism also became popular in Japan during this time, and people were eager for condiments to flavor their rather bland diet. Soldiers also found the transportability of the seasonings useful.

Soy sauce evolved from tamari and miso by adding wheat to the soybean fermentation mash. The Japanese modified the shoyu to include wheat to gentle the taste so that it did not overwhelm the delicate flavors of Japanese cuisine. Most households made their shoyu during the slack time in agricultural cycles. Families harvested grains in the fall and processed them into mash. The mash fermented beginning in October–December to January–March when the shoyu was pressed from the mash.

Regional differences among the soy sauces developed depending upon the mix of soybean, wheat, and fermentation techniques. Even in the last decade of the twentieth century, there were hundreds of local varieties of soy sauce available commercially in Japan.

Produced in the traditional way, soy sauce was a natural flavor enhancer. In the latter part of the twentieth century, ingredient-conscious consumers shied away from artificial flavor enhancers. Soy sauce responded to the challenge of finding ingredients to flavor foods. For vegetarian manufacturers, the "beefy" taste provided by the soy sauce without any meat extract was highly desirable.

There were two methods of manufacturing soy sauce—the traditional fermentation processed used by Kikkoman and the chemical method.

Soy Sauce through Fermentation—Kikkoman's Traditional Method

Kikkoman's process was the traditional one and involved processing soy and wheat to a mash. Kikkoman had developed an innoculum of seed mold that the company added. The seed mold produced a growth, the development of which was controlled by temperature and humidity. The resulting mash (koji) was discharged into fermentation tanks where selected microorganism cultures and brine were added. The product (moromi mash) was aerated and mixed, then aged. During this process, enzymes formed in the cells of the koji and provided the characteristics of the brewed sauce. The soybean protein changed to amino acid, and the enzymatic reaction that occurred between the sugar and amino acids produced the taste and color. Enzymes changed the wheat starch to sugars for sweetness, and a special yeast developed changing some of the sugars to alcohol. Fermentation changed other parts of the sugars to alcohol that produced tartness. The brewing process determined flavor, color, taste, and aroma. The brine added to the koji mixture stimulated the enzymes and produced the reddish brown liquid mash. This process resulted in umami—or flavor-enhancing—abilities, as well as the brewed flavor components. The final mash was pressed between layers of cloth under constant pressure. After a pasteurization process to intensify color and aromas, the shoyu was filtered again and bottled. There were not flavorings, coloring, additives, or artificial ingredients in the product. According to produce developers, these complex flavors were not present in brewed soy sauce.

Chemically Produced Soy Sauce

Nonbrewed soy sauce could be made in hours. Soybeans were boiled with hydrochloric acid for 15 to 20 hours. When the maximum amount of amino acid was removed from the soybeans, the mixture was cooled to end the hydrolysis action. The amino acid liquid was then neutralized, mixed with charcoal, and finally purified through filtration. Color and flavor were introduced via varying amounts of corn syrup, salt, and caramel coloring. The resulting soy sauce was then refined and bottled.

Case Index

Subject Index